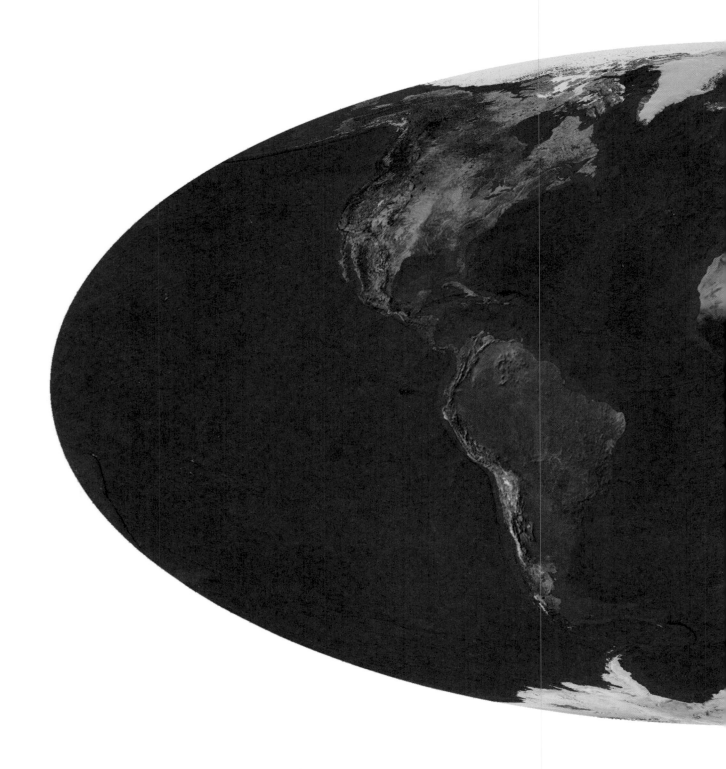

World Topography

YOUR ACCESS TO SUCCESS

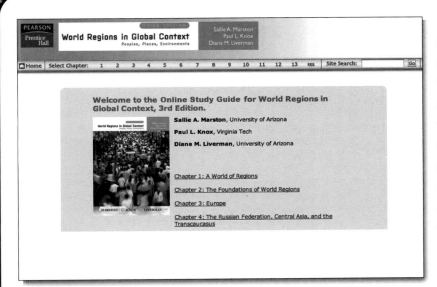

Students with new copies of Marston/Knox/Liverman, *World Regions in Global Context,* Third Edition have full access to the book's Online Study Guide—a 24/7 study tool with review exercises, web destinations, and other features designed to help you make the most of your study time.

Just follow the easy website registration steps listed below...

Registration Instructions for *www.prenhall.com/marston*

1. Go to *www.prenhall.com/marston*
2. Click the cover for Marston/Knox/Liverman, *World Regions in Global Context,* Third Edition.
3. Click "Register."
4. Using a coin (not a knife) scratch off the metallic coating below to reveal your Access Code.
5. Complete the online registration form, choosing your own personal Login Name and Password.
6. Enter your pre-assigned Access Code exactly as it appears below.
7. Complete the online registration form by entering your School Location information.
8. After your personal Login Name and Password are confirmed by e-mail, go back to *www.prenhall.com/marston*, click your book's cover, enter your new Login Name and Password, and click "Log In".

Your Access Code is:

P.

If there is no metallic coating covering the access code above, the code may no longer be valid and you will need to purchase online access using a major credit card to use the website. To do so, go to *www.prenhall.com/marston*, click the cover for Marston/Knox/Liverman, *World Regions in Global Context*, Third Edition, then click the "Get Access" button, and follow the instructions under "Students".

Important: Please read the Subscription and End-User License Agreement located on the "Log In" screen before using the Marston/Knox/Liverman, *World Regions in Global Context,* Third Edition, Online Study Guide. By using the website, you indicate that you have read, understood, and accepted the terms of the agreement.

Minimum system requirements

PC Operating Systems:

Windows 2000, XP

Pentium II 233 MHz processor. 64 MB RAM In addition to the minimum memory required by your OS.

Internet Explorer 6.0, Netscape Navigator 7.2, or Firefox 1.0.x

Macintosh Operating Systems:

Macintosh Power PC with OS X (10.2, 10.3)

In addition to the RAM required by your OS, this product requires 64 MB RAM, with 40MB Free RAM, with Virtual Memory enabled

Netscape Navigator 7.2, Safari 1.0, 1.3, or Firefox 1.0.x

Macromedia Shockwave(TM)

8.50 release 326 plugin

Macromedia Flash Player 6.0.79 & 7.0

Acrobat Reader 6.0.1

800 x 600 pixel screen resolution

Technical Support Call 1-800-677-6337. Phone support is available Monday–Friday, 8am to 8pm and Sunday 5pm to 12am, Eastern time. Visit our support site at *http://247.prenhall.com*. E-mail support is available 24/7.

World Regions in Global Context

Peoples, Places, and Environments

THIRD EDITION

Sallie A. Marston
University of Arizona

Paul L. Knox
Virginia Tech

Diana M. Liverman
Oxford University

PEARSON
Prentice
Hall

Upper Saddle River, NJ 07458

Library of Congress Cataloging-in-Publication Data

Marston, Sallie A.
  World regions in global context : peoples, places, and environments / Sallie A. Marston,
Paul L. Knox, Diana M. Liverman.—3rd ed.
    p. cm.
  Includes bibliographical references.
  ISBN 0-13-229835-X
  1. Geography. 2. Globalization. I. Knox, Paul L. II. Liverman, Diana M. III. Title.
G116.M37 2008
910—dc22   2007000493

Publisher: Daniel Kaveney
Editor-in-Chief, Science: Nicole Folchetti
Development Editor: Barbara Muller
Production Editor: Tim Flem, PublishWare
Associate Editor: Amanda Brown
Executive Managing Editor: Kathleen Schiaparelli
Assistant Managing Editor: Beth Sweeten
Marketing Manager: Amy Porubsky
Media Editor: Andrew Sobel
Creative Director: Juan Lopez
Art Director: Jonathan Boylan
Interior and Cover Design: John Christiana
Manufacturing Manager: Alexis Heydt-Long
Senior Managing Editor, Art Production and Management: Patricia Burns
Manager, Production Technologies: Matthew Haas
Managing Editor, Art Management: Abigail Bass
Art Production Editor: Xiaohong Zhu
Illustrations: Precision Graphics
Cartography: The GeoNova Group
Manufacturing Buyer: Alan Fischer
Editorial Assistants: John DeSantis, Jessica Neumann
Director, Image Resource Center: Melinda Patelli
Manager, Rights and Permissions: Zina Arabia
Interior Image Specialist: Beth Brenzel
Cover Image Specialist: Karen Sanatar
Image Permission Coordinator: Annette Linder
Photo Researcher: Jerry Marshall
Cover Photograph: Crowded streets of Mumbay, © Ladi Kirn/Alamy Ltd.

© 2008, 2005, 2002 Pearson Education, Inc.
Pearson Prentice Hall
Pearson Education, Inc.
Upper Saddle River, NJ 07458

Pearson Prentice Hall™ is a trademark of Pearson Education, Inc.

Printed in the United States of America

10 9 8 7 6 5 4 3 2

ISBN 0-13-229835-X

Pearson Education Ltd., *London*
Pearson Education Australia Pty., Limited, *Sydney*
Pearson Education Singapore, Pte. Ltd.
Pearson Education North Asia Ltd., *Hong Kong*
Pearson Education Canada, Ltd., *Toronto*
Pearson Educación de Mexico, S.A. de C.V.
Pearson Education—Japan, *Tokyo*
Pearson Education Malaysia, Pte. Ltd.

BRIEF CONTENTS

CONTENTS

CHAPTER 3
THE RUSSIAN FEDERATION, CENTRAL ASIA, AND THE TRANSCAUCASUS   106

CHAPTER 4
MIDDLE EAST AND NORTH AFRICA   152

CHAPTER 10
SOUTH ASIA   470

CHAPTER 11
AUSTRALIA, NEW ZEALAND, AND THE SOUTH PACIFIC   520

CHAPTER 12
FUTURE REGIONAL GEOGRAPHIES

APPENDIX: MAPS AND GEOGRAPHIC INFORMATION SYSTEMS

GLOSSARY

PHOTO CREDITS

INDEX

PREFACE

Bear in mind that the wonderful things you learn in your schools are the work of many generations, produced by enthusiastic effort and infinite labor in every country of the world. All this is put into your hands as your inheritance in order that you may receive it, honor it, add to it, and one day faithfully hand it on to your children. Thus do we mortals achieve immortality in the permanent things which we create in common.

From Albert Einstein's *Thoughts and Opinions*

World Regions in Global Context provides an introduction to world regional geography that will make exotic places, landscapes, and environments accessible and will reveal the familiar in new ways. To put it simply, to study world regional geography is to study the dynamic and complex relationships between people and the worlds they inhabit. This book gives students the basic geographical tools and concepts needed to understand the complexity of regions and to appreciate the interconnections between their own lives and those of people in different parts of the world.

OBJECTIVES AND APPROACH

This book has two primary objectives. The first is to provide a body of knowledge about how natural, social, economic, political, and cultural phenomena come together to produce distinctive territories with distinctive landscapes and cultural attributes: that is, world regions. The second is to emphasize that although there is diversity among world regions, it is important for us to understand the increasing interdependencies that exist among and between regions in order to build any real understanding of the modern world.

In an attempt to achieve these objectives, we have taken a fresh approach to world geography, reflecting the major changes that have recently been impressed on global, regional, and local landscapes. These changes include the global spread of new information technologies such as the World Wide Web, which brings distant people and places to our computer screens; the rise of global institutions like the World Trade Organization and the geopolitical and geoeconomic impacts that have resulted; and the global spread of new social movements that are pressing for reforms on a whole range of issues from global climate change to genocide. The approach used in *World Regions in Global Context* provides access not only to the new ideas, concepts, and theories that address these changes and many other changes but also to the fundamentals of geography: the principles, concepts, theoretical frameworks, and basic knowledge that are necessary to build a geographic understanding of today's world.

A distinctive feature of our approach is that it emphasizes the interdependence of places and processes at different scales and how regions are implicated in these processes. In overall terms, this approach is designed to provide an understanding of relationships between widespread processes that are affecting places throughout the globe as well as the way these processes are working out in particular places. Moreover, we are not only interested in understanding the internal dynamics of a world region; we are also interested in that region's relationship to other regions around the globe. One of the chief organizing principles of our approach is how globalization frames the social and cultural construction of particular places and regions at various scales.

This approach allows us to emphasize a number of important themes.

- *Globalization and the links between global and local—* Throughout the book, we stress the increasing interconnectedness of different parts of the world through common processes of economic, environmental, political, and cultural change. We approach the processes of globalization through a world-systems framework based on ideas about geographic cores, peripheries, and semiperipheries. A world economy has in fact been in existence for several centuries, and it has been reorganized several times. Each time it has been reorganized, there have been major changes not only in world geography but also in the character and fortunes of individual regions. In this book, we look not only at world regions as they exist in modern times but also at how each region has contributed to world history and has been affected by the role that it has played. Recently there has been a pronounced change in both the pace and the nature of globalization. There has been an intensification of global connectedness, a major reorganization of the world economy, and a radical change in our relationships to other people and other places.

- *The unevenness of political and economic development—* We also explicitly recognize the underlying diversity of the world. While there are a range of processes that are likely to be common to most regions—urbanization, industrialization, and population distribution—the way these processes are manifested will vary from region to region and even within regions. In short, there are important variations within places and regions at every scale: For example, social well-being varies and there can be affluent enclaves in poor regions and pockets of poverty in rich regions.

- *The connection between society and nature—*Inherent to the basic geographic concepts of landscape, place, and region are the interactions between people and the natural environment that shape landscapes and give places and regions their distinctive characteristics. In this book, we explore the nature–society and human–environment relationships that assist in our understanding of regional geography. We emphasize that human adaptation to Earth's physical environments has gone far beyond responses to natural constraints to produce significant modifications of environments and landscapes and widespread environmental degradation and pollution as well as global climate change.

- *The links among and between regions*—While the book explores a set of coherent world regions, we also make it clear that regions are not isolated areal units but exist in complex relationships to other regions. The world, in short, is an integrated whole, and the concept of regions allows us to break it up into more manageable units. Yet, it is often the case that some regions have stronger and more long-standing connections to other regions or that some sub-areas of a region—certain key cities or industrial areas—may actually be more connected to outside regions than to their own. This emphasis on the links among and between regions enables us to demonstrate the interdependence of the world and how that interdependence is unevenly produced.

THE GEOGRAPHY OF WORLD REGIONS

There is no standard way of dividing the world into regions. Textbooks, international organizations, and regional studies groups within universities, however, do divide up and make sense of the world in different ways. In this text we have divided the world into ten major regions—Europe; The Russian Federation, Central Asia, and the Transcaucasus; the Middle East and North Africa; Sub-Saharan Africa; the United States and Canada; Latin America; East Asia; Southeast Asia; South Asia; and Australia, New Zealand, and the South Pacific. Although we review the distinctive characteristics of every region at the beginning of each chapter, the changing and sometimes controversial process of defining world regions merits some discussion here.

Early Greek geographers divided their known world into Europe, Africa, and Asia, with the boundaries defined by the Straits of Gibraltar (dividing Africa and Europe), the Red Sea (dividing Africa and Asia), and the Bosporus Strait (dividing Europe and Asia). As Europeans began to explore the world, new regions were associated with major landmasses or continents, with the Americas usually split into North and South America and Australia and Antarctica added as the sixth and seventh continents. These divisions lumped together many different landscapes and cultures (especially in Asia) but served, in the minds of Europeans, to differentiate "us" from "them," and to provide a framework for organizing colonial exploration and administration. The colonial period produced many new nations and boundaries and transformed cultures and landscapes in ways that produced more homogeneous regions. For example, 400 years of Spanish and Portuguese colonization

of the region that stretches from Mexico to Argentina created a region of shared languages, religion, and political institutions that became known as Latin America. British colonization of what now constitutes Sri Lanka, India, Bangladesh, Pakistan, and Nepal interacted with local culture to produce a region frequently known as South Asia. In the Middle East and North Africa, the persistence of Muslim religion and tradition gave these regions an identity that separated them from Asia and from Africa south of the Sahara.

In the 20th century, new configurations of political power and economic alliances produced some reconfigurations of world regions. The most notable was the large block of Asia and eastern Europe associated with the socialist politics of the former Soviet Union centered on Russia, together with eastern European countries ranging from East Germany to Bulgaria.

In response to global conflicts and economic opportunities in the second half of the 20th century, governments and universities established programs and centers that focused on specific world areas and their languages. For example, in the United States, the Department of Education established university centers that focused on apparently coherent regions such as Latin America; the Caribbean; the Pacific; Europe; Africa; the Soviet Union and Eastern Europe; the Middle East; and East, South, and Southeast Asia.

At the beginning of the 21st century, these traditional divisions of the world into regions have been challenged by events, critics, and the latest phases of globalization. When the Soviet bloc disintegrated in 1989, some states reoriented toward western Europe and to the economic alliance of the European Union, whereas others remained closer to Russia or looked eastward to an identity with countries such as Afghanistan as part of central Asia. As we note in the relevant chapters, regionalizations have been criticized for being based on race or religion (for example, the Middle East and Sub-Saharan Africa), for being remnants of colonial thinking (for example, Latin America or Southeast Asia), or for being grounded only in physical proximity or environmental characteristics rather than on cultural or other human commonalities (for example, Australia, New Zealand, and the Pacific islands clustered in Oceania). We will also discuss a number of countries, such as Sudan, Cyprus, or Antarctica, that do not fit easily into the traditional regions or that fit into more than one region. Some scholars and institutions have proposed a dramatic rethinking of world regions. They suggest, for example, that all Islamic or oil-producing countries be treated together, or that countries be grouped according to their level of economic development or integration into the global economy. As another example, the World Bank commonly classifies nations into high-, middle-, and low-income countries, and this book identifies many regions and countries according to their relation to the core or periphery of the world-system.

Our own division of the world tries to take into account some of these changing ideas about world regions without deviating too radically from popular understandings or other texts or course outlines and by trying to create a manageable number and coherent set of chapters. Each chapter includes our rationale for treating the places in the chapter as a distinct region and a review of the limitations and debates about defining each region. In addition, each chapter emphasizes the links of the region under discussion to other regions and to processes of globalization that might be changing the nature and coherence of world regions.

CHAPTER ORGANIZATION

Two of the central challenges to writing a world regional geography text appropriate for the modern world involve balancing an emphasis on globalization and global processes with the traditional and important emphasis on individual places and in striking a balance between broad regional generalizations and overly divisive country-by-country regional descriptions. The internal structure of each of the regional chapters is critically important to achieving this balance. In order to strike such a balance, we divide each regional chapter into five standard categories.

Environment and Society in the Region:
We begin each of the chapters with a concise discussion of the physical and environmental context of the region, ending this section with an explanation of the region's environmental history. Our aim here is to demonstrate the links between people and nature and how the environment is shaped by and shapes the region's inhabitants over time.

The Region in the World-System: Consistent
with our aim to highlight the enduring interdependence of the world's regions, we provide a section that places each of the regions within the larger context of global history and geography.

The Peoples of the Region: In this section we
discuss the people who live in the region and their connections to other people around the globe.

Contemporary Challenges in a Globalizing World: This section outlines the contemporary
role of the region in the global context. This material contrasts to the more historical material emphasized in "The Region in the World-System."

Regional Development: One of our approaches is
to demonstrate the ways in which core, periphery, and semiperiphery are being transformed by globally extensive political and economic processes. To illustrate this point, we end each chapter with a section on regional change that describes how particular subregions within each of the world regions are being transformed. In addition, this section covers exploring and understanding some of the important rapidly growing cities within these subregions.

The organization of the book is pedagogically useful in several ways. First, the conceptual framework of the book is built on a single opening chapter that describes the basics of a regional perspective and introduces the key concepts that are deployed throughout the remaining regional chapters. In addition, this chapter highlights the importance of the globalization approach. The ten regional chapters that follow explore and elaborate the concepts and conceptual framework laid out in Chapter 1. We have also shortened each of the regional chapters and have used a new mapping program that is more accessible for students and instructors.

An important aspect of the book is the distinctive ordering of the chapters. The sequencing of the chapters is a deliberate move to avoid privileging any one region over any other or to cluster the regions according to any economic or political categorization. Rather, because the key conceptual framework of the book is the globalization of the capitalist world-system, we begin with the European region (Chapter 2) because that is the source of contemporary capitalism and many of the impulses for the contemporary world map. Following the initial appearance of this historically critical core region, however, we deliberately intersperse core, semiperipheral, and peripheral regions in order to signal the interdependence of each.

The final chapter provides a coherent summary of the text's main points through an elaboration of the possible futures of the world's regions. This chapter returns students to the conceptual foundations of the book and provides them with a sense of what the future of the globe—and the places and regions within it—might be like.

NEW TO THE THIRD EDITION

The third edition of *World Regions in Global Context* represents a thorough revision. Every part of the book has been examined carefully with the dual goals of keeping topics current and improving the clarity of the text and graphics. We have also shortened the book considerably. Chapters 1 and 2 have been combined and streamlined. In addition, we have dropped the "Core Regions and Distinctive Landscapes" sections from the previous edition and replaced them with more succinct "Regional Development" sections. Each chapter now includes a "Signature Region" feature, which replaces the last edition's "Sense of Place" box feature. We have also expanded upon quite a few topics, including the conflicts and tensions in the Middle East; the growing concern and scientific evidence around global climate change; the increasing political and economic importance of India and China; the implications of the growth of the world population to 6 billion people; the spread of new technology systems; the changes in the European Union and North Korea as a political hot spot; the Southeast Asian tsunami; Millennium Development Goals in Africa; and the Make Poverty History debt relief campaign. Last, the third edition of the book incorporates a comprehensive updating of all the data, maps, and illustrative examples and new striking panoramic photographs in each chapter.

FEATURES

This book takes a decidedly different approach to understanding world regions, and the features we use help to underscore that difference. The book employs a clean and accessible cartography program and three different boxed features (Geography Matters; Signature Regions; and Geographies of Indulgence, Desire, and Addiction), as well as more familiar pedagogical devices such as end-of-chapter review questions and exercises and a listing of the important films, music, and popular literature of for each region.

Geography Matters: This feature examines one of the key concepts of the chapter by providing an extended example of its meaning and implications through both visual illustration and text. The "Geography Matters" feature demonstrates to students that the focus of world regional geography is on real-world problems.

Signature Regions: This feature highlights specific subregions—places within the larger world region—with the intention of providing students with a more nuanced sense of what it is like to live in such a place. The "Signature Region" feature draws students closer to the textures of a specific regional geography.

Geographies of Indulgence, Desire, and Addiction: This feature links people in one world region to people throughout the world through a discussion of the local production and global consumption of one of the region's primary commodities. The "Geographies of Indulgence, Desire, and Addiction" feature helps students to appreciate the links between producers and consumers around the world, as well as between people and the natural world.

INSTRUCTIONAL PACKAGE

In addition to the text itself, the authors and publisher have been pleased to work with a number of talented people to produce an excellent instructional package. This package includes the traditional supplements that students and professors have come to expect from authors and publishers, as well as new kinds of components that utilize electronic media.

For the Professor

- *Instructor Resource Center on DVD* (0-13-225385-2): Everything instructors need where they want it. The Prentice Hall Instructor Resource Center helps make instructors more effective by saving them time and effort. All digital resources can be found in one, well-organized, easy-to-access place. The IRC on DVD includes:
  - JPEGs of all illustrations and photos from the text
  - Pre-authored PowerPoint™ slides, which outline the concepts of each chapter with embedded art and can be used as is for lecture or customized to fit instructors' lecture presentation needs
  - The TestGen software, questions, and answers
  - Electronic files of the *Instructor's Manual* and *Test Item File*
  - Link to the Online Study Guide

- *Transparencies* (0-13-229837-6): Images and illustrations pertaining to the text's core concepts have been selected and enhanced for optimal classroom presentations. All images within the transparency pack are also available

electronically on the *Instructor Resource Center on DVD* (0-13-225385-2).

- *Prentice Hall World Regional Geography Videos on DVD* (0-13-159348-X): This two-DVD set is designed to enhance any world regional geography course. It contains ten full-length video programs covering a wide array of issues affecting people and places in the contemporary world, including international immigration, the HIV/AIDS epidemic, urbanization, homelessness, poverty, and environmental destruction.

  These DVDs are designed to function in computer-based DVD drives in addition to traditional component DVD players. The videos included on these DVDs are offered at the highest quality to allow for full-screen viewing on your computer and projection in large lecture classrooms. Video programs include:

  DVD 1
  - *The Millennium Goals—Dream or Reality?*
  - *Cash Flow Fever*
  - *Sowing Seeds of Hunger*
  - *Yemeni Futures*
  - *Blue Danube?*

  DVD 2
  - *Cheated of Childhood*
  - *The Real Leap Forward*
  - *Slum Futures*
  - *Helping Ourselves*
  - *My Hanoi*
  Average length: 26 minutes

  The *Prentice Hall World Regional Geography Videos on DVD* are available as either a standalone product or at a very substantial discount when packaged with *World Regions in Global Context*. Please see your local Prentice Hall representative for details.

- *Instructor's Manual* (0-13-229804-X): The instructor's manual is intended as a resource for both new and experienced instructors. It includes a variety of lecture outlines, additional source materials, teaching tips, advice about how to integrate visual supplements (including the Web-based resources), and various other ideas for the classroom.

- *Test Item File* (0-13-240249-1): The *Test Item File* provides instructors with a wide variety of test questions for use in their exams.

- *TestGen* (0-13-229836-8): *TestGen* is a computerized test generator that lets instructors view and edit test bank questions, transfer questions to tests, and print the test in a variety of customized formats.

- *Course Management:* Prentice Hall is proud to partner with many of the leading course-management system providers on the market today. These partnerships enable us to provide our testing materials already formatted for easy importation into the powerful course management tools Blackboard and WebCT. Please contact your local Prentice Hall representative for details.

For the Student

- *Online Study Guide:* The online study guide gives students the opportunity to use the Internet to explore topics presented in the book. This Web site contains numerous review exercises (from which students get immediate feedback), exercises to expand students' understanding of world geography, and resources for **further** exploration. This Web site provides an excellent platform from which to start using the Internet for the study of geography. Please visit the site at **http://www.prenhall.com/marston.**

- *Goode's World Atlas* (0-13-612824-6): Prentice Hall and Rand McNally are pleased to announce that Prentice Hall is now distributing *Goode's World Atlas*—the number-one atlas used by college professors—to colleges and universities worldwide. *Goode's World Atlas* is the world's premiere educational atlas, and for good reason. It features nearly 250 pages of maps, from definitive physical and political maps to important thematic maps that illustrate the spatial aspects of many important topics. The current 21st edition of the atlas features fully updated content and has been vetted by an academic board comprising some of the most trusted names in geography today. Prentice Hall offers the atlas at a dramatically reduced price with *World Regions in Global Context.* See your local Prentice Hall representative for details.

- *Mapping Workbook and Study Guide* (0-13-229805-8): The *Mapping Workbook and Study Guide* features political and physical outline maps for each chapter, based on the maps in the text, ready for student use in identification exercises. Additionally, it helps students to identify important concepts from the text followed by vocabulary and review exercises. The *Mapping Workbook* can be packaged with the text at no extra charge.

CONCLUSION

One important outcome of recent reforms in post-secondary education has been the inclusion of geography as a core subject in the Goals 2000: Educate America Act (Public Law 103-227). Another was the publication of a set of national geography standards for K–12 education (*Geography for Life,* published by National Geographic Research and Education for the American Geographical Society, the Association of American Geographers, the National Council for Geographic Education, and the National Geographic Society).

More broadly, this book is the product of conversations among the authors, colleagues, and students about how best to teach a course on world regional geography. In preparing the text, we have tried to help students make sense of the world by connecting our conceptual materials to the most compelling current events. We have also been careful to represent the best ideas and concepts the discipline of geography has to offer by mixing cutting-edge and innovative theories and concepts with more classical and proven approaches and tools. Finally, we have also tried to make it clear that no textbook is the product of its authors alone but is instead built from the intellectual and pedagogical toils and triumphs of thousands of colleagues around the world. Our aim has been to show how a geographical imagination is important, how it can lead to a greater understanding of the world and its constituent places and regions, and how it has practical relevance in our everyday and professional lives.

ACKNOWLEDGMENTS

We are indebted to many people for their assistance, advice, and constructive criticism in the course of preparing this book. Among those who provided comments on various drafts of this book are the following professors:

Donald Albert, *Sam Houston State University*
Brad Baltensperger, *Michigan Technological University*
Max Beavers, *University of Northern Colorado*
Richard Benfield, *Central Connecticut State University*
William H. Berentsen, *University of Connecticut*
Keshav Bhattarai, *Central Missouri State University*
Warren R. Bland, *California State University, Northridge*
Brian W. Blouet, *College of William and Mary*
Jean Ann Bowman, *Texas A & M University*
John Christopher Brown, *University of Kansas*
Stanley D. Brunn, *University of Kentucky*
Michelle Calvarese, *California State University, Fresno*
Craig Campbell, *Youngstown State University*
David B. Cole, *University of Northern Colorado*
Jose A. da Cruz, *Ozarks Technical Community College*
Tina Delahunty, *Texas Tech University*
Vincent Del Casino, *California State University, Long Beach*
Cary W. de Wit, *University of Alaska, Fairbanks*
Lorraine Dowler, *Pennsylvania State University*
Ronald Foresta, *University of Tennessee*
Gary Gaile, *University of Colorado*
Roberto Garza, *University of Houston*
Jay Gatrell, *Indiana State University*
Mark Giordano, *Oregon State University*
Devon A. Hansen, *University of North Dakota*
Julie E. Harris, *Harding University*
Russell Ivy, *Florida Atlantic University*
Kris Jones, *Saddleback College*
Lawrence M. Knopp, *University of Minnesota, Duluth*
Debbie Kreitzer, *Western Kentucky University*
Robert C. Larson, *Indiana State University*
Alan A. Lew, *Northern Arizona University*
John Liverman
Max Lu, *Kansas State University*
Donald Lyons, *University of North Texas*
Taylor Mack, *Mississippi State University*
Chris Mayda, *Eastern Michigan University*
Eugene McCann, *Simon Fraser University*
Tom L. McKnight, *University of California, Los Angeles*
M. David Meyer, *Central Michigan University*

Sherry D. Moorea-Oakes, *University of Colorado, Denver*
Barry Donald Mowell, *Broward Community College*
Tim Oakes, *University of Colorado*
Nancy Obermeyer, *Indiana State University*
J. Henry Owusu, *University of Northern Iowa*
Rosann Poltrone, *Arapahoe Community College*
Jeffrey E. Popke, *East Carolina University*
Henry O. Robertson, *Louisiana State University, Alexandria*
Yda Schreuder, *University of Delaware*
Anna Secor, *University of Kentucky*
Daniel Selwa, *Coastal Carolina University*
Joseph Spinelli, *Bowling Green State University*
Liem Tran, *Florida Atlantic University*
Samuel Wallace, *West Chester University*
Gerald R. Webster, *University of Alabama*
Mark Welford, *Georgia Southern University*
Anibal Yanez-Chavez, *California State University, San Marcos*

Special thanks go to our editorial team at Prentice Hall, Dan Kaveney, Jeff Howard, and Jessica Neumann; to our developmental editor, Barbara Muller, and our copyeditor, Roberta

Dempsey; to Jerry Marshall for assisting with photo research; to art director Jon Boylan for his creative work with the design of the text; and to our production editor, Tim Flem. We would also like to thank our excellent research assistants, Sara Smith and Mary Thornbush; Elizabeth Cordova, receptionist in the University of Arizona Geography and Regional Development Department; and Liz Roberson, assistant to the dean, College of Architecture and Urban Studies, Virginia Tech. Finally, a number of colleagues gave generously of their time and expertise in guiding our thoughts, making valuable suggestions, and providing materials: Simon Batterbury, University of Melbourne; Jessie Clark, University of Arizona; Kenneth Jacobson, Anti-Defamation League; John Paul Jones III, University of Arizona; David Liverman, Memorial University, Newfoundland; Robert Merideth; David Preston; Paul Robbins, University of Arizona, and Charles Smith, University of Arizona.

Sallie A. Marston
Paul L. Knox
Diana M. Liverman

ABOUT THE AUTHORS

SALLIE A. MARSTON

Sallie Marston received her Ph.D. in Geography from the University of Colorado, Boulder. She has been a faculty member at the University of Arizona since 1986. Her teaching focuses on the historical, social, and cultural aspects of U.S. political geography, with particular emphasis on race, class, gender, and ethnicity issues. She received the College of Social and Behavioral Sciences Outstanding Teaching Award in 1989. She is the author of numerous journal articles and book chapters and serves on the editorial board of several scientific journals. In 1994/1995 she served as interim director of Women's Studies and the Southwest Institute for Research on Women. She is currently a professor in the Department of Geography and Regional Development at the University of Arizona.

PAUL L. KNOX

Paul Knox received his Ph.D. in Geography from the University of Sheffield, England. After teaching in the United Kingdom for several years, he moved to the United States to take a position as professor of urban affairs and planning at Virginia Tech. His teaching centers on urban and regional development, with an emphasis on comparative study. He has written several books on aspects of economic geography, social geography, and urbanization. He serves on the editorial board of several scientific journals and is co-editor on a series of books on world cities. In 1996 he was appointed to the position of University Distinguished Professor at Virginia Tech, where he currently serves as Senior Fellow for International Advancement and International Director of the Metropolitan Institute.

DIANA M. LIVERMAN

Diana Liverman received her Ph.D. in Geography from the University of California, Los Angeles, and also studied at the University of Toronto, Canada, and University College London, England. Born in Accra, Ghana, she is currently the director of Oxford University's Environmental Change Institute, where she also holds Oxford University's first established Chair of Environmental Science in the School of Geography. Prior to this, she taught geography at the University of Arizona, Penn State, and the University of Wisconsin. Her teaching focuses on global environmental issues and on Latin America. She has served on several national and international advisory committees dealing with environmental issues and climate change and has written recent journal articles and book chapters on such topics as natural disasters, climate change, and environmental policy.

A World of Regions

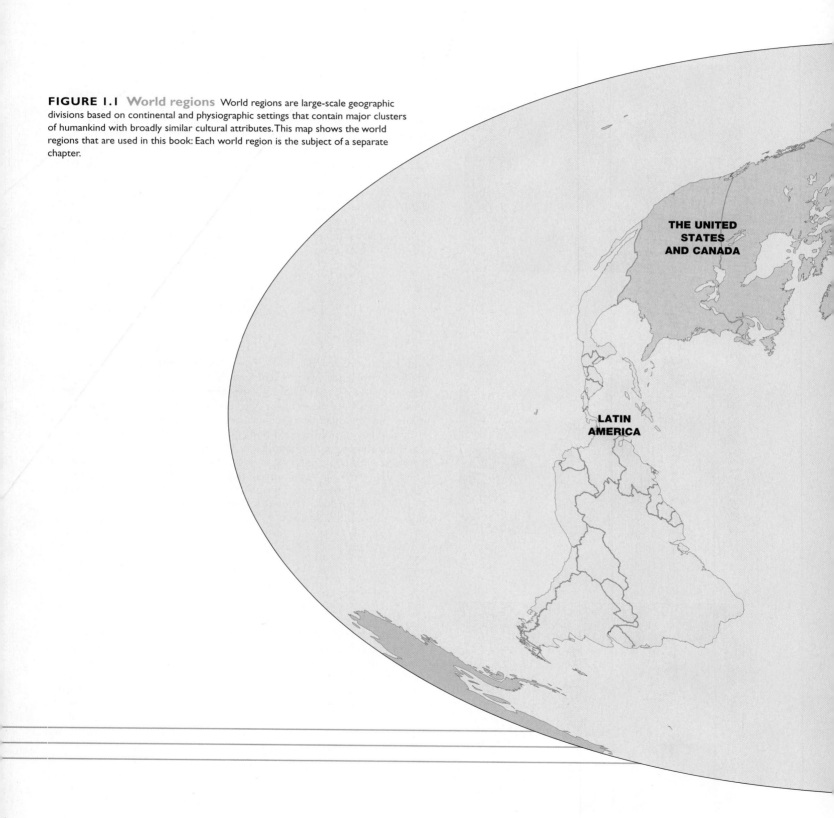

FIGURE 1.1 **World regions** World regions are large-scale geographic divisions based on continental and physiographic settings that contain major clusters of humankind with broadly similar cultural attributes. This map shows the world regions that are used in this book: Each world region is the subject of a separate chapter.

THE UNITED
STATES
AND CANADA

LATIN
AMERICA

THE RUSSIAN FEDERATION,
CENTRAL ASIA, AND
THE TRANSCAUCASUS

EAST ASIA

SOUTHEAST
ASIA

SOUTH ASIA

AUSTRALIA,
NEW ZEALAND, AND
THE SOUTH PACIFIC

EUROPE

MIDDLE EAST
AND NORTH AFRICA

SUB-SAHARAN
AFRICA

Will instantaneous global telecommunications, satellite television, and the Internet soon overthrow all but the last vestiges of geographic differentiation in human affairs? Will companies no longer need headquarters because they will be able to locate their activities almost anywhere in the world? Will workers labor as effectively from home, car, or beach as they could in the offices that need no longer exist? Will events halfway across the world be seen, heard, and felt with the same immediacy as events across town? Will national differences and regional cultures dissolve, as a global marketplace brings a uniform dispersion of people, tastes, and ideas?

The answer to such questions is an unequivocal "no." Even in the information age, geography still matters and may well become more important than ever. Places and regions will undoubtedly change as a result of the new global context of the information age. But geography will still matter because of transport costs, differences in resource endowments and access to capital, fundamental principles of spatial organization, people's territorial impulses, the resilience of local cultures, and the legacy of the past.

Today, major world regions (**Figure 1.1**) are increasingly dependent on one another, and it is important to know something about regional geography and to understand how places and regions affect, and are affected by, one another. Regional geography is about understanding the variety and distinctiveness of places and regions, without losing sight of the interdependence among them. Geographers learn about the world by finding out where things are and why they are there and by analyzing the spatial patterns and distributions that underpin regional differentiation and regional change. This chapter will introduce the basic tools and fundamental concepts that enable geographers to study the world in this way, and it will describe the conceptual framework that informs each of the subsequent chapters.

THE POWER OF GEOGRAPHY

As a subject of scientific observation and study, geography has made important contributions to the understanding of the world and to its development. And as the world becomes increasingly connected, geography continues to contribute to the understanding of a world that is more complex and fast-changing than ever before. With basic foundational knowledge of world regional geography, it is possible not only to appreciate the diversity and variety of the world's peoples and places but also to be aware of their relationships to one another and to be able to make positive contributions to regional, national, and global development.

The study of geography involves the study of Earth as created by natural forces and as modified by human action—an enormous amount of subject matter. Physical geography deals with Earth's natural processes and their outcomes. It is concerned with climate, weather patterns, landforms, soil formation, and plant and animal ecology. Human geography deals with the spatial organization of human activity and with people's relationships with their environments. This focus necessarily involves looking at physical environments insofar as they influence, and are influenced by, human activity. The result is that the study of human geography must cover a wide variety of phenomena. These phenomena include, for example, agricultural production and food security, population change, the ecology of human diseases, resource management, environmental pollution, regional planning, and the symbolism of places and landscapes.

Regional geography combines elements of both physical and human geography and is concerned with the way that unique combinations of environmental and human factors produce territories with distinctive landscapes and cultural attributes. Geographers apply the concept of **region** to large-sized territories (such as counties, provinces, and countries, or large sections of countries, such as the U.S. Midwest) that encompass many **places**, all or most of which share a set of attributes that differ from the attributes of places that make up a different region. What is distinctive about the study of regional geography is not so much the phenomena that are studied as the way they are approached. The contribution of regional geography is to reveal how natural, social, economic, political, and cultural phenomena come together to produce distinctive geographic settings.

A knowledge of regional geography is crucial to understanding international development. As the World Bank's *2006 Report* points out, national statistics fail to capture some of the most fundamental aspects of development, especially the inequities that exist both within and between regions and that make it impossible for all citizens to contribute equally to global development.[1] In the United States, a decade of debate in the 1990s about geography education resulted in a widespread acceptance that being literate in geography is essential in equipping citizens to earn a decent living, to enjoy the richness of life, and to participate responsibly in local, national, and international affairs. The importance of geography as a subject of study has in fact become more widely recognized in recent years as people everywhere have struggled to understand a world that is increasingly characterized by instant global communications, unfamiliar international relationships, international terrorism, and growing evidence of environmental degradation. Compared to just a decade ago, many more schools now require courses in geography, and the Educational Testing Service's College Board has added the subject to its Advanced Placement program. Meanwhile, many employers have come to realize the value of employees with expertise in geographic analysis and an understanding of the uniqueness, influence, and interdependence of places.

A WORLD OF REGIONS

Regions are dynamic, with changing properties and fluid boundaries that are the product of the interplay of a wide variety of environmental and human factors. This dynamism and complexity is what makes travel so fascinating for many people. It is also what makes regions so influential in shaping people's lives.

One of the most important tenets of regional geography is that regions are not just distinctive outcomes of geographic processes; they are part of the processes themselves. They are created by people responding to the opportunities and constraints presented by their environments. As people live and work in particular geographic settings, they gradually impose themselves on their environments, modifying and adjusting the environment to meet their needs and express their values. At the same time, people gradually accommodate to both their physical environments and to the people around them. There is thus a continuous two-way process, in which people create and modify regions while at the same time being influenced by the settings in which they live and work. Processes of geographic change are constantly modifying and reshaping regions, and the region's inhabitants are constantly coping with change (**Figure 1.2**). It is often useful to think of regions as representing the cumulative imprint of successive periods of change. For example, present-day Turkey embodies elements of Roman, medieval, Arabic, Persian, Ottoman, and modern European influences, among others. Following this approach, geographers look for superimposed layers of development. We show how some patterns and relationships last, while others are modified or obliterated. We show how different regions bear the imprint of different kinds of change, perhaps in different sequences and with different outcomes.

The Regional Approach

At the heart of geographers' concern with understanding how combinations of environmental and human factors produce regions with distinctive landscapes and cultural attributes is the belief that this "regional approach" is one of the best ways of organizing knowledge about the world. This, as with other branches of geography, depends on a working knowledge of one of geographers' basic tools:

FIGURE 1.2 Namdaemun gate and downtown Seoul, South Korea Old and new exist side by side in this landscape. The structure in the foreground was built in the 14th century and is currently the oldest wooden structure in the city. It is the entryway to a market that has been operating in Seoul for centuries. The gate is surrounded by an eight-lane highway; modern skyscrapers form the background.

[1]World Bank, *World Development Report*, Washington, DC: The World Bank, 2006.

maps (see Appendix 1). There are, however, different methods of regional analysis and different ways of identifying and defining regions. At the same time, place making and regional differentiation carry over to affect landscapes and people's **sense of place**, which are the feelings evoked as a result of the experiences and memories that people associate with a place.

Regionalization is the geographer's classification of individual places or areal units; it is the geographer's equivalent of scientific classification. The purpose of regionalization is to identify "regions" of one kind or another. There are several ways in which individual areal units can be assigned to classes (regions). One is that of *logical division*, or "classification from above." This involves partitioning a universal set of areal units into successively larger numbers of classes, using more specific criteria at every stage. Thus a world regional classification of national states might be achieved by first differentiating between rich and poor countries, then dividing both rich and poor countries into those countries that have a trade surplus and those that have a deficit, and so on. A second way in which individual areal units can be assigned to classes (regions) is that of *grouping*, or "classification from below." This involves searching for regularities or significant relationships among areal units and grouping them together in successively smaller numbers of classes, using a broader measure of similarity at each stage.

An implicit assumption in any type of classification of areal units into regions is that each unit is homogeneous with respect to the attribute or attributes under consideration. Where this assumption holds true, the result of regional classification is a set of formal regions. **Formal regions** are groups of areal units that have a high degree of homogeneity in terms of particular distinguishing features (such as religious adherence or household income). Few phenomena, however, exhibit such homogeneity over large areal units. For this reason, geographers also recognize **functional regions** (sometimes referred to as *nodal regions*)—regions that are defined and classified by patterns of spatial interaction or spatial organization. Functional regions are those within which, while there may be some variability in certain attributes (again, for example, religion and income), there is an overall coherence to the structure and dynamics of economic, political, and social organization. The concept of functional regions allows us to recognize that the coherence and distinctive characteristics of a region are often stronger in some places than in others. This point is illustrated by geographer Donald Meinig's *core-domain-sphere* model, which he set out in his classic essay on the Mormon region of the United States.[2] According to this model, in the core of a region, the region's distinctive attributes are very clear; in the domain, they are dominant, but not to the point of exclusivity; in the sphere, they are present but not dominant (**Figure 1.3**).

Geography and Interdependence

Different aspects of regional differentiation are best understood, and most effectively analyzed, at different spatial levels. At the same time, these different aspects are interrelated and interdependent, so that geographers have to be able to relate things on one level to things on another.

It is useful to think of these scales, or levels, as the site where real-world processes are played out—not simply as different levels of abstraction, or as convenient devices for zooming in and out from the global context to the detail of local settings. At any particular

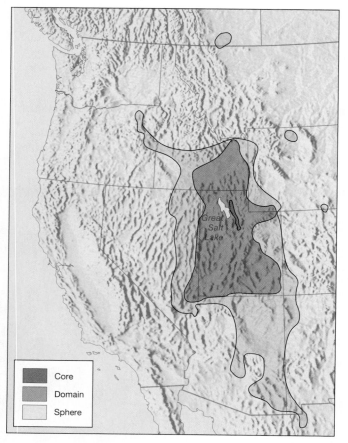

FIGURE 1.3 The Mormon culture region Cultural attributes often have no single, clear-cut boundary, but rather gradually shade from one region to another. Geographer Donald Meinig's work on the Mormon culture region of the United States identified a "core" region, which exhibits all the attributes of Mormon culture; a "domain," where not all these attributes may be present (or may be less intense); and a "sphere," where some attributes of Mormon culture are present but are often a minority within the attributes of another culture region. (*Source:* D. Meinig, "The Mormon Culture Region: Strategies and Patterns in the Geography of the American West," *Annals of the Association of American Geographers,* 55[1965], pp. 191–220.)

Great Salt Lake

Core
Domain
Sphere

[2]D. Meinig, "The Mormon Culture Region: Strategies and Patterns in the Geography of the American West," *Annals of the Association of American Geographers,* 55(1965), pp. 191–220.

moment we can thus identify a sequence of specific levels that represent significant confluences of geographic processes. In today's world, the largest one is represented by international regions, or world regions, extensive but relatively homogeneous territories with distinctive economic, cultural, and demographic characteristics (Figure 1.4). **World regions** are extensive geographic divisions based on continental and physiographic settings that contain major clusters of humankind with broadly similar cultural attributes. Examples would be Europe, Latin America, and South Asia, as shown in Figure 1.1. These regions are constructed, unraveled, and reconstructed as the realities of natural resources and technologies form a framework of opportunities and constraints to which particular cultures and societies respond.

Superimposed on these regions, sometimes with only an approximate fit, are the formal, *de jure* territories of national states (*de jure* simply means "legally recognized"). **States** are independent political units with boundaries that are internationally recognized by other states. A **nation** is a group of people often sharing common elements of culture such as religion or language, a history, or a political identity. Because of the inherent power of national governments, especially in relation to the flows of the goods, money, and information that underpin "reality," national states represent a geographic scale that is often very significant. Once their boundaries are set, principles of national sovereignty mean that these boundaries tend increasingly to become regarded by their inhabitants as somehow natural or immutable. National political boundaries are not fixed and unchanging, however. When economic circumstances change, national states may feel the need to adjust their boundaries or seek other means of accommodating economic reality, such as joining supranational organizations.

Supranational organizations are collections of individual states with a common goal that may be economic and/or political in nature and that diminishes, to some extent, individual state sovereignty in favor of the group interests of the membership. Examples of supranational organizations include the European Union (EU), the North American Free Trade Agreement (NAFTA), and the Association of South East Asian Nations (ASEAN).

The realm of experience, for most people, is encompassed at the level of human settlements—how people's lives are organized through their work, consumption, and recreation. It is also roughly coincident with *de jure* territories: local municipalities that provide the framework for public administration and the provision of certain goods and services (public transport, education, public housing, recreational amenities, and so forth).

Within the realm of experience, there are other significant sites. Of these, community is the most important but also the most difficult to pin down. It is the site of social interaction—of personal relationships and daily routine that depends a great deal on the economic, social, and cultural attributes of local populations. Much more sharply defined is the home, which is an important geographic site insofar as it constitutes the physical setting for the structure and dynamics of family and household. It also reflects, in its own spatial organization, the differential status accorded to men and women and to the young and the elderly.

Perhaps the most important conclusion we can draw from this discussion is that, while certain phenomena can be identified and understood best at specific spatial scales, regional geographies are very fluid phenomena, constantly being constructed, reinforced, undermined, and rebuilt. Similarly, although certain levels represent materializations of powerful real-world processes, the real world has to be understood, ultimately, as the product of interdependent phenomena among different levels. It follows that every world region should be seen in its diversity, comprising metropolitan cores and rural peripheries, each of which is part of a broader framework of interdependent places and regions within the global economy.

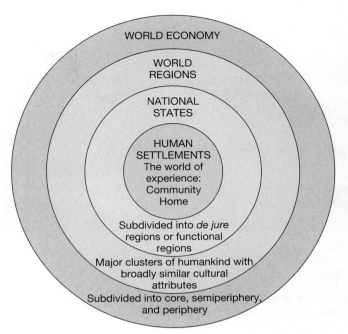

FIGURE 1.4 Spatial levels Geographic phenomena may be identified, analyzed, and understood at many levels. This diagram shows some of the principal ones that are commonly the focus of geographic research.

Boundaries and Frontiers

Boundaries allow claims on space to be defined and enforced and allow conflict and competition to be managed and channeled. The creation of boundaries is, therefore, a significant element in region building and place making. The key point is that, once established, *formal boundaries tend to reinforce regional differentiation.* This is partly because of the outcomes of the operation of different sets of rules, both formal and informal, that apply within different regions and territories. It is also partly because boundaries often restrict contact between people and so foster the development of stereotypes of "others." This restricted contact, in turn, reinforces the role of boundaries in regulating and controlling conflict and competition between territorial groups.

FIGURE 1.5 Israeli security fence Work began in 2002 on the first 110-kilometer stretch of a 350-kilometer-long, $250 million security fence with cameras, razor wire, and electronic sensors designed to protect Jewish settlers in the West Bank and to reduce the threat of Palestinian terrorism to Israel's security within the "Green Line" (Israel proper). The World Court declared the wall a violation of international law.

Boundaries   Boundaries can be established in many different ways, however, and with differing degrees of permeability. At one extreme are informal, implied boundaries that are set by markers and symbols but never delineated on maps or set down in legal documents. Good examples are the "turf" of a city gang, the "territory" of a salesperson, and the range of a pastoral tribe. At the other extreme are formal boundaries established in international law, marked on maps, demarcated on the ground, fortified, and aggressively defended—against the movement not only of people but also of goods, money, and even ideas. One striking example of this sort of boundary is the one between North and South Korea; another is the security fence erected by the Israeli government around Palestinian settlements in the West Bank (**Figure 1.5**). In between are formal boundaries that have some degree of permeability. The boundaries between the states of the European Union, for example, have become quite permeable, since people and goods from member states can now move freely between them, with no customs or passport controls.

Frontier Regions   Frontier regions occur where boundaries are very weakly developed or where population densities are especially low. They involve zones of under-developed human settlement, areas that are distinctive for their marginality rather than for their belonging. In the 19th century, for example, some vast frontier regions still existed, such as Australia, the American West, the Canadian North, and Sub-Saharan Africa—major geographic realms that had not yet been conquered, understood, and settled by the states claiming jurisdiction over them (though there were, of course, indigenous groups with no apparatus of formal state boundaries). All of these frontier regions are now formally occupied through individual land ownership or local and national governmental jurisdiction. Only Antarctica, virtually unsettled, exists today as a frontier region in this sense.

FIGURE 1.6 Basque region This area of France and Spain contains a large number of people with a strong sense of identity based on Basque culture and history; this culture constitutes a persistent movement in favor of political autonomy from the French and Spanish states.

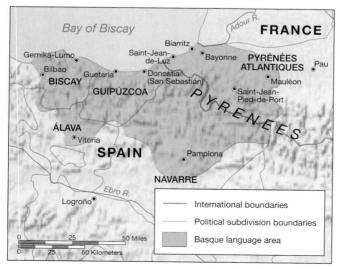

Regionalism and Sectionalism

Regionalism often involves ethnic groups whose aims include autonomy from a national state and development of their own political power. A good example is Basque regionalism, which has roots in the period at the turn of the 19th century. The Basque people of northeastern Spain and the southern part of Aquitaine in southwestern France (**Figure 1.6**) feared that cultural forces accompanying industrialization would undermine their traditions. To counter this trend, the Basque provinces of Spain and France sought autonomy from those states for most of the 20th century. Since the 1950s, agitation for political independence has occurred through terrorist acts—especially for the Basques in Spain. For more than 25 years, the French, Spanish, and more recently the Basque regional police have attempted to undermine the Basque Homeland and Freedom movement through arrests and imprisonments. Not even the Spanish move to parliamentary democracy and the granting of autonomy to the Basque provinces, however, has been able to slake the thirst for self-determination among the Basques in Spain. Elections in summer 2006 in Catalonia (a semiautonomous region in Spain) point to the possibility of increasing political independence from Spain for them as well as the Basques. Meanwhile, on the French side of the Pyrenees, although a Basque separatist movement does exist, it is neither as violent nor as active as the movement in Spain.

In certain cases, enclaves of ethnic minorities are claimed by the government of a country other than the one in which they reside. Such is the case, for example, of Serbian enclaves in Croatia, claimed by nationalist Serbs. The assertion by the government of a country that a minority living outside its formal borders belongs to it historically and culturally is known as **irredentism**. In some circumstances, as with Serbia's claims on Serbian enclaves in Croatia in the early 1990s, irredentism can lead to war.

Not to be confused with regionalism or irredentism is **sectionalism**, an extreme devotion to regional interests and customs. Sectionalism has been identified as an overarching explanation for the U.S. Civil War. It was an attachment to the institution of slavery and the political and economic way of life that slavery enabled that prompted the southern states to secede from the Union. The Civil War was fought to ensure that sectional interests would not take priority over the unity of the whole—that is, that states' rights would not undermine the power of the federal government. Although the Civil War was waged around the real issue of permitting or prohibiting slavery, it was also fought at another level, a level that dealt with issues of the power of the state. The election of Abraham Lincoln to the presidency in 1860 reflected the sectionalism that dominated the country: He received no support from slave states.

PLACES AND REGIONS IN AN INTERDEPENDENT WORLD

Today, in a world experiencing rapid changes in economic, cultural, and political life, geographic knowledge is especially useful. At a time when our fortunes and our ideas are increasingly bound up with those of other peoples in other places, the study of geography provides an understanding of the crucial interdependencies that underpin the lives of everyone on the planet. A recurring theme in this book is the interdependence of people, places, and regions. A key issue for regional geographers is to recognize these interdependencies and broad geographic patterns without losing sight of the individuality and uniqueness of specific places and regions.

Globalization

Globalization involves the increasing interconnectedness of different parts of the world through common processes of economic, environmental, political, and cultural change. A world economy has been in existence for several centuries, and with it has developed a comprehensive framework of sovereign national states and an international system of production and exchange. This system has been reorganized several times. Each time, there have been major changes, not only in world geography but also in the character and fortunes of individual regions.

Recently there has been a pronounced change in both the pace and the nature of globalization. New technologies, corporate strategies, and institutional frameworks have all combined to create a dynamic new framework for real-world geographies. New information technologies have helped create a frenetic international financial system, while transnational corporations are now able to transfer their production activities from one region of the world to another in response to changing market conditions. (The investments and activities of a **transnational corporation, or TNC,** span international boundaries, with subsidiary companies, factories, offices, or facilities in

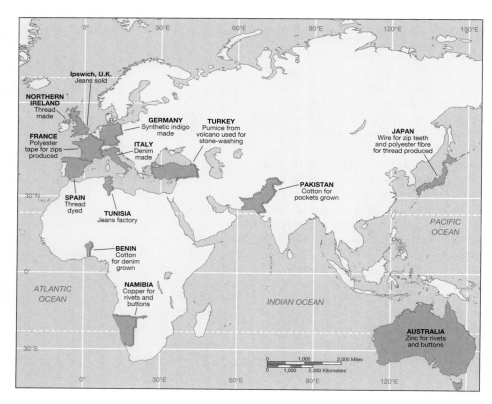

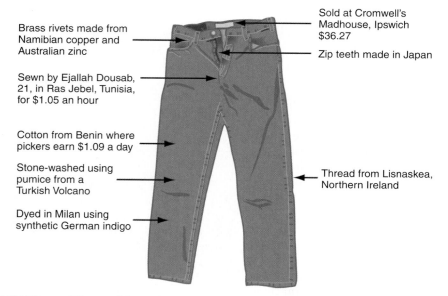

Brass rivets made from
Namibian copper and
Australian zinc

Sewn by Ejallah Dousab,
21, in Ras Jebel, Tunisia,
for $1.05 an hour

Cotton from Benin where
pickers earn $1.09 a day

Stone-washed using
pumice from a
Turkish Volcano

Dyed in Milan using
synthetic German indigo

Sold at Cromwell's
Madhouse, Ipswich
$36.27

Zip teeth made in Japan

Thread from Lisnaskea,
Northern Ireland

FIGURE 1.7 The making of a pair of Lee Cooper jeans The map shows the locations from which the various components of the jeans come. (*Source:* A. Hughes and S. Reimer [eds.], *Geographies of Commodity Chains.* New York: Routledge, 2004.)

several countries.) This locational flexibility has meant that there is now a high degree of functional integration between economic activities that are increasingly dispersed, so that products, markets, and organizations are both spread and linked across the globe. The foundation of the contemporary world economy is constituted through myriad commodity chains that crisscross global space. **Commodity chains** are networks of labor and production processes that originate in the extraction or production of raw materials and end with the delivery and consumption of a finished commodity. These networks often span countries and continents, linking the production and supply of raw materials, the processing of raw materials, the production of components, the assembly of finished products, and the distribution of finished products into vast global assembly lines (**Figure 1.7**).

This new framework for economic geography has already left its mark on the world's economic landscapes. It has also meant that the lives of people in different parts of the world have become increasingly intertwined. Some workers in industrialized countries are fearful of losing their jobs because of cheap exports from lower-cost producers. Others worry about companies relocating abroad in search of low wages and lax labor and environmental laws. In their attempts to adjust to this new situation, governments have sought new ways of dealing with the consequences of globalization, including new international political and economic alliances.

Global Stratification The interdependence associated with globalization operates in a multitude of ways. In many cases, interdependence is seemingly very unequal in nature—as, for example, in the case of a transnational firm based in one country taking advantage of low-cost labor in another. In some cases, interdependence can be seen to be to mutual advantage—as, for example, in the case of countries that share the costs and responsibilities of trans-border resource management. In almost every case, the outcomes of the increased geographic interdependence associated with globalization are very much open to interpretation. Who is advantaged and who is marginalized depends very much on one's perspective and the geographic scale.

In addition, there are very different interpretations of the overall process of globalization. The positive interpretation suggests that open markets and free trade and investment across global markets allow more and more people to share in the prosperity of a growing world economy. Economic and political interdependence, meanwhile, creates shared interests that help prevent conflict and foster support for common values. According to this view, democracy and human rights will spread to billions of people in the wake of neoliberal policies that promote open markets and free trade. **Neoliberal policies** are economic policies that are predicated on a minimalist role for the state, assuming the desirability of free markets as the ideal condition not only for economic organization, but also for political and social life.

The negative interpretation of globalization sees neoliberal policies as the agenda of wealthy countries and transnational corporations. According to this interpretation, economic interdependence involves intrinsically uneven relationships between places and regions, with the inevitable result being an intensification of economic inequality at every scale. The spread of common values is, effectively, Westernization. As such, globalization is seen by many to undermine the integrity of other cultures and is therefore repressive, exploitative, and harmful to most people in many places.

Globalization is also seen to have effects on population in terms of distribution, movement, and growth or decline. It is important to understand these effects in order to appreciate the potential for population change because of its impacts on a wide range of things from natural resource needs to cultural conflict.

Globalization and Population Change

As the world population density map demonstrates (**Figure 1.8**), some areas of the world are very heavily inhabited, others only sparsely. Almost all of the world's inhabitants live on 10 percent of the world's land. Most live near the edges of land masses—near the oceans or seas or along rivers with easy access to a navigable waterway. Approximately 90 percent live north of the equator, where the largest proportion of the total land area (63 percent) is located. Finally, most of the world's population live in temperate, low-lying areas with fertile soils.

In mid-2000 the world contained just over 6 billion people. The population division of the United Nations Department of Social and Economic Affairs projects that the world's population will increase by 1.2 percent annually to mid-century. This means that by the year 2050, the world is projected to contain nearly 9.3 billion people.

FIGURE 1.8 Population distribution As this map shows, the world's population is not evenly distributed across the globe. Such maps are useful in understanding the relationship between population distributions and the national contexts in which they occur.

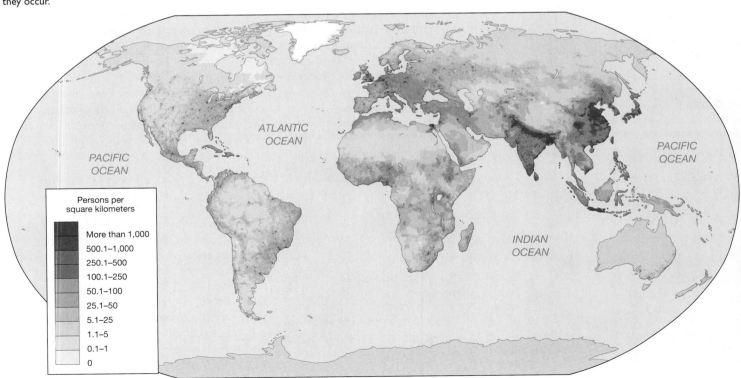

The distribution of this projected population growth is noteworthy. Over the next half-century, population growth is predicted to occur overwhelmingly in regions least able to support it. Just six countries will account for half the increase in the world's population: Bangladesh, China, India, Indonesia, Nigeria, and Pakistan. Meanwhile, Europe and North America will experience very low and in some cases zero population growth.

The history of demographic change in industrialized countries has prompted some analysts to suggest that many of the economic, political, social, and technological transformations associated with industrialization and urbanization lead to a demographic transition. The **demographic transition** is a model of population change when high birth and death rates are replaced by low birth and death rates. Once a society has moved from a preindustrial economic base to an industrial one, population growth slows. According to the demographic transition model, the slowing of population growth is attributable to improved economic production and higher standards of living brought about by changes in medicine, education, and sanitation.

As **Figure 1.9** illustrates, the high birth and death rates of the preindustrial phase (Phase 1) are replaced by the low birth and death rates of the industrial phase (Phase 4) only after passing through the critical transitional phase (Phase 2) and then more moderate rates (Phase 3) of natural increase and growth. The transitional phase of rapid growth is the direct result of early and steep declines in mortality while fertility remains at high, preindustrial levels.

The model suggests that countries inevitably will be stalled for a while in the transitional high-growth phase, which has been called a "demographic trap." The reasoning for this is that, while new and more effective methods for fighting infectious diseases have been advanced, social attitudes about the desirability of large families have only recently begun to change in response to lower mortality rates. It should be emphasized, though, that the demographic transition model is based on the actual experience of developed countries and is thought by many experts to be less useful in explaining the demographic trends affecting less-developed countries and regions, whose entire development experience is quite different from that of industrialized countries.

Policymakers now also recognize that a close relationship exists between women's status and fertility. Women who have access to education and employment tend to have fewer children because they have less of a need for the economic security and social recognition that children are thought to provide. In Botswana, for instance, women with no formal education have, on average, 5.9 children, while those with four to six years of school have just 3.1 children. In Senegal, women with no education give birth to an average of 7 children. In contrast, the average number of children born to a Senegalese woman with ten years of education drops to 3.6. The numbers are comparable for Asia and South America. Success at damping population growth in less-developed countries appears to be very much tied to enhancing the possibility for a good quality of life and to empowering people, especially women, to make informed choices.

Globalization and Cultural Change

Anyone who has ever traveled between major world cities—or, for that matter, anyone who has been attentive to the backdrops of movies, television news stories, and magazine photojournalism—will have noticed the many familiar aspects of contemporary life in settings that, until recently, were thought of as being quite different from one another. Airports, offices, and international hotels have become notoriously alike, and their similarities of architecture

FIGURE 1.9 Demographic transition This model of economic development is based on the idea of successive stages of growth and change. Each stage is seen as leading to the next, though different regions or countries may require different periods of time to make the transition from one stage to the next.

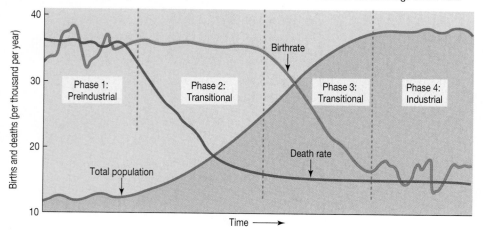

and interior design have become reinforced by near-universal dress codes of the people who frequent them. The business suit, especially for males, has become the norm for office workers throughout much of the world. Meanwhile, jeans, t-shirts, and sneakers have become the universal attire for both young people and those in lower-wage jobs. The same automobiles can be seen on the streets of cities throughout the world (though sometimes they are given different names by their manufacturers); the same popular music is played on local radio stations; the same movies shown in local theaters; and the same brand names show up in stores and restaurants.

These commonalities provide a sense of familiarity among the inhabitants of the more-developed world. From the point of view of cultural nationalism, the "lowest common denominator" of this familiarity is often seen as the culture of fast food and popular entertainment that emanates from the United States. Popular commentators have observed that cultures around the world are being Americanized, or "McDonaldized," which represents the beginnings of a single global culture that will be based on material consumption, with the English language as its medium.

However, neither the widespread consumption of U.S. and U.S.-style products, nor the increasing familiarity of people around the world with global media and international brand names, adds up to the emergence of a single global culture (where **culture** is understood to be a shared set of meanings that are lived through the symbolic and material practices of everyday life) (**Figure 1.10**). Rather, what is happening is that processes of globalization are exposing Earth's inhabitants to a common set of products, symbols, myths, memories, events, cult figures, landscapes, and traditions. People living in Tokyo or Tucson, Turin or Timbuktu, may be perfectly familiar with these commonalities without necessarily using or responding to them in uniform ways.

It is equally important to recognize that cultural flows take place in all directions, not just outward from the United States. Think, for example, of European fashions in U.S. stores; of Chinese, Indian, Italian, Mexican, and Thai restaurants in U.S. towns and cities; and of U.S. and European stores selling exotic craft goods from less-developed countries.

The answer to the question "Is there a global culture?" then, must be "no." While an increasing familiarity exists with a common set of products, symbols, and events (many of which share their origins in U.S. culture of fast food and popular entertainment), these commonalties become configured in different ways in different places, rather than constitute a single global culture. Sometimes, distant cultures come into close and enduring contact—as when British colonialists forced Indian indentured servants to work in the cane fields of Fiji in the 19th century—producing the hybrid culture of Indo-Fijian. Sometimes traditional, local cultures become the subject of global consumption; sometimes it is the other way around. Changes in cultural practices, however, are tied, not only to the circulation of products, symbols, and events, but also to the increasing mobility of the world's people.

FIGURE 1.10 McDonald's in Indonesia Workers in a McDonald's restaurant in Jakarta, Indonesia wear the traditional Muslim headscarf and hat as they serve customers.

The Increasing Significance of Places and Regions

At first glance, the emergence of transnational architectural styles, dress codes, retail chains, and popular culture on one hand and ubiquitous immigrants, business visitors, and tourists on the other might suggest a sense of placelessness and dislocation—a loss of territorial identity and an erosion of the distinctive sense of place associated with certain localities. Yet the common experiences associated with globalization are still modified by local geographies. The structures and flows of a globalized world are variously embraced, resisted, subverted, and exploited as they make contact with specific places and specific communities. *In the process, places and regions are reconstructed rather than effaced.* Often, this involves deliberate attempts by the residents of a particular area to create or re-create territorial identity and a sense of place. In short, regional geographies change, but they do not disappear.

The new mobility of money, labor, products, and ideas actually increases the significance of place in some very real and important ways:

> The more universal the diffusion of material culture and lifestyles, the more valuable regional and ethnic identities become.
> The faster the information highway takes people into cyberspace, the more they feel the need for a subjective setting—a specific region or community—that they can call their own.
> The greater the reach of transnational corporations, the more easily they are able to respond to place-to-place variations in labor markets and consumer markets, and the more often and more radically economic geography has to be reorganized.
> The greater the integration of transnational governments and institutions, the more sensitive people have become to localized cleavages of race, ethnicity, and religion.

All in all, globalization influences—and is influenced by—specific cultures and settings in very different ways. In the process, places and regions are modified, rather than being destroyed or homogenized.

Jihad vs. McWorld   Related to the question of global culture is an issue that has been characterized by political scientist Benjamin Barber as "Jihad vs. McWorld." In his characterization, "McWorld" is shorthand for the pop culture and shallow materialism that is part of Western capitalism and modernization. "Jihad" is shorthand for cultural values that are underpinned by religious fundamentalism, traditional tribal allegiances, and opposition to Western materialism. (The term *jihad* properly refers to a struggle waged as a religious duty on behalf of Islam.) Neither "Jihad" nor "McWorld" is conducive to a healthy democracy or civil society, argues Barber, while tensions between the two make for potentially volatile situations (**Figure 1.11**).

At the heart of these tensions is a marked disillusionment with the West, especially within traditional Islamic societies. Across much of the world, modernization is now taken to mean Westernization and, more specifically, Americanization. While most Americans think of modernization as necessary and good, many other people see it as having resulted in their exploitation and humiliation. In most less-developed countries, only a minority can enjoy Western-style consumerism, though the impoverished majority are acutely aware of the affluence of Western countries. While the gap between rich and poor countries has actually been widening for several decades, the U.S. aid budget—already low compared to the aid budgets of other developed countries—has been declining substantially. The United States, therefore, tends to be seen as a swaggering superpower, rigging the world-system in its own interests, but doing relatively little by way of economic or humanitarian aid.

In the Muslim world, the sense of grievance at such injustice, along with a sense of dismay at the way that modernization is undermining Islamic values and traditions, has been intensified by opposition to U.S. policy toward the Middle East, which is seen as being cynically geared to U.S. oil interests and support for Israel. In addition, there is widespread resentment at the injustices experienced by Palestinians, at the suffering of Iraqi civilians resulting from the U.S.-led war in Iraq, at the presence of U.S. troops in Saudi Arabia, and at the repressive and corrupt nature of U.S.-backed Persian Gulf governments.

Meanwhile, the world's richer and more powerful countries, acting on the confident assumption that people everywhere want Western-style modernization, have until recently failed to recognize the cultural resentment, the sense of injustice, and the genuine rejection of modernization that exists in many parts of the world. The terrorist attacks on the Pentagon and on New York's World Trade Center in September 2001 brought an end to such assumptions. In the aftermath of the attacks, it became clear that resentment toward the United States and its behavior around the world has bred widespread hostility and even hatred.

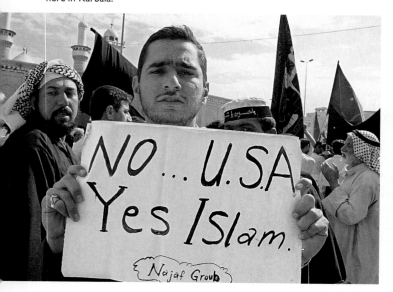

FIGURE 1.11 Anti-U.S. protest The war in Iraq has escalated anti-American sentiment among Iraqi Shia Muslims like the one pictured here in Karbala.

ECONOMIC DEVELOPMENT, TECHNOLOGY, AND SOCIAL WELL-BEING

Patterns of economic development are the result of many different factors. One of the most important is the availability of key resources such as cultivable land, energy sources, and valuable minerals. Key resources are unevenly distributed across the world. And particularly uneven in their distribution are the *combinations* of energy and minerals that are crucial to economic development. A lack of natural resources can, of course, be remedied through international trade (Japan's success is a prime example of this), but for most countries the resource base remains an important determinant of development.

A high proportion of the world's key industrial resources—basic raw materials and sources of energy—are concentrated in Russia, the United States, China, Canada, South Africa, and Australia. The biggest single exception to this pattern is the presence of vast oilfields in the Middle East. It is an exception that has enabled formerly less-developed countries such as Saudi Arabia to become wealthy and that has made the region a focal point of international politics.

The concentration of known resources in only a few countries is largely a result of geology, but it is also partly a function of countries' political and economic development. Political instability in much of post-colonial Africa, Asia, and Latin America has seriously hindered the exploration and exploitation of resources. In contrast, the relative affluence and strong political stability of the United States has led to a much more intensive exploration and exploitation of resources.

We should also bear in mind that the significance of particular resources is often tied to particular technologies. As technologies change, resource requirements also change, and the geography of economic development is "rewritten." One important example of this occurred early in the 20th century with the switch in industrial energy sources from coal to oil. When this happened, coalfield areas like central Appalachia found their prospects for economic development on indefinite hold, while oilfield areas such as west Texas suddenly had potential. Another example was the switch in the manufacture of mass-produced textiles from natural fibers such as wool and cotton to synthetic fibers in the 1950s and 1960s. When this happened, many farmers in the American South, for example, had to switch from cotton to other crops. Regions and countries that are heavily dependent on one particular resource are vulnerable to the consequences of technological change and the price for their products on the world market.

Technology Systems

Clusters of interrelated energy technologies, transportation technologies, and production technologies that dominate economic activity for several decades at a time, until a new cluster of improved technologies evolves, are known as **technology systems**. They have allowed a succession of expansions of economic activity in time and space; as a result, many existing industrial regions have grown bigger and more productive. Each major cluster of technological innovations tends to create new requirements in terms of natural resources as well as labor forces and markets. The result is that each major cluster of technological innovations has tended to favor different regions and different kinds of places.

What is especially remarkable about technology systems is that they have come along at about 50-year intervals. Since the beginning of the Industrial Revolution, four have occurred:

1790–1840: Early mechanization based on water power and steam engines, the development of cotton textiles and ironworking, and the development of river transport systems, canals, and turnpike roads

1840–1890: The exploitation of coal-powered steam engines, steel products, railroads, world shipping, and machine tools

1890–1950: The exploitation of the internal combustion engine, oil and plastics, electrical and heavy engineering, aircraft, radio, and telecommunications

1950–1990: The exploitation of nuclear power, aerospace industries, and electronics and petrochemicals; and the development of limited-access highways and global air routes

A fifth technology system, still incomplete, began to take shape in the 1980s with a series of innovations that are now being commercially exploited:

1990–: The exploitation of solar energy, robotics, microelectronics, biotechnology, advanced materials (fine chemicals and thermoplastics, for example), and information technology (digital telecommunications and geographic information systems, for example)

Each technology system has rewritten the geography of development as it has shifted the balance of advantages between regions (**Figure 1.12**). The contemporary economic structure of a country or region is often described in terms of the relative share of primary, secondary, tertiary, and quaternary economic activities. **Primary activities** are those that are concerned directly with natural resources of any kind. These include agriculture, mining, fishing, and forestry. **Secondary activities** are those concerned with manufacturing or processing. They involve processing, transforming, fabricating, or assembling the raw materials derived from primary activities, or reassembling, refinishing, or packaging manufactured goods. These include, for example, steelmaking, food processing, furniture making, textile manufacturing, and garment manufacturing. **Tertiary activities** are those that involve the sale and exchange of goods and services. These include warehousing, retail stores, personal services such as hairdressing, commercial services such as accounting and advertising, and entertainment. **Quaternary activities** deal with handling and processing knowledge and information. Examples include data processing, information retrieval, education, and research and development (R & D).

The economic structure of much of the world is dominated by the primary sector. In much of Africa and Asia, between 50 and 75 percent of the labor force is engaged in primary-sector activities. In contrast, the primary sector of the world's affluent countries is typically small, occupying only 5 or 10 percent of the labor force. The secondary sector is much larger in the developed countries, where the world's specialized manufacturing regions are located. The tertiary and quaternary sectors are significant only in the most affluent countries. In the United States, the primary sector accounts for less than 4 percent of the labor force, the secondary sector for about 22 percent, the tertiary sector for just over 50 percent, and the quaternary sector for 24 percent of the labor force.

Measuring Economic Development

Understanding the structure of the world's economies tells only part of the story of their levels of development. At the global scale, levels of economic development are usually measured by national economic indicators such as gross domestic product and gross national product (though national statistics of course tend to obscure within-country social and spatial inequalities). **Gross domestic product (GDP)** is an estimate of the total value of all materials, foodstuffs, goods, and services produced by a country in a particular year. To standardize for countries' varying sizes, the statistic is normally divided by total population, which gives an indicator, *per capita* GDP, that provides a good yardstick of relative levels of economic development. **Gross national product (GNP)** includes the net value of income from abroad—flows of profits or losses from overseas investments, for example.

In making international comparisons, GDP and GNP can be problematic. They are calculated using national currencies (the value of which can be distorted by speculation and government policies), and they do not include non-market goods and services. (A non-market good or service does not have an observable monetary value. Examples of the former include viewing wildlife or snorkeling at a coral reef. An example of the latter is the preparation of food for a family done by a parent.) Recently, it has become

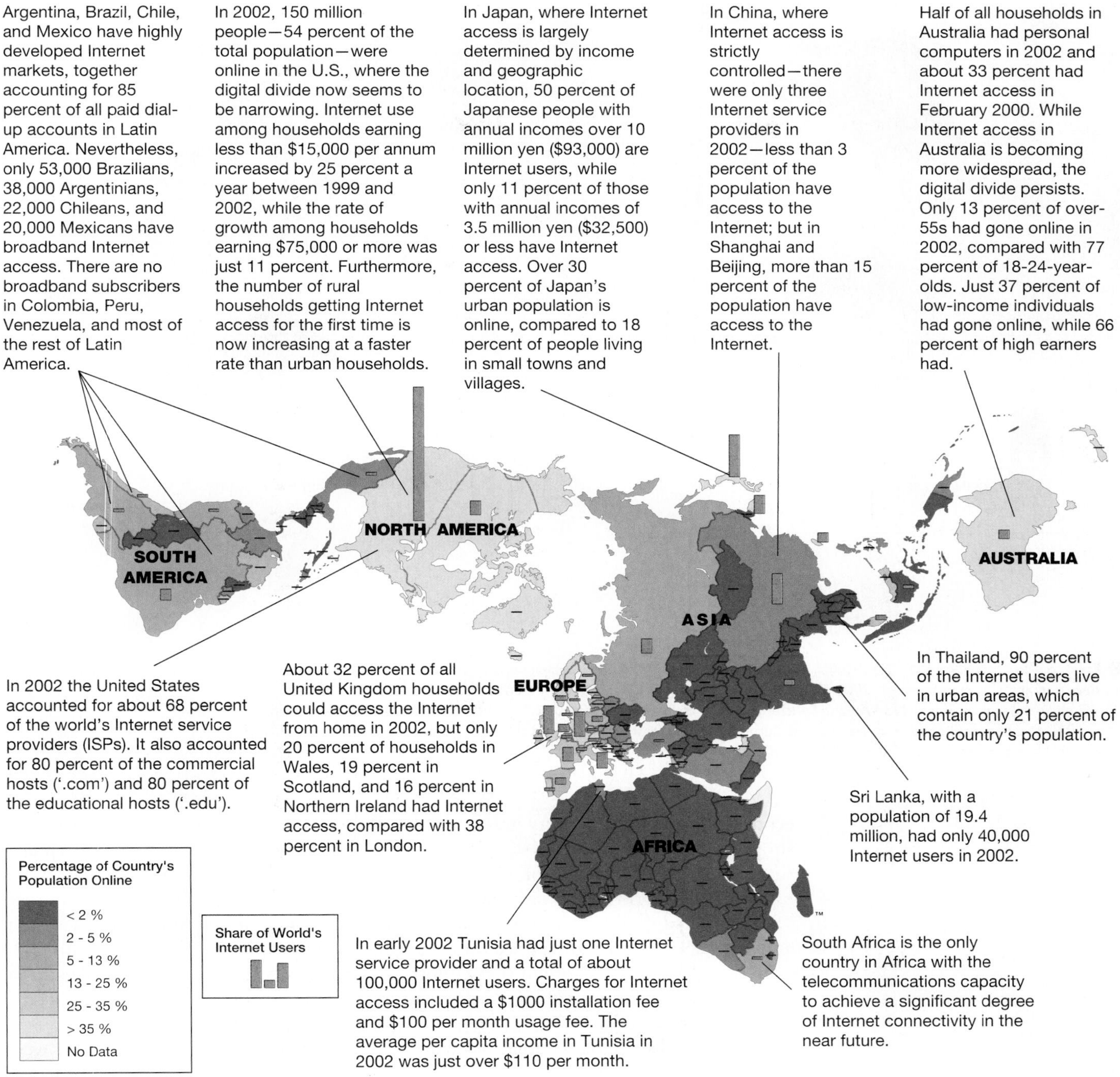

Argentina, Brazil, Chile, and Mexico have highly developed Internet markets, together accounting for 85 percent of all paid dial-up accounts in Latin America. Nevertheless, only 53,000 Brazilians, 38,000 Argentinians, 22,000 Chileans, and 20,000 Mexicans have broadband Internet access. There are no broadband subscribers in Colombia, Peru, Venezuela, and most of the rest of Latin America.

In 2002, 150 million people—54 percent of the total population—were online in the U.S., where the digital divide now seems to be narrowing. Internet use among households earning less than $15,000 per annum increased by 25 percent a year between 1999 and 2002, while the rate of growth among households earning $75,000 or more was just 11 percent. Furthermore, the number of rural households getting Internet access for the first time is now increasing at a faster rate than urban households.

In Japan, where Internet access is largely determined by income and geographic location, 50 percent of Japanese people with annual incomes over 10 million yen ($93,000) are Internet users, while only 11 percent of those with annual incomes of 3.5 million yen ($32,500) or less have Internet access. Over 30 percent of Japan's urban population is online, compared to 18 percent of people living in small towns and villages.

In China, where Internet access is strictly controlled—there were only three Internet service providers in 2002—less than 3 percent of the population have access to the Internet; but in Shanghai and Beijing, more than 15 percent of the population have access to the Internet.

Half of all households in Australia had personal computers in 2002 and about 33 percent had Internet access in February 2000. While Internet access in Australia is becoming more widespread, the digital divide persists. Only 13 percent of over-55s had gone online in 2002, compared with 77 percent of 18-24-year-olds. Just 37 percent of low-income individuals had gone online, while 66 percent of high earners had.

In 2002 the United States accounted for about 68 percent of the world's Internet service providers (ISPs). It also accounted for 80 percent of the commercial hosts ('.com') and 80 percent of the educational hosts ('.edu').

About 32 percent of all United Kingdom households could access the Internet from home in 2002, but only 20 percent of households in Wales, 19 percent in Scotland, and 16 percent in Northern Ireland had Internet access, compared with 38 percent in London.

In Thailand, 90 percent of the Internet users live in urban areas, which contain only 21 percent of the country's population.

Sri Lanka, with a population of 19.4 million, had only 40,000 Internet users in 2002.

In early 2002 Tunisia had just one Internet service provider and a total of about 100,000 Internet users. Charges for Internet access included a $1000 installation fee and $100 per month usage fee. The average per capita income in Tunisia in 2002 was just over $110 per month.

South Africa is the only country in Africa with the telecommunications capacity to achieve a significant degree of Internet connectivity in the near future.

Percentage of Country's Population Online

- < 2 %
- 2 - 5 %
- 5 - 13 %
- 13 - 25 %
- 25 - 35 %
- > 35 %
- No Data

Share of World's Internet Users

FIGURE 1.12 Global Internet connectivity Like all previous revolutions in transportation and communications, the Internet is effectively reorganizing space. Although often spoken of as "shrinking" the world and "eliminating" geography, the Internet is highly uneven in its availability and use. About 70 percent of all traffic on the Internet originates from, or is addressed to, North America. In contrast, some countries have almost no Internet connectivity. In others, the costs are prohibitive. Even in Europe, Japan, and North America, Internet connectivity is decidedly uneven in socioeconomic terms. This map shows the percentage of the total population in each country with access to the Internet (indicated by the density of shading) and the relative share of the world's Internet users accounted for by each country (indicated by the vertical bars). (*Source:* M. Zook, **http://www.zookNIC.com/**.)

possible to compare national currencies based on *purchasing power parity* (PPP). In effect, PPP measures how much of a common "market basket" of goods and services each currency can purchase locally, including goods and services that are not traded internationally. Using PPP-based currency values to compare levels of economic prosperity usually produces lower GDP figures in wealthy countries and higher GDP figures in poorer countries, compared with market-based exchange rates. Nevertheless,

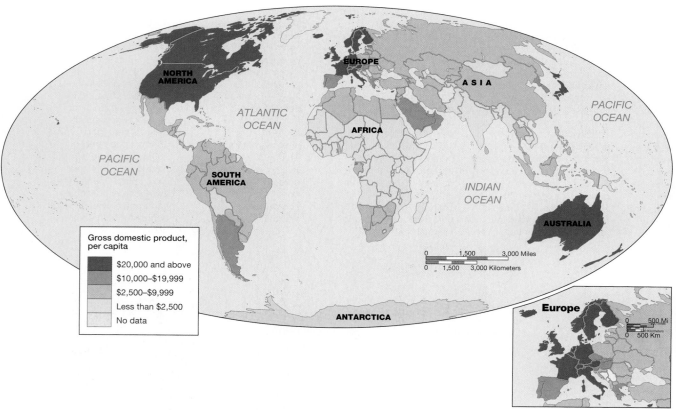

FIGURE 1.13 Gross domestic product (GDP) per capita GDP per capita is one of the best single measures of economic development. This map, based on 2003 data, shows the tremendous gulf in affluence between the developed countries of the world—such as the United States, Norway, and Switzerland, with an annual per capita GDP (in PPP "international" dollars) of more than $37,000—and less-developed countries such as Burundi, Tanzania, and Malawi, where annual per capita GDP was less than $650. The global average per capita GDP in 2003 was $8229.

economic prosperity is very unevenly distributed across countries. As **Figure 1.13** shows, most of the highest levels of economic development are found in northern latitudes (very roughly, north of 30° N), which has given rise to another popular shorthand for the world's economic geography: the division between the "North" and the "South." In the more-developed countries of Japan, the United States, and Canada, and almost all of northwestern Europe, annual per capita GDP (in PPP) in 2003 exceeded $20,000. The only other countries that matched these levels were Australia, Hong Kong, Singapore, and the United Arab Emirates, where annual per capita GDP in 2003 was $29,632; $27,179; $24,481; and $22,420, respectively.

The world's average annual per capita GDP (in PPP) is $8,229. The gap between the highest per capita GDPs ($62,298 in Luxembourg; $37,738 in Ireland; and $37,670 in Norway) and the lowest ($548 in Sierra Leone and $608 in Malawi) is huge: In 2000, the average of the bottom ten was about one-fiftieth of the average of the top ten.

Patterns of Social Well-being

This inequality is reflected—and reinforced—by many aspects of human well-being. Patterns of infant mortality, a reliable indicator of social well-being, show the same steep North–South gradient. For adults in the industrial countries, life expectancy is high and continues to increase. Life expectancy at birth in Japan in 2003 was 82 years, in Hong Kong it was 81.6, and in the United States it was 77.4. In contrast, life expectancy in the poorest countries is dramatically shorter. In 2003 in Zimbabwe, life expectancy at birth was 36.9 years; in Botswana it was 36.3, and in Swaziland it was 32.5. In most African countries, the average person can expect to live only to the age of 46.

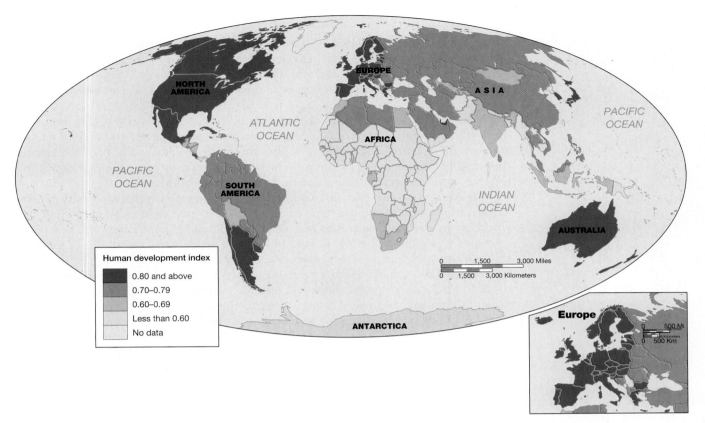

FIGURE 1.14 An index of human development, 2003 This index, calculated by the United Nations Development Programme, is based on measures of life expectancy, educational attainment, and personal income. A country that had the best scores among all of the countries in the world on all three measures would have a perfect index score of 1.0, while a country that ranked worst in the world on all three indicators would have an index score of 0. Most of the affluent countries have index scores of 0.9 or more, while the worst scores—those less than 0.4—are concentrated in Africa.

The United Nations Development Programme (UNDP) has devised an overall index of human development based on measures of life expectancy, educational attainment, and personal income. **Figure 1.14** shows the international map of human development in 2003. Norway, Iceland, and Australia had the highest overall levels of human development (0.96, 0.96, and 0.95, respectively), while Niger and Sierra Leone (0.30 and 0.28) had the lowest levels. The same fundamental pattern is repeated in terms of the entire array of indicators of human development: adult literacy, poverty, malnutrition, access to physicians, public expenditure on higher education, telephone lines, Internet users, and so on. Inequality on this scale poses the most pressing, as well as the most intractable, questions of national and international policymaking. It also raises important questions of **spatial justice**—the fairness of geographic variations in people's levels of affluence and well-being, given people's needs and their contributions to the production of wealth and social well-being.

These questions are underscored by some simple comparisons between the needs of people in less-developed countries and the spending patterns of those in the world's most affluent countries. The UNDP has calculated that the annual cost of providing a basic education for all children in less-developed countries would be in the region of $6 billion, which is less than the annual sales of cosmetics in the United States. Providing water and sanitation for everyone in less-developed countries is estimated at $9 billion per year, which is less than Europeans' annual expenditure on ice cream. Providing for basic health and nutrition for everyone in less-developed countries would cost an estimated $13 billion per year, which is less than the annual expenditure on pet foods in Europe and the United States. Reducing the military expenditures of affluent countries (in the region of $500 billion per year) by less than 10 percent each year would pay for basic education, water and sanitation, basic health and nutrition, and reproductive health programs for everyone in less-developed countries.

Development and Gender Equality

North–South patterns are also reflected in indicators that measure economic development in terms of *gender equality*. **Gender** refers to the social differences between men and women rather than the anatomical differences related to sex. Unequal gender relations are part of the broader issue of social inequality based on societal norms and values, but gender equality is of such pervasive significance that it deserves extra emphasis. In almost all countries, the majority of women and girls are disadvantaged in terms of their relative power and control over material resources, and they often face more severe insecurities (for example, after the death of a husband). Poor women are thus doubly disadvantaged. Moreover, the lack of autonomy of women has significant negative consequences for the education and health of children.

On average, women earn 30 to 40 percent less than men for the same work. This is in part a reflection of the dramatic gender disparities that exist in many parts of the world, particularly in South Asia and West, central, and North Africa. Of the world's estimated 854 million illiterate adults, 544 million are women, and of the 113 million children not attending primary school, 60 percent are girls.

The UNDP has established a gender-sensitive development index that adjusts the overall human development index for gender inequality in life expectancy, educational attainment, and income. According to this index, in no country are women better off than men. Perhaps most revealing is the UNDP's Gender Empowerment Index, which is based on measures of women's incomes; their participation in the labor force as administrators, managers, and professional and technical workers; and the percentage of parliamentary seats held by women. **Figure 1.15** shows the actual

FIGURE 1.15 An index of gender empowerment, 2005 The United Nations Development Programme's Gender Empowerment Index is based on measures of women's incomes, their participation in the labor force as administrators and managers and professional and technical workers, and the percentage of parliamentary seats they hold. As in the overall index of human development (Figure 1.14), a perfect score would be 1.0, with 0 representing the worst possible score (ranked worst on all measures). There is by no means a direct correlation between economic prosperity and gender empowerment; creating economic opportunities for women does not necessarily require high levels of economic development.

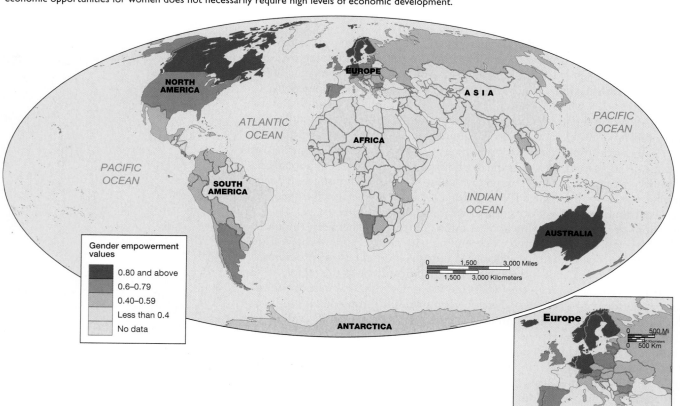

index values for 2005. The top countries were Scandinavian: Norway (0.93), Denmark (0.86), Sweden (0.85), Iceland (0.83), and Finland (0.83). The countries with the worst recorded gender empowerment index scores were Yemen (0.12), Bangladesh (0.22), and Saudi Arabia (0.25). Nevertheless, as Figure 1.15 demonstrates, high levels of economic development are not a prerequisite for creating economic opportunities for women. Namibia and Bulgaria, for example, both scored better than Italy and Japan.

Women do, in fact, play a central and increasing role in processes of development and change in the global economy. Women in Africa and Asia tend to work longer hours than men—12 to 13 hours a week more (counting both paid and unpaid work). In many less-developed countries, women constitute the majority of workers in the manufacturing sector created by the new international division of labor. In others, it is women who keep households afloat in a world economy that has resulted in localized recession and intensified poverty (**Figure 1.16**).

Globalization appears to lead to increasing levels of participation by women in the formal labor force. Large firms producing for export tend to employ women in assembly-line jobs because they can be hired for wages lower than those for men. But increasing participation does not always mean less discrimination. Women constitute a large share of workers in informal subcontracting—often in the garment industry—at low wages and under poor conditions. Globalization is also associated with increasing levels of home work, tele-work, and part-time work. In the United Kingdom, the share of workers in such positions rose from 17 percent in 1965 to 50 percent in 2001. Similar changes have taken place in many other countries, and in most of them women constitute 70 or 80 percent of home, tele-, and part-time workers. This is a mixed blessing. Informal work arrangements can accommodate women's care obligations in the family, but such jobs are typically precarious and underpaid.

FIGURE 1.16 Berber woman carrying firewood The lack of adequate fuel to cook and heat the home is one of the biggest challenges faced by women in peripheral parts of the world. In places where the land has been deforested, gathering wood can take many hours each day, as it does for this woman who lives in the High Atlas Mountains of Morocco.

THE FOUNDATIONS OF WORLD REGIONS

An essential foundation for an informed regional geography is an ability to understand places and regions as components of a constantly changing global system. In this sense, all regional geography is historical geography. Built into every place and each region is the legacy of a sequence of major changes in world geography. One of the key features of this aspect of geography, however, is that the sequence of changes has not been the same everywhere. We can best understand these changes and their consequences for different places and regions by thinking in terms of the world as a changing, competitive, political-economic system.

We need also to think of the changing world as an outcome of how we alter our physical environment through the economic, political, and sociocultural systems we create. The environment that surrounds us provides us with what we need to produce and enjoy the world in which we live. Understanding the limits and resources that the natural world furnishes is just as important as understanding the strengths and weaknesses of the social systems we have created to organize our lives.

The Earth System

The physical and biological characteristics of places make distinctive contributions to our understanding of regional geography because they provide constraints on, and opportunities for, human activities. Many geographers view physical and environmental conditions as highly dynamic and best understood if one thinks of Earth as a system in which humans play an important role. **Earth system science** is an integrated approach to global patterns of geology, climate, and ecosystems and how they have changed over time and space, producing a physical geography that is dynamically shaped by both natural forces and human actions. Physical geographers work with other Earth scientists to understand the functioning of the Earth system and with human geographers to interpret the interactions between the Earth system and social, cultural, economic, and political circumstances.

The fundamental Earth system processes that shape world regions are plate tectonics, atmospheric circulation, and ecosystem functioning. Plate tectonics explains the formation of continents and mountain ranges; atmospheric circulation shapes the pattern of world climates; and ecosystem characteristics affect the geography of vegetation, the cycling of key minerals, and the location of animals and other key organisms.

Plate Tectonics The theory of **plate tectonics** explains how Earth's crust is divided into large solid plates that move relative to each other and cause mountain-building, volcanic, and earthquake activity when they separate or meet. This layer, which is from 50 to 100 kilometers (31 to 62 miles) thick, is composed of about a dozen large "plates" of solid rocks floating on a layer of molten material. These plates move very slowly over the more fluid deeper layer and interact at their boundaries, where the resulting tensions are responsible for most of the world's volcanic, earthquake, and mountain-building activity (**Figure 1.17**). The continents sit on the plates and emerge from the oceans where Earth's crust is thicker or where the rocks are lighter and therefore more buoyant. At the core of each continent is a region of old (500 million years or older) crystalline rocks called a *continental shield*. Shield areas often contain many minerals.

Plate tectonics builds on theories about **continental drift**, the slow movement of the continents over long periods of time across Earth's surface (**Figure 1.18**). These theories are associated with Alfred Wegener (1880–1930), a German geophysicist who hypothesized nearly a century ago that over millions of years landmasses had moved relative to each other and across Earth's surface. He noted the remarkable fit of the South American and African continents and was also intrigued by plant and animal fossils found in both South America and Africa, organisms that he thought unlikely to have swum or to have been transported across the Atlantic Ocean by some other means. According to Wegener's theory, the earliest continent was a single landmass called Pangaea that formed where molten lava emerged from the ocean floor about 225 million years ago. This supercontinent slowly shifted

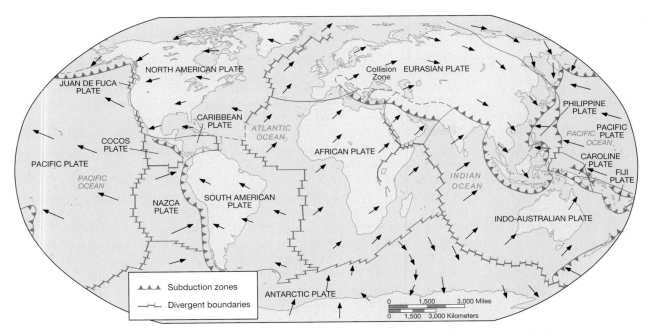

FIGURE 1.17 Major tectonic plates Earth's crust is broken into a dozen or so rigid slabs or tectonic plates that are moving relative to one another. Each arrow represents 20 million years of movement and the direction of movement. Longer arrows indicate that the Pacific and Nazca plates are moving more rapidly than others. The long jagged boundaries indicate areas where plates are moving away from each other. The triangles show subduction zones, where one plate sinks underneath another.

FIGURE 1.18 Plate tectonics and the creation of the Himalayas (a) The collision between the Indian and Eurasian plates has pushed up the Himalayas and the Tibetan Plateau. (b) These cross sections show the orientation of the two plates before and after their collision. The reference points (small squares) show the amount of uplift of an imaginary point in Earth's crust during this mountain-building process. (c) The Himalayas are among the highest mountains in the world, resulting from very active mountain building in the region.

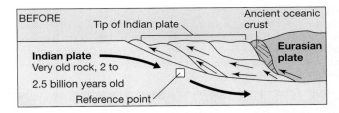

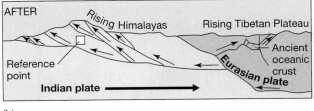

(b)

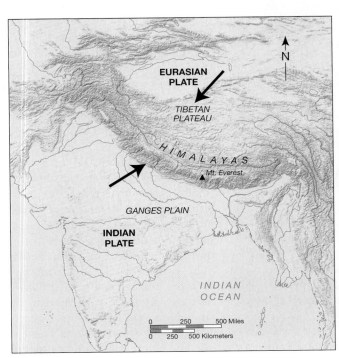

(a)

(c)

position, and about 200 million years ago it broke up into two pieces, Laurasia to the north and Gondwanaland to the south. Laurasia was eventually split by narrow ocean gaps into North America and the landmass of Europe and Asia. Gondwanaland split into South America, Africa, Antarctica, India, and Australia. As parts of Gondwanaland drifted north, they connected with Laurasia, most notably where India collided with Asia, causing the uplifting of the Himalayas (see Figure 1.18). The permanent connection between North and South America occurred around 5 million years ago.

Within the continents, more local processes—erosion, weathering, and sedimentation—create regional landforms. The study of landforms in geography is called **geomorphology**. *Erosion* occurs when water and wind move across the land surface, picking up material and transporting it to other locations. In some cases, heat and the characteristics of water or rocks cause chemical changes and breakdown of material in the process called *weathering*. Erosion has affected many of the world's great mountain ranges, moving material to lower regions and depositing it in a process called *sedimentation*. Extensive areas of deposited sediment occur in the large river basins, such as the Amazon, and across some of the vast plains, such as the North American prairies. Erosion and weathering have been critical in the development of better soils and, over the longer term, in the formation of layers of *sedimentary rock*. Over time, organic material in sedimentary basins can compress and form reserves of oil and coal. *Igneous rock* is formed when molten material approaches Earth's surface and solidifies and crystallizes. When existing sedimentary or igneous rock undergoes physical or chemical change under conditions of high temperature and pressure, *metamorphic rock*, which often contains valuable minerals, is formed.

FIGURE 1.19 Seasonal incidence of Sun's rays by latitude As Earth moves around the Sun, the angle at which sunlight hits Earth varies according to the seasons. The Sun's rays hit Earth most directly and focus the greatest solar energy and heat at the equator in March and September, at the latitude of the Tropic of Cancer (23.5° N) in the Northern Hemisphere in June, and at the latitude of the Tropic of Capricorn (23.5° S) in the Southern Hemisphere in December. (*Source: E. Aguado and J. E. Burt, Understanding Weather and Climate, 2nd ed. Upper Saddle River, NJ: Prentice Hall, 2001.*)

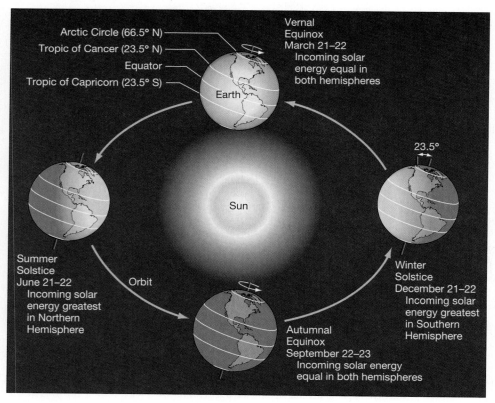

Atmospheric Circulation

Earth scientists have combined an understanding of basic physics with information about global patterns of temperature and precipitation to provide explanations of atmospheric circulation, the global movement of air that transports heat and moisture and explains the climates of different regions. Whereas **weather** is the instantaneous or immediate state of the atmosphere (for example, a rainy or freezing day) at a particular time and place, **climate** is the typical conditions of the weather expected at a place often measured by long-term averages of temperature and precipitation and at different seasons (for example, a place with wet, cool winters and hot, dry summers).

A simple model of atmospheric circulation is based on variations in the input of energy from the Sun and the configuration of the major continents and mountain ranges. The spherical shape of Earth, the tilt of its axis, and its revolution around the Sun mean that the sunlight does not hit all parts of Earth's surface at the same angle (**Figure 1.19**). As Earth moves around the Sun, the angle at which sunlight hits Earth varies according to the seasons. The Sun's rays hit Earth most directly and focus the greatest solar energy and heat at the equator in March and October, at the latitude of the Tropic of Cancer (23.5° N) in the Northern Hemisphere in June, and at the latitude of the Tropic of Capricorn (23.5° S) in the Southern Hemisphere in December.

The constant high input of solar radiation at the equator produces warm temperatures throughout the year, and this warmer air has a tendency to rise into the atmosphere, creating low pressure at ground level, and cooling and condensing into clouds that eventually generate heavy rainfall. This process is called *convectional precipitation* and is typical of the equatorial climate with high temperatures and rainfall year-round.

The cooler air rises high into the atmosphere, moves out from the equator toward the poles, and eventually sinks over tropical latitudes (about 30° north and south latitude), creating a zone of high pressure (**Figure 1.20**). As the air moves toward the surface, it becomes warmer and drier, holding so little moisture by the time it reaches ground level that these regions are characterized by the very low rainfall, sparse vegetation, and warm, dry conditions of desert climates.

When the sinking air reaches ground level, it diverges and some of the air flows back toward the equator, where it converges with the heated air and rises again.

FIGURE 1.20 Atmospheric circulation The general circulation of the atmosphere is based on air moving from regions of high to low pressure and on the vertical lift of air in the regions of highest heating over the equator at the intertropical convergence zone. Air that is heated by the Sun's direct rays at the equator rises and then moves north and south toward the poles high in the atmosphere, sinking in a high-pressure zone at about 30° north and south latitude and returning at the surface to the equator in a system called the *Hadley cell.* These major wind and pressure belts shift north and south with the seasons (north when the Sun is strongest in the Northern Hemisphere in June and south when the Sun is strongest in the Southern Hemisphere in December). (*Source:* R. W. Christopherson, *Geosystems: An Introduction to Physical Geography,* 6th ed. Upper Saddle River, NJ: Prentice Hall, 2005.)

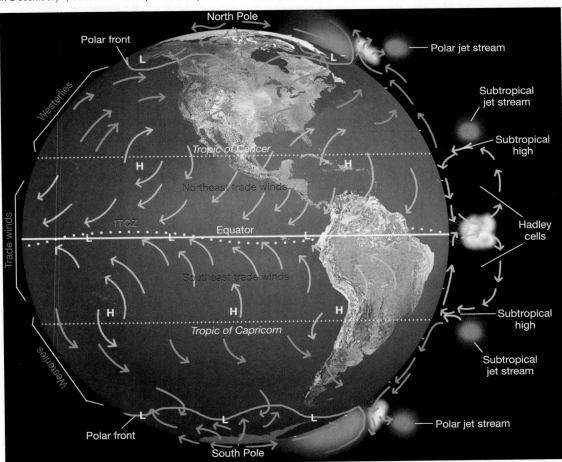

This vertical circulation of air from the equator to the tropics back to the equator is called a *Hadley cell*. The **intertropical convergence zone (ITCZ)** is the region where air flows together and rises vertically as a result of intense solar heating at the equator, often with heavy rainfall. It shifts north and south with the seasons (see Figure 1.18).

The rotation of Earth tends to drag air flowing back from the tropical latitudes to the equator into a more east-to-west flow, creating a major wind belt called the *trade winds* that blow from east to west between the dry tropics and the equator. Some of the air descending over the tropics also flows poleward and is pulled by Earth's spin into a major west-to-east flow called the *westerly winds*.

The seasonal variation associated with the tilt of Earth's axis and the changing orientation of the Northern and Southern Hemispheres toward the Sun (the Northern Hemisphere facing the Sun more directly in June than in December) means that the zones of rising and sinking air, and the major wind belts, move northward in June and southward in December, with corresponding shifts in the zones of rainfall and dry conditions. When winds blow across warmer oceans, they tend to pick up moisture, and when moisture-laden air encounters a landmass, especially coastal mountains, it condenses into rainfall or snow. Precipitation associated with mountains, called *orographic precipitation*, may result in the formation of a dry rainshadow region on the inland, or lee, side of the mountains, where sinking air that has lost its moisture becomes even drier. The trade winds flow across the oceans in tropical latitudes and frequently produce rain on east-facing coasts in what is sometimes called the *trade wind climates* (**Figure 1.21**).

Similarly, the westerly winds bring rain as they blow from the oceans onto western coasts. The regions on the margins of the trade winds, and on the margins of the equatorial rainfall zone, have highly seasonal climates with a distinct rainy season. Seasonal shifts in pressure and wind belts mean that the westerlies move nearer the equator in December and to the poles in June, resulting in distinct wet and dry seasons on the margins of the westerly circulation. When the global circulation shifts southward in December, storms spinning out of the Northern Hemisphere westerlies bring rain to the poleward margins of drier regions in the Northern Hemisphere.

This simple model of atmospheric circulation produces a pattern of global climate with regions of warmer temperatures nearer the equator, and of wetter regions at the equator, on east coasts in the tropics, on west coasts in temperate regions, and in the complex region where warmer air flowing toward the poles meets colder air flowing toward the equator along the polar front and the major jet stream. This general pattern helps explain the climates and the associated interaction with human activity of each of the major world regions (**Figure 1.22**).

FIGURE 1.21 Orographic rainfall on a trade wind coast Winds blowing across the oceans pick up moisture. When they rise over coastal mountains, cooling causes the moisture to condense and fall as rainfall or snow. Orographic rainfall is common where winds, such as the trades, cross warm oceans, such as the Caribbean, and rise over mountains near the coasts of countries such as Costa Rica. Heavy orographic rainfall also occurs where the westerlies rise over coastal mountains such as the Andes in Chile or where high mountains emerge from generally drier regions such as in East Africa and the western United States.

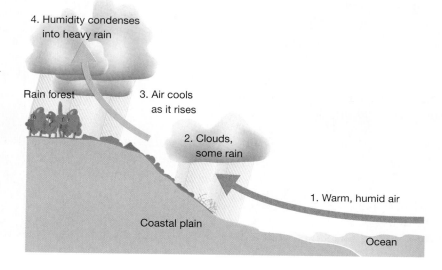

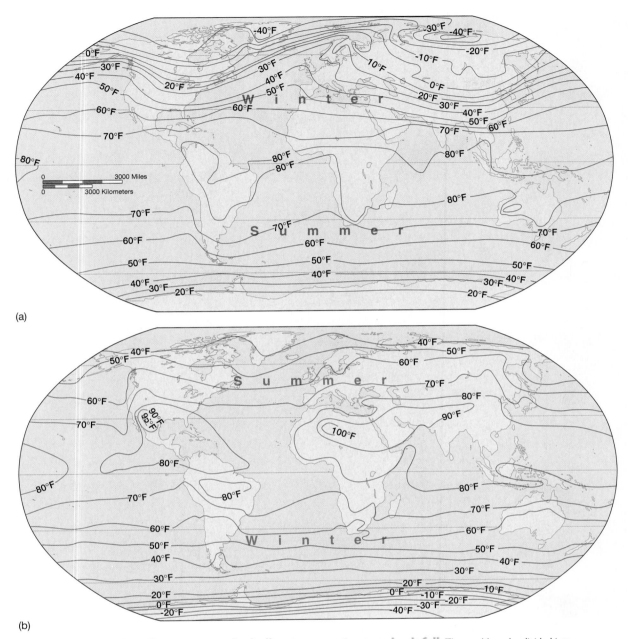

FIGURE 1.22 Major climate zones, including temperature and rainfall The world can be divided into very general climate zones based on temperature and on the total amount and seasonality of precipitation. (a) Average January sea-level temperatures and (b) average July sea-level temperatures show the global pattern of annual average temperature, with warmer conditions at the equator and cooler temperatures toward the poles and at higher altitudes. (*Source:* Modified from T. L. McKnight, *Physical Geography: A Landscape Appreciation,* 6th ed. Upper Saddle River, NJ: Prentice Hall, 1999, pp. 97, 160–61)

Ecosystems Functioning Atmospheric circulation and the associated patterns of world climates are the major influences on the global distribution of **ecosystems**—the complexes of living organisms and their environments in particular places. For example, U.S. and Mexican ecosystems include the Sonoran Desert ecosystem, with its characteristic species such as the saguaro cactus adapted to dry conditions, and the prairie ecosystem of tall grasses once grazed by bison. When ecosystems are grouped into larger classifications, defined by major vegetation type such as desert, forest, or grassland, they are known as **biomes,** which are the largest geographic biotic units.

Warmer temperatures and higher rainfall are generally associated with more abundant vegetation. For example, the high rainfall and warm temperatures of

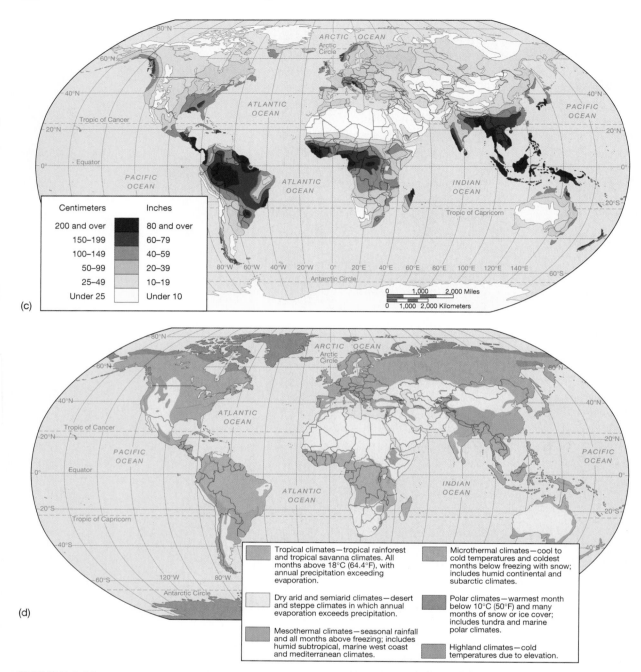

Centimeters	Inches
200 and over	80 and over
150–199	60–79
100–149	40–59
50–99	20–39
25–49	10–19
Under 25	Under 10

(c)

(d)

Tropical climates—tropical rainforest and tropical savanna climates. All months above 18°C (64.4°F), with annual precipitation exceeding evaporation.

Dry arid and semiarid climates—desert and steppe climates in which annual evaporation exceeds precipitation.

Mesothermal climates—seasonal rainfall and all months above freezing; includes humid subtropical, marine west coast and mediterranean climates.

Microthermal climates—cool to cold temperatures and coldest months below freezing with snow; includes humid continental and subarctic climates.

Polar climates—warmest month below 10°C (50°F) and many months of snow or ice cover; includes tundra and marine polar climates.

Highland climates—cold temperatures due to elevation.

FIGURE 1.22 *(Continued)* (c) The global pattern of average annual rainfall indicates regions of low and high precipitation (averages are usually based on 30-year climate "normals"; in this case, 1961–90). (d) The climate system of the world can be generalized into six major regions based on temperature and precipitation. This map is based on a simplification of the climate classification of German climatologist Wladimir Köppen. *(Source:* [c] Modified from T. L. McKnight, *Physical Geography: A Landscape Appreciation,* 6th ed. Upper Saddle River, NJ: Prentice Hall, 1999, pp. 97, 160–61; [d] Modified from R. W. Christopherson, *Geosystems,* 4th ed. Upper Saddle River, NJ: Prentice Hall, 2000, p. 268.)

the equatorial regions are associated with the lush vegetation of the tropical rainforest ecosystems or tropical forest biome. The hot, dry conditions of the desert ecosystems are associated with sparser shrubs and drought-adapted plants and animals of the desert ecosystem. Colder deserts with slightly more rainfall produce the short grasses that are typical of the *steppe* or prairie ecosystems. The cold, drier conditions of regions nearer the poles correspond to a landscape of frost-resistant mosses, shrubs, and grasses called *tundra.* Just to the equator-ward side of the tundra, as temperatures and rainfall increase slightly, are the evergreen conifer boreal forest ecosystems (sometimes called the *taiga*). In regions where the westerly winds are dominant, they produce wet coastal climates associated with the towering conifer forest ecosystems. Similarly, the trade winds in warmer regions produce tropical rain forests on the east coasts of many continents. **Figure 1.23** shows the world distribution of ecosystems.

In regions where precipitation is highly seasonal as a result of shifts in major wind and pressure belts, several distinctive ecosystems are possible. In warmer regions with a pronounced dry season (between the rain forests and deserts), we find the savanna ecosystem of extensive tall grasslands, mixed with deciduous trees toward the wetter margins. The Mediterranean ecosystem of scrub and dry forest is found in regions where the seasonal shift of the westerly winds brings rainfall only in the winter season.

The global pattern of ecosystems is also influenced by geology and soils. In all regions, high-altitude plateaus and mountains have distinctive ecosystems associated with cooler temperatures or higher rainfall. In other regions the physical structure or chemical composition of the soils produces particular ecosystems, and erosion and volcanic activity may promote or inhibit the overall growth of vegetation.

Geographers are interested in the spatial distribution of plants, animals, and ecosystems known as **biogeography**. They work with other scientists to examine global patterns and to understand the relative roles of climate and other factors in determining these patterns. Some of the most interesting questions in studying ecosystems and biogeography are those related to **biodiversity**—the differences in the types and numbers of species in different regions of the world. There is a general relationship between biodiversity and temperature, with tropical regions generally hosting a wider variety of species. Although there are broad similarities between the ecosystems of different tropical regions, such as Africa and Latin America, there are also considerable differences. Some of these differences relate to the ways ecosystem structure and composition are influenced by long-term processes of evolution and environmental change, including longer-term changes in climate, and by human modification of the environment. In regions where climate has remained stable over long periods of time, organisms have mutated, migrated, and interbred to form many different species and have adapted to local environmental conditions. If these regions are isolated from others, as in the case of islands such as Australia, the resulting species may be very different from those in other parts of the world. Where climate has changed dramatically, as in areas covered by ice sheets as recently as 10,000 years ago, there may be less diversity, as species may have only recently begun to migrate back into the region.

Climate Change Although Earth system scientists believe that the general circulation of the atmosphere tends to remain the same over centuries, considerable evidence suggests that global and regional climates have varied over time. Landscapes show evidence of wetter or drier conditions in the past through remains of animals, vegetation, landforms, and lakes associated with a different climate. Human history records periods of hotter and cooler climates and their impact on harvests and migrations. Most dramatically, the landscapes of many regions show the marks of ice cover, erosion, and deposition from periods when it was so cold that rivers of ice (called *glaciers*) or even larger masses (*ice caps*) covered much of the world. Earth system scientists believe that the ice ages were caused by slight changes in the tilt of Earth's axis and its orbit around the Sun and associated changes in the amount of solar radiation reaching Earth (**Figure 1.24**).

Global and regional climates have also been affected by tectonic activity, especially volcanic eruptions. The most explosive volcanic eruptions can blast ash and gases high into the atmosphere, blocking sunlight and changing the chemical composition of the air. For example, the explosion of the Krakatoa volcano near Java in 1883 caused a worldwide drop in temperatures and harvest failures in Europe during the "year without a summer."

FIGURE 1.23 World ecosystems This map shows the most general classification of global ecosystems into major biomes. Forests and woodlands are tree-dominated communities, generally in areas of high precipitation. Shrublands of short woody plants and bushes are found in slightly drier regions, and grasslands occur where precipitation is even less plentiful. Deserts are found in the driest regions and include bare ground and a variety of scattered grasses, succulent plants, and bushes. Tundra is found in cooler regions and can include a variety of shorter plants, including grasses. Wetland vegetation is found in wet and flooded areas and includes mangroves and marshlands. (*Source:* T. L. McKnight, *Physical Geography: A Landscape Appreciation,* 6th ed. Upper Saddle River, NJ: Prentice Hall, 1999.)

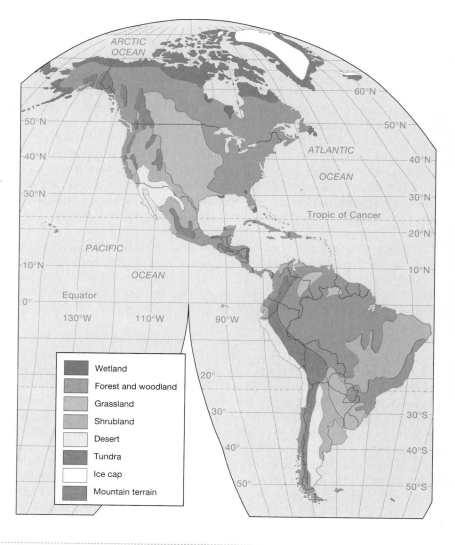

Legend:
- Wetland
- Forest and woodland
- Grassland
- Shrubland
- Desert
- Tundra
- Ice cap
- Mountain terrain

FIGURE 1.24 Major causes of climate changes This diagram, based on the work of the Intergovernmental Panel on Climate Change, shows the major causes of climate change, including volcanic activity, changes in land use, and alterations in the composition of the atmosphere, such as increases in moisture, greenhouse gases including carbon dioxide, and pollutants such as sulfur dioxide. For example, scientists have shown that sulfur dioxide and dust from major volcanic eruptions and industrial pollution are likely to cool the climate and that deforestation and increased carbon dioxide from fossil-fuel burning are likely to warm the climate.

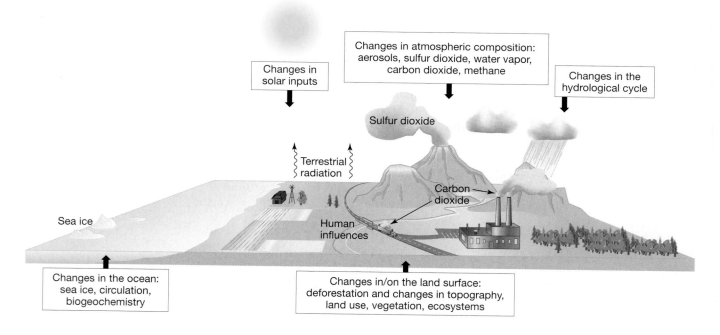

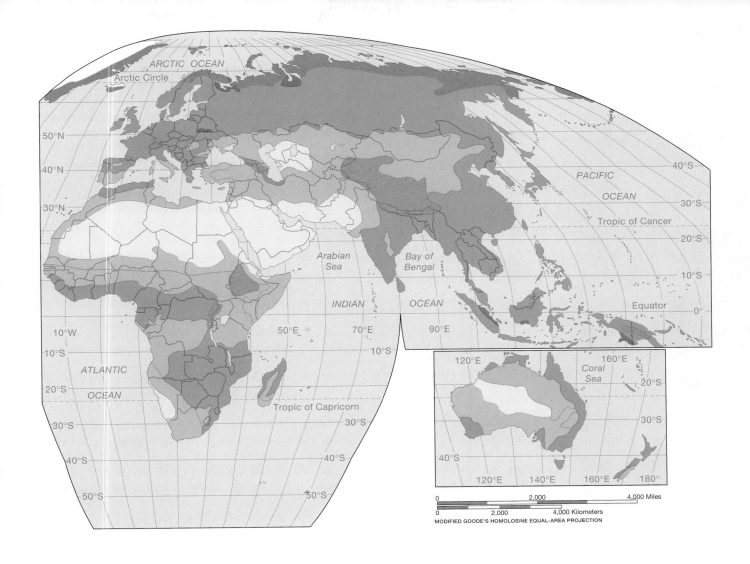

MODIFIED GOODE'S HOMOLOSINE EQUAL-AREA PROJECTION

Human activity can also change the climate through altering the composition of the atmosphere. Of greatest concern is the role that human activity is playing in causing **global warming,** an increase in world temperatures and change in climate associated with increasing levels of carbon dioxide and other gases resulting from human activities such as deforestation and fossil-fuel burning. Global warming is associated with the **greenhouse effect,** the trapping of heat within the atmosphere by water vapor and gases, such as carbon dioxide, resulting in the warming of the atmosphere and surface. Carbon dioxide is produced from burning fossil fuels, from cement production, and from deforestation, and the level of carbon dioxide in the atmosphere has increased dramatically with increases in human population and consumption over the last 100 years. Earth system scientists suggest that human-caused increases in carbon dioxide may result in an overall global temperature increase of about 3°C (5.5°F) over the next 50 years, as well as regional changes in the amount and distribution of precipitation. Evidence is accumulating that such changes are already occurring (**Figure 1.25**).

The World-System

The modern world-system was first established over a long period that began in the late 15th century and lasted until the mid-17th century. A **world-system** is an *interdependent* system of countries linked by political and economic competition. The term *world-system* is hyphenated to emphasize the interdependence of places and regions around the world.

29

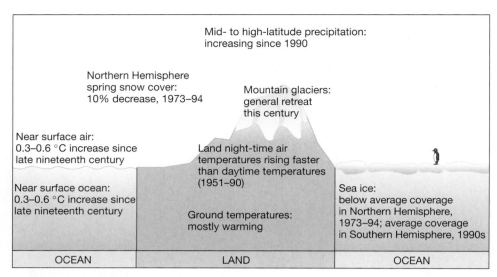

Mid- to high-latitude precipitation: increasing since 1990

Northern Hemisphere spring snow cover: 10% decrease, 1973–94

Mountain glaciers: general retreat this century

Near surface air: 0.3–0.6 °C increase since late nineteenth century

Land night-time air temperatures rising faster than daytime temperatures (1951–90)

Near surface ocean: 0.3–0.6 °C increase since late nineteenth century

Ground temperatures: mostly warming

Sea ice: below average coverage in Northern Hemisphere, 1973–94; average coverage in Southern Hemisphere, 1990s

OCEAN   LAND   OCEAN

FIGURE 1.25 Detected changes in climate This diagram, based on the work of the Intergovernmental Panel on Climate Change, summarizes the evidence for recent and observed changes in climate. Evidence includes a warming of ground, ocean, and near-surface air temperatures; a decline in sea ice and snow cover in the Northern Hemisphere; a retreat of mountain glaciers; and an increase in precipitation in high latitudes.

In parts of 15th-century Europe, exploration beyond European shores began to be seen as an important way of opening up new opportunities for trade and economic expansion. By the 16th century, new techniques of shipbuilding and navigation had begun to bind more and more places and regions together through trade and political competition. As a result, more and more people around the world became exposed to one another's technologies and ideas. But their different resources, social structures, and cultural systems resulted in quite different pathways of economic growth and change. Some societies were willingly incorporated into the new, European-based international economic system faster than others, some resisted incorporation, and some sought alternative systems of economic and political organization.

Since the 17th century, the world-system has been consolidated, with stronger economic ties between countries. It has also been extended, with all the world's countries eventually becoming involved, to some extent, in the interdependence of the capitalist system. **Capitalism** is a form of economic and social organization characterized by the profit motive and the control of the means of production, distribution, and exchange of goods by private ownership. There have, however, been many instances of resistance and adaptation, with some countries (Tanzania, for example) attempting to become self-sufficient and others (Cuba, for example) seeking to opt out of the system altogether in order to pursue a different path—communism. **Communism** is a form of economic and social organization characterized by the common ownership of the means of production, distribution, and exchange. Despite these exceptions, the overall result is that a highly structured relationship among places and regions has emerged. This relationship is organized around three tiers: *core*, *semiperipheral*, and *peripheral* regions. These broad geographic divisions have been created through a combination of processes of private economic competition and competition among states.

The Core The **core regions** of the world-system are those that dominate trade, control the most advanced technologies, and have high levels of productivity within diversified economies. As a result, they enjoy relatively high per capita incomes. The first core regions of the world-system were the trading hubs of Holland and England. Later, these were joined by manufacturing and exporting regions in other parts of western Europe and in North America, and later still, by Japan.

The success of the core regions depends on their dominance and exploitation of other regions. This dominance, in turn, depends on the participation of these other regions within the world-system. Initially, such participation was achieved by military enforcement, then by European colonialism, and finally by the sheer economic and political influence of the core regions. **Colonialism** involves the establishment and maintenance of domination—including political, economic, social, and cultural domination—by a state over a separate and alien society. This domination usually involves some **colonization** (that is, the physical settlement of people from the colonizing state) and always results in economic exploitation by the colonizing state.

The Periphery Regions that have resisted or remained economically and politically unable to participate in this process of incorporation into the world-system are peripheral to it. **Peripheral regions** are characterized by dependent and disadvantageous trading relationships, by inadequate or obsolete technologies, and by undeveloped or narrowly specialized economies with low levels of productivity.

In between core regions and peripheral regions are semiperipheral regions. **Semiperipheral regions** are able to exploit peripheral regions but are themselves exploited and dominated by the core regions. They consist mostly of countries that were once peripheral. This semiperipheral category underlines the fact that neither peripheral status nor core status is necessarily permanent. The United States and Japan both achieved core status after having been peripheral; Spain and Portugal, part of the original core in the 16th century, became semiperipheral in the 19th century but are now once more part of the core. Quite a few countries, including Brazil, India, Mexico, South Korea, and Taiwan, have become semiperipheral after developing a successful manufacturing sector.

An important determinant of these changes in status is the effectiveness of states in ensuring the international competitiveness of their domestic producers. They can do this in several ways: by manipulating markets (protecting domestic manufacturers by charging taxes on imports, for example), by regulating their economies (enacting laws that help establish stable labor markets, for example), and by creating physical and social infrastructures (spending public funds on such things as road systems, ports, and educational systems). Because some states are more successful than others in pursuing these strategies, the hierarchy of these three geographical tiers is not rigid. Rather, it is fluid, providing a continually changing framework for geographical transformation within individual places and regions, as illustrated in **Figure 1.26**, which shows the geography of the world economy over three time periods.

It is also important to recognize that core, peripheral, and semiperipheral regions are not monolithic geographies. In other words, there are peripheral areas within core regions and even within core cities, just as there are core areas within peripheral regions and peripheral cities. For example, North America is, generally speaking, a core region. Yet within both Canada and the United States there are extensive areas, such as Nunavut in Canada, that do not have widespread access to advanced technologies, have low levels of economic productivity (in the capitalist sense), and have very narrowly specialized economies. The same is true of the periphery, where some areas have more in common with the core regions than they do with the areas that immediately surround them. This is certainly the case with Rio de Janiero in Brazil or Jakarta in Indonesia, both of which are core cities in semiperipheral and peripheral countries.

Consolidation of the World Economy   The main outcome of economic globalization has been the consolidation of the core of the world economy. This core is now a close-knit triad of geographic centers (North America, Europe, and Japan) (**Figure 1.27**). These three geographic centers are connected through three main circuits, or flows, of investment, trade, and communication: between Europe and North America, between Europe and the Far East, and among the regions of the Pacific Rim. Within this core of centers and flows, a new hierarchy of regional specialization has been imposed through the strategies that transnational corporations and international financial institutions use to locate their operations.

While incorporating more of the world, more completely, into the capitalist world-system, globalization has intensified the differences between the rich and the poor. According to the United Nations Development Program, the gap between the poorest fifth of the world's population and the wealthiest fifth increased more than threefold between 1960 and the turn of the new century. Some parts of the periphery have almost slid off the economic map. In some countries—55 of them, in fact—per capita incomes actually fell during the 1990s. In Sub-Saharan Africa, economic output fell by one-third during the 1980s and stayed low during the 1990s, so that people's standard of living there is now, on average, lower than it was in the early 1960s. At the beginning of the 21st century, the fifth of the world's population living in the highest-income countries had:

FIGURE 1.26 The world-system core, semiperiphery, and periphery in 1800, 1900, and 2000 These three maps show the changing geography of the world-system as more and more regions were incorporated in a capitalist economic system.

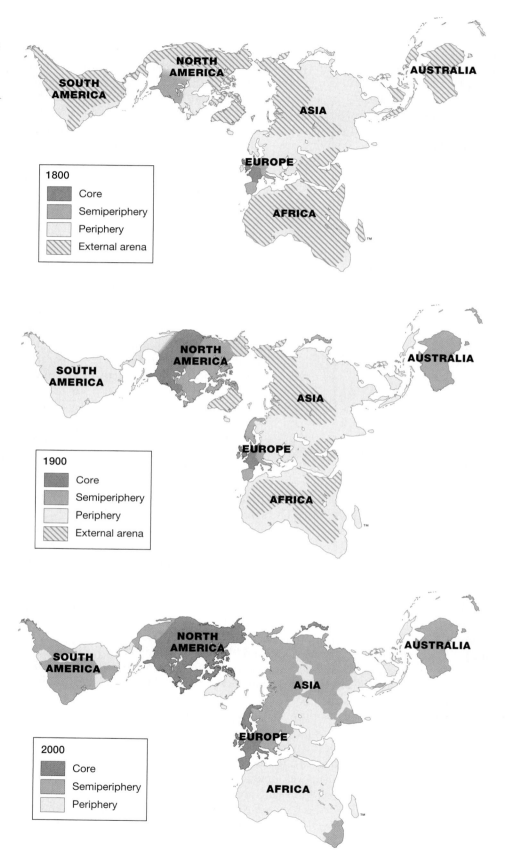

> 74 percent of world income—the bottom fifth had just 1 percent,
> 82 percent of world export markets—the bottom fifth had just 1 percent, and
> 74 percent of world telephone lines, today's basic means of communication—the bottom fifth had just 1.5 percent.

Such enormous differences lead many people to question the equity, or fairness, of geographical variations in people's levels of affluence and well-being. The concept of *spatial justice* is important in this context, because it requires us to consider the distribution of society's benefits and burdens, taking into account both variations in people's needs and in their contribution to the production of wealth and social well-being.

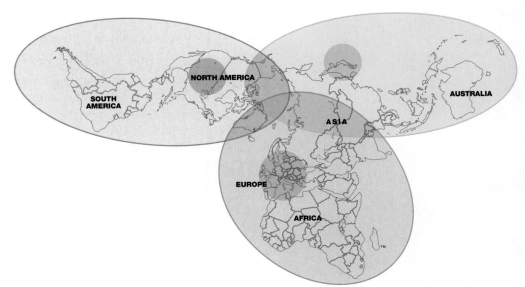

FIGURE 1.27 Triadic core In general terms, the world economy is now structured around a "core" with three centers: the United States, Japan, and the European Union. Most of the flows of goods, capital, and information are within and among these three centers. They dominate the world's periphery, with each center having particular influence in its own regional expansion zone—its nearest peripheral region.

Meanwhile, economic and cultural globalization has not been evenly matched by the growth of political globalization or a comprehensive system of government that can cope with these powerful forces. Policymakers, for the most part, lack an adequate framework for coping with the consequences of globalization. While institutions such as the World Criminal Court and the Kyoto Agreement constitute the beginnings of a global governance framework for crime and the environment, powerful nations like the United States have not joined them, so their effectiveness is somewhat limited. Further, trade policy has come to be governed by powerful transnational corporations, while national governments are unable to deal with transnational environmental issues. As a result, globalization has fueled global economic expansion but in the process it has widened the gap between rich and poor and made places and regions everywhere vulnerable to rapid and dislocating transformations.

This inequality resulting from globalization is reflected—and reinforced—by many aspects of human well-being. Patterns of infant mortality, a reliable indicator of social well-being, show a steep core-periphery gradient. For adults in the industrial core countries, life expectancy is high and continues to increase. In the year 2000, life expectancy at birth in Australia was 79 years; in Canada it was 79; and in the United States it was 77. In contrast, life expectancy in the poorest countries is dramatically shorter. In Namibia in 2000, it was 47; in Ethiopia it was 42; and in Sierra Leone it was 39. In most African countries, only 60 to 75 percent of the population can expect to survive to age 40.

ORGANIZING THE CORE

Beginning in the 15th century, the transformation of much of Europe, and later the United States, as core regions was predicated on complex innovations and institutions that stabilized and enabled capitalist political and economic organizations to flourish, particularly those central to trade and later industrialization. All of these institutions and innovations emerged prior to or during the mercantile period; they were stabilized and extended geographically during the industrial period in order to support the requirements of capitalist economic organization. **Mercantilism,** an economic policy prevailing in Europe during the 16th, 17th, and 18th centuries, is based on the idea that government should control industry and trade. Following are some of the primary factors that played critical roles in organizing and consolidating the core:

1. The division of labor enabled increased productivity.

2. The standardization of time, space, measure, value, and money allowed for more predictability and consistency in commerce and manufacture.

3. The forging of national identities affirmed the emergence of a unified and powerful state.

4. The controlling and commodifying of nature increased resources.

5. The development of internal physical infrastructures, such as railroads, canals, and communications systems, improved the movement of goods, people, and ideas.

The Division of Labor

All contemporary societies are organized around a division of labor, whether it is complex or simple. Furthermore, the division of labor has been a feature of human societies from the earliest times. A **division of labor** is the separation of productive processes into individual operations, each performed by different workers or groups of workers. For example, in many preindustrial societies, men hunt, trap, and fish while women manage household gardens and tend to children. When the separation of productive processes is based on gender, it is known as a **gender division of labor** (**Figure 1.28**). Other divisions of labor might be based on skill or vocation, as in the medieval period, when the system of social and economic organization was based on different groups of artisans and merchants organized into guilds. At one level, the division of labor is ingenious because it enables a substantial increase in individual and collective efficiency due to the increase in skill that specialization provides. At another level, however, the division of labor separates workers from the product of their labor so that they contribute only a small fragment to the whole and may come to feel meaningless in the larger scheme of production. The technical division of labor is a central institutional feature of the economic organization of the core. At the same time that it has enabled the core to be efficient in productive activities in an unprecedented way, it has also narrowed and segmented individuals' social identities, virtually equating a person's social identity with his or her role in the division of labor.

FIGURE 1.28 Gender division of labor Pictured here are female sales clerks and their male supervisor at the Mitsukoshi store in Tokyo, the oldest department store in the world. The majority of salespeople in Japan and elsewhere in the core are female. Relatively few hold management positions.

Standardizing Time, Space, Measure, Value, and Money

Standardization of timekeeping, measurement, currency, and value also became a central requirement for conducting transactions in the daily life of the core as well as in an increasingly interconnected world. At the level of everyday life, standardization of time, for instance, ensured that workers arrived each morning at the factory gate at the same time. Whereas previously national, regional, and local time standards, or just general daily and seasonal sensitivity to light and dark, shaped human activity patterns, the standardization of time meant that sharply defined work schedules and deadlines became part of factory life and daily habits. With the increasing interconnectedness of the globe, the standardization of space—a framework for determining relative location and distance—was also critical. The standardization of measure ensured that replacement parts for a machine would fit all the same machines in any factory anywhere in the world. Furthermore, the prices for goods could be fixed more precisely and consistently through an agreed-upon system of weights and measures. Moreover, value—how much a worker was paid and how much a product was worth—came to be defined in terms of money or currency, and the standardization of money simplified and extended the transactions of market exchange. The stabilization of credit—the ability to borrow money—was also an important accomplishment of core industrialization.

Forging National Identities and Constructing States

Another important aspect of the organization of the core was the increasing political significance of a national population unified around a strong state. As mentioned previously, a state is an independent political unit with territorial boundaries that are internationally recognized by other states; a nation is a community of people often sharing common elements of culture, such as religion or language, or a history or political identity. Nations were invented as part of the rise of the republic as a new form of government.

Following the overthrow or decline of monarchies in Europe in the late 18th to mid-19th centuries, a number of new republics were created. Republican government, as distinct from monarchy, requires the democratic participation and support of its population. Monarchical political power is derived from force and subjugation; republican political power derives from the support of the governed. By creating a sense of nationhood, the newly emerging states of Europe were attempting to homogenize their multiple and sometimes conflicting constituencies so that they could govern with their active cooperation according to a sense of a common purpose.

In addition to enabling the creation of a stable democracy, the construction of a nation also enables the organization of a more extensive and coherent market where buyers and sellers all speak the same language and all have an investment in the success of the economic enterprise. A national identity is built not only upon a common language but also upon a common sense of history and purpose such that individuals feel compelled to defend the nation and to further the objectives of the state.

The increasing interconnectedness of the world has meant increased population mobility and widespread dispersal of Earth's peoples. The spatial dispersion of a previously homogeneous group is known as a **diaspora**. Contemporary members of a nation recognize a common identity, but they need not reside within a common geographical area. For example, the Jewish nation refers to members of the Jewish culture and faith throughout the world regardless of their place of origin. The term **nation-state** is an ideal form consisting of a homogeneous group of people governed by their own state. In a true nation-state, no significant group exists that is not part of the nation. **Nationalism** is the feeling of belonging to a nation as well as the belief that a nation has a natural right to determine its own affairs (**Figure 1.29**).

Controlling and Commodifying Nature

Perhaps the most widespread conception of nature that informed the imperialist practices of the core—and one that has persisted under different labels for thousands of years—is that humans are the center of all creation and that nature in all its wildness was meant to be dominated by humans. Judeo-Christian belief insists that Man (meaning an ideal type, not necessarily masculine), made in the image of God, was set apart from nature and must be encouraged to control it.

The view that nature was to be controlled by humans was accompanied by the parallel idea that nature was a commodity to be exploited and produced. A **commodity** is anything that has a use value or that has some usefulness to someone. Sheep, rivers, and trees were all referred to as commodities because they could be used to sustain

FIGURE 1.29 Nationalism in Ukraine Pictured here are members of the Ukrainian nationalist movement who have masked themselves and march in protest against the government's plans to allow dual citizenship and introduce Russian as the state's second language.

and shelter life. With the rise of capitalism, the popular understanding of use value was replaced by that of exchange value, and a commodity came to mean anything useful that could be bought or sold. Production for sale in the marketplace is what makes commodities of things—whether foodstuffs, minerals, animals, even human beings. Capitalism has made it possible for everything and anything to be a commodity under certain conditions. For example, the international agreement signed in 1997 in Kyoto, Japan, has made the right to pollute the air a commodity that can be bought and sold.

The commodifying of nature that accompanied the rise of capitalism was feverishly pursued during the age of discovery as European explorers found new resources to exploit in new places. Unfortunately, the history of the capitalist pursuit of producing commodities often includes the destruction and substantial dislocation of whole social systems so that these commodities can be marketed and made profitable. Important for the development of the interconnectedness of world regions is the fact that turning nature into commodities has a history that is part of the history of the globalization of capitalism. In brief, any commodity has a history that is located in an origin and can be traced outward to other parts of the globe. A commodity is linked to the societies that first recognized its use value, then understood how to enhance that value by cultivating or processing it, and finally began to trade it. But the history of any commodity must also take into account the links that were created to connect it economically, politically, socially, and culturally to other parts of the world. Finally, the history of a commodity is not only about the commodity itself, such as wine, tobacco, sugar, oil, or diamonds—the history of those commodities will be discussed in the following chapters—but it is also the history of the billions of people who have produced, desired, and consumed the commodities.

ORGANIZING THE PERIPHERY

Parallel with the internal development of core regions were changes in the geographies of the periphery of the world-system. Indeed, the growth and internal development of the core regions simply could not have taken place without the foodstuffs, raw materials, and markets provided by the colonization of the periphery and the incorporation of more and more territory into the sphere of industrial capitalism.

As soon as the Industrial Revolution had gathered momentum in the early 19th century, the industrial core nations embarked on the inland penetration of the world's mid-continental grassland zones in order to exploit them for grain or stock production. This led to the settlement, through the emigration of European peoples, of the temperate prairies and pampas of the Americas, the *veld* in southern Africa, the Murray-Darling Plain in Australia, and the Canterbury Plain in New Zealand. At the same time, as the demand for tropical plantation products increased, most of the tropical world came under the political and economic control—direct or indirect—of one or another of the industrial core nations. In the second half of the 19th century, and especially after 1870, there was a vast increase in the number of colonies and the number of people under colonial rule.

The colonization that accompanied the expansion of the world-system was closely tied to the evolution of world leadership cycles. **Leadership cycles** are periods of international power established by individual states through economic, political, and military competition. In the long term, success in the world-system depends on economic strength and competitiveness, which brings political influence and pays for military strength. With a combination of economic, political, and military power, individual states can dominate the world-system, setting the terms for many economic and cultural practices and imposing their particular ideologies by virtue of their preeminence. This kind of dominance is known as hegemony. **Hegemony** refers to domination over the world economy, exercised—through a combination of economic, military, financial, and cultural means—by one national state in a particular historical epoch. Over the long run, the costs of maintaining this kind of power and influence tend to weaken the hegemon. This phase of the cycle is known as *imperial overstretch*. (**Imperialism** is the extension of the power of a state through the direct or indirect control of the economic and political life of other territories.) It is followed by another period of competitive struggle, which brings the possibility of a new dominant world power.

Imperialism and Colonialism

The incorporation of the external arena into the core was motivated by several factors, among them the basic logic of free trade, investment, and the desire for new territories. Although Britain was the leading world economic and military hegemon in the late 19th century, several other European countries (notably Germany, France, and the Netherlands), together with the United States—and later Japan—were competing for global influence. This competition developed into a scramble for territorial and commercial domination (**Figure 1.30**). The core countries engaged in preemptive geographic expansionism in order to protect their established interests and to limit the opportunities of others. They also wanted to secure as much of the world as possible—through a combination of military oversight, administrative control, and economic regulations—in order to ensure stable and profitable environments for their traders and investors.

The imprint of core expansionism on the geographies of the newly incorporated peripheries of the world-system was immediate and profound. The periphery became almost entirely dependent on European and North American capital, shipping, managerial expertise, financial services, and news and communications. As a consequence, the periphery also came to depend on European cultural products: language, education, science, religion, architecture, and planning. All of this ultimately was etched into the landscapes of the periphery in a variety of ways as new places were created, old places were remade, and regions were reorganized.

One of the most striking changes in the periphery was the establishment and growth of externally oriented port cities through which commodity exports and manufactured imports were channeled. Often, these major ports were also colonial administrative and political capitals, so that they became overwhelmingly important, growing rapidly to sizes far in excess of other settlements. Good examples include Georgetown (Guyana), Lagos (Nigeria), Luanda (Angola), Karachi (Pakistan), and Rangoon (Burma). Meanwhile, the interior geography of peripheral countries was restructured as smaller settlements were given new functions: colonial administration and commercial marketing. As with the interior development of the core countries, transport networks were vital to this process. Railroads provided the principal means of spatial reorganization, and in the colonies of Africa, Central America, and South and Southeast Asia, railroad lines evolved into linear patterns with simple feeder routes and limited interconnections that focused almost exclusively on major port cities.

An International Division of Labor

The fundamental logic behind imperialism and colonization was economic: the need for an extended arena for trade, an arena that could supply foodstuffs and raw materials in return for the industrial goods of the core. The outcome was an international division of labor, driven by the needs of the core and imposed through its economic and military strength. This **international division of labor** involved the specialization of different people, regions, and countries in certain kinds of economic activities. In particular, colonies began to specialize in the production of those foodstuffs and raw materials that fit the following criteria:

> materials for which there was an established demand in the industrial core
> materials for which colonies held a **comparative advantage**, in that their productivity was higher than for other possible specializations
> materials that did not duplicate or compete with domestic suppliers within core countries (tropical agricultural products such as cocoa and rubber, for example, simply could not be grown in core countries)

The result was that colonial economies were founded on narrow specializations that were oriented to, and dependent on, the needs of core countries. Examples of these specializations are many: bananas in Central America; cotton in India; coffee in

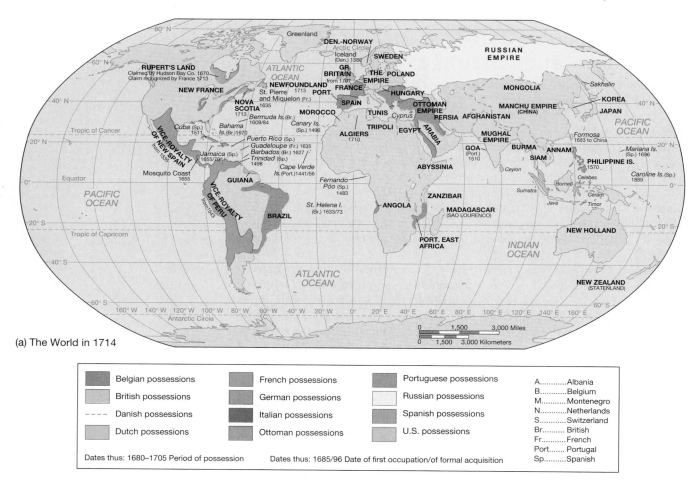

(a) The World in 1714

■ Belgian possessions	■ French possessions	■ Portuguese possessions	A............Albania
□ British possessions	■ German possessions	□ Russian possessions	B............Belgium
- - - - Danish possessions	■ Italian possessions	■ Spanish possessions	M...........Montenegro
□ Dutch possessions	■ Ottoman possessions	□ U.S. possessions	N............Netherlands
			S............Switzerland
			Br.......... British
			Fr...........French
			Port....... Portugal
			Sp..........Spanish

Dates thus: 1680–1705 Period of possession   Dates thus: 1685/96 Date of first occupation/of formal acquisition

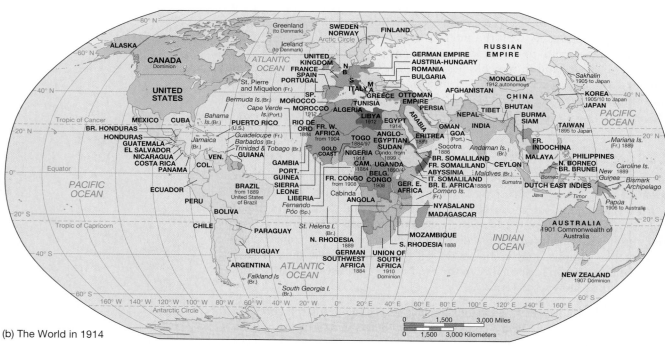

(b) The World in 1914

FIGURE 1.30 The world in 1714 and 1914 These two maps illustrate the transformation in the political geography of the globe that occurred during the 200 years that mark the most intense period of European global imperialism and colonialism. The maps show that imperialism in the Americas was effectively ended by the 19th century, whereas imperialism in Africa and Asia was in full swing. (a) In 1714, European possessions amounted to less than 10 percent of the world's land area and only 2 percent of the world's population. (b) By 1914, European colonies amounted to more than 55 percent of the world's land area and 34 percent of the world's population. (*Source:* Redrawn from B. Crow and A. Thomas, *Third World Atlas.* Milton Keynes: Open University Press, 1982, pp. 37, 41.)

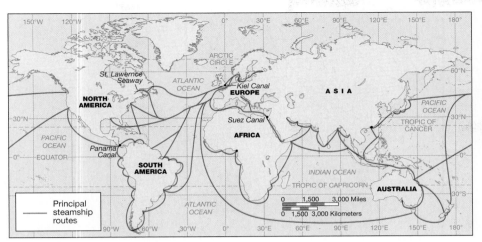

FIGURE 1.31 Principal steamship routes, 1920 The shipping routes reflect (1) the trans-Atlantic trade between the two core regions of the world-system at the time; and (2) the colonial and imperial relations between the world's core economies and the periphery. Transoceanic shipping boomed with the development of steam-turbine engines for merchant vessels and with the construction of shipping canals, such as the Kiel Canal, the Suez Canal, the St. Lawrence Seaway, and the Panama Canal. When the 82 kilometers (51 miles) of the Panama Canal opened in 1914, shipping could move between the Atlantic and the Pacific without having to go around South America, saving thousands of kilometers of steaming.

Brazil, Java, and Kenya; copper in Chile; cocoa in Ghana; jute in East Pakistan (now Bangladesh); palm oil in west Africa; rubber in Malaya (now Malaysia) and Sumatra; sugar in the Caribbean islands; tea in Ceylon (now Sri Lanka); tin in Bolivia; and bauxite in Guyana and Suriname. Most of these specializations have continued to the present. Thus, for example, 48 of the 55 countries in Sub-Saharan Africa still depend for more than half of their export earnings on only three products—tea, cocoa, and coffee.

This new world economic geography took some time to establish, and the details of its pattern and timing were heavily influenced by technological innovations. The incorporation of the temperate grasslands into the commercial orbit of the core countries, for example, involved successive changes in regional landscapes as critical innovations such as barbed wire, the railroad, and refrigeration were introduced. But the single most important innovation behind the international division of labor was the development of metal-hulled, oceangoing steamships. This development was in fact cumulative, with improvements in engines, boilers, transmission systems, fuel systems, and construction materials adding up to produce dramatic improvements in carrying capacity, speed, range, and reliability. The construction of the Suez Canal (opened in 1869) and the Panama Canal (opened in 1914) was also critical, providing shorter and less hazardous routes between core countries and colonial ports of call. By the eve of World War I, the world economy was effectively integrated by a system of regularly scheduled steamship trading routes (**Figure 1.31**). This integration in turn was supported by the second most important innovation behind the international division of labor, a network of telegraph communications (**Figure 1.32**) that enabled businesses to monitor and coordinate supply and demand across vast distances on an hourly basis.

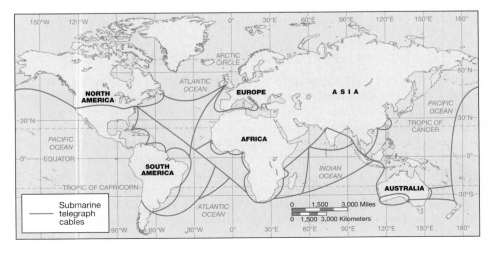

FIGURE 1.32 The international telegraph network, 1900 For Britain, submarine telegraph cables were the nervous system of empire. Of the global network of 246,000 kilometers (152,860 miles) of submarine cable, Britain had laid 169,000 kilometers (105,015 miles).

FIGURE 1.33 The British empire, late 1800s Protected by the all-powerful Royal Navy, the British merchant navy established a web of commerce that collected food for British industrial workers and raw materials for its industries, much of it from colonies and dependencies appropriated by imperial might and developed by British capital. So successful was the trading empire that Britain also became the hub of trade for other states. (*Source: After P. Hugill, World Trade Since 1431. Baltimore: Johns Hopkins University Press, 1993, p. 136.*)

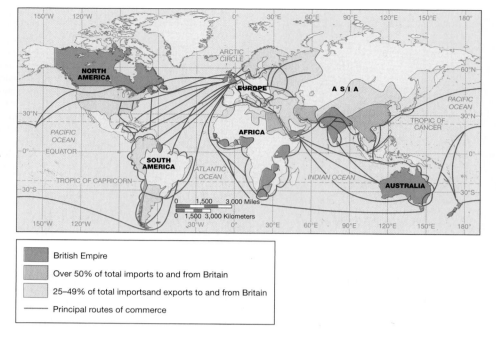

British Empire

Over 50% of total imports to and from Britain

25–49% of total importsand exports to and from Britain

Principal routes of commerce

The international division of labor brought about a substantial increase in trade and a huge surge in the overall size of the capitalist world economy. The peripheral regions of the world contributed a great deal to this growth. By 1913 Africa and Asia provided more *exports* to the world economy than either North America or the British Isles. Asia alone was *importing* almost as much, by value, as North America. The industrializing countries of the core bought increasing amounts of foodstuffs and raw materials from the periphery, financed by profits from the export of machinery and manufactured goods. Britain, the leading world power of the period, drew on a trading empire that was truly global (**Figure 1.33**).

Patterns of international trade and interdependence became increasingly complex. Britain used its capital to invest not just in peripheral regions but also in profitable industries in other core countries, especially the United States. At the same time, these other core countries were able to export cheap manufactured goods to Britain. Britain financed the purchase of these goods, together with imports of food from its dominion states (Canada, South Africa, Australia, and New Zealand) and colonies, through the export of its own manufactured goods to peripheral countries. India and China, with large domestic markets, were especially receptive. Thus there developed a widening circle of exchange and dependence, with constantly switching patterns of trade and investment.

Exploration and Exploitation

The scramble to incorporate the periphery into the world-system in the late 18th and early 19th centuries was aimed at acquiring territory and cultivating commercial opportunities. Colonialism was carried out through the processes of exploration and exploitation. Exploration is generally understood to mean the growth of knowledge of the globe that occurred as a result of voyages of discovery and scientific expeditions. It should be noted, however, that an alternative view is to see the encounter between the core and the periphery that took place during this period as, more accurately, one of invasion and conquest (**Figure 1.34**). Regardless of the moral issues behind the historical meeting of the core and periphery, clearly exploration and scientific discovery went hand-in-hand and that geography as a discipline contributed substantially to both (**Figure 1.35**).

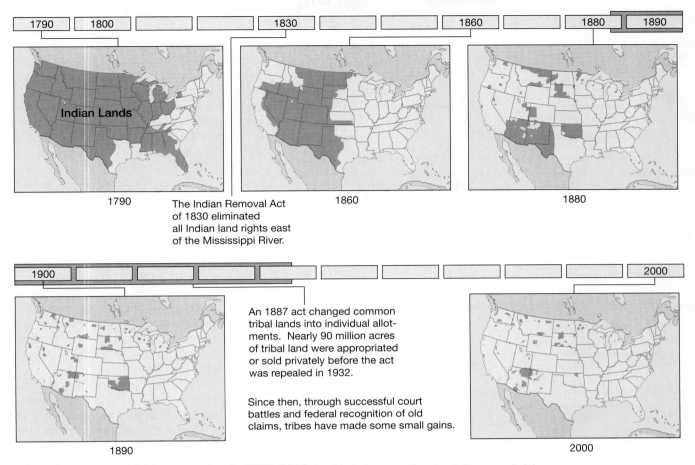

1790   1800   1830   1860   1880   1890

Indian Lands

1790
The Indian Removal Act
of 1830 eliminated
all Indian land rights east
of the Mississippi River.

1860

1880

1900   2000

An 1887 act changed common
tribal lands into individual allot-
ments. Nearly 90 million acres
of tribal land were appropriated
or sold privately before the act
was repealed in 1932.

Since then, through successful court
battles and federal recognition of old
claims, tribes have made some small gains.

1890

2000

FIGURE 1.34 Diminishing tribal lands, 1790–2000 Two hundred years ago American Indians controlled three-quarters of the present-day United States. Today the 358 federally recognized Indian reservations cover less than 2 percent of the United States. (*Source:* Bureau of Indian Affairs; Smithsonian Institution; *New York Times*, "Mending a Trail of Broken Treaties," June 25, 2000, Section WK, p. 3.)

The experience of the encounter between the core and the periphery was certainly complicated. It is uncontestable that the core countries—effectively those of western Europe—transformed existing lands and peoples to meet their own commercial, evangelical, and colonial motives. Furthermore, the encounter between the two worlds was framed by the view that Western civilization was superior to the barbaric rest of the

FIGURE 1.35 Exploration and geography The Royal Geographical Society helped fund the team of Laurence Oates, H. R. Bowers, Robert F. Scott, Edward A. Wilson, and Edgar Evans on their trip to discover the South Pole and claim it for Britain. A Norwegian team led by Roald Amundsen beat Scott's team to the Pole by one month in December 1911. And while Amundsen's team returned to Norway in good health, all five members of the British team died on their way back.

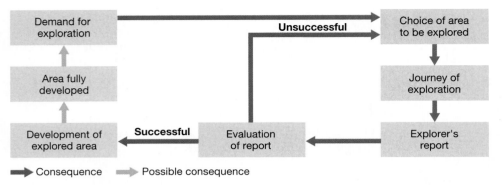

FIGURE 1.36 **Principal elements in the process of exploration** This diagram illustrates the main elements in the process of exploration, beginning with a need in the home country that prompts a desire to look outward to satisfy that need. Geographers have figured prominently in the process of exploration by identifying areas to be explored as well as actually traveling to these far-flung places, cataloging resources and people. Nineteenth-century geography textbooks are records of these explorations and the way in which geographers conceptualized the worlds they encountered. Exploration is one aspect of the process of imperialism; colonization is another. (*Source:* J. D. Overton, "A Theory of Exploration," *Journal of Historical Geography* 7, 1981, p. 57.)

world. Thus, the engagement between "the West" and "the rest" was as much a moral event as anything else. As a result, the core often attempted to "master" the periphery and ended up marginalizing, if not completely destroying, existing and highly developed social, cultural, and moral systems. The same thing was largely true of the core's impact on the natural world of the periphery.

Figure 1.36 provides a theorization of imperialism beginning with the process of exploration and culminating in either colonization or the exploitation of people and resources or both. At the beginning of the process, a state perceives a need for exploration. This need is often the result of a scarcity or lack of a critical natural resource. Broadly speaking, in the first phases of imperialism, the core exploits the periphery for raw materials. Later, as the periphery becomes developed, colonization may occur, and cash economies are introduced where none previously existed. The periphery may also become a market for the manufactured goods of the core. Eventually, though not always, the periphery—because of the availability of cheap labor, land, and other inputs to production—can become a new arena for large-scale capital investment.

The first cases of sustained encounter between the core and the periphery usually resulted in the establishment of trading relations, sometimes even trading settlements. This was the case with European contact with Africa during the 15th century, when the Portuguese explored the West African coastline and established a chain of trading settlements. These new opportunities for trade with Europe often dislocated the ongoing patterns of internal trade in the periphery and disrupted political life along with existing economic and religious systems.

After trading links were established, core states would often increase exploration and accelerate exploitation. For instance, by the late 18th century European countries had substantial and well-established trade with Africa. Over the next century, European colonization efforts in Africa, Asia, and South America expanded as domestic demand for certain agricultural and mineral products increased. Mining operations were established; European technology and crops were introduced into their colonies (**Figure 1.37**); other natural resources such as fish, animals, and wood products were harvested and shipped back to European markets; and an exchange economy based on money and profit evolved (**Figure 1.38**).

The classic institution of colonial agriculture was the **plantation**—an extensive, European-owned, operated, and financed enterprise where single crops were produced by local or imported labor for a world market. The first plantations are likely to have been started in the Caribbean only two decades after the first voyage of Columbus in the late 15th century.

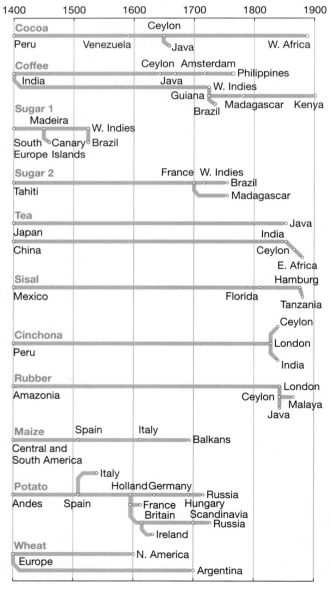

Chronology of the transfer of cash crops, 1400–1900

FIGURE 1.37 **Global transfer of crops, 1400–1900** This diagram depicts the timing of the transfer of crops as they were introduced around the globe. Perhaps the most significant impact of European imperialism beginning in the 16th century was the gradual incorporation of agriculture into one comprehensive world-system. The diagram illustrates the very important point that production, which began in one location, was moved to other locations where the climate was suitable, labor could be acquired, and production and trade could be managed. Thus agriculture became a globally organized system where crops were produced in numerous locations to feed world markets. (*Source:* B. Crow and A. Thomas, *Third World Atlas.* Milton Keynes: Open University Press, 1982, p. 29.)

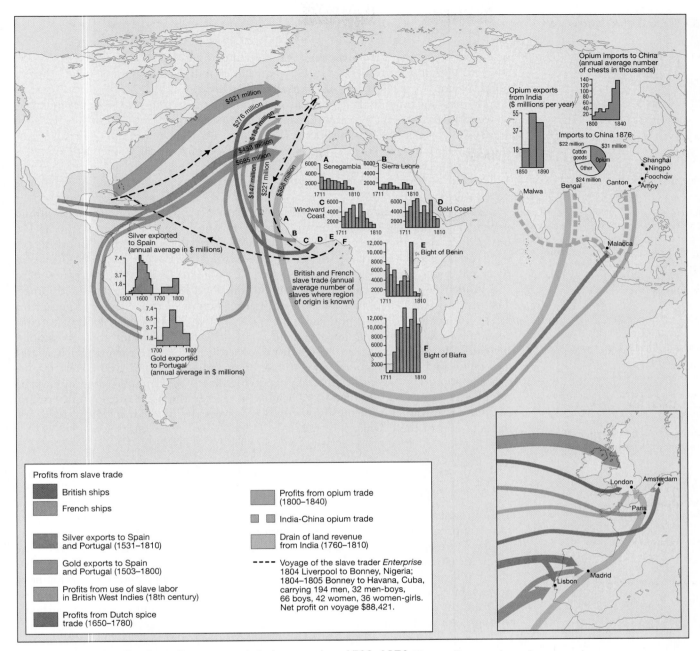

FIGURE 1.38 Profits from European global expansion, 1500–1876 This map illustrates the profits generated through European plunder of global minerals, spices, and human beings over more than three centuries. Silver and gold from the Americas, opium and tea from China, spices from the East Indies (Indonesia, Malaysia, and the Philippines), and slaves from Africa are represented.
(*Source:* Adapted from B. Crow and A. Thomas, *Third World Atlas*. Milton Keynes: Open University Press, 1982, p. 27.)

The first plantation crop was sugar, followed by other crops, both edible and nonedible—for example, coffee plantations in India and rubber plantations in Sri Lanka. Over time, some plantation crops were replaced by others as competition over the production of particular crops between colonies increased or crops in some locations became increasingly susceptible to pests.

GLOBALIZATION AND POLITICAL, ECONOMIC, AND CULTURAL CHANGE

The imperial world order began to disintegrate shortly after World War II. The United States emerged as the dominant state within the world-system core. This core came to be called the "First World." The Soviet Union and China, opting for alternative paths of development for themselves and their satellite countries, were seen as a "Second World," withdrawn from the capitalist world economy. Their pursuit of alternative political economies was based on radically different values.

By the 1950s many of the old European colonies began to seek political independence. Some of the early independence struggles were very bloody, but by the early 1960s the process of decolonization had become relatively smooth. The periphery of the world-system now consisted of a "Third World" of politically independent states, some of which adopted a policy of nonalignment vis-à-vis the geopolitics of the First and Second worlds. Nevertheless, in economic terms they were still highly dependent on the world's core countries.

As newly independent peripheral states struggled to be free of their economic dependence through industrialization, modernization, and trade from the 1960s onward, so the capitalist world-system became increasingly integrated and interdependent. The old imperial patterns of international trade broke down and were replaced by more complex patterns. Nevertheless, the newly independent states were still influenced by many of the old colonial links and legacies that remained intact. The result was a neocolonial pattern of international development. **Neocolonialism** refers to economic and political strategies by which powerful states in core economies indirectly maintain or extend their influence over other areas or people. Instead of formal, direct rule (colonialism), controls are exerted through such strategies as international financial regulations, commercial relations, and covert intelligence operations. Because of this neocolonialism, the human geographies of peripheral countries continued to be heavily shaped by the linguistic, cultural, political, and institutional influence of ex-colonial powers and by the investment and trading activities of their firms.

Deploying and Encountering Development

The rationale whereby the postwar world became more fully integrated was through a *set* of approaches to economic and political transformation known as development theory. **Development theory** is the analysis of the social changes that affect the economic progress of individual countries. Numerous authors, world leaders, and economic policies have been associated with development theory and the development project, but the centerpiece of all mainstream approaches to development is the aim to replicate the prosperity of the core in the periphery by encouraging economic growth through industrialization and modernization.

Theory and Critique   Development theory first came into being as the justification for the rebuilding of postwar Europe and as a weapon against the Cold War threat of communism and was soon after applied to the situation of newly emerging states in Africa, Asia, and South America struggling under the legacies of colonialism and post-colonialism. There were two underlying assumptions of the core's attitude about development: (1) that the periphery should aim to be like the core in its pathway to development, and (2) that the economic problems of development in the periphery are poverty and backwardness.

This overall relationship between the economy and levels of prosperity makes it possible to interpret economic development in terms of distinctive *stages*. Each region or country, in other words, might be thought of as progressing from the early stages of development, with a heavy reliance on primary activities (and relatively low levels of prosperity), through a phase of industrialization, and on to a "mature" stage of postindustrial development (with a diversified economic structure and relatively high levels of prosperity). This, in fact, is a commonly held view of economic development, conceptualized by a prominent economist, W. W. Rostow (**Figure 1.39**). Most development theorists and practitioners hew to this perspective and view the situation of peripheral and semiperipheral countries as one in which they must simply be helped to move along a clear path so that eventually they will "catch up" economically.

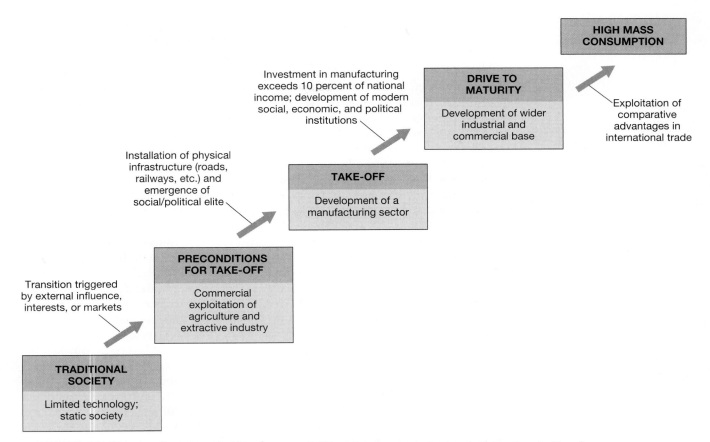

FIGURE 1.39 Stages of economic development This model of economic development is based on the idea of successive stages. Each stage is seen as leading to the next, though different regions or countries may take longer than others to make the transition from one stage to the next. As such, places and regions can be seen as following parallel courses within a world that is steadily modernizing.

In such a model, an economy is understood to consist of a modern sector(s) and a non-modern sector(s) with the latter characterized by low labor productivity. If the country or region with these conflicting economic sectors is to develop, then the non-modern sector must be transformed or modernized. In short, **modernization theory** states that economic development occurs when investment rates enable higher levels of industrialization, thus raising labor productivity and increasing the GDP per capita levels. The ultimate goal in this staged economic development model is an end period of high mass consumption.

The modernization version of development theory was not without its detractors. Chief among the critics were scholars and policymakers from the periphery who became part of the *dependency school of development*. The dependency theorists argued that it was not labor inefficiency or absence of modernization that was the root cause of the poverty in the periphery, but rather that the very nature of the core-periphery relationship was such that the core, through economic exploitation, had created a state of *underdevelopment* in the periphery. Thus the pathway to development was not the same for the periphery as it was for the core. The progression of the core from undeveloped to developed status was achieved at the direct expense of the periphery. The core had expressly underdeveloped the periphery by taking the economic surplus generated there and repatriating it to the core. Moreover, the process of underdevelopment in the periphery had rendered it dependent on the core for inputs of capital and technology. The solution, the dependency school theorists argued, was for the periphery to break off from the capitalist world-system in order to escape active underdevelopment and the status of economic dependence.

Another critique of development theory was launched by feminists in the 1970s. Their objection to mainstream development theory and policy was that it left out women, either by assuming that women had no role to play in development or by failing to recognize that women might experience development differently from men. This criticism came to be widely recognized as a legitimate one, and development theory and policies were revised not only to take account of the differential impact of development on women but to incorporate women directly into development projects. More recently, however, this approach has also been criticized by a new generation of feminists, who see it as failing to recognize that women's identities and access to power and resources are also shaped by other important identities, such as generation, ethnicity, religion, sexuality, and marital status, just to name a few.

Development theory, like most economic theories, rests on certain simplifying assumptions about the world. The real world is highly differentiated, not just in terms of natural resources, but in terms of demographics, culture, and politics. The assumptions in Rostow's model, for instance, fit the experience of some parts of the world, but by no means all of it. In reality, there are a variety of pathways to development, and a variety of different processes and outcomes of development. Indeed, this narrow construction of the pathway toward, and the existing conditions necessary for, development ultimately created serious challenges for modernization theory and its policy proponents. At the same time, dependency theory was also seen as seriously flawed. The result has been a reconsideration and restructuring of modernization theory and the emergence of the idea of sustainable development and alternative and critical theories of development advanced more recently by scholars from the periphery.

Neoliberalism and Development Neoliberal policies of development have emanated from the core and have been very much associated with the increasing influence of the World Bank and the International Monetary Fund over the last 25 years. The **World Bank** is a development bank and the largest source of development assistance in the world. Its goal is to help countries strengthen and sustain the fundamental conditions that will attract and retain private investment. The **International Monetary Fund (IMF)** provides loans to governments throughout the world. In order to obtain these loans, governments must submit to IMF conditions. This often means rewriting laws so that they are more favorable to foreign investment. Along with the World Bank, the IMF aims to help countries strengthen their banking systems.

There have been a number of means by which the World Bank and the IMF have attempted to shape and assist economic development in the periphery. These include neoliberal policies that emphasize privatization, export production, and limited restrictions on imports. The term *neoliberal* (new liberal) refers to the revival of ideas popular at the end of the 19th century promoting free trade and economic integration. Neoliberalism promotes a reduction in the role and budget of government, including reduced subsidies and the privatization of formerly publicly owned and operated concerns such as utilities. Like modernization theory, the goal of neoliberal development policies is to enable peripheral countries to achieve core economic standards of wealth and prosperity while recognizing that preexisting conditions will have to be taken into account to construct a place-specific development path. For the most part, neoliberal development is premised on policies of structural adjustment, focused on market-led economic growth, with the aim of duplicating the economic and political organization of the core. Mostly associated with the IMF, **structural adjustment policies** require governments to cut budgets and liberalize trade in return for debt relief.

In response to the revival of modernization theory in the guise of neoliberalism, critics have emerged who question whether the kind of development promulgated by neoliberalism is environmentally and socially sustainable. In practice, sustainable development policies argue for using renewable natural resources in a manner that does not eliminate or degrade them—by making greater use, for example, of solar and geothermal energy and by greater use of recycled materials. It means *managing* economic systems so that all resources—physical and human—are used optimally. It means *regulating* economic systems so that the benefits of development are distributed more equitably (if only to prevent poverty from causing environmental degradation). And it means *organizing* societies so that improved education, health care, and social welfare can contribute to environmental awareness and sensitivity and an improved quality of life. A final and more radical aspect of sustainable development is a move away from wholesale globalization toward increased "localization," a desire to return to a more locally based economy where production, consumption, and decision making can be oriented to local needs and conditions.

Since the 1980s, the apparent failure of existing development theory and policy to modernize the periphery has generated radical criticism by feminist, post-colonial, and other perspectives. The aim has been to reconceptualize development as violent imposition of core economic values upon the periphery and a means for the core to exercise control over the periphery. As geographers Philip Porter and Eric Sheppard have written, development in the periphery has been predicated on the initial "violence of colonialism, gunboat diplomacy and wars between superpowers; impoverishment; external control over domestic affairs; the dissolution of indigenous institutions and cultures; and environmental deterioration. In short, they [the periphery] have encountered rather than propagated development. . . . "[3] As a result of this radical refiguring of development theory and policy, contemporary theorists have called into question the whole grand notion of development. They argue instead for indigenous alternatives that empower grassroots movements and promote local knowledge and that can repair the damage done by core development projects. They have shown how the push to modernize is just one way to think about a very complicated reality, although one that has come to dominate as the only solution to social, cultural, economic, and political crises in the periphery.

The contemporary radical critique of mainstream development theory challenges the core's position that it knows best how to solve the problems of the periphery and further argues that the neoliberal goal of economic development for all states and nations of the world might even be called into question. These challenges are part of a broader critique that argues for the need to recognize the importance of social and cultural factors in the process of economic and political development. Focusing on women and other underrepresented groups, the radical critique of development theory contends that different groups in different places have different access to the power and resources that shape their daily lives. There has also been a growing understanding that development dramatically shapes the environment as well as people.

Sustainable Development   The global nature of environmental changes has led to calls for global solutions including international agreements to reduce pollution and protect species. A more benign relationship between nature and society has been proposed under the principle of **sustainable development,** a term that is now widely used but vaguely defined. One definition is that of the World Commission on Environment and Development, chaired by the former prime minister of Norway, Gro Brundtland, stating that sustainable development is "development that meets the needs of the present without compromising the ability of future generations to meet their own needs."[4] This definition incorporates the ethic of intergenerational equity, with its obligation to preserve resources and landscapes for future generations.

Geographers such as William Adams and Timothy O'Riordan consider sustainable development to include ecological, economic, and social goals of preventing environmental degradation while promoting economic growth and social equality. Sustainable development means that economic growth and change should occur only when the impacts on the environment are benign or manageable and the impacts (both costs and benefits) on society are fairly distributed across classes and regions. This means finding less-polluting technologies that use resources more efficiently and managing renewable

[3]P. W. Porter and E. Sheppard, *A World of Difference: Society, Nature, Development*, New York: Guilford Press, 1998, p. 97.
[4]World Commission on Environment and Development, *Our Common Future* (Brundtland Report), New York: Oxford University Press, 1987, p. 43.

resources (those that replenish themselves, such as water, fish, and forests) so as to ensure replacement and continued yield.

In practice, sustainable development policies of major international institutions, such as the World Bank, have promoted reforestation, energy efficiency and conservation, and birth control and poverty programs to reduce the environmental impact of rural populations. At the same time, however, the expansion and globalization of the world economy has resulted in increases in resource use and inequality that contradict many of the goals of sustainable development.

Six Key Factors of Globalization

The increasing integration of the world-system over the last 25 years has been informed by the theories and policies of development discussed above. The resulting level of globalization has been caused by dramatic changes in all aspects of economic life from production to consumption. The six key factors of globalization include a new international division of labor, an internationalization of finance, a new technology system, the homogenization of international consumer markets, the proliferation of the transnational corporation, and transnational economic integration.

A New International Division of Labor   The new international division of labor that has accompanied and enabled the most recent round of globalization has resulted in three main changes. First, the United States has declined as an industrial producer, relative to the spectacular growth of Japan and the resurgence of Europe as industrial producers. Second, the **new international division of labor** involves the decentralization of manufacturing production from all of these core regions to some semiperipheral and peripheral countries. In 1995 U.S.-based companies employed about 5.5 million workers overseas, 80 percent of whom were in manufacturing jobs. By 2000, the United States had lost nearly its entire manufacturing base to overseas employment. One reason for this trend has been the prospect of keeping production costs low by exploiting the huge differential in wage rates around the world.

A third result of the new international division of labor is that new specializations have emerged within the core regions of the world-system. These specializations include high-tech manufacturing and producer services—information services, insurance, and market research that enhance the productivity or efficiency of other firms' activities or that enable them to maintain specialized roles. The most significant reflection of this new international division of labor is that global trade has grown much more rapidly over the past 25 years than has global production, a clear indication of the increased economic integration of the world-system.

The Internationalization of Finance   The second factor contributing to today's globalization is the internationalization of finance: the emergence of global banking and globally integrated financial markets. These changes are of course tied in to the new international division of labor. In particular, they are a consequence of massive increases in levels of international direct investment. Between 1988 and 1996, the flow of investment capital from core to semiperipheral and peripheral countries increased 20-fold. These increases include transnational investments by individuals and businesses as well as cross-border investments undertaken within the internal structures of transnational corporations. In addition, the capacity of computers and information systems to deal very quickly with changing international conditions has added a speculative component to the internationalization of finance. All in all, about $100 billion worth of currencies are traded every day. The volume of international investment and financial trading created a need for banks and financial institutions that could handle investments on a large scale, across great distances, quickly and efficiently. The nerve centers of the new system are located in

FIGURE 1.40 Shrinking world This diagram illustrates how the interconnectedness of transportation systems around the globe has enabled travel times to shrink dramatically over the last 500 years of capitalist development. (*Source:* Redrawn from P. Dicken, *Global Shift.* London: Paul Chapman, 1998.)

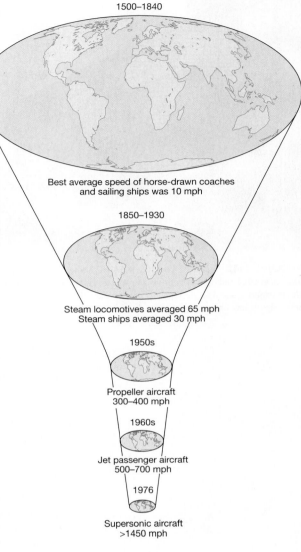

1500–1840

Best average speed of horse-drawn coaches and sailing ships was 10 mph

1850–1930

Steam locomotives averaged 65 mph
Steam ships averaged 30 mph

1950s

Propeller aircraft
300–400 mph

1960s

Jet passenger aircraft
500–700 mph

1976

Supersonic aircraft
>1450 mph

just a few places—London, Frankfurt, New York, and Tokyo, in particular. Their activities are interconnected around the clock, and their networks penetrate every corner of the globe.

A New Technology System The third factor contributing to globalization is a new technology system based on a combination of innovations, including solar energy, robotics, microelectronics, biotechnology, digital telecommunications, and computerized information systems. This new technology system has required the geographical reorganization of core economies. It has also extended the global reach of finance and industry and made for a more flexible approach to investment and trade. Especially important in this regard have been new and improved technologies in transport and communications: the integration of shipping, railroad, and highway systems through containerization; the introduction of wide-bodied cargo jets; and the development of fax machines, fiber-optic networks, communications satellites, and electronic mail and information-retrieval systems (**Figure 1.40**). Many of these telecommunications technologies have also introduced a wider geographical scope and faster pace to various aspects of political, social, and cultural change such as the introduction of 24-hour trading (**Figure 1.41**).

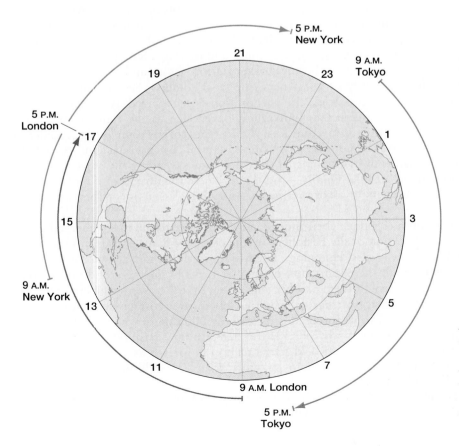

FIGURE 1.41 Twenty-four-hour trading between major financial markets Office hours in the most important financial centers—New York, London, and Tokyo—are nearly continuous from place to place because the three cities are situated in broadly separated time zones. This means that, among the three, they span the globe with 24-hour trading in currencies, stocks, and other financial instruments.

FIGURE 1.42 Global brand IKEA is a home furnishings store that first opened in Sweden in 1959 and now has outlets all over the globe, including Europe, the Middle East, North America, and Asia. Although its products are the result of individual designers, the IKEA brand signals low cost, contemporary design.

Homogenization of International Consumer Markets A fourth factor in globalization has been the growth of consumer markets. Among the more affluent populations of the world, similar trends in consumer taste have been created by similar social processes. A new and materialistic international culture has taken root in which people save less, borrow more, defer parenthood, and indulge in affordable luxuries that are marketed as symbols of style and distinctiveness. This culture is easily transmitted through the new telecommunications media, and it has been an important basis for transnational corporations' global marketing of "world products," including German luxury automobiles, Swiss watches, British raincoats, French wines, American soft drinks, Italian shoes and designer clothes, and Japanese consumer electronics (**Figure 1.42**). It is also a culture that has been easily reinforced through other aspects of globalization, including the internationalization of television—especially CNN, MTV, and Star Television—and the syndication of TV movies and light entertainment series.

The Transnational Corporation As we have discussed, the division of labor is one way to differentiate the workforce in order to introduce new efficiencies. The introduction of a division of labor during the mercantile period fostered a new form of commercial organization, which would enable the combination of resources and labor on a much larger scale than was possible with the individual or even partnerships. This new form of commercial organization was the corporation with limited liability. Although first appearing during the 15th century, limited liability corporations grew dramatically during the early days of the American republic when the developing nation had no banks or other established institutions to support economic growth. Groups of individuals incorporated in order to construct roads, create trading or mining groups, or build and operate factories.

The corporation as a form of business organization has a number of advantages. First, it exists independently of its owners (the stockholders). Second, in U.S. law, as well as in most other countries, the corporation is recognized as a *legal person* with many of the same rights that individuals have, such as the right to buy and sell property and to enter into contracts. Third, the corporation is an excellent device for raising vast amounts of business capital by pooling the financial resources of thousands of individuals, at the same time spreading the risks of a new venture among many people. Finally—and this is where the notion of limited liability comes in—the owners of a corporation are not liable for its debts beyond their investment.

As former colonies gained their independence and neocolonialism emerged as a new form of exploitation of the periphery by the core, the giant corporation, a new institutional form, was also emerging. These corporations had grown within the core countries through the elimination of smaller firms by mergers and takeovers. By the 1960s quite a few of them had become so big that they were transnational in scope, having established overseas subsidiaries, taken over foreign competitors, or simply bought into profitable foreign businesses. By 2005 there were 69,727 parent transnational corporations with 690,391 foreign affiliates around the world. In 2003 the top 100 TNCs together held $3.99 trillion in foreign assets, sold products worth $3 trillion abroad, and employed more than 7.2 million people in their foreign affiliates (**Table 1.1**).

Transnational corporations have been portrayed as imperialist by some geographers because of their ability and willingness to exercise their considerable power

TABLE 1.1 World's Top 10 Transnational Corporations, 2003

Ranking by:

Foreign assets	Corporation	Home economy	Industry
1	General Electric	United States	Electrical & electronic equipment
2	Vodafone Group Plc	United Kingdom	Telecommunications
3	Ford Motor Company	United States	Motor vehicles
4	General Motors	United States	Motor vehicles
5	British Petroleum Company Plc	United Kingdom	Petroleum
6	ExxonMobil Corporation	United States	Petroleum
7	Royal Dutch/Shell Group	United Kingdom/ Netherlands	Petroleum
8	Toyota Motor Corporation	Japan	Motor vehicles
9	Total	France	Petroleum
10	France Telecom	France	Telecommunications

Source: United Nations, *World Investment Report: Transnational Corporations and Export Competitiveness.* New York and Geneva: United Nations, 2005, p. 264

in ways that adversely affect peripheral states. They have certainly been central to a major new phase of geographical restructuring that has been under way for the last 25 years or so. This phase has been distinctive because an unprecedented amount of economic, political, social, and cultural activity has spilled beyond the geographic and institutional boundaries of states. It is a phase of *globalization*, a much fuller integration of the economies of the worldwide system of states and a much greater interdependence of individual places and regions from every part of the world-system. And the increasing integration of the world economy is increasingly predicated on nongovernmental corporate enterprises that operate at a worldwide scale.

Transnational Economic Integration A sixth factor in globalization is the long-term trend among the various national economies toward integrating national economic systems. What has happened is that the logic of the world economy has in many ways transcended, and in some ways undermined, nation-states. The rationale and institutions of contemporary states are not conducive to transnational integration, whether economic or political, but the outcomes of the new international division of labor have forced many states to explore cooperative strategies of various kinds. As a result, the world's economic landscapes now bear the imprint, in a variety of ways, of transnational economic and political integration.

The history and geography of transnational economic integration since 1945 is summarized in **Figure 1.43**. In practice, integration can be pursued in a variety of ways and at different levels. It can be *formal*, involving an institutionalized set of rules and procedures—for example, the United Nations Organization or the General Agreement on Tariffs and Trade (GATT)—or *informal*, involving coalitions of interests, such as UN voting blocs. It can be *trans*national, involving attempts to foster integration among nation-states—the North Atlantic Treaty Organization (NATO), the Organization of Asian Unity (OAU), or the World Trade Organization (WTO)—or *supra*national, involving a commitment to an institutionalized body with certain powers over member states—for example, the European Union (EU). It can be *economic* (WTO or the European Free Trade Association, EFTA), *strategic* (NATO or the Warsaw Pact), *political* (UN voting blocs), *sociocultural* (the United Nations Educational, Scientific, and Cultural Organization, UNESCO), or *mixed* (the EU or the OAU).

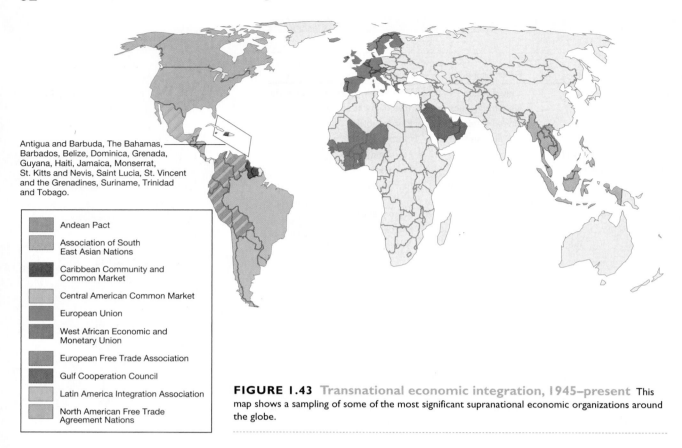

Antigua and Barbuda, The Bahamas, Barbados, Belize, Dominica, Grenada, Guyana, Haiti, Jamaica, Monserrat, St. Kitts and Nevis, Saint Lucia, St. Vincent and the Grenadines, Suriname, Trinidad and Tobago.

Andean Pact

Association of South East Asian Nations

Caribbean Community and Common Market

Central American Common Market

European Union

West African Economic and Monetary Union

European Free Trade Association

Gulf Cooperation Council

Latin America Integration Association

North American Free Trade Agreement Nations

FIGURE 1.43 Transnational economic integration, 1945–present This map shows a sampling of some of the most significant supranational economic organizations around the globe.

SUMMARY AND CONCLUSIONS

Regional geography combines elements of both physical and human geography and is concerned with how unique combinations of environmental and human factors produce territories with distinctive landscapes and cultural attributes. What is distinctive about the study of regional geography is not so much the phenomena that are studied as the *way* they are approached. The study of regional geography draws on several fundamental concepts. Understanding maps and concepts of location, spatial interdependence, sense of place, and landscape allows geographers to analyze the spatial patterns and distributions that underpin regional differentiation and regional change.

Geography matters because it is in specific places that people learn who and what they are and how they should think and behave. Places are also a strong influence, for better or worse, on people's physical well-being, their opportunities, and their lifestyle choices. Places also contribute to people's collective memory and become powerful emotional and cultural symbols. Places are the sites of innovation and change, of resistance and conflict.

Investigations of specific places must be framed within the compass of the entire globe, however, for two reasons. First, the world consists of a mosaic of places and regions that are interrelated and interdependent in many ways. Second, place-making forces—especially economic, cultural, and political forces that influence the distribution of human activities and the character of

places and regions—are increasingly operating at global and international scales. The interdependence of regions means that individual places are tied in to wider processes of change that are reflected in broader geographic patterns. An important issue for regional geographers is to recognize these wider processes and broad geographic patterns without losing sight of the individuality and uniqueness of specific places and regions.

While the regional approach provides a rich and intuitively appealing way of organizing knowledge about the world, there are various methods of regional analysis and different ways of identifying and defining regions. In this book, we emphasize the interdependence of regions, explaining and analyzing them as the outcomes, in different physical environments, of successive eras of human activity that have been organized on the basis of different economic, cultural, and political systems and successive phases of economic and technological development. We identify the world-system, based on the clusters of core, semiperiphery and periphery, as a highly effective way to comprehend integration, interdependence, and connectivity. And while we recognize that integration does tend to blur some national and regional differences as the global marketplace brings a dispersion of people, tastes, and ideas, the overall result has been an intensification of the differences between the core and the periphery.

KEY TERMS

biodiversity (p. 25)
biogeography (p. 25)
biome (p. 25)
capitalism (p. 30)
climate (p. 22)
colonialism (p. 30)
colonization (p. 30)
commodity (p. 35)
commodity chain (p. 8)
communism (p. 30)
comparative advantage (p. 37)
continental drift (p. 20)
core region (p. 30)
culture (p. 11)
demographic transition (p. 10)
development theory (p. 44)
diaspora (p. 35)
division of labor (p. 34)
Earth system science (p. 20)
ecosystem (p. 25)

formal region (p. 4)
functional region (p. 4)
gender (p. 18)
gender division of labor (p. 34)
geomorphology (p. 22)
global warming (p. 29)
globalization (p. 7)
greenhouse effect (p. 29)
gross domestic product
   (GDP) (p. 14)
gross national product
   (GNP) (p. 14)
hegemony (p. 36)
imperialism (p. 36)
international division of labor
   (p. 37)
International Monetary Fund
   (IMF) (p. 46)
intertropical convergence zone
   (ITCZ) (p. 24)

irredentism (p. 7)
leadership cycles (p. 36)
mercantilism (p. 33)
modernization theory (p. 45)
nation (p. 5)
nationalism (p. 35)
nation-state (p. 35)
neocolonialism (p. 44)
neoliberalism (p. 9)
new international division
   of labor (p. 48)
peripheral region (p. 31)
place (p. 2)
plantation (p. 42)
plate tectonics (p. 20)
primary activity (p. 14)
quaternary activity (p. 14)
region (p. 2)
regional geography (p. 2)
regionalization (p. 4)

secondary activity (p. 14)
sectionalism (p. 7)
semiperipheral region (p. 31)
sense of place (p. 4)
spatial justice (p. 17)
state (p. 5)
structural adjustment
   policies (p. 46)
supranational organization
   (p. 5)
sustainable development
   (p. 47)
technology system (p. 13)
tertiary activity (p. 14)
transnational corporation
   (TNC) (p. 7)
weather (p. 22)
World Bank (p. 46)
world region (p. 5)
world-system (p. 29)

REVIEW QUESTIONS

Testing Your Understanding

1. What distinguishes regional geography from physical geography and human geography?
2. What processes are involved in globalization? Does globalization always reduce the distinctiveness of places and regions?
3. Describe the relationship between a woman's access to education, employment, and/or health care and the number of children she is likely to have.
4. Distinguish among the following economic sectors: primary activities, secondary activities, tertiary activities, and quaternary activities.
5. Define gross domestic product (GDP), gross national product (GNP), purchasing power parity (PPP), and human development index (HDI).
6. How does the theory of plate tectonics explain the current configurations of continents, mountains, and volcanically active zones?
7. Describe the major elements of the atmospheric circulation (winds, rising and sinking air) and explain how they relate to the geography of global precipitation. What are the main factors that explain the pattern of average temperature? What features of the climate explain rainforest, desert, and tundra vegetation?
8. What is global warming and what is the evidence that it may be happening?
9. In today's world-system, what are the main characteristics that differentiate the core regions, the semiperiphery, and the periphery?
10. Define hegemony. How did dominance move from one state to another during the European colonial period? Which states were hegemons, when, and why?

11. According to the concept of the international division of labor, why do colonies specialize in the production of certain products? Give an example of international specialization and explain where specialization occurs (for example, the cocaine trade).
12. What is development theory? Describe the main elements of Rostow's model of economic development. What are some arguments against development theory?
13. How do the World Bank and the International Monetary Fund (IMF) support neoliberal policies of development?

Thinking Geographically

1. As the global marketplace becomes more accessible to more people worldwide, why will regional geography remain relevant? List at least five reasons why people will maintain their sense of place in an increasingly global economy.
2. How realistic is the concept of sustainable development? Please provide two arguments for and against it in your community.
3. Sketch out what happens to a society's birthrate, death rate, and technological level as it moves along the demographic transition from a preindustrial phase to an industrial phase. Where does a population explosion occur? Why is this a "demographic trap" for so many developing countries?
4. Issues of spatial justice and gender equity are becoming increasingly salient around the world. Please discuss at least one example of each, indicating how public perceptions of the issues have evolved over the past decade.

5. Over one month, collect news articles and provide a summary of articles that you believe provide evidence of global warming.

6. How did the international slave trade of the 1600s help establish the current world-system?

7. Why are some regions considered peripheral while others are semiperipheral? Provide and explain at least two examples of each.

FURTHER READING

Barber, B. R., *Jihad vs. McWorld. How Globalism and Tribalism Are Reshaping the World*. New York: Ballantine Books, 1995.

Barkawi, T., *Globalization and War*. Lanham, MD: Rowan and Littlefield, 2006.

Bouta, T., Frerks, G., and Bannon, I., *Gender, Conflict and Development*. Washington, DC: The World Bank, 2005.

Cardoso, F. H., and Faletto, R., *Dependency and Development*. Berkeley, CA: University of California Press, 1979.

Dehesa, G., *Winners and Losers in Globalization*. Malden, MA: Blackwell, 2006.

Dickinson, R. E., *The Regional Concept*. London: Routledge & Kegan Paul, 1976.

Dobson, A., and Bell, D. (eds.), *Environmental Citizenship*. Cambridge, MA: MIT Press, 2006.

Dryzek, J., and Schlosberg, D. (eds.), *Debating the Earth: The Environmental Politics Reader*. Oxford: Oxford University Press, 2006.

Elias, J., *Fashioning Inequality: The Multinational Company and Gendered Employment in a Globalizing World*. Aldershot, England: Ashgate, 2004.

Elliott, J. A., *An Introduction to Sustainable Development*. London: Routledge, 2006.

Escobar, A., *Encountering Development*. Princeton, NJ: Princeton University Press, 1995.

Frank, A. G., *World Accumulation, 1492–1789*. New York: Monthly Review Press, 1978.

Giddens, A., *Runaway World: How Globalization Is Reshaping Our Lives*. New York: Routledge, 2000.

Gilbert, A., "The New Regional Geography in English- and French-speaking Countries." *Progress in Human Geography*, 12(1988), 208–28.

Gregory, D., *Geographical Imaginations*. Oxford: Blackwell, 1994.

Jaquette, J. S., and Summerfield, G., *Women and Gender Equity in Development Theory and Practice: Institutions, Resources, and Mobilization*. Durham, NC: Duke University Press, 2006.

Kingma, K., and Sweetman, C., *Gender, Development, and Advocacy*. Oxford: Oxfam GB, 2005.

Lampel, J., Shamsie, J., and Lant, T. K. (eds.), *The Business of Culture: Strategic Perspectives on Entertainment and Media*. Mahwah, NJ: Lawrence Erlbaum, 2006.

Maira, S., and Soep, E., *Youthscapes: The Popular, the National, the Global*. Philadelphia: University of Pennsylvania Press, 2005.

Moghadam, V. M., *Globalizing Women: Transnational Feminist Networks*. Baltimore, MD: Johns Hopkins University Press, 2005.

Oishi, N., *Women in Motion: Globalization, State Policies, and Labor Migration in Asia*. Stanford, CA: Stanford University Press, 2005.

O'Loughlin, J., Staeheli, L., and Greenberg, E., *Globalization and Its Outcomes*. New York: Guilford Press, 2004.

Paavola, J., and Lowe, I. (eds.), *Environmental Values in a Globalising World: Nature, Justice and Governance*. London: Routledge, 2005.

Porter, P. W., and Sheppard, E., *A World of Difference: Society, Nature, Development*. New York: Guilford Press, 1998.

Robbins, J. T., and Hite, A. (eds.), *From Modernization to Globalization: Perspectives on Development and Social Change*. Malden, MA: Blackwell, 2000.

Rogers, A., Viles, H., and Goudie, A. (eds.), *The Student's Companion to Geography*. 2nd edition. Cambridge, MA: Blackwell, 2003.

Sacquet, A., *World Atlas of Sustainable Development: Economic, Social and Environmental Data*. London: Anthem, 2005.

Savage, M., Bagnall, G., and Longhurst, B., *Globalization and Belonging*. London: Sage, 2005.

Schulz, A. J., and Mullings, L., *Gender, Race, Class, and Health: Intersectional Approaches*. San Francisco, CA: Jossey-Bass, 2006.

Seager, J., *Atlas of Women in the World*. New York: Penguin, 2003.

Sen, A. K., *Identity and Violence: The Illusion of Destiny*. New York: W.W. Norton, 2006.

Shapiro, H. S., and Purpel, D. E., *Critical Social Issues in American Education: Democracy and Meaning in a Globalizing World*. Mahwah, NJ: Lawrence Erlbaum, 2005.

Sumner, J., *Sustainability and the Civil Commons: Rural Communities in the Age of Globalization*. Toronto: University of Toronto Press, 2005.

United Nations Conference on Trade and Development, *World Investment Report: Transnational Corporations and the Internationalization of R&D*. New York and Geneva: United Nations, 2005.

Wallerstein, I., *The Capitalist World Economy*. Cambridge, UK: Cambridge University Press, 1979.

Wallerstein, I., *The Politics of the World Economy*. Cambridge, UK: Cambridge University Press, 1984.

Watson, J. L., and Caldwell, M.L., *The Cultural Politics of Food and Eating: A Reader*. Malden, MA: Blackwell, 2005.

Wood, D., *Five Billion Years of Global Change: A History of the Land*. New York: Guilford Press, 2004.

More than 5 million

1–5 million

Fewer than 1 million

Capital cities are underlined

ARCTIC OCEAN

Arctic Circle

N

ICELAND

Reykjavík

ATLANTIC
OCEAN

SWEDEN

NORWAY

Bergen

Oslo

Stockholm

Eskilstuna

Karlskoga

Göteborg

Huskvarna

North
Sea

DENMARK

Turk

Aberdeen

Glasgow

Edinburgh

Belfast

UNITED
KINGDOM

Newcastle
upon Tyne

Dublin

Leeds

IRELAND

Liverpool

Manchester

Birmingham

Århus

Copenhagen

Malmö

Baltic Sea

RUSSIA

Kaliningrad

Gdansk

Hamburg

POLAND

NETH.

Hannover

Amsterdam

Weser

Bielefeld

Berlin

Warsaw

Thames

London

Rotterdam

Oder

Lodz

Portsmouth

Antwerp

Essen

Vistula

Bruges

Düsseldorf

Rye

Brussels

Köln

GERMANY

Katowice

Lille

Aachen

Meuse

BELGIUM

Frankfurt

Elbe

Paris

Luxembourg

Nürnberg

Prague

LUX.

Mannheim

CZECH REPUBLIC

Loire

Seine

Rhine

Stuttgart

SLOVAKI

BLACK
FOREST

Danube

Bratislav

Munich

Vienna

FRANCE

JURA

Bern

Zürich

LIECH.

AUSTRIA

Budapest

SWITZ.

Bordeaux

Garonne

Lyon

ALPS

DOLOMITES

Ljubljana

SLOVENIA

HUNGAR

Rhône

Turin

Milan

Venice

DINARIC ALPS

Zagreb

Lt. Lugano

Verona

PORTUGAL

Po

Florence

Belgrade

CROATIA

BOS. &
HERZ.

PYRENEES

Nice

Genoa

SPAIN

Ebro

Marseille

MONACO

Pisa

SAN
MARINO

Sarajev

Lisbon

Madrid

ANDORRA

Siena

Adriatic Sea

Toledo

Barcelona

Tiber

APENNINES

MONTENEGRO

Corsica

Rome

Tirana

Valencia

ALBANI

Seville

Benidorm

Balearic Islands

Sardinia

Naples

ITALY

Murcia

Mediterranean

PINDU
MTS

GIBRALTAR

Sicily

Sea

MALTA

0   200   400 Miles

0   200   400 Kilometers

FIGURE 2.1

Europe is the most intensively settled of the major world regions, with a population of 726 million, 75 percent of whom live in Europe's cities, 63 of which have populations of more than 500,000 (**Figure 2.1**). The western, northern, and southern limits of Europe as a whole are quite clearly defined, since they are formed by the Atlantic Ocean on the west, the Arctic Ocean on the north, and the Mediterranean Sea on the south. The eastern edge of Europe merges into the vastness of Asia and is less easily defined. The mountain ranges of the Urals are sometimes used by geographers to mark the boundary between Europe and Asia, but the most significant factors separating Europe from Asia are human and relate to race, language, and a common set of ethical values that stem from Roman Catholic, Protestant, and Orthodox forms of Christianity. As a result, the eastern boundary of Europe is often demarcated through political and administrative boundaries rather than physical features.

For a few decades, between 1945 and 1989, there was a significant geopolitical division within Europe into eastern and western Europe. These two subregions share a great deal in terms of physical geography, racial characteristics, and cultural values, but for a while they were divided by the Cold War territorial boundary that separated the capitalist democracies of western Europe from Soviet **state socialism**, a form of economy based on principles of collective ownership and administration of the means of production and distribution of goods dominated and directed by state bureaucracies. The result was what Winston Churchill called an "Iron Curtain" along the western frontier of Soviet-dominated territory: a militarized frontier zone across which Soviet and East European authorities allowed the absolute minimum movement of people, goods, and information.

Soviet influence to the east of the Iron Curtain created distinctive economic, social, and cultural conditions for a long enough period to have effected some modifications to the geography of eastern Europe. Since the collapse of the Soviet Union in 1991, however, its former **satellite states** in eastern Europe have reoriented themselves as part of the broader European world region. Meanwhile, most European states have joined together in the European Union, creating an extremely powerful economic and political force in world affairs. Europe as a whole still bears the legacy of a complex history of social and political development, but it has reemerged since World War II as a crucible of technological, economic, and cultural innovation.

ENVIRONMENT AND SOCIETY IN EUROPE

Two aspects of Europe's physical geography have been fundamental to its evolution as a world region and have influenced the evolution of regional geographies within Europe itself. First, as a world region, Europe is situated between the Americas, Africa, and the Middle East (see Figure 1.1). Second, as a satellite photograph of Europe reveals, the region consists mainly of a collection of peninsulas and islands at the western extremity of the great Eurasian landmass (**Figure 2.2**).

The largest of the European peninsulas is the Scandinavian Peninsula, the prominent western mountains of which separate Atlantic-oriented Norway from continental-oriented Sweden. Equally striking are the Iberian Peninsula, a square mass that projects into the Atlantic, and the boot-shaped Italian Peninsula. In the southeast is the broad triangle of the Balkan Peninsula, which projects into the Mediterranean, terminating in the intricate coastlines of the Greek peninsulas and islands. In the northwest are Europe's two largest islands, Britain and Ireland.

The overall effect is that tongues of shallow seas penetrate deep into the European landmass. This was especially important in the pre-Modern period, when the only means of transporting goods were by sailing vessel and wagon. The Mediterranean and North seas, in particular, provided relatively sheltered sea lanes, fostering seafaring traditions in the peoples all around their coasts. The penetration of the seas deep into the European landmass provided numerous short land routes across the major peninsulas, making it easier for trade and communications to take place in the days of sail and wagon. As we shall see, Europeans' relationship to the surrounding seas has been a crucial factor in the evolution of European—and, indeed, world—geography.

FIGURE 2.2 Europe from space This image underlines one of the key features of Europe: the many arms of the seas that penetrate deep into the western extremity of the great Eurasian landmass.

Europe's navigable rivers also shaped the human geography of the region. Although small by comparison with major rivers in other regions of the world, some of the principal rivers of Europe—the Danube, the Dneiper, the Elbe, the Rhine, the Seine, and the Thames—played key roles as routeways. Also, the low-lying **watersheds** (dividing ridges between drainage areas) between the major rivers of Europe's plains allowed canal building to take place relatively easily, thereby increasing the mobility of river traffic.

Landforms and Landscapes

The physical environments of Europe are complex and varied. It is impossible to travel far without encountering significant changes in physical landscapes. There is, however, a broad pattern to this variability, and it is based on four principal **physiographic regions** that are characterized by broad coherence of geology, relief, landforms, soils, and vegetation. These regions are the Northwestern Uplands, the Alpine System, the Central Plateaus, and the North European Lowlands (**Figure 2.3**).

Northwestern Uplands The Northwestern Uplands are composed of the most ancient rocks in Europe, the product of the Caledonian mountain-building episode about 400 million years ago. Included in this region are the mountains of Norway and Scotland and the uplands of Iceland, Ireland, Wales, Cornwall (in England), and Brittany (in France). The original Caledonian mountain system was eroded and uplifted several times, and following the most recent uplift, the Northwestern Uplands have been worn down again, molded by ice sheets and glaciers. Many valleys were deepened and straightened by ice, leaving spectacular glaciated landscapes. There are *cirques* (deep, bowl-shaped basins on mountainsides, shaped by ice action), glaciated valleys, and **fjords** (some as deep as 1200 meters—about 3900 feet) in Norway; countless lakes; lines of **moraines** that mark the ice sheet's final recession; extensive deposits of sand and gravel from ancient glacial deltas, and vast expanses of peat bogs that lie on the granite shield that forms the physiographic

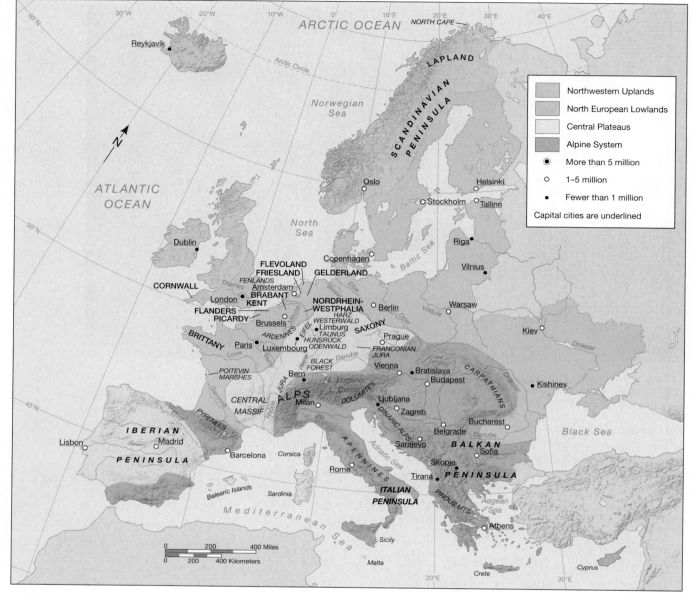

FIGURE 2.3 Europe's physiographic regions Each of the four principal physiographic regions of Europe has a broad coherence in terms of geology, relief, landforms, soils, and vegetation. (*Source:* Adapted from R. Mellor and E.A. Smith, *Europe: A Geographical Survey of the Continent.* London: Macmillan, 1979.)

foundation of the region. Since the last glaciation, sea levels have risen, forming fjords and chains of offshore islands wherever these glaciated valleys have been flooded by the rising sea (**Figure 2.4**).

This formidable environment is rendered even more forbidding in much of the region as a result of climatic conditions. In the far north, the summer sun shines for 57 days without setting, but the winter nights are interminable. Oslo sees a *total* of only 17 hours of sunshine in the whole month of December. Rivers and lakes in the far north are frozen from mid-October on, while even farther south in Norway they freeze at the end of November and remain frozen until May. Snow, which is permanent in parts of Iceland and Lapland, begins to fall toward the middle of September and covers much of the landscape from October through early April.

Much of the Northwestern Uplands is covered by forests. In the southern parts of the region, conifers (mostly evergreen trees such as pine, spruce, and fir) are mixed with birches and other deciduous trees; further north, conifers become

FIGURE 2.4 The Northwestern Uplands The northern parts of the region are characterized by deeply eroded glacial valleys that have been drowned by the sea, creating distinctive fjord landscapes such as this one at Reine Harbor in Norway's Lofoten Islands.

entirely dominant, and in the far north, toward the North Cape, the forest gives way to desolate treeless stretches of the **tundra**, with its gray lichens and dwarf willows and birches. Not surprisingly, forestry is a major industry. The forests supply timber for domestic building and fuel and produce the woods that are in greatest demand on world markets: pine and spruce for timber and for the paper industry; birch for plywood and cabinetmaking; and aspen for matches.

The farmers in these mountain subregions depend on **pastoralism**, a system of farming and way of life based on keeping herds of grazing animals, eked out with a little produce grown on the valley floors. In the less mountainous parts of Scandinavia, as in much of Baltic Europe, with their short growing season and cold, acid soils, agriculture supports only a low density of settlement. Landscapes reflect a mixed farming system of oats, rye, potatoes, and flax, with hay for cattle. Oats, the largest single crop, often has to be harvested while it is still green. More than half of the milk from dairy cattle is used to produce butter and cheese.

In these upland landscapes, farms and hamlets are casually situated on any habitable site, their buildings often widely scattered. The countryside is dotted with trim wooden houses, roofed with slate, tiles, shingles, or even sods of turf. Often, the buildings of a particular district are distinguished by some special stylistic feature. In some places, the old weatherboard houses that were used as shelters in bad weather still exist. They date back to the Middle Ages, as does the custom of storing reserve stocks of food or hay in a special isolated building, the *stabbur*, decorated with beautifully carved woodwork. The predominant color of the buildings is gray, the natural color that wood acquires with age. Nearer to towns, the houses are painted brighter colors: yellow, dark red, and mid-blue.

The more temperate subregions of the Northwestern Uplands (in Ireland and the United Kingdom) are dominated by dairy farming on meadowland, sheep farming on exposed uplands (**Figure 2.5**), and arable farming (mainly wheat, oats, potatoes, and

FIGURE 2.5 The Northwestern Uplands The southern part of the region is characterized by rounded hills and moorlands, with pasture land on glacial outwash plains. Shown here is Loch Earn, Scotland.

FIGURE 2.6 The Alpine System Jagged peaks and glaciated valleys are typical of the Alpine ranges. This photograph is of the central Alps, with the peak of the Matterhorn in the background and the ski resort of Zermatt in the foreground.

barley) on drier lowland areas. In these areas, dispersed settlement, in the form of hamlets and scattered farms, is characteristic, and stone is more often the traditional building material.

Alpine Europe The Alps occupy a vast area of Europe, stretching eastward for nearly 1290 kilometers (about 800 miles) across the southern part of Europe from the Pyrenees, which mark the border between Spain and France, through the Alps and the Dolomites and on to the Carpathians, the Dinaric Alps, and some ranges in the Balkan Peninsula. The Apennines of Italy and the Pindus Mountains of Greece are also part of the Alpine System. The Alpine System is the product of the most recent of Europe's mountain-building episodes, which occurred about 50 million years ago. Its relative youth explains the sharpness of the mountains and the boldness of their peaks. The Alpine landscape is characterized by jagged mountains with high, pyramidal peaks and deeply glaciated valleys (**Figure 2.6**). The highest peak, Mont Blanc, reaches 4810 meters (15,781 feet). Most of the rest of the mountains are between 2500 and 3600 meters (about 8200 and 11,800 feet) in height. Seven of the peaks in the western Alps exceed 4000 meters (13,123 feet) in height. Although the Alps pose a formidable barrier between northwestern Europe and Italy and the Adriatic, a series of great passes—including the Brenner Pass, the Simplon Pass, the Saint Gotthard Pass, and the Great Saint Bernard Pass—and longitudinal valleys have always provided transalpine routeways.

The dominant direction of the Alps and their parallel valleys is roughly southwest to northeast. The major Alpine valleys thus have one sunny, fully exposed slope that is suitable for vine growing and a shaded side rich with orchards, woods, and meadows. The mountains and valleys of the Alps proper are surrounded by glacial outwash deposits that provide rich farmland. The limestone of the Alpine region is widely quarried for cement, while mineral deposits—lead, copper, and iron—and small deposits of coal and salt have long been locally important throughout the region. In addition, the Alps are a valuable source of hydroelectric power: about 65 billion watt-hours in Switzerland (60 percent of the country's electricity consumption), about 72 billion watt-hours in France (15 percent of the country's electricity consumption), and about 45 billion watt-hours in Austria (85 percent of the country's electricity consumption).

The traditional staple of the economy, however, has been agriculture, and farming has given the Alpine region its distinctive human landscape (**Figure 2.7**). The Alpine rural landscape is a patchwork of fields, orchards, vineyards, deciduous woodlands, pine groves, and meadows on the lower slopes of the valleys, with broad Alpine pasture above. In these pastures, which are dotted with wooden haylofts and summer chalets, dairy cattle wander far and wide. Farmers attach bells around the necks of their animals in order to be able to locate them, and the consequent effect is a resonant pastoral "soundscape" of clanking cowbells. Farms and hamlets tend to cling to lower elevations, the chalet-style architecture drawing on timber or rough-cast stone construction, with overhanging eaves, tiers of windows, and painted ornamentation.

The landscapes of the Alpine fringes are more lush. Lavender and fruit have been introduced to enrich and give variety to the mixed farming system of the Alpine fringes, which features vine and wheat growing, along with dairy cattle. The higher slopes, which receive more rainfall, provide lush pastures that have made the region famous for its rich cheeses, such as Gruyère.

The principal industry of the Alpine region is tourism. Attractive rural landscapes, together with magnificent mountain scenery, beautiful lakes, and first-class winter sports facilities, have attracted tourists to this region since the 1800s. Lakeside resorts such as Lucerne and Lugano, Switzerland; mountain resorts such as Chamonix, France, and Innsbruck, Austria; and winter sports resorts such as Val d'Isere, France, and Davos, St. Moritz, and Zermatt, Switzerland, are all well established, with an affluent clientele from across Europe. With the growth of the global tourist industry, Alpine resorts have attracted a new clientele from North America and Japan.

FIGURE 2.7 Alpine landscapes The distinctive landscapes of the Alps juxtapose lush meadows and prosperous villages against jagged mountains, as in this photograph of the Pustertal in Italy's South Tyrol region.

Central Plateaus Between the Alpine System and the Northwestern Uplands are the landscapes of the Central Plateaus and the North European Lowlands. The Central Plateaus are formed from 250- to 300-million-year-old rocks that have been eroded down to broad tracts of uplands. Beneath the forest-clad slopes and fertile valleys of these plateaus lie many of Europe's major coalfields. For the most part, the plateaus reach between 500 and 800 meters (1640 and 2625 feet) in height, though they rise to more than 1800 meters (5905 feet) in the Central Massif of France. The Central Plateaus were generally too low to have been glaciated and too far south to have been covered by the great northern ice sheets of the last Ice Age. Rather, their landscape is characterized by rolling hills, steep slopes and dipping vales, and deeply carved river valleys.

In central Spain, the landscape is dominated by plateaus and high plains that go on for hundreds of miles, with long narrow mountain ranges—*cordillera*—stretched out like long cords along the edges. The flat landscape of the region is a result of immense horizontal sheets of sedimentary rock that cover a massif of ancient rock, with a general appearance of tables ending in ledges—hence the term *Meseta*, which is generally used to designate the center of Spain (**Figure 2.8**). These dry, open lands

FIGURE 2.8 The Central Plateaus The *Meseta* of Spain covers thousands of square miles in the center of the Iberian Peninsula.

FIGURE 2.9 Black Forest The town of Waldkirch, shown here, is typical of the market towns that are strung along the valley bottoms of the Black Forest.

are preeminently areas of grain crops and of flocks and herds of sheep and cattle that in summer are driven up to the cooler mountains. Olive trees dominate the shallow valley slopes, and in irrigated valley bottoms vines and prosperous market gardens flourish.

Further east—in the Massif Central in France; the Eifel, Westerwald, Taunus, Hunsruck, Odenwald, and Franconian Jura in Germany—where the climate is wetter, the landscape is dominated by gently rounded, well-wooded hills, with villages surrounded by neat fields and orchards in the vales. These hills rarely rise above 700 meters (2300 feet), and the landscape includes many attractive and fertile subregions of low hills and rounded hillocks planted with vines and shallow valleys with orchards and meticulously maintained farms. The hills are covered with beech and oak forests, interspersed with growths of fir. The Black Forest is much higher, its bare granite summits reaching 1493 meters (about 4900 feet) in the south. It is scored by steep, narrow valleys with terraces of glacial outwash. The northeastern reaches of the Black Forest form an immense, silent, solid mass of fir forests. To the southwest, near the River Rhine, there are small fields and meadows with prosperous farms at the edge of white fir forests and market towns nestling in tributary valleys (**Figure 2.9**). The Rhine has cut deep, scenic gorges through the higher plateau lands, but for much of its course across the central plateaus it is majestic and calm, with gentler slopes covered with vines and the bottomlands of the valley a busy corridor of prosperous towns surrounded by industrial crops and market gardens.

North European Lowlands The North European Lowlands sweep in a broad crescent from southern France, through Belgium, the Netherlands, and southeastern England and into northern Germany, Denmark, and the southern tip of Sweden. Continuing eastward, they broaden into the immense European plain that extends through Poland, the Czech Republic, Slovakia, and Hungary, all the way into Russia. Coal is found in quantity under the lowlands of England, France, Germany, and Poland and in smaller deposits in Belgium and the Netherlands. Oil and natural gas deposits are found beneath the North Sea and under the lowlands of southern England, the Netherlands, and northern Germany. Nearly all of this area lies below 200 meters (656 feet) in elevation, and the topography everywhere is flat or gently undulating. As a result, the region has been particularly attractive to farming and settlement. The fertility of the soil varies, however, so that settlement patterns are uneven and agriculture is finely tuned to the limits and opportunities of local soils, landscape, and climate.

FIGURE 2.10 The North European Lowlands The rolling plains of the North European Lowlands provide fertile and easily tilled soils that have given rise to lush agricultural landscapes. Shown here is the lowland farming landscape of Dorset, in southern England.

The western parts of the North European Lowlands are densely settled and intensively farmed, the moist Atlantic climate supporting lush agricultural landscapes (**Figure 2.10**). Further east, the Lowlands are characterized by a drier Continental climate and lowland river basins with a rolling cover of sandy river deposits and **loess** (a fine-grained, extremely fertile soil). The hills are covered with oak and beech forests, but much of the region consists of broad loess plateaus where very irregular rainfall averages around 40 centimeters—approximately 16 inches—a year. There are no woods and irrigation is often necessary to sustain the typical two-year rotation of corn and wheat. In some parts, several meters of loess and rich, sandy soil rest on the rocky substratum. Stone and trees are so scarce that houses are built of *pisé*, a kind of rammed-earth brick. The scarcity of trees forces storks to build nests atop chimneys and telegraph poles. The rich soils produce high yields of wheat and corn, together with hops, sugar beets, and forage crops for livestock.

The area also features residual regions of **steppe**: semiarid, treeless, grassland plains with landscapes that are infinitely monotonous. This land, which is too dry or too marshy to have invited cultivation, was once the domain of wild horses, cattle, and pigs, but today huge flocks of sheep find pasture there. The climate, though, is harsh, with seasonal extremes of burning hot and freezing cold, the winter easterlies blowing down from mid-continent Russia. Population densities are low, and there are few villages.

It should be stressed that, within these broad physiographic divisions, marked variations exist. The mosaic of regions and landscapes within Europe is both rich and detailed. Physical differences are encountered over quite short distances, and there are numerous specialized farming regions where agricultural conditions have influenced local ways of life to produce distinctive landscapes. In detail, these landscapes are a product of centuries of human adaptation to climate, soils, altitude, and **aspect** (exposure), and to changing economic and political circumstances. Farming practices, field patterns, settlement types, traditional building styles, and ways of life have all become attuned to the opportunities and constraints of regional physical environments, with the result that distinctive regional landscapes have been produced (see Signature Region: Mediterranean Europe, p. 66).

Climate

The seas that surround Europe strongly influence the region's climate. In winter, seas cool more slowly than the land, while in summer they warm up more slowly than the land. As a result, the seas provide a warming effect in winter and a cooling effect in summer. Europe's arrangement of islands and peninsulas means that this moderating effect is particularly marked, contributing to an overall climate that does not have great seasonal extremes of heat and cold. The moderating effect is intensified by the North Atlantic Drift, which carries great quantities of warm water from the tropical Gulf Stream as far as the United Kingdom.

Given its latitude (Paris, at almost 49° N, is the same latitude as Winnipeg and Newfoundland in Canada), most of Europe is remarkably warm. It is continually crossed by moist, warm air masses that drift in from the Atlantic. The effects of these warm, wet, westerly winds are most pronounced in northwestern Europe, where squalls and showers accompany the passage of successive eastward-moving weather systems. Weather in northwestern Europe tends to be unpredictable, partly because of the swirling movement of air masses as they pass over the Atlantic and partly because of the complex effects of the widely varying temperatures of interpenetrating bodies of land and water. Farther east, in continental Europe, seasonal weather tends to be more settled, with more pronounced extremes of summer heat and winter cold. In these interior regions, local variations in weather are influenced a great deal by the direction in which a particular slope or land surface faces and its elevation above sea level.

The Mediterranean Basin has a different and quite distinctive climate. In winter, low-pressure systems along the northern Mediterranean draw in rain-bearing weather fronts from the Atlantic. When low pressure over the northern Mediterranean coincides with high pressure over continental Europe, southerly airflows spill over mountain ranges and down valleys, bringing cold blasts of air. These events have local names: the *mistral*, for example, which blows down the Rhône Valley in southern France, and the *bora*, which blows over the eastern Alps toward the Adriatic region of Italy. In summer, hot, dry air masses from Asia and Africa dominate the Mediterranean Basin, producing dry, sunny conditions.

Environmental History

Temperate forests originally covered about 95 percent of Europe, with a natural ecosystem dominated by oak, together with elm, beech, and lime (linden). By the end of the medieval period, Europe's forest cover had been reduced to about 20 percent, and today it is around 5 percent. Between A.D. 1000 and A.D. 1300, a period of warmer climate, together with advances in agricultural knowledge and practices, led to a significant

Mediterranean Europe

Mediterranean Europe is an extensive region that stretches along the coastline of the Mediterranean Sea from southern Spain to eastern Greece, a distance of some 2414 kilometers (about 1500 miles). The distinctiveness of the region derives not only from its ties with the sea but also from its climate and vegetation and its long tradition of urban life. The watershed of rivers that drain into the Mediterranean provides a good approximation of the extent of the region (**Figure 1**).

The Mediterranean climate is such that winters are cool, with an Atlantic air stream that brings overcast skies and intermittent rain—though snow is unusual. In spring the temperature rises rapidly and rainfall is more abundant. Then summer bursts forth suddenly as dry, hot, Saharan air brings three months of hot, sunny weather. There is no rain save an occasional storm; the soil cracks and splits and is easily washed away in the occasional downpours. In October the temperature drops, and deluges of rain show that Atlantic air prevails once more.

In such conditions, delicate plants cannot survive. The Mediterranean climate precludes all plant species that cannot tolerate the range of conditions—cold as well as heat and drought as well as wet. The result is a distinctive natural landscape of dry terrain dotted with cypress trees, holm-oaks, cork oaks, parasol pines, and eucalyptus trees. These same conditions make agriculture a challenge. The crops that prosper best include olives, figs, almonds, vines, oranges, lemons, wheat, and barley. Sheep and goats graze on dry pastureland and stubblefields. Irrigation is often necessary, and in some localities it sustains high yields of fruit, vegetables, and rice.

In a few subregions, conditions are naturally more favorable, making for rich rural landscapes. In Tuscany, for example, a regional landscape has evolved that reflects an intensive and carefully developed system closely adapted to the land. On the better and well-watered soils of the valleys, there are artificial meadows that favor stock-breeding, along with fields of wheat, mulberries, and corn. On the hills around the scattered farms and villas, elegant cypress trees stand out against the silvery-green of olive trees, and in the fields there is a rich mixture of cereals, vegetables, fruit

FIGURE 2 Mediterranean landscapes The dry climate of the Mediterranean has led to distinctive landscapes, such as this Tuscan landscape near San Quirico d'Orcia, Italy.

FIGURE 1 The Mediterranean region Reference map showing principal physical features, political boundaries, and major cities of the Mediterranean region.

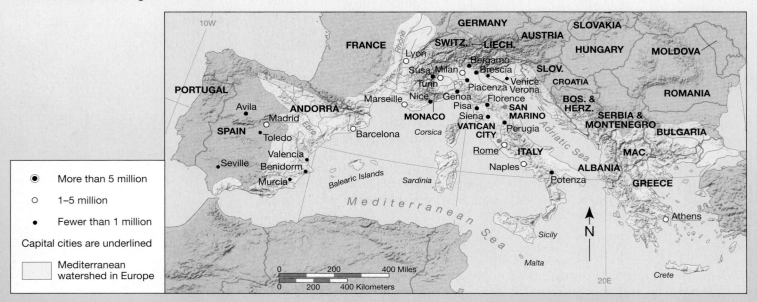

trees, and vines (for chianti wine). This classical Tuscan landscape (**Figure 2**), developed over centuries, became emblematic of Italy itself with the creation of modern Italy and the *Risorgimento* ("revival through unification," 1815–61) and has been the subject of landscape painters, romantic poets, and novelists ever since.

The landscapes of the Mediterranean reflect the imprint of successive cultures over a very long history. The fields themselves are a good example. Under Roman colonization, land was often subdivided into a checkerboard pattern of rectilinear fields. This highly ordered system was known as *centuriation*, and the pattern can still be seen in some districts today—in parts of the Po valley, for example. Elsewhere, across large tracts of the Mediterranean, the soil can be cultivated only on a large scale, and the poor quality of pastureland necessitates vast untilled areas being left for flocks and herds. In these areas, successive conquerors, from the Greeks, Phoenicians, and Carthaginians to the Ottoman Turks and Christian Crusaders, carved out huge estates, known as **latifundia**, on which they set peasants to work. Land that did not belong to these big estates was often subdivided by independent peasant farmers into very small, intensively cultivated lots, or **minifundia**, most of which are barely able to support a family.

Settlement patterns also reflect these influences. Both *latifundia* and *minifundia* systems tend to result in clustered settlements. In more productive districts, these can be quite large, with "villages" of 10,000–12,000 people, as in the huerta districts of southeastern Spain and the picturesque whitewashed villages of the Greek islands (**Figure 3**). The history of the Mediterranean, however, has made it above all a land of towns. Fears of invasion encouraged people to cluster together in easily defended sites: typically on steep-sided hills, as in Avila and Toledo in Spain and in Siena, Perugia, and Todi in Italy (**Figure 4**). Other towns naturally emerged at strategic locations: at the entrance to a valley (for example, Murcia, Spain, and Verona, Italy); and at bridging points (for example, Piacenza, Italy, and Seville, Spain).

More recently, the urban landscapes of the Mediterranean have been transformed by tourism and retirement migration. The classic landscapes, picturesque hill towns, and ancient cities of the Mediterranean have attracted affluent tourists and retirees from the rest of Europe since the late 1700s, but the advent of mass-market tourism after World War II has created resort towns and brought tourist amenities—hotels, restaurants, night clubs, bars, and so on—to much of the region's coastline. Benidorm, on Spain's Costa del Sol, was a fishing village of just 1500 inhabitants in the early 1950s. Today, it is a mass-market, package-tour resort with more than 30,000 hotel beds and 100,000 more in rental apartments. Similar transformations have taken place elsewhere, as millions of vacationers and retirees from the colder, industrialized regions of northern Europe have made Mediterranean beaches their destination.

FIGURE 3 Santorini, Greece The villages of the Greek island of Santorini still retain much of their old visual character. Fear of pirates was the compelling motive that led to original village sites on steep cliffs. Climate and topography led to high-density settlements with narrow streets and small, whitewashed buildings with thick walls.

FIGURE 4 Todi, Italy Todi's site, perched on a bluff high above the valley of the Tevere (Tiber), derives from the practical rationale common to northern Italian hill towns: It was easy to defend.

transformation of the European landscape. The population more than doubled, from around 36 million to more than 80 million, and a vast amount of land was brought under cultivation for the first time. By about 1200 most of the best soils of western Europe had been cleared of forest and new settlements were increasingly forced into the more marginal areas of heavy clays or thin sandy soils on higher ground and **heathlands**. (Heath is open land with coarse soil and poor drainage.) Many parts of Europe undertook large-scale drainage projects in order to reclaim marshlands. The Romans had already demonstrated the effectiveness of drainage schemes, reclaiming parts of Italy and northwestern Europe. In the 12th and 13th centuries there were extensive drainage and resettlement schemes in Italy's Po Valley, in the Poitevin marshes of France, and in the Fenlands of eastern England.

In eastern Europe, forest clearances were organized by agents acting for various princes and bishops who controlled extensive tracts of land. The agents would also arrange financing for settlers and develop villages and towns, often to standardized designs.

This great medieval colonization came to a halt nearly everywhere around 1300. One factor was the so-called Little Ice Age, a period of cooler climate which significantly reduced the growing season—perhaps by as much as five weeks. Another factor was the catastrophic loss of population during the period of the Black Death (1347–51) and the periodic recurrences of the plague that continued for the rest of the 14th century. The Little Ice Age lasted until the early 16th century, by which time many villages, and much of the more marginal land, had been abandoned.

The resurgence of European economies from the 16th century onward coincided with overseas exploration and trade, but domestic landscapes were significantly affected by repopulation, by reforms to land tenure systems, and by advances in science and technology that changed agricultural practices, allowing for a more intensive use of the land. In the Netherlands, a steadily growing population and the consequent requirement for more agricultural land led to increased efforts to reclaim land from the sea and to drain coastal marshlands. Hundreds of small estuarine and coastal barrier islands were slowly joined into larger units, and sea defense walls were constructed in order to protect low-lying land, which was drained by windmill-powered water pumps, the excess water being carried off into a web of drainage ditches and canals.

The resulting **polder** landscape provided excellent, flat, fertile, and stone-free soil. Between 1550 and 1650, 165,000 hectares (407,715 acres) of polderland was established in the Netherlands, and the sophisticated techniques developed by the Dutch began to be applied elsewhere in Europe—including eastern England and the Rhône estuary in southern France. While most of these schemes resulted in improved farmland, the environmental consequences were often serious. In addition to the vulnerability of the polderlands to inundation by the sea, large-scale drainage schemes devastated the wetland habitat of many species, while some ill-conceived schemes simply ended in widespread flooding.

These environmental problems were but a prelude to the environmental changes and ecological disasters that accompanied the industrialization of Europe, beginning in the 18th century. Mining—especially coal mining—created derelict landscapes of spoil heaps; urbanization encroached on rural landscapes and generated unprecedented amounts and concentrations of human, domestic, and industrial waste; and manufacturing, unregulated at first, resulted in extremely unhealthy levels of air pollution and in devastating pollution of rivers and streams.

EUROPE IN THE WORLD-SYSTEM

The foundations of Europe's human geography were laid by the Greek and Roman empires. Beginning around 750 B.C., the ancient Greeks developed a series of fortified city-states (called *poleis*) along the Mediterranean coast, and by 550 B.C. there were about 250 such trading colonies. **Figure 2.11** shows the location of the largest of these, some of which subsequently grew into thriving cities (for example, Athens and Corinth), while others remain as isolated ruins or as archaeological sites (for example,

Delphi and Olympia). The Roman Republic was established in 509 B.C. and took almost 300 years to establish control over the Italian Peninsula. By A.D. 14, however, the Romans had conquered much of Europe, together with parts of North Africa and Asia Minor. Most of today's major European cities had their origin as Roman settlements. In quite a few of these cities, it is possible to find traces of the original Roman street layouts. In some, it is possible to glimpse remnants of defensive city walls, paved streets, aqueducts, viaducts, arenas, sewage systems, baths, and public buildings. In the modern countryside, the legacy of the Roman Empire is represented by arrow-straight roads, built by their engineers and maintained and improved by successive generations.

The decline of the Roman Empire, beginning in the fourth century A.D., was accompanied by a long period of rural reorganization and consolidation under feudal systems, a period often characterized as uneventful and stagnant. In fact, the roots of European regional differentiation can be traced to this long feudal era of slow change. **Feudal systems** were almost wholly agricultural, with 80 or 90 percent of the workforce engaged in farming and most of the rest occupied in basic craft work. Most production was for people's immediate needs, with very little of a community's output ever finding its way to wider markets.

By A.D. 1000 the countryside of most of Europe had been consolidated into a regional patchwork of feudal agricultural subsystems, each of which was more or less self-sufficient. For a long time, towns were small, their existence tied mainly to the castles, palaces, churches, and cathedrals of the upper ranks of the feudal hierarchy. These economic landscapes—inflexible, slow-motion, and introverted—nevertheless contained the essential preconditions for the rise of Europe as the dynamic hub of the world economy.

Trade and the Age of Discovery

A key factor in the rise of Europe as a major world region was the emergence of a system of **merchant capitalism** in the 15th century. The immensely complex trading system that soon came to span Europe was based on long-standing trading patterns that had been developed from the 12th century by the merchants of Venice, Pisa, Genoa, Florence, Bruges, Antwerp, and the Hanseatic League (a federation of city-states around the North Sea and Baltic coasts that included Bremen, Hamburg, Lübeck, Rostock, and Danzig, as shown in **Figure 2.12**).

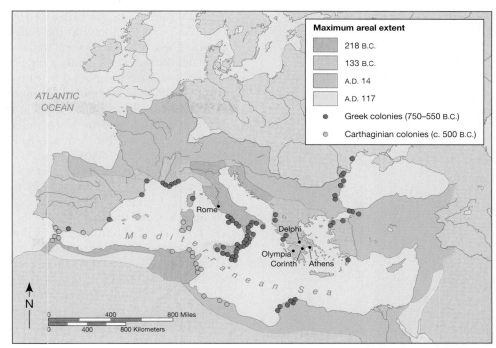

FIGURE 2.11 Greek colonies and extent of the Roman Empire This map shows the distribution of Greek *poleis* (city-states) and Carthaginian colonies and the spread of the Roman Empire from 218 B.C. to A.D. 117. (*Source:* Redrawn from R. King et al., *The Mediterranean.* London: Arnold, 1997, pp. 59 and 64.)

FIGURE 2.12 The Hanseatic League The Hanseatic League was a federation of city-states founded in the 13th century by north German towns and affiliated German merchant groups abroad to defend their mutual trading interests. The League, which remained an influential economic and political force until the 15th century, laid the foundations for the subsequent growth of merchant trade throughout Europe. (*Source:* Redrawn from P. Hugill, *World Trade Since 1431.* Baltimore: Johns Hopkins University Press, 1994, p. 50.)

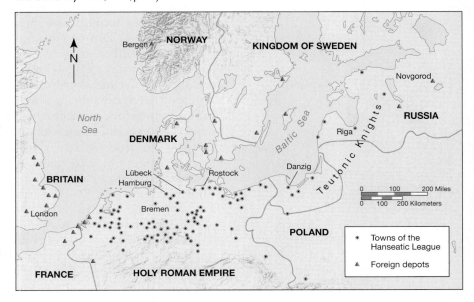

Innovations   In the 15th and 16th centuries a series of innovations in business and technology contributed to the consolidation of Europe's new merchant capitalist economy. These included several key innovations in the organization of business and finance: banking, loan systems, credit transfers, company partnerships, shares in stock, speculation in commodity futures, commercial insurance, and courier/news services. Meanwhile, technological innovations began to further strengthen Europe's economic advantages. Some of these innovations were adaptations and improvements of Oriental discoveries—the windmill, spinning wheels, paper manufacture, gunpowder, and the compass, for example. In Europe, however, there was a real passion for mechanizing the manufacturing process. Key engineering breakthroughs included the more efficient use of energy in water mills and blast furnaces, the design of reliable clocks and firearms, and the introduction of new methods of processing metals and manufacturing glass.

It was the combination of innovations in shipbuilding, navigation, and naval ordnance, however, that had the most far-reaching consequences for Europe's role in the world economy. In the course of the 15th century, the full-rigged sailing ship was developed, enabling faster voyages in larger and more maneuverable vessels that were less dependent on favorable winds. Meanwhile, Europeans developed navigational tools such as the quadrant (1450) and the astrolabe (1480) and acquired a systematic knowledge of Atlantic winds. By the mid-16th century, armorers in England, Holland, and Sweden had perfected the technique of casting iron guns, making it possible to replace bronze cannons with larger numbers of more effective guns at lower expense. Together, these advances made it possible for the merchants of Europe to establish the basis of a worldwide economy in less than 100 years after Portuguese explorer Bartholomeu Dias reached the Cape of Good Hope (the southern tip of Africa) in 1488.

Changing Patterns of Advantage   The geographical knowledge acquired during this Age of Discovery was crucial to the expansion of European political and economic power in the 16th century. In societies that were becoming more and more commercially oriented and profit-conscious, geographical knowledge became a valuable commodity in itself. Information about overseas regions was a first step to controlling and influencing them; this in turn was a step to wealth and power. At the same time, every region began to open up to the influence of other regions because of the economic and political competition unleashed by geographical discovery. Not only was the New World affected by European colonists, missionaries, and adventurers, but the countries of the Old World found themselves pitched into competition with one another for overseas resources.

Gold and silver from the Americas provided the first major economic transformation of Europe. The gold and silver bullion plundered by Spain and Portugal from the Americas created an effective demand for consumer and capital goods of all kinds—textiles, furniture, weapons, ships, food, and wine—thus stimulating production throughout Europe and creating the basis of a Golden Age of prosperity for most of the 16th century. Meanwhile, overseas exploration and expansion made available a variety of new and unusual products—cocoa, beans, maize, potatoes, tomatoes, sugarcane, tobacco, and vanilla from the Americas, tea and spices from the Orient—that opened up large new markets to enterprising merchants. Wine was one of the early luxury products that established the pattern of merchant trading within Europe, and when Europeans branched out to incorporate more of the world into the orbit of their world-system, they began organizing the production of wine wherever climatic conditions were encouraging: in warm temperate zones, roughly between latitudes 30° and 50° north and south (see Geographies of Indulgence, Desire, and Addiction: Wine, p. 72). Not least, the emergence of a worldwide system of exploration and trade helped establish the foundations of modern academic geography.

These changes had a profound effect on the geography of Europe. Before the mid-15th century, Europe was organized around two subregional maritime economies—one based on the Mediterranean and the other on the Baltic. The overseas expansions pioneered first by the Portuguese and then by the Spanish, Dutch, English, and French reoriented Europe's geography toward the Atlantic. The river basins of the Rhine, the

Seine, and the Thames rapidly became focused on a thriving network of **entrepôt** seaports (intermediary centers of trade and transshipment) that transformed Europe. These three river basins, backed by the increasingly powerful states in which they were embedded—the Netherlands, France, and Britain, respectively—then became engaged in a struggle for economic and political hegemony. Although the Rhine was the principal natural routeway into the heart of Europe, the convoluted politics of the Netherlands allowed Britain and France to become the dominant powers by the late 1600s. Subsequently, France, under Napoleon, made the military error of attempting to pursue both maritime and continental power at once, allowing Britain to become the undisputed hegemonic power of the industrial era.

Industrialization and Imperialism

Europe's regional geographies were comprehensively recast once more by the new production and transportation technologies that marked the onset of the Industrial Revolution (from the late 1700s). Production technologies based on more efficient energy sources helped raise levels of productivity and create new and better products that stimulated demand, increased profits, and generated a pool of capital for further investment. Transportation technologies enabled successive phases of geographic expansion that completely reorganized the geography of Europe. As the application of new technologies altered the margins of profitability in different kinds of enterprise, so the fortunes of particular places and regions shifted.

Waves of Industrialization There was in fact not a sudden, single Industrial Revolution but three distinctive transitional waves of industrialization, each having a different degree of impact on different regions and countries (**Figure 2.13**). The first, between about 1790 and 1850, was based on a cluster of early industrial technologies (steam engines, cotton textiles, and ironworking) and was highly localized. It was limited to a few regions in Britain where industrial entrepreneurs and workforces had first exploited key innovations and the availability of key resources (coal, iron ore, and water).

The second wave, between about 1850 and 1870, involved the diffusion of industrialization to most of the rest of Britain and to parts of northwest Europe, particularly the coalfield areas of northern France, Belgium, and Germany (see Figure 2.13). New opportunities were created as railroads and steamships made more places accessible, bringing their resources and their markets into the sphere of industrialization. New materials and new technologies (steel, machine tools) created opportunities to manufacture and market new products. These new activities prompted some significant changes in the logic of industrial location. Railway networks, for example, attracted industry away from smaller towns on the canal systems and toward larger towns with good rail connections. Steamships for carrying on coastal and international trade attracted industry to larger ports. At the same time, steel produced concentrations of heavy industry in places with nearby supplies of coal, iron ore, and limestone.

FIGURE 2.13 The spread of industrialization in Europe European industrialization began with the emergence of small industrial regions in several parts of Britain. As new rounds of industrial and transportation technologies emerged, industrialization spread to other regions with the right attributes: access to raw materials and energy sources, good communications, and large labor markets.

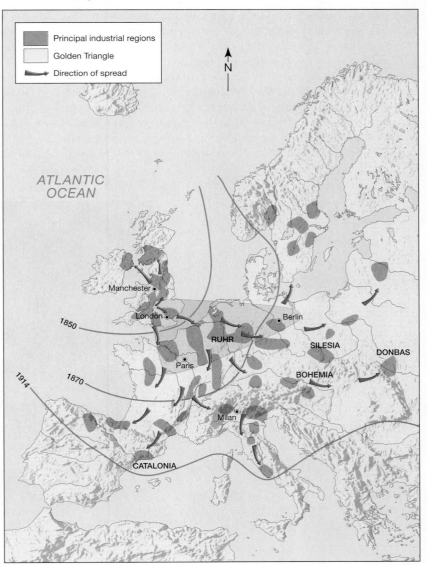

Wine

The production and consumption of wine reflects the evolution of the world-system. The original domestication of wine grapes (*Vitis vinifera*) seems to have taken place as early as 8000 B.C. along the mountain slopes of Georgia, eastern Turkey, and western Iran. Wine had symbolic and ritual significance in early civilizations of the eastern Mediterranean, partly because its ability to intoxicate and engender a sense of "other-worldliness" provided a means through which people could feel in contact with their gods, and partly because of the apparent death of the vine in winter and its dramatic growth and rebirth in the spring. Greek civilization established viticulture—the cultivation of grape vines for winemaking—as one of the staples of the Mediterranean agrarian economy, along with wheat and olives. By the sixth century B.C., Greek wine was being traded as far as Egypt, the shores of the Black Sea, and the southern regions of France.

Under the Roman Empire, viticulture spread west along the north shores of the Mediterranean and along the valleys of navigable rivers in France and Spain, while the wine trade extended north, to the North Sea and the Baltic. By the first century A.D., wine had become a commodity of indulgence, desire, and—for some—addiction throughout Europe. Viticulture and the art of winemaking survived (but did not prosper) through the Middle Ages, even in those parts of Mediterranean Europe that came under Islamic rule, where the consumption of alcohol was, theoretically, prohibited. Then, in the late medieval period, the growth of towns provided a substantial and increasingly affluent consumer market that led to the development of large, commercially oriented vineyards. Commercial viticulture spread to the south-east-facing slopes of the major river valleys in northern France and Germany, and merchant traders, drawing on innovations in finance, banking, and credit, facilitated the movement of vast quantities of wine, together with spices, perfumes, and silks, from the Mediterranean to England, Flanders, Scandinavia, and the Baltic. These northern European regions, meanwhile, paid for their luxury imports with the proceeds of exports of furs, fish, dairy produce, timber, and wool.

In the 16th century, Spanish and Portuguese overseas expansion saw the introduction of viticulture to the New World—to Mexico in the 1520s, Peru in the 1530s, Chile in the 1550s, and Florida in the 1560s. The British introduced viticulture to Virginia in the 1600s and the Dutch established vineyards in the Cape Colony of southern Africa in the 1650s. The first vineyards in California were established by Franciscan missions in the 1770s, in southeastern Australia in the 1790s, and in New Zealand in the early 1800s. Meanwhile, in Europe, demographic growth and increasing prosperity rapidly expanded the market for wine. Winemakers developed new types of wine (including champagne, claret, and port), began to specialize in particular varieties of grapes (red grapes such as Cabernet Sauvignon, Nebbiolo, and Pinot Noir, and white grapes such as Chardonnay, Riesling, and Sauvignon Blanc), and found ways of storing wine, so that especially good quality wines could be aged without spoiling. Vintage wines, carefully aged and stored, acquired special value for connoisseurs.

Disaster hit European winemakers in the 1860s in the form of an aphid, *phylloxera*, which had somehow been brought to

FIGURE 1 **The globalization of wine consumption** Imported wine for sale in one of the dozens of curbside stalls in Cholon, the ethnic Chinese quarter of Ho Chi Minh City, Vietnam.

Europe on American vines. Though American vines were immune to *phylloxera*, the aphid killed European species. Many European vineyards were devastated before it was discovered, in 1881, that grafting European vines onto American rootstock would produce high-quality and *phylloxera*-resistant plants.

On recovering from the *phylloxera* episode, the makers (and consumers) of fine wines faced other problems: Unscrupulous merchants and foreign competitors sought to pass off lesser wines as prestigious wines, supplies of good wines were watered to stretch limited supplies, and poor wines were adulterated with chemicals to improve their color or their shelf life. In response, the exclusivity of wines was protected by new systems of regulation. In France, for example, the *Appellation Contrôlée* system was introduced to guarantee the authenticity of wines, district by district. In Germany, the classification system was based not on geographic origin but on levels of quality and degrees of sweetness. Such regulations have been important in reinforcing the appeal of wine as a commodity of indulgence and desire.

Today, wine is one of the most widespread commodities of consumer indulgence. Fine wines denote affluence and distinction throughout the world's core regions and in the affluent enclaves of many of the metropolises of peripheral regions, while cheaper wines are consumed throughout much of the world (**Figure 1**). The globalization of viticulture and the more widespread consumption of wine have made branding an issue. Japanese supermarket shelves are lined with locally produced bottles with French-language labels that allude to nonexistent châteaus, while California wineries produce "Chablis," "Champagne," and "Burgundy."

Two of the most important changes in relation to wine production date from the mid-20th century and have contributed a great deal to the globalization of wine as a commodity of indulgence and desire. First, the deployment of scientific approaches and new technologies, combined with large-scale capital investment in the industry, allowed the development of first-class wines in North America, Australia, New Zealand, and elsewhere (**Figure 2**). Second, the hedonistic cultural shift of the 1960s in Western societies brought the consumption of wine firmly into the routine practices of the middle classes. The result is that the production and retailing of wine is now a significant component of the activities of large, conglomerate, and transnational corporations. The most successful of these are able to exploit and manipulate changing patterns of consumption, introducing profitable new products such as wine coolers in order to broaden the market.

FIGURE 2 The global distribution of viticulture In general, the best areas for viticulture lie between the 10°C and 2°C annual isotherms, equating approximately to the warm temperate zones between latitudes 30° and 50° north and south. In detail, the geography of viticulture is heavily influenced by soils and micro-climatic conditions. Where grapes are produced successfully nearer the equator, as in parts of Bolivia and Tanzania, it is usually because they are grown at higher altitudes. (*Source:* Adapted from T. Unwin, *Wine and the Vine*. New York: Routledge, 1996, pp. 35 and 219.)

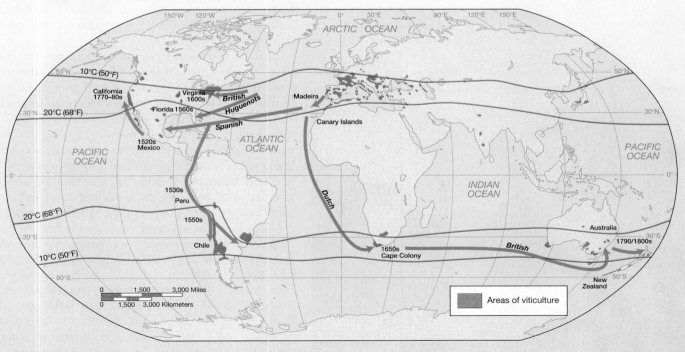

The third wave of industrialization saw a further reorganization of the geography of Europe as yet another cluster of technologies (including electricity, electrical engineering, and telecommunications) brought different resource needs and created more new investment opportunities. During this period, industrialization spread for the first time to remoter parts of the United Kingdom, France, and Germany and to most of the Netherlands, southern Scandinavia, northern Italy, eastern Austria, Bohemia (in what was then Czechoslovakia), Silesia (in Poland), Catalonia (in Spain), and the Donbas region of Ukraine, then in Russia. The overall result was to create the foundations of a core-periphery structure within Europe (see Figure 2.13), with the heart of the core centered on the "Golden Triangle" stretching between London, Paris, and Berlin.

The peripheral territories of Europe—most of the Iberian peninsula, northern Scandinavia, Ireland, southern Italy, the Balkans, and east-central Europe—were slowly penetrated by industrialization over the next 50 years. The environmental impacts of these changes were profound. Much of Europe's forest cover was cleared, while remaining forests and woodlands suffered from the **acid rain** resulting from heavy doses of atmospheric pollution. Many streams and rivers also became polluted, while the landscape everywhere was scarred with quarries, pits, cuttings, dumps, and waste heaps.

Imperialism and War   Several of the most powerful and heavily industrialized European countries (notably the United Kingdom, Germany, France, and the Netherlands) were by now competing for influence on a global scale. This competition developed into a scramble for territorial and commercial domination through **imperialism**—the deliberate exercise of military power and economic influence by core states in order to advance and secure their national interests. European countries engaged in preemptive geographic expansion to protect their established interests and to limit the opportunities of others. They also wanted to secure as much of the world as possible—through a combination of military oversight, administrative control, and economic regulations—to ensure stable and profitable environments for their traders and investors. This combination of circumstances defined a new era.

During the first half of the 20th century, the economic development of the whole of Europe was disrupted twice by major wars. The devastation of World War I was immense. The overall loss of life, including the victims of influenza epidemics and border conflicts that followed the war, amounted to between 50 and 60 million. About half as many again were permanently disabled. For some countries, this meant a loss of between 10 and 15 percent of the male workforce.

Just as European economies had adjusted to these dislocations, the Great Depression created a further phase of economic damage and reorganization throughout Europe. World War II resulted in yet another round of destruction and dislocation (**Figure 2.14**). The total loss of life in Europe this time was 42 million, two-thirds of whom were civilian casualties. Systematic German persecution of Jews—the Holocaust—resulted in approximately 4 million Jews being put to death in extermination camps such as Auschwitz and Treblinka, with up to 2 million more being exterminated elsewhere, along with gypsies and others. The German occupation of continental Europe also involved ruthless economic exploitation. By the end of the war, France was depressed to below 50 percent of its prewar standard of living and had lost 8 percent of its industrial assets. The United Kingdom lost 18 percent of its industrial assets (including overseas holdings), and the Soviet Union lost 25 percent. Germany lost 13 percent of its assets and ended the war with a level of income per capita that was less than 25 percent of the prewar figure. In addition to the millions killed and disabled during World War II, approximately 46 million people were dis-

FIGURE 2.14 Dresden, Germany Bomb damage during WWII.

placed between 1938 and 1948 through flight, evacuation, resettlement, or forced labor. Some of these movements were temporary, but most were not.

After the war, the Cold War rift between eastern and western Europe resulted in a further handicap to the European economy and, indeed, to its economic geography. Ironically, this rift helped speed economic recovery in western Europe. The United States, whose leaders believed that poverty and economic chaos in western Europe would foster communism, embarked on a massive program of economic aid under the **Marshall Plan**. This pump-priming action, together with the backlog of demand in almost every sphere of production, provided the basis for a remarkable recovery. Meanwhile, eastern Europe began an interlude of state socialism.

Eastern Europe's Interlude of State Socialism

After World War II, the leaders of the Soviet Union felt compelled to establish a **buffer zone** between their homeland and the major Western powers in Europe. The Soviet Union rapidly established its dominance throughout eastern Europe: Estonia, Moldova, Latvia, and Lithuania were absorbed into the Soviet Union itself, and Soviet-style regimes were installed in Albania, Bulgaria, Czechoslovakia, East Germany, Hungary, Poland, Romania, and Yugoslavia. In addition to the installation in 1947 of the Iron Curtain, which severed most economic linkages with the West, this intervention resulted in the complete nationalization of the means of production, the collectivization of agriculture, and the imposition of rigid social and economic controls within the eastern European satellite states.

Command Economies The economies of the former Soviet Union and its satellites were *not* based on true socialist or communist principles in which the working class had democratic control over the processes of production, distribution, and development. Rather, these economies evolved as something of a hybrid, in which state power was used by a bureaucratic class to create **command economies** in the pursuit of modernization and economic development. In a command economy, every aspect of economic production and distribution is controlled centrally by government agencies.

The Communist Council for Mutual Economic Assistance (CMEA, better known as COMECON) was established to reorganize eastern European economies in the Soviet mold—with individual members, each pursuing independent, centralized plans designed to produce economic self-sufficiency. This quickly proved unsuccessful, however, and in 1958 COMECON was reorganized. The goal of economic self-sufficiency was abandoned, mutual trade among the *Soviet bloc*—the Soviet Union plus its eastern European satellite states—was fostered, and some trade with western Europe was permitted. Meanwhile, Albania withdrew from the Soviet bloc in pursuit of a more authoritarian form of communism inspired by the Chinese revolution of 1949 (see Chapter 8); and Yugoslavia was expelled from the Soviet bloc (because of ideological differences over the interpretation of socialism) and allowed to pursue a more liberal, independent form of state socialism.

Industrialization of Command Economies The experience of the east European countries under state socialism varied considerably, but, in general, rates of industrial growth were high. As in western Europe, industrialization brought about radical changes in economic geography. In practice, however, the command economies of eastern Europe did not result in any really distinctive forms of spatial organization. As in the industrial regions of the West, the industrialized landscapes of eastern Europe came to be dominated by the localization of manufacturing activity, by regional specialization, and by core-periphery contrasts in levels of economic development.

The geography of industrial development under state socialism, as in democratic capitalism, was heavily influenced by the uneven distribution of natural resources and by the economic logic of initial advantage, specialization, and **agglomeration**

FIGURE 2.15 Socialist housing The socialist countries of eastern Europe eradicated a great deal of substandard housing in the three decades following World War II, rehousing the population in mass-produced, system-built apartment blocks. Although this new housing provided adequate shelter and basic utilities at very low rents, space standards were extremely low and housing projects were uniformly drab. This example is from Budapest, Hungary.

economies—the cost advantages that accrue to individual firms because of their location among functionally related activities. The most distinctive landscapes of state socialism were those of urban residential areas, where mass-produced, system-built apartment blocks allowed impressive progress in eliminating urban slums and providing the physical framework for an **egalitarian society**—one based on belief in equal social, political, and economic rights and privileges—though at the price of uniformly modest dwellings and strikingly sterile cityscapes (**Figure 2.15**).

Eventually, the economic and social constraints imposed by excessive state control and the dissent that resulted from the lack of democracy under state socialism combined to bring the experiment to a sudden halt. By the time the Soviet bloc collapsed in 1989 (see Chapter 3), Poland and Hungary had already accomplished a modest degree of democratic and economic reform. By 1992, East Germany (the German Democratic Republic) had been reunited with West Germany (the German Federal Republic); Estonia, Latvia, and Lithuania had become independent states once more; and the whole of eastern Europe had begun to be reintegrated with the rest of Europe. Only Kaliningrad, a small province on the Baltic between Poland and Lithuania, remains as part of the Russian Federation, retained as Russian territory because of its warm-water naval port.

THE PEOPLES OF EUROPE

A distinctive characteristic of Europe as a whole is the size and relative density of its population. With less than 7 percent of Earth's land surface, Europe contains about 13 percent of its population at an overall density of nearly 100 persons per square kilometer (260 per square mile). Within Europe, the highest national densities match those of Asian countries such as Japan, the Republic of Korea, and Sri Lanka. On the other hand, population density in Finland, Norway, and Sweden stands at about 15 persons per square kilometer, the same as in Kansas and Oklahoma (**Figure 2.16**). This reflects a fundamental feature of the human geography of Europe: the existence of a densely populated core and a sparsely populated periphery. We have already noted the economic roots of this core-periphery contrast.

While the population of the world as a whole is increasing fast, the population of Europe is roughly stable. Europe's population boom coincided roughly with the Industrial Revolution of the late 18th to late 19th centuries. Today, Europe's population is growing slowly in some regions, while declining slightly in others. The main reason for Europe's slow population growth is a general decline in birthrates (though certain subgroups, especially immigrant groups, are an exception to this trend).

It seems that conditions of family life in Europe, including readily available contraception, have led to a widespread fall in birthrates. The average size of families has dropped well below the rate needed for replacement of the population (about 2.1 children per family), to about 1.75 per family. A "baby boom" after World War II has been followed by a "baby bust." Meanwhile, life expectancy has increased, due to improved health care, medical knowledge, and healthier lifestyles. The effect is not sufficient to outweigh falling birthrates, but it has meant a dramatic increase in the proportion of people over the age of 65, from 9 percent in 1950 to nearly 17 percent in 2005. Germany's population (**Figure 2.17**) reflects these trends and shows the impact of two world wars.

The European Diaspora

The upheavals associated with the transition to industrial societies, together with the opportunities presented by colonialism and imperialism and the dislocations of two world wars, have dispersed Europe's population around the globe. Beginning with the

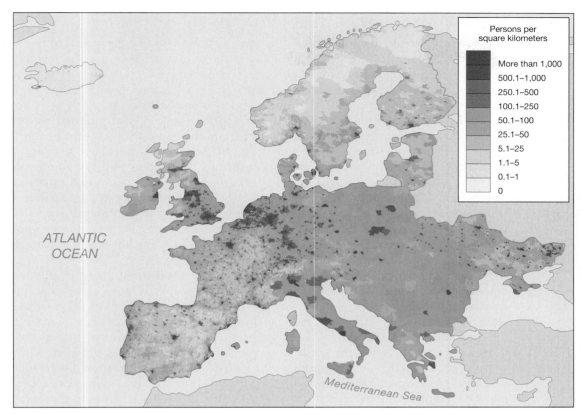

FIGURE 2.16 Population density in Europe The distribution of population in Europe reflects the region's economic history, with the highest densities in the "Golden Triangle," the newer industrial regions of northern Italy, and the richer agricultural regions of the North European Lowlands. (*Source:* Center for International Earth Science Information Network [CIESIN], Columbia University, *Gridded Population of the World* [GPW], Version 3. Palisades, NY: CIESIN, Columbia University, 2005. Available at http://sedac.ciesin.columbia.edu/gpw/.)

colonization of the Americas, vast numbers of people have left Europe for overseas. The full flood of emigration began in the early 19th century, partly in response to population pressure during the early phases of the demographic transition, and partly in response to the poverty and squalor of the early phases of the Industrial Revolution. The main stream of migration was to the Americas, with people from northwestern and central Europe heading for North America and southern Europeans heading for destinations throughout the Americas. In addition, large numbers of British left for Australia and New Zealand and eastern and southern Africa. French and Italian emigrants traveled to North Africa, Ethiopia, and Eritrea, and the Dutch went to southern Africa and Indonesia. The final surge of emigration occurred just after World War II, when various relief agencies helped homeless and displaced persons move to Australia and New Zealand, North America, and South Africa, and large numbers of Jews settled in Israel.

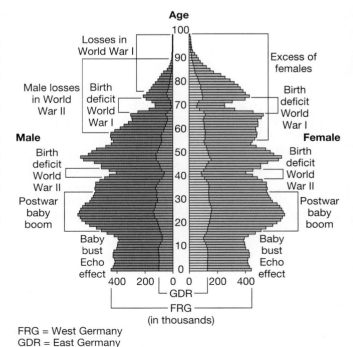

FIGURE 2.17 Population of Germany, by age and sex, 1989 Germany's population profile is that of a wealthy country that has passed through the postwar baby boom and currently possesses a low birthrate. It is also the profile of a country whose population has experienced the ravages of two world wars. (*Source:* J. McFalls, Jr., "Population: A Lively Introduction," *Population Bulletin,* 46[2], 1991, p. 1.)

Migration within Europe

Industrialization and geopolitical conflict have also resulted in a great deal of population movement within Europe. With the onset of industrialization, the regional redistribution of population within Europe followed the economic pattern. The three major waves of industrial development drew migrants from less-prosperous rural areas to a succession of industrial growth areas around coalfields.

As industrial capitalism evolved, the diversified economies of national metropolitan centers offered the most opportunities and the highest wages, thus prompting a further redistribution of population. In Britain this involved a drift of population from manufacturing towns southward to London and the southeast. In France, migration to Paris from towns all around France resulted in a polarization between Paris and the rest of the country. Some countries, developing an industrial base after the "coalfield" stage, experienced a more straightforward shift of population, directly from peripheral rural areas to prosperous metropolitan regions. In this way, Barcelona, Copenhagen, Madrid, Milan, Oslo, Stockholm, and Turin all emerged as regionally dominant metropolitan areas.

Wars and political crises have also led to significant redistributions of population within Europe. World War I forced about 7.7 million people to move. Another major transfer of population took place in the early 1920s, when more than 1 million Greeks were transferred from Turkey and half a million Turks were transferred from Greece in the aftermath of an unsuccessful Greek attempt to gain control over the eastern coast of the Aegean Sea. Soon afterward, more people were on the move, this time in the cause of ethnic and ideological purity, as the policies of Nazi Germany and fascist Italy began to bite. **Fascism,** of which Nazism was one variety, involves a centralized, autocratic government and values nation and race over the individual. Jews, in particular, were squeezed out of Germany. With World War II, there occurred further forced migrations involving approximately 46 million people.

These migrations, together with mass exterminations undertaken by Nazi Germany, left large parts of west and central Europe with significantly fewer ethnic minorities than before the war. In Poland, for example, minorities constituted 32 percent of the population before the war but only 3 percent after the war. Similar changes occurred in Czechoslovakia—from 33 percent to 15 percent—and in Romania—from 28 percent to 12 percent. Southeast Europe did not experience such large-scale transfers, and as a result many ethnic minorities remained intermixed, or surrounded and isolated, as in the former republic of Yugoslavia. The geopolitical division of Europe after the war also resulted in significant transfers of population: West Germany, for example, had absorbed nearly 11 million refugees from eastern Europe by 1961, when the Berlin Wall was built.

Recent Migration Streams

More recently, the main currents of migration within Europe have been a consequence of patterns of economic development. Rural-urban migration continues to empty the countryside of Mediterranean Europe as metropolitan regions become increasingly prosperous. Meanwhile, most metropolitan regions themselves have experienced a decentralization of population as factories, offices, and housing developments have moved out of congested central areas. Another stream of migration has involved better-off retired persons, who have tended to congregate in spas, coastal resorts, and picturesque rural regions.

The most striking of all recent streams of migration within Europe, however, have been those of migrant workers (**Figure 2.18**). These population movements were initially the result of western Europe's postwar economic boom in the 1960s and early 1970s, which created labor shortages in western Europe's industrial centers. The demand for labor represented welcome opportunities to many of the unemployed and poorly paid workers of Mediterranean Europe and of former European colonies. By the mid-1970s these migration streams had become an early component of the globalization of the world economy. By 1975, between 12 and 14 million immigrants had arrived in northwestern Europe. Most came from Mediterranean countries—Spain, Portugal, southern Italy, Greece, Yugoslavia, Turkey, Morocco, Algeria, and Tunisia. In Britain and France the majority of immigrants came from former colonies in Africa, the Caribbean, and Asia. In the Netherlands most came from former colonies in Indonesia. Most of these immigrants have stayed on, adding a striking new ethnic dimension to many of Europe's cities and regions.

Finally, it is estimated that more than 18 million people moved within Europe during the 1980s and 1990s as refugees from war and persecution or in flight from economic collapse in Russia and eastern Europe. Civil war and dislocation in the Balkans displaced more than 4 million people in the early 1990s, and by 2002 another 2.7 million had been displaced as a result of continuing conflict in the region (**Figure 2.19**).

European Cultural Traditions

The foundations of European culture were established by the ancient Greeks, who between 600 B.C. and 200 B.C. built an intellectual tradition of rational inquiry into the causes of everything, along with a belief that individuals are free, self-understanding, and valuable in themselves. The Romans took over this intellectual tradition, added Roman law and a tradition of disciplined participation in the state as a central tenet of citizenship, and spread the resulting culture throughout their empire. From the Near East came the Hebrew tradition, which in conjunction with Greek thought produced Judaism and Christianity, religions in which the individual spirit is seen as having its own responsibility and destiny within the creation. At the heart of European culture, then, are the curiosity, open-mindedness, and rationality of the Greeks; the civic responsibility and political individualism of both Greeks and Romans; and the sense of the significance of the free individual spirit that is found in the main tradition of Christianity.

When Europeans pushed out into the rest of the world in their colonial and imperial ventures, they took these values with them, imposing them onto some cultures and grafting them into others. By the 18th century they also carried the idea of **Modernity**, the genesis of which was in the changing world geography of the Age of Discovery. Modernity emphasized innovation over tradition, rationality over mysticism, and utopianism over fatalism. As Europeans tried to make sense of their own ideas and values in the context of those they encountered in the East, in Africa, in Islamic regions, and among Native Americans during the 16th and 17th centuries, many certainties of traditional thinking were cracked open. In the 18th century this ferment of ideas culminated in the **Enlightenment** movement, which was based on the conviction that all of nature, as well as human beings and their societies, could be understood as a rational system. Politically, the Enlightenment reinforced the idea of human rights and democratic forms of government and society. Expanded into the fields of economics, social philosophy, art, and music, the Enlightenment gave rise to the cultural sensibility of Modernity.

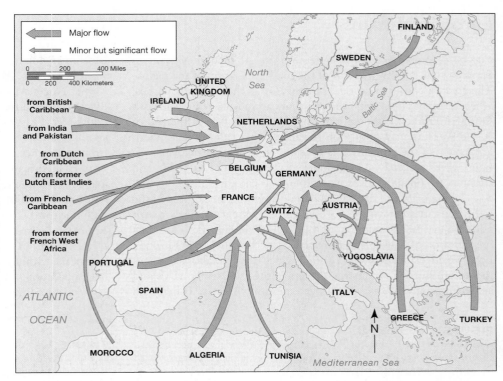

FIGURE 2.18 International labor migration This map shows the main international labor migration flows to European countries between 1945 and 1972. (*Source:* D. Pinder [ed.], *The New Europe: Economy, Society, and Environment.* New York: John Wiley & Sons, 1998, p. 265.)

FIGURE 2.19 Immigrants The demographic composition of many European cities contains a broad variety of immigrant groups. This photograph shows Albanian refugees arriving in Bari, Italy in 1991.

Europe's Muslims

Europe is home to approximately 15 to 20 million Muslims—between four and five percent of the total population of the region. The greatest concentrations of Muslims are in the Balkan countries, where Islam has been important for centuries, a legacy of the Turkish Ottoman Empire. Although the empire was dissolved at the end of World War I, Islamic culture has remained in place. In Albania, about 70 percent of the population is Muslim; in Bosnia-Herzegovina, the figure is 40 percent; in Macedonia, 30 percent; and in Serbia and Montenegro (including Kosovo), around 20 percent.

The majority of Europe's Muslims, however, are located in the industrial cities of western Europe, and they are a relatively recent addition to the population of the region (**Figure 1**). The mass immigration of Muslims to Europe was a consequence of Europe's post-World War II economic boom, which created labor shortages in western Europe's industrial centers in the 1960s and 1970s and spawned programs that encouraged migrant workers. The French Muslim population of between 5 and 6 million is the largest in western Europe. About 70 percent have their heritage in France's former North African colonies of Algeria, Morocco, and Tunisia. By contrast, Germany's Muslim population of around 3 million is dominated by people of Turkish origin. In the United Kingdom, significant numbers of Muslims arrived in the 1960s as people from the former colonies took up offers of work. Some of the first were East African Asians, while many came from south Asia. Permanent communities formed, and at least 50 percent of the current population of 1.6 million was born in the United Kingdom, with one third of the Muslim population currently aged 15 or less. Approximately one million Muslims live in the Netherlands, the majority with ties to the former Dutch colonies of Suriname and Indonesia. Other west European countries with significant Muslim populations include Austria (339,000, representing 4.1 percent of the total population), Belgium (400,000; 4 percent),

FIGURE 1 Europe's Muslims Immigrants from former colonies, recruited to Europe to solve labor shortages after World War II, have added a new cultural dimension to many of Europe's cities. These women in Copenhagen, Denmark, are immigrants from North Africa.

FIGURE 2 Leeds Grand Central Mosque, England Newly built amid the 19th-century housing of the city's Burley neighborhood, the mosque serves the city's Muslim population, most of whom are Pakistani in origin.

Radicalism In the late 20th century, after the decline of heavy industry and repeated episodes of economic recession; after two terrible world wars; after interludes of fascist dictatorships in Germany, Italy, Greece, Portugal, and Spain; after a protracted period of being on the front line of a Cold War that divided European geography in two; and after intermittent episodes of regional and ethnic conflict, it is not surprising that the culture of Europe is a culture of doubt and criticism, heavily influenced by a search for radical rethinking. In this search, Europeans have not only established a new cultural sensibility for themselves but they have also generated some powerful new ideas and philosophies that have begun to influence other cultures around the world. Dismay with the side effects of *laissez-faire* industrial capitalism and, later, horror at the results of fascism and Nazism gave a strong impetus to left-wing critiques that have been powerful enough to reshape entire national and regional cultures and, with them, some dimensions of regional geographies.

Denmark (270,000; 5 percent), Italy (825,000; 1.4 percent), Spain (1 million; 2.3 percent), and Sweden (300,000; 3 percent).

Many of these immigrant groups, now facing high unemployment and low wages as the postwar boom has leveled off, have settled in distinctive enclaves, where they have retained powerful attachments to their cultural roots. In the United Kingdom, Muslim populations have tended to concentrate in older inner-city neighborhoods (**Figure 2**), while in France the pattern is one of concentration in suburban public housing projects. Government policies in most European countries favor multiculturalism, an idea which, in general terms, accepts all cultures as having equal value. The growth of Muslim communities and their resistance to cultural assimilation, however, has challenged the European ideal of strict separation of religion and public life. By 2002, immigration had become a major electoral issue in Austria, Belgium, Denmark, France, and the Netherlands. In France, a ban on religious symbols in public schools provoked a major national row as it was widely regarded as being a ban on the Islamic headscarf. Although the U.S. wars against Afghanistan and Iraq received little popular support across much of Europe, Islamist terrorist attacks against west European targets have heightened fears and tensions between Muslim communities and host populations.

In March 2004 thirteen bombs on four packed commuter trains killed 191 people and wounded more than 1500 in Madrid, Spain. The attack was attributed to the Islamic militant group al-Qaeda. A few months later in the Netherlands a prominent filmmaker critical of Islam was murdered in 2004 by a radical Islamist. In July 2005, an Islamist attack on buses and underground trains in London left 52 dead. Later in 2005, the Danish newspaper *Jyllands-Posten* published a series of cartoons featuring the prophet Mohammad. Whereas European culture generally regards satire and caricature as accepted elements of free speech and democracy, Muslims regard visual representations of the prophet Mohammad as a profanity. The result was that the cartoons became a lightning rod for cultural tensions. Muslim leaders in Denmark were able to internationalize the issue, and a few months later a sudden wave of anti-Danish demonstrations swept across the Middle East and in Indonesia and Pakistan.

FIGURE 3 Paris riots Following the deaths of two teenage boys in an electrical sub-station after they had fled police in Clichy-sous-Bois in October 2005, there were extensive riots that spread to several other French cities with large immigrant populations.

Meanwhile, Muslim communities across Europe face increased resentment and hostility from host populations. In Muslim neighborhoods with high concentrations of unemployment, heavy-handed policing and racial discrimination can easily trigger civil disorder. This is what happened in the fall of 2005 in the Paris suburbs of Clichy-sous-Bois (**Figure 3**), where days of rioting followed the deaths of two teenagers who had been chased by police. The riots quickly spread to other French cities, including Lille, Lyon, Marseille, St Etienne, Strasbourg, and Toulouse; thousands of vehicles were burned and the French government was forced to order a state of emergency that extended until January 2006. Tensions remain high, and the cultural issues associated with Europe's Muslim population are likely to continue to be an important dimension of European politics, especially with the prospect of Turkey joining the European Union, which would add around 83 million Muslims to Europe's population.

The most profound influence of all was Karl Marx, whose penetrating critique of industrial capitalism (written in London and drawing heavily on descriptions of conditions in Manchester, England, supplied by his colleague Friedrich Engels) inspired both a socialist political economy in Russia and a fascist countermovement in Germany. After World War II, western European left-wing critique portrayed both fascism and Soviet-style socialism as essentially imperialist, while American-style capitalism was critiqued as being intrinsically exploitative in privileging the individual and property over the community and the public good.

Contemporary Europe has a distinctive set of social values, and the "European Dream" is quite distinctive from the "American Dream":

The European Dream emphasizes community relationships over individual autonomy, cultural diversity over assimilation, quality of life over the accumulation of wealth, sustainable development over unlimited material growth, deep play over unrelenting toil, universal human rights and the rights of nature over property rights, and global cooperation over the unilateral exercise of power.[1]

Present-day Europe also has a distinctive cultural cast. Intellectual debate—about the role of culture itself; about whether people's thoughts and lives should be understood in terms of the dynamics of the cultures in which they are embedded (structuralism) or in terms of individual consciousness (existentialism); and about whether any kind of single-viewpoint, big-picture understanding of the world is really possible (postmodernism)—has spilled over into literature, cinema, television, magazines, and newspapers. Thus contemporary European culture is marked by a critical awareness of the role of culture itself (see Film, Music, and Popular Literature, p. 104).

Gender and Inequality   Another powerful postwar movement deeply critical of the dominant structures of capitalist society was feminism, built on the ideas of Simone de Beauvoir in her 1949 book *The Second Sex*. The strong liberal component of European culture has meant that, compared with peoples in most other world regions, Europeans have been more willing to address the deep inequalities between men and women that are rooted in both traditional societies and industrial capitalism. Still, patriarchal society and the culture of *machismo* remain strong in Mediterranean Europe—especially in rural areas—and working-class communities throughout Europe are still characterized by significant gender inequalities.

It is in northwestern Europe—and especially in Scandinavia—that gender equality has improved most, as a result of both the progressive social values of the "baby-boom" generation and legislation that has translated these values into law. By the mid-1980s, younger men in much of northwestern Europe had acquired a new, progressive collective identity associated with ideals of gender equality—especially as they relate to men's domestic roles. More recently, however, a "men-behaving-badly" syndrome—known as "laddism" in the United Kingdom—has emerged in reaction.

In global context, Europe stands out as a region where women's representation in senior positions in industry and government is relatively high. Women in Europe generally have a significantly longer life expectancy than men and have comparable levels of adult literacy. Nevertheless, women in the European labor force tend to earn, on average, only 45 to 65 percent of what men earn. These statistics demonstrate a distinctly regional pattern. Broadly speaking, the gender gaps in education, employment, health, and legal standing are wider in southern and eastern Europe and narrower in Scandinavia and northwestern Europe. In part, this reflects regional differences in social customs and ways of life; in part, it reflects regional differences in overall levels of affluence.

Although Europe is a relatively affluent world region, there are in fact persistent and significant economic inequalities at every geographic scale. Annual per capita GDP (in PPP) in 2004 ranged from $2119 in Moldova to $63,609 in Luxembourg. Regional income disparities within many European countries are increasing. In northwestern Europe this is generally a result of the declining fortunes of "rustbelt" regions and the relative prosperity of regions with high-tech industry and advanced business services. In southern and eastern Europe it is a result of differences between regions dominated by rural economies (generally poorer) and those dominated by metropolitan areas (generally more prosperous). The resulting disparities are significant, with annual per capita GDP (in PPP) in 2004 ranging from $51,906 in central London and more than $30,000 in many major metropolitan regions to between $12,000 and $18,000 in many peripheral rural regions. Poverty and homelessness exist in every European country, though poverty as measured on a global scale ($1 or $2 a day per person) is virtually unknown within Europe.

---

[1]J. Rifkin, *The European Dream. How Europe's Vision of the Future Is Quietly Eclipsing the American Dream*, New York: Tarcher, 2004, p. 3.

Culture and Ethnicity, Nations and States

While European culture is distinctive at the global scale, it is also characterized by some sharp internal regional variations. In the broadest terms, there is a significant north–south cultural divide. Southern Europe has always been more traditional in its religious affiliations—not just in terms of the dominance of Roman Catholicism over Protestantism, but of the prevalence of the conservative and more mystical forms of Catholicism. The Roman Catholic Church, still one of the most widespread within Europe, emerged in the fourth century under the bishop of Rome and spread quickly through the weakening Roman Empire. Missionaries helped spread not only the gospel but also the use of the Latin alphabet throughout most of Europe. The Eastern Orthodox Church, under the auspices of the Byzantine Empire centered in Constantinople (present-day Istanbul), dominated the eastern margins of Europe and much of the Balkans, while Islamic influence spread into parts of the Balkans (present-day Albania, the European part of Turkey, and parts of Bosnia-Herzegovina) and, for a while, southern Spain. With the religious upheavals of the 16th and 17th centuries, Protestant Christianity came to dominate much of northern Europe. More recently, immigrants from the Middle East, Africa, and South Asia have reintroduced Islam to Europe, adding an important dimension to contemporary politics as well as culture (see Geography Matters: Europe's Muslims, p. 80).

Another distinctive aspect of southern European culture is its traditional patterns of family life, with larger, close-knit families that tend to stick together as a buffer against unemployment and poverty in societies with relatively underdeveloped social welfare systems. The western part of southern Europe also shares the Romance family of languages, the development of which was fostered by the spread of the Roman Empire. A second major group of languages, Germanic languages, occupy northwestern Europe, extending as far south as the Alps (**Figure 2.20**). English is one of the Germanic family of languages, an amalgam of Anglo-Saxon and Norman French, with Scandinavian and Celtic traces. A third major language group consists of Slavic languages, which dominate eastern Europe.

These broad geographic divisions of religion, language, and family life are reflected in other cultural traits: folk art, traditional costume, music, folklore, and cuisine. Thus there is a Scandinavian cultural subregion with a collection of related languages (except Finnish), a uniformity of Protestant denominations, and a strong cultural affinity in art and

FIGURE 2.20 Major languages in Europe Although three main language groups—Romance, Germanic, and Slav—dominate Europe, differences among specific languages are significant. These differences have contributed a great deal to the cultural diversity of Europe but have also contributed a great deal to ethnic and geopolitical tensions. (*Source:* Redrawn from R. Mellor and E. A. Smith, *Europe: A Geographical Survey of the Continent.* London: Macmillan, 1979, p. 22.)

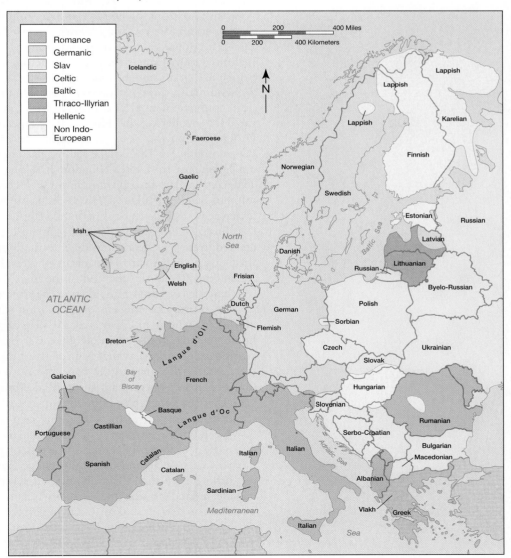

music that reaches back to the Viking age and even to pre-Christian myths. A second distinctive subregion is constituted by the sphere of Romance languages in the south and west. A third is constituted by the British Isles, bound by language, history, art forms, and folk music, but with a religious divide between the Protestant Anglo-Saxon and Catholic Celtic spheres. A fourth clear cultural subregion is the Germanic sphere of central Europe, again with mixed religious patterns—Lutheran Protestantism in the north, Roman Catholicism in the south—but with a common bond of language, folklore, art, and music. The Slavic subregion of eastern and southeastern Europe forms another broad cultural subregion, though beyond the commonalities of related languages and certain physical traits among the general population, there is considerable diversity.

It is, in fact, the cultural and ethnic diversity of Europe's peoples and their languages, religions, and cultures that is one of the most significant aspects of its geography. Europe's cultural diversity has made it vital and attractive; it has contributed in large measure to the modern ideal of national states; and it has also made it the theater of innumerable wars, including two world wars within a single generation.

Ethnicity and National Identity   Many of the countries of Europe are relatively new creations and the political boundaries of many have changed quite often. The whole idea of national states, in fact, can be traced to the Enlightenment in Europe, when the ferment of ideas about human rights and democracy, together with widening horizons of literacy and communication, created new perspectives on allegiance, communality, and identity. In 1648 the Treaty of Westphalia, signed by most European powers, brought an end to Europe's seemingly interminable religious wars by making national states the principal actors in international politics and establishing the principle that no state has the right to interfere in the internal politics of any other state.

Gradually, these perspectives began to undermine the dominance of the great European continental empires controlled by family dynasties—the Bourbons, the Hapsburgs, the Hohenzollerns, the House of Savoy, and so on. After the French Revolution (1789–93) and the kaleidoscopic changes of the Napoleonic Wars (1800–15), Europe was reordered, in 1815, to be set in a pattern of modern states. Denmark, France, Portugal, Spain, and the United Kingdom had long existed as separate, independent states. The 19th century saw the unification of Italy (1861–70) and of Germany (1871) and the creation of Belgium, Bulgaria, Greece, Luxembourg, the Netherlands, Romania, Serbia, and Switzerland as independent national states. Early in the 20th century they were joined by Czechoslovakia, Estonia, Finland, Latvia, Lithuania, Norway, and Sweden. Austria was created in its present form in the aftermath of World War I, as part of the carving up of the German and Austro-Hungarian empires. In 1921 long-standing religious cleavages in Ireland resulted in the creation of the Irish Free State (now Ireland), with the six Protestant counties of Ulster remaining in the United Kingdom.

The European concept of the nation-state has immensely influenced the modern world. As we saw in Chapter 1, the idea of a nation-state is based on the concept of a homogeneous group of people governed by their own state. In a true nation-state, no significant group exists that is not part of the nation. In practice, most European states were established around the concept of a nation-state but with territorial boundaries that did in fact encompass substantial ethnic minorities (**Figure 2.21**). The result has been that the geography of Europe has been characterized by regionalism and irredentism throughout the 20th century and into the 21st.

We have already cited the example of Basque regionalism in Spain and France (see p. 6 in Chapter 1). Other examples of regionalism include regional independence movements in Catalonia (within Spain), Scotland (within the United Kingdom), and the Turkish Cypriots' determination to secede from Cyprus. Examples of *irredentism* include Ireland's claim on Northern Ireland (renounced in 1999), the claims of Nazi Germany on Austria and the German parts of Czechoslovakia and Poland, and the claims of Croatia and Serbia and Montenegro on various parts of Bosnia-Herzegovina. Some cases of regionalism have led to violence, social disorder, or even civil war, as in Cyprus. For the most part, however, regional ethnic separatism has been pursued within the framework of civil society, and the result has been that several regional minorities have achieved a degree of political autonomy. For example, the United Kingdom created regional parliaments for Scotland and Wales.

Ethnic Conflict in the Balkans

Most cases of irredentism, on the other hand, have contributed at some point in history to war or conflict. Nowhere has this been more evident than in the troubled region of the Balkans. When 19th-century empires were dismantled after World War I, an entirely new political geography was created in the Balkans. Those political boundaries survived until the 1990s, when the breakup of Yugoslavia marked the end of the Great Powers' attempt to unite Serbs, Croats, and Slovenes within a single territory (**Figure 2.22**). The repeated fragmentation and reorganization of ethnic groups into separate states within the region has given rise to the term **balkanization** in referring to any situation in which a larger territory is broken up into smaller units, and especially where territorial jealousies give rise to a degree of hostility. In the Balkans themselves, the geopolitical reorganizations of the 1990s have left significant **enclaves**, culturally distinct territories that are surrounded by the territory of a different cultural group, and **exclaves**, portions of a country or of a cultural group's territory that lie outside its contiguous land area. These enclaves and exclaves remain the focus of continued or potential hostility. In Romania, for example, there are more than 1.6 million Hungarians, while in Bulgaria

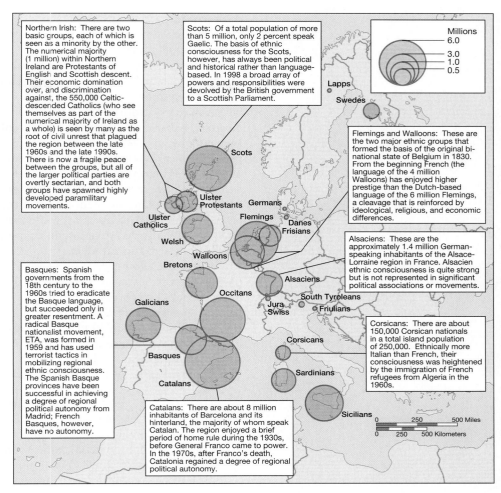

FIGURE 2.21 Minority ethnic subgroups in western Europe Regional and ethnic consciousness now represents a strong political factor in many European countries. Within Spain, for example, the dominant population—some 27 million—is Castillian, but there are between 6 and 8 million Catalans, almost 2 million Basques, and about 3 million Galicians. Belgium is divided into 4 million French-speaking Walloons and 6 million Flemings, whose language is Dutch-based. (*Source:* P. Knox, *Geography of Western Europe*. London: Croom Helm, 1984, p. 69.)

FIGURE 2.22 Changing political boundaries in the Balkans, 1878, 1919, and 2006

there are more than 800,000 Turks. Serbian nationalism, however, has provided the principal catalyst for violence and conflict in the region. In the 1990s, Serbian nationalism led to attempts at **ethnic cleansing**.

The most extreme example of ethnic cleansing was in the Kosovo region. In 1998, Yugoslavia's Serbian leader, Slobodan Milosevic, initiated a brutal, premeditated, and systematic campaign of ethnic cleansing that was aimed at removing Kosovar Albanians from what had become their homeland. Serbian forces expelled Kosovar Albanians at gunpoint from villages and larger towns, looted and burned their homes, organized the systematic rape of young Kosovar Albanian women, and used Kosovar Albanians as human shields to escort Serbian military convoys. In addition, Serbian forces carried out widespread summary executions, dumping bodies in mass graves in an attempt to destroy evidence, and systematically stripped Kosovar Albanians of identity and property documents, including passports, land titles, automobile license plates, identity cards, and other forms of documentation. By systematically destroying schools, places of worship, and hospitals, Serbian forces sought to destroy social identity and the fabric of Kosovar Albanian society.

International outrage at these human rights violations finally led to the declaration of war against Yugoslavia by NATO in March 1999. A 78-day bombing campaign pushed back Serb forces, and within a few weeks Slobodan Milosevic and other Serbian leaders were indicted in the International Court of Justice for their roles in human rights violations. Since 2000, many Kosovar Albanian refugees have returned to their homeland in Kosovo to attempt to rebuild their lives, but Kosovo remains under UN control and the ethnic Albanian community has expressed frustration at the length of time being taken to decide Kosovo's future status.

A "European" Identity?   Ethnic tensions and feelings of nationalism throughout Europe have been intensified by globalization. Globalization has heightened people's awareness of cultural heritage and ethnic identities. As we saw in Chapter 1, the more universal the diffusion of material culture and lifestyles, the more valuable regional and ethnic identities tend to become. Globalization has also brought large numbers of immigrants to some European countries, and their presence has further heightened people's awareness of cultural identities.

In the more affluent countries of northwestern Europe, immigration has emerged as one of the most controversial issues since the end of the Cold War. Although the economic benefits of immigration far outweigh any additional demands that may be made on a country's health or welfare system, fears that unrestrained immigration might lead to cultural fragmentation and political tension have provoked some governments to propose new legislation to restrict immigration from the former communist states of eastern Europe and from outside Europe. The same fears have been responsible for a resurgence of popular **xenophobia**—a hate, or fear, of foreigners—in some countries. In Germany, for example, right-wing nationalistic groups have attacked hostels housing immigrant families, while citizenship laws have prevented second-generation Gastarbeiter ("guest worker") families from obtaining German citizenship. In France, claims that immigrants from North Africa are a threat to the traditional French way of life have led to some success for the National Front Party. Asylum seekers, drawn to northwestern Europe from all parts of the globe in such large numbers that they have had to be accommodated in processing centers, have also provoked negative reactions (**Figure 2.23**). On the other hand, globalization has brought a degree of cosmopolitanism to many cities. London, in particular, has become a city with a global mix of populations and subcultures. Almost one-third of London's current residents—2.2 million people—were born outside England, and this total takes no account of the contribution of the city's second- and third-generation immigrants, many of whom have inherited the traditions of their parents and grandparents. Altogether, the people of London speak more than 300 lan-

FIGURE 2.23 Immigration concerns   Local residents of Lee-on-the-Solent, England, protest against a proposed asylum center for refugees.

guages, and the city has at least 50 non-indigenous communities with populations of 10,000 or more.

All this raises the question, "How 'European' *are* the populations of Europe?" European history and ethnicity have resulted in a collection of national prides, prejudices, and stereotypes that are strongly resistant to the forces of cultural globalization. Germans continue to be seen by most other Europeans as a little overserious, preoccupied by work, and inclined to arrogance. Scots continue to carry the popular image of a dour, unimaginative, ginger-haired people who love bagpipe and accordion music, dress in kilts and sporrans, live on whisky and porridge, and generally spend as little as possible. The English are seen as a nation of lager-swilling hooligans, well-meaning middle classes, and out-of-touch aristocrats. Norwegians and Danes continue to resent the Swedes' "neutrality" during World War II, and so on. In reality, such stereotypes are, of course, exaggerations that stem from the behaviors of a relative minority, and opinion surveys show that these stereotypes, prejudices, and identities are steadily being countered by a growing sense of European identity, especially among younger and better-educated persons. Much of this can be attributed to the growing influence of the European Union, which is discussed in the next section.

CONTEMPORARY CHALLENGES IN A GLOBALIZING WORLD

Contemporary Europe is a cornerstone of the world economy with a complex, multilayered, and multifaceted regional geography. In overall terms, Europe, with about 12 percent of the world's population, accounts for almost 35 percent of the world's exports, almost 43 percent of the world's imports, and 33 percent of the world's aggregate GNP. Europe's inhabitants, on average, now consume about twice the quantity of goods and commercial services they did in 1975. Purchasing power has risen everywhere to the extent that basic items of food and clothing now account for only about 30 percent of household expenditure, leaving more resources for leisure and consumer durables. Levels of material consumption in much of Europe approach those of households in the United States (**Figure 2.24**). The development of European **welfare states** (institutions with the aim of distributing income and resources to the poorer members of society) has helped maintain households' purchasing power during periods of recession and ensured at least a tolerable level of living for most groups at all times. Levels of personal taxation are high, but all citizens receive a wide array of services and benefits in return. The most striking of these services are high-quality medical care, public transport systems, social housing, schools, and universities. The most significant benefits are pensions and unemployment benefits.

Contemporary Europe is a dynamic region that embodies a great deal of change. Because of the legacies of European history and culture, and because modern regional development in Europe was so closely tied to the technology systems of the Industrial Revolution, economic globalization and new high-tech, information-based technology systems present immense challenges and opportunities to places and regions within Europe. Formerly prosperous industrial regions have suffered economic decline, while some places and regions have reinvented themselves to take advantage of new paths to economic development. Meanwhile, the former Soviet satellite states have been reintegrated into the European world region and much of Europe has joined in the European Union, a supranational organization founded to recapture prosperity and power through economic and political integration (see p. 88).

FIGURE 2.24 A German family with their material possessions The Pfitzner family from Köln, Germany, photographed with their possessions outside their home in the mid-1990s, represents a statistically average German family in terms of family size, residence, and income.

Growth, Deindustrialization, and Reinvestment

Europe provides a classic example of how long-term shifts in technology systems tend to lead to regional economic change (see Chapter 1). The innovations associated with new technology systems generate new industries that are not yet tied down by enormous investments in factories or tied to existing industrial agglomerations. Combined with innovations in transport and communications, this creates windows of opportunity that can result in new industrial districts and in some towns and cities growing into dominant metropolitan areas through new rounds of investment. Within Europe the regions that have prospered most through the onset of a new technology system are the Thames Valley to the west of London; the Île de France region around Paris; the Ruhr valley in northwestern Germany; and the metropolitan regions of Lyon–Grenoble (France), Amsterdam–Rotterdam (Netherlands), Milan and Turin (Italy), and Frankfurt, Munich, and Stuttgart (Germany).

Just as high-tech industries and regions have grown, the profitability of traditional industries in established regions has declined. Wherever the differential in profitability has been large enough, disinvestment has taken place in the less-profitable industries and regions. **Disinvestment** means selling off assets such as factories and equipment. Widespread disinvestment leads to deindustrialization in formerly prosperous industrial regions. **Deindustrialization** involves a relative decline (and in extreme cases, an absolute decline) in industrial employment in core regions as firms scale back their activities in response to lower levels of profitability. This is what happened to the industrial regions of northern England, South Wales, and central Scotland in the early part of the 20th century, and it is what happened to the industrial region of Alsace-Lorraine, in France, and to many other traditional manufacturing towns and regions within Europe in the 1960s and 1970s.

The European Union

The European Union (EU) had its origins in the political and economic climate following World War II. The idea behind the EU was to ensure European autonomy from the United States and to recapture the prosperity Europe had forfeited as a result of the war. Part of the rationale for its creation was also to bring Germany and France together into a close association, which would prevent any repetition of the geopolitical problems in western Europe that had led to two world wars. The first stage in the evolution of the EU was the creation in the 1950s of several institutions to promote economic efficiency through integration. These were subsequently amalgamated to form the European Community (EC), which was in turn expanded in scope to form the European Union (EU). EU membership has expanded from the six original members of the EC—Belgium, France, Italy, Luxembourg, the Netherlands, and West Germany—to 27 countries (**Figure 2.25**) with a population of nearly 457 million, and a combined gross domestic product (GDP) larger than that of the United States. It has developed into a sophisticated and powerful institution with a pervasive influence on patterns of economic and social well-being within its member states. It also has a significant impact on certain aspects of economic development within some non-member countries.

The origin of the organization that evolved into the EU was a compromise worked out between the strongest two of the original six members. West Germany wanted a larger but protected market for its industrial goods, while France wanted to continue to protect its highly inefficient but large and politically important agricultural sector from overseas competition. The result was the creation of a tariff-free market within the Community, the creation of a unified external tariff, and a Common Agricultural Policy (the CAP) to bolster the Community's agricultural sector.

Some of the most striking changes in the regional geography of the EU have been related to the operation of the CAP. Although agriculture accounts for less than 3 percent of the EU workforce, the CAP has dominated the EU budget from the beginning.

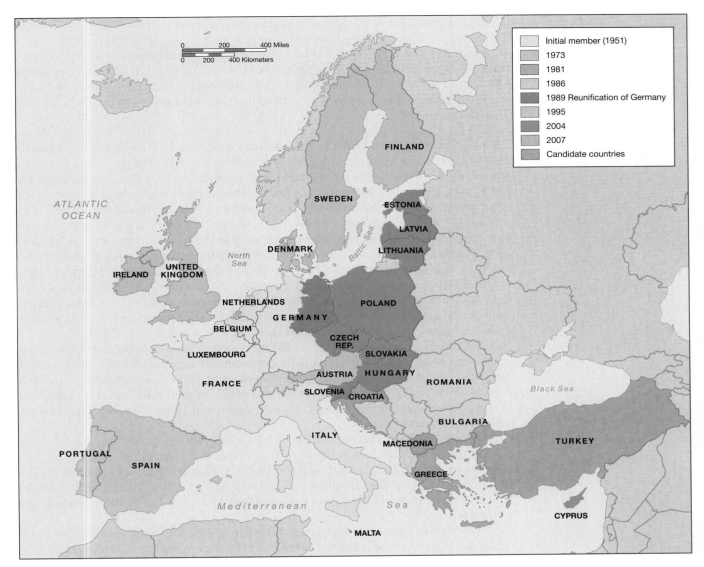

FIGURE 2.25 The expansion of the European Union The advantages of membership in the European Union have led to a dramatic growth in its size, transforming it into a major economic and political force in world affairs.

For a long time, it accounted for more than 70 percent of the EU's total expenditures, and it still accounts for more than 45 percent. Its operation has had a significant impact on rural economies, rural landscapes, and rural standards of living, and it has even influenced urban living through its effects on food prices.

The basis of the CAP is a system of EU support of wholesale prices for agricultural produce. This support has the dual effect of stabilizing the price of agricultural products and of subsidizing farmers' incomes. The CAP was originally designed to encourage farm modernization by securing higher incomes for farmers. An additional attraction of the policy, though, is that stable, guaranteed prices provide consumers with security and continuity of food supplies. Stable markets also allow trends in product specialization and concentration by farm, region, and country to proceed in an ordered and predictable fashion.

The overall result has been a realignment of agricultural production patterns, with a general withdrawal from mixed farming. Ireland, the United Kingdom, and Denmark, for example, have increased their specialization in the production of wheat, barley, poultry, and milk, while France and Germany have increased their specialization in the production of barley, maize, and sugar beet.

The reorganization of Europe's agricultural landscapes under the CAP brought some unwanted side effects, however, including environmental problems that have occurred as a result of the speed and scale of farm modernization, combined with farmers' desire to take advantage of generous levels of guaranteed prices for crops. Moorlands, woodlands, wetlands, and hedgerows have come under threat, and some traditional mixed-farming landscapes have been replaced by the prairie-style settings of specialized agribusiness.

The EU and Regional Interdependence   The Treaty of European Union of 1992 (the Maastricht Treaty) gave to the EU most of the major functions of a sovereign national state, including creation of a single currency (the euro, launched in 1999), coordination of economic policies, redistribution of wealth among regions, and management of a common external policy covering foreign relations and defense. This relaunching was an impressive achievement, particularly since it was undertaken at a time of major distractions: coping with the reunification of Germany and the breakup of the former Soviet empire in eastern Europe and, not least, having to deal with a resurgence of nationalism within Europe. Nevertheless, the EU's progress toward more comprehensive unification based on a common constitution has been called into question. A Constitutional Treaty, approved by the European Council in 2004 subject to ratification by all 25 member states, was put on hold after the negative results of referenda on the proposed constitution in France and the Netherlands in 2005.

The overall economic benefits of EU membership have been apparent for a long time. Not surprisingly, a growing number of countries seek membership. Bulgaria and Romania are set to join in 2007, while Croatia and Turkey are officially "candidate countries" whose membership negotiations depend on their fulfilling EU criteria concerning democracy, the rule of law, human rights, and respect for and protection of minorities (**Figure 2.26**).

EU membership brings regional stresses as well as the prospect of overall economic gain. Existing member countries have found that the removal of internal barriers to labor, capital, and trade has worked to the clear disadvantage of peripheral regions and in particular to the disadvantage of those farthest from the Golden Triangle, which is increasingly the European center of gravity in terms of both production and consumption.

This regional imbalance was recognized by the Single European Act (SEA) of 1985, which included "economic and social cohesion" as a major policy. The SEA doubled its

FIGURE 2.26 EU expansion The proposed addition of Turkey to the European Union has met with concerns about that country's ability to meet the EU's criteria on human rights.

grant funding for regional development assistance and established a Cohesion Fund to help Greece, Ireland, Portugal, and Spain achieve levels of economic development comparable to those of the rest of the EU. Regions eligible for these funds are shown in **Figure 2.27**. In its 2007–2013 budget cycle, the EU has allocated $406 billion—about one-third of the total EU budget—to projects and policies designed to improve economic and social cohesion within and among its member countries.

A New Infrastructure for an Integrated Europe

The economic integration of Europe, following fundamental geographic principles, leans heavily on policies designed to increase accessibility and spatial interaction. In 1996 the EU approved a far-reaching plan for a series of trans-European networks (TENs) to weld together Europe's patchwork of national transport systems. The plan centers on 30 priority projects for new or upgraded highways, rail lines, waterways, bridges, and airports that will improve linkages among states, boost economic efficiency, and reinforce the social and political cohesiveness of the EU. Improvements to Europe's railway infrastructure account for 22 of the EU's 30 priority projects and about 85 percent of the $275 billion budget.

With its relatively short distances between major cities, Europe is ideally suited for rail travel and less suited, because of population densities and traffic congestion around airports, to air traffic. Allowing for check-in times and accessibility to terminals, travel between many major European cities is already quicker by rail than by air. The high-speed London–Paris rail service—in direct competition with the airlines—has captured 60 percent of inter-city traffic since opening in 1994. The EU plans to coordinate and

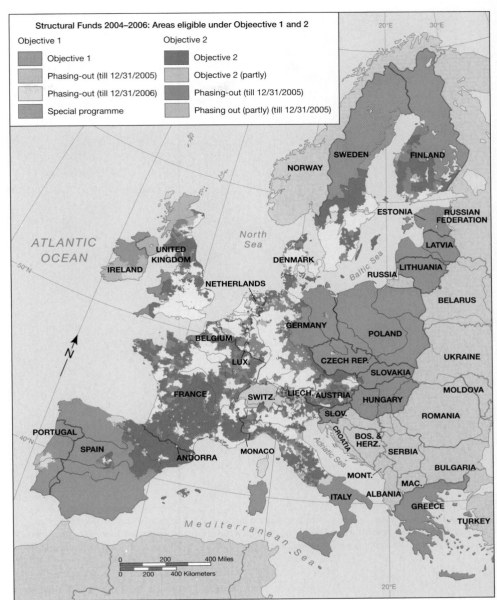

FIGURE 2.27 European Union regions eligible for aid, 2006 Just over half of the total population of the European Union lives in areas eligible for regional assistance from the European Regional Development Fund and Cohesion Fund. Most of the EU's regional aid is allocated to "lagging" regions (where per capita GDP is less than 75 percent of the EU average) and to declining industrial regions. (*Source:* EU Inforegio. European Commission, European Regional Development Fund and Cohesion Fund, 2002. Available at http://europa.eu.int/ comm/regional_policy/funds/prord/guide/euro2000–2006_en.htm.)

subsidize a $250 billion investment in 30,000 kilometers (almost 20,000 miles) of high-speed track to be phased in through 2012. The heart of the system will be the "PBKAL web," which will connect Paris, Brussels, Köln (Cologne), Amsterdam, and London, and which will be completed by 2007 (**Figure 2.28**).

Improved locomotive technologies and specially engineered tracks and rolling stock will make it possible to offer passenger rail services at speeds of 275 to 350 kilometers per hour (180 to 250 miles per hour). New tilt-technology railway cars, which are designed to negotiate tight curves by tilting the train body into turns to counteract the effects of centrifugal force, are being introduced in many parts of Europe to raise maximum speeds on conventional rail tracks. German Railways (DB), for example, introduced third-generation ICE (inter-city express) trains with a maximum speed of 330 kilometers per hour (205 miles per hour) in 2000.

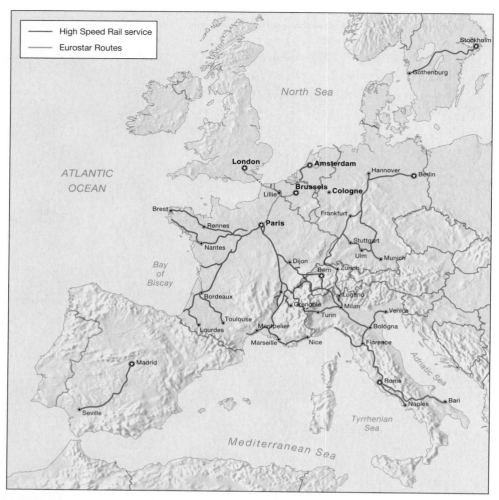

FIGURE 2.28 High-speed rail in Europe The European Union is promoting 30,000 kilometers (almost 20,000 miles) of high-speed track to be phased in through 2012. The heart of the system, the "PBKAL web," will lead to some restructuring of European geography. High-speed rail routes will have only a few scheduled stops; cities with no scheduled stops will be less accessible and, then, less attractive for economic development.

High-speed rail routes will cause some restructuring of the geography of Europe. They will have only a few time-tabled stops because the time penalties that result from deceleration and acceleration undermine the advantages of high-speed travel. Places that do not have scheduled stops will be less accessible and, then, less attractive for economic development. Places linked to the routes will be well situated to grow in future rounds of economic development.

Other trans-European network projects feature new tunnels through the Alps and the Pyrenees and under the city of Antwerp; new motorways across Greece (connecting Athens to the Bulgarian border), and between Lisbon (Portugal) and Valladolid (Spain); and improvements to the connections between Milan's Malpensa airport, the city, and the railway network. There are also numerous energy-related infrastructure projects aimed at increasing the efficiency and capacity of power stations and extending natural gas pipelines and electricity grids across member countries—and even into neighboring countries that have petitioned for EU membership, in order to help boost their economic efficiency before they join the EU. The most striking project of all is the Øresund Fixed Link, a 15-kilometer bridge and tunnel that opened in 2000, connecting Sweden and Denmark for the first time since prehistoric times (before the land link was breached by rising sea levels). The two sides of the Øresund Sound, hitherto entirely separate, will soon develop into a single functional economic region that will be well placed to form a commercial hub.

The EU and the Rest of the World The scale of the EU and its maintenance of a strongly protectionist agricultural policy has inevitably had a significant impact on non-member countries. The EU does extend favorable trading privileges to a large group of countries in Africa, the Caribbean, and the Pacific, most of them former colonial territories of EU member states. Nevertheless, sensitive products (that is, those that compete directly with EU agricultural and industrial products) are excluded from preferential treatment or are subject to seasonal restrictions.

Because the whole idea of the EU is based on improving Europe's competitiveness with the United States and Japan, it is not surprising that the EU's trade relations with those countries have been fractious. Other countries, especially those with strong traditional ties to European markets, have found themselves excluded by the EU's external tariff wall. New Zealand is a good example. The United Kingdom used to take nearly all of New Zealand's butter, cheese, and lamb. But after the United Kingdom joined the EU in 1972, New Zealand no longer had access to markets in the United Kingdom. As a result, New Zealand's agriculture had to be restructured, new products had to be developed—one notable success was the kiwi fruit—and new markets had to be developed in Latin America, India, and Japan (see Chapter 9). Meanwhile, the EU has become the biggest single donor of aid to less-developed countries.

The Reintegration of Eastern Europe

Between 1989 and 1992, all of the former satellite states of the Soviet Union in eastern Europe turned away from state socialism with command economies and began the process of establishing democracies with capitalist economies. In 1991 COMECON was abolished, and one by one, eastern European countries began a complex series of reforms. These included the abolition of controls on prices and wages, the removal of restrictions on trade and investment, the creation of a financial infrastructure to handle private investment, the creation of government fiscal systems to balance taxation and spending, and the **privatization** of state-owned industries and enterprises. After more than 40 years of state socialism, such reforms were difficult and painful. Indeed, the reforms are by no means complete in any of the countries, and economic and social dislocation is a continuing fact of life.

Nevertheless, the reintegration of eastern Europe has added a potentially dynamic market of 130 million consumers to the European economy. Within a capitalist framework, eastern Europe has the comparative advantage of relatively cheap land and labor. This has attracted a great deal of foreign investment, particularly from transnational corporations and from German firms and investors, many of whom have historic ties with parts of eastern Europe. In some ways, the transition toward market economies has been remarkably swift. It did not take long for Western-style consumerism to appear on the streets and in many of the stores in larger eastern European cities. On the flip side, it also did not take long for inflation, unemployment, and homelessness to appear. Overall, eastern Europe is increasingly reintegrated with the rest of Europe, but for the most part as a set of economically peripheral regions, with agriculture still geared to local markets and former COMECON trading opportunities and industry still geared more to heavy industry and standardized products than to competitive consumer products. Still very weakly developed are the service sector in general and knowledge-based industries in particular.

In detail, the pace and degree of reintegration varies considerably across eastern Europe. Ethnic conflict in Bosnia and Herzegovina, Croatia, and the former republic of Yugoslavia has severely retarded reform and reintegration, while Albania, Bulgaria, Macedonia, Moldova, and Romania suffer from the combined disadvantages of having relatively poor resource bases, weakly developed communications and transportation infrastructures, and political regimes with little ability or inclination to press for economic and social reform. In Ukraine, which has a much better infrastructure, a significant industrial base, and the capacity for extensive trade in grain exports and in advanced technology, reintegration has been retarded by a combination of geographical isolation from western Europe, continuing economic and political ties with Russia, and a surviving political elite that has little interest in economic and social reform.

The Baltic states of Estonia, Latvia, and Lithuania have been more successful in reintegrating with the rest of Europe. Their small size and relatively high levels of education have made them attractive as production subcontracting centers for western European high-technology industries. They are reviving old ties with neighboring Nordic countries, and in this regard Estonia is particularly well placed because its language belongs to the Finnish family, and it was part of the Kingdom of Sweden when it was annexed by the Russians in 1710. The best-integrated states of eastern Europe are the Czech Republic, Hungary, Poland, and Slovenia. All have a relatively strong industrial base, and Hungary has a productive agricultural sector. Poland and Hungary have been especially open to foreign direct investment and have been swift and vigorous in pursuing economic and institutional reform. They are among the principal contenders for membership in an expanded EU.

Regional Development

The economic and political integration of Europe has intensified core-periphery differences within the region. The removal of internal barriers to flows of labor, capital, and trade has worked to the clear disadvantage of geographically peripheral regions within

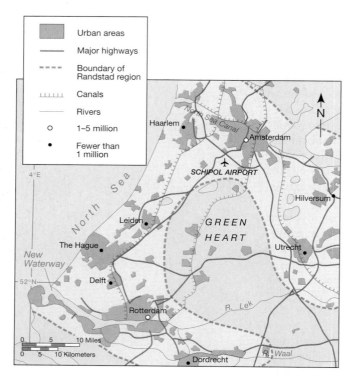

FIGURE 2.29 The Randstad region The Randstad is one of the world's most densely populated regions, and strict land-use planning has been required to protect agricultural resources and open spaces.

FIGURE 2.30 Amsterdam The central districts of Amsterdam are distinctive for their network of canals, tree-lined streets, and town houses.

the EU, while core metropolitan regions have benefited. The principal core region within Europe is the Golden Triangle, centered on the area between London, Paris, and Berlin. A secondary emergent core is developing along a north–south crescent that straddles the Alps, stretching from Frankfurt, just to the south of the Golden Triangle, through Stuttgart, Zürich, and Munich to Milan and Turin. Both cores are linked by the new trans-European high-speed rail system.

Europe's Golden Triangle The character and relative prosperity of Europe's chief core region, the Golden Triangle, stem from four advantages:

1. Its geographic situation provides access to southern and central Europe by way of the Rhine and Rhône river systems and access to the sea lanes of the Baltic Sea, the North Sea, and, by way of the English Channel, the Atlantic Ocean.
2. Within it are the capital cities of the major former imperial powers of Europe.
3. It includes the industrial heartlands of central England, northeastern France, and the Ruhr district of Germany.
4. Its concentrated population provides both a skilled labor force and an affluent consumer market.

These advantages have been reinforced by the integrative policies of the European Union, whose administrative headquarters are situated squarely in the heart of the Golden Triangle, in Brussels, Belgium. They have also been reinforced by the emergence of Berlin, Paris, and, especially, London, as world cities, in which a disproportionate share of the world's economic, political, and cultural business is conducted. As these world cities have come to play an increasingly central role in the world economy, so they have become home to a vast web of sophisticated financial, legal, marketing, and communications services. These services, in turn, have added to the wealth and cosmopolitanism of the region.

Agriculture within the Golden Triangle tends to be highly intensive and geared toward supplying the highly urbanized population with fresh dairy produce, vegetables, and flowers. Industry that remains within the Golden Triangle tends to be rather technical, drawing on the highly skilled and well-educated workforce. Most heavy industry and large-scale, routine manufacturing has relocated from the region in favor of cheaper land and labor found elsewhere in Europe or beyond.

In the Golden Triangle, a tightly knit network of towns and cities is linked by an elaborate infrastructure of canals, railways, and highways. The region has reached saturation levels of urbanization, as exemplified in Randstad Holland, the densely settled region of the western Netherlands that includes Dordrecht, Rotterdam, Delft, The Hague, Leiden, Haarlem, Amsterdam, Hilversum, and Utrecht (**Figure 2.29**). In addition to London, Paris, and Berlin, major cities of the Golden Triangle include Amsterdam (**Figure 2.30**), Antwerp, Birmingham, Brussels, Cologne, Dortmund, Düsseldorf, Hamburg (**Figure 2.31**), Hannover, Lille, Portsmouth, and Rotterdam. Nevertheless, the Golden Triangle still contains fragments of attractive rural landscapes, together with some unspoiled villages and small towns. These have survived partly because of market forces: They are very attractive to affluent commuters. Equally important to their survival, though, has been the relatively strong role of environmental, land use, and conservation planning in European countries.

FIGURE 2.31 Hamburg Germany's second-largest city, Hamburg is Europe's second-largest port and the commercial and cultural center of Northern Germany.

FIGURE 2.32 Bulb fields This photograph is from Enkhuizen in the Netherlands.

Surrounding the advanced city regions of the Golden Triangle are the fruit orchards and hop-growing fields of Kent, in southeastern England; the bulb fields of the Netherlands (**Figure 2.32**); the dikes and rectangular fields of the reclaimed marshland (polders) of North-Holland, Flevoland, and Friesland along the Dutch coastal plain (**Figure 2.33**); the pastures, woodlands, and forests of the upland plateaus of the Ardennes, the Eifel, the Westerwald, and the Harz; and the meadows and cultivated fields separated by hedgerows and patches of woodland that characterize most of the remaining countryside: Picardy in France; Flanders and Brabant in Belgium; Limburg, Nordrhein-Westphalia, and Saxony in Germany; and Gelderland in the Netherlands, for example. Embedded among these distinctive landscapes are hundreds of villages and scores of market towns. Those within the orbit of the metropolises and advanced city regions have lost a great deal of their character. A few, like Aylsham, in southeastern England (**Figure 2.34**), have been bypassed both by industrialization and by the post-industrial

FIGURE 2.33 Dutch landscape This photograph shows the landscape around Kinderdijk, in the Netherlands.

FIGURE 2.34 Market town Because of its off-center geography—situated in England's rural East Anglia region, and away from major rail and road routes—the market town of Aylsham has been affected very little by industrialization.

economy and have retained much of their traditional character. Some, like Bruges in Belgium, have traded on their legacy to become tourist stops. It is the metropolises and advanced city regions, however, that both define and dominate the Golden Triangle.

Major City: Berlin   If it were not for the geopolitical aftermath of World War II, Berlin would probably be a world city to rival Paris and London. Berlin is situated on a natural east–west commercial axis on the north European plain, with a favorable location on the river system that provides connections to the Elbe and Oder rivers. It is at once the most westerly city of eastern Europe and the most easterly city of western Europe. As such, it enjoys an excellent strategic location within continental Europe.

At the beginning of the 18th century, Berlin became the capital of the Hohenzollern dynasty of the Prussian monarchy. By the late 18th century it had a population of about 150,000, with soldiers and their families accounting for one in every five inhabitants. Berlin's position was further enhanced by the formation of the German Customs Union in 1834 and by the creation of the German Empire after the Franco-Prussian War (1871). The city is still graced by the monumental architecture of this period, although much was destroyed during World War II. With the Industrial Revolution, Berlin began producing machinery, chemicals, textiles, electrical goods, electronics, and clothing. It also became a hub in the central European transportation system and a major banking center. At its peak, in 1939, Greater Berlin had a population of 4.3 million. In physical terms, the building blocks of Berlin were *Mietskaserne* ("rental barracks"), four- or five-story apartment houses arranged around a courtyard and often extended by a series of rear courtyards, with access to the street only from the first court. With a new building ordinance in 1925, the classic *Mietskaserne* was effectively outlawed. The term continues to be used, however, for large-scale working-class housing developments.

Berlin was a cultural and intellectual center in the early part of the 20th century. It was a seedbed of avant-garde theater, film, cabaret, art, and architecture. World War II changed everything. By the end of the war, 34 percent of Berlin's housing had been destroyed, and another 54 percent was damaged. The city found itself embedded within the eastern, socialist part of a partitioned nation and was itself partitioned into eastern and western sectors. As a result, Berlin's dynamism was seriously disrupted.

West Berlin had to develop a new central business district, the old one having fallen within the eastern sector. In 1961 the division between the two half-cities was physically reinforced when East Germany built the Berlin Wall to stem the flow of migrants to West Berlin. After the wall went up, both East and West Berlin remained highly militarized, with troops and their equipment a very visible part of the urban landscape. Both also redeveloped their industry and refurbished their housing. East Berlin, with a population of just under 1.5 million by the late 1980s, was a showcase for the German Democratic Republic. Its economy was based on a mixture of industry including electrical engineering and electronics, metals, automobile production, textiles, printing, publishing, and beverages. It was, however, dominated by bleak modernist architecture. West Berlin, with a population of more than 2 million (of whom more than 250,000 were foreign workers and their families), developed a significant youth counterculture, partly because of its many institutions of higher education (which together account for more than 120,000 students), and partly because its residents were not required to perform military service in the army of the Federal Republic of Germany.

With the reunification of Germany in 1989, Berlin reassumed its prewar role as a national political and cultural center. The city experienced a surge of construction as the two parts of the city were reconnected, wired, and plumbed together again and as the federal government and investors raced to install new infrastructure, department stores, office blocks, hotels, and entertainment centers in keeping with the city's restored position in the world (**Figure 2.35**). Federal offices have been moved from Bonn to Berlin, and

FIGURE 2.35 Berlin Since the reunification of Germany in 1989, Berlin has experienced a major construction boom, reflecting the city's restored role as a world city. Shown here is Marlene Dietrich Platz.

Potsdamer Platz, once a no-man's land of barbed wire, tank traps, and mines, has been redeveloped with 111,000 square meters (about 1.18 million square feet) of apartment space, 310,000 square meters (about 3.3 million square feet) of office space, 57,000 square meters (about 613,500 square feet) of retail shops and restaurants, plus two Imax theaters, eight cinemas, a concert stage, an underground train station, and a shopping arcade.

Major City: London   London is a vast, sprawling city that covers more than 3900 square kilometers (about 1500 square miles) of continuously built-up area. It has a total population of just over 7 million (13 million including the metropolitan fringes). In the 19th and early 20th centuries, it was the center of global economic and geopolitical power. It dominates the economic and political life of the whole of the United Kingdom and remains the single most cosmopolitan city in Europe.

London grew up around two core areas: a commercial core centered on its port and trading functions and an institutional core centered on its religious and governmental functions. The commercial core has Roman roots: *Londinium* was the fifth largest Roman city north of the Alps, a major trading center that enjoyed the advantages of a deep-water port (on the River Thames) and a key situation facing the continental North Sea and Baltic ports. These same advantages helped London prosper with the resurgence of trade in the medieval period, when the wealth accumulated by wool merchants provided the economic foundation for growth. From this commercial nucleus grew an extensive merchant and financial quarter (**Figure 2.36**). The docks spread eastward from the financial precinct (the City), and specialized market areas grew to the north and east.

Today, this area remains the commercial core of the city. It contains the Stock Exchange, the Bank of England, the Royal Exchange, the Guildhall, and the Central Criminal Courts, as well as specialized commercial areas such as Fleet Street (the press/media precinct), Lincoln's Inn Fields (the legal precinct), and the sites of old marketplaces, such as Billingsgate (fish) and Smithfield (meat). Older docks, such as St. Katherine's next to Tower Bridge, have meanwhile been renovated and now boast yacht basins, hotels, a trade center, upscale pubs, bistros, specialty retail stores, galleries, and condominiums.

London's institutional core developed around Westminster Abbey, some 2.2 kilometers (2 miles) upstream from the commercial core (**Figure 2.37**). Early meetings of Parliament were held in the Abbey's Chapter House; the present Houses of Parliament date only from the 19th century. St. James's Palace was built as a London residence for the monarchy in the 16th century; Buckingham Palace, built for the Duke of Buckingham in 1703 and purchased by George III in 1762, became the royal residence during Queen Victoria's reign. To the north of the Houses of Parliament, along Whitehall, are government offices; between these and Buckingham Palace is St. James's Park; and to the north of the park are the palaces and mansions of the nobility, centers of culture (the Royal Academy, the National Gallery, and the Royal Opera House), the exclusive shops that cater to the city's elite, and the squares and townhouses of the rich and powerful.

London's population grew sixfold during the 19th century, reaching more than 6 million by 1900. As it grew, the two core areas merged together as part of a huge central business district. Downriver from the central business district, new docks and manufacturing industry attracted concentrations of low-income housing in the city's East End, while from around 1840 the railways triggered a process of suburbanization that created a mosaic of neighborhoods

FIGURE 2.36 London's financial core London's original river port trade gave rise to a commercial core that developed into a major financial hub in the district of London known as the City. Though the skyline of this financial precinct is still dominated by the dome of St. Paul's Cathedral, the City skyline has acquired a few high-rise buildings.

FIGURE 2.37 London's institutional core Westminster Abbey and the Houses of Parliament stand at the center of a distinctive district of government offices, royal palaces and parks, military barracks, and upscale residential neighborhoods.

of high-density terrace housing. These inner-city neighborhoods are now mostly obsolescent, and a good deal of the original housing has disappeared, replaced by **municipal housing** projects. In addition, the Dockland Development Corporation, established in 1981, has regenerated large tracts of formerly derelict docks and slums in the East End. Extensive areas of substandard housing remain in much of inner London, however—a mixture of older terraced housing and newer, but run-down, municipal housing.

London's outer suburbs are the product of extension of the city's underground rapid-transit system, establishment of a suburban railway network, and diffusion of the private automobile. These outer suburbs are relatively affluent and conservative, characterized by semidetached "villas" that form a broad ring about 11 kilometers (6.8 miles) deep, punctuated only by neighborhood shopping streets and industrial parks. The major problem for outer London is traffic, the whole region being swamped by a density of automobiles that is several times the capacity of the road system.

London's outer suburbs stop suddenly at the point they reached in 1947, when a strategic plan for the city established a greenbelt designed to halt suburban sprawl, protect valuable agricultural land, and provide an amenity for the city's population. Within the greenbelt, which covers some 2330 square kilometers (about 900 square miles) in a zone between 8 and 16 kilometers (5 and 10 miles) wide, development has been strictly policed by city planners, with the result that villages and small market towns have a picture-postcard quality that is much sought after by affluent commuter households.

Beyond the greenbelt is a metropolitan fringe that extends between 32 and 64 kilometers (20 and 40 miles) from the central area and contains nearly 6 million people. Within this zone are such older market towns as Luton, Reading, Guildford, and Maidstone, together with eight New Towns. These New Towns were established as part of the strategic plan for London and were designed to house "overspill" population and light industry as inner London was thinned out and rebuilt after World War II.

Major City: Paris   While London is the most cosmopolitan European city, Paris is the most urbane and the most spectacularly monumental. Paris is the unrivaled focus of political, economic, social, and cultural life in France. It is an industrial center as well as a major international financial center. It is, in short, *the* French city, and there are few cities in the rest of the world (perhaps only Tokyo) that so dominate their national urban systems, their national economy, their politics, and their culture. Paris is by far the largest city in France, with a central-city population of 2.2 million in 2002, compared to 808,000 in Marseille, 422,000 in Lyon, and 366,000 in Toulouse.

In Paris itself, this dominance is reflected in the monumental buildings of the central core, or Ville de Paris. The nucleus of this core is the Île de la Cité, a boat-shaped island about ten blocks long and five blocks wide, the site of the palace of the city's Roman governor and of the great cathedral of Notre Dame de Paris. The whole historic core is dominated by the river Seine, which runs some 9 meters (about 30 feet) below street level and is bordered by trees and shrubs, with another line of trees at street level, providing a sequestered setting in the heart of the city (**Figure 2.38**). Along the river are some of the greatest examples of urban design anywhere in the world. Beginning in the 17th century, royal sponsorship rebuilt and embellished the route from the Louvre (the old royal palace) through the Tuileries Gardens to the Champs-Élysées. In the 19th century, Napoleon built the Arc de Triomphe, giving a focal point to the far end of this axis. Napoleon took a particular interest in the development of Paris as a deliberate reflection of the power and glory of his empire. In addition to monumental embellishments such as the Arc de Triomphe, the church of the Madeleine, and the stylishly arcaded Rue de Rivoli, Napoleon initiated many public works and infrastructure improvements. However, it was his nephew, Napoleon III, who presided over the most comprehensive program of urban redevelopment and monumental planning. This work was directed by George Haussmann, Prefect of the Seine region between

FIGURE 2.38 Central Paris Central Paris is mostly low-rise, with only isolated skyscrapers.

1853 and 1870. Haussmann demolished large sections of old Paris in order to create a network of broad, new, tree-lined avenues that today form the basis of the most extensive one-way street system in Europe.

Despite this redevelopment, the continued growth of central Paris as a place of government, retail, office, and service employment has brought acute congestion that has fostered widespread conflict over land use and urban planning. The built environment has become a major focus of Parisian (and, indeed, French) politics. Some of the most intense and long-running conflicts have been focused on modernization projects—such as the redevelopment of Les Halles (the old produce market for Paris). More recently, however, the emphasis has been on conserving historic buildings and districts.

Beyond the historic core, suburban Paris extends for some 16 to 24 kilometers (10 to 15 miles), with another 16 kilometers (10 miles) or so of metropolitan fringe. The inner suburbs date from the 1880s. They are relatively high-density, by North American standards, with piecemeal development that now contains a mixture of middle- and high-rise apartment blocks and single-family homes. Many of the gaps left by earlier speculative development, along with much of the outer suburbs, are filled with *grands ensembles* of **social housing**. Built in haste to accommodate the city's postwar growth, these soon acquired a very negative reputation because of their uninspired architecture and lack of social facilities. The suburbs are heavily interspersed with industry, much of it large-scale and involving various kinds of electrical or mechanical engineering.

Managing the growth of the suburbs and metropolitan fringe while encouraging the decentralization of central Paris has been the principal concern of urban and regional planners. Central to their efforts has been the development of master plans. One early master plan sought to counteract the primacy of Paris by establishing eight growth centers, or *métropoles d'équilibre*, in other regions of France. Subsequently, planners sought to reduce the dominance of central Paris by establishing five new towns and encouraging nodes of commercial development outside the city center. The biggest and most successful of these suburban nodes is La Défense, a major set piece of modern planning (**Figure 2.39**). La Défense is a complex, multilevel, multiuse development with more than 1.39 million square meters (about 15 million square feet) of office space, 150,000 workers, and 20,000 residents. Still, the dominance of central Paris has become stronger than ever, with the new towns serving as dormitories for clerks and mid-level executives who are among the 1 million who commute to central Paris every day.

FIGURE 2.39 La Défense One of the largest and most successful growth centers within metropolitan Paris, La Défense was designed by planners to attract office development from the central core of the city.

FIGURE 2.40 Frankfurt am Main, Germany A city of global financial importance, Frankfurt is the seat of the European Central Bank and the Frankfurt Stock Exchange and is one of the most affluent cities in Europe.

The Southern Crescent Stretching south from the Golden Triangle is a secondary, emergent, core region that straddles the Alps, running from Frankfurt in Germany through Stuttgart, Zürich, and Munich, and finally to Milan, Turin, and northern Italy. The prosperity of this Southern Crescent is in part a result of a general decentralization of industry from northwestern Europe and in part a result of the integrative effects of the European Union. Some of the capital freed up by the deindustrialization of traditional manufacturing regions in northwestern Europe has found its way to more southerly regions, where land is less expensive and labor is both less expensive and less unionized. The cities of the Southern Crescent have become key to the spatial reorganization of the whole region. Frankfurt (**Figure 2.40**) and Zürich (**Figure 2.41**) are global-scale business and financial centers in their own right, while Milan is a center of both finance and design, and Munich, Stuttgart, and Turin are important centers of industry and commerce.

This Southern Crescent stretches across a great variety of landscapes, from the plateaus of central Germany, across the Alps, and into northern Italy and the Apennines. Overall, these landscapes are much less urbanized than are those of the Golden Triangle. However, the *rate* of urbanization is much higher.

Much urban growth is taking place in smaller towns and cities that are part of new-style industrial subregions that have benefited from the deindustrialization of northwestern Europe. They represent a very different form of industrialization based on loose spatial agglomerations of small firms that are part of one or more leading industries. Small firms using computerized control systems and an extensive subcontracting network have the advantage of being flexible in what they produce and when and how they produce it. Consequently, the new industrial districts with which they are associated are often referred to as **flexible production regions**. Within each of these regions, small firms tend to share a specific local industrial culture that is characterized by technological dynamism and well-developed social and economic networks.

Northern Italy provides examples of a number of flexible production regions (**Figure 2.42**). Here, regional networks of innovative, flexible, and high-quality manufacturers make products that include textiles, knitwear, jewelry, shoes, ceramics,

FIGURE 2.41 Zürich, Switzerland Switzerland's main commercial center is also a center of international banking and finance.

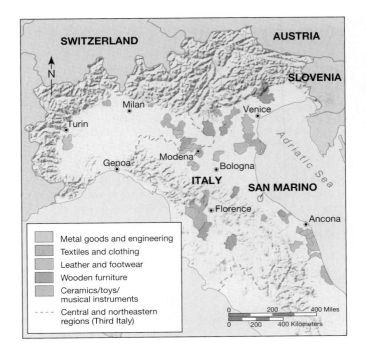

FIGURE 2.42 New industrial districts in northern Italy New industrial districts in the Southern Crescent are based on loose spatial agglomerations of small firms involved in a few key industries. There is a particular concentration of these new industrial districts in central and northeastern Italy—the so-called "Third Italy." (*Source:* D. Pinder [ed.], *The New Europe: Economy, Society, and Environment.* New York: John Wiley & Sons, 1998, p. 106.)

machinery, machine tools, and furniture. Other examples of flexible production regions based on a similar mixture of design- and labor-intensive industries include the Baden-Württemberg region around Stuttgart in Germany (textiles, machine tools, auto parts, and clothing) and the Rhône-Alpes region around Lyon in France.

The northern end of the Southern Crescent is dominated by the pastures, woodlands, and forests of the upland plateaus of the Hunsrück, the Taunus, the Odenwald, and the Franconian Jura. All of these uplands are crossed by rivers whose valleys contain prosperous, manicured landscapes of mixed farming, vineyards, and orchards. Farther south still are the rich meadows and dairy farms of the Alpine fringe, followed quickly by the spectacular mountains and lakes of the Alps themselves. Beyond the Alps is a belt of moraines that dam a series of sub-Alpine lakes (Maggiore, Lugano, Como, Iseo, and Garda) and form the hills upon which some of northern Italy's distinctive hill towns (such as Bergamo and Brescia) stand. The landscape then flattens out into a zone of low terraces that descend to the rich, broad floodplain of the River Po (**Figure 2.43**) before rising again toward the hills of the Apennines.

Major City: Milan Milan provides a good example of the prosperity of the Southern Crescent. Although Rome is the Italian capital and Naples is perhaps better known, Milan is the leading city of the country—the richest, the most fashionable, the most innovative, and the best governed. With only 7 percent of the country's population, it accounts for 28 percent of Italy's national income. If Milan were still an independent city-state, it would be richer than Switzerland. It has a diversified economic base that has expanded in recent years as, along with other cities in the European sunbelt, it has attracted a significant amount of foreign investment. Industries include automobile assembly, aircraft, motorcycles, electrical appliances, railroad materials, metal trades, chemical production, and graphics and publishing. Although parts of the industrial sector have declined—Pirelli, for example, closed its huge tire factory in the northern suburbs of the city in the 1980s—the

FIGURE 2.43 Rural landscapes of the Southern Crescent The rich floodplain of the Po River valley in Italy is one of the most distinctive agricultural regions within the Southern Crescent. Shown here is the area around Mantua.

FIGURE 2.44 Milan Milan has long been a major regional center and today has developed into a prosperous city of global importance in finance, fashion, and industrial design.

service sector is growing rapidly. For every manufacturing firm that closed down or moved out during the 1990s, three service firms were created. Services now account for 70 percent of the local economy, and Milan has gained international significance as a financial center and as a center for design—both industrial and fashion. The Milanese are hard-working and entrepreneurial, with a strong progressive streak that is vigorously pursued by the (traditionally socialist) city government. The city exudes an exhilarating combination of the historic and the modern, of industry and culture, and of the fast track and laid-back urbanity.

The center of the city owes its street pattern to the pattern of successive defensive walls. It is dominated by the Duomo (cathedral), begun in the 14th century and completed in the 19th, and the Castello Sforzesco, a 15th-century castle. They look out on a low-rise city center in which are tucked away such landmarks as the Piazza Mercanti (the center of activity in medieval times), the theater of La Scala facing the Piazza della Scala with its statue of Leonardo da Vinci, the church of Santa Maria delle Grazie with its mural of the Last Supper by Leonardo da Vinci, and the magnificent indoor shopping arcade of the Galleria Vittorio Emanuele (**Figure 2.44**). The narrowness of the streets in the center has precluded development of much industry; it is the suburbs, particularly to the north/northeast and south/southwest, that are the setting for Milan's industry. These suburbs are for the most part well built and well served. The pressure of population growth, however, has resulted in the expansion of slum housing and the appearance of shantytowns such as Brianza on the urban fringe.

SUMMARY AND CONCLUSIONS

Contemporary Europe is highly urbanized and is a cornerstone of the world economy with a complex, multilayered, and multifaceted regional geography. In overall terms, Europe accounts for almost two-fifths of world trade and about one-third of the world's aggregate GNP.

The rise of Europe as a major world region had its origins in the emergence of a system of merchant capitalism in the 15th century, when advances in business practices, technology, and navigation made it possible for merchants to establish the basis of a worldwide economy in the space of less than 100 years. These changes also had a profound effect on Europe's geography, reorienting the region toward the Atlantic and away from the subregional maritime economies of the Mediterranean and the Baltic. Since then, Europe's regional geographies have been comprehensively recast several times: by the new production and transportation technologies that marked the onset of the Industrial Revolution, by two world wars, and by the Cold War rift between eastern and western Europe.

The European Union emerged after World War II as a major factor in reestablishing Europe's role in the world. The EU is now a sophisticated and powerful institution with a pervasive influence on patterns of economic and social well-being within its member states. It has a population of more than 370 million,

with a combined GDP 10 percent larger than that of the United States. The reintegration of eastern Europe has added a potentially dynamic market of 130 million consumers to the European economy. Overall, eastern Europe functions as a set of economically peripheral regions, with agriculture still geared to local markets and former COMECON trading opportunities and industry still geared more to heavy industry and standardized products than to competitive consumer products.

The principal core region within Europe is the Golden Triangle, which stretches between London, Paris, and Berlin. A secondary, emergent core is developing along a north–south crescent that straddles the Alps, stretching from Frankfurt, just to the south of the Golden Triangle, through Stuttgart, Zürich, and Munich, to Milan and Turin.

Beyond Europe's core regions, major metropolitan areas, and specialized industrial districts, a mosaic of landscapes has developed around broad physiographic regions. In detail, these landscapes are a product of centuries of human adaptation to climate, soils, altitude, and aspect and to changing economic and political circumstances. Farming practices, field patterns, settlement types, local architecture, and ways of life have all become attuned to the opportunities and constraints of regional physical environments, producing distinctive regional landscapes.

KEY TERMS

acid rain (p. 74)
agglomeration economy (p. 75)
aspect (p. 65)
balkanization (p. 85)
buffer zone (p. 75)
command economy (p. 75)
deindustrialization (p. 88)
disinvestment (p. 88)
egalitarian society (p. 76)
enclave (p. 85)
Enlightenment (p. 79)

entrepôt (p. 71)
ethnic cleansing (p. 86)
exclave (p. 85)
fascism (p. 78)
feudal system (p. 69)
fjord (p. 59)
flexible production
 region (p. 100)
heathland (p. 68)
imperialism (p. 74)
latifundia (p. 67)

loess (p. 64)
Marshall Plan (p. 75)
merchant capitalism (p. 69)
minifundia (p. 67)
Modernity (p. 79)
moraine (p. 59)
municipal housing (p. 98)
pastoralism (p. 61)
physiographic region (p. 59)
polder (p. 68)
privatization (p. 93)

satellite state (p. 58)
social housing (p. 99)
state socialism (p. 58)
steppe (p. 65)
tundra (p. 61)
watershed (p. 59)
welfare state (p. 87)
xenophobia (p. 86)

REVIEW QUESTIONS

Testing Your Understanding

1. How has Europe benefited from its location and its major physical features?
2. Many European cultures have a strong history of seafaring. How did that become a crucial factor in European and world geography?
3. As the Roman Empire spread westward, what modifications did the ancient Romans make to the European landscape? How did people living in medieval feudal systems affect the landscape of Europe?
4. What key inventions during the period from 1400 to 1600 helped European merchants establish the basis of today's global economy? Why?
5. Which imports from the American colonies helped transform Europe? Focus on natural resources and new crops.
6. What was an entrepôt seaport? How have entrepôt functions affected a city like London?
7. What factors led to the end of the European colonial era?
8. What was the Cold War? Why did the Soviet Union establish a buffer zone in eastern Europe? Which two eastern European countries left the Soviet bloc to pursue alternate forms of state socialism?

9. How did the European Union (EU) develop? Why is the EU's Common Agricultural Policy (CAP) so important?
10. What are the main characteristics of Europe's two core regions? Please explain where these core regions are and why they are prosperous.

Thinking Geographically

1. Why was geographic knowledge and accurate mapmaking crucial to the growth of European power during the 1500s?
2. How did aid from the Marshall Plan and COMECON help rebuild Europe after World War II? Which regions or economies benefited first?
3. What migration patterns characterized Europe during the 19th and 20th centuries? Consider movement within Europe as well as movement to and from Europe.
4. From Greece to Portugal, many European countries pride themselves on their wine production and rely on income from their wine exports. How does the history of wine as a commodity reflect the history of Europe from classical Greece to the present day?

FURTHER READING

Dorling, D., *Human Geography of the UK*. London: Sage, 2005.

Dunford, M., and Smith, A., "Catching Up or Falling Behind? Economic Performance and Regional Trajectories in the 'New Europe'." *Economic Geography*, 76, 2000, 169–95.

Gibb, R., and Wise, M., *The European Union: Challenges of Economic and Social Cohesion*. London: Arnold, 2000.

Gowland, D., O'Neill, B., and Reid, A. (eds.), *The European Mosaic. Contemporary Politics, Economics, and Culture*, 2nd ed. London: Longman, 1999.

Graham, B. (ed.), *Modern Europe: Place, Culture, Identity*. London: Arnold, 1998.

Grove, A. T., and Rackham, O., *The Nature of Mediterranean Europe: An Ecological History*. New Haven: Yale University Press, 2001.

Hitchcock, W. I., *The Struggle for Europe: The Turbulent History of a Divided Continent*. New York: Doubleday, 2002.

Kazepov, Y. (ed.), *Cities of Europe*. Oxford: Blackwell, 2005.

Keating, M. (ed.), *Regions and Regionalism in Europe*. Northampton, MA: Edward Elgar, 2004.

King, R., Proudfoot, L., and Smith, B. (eds.), *The Mediterranean: Environment and Society.* London: Arnold, 1997.

McDonald, J. R., *The European Scene: A Geographic Perspective,* 2nd ed. Upper Saddle River, NJ: Prentice Hall, 1997.

McDonogh, G., *Global Iberia.* London: Routledge, 2006.

Ostergren, R. C., and Rice, J. G., *The Europeans. A Geography of People, Culture, and Environment.* New York: Guilford Press, 2004.

Pinder, D. (ed.), *The New Europe: Economy, Society and Environment.* New York: John Wiley & Sons, 1998.

Rifkin, J., *The European Dream: How Europe's Vision of the Future Is Quietly Eclipsing the American Dream.* Cambridge: Polity Press, 2004.

Standage, T., *A History of the World in Six Glasses.* New York: Walker & Co., 2005.

Tickle, A., and Welsh, I. (eds.), *Environment and Society in Eastern Europe.* London: Addison Wesley Longman, 1998.

Townsend, A. R., *Making a Living in Europe: Geographies of Economic Change.* New York: Routledge, 1997.

Tummers, L. J. M., and Schrijnen, P. M., "The Randstad." In R. Simmonds and G. Hack (eds.), *Global City Regions* (pp. 66–79). New York: Spon Press, 2000.

Turnock, D. (ed.), *Eastern Europe and the Former Soviet Union.* London: Arnold, 2001.

Unwin, T., *Wine and the Vine.* New York: Routledge, 1996.

Unwin, T. (ed.), *A European Geography.* London: Longman, 1998.

Wainwright, J., and Thornes, J. B., *Environmental Issues in the Mediterranean.* New York: Routledge, 2002.

FILM, MUSIC, AND POPULAR LITERATURE

Film

The Back Roads of Europe. PBS Home Video series, 1998. A three-tape travelogue through rural Europe.

Bend It Like Beckham. Directed by Gurinder Chadha, 2002. Set in London, this film is based on the life of a soccer-mad first-generation Asian immigrant teenage girl.

Bosnia: Peace Without Honor. BBC Production, 1999. This documentary traces the roots of the Bosnian conflict through the efforts of U.S. and British diplomats.

Diamonds in the Dark. Directed by Olivia Carrescia, 1999. This documentary tells the stories of ten Romanian women: how they lived under the old regime and how they are confronting the new problems of the post-communist era.

The Grand Canal. PBS Home Video Great Streets series, 2000. An intimate view of Venice, Italy, focusing on the Grand Canal.

In Search of Tuscany with John Guerrasio. PBS Home Video series, 1999. A tour of Tuscany with food critic and author John Guerrasio.

Jonah, Who Will Be 25 in the Year 2000 (Jonas qui aura 25 ans en l'an 2000). Directed by Alain Tanner, 1976. This movie captures the liberal aspirations of the European baby-boom population who had become 30-something by the mid-1970s.

Mondovino. Directed by Jonathan Nossiter, 2004. A documentary on the impact of globalization on the world's different wine regions.

One World: The Baltic States. PBS documentary by Ward Television Corporation, 1997. A documentary on the post-Soviet Baltic States, presenting multiple views on current issues, the Soviet heritage, ethnic minorities, and economic development.

Rome: Power and Glory. PBS Home Video series, 1997. A six-part documentary on the Roman Empire.

Music

Bocelli, Andrea. *Sogno.* Philips, 1999.

Bulgarian Women's Choir. *Voices of Life.* Globe Music Media Arts, 2000.

Chao, Manu. *Clandestino.* Uni/Ark, 1998.

Chumbawamba. *Tubthumper.* Universal Records, 1997.

Hardy, Francoise. *Ma Jeunesse Fout Le Camp.* Virgin, 2000.

Lien, Annbjorg. *Baba Yaga.* Northside, 2000.

Madredeus. *Antologia.* Blue Note, 2000.

Various Artists. *Paris Is Sleeping: Respect Is Burning.* Caroline, 1998.

Vasen. *Whirled.* Northside, 1997.

Popular Literature

Bryson, Bill. *Neither Here Nor There.* New York: Avon Books, 1992. Europe closely observed by an American writer who lived in Britain for 20 years.

Carhart, Thaddeus. *The Piano Shop on the Left Bank: Discovering a Forgotten Passion in a Paris Atelier.* New York: Random House, 2001. A novel set in present-day Paris describing an American's search for the ideal piano for his small apartment.

Davies, Norman. *Europe: A History.* New York: HarperCollins, 1998. A well-written and comprehensive history of Europe.

Doyle, Roddy. *The Barrytown Trilogy (The Commitments; The Snapper; The Van).* New York: Penguin USA, 1995. Three novels that depict working-class life in contemporary Dublin with humor and compassion. *The Commitments* was made into a hit movie (directed by Alan Parker, 1999).

Drakulic, Slavenka. *Cafe Europa: Life After Communism.* New York: Penguin, 1999. A collection of essays that explore life in various Eastern European countries since the fall of communism.

Epstein, Alan. *As the Romans Do: The Delights, Dramas, and Daily Diversions of Life in the Eternal City.* New York: William Morrow, 2000. An evocative book on the people, places, and everyday life of Rome.

Hall, Brian. *The Impossible Country: A Journey Through the Last Days of Yugoslavia.* New York: Penguin, 1995. A journalistic description of the last days of peaceful coexistence among Yugoslavia's religious and ethnic communities and the tensions and conflicts that would trigger the horrors of "ethnic cleansing" and war.

Kaplan, Robert D. *Balkan Ghosts: A Journey Through History.* New York: Vintage, 1994. A political travelogue that deciphers the Balkan landscapes and the people's ancient passions and intractable hatreds for outsiders.

Mayle, Peter. *Encore Provence.* New York: Vintage Books, 2000. A vivid and intimate description of one of France's most popular regions.

Mazower, Mark. *Dark Continent: Europe's Twentieth Century.* New York: Vintage Books, 2000. Explores the conflicts that dominated Europe in the 20th century and the social value systems that informed them.

Rackham, Oliver. *The Illustrated History of the Countryside.* New York: Sterling Publishing, 1994. A historical ecology of the British countryside, showing how everyday landscapes reflect past activities.

The Russian Federation, Central Asia, and the Transcaucasus

FIGURE 3.1

Bering Strait

Provideniya

ARCTIC
OCEAN

N

170°W

180°

80°N

170°E

Kolyma R.

RUSSIAN FEDERATION

Lena R.

Verkhoyansk

50°N

Sea of Okhotsk

160°E

PACIFIC
OCEAN

Lena R.

150°E

Yenisey R.

Bratsk

Krasnoyarsk

Lake
Baykal

Amur R.

40°N

Novokuznetsk

SAYAN MTS.

Angarsk Irkutsk

YABLONOVYY MTS.

KHINGAN MTS.

Vladivostok

Y MOUNTAINS

30°N

● More than 5 million

○ 1–5 million

• Fewer than 1 million

Capital cities are underlined

0   250   500 Miles

0   250   500 Kilometers

The Russian Federation (the principal successor state to the Soviet Union), together with neighboring Belarus and the former Soviet satellite states in Central Asia (Kazakhstan, Kyrgyzstan, Tajikistan, Turkmenistan, and Uzbekistan) and the Transcaucasus (Armenia, Azerbaijan, and Georgia) constitutes a vast world region (**Figure 3.1**). The Russian Federation alone stretches across 11 time zones, from St. Petersburg (just across the Gulf of Finland from Helsinki) in the west to Provideniya (just across the Bering Strait from Nome, Alaska) in the east. Altogether the Russian Federation amounts to 17,075,400 square kilometers (6,591,100 square miles)—roughly twice the size of the United States. The region as a whole amounts to a landmass of 21,024,210 square kilometers (8,115,340 square miles). This vast area is relatively sparsely settled, mainly because of harsh climate, poor soils, and difficult terrain. The bulk of the population, in fact, is concentrated in the southern parts of European Russia to the west of the Ural Mountains, which constitutes the heartland of the old Russian empire. Of the region's total population of 232 million, 69 percent live in urban areas, 43 of which have populations that exceed 500,000.

The region is bounded on the north by the icy seas of the Arctic and on the south by a mountain wall that stretches from the Elburz Mountains of northern Iran through the Pamir Mountains and Tien Shan ("Mountains of Heaven") along the southern borders of the Central Asian countries, to the Altay and Sayan Mountains, which separate Siberia from Mongolia, and the Yablonovyy and Khingan ranges, which separate southeastern Siberia from northern China. The boundary to the east is the Pacific Ocean, while to the west, as we saw in Chapter 2, the boundary is political rather than physical, the former Soviet republics in the Baltic and the former satellite states of eastern Europe having returned to their European orientation.

ENVIRONMENT AND SOCIETY IN THE RUSSIAN FEDERATION, CENTRAL ASIA, AND THE TRANSCAUCASUS

A satellite photograph (**Figure 3.2**) suggests several of the fundamental attributes of this vast world region. First, its sheer size: more than 10,000 kilometers (6200 miles) east–west and more than 2500 kilometers (1550 miles) north–south at its broadest. It takes a full week to traverse the region by train from Vladivostok in the east to St. Petersburg in the west. Second, its northerliness: Nearly half of the territory of the Russian Federation is north of 60° N. Moscow is approximately the same latitude as Juneau, Alaska, and Tbilisi, Georgia—one of the southernmost cities of the region—is approximately the same latitude as Chicago (42° N).

A third attribute suggested by Figure 3.2 is the region's restricted access to the world's seas. The northerliness of most of the region means that most ports are ice-bound during the long winter. Murmansk, on the Kola Peninsula in the far north, is a major exception. It benefits from its location near the tail end of the warm Gulf Stream and is open year-round. Some ports, such as Vladivostok, on the Sea of Japan in the far east, can be kept open by icebreakers. At least the Russian Federation has some warm-water ports, including Kaliningrad, a small province on the Baltic between Poland and Lithuania, retained as an exclave by the Russian Federation for its naval port. All of the other countries in the region are landlocked, with the exception of Georgia, which has access to international sea lanes by way of its Black Sea ports.

The Black Sea itself is an inland sea, connected to the Aegean Sea and the Mediterranean by way of the Bosporus, a narrow strait, the Sea of Marmara, and then another narrow strait, the Dardanelles. The many rivers that empty into the Black Sea give its surface waters a low salinity, but it is almost tideless, and below about 80 fathoms it is stagnant and lifeless. The Caspian Sea is the largest inland sea in the world, at 371,000 square kilometers (143,205 square miles—roughly the size of Germany). With the Black Sea and the Aral Sea, it once formed part of a much greater inland sea. Though perhaps dwarfed by the vastness of the region, there are several inland lakes of signifi-

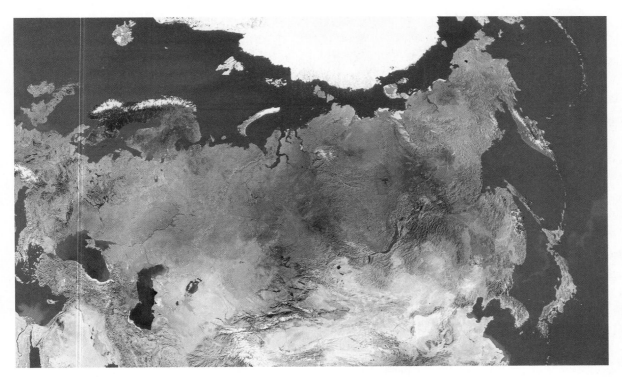

FIGURE 3.2 The Russian Federation, Central Asia, and the Transcaucasus from space This image underlines one of the key features of the Russian Federation, Central Asia, and the Transcaucasus: its sheer size.

cant size, including Lake Balkhash (17,400 square kilometers; 6715 square miles) and Lake Baykal (30,500 square kilometers; 11,775 square miles), which, with a depth of 1615 meters (5300 feet), is the deepest lake in the world.

The northerliness of the region limits the use of its rivers for navigation and for generating hydroelectric power. Many rivers are frozen for much of the year, while the mouths of some remain frozen through the spring, causing backed-up meltwater to flood extensive areas of wetlands. In May 2001, when the worst floods in a century rendered homeless tens of thousands of people along the Lena River, SU-24 supersonic bombers had to be deployed to break up a 30-kilometer (18-mile) ice floe on the river with 250-kilogram (550-pound) bombs. Nevertheless, the sheer size of the territory sustains several rivers of considerable size, all of which were used historically as transport routes, allowing for conquest, colonization, and trade. It takes some of the longest rivers on Earth to drain the huge Siberian landmass. Rising in the southern mountains of Central Asia, the Lena, Kolyma, Ob', and Yenisey flow north to the Arctic Ocean, while the Amur flows north to the Pacific. In the western part of the Russian Federation, the rivers flow south from the Central Region occupied by Moscow and Nizhniy Novgorod. The Dnieper flows to the Black Sea, the Don to the Sea of Azov (which in turn connects to the Black Sea), and the Volga to the Caspian Sea. In the modern period, the Volga has become particularly important as a navigable waterway and source of hydropower, with huge reservoirs built during the Soviet era to regulate the flow of the river, conserving spring floodwaters for the dry summer months.

Physiographic Regions

The most striking feature of the entire region is the monotony of its plains over thousands and thousands of kilometers. The reason for this monotony lies in the geological structure of the region. Two large and geologically ancient and stable shields of highly resistant crystalline rocks provide platforms for extensive plains of sedimentary material and glacial debris. In the west is the first shield, the Russian Plain, an extension of the Central European Plateau that runs from Belarus in the west to the Ural Mountains in the east and from the Kola Peninsula in the north to the Black Sea in the south (**Figure**

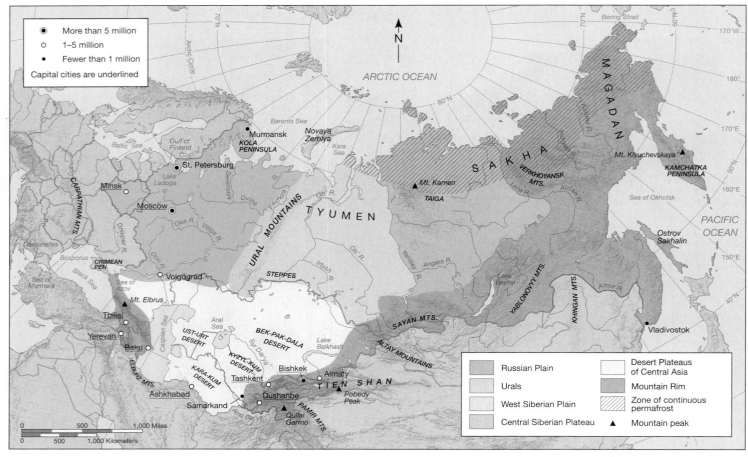

FIGURE 3.3 Physiographic regions of the Russian Federation, Central Asia, and the Transcaucasus The framework for the physical geography of the region consists of two stable shields on either side of the ancient Ural Mountains, with a wall of young mountains that runs along the southern and eastern margins of the shields.

FIGURE 3.4 The Russian Plain The Russian Plain is an extension of the Central European Plain. It is one of the most densely settled parts of the Russian Federation, with some of the best farmland.

3.3). East of the Urals is a second shield that extends as far as the Lena River. It is so vast that it is conventionally divided into several physiographic subregions: the West Siberian Plain, the Central Siberian Plateau, and the desert plateaus of Central Asia. The Urals themselves represent a third distinctive physiographic region, and a fourth is the mountain wall that runs along the southern and eastern margins of the two shields.

The Russian Plain (**Figure 3.4**) has a gently rolling topography, the hard crystalline rock shield providing a flat platform that is covered by several meters or more of sedi-

FIGURE 3.5 **The West Siberian Plain** This photograph of marshland near Primorye, western Siberia, shows very clearly the difficult, boggy conditions that prevail in much of western Siberia in summer.

mentary deposits. Much of the Russian Plain is poorly drained, boggy, and marshy, though the major rivers that drain it—the Dnieper, the Don, and the Volga—have eroded the sedimentary layer in places, resulting in more varied and attractive topography. The West Siberian Plain is even flatter and contains still more extensive wetlands and tens of thousands of small lakes. Poorly drained by the slow-moving Ob' and Irtysh rivers, the West Siberian Plain (**Figure 3.5**) is mostly inhospitable for settlement and agriculture, though it contains significant oil and natural gas reserves. The West Siberian Plain is distinctive for its absolute flatness: Across the whole broad expanse—more than 1800 kilometers (1116 miles) in each direction—relief is no more than 400 meters (1312 feet). The monotony of the landscape is captured in this quote from Russian writer A. Bitov, describing a train journey:

> Once I was traveling through the Western Siberian Lowlands. I woke up and glanced out of the window—sparse woods, a swamp, level terrain. A cow standing knee-deep in the swamp and chewing, levelly moving her jaw. I fell asleep, woke up—sparse woods, a swamp, a cow chewing, knee deep. I woke up the second day—a swamp, a cow. . . ."[1]

The Yenisey River marks the eastern boundary of this flat condition and the beginning of the Central Siberian Plateau, where the rock shield, having been uplifted by geological movements, averages about 700 meters (2297 feet) in elevation. Stretching between 800 and 1900 kilometers (496 to 1178 miles) west–east, the Central Siberian Plateau (**Figure 3.6**) has been dissected by rivers into a hilly upland topography with occasional deep river gorges.

[1]A. Bitov, *A Captive of the Caucasus*, Cambridge: Cambridge University Press, 1993, p. 50. Quoted in A. Novikov, "Between Space and Race: Rediscovering Russian Cultural Geography," in M. J. Bradshaw (ed.), *Geography and Transition in the Post-Soviet Republics*, Chichester: John Wiley & Sons, 1997, p. 45.

FIGURE 3.6 **The Central Siberian Plateau** The rock shield of the Central Siberian Plateau has been uplifted by geological movements; as a result, the land has been dissected by rivers into a hilly upland with occasional deep river gorges.

FIGURE 3.7 Urals landscape The mountains of the Urals are ancient and have been worn down to rounded landforms with thin soils that support small farms. Shown here is a small farming village near Kungur.

The Urals (**Figure 3.7**) consist of a once-great mountain range of ancient rocks that have been worn down over the ages. For the most part only 600 to 700 meters (1969 to 2297 feet) above sea level, and only in a few places rising above 2000 meters (6562 feet) in elevation, the Urals are penetrated by several broad valleys, and so they do not constitute a major barrier to transport. The Urals stretch for more than 3000 kilometers (1864 miles) from the northern frontier of Kazakhstan to the Arctic coast of the Russian Federation, the range reappearing across the Kara Sea in the form of the islands of Novaya Zemlya. The rocks of the Urals are heavily mineralized and contain significant quantities of chromite, copper, gold, graphite, iron ore, nickel, titanium, tungsten, and vanadium. As a result, a number of significant industrial cities, including Chelyabinsk, Magnitogorsk, Perm', Ufa, and Yekaterinburg have developed in the Urals, together forming a major industrial region (see p. 145).

The mountain wall that runs along the southern and eastern margins of the two stable shields on either side of the Urals is the product of geological instability. Younger, sedimentary rocks have been pushed up against the older and more stable shields in successive episodes of mountain-building, forming a series of mountain ranges of varying height, composition, and complexity. The highest ranges are those of the Caucasus (where Mt. Elbrus reaches 5642 meters, or 18,510 feet) and the Pamirs and Tien Shan ranges along the borders with Iran, Afghanistan, and China, where many peaks reach 5000 to 6000 meters, and two—Pobedy and Qullai Garmo (formerly Communism Peak)—exceed 7400 meters (24,278 feet). In the far east, the ranges of the Kamchatka Peninsula contain numerous active volcanoes (**Figure 3.8**), including Mt. Klyuchevskaya (4750 meters; 15,584 feet) and Mt. Kamen (4632 meters; 15,197 feet). Only in the western part of Central Asia does the mountain wall fall outside the region, running along the southern side of Turkmenistan's border with Iran and Afghanistan. North of this border, extending through Uzbekistan into Kazakhstan and beyond, is a huge geosyncline, a geological depression of sedimentary rocks. This syncline is of special importance as a source of energy resources, with oil reserves equivalent to

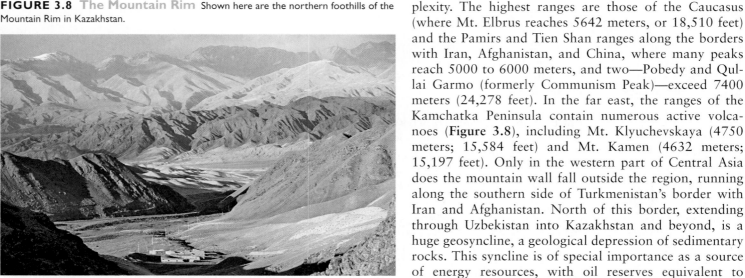

FIGURE 3.8 The Mountain Rim Shown here are the northern foothills of the Mountain Rim in Kazakhstan.

between 15 and 31 billion barrels—about 2.7 percent of the world's proven reserves—plus significant deposits of coal and about 7 percent of the world's proven reserves of natural gas.

Climate

The northerliness and vast size of the region exert strong influences on its climate. The absence of mountainous terrain, except in the far south and east, and the lack of any significant moderating influence of oceans and seas means that the prevailing climatic pattern is relatively simple. The region is dominated by a severe continental climate, with long, cold winters and relatively short, warm summers. The cold winters become colder eastward, as one moves away from the weak marine influence that carries over from the westerly weather systems that cross Europe from the Atlantic. Pronounced high-pressure systems develop over Siberia in winter, bringing clear skies and calm air. Average January temperatures in Verkhoyansk, a mining center in the middle of this high-pressure area, are in the region of −50°C (−58°F). The region's long and intense winters mean that the subsoil is permanently frozen—a condition known as **permafrost**—in more than two-thirds of the Russian Federation. In the extreme northeast, winter conditions can last for ten months of the year.

Summer comes quickly over most of Belarus and the Russian Federation, as spring is usually a brief interlude of dirty snow and much mud. Because many rural roads remain unpaved, they are typically impassable before the summer heat bakes the mud. As the landmass warms, low-pressure systems develop, drawing moist air across the western Russian Federation from Atlantic Europe and resulting in moderate summer rains. In late summer, the Chinese **monsoon** brings heavy rains to the southeastern corner of the far east. Across much of Siberia, though, summer rainfall is quite low. The summers become hotter southward, and drought is a frequent problem in the southwestern and southern parts of the Russian Federation. In Central Asia, aridity is a severe problem, with desert and semidesert covering much of Kazakhstan, Uzbekistan, and Turkmenistan.

In the Transcaucasus, climatic patterns are mainly a result of the presence of massive mountain ranges to the north and south and substantial bodies of water to both east and west. A lot of precipitation falls on the windward side of the mountains, though the Transcaucasus is also influenced by the warm, dry air masses that originate over the deserts of Central Asia. The most distinctive feature of climatic patterns in the Transcaucasus, however, is the subtropical niche of western Georgia, on the shores of the Black Sea—a unique and striking feature in a region of otherwise severe climatic regimes.

Natural Landscapes

The natural landscapes of the Russian Federation, Central Asia, and the Transcaucasus follow a strikingly straightforward pattern of seven long, latitudinal zones that run roughly from west to east. These zones are very closely related to climate, glacial geomorphology, and soil type and remain easily recognizable to the modern traveler, despite centuries (or, in places, millennia) of human interference and modification. The northernmost zone is that of the tundra, which fringes the entire Arctic Ocean coastline and part of the Pacific (see Figure 3.3).

The Tundra The tundra is an arctic wilderness where the climate precludes any agriculture or forestry. The tundra zone extends along the northern shores of the Russian Federation and includes its Arctic islands. Altogether, it amounts to 2.16 million square kilometers (833,760 square miles), representing almost 13 percent of the country. Almost all of it was sculpted by one or another of the great ice sheets of the Quaternary ice ages (between 1.7 million and 10,000 years ago). These, wrote geographer W. H. Parker, "scraped, polished, grooved, crushed or sheared the rocks in their advance, and dropped boulders and stones haphazardly on their retreat."[2] Frost action is still the main modifier of the landscape, as running water is almost entirely absent. For nine months or more, the

---

[2] W. H. Parker, *The Soviet Union*, Chicago: Aldine, 1969, p. 42.

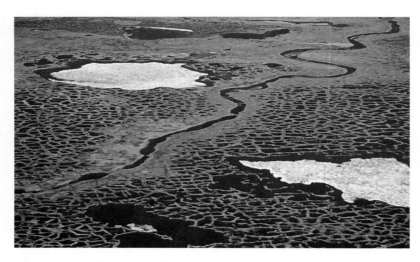

FIGURE 3.9 Tundra landscape The tundra landscape is bleak, with sparse vegetation and a surface strewn with rocks, which frost-heave action has arranged into geometric patterns. This photograph was taken in the Kolyma River Delta region.

FIGURE 3.10 Taiga landscape The taiga is a zone of boreal coniferous forest that stretches from the Gulf of Finland to the Kamchatka Peninsula. In much of the Siberian taiga, as in the example shown here, the dominant tree species is the larch.

landscape is locked up by ice and covered by snow, while during the brief summer, much of the melted snow and ice is trapped in ponds, lakes, boggy depressions, and swamps by permafrost that extends, in places, to a recorded depth of 1450 meters (4757 feet). Water seeps slowly to streams that drain into the slow-moving rivers that cross the tundra and drain into the Arctic (**Figure 3.9**).

During winter, the tundra landscape has a uniformity that derives from snow cover and the somber effect of long nights and weak daylight, the sun remaining low in the sky. There is little sign of life, apart from herds of reindeer or occasional polar bear or fox. In summer, vegetation bursts into bloom, and animals, birds, and insects appear. The days are long—in June the sun circles the horizon and there is no night at all. Mosses and tiny flowering plants provide color to the landscape, contrasting with the black, peaty soils and the luminous bright skies. Swans, geese, ducks, and snipe arrive on lakes and wetlands for their breeding season, as do seabirds and seals along the coast. From the forests to the south, wolves enter the tundra in search of prey that includes Alpine hare and lemmings (small, fat rodents that can produce five or six litters annually). Everywhere there are swarms of gnats and mosquitoes. Summer also brings a zonal differentiation to the region, with shrubs—blackberry, crowberry, and cowberry—and dwarf trees—birch, spruce, and willow—becoming more frequent as one moves south toward the taiga.

The Taiga South of the tundra is the most extensive zone of all—a belt of coniferous forest known as the *taiga*. The term **taiga** originally referred to trackless or virgin forest, though it is now used to describe the entire zone of boreal (northern) coniferous forest (spruce, fir, and pines, for example) that stretches from the Gulf of Finland to the Kamchatka Peninsula—more than 4.4 million square kilometers (1.3 million square miles) of territory (**Figure 3.10**). The underlying rock shield, having been steadily lifted

by geological movements, averages about 700 meters (2296 feet) in elevation and has been dissected by rivers into a hilly upland topography with deep river gorges that are cut 300 meters (984 feet) or more below the general level of the plateau. The steep sides of the valleys are notched by numerous terraces, marking successive stages in the uplift of the ancient crystalline rock plateau. This topography, though, is given uniformity by the distinctive forest cover of the region. The characteristic forest is made up of larches: hardy, flat-rooted trees that can establish themselves above the permafrost. Slow-growing and long-lived, they are able to counter the upward encroachment of moss and peat by putting out fresh roots above the base of the trunk. The larches can grow to 18 meters (59 feet) or more, allowing an undergrowth of dwarf willow, juniper, dog-rose, and whortleberry. The indigenous inhabitants of the taiga were hunters and gatherers, not farmers. Where the forest is cleared, some cultivation of hardy crops such as potatoes, beets, and cabbage is possible, but the poor, swampy soils and short growing season make agriculture chancy. The central Siberian taiga is one of the richest timber regions in the world. Overall, close to 90 percent of the territory is covered with forest, and more than a quarter of the Russian Federation's lumber production comes from the region. More recently the taiga has become commercially important for the fur-bearing animals whose luxuriant pelts are well adapted to the bitter cold, and for the forest itself, whose timber is now methodically exploited and exported.

Mixed Forest and Steppe Landscapes

This zone is a continuation of the mixed forests of central Europe that extend through Belarus and into the Russian Federation as far as the Urals, with discontinuous patches in Siberia and the far east. Here, firs, pines, and larches are mixed with stands of birch and oak. It quickly shades into another relatively narrow zone of wooded steppe. In this zone the grasslands of the steppe are interspersed with less extensive stands of mixed woodland, mostly in valley bottoms. Both the mixed forest and the wooded steppe were cleared and cultivated early in Russian history, providing both an agricultural heartland for the emerging Russian empire and a corridor along which Russian traders and colonists pushed eastward in the 16th and 17th centuries—through the middle Volga region to the southern Urals and eventually to the Pacific coast via the mixed forests of the Amur valley. The wooded steppe, in turn, quickly shades into the steppe proper (see Signature Region: The Steppes, p. 116).

Semidesert and Desert

South of the steppe are zones of semidesert and desert. They are largely a feature of Central Asia—covering most of Kazakhstan, Turkmenistan, and Uzbekistan—and they continue south of Siberia into Chinese and Mongolian territory. The semidesert is characterized by boulder-strewn wastes and salt pans (areas where salt has been deposited as water evaporated from short-lived lakes and ponds created by runoff from surrounding hills) and patches of rough vegetation used by nomadic pastoralists. The desert proper is characterized by bare rock and extensive sand dunes, though there are occasional oases and fertile river valleys. The climate is harsh: Total annual precipitation in the deserts is less than 18 centimeters (7 inches), shade temperatures can reach 50°C (122°F), and ground surfaces can heat up to 80°C (176°F). The scorching heat is aggravated by strong drying winds, called *sukhovey*, that blow on more than half the days of summer, often causing dust storms. In late summer and fall, the increasing temperature range between the hot days and the longer, cooler nights becomes so extreme that rocks exfoliate, or "peel," leaving the debris to be blown away by the wind. The landscapes of the northern zone of the desert region are arid plateaus with rocky outcrops, hillocks, and shallow depressions that have become crusted with salty deposits as a result of the evaporation of runoff from surrounding hills.

The two principal deserts here are the Ust-Urt and Bek-pak-Dala. Farther south is a zone of sandy deserts: the Kara-Kum (Black Sands) and the Kyzyl-Kum (Red Sands). Here, the landscape is dominated by long ridges of sand in crescent-shaped dunes called *barchans* and by vast plains of level sand punctuated by patches of sand hills and by isolated remnants of worn-down mountain ranges called

SIGNATURE REGION

The Steppes

The steppe belt stretches about 4000 kilometers (2486 miles) from the Carpathians to the Altay Mountains (see Figure 3.3), covering a total area of more than 4.25 million square kilometers (1.25 million square miles). The topography of the region is strikingly flat: yellow loess, several meters thick, has blanketed the underlying geology, creating a rolling landscape of unbounded horizons, punctuated here and there by incised streams and river valleys. The natural vegetation of tall and luxuriant feather grasses and steppe fescue have matted roots that are able to trap whatever moisture is available in this rather arid region (**Figure 1**). The accumulated and decayed debris of these grasses has produced a rich dark soil, known as black earth, or **chernozem**. These soils, along with related brown and chestnut soils, have high natural fertility, but when they are plowed, they are vulnerable to the aridity of the region and can easily degenerate into wind-driven dustbowl conditions. Trees and shrubs are restricted to valleys, where broadleaved woods of oak, ash, elm, and maple have established themselves; pinewoods and a low scrub of blackthorn, laburnum, dwarf cherry, and Siberian pea-trees grow in drier locations.

FIGURE I Steppe landscape A man cuts grass on the rolling steppe landscape of western Siberia.

For centuries, the steppe region was the realm of nomadic peoples, including Pechenegs, Kazakhs, Scythians, and Tatars. In the late 1700s, when the Turkish empire's hold on the steppes was broken, large numbers of colonists began to enter the western steppe. Along with Russians and Ukrainians came Armenians, Bulgarians, French, Germans, Greeks, Montenegrins, Serbs, and Swiss. Wheat growing rapidly expanded wherever transportation was good enough to get the grain to the expanding world market, but large flocks of sheep dominated most of the colonized steppe until the railway arrived. Then, German Mennonites began mixed farming on the rich soils, Greeks began tobacco farming, and Armenians specialized in business and commerce. Farther east, the flat steppe of northern Kazakhstan remained largely untouched until the 19th century, save for Kazakh nomads and their herds and a few Russian forts and trading posts. During the 19th century, settlers came from the west in increasing numbers—a million or more by 1900—displacing the Kazakh nomads, thousands of whom died in famines or in unsuccessful uprisings against the Russians.

The Soviet period brought significant modifications to the region and its landscape. The colonists' small farms were merged into collectives, linear shelter belts of trees were planted in an attempt to modify climatic conditions, and rivers were dammed to provide hydroelectric power and irrigation for extensive farming of wheat, corn, and cotton (**Figure 2**). In the 1950s, Nikita Khruschev announced that the "virgin and idle lands" of the eastern steppe would be plowed and farmed for wheat. The Soviet government organized state farms and built large villages of new wooden houses to receive an army of 350,000 immigrants from European Russia. The eastern steppe was quickly transformed by modern machinery, fertilizers, and pesticides, initially producing as much wheat, on average, as the annual wheat harvest of Canada or France. This extensive wheat farming quickly led to dust-bowl conditions, however. In response, dry-farming techniques and irrigation have been introduced. **Dry-farming** techniques allow the cultivation of crops without irrigation in regions of limited moisture (50 centimeters, or 20 inches, of rain per year). Such techniques include keeping the land free from weeds and leaving stubble in the fields after harvest to trap snow. Together with irrigation schemes, dry-farming techniques now allow for the cultivation of not only wheat, but also millet and

inselbergs. Several rivers—including the Amu Dar'ya, the Syr Dar'ya, and the Zeravshan—drain from the Tien Shan and Pamir mountain ranges across these deserts toward the Aral Sea. Dotted along their valleys are irrigated oases, while *tugay*—impenetrable thickets of hardy trees and thorny bushes—thrive in the rather salty soils of the valley floors.

Environmental History

The more open discourse that followed the breakup of the Soviet Union and the creation of democratic societies has revealed a legacy of serious environmental problems that stem from mismanagement of natural resources and failure to control pollution

sunflowers, together with silage corn and fodder crops to support livestock.

Today, the steppes are an agricultural region. Particularly productive is the North Caucasus, which receives more rainfall than elsewhere in the steppes. Nevertheless, the North Caucasus has traditionally been one of Russia's least economically developed regions. There are several large cities within or bordering the North Caucasus steppe, including Rostov-on-Don (population 1.05 million in 2005), Krasnodar (646,000), Grozny (364,000), and Stavropol' (342,000), but their industrial base is tied narrowly to agricultural processing and distribution, while the whole subregion has suffered acutely from the political instability and conflicts of the post-Soviet period. The economic vitality of the eastern steppe of northern Kazakhstan is similarly clouded. Aqmola (population 302,000) is the largest city of the eastern steppe, having become the capital of Khruschev's "virgin lands" scheme. In 1997 it replaced Almaty as the capital of Kazakhstan and is enjoying a small boom as a result. Elsewhere, though, the towns of the eastern steppe are bleak and impoverished. The area near Semey was the Soviet Union's chief nuclear-testing ground, the site of more than 450 underground nuclear detonations between 1949 and 1989. Most of the towns and cities of the eastern steppe are experiencing significant rates of out-migration, as Russians and other Slavs, seeing little likelihood of local economic development, are emigrating back to European Russia in search of better prospects.

FIGURE 2 Extensive agriculture on the steppes Beginning in the 1950s, the eastern steppes were transformed into an extensive wheat farming region through massive investments of modern machinery, fertilizers, and pesticides.

during the Soviet era. Soviet central planning placed strong emphasis on industrial output, with very little regard for environmental protection. Early Soviet ideology had propagated the view that it would be feasible to harness and transform nature through the collective will and effort of the people. Nature, it was asserted, is a dangerous force that needs to be subdued and transformed, and natural resources have no value in a socialist society until people's labor has been applied to them. As a result of this way of thinking, there was a tendency during the Soviet era to squander natural resources and to "take on" and "conquer" nature through ambitious civil engineering projects. Soviet authorities saw problems of pollution and environmental degradation as an inevitable cost of modernization and industrialization, and the people most affected—the general public—had no political power or means to voice environmental concerns.

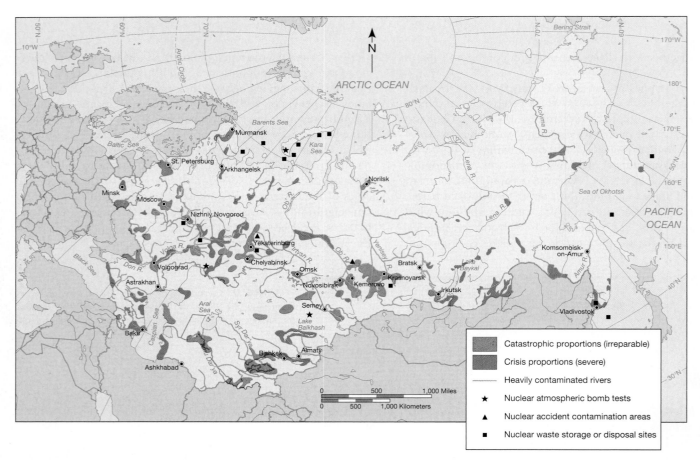

FIGURE 3.11 Environmental degradation Serious environmental degradation afflicts all parts of the Russian Federation, Central Asia, and the Transcaucasus. The range of issues is enormous, and the problems are so intense that they are likely to persist for several generations. (*Source:* Adapted from J. H. Bater, *Russia and the Post-Soviet Scene.* London: Arnold, 1996, p. 314.)

Today, serious environmental degradation affects all parts of the region (**Figure 3.11**), a legacy of Soviet problems that in many ways have been intensified by the transition to **market economies,** in which goods and services are produced and distributed through free markets. The ubiquitous corruption that has come to characterize the region during the post-Soviet transition means that environmental regulations are easily ignored or circumvented. In addition, economic problems in the Russian Federation have clearly limited the country's ability to address its environmental problems. The resulting legacy of environmental problems includes overcutting of forests, widespread overuse of pesticides, heavy pollution of many rivers and lakes, extensive problems of acid rain and soil erosion, and serious levels of air pollution in industrial towns and cities. Fragile environments at the margins of human settlement and on the peripheries of the Soviet empire have been among the worst affected. Across the far north, for example, air pollution produces a phenomenon known as "Arctic haze," seriously reducing sunlight and destroying delicate vegetation complexes that underpin fragile ecosystems. In the semiarid and arid regions of the south, the diversion of rivers for irrigation schemes aimed at boosting agricultural productivity have depleted water resources in some areas and led to widespread soil erosion and desertification.

Radioactivity Contamination by radioactivity is seen by many to epitomize the consequences of Soviet attitudes toward the environment. Both the large-scale civilian nuclear energy program and the military nuclear capability of the Soviet Union were developed in ways that have resulted in an alarming incidence of radioactive pollution. The 1986 disaster at Chernobyl, in the former Soviet republic of Ukraine, became emblematic of the Soviet nuclear legacy. Stories of radiation sickness and eventual ghastly deaths of the facility workers, firefighters, medical personnel, and other volunteers filled international newspapers for weeks following the meltdown. Less graphic and less well remembered are the invisible and enduring effects on the population of the area surrounding the power plant as well as on the natural environment. Radiation particles entered the soil, the vegetation, the human population, and the rivers, effectively contaminating the entire food chain of the region. Secondary radiation continues to be a problem. In the immediate area surrounding Chernobyl, all the trees were contaminated. As the trees slowly die, rot, and decay, radioactive material enters the physical system as "hot" nutrients. More than 3000 square kilometers (1161 square miles) of trees turned brown from radiation immediately following the accident, and it is still not clear how to decontaminate such a large area. Entire towns remain abandoned (**Figure 3.12**).

Meanwhile, economic stress has led the Russian Federation to agree to become a dumping ground for other countries' nuclear waste. All over the industrialized world, atomic power plant construction is significantly slowing down because of unresolved safety considerations and the failure to develop a safe, permanent means of disposing long-lived nuclear waste. In 2000 the Russian Federation volunteered to store 2000 metric tons (about 4.5 million pounds) of highly radioactive nuclear waste from Switzerland over the next 30 years for roughly $2 billion. Several more countries, including Germany, France, South Korea, Taiwan, and Japan, are likely to take advantage of the relatively low price charged by the Russian Federation for nuclear reprocessing. The risks, though, are appallingly high, given the Russian Federation's industrial inefficiency, corruption, and organized crime.

FIGURE 3.12 Pripet, Ukraine The entire town of Pripet was abandoned after the world's worst nuclear accident in 1986, the explosion of the number 4 reactor of the nearby Chernobyl nuclear power station.

The Aral Sea Radioactivity is only one of several major environmental problems that have left an enduring legacy to the Soviet Union's successor states. Soviet modernization programs brought large-scale irrigation schemes to the desert and semidesert regions of Central Asia, notably the Kara-Kum Canal, a 770-kilometer (478-mile) irrigation canal that diverts water from the Amu Dar'ya and irrigates 1.5 million hectares (4.7 million acres) of arable land and 5 million hectares (12.4 million acres) of pasture as it trails across southern Turkmenistan. Cotton was the dominant crop in these irrigated lands and remains so (**Figure 3.13**). In Turkmenistan, for example, more than half the arable land is devoted to cotton **monoculture**, while Uzbekistan is the world's fifth-largest producer of raw cotton and third-largest exporter of cotton.

In many ways, however, irrigated cotton cultivation has been harmful. Yields remain comparatively low, in spite of irrigation, due to soil exhaustion and salinization. **Salinization** is caused when water evaporates from the surface of the land and leaves behind salts that it has drawn up from the subsoil. An excess of salt in the soil seriously affects the yield of most crops. In addition to salt, residues of the huge doses of defoliants, pesticides, and fertilizers used on the cotton fields have found their way into the drinking-water systems of the region. Meanwhile, cotton monoculture has rendered the countries of the region heavily dependent on food imports.

The worst consequence of the Soviet program of irrigated cotton cultivation has been the effects of excessive withdrawals of water from the main rivers that drain into the Aral Sea. The Kara-Kum Canal alone took away almost one-quarter of the Aral Sea's annual supply of

FIGURE 3.13 Cotton cultivation Manual labor remains important in the extensive cotton farming on irrigated lands in Turkmenistan.

FIGURE 3.14 The Aral Sea Like this area near Aralsk, Kazakhstan, some 24,000 square kilometers (11,000 square miles) of former seabed in the Aral Sea have become a desert of sand and salt.

water. Overall, the Aral Sea has shrunk by more than 40 percent in surface area, and it continues to shrink. The level of the Aral Sea has already dropped by more than 10 meters (33 feet), and the desiccation of the former seabed, now littered with stranded ships (**Figure 3.14**), generates a constant series of dust storms that are thought to cause unusually high levels of respiratory ailments among the people of the region. The acute desiccation of the Aral Sea region has devastated its fishing industry and left ports such as Aralsk and Moynaq stranded more than 40 kilometers (25 miles) from the retreating lakeshore in the midst of a new "White Desert" of former lakebed sands.

Lake Baykal Another notorious example of environmental degradation is Lake Baykal, where the unique ecosystem has been threatened by industrial pollution. Lake Baykal is the world's deepest lake at 1615 meters (5300 feet—more than a mile) and contains about 20 percent of all the fresh water on Earth—more than North America's five Great Lakes combined. It has a unique ecology, with more than 2500 recorded plant and animal species, 75 percent of which are found nowhere else. These include the nerpa, Baykal's freshwater seal. Lake Baykal is also a place of incredible beauty—"The Pearl of Siberia"—that has become emblematic of the pristine wilderness of the region. But the lake's purity and unique ecosystem have been compromised by environmental mismanagement. In the 1960s, increasing levels of pollution were carried into the lake by the Selenga River, which supplies about half of the water that flows into the lake. The Selenga rises in mountain ranges to the south but collects agricultural chemicals such as DDT and PCB, as well as human and industrial waste from several large cities before entering Lake Baykal.

Meanwhile, the purity of the lake's waters caught the attention of Soviet economic planners, who began to see the lake as a good location for factories that needed plentiful supplies of pure water (**Figure 3.15**). When the huge Baikalsk Pulp & Paper Mill, which produces high-quality cellulose for the Russian defense industry, was opened in the early 1960s, Lake Baykal triggered the birth of Russia's environmental movement. It is estimated that over the past 40 years the mill has spewed more than a billion tons of waste into the lake.

FIGURE 3.15 Lake Baykal The purity of the deep waters of Lake Baykal has been compromised by industrialization along its shores and along the rivers that feed the lake.

As a result of unprecedented expressions of public concern, the Soviet government ordered the mill closed in 1986. But the government collapsed before the closure took effect, and since 1989 the mill has been partially privatized and now makes pulp for low-quality paper rather than cellulose. When thousands of the lake's freshwater seals began dying in 1997, the lake's fragile ecology came under international scrutiny, and in 1998 the lake was designated a World Heritage Site by UNESCO, the UN cultural agency. Nevertheless, it remains to be seen whether Russia can solve its environmental problems at a time when its economy is in disarray.

Forest Management Poor forest resource management also gives cause for concern. After decades of relentless Soviet exploitation, the Siberian taiga, once dense and practically impassable, has been cleared throughout much of the southern parts of the region and around all the larger towns and cities. Loggers are now moving farther and farther north to cut down century-old pines. The post-Soviet transition has intensified concern

FIGURE 3.16 Illegal logging More than 1.5 million cubic meters of oak, cedar, and ash are illegally logged in the far eastern Primorye region each year. Chinese traders pay $100 per cubic meter and resell the wood at prices of $400–$500 per cubic meter.

over forest resource management as privatization has attracted U.S., Korean, and Japanese transnational corporations to invest in "slash-for-cash" logging operations (**Figure 3.16**) in a loosely regulated and increasingly corrupt business environment. The future of the central Siberian taiga has become an issue of international concern because the taiga accounts for a significant fraction of the world's temperate forests, which absorb huge amounts of carbon dioxide gas in the process of photosynthesis, thereby removing a main contributor to global warming from the atmosphere.

THE RUSSIAN FEDERATION, CENTRAL ASIA, AND THE TRANSCAUCASUS IN THE WORLD-SYSTEM

As explained in the previous section, huge tracts of this world region are decidedly marginal. Agriculture and settlement have been greatly restricted by severe climatic conditions, highly acidic soils, poor drainage, and mountainous terrain. Even in the zone of rich chernozem soils, low and irregular rainfall rendered agriculture and settlement marginal until large-scale irrigation schemes were introduced in the 20th century. Only in the mixed forest and the wooded steppe west of the Urals were conditions suitable for the emergence of a more prosperous and densely settled population. It was this area, in fact—from Smolensk in the west to Nizhniy Novgorod in the east, and from Tula in the south to Vologda and Velikiy Ustyug in the north—that was the Russian "homeland" that developed around the principality of Muscovy from late medieval times. Long before then, however, the towns of Central Asia had become key nodes in the vast trading network known as the Silk Road.

Central Asia and the Silk Road

The **Silk Road** is the collective name given to a network of overland trade routes (see Figure 8.11) that connected China with Mediterranean Europe, facilitating the exchange of silk, spices, and porcelain from the East and gold, precious stones, and Venetian glass from the West. It had existed since Roman times and remained important until Portuguese navigators found their way around Africa and established the seaborne trade routes that exist to this day. Along the Silk Road stood the ancient cities of Samarkand, Bukhara, and Khiva (**Figure 3.17a**), places of glory and wealth that astonished Western travelers such as Marco Polo in the 13th century. These cities were east–west meeting places for philosophies, knowledge, and religion. In their prime they were known for their leaders in mathematics, music, architecture, and astronomy: scholars such as Al Khoresm (780–847), Al Biruni (973–1048), and Ibn Sind (980–1037). The cities' prosperity was marked by impressive feats of Islamic architecture (**Figure 3.17b**). Their civilization was overcome by Mongol Tatar horsemen, who ruled until the 14th century. Timur (Tamerlane), one of Genghis Khan's descendants and a convert to Islam, subsequently built up a vast Central Asian empire stretching from northern India to Syria, with its capital in Samarkand. The decline of Timur's empire in the 16th century saw the rise of nomadic peoples, who established three khanates, or kingdoms: in Bukhara, Khiva, and Kokand. They prospered as trading posts on the transdesert caravan routes until the late 19th century, when the three khanates fell to Russian troops.

Muscovy and the Russian Empire

Understanding the spread of colonization and the extension of political control by the peoples of the Russian homeland is key to understanding the present-day geography of the entire region. In the mid-15th century, Muscovy was a principality of approximately 5790 square kilometers (2235 square miles) centered on the city of Moscow. Over a 400-year period, the Muscovite state expanded at a rate of about 135 square kilometers (52 square miles) per day so that by 1914, on the eve of the Russian Revolution, the empire occupied more than 22 million square kilometers (roughly 8.5 million square

FIGURE 3.17 Khiva, Uzbekistan (a) The fortified walls of Ichan-Kala, the historic center of Khiva; (b) Kalta Minor Minaret.

(a)

(b)

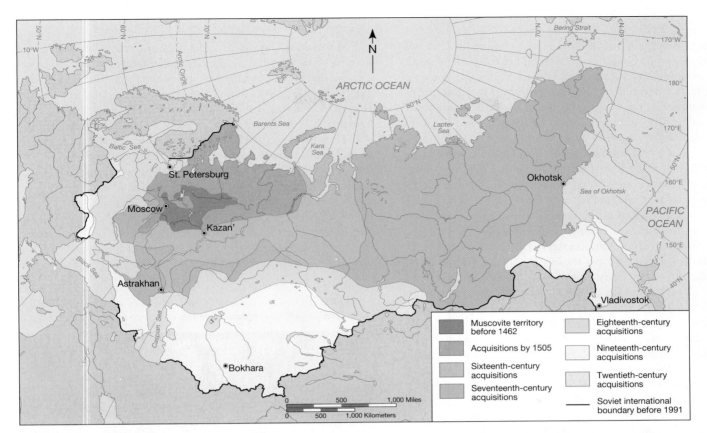

FIGURE 3.18 Territorial growth of the Muscovite/Russian state The Muscovite empire was vast and was conquered over the same period (15th century to the late 20th) that corresponds to the globalization of the world economy. What makes the Russian case unique is that the lands conquered were adjacent ones and not overseas. When the Bolsheviks came to power at the beginning of the 20th century, some of the territory was lost. Eventually, however, the Bolsheviks were able to control most of the territories formerly held by the tsars, and it was upon this that they also built the Soviet state. (*Source:* Redrawn from D. J. B. Shaw, *Russia in the Modern World.* Oxford: Blackwell, 1999, p. 7.)

miles), or one-seventh of the land surface of Earth (**Figure 3.18**). At first, Muscovy formed part of the Mongol-Tatar empire whose armies were known as the Golden Horde, and Russian princes were obliged to pay homage to the Khan, the leader of the Golden Horde. In 1552, under Ivan the Terrible, the Muscovites defeated the Tatars at the battle of Kazan'—a victory that prompted the commissioning of St. Basil's Cathedral in Moscow.

Colonization Desirous of more forest resources—especially furs (see Geographies of Indulgence, Desire, and Addiction: Furs, p. 124)—Muscovy expanded into Siberia. Gradually, more and more territory was colonized. By the mid-17th century, the eastern and central parts of Ukraine had been wrested from Poland. The steppe regions, though, remained very much a frontier region of the Russian empire because of the constant threat of attack by nomads. Early in the 18th century, Peter the Great (1682–1725) founded St. Petersburg and developed it as the planned capital of Russia. Beyond the wealth and grandeur of a few cities, however, Russia was very much a rural, peasant economy. In the latter part of the 18th century, under Catherine the Great (1762–96), Russia secured the territory of what would eventually become southern Latvia, Lithuania, Belarus, and western Ukraine. Then, with the defeat of the Crimean Tatars in the late 18th century, the steppes were opened to colonization by Russians and by ethnic and religious minorities—including Mennonites and Hutterites—from eastern and central Europe. It was during this period that Russia ousted the Ottoman Turks from the Crimean Peninsula and gained the warm-water port city of Odessa on the Black Sea.

Furs

From earliest times, fur has been a prized commodity. In cold regions, fur coats, hats, and boots are valued for their warmth and as a practical investment that is also a portable form of wealth. In Russia and Europe, fur has long had royal and aristocratic connotations and, as a result, became a status symbol for all who could afford it. In the world of women's fashion, furs have become synonymous with haute couture, and in much of the world fur is seen by status-conscious consumers as a fashionable luxury good, a clear marker of material wealth. Furs have, however, become a controversial luxury item. In Europe and North America in particular, the market for furs has been significantly affected by people's concern that certain animal species might be threatened with extinction and the realization that fur trapping and fur farming can involve unnecessary cruelty to animals.

European merchants began trading fur in the Middle Ages, and fur was the commodity that drew Russian trappers and traders to Siberia in the 16th century. In 1581, under sponsorship of the rich merchant family of Stroganov, a military expedition opened a routeway to Siberia for *promyshlenniks* (fur hunters), who were drawn eastward in search of sable and sea otter. The pelts of these animals were exchanged for Chinese and Indian goods, and the tax revenues from the trade were the mainstay of the Russian imperial treasury for the next 300 years. It became government policy to encourage the fur trade and to support the *promyshlenniks* in their ruthless displacement of indigenous peoples and their sustainable economies. By the reign of Peter the Great (1682–1725), the *promyshlenniks* had reached the Sea of Okhotsk, and fur hunting was coming to a saturation point. In response, Peter the Great sponsored maritime expeditions to the Kamchatka Peninsula and to the offshore islands of the northeast. After Vitus Bering's expedition to the Northern Pacific in 1741–42 established that the islands had abundant populations of sea otter, foxes, seals, and walruses, there was a "fur rush" that drew *promyshlenniks* all the way across the Bering Sea to Alaska.

Meanwhile, trade in fur pelts (beavers, muskrats, minks, and martens) had attracted Europeans' initial interest in North America. Beaver, trapped by Native Americans, was a main source of barter at trading posts that later grew into such cities as Chicago, Detroit, Montréal, New Orleans, Québec, St. Louis, St. Paul, and Spokane. The Hudson's Bay Company, founded in England in the mid-17th century to trade skins for guns, knives, and kettles, gained almost total control of the North American fur trade. For the company's first 200 years, its business consisted entirely of trading in furs. The company abandoned fur sales in 1991 but in 1997 started them again, largely because of a surge in demand from China and the other rapidly growing capitalist economies of Asia. Today, fur farming (raising animals in captivity under controlled conditions), rather than trapping, is the principal source of furs for the world market (**Figure 1**). Fur farming was started in

FIGURE 1 Russian fur farm Most of Russia's fur farms are located in remote settings, with few regulatory controls or inspections.

Empire Russia's imperial expansion followed the same impulses as other European empires. The factors behind expansion were the drive for more territorial resources (especially a warm-water port) and additional subjects. Different for Russia, however, was that vast stretches of adjacent land on the Eurasian continent were annexed, whereas other empires established new territories overseas.

The final phases of expansion of the Russian empire occurred in the late 18th and 19th centuries. Finland was acquired from Sweden in 1809. In the Transcaucasus, Georgians and Armenians were "rescued" from the Turks and Persians. In Central Asia, the Moslem Khanates fell one by one under Russian control: the city of Tashkent in 1865, the city of Samarkand in 1868, the Emirate of Bukhara in 1868, and the Khanate of Khiva in 1874. Meanwhile, in the far east, the weakening of the Manchu dynasty, which had ruled China since 1664, prompted the Russian annexation of Chinese territory, where colonization and settlement was aided by the construction of the Trans-Siberian Railroad in the final years of the 19th century. By 1904, when defeat in Manchuria by Japan brought a halt to Russian territorial expansion, the Russian empire contained about 130 million persons, only 56 million of whom were Russian. Of the rest, which included more than 170 distinct ethnic groups, some 23 million were Ukrainian, 6 million were Belorussian, more than 4 million were Kazakh or Kyrgyz, nearly 4 million were Jews, and nearly 3 million were Uzbek.

Canada in 1887 on Prince Edward Island. Through controlled breeding, animals with unique characteristics of size, color, or texture can pass on those characteristics to their offspring. The silver fox, developed from the red fox, was the first fur so produced.

Overall, the Scandinavian countries produce about 45 percent of the world supply of pelts, Russia 30 percent, the United States 10 percent, and Canada 3 percent. Retail sales of furs in the United States grew from less than $400 million in the early 1970s to $1.8 billion by the mid-1980s but fell off to between $1.0 billion and $1.2 billion annually in the 1990s. The reason for this leveling-off in sales during the sustained economic boom of that period was a shift in attitudes toward furs, led by animal rights activists. In the late 1980s, Greenpeace commissioned photographer David Bailey to work on an advertisement with the slogan, "It takes more than 100 dumb animals to make a fur coat, but only one to wear one." In the late 1990s, PETA (People for the Ethical Treatment of Animals) ran its "I'd Rather Go Naked Than Wear Fur" poster, featuring five supermodels—Naomi Campbell, Christy Turlington, Claudia Schiffer, Cindy Crawford, and Elle Macpherson—doing just that. Anti-fur demonstrations targeting designers, led by entertainment icons such as Charlize Theron, Stella McCartney, Pamela Anderson, and Martha Stewart, have captured widespread attention (**Figure 2**). Most leading designers dropped furs from their fashion lines in the mid-1990s, but furs have made a fashion comeback since 2001, led by designer labels such as Dolce & Gabbana and Louis Vuitton and promoted by celebrities such as Jennifer Lopez, Halle Berry, Posh Spice, and even some who once took part in anti-fur protests, such as Madonna, Cindy Crawford, Naomi Campbell, and Kate Moss.

Meanwhile, a number of well-publicized cases of maltreatment on fur farms has further reinforced the case of Western anti-fur activists. Some Russian fur farmers, faced with a combination of falling consumer demand because of economic recession,

higher taxes, and widespread corruption, let their animals go hungry. Western visitors to Siberian fur farms found starving animals in tiny cages with no bedding, no protection against the elements, and no veterinary care. Many Russian fur farmers have slaughtered most of their animals rather than watch them starve. Of the 200 fur farms in Russia in the early 1990s, only 40 were still operating in 2002. The others have closed or were gradually phasing out production. Nevertheless, Russian consumers have not been affected by Western activists' concerns. Many middle-class Russians own fur coats, and most consider them necessities in the harsh winter.

FIGURE 2 Anti-fur protest PETA (People for the Ethical Treatment of Animals) protesters hold signs protesting Jennifer Lopez's use of fur for her fashion line, May 2005.

To meet the challenge of different ethnicities under one state, Russia needed to apply binding policies and practices. Russia's strategies to bind together the 100-plus "nationalities" (non-Russian ethnic peoples) into a unified Russian state were oftentimes punitive and unsuccessful. Non-Russian nations were simply expected to conform to Russian cultural norms. Those who did not were persecuted. The result was opposition and, sometimes, rebellion and stubborn refusal to bow to Russian cultural dominance.

Revolution Meanwhile, since the time of Peter the Great, tsarist Russia had been seeking to modernize. By 1861, when Tsar Alexander II decreed the abolition of serfdom, Russia had built up an internal core with a large bureaucracy, a substantial intelligentsia, and a sizable group of skilled workers. The abolition of feudal serfdom was designed to accelerate the industrialization of the economy by compelling the peasantry to raise crops on a commercial basis; the idea was that the profits from exporting grain would be used to import foreign technology and machinery. In many ways, the strategy seems to have been successful: Between 1860 and 1900 grain exports increased fivefold, while manufacturing activity expanded rapidly. In 1906 further measures, known as the Stolypin Agricultural Reform, helped establish large, consolidated farms in place of some of the many small-scale peasant holdings. The consequent flood of dispossessed peasants to the cities created acute problems as housing conditions deteriorated and urban labor markets became inundated.

These problems, to which the tsars remained indifferent despite the petitions of desperate city governments, fueled deep discontent among the population. At the turn of the 20th century, Russia was in the grip of a severe economic recession. Inflation, with high prices for food and other basic commodities, led to famine and widespread hardship, but there was no real mechanism for legitimately voicing the concerns and aspirations of the majority of the population. Unions were illegal, as were strikes. Nevertheless, riots spread across the countryside and, in 1905, after an embarrassing military defeat by the Japanese in Manchuria the previous year, there was a revolutionary outbreak of strikes and mass demonstrations. A network of grassroots councils of workers—called *soviets*—emerged spontaneously not only to coordinate strikes but also to help maintain public order. The unrest was eventually subdued by brute force, and the soviets were abolished. But the discontent continued, intensified if anything by the flood of dispossessed peasants to cities after the Stolypin Agricultural Reform of 1906. World War I intensified the discontent of the population, as casualties mounted and the government's handling of both the armed forces and the domestic economy led to the socialist revolution of 1917.

The Soviet Empire

From the beginning, the state socialism of the Soviet Union was based on a new kind of social contract between the state and the people. In exchange for people's compliance with the system, their housing, education, and health care were to be provided by state agencies at little or no cost. This new social contract, though, had its roots in the traditional Russian traits of collectivism and authoritarianism. It was not the exploited peasantry or the oppressed industrial proletariat that emerged from the chaos of revolution to take control of this new system. It was the Bolsheviks, a dissatisfied element drawn from the former middle classes, whose orientation from the beginning favored a strategy of economic development in which the intelligentsia and more highly skilled industrial workers would play the key roles.

By the early 1920s, Nikolai Lenin, whose real name was Vladimir Ilich Ulyanov, the revolutionary leader and head of state, was also able to focus attention on the more idealistic aspects of state socialism. The Bolsheviks were internationalists, believing in equal rights for all nations and wanting to break down national barriers and end ethnic rivalries. Lenin's solution was recognition of the many nationalities through the newly formed Union of Soviet Socialist Republics (USSR). Lenin believed that this federal system, with each republic defined according to the geographic extent of ethnonational communities, would provide different nationalities with a measure of political independence.

Lenin was optimistic that once international inequalities were diminished, and once the many nationalities became united as one Soviet people, the federated state would no longer be needed: Nationalism would be replaced by communism. Lenin's vision was short-lived, and, following his death in 1924, the federal ideal faded. After eliminating several rivals, Joseph Stalin came to power in 1928 and enforced a new nationality policy, the aim of which was to construct a unified Soviet people whose interests transcended nationality. Although the federal administrative framework remained in place, nations increasingly lost their independence and by the 1930s were punished for displays of nationalism. **Figure 3.19** shows the administrative units and nationalities that were part of the USSR during Stalin's tenure as premier (1928–53). Figure 3.19 also shows how, during and immediately after World War II, Stalin expanded the power of the Soviet state westward to include Albania, Bulgaria, Czechoslovakia, the German Democratic Republic, Hungary, Poland, Romania, and Yugoslavia.

Socialist Planning Meanwhile, Soviet aspirations for an egalitarian society required the reshaping of the country's geography at every scale. Under Lenin, a number of visionary, utopian (and often impractical), architectural, and city-planning schemes emerged, together with hundreds of new standards and norms that were designed to

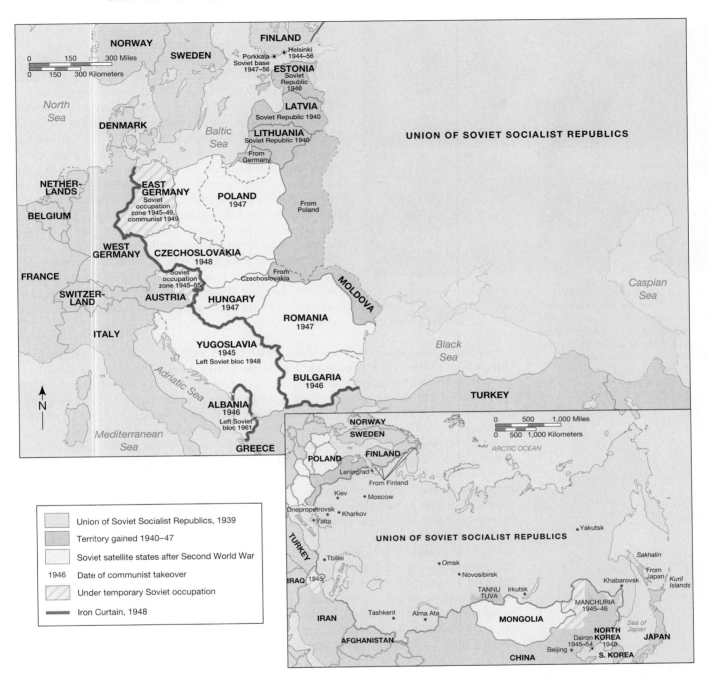

FIGURE 3.19 Soviet state expansionism, 1940s and 1950s World War II gave the Soviet state the pretext for moving westward for additional territories. Insisting that these countries would never again be used as a base for aggression against the USSR, Stalin retained control over Poland, East Germany, Czechoslovakia, Hungary, Romania, Bulgaria, Albania, Yugoslavia, and eastern Austria. In 1945 Stalin promised democratic elections in these territories. After 1946, however, Soviet control over eastern and central Europe became complete as noncommunist parties were dissolved and Stalinist governments installed. (*Source: Atlas of Twentieth Century World History.* New York: HarperCollins Cartographic, 1991, pp. 86–87.)

ensure an equitable allocation of resources. It was decided, for example, that there were to be 35 cinema seats per 1000 urban inhabitants; that the maximum journey-to-work time should be no more than 40 minutes; and that the optimal size of a city would be between 50,000 and 60,000 persons. Cities were to be planned in such a way as to provide a basic range of services to everyone, while at the same time engendering a sense of neighborliness and collective responsibility. The key organizational unit was to be the **mikrorayon**, a planned development with a radius of 300 to 400 meters (328 to 437 yards), accommodating 8000 to 12,000 people with a representative mix of the city's

FIGURE 3.20 Soviet-era prefabricated housing One of the Soviet era's great achievements was construction of an adequate supply of sound housing for Soviet citizens. Most of the housing, however, came from a very restricted range of prefabricated apartment block designs; as a result, places throughout the Soviet empire acquired the same drab appearance.

socioeconomic and ethnic groups, ample green space, perimeter thoroughfares with public transportation, day care, schools, sports and recreation facilities, and health services. Within each *mikrorayon*, the community would be organized into superblocks of 1000 to 1500 people living in standardized housing, with an allowance of 9 square meters of living space (97 square feet) per person.

While many of the utopian and visionary ideals of the 1920s were left on the drawing boards of Soviet planners, the *mikrorayon* concept was pursued vigorously: By the late 1980s, about one half of the Soviet urban population lived in a *mikrorayon*. The standardization of housing construction also left a distinctive mark on Soviet urban landscapes. One of the great achievements of the Soviet era was the accommodation of the bulk of the population, who formerly lived in miserable, substandard dwellings, in decent new sanitary housing. Nevertheless, the new prefabricated housing (**Figure 3.20**) was drab, uniform, and cramped, the norm of 9 square meters of living space per person remaining unchanged throughout the Soviet era.

Collectivization and Industrialization

Under Stalin's leadership, a major shift in power occurred within the Soviet Union. The New Economic Policy and its "bourgeois specialists" were replaced by a much more centralized allocation of resources: a command economy operated by engineers, managers, and *apparatchiks* (state bureaucrats) drawn from the membership of the Communist Party. With this shift, the Soviet Union chose to withdraw from the capitalist world economy as far as possible, relying on the capacity of its vast territories to produce the raw materials needed for rapid industrialization. The foundation of Stalin's industrialization drive was severe exploitation of the rural population. This involved the compulsory relocation of peasants into state or collective farms, where their labor was expected to produce bigger yields. The state would then purchase the harvest at relatively low prices so that, in effect, the collectivized peasant was to pay for industrialization by "gifts" of labor.

Severe exploitation required severe repression. Stalin employed police terror to compel the peasantry to comply with the requirements of the Five-Year Plans that provided the framework for his industrialization drive. Dissidents, along with enemies of the state uncovered by purges of the army, the bureaucracy, and the Communist Party, conveniently provided convict (*zek*) labor for infrastructure projects to support the industrialization drive. Altogether, some 10 million people were sentenced to serve in the *zek* workforce, to be imprisoned, or to be shot. The barbarization of Soviet society was the price paid for the modernization of the Soviet economy.

The Soviet economy *did* modernize, however. Between 1928 and 1940 the rate of industrial growth increased steadily, reaching levels of more than 10 percent per year in the late 1930s—growth rates that had never before been achieved and that since then have been equaled only by Japan (in the 1960s) and China (in the 1990s). An industrial revolution in the Western sense was achieved in just over a decade. When the Germans attacked the Soviet Union in 1941, they took on an economy that in absolute terms (though not *per capita*) had industrial output figures comparable with their own.

Satellite States

World War II cost the Soviet Union 25 million dead, the devastation of 1700 towns and cities and 84,000 villages, and the loss of more than 60 percent of all industrial installations. In the aftermath, the Soviet Union gave first priority to national security. The *cordon sanitaire* of independent eastern European nation-states that had been set up by the Western nations after World War I was appropriated as a buffer zone by the Soviet Union. Because this buffer zone happened to be relatively well developed and populous, it also formed the basis of a Soviet empire—the Soviet bloc—as an alternative to the capitalist world economy, thus providing economic as well as military security.

But the Soviet Union felt vulnerable to the growing influence and participation of the United States in world economic and political affairs, and in 1947 Stalin felt compelled to intervene more thoroughly in eastern Europe. In addition to the installation of the "Iron Curtain" that severed most remaining economic linkages with the West, this intervention resulted in the complete **nationalization** of the means of production, the collectivization of agriculture, and the imposition of rigid social and economic controls in all of the eastern European satellite states. The Communist Council for Mutual Economic Assistance (CMEA, better known as COMECON) was also established to reorganize the eastern European economies in the Stalinist mold—with individual members, each pursuing independent, centralized plans for economic self-sufficiency. This proved unsuccessful, however, and in 1958 COMECON was reorganized by Stalin's successor, Nikita Khruschev. The goal of economic self-sufficiency was abandoned, mutual trade among the Soviet bloc was fostered, and some trade with western Europe was permitted.

Growth, the Cold War, and Stagnation Meanwhile, the whole Soviet bloc gave high priority to industrialization. Between 1950 and 1955, output in the Soviet Union grew at nearly 10 percent per year, though it subsequently fell away to more modest levels. In addition to their desire for rapid growth, Soviet economic planners sought to follow three broad criteria in shaping the economic geography of state social-ism. First was the idea of technical optimization. Without free markets to provide com-petitive cost-minimization strategies, Soviet planners had to organize industry in ways that ensured both internal and external efficiencies. Perhaps the most striking result of this was the development of **territorial production complexes**, regional groupings of pro-duction facilities based on local resources that were suited to clusters of interdependent industries: petrochemical complexes, for example, or iron-and-steel complexes (**Figure 3.21**). Second was the idea of fostering industrialization in economically less-developed

FIGURE 3.21 Industrial regions of the Soviet Union Soviet planners gave a high priority to industrialization and sought to take advantage of agglomeration economies by establishing huge regional concentrations of heavy industry. (*Source:* Redrawn from P. L. Knox and J. Agnew, *The Geography of the World Economy,* 3rd ed. London: Arnold, 1998, p. 168.)

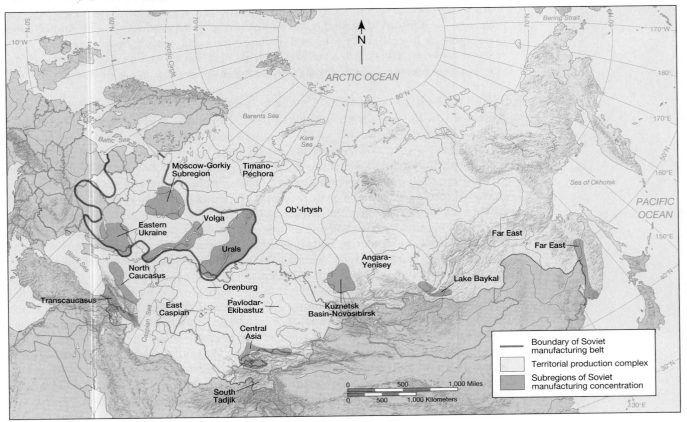

subregions, such as Central Asia and the Transcaucasus. A third consideration was secrecy and security from external military attack. This criterion led to some military-industrial development in Siberia and to the creation of scores of so-called secret cities—closed cities, where even the inhabitants' contacts with relatives and friends were strictly controlled because of the presence of military research and production facilities.

Soviet regional economic planners also sought to ameliorate many of the country's marginal environments through ambitious infrastructure schemes. *Stalin insisted that it must be feasible to harness and transform nature through the collective will and effort of the people.* As a result, plans were drawn up to reverse the flow of major rivers and divert them to feed irrigation schemes. There were also plans to ameliorate local climatic conditions in steppe regions through vast plantings of trees in shelter-belts. The prohibitive cost of these grandiose schemes kept most of them on the drawing board, but nevertheless the tendency to undertake civil engineering projects of heroic scale lasted through most of the Soviet era, resulting in some dramatic examples of the mismanagement of natural resources.

By the 1960s, the Soviet Union had clearly demonstrated its technological capabilities with its manned space program and the production of some of the world's most sophisticated military hardware. These successes were paralleled by the Soviet Union's geopolitical influence. The Soviet Union not only had an extensive nuclear arsenal but also an ideological alternative to the capitalist and imperialist ideology that had created peripheral regions throughout much of the world. Armed with these, the Soviet Union posed a very real threat to U.S. hegemony, waging a Cold War that between 1950 and 1989 provided the principal framework for world affairs. In that period, Soviet influence caused significant tension and a succession of geopolitical crises in many regions of the world, including Cuba, much of the Middle East, South Asia, East Asia, Southeast Asia, and parts of South America (Chile), Central America (Nicaragua and Panama), and Africa (Angola, Libya, and Egypt).

Yet throughout most of the Soviet Union itself, millions of peasants worked with primitive and obsolete equipment as they toiled to meet centrally planned production targets. Most nonmilitary industrial productivity was also constrained by technological backwardness and by cumbersome and bureaucratic management systems. A second economy—an informal or shadow economy—of private production, distribution, and sale emerged. It was largely tolerated by the government, mainly because without it the formal economy would not have been able to function as well as it did. By the 1970s the Soviet economic system was steadily being enveloped by an era of stagnation.

The Breakup of the Soviet Empire   By the 1980s the Soviet system was in crisis. In part, the crisis resulted from a failure to deliver consumer goods to a population that had become increasingly well informed about the consumer societies of their foreign enemies. Persistent regional inequalities also contributed to a loss of confidence in the Soviet system as an alternative mode of economic development. The cynical manipulation of power for personal gain by ruling elites and the drain on national resources from the arms race with the United States also undoubtedly played some role in undermining the Soviet model. The critical economic failure, however, was state socialism's inherent inflexibility and its consequent inability to take advantage of the new computerized information technologies that were emerging elsewhere.

Surprising even the most astute observers, the Soviet system unraveled rapidly between 1989 and 1991, leaving 15 independent countries as successors to the former USSR. The former states of Yugoslavia and Czechoslovakia were broken into smaller entities; East Germany was absorbed into Germany; Hungary, Poland, and the Baltic states (Estonia, Latvia, and Lithuania) were drawn rapidly into the European Union's sphere of influence; and Moldova and Ukraine began to show signs of a Western orientation. Belarus, the Russian Federation, and the states of Central Asia and the Transcaucasus continue to experience somewhat chaotic transitions, at different speeds, toward market economies. In the process, all local and regional economies have been disrupted, leaving many people to survive by supplementing their income with informal activities, such as street trading and domestic service.

New Realities

For the Russian Federation, the principal successor state to the Soviet Union, these changes have greatly weakened its position in the world. The Russian Federation is an elaborate hierarchy of administrative units. There are 21 republics, 10 autonomous areas (*okrugs)*, and 58 regional administrative districts (*oblasts*) and metropolitan districts (*krays*). Separate treaties of federation have resulted in a complex federal system in which these different administrative units have different sets of rights and privileges. The republics have elected presidents and written constitutions and have their own legislatures. Some republics have won special tax concessions and have come to agreements with the federal authorities on language and cultural rights. Nevertheless, the Russian Federation is still highly centralized in terms of real political power.

Economic Transformation and Social Disorganization

Restoring capitalism in countries where it had been suppressed for more than 70 years has proven to be problematic. Although still a nuclear power with a large standing army and a vast territory containing a rich array of natural resources, the Russian Federation is economically weak and internally disorganized. The latter years of the Soviet system left industry in the Russian Federation with obsolete technology and low-grade product lines, epitomized by its automobiles and civilian aircraft. Similarly, the infrastructure inherited by the Russian Federation's economy is poorly developed, shoddy, and often downright dangerous, as witnessed by the Chernobyl disaster of 1986, when a nuclear power plant in Ukraine exploded, causing a runaway nuclear reaction and widespread radiation pollution (see p. 118). Investment in the development of computers and new information networks was deliberately suppressed by Soviet authorities because, like photocopiers and fax machines, computers were seen as a threat to central control. As a result, the Russian Federation's economy now faces a massive task of modernization before it can approach its full potential.

Overall, the economy of the Russian Federation shrank by between 12 and 15 percent each year between 1991 and 1995, and by between 5 and 10 percent each year between 1996 and 2000. Foreign capital has flowed into the Russian Federation, but it has been targeted mainly at the fuel and energy sector, natural resources, and raw materials (which now account for about half of the Russian Federation's total exports) rather than manufacturing industry. By the end of the 1990s, the Russian Federation's economy was in crisis. About one half of the government's budget revenue was being absorbed by repaying debts to creditor nations; the rate of inflation had reached 100 percent; and economic output had plunged to about one half that of 1989.

At the same time that there looms the massive task of establishing the institutions of business and democracy after 70 years of state socialism, the Russian Federation has been unable to create some of the essential pillars of a **market economy**. In the institutional vacuum that followed the breakup of the command economy, there were no accepted codes of business behavior, no civil code, no effective bank system, no effective accounting system, and no procedures for declaring bankruptcy. Security agencies were disorganized, bureaucratic lines of command were blurred, and border controls between the new post-Soviet states were nonexistent. The absence of these key economic elements has provided enormous scope for crime and corruption and fostered regional ethnic *mafiyas*, including Chechen, Azeri, and Georgian *mafiyas*. Meanwhile, the purchasing power of most people's wages has already fallen to 1950s levels.

The Post-Soviet Republics In an attempt to counter some of the economic disruption caused by the political disintegration of the Soviet Union, several successor states agreed to form a loose association, known as the Commonwealth of Independent States (CIS). The CIS was designed to provide a forum for discussing the management of economic and political problems, including defense issues, cooperation in transport and communications, the creation of regional trade agreements, and environmental protection. The founding members were the Russian Federation, Belarus, and Ukraine; soon they were joined by the Central Asian states and some Transcaucasus states.

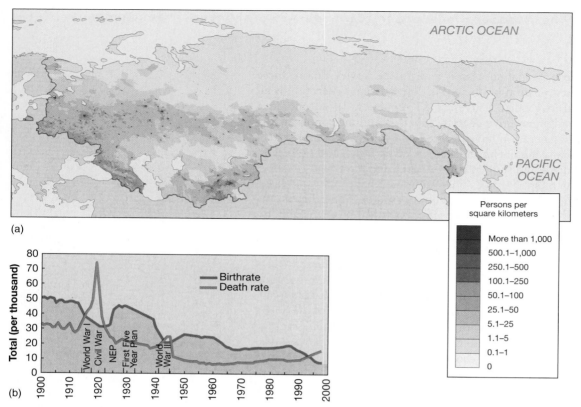

(a)

(b)

FIGURE 3.22 Population density and vital rates in the Russian Federation, Central Asia, and the Transcaucasus 1995 (a) The distribution of population in the Russian Federation, Central Asia, and the Transcaucasus reflects the region's economic history, with the highest densities in the industrial regions of the western parts of the Russian Federation and the richer agricultural regions of the Transcaucasus. (b) This graph shows the dramatic drop in the birthrate in Russia that characterized the 1960s and 1990s. Note also the sharp rise in death rates since 1990. (*Sources:* [a] Center for International Earth Science Information Network [CIESIN], Columbia University; International Food Policy Research Institute [IFPRI]; and World Resources Institute [WRI], 2000. *Gridded Population of the World [GPW]*, Version 3. Palisades, NY: CIESIN, Columbia University, 2005. Available at http://sedac.ciesin.columbia.edu/gpw/; [b] Updated from J. H. Bater, *Russia and the Post-Soviet Scene*. London: Arnold, 1996, p. 94.)

Meanwhile, however, the reorientation of the Baltic and eastern European states toward Europe and the imminent prospect of European Union and NATO membership for some of these states has not only undercut the economic prospects of the CIS (which has never really blossomed) but has also weakened the geopolitical security of the Russian Federation. In response, the leadership of the Russian Federation has asserted that country's claims to a special sphere of influence in what it calls the **Near Abroad,** the former components of the Soviet Union, particularly those countries that contain a large number of ethnic Russians.

The Russian Federation is clearly finding it problematic to adjust to a new role in the world. But although embarrassed by the disintegration of the Soviet Union and bankrupt by the subsequent dislocation to economic development, the Russian Federation is still accorded a great deal of influence in international affairs and may yet reemerge as a major contender for world power.

THE PEOPLES OF THE RUSSIAN FEDERATION, CENTRAL ASIA, AND THE TRANSCAUCASUS

A distinctive characteristic of this world region as a whole is the relatively low density of its population (**Figure 3.22a**). With a total population of some 232 million and almost 14 percent of Earth's land surface, the Russian Federation, Central Asia, and the Transcaucasus contains about 4.8 percent of Earth's population at an overall density of only 11 persons per square kilometer (28 per square mile). The highest national densities—123 per square kilometer in Armenia, 87 per square kilometer in Azerbaijan, and 79 per square kilometer in Georgia—approximate the population densities of Colorado, Kansas, and Maine. Within the Russian Federation there is an area of relatively high population density (between 40 and 60 per square kilometer) that corresponds to the region of mixed forest and the wooded steppe west of the Urals. In contrast, population density in much of the far north, Siberia, and the far east stands at less than 1 person per square kilometer, about the same as in the far north of Canada.

Levels of urbanization reflect this same broad pattern. Most large cities are in the European part of the Russian Federation and in the Urals. These include Moscow, Nizhniy Novgorod, St. Petersburg, Volgograd, and Yekaterinburg. Most of the other cities of any significant size are found in southern Siberia, on or near the Trans-Siberian Railway. Overall, both Belarus and the Russian Federation are quite highly urbanized, with 72 and 76 percent of their total populations living in cities, according to their respective census counts in the mid-1990s. The populations of the Transcaucasus are moderately urbanized (56 to 69 percent living in cities), while those of Central Asia are more rural (only 30 to 50 percent living in cities).

Overall, this is a world region with a relatively slow-growing population. Throughout the 20th century there was a general decline in both birth- and death rates (**Figure 3.22b**). In the 1990s the population began to register a decline as a result of more deaths than births. Viewed in greater detail, it is clear that this trend masks some important regional differences. In Belarus and the Russian Federation, population growth has for a long time been relatively modest, and it is in these countries that recent declines have been most pronounced. In contrast, in Central Asia and the Transcaucasus, birthrates have historically been relatively high, and rates of natural increase remain at a level comparable with those in South Asia and Southeast Asia.

Both World War I and World War II resulted in huge population losses that are still reflected in the age-sex profile of the Russian Federation (**Figure 3.23**). It was not until the 1960s, however, that rates of natural population increase in the Soviet empire began to decrease significantly on a long-term basis. At the beginning of the 1960s, birthrates fell sharply as a result of a combination of the legalization of abortion, a greater propensity to divorce, planned deferral of marriage among the rapidly expanding urban population, and a growing preference to trade off parenthood for higher levels of material consumption. At about the same time, there began a steady rise in death rates, which increased sharply after the breakup of the Soviet empire. The reasons for this increase in death rates are several. Deteriorating healthcare systems and the worsening health of mothers have contributed to an escalation of infant mortality rates. Meanwhile, public health standards have generally deteriorated, environmental degradation has intensified, and the rate of industrial accidents and alcohol-related illnesses has increased. By 2005 the average life expectancy of those born in the Russian Federation had slipped from the mid-1980s peak of 70.1 years to 65.4.

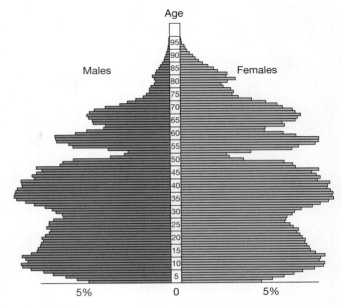

FIGURE 3.23 Age-sex pyramid for the Russian Federation This profile of the Russian Federation's population in the mid-1990s shows very clearly the effects of World War II (the relative lack of men and women in their early 50s and the reduced number of men aged 70 and older) and the reduced birthrates of the 1960s and 1990s. (*Source:* Updated from J. H. Bater, *Russia and the Post-Soviet Scene*. London: Arnold, 1996, p. 101.)

Languages and Ethnic Groups

The final census count of the Soviet Union in 1989 acknowledged 92 distinct ethnic groups. Dominant today throughout Belarus and the Russian Federation are Slavic peoples, among whom Russians represent one particular ethnic group. The hearth area of the original Slav tribes was in the Danubian Plains of present-day Hungary and Bulgaria. Between A.D. 300 and 600, these tribes spread outward to occupy a vast swathe of the continent, extending to the Elbe River in Germany, to the Baltic and Adriatic seas and the Gulf of Corinth, and eastward into the mixed forest and wooded steppe of present-day Ukraine, Belarus, and the Russian Federation. In the course of these great waves of migration, the Slavs split into three main branches: western

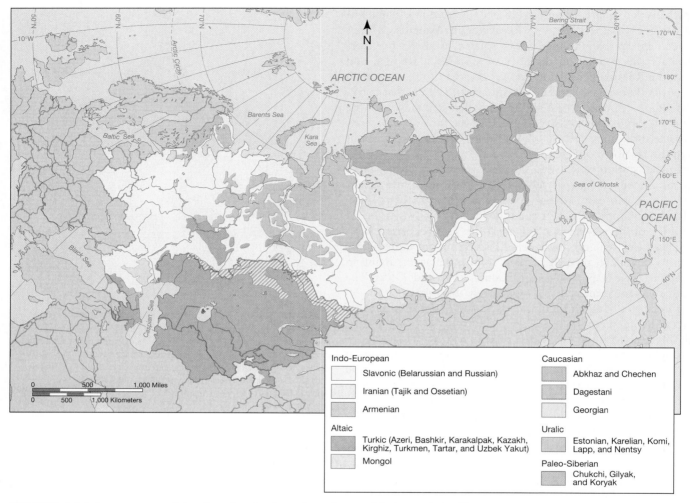

FIGURE 3.24 Languages of the Russian Federation, Central Asia, and the Transcaucasus More than 100 languages are spoken in the region, the majority by very small ethnic groups and hence unrecordable on any but the most detailed maps. The greatest diversity is seen in the Caucasus, especially in Dagestan on the northeastern flank of the range. (*Source:* Redrawn from R. Millner-Gulland and N. Dejevsky, *Cultural Atlas of Russia*, rev. ed. New York: Checkmark Books, 1998, pp. 26–27.)

(including Czechs, Poles, and Slovaks), southern (including Serbians, Serbo-Croats, and Slovenes), and eastern (the East Slavs, subdividing only in the late Middle Ages into Belarussians, Russians, and Ukrainians).

The Slavs are fundamentally defined by linguistic commonalities rather than territorial, racial, or other attributes. The Slavonic group of languages forms one of the major components of the great Indo-European language family, whose speakers range from north India (Hindi and Urdu) through Iran (Farsi) and parts of Middle Asia (Tajik) to virtually the whole of Europe. Written language came late to the Slavs, and when it did it was the deliberate effort of two missionaries—Constantine (later, as a monk, called Cyril) and Methodius—who were sent by the ninth-century Byzantine emperor Michael III to the Slavic nation of Greater Moravia (which occupied much of present-day Hungary, Germany, Slovakia, and the Czech Republic) to spread the Scriptures. The new alphabet that Constantine/Cyril devised in order to accommodate Slavonic speech sounds became known as the Cyrillic alphabet. As **Figure 3.24** shows, Slavonic-speaking peoples correspond to the most densely settled parts of the region, extending eastward along the zone of wooded steppe and steppe to the far east.

A second major language group is that of Turkic languages, which belong to the Altaic family of languages. These are spoken by the peoples of Central Asia and parts of the Transcaucasus and were spread into Russia itself through the Tatar invasion and period of rule (c. A.D. 1240–1480). Much of northern and eastern Siberia is occupied by peoples who speak other branches of the Altaic language group, while in the far east are peoples whose languages are part of the Paleo-Siberian language family, including Gilyak and Koryak. Finally, there are several smaller areas of Caucasian languages: Abkhaz and Chechen on the northern slopes of the Caucasus, and Georgian and Dagestani languages in the Transcaucasus.

The Russian Diaspora and Migration Streams

The spread of the Russian empire from its hearth in Muscovy took Russian colonists and traders to the Baltic, Finland, Ukraine, most of Siberia, the far east, and parts of Central Asia and the Transcaucasus. In the late 19th and early 20th centuries many Russians joined the stream of emigrants headed toward North America. Concentrations of Russian immigrants developed in Chicago, New York, and San Francisco. They were joined by others who fled the civil war and Bolshevik revolution of 1917. More recently, in the first five years after the breakup of the Soviet Union, the United States resettled nearly 250,000 refugees from the former Soviet Union, mostly from Russia. Over a quarter of these immigrants have settled in New York City, the majority in Brooklyn, where distinctive Russian exclaves, such as the Brighton Beach neighborhood of southern Brooklyn, have emerged as vital nodes in the Russian global diaspora.

With the rise of the Soviet empire, many Russians were directed and encouraged to settle in the Baltic, Ukraine, Siberia, the far east, Central Asia, and the Transcaucasus—partly in order to further the Stalinist ideal of a transcendent Soviet people and partly to provide workers needed to run the mines, farms, and factories required by Soviet economic, strategic, and regional planners. By the time of the breakup of the Soviet Union, 80 percent or more of the population of Siberia and the far east were Russian, and the Russian diaspora had become very pronounced in most of the Soviet Union's successor states beyond the borders of the Russian Federation.

In 1989, without any sense of ever having emigrated from their homeland, some 25 million Russians suddenly found themselves to be ethnic minorities in newly independent countries (**Table 3.1**). The largest number was in Ukraine, where more than 11.3 million Russians made up 22 percent of the population of the new state. In Kazakhstan, Russians represented nearly 38 percent of the population. Overall, the sudden collapse of the Soviet Union created havoc in the lives of many families, who suddenly found themselves living "abroad." During the 1990s, a good number of them decided to migrate back to the Russian Federation. In the Transcaucasus, where the proportion of Russians was generally lower than elsewhere, strongly nationalistic governments of the successor states quickly enacted policies that encouraged Russians to

TABLE 3.1 The Russian Diaspora		
Republic	Number of Russians	Russians as % of Total Population of Republic
Ukraine	11,356,000	22.1
Belarus	1,342,000	14.2
Estonia	475,000	30.3
Latvia	906,000	34.0
Lithuania	344,000	9.4
Moldova	562,000	14.0
Georgia	341,000	6.3
Armenia	51,600	1.6
Azerbaijan	392,000	5.6
Kazakhstan	6,228,000	37.8
Uzbekistan	1,653,000	8.3
Kyrgyzstan	917,000	21.5
Turkmenistan	334,000	9.5
Tajikistan	388,000	7.6

Source: D. B. Shaw, *Russia in the Modern World.* Malden, MA: Blackwell, 1999, p. 256.

leave—reducing the number of Russian-language schools, for example. In Central Asia too, nationalistic policies were enacted with similar effect. Kyrgyzstan, Turkmenistan, and Uzbekistan dropped the use of the Cyrillic alphabet, deliberately creating institutional barriers for Russian speakers. Civil war in Tajikistan led to the departure of 80 percent of that country's Russian-speaking population within just three years of its independence from the Soviet Union. About 17 percent of the Russian population of Kyrgyzstan departed in that same period, mainly because of the withdrawal of the Russian Federation's defense industry enterprises and military installations. Altogether, almost 4 million ethnic Russians migrated to the Russian Federation from the other Soviet successor states between 1989 and 1999.

Meanwhile, an even greater number of people emigrated from the Russian Federation and the other successor states to countries elsewhere in the world. The annual loss, at about 100,000 per year, is not particularly significant in terms of raw numbers. What is significant, however, is the fact that most are well-educated individuals, and some are among the most talented. The countries of the former Soviet Union have thus been suffering something of a "brain drain," with the principal beneficiaries being Germany, Israel, and the United States.

Nationalisms

The prelude to the breakup of the Soviet Union involved not only a massive restructuring of the Soviet economy through radical economic and governmental reforms (*perestroiyka*) but also the direct democratic participation of the republics in shaping these reforms through open discussions, freer dissemination of information, and independent elections (*glasnost*). Both *perestroiyka* and *glasnost* were initiated by Mikhail Gorbachev when he became the Soviet leader in 1985. *Glasnost* resulted in the removal of restrictions that had been placed on the legal formation of national identity by Stalin. By 1987, grassroots national movements were already emerging, first in the Baltic republics and later in the Transcaucasus, Ukraine, and Central Asia. In 1989 *perestroiyka* and *glasnost* together culminated in the breakup of the Soviet Union. The Soviet Union's federated structure enabled the relatively peaceful breakup of the country, but the demise of a strong central government and the exhaustion of state socialism as an ideology opened the way for a reemergence of nationalist political identities based on ethnic divisions. At the same time, the end of the Cold War meant that localized territorial disputes between ethnic groups no longer had to be suppressed for fear that they might spark a world war.

Within the Russian Federation, there are approximately 27 million non-Russians. This number encompasses 92 different ethno-national groups (though 25 of these groups include minority peoples of the north, who together number fewer than 200,000). Although most of the larger ethno-national groups enjoy a fair degree of administrative territorial autonomy within the Russian Federation, secessionist and irredentist claims are numerous (**Figure 3.25**). One of the most troubled regions is the North Caucasus, a complex mosaic of mountain peoples with strong territorial and ethnic identities. Soon after the breakup of the Soviet Union, Ingushetia broke away from the Chechen-Ingush Republic, and Chechnya promptly declared independence from the Russian Federation (see Geography Matters: Chechnya, p. 138). The Ingush themselves have irredentist claims to parts of neighboring North Ossetia; the autonomous *oblast* of South Ossetia, in Georgia, declared its intent to secede from Georgia and unite with North Ossetia in the Russian Federation—a move that resulted in a brief civil war in 1992. Beyond the North Caucasus, the two most powerful nationalisms are in Tatarstan (where Tartars have irredentist claims on neighboring Bashkortostan) and in the area around Lake Baykal (where ethnic Buryats have called for the reunification of the Ust'-Ordin and Agin Buryat autonomous *okrugs* with the Republic of Buryatia).

In the Transcaucasus, the big trouble spot is the region of Nagorno-Karabakh, in Azerbaijan. For many years, this region was dominated by Armenians. At one time the region's population had been about 90 percent Armenian. By the mid-1980s the population of Nagorno-Karabakh was still more than 75 percent Armenian, and *glasnost* brought the opportunity for them to formally petition for secession from Azerbaijan.

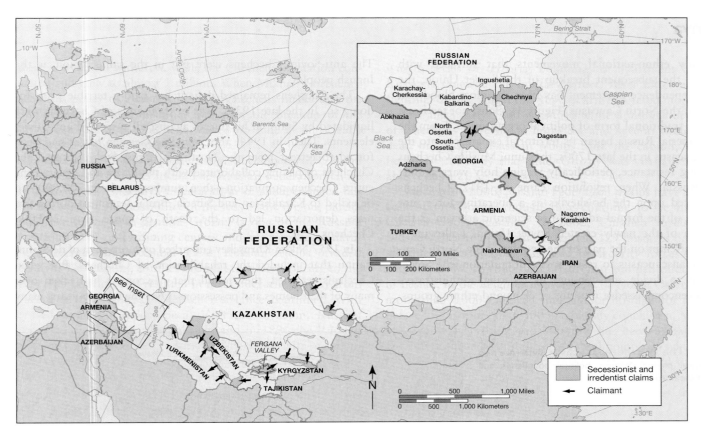

FIGURE 3.25 Secessionist and irredentist claims in the post-Soviet states The politics of multiculturalism is especially important in the Transcaucasus and Central Asia, where long-standing ethnic tensions, suppressed by the Soviet
regime, have found renewed energy and expression. (*Source:* Redrawn from G. Smith, *The Post-Soviet States: Mapping the Politics of Transition.*
London: Arnold, 1999, p. 129.)

When the petition was refused, pent-up anger was unleashed in both Azerbaijan and
Armenia against ethnic minorities from the other state. Riots, pogroms, and forced
migrations quickly led to civil war, the outcome of which
was that Armenian military forces secured Nagorno-
Karabakh and established a militarized corridor as a lifeline
to Armenia. Russian Federation armed forces were invited
to serve a peacekeeping role in the region, and today a tense
standoff prevails. The political situation in Azerbaijan is of
broad international interest because of the 1760-kilometer
(1094-mile) pipeline from Baku, Azerbaijan, to Ceyhan,
Turkey, that opened in 2005 to carry oil from U.S. and
European companies' oilfields in the Caspian Sea to Western markets via the Mediterranean (**Figure 3.26**).

Glasnost also led to an evanescence of ethno-national
movements in Central Asia. Tajikistan has been beset by
conflict between Tajik and Uzbek "patriots." A brief civil
war ended in 1993 when the ruling government accepted
intervention by the Russian Federation, acting to assert its
claims to a special sphere of influence in the Near Abroad.
Tajikistan now relies on the Russian Federation army to
defend its borders. Since 1993 there have been frequent
military skirmishes with a force of some 5000 rebels who
are based in Afghanistan with the tacit support of the
Afghan government and the active support of Islamic fun-
damentalists. Elsewhere in Central Asia, one of the most

FIGURE 3.26 Oil pipeline The BTC (Baku-Tbilisi-Ceyhan) Oil Pipeline was
opened in 2006. It was one of the most expensive oil projects in history, costing approximately $3.6 billion. The main backer was British Petroleum, in a consortium that included
Unocal and Turkish Petroleum Inc.

opening up of foreign trade and investment, and participation in international economic organizations. All of these require radical changes in institutional, organizational, and technological structures and processes, along with equally radical changes in political and cultural life and in the behavior and lifestyles of different socioeconomic groups.

The ethno-national movements described in the previous section represent one of the major regional dimensions of the problems involved in the transition from state socialism to market economies. If democracy is to flourish, the new states must be able to guarantee territorial integrity, physical security, and effective governance. In some regions, secessionist and irredentist tensions are clearly undermining these preconditions for democracy. A second and more widespread problem concerns the vitality of civil society. **Civil society** involves the presence of a network of voluntary organizations, business organizations, pressure groups, and cultural traditions that operate independently of the state and its political institutions. A vibrant civil society is an essential precondition for **pluralist democracy**—a society in which members of diverse groups continue to participate in their traditional cultures and special interests. The Soviet state did not tolerate a civil society. During the period of *glasnost*, autonomous social movements did emerge in some of the coalfield regions and cities of the Soviet Union, and they played a key part in challenging the legitimacy and moral authority of the Soviet state. Since the breakup of the Soviet Union, however, such movements have lost energy and focus, and civil society has begun to flourish only in parts of the former Soviet empire that have reoriented themselves toward Europe. In the countries covered in this chapter, civil society is emerging only slowly, and in some regions—especially in Central Asia—democratic reform has been so limited that the emergence of civil society has been hard to detect.

Problems of Economic and Social Transformation

One immediate consequence of the breakup of the Soviet Union was that the collective natural resource base was fragmented among the new states. The states of Central Asia and the Transcaucasus were particularly affected, their smaller territories and less varied physiography leaving each of them with a relatively narrow resource base—though the oil and natural gas reserves of Central Asia are a major asset. Kazakhstan has the bulk of the oil reserves, while the natural gas fields are mainly to the south, in Turkmenistan and Uzbekistan. Proven oil reserves in the Central Asian geosyncline, around and beneath the Caspian Sea, amount to between 15 and 31 billion barrels, but estimates of the potential reserves run between 60 and 140 billion barrels. Only the oilfields of the Persian Gulf states (see Chapter 4) and Siberia are larger. This represents a tremendous economic asset for the Central Asian states. Exploiting these assets is beset with difficulties, however. Most of the states involved are effectively landlocked, which means that expensive pipelines have to be constructed before the oilfields and gasfields can be fully developed. But pipeline construction and routing are both risky and contentious because of political tensions and instability in the region, along with the competing claims and interests of consumers and investors from different geographic markets—principally the Russian Federation vis-à-vis Europe and North America.

The Russian Federation has lost free access to these oil and gas reserves and to the large uranium reserves of Tajikistan and Uzbekistan. Nevertheless, Russia still has a broad resource base, with huge reserves of coal, lignite, vanadium, manganese, and iron. It also has substantial reserves of oil and gas and has shown that it is willing to use them in order to exert geopolitical influence on the Near Abroad—such as in early 2006 when it briefly cut off gas supplies to Ukraine and threatened a fourfold increase in gas prices in the wake of a pro-Western shift in Ukraine government.

In addition, a great deal of regional change has been triggered by the transformation from state socialism to market economies. It should be stressed that these changes have been very uneven in their impact, simply because market reform itself has been uneven, both from one economic sector to another and from one state to another. In broad terms, market reforms took place more rapidly, and were more extensive, in the Russian Federation. At the other extreme were the states of the Transcaucasus, where political leadership has been more conservative and less reform-minded. In Central Asia, economies remain effectively state-run.

Among the first components of post-Soviet economic systems to be privatized were retail trade and public food services. In the Russian Federation the tempo of privatization was left very much to the discretion of local authorities, who were the "owners" of these services under the Soviet system. The most rapid privatization took place in the largest cities, especially those in the western part of the federation, including Moscow and St. Petersburg. The privatization of the manufacturing industry took longer to organize, mainly because the Russian Federation wanted to avoid making state assets available to foreign investors at fire-sale prices. The privatization of industry has been very uneven. There remain significant pockets of collectively owned and state-run enterprises, many of them inefficient and undercapitalized. Meanwhile, the growing private sector in retailing and services has been only loosely regulated, resulting in some rapacious aspects of everyday life.

In the countryside, market reform has meant dismantling the collective and state farms, and in some regions large farms have been decollectivized and split into a multitude of small holdings of just a few hectares each, leading to significant changes in rural landscapes. A good example is the countryside surrounding the village of Chocti, in Georgia (**Figure 3.27**). In general, however, rural reform has been slow. Most of the land remains under some form of collective ownership, and there have been relatively few

FIGURE 3.27 The landscape of decollectivization This figure shows the layout of the village of Chocti in eastern Georgia (a) before and (b) after the decollectivization of the early 1990s. (*Source:* Bradshaw, M. J. [ed.], *Geography and Transition in the Post-Soviet Republics.* New York: John Wiley & Sons, 1997, p. 114.)

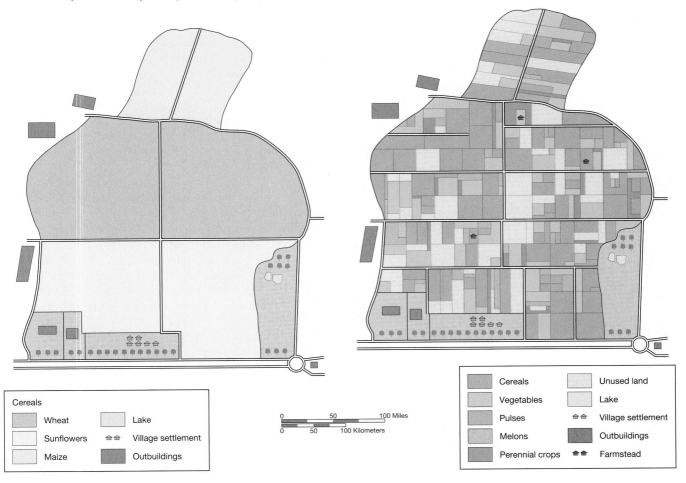

Cereals

Wheat	Lake
Sunflowers	Village settlement
Maize	Outbuildings

0   50   100 Miles
0   50   100 Kilometers

Cereals	Unused land
Vegetables	Lake
Pulses	Village settlement
Melons	Outbuildings
Perennial crops	Farmstead

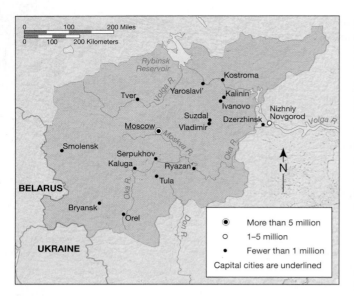

FIGURE 3.28 The Central Region Reference map showing principal physical features, political boundaries, and major cities of this region.

progressive changes in farming practice. Shortages of machinery are an obstacle to the modernization of agriculture. Output of agricultural products has fallen everywhere, as people have turned to semisubsistence forms of farming as an insurance against the risks of post-Soviet transition. A 1999 report issued by the Russian Federation's ministry of agriculture showed that the extent of farmland shrank by 35.2 million hectares, to 84.5 percent of the 1990 level. Years of out-migration by the young and enterprising have left behind a population that is frequently elderly and conservative, used to the Soviet way of doing things and unwilling or unable to take the risk of establishing private farms. Both politically and socially, the countryside remains very conservative and is still dominated by farm managers and officials who derive from the old regime.

Regional Development

Although the breakup of the Soviet Union and the transition toward market economies are beginning to modify patterns of regional development, at present the core regions of this world region remain broadly the same as under state socialism and, before that, Imperial Russia. The principal core region is the Central Region that extends for a radius of approximately 400 kilometers (248 miles) around Moscow. A secondary core area, developed around a long-standing industrial base, exists in the Urals. Between them, these core regions contain 11 of the 13 largest Russian Federation cities and about half of the total population of the Russian Federation.

The Central Region The Central Region (**Figure 3.28**) was the hearth of the Muscovite state, the base from which its growing power thrust along the rivers in all directions toward distant seas. The industrial roots of the region go back to the 1600s, when various early industries, drawing on local resources of flax, hemp, hides, wool, and bog iron, developed to serve the needs of the growing capital, Moscow. By the 1700s, the region had developed a specialization in textiles; and with the onset of Russia's industrial revolution in the 1800s, the textile industry expanded and was joined by a broad range of engineering and manufacturing. Although the Central Region has no significant sources of energy (apart from low-grade lignite and peat deposits that can be converted into electricity in power stations), Soviet economic planners regarded the region as pivotal to their industrialization policies. Significant imports of coal, oil, gas, and electricity were used to develop a broad economic base. The region was also key to the Soviet Union's drive for technological supremacy, and a considerable proportion of the country's leading scientific research and development institutes were established as part of the Central Region's massive military-industrial complex.

Today, the Central Region is highly urbanized, with about 85 percent of the population living in towns and cities. Moscow (population 9,300,000 in 2005) dominates the entire region, but other significant centers include Dzerzhinsk (285,000), Ivanovo (474,000), Nizhniy Novgorod (1,460,000), Ryazan' (536,000), Serpukhov (139,000), Smolensk (355,000), Tula (532,000), Vladimir (339,000), and Yaroslavl' (629,000). The region accounts for about 80 percent of the Russian Federation's textile manufactures. Cotton textiles are most important and are produced mainly in towns along the Klyazma valley between Moscow and Nizhniy Novgorod and at Ivanovo. Woolens are manufactured in and around Moscow; synthetic fibers are produced in Kalinin, Serpukhov, and Vladimir; and the ancient linen industry survives at Kostroma. Engineering, automobile and truck manufacture, machine tools, chemicals, electrical equipment, and food processing are also important. Overall the Central Region accounts for about 20 percent of the Russian Federation's industrial production.

In spite of the high degree of urbanization and industrialization, much of the region has a rural flavor. About 25 percent of the Central Region remains forested, and there are numerous lakes and marshy areas. The traditional staple crop of the region was rye, but when the railways made it possible to import cheaper grain, farmers

FIGURE 3.29 Moscow Red Square.

turned to industrial crops, such as flax, and to potatoes, sugar beets, fodder crops, dairying, and market gardening. Around rural settlements, there are orchards of apples, cherries, pears, and plums. Beyond these traditional rural landscapes, the geography of the Central Region is being significantly rewritten by the transition to an open, internationalized market economy. The effects of the transition are very uneven. On the positive side, the gateway situation of the Moscow region, with good transport and communication links to other regions and countries, is attracting a good deal of foreign direct investment, while the region's high-tech labor force and research institutes have also been attractive to investors. On the negative side, reduced domestic demand and competition from cheap imports have had severe adverse effects on the region's smokestack industries, especially textiles, machine building, and engineering. Among the places worst affected by deindustrialization are the eastern parts of the Moscow region, Bransk, Kostroma, Vladimir, and Yaroslavl'.

Major City: Moscow Moscow is situated at the center of the vast Russian Plain, on the Moskva River, a tributary of the Oka, which in turn leads to the Volga. The city's growth is reflected in its layout by a series of ring roads: the Boulevard Ring, the Garden Ring (both following the line of former fortifications), the Greater Moscow Ring Railway, and the Moscow Circular Beltway. Radial boulevards penetrate these ring roads, converging toward the ancient hub of the city, the Kremlin, built as a fortified palace complex in the 14th century and subsequently used as the seat of government for Russia, the Soviet Union, and, now, the Russian Federation. Next to the Kremlin is the famous Red Square, the ceremonial center of the capital that is anchored at its southern end by the Cathedral of St. Basil the Blessed, built between 1554 and 1560 by Ivan the Terrible to commemorate the defeat of the Tatars (**Figure 3.29**).

Moscow's inner city differs from large European and North American cities in that it does not contain any significant slums, nor does it contain a modern central business district. Rather, it contains a mixture of buildings representative of every period of the city's development: churches and institutional buildings from the 15th through the 19th centuries interspersed with Soviet-era offices, apartment buildings, squares, and boulevards that gradually replaced the city's slums and dilapidated buildings from the 1920s onward. Beyond the Garden Ring as far as the Ring Railway is a zone of 18th- and 19th-century development—including the principal railway stations and freight yards, factories, and associated housing—that has been the target of extensive urban renewal projects. Here also are many of the larger institutional buildings of the Soviet era, including most of the distinctive "wedding-cake" skyscrapers of the Stalinist period.

The outer zones of the city, beyond the Ring Railway, are almost entirely the product of the post-World War II growth, when the built-up area of the city increased more than tenfold (**Figure 3.30**). Immediately beyond the Ring Railway are the *mikrorayoni* of the 1950s, dominated

FIGURE 3.30 Suburban Moscow The suburbs of Moscow are dominated by apartment buildings, interspersed with small districts of light industry.

by five- to nine-story apartment buildings of yellowish brick. Farther out, larger factories and standardized high-rise apartment blocks of precast concrete dominate the cityscape, while in the outermost zones are scattered a series of satellite industrial towns amid open land and forest.

The transition to a market economy has already left its mark on Moscow in several ways. The combination of a newly emerging wealthy class, together with a chaotic planning situation, has sparked a spate of uncontrolled housing construction. Some has taken place within the borders of the city but a good deal of the recent growth has been in the forest protection belt, where speculative developments, mostly funded by foreign companies, have sprung up, providing expensive housing in community-style developments with tight security. New office buildings for transnational companies and new, Western-style stores have begun to appear in the center of the city, consuming many of the green sites created by Soviet planners. Meanwhile, a sharp rise in the number of private automobiles (from approximately 0.5 million vehicles in 1985 to almost 2 million by 2005) has led to an equally sharp rise in traffic congestion and unprecedented strain on the existing road infrastructure.

The greatest impacts of the transition to a market economy, however, are the social and economic consequences. Formerly a leading industrial center, by 2005 Moscow had slipped to 14th place among the Russian Federation's economic regions in terms of industrial production. The decline of the traditional industrial sector in Moscow has been mitigated largely by the rise of new sectors in the economy, particularly in tourism, retailing, and banking. Moscow has quickly developed as the Russian Federation's principal center for financial and business services, which in turn has attracted considerable foreign investment and many joint ventures. This has also led to the emergence of new culture and entertainment industries, while the overall climate of change has fostered a proliferation of small, private enterprises. The pace of change, however, has far outstripped the capacity of the city's authorities to regulate and control it, so that the positive aspects of transition have been accompanied by dramatic increases in social polarization and crime and a backlog in providing adequate infrastructure for ground and air transportation and telecommunications.

Major City: St. Petersburg   St. Petersburg is a large metropolitan area (population 5.14 million in 2005), located some 650 kilometers (403 miles) from Moscow, at the eastern end of the Gulf of Finland. As such, it falls well outside the Central Region proper. Nevertheless, it must be considered as an extension of the Central Region, an industrial, cultural, and administrative metropolis, closely tied to the regional development of Moscow and the Central Region. Most of the surrounding northwest region forms part of the original Russian homeland, though the area bordering on the Gulf of Finland was long disputed. When it was finally annexed to Russia by Peter the Great at the beginning of the 18th century, Peter decided to build a new capital city—St. Petersburg—on a swampy site at the mouth of the River Neva. Like Venice, Italy, St. Petersburg rests on countless wooden piles to prevent it from subsiding into its marshes. It was built at the cost of thousands of human lives, but the tsar was determined to create an imperial capital to rival those of continental Europe. He also wanted St. Petersburg to be Russia's "window on Europe," exposing Russia to new ideas and technology.

Connections to Moscow—first by canal, and later by railway—allowed St. Petersburg to flourish as Russia's chief trading port, and the city quickly became a cultural and intellectual center. With the Soviet revolution of 1917, however, Moscow was reinstated as the capital city. Anti-German sentiment, meanwhile, had caused St. Petersburg to be renamed as Petrograd. The city's trading function withered under state socialism's doctrine of national economic self-sufficiency, but Soviet planners quickly developed Petrograd—renamed again as Leningrad in 1924—into a key component of the Soviet military-industrial complex. During the Soviet era, the city was mostly a manufacturing center, the principal industries being electrical and power machinery, shipbuilding and repair, armaments, electronics, chemicals, and high-quality engineering. The city suffered terribly in World War II, with an estimated 1 million of its residents dying from hunger or disease while the city was under siege by the German army for 872 days.

In spite of seven decades of socialism and more than a decade of hardship and disorganization in the transition to a post-Soviet society, St. Petersburg remains impressive and inspiring. The city was home not only to Peter the Great but also to Dostoevsky, Nijinsky, and Lenin. The great composers Rimsky-Korsakov, Mussorgsky, Borodin, and Tchaikovsky are buried in the city's Tikhvin Cemetery. But it is the city's core of imperial architecture and urban design that provides its sense of place and symbolizes its sophistication. Often called "The Venice of the North" because of the opulence of its architecture and its canals, St. Petersburg was deliberately fashioned in the Grand Manner as a European-style capital city. The tsars' architects were able to lay out their work unrestricted by any legacy of old streets or buildings. Over two centuries, they collectively created a marvelous set piece of urban design, with imposing public buildings, imperial palaces, and churches in the baroque, rococo, and classical styles, all laid out around impressive plazas and along broad boulevards, all surrounded by large, fashionable residences (**Figure 3.31**).

FIGURE 3.31 St. Petersburg In a drive to make St. Petersburg Europe's most imposing capital, Catherine the Great (1762–96) and Alexander I (1801–25) commissioned dozens of elaborate projects in the center of the city.

Today, the city's imperial past is very visible in the Grand Design of the core area on the south bank of the River Neva—the Palace Square, the Admiralty building with its landmark elegant spire, and the Winter Palace, which now houses the Hermitage Museum, a treasure house of fine art of worldwide significance that originated in 1764 as the private collection of Catherine the Great. The Soviet past is visible, as in every other Russian city, in the extensive industrial and residential suburbs of standardized high-rise apartment blocks of precast concrete. Renamed once more as St. Petersburg, the city has faced a tough period of readjustment as its older military-industrial base experienced a sharp decline in fortune. Crime and corruption also emerged as striking features of the post-Soviet city. Nevertheless, St. Petersburg is once again poised to take advantage of its gateway situation, while its imperial legacy makes it an attractive international tourist destination. Already, the city handles about 35 percent of the Russian Federation's imports and about 30 percent of its exports. Although the city's infrastructure badly needs upgrading, its history and its European ambience are beginning to prove attractive not only to tourists but also to Western investors.

FIGURE 3.32 The Southern Urals Reference map showing principal physical features, political boundaries, and major cities of the southern Urals.

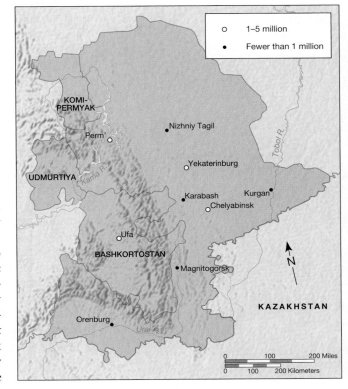

The Urals

The Urals have been economically important to Russia since the early 1700s, when Peter the Great established iron-smelting works in Yekaterinburg and Nizhniy Tagil using local ore and charcoal. In addition to iron ore, the Urals contain a wealth of mineral resources, including asbestos, bauxite, chromium, copper, magnesium and potassium salts, and zinc. The energy resources of the southern Urals include extensive low-grade bituminous coal and lignite deposits, the Volga-Urals oilfield (which extends southwestward from the western foothills of the Urals to the Saratov area in the Volga region), and a major natural gas field at the southern end of the mountains, near Orenburg (**Figure 3.32**).

The rise of the Urals as an economic core region can be traced to Stalin's industrialization drive of the late 1920s, when Soviet economic planners established a major industrial complex focused on mining, ferrous and nonferrous metallurgy, and heavy engineering. The discovery of the Volga-Urals oilfield in the 1930s added chemicals and petrochemicals as well as a new source of energy. At about the same time, Soviet planners decided to bring in high-grade coking coal from the Kuznetsk basin in central Siberia, 2000 kilometers (1240 miles) to the east, to fully exploit the vast reserves of iron ore in the Urals. Trains returning to the

Kuznetsk coalfields were loaded with iron ore from the Urals, thus facilitating the creation of an iron and steel complex in the Kuznetsk basin. This arrangement was known as the Urals-Kuznetsk Combine.

During World War II, a substantial amount of additional industry was moved to the Urals from European Russia so it would be safely out of range of German air attack. After the war, the Urals were further developed as a key region of the Soviet military-industrial complex, and most of the region was closed to foreigners until 1990. Five of the 10 secret cities of the Soviet Union's "nuclear archipelago" for weapons research and production were located in the Urals: Sverdlovsk-44, Sverdlovsk-45, Chelyabinsk-65, Chelyabinsk-70, and Zlatoust-36 (the numbers are their postal codes).

Today, the southern Urals remain a key component of the Russian Federation's economy. The region is highly urbanized: 75 percent of its 20 million people live in cities, the largest of which is Yekaterinburg (population 1.4 million in 2005), a railway, metallurgical, and heavy engineering center. Perm' (population 1.1 million) has a similar economic profile, while Ufa (1.1 million) is a center of oil refining, chemical manufacture, and heavy engineering. Chelyabinsk (1.2 million), Nizhniy Tagil (409,000), and Magnitogorsk (427,000) are all iron and steel centers with associated heavy engineering complexes. Many of these industries, however, have fared poorly in the transition from state socialism to market capitalism. Nonferrous metallurgy, petrochemicals, and the oil industry have attracted foreign investment and provided a source of export revenues for the Russian Federation, but the iron and steel and heavy engineering industries, with their obsolescent plants, have been noncompetitive and unattractive. Many of the defense-related industries, meanwhile, have suffered as a result of the inability of the Russian Federation to fund them at a level comparable to that of the Soviet era.

In many communities, the economic hardship resulting from the decline of smokestack industries has been compounded by the legacy of pollution. Take, for example, the small town Karabash (population 15,000 in 2005), about two hours south of Yekaterinburg in the foothills of the Urals. The Karabash Copper Smelting Works, established in the 1940s to produce copper for ammunition, went on to produce copper for electrical equipment until 1987, when it was closed by the government because the plant's productivity was too low and its hazardous emissions too high. But the plant was reopened in 1998, when the town's residents had become desperate for jobs and the government had become desperate for tax revenues from the region's copper. Air pollution has returned, compounding the environmental hazards from the 15-meter (49-foot) heaps of slag that line the main road, encircle the factory, and spill over into backyards. Slag, laced with lead, arsenic, and cadmium, is the waste from the copper smelting furnaces after raw copper is extracted from ore. Two-thirds of the children in Karabash suffer from lead, arsenic, or cadmium poisoning, and a 1995 government study found that they also suffer from at least twice the rates of congenital defects; disorders of the central nervous system; and diseases of the blood, glands, and the immune and metabolic systems compared with children in nearby towns.

Gender and Inequality

When the Soviet system collapsed in 1989, economic liberalization produced chaos, hyperinflation, and industrial collapse; the usual social and economic safety nets were dismantled; and social and economic upheaval was accompanied by an intensification of inequality. In the early 1990s, industrial production in Russia fell by nearly half, while hyper-inflation devalued people's savings, leaving many destitute. Then in the late 1990s there was a deep crisis of national finance as a result of Russia's weak trading record. The consequences for many parts of the Russian population included rising mortality rates, especially among older men, attributed in part to the stresses surrounding economic dislocation, in part to increasing poverty, and in part to the decline in the provision of health care in post-Soviet Russia. There has been an increase in the rate of industrial accidents and alcohol-related illnesses, and a rapid escalation of infant mortality rates. Today, the modest levels of material welfare to which families became accustomed under state socialism (**Figure 3.33**) are increasingly difficult to sustain. For people throughout the region, real income has fallen significantly, and personal savings have been eroded or disappeared altogether. For many, employment has become a part-time or informal affair.

Amid this upheaval, the role of women changed significantly. Women, together with all other groups discriminated against under the tsars, were "freed" by the 1917 Bolshevik revolution, which declared them equal and granted them all social and political rights. In reality, however, the Soviet political system became male-dominated, its legislative organs developing into a rigid structure based on proportional representation. After the collapse of the Soviet system, many women began to take up new opportunities presented by the transition to a market economy, venturing into small trade and opening their own businesses. Some women also took advantage of opportunities in newly established firms, quickly climbing through the ranks to become managers. Today, the number of women holding full-time jobs (about 45 percent) in Russia is on par with the developed countries. Nevertheless, while women's wages had been, on average, about 70 percent of men's during the 1980s, they had dropped to 52 percent by 1999, recovering only to 64 percent by 2005. If any group has borne the brunt of falling living standards and quality of life, it has been women. The transition to new market economies has cost women many of the benefits they enjoyed under state socialism—such as child care, health care, equal pay, and political representation. Between 1985 and 2005, the number of working women in the Russian Federation fell by 24 percent. Another area in which the women of the region have clearly regressed is political representation. Under state socialism, quotas ensured that one-third of the seats in parliament went to women. In 2005, only 3.4 percent of the seats in the Russian Federation's upper parliament were held by women, and there were no women in government at the ministerial level.

Many women who might have hoped for a clerical or professional job under state socialism now find themselves forced into unskilled work in order to make ends meet while caring for children and keeping their family together. Often, this means working in the unprotected realm of the informal economy. For some, it means being drawn into the illegal activities of the informal sector. A great deal of media attention has been given to the fact that tens of thousands of women have been forced into prostitution, often after being trafficked abroad on the pretense that they would work as maids or waitresses.

Regional Inequality The transition to market economies has meanwhile intensified regional inequality. Regional inequality was in fact part of the legacy of the Soviet era. Soviet patterns of economic development came to be characterized by regional specialization and by core-periphery contrasts. One reason for this was that principles of scientific rationality and the primacy of national economic growth took precedence over ideological principles of spatial equality. As a result, Soviet planners revised upward the optimal size of cities and applied the logic of agglomeration economies to regional planning, developing territorial production complexes. Another reason was that centralized economic planning was unable to redress the resulting regional inequalities because of conservatism and compartmentalization throughout the Soviet economic system. Regional resource allocations were guided not by principles of equity or efficiency but by *incrementalism*, whereby successive rounds of budgeting were based on previous patterns of funding.

The transformation to market economies has intensified the unevenness of patterns of regional economic development. Market forces have introduced a much greater disparity between the economic well-being of regional winners

FIGURE 3.33 A Russian family with their material possessions The Kapralov family from Suzdal, Russia, photographed with their possessions outside their home in the mid-1990s, represents a statistically average Russian family in terms of family size, residence, and income. Less than a month after Eugeny Kapralov posed for this photograph with his family and possessions, he was beaten to death by unknown assailants who smashed the windows of his car in what was presumed to be a robbery.

FIGURE 3.34 Prigorsk, Siberia Two men sit in the sun, most likely drunk and with no hope of employment. The town was built in the early 1980s around a top-secret uranium-processing plant, but with the collapse of the Soviet Union the plant closed. Eighty percent of the town's population has left, and the remainder have few prospects. Apartment blocks stand abandoned with no water, windows, or heating in a region where the temperature reaches –30°C in winter.

and losers while at the same time allowing for the more volatile spatial effects of the ebbs and flows of investment capital. After 17 years of transition, many of the regional winners are the same as under state socialism. This is partly because of the natural advantages of certain regions and partly because of the initial advantage of economic development inherited from Soviet-era regional planning. Four different kinds of regions have prospered through the transformation to date: gateway regions, natural resource regions, rich agricultural regions, and established high-tech manufacturing regions.

Gateway regions are those centered on metropolitan areas that have inherited good transportation and communication links not only within the former Soviet empire but also with Europe and beyond. Moscow and St. Petersburg are the most important, but most major metropolitan regions are also in this category, as are Vladivostok, on the Pacific coast, and Kaliningrad, on the Baltic. Prosperous natural resource regions include the oil-rich geosyncline of Central Asia, Magadan (northeastern Siberia), Sakha (Yakutia), and Tyumen' (western Siberia). The best-endowed agricultural regions have also prospered, partly because of their natural advantages of better soils and climate and partly because these attributes have attracted the greatest levels of privatization and capital investment. These regions are mostly in the mixed forest and the wooded steppe west of the Urals and in the niche of subtropical farming in western Georgia, on the shores of the Black Sea. Finally, the established high-tech manufacturing regions that have prospered most are those with major research institutes and other facilities associated with the Soviet military-industrial complex. Many of these were located in the gateway regions of Moscow, St. Petersburg, and Nizhniy Novgorod, but others include Chelyabinsk, Samara, Saratov, and Voronezh.

In contrast, three different kinds of regions have experienced decreasing levels of prosperity through the transformation to date. The first consists of regions of armed territorial conflict (such as North Ossetia, Ingushetia, and Chechnya in the North Caucasus; Nagorno-Karabakh; and Tajikistan). A second consists of resource-poor peripheral regions—mainly in the European north, Siberia, and the far east (**Figure 3.34**). The third consists of "smokestack" regions of declining heavy industry. These include many of the core industrial regions of the old command economy, including much of the Central Region—the area that extends about 400 kilometers (248 miles) from Moscow in all directions—Volga-Vyatka (the Volga region), the Urals, and southern Siberia.

SUMMARY AND CONCLUSIONS

The Russian Federation, Central Asia, and the Transcaucasus is a world region very much in transition. After more than seven decades under the Soviet system, the Russian Federation, Belarus, and the Soviet Union's other successor states in Central Asia and the Transcaucasus are now experiencing transitions to new forms of economic organization and new ways of life. These transitions are taking place at different speeds in different places, and with rather uncertain outcomes. It is clear, though, that the process is having a significant impact on local economies and ways of life throughout the region. The region itself, meanwhile, is still struggling to find its new place in the world economy. Some of the old ties among the countries of the region have been weakened or reorganized, as have the interdependencies with Ukraine, Moldova, and the Baltic states. All of the new, post-Soviet states have joined the capitalist world system in semiperipheral roles, and all of them have to find markets for uncompetitive products while at the same time engaging in domestic economic reform. Inevitably, patterns of regional interdependence have been disrupted and destabilized.

The Russian Federation, as the principal successor state to the Soviet Union, remains a nuclear power with a large standing army, but its future geopolitical standing remains uncertain. It has a formidable arsenal of sophisticated weaponry; a large, talented, and discontented population; a huge wealth of natural resources;

and a pivotal strategic location in the center of the Eurasian land-mass. Now freed from the economic constraints of state social-ism, the Russian Federation stands to benefit a great deal by establishing economic linkages with the expanding world econ-omy. Similarly, the collapse of the Communist Party has removed a major barrier to domestic economic and political development. The Russian Federation also has an ample labor force and a domestic market large enough to form the basis of a formidable economy. At present, the Russian Federation's economy is shrink-ing as it withdraws from the centrally planned model. Yet, although embarrassed by the disintegration of the Soviet Union and bankrupt by the subsequent dislocation to economic develop-ment, the Russian Federation is still accorded a great deal of influence in international affairs. The embarrassment and insol-vency may also prove in the long run to spur the Russian Federa-tion once again to contend for great-power status.

Nevertheless, it will be some time before the Russian Federa-tion can contend for world-power status. The latter years of the Soviet system left its industry with obsolete technology, low-grade product lines, and a shoddy infrastructure. The economy now faces a massive task of modernization before it can approach its full potential. The Russian Federation must also renew civil society and the institutions of business and democracy after 70 years of state socialism. The partial breakdown of constitutional order has under-mined respect for the law, and organized crime has flourished amid the factionalism and ideological confusion of the government. These problems could have serious implications for the future world order: A weak Russian Federation invites geopolitical instability.

KEY TERMS

chernozem (p. 116)
civil society (p. 140)
dry farming (p. 116)
market economy (p. 131)

mikrorayon (p. 127)
monoculture (p. 119)
monsoon (p. 113)
nationalization (p. 129)

Near Abroad (p. 132)
permafrost (p. 113)
pluralist democracy (p. 140)
salinization (p. 119)

Silk Road (p. 122)
taiga (p. 114)
territorial production
   complex (p. 129)

REVIEW QUESTIONS

Testing Your Understanding

1. How does the Russian Federation suffer from its location, physical features, and climate? What is unique about the Transcaucasus area in terms of climate?
2. Define: permafrost; tundra; taiga; steppe; chernozem.
3. Why is fur far more than an indulgence in Russia? What role did the fur trade play in the expansion of Russia?
4. Define: soviet; Bolshevik; *perestroika*; *glasnost*.
5. Under Stalin's rule, how did peasant farmers pay for Russia's industrialization and modernization?
6. How did the establishment of the Soviet bloc aid develop-ment of the Soviet Union following World War II? Discuss with regard to technical optimization, industrialization, and military security.
7. What factors led to the breakup of the Soviet empire?
8. What is the Near Abroad? List significant areas.
9. What challenges currently face the Russian Federation?
10. Explain the tensions in Nagorno-Karabakh. What is Russia's role there today?
11. What is a civil society and what does it need in order to flourish?
12. Which flaws in Soviet economic-development practices led to regional inequality? How do market forces reinforce regional inequality today? Which regions benefit as a result?
13. In 1986, what happened at Chernobyl? Today, what policy does the Russian Federation have regarding the storage of nuclear waste?
14. During their transition to a market economy, how are Moscow and St. Petersburg changing in terms of city plan-ning, economic sector activity, and cultural life?

Thinking Geographically

1. How have climate and physical geographic features spurred Russia's imperial expansion?
2. Why was the loss of Ukraine in the west and Georgia in the south so devastating for the Russian Federation? How is the Russian Federation responding to fill its agricultural needs without them? What are the implications for the ongoing conflict in Chechnya?
3. Discuss the environmental degradation of Lake Baykal and the Aral Sea.
4. How do population dynamics in the Transcaucasus or Cen-tral Asian areas of the former Soviet Union compare to those in the Russian Federation? What cultural factors may explain the disparities? What role does voluntary migration play? What might occur to the Russian Federation's dominance of the region if current trends continue?
5. What are some economic and social problems facing the post-Soviet Russian Federation?
6. During the Soviet era, the human population of Siberia's tun-dra and taiga rose sharply. Currently people are leaving the area. Discuss migration in and out of Siberia with regard to natural resource development, industrialization, forced labor, military strategy, and free market forces.
7. Ethnic diversity in Central Asia contributed to the breakup of the Soviet Union. How have national identities been asserted in the decade since the Central Asian republics became inde-pendent countries? What cultural factors serve to unify or separate the states in this region?

FURTHER READING

Bater, J. H., *Russia and the Post-Soviet Scene: A Geographical Perspective*. London: Arnold, 1996.

Billington, J. H., *Russia in Search of Itself*. Washington, DC: Woodrow Wilson Center Press, 2004.

Bradshaw, M., *A New Economic Geography of Russia*. New York: Routledge, 2006.

Brown, A., Kaser, M., and Smith, G. S. (eds.), *The Cambridge Encyclopedia of Russia and the Former Soviet Union*. Cambridge: Cambridge University Press, 1994.

Gilbert, M., *The Routledge Atlas of Russian History*, 3rd ed. New York: Routledge, 2002.

Gwynne, R. N., Klak, T., and Shaw, D. J. B., *Alternative Capitalisms. Geographies of Emerging Regions*. London: Arnold, 2004.

Hønneland, G., *Centre-Periphery Relations in Russia. The Case of the Northwestern Regions*. Burlington, VT: Ashgate, 2001.

Hunter, S. T., *The Transcaucasus in Transition: Nation Building and Conflict*. Washington, DC: Center for Strategic and International Studies, 1994.

Jordan, B. B., and Jordan-Bychkov, T. G., *Siberian Village. Land and Life in the Sakha Republic*. Minneapolis: University of Minnesota Press, 2001.

Marples, D. R., *Belarus: A Denationalized Nation*. London: Harwood Academic, 1999.

Milner-Gulland, R., and Dejevsky, N., *Cultural Atlas of Russia and the Former Soviet Union*. New York: Checkmark Books, 1998.

Oldfield, J., "The Environmental Impact of Transition—A Case Study of Moscow City." *Geographical Journal* 165(1999), 222–31.

Parker, W. H., *The World's Landscapes. The Soviet Union*. Chicago: Aldine, 1969.

Pryde, P. R. (ed.), *Environmental Resources and Constraints in the Former Soviet Republics*. Boulder: Westview Press, 1995.

Service, R., *A History of Modern Russia: From Nicholas II to Vladimir Putin*. Cambridge, MA: Harvard University Press, 2005.

Shaw, D. J. B., *Russia in the Modern World: A New Geography*. Oxford: Blackwell, 1999.

Smith, G. (ed.), *The Nationalities Question in the Post-Soviet States*. London: Longman, 1996.

Smith, G., *The Post-Soviet States: Mapping the Politics of Transition*. London: Arnold, 1999.

Stenning, A., and Bradshaw, M. J., "Globalization and Transformation: The Changing Geography of the Post-Socialist World." In J. Bryson, N. Henry, D. Keeble, and R. Martin (eds.), *The Economic Geography Reader* (pp. 97–107). New York: John Wiley & Sons, 1999.

Stewart, J. M. (ed.), *The Soviet Environment: Problems, Policies and Politics*. Cambridge: Cambridge University Press, 1992.

Turnock, D. (ed.), *Eastern Europe and the Former Soviet Union*. London: Arnold, 2000.

FILM, MUSIC, AND POPULAR LITERATURE

Film

Anna Karenina. Directed by Bernard Rose, 1997. Dramatization of Tolstoy's classic novel.

Baikal—Blue Eye of Siberia. Directed by Iurii Beliankin for Channel Four (U.K.), 1992. Describes the lake and its environmental problems.

Chechnya: A Russian Nightmare. Produced by Jenny Bristow, for Assignment, BBC, 1995. An account of the early years of ethnic strife in Chechnya.

The Cold War. BBC, 1998. Deals with the geopolitics of the Cold War period, 1950–89.

Dirty Money. Produced by Peter Molloy for the BBC, 1994. Documentary on Russia's gangster capitalism.

Dr. Zhivago. Directed by David Lean, 1965. Set just before and during the years following the Bolshevik Revolution in Russia, the film follows the life of Dr. Zhivago as he marries, raises a family, and has his life totally disrupted, first by World War I and then by the revolution.

Journey to Hell. Directed by Basile Grigoriev, for Dispatches, Channel Four (U.K.), 1995. Documentary on Krasnoyarsk 26 and plutonium pollution.

Kazakhstan. Directed by Mark Kidel and Tony Harrison for Channel Four (U.K.), 1994. Describes the land and peoples of Kazakhstan.

Russia: Land of the Tsars. 2003. A 2-hour documentary written for the History Channel by Don Campbell.

Russian Ark. Directed by Aleksandr Sokurov, 2002. The story of a 19th-century French aristocrat, notorious for his scathing memoirs about life in Russia, who travels through the Russian State Hermitage Museum and encounters historical figures from the last 200 years.

Russian Empire. Directed by Leonid Parfyonov, 2004. A series of documentaries made for Russian television to celebrate the tricentennial of the Russian Empire.

Where the Sky Meets the Land. Directed by Frank Müller (2000). Daily life and landscapes in Kyrgyzstan.

Music

Black Pearl. *Air Mail Music: Russian Gypsy Music.* Playasound, 2000.

Ensemble Kolkheti. *Batonebo.* Pan, 1996.

Inna and the Farlanders. *The Dream of Endless Nights.* Shanachie, 1999.

Kino. *Istoria Etogo Mir.* Musicrama, 2000.

Pugacheva, Anna. *Primadonna.* Sintez, 1997.

T.A.T.U. *200km/h in the Wrong Lane.* Interscope, 2002.

Tuva. *Voices from the Center of Asia.* Smithsonian Folkways, 1990.

Usmanova, Yulduz. *The Selection Album.* Blue Flame, 1997.

Popular Literature

Hopkirk, P. *The Great Game. The Struggle for Empire in Central Asia.* New York: Kodansha International, 1992. Tells the story of the 19th-century imperial struggle between agents of Victorian Britain and Tsarist Russia for strategic and economic supremacy over an area stretching from the Caucasus to China.

Kaplan, Robert. *Eastward to Tartary: Travels in the Balkans, the Middle East, and the Caucasus.* New York: Random House, 2000. Geopolitical journalism from one of the best writers in the genre, who is adept at conveying both a sense of place and of the history of the places he describes.

Legg, Stuart. *The Heartland.* New York: Dorset, 1990. An epic history of the grassland empires of inner Asia.

Remnick, David. *Lenin's Tomb.* New York: Vintage Books, 1994. Pulitzer prize-winning account of the Gorbachev era.

Rutherford, E. *Russka: The Novel of Russia.* New York: Ballantine, 2005. An epic novel that tells the story of Russia as it traces the personal stories of successive generations of inhabitants.

Rzhevsky, Nicholas (ed.). *An Anthology of Russian Literature from Earliest Writings to Modern Fiction: Introduction to a Culture.* New York: M. E. Sharpe, 1997. A useful anthology that includes information on related film, video, music, and art collections.

Solzhenitsyn, Alexandr. *The Gulag Archipelago* (3 volumes). New York: Harper and Row, 1974–78. An influential novel that describes the fate of political prisoners in the Soviet Union.

Stewart, John M. *The Nature of Russia.* London: Boxtree, 1992. A comprehensive volume on the natural history of Russia, with coverage of many environmental issues.

Taplin, Mark. *Open Lands: Travels Through Russia's Once Forbidden Places.* New York: Steerforth Press, 1998. An informed travelogue by one of the first writers to visit places and regions that were newly accessible to foreigners after the collapse of the Soviet Union.

Thubron, Colin. *In Siberia.* New York: HarperCollins, 1999. One of the first travel books to explore Siberia after it was opened to Western travelers.

Troiëtìskiæi, Artemy. *Back in the USSR: The True Story of Rock in Russia.* New York: Omnibus Press, 1998. The definitive history of Russian rock music up to the late 1980s.

chapter 4

Middle East and North Africa

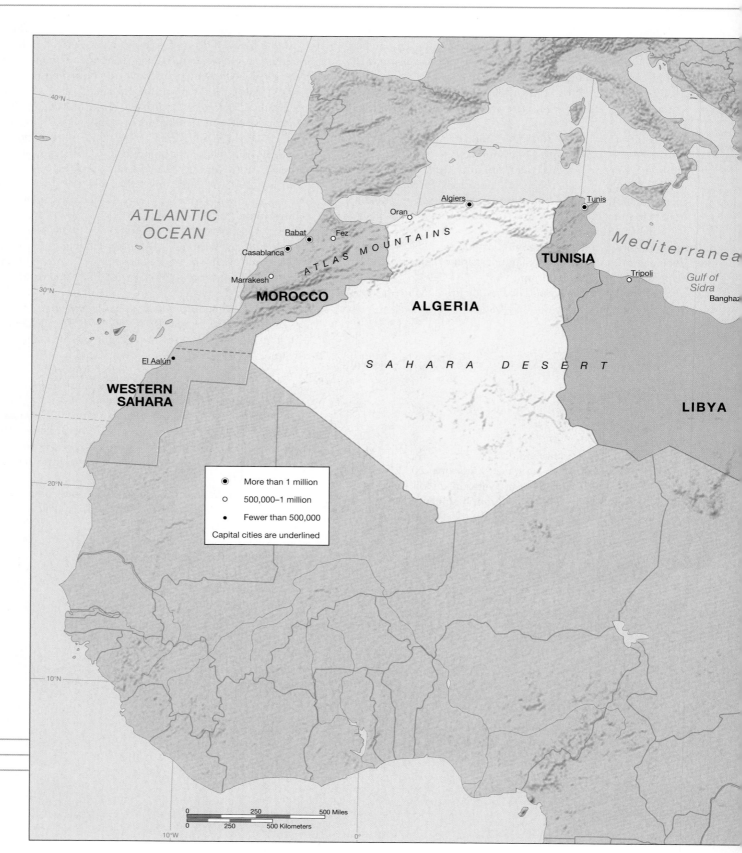

ATLANTIC OCEAN

40°N

Algiers
Oran
Tunis

Rabat
Fez
Casablanca

TUNISIA

Mediterranea

Tripoli

Gulf of Sidra

Marrakesh

30°N

MOROCCO

A T L A S   M O U N T A I N S

ALGERIA

Banghaz

El Aalún

S A H A R A   D E S E R T

WESTERN SAHARA

20°N

LIBYA

- ● More than 1 million
- ○ 500,000–1 million
- • Fewer than 500,000

Capital cities are underlined

10°N

0   250   500 Miles

0   250   500 Kilometers

10°W   0°

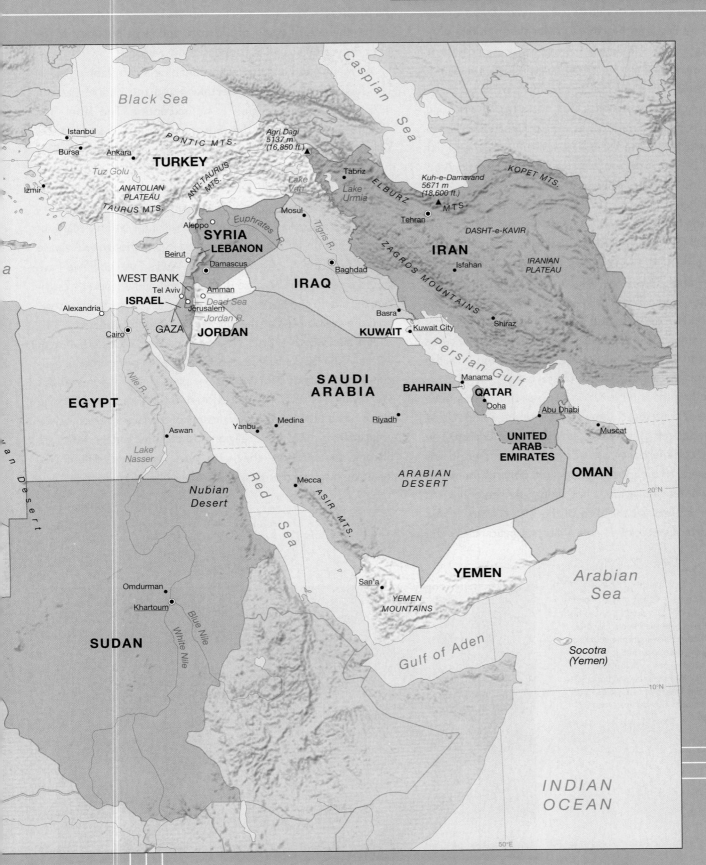

Black Sea

Istanbul
Bursa
Ankara
Izmir
Tuz Golu
PONTIC MTS.
ANATOLIAN
PLATEAU
TAURUS MTS.
ANTI-TAURUS MTS.
TURKEY

Agri Dagi
5137 m
(16,850 ft.) ▲

Lake
Van
Tabriz
Lake
Urmia

Caspian Sea

Kuh-e-Damavand
5671 m
(18,600 ft.) ▲
ELBURZ MTS.
Tehran
KOPET MTS.

DASHT-e-KAVIR

Mosul
Aleppo
SYRIA
LEBANON
Beirut
Damascus
Euphrates
Tigris R.

IRAQ

Baghdad

ZAGROS MOUNTAINS

IRAN

Isfahan

IRANIAN
PLATEAU

WEST BANK
Tel Aviv
ISRAEL
Alexandria
Jerusalem
Dead Sea
Jordan R.
Amman
GAZA
JORDAN

Cairo

Basra
Shiraz

KUWAIT
Kuwait City

Persian Gulf

EGYPT

Nile R.

Aswan

Lake
Nasser

Yanbu
Medina

SAUDI
ARABIA

Riyadh

BAHRAIN
Manama
QATAR
Doha

Abu Dhabi
Muscat

UNITED
ARAB
EMIRATES

OMAN

20°N

Nubian
Desert

Red
Sea

ASIR MTS.

Mecca

ARABIAN
DESERT

Omdurman
Khartoum
Blue Nile
White Nile

SUDAN

San'a
YEMEN
MOUNTAINS

YEMEN

Arabian
Sea

Gulf of Aden

Socotra
(Yemen)

10°N

FIGURE 4.1

INDIAN
OCEAN

50°E

153

Located at the intersection of Europe, Asia, and Africa, the Middle East and North Africa together constitute a complex region linked by broad similarities of climate, religion, and culture. Physically, the Middle East and North Africa form something of an east-to-west arc. Iran and Turkey compose the northeastern tier. Southward are the Arab states of Lebanon, Jordan, Syria, and Iraq and the Jewish state of Israel. The southernmost boundary includes Saudi Arabia and the small Gulf states (Kuwait, Bahrain, Qatar, the United Arab Emirates) as well as Oman and Yemen. Moving westward from the Saudi Arabian Peninsula, the North African states of Egypt and Sudan, as well as Libya, Tunisia, Algeria, Morocco, and Western Sahara complete the region.

The region is bordered by several major bodies of water—among them the Mediterranean, the Black Sea, the Red Sea, and the Persian Gulf (**Figure 4.1**). To the west is the Atlantic Ocean, and to the southeast the Arabian Sea. The region encompasses vast deserts—among them the Sahara, the Arabian, the Syrian, and the Nubian—and overall has low levels of precipitation. The Middle East and North Africa also contain impressive mountain ranges—from the Atlas Mountains in the west to the Zagros Mountains in the east—and such critical rivers as the Nile, the Tigris, the Euphrates, and the Jordan (**Figure 4.2**).

The Middle Eastern and North African region has long been called a "cradle of civilization," the birthplace of the world's three great monotheistic religions (Islam, Christianity, and Judaism). The region was the commercial crossroads of the ancient world and the base of several of the most sophisticated empires the world has ever known. Yet the region is not simply the site of ancient ruins and source areas. At the turn of the 21st century, it also possesses enormous economic and political significance as the site of most of the world's petroleum reserves and some of the world's most volatile and seemingly intractable political conflicts. As the Israeli-Palestinian conflict and the U.S. war in Iraq demonstrate, the fate of much of the core and large portions of the periphery is tied to what happens in the region.

As mentioned in the Preface, defining a geographic region is a highly problematic undertaking and the Middle Eastern and North African region is no exception. The label "the Middle East" reflects the European colonial experience. Grouping several North African states with the Middle East further complicates the regionalization.

Critics of the *Middle East* label argue that because it is the name given to the region by European and later U.S. imperialists, it carries colonial or post-colonial implications. Many of those critics prefer the label *Southwest Asia*. Although well aware of the progressive criticisms of the *Middle East* label, we have opted to employ it because it is used and understood throughout the world and because it connotes the central and strategic role the region plays at the interface of three continents.

It is also worth explaining why we decided to include North Africa in the label. Many textbooks as well as government agencies simply include North Africa as part of the region without identifying it as such. We have chosen to label it as a signal to the reader that although the two subsets of the larger region have a great many similarities—religion and to some extent language, history, and climate—they also have significant differences, including history, cultural systems, and political aspirations.[1]

---

[1]This discussion is adapted in part from C. C. Held, *Middle East Patterns: Places, Peoples, and Politics*, 3rd ed., Boulder: Westview Press, 2000, pp. 7–9.

FIGURE 4.2 Middle East and North Africa from space This satellite photo highlights the extreme aridity of the Middle East and North Africa. The deserts dominate the southern part of the map. Along the coasts and in the mountains, high plateaus, and steppes, greater moisture availability means that more plants (and humans) can survive and thrive. Few rivers and lakes exist in the region but the ones that do are crucial to human, plant, and animal life.

ENVIRONMENT AND SOCIETY IN THE MIDDLE EAST AND NORTH AFRICA

The Middle Eastern and North African region is environmentally complex. The popular image of the region is fostered largely by the entertainment industry in commercial films showing vast, blazing hot deserts dotted with lush, but far-flung, oases. The deserts of the region are certainly impressive. The Sahara, the largest desert in the world, has an average annual rainfall of less than 25 millimeters (1 inch). Incorporated within the larger framework of the Sahara are the Libyan and Nubian deserts of Egypt and northern Sudan. The other important desert of the region is known by two names: the Eastern Desert and the Arabian Desert. Although this desert lies between the Nile River and the Red Sea, the label *Arabian Desert* is also applied to the Rub al-Khali, or the Empty Quarter, a seemingly endless expanse of barren sand dunes that occupies a substantial part of the Arabian Peninsula.

While deserts and oases like those portrayed in film do exist, in reality they make up only a small percentage of the total land area of the Middle East and North Africa. The predominant landscape of the region is vast grass plains, which receive substantially more precipitation than the deserts. Towering mountain ranges and extensive, treeless plateaus are also common. Trapped among these more predominant landscapes are the isolated deserts, some of which are really vast seas of sand. As in other arid lands throughout the world, summers in the lowland areas of the Middle East and North Africa are extremely hot and dry, with daily high temperatures often at 38°C (100°F). The highland areas, such as the Atlas Mountains; the Iranian and Anatolian plateaus; and coastal areas of the Atlantic Ocean and the Mediterranean, Caspian, Arabian, Red, and Black seas experience more moderate daily summer temperatures and a predictable influx of visitors escaping the searing heat elsewhere. Winter temperatures, as would be expected, are more moderate in the lowlands and colder in the highlands.

The single most important climatic variable unifying the region is **aridity**, in that the climate lacks sufficient moisture to support trees or woody plants. This environmental characteristic is so pervasive that early geography textbooks labeled the Middle East and North Africa "the dry world." The result of aridity is landscapes with great stretches of little or no vegetation (**Figure 4.3**). Such landscapes are largely uninhabitable by humans unless substantial and expensive technologies are available to provide a dependable water supply.

FIGURE 4.3 Sahara Desert Geological evidence suggests that between 50,000 to 100,000 years ago, the Sahara possessed a system of shallow lakes that sustained extensive areas of vegetation. Though most of these lakes had disappeared by the time the Romans arrived in the region, a few survive in the form of oases. Pictured here is a grid fence that has been erected to slow the advance of migrating sand dunes into an ancient oasis.

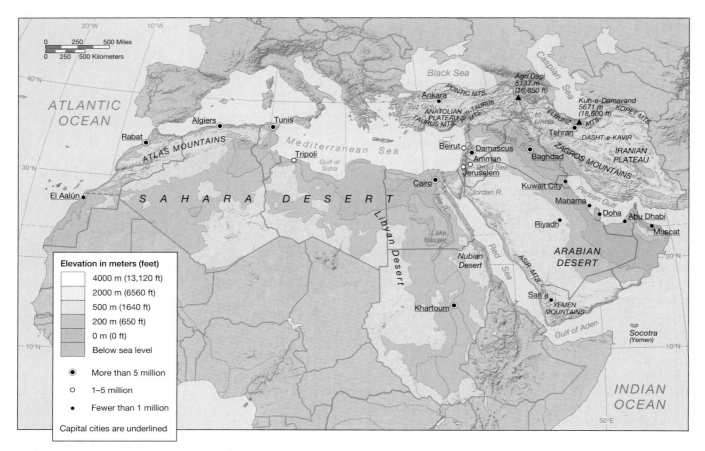

FIGURE 4.4 **Physiographic features of the Middle East and North Africa** Perhaps the most consistent feature of the physiographic map of the region is the way that land and water features seem to alternate in a somewhat regular pattern. Also significant is the scattering of plateaus and mountain ranges that punctuate the vast lowland areas of desert and coastal plains.

To fully understand the environmental complexity of the region, one must first accept the principle that dryness is not synonymous with dullness or absence of diversity. Although the Middle East and North Africa share a climatic variable, the countries and subregions contained within this world region exhibit a wide range of remarkable landscapes shaped by some small and some significant differences in the amount of surface water and annual precipitation. The absence or presence of water has strongly influenced the history of the interaction of peoples and environments of the Middle East and North Africa.

Landforms and Landscapes

The Middle East and North Africa contain a wide variety of physical landforms (**Figure 4.4**). The region is interspersed with seas, and an ocean hems its western flank. There are substantial mountain ranges, and two major river systems drain through its center. And while the region possesses the gamut of landscapes from tranquil beaches to towering mountains, the landscapes most heavily occupied by humans are the highland plateaus and the coastal lowlands, as well as the floodplains of the major rivers, where rain and surface water are most dependable. As **Figure 4.5** shows, the region is located at the conjunction of three continental landmasses, where active plates make the area highly prone to earthquakes.

Mountain and Coastal Environments The Arabian Peninsula, which is a tilted plateau that rises at its western flank on the Red Sea and slopes gradually to the Persian Gulf on its eastern flank, is part of the Arabian tectonic plate. It is not hard to recognize that the Arabian Peninsula was once part of the

African Plate tucked against the coastal areas of present-day Egypt, Sudan, and Eritrea. The separation of the Arabian Plate as it moved eastward from the African Plate millions of years ago resulted in the creation of the Red Sea, which initially formed as a rift valley and later filled with water. Both the African and the Arabian plates rub up against the Eurasian Plate along the Mediterranean Sea and at the mountains that separate the Arabian Peninsula from the Anatolian and Iranian plateaus. The mountain ranges of Turkey, Iran, and the Transcaucasus radiate out from this feature. Crustal plate contact also means that the subregion surrounding the contact zone is prone to severe earthquakes like the one that shook Turkey in August 1999, killing close to 15,000 people and causing tens of billions of dollars of property damage.

Three mountain ranges dominate the region. While impressive in terms of their beauty and ruggedness, these ranges, more importantly, generate rainfall and are the source of rivers and runoff for the arid region. The first set of ranges, which contains the most extensive and highest mountains, is the result of contact between the African, Arabian, and Eurasian plates at the center of the region (see Figure 4.5). These include the Taurus and Anti-Taurus mountains in Turkey and the Elburz and Zagros mountains in Iran. These ranges are higher than any in the continental United States and include Kuh-e-Damavand in Iran, which soars to 5671 meters (18,600 feet), and Agri Dagi, also known as Mount Ararat, which is only slightly less impressive at 5137 meters (16,850 feet). The second mountain range in the region is the Atlas Mountains of northwest Africa, which stretch along the southern edge of the Mediterranean from Morocco to Tunisia. A continuation of the European alpine range, these mountains are composed of a complex series of folded ridges separated by wide interior plateaus. The third set of mountains are those that border both sides of the Red Sea and are known as the Central Highlands or the High Yemen Mountains (**Figure 4.6**). These mountains are especially dramatic in Yemen, where the highest peaks are more than 3750 meters (12,300 feet) high.

In addition to being sources of precious water, the mountains provide homes for many people in the region. Though mountain environments can present substantial challenges to human habitation, the availability of moisture means that these environments can support agriculture over a somewhat shortened growing season. Historically, the mountains have also often provided safe havens for minority populations fleeing persecution and discrimination. The Druze in Syria and the Zayidis in Yemen are two such peoples who have sought mountain refuge from their oppressors.

While the highland areas are home to a small portion of the people of the Middle East and North Africa, many of the coastal areas, the floodplains, and the plateaus are the most densely populated landscapes of the region. The clustering of populations in these landscapes is hardly surprising given that they are the ones where water is most abundant and the environments are the least harsh. The Iranian and Anatolian plateaus are the most obvious examples of these landforms. But the highland plateau of Yemen also contains a sizable population. The coastal areas and floodplains of the region, excluding the coastal areas of the Persian Gulf, are equally attractive to human habitation and constitute some of the most remarkable, highly engineered, and scenic of the region's landscapes.

Riverine Landscapes
There are only two major river systems in the Middle East and North Africa—the Nile River system and the integrated Tigris and Euphrates rivers system. These systems are

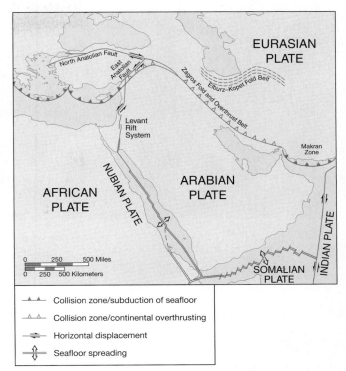

FIGURE 4.5 Generalized tectonics of the Middle East This generalized map shows the concentration of activity in eastern Turkey. The African and Arabian plates are made of ancient rock and are stable; little tectonic activity occurs there. Along the Eurasian plate are folded and faulted mountains extending from western to eastern Anatolia and then south across Iran and eastward again into the Himalayas. These mountains are the result of active plates colliding. (*Source:* Redrawn from C. C. Held, *Middle East Patterns: Places, Peoples and Politics*, 3rd ed. Boulder: Westview Press, 2000, p. 38.)

FIGURE 4.6 High Yemen Mountains experience winter rainfall and contain a wide range of bird, plant, and animal life.

FIGURE 4.7 The Euphrates River is a critical source of water for Iraq and Syria. It is shown here behind the ruins of an ancient city and fortress, Doura Europos, which is an important archaeological site in Syria.

essential to the continued growth of the countries through which they flow and, not surprisingly, are also the source of conflict—largely over access—because of the precious resource they deliver. The Nile is the world's longest river. Its source is in the mountains of Ethiopia and East Africa. From the Ethiopian Plateau, the Blue Nile flows northward across the Sahara Desert, where it joins the White Nile at Khartoum, Sudan. It proceeds northward as the Nile River, finally emptying into the eastern Mediterranean north of Cairo. Once the flow is joined by another of its tributaries, the Atbara River in northern Sudan, the Nile system flows through some of the driest terrestrial conditions on the planet, where no additional moisture is added and high evaporation occurs.

The Tigris and Euphrates system supported the development of a hearth area for the first agricultural revolution. The Tigris River originates in the Anatolian Plateau of Turkey and flows through Iraq. It is joined by the Euphrates River, which flows through Syria, in lower Iraq, where it eventually empties into the Persian Gulf in Iran (**Figure 4.7**).

It is no exaggeration to call these two river systems the lifeblood for millions of the region's inhabitants. While they are the major source of water for a large proportion of the region's population, there are other sources, though many are highly undependable. In the Sahara Desert, for example, runoff from the Atlas Mountains collects underground in porous rock layers deep below the desert surface. In some places, known as **oases**, land erosion and a high water table have enabled some of the underground water to percolate to the surface. Oases exist in sharp contrast to the dry, largely uninhabitable desert that surrounds them. Oasis soils are usually quite fertile, and animal and plant life are abundant. Agriculture is frequently undertaken here; dates are a highly successful cash crop due in part to their tolerance of saline soils in oases. Oases also play an economic role in the region when they serve as stopping points for caravans carrying commercial goods across the vast deserts.

Other sources of water in the region include natural springs, perennial streams, and wells drilled largely for irrigation, though some water holes have been drilled to create artificial oases. One of the most ingenious methods for mining water is a system of low-gradient tunnels that collect groundwater and bring it to the surface through gravity flow. The gravity system of water mining is known as *qanat* in Iran, *flaj* on the Arabian Peninsula, and *foggara* in North Africa (**Figure 4.8**). The system is restricted to piedmont—meaning, literally, the foot of the mountains—areas where runoff from orographic rain and snowmelt begins to percolate below ground level. Under ideal circumstances, where the *qanat* system and its regional relatives are carefully practiced, they provide a highly dependable source of water enabling year-round irrigation.

Because of its scarcity and the difficulties that must be met to secure adequate supplies of it, water is a highly politically charged resource in the region, and access rights to water are the source of much conflict. Syria and Iraq, for instance, have called on Turkey to halt construction of a dam on the Euphrates River, and Egypt has threatened military intervention in the Sudan should that country attempt to limit downstream flow of the Nile. A third conflict involves Israel and Jordan, both of which inhabit the Jordan River valley and have access to its waters. A shallow, slow-moving river, the Jordan is nonetheless highly engineered through dams and diversions, and at times its flow is little more than a trickle. As geographer Aaron Wolf has pointed out, access to its water is crucial to both countries, and conflicts and national complaints over access are routine.

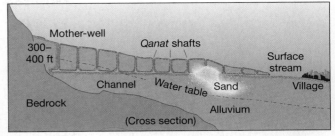

FIGURE 4.8 Simplified diagram of *qanat* irrigation Through a series of low-gradient tunnels, the *qanat* collects groundwater, bringing it to the surface by way of gravity. The diagram shows the shafts drilled into the loose soil and gravel at the foot of the mountain to reach the water table below. The water is drawn up through these shafts and directed out for use through pipes. (*Source:* Redrawn from P. English, *City and Village in Iran.* Madison: University of Wisconsin Press, 1966, p. 31.)

Climate

As in any region, the variables of temperature, humidity, and rainfall as they interact with topography and large water bodies are central to comprehending climate patterns and characteristics. In the Middle East and North Africa, temperatures vary dramatically by season and location, and in the desert areas, temperatures exhibit extreme variation between night and day. Humidity and rainfall are also variable across the region. As **Figure 4.9** illustrates, the Middle East and North Africa—though clearly dominated at midsection by a continuous swath of dry lands from western Morocco to eastern

FIGURE 4.9 Climate in the Middle East and North Africa Although aridity is the dominant climate characteristic of the Middle East and North Africa, there is actually a significant amount of climatic variation in the region. *Aridity* is a relative term: Some areas are hyper-arid and others, mildly so. Coastal areas possess Mediterranean climates that mean dry summers and wetter winters. The highland areas experience rain and snow throughout the year. Southern Sudan has a humid subtropical climate, while the north is dry.

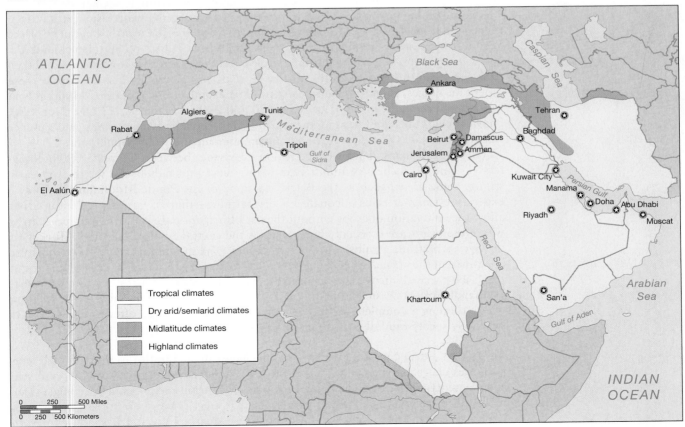

FIGURE 4.10 Algiers, Algeria Algiers is the capital and largest city of Algeria. Moderate climate and its Mediterranean location have made it the leading port in North Africa, serving chiefly as a shipping center and refueling station. The lower part is the modern city, built by the French, with wide boulevards, theaters, cathedrals, museums, an opera house, and many educational institutions. The upper part is the old city, with narrow, twisting streets dominated by the Kasbah, a 16th-century fortress built by the Turks.

Sudan—is a latitudinally broad region that stretches from the winter cold climes of northern Turkey to the summer wet, subtropical climes of southern Sudan. The moderating effect of large bodies of water on the coastal areas, as previously mentioned, also adds to climatic variation in the region, producing milder year-round climates with wet winters in those places (**Figure 4.10**).

Arid Lands Except in the coastal mountain areas, precipitation in the Middle East and North Africa is low and highly variable. Nearly three-quarters of the region experiences average annual rainfall of less than 250 millimeters (10 inches), which means that agriculture, where it occurs, must be irrigated. Scarce rainfall also means the soils in the region tend to be thin and deficient in a wide range of nutrients. In contrast, agriculture along the coastal plains and lowlands of Turkey and the floodplains of the Nile is able to take advantage of fertile soils. Other exceptional locations with respect to moisture include southern Sudan, which, because of its tropical location in Sub-Saharan Africa, experiences the wet spring and summer effects of the moisture-bearing storms of the intertropical convergence zone (see Chapter 1, p. 24), and the Central Highlands of Yemen, which experience abundant rainfall in the summer due to the Indian Ocean monsoon system.

Most of the rain that does fall in the region is affected in some way by numerous mountain ranges. For instance, the winter and spring storms that bring rainfall to the coastal areas of the Mediterranean Sea are orographic in nature (see Chapter 1, p. 24). Moisture-bearing air masses move in from the Atlantic in the west, rise over a coastal range—such as the Atlas Mountains in Morocco or the Judaean hill country of the Levant (the eastern Mediterranean, including Syria, Lebanon, and Israel and the Palestinian territories), where the air is cooled and the moisture is condensed—and then drop their moisture as rain as the air masses rise over the mountains. In some of these mountain ranges, rainfall is quite plentiful. For example, in the Zagros Mountains in Iran annual rainfall can range between 600 and 2000 millimeters (23 and 80 inches). Snowcapped peaks are found in Turkey, Iran, and Lebanon, where spring and summer snowmelt provides water for lowland human, animal, and plant populations.

Most of the coastal areas of the region experience between 375 and 1000 millimeters (15 and 40 inches) of rain a year. While most rain falls in the winter and early spring, some areas, such as the Black Sea slope of the Pontic Mountains in Turkey, experience summer rains adequate for dry farming—that is, farming techniques that allow the cultivation of crops without the use of irrigation. In some mountainous areas where the peaks are especially high, such as the central Anatolian Plain in Turkey or the Syrian plateau, a rainshadow effect occurs: The mountains cause most moisture contained in the air masses passing over them to condense and fall as rain before it can reach the parched interior deserts of the region. This occurs, for instance, in southeastern Saudi Arabia, western Oman, and Dasht-e-Kavir (the Great Salt Desert) of Iran, where there is a complete absence of vegetation and there are often successive years with only spotty rainfall or none at all.

Adaptation to Aridity People have adapted to the aridity and high temperatures characteristic of the region through architecture, patterns of daily and seasonal activity, and dress. The typical regional architecture features high ceilings, thick walls, deep-set windows, and arched roofs that enable warm air to rise away from human activity. The practice of locating living quarters around a shady courtyard enables residents to move many activities to cooler outdoor spaces that are also highly private. The clothing worn by Middle Eastern and North African peoples is also an adaptation to the heat and dryness. Head coverings and long, flowing robes made from fabrics of light color lower body temperatures by reflecting sunlight. They also function to inhibit perspiration and thus diminish moisture loss.

Some populations, such as the Berber of North Africa, migrate to mountainous areas in the summer and warmer lowlands in the winter to avoid the extremes of temperature. Plants and animals also have adaptive strategies to deal with the intense heat and aridity. For example, native plant species are typically able to store water for long periods of time or survive on very small amounts of water by keeping their leaves and stems very small or developing an extensive root system. Animals adapt by lowering their body temperature through sweating or by being active only at night.

Environmental History

For much of the early history of the Middle Eastern and North African region, *adaptation* was an appropriate term for understanding the relationships among people, plants, and animals and their environments. Perhaps the most pivotal event in the environmental history of the region was the domestication of plants that occurred between 7000 and 9000 B.C. (We discuss this key agricultural revolution in a later section of this chapter; note here that the region has been cultivated for millennia.) From the agricultural practices they have developed to the cities they have built, the inhabitants of the region have been ingenious in adapting to environmental constraints.

Human-Environment Interactions After thousands of years of human occupation and the increasing pressures that population growth has created, the key term for describing human-environment interaction in the region today is *overexploitation*. In the long transition from adaptation to overexploitation, the landscape of the region has been dramatically transformed, in some cases so much so that entire species have been eliminated. The environmental history of the Middle East and North Africa, therefore, is a long history that has changed as new technologies have been introduced and more human beings have placed greater pressures on the existing resource base.

It is not surprising that most of the plant and animal life is found where most of the people are: where the climate offers sufficient moisture. In fact, dense and extensive forests used to exist throughout Turkey, Syria, Lebanon, and Iran. Today, after several thousand years of woodcutting and overgrazing, the forests of Turkey and Syria are nearly entirely denuded, with only a few small remnant areas remaining. While large areas of Lebanon have also been deforested, the Horsh Ehden Forest Nature Reserve, in the northern mountainous part of the country, is one place that has not, and it is home to several species of rare orchids and other flowering plants. Sadly, Lebanon's famous cedars continue to grow only in a few high-mountain areas (**Figure 4.11**). Iran retains a substantial expanse of its deciduous forests, particularly in the Elburz Mountain region. The forests of the Atlas Mountains of Morocco and Algeria continue to be harvested for commercial purposes.

Animal life has been greatly affected by the millennia of human occupation as well as by more recent increases in human population. At one time, and because of the region's location at the crossroads of three continents, a wide variety of large mammals inhabited the region's forests, including leopard, cheetah, oryx, striped hyena, and caracal; crocodiles thrived in the Nile; and lions roamed the highlands of Persia (present-day Iran). Nearly all of these species are now extinct or near extinction, with domesticated camel, donkey, and buffalo being the most ubiquitous mammals today. The highland areas of Turkey and Iran still contain a fairly wide variety of mammals similar to those found in parts of Europe,

FIGURE 4.11 Cedars of Lebanon For millennia, this coniferous tree has been significant to the region for trade, medicine, religion, and habitation. The national symbol of Lebanon, overexploitation has almost completely eliminated the once abundant cedar forests. Reforestation programs are under way, however, in both Lebanon and Turkey. Pictured here is the last remaining cedar forest in Lebanon.

GEOGRAPHY MATTERS

Environment and Tourism in Jordan

For a long time, tourism development has been a highly uncomfortable proposition in various countries across the Middle East and North Africa.* Countries like Jordan (which possesses more than 75 biblical sites) found distasteful the idea of promoting their numerous sacred sites to foreigners and simply refused to do so. In 1998, however, Jordan created a national tourism board with the intention of not only expanding its economic base beyond agriculture and mineral exploitation and processing, but also exerting greater control over protecting its natural and cultural resources by providing an upscale tourism experience.

The cultural features that Jordan is promoting relate to its history as the site of the birth of Christianity more than 2000 years ago. For instance, recently excavated was a seventh-century Byzantine church that is believed to have been built on a site traditionally thought to be the birthplace of the prophet Elijah. The site that promises to be the most significant, however, is one—still under excavation—where some archaeologists believe they have found evidence to support the legend that Jesus may have been baptized there (**Figure 1**). Jordan approached the promotion of this site very cautiously. Because this and other ancient sites are so vulnerable to damage from excessive numbers of visitors, the government has created a royal commission made up of Jordanians and citizens of other countries whose task is to oversee its protection and development.

While sacred sites feature prominently in Jordan's tourism plans, even more attention is being paid to developing ecotourism and spa tourism in the region. This sort of development must be undertaken with special care because the ecosystems of the surrounding desert and Dead and Red seas are especially fragile. One of the largest spas in the Middle East is Jordanian. On the shores of the Dead Sea and operated by a Swiss company, this five-star hotel and spa is meant to compete with the numerous Israeli resorts that have already been built on the opposite shore of the Dead Sea.

The Dead Sea is a salt lake, about 397 meters (1300 feet) below sea level, between Israel and Jordan. It is the lowest point on Earth and one of its saltiest water bodies. It lies between the hills of Judea to the west and the Transjordanian plateaus to the east (**Figure 2**). It is fed by local springs and the Jordan River, which flows into it from the north. For centuries the healing powers of the Dead Sea have attracted people from all over the world, and the current wave of spa resort development is just one manifestation of the sea's enduring attractions.

FIGURE 1 Church of Bethabara Ruins of this church have recently been discovered in Jordan along with artifactual evidence that leads some archaeologists to believe that Jesus was baptized here. However, this claim has been made by at least two other places in the area. One is downstream on the Jordan River and another is in Israel south of Lake Tiberias.

FIGURE 2 Dead Sea This aerial photo of the Dead Sea shows the Jordanian salt evaporation ponds at the southern end of the sea. Salt-evaporation works are expanding throughout the world in response to increased manufacturing demand.

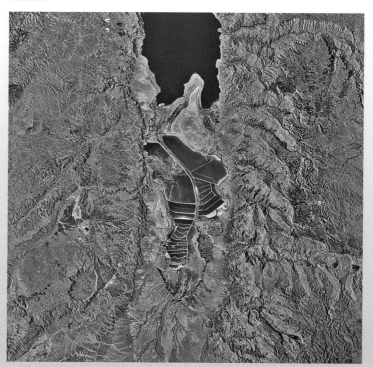

including bear, deer, jackal, lynx, wild boar, and wolf. Birds are also plentiful in the region, with different ecosystems supporting a wide variety of species.

Environmental Problems At the same time that the elimination of plant and animal species has been widespread throughout the region, different parts of it are experiencing pressing environmental problems. Some of these problems are particularly

Unfortunately, since the 1960s, the Dead Sea's ecology has begun to experience serious transformations, and according to the Royal Jordan Geographical Center, it is undergoing a slow and painful death. The main inflow into the sea is from the Jordan River, a water source that is heavily canalized and dammed for irrigation and general-purpose water uses by Israel, Jordan, and Palestine. The decrease of inflow and the development of the salt processing industry are causing the sea's shoreline to undergo very fast and dynamic changes. Geographer Jihad Hijazi believes that deviations from the water flow of the Jordan River have broken the natural replenishment cycle of the Dead Sea.

The threat to the shoreline and regional flora and fauna that thrive on the Dead Sea's proximity is enormous. While no life beyond bacteria actually inhabits the sea, 25 species of amphibians and reptiles, 24 species of mammals, and 6 species of fish live near the sea. Many freshwater sources and oases occur along the shores of the Dead Sea, providing habitat for species such as the indigenous Dead Sea sparrow and animals such as the leopard, hyrax, ibex, hyena, bat, fox, wolf, and mongoose. Many other endangered mammal species can be found there. There are 400 to 500 plant species that flourish around the shores of the Dead Sea. More than 90 species of birds have been identified in the Dead Sea region due largely to its location on a major migration route between Eurasia and Africa.

Because of excessive withdrawal of water from the Jordan River in the north and dams and industrial development in the south, the Dead Sea is facing an environmental crisis of disastrous proportions. Industry, agriculture, and tourism need more and more water. As a result, one-third of the world's saltiest lake has already been drained. While much of this water is being used for basic domestic consumption, most goes toward highly subsidized and inefficient agriculture.

The Dead Sea is not the only natural environment in Jordan that is being exploited for tourism. And, there is at least one success story to celebrate. A second, smaller area of tourist development is the Dana Biosphere Reserve in central Jordan, where the landscape drops dramatically from 1600 meters (5200 feet) above sea level to 200 meters (650 feet) below sea level, as lush slopes on top become sparse woodlands and eventually arid deserts below. Here, Jordanians are protecting indigenous birds—such as eagles, falcons, kestrels, and vultures—as well as mammals—including wildcats, hyenas, wolves, and porcupines—and several types of snakes and lizards.

Supported by additional funds from the World Bank and the United Nations, the Dana Biosphere Reserve is a system of wadis (streambeds that only carry water during the rainy sea-son) and mountains that extend from the top of the Rift Valley down to the desert lowlands of Wadi Araba. Hundreds of plant, animal, and bird species occupy the multiple biogeographical zones represented there. The reserve combines the conservation of nature with a socioeconomic program in Dana Village where in the 1990s a group of women started renovating the village with the financial support of Jordan's Royal Society for the Conservation of Nature (RSCN). Their aim was to create sustainable ecotourism, coupled with local economic development. Farmers in the village sell their figs, grapes, and olives to the RSCN, which in turn employs villagers to produce organic jams and olive oil soaps. Local herbs and handmade jewelry are available in a small shop in the village. Villagers provide accommodation for biosphere tourists in small guest houses and act as hiking guides in the reserve. Dana Biosphere Reserve and Dana Village are examples of the successful combination of scientific research, social revitalization, and sustainable ecotourism that is a bright light in the increasing development of tourism among countries in the Middle East and North Africa (**Figure 3**).

FIGURE 3 Dana Biosphere Reserve Shown here is Dana Village as well as the rugged topography of the reserve.

*This discussion is adapted in part from N. Swengley, "You've Got to Excavate to Accumulate," *High Life*, October 2000, pp. 110–16.

severe because national governments lack the resources either to prevent or mitigate them. All the states in the region are experiencing serious problems related to water quality, accessibility, and the impact of hydrotechnology on surrounding areas. In many states, excessive drawing of water from oasis wells has been occurring for such a long period that oases, such as the Azraq in north central Jordan, are actually dying. All of the states, but especially those in the Persian Gulf, are faced with severe shortages of fresh water and the effects of oil and industrial pollution on air, land, and water. Water control schemes, such as those in Iraq, are destroying the natural habitat of wildlife. In Egypt, Nile irrigation is increasing the amount of salt in the soil, thus decreasing soil fertility. Coastlines along the Persian Gulf are also experiencing erosion and degradation of marine habitats caused by oil spills and the discharge of ships and industry. And in every state of the region except Turkey, desertification—the process by which arid and semiarid lands become degraded and less productive, leading to more desertlike conditions—is an especially troubling problem as precious forests are lost due to overcutting and arable land is lost due to overfarming. Tourism, a source of income for many of the states of the region, is worsening many of these environmental problems. For example, increased coastal development in Lebanon is causing the loss of precious wetlands, and heavy shipping traffic is damaging the coral reefs in the Red Sea.

There is no question that the Middle East and North Africa face severe environmental problems. However, even though the region as a whole has little surplus capital to invest in environmental protection or preservation, some important efforts have been made. Egypt and Jordan recently appointed environmental ministries, and efforts have been made to establish protected areas (see Geography Matters: Environment and Tourism in Jordan, p. 162). Reforestation and **afforestation**—converting previously unforested land to forest by planting seeds or trees—programs are under way in several Middle East states. Oman and the United Arab Emirates have begun to take a deliberate stand against desertification, and greenbelts are being planted. Israel has introduced active breeding programs to encourage the regeneration of endangered animal species. Still, the state of the environment in the Middle East and North Africa is seriously challenged. Structural problems, such as burgeoning populations of very poor people, make the solutions extremely difficult to implement.

FIGURE 4.12 Fertile Crescent This map shows the ancient sites found within the Fertile Crescent. Changing climate conditions after 9000 B.C. transformed the environment of the area, encouraging an increase in human population as well as the wild plants and animals that were critical to their food supply. Early forms of wheat and barley flourished here and were gradually domesticated by the Stone Age people. (*Source:* Redrawn from C. C. Held, *Middle East Patterns: Places, Peoples and Politics,* 3rd ed. Boulder: Westview Press, 2000, p. 16.)

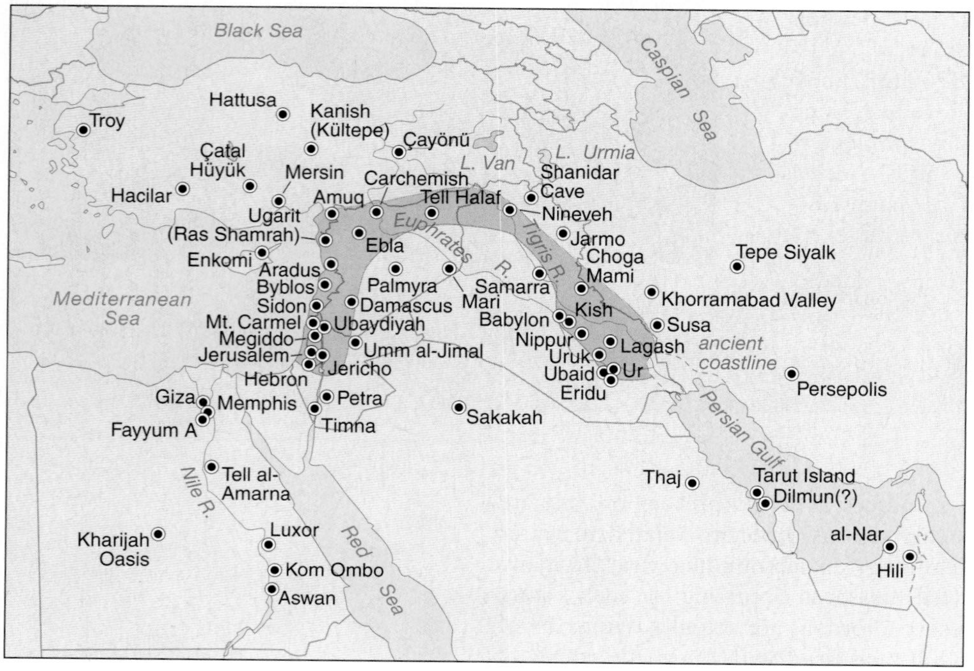

THE MIDDLE EAST AND NORTH AFRICA IN THE WORLD-SYSTEM

The Middle East and North Africa have long influenced growth and change in the rest of the world. As mentioned previously, the Middle East and North Africa are widely known as a "cradle of civilization." This title derives from the fact that the first known humans to settle there were ultimately responsible for domesticating plants such as wheat, producing some of the earliest integrated civilizations, establishing large cities and networks of villages and towns, and organizing complex religious-political systems. The geographical center of all these accomplishments was the Fertile Crescent, a region arching across the northern part of the Syrian Desert and extending from the Nile Valley to the Mesopotamian Basin in the depression between the Tigris and Euphrates rivers (**Figure 4.12**). Ideas and technologies generated in the Fertile Crescent diffused outward to similar nearby environments and then beyond the area. Inhabitants of the Mesopotamian area appear to have developed the earliest known writing and complex understandings of science and mathematics.

Early Empires and Innovation

Perhaps what is most impressive about the Middle Eastern and North African region is the number of culturally rich and intellectually sophisticated empires that have emerged and flourished in key areas over the last 4000 years. The most famous empires include the Babylonian, Hittite, Egyptian, Assyrian, Chaldean, Persian, Seleucid, Ptolemaic, Byzantine, Parthian, Sassanian, Umayyad, Abbasid, and Ottoman. Smaller empires include the Aramaean, Phoenician, Sabaen, and Nabatean. The Roman Empire also extended into this region (**Figure 4.13**). Mesopotamia, Asia Minor, the Nile Valley, and the Iranian Plateau all functioned as centers for the major empires, such that at any one time, each major part of the region was able to extend its control to the rest of the region and, in turn, has been controlled by some other part of the region.

The interaction of dominance and subordination among the various subregions meant that the exchange of ideas, goods, people, and belief and value systems helped tie the region together and promote a more or less unified regional identity. It also meant that a great deal of social stimulation for developing new ideas and practices existed and enabled technological innovations and cultural revolutions to take place, especially with respect to religion and culture but also related to plant domestication, trade, and the growth of cities.

Source of World Religions Christianity, Islam, and Judaism all developed among the Semitic-speaking people of the deserts of the Middle East. Like Hinduism and Buddhism, originating from the Indo-Gangetic plains (see Chapter 10, p. 495), these three **world religions**—belief systems that have adherents worldwide—are related. Judaism originated about 3500 years ago, Christianity about 2000 years ago, and Islam about 1300 years ago. Judaism developed out of the cultures and beliefs of Bronze Age peoples and was the first monotheistic religion (a religion that believes in one God). Although Judaism is the oldest monotheistic religion and one that spread widely and rapidly, it is numerically small because it does not seek new converts. Christianity developed in Jerusalem among the disciples of Jesus, who proclaimed that he was the Messiah expected by the Jews. As Christianity moved east and south from its hearth area, its diffusion was helped by missionizing and by imperial sponsorship. Islam is the dominant religion and culture of the region deeply penetrated by the Arabic language (although Turkish is the dominant language in Turkey and Persian is the dominant language in Iran).

These three religions have had an enormous impact on the rest of the world. For instance, zealous Christianity was responsible for the Crusades, military expeditions undertaken through papal sanction by European Christians in the 11th, 12th, and 13th centuries to recover the Holy Land from the Muslims. The Crusades brought Europeans to the Middle East, where they had a modest impact. As geographer Colbert Held points out, the reverse impact was momentous: The Crusades were a major stimulus for the European Renaissance, because crusaders returned to Europe with new ideas and practices related to architecture, art, literature, and the sciences (**Figure 4.14**). In addition, the spread of Christianity to Europe is seen by many, including the eminent sociologist Max Weber, as one of the primary foundations for the spread of capitalism following the Renaissance. Capitalism and Christianity were linked in the motivations for conquest by the European colonizers. Spanish colonialism in North and Latin America, for example, was undertaken in the name of the Christian god as missionaries converted

FIGURE 4.13 Empires of the Middle East from 1000 B.C. to the rise of Islam Various empires rose and fell in the Middle East and North Africa and encouraged the interaction of people and ideas from across Asia, Africa, and Europe. The four maps show the extent of the most powerful regional empires. An interesting aspect of the many empires that have existed in the region is that they fostered a great deal of interaction between the region and areas beyond. (*Source:* Redrawn from C. C. Held, *Middle East Patterns: Places, Peoples and Politics*, 3rd ed. Boulder: Westview Press, 2000, p. 23.)

(a)

(b)

FIGURE 4.14 Influence of the Middle East and North Africa on Venetian architecture
Architecture and art diffused out of the Middle East and North Africa to shape the landscapes and arts of Europe for centuries but most widely during the Crusades. La Serenissma, or the Serene Republic of Venice, was one Mediterranean location clearly affected by Islamic aesthetics. (a) The Basilica of San Marco distinctly reflects the influence of the Byzantine Empire, the eastern portion of the Roman Empire that flourished in the Middle East from A.D. 330 when Emperor Constantine I rebuilt Byzantium and made it his capital. (b) The Ducal Palace also clearly bears an Islamic imprint particularly with respect to its courtyard, mosaic floors, and façade.

the indigenous peoples with whom they came into contact and trade networks were opened for European markets.

The impact of Islam has been equally substantial. At the opening of the 21st century, Islam is second only to Christianity in the number of adherents worldwide—about 1 billion. **Figure 4.15** illustrates the extent of the contemporary Islamic world. As the

FIGURE 4.15 The Islamic world The distribution of Islam in Africa, Southeast Asia, and South Asia that we see today testifies to the broad reach of Muslim cultural, colonial, and trade activities that carried Islam throughout these regions. (*Source:* Redrawn from D. Hiro, *Holy Wars*. London: Routledge, 1989, frontispiece.)

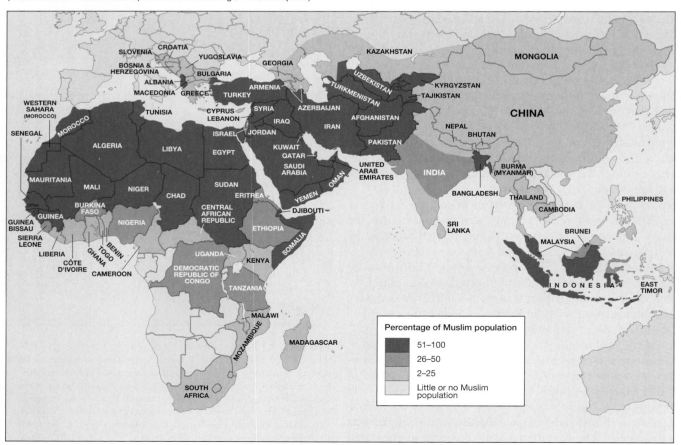

map makes clear, the Islamic world includes very different societies and regions from Southeast Asia to Africa. Muslims represent more than 85 percent of the populations of Afghanistan, Algeria, Bangladesh, Egypt, Indonesia, Iran, Iraq, Jordan, Pakistan, Saudi Arabia, Senegal, Tunisia, Turkey, and most of the newly independent republics of Central Asia and the Transcaucasus (including Azerbaijan, Turkmenistan, Uzbekistan, and Tajikistan). In Albania, Chad, Ethiopia, and Nigeria, Muslims make up 50 to 85 percent of the population. In India, Burma (Myanmar), Cambodia, China, Greece, Slovenia, Thailand, and the Philippines, significant Muslim minorities also exist.

Plant Domestication

As mentioned in Chapter 1, the emergence of seed agriculture through the domestication of crops, such as wheat and barley, and animals, such as sheep and goats, replaced hunting and gathering as a way of living and sustaining human life. As cultural geographer Carl Sauer pointed out in his book *Agricultural Origins and Dispersals* (1952), these agricultural breakthroughs could take place only in certain geographic settings. In these settings natural food supplies were plentiful; the terrain was diversified (thus offering a variety of habitats and a variety of species); soils were rich and relatively easy to till; and there was no need for large-scale irrigation or drainage. The emergence of seed agriculture occurred during roughly the same period (between 9000 and 7000 B.C.) in several regions around the world, including the Middle East, parts of Latin America (Chapter 7, p. 335), South Asia (Chapter 10, p. 483), and East Asia (Chapter 8, p. 382), as well as East Africa (Chapter 5, p. 220). In the Middle East, Mesopotamia was the source area. In North Africa, the Nile Valley in Egypt was a second site of agricultural innovation.

Before the first agricultural revolution, in prehistoric times, hunting-and-gathering minisystems were finely tuned to local physical environments. (A **minisystem** is a society with a single cultural base and a shared social system and economy.) They were all highly vulnerable to environmental change. Because they did not have the ability (or the need) to sustain an extensive physical infrastructure, they were also limited in geographic scale. The domestication of plants and animals represented a transition from hunting-and-gathering minisystems to agriculturally-based minisystems that began in the early Stone Age, a period between 9000 and 7000 B.C. The transition was based on a series of technological preconditions: the use of fire to process food, the use of grindstones to mill grains, and the development of improved tools to prepare and store food.

This transition to food-producing systems had several implications for the long-term evolution of the world's geographies. First, it allowed much higher population densities and encouraged the proliferation of settled villages. Second, it brought about a change in social organization, from loose communal systems to systems that were more highly organized on the basis of family ties. Extended family groups provided a natural way of assigning rights over land and resources and of organizing patterns of land use. Third, it allowed some specialization in nonagricultural crafts, such as pottery, woven textiles, jewelry, and weaponry. This specialization led to a fourth development: the beginnings of barter and trade among communities, sometimes over substantial distances. **Figure 4.16** illustrates the routes of the incense and spice trade that criss-crossed the region when the Greeks and Romans dominated. From precious metals, including silver and mercury, and precious stones; to foodstuffs, including spices, fruits, rice, and dates; to textiles, carpets, brass, iron, and steelware; to more luxurious items, such as perfume, ebony, ivory, amber,

FIGURE 4.16 Incense and spice trade routes in the Greco-Roman world For several hundred years before and after the birth of Jesus, the southern rim of the Arabian Peninsula, within current-day Yemen and Oman, was a transshipment area for the Middle East and North Africa. Goods that arrived from India, China, Ethiopia, and elsewhere were packed off by camel caravan to Egypt, Persia, Syria, and even Rome. Incense and spice were two of the most valuable commodities traded.

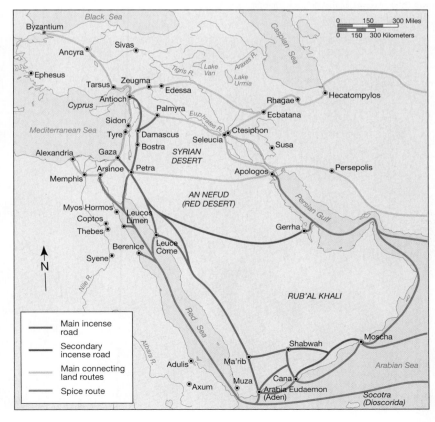

incense, and fur—a wide range of goods circulated through the region's thousands of trading centers. We discuss the influence of trade on urbanization in more detail in the following section.

Irrigation was the key to the success of the many agriculturally based minisystems that emerged in the Middle East and North Africa when farmers there minimized their dependence on rainfall. Archaeologists and other scholars of the region argue that settled minisystems that were able to control irrigated farming across large areas were able also to control weaker minisystems. By using food as a weapon of control, some minisystems were able to thrive, while others failed or were incorporated into stronger minisystems. An example is Babylon, which began as one of a number of regional minisystems in Mesopotamia but was able to turn itself into an enduring empire. Babylon's nearly 4000 years of dominance was achieved by systematically increasing control over regional agricultural production, through a buildup of its military strength (including a walled and fortified city center), the elaboration of a long-distance trade network (through extensive port facilities), and organizing extensive religious and symbolic political control. Evidence of a walled and fortified city, port facilities, and numerous temples and palaces demonstrates the extensive and well-established power and control of Babylon, which was, for a long period in its 4000-year history, the largest city in the world.

Cities and Trade In the Middle East and North Africa, key urban centers, like Babylon, located at crucial points along natural and well-traveled human routes, were the organizational anchors of the region, shaping distinctive land-use patterns and serving as crucibles for significant cultural developments. In the Nile Valley, for instance, the urban-based Egyptian empire emerged, influenced by the cultures of Mesopotamia at the same time that it developed its own unique way of life. For instance writing, originated simultaneously in Mesopotamia and Egypt for the purposes of recording inventories and trade transactions as well as for religious and royal inscriptions. (Writing also originated in Mesoamerica at about the same time.)

Like their neighbors, Egyptians were active city-builders, and they constructed monumental tombs, temples, and palaces, the engineering of which still baffles architectural historians (**Figure 4.17**). The culture was also premised on elaborate rituals and sophisticated body adornments that required significant quantities of gold, cedar, ebony, and turquoise. As a result, the Egyptians entered into active trade with settlements in the northern Red Sea, the upper Nile, and the eastern Mediterranean. These trade relations enabled the transfer of ideas and improvement of technologies that enriched all of the cultures of the Middle East and North Africa, as well as Greece and Rome (see Signature Region: The Maghreb, p. 170).

Considerable evidence suggests that the oldest cities on Earth were constructed along the valleys of the Tigris and Euphrates rivers as well as the Nile River (and possibly in the Indus River valley; see Chapter 10, p. 478) sometime during the fourth millennium B.C. The availability of the rivers for transportation and irrigation and the use of wheeled vehicles probably allowed the concentration of a surplus at a few regional centers. The need to protect

FIGURE 4.17 Pyramids of Giza, Egypt The ancient Egyptians' belief in the continuity and stability of the cosmos was supported by a range of cultural activities from the preservation of wood, cloth, people, and animals to the construction of large-scale monuments. The pyramids are one example of this monumental architecture, which represents Egyptians' view that life continues after death.

inhabitants from flooding and to channel river water for irrigation suggests that populations concentrated to take advantage of these opportunities. Walled towns began to appear in Mesopotamia at least as early as 4500 B.C. These early cities probably contained between 7000 and 25,000 inhabitants, and the major producers were fishers and farmers who supported a non-producing class of priests, administrators, and traders. Artisans also were clearly city dwellers. Houses for the producers, the lowest class of inhabitants, were likely to have been of mud construction. But the more elite urban dwellers probably lived in elaborate houses, many with courtyards and two stories. These houses were outfitted with systems for delivering fresh water and removing sewage. While some of the earliest cities were clearly planned, others were more randomly organized. What seems to be consistent across all of these early cities are three main elements: city walls; a commercial district; and suburbs, including houses, fields, groves, pastures, and cattle folds. As the historical evidence of urban commercial districts throughout the region suggests, trade was an essential part of life in these early cities. It not only helped spread ideas, it was a factor in encouraging and sustaining urban growth.

Many other powerful civilizations constructed cities and facilitated trade. The Egyptians had well-established trade relations with Crete, with cities along the Levant coast, with Anatolia in present-day Turkey, and with the people of the Sinai. The ruins of temples, pyramids, and related monumental works attest to the sophisticated engineering skills of the ancient Egyptians. When Egyptian rule declined after about 1090 B.C., other civilizations—among them the Assyrian, Persian, Roman, and the rule of Alexander the Great—all left their imprint on the region, from Roman roads, aqueducts, and theaters to Assyrian palace complexes at Khorsabad and Nimrud.

More recently, Islamic rule has certainly had the most visible impact on contemporary urban patterns in the region. At its greatest extent, Islamic rule and influence under different dynasties reached westward as far as Tours in France and eastward beyond Turkey and the Iranian Plateau into Afghanistan, Pakistan, and India, and southward into North and West Africa, throughout which local variations of the Islamic city can be found today. From the 7th to the 15th centuries A.D., Islamic trade networks were so vast that they linked Mediterranean Europe to parts of the Transcaucasus, Pakistan, and China. Such extensive trade networks are evidence that parts of the world were highly integrated—politically, economically, and culturally—long before contemporary globalization occurred.

The Ottoman Empire, European Colonialism, and the Emergence of Modern States

The Ottoman Empire, based on the Anatolian Plateau in Turkey, and with its capital in Istanbul was a successor to the Byzantine Empire. In power for more than 600 years, its influence began to decline in the Middle East and North Africa at the end of the 19th century. The Ottomans were Turkish Muslims who had replaced the Christian Greeks as the political power of the region after A.D. 1100. At its height, the Ottoman Empire (named after the founder of the Ottoman dynasty, Osman) extended from the Danube River in southeastern Europe (including present-day Hungary, Albania, Bosnia, and Kosovo) to North Africa and to the Arab lands of the eastern end of the Mediterranean. Within the region, only the Persian Empire, based on the Iranian Plateau, the central Arabian Peninsula, and Morocco, had been able to resist direct Ottoman control.

By the mid-19th century, Ottoman rule was under siege from Europe through the legacy of the French political revolution and the British Industrial Revolution. By the early 20th century the edges of the empire were being nibbled away. Egypt was occupied by Britain, and Algeria and Tunisia by France. By the eve of World War I, the Balkans and the remaining European possessions were lost, and the empire had been

The Maghreb

The Maghreb is the region of northwest Africa that contains the coastlands and Atlas Mountains of Morocco, Algeria, and Tunisia, and the mostly desert state of Libya. Its people, history, and geography make it distinctive. Part of the Maghreb includes a coastal plain along the Mediterranean Sea (see Figure 4.38). Within this narrow band, the region enjoys a moderate, Mediterranean climate, with cool, wet winters and hot, dry summers. Agriculture and tourism thrive here. Within the Maghreb are located the famous cities of Tripoli, Casablanca, Tangier, Marrakech, and the Barbary Coast—places of heroics and legend and Hollywood-style glamour that conjure in the imagination a landscape of mythic and romantic appeal.

The Maghreb's history differentiates it not only from the rest of Africa but also from the Middle East. In ancient times, the region was influenced by the Phoenicians, Carthaginians, Romans, Christians, Vandals, and Byzantines and then finally by the Arabs, who in the late ninth century A.D. converted the populace to Islam. While much of the material remains of that period have been destroyed or built over, remnants have survived. For instance, in Tunisia, Phoenician merchants founded a number of trading posts several thousand years ago. The most important one was Carthage, founded in 814 B.C. When the Romans defeated the Phoenicians, this area was incorporated into the Roman Empire, providing wheat and other commodities to the population in Rome. The ruins of Carthage lie in a suburb of present-day Tunis, the capital of Tunisia (**Figure 1**).

During the most recent period of imperialism, from the mid-19th to the mid-20th century, millions of Europeans, primarily French but also Spanish and Italian, flocked to the Maghreb and influenced its government, architecture, and language, especially in the city of Algiers, which is where most of the colonial Europeans lived. Significant numbers of Europeans also inhabited Casablanca and Tunis and formed a professional class that introduced many of the local elites to European cultural practices. In the early to mid-20th century, thousands of young people from the Maghreb went to the continent for university educations. They returned to the Maghreb with the seeds of nationalist ideology planted in their hearts and minds. Many of these individuals played roles in the independence movements that occurred throughout the Maghreb.

In addition to possessing material remnants of the ancient world, the region is home to the Berber, a people of ancient origin who preceded the Carthaginians and the Romans (see Figure 4.22). The Berber appear to have been indigenous to the Maghreb region, though in more recent times, those who are attempting to maintain their traditional ways of life have tended

FIGURE I Carthaginian ruins in Tunis Carthage was one of the great cities of the ancient world. Artifacts unearthed by archaeologists suggest the city was probably established as a trading post by Phoenicians toward the end of the ninth century B.C. Pictured here are the Roman Baths of Carthage.

carved up by various European powers, as well as Russia (**Figure 4.18**). European occupation exposed the various subregions to continental ideas about democracy, and as a result **nationalist movements** erupted—groups of people, sharing common elements of culture such as language, religion, or history, who wished to determine their own political affairs. The nationalist movements were particularly problematic for the polyglot Ottoman Empire, which had previously held itself together through an elaborate imperial legal and administrative structure that tended to allow for cultural differences. Already weakened by internal conflicts and external challenges, the Ottoman military, which had aligned with Germany, Austro-Hungary, and Bulgaria, was defeated by the Allied powers during World War I, resulting in the radical restructuring of the Ottoman Empire.

The Mandate System As part of the spoils of war, the Arab provinces of the Ottoman Empire were carved up and were neither colonized nor allowed to be entirely independent. Instead they became **mandates**—areas generally administered by a European power, with a promise and preparation for self-government and future indepen-

to live in the mountains and deserts, away from the increasingly populated coastal area. The Tuareg, once a largely nomadic Berber people, live in Algeria. For centuries the Tuareg were known as the "lords of the desert" because they patrolled the caravan routes on their camels and acted as guides for caravaneers. The word *Tuareg* literally means "blue men," and the group was given the name because their indigo robes darken their skin blue (**Figure 2**). Like many other Berber peoples, the Tuareg are for the most part no longer nomadic and are more likely to be oil or service workers. Another aspect of Berber culture can be found in a number of place-names in the Maghreb. The Barbary Coast, for instance, is a name derived from the word *Berber*. It became famous as a base of Arab and Berber pirates who launched attacks on Spanish and other European fleets as well as, at one point, on vessels of the United States.

The Maghreb region has a relatively strong economy based largely on oil and mineral exploitation, agriculture, and tourism. Algeria's oil industry provides nearly 90 percent of its export revenues. Libya too has substantial, high-quality petroleum reserves. Both Tunisia and Morocco are significant globally for their phosphate industries. All of the Maghreb countries are also agricultural producers, though none is self-sufficient. The most important agricultural products of the region include wheat, barley, olives, dates, citrus fruits, almonds, peanuts, beef and poultry, and vegetables.

Hugging the southern coastline of the Mediterranean with rugged mountains rising up from the coastal plains and then trailing off to the desert, the Maghreb is a spectacularly beautiful setting for tourists. The region offers a range of tourist experiences, in both luxury and economy style—from lying on the beautiful beaches to trekking into the Atlas Mountains or the Sahara Desert to visiting ancient archaeological ruins. Europeans are frequent visitors to the Maghreb because a short flight brings them to warm temperatures, exotic landscapes, and inexpensive and sumptuous food.

Algeria and Morocco are two of the fastest-growing economies in North Africa, with Libya and Tunisia making substantial strides as well. Links across the Mediterranean with the European Union through the Euro-Med agreements discussed earlier are likely to boost all sectors of the Maghreb economy, from resources to tourism. In the next 10 years or so, it is certainly possible that despite its strong Islamic history and resultant ties to the Middle East, the Maghreb may once again become especially close to Europe. This transformation is something of a tall order, however, as it requires the different states of the Maghreb to overcome their anxieties and animosities as former colonies or occupied territories and learn to wield power alongside their former colonizers and occupiers: Spain, Italy, and France.

FIGURE 2 Tuaregs crossing the Sahara A Tuareg man and his children, dressed in traditional blue robes, cross the Sahara's Erg Chebbi area with camels.

dence. Syria and Lebanon were mandates of the French; the British took Iraq and Palestine and turned part of the latter into Transjordan. The rationale for this sort of political arrangement—neither colony nor independent state—was heavily influenced by U.S. President Woodrow Wilson, who advocated self-determination and freedom over unmitigated colonization. The result was that a new form of external political control was created that legitimized French and British government dominance over their Middle Eastern and North African possessions. The mandate differs from outright colonial status because it requires the mandate holders to submit to internationally sanctioned guidelines. These guidelines require that constitutional governments be established as the first step in preparing the new states for eventual independence.

One of the most consequential mandates was the one determining the future of Palestine. As the mandate holder, Britain was obliged by treaty in 1917 to implement the provisions of the **Balfour Declaration**, named after British foreign secretary Arthur James Balfour, which committed Britain to the establishment of a Jewish national homeland in Palestine.

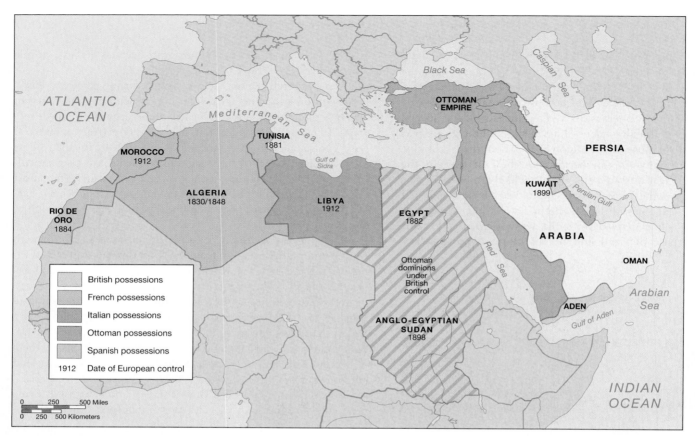

FIGURE 4.18 Europe in the Middle East and North Africa in 1914 The colonial presence of Europe in the Middle East and North Africa was short-lived—only about 50 years—but significant. The redrawing of boundaries in Israel/ Palestine, Jordan, Lebanon, and Iraq continues to be the source of political conflict that is often about access to land and other resources such as water. Many of the most politically contentious areas of the world are in the Middle East and North Africa. (*Source:* Redrawn from *Hammond Times Concise Atlas of World History.* Maplewood, NJ: Hammond, 1994, pp. 100–1.)

The political order that was imposed on the Middle East and North Africa following World War I was seriously challenged throughout the region. Egypt, Iraq, Syria, and Palestine, for instance, all revolted violently against the European presence in the region, though none was formally colonized. And while Turkey and Iran were able eventually to establish independent republics, by the mid-1920s, Britain and France exercised control—often somewhat tenuous—over the rest of the Middle East and North Africa.

Due to the mandate system of external control, strictly speaking, there were only five true colonies—Aden (British); Libya (Italian); and Algeria, Tunisia, and Morocco (French)—in the Middle East and North Africa in the 20th century. But a pattern of control did emerge such that the new states were heavily influenced, and in many cases, overly dominated, by their mandate holder.

The negative impact of the mandate system helped foment increasing regional dissatisfaction with outside dominance, and by the mid-20th century, aided by the crushing blows that World War II dealt to Europe, all of the states of the Middle East and North Africa had gained their independence. However, winning independence from colonizers who have effectively lost interest in their colony is not the same as gaining the allegiance of the diverse collection of new citizens. Many of the challenges that the new states of the Middle East and North Africa faced at mid-20th century continue to plague them in the 21st.

Independence and Economic Challenges The contemporary integration of the region into the global capitalist economy has brought increased wealth for some but also increased poverty or reduced living standards for many others, even in the wealthy oil-producing states. In the 1930s, entrepreneurial states such as Turkey adopted policies of **import substitution**, whereby domestic producers provide goods and services that were formerly bought from foreign producers. After World War II, more comprehensive and aggressive approaches to state-led development were also undertaken, often in response to nationalist movements and anti-imperialist sentiments. Iran, Turkey, Egypt, Syria, Iraq, Tunisia, and Algeria were foremost among the Middle East and North African states that adopted **nationalization** of economic development, which involves the conversion of key industries from private operation to governmental operation and control.

The explicit goal of nationalizing private enterprises was to improve the standard of living of working people, especially peasants in rural communities. Unfortunately, while the nationalization policies in the region did help expand the public sector, they had an urban bias. As a result, the main beneficiaries were urban industrial, clerical, and service workers. While some middle-class peasants did benefit from land reforms that helped expand their holdings, the condition of poor rural peasants either stayed the same or deteriorated.

Eventually, states in the Middle East and North Africa began to turn away from the nationalization of industries as their economies began to stagnate, standards of living declined, and national debt skyrocketed. Pressured by the International Monetary Fund (IMF), the World Bank, and the U.S. Agency for International Development, states of the region were forced to initiate stabilization and structural-adjustment programs in order to qualify for new loans and to reschedule old debts. These programs, also known as neoliberal policies (see Chapter 1, p. 9), often raised the cost of food and other necessities, cut government spending on social programs, and generally reduced investments in the public sector. The impact of these programs was felt most directly and significantly by urban workers, government bureaucrats, and people on fixed incomes.

Although the rural peasantry was supposed to benefit most from these neoliberal policies as consumer subsidies were dismantled and markets were privatized (allowing peasants market-based prices for goods and the opportunity to market crops more freely), capitalist farmers have been the main beneficiaries of neoliberalism. Thus, the impact of neoliberal policies has been to put into motion a whole new set of forces in the Middle East and North Africa that have improved the lives of some but have mostly lowered the living standards of both urban workers and peasants. This outcome is especially troubling; populations in the region are becoming increasingly urbanized as rural people move to the cities to find employment. Unfortunately, when they arrive they are confronted with decreased public services, not only in terms of schools and health care but also in terms of the most basic necessities, such as adequate housing and clean water. As a result, many people are forced to live in squatter settlements without sanitation. They are also often forced to eke out a living in the **informal economy**—that is, economic activities that take place beyond official record and are not subject to formalized systems of regulation or remuneration, such as unregulated taxi driving and street vending.

PEOPLES OF THE MIDDLE EAST AND NORTH AFRICA

The distinctive pattern of population distribution in the Middle East and North Africa reflects the influences of environment, history, and culture (**Figure 4.19**). Environment is clearly a key factor in that populations concentrate near rivers, streams, and oases or in areas of dependable precipitation. As a result, the population is heavily concentrated in coastal areas; the floodplains of the Tigris, Euphrates, and Nile rivers and smaller streams; and highland settings such as the Atlas Mountains. Other population clustering occurs around the region's cities, which have been well established for centuries but have grown especially rapidly since the independence period of the 1950s. Even though the Middle East and North Africa is more urbanized than is popularly assumed, many of the people of the region still live in rural villages (**Figure 4.20**).

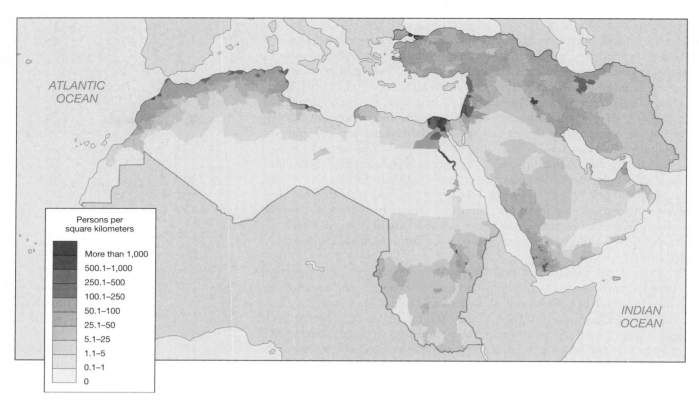

FIGURE 4.19 Population distribution in the Middle East and North Africa 1995 Population distribution is heavily influenced by the availability of water. The intensity and unusual linear pattern of population concentration along the Nile River valley is a perfect illustration of this point. Other concentrations, such as along the eastern end of the Mediterranean, the northern edge of Algeria, and the northern parts of Iran, Iraq, and Turkey, also reflect higher availability of fresh water. (*Source:* Center for International Earth Science Information Network [CIESIN], Columbia University; International Food Policy Research Institute [IFPRI]; and World Resources Institute [WRI], 2000. Gridded Population of the World [GPW], Version 2. Palisades, NY: CIESIN, Columbia University. Available at **http://sedac.ciesin.org/plue/gpw/index.html?main.html&2.**)

FIGURE 4.20 Gathering hay in northern Iraq In this Kurdish region of Iraq, most of the people are involved in agricultural activities and live in small villages or towns.

The total population of the 21 countries that make up the Middle East and North Africa is well over 350 million, but given the inaccuracy, infrequency, and inconsistency of national censuses in the region, this number is only an approximation. Although most of the region's states have recently conducted censuses that are considered by population experts to be accurate and reliable, others, such as Turkey, tend to underestimate their minority populations (the Kurds in particular) for political reasons. Despite the fact that fertility rates have fallen over the last four decades, the region is currently experiencing rapid population growth. Through both natural increase and immigration, many places in the region, such as Libya (where traditional ways of life support the promotion of large families) and Iraq (where the government promotes high rates of fertility) are among the fastest growing in the world. For a number of the most populated countries in the region, including Egypt, Algeria, and Turkey, a large part of the population is younger than 15 years of age, meaning that the populations of these countries will continue to grow as these individuals reach their reproductive age.

Religion

The Middle East and North Africa are infused with especially active religious practices and belief systems. Unlike many parts of the global core, where societies have become increasingly secular, religion in this complicated region is a central feature of everyday life for the vast majority of the inhabitants. Yet, the geography of religion is not uniform and significant differences in religious practice are likely to occur from the regional level to the neighborhood level. For instance, although Iran is widely recognized as a state that is passionately committed to Islam, so much so that there is little separation between the state and the Islamic religion, in Tehran, the capital city of more than 7 million inhabitants, many upper- and middle-class households are likely to be secular and more aligned with Western values than with the teachings of Islam.

About 96 percent of the population of the Middle East and North Africa is Islamic. The religion with the second largest number of followers is Christianity (about 3 percent), with Judaism ranking third (less than 1 percent). There are also a number of additional religions with much smaller numbers of adherents.

Islam   **Islam** is an Arabic term that means "submission to God's will." A **Muslim** is a member of the community of believers whose duty is obedience and submission to the will of God. As a revealed religion (a religion founded primarily on the revelations of God to humankind), Islam recognizes the prophets of the Hebrew and Christian Testaments of the Bible, but Muhammad is considered the last prophet and God's messenger on Earth. The Qur'an, the principal holy book of the Muslims, is considered to be the word of God as revealed to Muhammad by the Angel Gabriel beginning in about A.D. 610.

There are two fundamental sources of Islamic doctrine and practice: the Qur'an and the Sunna. Muslims regard the Qur'an as directly spoken by God to Muhammad. The Sunna is not a written document but a set of practical guidelines for behavior. It is effectively the body of traditions derived from the words and actions of the prophet Muhammad. While Islam holds that God has four fundamental functions—creation, sustenance, guidance, and judgment—the purpose of people is to serve God by worshiping him alone and adhering to an ethical social order. The actions of the individual, moreover, should be to the ultimate benefit of humanity, not the immediate pleasures or ambitions of the self. A Muslim must fulfill five primary obligations, known as the five pillars of Islam: repeating the profession of the faith ("There is no god but God; Muhammad is the messenger of God."); praying five times a day facing Mecca; giving alms, or charitable giving; fasting from sunup until sundown during the holy month of Ramadan; and making at least one pilgrimage, or **hajj**, to Mecca if financially and physically able.

The emergence and spread of Islam is linked to the commercial history of the Middle East and North Africa. The geographical origin of Islam is Mecca, in present-day Saudi Arabia (**Figure 4.21**). When Islam first emerged, Mecca, where Muhammad was born in A.D. 570, was a node in the trade routes that at first connected Yemen and Syria and eventually linked the region to Europe and all of Asia. Today Mecca is the most important sacred city in the Islamic world. It also continues to be a commercial center. Eventually Medina also became a sacred city because it was the place to which Muhammad fled when he was driven out of Mecca by angry merchants who felt his religious beliefs were a threat to their commercial practices.

Disagreement over the line of succession from the prophet Muhammad occurred shortly after his death in 632 and resulted in the split of Islam into two main sects, the Sunni and the Shi'a. The central difference between them revolves around the question of who should hold the *political* leadership of the Islamic community and what the *religious* dimensions of the leadership should be. The Shi'a contend that political leadership must be divine and therefore must derive from descendants of the Prophet. The Sunni faction, which argued that the clergy (with no divine power) should succeed Muhammad, gained the upper hand and became dominant. In specific countries, however, the pattern varies. The majority of Iran's 60 million people follow Shi'a, the official state religion of the Islamic Republic of Iran, founded in 1979. The majority

FIGURE 4.21 Mecca, Saudi Arabia
Pictured here is an Indonesian pilgrim who has come to Mecca to fulfill her religious obligation. Every year, during the last month of the Islamic calendar, more than 1 million Muslims make a pilgrimage, or *hajj*, to Mecca. In addition to the required pilgrimage, Islamic traditions require Muslims around the world to face Mecca during their daily prayers.

of Iraq's population is also Shi'a, even though the government that was headed for twenty-four years by Saddam Hussein was Sunni. It is also important to keep in mind that Islam is practiced differently in many different locales throughout the Middle East and North Africa and that Muslims who have migrated out of the region—to Europe and the United States, for instance—are shaped by and shape the practice of Islam in the Middle East and North Africa.

Perhaps one of the most widespread cultural counterforces to globalization has been the rise of **Islamism**, which is more popularly, although incorrectly, known as Islamic fundamentalism. Whereas *fundamentalism* is a general term that describes the desire to return to strict adherence to the fundamentals of a religious system, Islamism is an anti-Western, anti-imperial, and overall anti-core political movement. In Muslim countries, Islamists resist the core, especially Western, forces of globalization—namely modernization and secularization. Not all Muslims are Islamists; Islamism is the most militant movement within Islam today.

The basic intent of Islamism is to create a model of society that protects the purity and centrality of Islamic precepts through the return to a universal Islamic state—a state that would be religiously and politically unified by including principles from the sacred law of Islam into state constitutions. Most Islamists object to secularization because they believe the corrupting influences of the core place the rights of the individual over the common good. They view the popularity of Western ideas as a move away from religion to a more secular (nonreligious) society.

Another aspect of the Islamist movement is the concept of **jihad**, a complex term derived from the Arabic root meaning "to strive." Current use of the term connotes both an inward spiritual struggle to attain perfect faith as well as an outward material struggle to promote justice and the Islamic social system. *Qital* (fighting or warfare) is one form of jihad and, according to the Qur'an, means a war of conquest or conversion against all nonbelievers. When a war directed against the enemies of Islam occurs, it can be interpreted as a holy war. But jihad can also be a more peaceful struggle to establish Islam as a universal religion through the conversion of nonbelievers. One example of jihad today is the struggle of Shi'ite Muslims for social, political, and economic rights within Sunni-dominated Islamic states.

Christianity, Judaism, and Other Middle Eastern and North African Religions   Although Islam is the most widely practiced religion in the Middle East and North Africa, it is by no means the only religion of political, cultural, or social significance. There are more than a dozen Christian sects—among them Coptic Christians in Egypt, Maronites, the Chaldean Catholic Church, and various orthodox affiliations, including Armenian, Greek, Ethiopian, and even some Protestant faiths. Faiths not associated with any of the three world religions are largely concentrated in Iran and include Bahaism and Zoroastrianism. Generally, Jews in the Middle East and North Africa are secular, observing some Jewish traditions. A small percentage are Orthodox or Hasidic and there also exists an offshoot of Judaism, known as Samaritanism, the adherents of which are largely concentrated in the West Bank.

The three regionally predominant religions have helped shape the peoples and the landscape of the region. The most obvious and enduring landscape influences have been places of worship and sacred spaces more generally. Nowhere is the enduring interrelationship of the three religions more apparent than in the ancient city of Jerusalem. The centrality of Jerusalem as an ancient religious space, as well as its contemporary significance as a place of pilgrimage for Jews and Christians, is very much tied up with Arab-Israeli conflicts. Modern constructions of the state that link territory with nationality are ill-equipped to deal with the religious significance of Jerusalem to Christians, Jews, and Muslims.

Culture and Society

The social organization of the Middle East and North Africa is as complex as that of any other region of the globe, with the social categories of gender, tribe, nationality, kinship, and family figuring prominently. Global media technologies such as satellite television and the Internet are increasingly penetrating the region, however, with the potential for new social forms to emerge and old ones to be reconfigured. Generally, the predominant forms of social organization in the region have persisted for hundreds of years. Both subtle and dramatic changes within these forms have already occurred.

Kinship and Family   To understand Middle Eastern and North African society, it is important to understand ideas of kinship, family, and other personal relationships. **Kinship** is normally thought of as a relationship based on blood, marriage, or adoption. However, this definition needs to be expanded to include a shared notion of relationship among members of a group. Not all kinship relations are understood by social groups to be exclusively based on biological or marriage ties. Although in the Middle East and North Africa, biological ties, usually determined through the father, are important, they are not the only ties that link individuals and families. In fact, though kinship is often expressed as a "blood" tie among social groups throughout the Middle East and North Africa, it is often the case that neighbors, friends, and even individuals with common economic or political interests are considered kin. Kinship is such a valued relationship for expressing solidarity and connection that it is often used to assert a feeling of group closeness and as a basis for identity even where no "natural" or "blood" ties are present.

For many Middle Easterners and North Africans, kinship helps shape a whole range of social relationships from business to marriage to politics. This is true in ordinary households in urban and rural areas as well as in the monarchies of the region, such as those of Saudi Arabia, Oman, and Morocco. Kinship also figures largely in other states, such as in Iran, Egypt, Syria, Turkey, and Lebanon, where it is not unusual to find that the holders of many government offices are close relatives. The underlying assumption of such arrangements is that appointments based on kinship are not an abuse of political authority but a guarantee of loyalty.

Kinship is even an important factor in shaping the spatial relationships of the home as well as outside the home, determining who can interact with whom and under what circumstances. This is especially the case for the interaction of gender and kinship, where women's and men's access to public and private space is sharply differentiated.

Social Order and Loyalty   The idea of the tribe is central to understanding the sociopolitical organization of the Middle East and North Africa. Moreover, the term *tribe* is a highly contested concept and one that should be treated carefully. For instance, it is often seen as a negative label applied by the colonizers to suggest primitiveness in social organization. Where it is adopted in the Middle East and North Africa, however, *tribe* is not seen as a primitive form of social organization but rather a valuable element in sustaining modern national identity.

Generally speaking, a **tribe** is a form of social identity created by groups who share a common set of ideas about collective loyalty and political action. Tribes are grounded in any combination or single expression of social, political, and cultural identities created by those who share them. The result of shared tribal identity is the formation of collective loyalties that result in a primary allegiance to the tribe. External groups may recognize the existence of these self-defined tribal groups and may seek to undermine or encourage their persistence. For instance, in early 20th-century Iran, the state ruthlessly and systematically attempted to eliminate tribal affiliations. In contrast, during the European colonial period in Sudan and Morocco, tribes were seen as forms of social organization that might inhibit nationalist movements, so they were largely promoted and supported by the colonial state.

One Middle Eastern and North African group that is frequently and proudly tribal is pastoralists. Pastoralism is a subsistence activity that involves breeding and herding animals to satisfy the human need for food, shelter, and clothing. Usually practiced in marginal areas where subsistence agriculture cannot be practiced, pastoralism can be either sedentary or nomadic. Sedentary pastoralists live in settlements and herd animals in nearby pastures, while nomadic pastoralists travel with their herds over long distances,

FIGURE 4.22 Berber shepherd campsite The Berber have lived in North Africa since ancient times. *Berber* is the name applied to the language and people belonging to a number of tribes who currently inhabit large sections of North Africa. Pictured here is a Berber shepherd campsite in the High Atlas Mountains, where great herds of sheep are tended. Increasing numbers of Berbers are raising crops, a practice that signals the erosion of their nomadic practices.

never settling in any one place for very long (**Figure 4.22**). Most nomadic pastoralists practice **transhumance**, the movement of herds according to seasonal rhythms. Flocks are kept in warmer, lowland areas in the winter and in cooler, highland areas in the summer.

Although the herds are occasionally slaughtered and used directly for food, shelter, and clothing, often they are bartered with farmers for grain and other commodities. Female and younger members of pastoralist groups may farm small plots. In such cases, mostly women and children split off from the larger group and plant crops at fixed locations in the spring. They may stay sedentary for the growing season, tending the crops, or they may rejoin the group and return to the fields when the crops are ready for harvesting.

Gender Although gender differences play a part in shaping social life for men and women in the Middle East and North Africa, as elsewhere around the globe, there is no single Islamic, Christian, or Jewish notion of gender that operates exclusively in the region. Many people have formed stereotypes about the restricted lives of Middle Eastern and North African women because of the operation of rigid Islamic traditions. These stereotypes do not capture the great variety in gender relations that exist in the Middle East and North Africa across lines of class, religion, generation, level of education, and geography (urban versus rural origins, for instance). What pervades the Middle East and North Africa, as well as many other societies throughout the world, is an ideological assumption that women should be subordinate to men. This view is held by both men and women in many Middle Eastern and North African societies. Interestingly, it seems that men regard women's subordination as something natural, something that is effectively determined by biology. In contrast, most women in the Middle East and North Africa tend to regard their subordination as something that is the product of the society in which they live and operate, and therefore something that can be negotiated and manipulated. The gender systems that operate in a wide variety of contexts in the Middle East and North Africa are derived in large part from some of the same notions about men and women that inform gender systems in Western societies. Although this view is being increasingly critiqued and has begun to be dismantled in the West, it is still powerful there as well as in the Middle East and North Africa. Control over women in the Middle East and North Africa is frequently exercised by restricting their access to public space and secluding them within private space (**Figure 4.23**).

FIGURE 4.23 Gendered architecture Islamic architecture reflects gender differences within the culture, and in different places within the Middle Eastern and North African region these differences can be either strictly or more loosely observed. A classic aspect of Islamic architecture is the screen placed across windows in the women's parts of the houses and in the interiors of some public buildings. The screens pictured here are from Tunisia. They allow women to watch activities outside their windows without being seen.

Sexuality and gender roles affect how men and women see themselves and represent themselves publicly in the Middle East and North Africa. Some societies, such as in Yemen and Bahrain, exercise very strict control over women's public movements, and women are expected to cover themselves with veils and long, dark clothing when out on the streets. In some more generally secular of the region's societies, such as Turkey and Egypt, women's public movements are much less strictly regulated. The veil—from the all-encompassing full body garment, known as a **chador**, to a simpler head covering—has become the means by which women are able to effectively operate in public and yet remain in their personal space.

National-level policies and practices vary with respect to women's access to, and behavior in, public space (**Figure 4.24**). Subnational and local variations do exist, particularly differences in urban versus rural practices and even according to class differences within urban areas. Generally, urban women's public movements tend to be more restricted than those of rural women. This is largely because rural villages are usually composed of kin, and women can operate relatively freely among them, while urban women must move about in a world of both kin and strangers. In some cities middle- and upper-class women tend to have more constraints on their public social behaviors than poorer women. Again, the strictures placed on women's movements vary throughout the region and even within particular countries and subregions within countries.

The most important aspect of gender systems in the Middle East and North Africa is that social reality is not fixed and that cultural assumptions and practices around

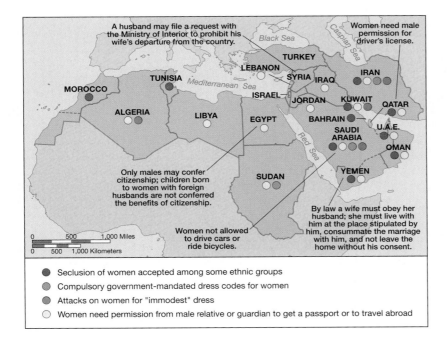

A husband may file a request with the Ministry of Interior to prohibit his wife's departure from the country.

Women need male permission for driver's license.

Only males may confer citizenship; children born to women with foreign husbands are not conferred the benefits of citizenship.

Women not allowed to drive cars or ride bicycles.

By law a wife must obey her husband; she must live with him at the place stipulated by him, consummate the marriage with him, and not leave the home without his consent.

- ● Seclusion of women accepted among some ethnic groups
- ● Compulsory government-mandated dress codes for women
- ● Attacks on women for "immodest" dress
- ○ Women need permission from male relative or guardian to get a passport or to travel abroad

FIGURE 4.24 Women's mobility Although Islamic law imposes restrictions on women's movements and dress in public space, there is a great deal of variation across the region with respect to adherence to these legal strictures.

gender are subject to negotiation and change. Although the predominant gender theme in the Middle East and North Africa is that women are subordinate to men, women can and do exercise a great deal of household as well as political influence and independence across a range of societies in this region.

Migration and the Middle Eastern and North African Diaspora

For thousands of years in the Middle East and North Africa, populations have moved around within the region, at times as refugees, at other times voluntarily. They have also moved out of the region, settling all over the world. Generally speaking, migration into and out of the region since the end of the colonial period has largely been related to several factors that have pulled immigrants to the region and forced many others to leave (**Figure 4.25**). Internal regional and national migration has also been significant and is almost always related to the draw of urban economic opportunity as rural areas experience population increase or economic decline.

Pull Factors   The strongest force drawing migrants to the Middle East and North Africa in the last 50 years has been the phenomenal growth of the oil economy. Oil is not the only attractive force, however; other factors have also attracted migrants. For instance, the founding of the state of Israel at mid-century drew large numbers of European Jews to the region, particularly during and after World War II. More recently, Ethiopian and Russian Jews have also migrated, in the former case due to civil war and in the latter due to the end of the Cold War. Non-oil-related economic growth has fostered migration to places like Beirut in Lebanon, Cairo in Egypt, and Istanbul in

FIGURE 4.25 Kurdish and Lebanese diaspora, 1990   The most significant diasporic populations of the Middle East and North Africa during modern times are the Palestinians, the Lebanese, and the Kurdish peoples. (Of course, Jews are also a diasporic population, but recently they have returned to—rather than left—the Middle East in very large numbers.) This map shows the scattering of the Lebanese and the Kurds. (The dispersal of the Palestinians is shown in Figure 4.28.) Over the last century, Lebanon has experienced various waves of diasporic migration due largely to war and the tensions within this multiethnic, multireligious society. Many Kurds moved to different parts of the region or left it altogether during the 20th century because of military aggression, persecution, and the repeated failure to establish a Kurdish state. (*Source:* Redrawn and modified from A. Segal, *An Atlas of International Migration.* London: Hans Zell, 1993, pp. 95 and 103.)

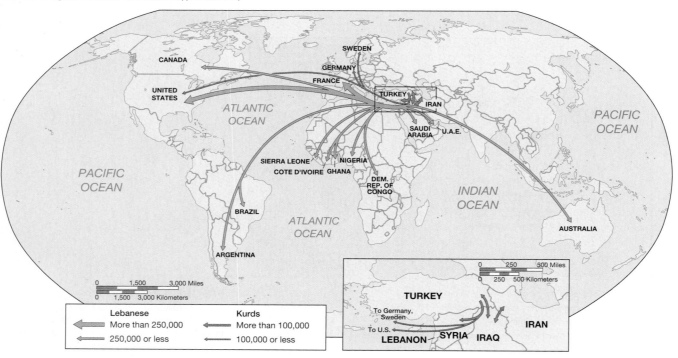

Turkey, all of which have increased their importance as core cities in the regional economy following the spread of political independence throughout the region.

Still, the most prominent attractive force has been the job opportunities made possible through the wealth generated by the continued development of the petroleum industry (**Figure 4.26**). In the states of the Arabian Peninsula, several factors—small populations, lack of skill, and a lack of interest in or possibly cultural resistance to the kinds of jobs made available through the oil economy—have meant that workers had to be imported. Nearly three-quarters of the labor force in the Gulf states are **guest workers**, brought in to work in all aspects of oil production, from exploration and well development to drilling, refining, and shipping (**Figure 4.27**). And because oil revenues have been widely reinvested in economic development projects in the region, even more jobs have been created outside the petroleum industry, ranging from service-sector positions to jobs in the building and construction industry.

To lessen the potentially dislocating impact of foreign workers on local social and cultural systems, immigration policy among the oil-producing states of the Arabian Peninsula has favored Muslim applicants. Within the region, large numbers of guest workers from Syria and Egypt, as well as Palestinian refugees, have come to participate in the Arabian Peninsula oil economy, filling both skilled and unskilled positions. Many additional guest workers have arrived from outside the region, especially from India, Indonesia, the Philippines, and Pakistan. Most of the migrants who have come from other Middle Eastern and North African countries have been male, although a significant number of the labor migrants from Indonesia and the Philippines have been female.

Push Factors The most consistent forces pushing migrants out of the Middle East and North Africa have been war, civil unrest, and the lack of economic opportunity. Often the latter two have either been fostered or exacerbated by the imposition of the core's political system of territorially bounded nation-states on populations previously organized around very different sociopolitical systems. The case of Lebanon is an illustration. At the beginning of the period of European imperialism in the region, Lebanon became a French mandate under the League of Nations. Instead of promoting national unity among the many ethnic and religious groups of the Greater Lebanese mandate, France created a political administrative system of divide-and-rule that promoted fragmentation and increased the probabilities of sectarian conflict.

During World War II, Lebanon was allowed to become fully independent of France. The way that independence was established, however, was especially problematic. Through an informal 1943 National Pact, power sharing in the newly sovereign Lebanon was to be distributed among the various ethnoreligious groups according to their share of the population. A form of proportional representation, this political arrangement enabled France to award the key political positions (the presidency and the commander of the armed forces) to the right-wing Maronite Christians who had been arbitrarily turned into the single largest religious community by redrawing Lebanon's territorial boundaries to include a Christian part of Syria. Predictably, after independence Lebanon was beset by sectarian divisions, including rebellions, external attacks by Israel, and civil war between factions of Christian and Muslim militias and even within different Christian and Muslim groups. This civil instability compelled tens of thousands of Lebanese people—both Christians and Muslims—to

FIGURE 4.26 Labor migrants Many immigrant workers live in the oil-rich countries of the Middle East and North Africa. In some countries, these workers make up 80 or 90 percent of the workforce largely because there are so few local people to fill the jobs. These construction workers are at the site of an apartment complex of 40 skyscrapers on the outskirts of Dubai, UAE.

FIGURE 4.27 Internal migration in the Middle East and North Africa Internal migration on a massive scale is a fairly recent phenomenon in the region. Until the decline of the Ottoman Empire, most residents of the region lived and died close to where they were born. European colonialism and imperialism in the early 20th century resulted in some migration. But the most significant impetus for mass internal migration really began with the expansion of oil production in the Oil States in the 1950s.

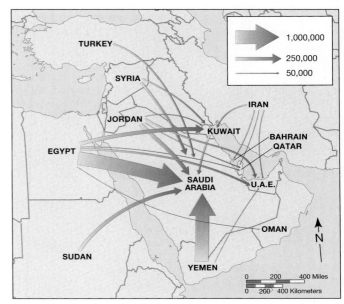

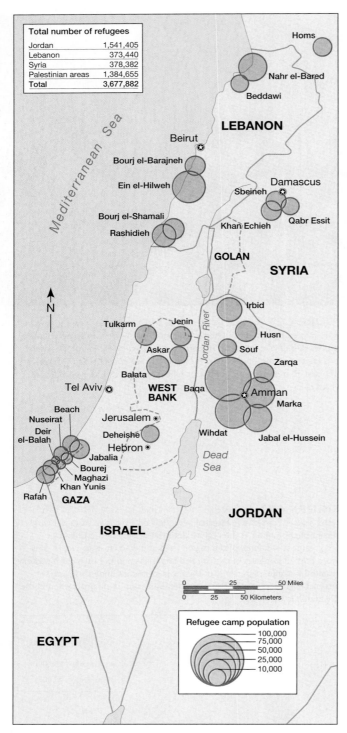

Total number of refugees	
Jordan	1,541,405
Lebanon	373,440
Syria	378,382
Palestinian areas	1,384,655
Total	3,677,882

FIGURE 4.28 Palestinian refugees in the Middle East
This map shows the dispersion of Palestinian refugees—in camps and elsewhere—in the states around Israel and in the West Bank, Gaza, and the Occupied Territories. One of the biggest obstacles in the Israeli-Palestinian peace talks has been the question of refugee return and where Palestinians will be allowed to settle. (*Source:* Adapted from *The Guardian,* October 14, 2000, p. 5.)

flee the country to escape violence. At the beginning of the new century, more Lebanese live outside Lebanon than in it. By the late 1990s and during the early years of the 21st century, Lebanon had begun to enjoy a period of relative civil tranquility and sustained economic growth, with the 2002 presidential election occurring in the absence of any violence. Unfortunately, all this changed in July 2006, with retaliatory missile attacks by Israel on southern Lebanon. We discuss the deterioration of this political and economic stability later in this chapter (p. 187).

British and U.S. political involvement in Iran also caused many Iranians to flee the country. With the beginning of the Cold War between Western countries and the Soviet Union following World War II, Iran's oil reserves were considered to be of great strategic importance to Britain and the United States. In the early 1950s, the United States and Britain feared that their access to Iranian oil reserves was threatened by Iran's democratically elected but mildly anti-Western Prime Minister Mohammad Mossadegh, because he had plans to nationalize the oil industry. Fearing that a nationalized industry would cut off Britain, which had controlled Iran's oil through the Anglo-Iranian Oil Company, Britain appealed to the United States to help oust Prime Minister Mossadegh from office. The ouster was supported by President Eisenhower and carried out by the U.S. Central Intelligence Agency and British intelligence operators. The virulent anti-Western fervor that has circulated in Iran since the coup that ousted Mossadegh in 1953, and the revolution in 1979 that eventually deposed Shah Mohammad Reza Pahlavi, are partly perceived to be the result of the interference of Britain and the United States in Iranian politics. Both events, but especially the fall of the shah, resulted in the exodus of tens of thousands of pro-Western Iranians to the United States, Britain, and Europe, as well as to several Middle Eastern countries such as Egypt.

Other significant instances of migration created in the post-colonial Middle East and North Africa are the Algerians, Tunisians, and Moroccans, who have migrated mostly to Europe; Turks, who have followed a historical migration route to the Balkans and more recently to Germany; and Egyptians who have migrated to other Arab countries in the region as well as elsewhere in the world. The migration of better-educated as well as low-skilled Turks and Egyptians has both pull and push dimensions to it. The push factor has occurred as educated and skilled workers have had to leave because economic growth has not been able to keep up with population growth by providing high-paying jobs. The pull factors include European policies that enable temporary workers to come and take up low-paying, low-skill jobs that are not economically attractive to Europeans. The artificial boundaries that the British drew around independent Iraq in 1932 created fierce cultural tensions between the Shi'ite and Sunni Muslim sects. These tensions have been the source of nearly 50 years of enduring political instability in the country and the cause of out-migration there.

The most dramatic instance of massive emigration in the Middle East and North Africa is that of the Palestinians, which began to occur when Israel became a state in 1948. Today Palestinians form the most widely scattered diasporic population in the world, with millions living outside the region altogether, while others live in various parts of the region, often in refugee camps (**Figure 4.28**). We discuss more of the background to the Palestinian diaspora and the current situation in Israel and the Occupied Territories later in this chapter (pp. 187–190).

The Diaspora The circulation of Middle Eastern and North African populations throughout the world has also resulted in the widespread distribution of their cultural practices, transforming the landscapes—in terms of buildings, tastes, sounds, and smells—of the places in which they have settled. The cuisine of the eastern Mediterranean, especially that of Lebanon and Syria, as well as of Turkey, Egypt, Iran, Morocco, Tunisia, and Algeria, is available in many large cities in most of the world's regions. In the United States and Europe, it is often available in smaller urban places as well. For example, many young Middle Eastern and North African men and women have gone to study at universities in the United States and Europe where cafés offering strongly brewed coffee and regional cuisine have sprung up to serve them.

The types of food available from this region include what are known as *meze dishes*, which are predominantly subtly spiced appetizers or small dishes. The range of meze dishes broadly reflects the tastes and ingredients of a particular country or subregion within that country. Some of the most popular meze dishes include *baba ganoush*, a puree of toasted eggplant, sesame seeds, and garlic; *falafel*, a mixture of spicy chickpeas rolled into balls and deep fried; *fuul*, brown broad beans seasoned with olive oil, lemon juice, and garlic; and *tabouleh*, a salad of bulgur wheat, parsley, mint, tomato, and onion. The region also specializes in grilled meats, especially lamb and chicken, often served with rice.

A second cultural contribution of the Middle Eastern and North African region is music and dance. The most widespread of the region's dances is the traditional belly dance, a women's erotic solo dance done for entertainment. The dance is characterized by undulating movements of the abdomen and hips and by graceful arm movements. Belly dancing is believed to have originated in medieval Islamic culture, though some theories link it to prehistoric religious fertility rites. Middle Eastern and North African music has also become a staple of the contemporary world music scene. For instance, Googoosh is a celebrated female vocalist from Iran who has a huge following among Iranian emigrants in Europe, the United States, Australia, and Japan, where her concerts are sold out. The audience often weeps as she sings a blend of traditional Persian and Western pop music. In contrast is another musical superstar, Cheb Khaled, an Algerian and multi-instrumentalist who sings rai (traditional Algerian music that derives from Arabic poetry and Bedouin folk music) with influences from flamenco to Elvis. His following includes fans in Europe, Asia, and Latin America. Also from Algeria is Souad Massi, a Muslim woman who is a romantic pop vocalist influenced by western rock, folk, and country music, as well as the chaabi and classical Andalusian music. The target of fundamentalist militias in her native Algeria, she was eventually able to travel to Paris, where she was catapulted into international stardom (**Figure 4.29**). The list goes on to include rap stars like Ceza in Turkey and Subliminal in Israel and, from the diaspora, Canadian-Israeli rapper SHI (Supreme Hebrew Intellect), the son of Jewish refugees from Morocco, who raps in Hebrew, Arabic, English, and French!

Perhaps the most substantial if more silent evidence of the globalization of Middle Eastern and North African culture is the appearance of mosques throughout the world. Mosques serve as the main place of worship for Muslims, but they also serve many social and political needs as forums for many public functions. Mosques also function as law courts, schools, and assembly halls. Adjoining chambers often house libraries, hospitals, or treasuries.

FIGURE 4.29 Souad Massi at a music award ceremony in Paris, where she was nominated for the best world music album of the year in 2006.

Cities and Human Settlement

The predominant pattern of settlement in the Middle East and North Africa is a relatively small number of very large cities, a substantial number of medium-sized cities, and a very great number of small rural settlements. Variation on this broad generalization among countries in the region is dramatic. Israel is mostly an urban country with 90 percent of its population living in cities. Sudan is largely a rural country with only about 30 percent of the population living in cities. Cities in the region are growing dramatically each year, as more and more migrants come to live in them. Only about 50 years ago, most people in the region lived in small scattered rural settlements, but since then political independence and the development of the oil economy have been underlying factors in the increasing urbanization of the population.

Table 4.1	Ten Largest Cities in the Middle East and North Africa, 2005
City	Population (in millions)
Cairo, Egypt	11.1
Istanbul, Turkey	9.7
Tehran, Iran	7.3
Baghdad, Iraq	5.9
Khartoum, Sudan	4.5
Riyadh, Saudi Arabia	4.2
Alexandria, Egypt	3.8
Ankara, Turkey	3.6
Algiers, Algeria	3.2
Casablanca, Morocco	3.1

The Middle East and North Africa have a long and distinguished urban history. Beginning with the period of early empires, cities here have been centers of religious authority, have played pivotal roles in trade networks, and have reflected the complex culture that created them. In the early 21st century, cities in the region continue to play central administrative roles—though today their political significance is as strong, if not stronger, than their religious significance. Even though trade continues to be crucial to city building—especially oil-related trade—other economic sectors stimulate urbanization, including processing and manufacturing and services. What has been most remarkable about contemporary urbanization in the region is that its rapid pace has led to the emergence of one or two very large cities in each country that contain a large proportion of the country's population and disproportionately wield political and economic influence. The rapid pace and extreme degree of urbanization in the region can be traced to the migration of rural people in search of economic opportunity in the city as well as to natural increase among resident urban dwellers. **Table 4.1** lists the major cities of the Middle Eastern and North African region. Cities like Cairo, with more than 11 million inhabitants; Istanbul, with nearly 10 million; and Tehran, with 7.5 million, are among the world's most populous cities.

One of the most widespread problems of rapid urbanization in the periphery is the inability of governments to meet the service and housing needs of growing urban populations. As a result, there are inadequate and often poor-quality water supplies, electricity, sewer systems, clinics, and schools as well as air pollution and severe traffic congestion. Most critically, governments seem unable to provide housing for all who need it and squatter settlements have been assembled on unclaimed or unoccupied urban land (**Figure 4.30**). Unfortunately, the very largest cities in the region continue to attract even more migrants who see the most well-known places as possessing the best opportunities for a better life. These primate cities continue to grow in disproportion to other urban places, compounding the severity of their problems.

On the other hand, rapid urban growth—directly and indirectly related to the growing oil industry—in a few of the very wealthy oil-producing countries such as Jubail (Saudi Arabia) and Doha (Qatar) has resulted in impressively modern cities with few of the urban problems of their neighbors. Their enormous wealth coupled with their very low populations has made the growth of some of their urban places relatively uncomplicated. Many other cities of the oil-producing region, including Jeddah (Saudi Arabia) and Basra (Iraq), however, have not escaped the erection of shantytowns and the difficult social problems that accompany this type of urban change.

The highly diverse peoples of the Middle East and North Africa occupy an ancient region with a complex history and environment. As mentioned earlier, water is a critical variable in shaping where people live. Religion is a central force in shaping social interactions; kinship, tribe, and gender play roles. Many important cities and several very large ones connect the region to the world-system. Just under half the population still lives in rural settlements, but even with this large proportion of rural dwellers, the Middle East and North Africa is more urbanized than some other

FIGURE 4.30 Squatter settlements in Istanbul, Turkey In Istanbul, squatter settlements are knows as *gecekondu*, a Turkish word meaning that the settlements were built after dusk and before dawn. Geographer Paul Kaldjian's research in Turkey has shown that many residents of these settlements actually own land in the countryside, where they grow some of the food that sustains their lives in the city. With no employment opportunities there, these individuals have been forced to migrate to the city in search of work. Relatives of the urban migrants often stay behind and maintain the family gardens during the growing season. At harvest time, the urban residents return to the countryside to help gather and divide up the crops.

world regions, including South Asia and Sub-Saharan Africa. With a large population that derives its livelihood mostly from agriculture, the region, generally speaking, is most heavily involved in international trade around primary products such as minerals and agricultural goods (especially cereals and grains, cotton, and fruits and nuts). The most important of these products, as we shall see in the following section, is oil. The Middle East and North Africa possess and trade more oil on the world market than any other region of the world. Despite its fantastic oil wealth, which is by no means widely distributed across the region, the Middle East and North Africa is still predominantly a peripheral region in the world economy.

CONTEMPORARY CHALLENGES IN A GLOBALIZING WORLD

During the 20th century, the countries of the Middle East and North Africa emerged from their colonial and dependent status with a range of economic and political problems. Many Middle East and North Africa experts believe that most of the political and economic problems of the region are a direct result of artificial political boundaries that united peoples who were previously antagonistic or divided peoples who were once unified. In fact, while the region has experienced wars and conflict for hundreds, if not thousands, of years, and certainly well before the Europeans arrived, it is generally agreed that most of its present conflicts stem directly from either of two things. The first involves the boundaries and borders created by the colonial powers; the second is the strategic importance of the Middle East and North Africa to the political and economic interests of the core countries of the world economy.

Remarkably, at the same time that the region has been the site for bitter and, in some instances, seemingly irresolvable conflicts, it has also been the site for a great deal of broad and sustained cooperation. The most significant unifying forces have been the religion of Islam and the Arabic language that have helped the vast majority of people appreciate and nurture their common cultural heritage. Moreover, these unifying forces have helped many of the peoples of the region to recognize that they have common political and economic goals.

New Political Geographies and Regional Conflicts

The post-colonial political geography of this region is seen as one of the most serious challenges to stability and peace there. Extreme stereotypes suggest that the inhabitants of the region are naturally bellicose people. While terrorist organizations do exist in the region (as they do in all regions of the world) and armed conflict has been a sad reality of life in many parts of the region, such characterizations are fundamentally false at the same time that they grossly simplify the region's political, economic, and social history. Both conservative and more radical observers of the region agree that the boundaries drawn by Britain, France, Spain, and Italy in the Middle East and North Africa have been the single major source of contemporary conflicts in the region, many of which are decades old. Our treatment of these conflicts in this text is meant to expose their structural sources so that they might be better understood not as stemming from the personal characteristics of the people who inhabit the region but from the difficult political situations they have inherited.

Tensions and Conflict: Iran, Iraq, and Kuwait The tensions that exist and the conflicts that have erupted between Iran and Iraq over the last 30-plus years are the result of a number of factors. One factor is the cultural differences between Persians (Iranians) and Arabs (Iraqis). Though the majority of both Persians and Arabs are Muslim, their ethnic origins, languages, geographies, and histories are distinctly different. Furthermore, the Persians were unceremoniously conquered by the Arabs in the seventh century and converted to Islam beginning in the ninth century.

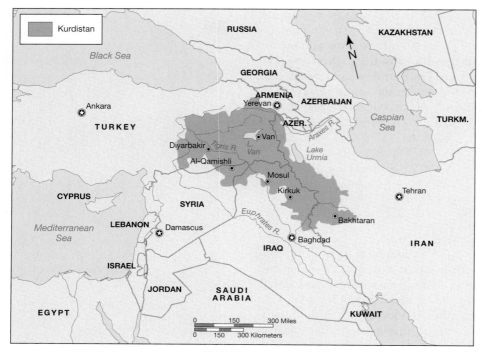

FIGURE 4.31 Kurdistan means the "land of the Kurds," and this map shows both the area where the Kurdish population is currently dominant as well as its traditional home. While not an independent state, the map does provide a sense of the boundaries that (from the Kurdish perspective) it might ideally encompass. (*Source:* University of Texas, **http://www.lib.utexas.edu/maps/middle_east_and_asia/ kurdish_lands_92.jpg**, accessed September 23, 2006.)

FIGURE 4.32 Shatt-al-Arab, Iran and Iraq This map shows one of the areas of dispute that fuel the territorial conflict between Iran and Iraq. A shift in the boundary along the Shatt-al-Arab from the east bank to the deepest part of the channel in 1975 was one reason war erupted between the two states. The enmity between the two countries goes back centuries, and the territories in question provide contemporary opportunities to ignite the ages-old antagonism. (*Source:* Redrawn from T. Y. Ismael, *Iraq and Iran: Roots of Conflict.* Syracuse: Syracuse University Press, 1983, p. 23.)

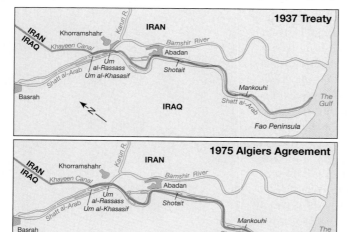

Since then both countries have a very long history of animosity that has more recently been complicated by their different dependent relationships with Britain and, later, the United States. The conflicts between Iran and Iraq remain unresolved today and are a source of continuing concern for the international community because both countries are important in global petroleum production.

Another source of conflict is the result of the transfer of three small islands at the mouth of the Persian Gulf to the United Arab Emirates (UAE) by the British after the UAE became independent in 1971. The islands had historically been part of Iran, however, and later in 1971 Iran seized them. Iraq pronounced this seizure an act of aggression and a violation of Arab sovereignty. Iraq unsuccessfully attempted to agitate the Arab population of Iran's Khuzestan Province to revolt against Iran. In 1980, war broke out between the two countries when Iraqi forces occupied most of the same Iranian province in retaliation for Iranian artillery attacks and propaganda broadcasts against Iraq.

Other points of tension have occurred around Iran's support of the Kurdish guerillas who have been fighting the Iraqi government for autonomous control over their mountainous region. The Kurds are a non-Arabic people, mostly Sunni Muslims, who have been subjugated by their neighbors for most of their history. About 20 million Kurds live in the mountainous areas along the borders of Iran, Iraq, Syria, Turkey, and a small area in Armenia, called Kurdistan by Kurds, (**Figure 4.31**). About 8 million live in southeastern Turkey. Throughout the 20th century and into the present one, the Kurds as an ethnic minority have faced repression and discrimination in the countries in which they live. Many Kurds have agitated peacefully as well as in armed rebellion for outright independence or autonomy. A large number of Kurds have left the region entirely and now live in western Europe, an important source of financial support for the resistance movement.

In Iraq, Peshmerga is a Kurdish group that has engaged in armed conflict to secure an independent Kurdish state. Another militant group, the Kurdistan Workers Party (PKK), has engaged in armed fighting in Turkey, Iraq, Syria, and Iran for more than 30 years. In Turkey, more than 30,000 Turkish and Kurdish people have died as a result of the war between the state and the PKK, with alleged atrocities being committed by both sides. In Iran, throughout the 1990s and continuing today, there has been ongoing government repression and unrest among the Kurdish population. Because of Kurdish determination for independence and the desire of the four governments to retain them, Kurdistan is one of the most militarized areas on Earth.

Yet another source of conflict has been a territorial dispute over the Shatt-al-Arab, a 204-kilometer (127-mile) stretch of water that connects the junction of the Tigris and Euphrates rivers to the Persian Gulf. Iraq controlled that part of the waterway, but Iran claimed it. Iraq eventually ceded it to Iran in a treaty that forced Iran to cease supporting the Iraqi Kurds (**Figure 4.32**). Not long after the ceding of the Shatt-al-Arab by Iraq to Iran, however, former President Saddam Hussein of

Iraq came to regard it as an incident of humiliation, and he vowed to force Iran to return it. Years of attacks and counterattacks have ensued over the Shatt-al-Arab and other issues. For instance, the 1991 Persian Gulf War is seen as the latest continuation of the animosity between the two countries. During this brief encounter, U.S. forces—along with troops from other countries, including some Arab states—retaliated against Iraq's invasion of Kuwait (which Iraq has argued was historically part of Iraq). Following the war, the international community has continued to be concerned over the conflictual relationship between Iraq and Iran and Iraq and Kuwait, because together these three states possess one of the world's richest oil reserves.

Recently, Iran caught the alarmed attention of the West by declaring its inalienable right to pursue uranium enrichment. While it is too soon to determine the regional impact of this declaration, it is important to point out that in response, the United States and the European Union, along with the International Atomic Energy Commission, called for Iran to suspend its nuclear program for fear that it is actually targeted for arms production. In late July 2006 the UN Security Council passed a resolution giving Iran one month to suspend uranium enrichment and allow inspections or face possible sanctions. Iranian President Mahmoud Ahmadinejad, with apparent support from the Iranian people, has said no matter what action the United Nations takes, Iran will proceed with its nuclear program. With a large part of the Middle East already in turmoil, Iran's persistence in carrying out a nuclear program is seen as a further threat to the stability of the region.

The Israeli-Palestinian and Israeli-Lebanon Conflicts

The history of the Israeli-Palestinian conflict is complex and the situation is highly volatile, despite persistent local and international efforts to bring peace to the region. The violence that re-erupted in the fall of 2000, just as the peace process seemed to be most promising, underscores the complexity of the problem and the difficulty of resolution. As with the Iran/Iraq/Kuwait case, the chief factors that have inflamed this seemingly intractable political problem were exacerbated by British partitioning of the region.

The official Jewish state of Israel is a mid-20th-century construction that has its roots in the emergence of **zionism**, a late 19th-century movement in Europe. Zionism's chief objective has been the establishment of a legally recognized home in Palestine for the Jewish people. Thousands of European Jews, inspired by the early Zionist movement, began migrating to Palestine at the turn of the 19th century. When the Ottoman Empire was defeated in 1917, the British gained control over Palestine and the Transjordan area and issued the Balfour Declaration. The Balfour Declaration was highly problematic, however, because a people, the Palestinians, already occupied the area. They viewed the arrival of increasing numbers of Jews and European sympathy for the establishment of a Jewish homeland as an incursion into the sacred lands of Islam. In response to increasing Arab-Jewish tensions in the area, the British decided to limit Jewish immigration to Palestine in the late 1930s through the end of World War II. In 1947, with conflict continuing between the two groups, Britain announced that it despaired of ever resolving the problems and would withdraw from Palestine in 1948, turning it over to the United Nations at that time. The United Nations, under heavy pressure from the United States, responded by voting to partition Palestine into Arab and Jewish states and designated Jerusalem as an international city, preventing either group from having exclusive control. Of the mandate of Palestine, the Jewish state was to have 56 percent and an Arab state was to have 43 percent; Jerusalem, a city sacred to Jews, Muslims, and Christians, was to be administered by the United Nations. The proposed UN plan was accepted by the Jews and angrily rejected by the Arabs, who argued that a mandate territory could not legally be taken from an indigenous population.

When Britain withdrew in 1948, war broke out. In an attempt to aid the militarily weaker Palestinians, combined forces from Egypt, Jordan, and Lebanon, as well as smaller units from Syria, Iraq, and Saudi Arabia, confronted the Israelis. Their goal was not only to prevent the Israeli forces from gaining control over additional Palestinian territory but also to wipe out the newly formed Jewish state altogether. This war, which came to be known as the first Arab-Israeli War, resulted in the defeat of the

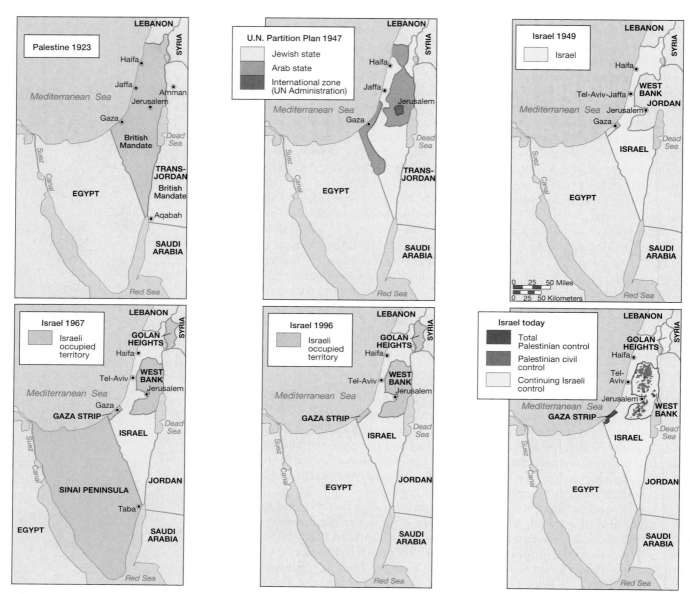

FIGURE 4.33 Changing geography of Israel and Palestine, 1923–2003 Since the creation of Israel out of part of the former Palestine in 1947, the regional political geography has undergone significant modifications. The changing map shown here is the result of a series of wars between Israelis and neighboring Arab states and a number of political decisions regarding how to cope with both resident Palestinians and large numbers of Jewish people immigrating to Israel from around the world. (*Source:* J. M. Rubenstein, *The Cultural Landscape: An Introduction to Human Geography,* 5th ed. Upper Saddle River, NJ: Prentice Hall, 1996, p. 233.)

Arab forces in 1949, and later armistice agreements enabled Israel to expand beyond the UN plan by gaining the western sector of Jerusalem, including the Old City. In 1950 Israel declared Jerusalem its national capital, though very few countries have recognized this.

Israel maintained the new borders gained during the first Arab-Israeli War for another 18 years until the Six-Day War in 1967, which resulted in further gains for Israel, including the Sinai Peninsula and the Golan Heights, the southwestern corner of Syria. The eastern sector of Jerusalem and the West Bank, previously held by Jordan, were also annexed during the Six-Day War. As **Figure 4.33** shows, a long period of relatively little territorial change occurred until the 1970s and 1980s, when Israel moved toward reconciliation with Egypt through a series of withdrawals that eventually returned all of the Sinai to Egyptian control by 1988.

The territorial expansion of Israel has meant that hundreds of thousands of Palestinians have been driven from their homeland, and the landscape of Palestine has been dramatically transformed. Today Palestinians live as refugees either in other Arab countries in the region, abroad, or under Israeli occupation in the West Bank, the Golan Heights, and the Gaza Strip (also known as the "Occupied Territories"). The Arabs of the Middle East and North Africa and many other international observers are convinced that Israel has no intention of allowing the diasporic Palestinian population to return to its homelands. By the late 1980s, in fact, Palestinians who had remained in their homeland had become so angered by Israeli territorial aggression that they rose up in rebellion. This rebellion, known as the **intifada** (the violent uprising of Palestinians against the rule of Israel in the Occupied Territories), has involved frequent clashes between fully armed Israeli soldiers and rock-throwing Palestinian young men. The intifada is mostly a reaction against 35 years of Israeli occupation of the Palestinian homeland and increasing Israeli settlement, particularly in the West Bank and the Gaza Strip.

In addition to the intifada, other Palestinian groups have coalesced in opposition to the Israeli occupation. The Palestine Liberation Organization (PLO) was formed in 1964 as an organization devoted to returning Palestine to the Palestinians. Since its official recognition, the PLO has become the Palestinian Authority. The Palestinian Authority, the first chairman of which was Yassar Arafat, is seen as the only legitimate representative of the Palestinian people. However, other, more extreme groups claim to represent the Palestinian cause. One of the most well-known is Hamas (Harakat al-Muqawama al-Islamiyya, or the Islamic Resistance Movement), whose militant activities are largely centered in the West Bank and Gaza Strip. Another is Hezbollah, whose activities are centered in southern Lebanon.

Since the mid-1990s, hopes for peace in the region have risen and fallen. In October 2000, after weeks of very difficult, but promising, U.S.-sponsored peace negotiations between Yassar Arafat and Ehud Barak, then Israeli prime minister, violence broke out again in the West Bank. This new violence left little hope in Israel, the Occupied Territories, or elsewhere that the Israeli-Palestinian conflict will be resolved any time in the near future. More recently, although this second intifada and Israeli encroachment into the Occupied Territories continue, a new glimmer of hope appeared through the Geneva Accord (drafted in November 2003), which was advanced with the aim of bringing peace to the region. The Geneva Accord, along with the other plans and accords that have preceded it, such as the Oslo Accord, are known as the "Road Map." The Road Map specifies how contested issues will be resolved—such as who will control Jerusalem, what will happen to the Jewish settlements in the Occupied Territories, whether the Palestinian refugee population will be allowed to return to Palestine—as well as how peace might be maintained, how disputes will be settled, and how economic relations between Israel and Palestine will be organized.

In a show of support for the Road Map, in summer 2005, Israel began to cede territory back to Palestine. As Israeli settlers moved from homes that they had inhabited, in most cases, for decades, critics argued that the return of land was a hollow gesture as Israel continued the construction of physical barriers between Israelis and Palestinians. The Gaza Strip barrier consists of 52 kilometers (30 miles) of mainly wire fence with posts, sensors, and buffer zones. Israel argues that the barrier is essential to protect the security of its citizens from Palestinian terrorism. Palestinians and other opponents of the barrier contend that its purpose is geographical containment of the Palestinians in order to pave the way for an expansion of Israeli sovereignty and to preclude any negotiated border agreements in the future. But Israel argues that the fence is purely a security obstacle, not a part of a future border. With the Gaza Strip security wall complete, in 2002 the West Bank wall was begun. When completed, that wall will seal off another portion of the Palestinian territories from Israel (**Figure 4.34**). These barriers continue to uproot and destroy Palestinian settlements and separate them from their livelihood. In October 2003, the

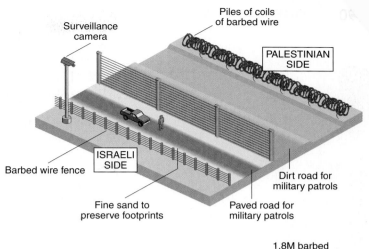

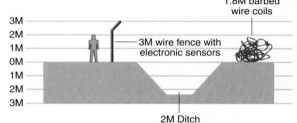

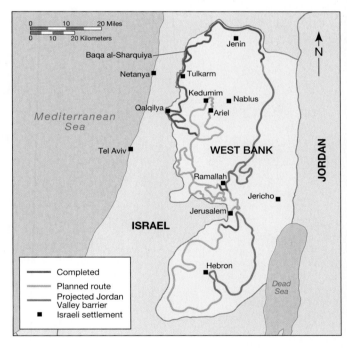

FIGURE 4.34 Israeli security fence, 2005 Shown are the planned and completed portions of the security fence, called "the wall" or the "apartheid wall" by Palestinians and other opponents. It is a physical barrier consisting of a network of fences, walls, and trenches. Israel's stated purpose in constructing it is to create a zone of security between itself and the West Bank. (*Source:* BBC News, Web edition; **http://news.bbc.co.uk/1/hi/world/middle_east/ 3111159.stm**; accessed July 4, 2005.)

UN General Assembly voted 144–4 that the West Bank wall was "in contradiction to international law" and therefore illegal. Israel called the resolution a "farce."

In January 2005, following the death the previous November of Yassar Arafat, Mahmoud Abbas was elected president of the Palestinian Authority by voters in the West Bank and Gaza. It was the first Palestinian election held since 1996. A year later, Palestinians again went to the polls to determine representatives for parliamentary seats. In a surprise victory, the terrorist organization, Hamas, took a majority of the 132 seats. The election has caused a new round of conflict as Israel has refused to negotiate with a Palestinian Authority that includes Hamas. The United States and the European Union have cut off funding to the Authority, which provides jobs to 25 percent of the people of the West Bank and Gaza.

In July 2006, a 19-year-old Israeli soldier was captured by Hamas. In retaliation, Interim Prime Minister Ehud Olmert ordered renewed missile strikes in Gaza and the West Bank and the Israeli Army has re-entered central Gaza. At present, Israel continues to occupy northern Gaza as the United Nations alerts the world to the possibility of a humanitarian crisis there for a population with inadequate food, water, and fuel.

In late July 2006, in response to the kidnapping of two Israeli soldiers by Hezbollah militias, the Israeli army began sea and air strikes against and ground incursions into southern Lebanon. The context for this most recent conflict is complex, but it can be traced in part to the end of the 1967 Arab-Israeli War, when Palestinians began to use Lebanon as a base from which to launch attacks on Israel. Over the rest of the twentieth century, despite periods of relative calm, Lebanon—especially the south as well as the cities of Beirut and Biqa—has been a target for Israeli attacks as Hezbollah and Palestinian guerillas continue to make their bases there.

There was some hope that the 21st century would be a more peaceful and prosperous one for Lebanon. The bloody civil war had ended in 1990; Israeli troops withdrew in 2000; and Syria withdrew its troops in 2005, marking the end of almost 30 years of occupation. But Israel's attacks in 2006 against Hezbollah have plunged the country back into open political and economic turmoil as widespread civilian casualties, the massive destruction of key infrastructure and thousands of homes, and the displacement of approximately one million people have derailed the fragile peace.

The U.S. War in Iraq   The United States responded to the terrorist attacks of September 11, 2001, by declaring a global war against terrorism and identifying the greatest threats to U.S. security as first Afghanistan and then Iraq. Although evidence of involvement in the 9/11 attacks by Iraq and its leader, Saddam Hussein, was highly questionable, on March 19, 2003, after amassing more than 200,000 U.S. troops in the Persian Gulf region, U.S. President George W. Bush ordered the bombing of the city of Baghdad. The declaration of war and invasion occurred without the explicit authorization of the UN Security Council, and some legal authorities take the view that the action violated the UN Charter. Some of the United States' staunchest allies (Germany, France, and Canada) as well as Russia opposed the attack. Moreover, throughout the world hundreds of thousands of anti-war protesters repeatedly took to the streets for the weeks and months preceding and following the onset of war, launched by a coalition of forces led by the United Kingdom and the United States. The motivation for the war, as expressed by Prime Minister Tony Blair and George W. Bush, was that Iraq had stockpiled "weapons of mass destruction"—chemical and biological weapons capable of massive human destruction. In the days leading up to the war, the UN weapons inspector, Hans Blix, and his team were unable to locate any weapons despite an intensive search of the country. President Bush, however, proceeded to justify a dramatically stepped-up "war on terrorism" (following the war in Afghanistan) on the grounds that "neutralizing" Iraq's leader, Saddam Hussein, was necessary to global security.

On May 1, 2003, after landing in a Lockheed S-3 Viking fighter plane on the aircraft carrier USS *Abraham Lincoln*, President Bush announced the end of major combat operations in the Iraq war. The fact that "major combat" has ended, however, does not mean that peace has returned to Iraq. Iraq continues to experience violent conflict between U.S. and Iraqi soldiers and forces described by the occupiers as insurgents. Additionally, sectarian violence has surged dramatically with Sunni and Shi'a in conflict. The tactics in use include mortars, suicide bombers, roadside bombs, small arms fire, and rocket-propelled grenades, as well as sabotage against the oil infrastructure of the country. Kidnappings are also rampant as insurgents disguised as members of the Iraqi Civil Defense Force or Iraqi police easily enter homes, offices, and even hospitals or simply grab their victims off the street. Kidnapping victims are usually tortured and killed.

As of winter 2007, the total number of casualties among U.S. soldiers as a direct result of the Iraq invasion reached 2940 dead and 22,057 wounded, most of whom are young men between the ages of 18 and 22 (**Figure 4.35**). Of these, more than 2440 were killed or died in accidents after President Bush announced the end of major combat. Not surprisingly, there is a wide range of estimates of Iraqi dead, as the count is both difficult to ascertain and is a highly political issue. A controversial study that appeared in the highly regarded British medical journal *The Lancet* in 2006 estimated 655,000 Iraqi deaths from all causes, including both civilians and military personnel, and above the number that would be expected in a non-conflict situation. In contrast, Iraq Body Count, an independent organization based in London that tracks and cross-checks Iraqi civilian deaths, indicated in February 2007 a minimum number of 55,441 and a maximum of 61,133 over the course of the occupation.

In early 2004, the 9/11 Commission (more formally known as the National Commission on Terrorist Attacks Upon the United States) concluded that there was no credible evidence that Saddam Hussein, the now-executed, former president of the country, had assisted the terrorist organization Al Qaeda in preparing for or carrying out the 9/11 attacks. There is also general agreement among U.S. intelligence and military personnel that Iraq had most likely completely destroyed its programs for biological and chemical weapons production, before the UN team began its inspection.

FIGURE 4.35 U.S. fatalities in Iraq, 2005 Produced by the Major Visibility Project, this map shows the fatalities of U.S. service people in Iraq as of late summer 2005. Their Web site also provides monthly totals up to the present. (*Source:* **http://www.iraqbodycount.net/database/**; last accessed 21 September 2006).

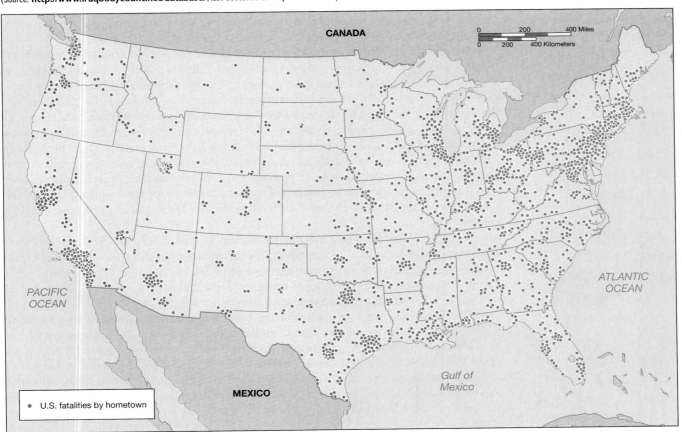

Genocide in Darfur   The conflict that began in early 2003 and continues to unfold in western Sudan has its roots in persistent social, political, and economic inequality between the country's core, centered around the Nile Valley, and the periphery represented by the western province of Darfur (an area about the size of Texas). With more than 450,000 dead and more than 2.5 million displaced either living in refugee camps or having fled the country altogether, the United Nations has called the events in Darfur a humanitarian crisis. Although the Bush administration has called it genocide, it has taken no protective action. And with another 7000 dying each month, there seems no end in sight to the atrocity.

The brutal violence that has been occurring in Darfur began when native Africans in the province looking for a measure of freedom revolted against Sudan's authoritarian Islamic government. Media reports indicate that the government aimed to end the rebellion by wiping out all the tribal Africans in the area so that Arabs could take over the land. The government provided support for a militia of African Arabs, who call themselves the Janjaweed, to undertake one of the most brutal campaigns of ethnic cleansing that Africa has ever seen.

Survivors say the attacks usually start at dawn, with bombs falling from Sudanese Air Force planes. The Janjaweed then come in on camel or horseback shooting and setting fire to villages, raping women and girls, and killing the men and boys. Later, government ground forces arrive (or helicopters are dispatched) to chase, capture, or kill those who remain. In May 2006 a peace agreement was brokered after intervention by the United States and Great Britain. Yet, as of winter 2007, reports indicate that the government-sponsored violence in Darfur continues and the possibility for providing security for those who remain is extremely difficult. It also appears that the government continues to obstruct the delivery of humanitarian aid, creating famine conditions for the vulnerable population.

The Western Sahara   Western Sahara is a former Spanish colony that did not gain independence, as did most of the other former colonies or mandate territories of the region in the mid-20th century, but instead was handed over to Morocco by Spain. It was incorporated as a province by the Moroccan state, partially in 1976 and completely in 1987. The population of this coastal area is just 200,000. The landscape is a windswept, flat, and monotonous desert where temperatures routinely reach 45°C (120°F) in the summer. Before the 20th century, Western Sahara was outside the control of any central political or military authority and was considered a geographical backwater. Except for some phosphate deposits and offshore fishing rights, Western Sahara would seem to be a generally resource-poor area and not obviously desirable as a territorial acquisition. Yet the Moroccans are aggressively determined to keep possession of Western Sahara, just as the Saharawis, as the people of Western Sahara are known, are determined to become independent (**Figure 4.36**). As in the Maghreb, a few Saharawis went to Spain in the early 20th century, received a modern university education, and came back to the region with ideas of national independence. At present, the Western Saharan resistance movement operates under the aegis of the Polisario Front (an acronym for the Popular Front for the Liberation of Saguia al-Hara and Rio de Oro, the two divisions of the former Spanish colony).

In 1976, Polisario declared the formation of the Saharawi Arab Democratic Republic (SADR), "a free, independent, sovereign state ruled by an Arab democratic system of progressive unionist orientation and of Islamic religion." Since then, while many African states have officially recognized the Sahrawi Republic, Morocco has refused to acknowledge it or to renounce control over it.

Western Sahara has been a valued acquisition for Morocco because of its phosphate reserves. The rock phosphates found in Western Sahara (and in other parts of the Maghreb) are converted to phosphoric acid and used in rustproofing metals and as an ingredient in soft drinks and dental cements. A variant, trisodium phosphate, is used as a detergent and water softener. Phosphates are globally significant in both industrial production and household use, and Morocco appreciates the economic value of Western Sahara to its development goals. Although Morocco is anxious to develop the phosphate reserves of Western Sahara, the political situation has prevented even a full-scale

FIGURE 4.36 Saharawi landmine victims Areas of Western Sahara were littered with landmines during the occupations by Morocco and Mauritania. Many of these mines are still in place, unexploded, a situation that takes its toll on the Saharawi people who must live, work, or travel across these dangerous areas.

exploration to proceed in the face of Polisario's determination to free itself from Moroccan control.

Because the international community has recognized Polisario's claims, the United Nations has been working to deal with the conflict by providing a framework for Western Sahara's autonomy under Morocco's sovereignty, but the process currently remains unresolved. One bright spot has been the confidence-building measures undertaken by Morocco and Polisario and promoted and supported by the United Nations. For the Saharawis, these measures have meant the facilitation of visits and phone and mail communications between refugees and persons in the territory. Many Saharawis have been able to see close relatives from whom they have been separated for 30 years. For the Moroccans, all of the Moroccan prisoners of war held by Polisario have been released. Meanwhile, the questions of independence or self-determination for Saharawis is still an open one, but both parties are now more open to the possibility of a negotiated settlement.

Regional Alliances

The Middle East and North Africa is a region with more than its share of conflict, yet it is also one where a great deal of cooperation, coordination, and joint action exists. Many political, economic, and cultural cooperative organizations are operating in the region.

The Arab League is a voluntary association of Arab states whose peoples speak mainly Arabic. Formally known as the League of Arab States, it is the most unifying of all the Middle Eastern and North African regional organizations. The stated purposes of the Arab League are to strengthen ties among member states, coordinate their policies, and promote their common interests. The league is involved in various economic, cultural, and social programs, including literacy campaigns and programs dealing with labor issues. It is also a high-profile political organization that acts as a sounding board on conflicts in the region, such as the 1991 Persian Gulf War and the Arab-Israeli conflict.

The league was founded in 1945 by Egypt, Iraq, Lebanon, Saudi Arabia, Syria, Transjordan (Jordan, as of 1948), and Yemen. Other countries of the Middle East and North Africa that later joined the Arab League are Algeria (1962), Bahrain (1971), Kuwait (1961), Morocco (1958), Oman (1971), Qatar (1971), Sudan (1956), Tunisia (1958), and the United Arab Emirates (1971). The PLO was admitted in 1976. In 1979 Egypt's membership was suspended after it signed a peace treaty with Israel, but it was readmitted 10 years later.

Another central and widely known regional organization, this one based on economic interests, is the Organization of Petroleum Exporting Countries (OPEC). Whereas organizations like the Council of Arab Economic Unity deal with every aspect of economic development and change, OPEC, as its name suggests, is a specialist economic organization. OPEC's central purpose is to coordinate the crude-oil policies of its member states. Founded in 1960, OPEC has 12 members—Algeria, Gabon, Indonesia, Iran, Iraq, Kuwait, Libya, Nigeria, Qatar, Saudi Arabia, United Arab Emirates, and Venezuela—four of which (Gabon, Indonesia, Nigeria, Venezuela) are not part of the Middle Eastern and North African region. As is clear from the list, however, Middle Eastern Arab states dominate the membership. OPEC originally was formed in response to the dropping price of oil in the 1950s, when supply greatly outstripped demand. In the 1970s, as oil supplies in non-OPEC countries were reduced, the organization lowered production, which had the effect of raising the price of oil. OPEC also sets production ceilings that specify how much oil may be produced by each member state. This practice ensures that the price per barrel does not fluctuate dramatically due to market gluts or scarcity.

Complementing as well as contrasting with the goals and objectives of OPEC is the Gulf Cooperation Council (GCC). The GCC coordinates political, economic, and cultural issues of concern to its six member states—Saudi Arabia, Kuwait, Bahrain, Qatar, the United Arab Emirates, and Oman. The members of the GCC have come together to coordinate the management of their substantial income from their oil reserves, problems of economic development, and social problems, trade, and security issues. All six of the states in the GCC are politically conservative monarchies wary of the revolutionary republican urges that have swept the region and transformed the previous monarchies of Egypt, Iran, and Iraq, for instance. The GCC has made very large sums of money available to all Arab countries for economic development as well as military protection during political crises.

Many other regional and international organizations have been established in the Middle East and North Africa. New regional alliances are being proposed. The Arab Common Market is one such proposed alliance that has a great deal of support in the region. Additionally, some individual states have begun to attempt to make connections with organizations beyond the region, tying the Middle East and North Africa more securely to the rest of the globe. For instance, Turkey, already a member of NATO, has applied for full membership in the European Union (an organization of European states dedicated to increasing economic integration and cooperation in Europe—see Chapter 1, p. 5), despite significant political barriers. Morocco, Tunisia, Jordan, and Israel have also signed agreements, so-called "Euro-Med" agreements, with the European Union that are leading to increased transnational integration beyond the region. While some critics argue that alliances with organizations outside the region may erode unique regional identities or diminish local control over local processes, others argue that transnational integration beyond the region may increase political stability and decrease conflict. At this point it is unclear whether either or both might be true. What is true is that the cooperation brought on by the vast oil wealth of some states as well as the conflict brought on by cultural differences has helped widen the gap between rich and poor in the region.

New Economies and Social Inequalities

The Middle East and North Africa is a region of extreme contrasts of wealth and poverty. For example, in 2005 the United Arab Emirates had the highest per capita income in the region ($23,770), while Sudan had the lowest ($550). Not surprisingly, however, national statistics like per capita income hide all sorts of variation—for instance, between the city and the rural areas and within the same area, where dramatic variation can occur between one urban neighborhood and the next. Most of the extreme wealth of the region comes from oil-based revenues to the states of Saudi Arabia, Kuwait, Iran, Iraq, Oman, Qatar, Libya, and the United Arab Emirates (**Table 4.2**). States with the largest populations tend to have the lowest levels of wealth. Despite the phenomenal wealth generated from oil production for some parts of the region, most

Table 4.2	Richest and Poorest States (in 2005 $)		
Richest			
Israel	23 (high)	17,360	20,033
Qatar	40 (high)	N/A	19,844
UAE	41 (high)	23,770	22,420
Bahrain	43 (high)	14,370	17,479
Kuwait	44 (high)	22,470	18,047
Poorest			
Syria	106 (medium)	1,230	3,576
Egypt	119 (medium)	1,250	3,950
Morocco	124 (medium)	1,570	4,004
Sudan	141 (medium)	530	1,910
Yemen	151 (low)	550	889

(Source: The World Bank, *Key Development Data and Statistics*, 2005, at **http://web.worldbank.org/WBSITE/EXTERNAL/ DATASTATISTICS/0, contentMDK:20535285˜menuPK: 1192694˜pagePK: 64133150˜piPK:64133175˜the- SitePK:239419,00.html**, last accessed 6 August 2006; and United Nations Development Program, *Human Development Reports*, 2005, at **http://hdr.undp.org/statistics/** last accessed 6 August 2006).

of the Middle East and North Africa remains poor and highly dependent on an increasingly marginalized agricultural sector.

Neoliberalism has increased the levels of inequality in the region, and other forces limit the life chances and standards of living of the region's population. For example, refugees and many migrant workers face very difficult economic circumstances. We have mentioned the difficult situation of Palestinian refugees living in temporary camps throughout the region. Since the first refugees left Palestine in 1948, as many as 2 million Palestinians have been displaced to refugee camps in Lebanon, Syria, Jordan, the West Bank, and the Gaza Strip. Many persons are born and grow up in these camps, originally intended as temporary settlements, where basic provisions are poor. Other large refugee populations live in camps in Iran, which shelters 1.5 million Afghan refugees and 600,000 Iraqis; Sudan, where 4 million displaced Sudanese people live outside their home territories; Turkey and Iran with up to 1 million displaced Kurds; as well as tens of thousands of Iraqis displaced because of the war and its aftermath.

Sudan, Turkey, and Iran illustrate the recent emergence of a new refugee status category, that of **internally displaced persons** (IDPs), individuals who are uprooted within their own countries due to civil conflict or human rights violations, sometimes by their own governments. **Figure 4.37** provides a snapshot of the refugees and IDP situation in the region as of 2005. Note that IDPs (both returned and outstanding) outnumber refugees. Moreover, the plight of IDPs is actually worse than refugees because their own governments are either unable or unwilling to provide them with the protection or assistance they have a right to expect. Inequality is also a problem for migrant workers imported into the oil-rich states of the Persian Gulf as guest workers, because, although they receive much higher wages than they would in their home countries, they have substantially lower standards of living than the resident Arab populations.

Finally, the many conflicts that have occurred and are occurring throughout the region can also economically dislocate resident populations and increase the plight of those who are socially or politically weak.

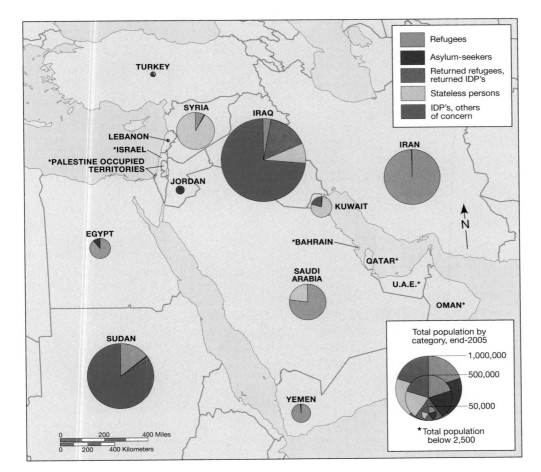

FIGURE 4.37 Refugees and internally displaced persons, 2005 Civil war and international conflict have created a huge refugee and internally displaced person problem in the region. Those driven from their homes by such conflict are shown here. Included as well are stateless persons, such as the Kurds, who have also been displaced in large numbers.

Regional Development

The Middle East and North Africa is a region of dramatic contrasts, with high-technology industrial production existing alongside ancient agricultural techniques. The most rapidly developing subregions within the Middle East and North Africa are those whose economies are the most dynamic and productive and effectively set the pace economically, and to some extent politically, for the rest of the region. These are the Oil States and the Eastern Mediterranean Crescent (**Figure 4.38**).

The Oil States   The Oil States subregion of the Middle East and North Africa includes Bahrain, Iran, Iraq, Kuwait, Oman, Qatar, Saudia Arabia, and the United Arab Emirates. Although Yemen, Algeria, and Libya also produce oil, their situations are substantially different. Yemen's oil reserves are only newly discovered, and the country has not yet exploited them to the level that its Arabian Peninsula neighbors have. Algeria has substantial oil and gas reserves but a far more mixed economy than the states along the Persian Gulf. Its history as a French colony also sharply differentiates it from the others. Libya, like Algeria, has an economy that is not solely oil-based, and its colonial and modern political history make it an exceptional case. Whereas the once active agricultural economies of the Oil States have been largely eroded by an emphasis on petroleum production, Algeria and Libya continue to possess productive agricultural sectors in addition to profiting from their oil reserves.

Generally speaking, the Oil States tend to be among the most culturally conservative in the region. Of all the countries of the Middle Eastern and North African region, the Oil States are the most committed to a strict interpretation of Islamic law. As a

FIGURE 4.38 Middle Eastern and North African subregions This map shows several of the subregions mentioned throughout the chapter. As with world regions, the boundaries of these are somewhat arbitrary and are subject to future alterations when conditions change. For instance, the Oil States may lose their coherence when oil reserves are depleted sometime in the early 21st century.

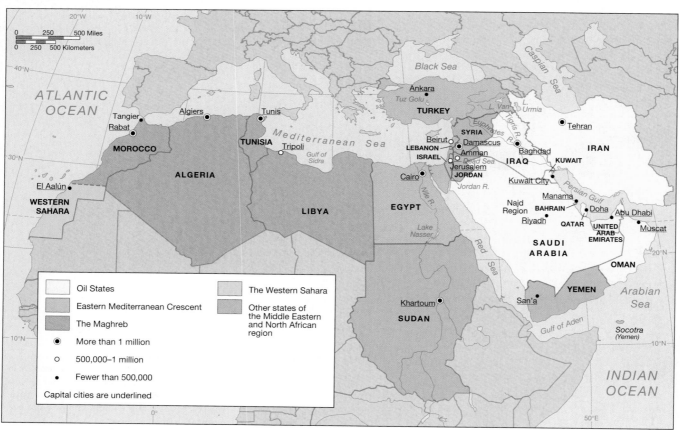

result, women's public movements are highly restricted. Socializing among middle- and upper-class women tends to take place in private spaces—in homes and sequestered spaces in restaurants. Religious police—charged with enforcing Islamic orthodoxy—can be found on the city streets of Saudi Arabia and Iran, for instance, ensuring that public telephones are not used during prayer time, and that women, especially tourists, are properly dressed (for instance, no skirts above the knee, no sleeveless tops).

Broad generalizations such as these gloss over the rich cultural and social life that exists among the eight states of this subregion. So, for example, while Saudi Arabia and Iran are especially conservative Islamic states, other states like Kuwait and Bahrain are more open and possess a relatively more lively public culture of cafés, horse racing, camel racing, and soccer, where both women and men are spectators. Overall, poor people in the region, especially the guest workers who have come to work in the oil economies, have a social experience very different from the other classes.

Amid social and cultural differences, the one thing that unites the region is oil and oil wealth. A visit to most of these countries will provide opportunities for partaking in activities that cater especially to the wealthy, including shopping in flashy new malls for luxury goods, attending sporting events, or participating in socially elite sporting activities (yacht clubs, golf courses, and the Dubai Cup, the horse race with the largest purse in the world). At some luxury hotels, spacious suites that are really more like lavishly appointed condominiums can cost up to $10,000 a night.

The Arabian Peninsula, which includes all but two of the Oil States (Iran and Iraq), is an area that is heavily dominated by the presence of huge reserves of oil—so huge, it is estimated, that Saudi Arabia alone may possess one-quarter of the world's known reserves. Saudi Arabia is the controlling political and economic force on the peninsula that, until the early 20th century, was occupied mostly by rural villagers and nomadic peoples. After Saudi Arabia, Iraq possesses about 10 percent of the world's known reserves, Kuwait about 9 percent, the United Arab Emirates 7 percent, and Iran about 6 percent. Oil production is the mainstay of each of the Oil States' subregional economies and contributes substantial revenues to each of the national economies. In some of the individual Oil States, revenues from oil production are so substantial that their respective national governments have a difficult time determining where to spend them.

An embarrassment of oil riches hardly seems a problem. Yet it is a problem, and one with a number of different facets. One facet is that a nearly exclusive dependence on one economic sector, and only one product within that sector, leaves the economy of a state highly vulnerable to fluctuations in the demand for oil. For example, in the 1980s, a period of sustained expansion in the oil economy came to an end as more fuel-efficient vehicles were developed, energy-conservation measures were taken, and cheaper fuels were substituted for oil. At the same time the world entered a period of economic recession, partly in response to high oil prices. As a result, oil profits fell dramatically, with implications for the Oil States moving like a wave through their economies. When prices fall in an exclusively oil-based economy, there is nothing to fall back on; there is no way to bring in new revenues to supplement the decreasing profits from oil.

For much of the early history of oil production in the region, the Oil States were content to use their wealth to benefit the kin of the ruling elite. Instead of investing in national infrastructure or developing human resources, these groups invested their wealth abroad or spent their money on luxurious living. As a result, until fairly recently, the economies of the subregion have been exceedingly vulnerable to falling oil prices. Recognizing this, all of the Oil States on the Arabian Peninsula have begun to diversify their economies (**Figure 4.39**). Some are attempting to introduce new industries, such as textile production and food processing plants. Others are developing port facilities. Still others are resuscitating or introducing agriculture, though the scarcity of water makes irrigation an enormous technological challenge for all except Iraq and Iran. Yet, while large-scale, irrigated agriculture is a costly undertaking for any of the

FIGURE 4.39 Tourism development in Dubai Pictured in the foreground is Madinat Jumeirah Resort and in the background Burj Al Arab Hotel in Dubai, the UAE. Tourism is rapidly gaining popularity as a way of diversifying the economies of oil rich countries. Besides the UAE, Qatar is also involved in the tourism boom, and more than 100 buildings and towers are being erected in Doha, its capital. Both places are striving to become the leisure destination of the world's business class.

Petroleum

Petroleum, more commonly known as *oil*, is a naturally occurring liquid composed of various organic chemicals. *Petroleum* usually refers just to crude oil, but the term can also apply to natural gas and shale oil. Petroleum is most widely used as an energy source for industry, commerce, government/military, and residences. Without petroleum, life as we know it in the core of the world-system would collapse and life in the semiperiphery and periphery would be deeply disabled. In fact, semiperipheral countries base their development goals on petroleum availability.

While contemporary society is utterly dependent on petroleum, ancient peoples also knew about petroleum and made use of surface deposits for waterproofing and as fuel for torches. Later, they learned to distill it and came to use oil as a lubricant and for medicinal purposes. In the 19th century, kerosene was extracted from petroleum and used as a cheap fuel for lamps and lanterns. Recognizing that the crude oil itself might have value, in the mid-19th century drilling began in the state of Pennsylvania, marking the beginning of the modern petroleum industry. The invention of the internal combustion engine and World War I helped establish the petroleum industry as a foundation of industrial society.

The organization of the petroleum industry took several decades to consolidate. It was more or less complete by the early decades of the 20th century. The U.S. petroleum industry, through its five leading companies, along with two companies in Britain, dominated the petroleum industry worldwide throughout much of the 20th century. In its early stages, the world petroleum market was organized by these seven companies, which produced and distributed abundant cheap oil first drilled around 1907 in Iran, by the 1920s in Iraq, and not until the 1930s in Bahrain and Saudi Arabia. In the United States, Standard Oil was the most prominent oil company, which by mid-century controlled 95 percent of the U.S. petroleum industry. In Britain, Shell Oil dominated.

In the middle decades of the 20th century, the Middle East first experienced rumblings of resistance to foreign companies dominating their oil supply. Iran was the first to resist, and by the 1960s, enraged by the unilateral cuts in oil prices made by the seven big oil companies, the major oil-exporting countries formed the Organization of Petroleum Exporting Countries (OPEC) with the goal of controlling the price of oil. The "Oil Crisis" of 1973 dealt a major shock to the global economy when panic over supply led to wild speculation, and OPEC cut back on production and thus raised the barrel price in order to cash in on the panic. A worldwide recession resulted, and the oil market suffered greatly due to decreased demand. In 1978, the Middle East oil supply was disrupted during the Arab-Israeli War and the Iranian revolution, the latter being directly connected to the core's thirst for oil.

The conflicts and economic problems that emerged around the global oil supply in the 1970s made it very clear to the core that oil was a political issue that had to be monitored closely and carefully. The Persian Gulf War in 1990–91 is an illustration of the strategic importance of oil to international relations and its central role in foreign policy. Critics of the 2003 U.S. war in Iraq have also argued that the main reason for the attack by the United States was to gain control over the region's oil production. And oil prices have surged since the war began (**Figure 1**).

Every day a globally coordinated system moves more than 60 million barrels of oil from producers to consumers. Although petroleum allows the core to enjoy a very high standard of living, there are serious implications to the widespread and increasing use of petroleum worldwide. The most critical problem is

Arabian Peninsula Oil States, the prevailing sentiment among them is that food—like oil—is an important security issue.

Another less obvious problem that the abundance of oil wealth has generated in the Oil States is the dislocation of traditional social and economic systems. Western ideas have penetrated the region through the introduction of television and other consumer goods. The importation of migrant labor from other parts of the Middle East and North Africa to work in the oil industry or in related jobs has also tended to disrupt the local traditions, as new migrants have brought their rather different cultures with them. As participation in the Oil States' increased global economy has brought the region into closer contact with the West, the stress exerted on the local culture has sometimes intensified existing conservative interpretations of Islam.

The enormous wealth of the Oil States has made them a global economic player. Understanding the power that status conveys, the Oil States have spent at least two decades augmenting it with more military strength by improving their armies and purchasing sophisticated weaponry on the world arms market. Israel is perhaps the most heavily armed state in the region. When its military might is included, it becomes clear that the Middle East and North Africa in general and the Oil States in particular are major players in the world military theater. Thus far, however, the new sophisticated weaponry has tended to be used largely within the region, against old rivals, rather than beyond the region.

FIGURE 1 What does your gas cost? This sign, from Dallas, Texas, reflects a growing sentiment in the United States about the increases in pump prices.

than three times the quantity coming from all tankers and other ships travels to the ocean by way of the world's rivers.

The world's reserves of crude oil add up to about 700 billion barrels, more than half of which are in the Middle East and North Africa. Many energy policy experts believe that the utilization of oil as a major source of energy will end up being a very brief affair, lasting little more than a century (**Figure 2**). Present estimates indicate that the supply of crude oil will probably be entirely exhausted sometime toward the middle of the 21st century, although new discoveries of oil continue to extend this deadline. We discuss the growing movement toward alternative energy sources in the final chapter.

FIGURE 2 Hydrogen alternatives As gas prices increase and concern for the environment grows, more and more people in the United States are purchasing hybrid automobiles—ones that operate on either gasoline or hydrogen.

environmental pollution of both the air and the water. Air pollution generated from industries and vehicles burning petroleum or any of its products is significant but varies from region to region, according to factors such as the amount of petroleum-based energy consumed or the pollution-control system in place. The impact of oil pollution on Earth's oceans and rivers is substantial. The amount of petroleum products ending up in the ocean is estimated at 25 percent of world oil production. About 6 million tons per year are discharged by tankers, passenger ships, and freighters. But the greatest volume of petroleum products dumped into the ocean is carried there by rivers. Through the discharge of industry, storage installations, refineries, and local gasoline stations, more

The Oil States are pivotal in the global economy for at least two additional reasons. First, many of the world states are highly dependent on them for oil. Without petroleum from the Oil States, the ability of a large portion of the rest of the world to maintain productive economies would be severely hampered. Second, the impact of **petrodollars**—revenues generated by the sale of oil—is especially significant for the core economies of the world-system where they are spent, invested, and banked. The Oil States of the Middle East are likely to continue to occupy a central role in the affairs of the region as well as the affairs of the core countries, where guaranteeing a secure supply of oil is absolutely central to the smooth functioning of the global economy (see Geographies of Indulgence, Desire, and Addiction: Petroleum, p. 198).

Major City: Riyadh Riyadh is the capital city of Saudi Arabia, one of the world's top three oil producers. A modern city—built on the ruins of an old walled city—Riyadh is situated on a high plateau in the Najd region of the central Gulf Peninsula (**Figure 4.40**). Although designated as the capital of the Sa'ud dynasty in 1824, the city lost this status in 1881 when the Rashid family extended its control over the Najd. Ibn Sa'ud regained control of Riyadh in 1902, and he used the city as the command center for his eventual conquest of all of Arabia, which he completed in 1930. The unified Kingdom of Saudi Arabia was proclaimed in 1932, and Riyadh became its capital. Although it has officially been the capital for nearly 70 years, only in the last generation has Riyadh truly

FIGURE 4.40 Riyadh, Saudi Arabia The capital of Saudi Arabia, Riyadh, is a modern city serving as the political and economic center of the oil industry in the kingdom. Shown in the center of the image is the Kingdom Tower, the tallest building in and an icon of Saudi Arabia. Located in central Riyadh, the tower's occupants include a five-star hotel, a major bank headquarters, a sports club, a wedding and conference center, and a luxury condominium and apartment complex.

functioned as the capital, having been eclipsed by Jidda, formerly the premier Saudi city. In the last three decades, the headquarters of the Saudi government have been moved to Riyadh, helping to confirm it as the practical as well as the symbolic center of the largest country in the Persian Gulf.

The discovery of vast petroleum deposits in Saudi Arabia in the 1930s helped generate the wealth that transformed Riyadh from an old provincial town into a modern urban place. Once a cluster of mud-brick dwellings in a desert oasis, Riyadh is now home to more than 3.5 million people occupying a sprawling city of flashy contemporary buildings, wide boulevards, modern hospitals and schools, and huge shopping centers that blend U.S.-style malls and Middle Eastern and North African *suqs*. Because Riyadh is at the epicenter of the Saudi oil economy, its population, once exclusively Najdi, is now quite cosmopolitan and includes a large number of other Arab nationals, Europeans, Americans, and Afro-Asians. In fact, although the most prestigious jobs are held by Saudis, most of the remainder of the private sector and government jobs are held by foreigners. Riyadh is a classic example of the impact of oil wealth on urbanization in the region. Other cities demonstrating this pattern include Abu Dhabi (UAE), Doha (Qatar), and Kuwait City (Kuwait).

Riyadh is also the kingdom's commercial and higher educational center, with an industrial base devoted almost entirely to oil production. As a commercial hub in the region, Riyadh possesses one of its most important markets, the camel market located about 30 kilometers (about 19 miles) from the city center. As the largest camel market in the Middle Eastern and North African region, this is a key commercial site where the tenor of peak trading in the late afternoon resembles that in the pit of the Chicago Mercantile Exchange right before the closing bell.

Major City: Tehran   Tehran is the capital, the largest city, and the political, cultural, and economic center of Iran. Its rapid growth, especially over the last 50 years, has been the result of its role in administrating and centrally investing the massive inflows of capital from the sale of oil, agricultural products, and foreign trade. Tehran is located in the northern part of the country, on a high, sandy plateau surrounded on the north by the majestic, snow-covered Elburz Mountains. To the south, east, and west are deserts. The city gradually rises in elevation to meet the mountains from roughly 1160 meters (3480 feet) in the south to 1800 meters (5400 feet) in the north. Its climate is arid but temperate, with summer temperatures averaging around 22.6°C (around 73°F) and winter temperatures averaging around 11.5°C (around 52°F). In terms of land area, the city occupies about 600 square kilometers (232 square miles).

Tehran first became an important place in 1220 when it survived the sacking of the ancient city of Rayy by the Mongols. At the time, Tehran was a small suburb of Rayy, probably founded around A.D. 300. Over the centuries Tehran grew slowly but steadily. In 1788 Agha Mohammad Khan, founder of the Kajar dynasty, made Tehran the capital of Persia. Beginning in 1925, when the Pahlavi dynasty came to power in Iran, Tehran became modernized, industrialized, and considerably rebuilt (**Figure 4.41**). Although a modern city, there are areas of the central and southern sections where traditional inward-looking structures with courtyards are more typical than the high-rise apartment structures found in the north. Unfortunately, conservation of old buildings in the city core has not been a priority, and a more systematic plan of conservation and restoration is needed to guarantee that areas such as these beautiful squares will be maintained.

FIGURE 4.41 Tehran, Iran The predominance of modern structures in Tehran is evidence of efforts by the Pahlavi dynasty to put the city on the world stage. The Iranian revolution in the 1970s slowed this process, but recent political changes have resulted in new development as well as redevelopment throughout the urban area. The older parts of Tehran contain some distinctive architecture dating back to the 18th century.

The northern part of the city is mainly residential, and the southern part contains a mix of residential, industrial, and commercial buildings. The southern and northern sections also reflect rather extreme social differences, with the north containing newer and mostly spacious middle- and upper-class neighborhoods, while the south contains densely occupied and underserviced poor and working-class neighborhoods. Today, the population of metropolitan Tehran exceeds 7 million. In the last two or three decades it has experienced rapid growth, resulting in a number of serious problems, including traffic congestion, air pollution, water shortages, and inadequate housing. Transportation may be the biggest problem, as lack of planning has resulted in too many vehicles on too few thoroughfares. The large number of vehicles, many of them older and with no emission controls, has also created serious pollution problems. According to World Health Organization reports, the levels of carbon dioxide found in the air are often four times that of safe levels.

Water shortages are also a problem in this arid region where periodic droughts occur. Although three large dams were built in the 1960s to help provide an adequate and more dependable water supply, population growth over the last three decades has begun to put new pressures on the water supply. There are also problems with water quality, particularly in the southern part of the city, where industrial pollutants have seeped into the water table.

The government has assumed an active role in attempting to provide housing for poor Tehranis. Still, the rapid growth in population has made it difficult for the government to keep pace, and squatter settlements and shantytowns have grown up in the southern section of the capital. On a more positive note, since 1990 the city government has been actively committed to creating and maintaining parks and green space throughout the city and has been remarkably successful in achieving this goal.

The Eastern Mediterranean Crescent The Eastern Mediterranean Crescent, made up of Egypt, Turkey, Lebanon, and Israel, constitutes something of an awkward but compelling clustering of states (see Figure 4.38). It is awkward largely because none of the states views itself as regionally coherent with the others. It is compelling because among them, the four states have the potential to be—or already have become—regional economic success stories. The greatest differences exist between Israel and the other three states. For example, Egypt, Turkey, and Lebanon have had strong agricultural bases for hundreds, if not thousands, of years (**Figure 4.42**). Israel's commitment to agriculture is more recent. Furthermore, while the former three employ agriculture as a major source of export revenues, for Israel, agricultural production is more about achieving national food security, though foodstuffs are also exported. Finally, while Egypt, Turkey, and Lebanon are just beginning to encourage more industrial development—some more successfully than others—Israel already possesses a strong industrial base that is fairly diverse but receives a large share of its income from high-technology production.

Why include Israel, if it is really more different from than similar to the other three states? Israel does not really fit comfortably into any subregion. It is a Jewish state in a predominantly Arab region (though neither Turkey nor Iran is Arabic). Its economy generates the highest GNP in the region, higher than any of the Oil States. It possesses a military that is as highly trained and technologically equipped as that of any European state. Yet, while Israel is really not like any of its neighbors, it is too important politically, culturally, and economically to be ignored. One reason for including Israel in the Eastern Mediterranean Crescent is that it functions as a kind of pacesetter for the other three, who are anxious to be more active players in the contemporary global economy.

There are similarities among the four states. For instance, all four possess more of a European orientation than many of their neighbors, certainly more so than the Oil States. All four have a sizable middle class that has been important to their political stability. And all four have the potential, because of their resource endowments, to continue

FIGURE 4.42 Agriculture in Turkey Much of Turkey's climate is conducive to agriculture, and the country contains numerous farming regions. Cotton is a major export crop; Turkey is also the world's largest exporter of sultana raisins and hazelnuts. Other crops are tobacco, wheat, sunflower seeds, sesame and linseed oils, and cotton-oil seeds. Opium was once a major crop, but its exportation was banned by the government in 1972. The ban was lifted two years later as poppy farmers were unable to adapt their land to other crops. The government now controls the production and sale of opium.

to build a diverse economic base. While Israel, coupled with any of the other three states, would make strange bedfellows, and strong political and cultural differences have tended to prevent all four of these countries from acting in concert, there is much to suggest that cooperation would be mutually beneficial. The main reason for clustering these four countries is that they appear to possess the necessary ingredients to participate in the world economy because of their histories, their economies, and their roles in regional politics.

Turkey and Egypt once controlled long-lasting, influential, and extensive world empires. Although neither was colonized by Europe, both labored under the conditions of a foreign bureaucracy—Egypt longer than Turkey. Presently, both states have similarly sized populations—Egypt with around 67 million and Turkey with around 65.5 million—and both are burdened with the problems that large national populations present to economic development. While Turkey possesses a fairly diversified economy with a strong agricultural sector and substantial mineral wealth, national agriculture in Egypt is built on a fairly narrow base, largely due to the environmental constraints of the desert. Both states have significant manufacturing capacity across a range of products from food processing to heavy machinery.

Lebanon possesses a strong agricultural base and, for many years before its civil war, was a banking and financial center for the Middle East and North Africa, connecting it to the core of Europe and North America. It was not until the early 1990s, however, that Lebanon began to recover from the serious political problems that civil war unleashed. It is still unclear what impact the 2006 conflict with Israel will have on agricultural productivity in Lebanon, but it is safe to say that it will be significantly reduced.

Finally, the four states of the Eastern Mediterranean Crescent possess the major cities of the Middle East and North Africa. Cairo in Egypt, Istanbul in Turkey, Beirut in Lebanon, and Tel Aviv in Israel are all critical nodes in the urban system of the world economy, enabling capital, ideas, and people to come together. We focus here on Cairo as one example of highly urbanized capital investment under the current conditions of globalization in the Middle East and North African region.

Major City: Cairo   "Cairo is Egypt": So say all the travel guides. This so-called "Mother of the World" is the capital of Egypt and the largest city in North Africa and the Middle East. Located on both sides of the Nile River near its delta in northern Egypt, Cairo is a city that visitors either love or hate, but few are ever indifferent.

The history of Cairo reflects the history of the region, which is one of conquest and change. The origins of Cairo go back to the early fourth millennium B.C., when Memphis, located on the site of present-day Cairo, was the capital of Egypt. As the city of Memphis grew, it spread along the east bank of the Nile. Later, Roman conquerors constructed the city of Babylon on the Memphis site. When the Fatimids, a dissident branch of Muslims, conquered Egypt in A.D. 969, they too established their headquarters at Al Qahira (Cairo), "the city victorious." When the Mamelukes rose to power in the region in the 13th century, they took Cairo as their capital, and the city became renowned throughout Africa, Europe, and Asia. In 1517 the Ottomans conquered Cairo and ruled Egypt from there until 1798, when Napoleon I took possession of it. The Ottomans were able to regain control of Cairo in 1801, but by the late 19th century, Egypt's sizable foreign debt and the increasing dissolution of the Ottoman Empire paved the way for British influence in the region until 1952, when, after much agitation and a revolution, Egypt became an independent republic.

Metropolitan Cairo is home to 16 million people, overburdening the urban region with the world's highest density of people per square kilometer. In central Cairo, traffic crawls along the city's narrow streets; building pediments hug the street's edge, leaving little room for pedestrians to pass; and in the narrow walkways between buildings, pedestrians jostle for space. In addition to being the administrative capital of Egypt, Cairo is also a port and the chief commercial and industrial center of a country that produces cotton textiles, food products, construction supplies, motor vehicles, aircraft, and chemical fertilizers. It is also the cultural center of Egypt.

At the center of the city is the river island of Zamalik. Three bridges link the island to the mainland on both sides of the river's bank. Scores of novels about Cairo have used this backdrop as the setting for passionate scenes—both political and personal. Though located within close range of the pyramids, Cairo was built not by the pharaohs but by the Fatimid dynasty, beginning just over 1000 years ago. Much of the city that the Fatimids built has survived, including the Fatimid mosque, Al-Azhar University (the oldest in the Islamic world), and the three great city gates of Bab An-Nasr, Bab al-Futuh, and Bab Zuweila.

The neighborhoods of Islamic Cairo are located on the east bank of the Nile, where the streets are especially narrow and the bazaars especially crowded. Hundreds of mosques populate the neighborhoods of Islamic Cairo, which is perhaps why the area is known as such, since it is no more or less Islamic than the rest of the city. To the south of Islamic Cairo is Old Cairo, home to many of the oldest architectural monuments in the city. Cairo's Coptic Christian community also occupies much of Old Cairo, where mosques are scarce and Coptic churches dominate the landscape (**Figure 4.43**).

Although a world city for political and economic reasons, Cairo faces very serious social problems. The monthly arrival of thousands of new migrants from rural areas as well as from other parts of the region has been unanswered by any sort of additional housing provision. The city and the country have been unable to meet the land and

FIGURE 4.43 Cairo, Egypt (a) Coptic Cairo. The architecture generally associated with the Copts, or Egyptian Christians, dates from about the 3rd to the 12th centuries. Monasteries and churches, scattered throughout Egypt, were built of unbaked brick on the basilica plan inherited from the Greco-Roman world. Characteristic features include heavy walls and columns and vaulted roofs. (b) Islamic Cairo. In Islamic architecture, almost all mosques repeat the plan of the house of the prophet Muhammad, founder of Islam, and are composed essentially of an enclosed courtyard, a building at one end for prayer, arcades on the sides, and a minaret used to call the faithful to prayer. (c) Modern Cairo. Modern Cairo could easily be mistaken for any number of core cities with skyscrapers; broad streets packed with automobiles, trucks, and buses; and busy sidewalks loaded with pedestrians and

(a)

(b)

(c)

housing needs of migrants, as well as the need for schools, hospitals, and other social services. As a result, new arrivals to the city must find alternatives to traditional housing. Some sleep on the streets. Others take over abandoned buildings or land that is underutilized. The most famous example of alternative uses is the thousands of people who live among the tombs of one of Cairo's oldest cemeteries. Known as the City of the Dead, this cemetery, intermingled with houses and apartment buildings, is now occupied by nearly 1 million living residents. Cairo's urban planners are well aware of the many problems such a large city faces and are implementing a wide range of plans. The subway system that was expanded during the 1990s has helped ease some of the extreme traffic problems in the city, and new urban centers are being built to house some of the population away from central Cairo.

Today, Cairo continues to maintain its regional significance as the largest city in the Islamic world. As such, its influence also projects outward, connecting the rest of the world to the Middle East and North Africa.

SUMMARY AND CONCLUSIONS

In this chapter we examined the complex Middle Eastern and North African region. We discussed the region's unique physical geography and environmental history, its ancient origins, the power of Islam and other religions, the particular cultural and gender systems that have emerged there, and the special political tensions that exist there.

The significance of the Middle East and North Africa to the rest of the world is substantial. This region is *a* primary, if not *the*

primary, site of the origins of Western civilization, and its influence on world culture, politics, and technology has been phenomenal. As the possessor of the largest share of the world's oil reserves, the region is also critical to the continued function of the global economy. While the region appears to be in a state of economic transition, it is hard to predict what role political conflict might play in influencing its progress.

KEY TERMS

afforestation (p. 164)
aridity (p. 155)
Balfour Declaration
  (p. 171)
chador (p. 179)
guest worker (p. 181)
hajj (p. 175)

import substitution (p. 173)
informal economy (p. 173)
internally displaced person
  (p. 195)
intifada (p. 189)
Islam (p. 175)
Islamism (p. 176)

jihad (p. 176)
kinship (p. 177)
mandate (p. 170)
minisystem (p. 167)
Muslim (p. 175)
nationalist movement
  (p. 170)

nationalization (p. 173)
oasis (p. 158)
petrodollar (p. 199)
transhumance (p. 178)
tribe (p. 177)
world religion (p. 165)
zionism (p. 187)

REVIEW QUESTIONS

Testing Your Understanding

1. How has the scarcity of water affected the cultural, economic, or political history of this region?
2. How do the people of this region adapt to the generally hot, dry environment through their housing and clothing preferences?
3. How are Judaism, Christianity, and Islam linked? Why is Judaism so much smaller numerically than the other two religions?
4. Name the five pillars of Islam. What are the Qu'ran and the Sunna?
5. What is pastoralism? What is transhumance?

6. What factors bring migrants into this region? What factors motivate migration out?
7. In a few sentences each, discuss the Balfour Declaration (1917), British Mandate (1922), UN Partition of Palestine (1947), the Camp David Accords (1978), and intifada (1980s–present).
8. How does the Palestinian Authority (PA) differ from the Palestine Liberation Organization (PLO) and from Hamas?
9. What are the Arab League and OPEC? In which ways are the goals of these groups the same as or different from each other?
10. How have structural adjustment policies in the Middle East and North Africa affected urbanization there?

Thinking Geographically

1. Using the Jordan River as an example, how well do countries in this region manage and share their water resources?

2. How is kinship viewed in this region? How do these views affect local government and society?

3. How do views about gender affect the use of public and private space? Are rules concerning the veiling of women uniform throughout the region? If not, how do they vary geographically?

4. Guest workers migrate both into and out of this region. Why do so many guest workers in the Oil States come from predominantly Muslim countries worldwide? Why do guest workers from Turkey and North Africa primarily seek work in Europe?

5. Describe the geographic distribution of Palestinians within the Middle East. How have colonial and post-colonial policies in the Middle East left Palestinians with no state of their own?

6. The Middle East and North Africa are becoming highly urbanized. What factors are driving urban growth in this region? How are cities with considerable oil wealth handling their rapid urbanization?

7. Why is the Maghreb a geographically distinct area within this region? What sort of tensions exist between indigenous populations who are trying to maintain their traditions and European-influenced populations who are trying to establish their national independence? Why is the Western Sahara a flashpoint for these tensions?

FURTHER READING

Abdul-Jabar, F., and Dawod, H., *Tribes and Power: Nationalism and Ethnicity in the Middle East*. London: Saqi, 2003.

Amery, H. A., and Wolf, A. T. (eds.), *Water in the Middle East: A Geography of Peace*. Austin: University of Texas Press, 2000.

Amin, C., Fortna, B. C., and Frierson, E. B. (eds.), *The Modern Middle East: A Sourcebook*. Oxford: Oxford University Press, 2006.

Bianco, S., *Urban Form in the Arab World: Past and Present*. New York: Thames and Hudson, 2000.

Bonine, M. (ed.), *Population, Poverty, and Politics in Middle East Cities*. Gainesville, FL: University Press of Florida, 1997.

Brandell, I. (ed.), *State Frontiers: Borders and Boundaries in the Middle East*. London: IB Tauris, 2006.

Cleveland, W. L., *A History of the Modern Middle East*, 3rd ed. Boulder: Westview Press, 2004.

Emadi, H., *Politics of the Dispossessed: Superpowers and Developments in the Middle East*. Westport, CT: Praeger, 2001.

Esposito, J. L., and Ramazani, R. K. (eds.), *Iran at the Crossroads*. New York: Palgrave, 2001.

Falah, G. W., and Nagel, C. (eds.), *Geographies of Muslim Women: Gender, Religion, and Space*. New York: Guilford Press, 2005.

Fawaz, L. T., and Bayly, C. A. (eds.), with the collaboration of R. Ilbert, *Modernity and Culture: From the Mediterranean to the Indian Ocean*. New York: Columbia University Press, 2002.

Gerner, D. J., and Schwedler, J. (eds.), *Understanding the Contemporary Middle East*. Boulder: Lynne Rienner Publishers, 2004.

Halliday, F., *Islam and the Myth of Confrontation: Religion and Politics in the Middle East*. London: I. B. Tauris, 2003.

Held, C. C., *Middle East Patterns: Places, Peoples, and Politics*, 4th ed. Boulder: Westview Press, 2005.

Hillel, D., *Rivers of Eden: The Struggle for Water and the Quest for Peace in the Middle East*. Replica Books, 2000.

Hourani, A., and Ruthven, M., *A History of the Arab Peoples: Second Edition*. Cambridge, MA: Harvard University Press, 2003.

Kheirabadi, M., *Iranian Cities: Formation and Development*. Syracuse, NY: Syracuse University Press, 2000.

Laqueur, W., and Rubin, B. (eds.), *The Israel-Arab Reader: Documentary History of Middle East Conflict*, 6th ed. New York: Penguin, 2001.

Long, D. E., *The Government and Politics of the Middle East and North Africa*. Boulder: Westview Press, 2002.

Peters, R. (ed.), *Jihad In Classical and Modern Islam: A Reader*, 2nd ed. Princeton, NJ: Markus Wiener Publishers, 2005.

Roy, O., *The Failure of Political Islam*. Trans. C. Volk. Cambridge, MA: Harvard University Press, 1998.

Spenser, W., *Global Studies: The Middle East*, 11th ed. Guilford, CT: McGraw-Hill/Dushkin, 2006.

Wedeen, L., *Ambiguities of Domination: Politics, Rhetoric, and Symbols in Contemporary Syria*. Chicago: University of Chicago Press, 1999.

Yambert, K., with special contributions from S. Telhami and A. Goldschmidt. *The Contemporary Middle East*. Boulder, CO: Westview Press, 2006.

Yiftachel, O., *Ethnocracy: Land and Identity Politics in Israel/Palestine*. Philadelphia: University of Pennsylvania Press, 2006.

FILM, MUSIC, AND POPULAR LITERATURE

Film

Battle of Algiers. Directed by Antonio Musu, 1993. Dramatization of the conflict between Algerian nationalists and French colonists that culminated in independence for Algeria in 1963.

Blackboards. Directed by Mezssam Makhamlbaf, 2000. Itinerant teachers wander the Iran–Iraq border searching for a village of children to teach.

Control Room. Directed by Jehane Noujaim, 2004. Explores the nature of truth and ethics in the popular media, with particular focus on the primary satellite news network to the Arab world, Al Jazeera.

Coup. Directed by Elif Savas, 1999. Documentary about the 1960, 1971, 1980, and 1997 military interventions and coups d'état in Turkey.

The Day I Became a Woman. Directed by Marzieh Meshkini, 2001. Three stories about women's struggles in Iran as the country moves toward democracy.

Days of Democracy. Directed by Ateyyat El Abnoudy, 1996. Interviews with women running for Egypt's parliament.

The English Patient. Directed by Anthony Minghella, 1996. The story of Count Almasy, a Hungarian mapmaker employed by the Royal Geographical Society to chart the vast expanses of the Sahara Desert.

Frontiers of Dreams and Fears. Directed by Mai Masri, 2001. The story of two Palestinian girls growing up in refugee camps in Lebanon and the Occupied Territories.

Grand Theatre: A Tale of Beirut. Directed by Omar Naim, 1999. A documentary viewing the Lebanese Civil War, as well as its roots and aftermath, through the eyes of an old theater.

Gunese Yolculuk. Directed by Yesim Ustaoglu, 1999. Depicts the discrimination and violence directed against the Kurdish minority in Turkey.

Lawrence of Arabia. Directed by David Lean, 1962. Story of T. E. Lawrence and his influence on the political history of Saudi Arabia.

Paradise Now. Directed by Hany Abu-Assad, 2005. An enthralling drama about the possible motivations and actions of two suicide bombers.

Private. Directed by Saverio Costanzo, 2004. A minimalist psychological drama about a Palestinian family of seven suddenly confronted with a volatile situation in their home that in many ways reflects the larger ongoing conflict between Palestine and Israel.

The Message. Directed by Moustaffa Akad, 1976. The story of Islam.

The Syrian Bride. Directed by Eran Riklis, 2004. A powerful film about physical, mental, and emotional borders and the courage it takes to cross them.

Syriana. Directed by Stephen Gaghan, 2005. An epic about the global politics of oil in the Middle East.

A Time for Drunken Horses. Directed by Bahman Gohbadi, 2003. A story about Kurds on the Iran–Iraq border.

turtles can fly. Directed by Bahman Ghobadi, 2005. On the Iraqi-Turkish border, enterprising 13-year-old "Satellite" is the de facto leader of a Kurdish village, thanks to his ability to install satellite dishes and translate news of the impending U.S. invasion.

Wall. Directed by Simone Bitton, 2005. Follows the separation fence that is destroying one of the most historically significant landscapes in the world, while imprisoning one people and enclosing the other.

Music

Al Madfai, Ilham. *Baghdad.* EMI International, 2003.

Brahem, Anouar. *Le Voyage de Sahar.* ECM Records, 2006.

The Gnoua Brotherhood of Marrakech/The Master Musicians of Joujouka. *SUFI: Moroccan Trance Music II.* Sub Rosa, 1996.

Khaled, Cheb. *Aiyesha.* Movie Play Gold, 2000.

The Master Musicians of Jajouka, featuring Bachir al-Attar. *Apocalypse Across the Sky.* Axiom/Island, 1992.

Massi, Souad. *Mesk Elil.* Wrasse Records, 2005.

Ramzy, Hossam. *Sabla Tolo: Journeys into Pure Egyptian Percussion.* Arc Music, 2000.

Soleimani, Haj-Ghorban. *Music of the Bards from Iran.* Kereshmeh, 1995.

Subliminal. *The Light and the Shadow.* Helicon, 2003.

Sultan, Sa'ida. *Danna International.* IMP Dance, 1993.

Taha, Rachid. *Made in Medina.* Ark 21, 2001.

Various Artists. *Best of Bellydance from Egypt and Lebanon.* Arc Records, 1996.

Various Artists. *Legends of Arabic Music*. Arc Records, 1998.

Various Artists. *The Music of Islam, Volume 11: Music of Yemen*. Celestial Harmonies, 1998.

Various Artists. *Samar: Music from Yemen Arabia*. Rounder Select, 1999.

Various Artists. *Traditional Music from Turkey*. Arc Records, 2000.

Popular Literature

Aboulela, L. *Minaret: A Novel*. New York: Grove Press, Black Cat, 2005. Written in the voice of Najwa, an upper-class Sudanese woman, the book covers, episodically, 20 years of her life as a Khartoum teenager and as an immigrant in London.

Al Aswany, Alaa. *The Yacoubian Building*. New York: American University in Cairo Press, 2005. The story of a building and a street, but more importantly, a country and the currents that have shaped it over a generation.

Alavi, Nasrin. *We Are Iran: The Persian Blogs*. New York: Soft Skull Press, 2005. This collection of blog reviews functions not only as an archive of Iranians' thoughts on their country, culture, religion, and the rest of the world, but also as an alternative recent history of Iran.

Al-Shaykah, Hanan. *Beirut Blues: A Novel*. New York: Doubleday, 1995. Story about a well-to-do Lebanese woman who must decide whether to abandon war-torn Beirut, the city she loves, or stay and suffer the demeaning and difficult consequences of the civil war.

Anderson, Terry. *Dens of Lions: Memoirs of Seven Years*. New York: Del Rey, 1994. Moving account by the Associated Press's former chief Middle East correspondent of his 2454 days as a hostage of the Islamic terrorist organization Hezbollah.

Bahrampour, Tara. *To See and See Again: A Life in Iran and America*. New York: Farrar, Straus & Giroux, 1999. Memoir of the daughter of an American singer and an Iranian architect that does justice to both sides of her complex heritage.

Bowles, Paul. *The Sheltering Sky*. New York: Signet, 1955. The desert is itself a character in this book, which is about three young Americans of the postwar generation who go on a walkabout into Northern Africa's arid "heart of darkness."

Hodgson, Barbara. *The Tattooed Map*. San Francisco: Chronicle Books, 1995. An intriguing story of a traveler who wakes up somewhere in North Africa with a map tattooed on her hand and then follows the map to solve a mystery.

Kalifeh, Sahar. *Wild Thorns*. New York: Interlink, 1999. A portrait of everyday Arab life in the West Bank and Gaza Strip that describes the difficulties of survival under Israeli oppression.

Mahfouz, Naguib. *The Cairo Trilogy: Palace Walk; Palace of Desire; Sugar Street*. New York: Doubleday, 1988, 1991, 1992. (Winner of the Nobel Prize, 1988.) The engrossing saga of a Muslim family in Cairo during Egypt's occupation by British forces in the early 1900s.

Manning, Olivia. *The Levant Trilogy*. New York: Penguin, 1982. Powerful political and romantic story of the role that the Levant played in World War II as Italy, Britain, and Germany used the region to launch various campaigns.

Munif, Abdelrahman. *Cities of Salt: A Novel*. New York: Vintage Books, 1993. A tale of indigenous people's exploitation and oppression by corporations and colonialists, set against the background of the range of identity issues affecting the peoples of modern Saudi Arabia.

Said, Edward. *End of the Peace Process: Oslo and After*. New York: Pantheon, 2000. A collection of 50 impassioned, damning essays on the consequences of the Middle East peace process.

Soueif, Ahdaf. *Map of Love*. London: Bloomsbury, 1999. A massive family saga that draws its readers into two moments in the complex, troubled history of modern Egypt: the late 19th and the late 20th centuries.

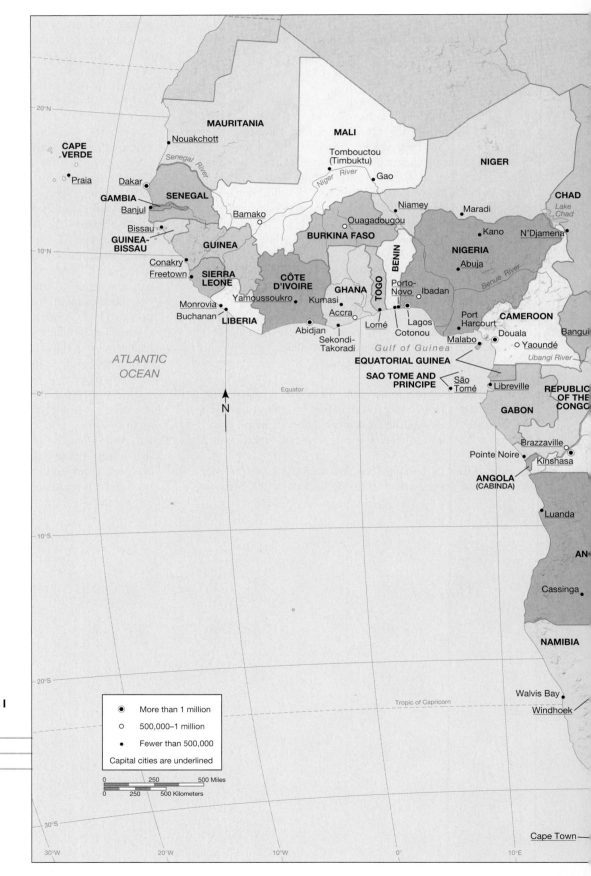

FIGURE 5.1

◉	More than 1 million
○	500,000–1 million
•	Fewer than 500,000

Capital cities are underlined

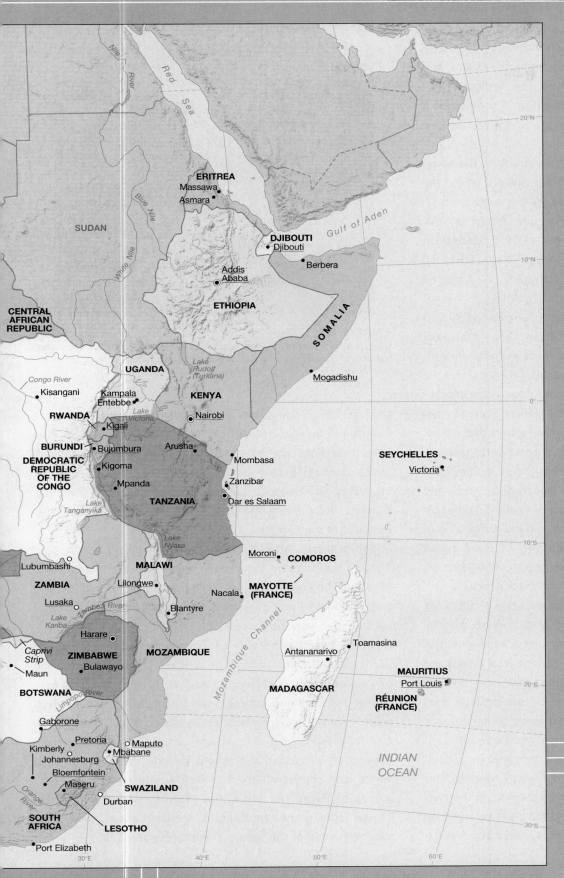

SUDAN

Nile River

Blue Nile

White Nile

Red Sea

20°N

ERITREA
Massawa
Asmara

DJIBOUTI
Djibouti

Gulf of Aden

10°N

Addis
Ababa

Berbera

ETHIOPIA

**CENTRAL
AFRICAN
REPUBLIC**

S O M A L I A

Lake
Rudolf
(Turkana)

UGANDA

Congo River

Kisangani

Kampala
Entebbe

KENYA

Mogadishu

RWANDA
Kigali

Nairobi

0°

BURUNDI
Bujumbura

Arusha

**DEMOCRATIC
REPUBLIC
OF THE
CONGO**

Kigoma

Lake
Victoria

SEYCHELLES
Victoria

Mpanda

Mombasa

TANZANIA

Zanzibar

Dar es Salaam

Lake
Tanganyika

10°S

Lake
Nyasa

Moroni

COMOROS

Lubumbashi

MALAWI

**MAYOTTE
(FRANCE)**

ZAMBIA

Lilongwe

Nacala

Lusaka

Zambezi River

Blantyre

Mozambique Channel

Lake
Kariba

Harare

Toamasina

*Caprivi
Strip*

ZIMBABWE

MOZAMBIQUE

Antananarivo

Bulawayo

MAURITIUS
Port Louis

Maun

Limpopo River

MADAGASCAR

20°S

**RÉUNION
(FRANCE)**

BOTSWANA

Gaborone

Pretoria

Maputo

Kimberly

Mbabane

Johannesburg

*INDIAN
OCEAN*

Bloemfontein

Orange River

Maseru

SWAZILAND

Durban

**SOUTH
AFRICA**

LESOTHO

30°S

Port Elizabeth

30°E

40°E

50°E

60°E

209

Africa is a large, complex, and often misunderstood continent. Perceptions range from a fertile tropical forest rife with exotic diseases to an idyllic game reserve, or from a harsh landscape devastated by war and drought to a place where rich cultural traditions reach back to the dawn of humanity. Africa has considerable mineral wealth and agricultural potential, but on almost all indicators of economic development and social and health conditions, it is ranked lowest and considered most peripheral among world regions.

The continental landmass called Africa straddles the equator, stretching 8000 kilometers (5000 miles) from the Mediterranean Sea in the north to the southern tip in South Africa at about 35 degrees south latitude. At its widest, Africa spans 7400 kilometers (4600 miles) from Senegal on the Atlantic coast to Somalia on the Indian Ocean. The total area is about 30.4 million square kilometers (11.7 million square miles).

Some geographers argue that the countries of North Africa that border the Mediterranean Sea—Morocco, Algeria, Tunisia, Libya, and Egypt—have more in common with the Middle East than with the countries of Africa that lie south of the Sahara Desert. North Africa does share characteristics with the Middle East, including similar physical environments of dry climates and human geographies that reflect a dominant Arabic language and ethnicity and Islamic religion.

Sub-Saharan Africa (**Figure 5.1**) has been defined and divided from North Africa based on historical, physical, and social characteristics that include a legacy of European colonialism and slavery, a mostly tropical climate, and the darker skin of many inhabitants. The race-based definition of Sub-Saharan Africa is very controversial but has been used by both Africans and non-Africans to identify the region as "Black Africa."

In this text, we discuss North Africa with the Middle East because of shared characteristics and because one chapter on the whole of Africa would be very long. However, the physical and human links across the continent of Africa are such that several sections of this chapter, including the section on humans and the environment, discuss broader patterns across the whole continent and refer to Africa as a whole rather than to Sub-Saharan Africa specifically.

The geographical, racial, ethnic, and religious bases for dividing Africa into two world regions is artificial, oversimplifying both the cultural and historical distinctiveness of the two regions, the overlaps between them, and the great variety they contain. For example, the Sahara Desert is a large area, rather

FIGURE 5.2 Satellite image of Africa This satellite image clearly shows the major landform regions of the Sahara Desert, the Congo rain forests, the highlands of Ethiopia, and the line of lakes along the East African Rift Valley, including Lake Victoria. The large island of Madagascar is also clearly visible.

than a clear dividing line, and includes territory from both North and Sub-Saharan African countries (**Figure 5.2**). The Nile River links the North African countries of Egypt and Sudan through a long fertile corridor to the Sub-Saharan countries of Ethiopia, Uganda, Kenya, Tanzania, Rwanda, Burundi, the Central African Republic, and the Democratic Republic of the Congo.

Sub-Saharan Africa includes 42 mainland countries, 6 island nations, and the French territories of Réunion and Mayotte. The region includes large populations growing their own food and living in small rural villages; less than 40 percent of the population lived in urban areas in 2003. Sub-Saharan Africa has an area of 22 million square kilometers (8.5 million square miles) and a 2003 total population of 674 million. The world region of Sub-Saharan Africa is frequently divided into subregional clusters of countries that share common geographical characteristics and have some distinctive landscapes that include parts of several countries. Commonly discussed subregions include West Africa, East Africa, and southern Africa as well as the distinctive landscapes of Equatorial Africa, the Horn of Africa, the Indian Ocean islands, and the Sahel, a semiarid zone across the southern edge of the Sahara Desert (**Figure 5.3**).

Sub-Saharan Africa is home to considerable populations of Arab and European ethnic groups and of Muslims, and North Africa hosts significant numbers of black Africans and non-Muslims. Traders have linked the economies of North and Sub-Saharan Africa for centuries, and the Organization of African States includes members from throughout the continent. Sudan (discussed in Chapter 4) exemplifies the challenges of treating Africa as two distinct world regions because the north part of the country is dominated by an Islamic and Arabic culture, whereas the south hosts a predominantly black and Christian population.

FIGURE 5.3 Major subregions and mineral resources of Africa Africa is commonly divided into several major regions, including southern, East, West, Equatorial, and North Africa as well as the distinctive landscapes of the Sahel, Horn of Africa, and Indian Ocean islands. The map also shows the location of the most important regions of mineral development in Africa, including oil, gold, and diamonds. South Africa, Zambia, and Sierra Leone are particularly rich in minerals, and Nigeria is a major oil producer.

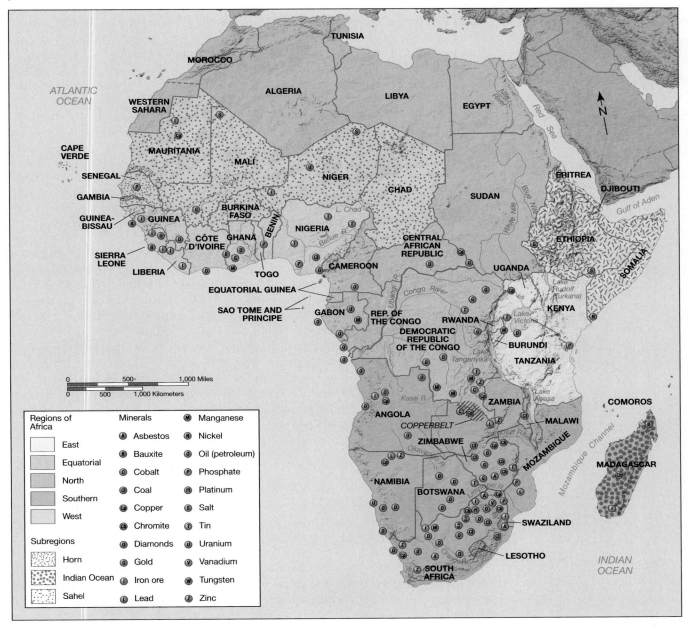

ENVIRONMENT AND SOCIETY IN SUB-SAHARAN AFRICA

The continent of Africa is the heart of the ancient supercontinent called Pangaea, the southern part of which broke off to form Gondwanaland about 200 million years ago (see Chapter 1, p. 22). The theory of plate tectonics explains that when the regions we now call Latin America and Asia broke away from Gondwanaland, the high plateau that remained became the continent of Africa.

Half of the continent is composed of very old crystalline rocks of volcanic origin that hold the key to Africa's mineral wealth. Ancient tropical swamps formed sedimentary rocks containing oil and other fossil fuels. These include coal in southern Africa and Nigeria and oil and gas in West Africa, particularly Nigeria and Gabon. Iron and manganese are found in western and southern Africa, and most of the world's known chromium is found in southern Africa, especially in Zimbabwe and South Africa. Vast copper reserves are located in the southern Congo and in the copper belt of Zambia, where cobalt is also found; bauxite, which is used in making aluminum, is found in a belt across West Africa, and uranium is found in Niger. These minerals are critical to industrial production elsewhere in the world.

Gold is found in several regions of Africa, including Ghana and Zimbabwe, and in South Africa, where as much as half of the world's gold reserves lie in the region around Johannesburg. South Africa is famous for diamonds, which are also found in Botswana and Namibia in southern Africa, at the edges of the Congo basin, and in Sierra Leone in West Africa. Although these resources bring billions of dollars into Africa, they also make national and regional economies vulnerable to fluctuations in world market prices, especially where minerals dominate exports. In Africa as a whole, exports of mining products in merchandise trade were valued at $95 billion in 2003, about 55 percent of total exports.

These mineral resources have played important roles in African history. Salt was a key commodity in trans-Saharan trade from the 10th century to the present day. Gold was valued in West Africa from early times and was worn and traded by kings and leaders; Mansu Musa, the emperor of Mali, carried and traded so much gold on a pilgrimage to Mecca in 1324 that his actions depressed gold prices worldwide. Gold and diamonds spurred European colonial grabs for Africa and conflicts between the core colonial powers. They also created conflicts with indigenous groups after the discovery of diamonds in 1867 at Kimberly and gold in 1886 on the Rand, a range of hills to the west of Johannesburg, in South Africa. Gold and diamonds, together with oil, continue to incite conflict within Africa and to amplify interest in African economies on the part of other states and multinational corporations (see Geographies of Indulgence, Desire, and Addiction: Diamonds, p. 216).

The distribution of mineral wealth is uneven between and within countries, with South Africa (gold and diamonds) and Nigeria (oil) accounting for more than half of total value. Sub-Saharan countries with mineral exports accounting for more than one-half of total earnings in 2004 include Angola (89 percent, oil), Botswana (88 percent, diamonds), Congo (82 percent, diamonds and copper), Gabon (98 percent, oil), Nigeria (98 percent, oil), and Zambia (66 percent, copper).

Landforms and Landscapes

Where the continental plates tore away from Africa during the breakup of Gondwanaland, they left steep slopes (called *escarpments*) that fell from the high plateau to the new oceans. Geologic tensions created trenches and volcanic activity. Most of the rivers that had previously drained into the inland lakes of the supercontinent eventually found outlets to the sea.

Africa is still mainly a plateau continent, with elevations ranging from about 300 meters (approximately 1000 feet) in the west, tilting up to more than 1500 meters (approximately 5000 feet) in the eastern part of the continent (**Figure 5.4**). There are some significant mountain ranges in western Africa, including the Cameroon mountains and Fouta Diallon highlands, with rivers flowing from the uplands. Steep slopes, especially on the western edge of the plateau, drop to narrow coastal plains. Where rivers descend to the coast, they often cut deep valleys back into the plateaus and drop over rapids and waterfalls, such as Victoria Falls on the Zambezi River in southern Africa. This poses a serious problem for navigation by boat into the continent but also offers the potential for hydroelectric development. This potential has been realized through major dams on many rivers in Africa, including the Kariba on the Zambezi, Akosombo on the Volta, and Aswan on the Nile (see Geography Matters: Dams and Development in Africa, p. 218).

Both Kariba and Akosombo have been affected by drought in recent years and have cut back on the amount of electricity they supply as a result. The slower flow of the river and the resulting stagnant water behind the dams have increased the incidence of several diseases, including schistosomiasis and malaria.

FIGURE 5.4 Map of major landforms in Africa Africa is a plateau continent surrounded by steep escarpments, with rivers that often flow through inland deltas on the plateau or drop over waterfalls at the edge of the escarpment. One of the most significant features is the East African Rift Valley, filled with elongated lakes and several active volcanoes. (*Source:* Adapted from S. Aryeetey-Attoh [ed.], *The Geography of Sub-Saharan Africa.* Upper Saddle River, NJ: Prentice Hall, 1997, p. 5.)

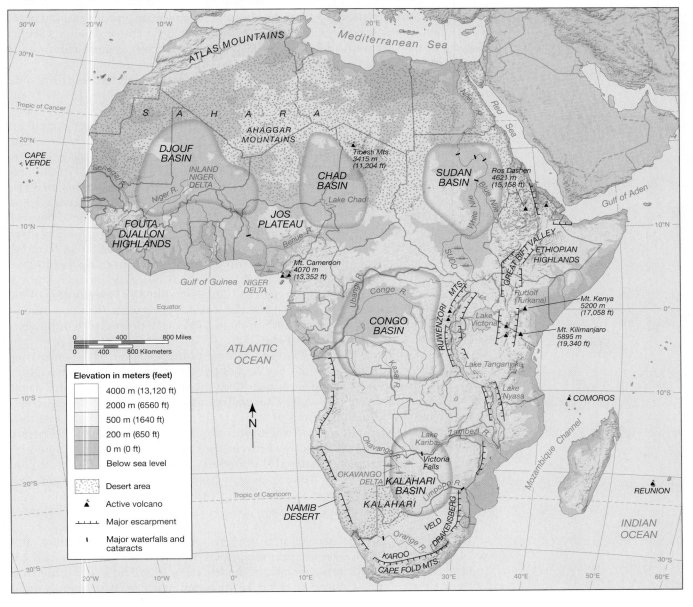

FIGURE 5.5 Great Rift Valley
Elongated lakes line the bottom of the Great Rift Valley. Lake Bogoria, Kenya, shown here, has several geothermal hot springs as a result of the tectonic activity and a large population of flamingoes colored pink from the organisms that live in the lake.

The routes of Africa's major rivers reflect the legacies of inland drainage on the supercontinent, because many of them flow away from the coast and into inland wetlands and deltas before shifting back toward the ocean. For example, the immense Congo River, second only to the Amazon in terms of overall discharge, flows north before turning west toward the rapids that bring it down to the Atlantic. The Niger River flows north toward the Sahara into a large inland delta, before turning south toward its exit to the Atlantic in Nigeria. The Nile, discussed in more detail in Chapter 4, flows into the vast wetland known as the *Sudd*. Several river systems still drain to inland basins, including the Okavango River of southern Africa and the Chari-Logone river system, which drains into Lake Chad in the Sahel. These inland deltas create some of the richest ecosystems in the region, providing habitat for wildlife, fisheries, and grazing and irrigated land for human activities.

The higher areas of the plateau, whose cooler temperatures and higher rainfall are hospitable to humans, include the High Veld of southern Africa, the highlands of Kenya and Ethiopia, and the Jos plateau of West Africa. Volcanic peaks such as Kilimanjaro (5895 meters, 19,340 feet), Kenya/Kirinyaga (5200 meters, 17,058 feet), and the Virungas (4507 meters, 14,787 feet) rise from the eastern plateau, which is also split by a deep trough where tectonic processes continue to pull the eastern edge of Africa away from the rest of the continent. This block of land that dropped between two others, forming a steep-sided trough, often at faults on a divergent plate boundary, runs more than 9600 kilometers (6000 miles) from Jordan and the Red Sea in the north to Mozambique in the south, and is called a rift valley; it ranges from 50 to 100 kilometers (30 to 60 miles) wide. The African Rift Valley has two major branches and is filled with deep elongated lakes, including Lake Tanganyika at 1473 meters deep (4832 feet). Lake Victoria, the third largest lake in the world, lies between the two branches of the rift valley. The age, size, and depth of these lakes make them diverse freshwater ecosystems with important fisheries (**Figure 5.5**).

African soils tend to be of low fertility because of the great age of the underlying geology and because of high rainfall that leaches (washes out) nutrients from exposed soils. Soil fertility tends to be higher in regions of recent volcanic activity, such as the East African highlands, and in wider river valleys where sediments settle and create alluvial (river) soils. The tropical soils of wetter zones, such as central Africa, lose their fertility rapidly once the forest is cleared and the soil is exposed to the elements. Between the dry and wet zones, such as between the coastal and Sahel regions of West Africa, soils have more organic material and support crops and pasture. Desert regions can have saline or alkaline soils that are toxic to crops. High iron and aluminum content is also poisonous to plants and crops in some regions.

Climate

Most of Sub-Saharan Africa lies between the tropics of Cancer and Capricorn and has a tropical climate with warm temperatures (higher than 20°C, 70°F) and little frost except in highland areas (**Figure 5.6**). The climate is dominated by two major features of the atmospheric circulation—the intertropical convergence zone (ITCZ) and the subtropical high (see Chapter 1, p. 23). As in Latin America and Asia, the ITCZ is a region where air flows together and rises vertically as a result of intense solar heating at the equator, often with heavy rainfall, and shifts north and south with the seasons. In Africa the ITCZ produces intense rainfall of more than 1500 millimeters (60 inches) a year over the Congo basin. The subtropical high is a zone of descending air, resulting in dry, stable air that causes desert conditions over the Sahara and Kalahari. The regions between these two features experience seasonal rainfall as the ITCZ and subtropical high shift northward in April through September and southward in October through March. During December the southward shift of the ITCZ low pressure brings hot dry

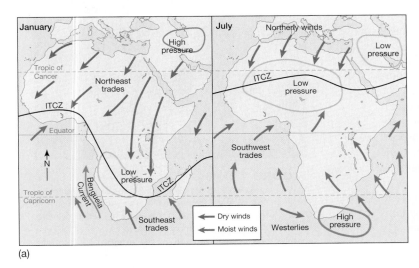

(a)

FIGURE 5.6 Climate and vegetation zones of Africa   (a) The major wind and pressure patterns over Africa in January and July are shown here. Atmospheric circulations include the West African monsoon in July and the dry harmattan winds in December. Precipitation occurs generally to the south of the intertropical convergence zone (ITCZ); seasonal movement is shown on the map. (b) The tropical forest regions near the equator receive most of the continent's rainfall, and deserts occur where dry, descending air and cold, offshore climates inhibit rainfall. Southern Africa receives rainfall from storms in the westerly winds from April to August and has a winter rainfall maximum typical of a Mediterranean climate and vegetation. Climate and vegetation zones overlap closely in Africa. They depend mostly on the amount and seasonality of precipitation. Large areas of Africa are covered with savanna vegetation and by deserts. (c) A camel caravan carries salt across the desert landscape in Niger. (*Source:* Adapted from W. M. Adams, A. S. Goudie, and A. R. Orme, *The Physical Geography of Africa*. London: Oxford University Press, 1999, Fig. 10.5.)

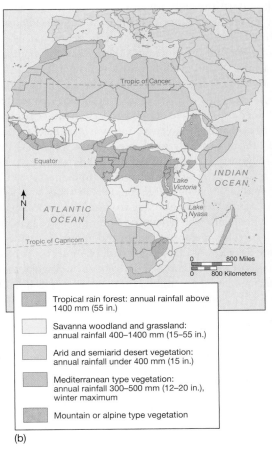

▨	Tropical rain forest: annual rainfall above 1400 mm (55 in.)
▢	Savanna woodland and grassland: annual rainfall 400–1400 mm (15–55 in.)
▨	Arid and semiarid desert vegetation: annual rainfall under 400 mm (15 in.)
▨	Mediterranean type vegetation: annual rainfall 300–500 mm (12–20 in.), winter maximum
▨	Mountain or alpine type vegetation

(b)

(c)

Diamonds

For many consumers around the world, diamonds are associated with love and luxury, the symbol of engagement to marry and of wealth and sophistication. Larger diamonds, after grading, cutting, polishing, and setting in gold or other metals, are sold for high prices in jewelry stores, with about half of all purchases made in the United States. These glittering stones also have considerable industrial value because of their hardness, forming a strong, sharp cutting edge.

Africa is a major source of the world's diamonds. About two-thirds of the world diamond trade is controlled by a South African conglomerate, De Beers. The virtual monopoly held by De Beers permits careful control of diamond markets to ensure that prices remain high and the supply stable, and the company has worked hard through advertising to maintain the romantic image of diamonds. Eighty percent of all diamonds are traded through the Diamond Center in Antwerp, Belgium.

Most diamond production takes place in South Africa, Botswana, and Namibia and contributes significantly to export revenue and local employment (see Figure 5.3). In Angola, the Democratic Republic of the Congo, and Sierra Leone, diamonds are also mined or smuggled across borders and have become associated with corruption, violence, and warfare. Easy to transport, diamonds are increasingly used to purchase weapons, and some analysts suggest that these "blood diamonds" may now make up as much as 10 percent of all global trade in diamonds.

Diamonds are mined in large commercial mines such as those in South Africa, but they are also dug from mud and streams by hundreds of individuals who dream of finding a large gem that will make their fortunes (**Figure 1**). Mines and miners in Angola and the Democratic Republic of the Congo are often under the protection of armed guards or military forces. For example, in Angola, the Catoca mine, which produced 1.5 million carats of diamonds in 2001, paid

FIGURE 1 Diamond diggers Hundreds of people have come to work in the diamond regions of the Democratic Republic of the Congo, where they work deep in the mud of streambeds to sift sediment with the dream of finding especially valuable diamonds. However, the diggers receive only a small portion of the eventual value of the diamonds on the world market and are sometimes harassed by the military or others who use violence to gain access to the diamonds.

winds called the **harmattan** out of inland Africa. These winds carry large amounts of dust and create stress for humans and animals. In July, the northward shift allows the southwestern trade winds to blow onto the coast of West Africa, bringing seasonal rains to inland countries such as Mali.

This general pattern is modified by the regional effects of mountains, lakes, and ocean currents. The cold Benguela current creates cool, dry conditions along the coasts of Angola and Namibia and promotes the desert conditions of the Kalahari (**Figure 5.6a**). Cold water and stable winds that blow along, rather than across, the coast also promote dry conditions in countries such as Somalia in the Horn of Africa. High-altitude regions, such as the East African highlands, have higher rainfall and more moderate temperatures, which are favorable to agriculture and human settlement. South Africa is located in more temperate latitudes and experiences a mild Mediterranean climate with dry conditions from October to March and rainfall from the westerly wind belt from April to August.

The semiarid regions of Africa have highly variable rainfall and frequent droughts, which pose great challenges to agriculture and water resources management. Some of this variation is connected to the changes in Pacific Ocean temperatures known as El Niño. El Niño is the periodic warming of sea surface temperatures in the tropical

$500,000 a month to the Angolan army for security against the rebel group UNITA (the National Union for the Total Independence of Angola), which used to control the region. Money associated with diamond mines has funded an increase in number and magnitude of arms on every side of conflict in Angola, including the purchase of land mines that have maimed thousands of civilians. UNITA, for instance, has used its control of diamond mines in the Lunda provinces to finance a guerrilla struggle against the MPLA government (representing the popular movement for the liberation of Angola). Dr. Jonas Savimbi, who heads the UNITA, has left the country covered with 10 to 20 million land mines in a 20-year war against the MPLA over control of Angola's diamonds. In 1994, the Lusaka Peace Protocol called for a cease-fire, so that today an uneasy peace remains in anticipation of another civil war because of UNITA's unwillingness to relinquish its diamond mines to the Angolan MPLA government under President Eduardo Dos Santos.

The Democratic Republic of the Congo has also become a pawn in the struggle for diamonds, with Angola, Namibia, and Zimbabwe sending troops to protect the government, and Burundi, Rwanda, and Uganda assisting rebels. The area around the diamond zone near Kisangani in the eastern Democratic Republic of the Congo has been abandoned to fighting, and Zimbabwe and Rwanda have struggled to obtain access to diamond deposits in the southern Democratic Republic of the Congo. Diamonds have also funded a brutal civil war in Sierra Leone, where rebels have chopped off people's limbs with machetes to intimidate residents into leaving the eastern diamond zones. Rebels account for more than 20 percent of the diamonds supplied to the global market. "Conflict diamonds" from Liberia are being smuggled into neighboring countries for export, and diamonds from the Ivory Coast are finding their way to the British and European markets. Pressure from human rights groups has led De Beers to refrain from purchasing diamonds that originate in conflict zones. De Beers has also agreed to support research and development of a system to fingerprint diamonds based on chemical signatures that can identify legitimate areas of origin.

In contrast, Botswana is producing diamonds under peaceful conditions and with the guidance of traditional leaders. The mines employ more than 25 percent of the population and are responsible for a gross national product per capita and standard of living that is much higher than the average for Sub-Saharan Africa. In February 2002, however, Survival International claimed that the Botswanan government cut off water supplies to the Central Kalahari Game Reserve to drive the Gana and Gwi Bushmen off their ancestral land. Diamonds have been implicated in this action to exploit the reserve's diamond resources.

On January 1, 2003, the Kimberley Process came into effect with its chief aim of eliminating the use of diamonds to finance armed conflict. In 2000 the diamond-producing countries of southern Africa had established the Kimberley Process Certification Scheme (KPCS) to protect their legitimate diamond industry; however, the main target of the KPCS was to highlight the illicit trade of rough diamonds, which has fueled much conflict. Canada, a major diamond-producing country, was made responsible for chairing the KPCS at the end of 2003. The mandate is for the global trade of rough diamonds in an open and transparent manner and through legitimate markets. The KPCS continues to gain widespread and growing support and now represents all countries involved in the production, processing, and trading of diamonds. It is recognized as a unique partnership between governments, the diamond industry, and civil society. Although the battle against conflict diamonds is far from over, the Kimberley Process is an international attempt at contributing to and promoting international peace and security.

Source: Adapted from B. Harden, "Diamond Wars: A Special Report. Africa's Gems: Warfare's Best Friend," *New York Times*, April 6, 2000.

Pacific off the coast of Peru that results in worldwide changes in climate, including severe droughts in southern Africa. There is also some evidence that Africa is being affected by global warming with drying trends in the Sahel and southern Africa.

Environmental History

Ecosystems African ecosystems, as in the rest of the world, are closely tied to climate conditions but also reflect a complex evolutionary history and physical geography that has produced great diversity, unique plants, and perhaps the world's most charismatic community of animal species. The Congo basin hosts Earth's second largest area of rain forest (after the Amazon), covering almost 2.6 million square kilometers (1 million square miles). Other forests are found along the West African coasts, the coast of Kenya, and on the island of Madagascar. Forests make up about 20 percent of the African land area. These forests have great biodiversity, including monkeys and apes such as chimpanzees and gorillas and tropical hardwoods of significant economic value such as mahogany. The forests are threatened by demands for timber and firewood, by poaching and foraging, and by conversion of natural habitats to cropland.

Dams and Development in Africa

The rivers of Africa, especially where they descend over the coastal escarpment, provide considerable potential for hydroelectric development and examples of the geographic impact of water resources development. Several large projects were initiated around the time of transition to independence in the 1950s to harness the energy of the rivers, to provide electricity to industry and cities, and to irrigate agricultural fields (**Figure 1**). The successes and failures of these projects are an important illustration of the need to understand both physical and social factors in the context of specific places in the assessment of development.

The Federation of Rhodesia and Nyasaland (now the countries of Zimbabwe and Zambia) completed the Kariba Dam on the Zambezi at Kariba gorge in 1959 (**Figure 2**). This dam, which produces inexpensive electric power for this region of southern Africa, created Lake Kariba. This required the resettlement of 57,000 people and the evacuation of thousands of wild animals isolated as the waters rose behind the dam through "Operation Noah." The areas to which people were moved were infested with the tsetse fly, and many were exposed to the sleeping sickness it carries. Because of poor planning, some people ended up in places resembling refugee camps. The hygiene in these camps was very

FIGURE 2 Kariba Dam The Kariba Dam on the Zambezi River supplies electricity to Zimbabwe and Zambia. It has become a destination for tourists, who come to view game in the parks that line the shores of Lake Kariba.

poor, and epidemics flourished. On the positive side, however, some of the unanticipated benefits include development of a tourist industry and lush animal habitat around the new lake and a productive fishery. The electricity produced by the dam supports the copper-mining industry in Zambia.

The Akosombo Dam, completed on the Volta River in 1965, was funded by the governments of Ghana, the United Kingdom, and the United States and by the World Bank. The electricity was targeted for a large aluminum smelter on the coast at Tema, which was supposed to use West African bauxite. This operation is now U.S.-owned and consumes about 45 percent of the electricity the dam generates; the smelter pays very low taxes, has imported cheap bauxite from the Caribbean, and is thereby able to keep aluminum prices low. The remainder of the electric power either goes to urban domestic consumption or is exported to Togo and Benin.

The construction of the Akosombo Dam had a number of social and environmental effects. The huge reservoir behind the dam, Lake Volta, reaches 400 kilometers (250 miles) northward and is the largest human-made lake in Africa. The area now under water included 15,000 homes and more than 700 villages, and 78,000 people had to be resettled to make way for the lake. Many were unhappy with the quality of their new houses and land and have returned to live near the lake.

Prior to the construction of the dam, floodplains downstream had benefited from the annual renewal of sediment, and cattle had grazed on the lush grasses along the river. When the river flow declined and releases from the dam became more sporadic, agriculture and livestock production declined in the area below the dam. Sediment is now building up behind the dam, reducing storage, electrical potential, and the potential lifetime of the dam.

FIGURE 1 Dams in Africa This map shows the location of major dams and irrigation schemes in Africa.

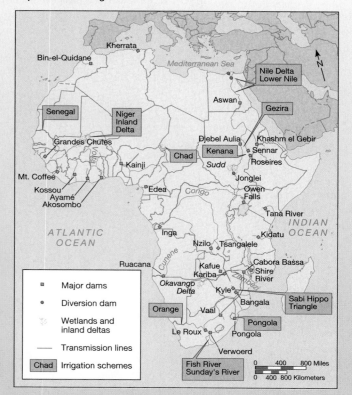

FIGURE 5.7 Ngorongoro Crater, Tanzania Wildebeest and zebra graze on the savanna grasslands of East Africa with baobab trees dotting the landscape.

Drier regions have mixed woodlands and grasslands (covering about 40 percent of Africa) with open stands of trees interspersed with shrubs and grasses. The baobab tree is a symbol of this landscape, which is found in West Africa centered on Guinea and in southern Africa near the Zambezi (**Figure 5.7**). The **savanna** grassland vegetation is found in tropical climates with a pronounced dry season and periodic fires. Savannas provide expansive grazing areas for both wildlife and livestock. Grassy plains such as the Serengeti of Tanzania have some of the densest concentrations of wild, hoofed, grazing mammals (called *ungulates*) in the world, together with their predators such as the big cats—lion, leopard, and cheetah. The larger herbivores include elephants, giraffes, zebras, and rhinoceroses.

Desert regions (38 percent of Africa) have very sparse and seasonal vegetation for the most part, with drought-resistant vegetation such as acacias and woody scrub. The Mediterranean climates of South Africa have produced a unique ecosystem dominated by *fynbos* shrubland, the vegetation of which is characterized by waxy or needlelike leaves and long roots that help plants survive long dry periods. Finally, the highland, or montane, vegetation is found on mountain ranges such as the volcanoes of East Africa or the Drakensberg highlands of southern Africa.

As in other world regions, African ecosystems such as those on Mount Kenya show clear altitude zonation, with a vertical change in environment and land use according to elevation based mainly on changes in climate and vegetation from lower (warmer) to higher (cooler) elevations. The popular tourist hikes up the slopes of Mount Kenya or Kilimanjaro reveal how vegetation and human land use change along these environmental gradients. The base of the mountains is nested in grasslands of the savanna, while rocky peaks are covered with snow and ice (now disappearing as a result of climate change). In between, a hiker would pass through zones of dry forest, bamboo forest, heathland, and alpine moorland.

Diseases and Insect Pests Africa's ecologies are notable for several pests and diseases that can have a devastating impact on human populations. Several of these diseases have reservoirs in certain wild species and are then transferred to

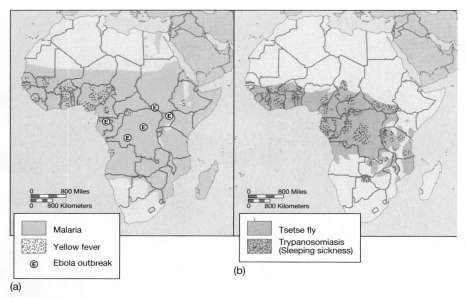

(a)

(b)

FIGURE 5.8 Maps of tropical infectious diseases and pests These maps show the distribution of some of the more serious tropical diseases in Africa. (a) Malaria and yellow fever. Yellow fever has a mosquito vector and a reservoir in monkey populations. Mortality in Africa has been reduced through immunization, but many who are poor or live in remote regions still do not have access to vaccines, and as many as 20,000 people died in an outbreak of yellow fever in Senegal in the 1960s. (b) The tsetse fly, which lives in African woodland and scrub regions, is a vector for a virus with a reservoir in wild animals. It is associated with both human and livestock diseases. In humans, the fly's bite causes sleeping sickness, or trypanosomiasis, with fever and infection of the brain that causes extreme lethargy and may end with death of the victim. Half a million people are infected in Sub-Saharan Africa. Sleeping sickness can be treated in early stages and can be prevented by a variety of pest-control measures, including burning brush, spraying with pesticides, and removing wild animals (including rodents) that serve as reservoirs for the disease. In domestic animals such as cattle and horses, the tsetse fly causes a disease called *nagana*, which is similar to sleeping sickness and causes fever and paralysis. This disease prevented the introduction of livestock into many parts of Africa and as a result preserved habitats for wild species. Areas with an elevation above 150 meters (480 feet), those with a long dry season, and those with sparse or no woodland are free from tsetse flies.

(*Source:* Modified from I. L. L. Griffiths, *An Atlas of African Affairs.* New York: Methuen, 1985, pp. 20–21.)

humans or their domesticated animals by vector (transmission) organisms such as mosquitoes, flies, and snails. Malaria, a disease transmitted to humans by mosquitoes, causes fever, anemia, and often fatal complications. It affects about 400 million people in Sub-Saharan Africa each year, killing more than 1.5 million, many of them children (**Figure 5.8a**). Early European explorers and settlers were highly vulnerable to malaria and suffered as much as 75 percent mortality in some regions. The discovery in 1820 that quinine—an extract from the cinchona tree, thought to have been brought to Europe from Peru by Jesuit priests—could partly control malaria facilitated colonialism and also allowed treatment of some local residents. But it did not cure the disease, and after World War II several synthetic drugs, such as chloroquine, became popular cures. Unfortunately, several strains of the malaria parasite have developed resistance to these drugs and there is still no certain and cheap cure for the disease although cheap mosquito nets can help.

Schistosomiasis (also called *bilharziasis*) is associated with a parasite that causes gastrointestinal diseases and liver damage. It is passed to humans who are exposed to a snail vector by working or bathing in slow-moving water, such as that in marshes, reservoirs, or irrigation canals. The disease is not fatal but reduces general health and energy levels. The United Nations World Health Organization (WHO) estimates that 160 million people are infected in Sub-Saharan Africa. River blindness (onchocerciasis) is transmitted by the bite of the black fly, which passes on small worms whose larvae disintegrate in the human eye and cause blindness. The eradication of river blindness has been relatively successful in West Africa by controlling fly populations with pesticides and treating victims with drugs. WHO estimates that 18 million people are infected, and 250,000 are blind as a result of this disease in Sub-Saharan Africa. Other serious diseases include yellow fever, onchocerciasis (river blindness), and sleeping sickness associated with the tsetse fly (**Figure 5.8b**).

Many of these debilitating diseases are associated with the tropical climate and diverse ecologies of Africa. Their spread may have been facilitated by the expansion of human populations and the transformation of natural environments through deforestation and irrigation. Reducing the human toll from these diseases is a major challenge for scientific research, African governments, charitable organizations, and the World Health Organization, which has targeted Africa for extra funds and programs. The Bill and Melinda Gates Foundation has committed more than $750 million to fighting malaria, including the development of a malaria vaccine, and has spurred a multibillion-dollar global health initiative aimed at achieving major reductions in disease in poor countries, especially in Africa.

Agricultural and Environmental History The United Nations Food and Agricultural Organization (FAO) has estimated that less than 30 percent of the soils in Sub-Saharan Africa are suitable for agriculture. In addition, agriculture is hindered by an unsuitable climate and an environment that is prone to pests and diseases. However, Africa, as the birthplace of the human species, is also the region where humans first adapted to the constraints of the physical environment, finding sustenance through hunting wild animals, fishing, gathering plants, and domesticating a number of crop and livestock species.

There is some disagreement about whether cattle were domesticated in Africa or introduced from the Middle East and Asia about 8000 years ago. Archaeological sites from this period have provided evidence of livestock living along with humans and also of domesticated and cultivated grains, including sorghum. The highlands of Ethiopia are considered one of the centers of **domestication**, producing coffee, millet, and an important local cereal called *teff*. Other crops domesticated in Africa include yams, oil palm, cow pea, and African rice.

Traditional peoples developed several strategies for adapting to low soil fertility, including **shifting cultivation**, which involves moving crops from one plot to another to preserve soil fertility. As in other regions of the tropical world, one form of shifting cultivation is **slash and burn** agriculture, used to clear patches of forest, shrubs, or grassland through burning and then take advantage of the ash to fertilize crops. When, after a few years, the nutrients are exhausted, farmers move on to a new area and leave the previous plot to return to forest or other vegetation. After a long fallow (rest) period, they return and clear and burn the land again. A modification of shifting cultivation is **bush fallow,** by which crops are planted around a village and plots are left fallow for shorter periods than in the slash and burn system. Soil fertility is often maintained through fallow periods or by applying household waste to the fields. Where household compost is used to grow crops within the village, the technique is called "compound farming" and is popular in forest environments as well as in some urban areas.

Intercropping—planting several crops together—is a technique for keeping the soil covered to reduce erosion, evaporation, and the leaching of nutrients. Where one of the crops, such as beans, can capture nutrients such as nitrogen, intercropping also improves soil fertility. Floodplain farming (**Figure 5.9a**) is used in regions such as the inland delta of the Niger River and the Sudd wetlands along the Nile River in the Sudan.

Pastoralism—a way of life that relies on livestock raising—is the human activity best adapted to drier regions of Africa. Nomads, such as the Bedouin, migrate with their animals in search of pastures in the arid landscapes of the Sahel and North Africa. Other groups, such as the Fulani of West Africa, practice a system of seasonal herd movements called *transhumance*. They move their herds to wells and rivers in the dry season and drive them northward to take advantage of new pastures in the wet season. In some regions, farmers let pastoralists graze their herds on harvested fields in the dry season, thereby fertilizing the land with animal manure in a mutually beneficial (symbiotic) relationship with the pastoralists, and in other regions pastoralists are also farmers. Cattle are traded at regional markets and are a family investment for the future in regions where there are few secure ways of accumulating capital (**Figure 5.9b**).

Environmental Issues

Conservation The rich biodiversity of Africa is valued by local residents, tourists, and international environmental groups alike, but differing views about its protection have resulted in many controversies about conservation. Traditional African societies hunted and gathered wild species for food and also incorporated wildlife into spiritual beliefs. While human populations were low and hunting technologies were less effective,

(a)

(b)

FIGURE 5.9 Traditional agriculture in West Africa
(a) The shores of the Niger River and its tributaries are agricultural regions. More than 500,000 people make a living from floodplain farming of crops, grazing livestock, and fishing along the Niger, adjusting their activities as the flooded area expands from 5000 to 25,000 square kilometers (3100 to 15,500 square miles) during and following the wet season. These traditional fields near Timbuktu in Mali are shown in the dry season. (b) This cattle market in Rifisque illustrates the significance of pastoralism in drier countries such as Niger.

populations ranged naturally where climate, vegetation, and terrain were most suitable. As population, technology, and land use changed, especially after colonialism, human activity began to modify habitat, and wildlife populations shifted. Europeans contributed to the decimation of African wildlife through indiscriminant hunting expeditions, the elimination of animals along railroads and near farms, and resettlement of local people into regions where they came into conflict with wildlife that encroached on their herds and fields.

Currently about 100 million hectares (5 percent) of Sub-Saharan Africa are under some sort of protected status, and there are more than 1000 protected areas, more than half in southern Africa (**Figure 5.10a**). The major parks in East Africa and southern Africa, such as Serengeti in Tanzania and Kruger in South Africa, have become high-profile international tourist destinations, bringing in millions of dollars to national economies and employing many local people. The parks are not without problems or criticism. Parks have been criticized for providing inadequate benefits to local people who may have been displaced or who lost traditional grazing and hunting rights or whose crops are destroyed by marauding wildlife. In some parks, too much tourism and high animal densities have destroyed fragile habitat, or poaching has pushed some species close to extinction (**Figure 5.10b**). The case of elephant and rhino conservation provides an illustration of debates about conservation in Africa and the related international attention and intervention.

Declining Population of Elephants and Rhinos

Elephants draw attention because of their size, intelligence, and the value of ivory and meat. Hunting elephants for their ivory tusks and trade in this precious commodity—known as "white gold"—has carried on for centuries. In Africa, herds had been hunted to extinction in the north of the continent hundreds of years before Europeans arrived with their guns. Pressure on herds in East and southern Africa grew with 19th-century colonialism. In Victorian England, many middle-class drawing rooms were filled with ivory knick-knacks, while "the ivories" became a slang term for dice and piano keys. By the end of the 19th century, some of Africa's elephant populations were significantly diminished.

A second surge in demand occurred in the 1970s, when prices for ivory soared with international financial instability and growing demand in Asia. Worldwide exports rose from 220 tons in the 1950s to nearly 1100 tons, especially from Burundi, Congo, Kenya, and Zaire, in the 1980s. The precipitous decline in most African elephant populations was a direct consequence of illegal killing, fueled by the ivory trade (**Figure 5.10c**). It has been estimated that 70,000 elephants were killed every year from the mid-1970s through the 1980s. The situation was aggravated by war and civil unrest, especially as firearms became available to unpaid soldiers and desperate refugees in regions where herds lacked strong protection. The population of elephants in Sub-Saharan Africa dropped from an estimated 2.5 million in 1970 to fewer than 500,000 in 1995, mainly as a result of poaching for ivory, but also because of competition between people and elephants for land, including areas opened up for agriculture and made available for human occupance and cattle by eradication of the tsetse fly.

In 1997 elephants were listed under the Convention on International Trade in Endangered Species (CITES) as a Category 2 species, in need of protection. But in 1990 mounting international pressure against the perceived slaughter of elephants resulted in moving elephants to Category 1, the most serious danger of extinction, and in a worldwide ban on the sale of ivory. The ban was opposed by countries in southern Africa, which had seen a less serious decline in elephant populations and were funding parks and conservation from the money earned from ivory and hide sales. In southern Africa, park managers culled elephants to protect habitat for other species but could not sell the ivory that they obtained from culling or catching poachers. In 2004, the UN granted permission to South Africa, Botswana, and Namibia to sell 60 tons of ivory even though there has been a ban on international sales of African ivory since 1989. The rhino is under much greater threats, especially from poachers who hope to sell rhino horn for dagger handles in the Middle East, especially in Yemen, and for highly valued medicinal powders in Asia. Protecting the rhino from poachers who can make thousands of dollars from selling a horn is a full-time and costly enterprise (**Figure 5.10d**).

FIGURE 5.10 National parks and conservation in Africa (a) National parks are concentrated in southern and eastern Africa, where millions of tourists are attracted by wildlife-viewing opportunities. (b) Cheetahs clamber onto a tour truck in the Masai Mara reserve in Kenya. (c) Impounded ivory from poached elephants at the Kenya Wildlife Service headquarters in Nairobi. (d) Many rhinos now have their own bodyguards, such as this group in Kenya's Masai Mara game reserve. Rhino horns may be removed by wildlife experts and replaced by bright plastic horns to reduce their attractiveness to poachers.

Biodiversity and Deforestation in Madagascar Currently more funds are being directed at conservation on the large island of Madagascar than in any other part of Africa. Rising to more than 3000 meters (10,000 feet), the island of Madagascar emerges from the Indian Ocean about 400 kilometers (250 miles) from the east coast of Africa (**Figure 5.11a**). Madagascar is the fourth largest island in the world—after Greenland, New Guinea, and Borneo—with an area of 587,000 square kilometers (226,650 square miles). Madagascar is almost a continent in miniature, with habitats that range from tropical forests to dry deserts in the rain shadows of mountains that have snow in winter. The island has one of the world's richest ecologies with 25 percent of all the flowering plants in Africa, including the rosy periwinkle, used to treat the disease leukemia, and unique fauna that include 33 species of lemurs, 800 species of butterflies, and numerous chameleons, cacti, and corals (**Figure 5.11b**).

The most serious environmental problem in Madagascar is deforestation, which has a long history and is associated with clearing land for rice production, sugar plantations, and cattle ranches and cutting trees to export tropical hardwoods. Madagascar

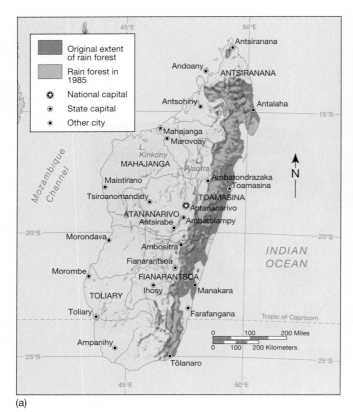

(a)

(b)

FIGURE 5.11 Madagascar (a) Map showing severe loss of rain forest; the original extent of rain forest is indicated by both shades of green and the 1985 extent by light green only. (b) Lemurs in the forest.

is currently one of the world's poorest nations, with a per capita income of approximately $760 per year. About 80 percent of the population are subsistence farmers who use a slash and burn technique called *tavy* to clear forests.

Less than 15 percent of the original forests remain. These are of great concern to conservationists worldwide because of their unique ecology. Deforestation on steep slopes has also placed human populations directly at risk from soil erosion, landslides, and floods. For example, more than 100 people were killed and 10,000 made homeless by floods associated with cyclones in 2000. Other threats to biodiversity include fires, introduction of non-native species, and hunting; it is clear that one key to protection is the reduction of poverty.

Recently Madagascar has established eight new protected areas totaling 6809 square kilometers (2630 square miles). The country's new National Association for Protected Area Management has taken over several of the key national parks for ecotourism (environmentally oriented tourism designed to protect the environment and often to provide economic opportunities for local people) in areas such as Ranomafana, Isalo, and Montagne d'Ambre. Other sources of conservation funding include major corporations (including Rio Tinto which has extensive mining operations) and carbon credits associated with climate change mitigation.

Land Degradation One of the critical environmental concerns in the drier regions of Africa is the loss of soil and vegetation from land degradation. This has often been called **desertification** and occurs when human activities transform land surfaces through overgrazing, deforestation, surface land mining, and poor irrigation techniques (leading to salinization). Although population growth has been blamed for both soil erosion and desertification, some researchers have argued that more people may actually reverse land degradation.

Sahel The Sahel region of west Africa has become an international focus for concern about desertification and for debates about the role of climate and human pressures in land degradation. The Sahel is a region on the southern border of the Sahara Desert in west Africa that has highly variable rainfall and a human population dependent on pastoralism (**Figure 5.12a**).

A limited network of meteorological stations provides data that show that rainfall is quite variable across the Sahel, but that wetter conditions seem to have occurred in the 1950s and early 1960s. Rather than adjust their herds to average conditions, Sahelian pastoralists tend to be opportunistic, building up their herds in good years because their livestock are the best way of accumulating wealth and investing capital. Overgrazing leads to soil erosion through the reduction of a vegetative cover as well as trampling and compaction. The destruction of perennial shrubs by grazing and their replacement by annuals, which were grazed out and left bare soil, led to the washing away of topsoil, leaving rocks and hard layers of silt that cannot be penetrated by plant roots when the rains return.

Beginning in 1968, it appears that the rains failed in most parts of the Sahel for up to seven years. As herds began to die off, images of the drought and starving refugees began to appear in the international media, resulting in a relief effort and anguished debates among researchers and policymakers about what had gone wrong and what could be done to avoid future tragedy. Between 1968 and 1973, as many as 3.5 million cattle died, and 15 million farmers lost more than half their harvests. A quarter of a million people died from famine before food relief could reach them.

Some researchers blamed nature and the irrational buildup of herds in the face of regular drought cycles in the Sahel. However, others argued that the roots of the crisis

FIGURE 5.12 The Sahel (a) The Sahel region, showing the degree of food insecurity in 1999. (b) Spreading desertification threatens one-third of Africa. (c) Goats feeding on acacia in Sahelian desert landscape.

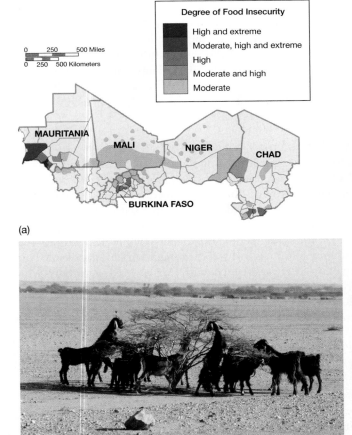

(a)

(c)

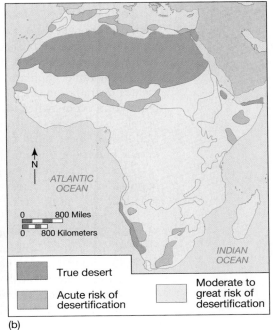

(b)

lay in changes in Sahelian political economy stemming from colonial structures and continued overreliance on export cropping. Geographer Michael Watts, for example, showed how in northern Nigeria people lost access to land and their drought-coping strategies because of the loss of traditional self-help institutions, colonial policies, and the marginalization of poorer farmers.

Others argued that decades of peanut and cotton production, particularly in Senegal and Mali, exhausted the soil and left it unproductive. Climatologists suggested that deforestation and overgrazing increased the reflectivity of the land surface, which meant less warm air rising to form clouds, or that increased atmospheric dust was reducing the uplift of air. Both processes reduce rainfall.

International efforts to respond to the 1970s drought focused initially on food relief but then turned to longer-term technical efforts to reduce risk, including drilling deep wells for cattle herds. Unfortunately, so many thirsty cattle gathered around the wells that all possible forage vegetation was consumed, and the herds starved. When food aid arrived in communities where some farmers still had crops to sell, food prices dropped, and farmers could not make a living.

In 1977 the United Nations held a conference on desertification to discuss the problems of the Sahel and other regions where the deserts appeared to be spreading into previously productive areas (**Figure 5.12b**). Desertification has a variety of meanings but is most generally viewed as the process by which arid and semiarid lands become degraded and less productive, leading to more desertlike conditions through drying, erosion, compaction, buildup of salts, and loss of fertility and vegetation. Although the United Nations gave a high priority to monitoring desertification, differences in definition and measurement resulted in widely varying estimates of the area affected over the next few decades. And while some sources reported that the desert had advanced hundreds of kilometers into the Sahel, others saw no long-term trend but only year-to-year variations in the vigor of vegetation. There were also disagreements about the relative role of different factors in causing desertification. The main culprits were seen as climate change, overgrazing, overcultivation (including cash cropping), deforestation for wood fuel, and unskilled irrigation that results in the buildup of salt in the soil (salinization) (**Figure 5.12c**).

Whether or not desertification is actually occurring on a large scale, a number of development projects have attempted to reduce the vulnerability of Sahelian people and landscapes to degradation. Reforestation projects in Mali have successfully created erosion barriers, forage for animals, and wood for fuel. Traditional rainwater-harvesting techniques using stone barriers to trap moisture have diffused from one community to another.

More People, Less Erosion in Machakos, Kenya

In the 19th century, when Thomas Malthus argued that population was growing faster than food supplies, he established a basis for what is now termed *Malthusian thinking* about the relationship between population growth and environment. Malthusians tend to argue that rapid population growth is associated with resource scarcity and environmental degradation, including soil erosion, deforestation, and food shortages. Overpopulation occurs when there are too many people for the environment to sustain and people are forced to overexploit resources or suffer hunger and destitution. This Malthusian specter has frequently been associated with Africa, and especially with famine and soil erosion in drier regions.

The case of Machakos, Kenya, has been used to argue against this negative view of population growth by researchers who found an improvement in environmental and economic conditions during a period of rapid population increase. The population grew fivefold from 1932 to 1990—from 240,000 to 1,400,000 (**Figure 5.13a**). The Machakos district is about 50 kilometers (30 miles) southeast of Kenya's capital Nairobi and stretches another 300 kilometers (180 miles) halfway to the coast. Rainfall is variable, soils have low fertility, and the hilly topography creates significant risks of soil erosion. Under British colonial administration, beginning about 1930, the local Akamba people were contained in a small reserve to allow white farmers to use the region for grazing. This resulted in more intense use of land by locals and the establishment of the Soil Conservation Service by the colonial government to promote conservation and prevent erosion. Compulsory labor, often by women, was required to build terraces and plant grass on hillslopes. Locally organized community work teams replaced compulsory labor in the 1950s, and the technique of terracing spread rapidly as local people observed the better soil and moisture and associated greater yields on the terraced fields. In some parts of the district, almost all of the farmland was terraced by 1980, encouraged by support from European governments and charities (**Figure 5.13b**).

FIGURE 5.13 Machakos, Kenya (a) The location of the Machakos district, and two maps that show large increases in population density in the district from 1932 to 1979. (b) These maps show how sloped land was converted to terraces in the Masii area of the Machakos district between 1948 and 1978. (c) From 1930 to 1987, agricultural production increased, with a shift to the production of cash crops and horticulture. (*Source:* [a] and [b] Redrawn from M. Mortimore and M. Tiffen, "Population and Environment in Time Perspective: The Machakos Story," in T. Binns [ed.], *People and Environment in Africa*, pp. 69–89. New York: John Wiley & Sons, Figs. 7.3 and 7.11; [c] M. Mortimore and M. Tiffen, "Population and Environment in Time Perspective: The Machakos Story," in T. Binns [ed.], *People and Environment in Africa*, pp. 69–89. New York: John Wiley & Sons, Fig. 7.6.)

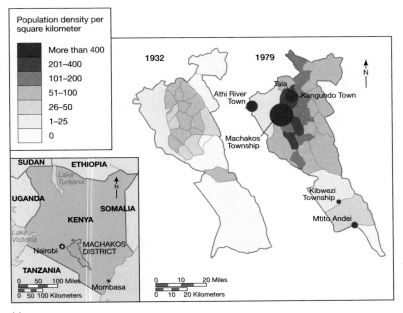

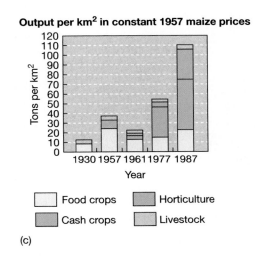

(a)

(c)

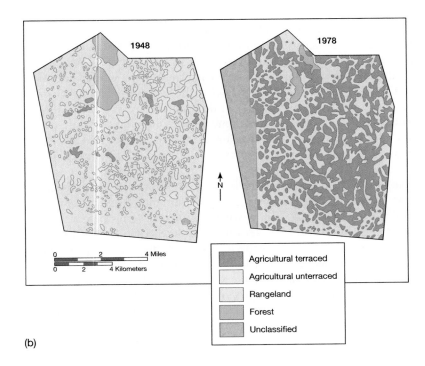

(b)

Production also benefited from adoption of ox-drawn plows and from fertilization by manure from livestock mostly fed fodder while kept in stalls rather than allowed to roam freely. People seem to have maintained and replanted trees while using dead wood and hedge cutting for fires.

Agriculture changed in the district from one based on subsistence cultivation of maize, beans, and pigeon peas to a more diverse crop mix that included coffee and, more recently, fresh vegetables for sale in Nairobi, to the canning industry, and even for export to Europe. In all but the driest years, food production per capita was maintained. As **Figure 5.13c** shows, overall output per square kilometer increased from about 10 tons in 1930 (mostly food crops) to 11 tons in 1987 (75 percent cash crops and horticulture).

Machakos provides a classic case of agricultural intensification, where, according to the theories of economist Esther Boserup, population increases provide the labor and the incentive to apply more labor and capital to produce more on the same area of land. Population increase resulted in better environmental management and an increase in agricultural production, rather than soil erosion and impoverishment as predicted by a Malthusian perspective. Researchers Michael Mortimore and Mary Tiffen and other colleagues suggest that several factors help explain the relative success of Machakos. These include security of land titles, proximity to off-farm employment in Nairobi (which provided capital for improvements), complementary efforts of husbands and wives, women's leadership in organizing community work teams, and improving educational levels.

SUB-SAHARAN AFRICA IN THE WORLD-SYSTEM

Sub-Saharan Africa's role in the world begins with evidence of human origins on the continent more than 2 million years ago and continues with the development of major trading societies about 5000 years ago and the incorporation into a European-dominated colonial system about 500 years ago. Colonialism included the worldwide trade in African slaves, resulting in a diaspora of African peoples that has continued to influence the culture and societies of other world regions. It also resulted in political boundaries that split ethnic groups across territories or clustered enemies within one territory.

Peoples from other world regions, including Europe and Asia, came to Africa under colonial rule and created hierarchies of power and politics. These hierarchies included the racial discrimination associated with apartheid in South Africa and tensions over land distribution in southern and eastern Africa, where countries gained independence and white farmers continued to hold the best land. Most of Sub-Saharan Africa was under European colonial domination by 1900 and did not become independent until after 1950. Independence also coincided with the height of Cold War tensions between the United States and the former Soviet Union and the consequent interventions of the superpowers in African political struggles and civil wars.

At the end of the 20th century, much of Sub-Saharan Africa was still struggling with the transition to independent and democratic government and with economies that rely on a narrow set of exports to other world regions. A series of natural disasters, development failures, and wars has seriously hindered the ability of agricultural production to meet the food needs of growing populations, with large numbers of poor people unable to grow or purchase food or to find alternative employment. Yet, as we will see, some countries and some sectors within those countries have been able to make considerable progress in improving economic and social conditions and are actively debating the most appropriate way to participate in the global economy.

Human Origins and Early African History

Africa is often called the "cradle of humankind" because archaeologists have shown that the earliest evidence of the human species (*Homo sapiens*) is found in Africa. Fossilized footprints of an earlier ancestor, the hominid (humanlike) *Australopithecus*, were found by archaeologist Mary Leakey at Laetoli in Tanzania and dated to 3.7 million years ago. Two-million-year-old stone tools have been found at several sites in Ethiopia and East Africa, including the famous site at Olduvai Gorge in Tanzania (**Figure 5.14**). Anatomically modern humans, who walked upright and had larger brains, have been dated to at least 100,000 years ago from sites in southern Africa and along the Rift Valley, and many scholars now believe that these humans are the genetic ancestors of all modern humans and thus the most basic link between Africa and the world.

For most of human history in Africa, the only record of history is from scattered archaeological sites. More detailed written accounts begin with the development of complex societies in the Nile Valley, about 5000 years ago, with sophisticated irrigation systems, hieroglyphic writing, and the hierarchical social organization of the Egyptians under their king or pharaoh (see Chapter 4).

From this time onward, explorations, military campaigns, and European trading begins with Sub-Saharan Africa from bases in the Nile Valley and North African coast, such as the Phoenician city of Carthage (in today's Tunisia). About 2500 years ago the famous Greek geographer Herodotus described accounts of Saharan trade in salt and of kingdoms to the south of Egypt, and by 2000 years ago the Roman Empire had extended to most of North Africa. By A.D. 500 some Indonesians had settled on the island now known as Madagascar, introducing yams and bananas to mainland Africa, and a strong kingdom had emerged at Aksum in Ethiopia and had adopted Christianity. Sub-Saharan Africa was settled as the Bantu people spread from West Africa bringing with them technologies such as iron smelting. Between A.D. 500 and 1000, several power centers with links to Roman and Arabic empires developed, including the kingdom of Ghana (centered in present-day Mali), where gold was mined and traded with Berber merchants from the Sahara and North Africa in exchange for salt. Trade also linked the Mediterranean coast with the kingdoms of Gao, Songhai (located in Niger), Kanem (near Lake Chad), and Mali, and this trade led to the conversion of many in these empires to the Islamic faith. The east coast of Africa was brought into the Arab system around A.D. 1100 through a series of trading posts that included Mogadishu, Malindi, Mombasa, and Zanzibar, cities that still exhibit the

FIGURE 5.14 Map of African history Sub-Saharan Africa had a rich historical heritage prior to European arrival in the region. The oldest human remains were found at Olduvai Gorge in present-day Tanzania. This map shows some of the locations and dates of the great kingdoms as well as the early migrations of Bantu people and Arab traders. (*Source:* Adapted from I. L. L. Griffiths, *An Atlas of African Affairs.* New York: Methuen, 1985; D. L. Clawson and J. S. Fisher (eds.), *World Regional Geography: A Developmental Approach.* Upper Saddle River, NJ: Prentice Hall, 1998, Fig. 23.2; and C. McEvedy, *The Penguin Atlas of African History.* New York: Penguin Books, 1995.)

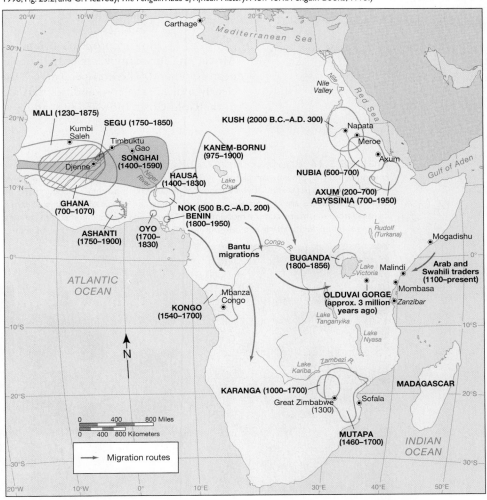

FIGURE 5.15 Zanzibar The island of Zanzibar, just off the coast of Tanzania, has a distinct history and culture as a key port on the Indian Ocean trading with the Middle East and Africa. Historians believe that Zanzibar was first inhabited by fisher people who traveled to the island from mainland Africa around 4000 B.C. By 1000 B.C., Zanzibar and the islands off the coast of East Africa were familiar to the Egyptians, Phoenicians, Greeks, and Romans. As these Mediterranean empires extended their trade routes to the south and east, Zanzibar became one of several major commercial ports along the East African coast. Around the third century A.D., the trade in goods attracted the attention of merchants from southwestern Arabia, who also began trading with the island residents, bringing weapons, wine, and wheat to barter for ivory and other luxury goods. The Arabs brought the religious traditions of Islam; the local language, Swahili, has many Arabic words and became the trade language for eastern Africa.

legacy of Arab and Islamic culture in their architecture, language, and religious traditions (**Figure 5.15**).

The European and colonial tendency to discount indigenous achievements has been especially unfair in the case of Africa. This stems partly from explorers' accounts of Africa in which they constructed a vision of Africa as the "dark" continent by using words such as *uncivilized, savage,* and *primitive* to describe the landscapes and societies of Africa. Great Zimbabwe is an example of a highly complex African society that existed prior to contact with Europe (**Figure 5.16a**). Other early cities include several in the Sahel, such as Timbuktu and Djenné, which were centers of trade, religion, and scholarly learning (**Figure 5.16b**).

The Colonial Period in Africa

With the development of faster and larger ships in the 15th century, contacts with Spain, Portugal, and China were added to the regular interaction between the Middle East and Africa. The Portuguese traded for gold from coastal settlements in West Africa, and in 1497 the Portuguese explorer Vasco da Gama rounded the Cape of Good Hope at the southern tip of the African continent en route from Portugal to India. During the 1500s, Portugal traded along the west and southeast coasts of Africa and had made contact with empires in West Africa, Congo, and Zimbabwe. In return for salt, horses, cloth, and glass, Sub-Saharan Africa provided gold, ivory, and slaves through Portuguese and Arab traders. For several centuries African slaves had been in demand among the Arabs, who used the slaves as servants, soldiers, courtiers, and concubines.

European colonialism took some time to establish control in Africa, and for many years only the coastal ports and trading posts were under European command. The European names for coastal regions along the west coast of Africa clearly indicate the commodities that they provided, from the Ivory Coast in the west to the Gold Coast (now Ghana) and Slave Coast (Nigeria and Benin) to the east. One

FIGURE 5.16 Pre-European architecture (a) Great Zimbabwe is the most famous of a large group of stone-walled enclosures on the Zimbabwean plateau. In the 14th century, this city, constructed of massive stonework, housed up to 20,000 members of the Shona population. It was a center of metalworking, pottery production, and religion and traded gold with coastal ports. The ruins of the city are now a major tourist attraction and source of pride in southern Africa. The modern Zimbabwe nation took its name from this major cultural monument. (b) Djenné was founded in the 13th century near the Niger River in southern Mali and became a center for scholarly and religious learning. The market is in front of the famous mosque that was built from baked mud.

(a)

(b)

of the main reasons for European reluctance to move inland was the reputation of Africa as the "White Man's Grave" because so many Europeans were rapidly killed by malaria, yellow fever, and sleeping sickness, diseases against which they had no natural immunity. In addition, African armies attacked ports and resisted European attempts to move inland.

Slavery Even in the face of native resistance and the ravages of disease, the coastal regions generated enormous profits for European traders. The Portuguese started to take slaves for their own use on new sugarcane plantations on the Atlantic islands of Madeira and Cape Verde, and in 1530 the first slaves were shipped to the Americas to work on plantations in Brazil. By 1700, 50,000 slaves were being shipped each year to the Americas to provide labor on colonized lands and new plantations whose potential indigenous labor supply had been decimated by European diseases (see Chapter 6, p. 282). Slavery was an important income source for some African coastal kingdoms, such as Dahomey and Benin, who captured their enemies or residents of inland villages and sold them to the slave traders. It is estimated that more than 9 million slaves were shipped to the Americas from Africa between 1600 and 1870, with at least 1.5 million slaves dying during the journey (**Figure 5.17**). Most slaves were male, and the conditions of capture and transport were inhuman. Hundreds of slaves were packed into the holds of ships with little food and water and were brutally abused by traders.

Beginning at the end of the 18th century, in Britain and the United States, members of the Quaker community led movements to abolish slavery. The British abolished the

FIGURE 5.17 The slave trade Millions of slaves were exported from Africa between about 1600 and 1870, mainly from the west African coast. Some local leaders acted as suppliers in return for guns and manufactured goods. Slaves were sent to work in plantations in the Americas, which then sent sugar, rum, and other products back to Europe in a triangular trade. (*Source:* Adapted from A. Thomas and B. Crow [eds.], *Third World Atlas.* Buckingham, UK: Open University Press, 1994, p. 28; and J. F. Ade, A. Crowder, M. Crowder, P. Richards, E. Dunstan, and A. Newman [eds.], *Historical Atlas of Africa.* Harlow, Essex, UK: Longman, 1985, p. 67.)

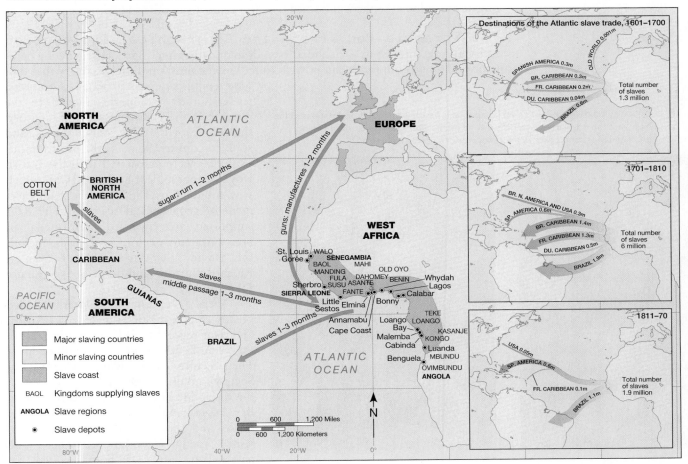

slave trade with their colonies in 1807 and emancipated (freed) slaves in the Caribbean in 1834. Slavery in the Americas was abolished in most countries by the 1850s, and the slavery issue was key in the U.S. Civil War. Slavery was abolished in the United States in 1863 by the Emancipation Proclamation (see Chapter 6, p. 282).

Banning of slavery in Britain in 1772 resulted in freeing slaves in several regions under British control. A large group of liberated slaves was shipped back to Africa to settle in Freetown, the present capital of Sierra Leone. The American Colonization Society subsequently settled 12,000 freed American slaves in 1822 at Monrovia, in Liberia. The British continued to intercept slave ships in the 19th century and settled the slaves in Sierra Leone. The descendants of these settlers, who were from many different regions of Africa, retained a separate identity from local cultural groups, and tensions between them and the locals emerged in civil wars in Liberia and Sierra Leone.

European Settlement in Southern Africa European settlement was encouraged in southern Africa by the more temperate climate and the strategic significance of the trading routes around the southern tip of the continent. In 1652, the Dutch established a community at Cape Town, which became surrounded with small farms growing wheat and raising cattle for supplying ships and the "Cape" communities, as the region around the Cape of Good Hope was called. As their language, the settlers evolved Afrikaans, a modified version of Dutch; they belonged to the strict puritan Christian Calvinist religion, saw themselves as superior to black Africans, and became known as the *Boers* (Dutch for "farmer"). As their military and trading power grew in the 1800s, the British took control of the Cape trading route, and British immigrants were encouraged to settle in the Cape region from about 1820, mainly in Cape Town and Durban. When the British imposed laws on the Boers, including banning slavery in 1834, the Boers moved north of the Orange River in a great trek, settling on the high pastures called the *veld* in what is now known as the Free State. Some Boers also migrated eastward into the Natal region, where they came into conflict with the powerful Zulus. As we will see, the geography of this colonial settlement framed the 20th-century politics of South Africa.

The Scramble for Africa and Geographical Exploration International interest in Africa increased dramatically after 1850, with growing competition among core European powers for colonial control and the discovery that quinine could suppress malaria. Explorers, traders, and missionaries moved to the interior of the continent seeking territory, the source of the Nile, commodities, and souls to convert. Some of the most famous explorers were associated with the British Royal Geographical Society (RGS), which was founded in 1830 for the "advancement of geographical science." The RGS supported and awarded their medal of honor to many explorers of Africa, including David Livingstone, Henry Stanley, Richard Burton, and John Speke (**Figure 5.18a and b**).

These Victorian explorers added greatly to geographic knowledge of Africa, and their reports fueled colonial interest in the continent's resources and peoples. Their lectures at the Royal Geographical Society and elsewhere increased interest in the discipline of geography and its role in Britain's colonial enterprise. However, their books and those of other explorers contained many Victorian prejudices and paternalistic attitudes that fostered the

FIGURE 5.18 Colonial explorers (a) David Livingstone is best known for his explorations of the Zambezi and his encounter with the magnificent waterfalls that he named after Queen Victoria. (b) Henry Stanley, a journalist sent to find Livingstone, poses as the conqueror of a hostile continent.

(a)

(b)

popular imagination of Africa as a barbarous and exotic continent in need of civilization and colonial supervision.

By 1880, new knowledge of African resources—including gold and diamonds, competition among European powers to dominate global empires and markets, and reduced risk of African diseases further increased interest in the continent. In 1882 the British claimed Egypt, prompting the French to exert their dominion over West Africa in Senegal and Gabon (**Figure 5.19**). The Portuguese made efforts to consolidate their holdings in Mozambique and Angola, and the Spanish did so in Equatorial Guinea. Inspired by the reports of explorer Henry Stanley, the personal crusade of King

FIGURE 5.19 The scramble for Africa Between about 1880 and 1914, European powers, especially the British, French, and Belgian governments, aggressively moved to colonize Africa. This map shows the routes and dates of the takeover of Africa. The British claimed what are now known as Gambia, Ghana, Nigeria, and Sierra Leone in West Africa; Kenya, Uganda, Sudan, and part of Somalia in East Africa; and southern Africa, except for German South West Africa (Namibia), Portuguese Mozambique, the Cape Verde Islands, Angola, and the independent Boer region of South Africa. Germany claimed German East Africa (Tanzania) and Cameroon; Portugal claimed the Cape Verde Islands; and France and Belgium split the Congo. Italy took Somalia, Djibouti, and Eritrea and coastal regions of Libya, with ambitions for Abyssinia (now Ethiopia). The Spanish obtained a small coastal region of northwest Africa and Equatorial Guinea. Most of the remaining territory of West and North Africa was allocated to or taken by the French. (*Source:* Adapted from A. Thomas and B. Crow [eds.], *Third World Atlas.* Buckingham, UK: Open University Press, 1994, p. 35.)

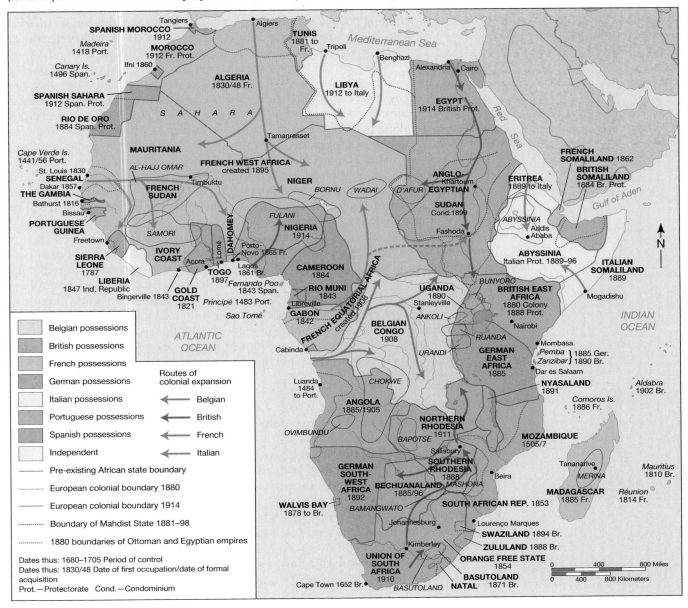

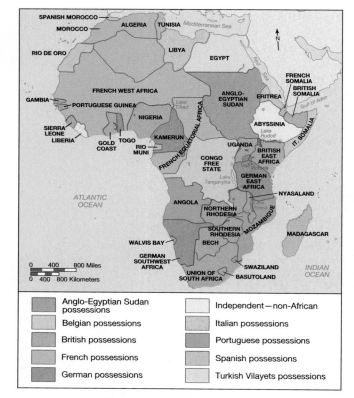

FIGURE 5.20 Map of colonial Africa 1914 This map shows colonial Africa in 1914, at the beginning of World War I. Between 1884 and 1914, the colonial powers consolidated their territory and drew boundaries. (*Source:* A. T. Grove, *The Changing Geography of Africa.* Oxford: Oxford University Press, 1994, Fig. 7.1.)

Leopold II of Belgium to establish colonies in Africa focused attention on the Congo basin; Germany sought colonies where it had missionaries in what are now Togo, Cameroon, Namibia, and Tanzania. Pressure from commercial companies and even missionaries drove these imperial ambitions and incorporated Africa into the emerging global capitalist economy.

The role of private companies in the colonization of Africa was important because European governments granted exclusive concessions for trade and resource exploitation in Africa. These companies, which were often given the right to police, to conscript, and to tax local populations, included the Royal Niger Company and British South Africa Company, both of which received royal charters in the late 1800s.

This hasty "scramble for Africa" culminated in the **Berlin Conference** of 1884–85, a meeting convened by German chancellor Bismarck in 1884–85 to divide Africa among European colonial powers. The 13 countries represented at this conference did not include a single African representative from any state in Sub-Saharan Africa, even though more than 80 percent of Africa was at that time under African rule. The Berlin Conference allocated African territory among the colonial powers, according to prior claims, and lay down a set of arbitrary boundaries that paid little respect to existing cultural, ethnic, political, religious, or linguistic regions (**Figure 5.20**).

The next 20 years saw some rearrangement and consolidation of the European colonies. The British created protectorates in what are now Botswana, Zambia, Zimbabwe, and Malawi and expanded their control over the Sudan. The French took control of many regions along the Niger, and the Italians unsuccessfully invaded Abyssinia. In southern Africa, British entrepreneurs, including the ambitious Cecil Rhodes, responded to the discovery of gold and diamonds between 1867 and 1886 by acquiring the mines at Kimberly and the Rand and sparking a gold and diamond rush. Growing tensions between the British and Afrikaners resulted in the Boer War (1899–1902), which gave control of much of southern Africa to the British.

By 1914 almost all of Africa was under European colonial control except for Abyssinia, Liberia, and some interior regions of the Sahara Desert. A number of battles were fought in Africa during World War I, but Germany's eventual loss redistributed the German colonies to Britain, France, and Belgium. Tanzania and South West Africa were assigned to the British, Rwanda and Burundi to Belgium. Togo and Cameroon were each split between Britain and France. Italy's long-standing imperial ambitions in Africa were temporarily achieved with Mussolini's conquest of Abyssinia (Ethiopia) in 1936, but the British soon moved to evict Italy from Africa, returning Ethiopia and Libya to independent rule by monarchy and taking over the Italian portion of Somalia.

The Impact and Legacy of Colonialism All of this reshuffling of African territory among European states can overshadow the considerable and everyday impact of colonial rule on African landscapes and peoples. The most general and enduring effects of colonialism include establishment of political boundaries; reorientation of economies, transport routes, and land use toward the export of commodities; improved medical care; and introduction of European languages, land tenure systems, taxation, education, and governance. As noted earlier, many of the new colonial boundaries divided indigenous cultural groups and in some cases placed traditional enemies within the same country. For example, the Yoruba were divided between Nigeria and Benin, and Nigeria itself comprised several competitive groups, including the Yoruba in the southwest, the Ibo in the southeast, and the Hausa in the north.

Mining activities were expanded in many regions, especially in southern and central Africa, with large amounts of gold, diamonds, and copper extracted and exported by European companies. New roads and railways were constructed from inland to the coasts to speed the export of crops and minerals, but few efforts were made to link regions within Africa. The resulting infrastructure facilitated trade beyond but not within Africa (**Figure 5.21**).

Colonists established plantations to produce crops, such as rubber, and used a variety of means, including taxation and intimidation, to persuade peasant farmers to produce peanuts, coffee, cocoa, or cotton for global markets. In the temperate climates of the East African highlands and southern Africa, areas that were more attractive to European immigrants, the best land was taken by white settlers for tea and tobacco plantations, livestock ranches, and other farming activities. By 1950, the geography of African agriculture illustrated this export orientation, with vast rubber plantations owned by the Firestone Corporation in Liberia, cocoa dominating the cropland of Ghana and the Ivory Coast, cotton in Sudan, peanuts in French West Africa, and tea and coffee in East Africa (**Figure 5.22**). Traditional African land-tenure systems of communal land and flexible boundaries were forced into privately owned and bounded plots, and traditional decision-making and legal systems were often replaced with European managers and courts.

The effects and process of colonial rule varied among European powers. The British chose a paternalistic indirect rule for most of their African colonies, making preexisting power structures and leaders responsible to the British Crown and colonial administrators in a decentralized and flexible administrative structure. For example, local leaders were required to collect taxes—sometimes a hut tax based on the number of dwellings in a community, sometimes a poll tax based on the number of residents. In order to obtain money to pay taxes, people had to produce crops for sale to the Europeans, an indirect way of transforming economies and land use to commodity production. Foreign ownership of land was prohibited in some cases, and traditional legal systems were used to resolve local conflicts. The British, preceded by missionaries, also introduced some European-style schools, and by the 1940s a select group of Africans were attending overseas universities and given posts in government administration.

The French colonial policy was one of assimilation, encouraging elites to evolve into French provincial citizens with allegiance to France, but with agriculture and mining under close supervision from the French capital in Paris. By 1946 there were about 20 Africans, elected from West Africa, in the French parliament. The Belgian and Portuguese modes of colonialism are described as much harsher, with direct rule and often ruthless control of land and labor. In the Congo, local people were forced to gather rubber, kill elephants for ivory, and build public works under threat of death or severe punishment. These authoritarian forms of control—with little political participation, dominating official ideology, and frequent use of armed force—provided an unfortunate model for leadership in independent Africa.

Given the dramatic impact of the colonial period on contemporary Africa, it is significant that in most of Africa, formal colonialism only lasted 80 years, from about 1880 to 1960. The legacies of the colonial period in specific regions and sectors will be discussed in more detail shortly.

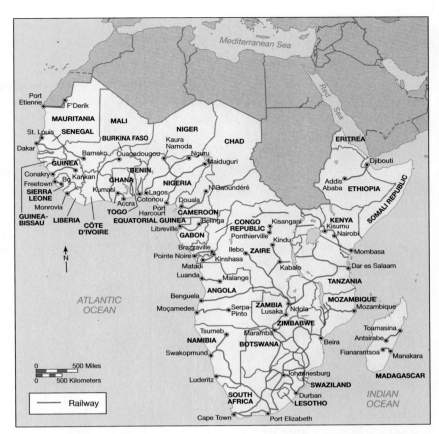

FIGURE 5.21 African rail network in 1970s The railway network of Africa still shows the legacy of the colonial period, when railways were constructed from the interior to the coasts, originating especially from mining and cash-crops areas. For example, a rail line from St. Louis to Dakar facilitated the export of peanuts from Senegal, and another from Kumasi to the coast speeded the export of labor, gold, and cocoa from the Gold Coast (Ghana). The line from Mombasa via Nairobi to Kisumu on Lake Victoria in Kenya linked the inland to the coast.

(a)

(b)

(c)

FIGURE 5.22 Export crops in Africa (a) Sisal is grown as a cash and export crop over large areas of Kenya and Tanzania and is used as a fiber for mats, sacks, and baskets. The sacks were used as containers for other export crops such as coffee and tea but are being replaced by synthetic fibers. (b) A child carries a peanut plant near Djiffer, Senegal. Peanuts were introduced as a cash crop in French West Africa during the colonial period. (c) Cocoa is still grown in West African countries such as Ghana and Nigeria in response to a love of chocolate that flourished in the colonial era. Charles Akinola, an agricultural specialist, splits open a cocoa pod on a southern Nigerian cocoa plantation.

Independence

Decolonization in Sub-Saharan Africa was rapid and ranged from relatively peaceful handovers of leadership to well-prepared African leaders to more violent transitions of power to divided or unprepared local leadership. South Africa was consolidated as an early independent state—the Union of South Africa—in 1910. African hopes for independence were encouraged by the British decision to grant India and Pakistan independence in 1947 and demanded by the almost half a million Africans who fought with the allies in World War II. The independence movement was led by several foreign-educated activists, such as Kwame Nkrumah of Ghana and Jomo Kenyatta of Kenya (**Figure 5.23**) and fostered by organized nationalist groups or African Unions within such key African countries as Tanganyika, Zimbabwe, and Kenya. These groups provided the basis for political parties. A Pan-African movement, led by black activists in the United States—including W. E. B. DuBois and Marcus Garvey—and others in the West Indies also promoted independence. The sixth Pan-African Congress of 1945, held in Manchester, England, brought together leading African nationalists, including Nkrumah and Kenyatta, to discuss independence. In 1957, Ghana became the first country in Sub-Saharan Africa to have power handed over to local populations; three years later, Nigeria gained its independence.

Although most of the British handovers were relatively peaceful, countries with significant white settler populations endured more violent transitions. In Kenya, about 3000 white settlers controlled more than 2.6 million hectares (6.4 million acres) of the best land, especially in the highlands, adjacent to overpopulated indigenous Kikuyu farms. Whites also dominated the government and set policy in the interests of the 60,000 white residents. The Mau-Mau rebellion between 1952 and 1956 resulted in the deaths of 100 whites and more than 10,000 black Africans. Kenya became independent in 1963. In Southern Rhodesia (now Zimbabwe) the population of about 250,000 white settlers, led by Ian Smith, made a Unilateral Declaration of Independence (UDI) in 1965 rather than consider the possibility of rule by the 6 million black Africans. Only after 15 years of conflict and international trade embargoes did an independent Zimbabwe finally emerge in 1980, with a mostly black government and a legacy of resentment against white residents.

In French West Africa and French Equatorial Africa the transition occurred dramatically in 1960, with France recognizing all the independent countries of Mauritania, Mali, Niger, Senegal, Upper Volta (now Burkina Faso), Ivory Coast (now Côte d'Ivoire), Togo, Dahomey, Chad, the Central African Republic, Cameroon, Gabon, and the Congo. In most cases, strong economic and cultural ties were maintained with France, the franc remained the currency, and French troops were stationed in most countries. One of the groups to benefit most from decolonization were the transnational corporations that preferred to deal directly with African economies rather than through the mediation of colonial powers and their monopoly companies and marketing boards.

Belgium left the Belgian Congo suddenly in 1960, with chaos following as the army mutinied; separatist groups tried to form governments in the wealthier provinces; and a

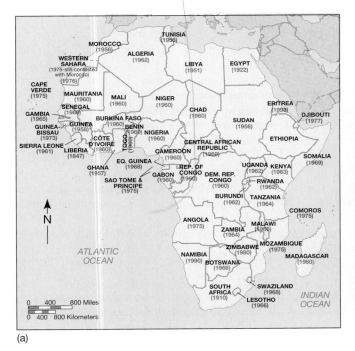

(a)

(b)

FIGURE 5.23 African independence (a) Dates of independence in Africa. (b) Leaders of independent Africa: (left to right) Dr. Kenneth Kaunda, Northern Rhodesian Premier; President Julius Nyerere, United Republic Tanganyika and Zanzibar; Jomo Kenyatta, Kenya Premier; and Dr. Milton Obote, Uganda Premier. (*Source:* (a) Adapted from I. L. L. Griffiths, *An Atlas of African Affairs.* New York: Methuen, 1985.)

U.S.–sponsored army officer, Joseph Mobutu, won a military coup to depose and assassinate independence leader Patrice Lumumba. In Rwanda and Burundi, independence from Belgium in 1962 left a legacy of tension between ethnic groups because the Belgians had favored the Tutsi minority over the Hutu majority. Portugal hung onto its colonies of Angola and Mozambique until 1974, by which time some groups demanding independence had come under the influence of the Soviet Union and Cuba. Independence groups in Angola, Mozambique, and Guinea also sought help from the United Nations in freeing themselves from colonial rule, while Namibia sought freedom from the control of South Africa. The best-known underground independence movements were the MPLA (People's Liberation Movement of Angola), FRELIMO (Mozambique Liberation Front), and SWAPO (the South West African People's Organization).

South African History and Apartheid

The case of South Africa merits particular attention because of the policies of **apartheid**, a policy of racial separation that prior to 1994 structured space and society to keep black, white, and colored populations apart through control of the movement, employment, and residences of blacks. The goal of apartheid was separate development of the races within South Africa.

The history of racial segregation in South Africa is long, dating back to the establishment of a supply station by the Dutch East India Company in Cape Town in 1652. The Dutch, whose settlement developed slowly at first, were segregationists and attempted to prevent contact between whites and native peoples, although they did hold Africans as slaves. The Dutch grew wheat, planted vines, and introduced livestock, moving northward and displacing African native communities as the frontier expanded in the search for more pasture land. In 1806 Britain seized political control over the Cape in order to control the route to its empire in India. Like the Dutch, the British set about expropriating land and creating defendable boundary lines between the European immigrant settlements and the largely Bantu-speaking Nguni and Sotho people.

The Boer policies of strict racial segregation between blacks and Afrikaners (as the Dutch farm settlers were called) included the establishment of native reserves and the mandate that blacks needed permission to enter or live in white areas, restrictions known as the *pass laws*. Native peoples were incorporated into the economy as servants, squatter tenants, or semi-feudal serfs. Ultimately, the "Fundamental Law," established in 1852, legally enshrined the inequality of blacks and whites. The first half of the 20th century witnessed the strengthening and extension of the Boer principles of racial segregation through territorial segregation. Black ownership of land was restricted, as was black settlement activity. In addition, the permanent residence of blacks in white urban areas was prohibited. The Natives (Urban Areas) Act codified this latter restriction, defining blacks as temporary urban residents who were to be repatriated to the tribal reserves if not employed. The act also required that blacks, while within urban areas, were to be physically, socially, and economically separated from the white population.

The Afrikaners imposed strict racial separation policies, transforming apartheid from practice to rule. Laws included the Group Areas Act of 1950, which established residential and business sections in urban areas for each race, and the Land Acts of 1954 and 1955, which effectively set aside more than 80 percent of South Africa's land for the white minority. In addition, the pass laws that required nonwhites to carry permits when in white areas were reinforced. The 1950 Population Registration Act classified all South Africans as either Bantu (black), colored (mixed race), or white. "Asian" was later added as a category. Segregation was enforced through regulations to prevent social contact and marriage between races, establishment of separate education standards and job categories, and provision for separate entrances to public facilities such as stations and hotels. Large-scale segregation was established in 1959 through the creation of ten **homelands**, a new version of tribal reserves (**Figure 5.24**). The homelands were areas set aside as tribal territories where black residents were given limited self-government but no vote and limited rights in the general politics of South Africa.

For nearly 40 years, apartheid was the method by which a white minority controlled a black majority through processes that were fundamentally geographical. Protests against apartheid were quickly and ruthlessly repressed, with African National Congress leaders such as Nelson Mandela jailed and activists such as Steven Biko killed. Enforcement of the requirement that black students use the Afrikaans language led to riots in Soweto in 1976.

The 1990s saw the end of apartheid in South Africa—Nelson Mandela was freed from jail and President F. W. de Klerk agreed to sharing political power between blacks and whites. International pressure contributed to the end of apartheid. Sports boycotts threatened white South Africa's passionate devotion to rugby and cricket. South Africa was forced to withdraw from the British Commonwealth, and economic and trade sanctions as well as voluntary investment bans were instituted by some major international corporations. A number of white South Africans were also vocal in their opposition to the system. In 1994 South Africa held the first election in its history in which blacks were allowed to vote, and Nelson Mandela was elected the first black president. The 1997 post-apartheid constitution includes one of the world's most comprehensive bills of rights and prohibits discrimination based on race, gender, pregnancy, marital status, ethnic or social origin, color, sexual orientation, age, disability, religion, conscience, belief, culture, language, and birth.

The Cold War and Africa

Independence movements and transitions in Africa coincided with the global tensions associated with the Cold War between the United States and the Soviet Union. Several African independence leaders had been introduced to socialist ideas during education overseas, and many other Africans found communist and socialist ideas of equity and state ownership appealing after the repression, foreign domination, and inequality of

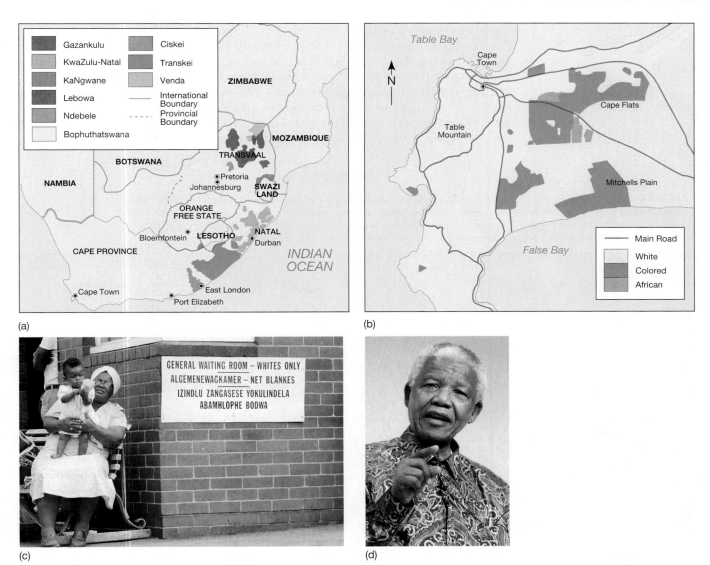

(a)

(b)

(c)

(d)

FIGURE 5.24 The different scales of apartheid (a) Map of the system of South African homelands. Comparisons have been drawn between the homelands policy and the establishment of Indian reservations in North America, especially where the land provided was also of poor quality. In 1970 each black South African was made a citizen of one of these homelands, which were given limited independence in lieu of giving citizens general voting rights. Three million black South Africans were forced to resettle in their homelands. (b) Map of residential areas in Cape Town designated for different race groups prior to 1994. (c) Black woman sits outside a "whites only" waiting room in a train station. (d) Nelson Mandela in 1994. (*Source:* [a, b] Redrawn from D. M. Smith [ed.], *Living Under Apartheid*. London: Allen & Unwin, 1982; Figs. 2.1, 2.3, and 2.5.)

colonial rule. In Tanzania, President Julius Nyerere developed the concept of an African socialism based on the traditional values of communal ownership and kinship ties to extended family expressed as *ujamaa* (familyhood). He believed that a socialist system of cooperative production would be more compatible with African traditions than would individualistic capitalism.

In Angola and Mozambique, where the Portuguese fiercely repressed independence movements, revolutionary movements espousing leftist ideals attracted the interest of the Soviet Union, China, and Cuba, which provided military and economic assistance and trained young Africans in their universities. In Angola, after the Portuguese colonial government fell in a coup in 1974, and a three-party governing coalition of independence movements collapsed, Angola became a focus for a Cold War power struggle.

The United States provided funds to the pro-Western groups, and the Soviet Union and Cuba continued to support the Marxist-Leninist government (**Figure 5.25**).

Tensions escalated after South Africa responded to Angolan support for rebels in Namibia (at that time under South African control) by sending troops toward Angola and supporting anti-government and anti-communist rebels in the mid-1970s. Angola reacted by moving further into the Soviet sphere, and by the 1980s, 50,000 Cuban advisors and troops and millions of dollars' worth of Soviet military aid were flowing into the region. Only when South Africa agreed to grant Namibia independence did

FIGURE 5.25 Conflict and intervention in Africa Africa has experienced many wars and conflicts since independence, some of them fueled by foreign intervention, including Cold War politics involving the Soviet Union, Cuba, and the United States. France and Britain have continued to provide some military assistance in former colonies, and countries such as South Africa, Liberia, Libya, Uganda, and Angola have provided military support for groups in neighboring countries.

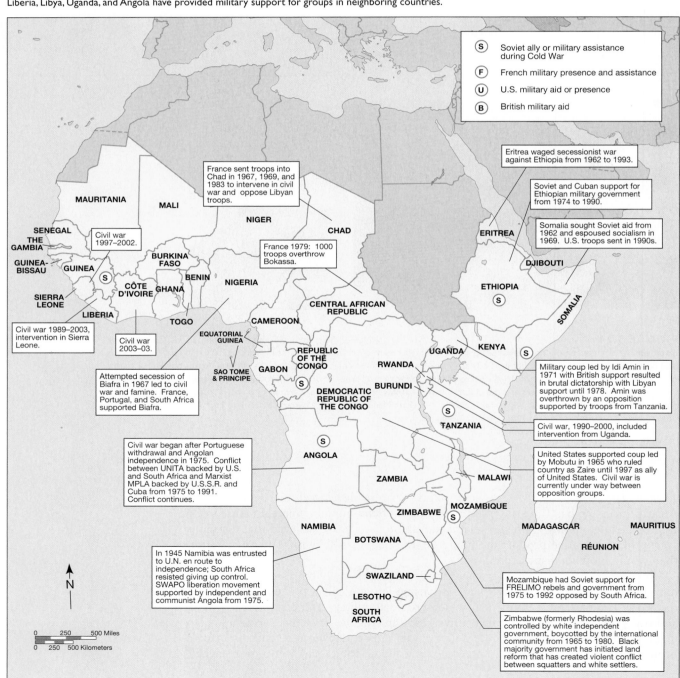

Angola agree to reduce Cuban and Soviet presence and to seek peace with the pro-Western rebel groups.

The Cold War had a different manifestation in the Horn of Africa, where independent countries came into conflict and sought arms and assistance from the superpowers. Somalia had sought Soviet aid as early as 1962, because the United States supported Ethiopian and Kenyan regimes that were resisting Somali expansion into adjacent territories with large Somali populations (a process called *irredentism*—the assertion by the government of a country that a minority living outside its borders belongs to it historically and culturally). In Ethiopia, Emperor Haile Selassie had ruled for more than 40 years over an economy, organized on semifeudal lines, in which the concentration of land and wealth contributed to periodic famines. Growing demands for reform grew during the 1960s, culminating in 1974 in a takeover by a council of junior military officers (the "Derg"), who promoted an Ethiopian socialism of self-reliance and widespread land reform in support of peasants and workers.

Africa provided fertile soil for Cold War rivalry as newly independent nations searched for political ideals, dealt with civil wars and incursions from their neighbors, and sought assistance to develop their economies. In many countries, millions of dollars were expended on arms and other military assistance, thousands were killed, and rural areas were abandoned because of land mines.

Development, Debt, and Foreign Aid

Development Theories   Development theorists agonized over prescriptions for African development in the late 20th century. Modernization theory was seen as a solution in the 1950s, explaining African underdevelopment in terms of the lack of industrialization and proposing solutions of technology transfer, training, and large projects for power generation, often supported by international assistance. Modernization projects included road construction, the Volta and Aswan dams, and harbors such as Tema in Ghana.

The dependency theory perspective (see Chapter 1, p. 45), which argued that African resources had been exploited by the colonial powers, was represented by Walter Rodney's classic 1972 text *How Europe Underdeveloped Africa* and by the analysis of famous Egyptian economist Samir Amin, including his 1971 book about neo-colonialism in West Africa. These texts argued that the dominant core capitalist powers of England and other European colonial powers transformed the political and economic structures of Africa to serve their interests in obtaining cheap raw materials, and in doing so undermined local agriculture and social development. Many countries emerged from colonialism with their economies and trade dependent on just a few products.

The terms of trade for products from African countries, including minerals and export crops such as cocoa and coffee, deteriorated over the last part of the 20th century. This meant that their value on the world market decreased in comparison to manufactured items and other goods being imported by African countries. In 1990, for example, a farmer had to produce twice as much coffee as in 1960 to earn the money needed to purchase a bag of fertilizer.

For dependency theorists the remedy was to reduce the dependency on export revenue and avoid the high costs of imports. This could be done by creating local capacity to produce goods that would replace those previously imported from other countries, especially manufactured industrial products (a policy called *import substitution*). Several African nations adopted strict import substitution policies that included subsidization of local industry and protection against foreign imports through tariffs and other mechanisms. As in Latin America (Chapter 7), import substitution was a mixed success and faced greater challenges because of Africa's generally low level of infrastructure, skills, domestic markets, and investment capital. While it fostered the development of some industries, particularly small-scale manufacturing in African capitals, it also led to inefficiency and poor quality.

Debt   Both modernization and import substitution required capital funds that were not easily available in Africa, and many countries looked outside the region to borrow money. Because many African countries had poor credit ratings with commercial banks, most loans were made from other governments such as the United States or through international agencies such as the World Bank instead of on the private market. Although some funds were invested in infrastructural, industrial, and agricultural development, considerable sums were used to purchase arms or were diverted by ruling elites, increasing their own personal fortunes as overall debt increased.

The total debt of Sub-Saharan Africa stood at $231 billion in 2003, only one-third of that of Latin America and Asia, but it is huge as a percentage of GNP in most African countries. In Angola, both Congos, Côte d'Ivoire, Guinea-Bissau, Liberia, Mauritania, Sierra Leone, and Zambia, the total debt exceeded GNP in 2003. Several countries were paying more than five times the value of their exports to service their debt each year.

Structural Adjustment and Debt Relief   As in other regions, the multilateral agencies such as the International Monetary Fund and World Bank responded to the debt crisis by first controlling the spiraling size of the loans through extending payment periods and adjusting interest rates, and then by demanding structural adjustment policies. These economic policies, mostly associated with the International Monetary Fund (IMF), required governments to cut budgets and liberalize trade in return for debt relief. In many parts of Africa this required devaluation of currencies (to make exports cheaper and thus more attractive to foreign purchases), liberalization of trade (by removing tariffs), reduced public spending, and the privatization of government-held companies.

The first country to accept structural adjustment was Ghana in 1983. By 1990, 30 African countries had implemented programs with the insistence of the IMF. In many of these countries, the impact of structural adjustment was severe, sending food prices spiraling and increasing unemployment as governments cut public-sector jobs. Kenya and Nigeria both fired more than 150,000 government employees in response to IMF policies. Some critics suggested that IMF should be renamed "Imposing Misery and Famine."

The structural adjustment programs fit within the broader program of neoliberalism, promoted particularly by the United States, that includes reducing government subsidies for social and agricultural programs, removing barriers to trade, and privatizing publicly owned land and corporations (see Chapter 7 for a discussion of similar policies in Latin America). But neoliberal policies of free trade clashed with the special concessions that had been granted to Africa by the European Economic Community (EEC). The Lomé Convention, named after the capital of Togo where it was first signed in 1975, is an agreement between the EEC and 66 countries, 43 of which are in Sub-Saharan Africa. In it, the EEC provides economic assistance and trade concessions to promote exports of certain key commodities. The convention includes access to European markets, stabilization of export earnings on selected commodities, industrial technology transfer, project financing, and development aid. However, such preferential treatment has been criticized by the United States and nations in other regions who seek to compete for European markets.

The destitution created in Africa by economic crises, structural adjustment, and war prompted international agencies and others to try to cushion the impact of restructuring in Africa by providing programs for alleviating poverty. This assistance is built on several decades of humanitarian and economic assistance to those regions of Africa suffering from disasters and war. Africa is the largest recipient of what is called foreign aid, receiving one-third of the global total, equivalent to about 10 percent of the region's total GNP and averaging about $20 per person.

As the 20th century drew to a close, an international campaign was organized to pressure for debt relief, especially for the poorest countries in Africa. Official recognition that many of the countries had debt burdens that would permanently cripple development led to several debt-relief programs. In 1996 the World Bank and IMF introduced the Heavily Indebted Poor Countries (HIPC) initiative to restructure and forgive part of the debt of poor countries that, over a five-year period, showed a willingness to pursue neoliberal economic policies of reduced government spending and free trade. Mozambique was one of the first of about 20 African countries that qualified for this form of debt relief. The HIPC program was severely criticized because it was very specific about changes in policy and told countries how to run their economies and because the debt reductions were too small. An international protest movement, called the Jubilee initiative, petitioned to cancel the majority of debts owed by poorer countries by the year 2000. In 2000 several European countries and the United States did move to cancel the debts owed to them by many countries in Africa, and the IMF increased the amount of debt relief under HIPC.

Sub-Saharan Africa has a very low level of economic development compared with other regions. The region had a total GNP of $523 billion in 2004, only about 1 percent of total global GNP, and an average per capita GNP of $601 compared to world average per capita GNP of $6329. Africa is also singled out for attention by many international agencies and receives the highest amount of development assistance per capita of any world region. The World Bank, for example, identifies Sub-Saharan Africa as "the most important development challenge of the twenty-first century."

More recently, the "Make Poverty History" movement, supported by popular musicians such as Bono of the band U2, have called for action and organized public concerts such as "Live 8" to do more for Africa and debt relief (**Figure 5.26**). Pressure to relieve debt focused on the leaders of the wealthy "G8" countries (Canada, France, Germany, Italy, Japan, Russia, United Kingdom, and the United States), who control much of the debt. In 2005 representatives of the countries who assembled at the G8 summit held in Gleneagles, Scotland, agreed to double annual aid to the developing world by $50 billion and to write off the debts of the world's 18 poorest countries, 12 of them in Africa. But Zambian Deputy Finance Minister Felix Mutati pointed to the additional need for fair trade so that African farmers can better compete with the West in a global market. He also expressed concern for climate change as posing serious problems for Africa.

FIGURE 5.26 Concerts for African Debt Relief The Live 8 concerts in London, Washington, Berlin, and other cities were broadcast around the world with calls to political leaders for more aid, debt relief, and fair trade. This is the U.S. poster for the event.

PEOPLES OF SUB-SAHARAN AFRICA
Population and Fertility

The total population of Sub-Saharan Africa was estimated at about 752 million in mid-2005. The average birthrate, at more than 41 births per 1000 population per year, is higher than any other continent. The overall population growth rate was about 2 percent a year, with a doubling time of about 29 years. The Population Reference Bureau has projected the 2025 population at about 1.15 billion.

Nigeria is the most populous country in Africa, with a 2003 population of 126 million, followed by Ethiopia with 74 million, the Democratic Republic of the Congo with 54 million, South Africa with 47 million, Tanzania with 37 million, and Kenya with 34 million. Some populations, such as Nigeria, have not been reliably censused for many years and the estimates are approximate. Overall population density is relatively low, at 30 people per square kilometer (77 people per square mile), about half the global average density. The only countries in the region with population densities higher than the global average are the Indian Ocean islands and the Central African countries of Rwanda and Burundi (**Figure 5.27**).

The density of population per unit of arable land is sometimes considered a better indicator of population pressure on land resources because it measures the ability of land to support its population, or its carrying capacity. By this measure Sub-Saharan

FIGURE 5.27 Africa population density Africa's population is mostly a scattered rural population, with the greatest density along the West African coast, the southeast coast of South Africa, the highlands of East Africa, and along major rivers. Population concentrations tend to be associated with better soils and climate, with colonial centers for mining and export crops, and with coastal ports. For a view of worldwide population density and a guide to reading population-density maps, see Figure 1.8. (*Source:* Center for International Earth Science Information Network [CIESIN], Columbia University; International Food Policy Research Institute [IFPRI]; and World Resources Institute [WRI]. *Gridded Population of the World* [GPW], Version 2. Palisades, NY: CIESIN, Columbia University, 2000. Available at **http://sedac.ciesin.org/plue/gpw/index.html?main.html&2**.)

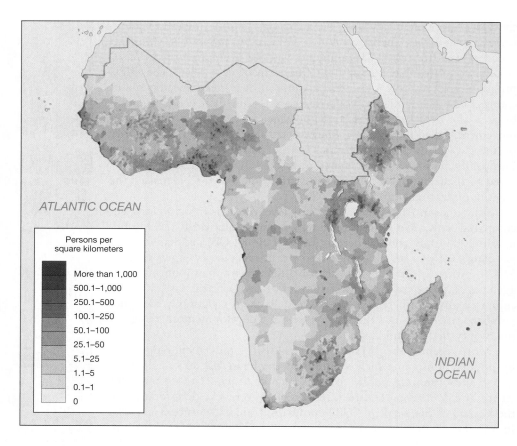

Fertility, contraceptive use, and women's education in Botswana and Nigeria, 1988 and 1990

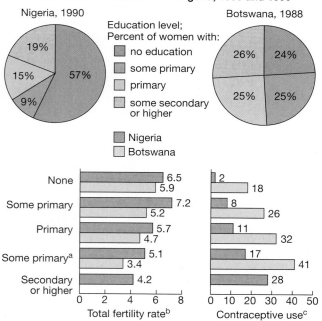

Nigeria, 1990

Education level; Percent of women with:
- no education
- some primary
- primary
- some secondary or higher

Nigeria, 1990: 19%, 15%, 57%, 9%

Botswana, 1988: 26%, 24%, 25%, 25%

- Nigeria
- Botswana

Total fertility rate[b]

Education	Nigeria	Botswana
None	6.5	5.9
Some primary	7.2	5.2
Primary	5.7	4.7
Some primary[a]	5.1	3.4
Secondary or higher	4.2	

Contraceptive use[c]

Education	Nigeria	Botswana
None	2	18
Some primary	8	26
Primary	11	32
Some primary[a]	17	41
Secondary or higher		28

[a] Secondary or higher for Botswana.

[b] Average total number of children per woman given current birth rates.

[c] Percentage of married women ages 15 to 44 using contraception.

Africa appears much more densely populated, with an average of 31 people per square kilometer (80 people per square mile) of arable land, which is just about equal to the global average. The total fertility rate (the average number of children born to a woman during her lifetime) is high in most of Sub-Saharan Africa, averaging 5.0 in 2004 and reaching more than 6 children per woman in many regions. As a result, between 42 percent of the African population is under age 15. This has major implications for future population growth and its effects, as this group starts to have children and makes demands on education and employment systems. Fertility rates are lower in southern Africa.

What are the reasons for high fertility and birthrates in Africa, and what are the prospects for slowing population growth? Population geographers and other researchers have focused on the study of African demography in response to these questions. They have found that although religious prohibitions of contraception and lack of access to contraceptive devices may play a small role, other factors are much more important.

Children are valued in Africa for many logical reasons, including their ability to work in agricultural fields and as herders, to help with household work, and to care for younger siblings. Children are also the possible source of financial or other gain when they marry. Children are the main source of security for elderly people in countries where there are

FIGURE 5.28 Status of women and fertility in Africa Use of contraceptives is generally lower in Nigeria than Botswana, partly as a result of larger Islamic populations and the Islamic prohibitions on the use of contraceptives. Women with more education in Nigeria and Botswana tend to have fewer children and are more likely to use contraceptives. (*Source:* Population Reference Bureau. Available at **www.prb.org**.)

few pensions or public services for the aged, and it is traditional for younger generations to respect and care for their elders. Large families are also often perceived as prestigious, a spiritual approach to linking past and present, and a way of ensuring family lineage. In regions of ethnic strife, children represent a way of securing votes, warriors, or political power. Even though infant mortality rates have improved with better nutrition and health care in much of Africa, many African families have internalized the need to have many children in order to ensure that some survive to adulthood.

Many studies have also shown that conditions for women have a strong influence on fertility rates, with lower age of marriage, minimal female education and literacy, and low rates of female employment all contributing to higher fertility rates (**Figure 5.28**). Fertility rates tend to be lower in urban areas with high rates of female education, employment, and later ages for marriage. In Kenya, for example, women with secondary or higher education have a total fertility rate of 4.9 compared to a rate of more than 7.0 for women with little or no schooling, and in Nigeria the fertility rate is 4.2 for better-educated women compared to 7.2 for women with little education.

Population projections for several African countries have been revised downward because of the high mortality and infection rates associated with the AIDS epidemic. In Zimbabwe and Botswana, where infection rates are more than 30 percent, estimates of average life expectancy have been revised down by 20 years, and population growth rates have been reduced or even reversed. Overall population projections for Africa for 2025 have been adjusted down by 200 million people.

HIV/AIDS

Today, the most serious disease affecting Sub-Saharan Africa—one that is thought to have emerged in central Africa—is HIV, the human immunodeficiency virus that causes fatal acquired immunodeficiency syndrome, or AIDS. Sub-Saharan Africa is more severely affected by AIDS than any other part of the world. African adult rates of HIV in 2003 were highest in Botswana, where 37 percent of the population was infected. The United Nations reports more than 28.5 million people in Africa infected with HIV in 2001—70 percent of the worldwide total. The infection rate is estimated at 9 percent of all adults compared to the 1 percent world rate, and more than 14 million Africans have lost their lives to AIDS since it was identified in 1981. It has become the main cause of death in Africa, killing more people than malaria and warfare (**Figure 5.29**).

The geography of AIDS in Africa varies by country, by regions within countries, and by social groups. Unlike in other regions, more women than men have AIDS in Sub-Saharan Africa, and mothers often transmit the disease to their children. Frequently, married couples are both infected with AIDS and die from it—a situation that has created as many as 11 million orphans.

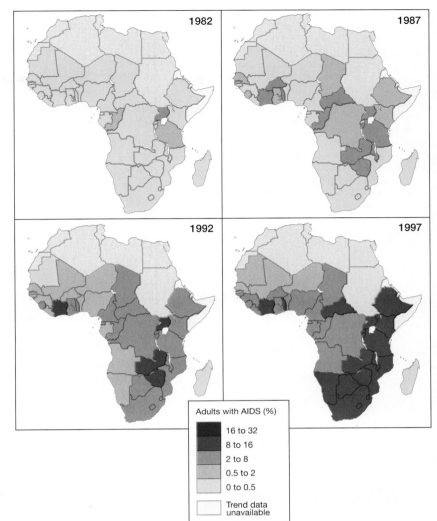

FIGURE 5.29 AIDS in Sub-Saharan Africa These maps of the progression of the HIV epidemic in Africa from 1982 to 1997 show the increasing percentage of adults infected. The highest rates of infection were in eastern Africa in the early 1980s but have now shifted to southern Africa, especially Botswana, Zambia, and Zimbabwe, where more than 30 percent of adults are infected. Urban dwellers who have multiple sex partners, including young office workers and migrant workers, have a higher infection rate, as do women who work in the commercial sex trade and the wives and children of migrant workers. The incidence is lower in rural areas except along major truck routes and in areas where there are a lot of soldiers. The road from Malawi to Durban, where 92 percent of truck drivers were infected, has been called "the highway of death." Migrant workers have taken the disease back to their homes. The death of skilled farm laborers has resulted in a decline in agricultural output, and many young professionals crucial to the region's future have left their jobs because they have AIDS. Major industries and companies in southern Africa, such as diamond mines and banks, estimate that absence and loss of employees to AIDS is costing them more than 5 percent of their profits. AIDS is having a serious impact on life expectancy and population size and composition in Africa. Countries such as South Africa and Zimbabwe have adjusted projections of population and economic growth down to take account of the serious negative impact of AIDS on mortality and economic productivity. (*Source:* From the World Bank Group, "Intensifying Action Against HIV/AIDS in Africa: Responding to a Development Crisis," 1998. Available at **http://www.worldbank.org/html/extdr/ offrep/afr/aidstrat.pdf**.)

Poverty exacerbates the AIDS problem in Sub-Saharan Africa because most Africans cannot afford prevention (for example, through the use of condoms), testing, or medicines that prolong the lives of those with HIV/AIDS. Governments have low healthcare budgets and may not admit to the severity of the AIDS epidemic. Few people have health insurance, diagnosis and treatment are often delayed, and interaction with other diseases such as tuberculosis increases mortality rates.

Some countries have had success in combating AIDS. Uganda and Senegal have promoted aggressive and successful AIDS education and prevention campaigns and have cut infection rates in half. Unprecedented international agreements with drug companies in combination with new assistance programs from the World Bank, charities, and donor countries are helping lower the cost of drugs.

There is great concern about the potential impact of some other emerging viruses in central Africa, specifically Ebola fever, which causes severe bleeding and kills more than 50 percent of its victims. So far, outbreaks such as the ones in the Congo in 1995 and in Uganda in 2000 have been contained, but only after killing more than 200 people in each case.

Urbanization

Although Africa is the most rural of world regions, it has been urbanizing rapidly over the last 40 years. In 1960 the urban population of Sub-Saharan Africa was only 17 million people, about 20 percent of the overall regional population. By 2000, the urban population had reached 220 million people, 35 percent of the total, and was growing at about 5 percent per year. This is more urban than most of Asia, but much less urban than Europe or the Americas. The level of urbanization varies greatly by country, from South Africa with 51 percent of its people living in urban areas, to Ethiopia at 18 percent and Uganda at 14 percent. East Africa has a lower level of urbanization (19 percent) than does southern (46 percent) or West Africa (33 percent).

About 30 percent of Sub-Saharan Africa's population lives in the largest city in their country. Lagos and Johannesburg are the two largest cities with populations of about 13 million and 3.2 million, respectively. Geographer David Simon has used several indicators to identify African cities of greatest regional importance and links to the global system, including the presence of stock markets, large numbers of embassies, air traffic, and headquarters of international or regional organizations and corporations. According to these criteria, Johannesburg, South Africa; Nairobi, Kenya; and Lagos, Nigeria, lead with more than 70 embassies and 40 regional or international headquarters in each city.

Major City: Johannesburg, South Africa Johannesburg was founded in 1886, following the discovery of gold in the Witwatersrand, or Rand, a range of hills to the west of the present city that overlays the world's richest gold deposit. The city sits on the high *veld* or plateau in the province of Gauteng (meaning "place of gold," formerly the southern Transvaal) that stretches from Pretoria southwest toward Kimberly.

The city of Johannesburg still bears the spatial mark of apartheid, although racial segregation is slowly being replaced by a residential pattern based more on economic status, and white residents have abandoned the city center. The majority (70 percent) of the population are black and live in "townships" such as Soweto, a community of 1.5 million people about 16 kilometers (10 miles) southwest of the city center. Here most people live in small houses and commute into the city to work (**Figure 5.30**). Soweto became famous for demonstrations and rent strikes during the struggle against apartheid and for the stark contrasts between the poverty of its residents and the wealth of white neighborhoods in the northern suburbs.

Major City: Lagos, Nigeria Nigeria is the giant of the region, with a population estimated at 120 million and the largest GDP in West Africa. Lagos—the colonial capital until the capital was changed to Abuja in the interior in 1992—has a metropolitan population of more than 13 million people (**Figure 5.31**). Sited on a natural harbor, Lagos was developed by the British as a rail terminus beginning about

1880. It also became a leading cargo port, industrial area, and center for production of consumer goods. About 80 percent of Nigeria's trade goes through Lagos, although some is shifting to the oil regions to the east. The city region includes 53 percent of Nigeria's manufacturing, 62 percent of the gross industrial output, and 22 industrial estates. When structural adjustment caused food price increases and unemployment after 1989, city residents expressed their frustrations by rioting. Lagos is also a cultural center, the original home of prize-winning writers Chinua Achebe, Ben Okri, and Wole Soyinka and of world-famous musicians Feli and Femi Kuti and King Sunny Adé.

Lagos is infamous for its traffic and crime problems. The average commute to work is more than 90 minutes in polluted air and tangled traffic jams, made worse by inadequate bridges between islands. Electricity and other services are also insufficient; as a result of interruptions and lack of service, the National Electric Power Administration (NEPA) has been given the nickname of "Not Expecting Power Anytime."

Although urban growth is partly driven by overall population, cities have been growing twice as fast as overall populations. Fertility rates tend to be lower in urban areas. As in many other regions, the major driver of urban growth is migration from rural areas to the cities, and the factors pushing people from rural areas and pulling them to the cities are somewhat similar. People are leaving rural areas because of poverty, lack of services or support for agriculture, scarcity of land, natural disasters, and civil wars. Urban areas are more attractive because they offer jobs, higher wages, better services (including education and electricity), and entertainment. Urban areas have benefited from the "urban bias" of both colonial and independent governments in Africa, which tended to invest disproportionately

FIGURE 5.30 Johannesburg, South Africa Johannesburg at dawn with the high-rise downtown headquarters for major mining corporations such as Rand Mines, the Johannesburg Stock Exchange, and the smoke drifting in from the townships on the outskirts, such as Soweto. Many townships do not have adequate electricity and water supplies, and residents must use wood or coal for heat during the chilly winter season, casting a pall of polluting smoke over the townships that contributes to health problems and high infant mortality rates.

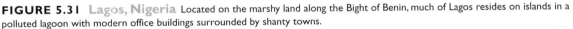

FIGURE 5.31 Lagos, Nigeria Located on the marshy land along the Bight of Benin, much of Lagos resides on islands in a polluted lagoon with modern office buildings surrounded by shanty towns.

in capital cities that housed centralized administrative functions. In addition, food prices were kept down in the cities to reduce wage demands and to decrease the risk of civil unrest.

The Sub-Saharan African Diaspora

Migration to and from Africa

Migration into Africa from other regions is overwhelmed by the immense African diaspora and emigration from Africa to other regions. Millions of black Africans were captured and sent as slaves, initially to the Middle East, but more significantly to the Americas, where their descendants represent a high percentage of the populations in Brazil, the Caribbean, and the United States. A second wave of emigration was associated with the aftermath of colonialism, a time when many Africans retained British Commonwealth passports or French citizenship and moved to Britain and France (or other Commonwealth countries such as Canada) in search of work. This included many people living in the Caribbean, often the descendants of slaves, who then were part of a secondary migration back to England or to Canada and the United States. Another secondary migration, of Asians who had settled in East Africa, was associated with Ugandan dictator Idi Amin's decision in 1972 to evict all Asians from Uganda because of their dominant role in commerce.

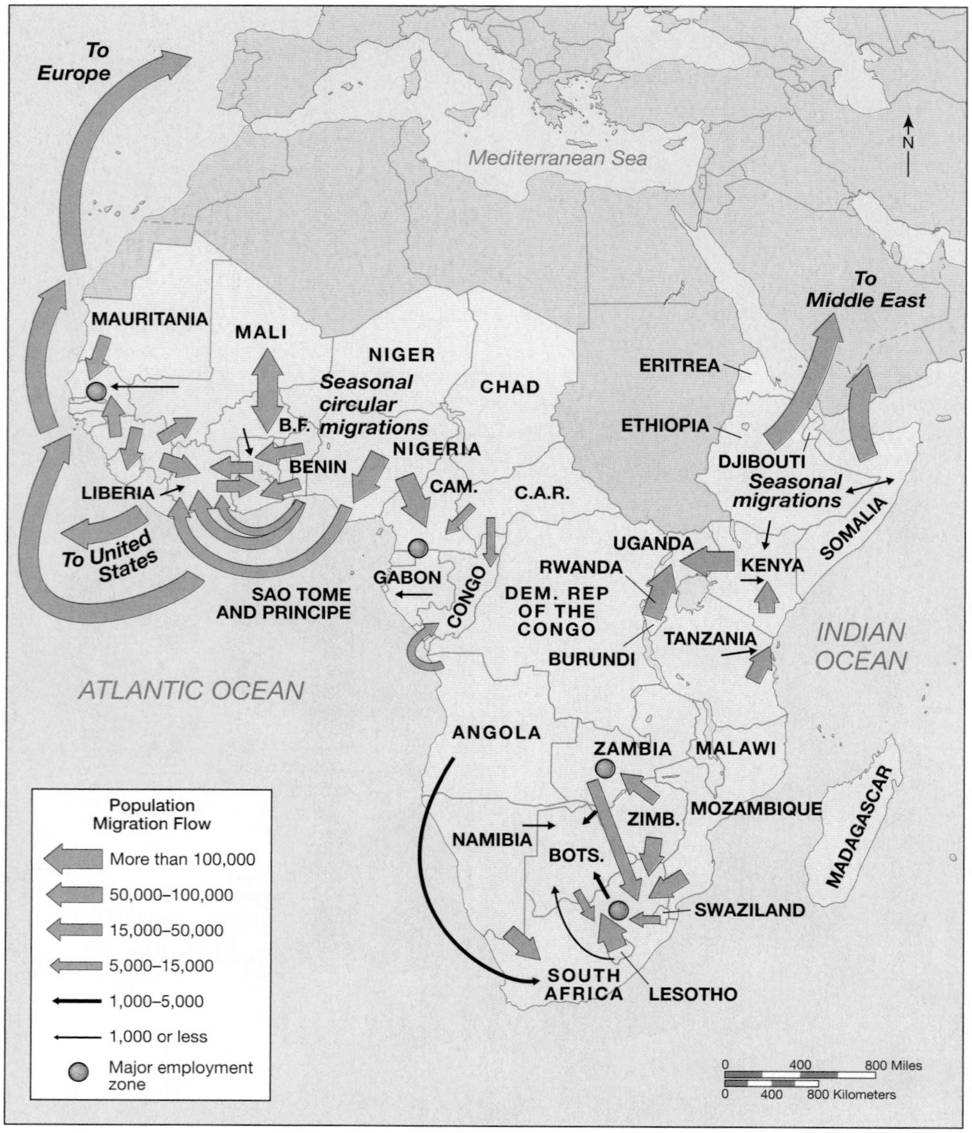

Other recent emigrations from Africa include movements of white populations from South Africa and other countries to Europe, North America, and Australia and a "brain drain" of 20,000 African students and professionals, especially doctors, per year to universities and companies in the core regions of Europe and the Americas. There are also African refugee populations in several world regions.

Migration within Africa

Contemporary migration within Africa is mainly associated with movements in search of work and with refugees fleeing famine, floods, and violent conflict (**Figure 5.32**). Labor migrations emerged during the colonial period when loss of traditional land to colonists and high taxes forced people to look for other work, and employment became available in mines and on plantations. For example, Sahelian residents migrated to work in peanut-, cotton-, and cocoa-producing areas in Senegal, Côte D'Ivoire, Nigeria, and Ghana; in East Africa, Hutu and Kikuyu migrated to work on Kenyan and Ugandan coffee and tea plantations and European farms. The most significant labor migration of the last 100 years is from southern Africa, especially Botswana and Zimbabwe, into South Africa to work in the mining industry. In 1960 more than 350,000 foreign workers were employed in South Africa. These migrations have disrupted family life, but the remittances that are sent back by workers have become an important contribution to local and, in the case of

FIGURE 5.32 Interregional migration in Africa Africans are moving within and beyond Africa in response to employment opportunities. Major flows include those into the mining zones of southern Africa, the oil regions, and the export-crop production zones of West and East Africa. Some of these are circular migrations for seasonal temporary work. Africans are moving from Africa to Europe, the United States, and the Middle East. (*Source: Redrawn from S. Aryeetey-Attoh [ed.], The Geography of Sub-Saharan Africa. Upper Saddle River, NJ: Prentice Hall, 1997, p. 136.)*

countries such as Botswana and Lesotho, national economies. Labor migration also continues from inland West Africa to coastal cities such as Abidjan.

Geographer David Rain has documented more traditional and long-standing **circular migrations** that respond to seasonal availability of pasture, droughts, and wage employment. In Niger, many people move to regional centers such as Maradi in the dry season and return to their villages to plant crops when the rains begin. Pastoralists move their herds south in the dry season seeking water, pasture, and the possibility of grazing on harvested cropland or on wetlands. These migrations are a rational response to the spatial and seasonal variations in environmental conditions.

Refugees The United Nations High Commission on Refugees (UNHCR) estimated that as of January 2003 there were more than 4.5 million refugees in Sub-Saharan Africa, more than one-third of the world total and the largest number of any world region. UNHCR reports that 3.3 million were official international refugees—involuntary migrants who have crossed a national frontier—with the remainder displaced within their countries. Wars in Liberia and Sierra Leone drove more than 685,000 people into neighboring countries, and civil war and famine have forced more than 400,000 Somalis and 300,000 Eritreans from their homes. Other refugees include those from conflicts in Rwanda and Burundi, although many of these have been recently repatriated, contributing to an overall modest decline in the refugee population.

Africa continued to host one-third of the world's refugee population in 2005. Although West Africa experienced a reduction in its number of refugees, East and Horn of Africa had a marginal increase. The Republic of Tanzania, followed by the United States, was the world's fourth largest asylum country. Five countries that produced more than 10,000 refugees in 2005 included Togo (39,100), Sudan (34,500), the Democratic Republic of the Congo (15,600), Somalia (13,600), and the Central African Republic (11,500).

The refugee populations place serious burdens on neighboring countries that lack the resources to feed and resettle the impoverished and starving arrivals. Guinea, for example, absorbed almost half a million refugees from Liberia and Sierra Leone, and Tanzania took in a similar number from Burundi. Most international refugees are housed in camps, supported by international organizations and charities (**Figure 5.33**). Disease spreads rapidly in the crowded conditions of the camps, and food supplies are sometimes interrupted or diverted by military groups and governments. Refugees are often accused of spreading HIV and other diseases, but excluded from HIV/AIDS programs. Long-standing conflicts and loss of livelihoods at home mean that many refugees spend long periods in the camps with little hope of return. However, more peaceful conditions and carefully monitored repatriation have resulted in the return of refugee populations to countries such as Rwanda and Mozambique.

People forced to move within their own countries, because they do not fall under international definitions or assistance for refugees, are some of the most desperate migrants. UNHCR estimates that there are 500,000 internally displaced people in the Democratic Republic of the Congo, most of them inaccessible to relief organizations.

FIGURE 5.33 Refugees in Africa Millions of Rwandans fled the country in the 1990s to camps such as this in Katale, Democratic Republic of the Congo.

Religion

Traditional African religions have been described as animist (worship of nature and spirits), but this overgeneralizes the wide variety of local religious beliefs in Africa. While natural symbols, sacred groves of trees, and landforms may have religious significance, many African religions also feature a belief in a supreme being, several secondary gods or guardians, good and evil spirits, and ancestor worship. Ancestors, priests, or witch doctors mediate and interpret the wishes of the gods and spirits, and rituals ensure the stability of society and relations with the natural world. More than 70 million people (about 10 percent of the total population) are reported to practice traditional religions in the continent of Africa.

Christianity spread into Sub-Saharan Africa via North Africa and Ethiopia from about A.D. 300, but the pace of conversion accelerated rapidly under European colonial rule and European missionaries. Dutch Calvinism in southern Africa; Catholicism in French, Spanish, and Portuguese colonies; and Anglican beliefs in the British colonies all had strong influences. Of the 360 million estimated Christians in all of Africa, there are about 125 million Roman Catholics and 114 million Protestants.

Islam is another major religion in Africa as a whole, with 308 million adherents, and it is predominant in the Sahel, North Africa, and some East African coastal communities. It was spread by traders and drew some fierce defenders among West African groups, such as the Fulani, who went to war to eradicate animistic beliefs. As in Latin America, traditional religion has blended with Christianity and Islam to create forms in which local traditional rituals are incorporated into religious services. Another parallel to Latin America is the recent rapid spread of evangelical Christianity in many regions of Africa.

Religious differences have fueled political conflict in some regions of Africa, most notably where Muslims and Christians were forced into the colonial national boundaries. In West African countries bordering the Sahel, such as Nigeria, tensions exist between northern Islamic groups, such as the Hausa, and southern Christians.

Language and Ethnicity

The geography of languages in Africa is incredibly complex, with more than 800 living languages, 40 of them spoken by more than 1 million people (**Figure 5.34**). The dominant indigenous languages, spoken by 10 million or more, are Hausa (the Sahel), Yoruba and Ibo (Nigeria), Swahili (East Africa), and Zulu (southern Africa). Hausa and Swahili are known as trade languages (or *lingua franca*), spoken as second languages by many groups to facilitate trade. English, French, Portuguese, and Afrikaans are also spoken in regions of recent colonial control and education systems or white settlement, and Arabic is common toward northern Africa. Arabic has strongly influenced Swahili along the east coast of Africa. Because most countries have no dominant indigenous African language, they have often chosen a European language for official business and school systems. The countries with the most coherent overlap between their territory and a dominant African language are Somalia (Somali), Botswana (Tswana), and Ethiopia (Amharic).

The multiplicity of languages and dialects reflects the large number of distinct cultural or ethnic groups in Africa. Some writers use the term *tribe* to define these groupings and describe Africa as a *tribalist* society. The term *tribe* describes a form of social identity created by groups who share a common set of ideas about collective loyalty and political action, with group affiliation based on shared kinship, language, and territory. While it is used by many groups to identify themselves, other groups see the term as negative (related to colonial perceptions of savagery) and now prefer to use the term *ethnic group*.

The largest ethnic groups in Africa are associated with the dominance of certain languages, such as Hausa, Yoruba, and Zulu, but almost all groups were either split geographically by colonial national boundaries or grouped together with their neighbors, enemies, or others with whom they shared no affinity. Attempts to consolidate ethnic groups across boundaries and struggles for power between groups within countries are a major cause of conflict in contemporary Africa.

For example, tensions between the Ibo and Yoruba in Nigeria led to civil war when the Ibo declared the independence of eastern Nigeria as Biafra in 1967. The conflict, which drew international attention and intervention because of starvation in Biafra and the presence of oil in the region, resulted in as many as 1 million deaths (mainly from hunger and disease) and lingering ethnic resentments after Nigeria was reunited. Ethnic and tribal tensions are also high in the Horn of Africa, especially in Somalia where tribal warfare frustrates attempts at peace.

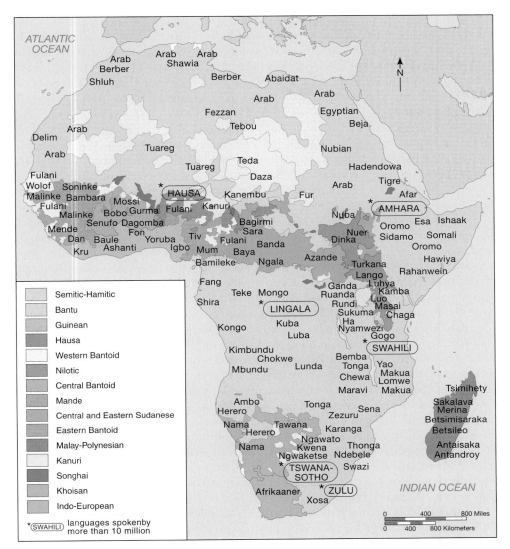

FIGURE 5.34 Language map of Africa The cultural complexity of Africa is clearly demonstrated in the variety of indigenous languages shown on this map. The indigenous languages of Africa can be grouped into larger language families, including the Afro-Asiatic languages of North Africa such as Somali, Amharic, and Tuareg; the Nilo-Saharan languages such as Dinka, Turkana, and Nuer in East Africa; and the largest Niger-Congo group, which includes Hausa, Yoruba, Zulu, Swahili, and Kikuyu. A small family are the Khoisan languages spoken by the bushmen of southern Africa, which have a distinctive "click" vocalization. Swahili and Hausa are spoken by millions as the trade languages of East and West Africa, respectively. (*Source:* Redrawn from S. Aryeetey-Attoh [ed.], *The Geography of Sub-Saharan Africa.* Upper Saddle River, NJ: Prentice Hall, 1997, Fig. 4.6.)

Culture

It is hard to draw cultural generalities from a continent as large and diverse as Africa. Those who do generalize highlight the importance of the extended family, ties to the land, oral tradition, village life, and music in traditional African culture. The importance of the extended family is linked to the supremacy of kinship ties in social relations and obligations and to a widespread respect for elders as sources of wisdom. Kinship ties going back multiple generations in the same region may define "clan" allegiances and may drive primary loyalties, as in contemporary Somalia, where interclan conflict has dominated recent political events. Different extended families are often linked through intermarriage, with a transfer of wealth, sometimes in the form of cattle, from the husband to the wife's family as a mark of respect and value of the woman's labor and companionship.

The tie to the land is connected to traditional forms of land tenure in Africa, where in many regions land was viewed as given by the spirits or held in trust for ancestors and future generations. The Elesi of Odogbolu (a traditional leader) in Nigeria expressed this view in these words: "The land belongs to a vast family of which many are dead, few are living, and countless members are still unborn." This gives land a communal nature such that it could not be bought or sold by individuals. In some cases, land rights are held by the extended family or the community rather than by the individual, and in other societies the chief or king controls land. Traditions of reciprocity, where a gift is given in order to obtain a favor, and of helping family members are a major source of cultural confusion, according to African historian Ali Mazrui. He suggests that these traditions provide an explanation for the way in which some leaders have favored family members with jobs in their administrations and for the use of bribes when making requests from government officials. He also notes that under colonialism, local residents viewed stealing from the government as a legitimate form of resistance because they felt that foreigners were robbing Africa of resources and funds through taxation.

Africa is associated with a rich tradition of music and the arts that has increasingly influenced other regions of the world. Slavery was one way in which African musical, artistic, and food customs spread around the world, especially to the Americas. Traditional music of the West African Sahel may have influenced the development of American blues, and West African coastal traditions influenced Afro-Caribbean music styles such as the Cuban rumba.

Africa is often associated with music from percussion instruments, especially drums. Other instruments with metal keys that are plucked or tapped, as well as flutes and harplike stringed instruments, are also commonly used in traditional and popular music. Such musical traditions vary widely across the continent and include the complex rhythms of women drummers in Tanzania and of xylophone players in Uganda, and the chanting of the Zulu of southern Africa. In West Africa, oral traditions are associated with the singers and storytellers, some of whom receive the respected name of *griots*.

African popular music mixes indigenous influences with those of the West, especially those of the United States and the Caribbean. For example, the highlife music of West Africa derived from Caribbean calypso and military brass bands, adding stronger percussion, soul influences, and exchange between lead and background singers to emerge as the now internationally popular *juju* or Afrobeat sounds of Nigeria's King Sunny Adé and Fela Kuti. In French West Africa, singers such as Youssou N'Dour blend traditional African beats with powerful vocals, and in South Africa, singers such as Miriam Makeba received international recognition in the 1950s, presaging the popularity of the a cappella style of South African black musicians such as Ladysmith Black Mambazo. Popular musicians have often expressed political opinions against apartheid or corruption, and Senegalese musician Youssou N'Dour campaigns to combat malaria (**Figure 5.35a**).

African art is also incredibly varied and includes painting, metalwork, and sculpture. In traditional Africa, artists were valued specialists, often under the patronage of kings and producing works of spiritual value. The masks and wood sculptures of the

FIGURE 5.35 African musicians and crafts (a) Senegalese musician Youssou N'Dour sings at the Africa Live concert to fight malaria. (b) Traditional Kente cloth from northern Ghana has become popular worldwide, especially in North America.

(a)   (b)

Dogon and Bambara peoples of West Africa are now collected around the world while maintaining cultural significance within the region. Kente cloth designs from northern Ghana have become meaningful in African-American identity and clothing (**Figure 5.35b**). As interest in travel and world culture has grown, artists and others have started to produce items for sale to tourists and to international distributors, including some organizations that try to ensure fair trading principles of returning as much value as possible to local people.

CONTEMPORARY CHALLENGES IN A GLOBALIZING WORLD

Contemporary Africa faces challenges as a world region and as a collection of diverse countries and communities. The most urgent issues include political stability, economic and social inequality, agricultural capacity, environmental conservation and degradation, and health (especially AIDS). Intertwined among these issues are interregional questions about economic integration, refugee flows, and development strategies.

Politics and Peace

The search for peace in Africa has been frustrated by the legacies of colonial frontiers and the Cold War, ethnic rivalries, and the special interests of powerful individuals and sectors. While some countries were able to create (or re-create) a sense of national identity following independence, others are still coping with internal struggles, contested nationalisms, and claims on land beyond their current borders. Although the end of the Cold War and the end of apartheid in South Africa opened new prospects for peace and cooperation, there are continuing wars and precarious coalitions in several regions of Africa.

The cost of wars in Sub-Saharan Africa has been a hindrance to investments in development. The Stockholm International Peace Research Institute reports that military expenditures by governments in Sub-Saharan Africa ranged between $6.6 and $9.5 billion in the 1990s and that many governments were spending more on arms and the military than on education or health.

Geographers Samuel Aryeetey-Attoh and Ian Yeboah identify multiple causes for continuing political instability in Africa, including ethnic conflict, poor leadership, outside interference, and the legacies of recent independence struggles and racist government. They note the frequency of military coups, with Ghana, Nigeria, and Uganda all experiencing at least five coups since independence about 50 years ago. They are also concerned about the number of elected leaders who eventually drifted toward one-party states and dictatorships, with accompanying repression and restrictions on freedom of speech. Yeboah and Aryeetey-Attoh see signs of optimism emerging in the political geography of Africa, as many countries moved toward democratic elections in the 1990s, and as political and ethnic tensions were reduced with the end of the Cold War and of apartheid in South Africa. They and others point to the relative success of Botswana, where after independence, government structure included a strong role for traditional chiefs and public input into government. Economic growth, especially in the diamond and beef industries, the lack of civil unrest, and relatively democratic decision making have all contributed to improved social conditions, with literacy at 70 percent and per capita incomes averaging $3000.

Rwanda and Burundi   The scars of conflict and genocide are still evident in Rwanda and Burundi, where tensions between the majority Hutu and powerful Tutsi peoples erupted into civil war in 1994. The ethnic divisions between these two groups were created or exacerbated by Belgian colonists, who gave the Tutsis control over the Hutus, who were mostly peasant farmers. The Tutsis received education, training, and other benefits, while the Hutus were taxed heavily and given few privileges. The rapid withdrawal of Belgium resulted in a Hutu majority government in Rwanda and a population that harbored resentment against the Tutsi minority (about 20 percent of the population of the two countries). In Burundi, the Tutsis maintained power until the late 1980s, but with several internal military coups and severe repression of Hutu uprisings.

Burundi finally moved toward multiparty and multiethnic government in 1993, but the new president, Melchior Ndadaye, was killed in a coup, and subsequent ethnic violence killed more than 200,000 and sent 800,000 refugees into neighboring countries. When in 1994 a plane crash killed the presidents of Burundi and Rwanda (Cyprien Ntaryamira and Juvenal Habyarimana), some Hutus blamed Tutsis and moderate Hutus. They initiated a massacre in which more than 500,000 died in Rwanda, and many Tutsis fled to neighboring countries where rebel forces were organized. When these Tutsi rebels won control of Rwanda and Burundi, thousands of Hutus fled to avoid retribution. Two million refugees ended up in Zaire (now the Democratic Republic of the Congo) and thousands in Uganda, Kenya, and Tanzania.

The challenge of reconciliation in these two countries is enormous because the memories of violence are so fresh and the divisions so deep. The international community has been accused of ignoring signs of imminent massacres and then delaying their response to the misery of refugees in need of humanitarian intervention. Since 2000 considerable energy has been focused on reconciliation and peace, thanks to the mediation of respected leaders such as Nelson Mandela of South Africa and Julius Nyerere of Tanzania. In Rwanda there has been an effort to bring to justice those most responsible for the genocide, to encourage forgiveness, and to de-emphasize ethnicity in politics.

In April 2005, the Rwandan rebel group Democratic Forces for the Liberation of Rwanda (FDLR) announced that it would cease its armed struggle to bring Rwanda back under its control. Early in 2006, The Security Council adopted Resolution 1653, which called on the Governments of Uganda, Rwanda, Burundi, and the Democratic Republic of the Congo to disarm and demobilize militias and armed groups, especially northern Uganda's Lord's Resistance Army.

Liberia and Sierra Leone Other conflicts seemed even harder to resolve. In Liberia and Sierra Leone, civil wars and authoritarian leadership produced conditions of anarchy in the late 1990s. The economies of these two countries depend on a very narrow range of exports with volatile prices—rubber in Liberia and cocoa in Sierra Leone. Resettlement of freed slaves from other regions, who saw themselves as an elite, has also caused conflict with the indigenous residents. There is considerable resentment of urban wealth by rural residents. In the 1990s, struggles for power between opposition power groups within the countries were fueled by arms and capital obtained through the sale of diamonds, with many ordinary people fleeing as refugees. Peace was established in Sierra Leone in 2002 as UN forces disarmed rebels and militias, and in 2003 hopes for peace in Liberia were encouraged by new leadership that sought to disarm rebels and control military violence. In 2006 U.S.-educated economist Ellen Johnson-Sirleaf won the Liberian presidential elections vowing to sustain democracy and became Africa's first elected woman head of state.

Peacekeeping These conflicts are occurring within the context of a new post–Cold War international political geography in which the United Nations, African regional security forces, and the United States are all playing new roles. The United Nations Peacekeeping Forces operate under the authority of the United Nations Security Council to help establish and maintain peace in areas of armed conflict with the permission of disputing parties. In Africa, UN forces, with their distinctive pale blue helmets, have been deployed in Angola, the Democratic Republic of the Congo, Sudan, Ethiopia, Eritrea, Rwanda, Namibia, Somalia, Sierra Leone, Liberia, and Mozambique (**Figure 5.36a**).

After initial success in monitoring transitions to peace in Mozambique and Namibia, the success of these missions has been mixed. UN forces failed to prevent massacres in Rwanda and Sierra Leone, were unable to establish peace in Somalia and the Democratic Republic of the Congo, and had inadequate human or financial resources to sustain several operations. The United States has been reluctant to send troops to Africa after negative publicity about its involvement in Somalia, and UN forces are increasingly composed of soldiers from poorer countries. The United States has been widely criticized for allowing foreign aid to be used for arms sales and for refusing to ban the sale of military hardware, including land mines. African leadership—especially from South Africa and Nigeria—in promoting peace within the region is of growing importance, including negotiations led by former South African president Nelson Mandela and a West African peacekeeping force and monitoring group, ECOMOG, led by Nigeria under the auspices of the Economic Community of West African States (ECOWAS). The recent head of the United Nations, Kofi Annan, was from Ghana and was particularly concerned with improving conditions in Africa (**Figure 5.36b**).

Regional Organizations ECOWAS is one example of programs for economic integration and political cooperation in Sub-Saharan Africa, established in 1975 to promote trade and cooperation with West Africa. ECOWAS includes the countries of Benin, Burkina Faso, Cape Verde, Côte d'Ivoire, Gambia, Ghana, Guinea, Guinea-Bissau, Liberia, Mali, Mauritania, Niger, Nigeria, Senegal, Sierra Leone, and Togo. African integration was the dream of several independence leaders, most notably Kwame Nkrumah of Ghana, who called for a Union of African States in his famous 1961 speech, "I Speak of Freedom." Nkrumah believed that only by joining together could independent Africa reach its full potential. Unable to convince others that complete unity was desirable, Nkrumah was able to lead the establishment of the Organization of African Unity (OAU) in 1963. The OAU, now called the African Union and based in Addis Ababa, Ethiopia, promotes solidarity among African states, the elimination of colonialism, and cooperative development efforts. It was successful in mediating boundary disputes between Ethiopia and Somalia in the 1960s and in pressing for the end of the apartheid regime in South Africa.

In southern Africa, economic integration has been promoted since 1979 through the Southern African Development Community (SADC), which promotes trade and development coordination, especially improvement of transport links. Members include Angola, Botswana, Lesotho, Malawi, Mauritius, Mozambique, Namibia, Swaziland, Tanzania, Zambia, and Zimbabwe. South Africa finally joined in 1994 with the advent of black majority rule. Similar regional programs have included the East African Cooperation (EAC) and East African Economic Union between Kenya, Uganda, and Tanzania, and the larger Common Market for East and Southern Africa (COMESA), which replaced the Preferential Trade Area (PTA) in 1993.

Social and Economic Inequality

The roots of political unrest in Africa also lie in the large regional and social inequalities in many countries. Sub-Saharan Africa ranks low on many measures compared to other world regions. Life expectancy averages 19 years below the world average of 67 years and is lower than in any other world region. GDP per capita is about $601 compared to a $6329 world average. The United Nations estimates that 40 percent of Sub-Saharan Africans are poor as measured by income and 40 percent according to the more general measure of human poverty, which combines life expectancy, literacy, and access to basic services such as clean water. Conditions in Africa are also difficult for children, who have an infant mortality rate of 94 deaths per 1000 children born (almost double the world average) and low levels of nutrition and immunization.

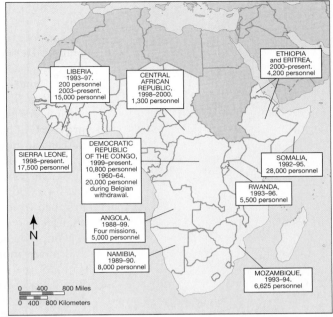

LIBERIA, 1993–97. 200 personnel 2003–present. 15,000 personnel

CENTRAL AFRICAN REPUBLIC, 1998–2000. 1,300 personnel

ETHIOPIA and ERITREA, 2000–present. 4,200 personnel

SIERRA LEONE, 1998–present. 17,500 personnel

DEMOCRATIC REPUBLIC OF THE CONGO, 1999–present. 10,800 personnel 1960–64. 20,000 personnel during Belgian withdrawal.

SOMALIA, 1992–95. 28,000 personnel

RWANDA, 1993–96. 5,500 personnel

ANGOLA, 1988–99. Four missions, 5,000 personnel

NAMIBIA, 1989–90. 8,000 personnel

MOZAMBIQUE, 1993–94. 6,625 personnel

N

0 400 800 Miles
0 400 800 Kilometers

(a)

(b)

FIGURE 5.36 UN peacekeeping in Africa (a) This map shows the dates and locations of UN peacekeeping missions in Sub-Saharan Africa. (b) Former UN Secretary-General Kofi Annan of Ghana. In October 2001, Kofi Annan and the United Nations were awarded the 2001 Nobel Peace Prize.

Within Africa, these generally gloomy average statistics do hide some regions with much better conditions. For example, the United Nations ranks Madagascar, South Africa, Swaziland, Botswana, Gabon, Ghana, Zimbabwe, and Lesotho higher on the Human Development Index (life expectancy, literacy, education, and GDP per capita) than other countries of Africa. Life expectancies in these countries are generally above 50, although many, including Botswana, Zimbabwe and South Africa, have dropped as a result of life expectancies shortened by HIV/AIDS. Levels of literacy, education, and income are also higher than the regional averages. These countries tend to have better provision of basic services. For example, in South Africa, Zimbabwe, and Botswana, 80 percent or more of the population has access to safe drinking water. In almost all countries life expectancy, incomes, and services are better in urban areas than in rural ones.

Generally, conditions have improved over the last 25 years. For example, from 1970 to 2000 life expectancy has increased from 45 to 49, and infant mortality has dropped from 138 to 89 deaths per 1000 children born. Literacy has shown dramatic changes, increasing from 38 percent in 1980 to 61 percent in 2000.

Improvements in conditions in specific countries are reflected in life expectancy and infant mortality changes. In Ghana, for example, life expectancy increased from 45 to 57 years and infant mortality decreased from 131 to 62 deaths per 1000 children. But war and AIDS have also affected Africa. For example, life expectancy in Botswana and Zambia started to drop in the 1990s as a result of AIDS and in Rwanda as a result of war and genocide. In 1998 AIDS was also mostly responsible for infant mortality increases in Botswana, Kenya, Zambia, and Zimbabwe.

The lowest 24 countries on the Human Development Index are all in Africa. Sierra Leone, for example, has a life expectancy of only 41 years and an annual GDP per capita averaging $149, mainly as a result of the loss of life and economic collapse associated with civil war. Low levels of life expectancy reflect some of the deficiencies in service provision in Africa, where an average of 42 percent of the population lack access to safe drinking water and 52 percent lack sanitation. Two-thirds of the population lacks safe drinking water in Ethiopia, Angola, Democratic Republic of the Congo, and Sierra Leone.

Economic and social conditions show great geographical and social variation within African countries. People in the core locations—urban areas, the formal sector, and producers of cash crops—generally have longer life expectancies, better service access, and higher incomes than those in the periphery, which includes rural areas and the informal and subsistence agricultural sectors.

Income concentration is high in many parts of Sub-Saharan Africa, with the richest 20 percent of the population receiving more than 60 percent of overall income in most of southern Africa, the Central African Republic, and Sierra Leone. More than 50 percent of the population earns less than $1 a day in most of West Africa, except Côte d'Ivoire.

Women and Development

Women in Africa tend to have less education and lower incomes than men, but in most countries they live slightly longer. The average female annual income is about $1000 less than for men, and literacy rates are 56 percent for women compared to 71 percent for men. Gender differences in Africa demonstrate the process of the **feminization of poverty**, whereby more than two-thirds of all people who join the ranks of the poor are women. African women are more likely to be poor, malnourished, and otherwise disadvantaged because of inequalities within the household, the community, and the country. Women are less likely to receive an education, and overall pay rates are lower in the workplace. Patriarchy and cultural traditions mean that women may be required to eat less than men and only after the men in the family have eaten, and women bear disproportionate responsibility for heavy household work such as collecting fuel wood and water (**Figure 5.37a**). The tradition of female circumcision has become a controversial struggle between those who see it as a human rights abuse involving brutal genital mutilation and health risks and others who see it as an important religious and symbolic experience. More than 100 million women in Africa are estimated to have undergone the ritual.

Women are also disadvantaged by many traditional and modern institutions that define property rights. Land may be passed on only to male children, and new land titles are often granted to male household heads. Development policies for agricultural training and technology to make work easier have been directed at men, and new projects for tree planting or cash crops often focus on men. Although some African governments and development agencies have recognized these disparities and established programs meant to improve conditions for women, poverty reduction among women has been patchy and partial.

There are places in Africa where significant numbers of women are seen as powerful, especially in urban areas where female entrepreneurs have been successful (**Figure 5.37b**). The best-known examples are the women who control the markets in Ghana and the women who control the cloth trade in Togo—women who are called the Mama Benz because of the expensive cars they own.

An early call for more attention to the role of women in Africa was that of economist Esther Boserup, whose 1970 book *Women's Role in Economic Development* documented the importance of women as farmers and resource managers in Africa. Geographers, among others, subsequently documented the work of African women in meeting the basic needs of families through preparing food and collecting wood and water, as income generators in crafts and community work, and as agricultural producers in both subsistence and commercial sectors. They also showed distinctly gendered spaces in the African landscape, with parts of the home, the market, and certain trees and crops reserved primarily for women's lives and work. A 1996 study by the United

FIGURE 5.37 Women's work in Africa (a) This graphic from the United Nations Food and Agricultural Organization shows the typically large burden of work carried by many African women. (b) Market women sell batik cloth in Bamako, Mali. (c) Ethiopian women carry heavy loads of firewood. (d) Woman drawing water from a well in Senegal. (*Source:* (a) "One Woman's Day in Sierra Leone," Food and Agricultural Organization of the United Nations, 1997. Available at http://www.fao.org/NEWS/FACTFILE/FF9719-E.HTM.)

One woman's day in Sierra Leone

21:00 to 23:00 converse around fire while shelling seeds and making fishnets

20:00 to 21:00 clean dishes, clean children

18:00 to 20:00 process and prepare food, cook dinner

17:00 to 18:00 fish in local pond

15:00 to 17:00 work in the gardens

14:00 to 15:00 wash clothes, carry water, clean and smoke fish

12:00 to 14:00 process and prepare food, cook lunch, wash dishes

11:00 to 12:00 collect berries, leaves and bark, carry water

8:00 to 11:00 work in the rice fields with four-year-old son and baby on back

6:00 to 8:00 light fire, heat washing water, cook breakfast, clean dishes, sweep compound

4:00 to 5:30 fish in local pond

(a)

(b)

(c)

(d)

Nations Food and Agriculture Organization (FAO) found that women's contribution to the production of food crops ranges from 30 percent in Sudan to 80 percent in the Republic of the Congo and that women in Sub-Saharan Africa are responsible for 70 percent of overall food production, 100 percent of food processing, 50 percent of animal husbandry, and 60 percent of agricultural marketing (**Figure 5.37c** and **Figure 5.37d**).

Those who understood the role of women's work in African communities and economies criticized development policies that ignored, undervalued, or displaced women. They also showed how women were often disproportionately affected by environmental degradation, as deforestation and drought made more difficult the work of collecting wood, water, and food.

Development policies gradually began to incorporate these ideas. The "Women in Development" (WID) approach focused on women's productive roles with projects that provided technology, credit, and training to women. This approach was in turn criticized for ignoring women's reproductive roles and the larger social processes such as discriminatory land-tenure policies that shape women's lives. In the 1980s the **gender and development (GAD)** approach was promoted as better linking women's productive and reproductive roles and trying to understand the gender-related differences and barriers to better lives of both men and women. Development agencies such as the World Bank incorporated elements of both approaches into programs that supported education, credit, and land-titling programs for women, women's organizations, and recognition of women's work.

Other Development Strategies

Africa provides an arena for struggles over development and the case studies for some of the best-known failures and successes of development. As discussed earlier, Sub-Saharan Africa was a focus of modernization in the pre- and post-independence periods, with many development projects that sought to transfer modern technology into Africa, including large dams and Green Revolution technologies. African countries such as Nigeria and Zambia then sought to reduce their dependency on expensive imports by seeking to develop national manufacturing industries and protectionist policies. In the most recent era of development thinking, Africa has shifted to the more neoliberal policies of free trade and demand for economic restructuring coming from international agencies and financial and trading partners such as the United States.

Microfinance   Another trend in development thinking in Africa is the promotion of **microfinance programs**, which provide credit and savings to the self-employed poor, including those in the informal sector, who cannot borrow money from commercial banks. Based on the demonstrated success of the Grameen Bank program in Bangladesh (see Chapter 10, p. 506), which provided small loans to thousands, African microfinance projects offer loans and secure savings opportunities to people who want to start or expand their businesses. Examples include loans to purchase sewing machines, food-processing equipment, agricultural supplies, and shop inventories.

Governments and development agencies have also realized that development requires more than purely financial capital. Projects seem to be most successful in communities that have high levels of **social capital**—networks and relationships that encourage trust, reciprocity, and cooperation that share and expand on initial investments.

Indigenous Technology   Another shift in development thinking has been the increasing appreciation of indigenous technology, especially in agriculture. Researchers such as Paul Richards and Robert Chambers documented how colonial administrators and development institutions systematically devalued local knowledge, substituting imported European ideas about the appropriate management of soil and forests. Case studies showed how substituting new single-crop permanent systems for traditional shifting, multiple cropping resulted in increases in soil erosion, pest damage, and nutrient losses. These criticisms also emerged in attempts to transfer the Green Revolution packages of improved seeds, irrigation systems, and agricultural chemicals to Sub-Saharan Africa. Many farmers could not afford the new technologies, or they wished to grow basic crops such as millet, yams, and sorghum for which improved varieties had not yet been developed. However, others, in Zimbabwe for example, were able to increase their yields of maize and to benefit from the new technologies.

New approaches to agricultural development take more account of local expertise, asking farmers how they cope with climate variability and soil management. Local knowledge has also been valued in health programs where indigenous healers can make important contributions to the treatment of disease.

Sustainable Development and African Agriculture   Sustainable development (see Chapter 1, p. 47) is a priority for Africa, because past development projects have caused serious environmental problems and because so many people depend directly on renewable resources, especially the productivity of agriculture, and on safe water supplies. The definition of sustainable development in Africa has ranged from narrow criteria of either development that does not damage the environment for future generations or development that is economically efficient to broader conceptions of development that is equitable and ecologically beneficial.

The challenges of agricultural development are a theme across all of Sub-Saharan Africa, where most people still work in agriculture, thereby providing the foundation of food supplies and export earnings. Agriculture employs about 62 percent of the labor force in Africa and produces more than 40 percent of the regional GDP and up to 95 percent of the export revenue in some countries. Per capita agricultural production has fallen in the last 20 years because growth in agricultural production has not kept up with the growth in population and increased demand from urban populations. Of even greater concern is the fact that the benefits of agricultural progress have not raised the incomes or improved the nutrition of many of Africa's residents. Many regions have become dependent on food aid, and exports have declined relative to imports.

Blame for agricultural problems in Sub-Saharan Africa has been attributed to environmental degradation, lack of infrastructure, government policy, and international market structures. Region-wide challenges, identified by geographer Godson Obia, include improving infrastructure for roads and storage and providing adequate incentives and rewards to local producers. Difficulties of getting crops to the market on Africa's dirt roads and tracks, especially in the rainy season, mean that farmers risk having to store grain and other products in granaries that are vulnerable to pests and molds.

Governments have controlled food prices to keep down wages and unrest in urban areas, and this has reduced the prices paid to farmers. In Zimbabwe, maize (corn) prices paid to black farmers were suppressed in order to benefit the mostly white commercial maize producers, and farmers were also banned from planting crops in wetland areas. When these restrictions were removed, maize production in Zimbabwe soared to levels that allowed export to neighboring Mozambique.

The marketing boards established by colonial powers have smoothed out price fluctuations, but they have also kept the profits when world prices are good. International market volatility and a lack of information have made it difficult for farmers to move into new types of crops, and the general decline in the price of agricultural products in comparison to needed imports has also made it difficult to make a living in agriculture.

Parts of Kenya have seen increases in agricultural production and reductions in soil erosion that contradict the often-gloomy picture of African agriculture (see Signature Region: Nairobi and the East African Highlands, p. 262). One often-overlooked success story is urban agriculture in Africa. In cities such as Nairobi (Kenya), Lusaka (Zambia), Kano (Nigeria), and Kinshasa (Zaire), more than half of the residents cultivate gardens, either at their homes or on unused land in the city (**Figure 5.38**). Kinshasa has been described as a giant garden plot, with crops growing at every roadside, on traffic islands, and on the airport perimeter. Crops from these urban plots contribute to urban food security and incomes.

FIGURE 5.38 Urban agriculture in Africa Urban agriculture along roadsides contributes to food security for residents of cities such as Kampala, Uganda, shown here.

The Millennium Development Goals and Africa African development is increasingly driven by a new set of eight targets established by the United Nations called the **Millennium Development Goals (MDGs)**, which aim to eradicate extreme poverty and hunger; achieve universal primary education; promote gender equality and empower women; reduce child mortality; improve maternal health; combat HIV/AIDS, malaria, and other diseases; ensure environmental sustainability; and develop a global partnership for development (**Table 5.1**). Sub-Saharan Africa is in crisis, with continuing food insecurity, a rise of extreme poverty, stunningly high child and maternal mortality, large numbers of people living in slums, and a widespread shortfall for most of the MDGs. Some of the MDG indicators have shown progress since 1990. There have been slight improvements in food availability and women's employment and significant improvements in children's schooling, literacy, infant mortality, clean drinking water, national debt, and access to technology. But indicators have become worse for poverty, infectious diseases, forest cover, and slum dwellers, and almost all indicators for Sub-Saharan Africa are a long way from the 2015 targets. Millennium Villages have been established to end extreme poverty by working with the poor, village by village throughout Africa, providing affordable and science-based solutions to help people out of extreme poverty.

Regional Development

Southern Africa One of Southern Africa's problems is the lack of trade flows between countries of the region. The presence of economic powerhouse South Africa has provided an opportunity to improve regional links and development within Southern Africa. The Southern African Development Community (SADC) consists of Angola, Botswana, the Democratic Republic of Congo, Lesotho, Madagascar (membership pending), Malawi, Mauritius, Mozambique, Namibia, Seychelles, South Africa, Swaziland, Tanzania, Zambia, and Zimbabwe. In March 2004, a strategic plan was set for economic integration of the region with outlined measures, such as the creation of a SADC regional development fund and self-financing mechanism by 2005 and of a free trade area by 2008; establishment of a SADC customs union and implementation of a common external tariff by 2010; establishment of a SADC central bank and preparation for a single SADC currency by 2016; and a common market pact by 2012. The combined GDP for Southern Africa in 2004 was $296 billion. South Africa is the region's most developed economy, contributing a GDP in 2004 of $213 billion, which is more than double the combined GDP of the other Southern African countries.

South Africa produces more than one-third of the continent's manufactured goods with the highest overall gross domestic product (GDP). The historical core of southern Africa's economy is the region around the city of Johannesburg now called Gauteng. The region contains large reserves of uranium, platinum, tin, and nickel, as well as diamonds and coal. Manufacturing in the Gauteng region makes up half of South Africa's industry and includes iron and steel (using coal from the local area and iron from northeast and central South Africa) and textiles. Since the 1990s informal occupations of taxi driving, haircutting, small-scale manufacturing, urban farming, and street selling have boomed, and it has been estimated that more than 1.2 million people in Gauteng province are now active in the informal sector. The causes of this boom include unemployment, reduced regulation, and an increase in contracting work, such as sewing and childcare, to women working in their homes.

Development challenges for the Southern African region as a whole have been identified as post-war disarmament and reconstruction (in Angola and the Democratic Republic of the Congo), and continuing internal strife (in Zimbabwe), which have already adversely affected economic performance in these states. Peace agreements in Angola and the Democratic Republic of the Congo have led to GDP growth. In 2004 Angola had a GDP of $20 billion, the second greatest GDP (after South Africa) in the region and the highest real GDP growth rate of 12 percent. On January 1, 2004, Angola became the 37th country in Sub-Saharan Africa to become eligible for tariff preferences under the Africa Growth and Opportunity Act (AGOA) for its continued

TABLE 5.1 Millennium Development Goals

	Target	Sub-Saharan Africa 1990	Sub-Saharan Africa 2001/04
1. Eradicate extreme poverty and hunger	Halve, between 1990 and 2015, the proportion of people whose income is less than $1 a day		
	Proportion of people living on less than $1 a day, %	44.6	46.4
	Halve, between 1990 and 2015, the proportion of people who suffer from hunger		
	Proportion of people living with insufficient food, %	36	33
2. Achieve universal primary education	Ensure that, by 2015, children everywhere, boys and girls alike, will be able to complete a full course of primary schooling		
	Net enrollment ratio in primary education	53	64.2
	Literacy rate of 15–24-year-olds, %	67.4	73.1
3. Promote gender equality and empower women	Eliminate gender disparity in primary and secondary education, preferably by 2005, and in all levels of education no later than 2015		
	Girls' primary school enrollment ratios in relation to boys' (Girls per 100 boys)	76	85
	Women in wage employment in the non-agricultural sector	32.4	35
4. Reduce child mortality	Reduce by two thirds, between 1990 and 2015, the under-five mortality rate		
	Under-five mortality rate per 1,000 live births, %	185	168
	Infant mortality rate, %	111	100
5. Improve maternal health	Reduce by three quarters, between 1990 and 2015, the maternal mortality ratio		
	Maternal mortality ratios per 100,000 live births 2000		920
	Proportion of births attended by skilled health personnel	42	46
6. Combat HIV/AIDS, malaria, and other diseases	Have halted by 2015 and begun to reverse the spread of HIV/AIDS		
	HIV prevalence in adults aged 15–49, %	3	7.3 (2001) 5.8 (2004)
	Have halted by 2015 and begun to reverse the incidence of malaria and other major diseases		
	Number of new tuberculosis cases per 100,000 population (excluding people who are HIV-positive)	148	281
7. Ensure environmental sustainability	Integrate the principles of sustainable development into country policies and programs and reverse the loss of environmental resources		
	Proportion of land area covered by forests, %	29.2	26.5
	Halve, by 2015, the proportion of people without sustainable access to safe drinking water and basic sanitation		
	Proportion of population using improved sources of drinking water, %	49	56
	By 2020, to have achieved a significant improvement in the lives of at least 100 million slum dwellers		
	Number of urban dwellers living in slums (millions)	101	166
8. Develop a global partnership for development	Address the special needs of the least developed countries, landlocked countries, and small island developing states		
	Develop further an open, rule-based, predictable, non-discriminatory trading and financial system		
	Deal comprehensively with developing countries' debt		
	Debt service as a percentage of exports of goods and services	11.5	5.8
	In cooperation with developing countries, develop and implement strategies for decent and productive work for youth		
	Youth unemployment rates, %	18	18.3
	In cooperation with the private sector, make available the benefits of new technologies, especially information and communications		
	Telephone lines and cellular subscribers per 100 people	1	8.2

Nairobi and the East African Highlands

Less than 20 minutes after leaving the international airport outside Nairobi, a visitor can be watching leopards hunting zebra across the grasslands in a national park while the high-rise buildings of downtown Nairobi glimmer on the horizon. Driving into the city, glimpses of former colonial mansions and luxury hotels surrounded by flowers shift rapidly to views across valleys crowded with slum housing and of a city center where business and government leaders drive luxury cars through streets crowded with traders, pickpockets, street children, and tourists (**Figure 1**).

Nairobi is the commercial and communications center of East Africa. The city of 2 million is at an altitude of 1800 meters (5900 feet) on the high plateau adjacent to Mount Kenya and the East African Rift Valley. Originally established at a railroad stop where there was a spring and low incidence of malaria, Nairobi became the center of British colonial rule and white settlement in

East Africa. The temperate highlands and rich soils north of Nairobi were assigned to European farmers who raised wheat, vegetables, and fruit and developed extensive plantations of tea and coffee for export. Cattle, sisal (a fiber), and food crops were also produced on white-owned estates in the Rift Valley to the west. While the lives of colonial settlers have been romanticized by films and books such as *Out of Africa*, their paternalistic treatment of black Africans and the eviction of people from their traditional lands eventually led to rebellions and then independence in 1963.

Nairobi's population and manufacturing sector is smaller than that of other major African cities, such as Lagos, but it is a service center with headquarters of international companies, agencies, and nongovernmental organizations, including the United Nations Environment Programme (UNEP). Manufacturing includes an automobile plant and textile, canning, and small

FIGURE 1 The squatter settlement of Mathare Valley in Nairobi and the skyline of downtown Nairobi, including the distinctive tower of the Kenyatta Conference Center.

FIGURE 2 Women from Kenya's Green Belt Movement meet to discuss tree planting.

progress toward a market-based economy, the rule of law, free trade, economic politics that will reduce poverty, and protection of workers' rights.

Zimbabwe has experienced a deteriorating economy, with real GDP contracting by about 30 percent in the last five years and inflation reaching 600 percent in 2003, before dropping to 124 percent in 2005. Many of the problems in Zimbabwe stem from conflicts about land tenure. The allocation of land is very skewed in many African countries, with a few people owning large areas of better land.

At independence in 1980, President Robert Mugabe of Zimbabwe promised to redistribute land owned by more than 5000 farmers, a large number of whom were white (**Figure 5.39**). According to government figures in 2000, some 4400 whites owned 32 percent of Zimbabwe's agricultural land—around 10 million hectares (almost 25 million acres)—while about 1 million black peasant families farmed 16 million hectares (almost 40 million acres) in plots mostly less than one hectare. Although title to the lands was given to white settlers by the colonial governments, many black Africans believe that these lands were seized unfairly and should be returned to the indigenous owners. In 2000, Mugabe's threat to confiscate the land was accompanied by invasions

metal-goods factories, mainly to the east of the city. Most of the population works in manufacturing, construction, or services, and thousands of poorer residents work in the informal sector selling food, household goods, and crafts on the street or from small kiosks. The city lacks adequate public transportation and relies on the infamous private minibuses called *matutus*. Overloaded with passengers, they swerve along the streets and contribute to Kenya's high motor vehicle accident rate. Nairobi is also a tourist center, serving as the hub for numerous tours to see the wildlife, culture, and landscapes of Kenya and adjacent countries such as Tanzania.

As in many other African cities, poorer communities in and around Nairobi have limited access to electricity, gas, or petroleum fuels for heating and cooking and rely on wood or charcoal as their major energy source. The increasing wood and charcoal demands of Nairobi have had a tremendous impact on forests in the region, with serious deforestation tied to the city's energy needs occurring as far as 200 kilometers (124 miles) away. The difficulties of finding firewood and the increases in prices have disproportionately affected women, who traditionally collect the wood and are responsible for cooking and heating the homes. Projects to reduce energy demands by using scrap metal to make more efficient stoves have complemented the efforts of female-led nongovernmental organizations to protect trees in and around Nairobi. The best-known social movement is the Green Belt Movement, which counts 50,000 women as members. Led by Nobel Prize-winning environmental and political activist Wangari Maathai, Green Belt has planted thousands of trees around Nairobi and has been the model for similar groups elsewhere in Africa and the world (**Figure 2**).

The East African Highlands and the adjacent rift valley are important agricultural production zones, serving urban demand in Nairobi and exporting coffee, tea, and sisal. The most rapidly growing export sector is fresh vegetables and cut flowers for export to Europe. Relying on refrigerated air transport out of Nairobi airport, Kenya now provides 40 percent of the European Union imports of fresh vegetables, sending more than $100 million worth of vegetables and fruit to Britain in 2002 (**Figure 3**). The flower industry, centered on Lake Naivasha, sends more than 1 billion cut blooms to Europe each year, including carnations and roses, and is now the fourth largest flower producer in the world, after the Netherlands, Colombia, and Israel. While these new industries provide employment and higher wages than some other sectors, the strict quality standards, perishability, and need for air transport mean that small producers find it difficult to compete. There are also concerns about pesticide risks to workers in the growing and packing sectors. This has led to a growing fair trade movement in which producers are paid a reasonable wage, and crops are produced more sustainably, including flowers, coffee, and crafts.

FIGURE 3 Sorting green beans for export in Nairobi, Kenya.

of squatters onto more than 500 farms and by international and internal attempts to resolve the conflicts by compensation for land that is transferred. Critics of Mugabe argue that previous land redistribution failed because peasant farmers did not have the knowledge or resources to succeed in commercial and export-oriented farming and that many farm workers are at risk of losing their jobs. But resentment at colonial land expropriation and racially based land policies is widespread, and several other African governments supported Mugabe's policies.

New post-apartheid governments in South Africa have faced similar challenges in deciding how to provide better land to black peasant farmers without provoking serious conflicts with long-standing white landholders. More than 50,000 households have acquired land through government subsidies in South Africa, in some cases through buying shares in farms where they were formerly workers.

West Africa The West African coast, with its warm, humid climate, lush forests, and abundant mineral resources, has been a center of traditional leadership, culture, trade, and population for centuries. The focus of the early slave trade and then

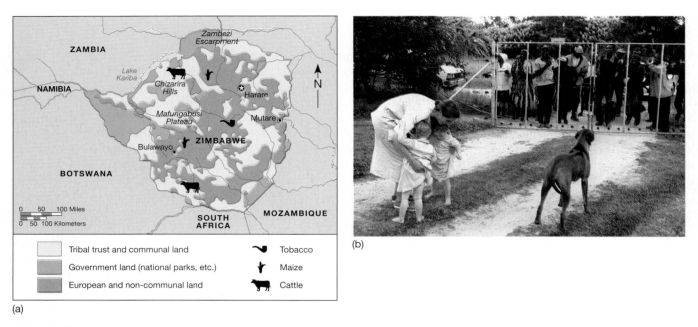

FIGURE 5.39 Land conflicts in Zimbabwe (a) In Zimbabwe, white farmers retained the better cropland after independence, growing tobacco and other cash crops. Most of the crop area highlighted in yellow was in white ownership. (b) Expectations were high for land reform under black majority rule, and squatters have invaded white farms, in some cases with the tacit support of the government. (*Source:* [a] Map from **http://europe.cnn.com/interactive/world/0008/farm.map/land.html**.)

of British and French colonialism, the West African coast is one of the most densely populated regions of Sub-Saharan Africa. The Europeans sited some of their trading ports and settlements near locations of earlier cities and took advantage of existing social and political hierarchies to obtain slaves and gold, and subsequently taxes and export crops, from the region.

Oil in Nigeria   The landscape of the West African coast was massively transformed by plantation agriculture in the 19th and early 20th centuries, with thousands of hectares of land converted from indigenous cropland and forest into cocoa, oil-palm, and rubber trees for export. Mining and energy development have also dominated the economy. In the 1960s the Niger delta became the core of an oil-producing region that triggered the secessionist Biafra war (the Ibo seceded from the mostly Yoruba Nigerian government) and promised an economic boom for Nigeria. As Nigeria has become even more dependent on oil exports, which are more than 90 percent of all exports by value, political unrest has continued in the oil region. While some unrest still arises from ethnic conflict between Ibo and Yoruba and from resentment that oil wealth is not benefiting the residents of the oil region, the most recent tensions relate to environmental pollution of the lands and waters of the delta (**Figure 5.40a**). The Nigerian government's hanging of Ken Saro-Iwa—a novelist and activist who protested oil spills in the area occupied by 500,000 Ogoni people—for his alleged role in political unrest in 1995 provoked international outrage and sanctions against the government (**Figure 5.40b**).

Although in the 1990s Nigeria experienced military coups, corruption and brutal repression, civilian rule and democratic elections have brought modest improvements since 1999. Crime is still a serious problem, including international Internet and phone scams. Ethnic tensions are still widespread in the Delta and between the Islamic north and Christian south. Nigeria's media is the most vibrant in Africa with dozens of radio and TV stations, and the emergence of the internationally popular "Nollywood" film industry based in the cities of Lagos and Abuja.

(a)

(b)

(c)

FIGURE 5.40 Nigeria (a) An oil fire near Lagos killed 60 poor fishermen in 2000. (b) Activist Ken Saro-Iwa, hanged for his opposition to oil development in eastern Nigeria. (c) Women workers in Accra, Ghana, process U.S. health insurance data.

Ghana Ghana is often promoted as a model for political stability and economic development in the West African region, with per capita economic productivity double that of the other countries in the subregion and open and democratic elections. The economy is based on exports of cocoa, timber, and gold, and an English-speaking, educated urban workforce that is beginning to participate in information technology activities. These include entering health insurance claims for the United States and operating call centers for international telecommunications companies (**Figure 5.40c**).

SUMMARY AND CONCLUSIONS

The future of Sub-Saharan Africa is difficult to forecast because there are both positive and negative signs throughout the region. While some countries have improved living standards, established democratic governments, and increased food and economic production, others are mired in conflict over resources and political futures or face forbidding health challenges of malaria and AIDS. Social inequalities persist in many regions and contribute to migration, unrest, and famines. Although some Africans maintain rural subsistence lives, almost totally disconnected from the world economy, others are working in transnational corporations or are producing new exports for the global market.

The region is still adjusting to the enduring legacies of colonialism that include economies dependent on mineral or agricultural exports, unequal land distribution, and boundaries that divide or cluster groups with little attention to cultural values or political expediency. Many countries are also struggling with the transition to independence and the creation of representative governments, with over-reliance on foreign assistance. Sub-Saharan Africa has many connections to other world regions and to global systems through trade, migration, and the diffusion of rich and varied cultures, yet it is often overlooked by the media and the core economies and portrayed only through negative images of poverty, war, and disease or as a vast nature reserve. Whatever the future may hold for Sub-Saharan Africa, it is a region that the rest of the world can ill afford to ignore.

KEY TERMS

apartheid (p. 237)
Berlin Conference (p. 234)
bush fallow (p. 221)
circular migration (p. 249)
desertification (p. 224)

domestication (p. 221)
feminization of poverty (p. 256)
G8 (p. 243)
gender and development
  (GAD) (p. 258)

harmattan (p. 216)
homelands (p. 238)
microfinance programs (p. 258)
Millennium Development
  Goals (MDGs) (p. 260)

savanna (p. 219)
shifting cultivation (p. 221)
slash and burn (p. 221)
social capital (p. 258)

REVIEW QUESTIONS

Testing Your Understanding

1. Why does Sub-Saharan Africa have such large regions of poor soils and hot, dry climates? Which regions have the more temperate climates and better conditions for agriculture, and why?

2. What major crops or animals were domesticated in Sub-Saharan Africa, and what are the traditional agricultural adaptations to low soil fertility and seasonal rainfall?

3. Where did modern humans originate? Prior to 1600, what were some of the major centers of African empires and trade within Africa?

4. Where did the Arabs, Portuguese, British, French, and Dutch begin their colonization and settlement of Sub-Saharan Africa? What was the role of slavery before and after European colonization? Who were some of the main European explorers and what image did they promote of the African interior?

5. How does Africa's dependency on mineral exports relate to the colonial period, the geographic pattern of roads and railways, and contemporary conflicts?

6. How do modernization theory, dependency theory, import substitution, and structural adjustment differ in their approaches to development, and what have been their positive and negative effects in Sub-Saharan Africa?

7. What hope do the following policies hold for the future in Sub-Saharan Africa: debt relief, women and development programs, microfinance programs, sustainable development, indigenous technology, social capital?

8. What factors may have led to continued political instability, warfare, and corruption in many Sub-Saharan African states? Which African countries are most seriously affected by conflict and to what extent does this explain their ranking on social indicators lists such as the Human Development Index? What role do organizations for regional cooperation and the United Nations play in the resolution or reduction of these conflicts?

9. Why has wildlife conservation become a priority in some regions of Sub-Saharan Africa and what strategies have been used to protect wildlife? Which countries opposed the ivory ban and why? What are the main causes of deforestation and associated wildlife depletion in Madagascar?

Thinking Geographically

1. What are the arguments for and against treating Sub-Saharan Africa as a major world region?

2. How does plate tectonics help explain the age, high elevation, and steep escarpments around much of Africa and the major feature of the East African Rift Valley? What are the

implications for human activities, including mining, settlement, river navigation, energy production, and freshwater fisheries?

3. Identify the major pests and diseases in Sub-Saharan Africa and their geographical distributions. How have they limited human activity? What has been done to reduce the spread and incidence of these pests and diseases?

4. How did Europe divide up Africa after the Berlin Conference? What were the legacies of this geographical division in terms of languages, boundaries, land tenure, and forms of rule? How did indigenous peoples respond to or resist European rule?

5. How do the following affect the geographical distribution of population in Sub-Saharan Africa and/or population growth rates: high infant mortality, high HIV/AIDS rates, education levels of women, coastal ports, highland areas, mineral deposits?

6. Using examples from at least two major urban areas in Africa, discuss what attracts people to these cities and some of the cities' social and environmental problems.

7. What are the major patterns of migration between and within African countries and how do they relate to employment opportunities, natural disasters, and warfare?

8. How do the cases of the West African Sahel and Machakos, Kenya, illustrate the debates about the causes of environmental change in Africa? For example, what arguments have been made about the role of human activity in causing desertification or soil erosion?

9. How is Sub-Saharan Africa progressing in achieving some of the targets set out in the UN's Millennium Development Goals?

FURTHER READING

Adams, W. M., Goudie, A. S., and Orme, A. R. (eds.), *The Physical Geography of Africa*. Oxford University Press, 1999.

Anderson, D., and Grove, R. H. (eds.), *Conservation in Africa: Peoples, Policies and Practice*. Cambridge: Cambridge University Press, 1990.

Aryeetey-Attoh, S. (ed.), *The Geography of Sub-Saharan Africa*, 2nd ed. Upper Saddle River, NJ: Prentice Hall, 2002.

Binns, T., *Tropical Africa*. London: Routledge, 1994.

Boserup, E., *Women's Role in Economic Development*. London: Allen & Unwin, 1970.

Chambers, R., *Rural Development: Putting the Last First*. New York: Longman, 1983.

Christopher, A. J., *The Atlas of Changing South Africa*. London: Routledge, 2000.

Gourevitch, P., *We Wish to Inform You That Tomorrow We Will Be Killed with Our Families: Stories from Rwanda*. New York: Farrar, Straus, and Giroux, 1998.

Griffiths, I. L. L., *An Atlas of African Affairs*, 2nd ed. New York: Routledge, 1994.

Grove, A. T., *The Changing Geography of Africa*. Oxford: Oxford University Press, 1994.

Jarosz, L., "Defining and Explaining Tropical Deforestation: Shifting Cultivation and Population Growth in Colonial Madagascar," *Economic Geography*, 64(1993): pp. 366–80.

Leach, M., and Mearns, R., *The Lie of the Land: Challenging Received Wisdom on the African Environment*. Portsmouth, NH: Heinemann, 1996.

Lewis, L. A., and Berry, L., *African Environments and Resources*. Boston: Allen and Unwin, 1988.

Mazrui, A. A., *The Africans: A Triple Heritage*. London: BBC Publications, 1986.

Mortimore, M., and Tiffen, M., "Population and Environment in Time Perspective: The Machakos Story," in T. Binns (ed.), *People and Environment in Africa* (pp. 69–89). New York: John Wiley & Sons, 1995.

Moseley, W. G., *Taking Sides: Clashing Views on Controversial African Issues*. New York: McGraw Hill, 2003.

Neumann, R. P., *Imposing Wilderness: Struggles over Livelihood and Nature Preservation in Africa*. Berkeley: University of California Press, 1998.

Oliver, R., and Crowder, M. (eds.), *The Cambridge Encyclopedia of Africa*. Cambridge: Cambridge University Press, 1981.

Peil, M., *Lagos: The City Is the People*. Boston: G. K. Hall, 1991.

Rain, D., *Eaters of the Dry Season: Circular Labor Migration in the West African Sahel*. Boulder: Westview Press, 1999.

Rakodi, C. (ed.), *The Urban Challenge in Africa: Growth and Management of Its Large Cities*. Tokyo: United Nations University Press, 1997.

Reader, J., *Africa: A Biography of the Continent*. London: Penguin, 1997.

Richards, P., *Indigenous Agricultural Revolution: Ecology and Food Production in West Africa*. Boulder: Westview Press, 1985.

Rodney, W., *How Europe Underdeveloped Africa*. Washington, DC: Howard University Press, 1974.

Simon, D., *Cities, Capital, and Development: African Cities in the World Economy*. New York: Halstead Press, 1992.

Stock, R. F., *Africa South of the Sahara: A Geographical Interpretation*. New York: Guilford Press, 2004.

Watts, M., *Silent Violence: Food, Famine, and Peasantry in Northern Nigeria*. Berkeley: University of California Press, 1983.

World Bank, *Intensifying Action Against HIV/AIDS in Africa: Responding to a Development Crisis, Africa Region*. Washington, DC: The World Bank, 2000.

FILM, MUSIC, AND POPULAR LITERATURE

Film

Chinua Achebe: A World of Ideas. Directed by Bill Moyers, 1989. An interview with the Nigerian author about African literature.

Cry Freedom. Directed by Richard Attenborough, 1987. A white South African journalist investigates the death of black activist Steve Biko during the era of apartheid.

Everyone's Child. Directed by Tsitsi Dangarembga, 1996. The tragic story of one Zimbabwean family devastated by AIDS.

From Sun Up. Directed by Flora M'mbubu, 1987. The dawn-to-dusk, life-sustaining efforts of the women of black Africa to survive and prosper.

Hotel Rwanda. Directed by Terry George, 2004. Based on the true story of the remarkable Paul Rusesabinga, a hotel manager who saved hundreds of lives in the midst of genocide.

Mama Africa: Growing up Urban. Various Directors, 2002. Films by and about women in Nigeria, Namibia, and South Africa.

Mister Johnson. Directed by Bruce Beresford, 1991. An educated black man tries to succeed in colonial Nigeria.

Mountains of the Moon. Directed by Bob Rafaelson, 1990. John Hanning Speke and Sir Richard Francis Burton's quest to find the source of the Nile River during the mid-19th century.

Out of Africa. Directed by Sydney Pollack, 1985. The life of Karen Blixen, who established a plantation in Kenya.

Tsotsi. Directed by Gavin Hood, 2005. Based on a novel by Athol Fugard, this award-winning film depicts the life of a young man in Johannesburg.

Yeelen. Directed by Souleymane Cissé, 1987. Adaptation of the great oral epic of the Bambara people of West Africa during the Mali Empire of the 13th century.

Music

Adé, King Sunny. *Juju Music.* Uni/Mango, 1982.

Cabo Verde. *Cesaria Evora.* RCA Victor, 1999.

Kuti, Fela. *Best of Fela Kuti.* Uni/MCA, 2000.

Ladysmith Black Mambazo. *Best of Ladysmith Black Mambazo.* Shanachie, 1992.

Makeba, Miriam. *Homeland.* Putumayo, 2000.

N'Dour, Youssou. *Immigres*. Earthworks, 1998.

Sangare, Oumou. *Moussoulou*. Wea/Atlantic, 1999.

Various Artists. *The Indestructible Beat of Soweto*. Shanachie, 1986.

Popular Literature

Achebe, Chinua. *Things Fall Apart*. Portsmouth, NH: Heinemann, 1996. Nigerian tribal life before and after the coming of colonialism.

Conde, Maryse. *Segu*. New York: Penguin USA, 1998. Epic story of 18th-century Bambara kingdom.

Emecheta, Buchi. *The Slave Girl: A Novel*. London: Allison and Busby, 1977. An Ibo woman writes of tribal life and those of African women.

Farah, Nurridin. *Maps*. New York: Penguin USA, 2000. The story of Askar, a man coming of age in the turmoil of modern Africa.

Gordimer, Nadine. *Burgher's Daughter*. New York: Viking, 1980. The impact of the South African political climate under apartheid.

Lessing, Doris. *Going Home*. New York: Harper, 1996. An account of a writer's return to her childhood home in what is now Zimbabwe.

Mandela, Nelson. *The Long Walk to Freedom*. Boston: Little, Brown, 1995. Autobiography of South Africa's first black president, who was imprisoned for 27 years by apartheid governments.

Matthiessen, Peter. *The Tree Where Man Was Born*. New York: Penguin USA, 1995. Vivid description of the East African landscape.

Ngugi, James. *Grain of Wheat*. London: Heinemann, 1967. A story about Kenya on the cusp of independence.

Paton, Alan. *Cry the Beloved Country*. New York: Milestone, 1959. Story of a Zulu pastor and his son during the apartheid era in South Africa.

Soyinka, Wole. *Ake: The Years of Childhood*. London: Rex Collings, 1981. Autobiography of the writer's childhood in Nigeria.

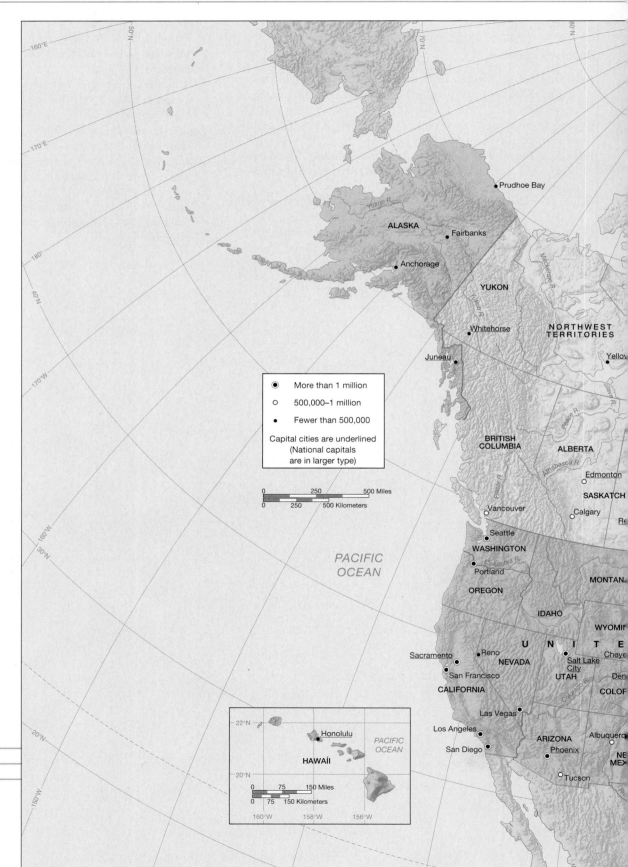

FIGURE 6.1

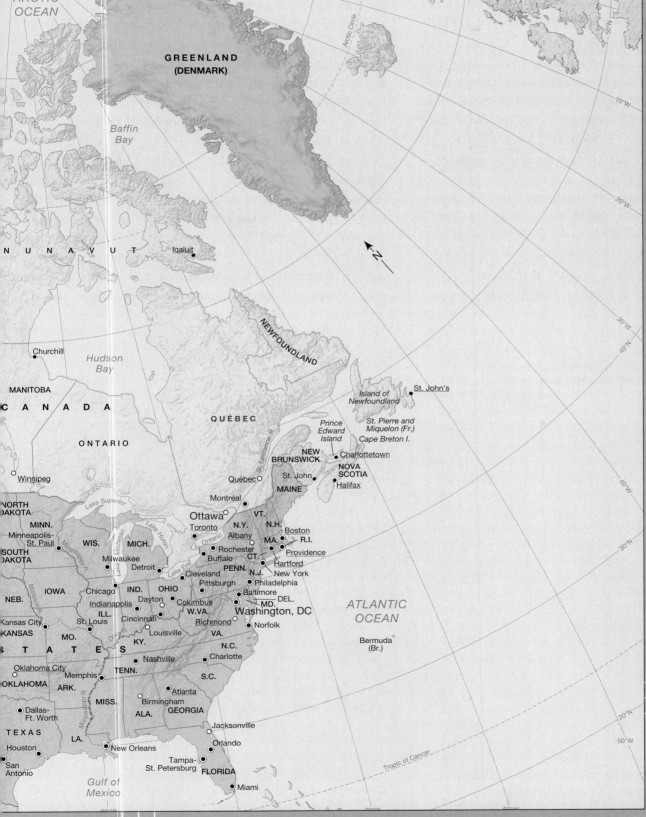

ARCTIC
OCEAN

GREENLAND
(DENMARK)

*Baffin
Bay*

N U N A V U T

• Iqaluit

NEWFOUNDLAND

Churchill •

*Hudson
Bay*

MANITOBA

C A N A D A

• St. John's

*Island of
Newfoundland*

QUÉBEC

St. Pierre and
Miquelon (Fr.)

ONTARIO

*Prince
Edward
Island*

Cape Breton I.

Winnipeg •

• Charlottetown

NEW
BRUNSWICK

NOVA
SCOTIA

St. Lawrence R.

NORTH
DAKOTA

Québec •

St. John •

• Halifax

MINN.

Montréal •

MAINE

Minneapolis-
St. Paul •

Ottawa

VT.

N.H.

SOUTH
DAKOTA

WIS.

MICH.

Toronto

Albany

• Boston

R.I.

Milwaukee •

Rochester

MA.

• Providence

Lake Superior

Lake Michigan

Lake Huron

Buffalo

CT.

Hartford

Detroit •

Lake Erie

PENN.

N.J.

New York

IOWA

Chicago •

IND.

OHIO

Cleveland •

Pittsburgh •

Philadelphia

NEB.

Indianapolis

Dayton

Columbus

Baltimore •

DEL.

MD.

Kansas City •

St. Louis •

ILL.

Cincinnati

W.VA.

Washington, DC

KANSAS

MO.

Louisville •

Richmond

S T A T E S

KY.

VA.

Norfolk

Nashville •

N.C.

*ATLANTIC
OCEAN*

Oklahoma City

Memphis •

TENN.

Charlotte •

Bermuda
(Br.)

OKLAHOMA

ARK.

S.C.

Dallas-
Ft. Worth •

MISS.

Birmingham •

Atlanta •

GEORGIA

Mississippi R.

ALA.

T E X A S

LA.

Jacksonville •

Houston •

New Orleans •

Orlando •

San
Antonio •

Tampa-
St. Petersburg •

FLORIDA

*Gulf of
Mexico*

• Miami

Tropic of Cancer

The United States and Canada constitute the predominantly English-speaking countries of the North American continent (**Figure 6.1**). The United States covers about 9,666,861 square kilometers (3,732,397 square miles), including 48 contiguous states and two noncontiguous states: Alaska (northwest of Canada) and the volcanic islands of Hawai'i, 3220 kilometers (2000 miles) southwest of the North American continent in the Pacific Ocean. Canada covers about 9,970,610 square kilometers (3,849,652 square miles), including 10 provinces and 3 territories, and is the world's second largest country after the Russian Federation. Most Canadians live in a 322-kilometer-wide (200-mile-wide) band along the 5635-kilometer (3500-mile) U.S.–Canadian border with significant population concentrations in large cities (**Figure 6.2**).

Canada stretches from 49° N latitude to a few degrees beyond the Arctic Circle (66.5° N), making it mostly a high-latitude, or "northern," country. The continental landmass of the United States (excluding Hawai'i and Alaska) is predominantly a midlatitude country that extends southward from Canada to the tip of Florida, a few degrees above the Tropic of Cancer (23.5° N). The two countries share many physical features of rugged mountains in the west; older, more eroded ones in the east; vast plains; and extensive coastlines on three oceans (the Atlantic, Pacific, and Arctic). Both are established democracies modeled on European political traditions. Both have significant populations of native peoples. Both consolidated their leadership roles in the world economy early in the 20th century. The United States and Canada are certainly integral to, if not the hub of, the contemporary world-system.

As with other New World lands, much of the recent history of these two countries is the result of European colonization. Because of this and their comparable economic status, academics as well as policymakers and government agencies treat the two countries as constituting a coherent region. But, as discussed in Chapter 1, we are in a period of dramatic and rapid change as the world's political borders are being dismantled or rearranged around the new economic relationships wrought by the accelerating globalization of capitalism. It is impossible to know what these new relationships will mean for the future of today's world

FIGURE 6.2 Population distribution of the United States and Canada The U.S. population is distributed thinly across the country, with the heaviest concentrations across the east and west coasts; the Canadian population has coastal clusters but only a thin band of settlement from east to west, hugging the U.S.–Canada border. (*Source:* Center for International Earth Science Information Network [CIESIN], Columbia University; International Food Policy Research Institute [IFPRI]; and World Resources Institute [WRI]. 2000. *Gridded Population of the World* [GPW], Version 2. Palisades, NY: CIESIN, Columbia University. Available at **http://sedac.ciesin.org/plue/gpw**.)

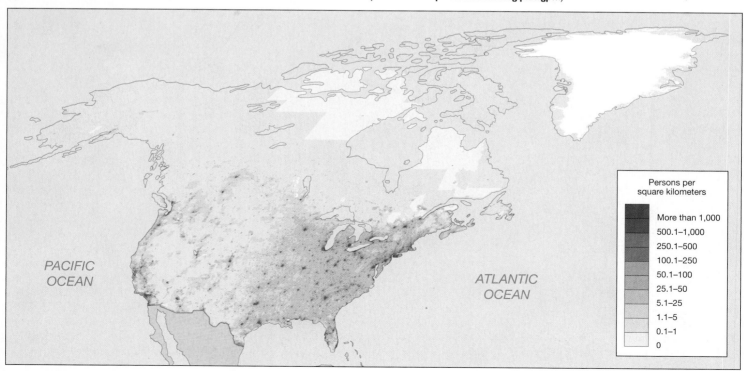

regions. For example, although the regionalization framework for this book locates Mexico with Latin America, despite the fact that it too occupies the North American continental landmass, it is not inconceivable that in 20 years or so, a new regionalization will combine Mexico (and possibly other countries in Central America) with the United States and Canada because of immigration, internal demographic changes, or the impact of economic alliances such as the North American Free Trade Agreement (NAFTA). For the present, however, the United States and Canada persist as a world region in the public imagination as well as in more formal political and economic frameworks.

ENVIRONMENT AND SOCIETY IN THE UNITED STATES AND CANADA

The United States and Canada possess a physical geography that contains a bounty of resources, from the whole range of minerals to vast forests; fertile, highly productive land; extensive fisheries; varied and abundant wildlife; and magnificent and unique physical beauty (**Figure 6.3**). Accompanying this extensive physical wealth has been the technological capability and the drive to exploit these resources to an extent achieved by few other regions on Earth. One result of this combination of physical resources and human ingenuity is a region that experiences an extraordinarily high quality of life. A second result is a high level of material consumption that results in a region with elevated levels of air and water pollution, numerous sites—often on the fringes of major urban settlements—of soil contamination, an ongoing problem of nuclear waste disposal, acid rain, extinct and endangered species, and increasingly frequent reports of insect and animal genetic mutations.

FIGURE 6.3 The United States and Canada from space This image shows a region surrounded by oceans, gulfs, and bays with vast interior plains and high mountains on the east and west coasts. The region also contains vast mineral wealth, extensive forests and supplies of clean water, and high agricultural productivity.

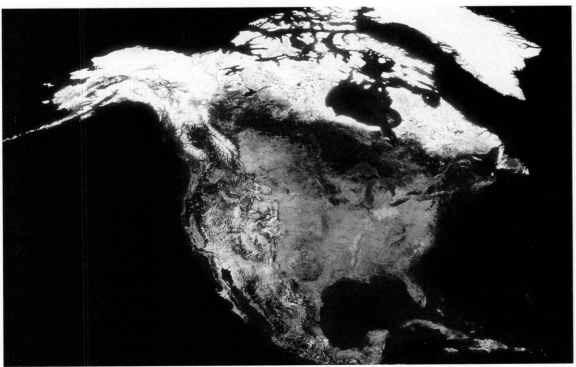

The physical geography of the region is the context for, and an inescapable reminder of, the enormous benefits and the sometimes devastating costs of the "American way of life." For instance, the Mississippi–Missouri river system is the most extensive and navigable river system in the world. This, along with the five Great Lakes (Superior, Michigan, Huron, Erie, and Ontario), undeniably enabled the early and formidable growth of the interior of the United States in ways that no railway system could have. However, the engineering that has been applied to the Mississippi–Missouri system (including its major tributaries) over a century or more has also irretrievably altered its ecosystem and exposed vast numbers of human settlements to extreme danger from flooding.

The impact of Hurricane Katrina on New Orleans in late August 2005 is a disturbing demonstration of the disastrous potential of riverine engineering. Built on the delta marshland of the Mississippi River, New Orleans has been a city of levees, floodwalls, and drainage canals since the 19th century, and nuisance flooding has been a perennial problem in the city. Hurricane Katrina was different, however, and far more destructive; high winds and rising water, combined with flawed levee design and lack of critical maintenance, caused widespread breaching or failure, subjecting 80 percent of the population to flooding. There were more than 1500 deaths related to the flooding. More than a million people were evacuated and tens of thousands have been rendered homeless. As of summer 2006, the levees have been restored but the possibilities for recovery and rebuilding are still unclear. Key social infrastructure is still not functioning at anything like pre-hurricane levels—including the public schools, hospitals, the fire and police departments, public housing, judicial system, and water system, among others—and the most severely devastated parts of the city are still not habitable and may never again be so. A recent U.S. census of the city found that its population has been reduced by 64 percent. One of Katrina's key lessons is that despite the awesome technological power that humans have developed, the physical environment remains a centrally significant factor in shaping lives and livelihoods in the region.

Landforms and Landscapes

As **Figure 6.4** shows, the United States and Canada are centered on a vast central lowland that includes the Canadian Shield, the Interior Lowlands, and the Great Plains. To the east of this central lowland are the Appalachian Mountains, which descend gradually to the Gulf-Atlantic Coastal Plain, which becomes more broad as one travels farther south and southwest. To the west of the central lowland are three distinct topographical regions. Moving from west to east are the mountains and valleys of the Pacific coastal ranges; then an **intermontane**—lying between mountains—set of basins, plateaus, and smaller ranges; and finally the great Rocky Mountain range, which rises steeply and imposingly at the western edge of the central lowland.

The western coastal formation sits along the fault line of two active crustal plates, the Pacific Plate and the Juan de Fuca Plate (see Figure 1.17, p. 21). Both plates are moving northward, rubbing against the more stationary North American Plate upon which the continental landmass sits. As a result of this friction, the coastal area from San Diego through British Columbia to Alaska is subject to frequent tremors. Extreme and devastating earthquakes have occurred in the past and are likely to occur again in the near future. The extraordinary views of the Pacific Ocean provided by the mountainous topography of the Pacific coastal region have attracted a great deal of home development on mountain slopes, and past earthquakes have destroyed many of these homes. The extensive rainfall in this area has also wreaked havoc, despite extraordinary feats of engineering that have placed multimillion-dollar homes on steep mountainsides. When the soil becomes saturated with rainwater, liquefaction occurs, and the soil literally moves in one massive slump, carrying very large structures along with it.

In the western United States, the intermontane basin and plateau formation between the Pacific coastal range and the Rockies includes four major physiographic provinces: the Columbia Plateau to the north, which begins at the headlands for the Columbia River; the Colorado Plateau in the south, which includes the erosional landscape of the Grand Canyon; in between, the Great Basin in Nevada and Utah, which includes extinct lakes as well as the Great Salt Lake; and the

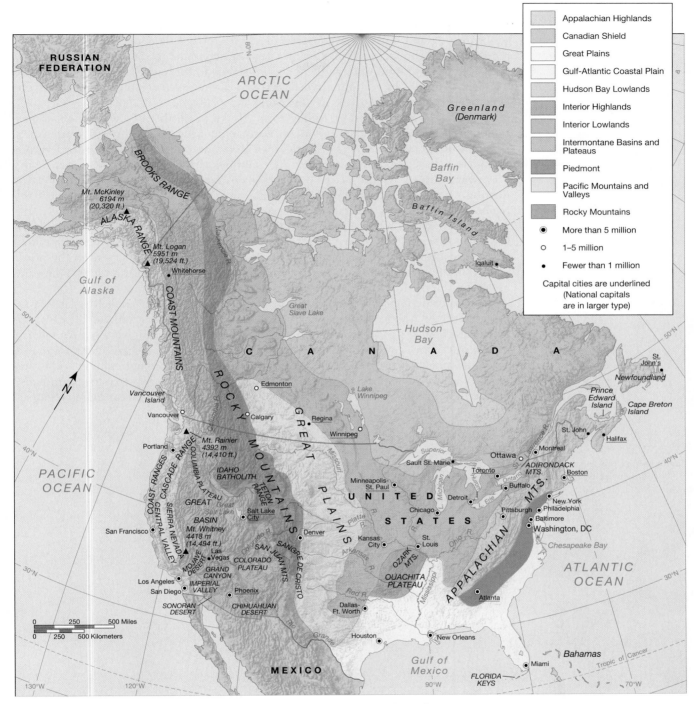

FIGURE 6.4 **Physiographic regions of the United States and Canada** The Interior Lowlands and Great Plains are central to agricultural production. The mountain ranges in the west are significantly higher and steeper due to their more recent emergence, while the Appalachian Mountains in the east are lower and more sloping due to their greater age and the effects of erosion. While the eastern coastal region slopes toward the sea, the West Coast is characterized by steep cliffs and fairly narrow beaches. Waves are also more dramatic in the west, as the steep land/sea interaction creates the conditions that push the advancing surf higher and steeper. The western seashore is more dangerous and prone to riptides and deadly undertows.

southwestern deserts (Mojave, Sonoran, and Chihuahuan). Its landscape has many contrasts, with spectacular scenery that includes deep canyons, majestic mountains, and unique deserts. It occupies an area of dry climates and thin vegetation and a general absence of many perennial surface streams. Wildfires, droughts, floods, and landslides are a continuing threat in the region. As geographer William Riebsame

Travis has demonstrated cartographically, fully one-half of this region is made up of federal land, one-quarter of which is national forest (**Figure 6.5**).

Ranching and mining have historically characterized the Great Basin region, but recreation and tourism now make up the leading economic sector. Copper mining and oil, gas, coal, and uranium mining are still primary-sector activities in this region (see Chapter 1, p. 00). In addition, hydroelectricity is generated for much of the western United States from many dams in this region.

The Rocky Mountains, extending from Alaska to northern New Mexico, constitute the eastern edge of the intermontane basin and plateau region. A significant aspect of both western and eastern North American mountain ranges is that their north–south orientation does not form a barrier to the southward flow of polar air masses or the northward flow of tropical ones. For places like Arizona and New Mexico, northward-flowing air masses bring summer monsoonal precipitation patterns that support the region's unique desert vegetation. The summer and winter rains there allowed the ancestors of contemporary Native Americans to cultivate beans, squash, and corn using sophisticated irrigation systems in a landscape that would otherwise seem inhospitable to subsistence agriculture. The absence of mountainous barriers to the north means that polar air sweeps down regularly in the winter months all the way into the midsection of the Interior Lowlands.

The lowland region that extends from the mouth of the Mackenzie River in Alaska to the Gulf of Mexico can, as mentioned earlier, be further subdivided into three provinces. The first of these is the Canadian Shield, a geologically very old region rich in minerals. The second is the Interior Lowlands, a glaciated landscape with fertile soils and abundant lakes and rivers. This region is devoted mostly to agriculture, with some industry as well. The third subdivision is the Great Plains, an area that slopes gradually upward as you move west toward the Rocky Mountains. The Great Plains region is

FIGURE 6.5 Public lands in the New West The largest landowner in the New West is the federal government. Much of the land in this region has been stewarded by the government for public use. Other lands have been leased to ranchers for grazing cattle. These two uses often pit environmentalists against ranchers over the best use of the land. (*Source:* W. Riebsame Travis, *Atlas of the New West.* New York: W.W. Norton, 1997, p. 58.)

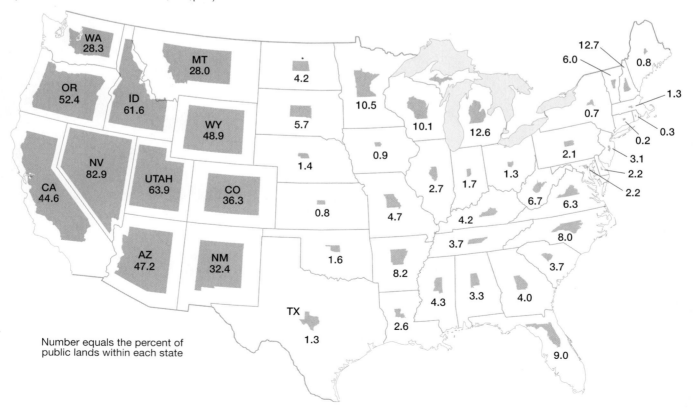

Number equals the percent of public lands within each state

also delimited by the fact that it experiences more rainfall than the regions surrounding it. This is an area of extensive gently rolling and flat terrain with excellent soils and some of the world's most productive farms. Beef, pork, corn, soybeans, and wheat are produced here.

The major landform feature of the eastern United States and Canada is the Appalachian mountain chain. Surrounding it in its eastern and southern flanks is a coastal plain that can be divided into two subregions, the Piedmont area of hills and easterly sloping land and the Gulf-Atlantic Coastal Plain, a lowland area that extends from New York to Texas. The coastal plains are generally level, with soils that are sandy and relatively infertile. Where agriculture does occur, it is intensive and scattered. For instance, the lower Mississippi is an area of good soils and intensive agriculture. The Piedmont is the historic region of plantation agriculture—cotton, tobacco, and corn—but much of the soil in this region is depleted or eroded from overfarming.

Climate

Because temperature, precipitation, and terrain patterns combine to influence vegetation, and to some extent soil, it is important to understand the role that climate plays in the subregions of North America. Temperatures range from those in the Arctic Circle in the north, where it is very cold for most of the year, to those where the United States extends close to the Tropic of Cancer in the south. Here, warmer, tropical temperatures are the norm. In short, the United States and Canada contain nearly every type of climate condition possible, with temperatures varying quite dramatically on any one day of the year from north to south. Of course, within-region differentials also occur due to the moderating influence of the oceans on three sides, the Gulf of Mexico, and the interior Great Lakes, as well as mountains and plateaus. Central United States and Canada experience the most dramatic temperature ranges, while the coasts have a far narrower range due to the influence of the oceans.

Variations in amounts of precipitation also have a profound effect on climate. While the east and west coastal areas tend to be mild and moderately wet, the interior is largely arid as the north–south mountain chains prevent moisture-bearing clouds from moving inland to drop their moisture. Because of this, a moisture gradient exists that declines slowly but continuously from east to west as far as the three significant mountain ranges—the Rockies, Sierra Nevadas, and Cascades (see Figure 6.4). Once beyond these mountains, the moisture gradient rises dramatically toward the Pacific.

In the southeastern part of the United States, where no significant coastal ranges exist, moisture-bearing clouds are able to more readily condense into rain. In the Arctic north, annual precipitation approximates desert conditions due to the dominance of very stable air masses with low moisture content. The jet stream (see Chapter 1, p. 24) brings precipitation to most of the continent in the winter months. While the warmer parts of the region—in the southern United States—experience this precipitation as rain, the colder, more northerly parts experience snow. In areas around the Great Lakes, the warming effects of these large bodies of water add even more moisture to the mix, bringing especially heavy snowstorms (called "lake-effect" snow) to places like Buffalo, New York, on the northeastern tip of Lake Erie, and Sault St. Marie, Ontario, on the channel between Lake Superior and Lake Huron.

As described in Chapter 1, climate is directly linked to vegetation and soil and the conditions for agriculture and forest growth. Overall conditions are very good for agriculture as one moves eastward until the precipitation gradient drops to a very low level just beyond the Interior Lowland and Great Plains regions. Beyond that point, soil fertility is low and rainfall is limited and infrequent. Conditions then become favorable again in the valleys along the Pacific Coast. Most of the agricultural productivity of the United States and Canada is concentrated in the Interior Lowland and Great Plains regions. Although natural conditions favor these subregions for the highest agricultural productivity, other parts of the region are also important agriculturally, largely because farmers there have overcome the natural barriers to production through fertilizers, irrigation, pesticides, and other technological applications. This is the case in the Pacific valley areas, for instance, where irrigation water drawn from the Colorado River enables agriculture to flourish, and in the Southwest, where intensive irrigation supports significant cotton and citrus production.

Environmental History

The Europeans who arrived on the Atlantic Coast of the United States and Canada beginning in the late 15th century encountered an environmentally diverse landscape thinly populated by native peoples. These were the peoples who first "discovered" the continent, having traveled as hunters and gatherers across the broad, low-lying belt of tundra known as the Bering Strait land bridge when sea levels dropped and exposed land. It is estimated that more than 30,000 years ago these peoples began the process of populating the continent and altering (and permanently changing) the environments they encountered. Despite what written accounts of initial contact between European explorers and native peoples record, Europeans did not discover a "pristine" or "virgin" land but one that had already been transformed by tens of thousands of years of human settlement.

Most archaeologists, anthropologists, historians, and geographers believe that during the last great ice age, the huge ice sheet that had once covered much of the continent gradually retreated. This enabled the first group of Arctic hunters to cross from Siberia into present-day Alaska, between 20,000 and 35,000 and possibly up to 60,000 years ago (**Figure 6.6**). They moved into the United States and Canada by traveling southward along the western edge of the continental icecap. Because Canada was probably entirely covered by ice during this period, it is likely that people settled the southern part of the continent. It is also likely that the Inuit, who currently live in Canada's Arctic region, were the last of the aboriginal people to arrive. These neolithic, or Stone Age, hunters probably originally came from northern China and Siberia. Descendants of these first hunters gradually moved farther and farther southward into the continental landmass, advancing eventually into Mexico.

Abundant evidence suggests that the ancestors of the neolithic hunters eventually spread throughout North America (as well as Central and South America) and adapted their ways of life to the particular conditions they encountered as they moved and settled. As they began to settle, different native groups introduced agriculture in different places. With game, fish, and wild and cultivated foodstuffs available, an economic system based on subsistence production and trade took form. The cultivation of maize spread to wherever it could be grown, and new wild foods, like potatoes and tomatoes, were eventually domesticated.

In New England, prior to European contact, hunting, gathering, and some shifting cultivation existed among the indigenous peoples. Hunter-gatherers were mobile, moving with the seasons to obtain fish, migrating birds, deer, and wild berries and plants. Shifting agriculture was organized around planting and harvesting corn, squash, beans, and tobacco. For both hunters and gatherers and shifting cultivators, a wide range of resources was identified and used. The economy was based on need. Need was met by planting or foraging or through barter (for example, trading corn for fish). Moreover, the prevailing practice was to take only what was needed to survive. In addition to native peoples having no concept of private property or land ownership, there is also no evidence that a profit motive existed before contact with Europeans. Land and resources were shared. Still, while New England native peoples did appear to live in something of a balance with the natural resources they exploited, substantial vegetation change occurred as a result of their settlement and hunting activities (often using fire), which resulted in some species depletion.

Geographer and environmental historian William Cronon has shown that Europeans saw the natural world they encountered in the United States and Canada much differently from how native peoples saw it. Most importantly, they viewed resources as commodities to be accumulated, not necessarily for personal use but to be sold for profit or export. The arrival of the Europeans meant that pressures on natural resources were hugely accelerated, especially for wood, furs, and minerals. In the Atlantic region, where European settlement first occurred, there was extreme

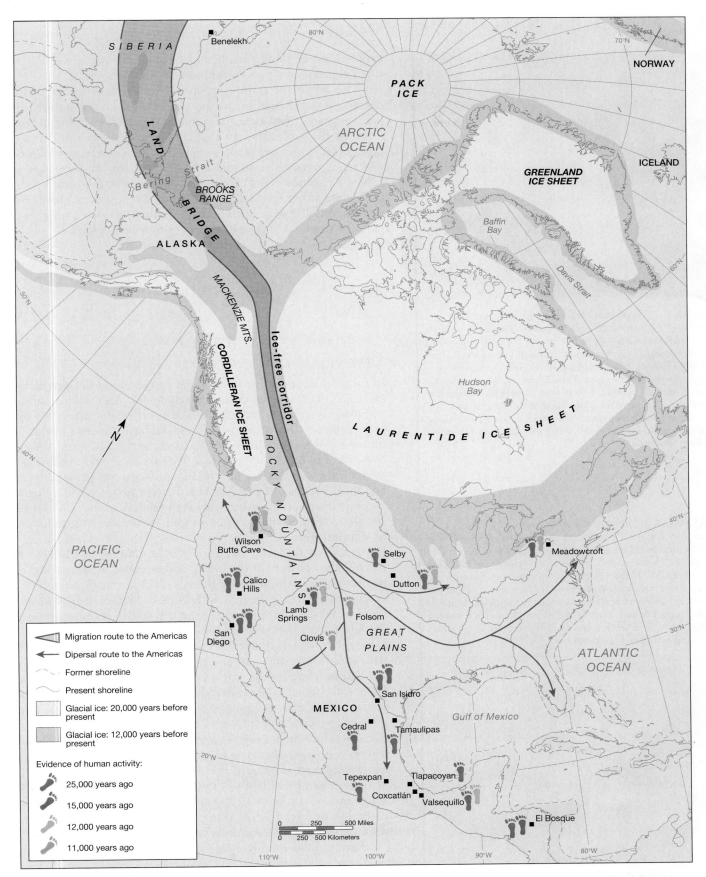

FIGURE 6.6 Migration of neolithic hunters into the Americas It is believed that the first humans to enter the North American continent by way of the Bering Strait land bridge, which had been exposed through the gradual retreat of ice sheets, were hunters pursuing large mammals and mastodons. When these animals grew scarce, the small bands of hunters moved on, looking for new prey. They also fed themselves with roots, plants, and berries and learned to fashion clothing, weave baskets, and construct fishing nets. Because of the limits of the environment, the bands tended to remain small, and as the population grew, small groups would break off and move on to increase their chances of survival in more plentiful surroundings as yet unoccupied or hunted. (*Source:* Redrawn and adapted from E. Homberger, *The Historical Atlas of North America*. London: Penguin, 1995, p. 21.)

exploitation of white pine, hemlock, yellow birch, beaver, and whales that led ultimately to deforestation and extinctions.

The arrival of Europeans in the region also meant a dramatic change in prevailing social understandings of the nature of land. Native perspectives about the communality and flexibility of land were replaced by European views of land as private and as having fixed boundaries. European settlers wanted to own and fence a plot of land, which led eventually to the concentration of land in large private farms, plantations, and haciendas. Increasingly, the native peoples of the United States and Canada were forced onto less productive land or reservations and were prohibited from hunting or gathering on private lands or from moving with seasons as they had before.

FIGURE 6.7 Norse settlement in L'Anse aux Meadows, Newfoundland The earliest contact between the old world and the new is likely to have been in the tenth century when seaborne Norse adventurers reached Greenland and ventured to the coast of North America, establishing themselves at L'Anse aux Meadows on the northern tip of the island of Newfoundland. This photo shows the remains of what are believed to be as many as three Norse settlements. According to available evidence, the Norse settlers and the Inuit at first fought each other, but then established a regular trading relationship. The Norse settlements were soon abandoned, probably as the Norse withdrew from Greenland.

FIGURE 6.8 Subsistence practices of U.S. and Canadian native peoples around 1600 This map, which shows the subsistence practices of indigenous peoples of the region at the point of European contact, testifies to the extensive spread of native population on the continent before the Europeans began to colonize. The geographic distribution of different tribes indicates their relationship to cultures and subsistence practices developed by the ancient people who preceded them. Compare this map to Figure 6.6 for an understanding of the long history of human occupation before the arrival of Europeans and their current settlement distribution.

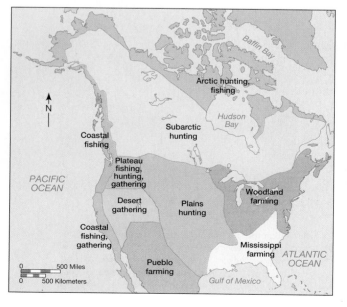

THE UNITED STATES AND CANADA IN THE WORLD-SYSTEM

The Region before the Europeans

In the 15th century European views of the world did not include the existence of the North American landmass. And while 16th-century Spanish missionaries and explorers identified the southernmost section of present-day United States and Mexico as of interest to their exploration and missionizing efforts, most of the rest of North America was considered to be of little consequence because it presented none of the appearances of grandeur and resource potential that the Aztec, Maya, and Inca empires of Latin America did (see Chapter 7 and **Figure 6.7**).

The distribution and subsistence practices of the native peoples of the United States and Canada around 1600 reflect the great diversity of cultural groups that occupied the continent (**Figure 6.8**). When Christopher Columbus arrived in the Caribbean, he assumed he had reached the Far East, or the Indies, and he called the aboriginal peoples he encountered *los indios*, or indians. And just as thousands of native languages existed at the time of European contact, there was no single word of self-description common to the diverse peoples who occupied the continent. As a result, the word *Indian* has endured as an extremely misleading and sometimes derogatory term for describing a wide range of regional cultural groups.

The estimates of the native population of the region at the point of European contact range widely, between 1 million and 18 million individuals. More than anything, the differing estimates indicate how little is known about the peoples who were thriving in the United States and Canada before the Europeans arrived. What is well known is that there was no common culture, particularly no common language, among the many who first populated the region. Native American scholar Jay Miller estimates that in 1492 the indigenous inhabitants of the United States and Canada spoke 2200 different languages, with many regional variations as well. Tribal culture and local environmental conditions were the frameworks within which daily life was governed and lived.

Europeans originally made contact with various individuals and tribes for help with extracting resources, including animal furs; naval stores, such as tar and turpentine for shipbuilding; fish; and other primary-sector products that would be exported back to the continent. The experiences of the Dutch, French, and English in North America also differed substantially from that of the Spanish in Latin America (Chapter 7). The Spanish conquistadors vanquished sophisticated civilizations in order to plunder their gold and silver treasuries and make themselves irresistibly rich in the process. While the Dutch, French, and English were also interested in improving their financial situations, they encountered a very different set of cultures with no centralized system of social control that they could exploit as the Spanish had done with the Aztecs in Mexico. Instead, the eastern tribes that Europeans first encountered in the United States and Canada were small, autonomous groups, possessing a lively sense of rivalry and competition with their neighbors. While the Spanish were interested in massive occupation and exploitation, the Dutch, French, and English considered exploration and colonization to be commercial ventures.

Colonization and Independence

No other landmass already occupied by a diverse range of complex and widely distributed societies, with the possible exception of Australia, has undergone such a dramatic transformation in such a short period of time. Moreover, lumping the settlers into one category of Europeans vastly simplifies the very complicated process of settlement that different peoples from different parts of Europe brought with them to the United States and Canada. So, while the occupation by missionaries and settlers who came to the region in the 16th and 17th centuries is widely known as the period of **europeanization,** the process was actually highly selective. Only a few western European countries—France, Spain, the Netherlands, and Great Britain—dominated colonization in the United States. In Canada, the European colonizers were predominantly Britain and France. In both Canada and the United States, Great Britain was by far the most influential of the four, though others did have substantial impacts, particularly the French in Canada and the Spanish in the United States.

Even within the four countries that dominated colonization, different groups from different regions settled in different parts of the United States and Canada. The unusual individuals and groups who assumed great risks in coming to the region represented only a small sample of their national cultures. As a result, the europeanization process, as it unfolded along the Atlantic seaboard of the United States and Canada, was accomplished through mixing a very wide range of native and imported traditions that eventually created distinct colonial cultures and societies in different places.

The process of European settlement routinely resulted in the overwhelming exploitation and abuse of the native peoples by colonists and later citizens. The history of colonial settlements, while at first peaceful, over time erupted into disputes over land claims that ended in violence and often outright massacres on both sides. After a time, moreover, not only were there conflicts between tribal people and colonists, but direct conflict emerged among the various European groups that vied for control over land. Additionally, colonists fanned the flames of rivalry between opposing tribal groups by providing them with arms, thus elevating the level of technology and intensifying the degree of violence in armed conflict. Finally, as has been widely documented, exposure to the Old World diseases that the colonists brought with them had a devastating impact on native populations (see Chapter 7, p. 344). As native populations were decimated, defeated, or demoralized and pushed farther into the interior of the continent, the various European groups increasingly came into direct conflict leading eventually to the Seven Years' War (1756–63), the U.S. phase of which is known as the French and Indian War (1754–63). This war left the British more or less triumphant over the whole of the European-inhabited territory of the United States and Canada.

In the following two decades, residents of the original 13 colonies of the United States became disillusioned with their administrators in Britain—who were taxing them to help recoup the high cost of the Seven Years' War—and launched their own war, leading to the creation of a new, independent nation in the late 18th century. In Canada, a bloodless separation from Great Britain would not occur until well into the 19th century.

Even before the American Revolution, however, a process of **americanization** had begun as a generation of individuals of European parentage born in the U.S. colonies felt less loyalty and fewer cultural ties to the mother country. As a result, a new ethos of liberalism, individualism, capitalism, and Protestantism emerged, gained currency, and ultimately came to define a U.S. national character. The successful outcome of the Revolutionary War with Britain (1775–83) left the continent with a robust new nation dominated by Anglo-American institutions and with the addition of slavery. Canada remained a colony, under British control, composed of both French- and English-speaking settlers.

The Legacy of Slavery in the United States

Although the impact of European colonization in the 16th and 17th centuries was felt all along the Atlantic seaboard of the United States and Canada, development of the U.S. South following the end of the revolutionary period differed dramatically from that of its northern neighbors. Before the arrival of the Europeans, the area that now forms the southeastern United States was inhabited by a wide range of native tribes, among them the Cherokee, Choctaw, Chickasaw, Creek, and Seminole peoples. Early on, the region was occupied by military personnel living in scattered outposts like Jamestown in Virginia. However, by the mid-17th century the military outposts had given way to tobacco farms (see Geographies of Indulgence, Desire, and Addiction: Tobacco, p. 284). At first, **indentured servants**—individuals bound by contract to the service of another for a specific term—from Britain were the primary source of labor on the tobacco and later indigo and cotton plantations. Increasingly, however, servants earned their freedom and were replaced by slaves from Africa, at the same time that disease, armed conflict, and demoralization reduced the native populations that would have been another source of laborers.

African slaves had been a well-established commercial staple of the Mediterranean well before the Spanish and Portuguese introduced them to their newly captured territories in Latin America and the Caribbean, thereby establishing the Atlantic slave trade. By the early 15th century, Dutch and English raiders attacking Spanish and Portuguese ships were able to take control of the slave trade. By the early 17th century, England became the dominant slaving nation. As a result, slaves were a part of the social and economic system of the American colonies beginning, practically simultaneously, with their founding. As an institution of formal social and economic organization, slavery endured in the South for more than 250 years, ending officially in 1870 following the end of the U.S. Civil War (1861–65). Its legacy, however, continues to shape the landscape and identity of the region.

FIGURE 6.9 Canadian settlement patterns In Québec the first settlers laid out long, narrow lots from the shores of the St. Lawrence River into the interior, as shown. As settlement moved farther inland, roads were built parallel to the waterways with narrow lots extended on either side. The pattern is duplicated in the Red River valley of Manitoba, where the early settlers were also French. In Ontario and the eastern townships of Québec, land subdivision was made according to preconceived plans. Although the townships were more or less square, the grid became irregular because it was started from a number of different points, each of which used a differently oriented base. In the prairies the grid is much more regular, partly as a result of the topography, partly because a plan for the subdivision of the whole region was laid out in advance of settlement.

European Settlement of the United States and Canada

With the creation of new nations and the transformation of colonies into states, the relentless European settlement of the North American continent accelerated, more so in the United States than in Canada. By the middle of the 19th century, settlement in the United States had pushed beyond the Appalachian Mountains into the Interior Lowlands, including the upper Ohio and Tennessee river valleys and the interior South. France lost control of Canada to Britain in 1763, which had little impact on new settlement there. By the end of the century, however, southern Ontario, in and around present-day Toronto, became attractive to settlers (**Figure 6.9**).

Historians have argued that frontier settlement involved a continual process of national and personal reappraisal as well as of increasing geographical divergence as new settlers encountered new landscapes. It was also a process of sustained mobility, so much so that mobility has come to be seen as characteristic of the region's inhabitants, especially in the United States. There the movement of the frontier was continuous *and* mostly contiguous, at least until settlers reached the Great Plains in the middle of the 19th century and confronted significant mountain ranges at its western edge. In Canada, westward expansion was interrupted early on by the vast, generally infertile, though heavily forested Canadian Shield, which separated Ontario from the prairies. As Figure 6.2 shows, many Canadian settlers leapfrogged across to the northern midsection of the country to acquire suitable farmland.

In the United States the pace of westward expansion was accelerated by the federal government's decision in the late 1780s to sell public lands cheaply to citizens. By 1850, the development of the railroads reoriented the pace and direction of continental settlement—eastward from the Pacific Coast to the interior west rather than from the East Coast westward—at the same time that it diminished the previous isolation of pioneer settlements. By the close of the 19th century, the frontier process had resulted in a set of rural and agrarian regions and subregions that stretched across the continent. Each region was defined by its own experiences of the history and particular conditions of settlement and by its distinctive regional economic development.

The regional economy during this period was oriented to agro-mercantile activities. This means that trading agricultural crops and primary resources, such as fish, timber, and minerals, provided an economic base for the expanding population. Yet in the United States by the mid-19th century, a new economy based on manufacturing was rapidly gaining momentum along the northern Atlantic seaboard, especially in and around southern New England and New York. At the same time, the rest of the United States and Canada was being settled by European immigrants or their descendants, making their livelihoods largely by farming.

By the early 20th century, however, with the continent occupied from east to west mostly by Europeans and Euro-Americans, the industrialization of the U.S. economy was well on its way to transforming the landscape from one of rural agricultural settlement to one of urbanization and industrialization. The 1920 census documented for the first time in U.S. history that there were as many people living in cities as there were in rural areas. From that point onward, the United States and, soon after, Canada became increasingly urbanized. By the late 20th century, 75 percent of the U.S. and Canadian population lived in cities, up from 25 percent in the mid-19th century.

Urbanization, Industrialization, and Conflict

Long before explorers and colonists arrived, native peoples built cities in the regions that would become the United States and Canada. However, a far more extensive and intensive urbanization process began in earnest during the colonial period. The Europeans who colonized the United States and Canada were usually part of commercial urban systems in their home countries. As they colonized the new lands, they responded to the need for central places for organizing commerce, defense, communication, and, later, administration and worship by building cities (**Figure 6.10**). In Florida and in the southwestern United States, the Spanish founded cities, which became symbols of political and military authority. French explorers came not to settle but to reap commercial rewards, and they established urban centers to facilitate the exchange of goods. The Dutch also established urban settlements for trading centers, including for furs and slaves.

With few exceptions, however, the British played the largest role in shaping U.S. urbanization and urban life. Sustained by trade based on an agrarian economy, the U.S. Atlantic coastal cities established by the English colonists were also oriented toward a kind of corporate communalism tempered by notions of social and religious harmony. As geographer Alan Pred has shown, in addition to being

FIGURE 6.10 Fort Matanzas, St. Augustine, Florida
Military defense sites were an important part of the early settlement of North America by Europeans as they fought each other for control of the territory. *Matanzas* means slaughter in Spanish and refers to the massacre of nearly 250 French Huguenots at the hands of the Spanish at the site, 175 years before the fort was constructed.

Tobacco *Written by Jamey S. Essex*

The global spread of tobacco cultivation, manufacturing, and consumption over the past five centuries has made tobacco one of the world's most widespread agricultural products. Tobacco's development as a global commodity presents an excellent example of the diffusion and diversification of social practices and values.

Based on evidence such as clay pipes found at several prehistoric sites, archaeologists believe indigenous peoples domesticated the wild tobacco plant more than 5000 years ago. Native cultivators grew two main types of tobacco, *Nicotiana rusticum* in the northeastern United States and Canada and *Nicotiana tabacum* in Central and South America. Practically all of the tobacco produced today is of the *tabacum* species. Native populations ascribed to tobacco a number of economic, social, and cultural purposes, and by the time of sustained European contact in the 15th century, tobacco use was ubiquitous in the Americas.

Native peoples also developed all of the principal means of tobacco consumption—smoking, inhaling, and chewing—before European contact. Sailors and merchants carried these customs back to Europe during the 16th century, where tobacco found favor in the ports and royal courts of Spain and Portugal. From the ports of these early colonial powers, tobacco use spread along trade routes to Africa, Asia, and the rest of Europe. By the end of the 17th century, the tobacco trade formed one of the most important parts of the colonial economy connecting the Old and New worlds.

With the constant spread of tobacco consumption came the extension of tobacco cultivation. Tobacco is a highly adaptable plant that can grow in a wide range of climatic and soil conditions. It has been successfully cultivated as far north as Sweden and as far south as New Zealand (**Figure 1**). Despite its adaptability, tobacco is also quite sensitive to climatic and soil conditions. The result has been the development of hundreds of different tobacco types, each with its own regional complex of production and specific commodity uses based on the leaf's subjective qualities, such as taste and aroma. Tobacco types have changed, evolved, and even disappeared over the centuries of cultivation and use, with changes in consumer preference and market structure. The history of one particular tobacco commodity, cigarettes, illustrates the changing social and economic geography of tobacco production and consumption (**Figure 2**).

The modern cigarette did not enjoy widespread popularity until the middle of the 20th century. Spanish and French consumers were the first to take up cigarette smoking in the early 19th century, and British soldiers brought Turkish cigarettes (probably developed from Spanish and French varieties) back with them from the Crimean War in the late 1850s. From the fashionable officers' clubs of London, cigarette smoking spread to New York's social elite in the 1860s. Manufacturers sprang up across Britain and the United States to feed and expand the growing demand for cigarettes, but several obstacles stood in the way of large-scale production and consumption. These early cigarettes required imported Turkish tobacco and expensive skilled labor to roll and package the finished product. In general, cigarettes were an upper-class urban luxury item, too expensive for the common consumer. In the United States, many considered cigarettes a passing fad, too expensive, European, and effeminate to be a viable long-term commodity.

The mechanization of cigarette production in the United States during the 1870s and 1880s made cigarettes available and affordable to most tobacco users. Large-scale mechanized production reduced labor and material costs and changed the structure of the entire tobacco industry, encouraging makers to expand production and create demand through intensive advertising campaigns, brand-name recognition (brand names often referred to British aristocracy or Middle Eastern luxury), and worldwide sales distribution. By the beginning of the 20th century, American and British producers had pushed into markets from Shanghai to Cairo. Cigarettes became an increasingly globalized commodity.

By 1910, the tobacco industry had developed into a "big business" dominated by the American Tobacco Company and its subsidiaries and partners around the world. The Supreme Court dissolved this monopoly in 1911 and divided the tobacco industry among a handful of successor companies carved from American Tobacco. The dissolution sparked a new round of market competition and brand innovation, the most important of which was the development of the blended American cigarette. This new product added sweetened Kentucky burley tobacco to the Turkish tobacco and Virginia and North Carolina bright tobacco that had originally filled mass-produced cigarettes. The contours of the modern industry developed at this time, with

FIGURE 1 Tying tobacco leaves on a farm in China The world's three largest multinational cigarette companies grow tobacco in scores of countries throughout the world. China is the world's largest producer and one of the many countries that has a favorable climate for tobacco production.

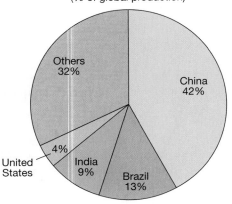

Top five tobacco–producing countries, 2005
(% of global production)

Others 32%
China 42%
4%
United States
India 9%
Brazil 13%

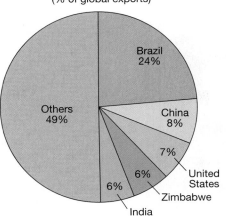

Top five tobacco–exporting countries, 2004
(% of global exports)

Brazil 24%
Others 49%
China 8%
7%
United States
6%
Zimbabwe
6%
India

FIGURE 2 Tobacco-producing and tobacco-exporting countries, 2005 (a) Global tobacco production serves 1.1 billion smokers. In China, which is the largest producer, 63 percent of males between the ages of 15 and 69 smoke. Only 3.8 percent of Chinese women smoke. (b) Despite the fact that cigarettes are a multibillion-dollar industry worldwide, in only four countries—Kyrgyzstan, Macedonia, Malawi, and Zimbabwe—do tobacco exports amount to more than 5 percent of total export earnings. (*Source:* UN Food and Agricultural Organization, "FAOStat," 2005, **http://apps.fao.org/page/collections?subset= agriculture**.)

several current manufacturers and their associated brands appearing in the aftermath of the Supreme Court's decision.

Through the 20th century, the cigarette has become the most popular and widespread tobacco product, constituting more than half of British tobacco sales in 1920 and more than half of U.S. sales in 1941. Some of this market expansion came at the expense of other tobacco commodities but much also came during the 1920s when the gendered constructions of cigarette smoking changed and large numbers of urban women took up the habit. Manufacturers diversified their brands and advertising strategies accordingly, a process they have repeated to tap growing markets in the countries of the periphery. Today an estimated 46 million U.S. residents smoke cigarettes, while worldwide estimates place the number of adult smokers at more than 1 billion (**Figure 3**).

Even as cigarette makers have opened new markets and realized astounding profits, they have had to answer to concerns about their products' social costs, particularly in relation to the impact on public health. Several state- and federal-level legal battles in the past decade have forced "Big Tobacco" to reassess its product and marketing strategies and pay out billions of dollars to cancer victims. These court decisions have set off further political debates about corporate responsibility, public health, and the allocation of settlement money. The trend of litigation against tobacco companies within the United States may set precedents for makers in other countries as well and has forced a reassessment of tobacco's social value.

Jamey S. Essex, Ph.D., University of Windsor

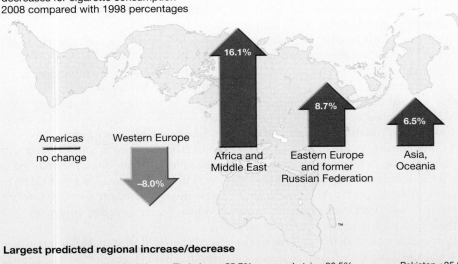

Projected regional increases and decreases for cigarette consumption 2008 compared with 1998 percentages

16.1%
8.7%
6.5%

Americas — no change
Western Europe −8.0%
Africa and Middle East
Eastern Europe and former Russian Federation
Asia, Oceania

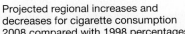

Largest predicted regional increase/decrease

| Brazil +40.2% | Norway +30.5% | Zimbabwe +55.7% | Latvia +26.5% | Pakistan +35.9% |
| USA −13.0% | UK −21.6% | South Africa −17.3% | Czech Republic −2.5% | New Zealand −24.9% |

FIGURE 3 Projected increases in smoking by region to 2008 As this figure shows, nearly all of the increase in smoking over the next three years is expected to occur in the semiperiphery and periphery. The difference between core and periphery suggests that there is an inverse relationship between smoking and level of development.

FIGURE 6.11 Waterwheel, Plymouth, Massachusetts
One advantage of locating new factories in New England was the abundance of rivers and streams with rapid and steadily moving water and waterfalls. Massive wheels were placed in the streams, where their buckets or paddles could catch the current and turn the wheel. The wheel turned a crankshaft that was connected through gears to other equipment. This method of producing energy was used for producing textiles throughout New England for the first several decades of the Industrial Revolution.

administrative centers, Boston, Providence, Baltimore, Philadelphia, Charleston, and Savannah were also ports and key nodes in a globally expanding mercantile system. As such, they enabled the transfer of resources, goods, and people, not only from the interior hinterland into the cities but also outwardly to Europe. At the same time, these cities received goods from England for U.S. consumer markets. Colonists saw their burgeoning cities not only as commercial centers but also as places where new ideas could be hatched and nurtured and as hearths of "civilization," where Old World cultural practices confronted those of the New World, creating in the process uniquely North American urban places.

As sites of innovation and cradles of culture, by the early 19th century cities were also largely the places where a new economy based on manufacturing was born and flourished. At first factories were located along the waterways of New England to take advantage of the power that could be harnessed from steep waterfalls (**Figure 6.11**). By the mid-19th century, manufacturing sites were springing up along the Atlantic seaboard from north of the Chesapeake Bay to Maine, and in the interior, in southern Ontario and southern Québec along the St. Lawrence River. By the end of the 19th century, the geography of manufacturing had spread westward to Cleveland, Detroit, Cincinnati, St. Louis, and Chicago in the United States and to Windsor, Hamilton, and Toronto in Canada. The New England, Mid-Atlantic, and upper midwestern areas in the United States interpenetrated with the lower central Canadian manufacturing sites and eventually became known as the U.S./Canadian Manufacturing Belt because of the high investments of labor, capital, and land in industrial activities from textiles to steel.

While industrialization was fueling the economies of the northern and midwestern United States, by the mid-19th century the differences between the northern and southern regions of the United States had become increasingly pronounced. The commerce and industry fueling the national economy made the cities of the North the most important ones economically. Although Charleston, Savannah, and Norfolk in the South were all ports, only Charleston was a deep-water port. More importantly, the southern ports were less crucial as transfer points than were those in the North because the South had many navigable inland rivers. Ships could simply pick up agricultural products and raw materials or drop off their own cargoes by way of the rivers, thereby eliminating the need to stop at the coastal ports.

While the North's economy was more diversified—based on commerce, agriculture, and industry—the South's was more simply tied to staple crop agriculture. Because the southern plantations produced much of the food and clothing for the region, and because most of the capital was invested in slave labor (which was unpaid and thus had no income to stimulate commercial exchange), the economy, as well as society and culture, made the South very different from the North and Canada. All of these differences—especially slavery and the economic issues that surrounded it—divided the southern states from the northern ones in highly volatile ways. By 1861 the division was so deep that the South formed a new government, the Confederate States of America, and attempted to secede from the United States in order to protect slavery and their agricultural economy. Civil war ensued.

With the South in defeat following the end of the Civil War in 1865, territories in the West joined the Union as free states, contributing people, resources, and capital to the burgeoning U.S. economy. Fearing that the United States, emboldened by its Civil War victory, might launch an invasion of Canada and responding to agitation among the French-speaking minority, the British Parliament passed the North America Act of 1867. The result was the creation of the Dominion of Canada, dissolving its colonial status and effectively establishing it as an autonomous state within the world-system, with its own constitution and parliament. All of the existing Canadian colonies joined the new confederation except British Columbia, which waited until 1871; Prince Edward Island, which joined the dominion in 1873; and Newfoundland, which remained independent until 1949.

The Emergence and Consolidation of U.S. Hegemony

By the end of the 19th century, the core of the world-system had been extended to include Canada and the United States, though Canada's incorporation was less clear-cut. The United States, politically independent just before the onset of the Industrial Revolution, was able to make the transition from periphery to the core because of several favorable circumstances. Vast natural resources of land and minerals provided the raw materials for a wide range of industries that could grow and organize without being hemmed in and fragmented by political boundaries. Populations, which were growing quickly through immigration, provided a large and expanding market and a cheap and industrious labor force. Cultural and trading links with Europe provided business contacts, technological know-how, and access to markets and capital (especially British capital) for investment in a basic infrastructure of canals, railways, docks, warehouses, and factories.

Canada's Staples Economy Canada's path to core status was distinctive, and some argue that Canada is not unequivocally a core country even now. While most of its population enjoys a high quality of life and high levels of economic productivity, Canada is certainly an atypical core country. It has never been highly industrialized, and the primary sector (see Chapter 1, p. 14) continues to be central in its economic structure. When industry did begin to grow and flourish in Canada after World War I, most of it occurred in the midsection of the country along a swath of land at the U.S.–Canadian border. A substantial proportion of the industries built there were branch plants of U.S. manufacturers. Furthermore, Canada's major trading partner is the United States, which imports more than half of all Canadian exports. What has been most remarkable about Canada's place in the world economy is that it has been so successful as a **staples economy**, meaning it is based on natural resources that are unprocessed or only minimally processed before they are exported to other areas where they are manufactured into end products. When staples are the centerpiece of an economy, the result is a resource-based strategy of economic growth that relies on international markets for those resources.

Canada's success as a core country has been largely the result of its staples-based links with more core economies like the United States and Britain. As a result, although Canada is part of the core, it is a somewhat weak competitor compared to the United States, which, in fact, derives a lot of its strength from exploiting the uneven relationship between itself and Canada. In the last decade or so, the Canadian economy has become more diversified through the development of the service sector (Table 6.1).

Industrialization in the United States and Canada largely developed around preexisting centers of urbanization and population and was shaped by the resource needs and market opportunities of successive clusters of technology (see Chapter 1, p. 33). The region's industrial strength was established at the beginning of the 20th century

TABLE 6.1 Canadian Labor Force Participation, 1961, 1991, and 2006						
	1961		1991		2006	
	Number	%	Number	%	Number	%
Primary	907,331	14.0	868,015	6.1	680,100	4.1
Secondary	1,835,958	28.4	3,017,540	21.2	3,339,700	20.3
Tertiary	3,728,561	57.6	10,334,680	72.7	12,398,600	75.5
Total	6,471,850		14,220,235		16,418,400	

Source: Based on data from Census of Canada, 1961, 1991, 2006.

with the development of a new cluster of technologies that included the internal combustion engine, oil and plastics, electrical engineering, and radio and telecommunications. Because of its awesome industrial capacity, by the early 20th century the United States became the world hegemon (see Chapter 1, p. 36), displacing nearly two centuries of British dominance.

The United States: The Global Hegemon In addition to its economic strength, the United States achieved world hegemony through its political and military strength. The first sign of the United States flexing its political and military muscle came with the Monroe Doctrine, which, although issued by President James Monroe in 1823, eventually became the foundation of U.S. foreign policy in Latin America. Monroe contended that European powers could no longer colonize the American continents and should not interfere with the newly independent Spanish-American republics. So long as Europe stayed out of the Americas, Monroe promised that the United States would not interfere with existing European colonies or with Europe itself.

In 1846 the United States used the Monroe Doctrine to justify war with Mexico, which resulted in the annexation of territory west of Texas and expansion into California and Oregon. During the 1870s and 1880s the United States began to interpret the Monroe Doctrine both as prohibiting the transfer of American territory from one European power to another and as granting the United States exclusive control over any canal connecting the Atlantic and Pacific oceans through Central America.

In 1904 President Theodore Roosevelt, in what became known as the Roosevelt Corollary—a reassertion of the Monroe Doctrine of 1823—claimed that the United States could intervene in any Latin American nation guilty of internal or external misconduct. Other presidents used the Roosevelt Corollary to justify subsequent intervention in the Caribbean. Although reduced in scope from the 1920s through the 1940s, the United States used the Monroe Doctrine and the Roosevelt Corollary to launch joint interventionist actions with other American republics. Subsequently, fearing the spread of communism in Latin America, the United States resumed unilateral actions without consulting its Latin American allies.

Although desirous of new territories for commercial potential, and often urged to war or other acts of aggrandizement by business leaders, U.S. militarism did not extend to an eagerness to get involved in European affairs, and the country only reluctantly entered World War I in 1916. Stunned by the nearly 5 million war casualties and the horror of the first highly technological engagement in history and eager to protect its growing economy, the United States subsequently entered a period of relative isolationism, rallying around the slogan of "America First." Although President Franklin Roosevelt declared U.S. neutrality with respect to the European war in 1939, by 1942 the country had entered World War II. The end of the war in 1945 marked a turning point in U.S. political and economic prowess as U.S. loans helped rebuild war-torn Europe and Japan. Allied victory and U.S. participation in the war effectively solidified the country's status as a world hegemon and ensured the dominant participation of the United States in a number of subsequent wars, including those fought in the Persian Gulf, Korea, and Vietnam.

All of these wars were fought in the name of the Cold War, which pitted the capitalist United States and western Europe against the communist Soviet Union for the hearts, minds, and territories of peoples throughout the globe. The Cold War came to an end with the disintegration of the Soviet Union in 1991. A new era of global cooperation dawned, with the U.S. government and U.S. transnational corporations still leading the way, though with markedly less militaristic fervor. The recent wars on terrorism in Afghanistan and Iraq have halted the brief hiatus in significant U.S. military involvement in global affairs, however (**Figure 6.12**). Indeed, the two wars

FIGURE 6.12 U.S. war in Iraq Military operations to remove Saddam Hussein from power began in mid-March 2003. Major combat operations were terminated by mid-April, although hostilities between the coalition forces and Iraqis continue. The war, prompted by the Bush administration's assertion that Iraq possessed weapons of mass destruction that could be employed for terrorist ends, is an illustration of the new belligerence displayed by the United States on the world stage. As of September 9, 2006, nearly 2700 American troops have died and 19,945 have been wounded in the war. Pictured here is an American mother viewing the photograph of her son at the "Faces of the Fallen" exhibit at Arlington National Cemetery. (*Source for casualty figures:* **http://www.antiwar.com/casualties/**.)

demonstrate a new phase in U.S. military history, with the president willing to enter into battle without the widespread support of traditional allies. The United States continues to be the globe's hegemon, and its new militarism should not be underestimated.

PEOPLES OF THE UNITED STATES AND CANADA

The 2004 census update officially set the U.S. population at 296,496,649 people. Whites constitute nearly three-quarters of that total; African Americans, about 13 percent; Asians and Pacific Islanders, about 4 percent; and Native Americans, about 1 percent. Hispanics, who may also be counted among other groups, make up about 14 percent of the total U.S. population. The main language is English, although Spanish is also widely spoken. Although the United States is popularly considered a Protestant country (including large numbers of Baptists, Methodists, Presbyterians, Lutherans, Pentecostals, and Episcopalians), Roman Catholics form the largest single religious group. The largest non-Christian religion is Judaism and other non-Christian religions, such as Islam, Buddhism, and Hinduism, also have substantial followings.

A significant aspect of the geography of U.S. religion is its regional variation. For example, the Bible Belt, which stretches from Texas to Missouri, is dominated by Protestant denominations, many of them fundamentalist and evangelist. Mormons, or members of the Church of Jesus Christ of Latter-day Saints, are concentrated in Utah, where more than 75 percent of the population are adherents. Large Catholic communities exist throughout the Southwest.

Canada has a population of roughly 33 million people. Canadians are predominantly of British origin (about 33 percent). The second largest majority is people of French origin, who make up about 25 percent of the population. There is also a large population of mixed British and French origin. The remaining population groups are small, with blacks making up less than 2 percent and indigenous peoples making up nearly 4 percent. Whereas the U.S. population is distributed widely, if somewhat thinly, across the country from east to west and north to south, with heavy concentrations along the coastal areas and in parts of the Midwest, Canada's population distribution reflects difficult environmental constraints and crucial U.S. economic connections. Nearly 75 percent of the population inhabits a narrow belt along the U.S. border.

Canada's largest religious denomination is Roman Catholic, with nearly half of that population living in Québec as a result of early French influence. The largest Protestant denomination is the United Church of Canada, followed by the Anglican Church of Canada. There is also a substantial Jewish population in Montréal. Ukrainian Orthodox communities are clustered throughout the provinces of Alberta, Saskatchewan, and Manitoba, and Buddhists and Hindus are concentrated mostly in the Canadian cities where large numbers of Asian immigrants have settled, such as Vancouver and Toronto.

As mentioned, the European settlers who colonized the United States and Canada largely displaced the indigenous groups who were already occupying the continent. Through colonization and later westward expansion, indigenous groups were reduced in number and pushed into new and usually more marginal areas of occupation. In the United States, native peoples were mostly settled onto reservations through treaties with the U.S. government; living on reservations granted native peoples a form of limited political sovereignty (**Figure 6.13**).

In Canada, native peoples, known as the First Nations or aboriginals, were also settled onto more than 2250 separate pieces of land known as *reserves*. The interactions between immigrants and the native peoples of Canada were little better than they were in the

FIGURE 6.13 Blackjack dealer at Hollywood Casino, Pueblo San Felipe, New Mexico Aboriginal lands in the United States and Canada were repeatedly taken over by government and private interests for most of the early history of both countries. More recently, native people have gained increasing control over their resources and economic well-being. Economic development projects abound on reservations in the United States and Canada. Pictured here is a gambling casino on a Native American pueblo in New Mexico. Gaming is an important source of revenues for Native Americans in many parts of the United States, from Connecticut to California.

United States. Encounters between aboriginals and Europeans in Canada began to increase in the 16th century through trade deals, the exchange of goods, intermarriage, and friendships. Contact between the Old World and the New resulted in high rates of mortality for the First Nations, as diseases (typhoid, influenza, diphtheria, plague, measles, tuberculosis, and scarlet fever) ravaged the vulnerable populations. It is estimated that after nearly 200 years of European contact, which began in the 17th century, the aboriginal population of Canada was reduced by as much as 95 percent.

During the second half of the 20th century, many members of the Canadian First Nations organized to protect their cultural rights and reclaim land that was taken from them. New treaties were signed and vast areas of territory were returned, as hunting and fishing rights were also restored (see Signature Region: The Northern Frontier, pp. 292). Over the last several decades, as in the United States, a free-enterprise economy has grown among Canada's aboriginal groups. Many are now involved in various sectors of the economy—from oil production to tourism. For many First Nations people, the future has some bright spots.

In the province of Québec, the Québeçois have organized to protect their cultural heritage. Their political movement, which seeks to separate Québec from the rest of Canada, is premised on a deep desire to preserve and enrich Québeçois culture. Since 1980, the province has attempted twice to secede from Canada; both efforts have failed. Lately the talk is less of secession and more about extending Québec's ties to Europe through the North American Free Trade Agreement. In short, globalization seems to be opening up new opportunities for Québec to maintain its distinct identity, prosper economically, and control more of its own destiny without having to secede from Canada.

Immigration

As societies founded upon European colonization and settlement, both the United States and Canada have varied and extensive immigration histories. The history of U.S. immigration is frequently discussed in terms of waves, because the numbers and types of immigrants ebbed and flowed over time (**Figure 6.14**). It is generally agreed that there have been three major waves of immigration into the United States, with the first occurring between 1820 and 1870, the second between 1870 and 1920, and the third beginning in 1970 and continuing through the present. In between these waves is an extended period of declining immigration that lasted from the mid-1930s to the 1970s. At the beginning of the 19th century, the population of the new nation was largely dominated by English colonists and African slaves. There were small numbers of Irish, Dutch, French, and Germans.

Waves of Immigration to the United States
The first large wave (1820–70), in which overall immigration rose sharply to 2.8 million individuals, involved large numbers of Irish and German immigrants. The number of English immigrants declined. The newly arriving Irish were mostly peasants who fled the potato famine that had devastated the Irish economy and daily life. The Germans who came were mostly skilled craft workers who were seeking new opportunities in a burgeoning country (**Figure 6.15**).

In the second wave (1870–1920), in addition to the continuing stream of "old" immigrants from northern and western Europe, "new" immigrants from southern and eastern Europe joined the flow into the United States. Between the 1870s and the 1880s, the absolute number of immigrants rose dramatically from 2.8 million to 5.2 million. Widespread economic depression in Europe and North America in the 1890s led to a decline in absolute numbers of immigrants (3.6 million). The numbers rose again in the first decade of the 20th century to an all-time high of 8.8 million. This wave carried peasants, skilled workers, and successful merchants.

The second wave of immigrants caused widespread backlash from first-wave immigrants. By the early 20th century, anti-Catholicism flared up against immigrants from Italy, Sicily, Poland, and Ireland. The new immigrants were blamed for everything from causing economic depression to destroying the character and moral fiber of the U.S. worker. Viewing immigrants as dangerous to U.S. values, Congress passed the Johnson-

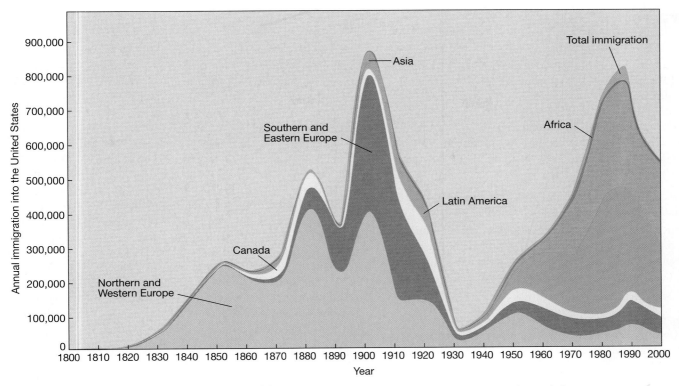

FIGURE 6.14 U.S. immigration, 1800–2000 Immigration often is conceived as a series of waves, as the graph shows very dramatic peaks and troughs over this 200-year period. However, numerous groups object to the term *waves*, which they feel reduces people to the flotsam and jetsam of oceanic movements. In their view, immigration can be undertaken for any number of reasons, but none of them is as impersonal or random as a debris-saturated wave. (*Source:* Modified from J. M. Rubenstein, *The Cultural Landscape: An Introduction to Human Geography*, 8th ed. Upper Saddle River, NJ: Prentice Hall, 2004.)

Reed Immigration Act in 1924 and imposed quotas on the numbers of new immigrants who would be allowed to enter the United States. The intention of the quotas was explicitly racial, and the impact was to reduce by half the foreign-born population. The "national origins" quota system remained in force until 1965, when the Hart-Cellar Act restructured the entire immigration system.

The third immigration wave (1970–present) is substantially different from the other two in that large numbers of migrants have been coming from Asia and Latin America. While Asians have been part of U.S. immigration history since the mid-19th century, Latin American migration to the United States is a 20th-century phenomenon that has increased since the changes brought about by the Hart-Cellar Act and the Immigration and Reform and Control Act of 1980. By 1990, Mexico had become

FIGURE 6.15 Second-wave immigrants in the United States Pictured here are Russian and German immigrants greeting President Theodore Roosevelt as he arrives in Victoria, Kansas, in 1903. Many German and eastern European immigrants settled agricultural communities in the Midwest moving beyond the more heavily populated states in the East.

SIGNATURE REGION

The Northern Frontier

The Northern Frontier sits at the apex of the North American continent. It is a vast area, including the new territory of Nunavut (created in 1999 out of the eastern portion of the Northwest Territories and turned over to the control of the region's First Nations). Although it occupies about one-third of Canada (an area roughly the size of India), it is home to only 60,000 people, nearly half of whom live in or around the settlement of Yellowknife (See **Figure 6.26**). The distinctiveness of the Northern Frontier landscape is reflected in a few key facts:

- wildlife vastly outnumber people (and in the most northerly parts, human habitation is impossible)
- much of the region is beyond the tree line, while mountain chains in the east and west rise majestically from the slope and sedimentary plain of the interior of the region
- short growing seasons make it impossible to sustain agriculture
- ice, snow, or permafrost are the norm

The Northern Frontier is a place of incredible, near-unimaginable beauty with relatively little impact from humans across its vast extent.

Nunavut, the largest territorial unit within Canada, is home to about 22,000 people, most of whom are Inuit, contributing to the uniqueness of the Northern Frontier (Figure 1). In response to claims by native peoples for land and political power, the Canadian government began to negotiate settlements beginning in the 1970s, and over the last 25 years has ceded to native peoples millions of acres of land and control over it. Nunavut stands out as a monumental concession and an indication of Canada's ability to make substantial reparations for its imperial past.

Until its transfer to native peoples, Nunavut was the central and eastern part of the Northwest Territories. Covering about 2 million square kilometers (about 772,000 square miles), Nunavut includes Baffin and Ellesmere islands and the surrounding region, stretching almost to the North Pole. For the most part, Nunavut is a flat tundra where average temperatures range from −32°C (−25°F) in January to 5°C (41°F) in July. Abundant wildlife includes white fox, caribou, and seals (**Figure 2**). Geological surveys have shown that Nunavut is rich in copper, lead, silver, zinc, and iron. But the severity of the climate prohibits any kind of large-scale mining. The settlement pattern of the Inuit is along the coast of Hudson Bay and the Labrador Sea.

Although the northern portion of the Northern Frontier is sufficiently inhospitable to deter human settlement, the southern part is inhabited and is a destination for adventure tourists. For instance, the area in and around the settlement of Yellowknife, the largest city in the Northern Frontier, is relatively developed with transportation linkages and other aspects of urban infrastructure. The area around Yellowknife is also home to native peoples, the Dene Nation, who are attempting to fight off the encroachment of any additional development in the region in order to protect their culture.

FIGURE 1 Inuit Muktar Akumalik Representing the people of the Canadian Arctic at the United Nations Climate Change Conference in Montreal in December of 2005, Akumalik accused the U.S. government of failing to adequately address the thawing of Arctic ice.

FIGURE 2 Musk ox bull, Ellesmere Island In addition to about 30,000 people, Nunavut is also home to a wide variety of wildlife, including caribou, polar bears, Arctic foxes, whales, and seals. The fur and skin of these animals is used for clothing and their flesh for food. Tourists also come to fish, hunt, and camp in this land of austere beauty.

the largest source of immigrants to the United States. The 2000 census shows that Mexicans now make up 7.3 percent of the U.S. foreign-born population (Figure 6.16). Most recent Mexican immigration into the United States has been to California, Texas, and Arizona, although there is a sizable Mexican population in Chicago and in many smaller cities because Mexican workers have been hired to harvest fruits and vegetables and to work in the meatpacking industry of the Midwest.

The most recent wave of immigration is largely the result of the dislocating effects of contemporary globalization and the attraction of the United States as a mythical place to live out a dream where the rewards of hard work and self-improvement are a better life for the current generation and an even better one for the next. While over time the "new" immigrants of the second wave have largely been assimilated into mainstream U.S. life, experiencing increasing prosperity and social mobility in later generations, third-wave immigrants continue to confront racism and bigotry. They have been frequent victims of **hate crimes**, acts of violence committed because of prejudice against women; ethnic, racial, and religious minorities; and homosexuals. In both the United States and Canada, racist and hate-motivated criminal behaviors have been linked to groups such as the Aryan Nation.

FIGURE 6.16 Protesting immigration reform Throughout the spring of 2006, hundreds of thousands of people took to the streets in cities across the United States to protest a federal immigration reform bill—H.R.-4437—sponsored by Congressmen Dennis Hastert and James Sensenbrenner. This pro-immigration rally took place in Chicago in March.

Immigrant Canada The immigration history of Canada is very similar to that of the United States, with one significant difference. The French dominated the settler stream into Canada well into the 18th century, but by around 1750, other immigrant groups from Britain and Ireland joined the stream as they had in the United States. In addition, Canada received some immigration from the United States at least until 1810, when restrictive British policies made it difficult for Americans to immigrate. By the beginning of the 20th century, Canada and the United States had very similar experiences of immigration, including the restrictions that curtailed inflows of new migrants until the late 20th century. Today, Canada is a primary destination for Asian migrants who make up nearly 50 percent of the immigrant stream.

As with all European settler societies, including those in Australia and South Africa, the range of ethnic groups that have migrated—whether voluntarily or not—creates a complex and diverse culture. Both Canada and the United States have experienced migration streams from all over the world. For example, in the populations of Los Angeles, New York, Toronto, and Vancouver—all popular destinations for aspiring immigrants—the number of nationalities represented is impressive. In Garden Grove, California, a city that has one of the highest immigrant populations in Los Angeles County, the school system must deal with a total of 65 different foreign languages among its student population. While the variety and range of national groups can potentially contribute to rich and interesting local and national expressions of culture, culture difference can also be seen as threatening to those who wish to protect a particular view of what it means to be American or Canadian.

Assimilation Versus Multiculturalism It is widely held that the United States and Canada, though sharing a similar immigration history, have reacted quite differently to the new immigrant groups in their midst. In the United States the dominant metaphor for the absorption of immigrants into the nation has been *the melting pot*. According to this metaphor, the integration of immigrants occurs through the intermingling of diverse ethnicities into a single national "alloy." The melting-pot process is another word for **assimilation**, the process by which peoples of different cultural backgrounds who occupy a common territory achieve sufficient cultural solidarity to sustain a national existence. The melting-pot metaphor implies first that the products of the melting pot will become culturally indistinguishable, with all members sharing a blended cultural composition. It also implies that natives will be irreversibly changed by their contact with newcomers in the melting pot. The result is a U.S. national identity that transcends the particularities of each of its components, such that out of the vast ethnic diversity of the United States emerges a single, culturally unified people.

The melting-pot metaphor and the public policies it has created have come under a great deal of criticism. In the United States the melting pot is increasingly being overshadowed by the liberal belief that all groups have a right to formal recognition of, and respect for, their cultures. Despite such demands, in the United States the process of immigrant incorporation has been to blend the U.S. culture with immigrant cultures, with U.S. culture dominating the mix.

In Canada, where there are two official languages (English and French), the situation for immigrants has always been somewhat different from assimilation. Canadian popular opinion and public policy have advocated something more akin to **multiculturalism**, the right of all ethnic groups to enjoy and protect their cultural heritage. Multiculturalism in practice includes protection and support of the right to function in one's own language, both in the home as well as in official or public realms. The ideal form of multiculturalism is premised on the belief that immigrants should not have to give up any of their original cultural attributes or practices. Under multiculturalism, the emergence of a single unified national identity, to which all Canadians could relate, is not technically possible. Instead, multiculturalism leads to ethnic coexistence, in which diverse groups share the same national space but not the same cultural systems.

Internal Migration in the United States and Canada

In addition to foreign immigration, **internal migration**—the movement of populations within a national territory—has also played a role in both countries. In the United States three overlapping waves of internal migration over the past two centuries have altered the population geography of the country. These three major migrations were tied to broad-based political, economic, and social changes.

Waves of Internal Migration   The first wave of internal migration began in the mid-19th century and increased steadily through the 20th century. This wave has two aspects: (1) a massive rural-to-urban migration associated with industrialization and (2) a large movement of people from the settled eastern seaboard and Europe into the interior of the country. Westward expansion took off in the early 19th century, when an official settlement policy was created (**Figure 6.17**). The federal government thereby encouraged migration over the course of more than a century as part of the country's expansionist strategies. The idea was to alleviate urban crowding and offset economic pressures in burgeoning eastern areas by promoting the idea of the self-sufficient farmer.

Despite this emphasis on western expansion and rural settlement, between 1860 and 1920 the United States was transformed from a rural to an urban society. Industrialization created new jobs, and unneeded agricultural workers (along with foreign immigrants) moved to urban areas to work in the manufacturing sector. Since the 1920s, this pattern of urbanization has continued, and in 2000, 80 percent of Americans lived in metropolitan areas.

The process has been quite similar for Canada, making urbanization the dominant settlement process. Additionally, there was large-scale internal migration westward in Canada, mostly during the early decades of the 20th century. But important differences in the immigration history of the United States and Canada also exist. During the colonial period, most of the immigrants arriving in Canada were British and French, whereas the immigrant stream to the United States was more broadly based. Moreover, while immigrants from all parts of Europe migrated to Canada during the late 19th and early 20th centuries, the number of people immigrating to Canada was smaller than

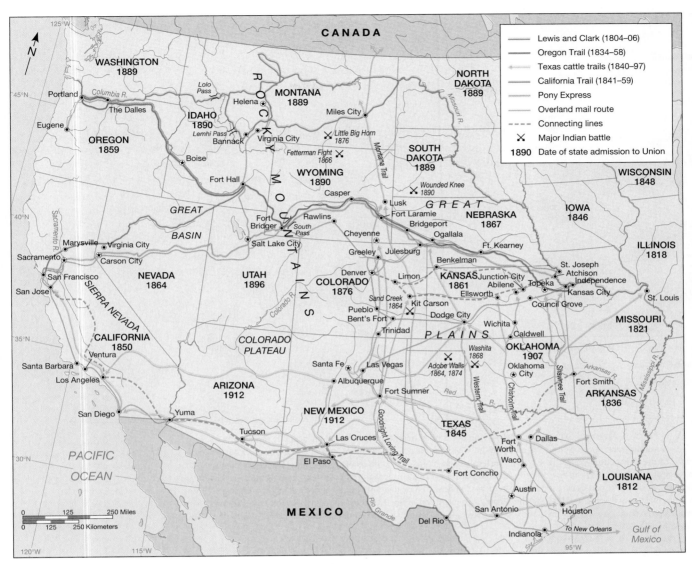

FIGURE 6.17 U.S. frontier trails, 1834–97 The frontier was part of the history and mythology of the United States (and Canada), and the paths individuals traveled to move westward suggest the many ways in which they experienced the passage. The topography of the land west of the Mississippi was intimidating, with vast grasslands, arid plains, searing deserts, and unimaginable insects and animals, like the vast herds of buffalo that the pioneers encountered. As more and more European and American migrants moved westward, the American Indians, the native inhabitants of these regions, saw their ways of life being threatened by these new-comers and often attacked their wagon trains. The westward travelers who successfully navigated all the dangers and hardships of the trail then had to confront the seemingly insurmountable obstacle of the Rocky Mountains. (*Source:* E. Homberger, *The Historical Atlas of North America.* London: Penguin, 1995, pp. 88–89.)

the number immigrating to the United States. Finally, there has long been migration interaction between the two countries, with many Americans immigrating to Canada during the American Revolutionary War. In the 20th century, Canadian immigration to the United States exceeded American immigration to Canada, as Canadians sought to secure a higher standard of living south of the international border.

The second wave of internal U.S. migration, which began early in the 20th century and continued through the 1950s, was the massive and very rapid movement of mostly African Americans out of the rural South, where they had made livelihoods picking cotton, to cities in the South, North, and West (**Figure 6.18**). Although African Americans already formed considerable populations in cities such as Chicago and New York, large numbers of blacks moved out of the rural areas when mechanization of cotton picking reduced the number of jobs available. At the same time, pull factors attracted African Americans to the large cities. In the early 1940s, for example, large numbers of

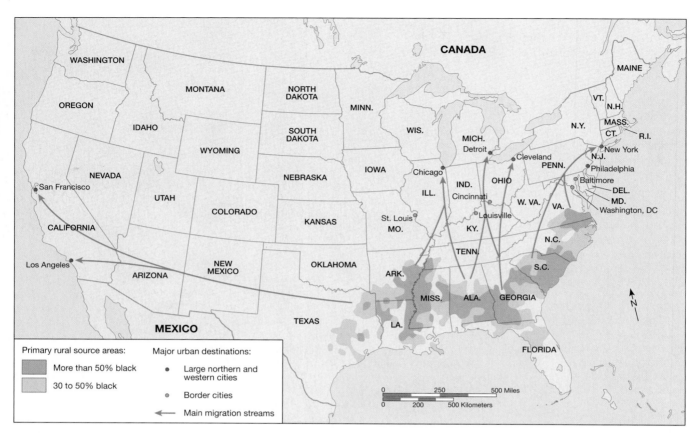

FIGURE 6.18 African-American migration The northward migration of African Americans in the early part of the 20th century was nothing new in the United States. Since the Civil War, blacks had been leaving the South in a slow but steady stream. By the turn of the new century, "Jim Crow" laws that legalized segregation and discrimination against blacks had been enacted; the boll weevil had devastated the cotton crop; and the cotton gin (which mechanized cotton processing and put tens of thousands of pickers out of work) had been introduced. An increased flow of new migrants joined already established black communities in most major northern cities. Despite the bigotry and exclusion in northern cities, employment and educational opportunities were better than they were in the South. (*Source:* Redrawn and adapted from E. Homberger, *The Historical Atlas of North America.* London: Penguin, 1995, pp. 106–7.)

new jobs in the defense-oriented manufacturing sector became available, because many urban workers left their jobs and entered the military when the United States entered World War II. This second wave of migration can be seen as part of a wider pattern of rural-to-urban migration among agricultural workers as industrialization spread globally. After the war, a more important catalyst drove this migration: the increasing emphasis on high levels of mass consumption, which reoriented industry toward production of consumer goods, and which in turn stimulated large increases in the demand for unskilled and semiskilled labor. The impact on the geography of racial distribution in the United States was profound.

The third wave of internal migration began shortly after World War II ended in 1945 and continued into the 1990s. Between the end of the war and the early 1980s—and directly related to the impact of governmental defense policies and activities on the country's politics and economy—the region of the United States now commonly called the Sunbelt (because of the year-round warm weather), and including most of the states of the U.S. South and Southwest, experienced a 97.9 percent increase in population. During the same period, the Midwest and Northeast, known as the Snowbelt (because of the cold winters) or Rustbelt (because of the aging factories that once peppered its landscape), together grew by only 33.3 percent. **Figure 6.19** shows suburban development in a Sunbelt city that experienced phenomenal growth from the postwar period into the new century. Although Santa Fe, New Mexico, has not grown as dramatically as, say, Houston or Phoenix or Las Vegas, it still manifests the low-density, low vertical profile, and geographically extensive form expressed in most Sunbelt cities.

Urban to Suburban Migration The first evidence of **suburbanization**—the growth of population along the fringes of large metropolitan areas—can be traced back to the late 18th and early 19th century, when real estate developers looked beyond the city for investment opportunities and wealthy city-dwellers began seeking more scenic residential locations. Later, residents fled to the suburbs to get away from the new immigrants and their increasing hold over urban machine politics.

The process was rapidly accelerated, however, with the introduction of new transportation technologies—first horse-drawn streetcars, then commuter rail services, and, finally, automobiles. Each innovation in transportation allowed people to travel longer distances to and from work within the same or shorter time period. North Americans chose to move to the suburbs in massive numbers, not in the least because the suburbs were, arguably, considered by many to be more healthful places to raise a family. Suburbanization continues today in both the United States and Canada with a new wrinkle—a slight reversal of migration from urban to rural areas, as retirees especially search out the good life on the far fringes of the metropolitan core in small towns like Bisbee, Arizona, and the Okanagan Valley in British Columbia (**Figure 6.20**).

The most compelling explanation for the large-scale population shift characteristic of the third migration wave is the pull of economic opportunity. Rather than reinvesting in upgrading the aged and obsolescent urban industrial areas of the Rustbelt, venture

FIGURE 6.19 Sunbelt city: Santa Fe, New Mexico While the residential architecture and design varies from place to place in the Sunbelt, the overall layout of residences set up side by side in numbing repetition is a classic manifestation of urban growth there. This mass production approach enables builders to keep construction costs low as materials can be ordered en masse and the building process broken down into separate tasks.

FIGURE 6.20 Okanagan Valley, British Columbia Pictured here is the town of Kelowna on Lake Okanagan. This town and the valley surrounding it has become an attractive site for retirement living for Canadians because of its sunny climate and the wide range of outdoor activities available, including hiking and fishing. The region is also a cultural attraction because of its First Nations history.

capital was invested in Sunbelt locations, where cheaper land and lower labor costs made it more profitable to introduce manufacturing and service-sector activity. The 2000 census shows a decrease in the rate of in-migration to the Sunbelt, but the changes in the geography of population at the beginning of the 21st century are dramatically different from the patterns of 150 years ago. This new population distribution illustrates the way political and economic transformations play an especially significant role in shaping individual choice and decision making.

The Cultures of the United States and Canada

Despite the discrimination and bigotry that immigrants have experienced in becoming members of U.S. and Canadian societies, they have made significant and transformative contributions to enriching global culture and influencing taste around the world. Music, art, literature, dance, architecture, film, photography, sports, fashion, journalism, and cuisine, not to mention science, medicine, and technology, have all been shaped by the contributions of immigrants. The influence of immigrants on music has been particularly impressive. Country, bluegrass, jazz, the blues, and rap all originated in the United States but have deep roots in the Old World. From jazz to rap, African Americans have been responsible for musical innovations that have been widely accepted, applauded, and imitated throughout the world.

Arts, Music, and Sports   The early 20th century origins and particularly U.S. expressions of jazz have been influential worldwide at the same time that they reveal a complex but clear lineage back to the African musical roots. Slaves left these roots behind in the wake of their terrible Atlantic passages. West African folk music forms one of the central foundations of jazz. But jazz was also influenced by European popular and light classical music of the 18th and 19th centuries. The earliest documented jazz style was Dixieland jazz, which emerged from New Orleans and was played by white musicians who recorded the new music form on phonograph records. The spread of these recordings helped jazz become a sensation in the United States and Europe.

Soon African-American jazz groups—the originators of the jazz style that was expressed through the related styles of ragtime, marches, hymns, spirituals, and the blues—were able to capitalize on the popularity of white Dixieland largely through the improvisational style of trumpeter Louis Armstrong. Armstrong migrated to Chicago in the 1920s, influencing local musicians and stimulating the evolution of the Chicago style.

About the same time that jazz caught on in Chicago, Harlem was emerging as a center for jazz, organized around a highly technical, hard-driving piano style. Regional variations on the original Dixieland style emerged in the urban areas, where significant populations of African Americans had settled. Jazz continued to flourish from the 1930s through the 1950s. In the 1960s jazz began to lose popularity as audiences embraced mainstream rock and roll, which had itself been influenced by jazz and the blues. In the 1980s, jazz experienced a revival as a serious form of music, which it continues to enjoy today. Other distinctly U.S. musical and performance styles include rap, bluegrass, and musical theater, the last having roots in European opera. Native populations in both the United States and Canada have also made significant cultural contributions to music, handicrafts (especially basketry, rugs, jewelry, and pottery), and contemporary literature. People from all over the world travel to visit First Nations and Native American sites to view and collect their distinctive commercial products such as Navajo rugs from the U.S. Southwest and the wood carvings of the Haida people of Pacific Canada.

The game of baseball is another U.S. innovation, and it too has enjoyed widespread popularity beyond the national boundaries, especially in Caribbean countries like the Dominican Republic, Venezuela, and Cuba, but also in Europe and Japan, among other places. The composition of many U.S. and Canadian major league baseball teams (one—the Toronto Blue Jays—are Canadian) demonstrates just how popular this sport has become worldwide. As a high-stakes commercial enterprise, baseball has traveled well. Consider the following: At the opening of the U.S. baseball season in 2006, more than a

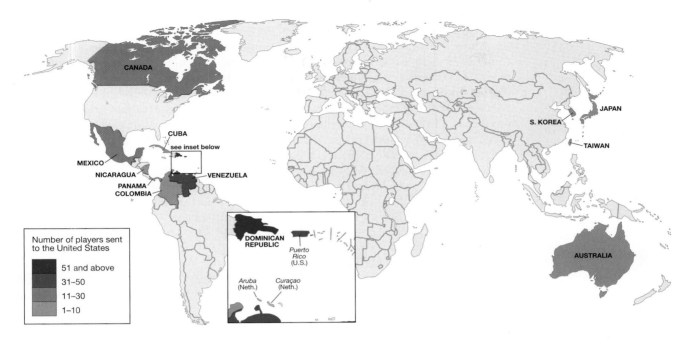

FIGURE 6.21 The globalization of U.S./Canadian major league baseball, 2006 The old saying that something is as "American as baseball or apple pie" may need revision given the dramatic transformations that have occurred over the last ten years in the demographics of players on major league baseball teams.

quarter (27.4%) of all the players on the 30 team rosters were from countries and territories other than the United States. These include Aruba, Australia, Canada, Colombia, Cuba, Curaçao, Dominican Republic, Japan, South Korea, Mexico, Nicaragua, Panama, Puerto Rico, Taiwan, and Venezuela. The New York Mets, Los Angeles Dodgers and the Los Angeles Angels of Anaheim led all major league teams with 15, 14, and 13 non-North American players, respectively (**Figure 6.21**).

Canadian Cultural Nationalism Canadian culture tends mostly to represent a mix of immigrant and British settler influences. One of the most significant aspects of Canadian culture is the fact that it has had to battle the tremendous influence of commercialized U.S. culture, which, because of its geographical proximity, has been enormously difficult to resist. Canada has been very aggressive in its attempt to ward off the invasion of U.S. cultural products and has developed an extensive and very public policy of cultural protection against the onslaught of music, television, magazines, films, and other art and media forms.

Government bodies, such as the National Film Board of Canada and the Canadian Radio and Television Commission, actively monitor the media for the incursion of U.S. culture. For example, 30 percent of the music on Canadian radio must be Canadian. Nashville-based Country Music TV was discontinued from Canada's cable system in the early 1990s and replaced with a Canadian-owned country music channel. Besides regulating how much and what type of culture can travel north across the border, the Canadian government also sponsors a sort of "affirmative action" grant program for its own culture industries, including music, radio, and the print media (**Figure 6.22**).

Although they are heavily exposed to U.S. cultural products, Canadians have been able to produce distinctively Canadian film and literary pieces. Some of the most highly regarded authors among anglophone audiences are Canadians. These include Michael Ondaatje, *The English Patient* and *Anil's Ghost*; Alice Munro, *Runaway*; Robertson Davies, *Deptford Trilogy*; Leonard Cohen, *Book of Longing*; Yann Martel, *Life of Pi*; and Margaret Atwood, *The Tent* and *Penelopiad*. Prominent francophone writers in Canada include Michel

FIGURE 6.22 The Arcade Fire Popular Canadian musical exports include a wide range of vocalists, such as Avril Lavigne, Kevin Parent, and Diana Krall, as well as rock groups like Barenaked Ladies and The Arcade Fire, pictured here on the cover of *Time Magazine*, April 4, 2005.

Tremblay, *Les Chroniques du Plateau Mont-Royal*; Louis Hémon, *Maria Chapdelaine*; and Gabriel Roy, *Bonheur d'occasion.*

Many scholars argue that "globalization" is really just a euphemism for "americanization," and it is difficult to argue against this perspective. It is also important to recognize, however, that just as U.S. culture is circulating intensively beyond its national borders, other cultures have come to influence U.S. culture in numerous and distinctive ways. The following examples help illustrate the fact that the globalization of culture, though largely dominated by the United States, is not exclusively so. For decades, other core countries have been exerting important cultural influences on the United States, especially Japan. After the rage of Japanese *Pokémon* trading cards in the late 1990s, for example, *Yu-Gi-Oh!* trading cards became wildly popular among U.S. children. Gwen Stefani recently toured with *harajuku* girls, the name given to teenage girls who dress up in trendy clothes and hang out in the area around Tokyo's Harajuku Station. But it's not just Japan that is influencing U.S. culture. Other countries are as well. Britain continues to deliver on the Harry Potter children's fiction series in both film and literary form, and while it is clearly a children's genre, it captivates adults and children alike. The *No. 1 Ladies Detective Agency* series is about a quirky female detective in Botswana; books from the series are best-sellers in the United States. They are written by Zambian-born Alexander McCall Smith who resides in Edinburgh, Scotland. And, very popular in the United States, of course, are the Hong Kong action movies, including *House of Flying Daggers* (2004) and *Hero* (2002), as well as *Kung Fu Hustle* (2004).

Peripheral countries influence U.S. culture as well. For instance, the film industry in India, Bollywood, is increasingly coming to shape U.S. film in both its content and look. Depending on one's viewpoint, the very popular film *Moulin Rouge* (2001) either imitated or stole Bollywood formats and dance sequences. Clearly, globalization has made it possible not only for U.S. and Canadian culture to circulate widely but for cultural products from other parts of the world to penetrate the region.

CONTEMPORARY CHALLENGES IN A GLOBALIZING WORLD

Today the United States and Canada together produce more than one-quarter of the world's GNP. The United States has the world's largest economy, Canada the ninth largest. Their resources are extensive and varied, and their ability to exploit them is high. As part of the recent restructuring of the global economy discussed in Chapter 1, the various regions of both the United States and Canada have experienced significant transformations in their economies, societies, political institutions, and even their physical environments. In this section we examine those changes and their implications, paying particular attention to the ways in which the economy and politics have been reorganized to facilitate contemporary globalization and how social groups and the physical environment have shaped—and in turn have been shaped by—these changes.

Transforming Economies

Political, economic, and social geographers would agree that the most important regional transformation of the last 25 years has been the rise of the service economy and the relative decline of the manufacturing employment sector in the United States and Canada. In the United States, the most recent wave of internal migration, the movement of U.S. residents from the Rustbelt to the Sunbelt, was part of this shift. The rise of the U.S. Sunbelt is a classic case of how regional core-periphery patterns are modified to facilitate the accumulation of capital (as discussed in Chapter 1, p. 30). During the 1960s and the 1970s, the historic core of North American industrialization, the Manufacturing Belt, began to experience economic problems in the form of high labor costs and aging infrastructure, mostly manifested in outdated technology systems. Once-peripheral regions of the country, the South and Southwest, began to attract investors. The military had invested in this region during World War II, establishing bases and holding training exercises. Following the war, the government continued to invest in this region as it built up its military capacity during the Cold War. Thus, by the 1960s, the South and the Southwest had substantial infrastructural development and a high level of technological sophistication organized around military applications—which have historically preceded the application of technology for civilian purposes.

Shifting Balances As the computer age dawned, numerous places in the South and the Southwest were ripe for civilian investment opportunities, possessing abundant land and labor forces that were highly educated. Labor was also unused to unions and high wage rates. The result was a shift, which has since been rebalanced, in the core-periphery patterns of the United States as the profitability of old, established industries in the Manufacturing Belt—or the Rustbelt, as it came to be called—declined compared to the profitability of new industries in the fast-growing new industrial districts of the Sunbelt. Once the profitability differentials between the two places became significant, disinvestment began to occur in the Rustbelt. Manufacturers there began to reduce their wage bill by cutting back on production; to reduce their fixed costs by closing down and selling off some of their factory space and equipment; and to reduce their spending on research and development for new products. This disinvestment, in turn, led to deindustrialization in the formerly prosperous industrial core regions of the Midwest and Northeast.

Deindustrialization involves a relative decline (and in extreme cases an absolute decline) in industrial employment in core regions as firms scale back their activities in response to lower levels of profitability (**Figure 6.23**). In effect, technological innovations in computerized production systems facilitated new industrial applications, and investors and manufacturers began to look around for new places in which to invest and build. Innovations in transport and communications technology, combined with these production innovations, created windows of locational opportunity. The result was the movement of capital investment in manufacturing away from the old industrial districts of the Manufacturing Belt and into small towns and cities in the Sunbelt, to suburban fringe areas near some of the old industrial districts, and offshore to countries that had lower-cost workforces.

Meanwhile, the capital made available from disinvestment in the Rustbelt became available for investment in new ventures based on innovative products and production technologies. Old industries and a large proportion of an established industrial region were "dismantled" to help fund the creation of new centers of profitability and employment. This process is often referred to as **creative destruction**, something that is inherent to the dynamics of capitalism. Creative destruction provides us with a powerful image to understand the need to withdraw investments from activities (and regions) yielding low rates of profit and to reinvest in new activities (and, often, in new places).

Creative destruction does not stop there, however. If the deindustrialization of the old core regions is severe enough, the relative cost of their land, labor, and infrastructure may decline to the point where they once again become attractive to investors. As a result, a seesaw movement of investment capital occurs, which over the long term tends to move from developed to less-developed regions—then back again, once the formerly developed region has experienced a sufficient relative decline. "Has-been" regions can become redeveloped and revitalized, given a new lease on life by the infusion of new capital for new industries. This is what happened, for example, to the area in and around Pittsburgh in the 1980s, resulting in the creation of a postindustrial economy out of a depressed industrial setting. The USX Corporation, a worldwide producer of steel and oil and natural gas products,

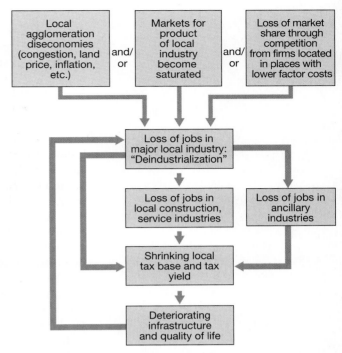

FIGURE 6.23 Spiral of deindustrialization When the locational advantages of manufacturing regions are undermined for one reason or another, profitability declines and manufacturing employment falls. This can lead to a downward spiral of economic decline, as experienced by the traditional manufacturing regions of North America during the 1970s and 1980s. (*Source:* P. L. Knox, *Urbanization.* Upper Saddle River, NJ: Prentice Hall, 1994, p. 295.)

reduced its workforce in the Pittsburgh region from more than 20,000 to fewer than 5000 between 1975 and 1995. These losses have been more than made up, however, by new jobs generated in high-tech electronics, specialized engineering, and finance and business services.

Reorganization of Regional Landscapes The dramatic and often very painful changes that occurred around the decline of the Rustbelt and the rise of the Sunbelt have resulted in a major reorganization of the U.S. regional landscape. The new technology systems—using robotics, telematics, biotechnology, and other knowledge-based systems that have emerged and been refined and improved over the last 25 years—have helped encourage the growth of new regions with very different economic bases than they possessed only 25 years ago. While the Rustbelt experienced crippling decline in the 1970s and early 1980s, by the mid-1990s it was again booming, having reorganized its economy and political institutions around service-related employment. The Sunbelt has maintained its strong economy and has continued to experience phenomenal population growth into the 21st century. Its economic base is a rich mix of sectors from resource extraction to knowledge-based industries.

The new regional geographies of the United States have resulted in massive population redistribution. More than 50 percent of the U.S. residents now live west of the Mississippi River, whereas 100 years ago the reverse was true. In the last 15 years, as a result of the dramatic changes brought about by the emergence of a fifth technology system based on solar energy, robotics, microelectronics, biotechnology, advanced materials, and information technology (see Chapter 1, p. 14), a "new economy" has emerged in the United States and Canada (see Geography Matters: The New Economy, p. 304). The new economy, though caused by the practical implementation of the fifth technology system, is also about the dramatic transformation of work and the labor force, markets, and the nature of competition among regions. In addition to reshaping regional economies, this new economy effects great changes in local and regional politics as well as in the relationship between regional and national politics, particularly in federal elections.

Restructuring the State

The United States and Canada are **federal states**, part of a form of government in which power is allocated to units of local government (province/state, county, and city/town government) within the country. Federalism leaves many political decisions to the local governments. During the first 100 years of the U.S. republic, the federal government spent most of its time regulating commerce. But beginning in the late 19th century, urged by constituents across the country, the federal government began to take an increasingly active and direct role in regulating and supporting all aspects of U.S. social and economic life, particularly with respect to providing for social welfare; developing infrastructure, such as dams and highways; and transferring large amounts of tax dollars to contractors for the buildup of U.S. defense systems, especially during the Cold War.

Because the state was so heavily invested in all aspects of U.S. society, but especially in the economy, when the global economy experienced shock waves during the 1970s, the government was hit very hard. And as corporations and business in the United States and elsewhere searched for remedies to their economic problems, the government did likewise and imposed dramatic restructuring on its own operations and programs.

The recent restructuring of the national and global economy has been brought about by changes in core-periphery patterns of U.S. regions. The changes were facilitated by state intervention and retrenchment as well as by changes in the popular understanding of the role of government. The view that government's primary responsibility was as a guarantor of social welfare had dominated popular understanding since the 1930s. By the 1970s and 1980s, as local governments in the Rustbelt were declaring bankruptcy and the federal government was accumulating massive debt, popular opinion changed and the role of government was reconfigured. Since the late

1980s, it has become routine for local governments to act more as entrepreneurs than as managers of the social welfare. As deindustrialization accelerated in the Rustbelt, government agencies in the Sunbelt helped lure investment to the region by offering tax breaks, creating needed infrastructure, and providing subsidies for private investment.

As a way to reduce its mounting debt, the federal government began to shed its responsibilities for social welfare, passing these responsibilities on to state governments. The federal government also began to shut down military bases throughout the country as the fall of the Berlin Wall signaled the end of the Cold War. With decreased responsibilities for social welfare and lower military spending until the recent military campaigns in Iraq and Afghanistan, the federal government has oriented its role toward more actively facilitating the free flow of trade and the operations of transnational corporations abroad.

Since independence, Canada has fostered a government that has been far more inclined to guarantee social welfare than has the United States, though Canada also has a tradition of entrepreneurialism in government. Many scholars of Canadian history believe that federation of the former Canadian colonies into the Dominion of Canada was driven by capitalists interested in supporting the burgeoning industrialization of the country. More recently, in addition to continuing its tradition of providing social welfare, the state in Canada has accelerated its entrepreneurialism by directing support to expanding its tertiary sector (activities involving the sale and exchange of goods and services) and quaternary sector (activities involving the handling and processing of knowledge and information), particularly with respect to high-technology development.

Wealth and Inequality

While globalization and the new economy have helped improve the employment opportunities and level of wealth of many in the United States, it has also seriously set back many others (**Table 6.2**). From the impact of transnational agribusiness corporations on U.S. farmers to the impact of increasing wealth for some on the cost of housing for everyone, the structural transformations in the U.S. economy have left behind many people. In 2004, 37 million in the United States (12.7 percent of the population) lived in families that did not earn enough to rise above the official poverty threshold. Furthermore, according to the U.S. Census Bureau, the 2000–01 poverty rate increase was the first year-to-year increase since 1991–92; and since that time, the rates have continued to increase each year.

In 2004, the poverty line for a family of two adults and two children was set at $19,157. The poverty rate among children was 17.8 percent. Statistics such as these underscore the likelihood that up to 40 percent of U.S. children will experience poverty at one time or another, because many families move in and out of poverty over time. According to a United Nations survey, the United States has the highest child poverty rate of 18 industrialized nations. One reason is that the United States also has the lowest government benefits to families with poor children. Another reason is the stagnation of wages at the lower end of the wage spectrum.

Another implication of inequality for the U.S. population is the impact that it has on health. The United States leads the world in healthcare spending. Yet some countries

TABLE 6.2 Growing Income Disparity in the United States

Household Groups	Share of All Income			Average After-Tax Income (Estimated)			Change	
	1977	1999	2004	1977	1999	2004	1977–99	1977–2004
One-fifth with lowest income	5.7%	4.2%	3.4%	$10,000	$8,800	$10,264	−12.0%	2.64%
Next lowest one-fifth	11.5	9.7	8.7	22,100	20,000	26,241	−9.5	18.7
Middle one-fifth	16.4	14.7	14.7	32,400	31,400	44,455	−3.1	37.2
Next highest one-fifth	22.8	21.3	23.2	42,600	45,10	70,085	5.9	64.5
One-fifth with highest income	44.2	50.4	50.1	74,000	102,300	151,593	38.2	105.0
1 percent with highest income	7.3	12.9	21.8	234,700	515,600	264,387	119.7	12.6

Source: U.S. Census Bureau, 2000 and 2004 Population Survey, Annual Demographic Supplements.

GEOGRAPHY MATTERS

The New Economy

In the last decade and a half, a new economy has emerged in the core, and especially in the United States and Canada, that has fundamentally transformed industries and jobs through information technologies (IT). These changes have been facilitated by a high degree of entrepreneurialism and competition, transforming the United States and Canada as well as many other regions around the globe. But the new economy was born in the United States, sired by the technological changes that emerged from Silicon Valley, California, nearly 50 years ago.

It is generally agreed that the previous economic order, the "old economy," lasted from 1938 to about 1974. The year 1974 was a critical year in economic history: Oil prices were skyrocketing and the corporate rate of profit was falling in the core. That economy's foundation was manufacturing geared toward standardized, mass-market production and run by stable, hierarchically organized firms focused on the U.S. market. Massive political and economic restructuring rocked core regions, the United States and Canada among them. Many regard 1975–90 as the transitional period, from the old manufacturing-based economy to the new IT economy (**Table 1**).

The new economy, however, is about more than just new technology. It is also about the application of new technologies to the organization of work—from the impact of biotechnology on farming to the impact of IT on organizing management hierarchies in the insurance industry. In short, the new economy has applied IT to transform the organizational practices of firms and industries. Dynamism, innovation, and a high degree of risk are at the center of the new economy.

For instance, while in 1990 it took six years to produce an automobile—from conceptualization to final production—it now takes two years. Technological innovation has become remarkably rapid, and change is now measured in "web years" (which amounts to roughly one fiscal quarter) rather than in calendar years. Moreover, new jobs are being created largely by firms that did not even exist five years ago. But the dynamism and innovation of the new economy is premised on a great deal of risk. Many ventures fail, and almost a third of all jobs are in flux every year (which means that these jobs have only recently been added or will soon be eliminated from the economy). In this high-risk economy, failure has become a badge of honor, signaling the willingness to jump headlong into a fast-break economy where firms come and go in the click of a computer mouse.

Figure 1 illustrates how well the 50 states of the United States are performing in the new economy with respect to investment in Research and Development (R&D). Gross state product, as contrasted with gross domestic product (see Chapter 1, p. 14), is a measure of the total value of all materials, foodstuffs, goods, and services produced by a state in a particular year. This map shows the ratio of expenditures on research and development to the total gross state product. The higher ratio (the darker the color and the larger the state size) means that more of the gross state product is derived from R&D. R&D investment indicates how much states are involved with new economy innovation in terms of everything from computer and electronics product manufacturing—where the states of California, Massachusetts, and Texas are the leaders—to automobile design and

TABLE 1	Keys to the Old and New Economies	
Issue	Old Economy	New Economy
Economy-wide Characteristics		
Markets	Stable	Dynamic
Scope of competition	National	Global
Organizational form	Hierarchical, bureaucratic	Networked, entrepreneurial
Potential geographic mobility of business	Low	High
Competition between regions	Low	High
Industry		
Organization of production	Mass production	Flexible production
Key factor of production	Capital/labor	Innovation/knowledge
Key technology driver	Mechanization	Digitization
Source of competitive advantage	Lowering cost through economies of scale	Innovation, quality, time to market, and cost
Importance of research/innovation	Moderate	High
Relations with other firms	Go it alone	Alliances and collaboration
Workforce		
Principal policy goal	Full employment	Higher wages and incomes
Skills	Job-specific skills	Broad skills, cross-training
Requisite education	A skill	Lifelong learning
Labor-management relations	Adversarial	Collaborative
Nature of employment	Stable	Marked by risk and opportunity
Government		
Business-government relations	Impose requirements	Assist firms' innovation and growth
Regulation	Command and control	Market tools, flexibility

Source: R. D. Atkinson, R. H. Court, and J. M. Ward, *The State of the New Economy Index: Benchmarking Economic Transformations in the States.* Washington, DC: Progressive Policy Institute, 1999, p. 5.

manufacturing—where Michigan dominates. New Jersey and Pennsylvania are front-runners with respect to chemical manufacturing. The top ten states in terms of R&D expenditure are, in order, California, Michigan, Massachusetts, Texas, New York, New Jersey, Washington, Illinois, Maryland, and Pennsylvania.

The percentage of adults with Internet access in each state is a significant indicator of which regions of the United States participate most actively in the digital economy (**Figure 2**). In 1997, 25 percent of households were online across the United States; by the end of 1998, the percentage was up to 33; in the year 2003, it was close to 50 percent. And while the average income of Internet users is dropping, as is the average education level, there are still huge disparities in online access between blacks and whites in the United States.

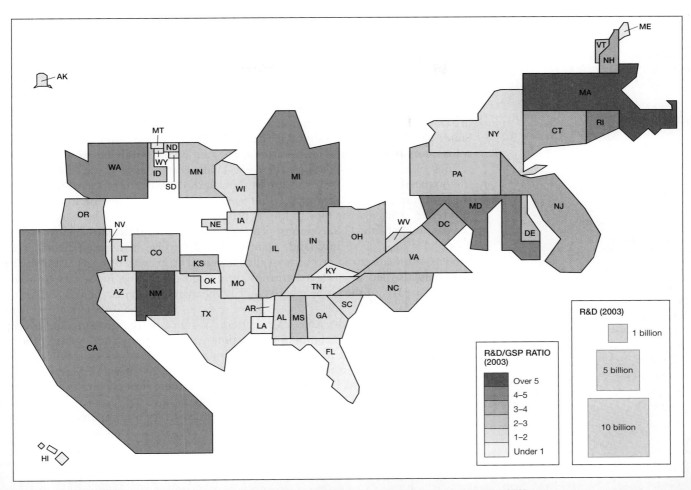

FIGURE 1 Research and Development (R&D) expenditures and R&D/gross state product ratios by state for 2003

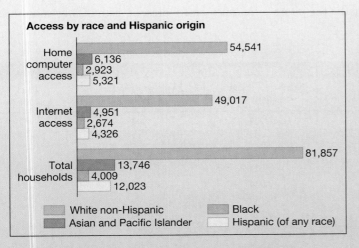

Access by race and Hispanic origin

Home computer access: 54,541 / 6,136 / 2,923 / 5,321

Internet access: 49,017 / 4,951 / 2,674 / 4,326

Total households: 81,857 / 13,746 / 4,009 / 12,023

White non-Hispanic
Asian and Pacific Islander
Black
Hispanic (of any race)

FIGURE 2 Computer use by race and ethnicity, 2003 As this figure indicates, race and ethnicity are significant variables in computer use and Internet access. Though the gap between whites and Asians and other minorities is beginning to narrow, the graph shows that blacks and Hispanics have less access to home computers as well as Internet access more generally. (*Source: Computer and Internet Use in the United States: 2003*, U.S. Census Bureau, Special Studies, 2005, p. 2.)

that spend substantially less have healthier populations. The reasons for this have to do with deep inequalities in the population based on access to health insurance coverage, income, race, ethnicity, and geographic factors like access to healthcare. For example, since 2000, the rate of infant mortality, which had been declining for more than 50 years in the United States, began to increase and is now higher than for many other core countries and equal to that of Malaysia.

Rural Poverty   Although the poor are found throughout the U.S. population, they can be roughly categorized into two geographic groups: the rural poor and the urban poor. Widespread instances of rural poverty and reduced income in the United States can be traced directly or indirectly to the transformation of family farms into transnational agricultural corporations. The number of family farms that have been in serious financial difficulty since the early 1980s continues to grow. The **farm crisis**—the financial failure and foreclosure of thousands of family farms across the U.S. Midwest—has not ceased, although it no longer gets the media attention it once did. Fewer and fewer farms are the type of family businesses that were once believed to constitute the backbone of the U.S. economy. Transnational corporations are able to use massive economies of scale to buy land, plant seed and fertilize it more efficiently, and then process and market the products of the harvest. The growth of transnational corporations has also led to the departure of rural food processing industries to other U.S. regions or parts of the globe where labor is cheaper and environmental regulations are less stringent.

So while most of the American economy is buoyant and growing and food prices are lower thanks to transnational production practices, many rural areas in the United States are experiencing a painful restructuring. Large numbers of small farmers and ranchers are being pushed into poverty and large parts of rural America are being depopulated as land is sold off to corporations, forcing farmers and ranchers to move into towns and cities to seek other ways of making a living. Canada has also experienced a precipitous drop in the number of farms, with the accompanying social distress (**Table 6.3**).

Urban Poverty   Urban poverty is just as grinding and difficult as rural poverty, though the causes and outcomes may differ. While rural poverty tends to affect poor whites, urban poverty tends to affect poor people of color. A particularly pressing component of contemporary urban poverty is the high cost of urban housing. For instance, the median price of a house in New York City is $472,000 with the median income at $59,200; for Los Angeles it is $500,000 and $56,200, respectively. For the top-ranked Canadian cities the median house price in Toronto is $290,400 with median income at $66,500; for Montréal it is $169,400 and $48,400, respectively. In both the United States and Canada the most expensive cities present astounding numbers. In San

TABLE 6.3 The Canadian Agricultural Landscape, 2001

Province	Number of Farms in 2001	Average Farm Size in 2001 (ha)	Area in Farmland in 2001 (ha thousands)
Canada	246,923	273	67,502
Newfoundland	643	63	40
Prince Edward Island	1,845	142	261
Nova Scotia	3,923	104	407
New Brunswick	3,034	128	388
Québec	32,139	106	3417
Ontario	59,728	92	5466
Manitoba	21,071	361	7602
Saskatchewan	50,598	519	26,266
Alberta	53,652	393	21,067
British Columbia	20,290	128	2587

Source: Statistics Canada. Available at **http://www.statcan.ca:80/english/Pgdb/econ124k.htm**.

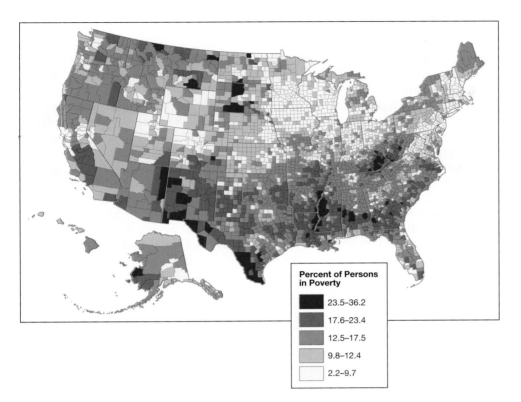

FIGURE 6.24 Poverty in the United States, 2004 One of the most startling aspects of this map is the geographical proximity of astronomical wealth and debilitating poverty. Some of the richest individuals in the country live side by side with some of its poorest. It is perhaps one of the most challenging paradoxes that in a "land of plenty," the plenty is concentrated among so few. (*Source: Demographic Profiles: 100 Percent and Sample Data.* Washington, DC: U.S. Census Bureau, 2004.)

Percent of Persons in Poverty

■	23.5–36.2
■	17.6–23.4
■	12.5–17.5
■	9.8–12.4
□	2.2–9.7

Francisco the median price of a house is $745,000 with median income at $91,200 and in Vancouver it's $373,000 and $56,000, respectively.

The gap between rich and poor in the United States is widening. Between the mid-1980s and 1990s, average household income (in real terms) rose by less than 1 percent. But the average income of the poorest one-fifth of households in the United States increased by only 0.1 percent, while the average income of the top one-fifth of households jumped by 20 percent. In the late 1990s, 5 percent of the population held 21 percent of the wealth. In 1999 the bottom 80 percent of the population claimed only 50 percent of the wealth. One reason is that nine-tenths of the growth in wealth went to the richest 1 percent of households, whose annual income in 1999 averaged $515,600 after taxes. With respect to these inequalities, it is already clear that recent changes in federal taxation will further boost income inequality. For example, for households in the top 1 percent of the income scale, the full savings from the tax cuts that were made from 2001 to 2003 were about $67,000. In contrast, for middle-income families, the cuts amounted to just under $600; and for the lowest 20 percent, the savings was $61.

Figure 6.24 illustrates the enormous wealth disparity that characterizes U.S. society. The map shows that poverty is greatest in rural areas—along the U.S.–Mexico border, in Appalachia, and in the Deep South and in the rural areas of the North/Northwest. Wealth is more typically concentrated in urban/suburban areas in the Midwest and Northeast and West.

Environmental Challenges

Decades of federal environmental protection legislation have forced U.S. industries to curtail much of their polluting processes or move to manufacturing sites outside the United States. Nonetheless, various regions of the country still face serious and persistent environmental challenges. Acid rain, generated by industrial processes and automobile emissions, continues to pose a challenge around the Rustbelt on both sides of the U.S.–Canada border. Along the U.S.–Mexico border, air and water pollution from the maquiladora industry is also a problem. Ironically, many manufacturing concerns migrated to the Mexican side of the border to escape the strict environmental regulations imposed by the U.S. government on industries. Able to pollute with very little restriction, these firms are dumping toxins into regional rivers and airsheds. Pollution does not recognize national boundaries, and much of the pollution generated by these U.S. firms operating in Mexico crosses the border back into the United States via northward-flowing rivers and airsheds that straddle the border between the two countries.

The legacy of past pollution-generating industrial practices also remains a problem. The U.S. government currently is overseeing the cleanup of hundreds of **superfund sites,** locations officially deemed by the federal government as extremely polluted and requiring extensive, supervised, and subsidized cleanup. The Rocky Flats defense weapons manufacturing site is a prime example. Approximately 13 kilometers (8 miles) outside of the city of Boulder, Colorado, the site is highly contaminated with plutonium, a radioactive substance used in the construction of missile systems.

The most serious environmental challenge Canadians and Americans face is their seemingly insatiable appetite for resources, especially energy resources. The set of images in **Figure 6.25** illustrates the high pattern of U.S. consumption. What is implied

FIGURE 6.25 Energy consumption, United States and Haiti The differential impact of core and peripheral countries on energy consumption is dramatic. Pictured here are families from one of the world's richest countries and one of its poorest. The Skeen family in the U.S. photo (a) appears to own only possessions that require large amounts of nonhuman or animal energy to produce and operate. In contrast, the Delafort family in the Haiti photo (b) owns a preponderance of possessions made by human hands and requiring little or no fossil-fuel energy to operate. The very different economic situations of the two families are portrayed clearly in the accompanying table. (*Source:* P. Menzel, *Material World: A Global Family Portrait.* San Francisco: Sierra Club Books, 1994, pp. 154–55 and 136–37.)

	Number in Family	Size of Dwelling	Work Week	Number of	Annual Per Capita Income ($U.S.)	Percentage of Income Spent on Food
Delaforts	6	30 square meters (325 square feet)	Father: 60 hours Mother: 55 hours Children: 30 hours each	Radios: 0 Stereos: 0 Phones: 0 TVs: 0 VCRs: 0 Vehicles: 0	$374	80%
Skeens	4	149 square meters (1600 square feet)	Father: 40 hours Mother: 20 hours (not including housework)	Radios: 3 Stereos: 3 Phones: 5 TVs: 2 VCRs: 1 Vehicles: truck, car, dune buggy	$22,356	9%

(a)

(b)

by these images is the amount of energy consumed, both to manufacture all these products and to operate and maintain them. The impact of the high level of energy consumption among core countries such as the United States, combined with increasing energy consumption among newly industrializing countries, will create serious challenges to Earth's supply of energy resources.

One particularly bright light in the movement to reduce energy consumption in the United States is that rising gasoline prices, worries about global warming, and a growing consumer interest in sustainability have created a large and growing market for environmentally-friendly—also known as "green"—goods and services. In fact, leading corporations such as the large automobile manufacturers and energy companies like General Electric and Shell Oil are making substantial investments in energy efficiency and energy technology; and consumers are responding positively. A good example is the largely unexpected growth in the purchase of hybrid cars. Booz Allen Hamilton, a highly respected global strategy and technology marketing firm, predicts that by 2015, 80 percent of all cars sold in the United States will be hybrid, as consumers choose from more than 50 models. Cities and counties are converting their fleets to hybrids along with large corporations like Federal Express (FedEx). And green technology is not only reshaping automobile supply and demand. It is also affecting architecture, furniture, and clothing and other consumer items, as well as urban and regional planning.

Regional Development

In the last 25 years, the different subregions of the United States and Canada have shifted and been restructured (**Figure 6.26**). As older subregions have reconfigured their economic bases, new regions have emerged on the cutting edge of technology and related industries. Even subregions that have been less pivotal to the U.S. and Canadian economies have reorganized their economies to some extent so they can participate more actively in the revolutionary changes that are underfoot. Three subregions are the clear pacesetters in innovation and dynamism: the Pacific Rim (western California); Cascadia (the northwestern United States, Alaska, and parts of Canada); and the U.S.–Canadian Core (the old Manufacturing Belt consisting primarily of the region around New York, Chicago, Toronto, and Montréal, and including the corridor between Boston and Washington, DC). In these regions the population has concentrated in large cities, manufacturing products and providing services for the areas surrounding them.

Beyond the U.S.–Canadian core regions and principal metropolitan areas lie numerous other landscapes and regions whose relationship to the environment, history, economic contribution, or political background makes them distinctive. The Prairie Provinces of Canada are critical to the world wheat market and to Canada's strong economy. Most importantly, this subregion produces more agricultural output than any other place of comparable size on Earth. While the U.S. portion of the Plains and Prairies tends also to include large-scale industry, the Canadian side is involved in mineral and oil extraction.

The New West, or Intermountain West, an area known historically for ranching and other primary-sector activities, has expanded its economy to include more service-based activities by mixing tourism and recreational activities with product-support service activities, as well as second-home and retirement residential developments. Some high-technology development is also part of the mix, especially in and around the places where universities are located, such as the Denver, Colorado, and Albuquerque, New Mexico, metropolitan regions.

New England and the Maritime Provinces are not only visually charming, as they reflect some of the earliest impacts of colonial architecture, but they are economically and politically significant for both historical and contemporary reasons. New England contains important high technology research and development centers and the universities needed to sustain them. The Maritime Provinces are increasingly developing their economies around call centers and related service-sector employment.

FIGURE 6.26 U.S. and Canadian subregions The most central and most widely known subregions of the United States and Canada are shown. It is a fairly consistent phenomenon of U.S. journalism that every five or so years, another popular book on America's new subregions is published. This phenomenon of serial publication reflects the fact that capital and people are increasingly mobile, thereby creating new subregions as they participate in contemporary economic transformations; it also reflects the public's hunger for new ways to think about themselves.

The U.S. South is also distinctive in terms of environment, history, politics, and culture. Even within the region there is a great deal of variation, particularly with respect to coastal and inland areas as well as the Deep South (the states of Alabama, Georgia, Louisiana, Mississippi, and South Carolina) and the other Southern states (Kentucky, Florida, North Carolina, Tennessee, Virginia, West Virginia, and sometimes Texas). Whereas the Deep South is often called the Bible Belt because of the attachment of much of the population to Protestant fundamentalism, states like Florida, for

FIGURE 6.27 Landscapes of the U.S. South The U.S. South is a varied subregion of the country with large, cosmopolitan cities and vast areas of beautiful scenery, much of it coastal. (a) Atlanta (b) Miami (c) Bayous of the Louisiana coast (d) Everglades National Park in south Florida.

instance, hardly qualify as part of the southern region as their populations are ethnically diverse and their orientation is more cosmopolitan than rural (**Figure 6.27**). Hawai'i, disconnected from the mainland United States far off in the Pacific, is also unique. A thick gloss of americanization overlies Polynesian cultural roots, and a strong connection to East Asia, especially Japan, also exists.

The Pacific Rim and the New Economy The Pacific Rim encompasses the western portion of the state of California, oriented around the three key coastal cities of San Francisco, Los Angeles, and San Diego and the inland state capital of Sacramento. More generally, the Pacific Rim includes all the nations bordering the Pacific Ocean as well as the island countries situated in it. As a global region, the Pacific Rim has grown dramatically, both economically and politically, over the last 20 years. In an attempt to improve trading relations among the many countries that are part of the Pacific Rim, the Asia-Pacific Economic Cooperation was established in 1989. Both the United States and Canada are members.

The U.S. Pacific Rim core region extends from the Pacific Ocean eastward to the Sierra Nevada mountain chain that runs the length of the state of California (see Figure 6.26). This region is the birthplace of the new economy conceived in Silicon Valley and now widely dispersed throughout many parts of the region. Through flows of trade, information, capital, and people, the global Pacific Rim region connects the U.S. economy to the diverse and growing economies of East, Southeast, and South Asia and the many Pacific island nations thousands of kilometers across the Pacific Ocean.

While it might seem odd to consider a part of one state to be a core region, it is important to be aware of just how productive, dynamic, and central the California economy is to the rest of the continent. California's gross state product in 2005 was an unbelievable $1.62 billion with a population of 36,132,147. This makes it the sixth largest economy in the world after, in rank order, the United States, Japan, Germany, the United Kingdom, and France.

For a long time in U.S. regional history, California was part of a distant frontier, a sleepy and economically inconsequential realm that contributed little to the national economy. Since the Gold Rush of 1849 and the massive migration of population to California in the 20th century, the U.S. Pacific Rim has matured into a region that contains more than one-fifth of all the Fortune 500 companies; numerous outstanding public and private universities, each containing a respectable share of prize-winning faculty; a unique culture that is premised upon wealth, health, and an active lifestyle built upon pleasant weather; and a variety of natural environments from oceans to mountains. It is certainly the open attitude, the willingness to take risks, and the proximity of excellent institutions of higher learning that have helped catapult this once rather marginal realm into the forefront of dynamism and change in the U.S. economy.

The urban system of this region links the various sections of its geographical vastness into a coordinated whole. In addition to the four key cities mentioned above, the region contains the knowledge industry and high-technology landscapes of Silicon Valley and key universities, including the University of California (UC) Berkeley, Stanford, UCLA, UC San Diego, Cal Tech, and UC Santa Cruz. It also contains agricultural landscapes in the Central and Imperial valleys that are linked to other knowledge-based institutions, such as the agricultural program at UC Davis. Important transformations in biotechnology and other agricultural innovations have been fostered in the Pacific Rim. These changes have helped transform the practice and output of agriculture around the world, while at the same time reconfiguring the U.S. food system and cultural tastes with respect to food. The Pacific Rim region also contains a respectable share of manufacturing activities, from textile and clothing production to aerospace and automobile manufacturing. Finally, the region is heavily involved in tertiary and quaternary sector activities (see Chapter 1, p. 14). The main core cities contain an array of banking, real estate, and insurance functions as well as legal and related services. And, of course, Hollywood, near Los Angeles, is the main home of the U.S. film industry.

FIGURE 6.28 Los Angeles, California Los Angeles is a key city on the Pacific Rim. Its port connects the United States to Asia, and its economy includes a strong manufacturing base, extensive service sector employment, and tourism. Because of its burgeoning economy, Los Angeles is the destination for hundreds of thousands of immigrants.

Major City: Los Angeles Geographers and planners at UCLA and the University of Southern California, including Michael Dear, Ed Soja, Jennifer Wolch, Mike Davis, Laura Pulido, Ruth Gilmore and Allen Scott, have provided a rich array of writing on Los Angeles, including its remarkable success stories as well as its darker underside of poverty and racism. In the process, they have created a school of academics who are committed to understanding Los Angeles as the prototypical North American city of the 21st century (**Figure 6.28**).

Los Angeles is a fairly old U.S. city, however, having been founded in 1781. Today it is the second-largest city in the United States with a 2004 population of 17,199,115 in the metropolitan area. It is also one of the most multiethnic of all U.S. cities. For most of its early years, Los Angeles was part of Mexico and existed as a small village surrounded by agricultural estates called *ranchos*. In 1850, when California became a state, Los Angeles was still a small settlement with a population under 2000. When the Southern Pacific Railroad tied into Los Angeles in 1872, the city was launched into a growth phase that has continued to the present.

Perhaps the most central story of the growth of Los Angeles is a twinned one: the story of water and transportation. The Los Angeles basin is a semiarid realm with nearly all of its rain falling in the winter and spring. Without a secure and substantial supply of water, people could migrate but they could not survive. Roman Polanski's 1974 *film noir, Chinatown*, captures the intrigue and political machinations that surround the story of building a massive aqueduct that would transport water from the Owens Valley, in the Mojave Desert, hundreds of miles away, across the San Gabriel Mountains and into the Los Angeles basin. Other water-supply projects have enabled Los Angeles to maintain its awesome pace of growth throughout the 20th century.

A second feature of Los Angeles is its low-lying, decentralized urban form, which was made possible by the introduction of the electric streetcar and interurban rail lines during the early years of the 20th century. These forms of urban transportation encouraged decentralization by allowing people to move out to suburban tracts and still easily commute to the central business district or to other employment sites. From 1900 to 1940, Los Angeles was the fastest-growing city in the United States. When the truck and the automobile were introduced during this period, they helped fuel decentralization even more. And by mid-century, Los Angeles already had an extensively developed freeway system.

Much of the economic structure of Los Angeles has been built on manufacturing. In addition to the motion picture industry, the metropolitan area manufactures garments, furniture, and defense and aerospace products. World War II and the Cold War made Los Angeles one of the largest weapons-manufacturing centers in the nation. The Los Angeles area also has a strong service economy. If the Los Angeles metropolitan region were a separate country, it would possess the world's 11th-largest economy based on its GNP, surpassing those of Austria and India.

Los Angeles persists as a gateway for immigrants, with more than 25 percent of the nation's immigrants settling in the metropolitan region. It is probably the most ethnically diverse metropolitan region in the United States as well, with whites now representing less than 40 percent of the total population. Fully 50 percent of Los Angelenos speak a language other than English at home. The fashion district in downtown Los Angeles is a prime example of the implications of these transformations in the demography of the metropolitan region.[1] Once the stronghold of Jewish garment merchants and manufacturers who migrated from New York in the 1950s to establish Los Angeles as the nation's leading center for sportswear and women's apparel, the fashion district is now dominated by Middle Eastern immigrants. Home to 5000 companies employing more than 50,000 people, the garment district takes in about $8 billion a year in wholesale and retail sales. Clearly, fortunes are being made here, and savvy new immigrants are making them. But the fashion district, as in the past, also has a reputation for low wages and sweatshop working conditions. As a consequence, the fashion industry was the object of demonstrations at the Democratic Convention held in Los Angeles in 2000.

Los Angeles is a metropolitan region of dramatic contrasts, where television stars make millions of dollars per episode as garment workers who speak little or no English struggle to make ends meet. It is also an important reminder that at the local scale, even in a region of enormous wealth, the periphery can exist side by side with the core.

Cascadia and Internationalism A second U.S.–Canadian Core region is north of the Pacific Rim. This is Cascadia, which includes Alaska, parts of the Canadian Yukon and Northwest Territories, British Columbia, and Alberta, as well as parts of the states of Washington, Oregon, and California. The Cascadian region's

---

[1]J. Kotkin, "Casbah for Clothes Is Bustling in California," *New York Times*, Business Section, August 20, 2000, p. 6.

FIGURE 6.29 Seattle, Washington The West Coast cities of the region are interesting and enchanting for very different reasons, but they share an attractive mix of natural beauty, dynamic culture, and prosperous economies. Seattle's role in the Cascadian region complements, and in some areas surpasses, that of Vancouver. Seattle is a city known to most twenty-somethings as the hip and quirky home of "grunge" music, the last stand of Kurt Cobain, and a mecca for the coffee-obsessed. In addition to being all of those things, Seattle is also one of the fastest-growing metropolitan regions in the region, with a diverse economic structure based on trade, manufacturing, high technology, tourism, and the whole range of quaternary-sector economic activities.

name comes from the Cascade mountain range, which runs from northern California through Oregon and Washington and into southern British Columbia. At its core are the key cities that anchor the populous corridor—Vancouver, Seattle, and Portland (**Figure 6.29**). Cascadia is a relatively new and dynamic region oriented around high technology. An important additional hallmark of Cascadia is its internationalism, which is manifested in ignoring, if not actually erasing, the cultural, political, and economic borders of three northwestern states, two Canadian provinces, and two territories (see Figure 6.26).

Cascadia is unique in that it is an unusually unified international region that has a global outlook. Cascadia is physically larger than the European Union, and, if it were an independent nation, it would rank as the world's tenth largest economy in terms of its annual GDP. The region employs more than 8 million people with a steady rate of employment growth. The Washington–British Columbia border is the busiest of any along the U.S.–Canada border, and the region contains four exceptional ports (Portland, Tacoma, Seattle, and Vancouver). Seattle is the leading West Coast container port; Vancouver is the busiest in terms of volume shipped. Most importantly for its global positioning, the region is the closest place in North America to Japan, Hong Kong, and China.

The diverse economic structure of the region includes a large aerospace industry. Cascadia is home to the third-largest computer software development center in North America, with more than 1000 software companies, including Microsoft, the largest in the world. The region is a growing center for environmental technology and biotechnology, as well as a very popular destination for outdoor tourism, from skiing to sea kayaking. Within the next few years, tourism is expected to be the largest employer and generator of foreign currency in the Pacific Northwest.

As geographer Matthew Sparke has written, despite all this international cooperation and phenomenal economic growth, there are fears that there may be too much growth in Cascadia. For instance, many fear that so much growth will unbalance the region as cities grow at the expense of their hinterlands, or that the Vancouver metropolitan area could become extraordinarily prosperous while Idaho languishes. Worse, Vancouver might be subsumed under the dominant orbit of Seattle. There is also very real and widespread concern that so much growth—more people, more cars, more houses, more roads—will add to the existing problems of crime, pollution, traffic congestion, and water supply in the burgeoning urban regions.

The Cascadian region is a young region, so it is too soon to tell what its future will be. Clearly, however, it is a serious competitor to the other two core regions of the United States and Canada in terms of its influence over global economic and cultural processes.

Major City: Vancouver Perhaps the most spectacularly beautiful city in North America, Vancouver is also one of its most atmospheric (**Figure 6.30**). Located along the west coast of Canada, where the Fraser River cuts across the Coast Mountains and empties into the Strait of Georgia, Vancouver is the metropolitan center of the province of British Columbia and a key node in the urban hierarchy of Cascadia. Nestled between the ocean and snowcapped mountains, Vancouver's downtown cozily fills a narrow sloping peninsula. The urban region possesses waterfront views, charming beaches, an expanse of parkland, and mirrored skyscrapers that twinkle beguilingly by night and reflect the bustling life of the city and harbor by day. To the southeast, Vancouver sprawls outward and upward to the forested slopes of the Coast Mountains and the vast wilderness of the British Columbia interior.

Only 22 kilometers (about 13.5 miles) from the U.S.–Canada border, Vancouver is Canada's closest major urban center to the United States. It is also Canada's third-largest

FIGURE 6.30 Vancouver, British Columbia Vancouver is the key Canadian city of Cascadia, with strong links to the United States as well as to the various regions of Asia.

city and its fastest-growing one, due in large part to the volume of traffic through its port facilities. The Port of Vancouver ships raw materials from the Canadian interior—lumber, wheat, and minerals—handling more dry tonnage than the ports of Seattle, Tacoma, Portland, San Francisco, and San Diego combined. Vancouver claims the title of "gateway to the Far East." The region plays a pivotal role in linking the North American continent to the Pacific Rim. Vancouver's commercial connections to the Pacific Rim have been reinforced, as geographer Katharyne Mitchell has shown, by the large influx of wealthy Hong Kong Chinese, the so-called "yacht people," who have migrated to Vancouver in extraordinary numbers. With impacts on all aspects of everyday life—schools, religion, food, and shopping among them—the most-talked-about impact of the Hong Kong migration to Vancouver has been on property values, which have skyrocketed since the mid-1980s, making Vancouver one of North America's most costly cities.

Despite the astronomical increases in real estate prices, Vancouver continues to be an attractive destination for migrants from all over the world. Between 1987 and 1992 the population increased by 17 percent. By the end of 2010, the population is expected to have grown by a phenomenal 50 percent. Culturally, the Vancouver region contains both high art and counterculture. It possesses a world-class museum and symphony orchestra, as well as dance and theater companies on the cutting edge of contemporary art. In terms of popular culture, it is now North America's largest film and television production center after Los Angeles and New York.

Vancouver also has a counterculture that nurtures avant-garde art galleries, clubs, and bars. One of the most irritating aspects of the counterculture for the U.S. Drug Enforcement Agency is the lax attitude Vancouver authorities have toward marijuana—particularly the growing of it. Attitudes among Vancouver residents about marijuana have turned the region into a major North American producer for some of the drug's strongest strains. While pot farmers in the United States and Mexico grow marijuana plantation style, the cooler climes of British Columbia require an indoor growing regime where plants have been genetically modified to reach potency levels ten times that of Woodstock-era weed. The Royal Canadian Mounted Police estimate that there are about 10,000 marijuana "grow operations" in Vancouver, supporting a $6-billion-a-year industry, making it British Columbia's number one crop.

[2]J. Brooke, "Home-Grown Drug Business Boom in Vancouver," *New York Times*, International Section, August 27, 2000, p. 3.

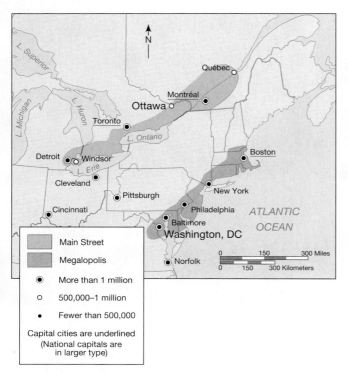

FIGURE 6.31 Megalopolis and Main Street The term *megalopolis* was originally coined by the Greeks to refer to places where people lived, rather than just to abstract space. French geographer Jean Gottman resuscitated the term to describe the dense, extended, and connected urban settlements, a "super-metropolitan" conurbation, along the coast of the eastern United States; hence, the proper name "Megalopolis." Main Street is Canada's answer to Megalopolis. Also a heavily urbanized corridor, Main Street connects some of Canada's major cities. The two terms are also interesting in their contrast, with Main Street suggesting a homey, familiar space, and Megalopolis implying something of extraordinary scale.

The booming marijuana industry is evidence of some of the negative effects of Vancouver's phenomenal recent growth. Taxes are the highest of any city in the United States or Canada. Coupled with extraordinarily high real estate prices, finding a reasonably priced place to live is extremely difficult in most parts of the metropolitan region. There is high unemployment and underemployment among young people as a lot of low-wage jobs, largely in tourism, dominate employment opportunities. With "B.C. Bud" prices more than triple on the U.S. side of the border, marijuana farming offers a lucrative alternative to low wages or no job at all. Add permissive attitudes to the fact that technical support for marijuana growing is widely available throughout the region, and all the ingredients are available for a boom industry.

The U.S.–Canadian Core Moving east across the middle of the continent, a third key subregion is the old Manufacturing Belt encompassing the realm primarily around the key cities of New York and Chicago, as well as Montréal and Toronto. The U.S.–Canadian Core also encompasses the most populous corridor in the United States that runs from Washington, DC, to Boston, known as **Megalopolis**, and a similar one that runs from Windsor to Québec City in Canada, known as **"Main Street"** (**Figure 6.31**). Although dubbed *the Manufacturing Belt* in the late 19th and early 20th centuries because it constituted the industrial powerhouse of the two countries, the label at the beginning of the 21st century is a misnomer. Manufacturing employment has dropped dramatically since the 1960s and quaternary economic employment now dominates the region. We call this the core of the core: the U.S.–Canadian Core.

The history of this subregion is instructive because it embodies the damage as well as the new growth that cycles of capital investment and disinvestment can visit upon people and place. The cities of the old Manufacturing Belt (New York, Chicago, Toronto, Boston, Montréal, Philadelphia, Baltimore, Chicago, Detroit, Windsor, Hamilton, Québec City, Cincinnati, Minneapolis, Milwaukee, St. Louis, and Cleveland, to name the most populous ones), already thriving industrial centers in the late 19th century, were connected through the early railroad network (**Figure 6.32**). As a result, they were well placed to take advantage of crucial economic shifts that broke upon the two countries between 1880 and 1920. These included the general upsurge in demand for consumer goods, the increased efficiency of the telegraph system and postal services, advances in manufacturing technologies, and the opening up of the national market through the continued extension of the railroad. Individual cities specialized in particular industrial products (for example, grain milling in Minneapolis, agricultural tools and equipment in Chicago, brewing in Milwaukee and St. Louis, coach building and furniture in Cincinnati), producing in volume for the national market rather than local ones (**Figure 6.33**). This specialization in turn required an increase in commodity flows between the cities of the old Manufacturing Belt, which bound the region even more closely together.

By the mid-20th century, however, the requirements of a new technology system—using robotics, telematics, biotechnology, and other knowledge-based systems—overwhelmed the ability of the region to respond, and disinvestment in the form of deindustrialization occurred (see Figure 6.23). For much of the 1970s and 1980s, the old Manufacturing Belt suffered population loss and capital flight as workers, entrepreneurs, and investors went to other parts of the region and the world to take advantage of more attractive employment and investment opportunities. But by the early 1990s, the old Manufacturing Belt was showing signs of recovery and by the middle of the decade it had regained its dominance. As Table 1 on page 304 shows, the key indicators of the new economy substantiate that many of the states in this subregion are especially active participants in the new economy as they hold the largest share of the top places. Of the top ten ranked states, seven are U.S. Core states (Massachusetts, Maryland, New Jersey, Connecticut, Virginia, Delaware, and New York), and the other three are from the fast-growing and relatively newer regions: Cascadia, the Pacific Rim, and the New West.

We can therefore claim that the U.S.–Canadian Core, with the metropolitan region of New York as its primary city, is also the primary core subregion of North America. While Cascadia and the Pacific Rim possess dynamic and complex economic structures with growing populations and lively cultures, they have not yet superseded the power—economic, political, and cultural—that the U.S.–Canadian Core commands. While the U.S.–Canadian Core has been built on urban regions, all of which experienced significant and wrenching declines due to the economic crises of the mid-1970s, it has all also enjoyed remarkable renewal. Former heavy industrial urban areas have replaced the outmoded components of the old economy (crumbling physical infrastructure, heavy dependence on unionized labor, inflexible production systems) with the more effective and leaner components of the new economy (high-technology and knowledge-based jobs, high levels of venture capital investment, a nonunionized workforce).

Although the U.S.–Canadian Core is once again prosperous, having remade itself as a key player in the new economy, not all areas of the region are enjoying that prosperity. Newark, New Jersey, a city that sits across the Hudson River in the long shadow of New York City, is still surrounded by pockets of extreme poverty, despite other pockets of progress and prosperity. Newark was the site of riots in the very hot summer of 1967 when other cities, also with large African-American populations, violently erupted to protest the institutionalized racism of U.S. society epitomized in the extreme poverty of too many of its black citizens. More than three decades later, Newark is hardly better off than it was in 1967, as more and more manufacturing jobs disappear and its population declines. Those who remain are more likely than ever to be poor.

Major City: New York City New York City has been the premier urban center of the United States since the early 19th century, eclipsing Boston at the end of the Revolutionary War. Over the last two centuries New York has attracted the largest population (21,524,931 in the metropolitan area in 2004)—and usually highly polyglot—and the most advanced and dynamic economy of any of its competitors in the United States, Canada, and abroad. A series of forces enabled New York to catapult to the top of the national urban hierarchy and, by 1920, to the top of the global urban hierarchy. In the 19th century New York proved especially hospitable to innovation and new commercial elites, and its port become the primary center for trade with Europe. The Erie Canal (1817–25) expanded the city's hinterlands to the far western end of the Great Lakes. By 1867, the Canal carried nearly 70 percent of all commerce, double that of all the national and regional railroads combined, thereby turning New York into the United States' entrepôt, a center for the storage and transshipment of goods. By 1850, 70 percent of imports and exports passed through the port of New York. With such an enormous volume of trade under its control, the urban region naturally also attracted bankers, financiers, stock, produce, and cotton exchanges, shippers, warehousing, law practices, insurance companies—in short, the full range of economic institutions.

The economic base of New York gradually shifted from commerce to light manufacturing over the course of the 19th century. Between 1850 and 1950, clothing and garment manufacturing employed nearly 50 percent of the population. The predominance of light manufacturing attracted cheap labor, most of whom were immigrants from Europe. By 1860, the foreign-born constituted nearly 50 percent of the population. The explosive growth in population and in the economy resulted in dramatic physical development. Because the core of the New York metropolitan region,

FIGURE 6.32 Philadelphia, Pennsylvania Founded by William Penn in 1682, Philadelphia links the midsection of the United States to the Atlantic coast. Once a center of transatlantic commerce, the city is currently dominated by service-sector employment.

FIGURE 6.33 Minneapolis, Minnesota Minneapolis is the largest city in Minnesota and one of the key points along the Mississippi River. The city's economy developed largely around the processing of grain from the Great Plains where companies like General Mills and Pillsbury became giant corporations. Today Minneapolis is more noted for its medical facilities and financial institutions.

FIGURE 6.34 World Trade Center The financial heart of New York City, the twin towers of the World Trade Center were proud symbols of the heart of global capitalism. On September 11, 2001, a terrorist attack completely destroyed the towers, other parts of the complex, and surrounding buildings, killing thousands of people, paralyzing the city and the region, and profoundly disrupting the U.S. economy. The attacks caused changes in U.S. politics at home and abroad, leading to a war on terrorism in Iraq as well as one at home. The war on terrorism in the United States has affected immigration, air travel, and a wide range of everyday practices. It is also responsible for the creation of a new federal initiative, called "homeland security," that reaches from Washington, DC, into the neighborhoods of cities and towns across the country.

Manhattan, is a long narrow island—20.9 kilometers (13 miles) north to south, 3.2 kilometers (2 miles) east to west—building had to reach skyward to accommodate growth for both residences and economic activity. Tall buildings are emblematic of New York, so much so that at various times over the last century, the world's tallest building was in New York: The Park Row Building (1899), the Singer Tower (1908), the Metropolitan Life Tower (1909), the Woolworth Building (1931), and the Empire State Building (1931). In 1974 New York had as many 60-story buildings as all of the rest of the world combined and twice as much office space in its central business district as any other CBD on Earth (Figure 6.34). With building densities intensifying in Manhattan as the New York economy continued to prosper, by 1950, the resident-per-square-mile density for Manhattan was a staggering 86,730 as compared with Chicago at 16,165 and Los Angeles at 4391.

The 1950s was also the beginning of the end of manufacturing as the primary economic base for New York. Between 1950 and 1990, New York lost 70 percent of its manufacturing jobs. Approximately 250,000 jobs in wholesale and retail were also eliminated. As industry declined and took related jobs with it, growth occurred in the service sector, a significant proportion of which was in finance, insurance, and real estate. But many banking jobs were also lost in the late 1980s and early 1990s as large corporations downsized their workforces or left the metropolitan region altogether. As a result of a declining tax base with the departure of jobs and people, the New York City government experienced fiscal crises as increasing demands for services, expanding welfare rolls, and deteriorating infrastructure placed a heavy burden on a shaky budget. In 1975 the city nearly went bankrupt but was saved when the state of New York intervened. New York City's municipal debt was $22.5 billion in 1995.

Since 1995, however, the economy of New York, as throughout North America, has improved dramatically. At the beginning of the 21st century, New York and its economic institutions are strong. The city has a highly transnational population, with more than 150 nations represented among its documented immigrants. For the first time in the city's history, no single ethnic group constitutes a majority of the population. A prosperous population of highly educated and skilled workers has increased the demand for housing and raised the value of real estate to astronomical levels in Manhattan. Geographer Neil Smith has shown that the housing market has responded by renovating areas of the city that were traditionally occupied by lower-income workers and immigrants. The result is **gentrification**, the process whereby the middle class, also known as the *gentry*, move into areas where real estate values have plummeted because of political and economic disinvestment. Gentrifiers transform the housing stock, which is usually architecturally interesting and structurally sound, making it difficult for the residents who first lived there to afford the higher rents or taxes that ensue from redevelopment.

SUMMARY AND CONCLUSIONS

The histories of the United States and Canada are parallel in many ways, yet there are important differences. Differences in the type of early European settlement, political independence, and economic history and structure have helped shape differences in political and economic structure, among other things. The same is true of subregional differences. And while the differences between the two countries are many and there have even been episodes of outright conflict, there is also a long history of cooperation. Still, many critics of U.S.–Canada relations would argue that "cooperation" is a euphemism for the heavy-handed dominance that the United States exerts over much of Canadian economic, cultural, and social life.

Canada and the United States continue to enjoy a strong relationship despite the friction that regularly emerges between them. The United States continues to be the largest importer of Canadian exports, and Canada continues to import a significant amount of U.S.–produced goods. The United States and Canada also have a reciprocal relationship when it comes to capital, with the United States investing large amounts in Canadian industry and new economy ventures and Canada investing in U.S. real estate, among other things. The trade alliances that created one market between the two countries continue to unite them.

The influence of the U.S.–Canadian region on the world continues to be substantial. While U.S. economic, cultural, and political ideas are likely to dominate the processes of globalization, Canada will remain a player in the development of the Pacific Rim and in peaceful resolution of international conflict.

KEY TERMS

americanization (p. 281)
assimilation (p. 293)
creative destruction (p. 301)
europeanization (p. 281)
farm crisis (p. 306)

federal state (p. 302)
gentrification (p. 318)
hate crime (p. 293)
indentured servant (p. 282)
intermontane (p. 274)

internal migration (p. 294)
Main Street (p. 316)
Megalopolis (p. 316)
multiculturalism (p. 294)
staples economy (p. 287)

suburbanization (p. 297)
superfund site (p. 308)

REVIEW QUESTIONS

Testing Your Understanding

1. Which mountains, rivers, and lakes contribute most to the prosperity of the United States and Canada? What role do the Great Plains play in regional economic development? How does the abundance of water moderate climate in the region?

2. Describe the process of human settlement in the United States and Canada.

3. How did indigenous peoples in the United States and Canada view concepts such as private property and land ownership? How culturally uniform were indigenous peoples at the time of European contact?

4. When and where did the first Europeans settle in the United States and Canada? Centuries later, while Spain colonized Florida, which other European powers followed to colonize other parts of the United States and Canada? How did europeanization differ from americanization?

5. Why did European colonists arm indigenous peoples? How did disease and demoralization affect native populations?

6. How did the U.S. government encourage mobility and manifest destiny along a steadily moving frontier from the late 1700s to the mid-1800s?

7. What factors led to the establishment of the Confederate States of America in 1861 and the Dominion of Canada in 1867?

8. Why was the United States able to make the transition from a periphery to a core state by 1900? Why, at that time, was Canada unable to do the same?

9. How does Canada protect its own distinct national culture?

10. Describe the Rustbelt and the Sunbelt.

11. What factors influence rural and urban poverty in the United States and Canada today?

Thinking Geographically

1. Which areas of the United States and Canada suffer most from acid rain, deforestation, chemical or nuclear toxic waste, and flooding? What can be done to reduce or remedy ecological damage?

2. Describe the factors that make Québec unique. Why do so many Québeçois want to secede from Canada? How might increasing globalization affect Québec?

3. Discuss the three main waves of immigration into the United States. When did they occur and where did the immigrants come from? Discuss the three main waves of internal migration within the United States. How were African Americans, many of whose ancestors were brought to the United States long before other immigrant groups arrived, generally affected by immigration and internal migration?

4. Which areas have been primarily Hispanic since their incorporation into the United States? Which areas have seen a large increase in Hispanic population over the past 30 years, and why?

5. Contrast and compare the changing geography (since 1980) of the Pacific Rim, Cascadia, and the North American Core. What factors make Silicon Valley, Vancouver, and New York City distinctive?

6. What factors make the Prairie Provinces/States, New England States–Maritime Provinces, and U.S. South peripheral to the core regions?

7. What concerns accompany rapid urbanization in the New West? What pull factors bring new migrants into the area?

FURTHER READING

Ayers, E. L., and Mittendorf, B. C., *The Oxford Book of the American South: Testimony, Memory, and Fiction*. Oxford: Oxford University Press, 1997.

Baker, L. D. (ed.), *Life in America: Identity and Everyday Experience*. Oxford: Blackwell Publishing, 2004.

Berry, K. A., and Henderson, M. L., *Geographical Identities of Ethnic America: Race, Space, and Place*. Reno: University of Nevada Press, 2002.

Birdsall, S. S., Palka, E. J., and Malinowski, J. C., *Regional Landscapes of the United States and Canada*, 6th ed. New York: John Wiley & Sons, 2004.

Bottles, S., *Los Angeles and the Automobile: The Making of the Modern City*. Berkeley: University of California Press, 1987.

Cameron, D., and Watkins, M., *Canada Under Free Trade*. Toronto: James Lorimer, 1993.

Carment, D., Stack, J. F., and Harvey, F. P. (eds.), *The International Politics of Quebec Secession: State Making and State Breaking in North America*. Westport, CT: Praeger Publishers, 2001.

Christian, S., "Hispanic Workers Revitalize a Town," *New York Times*, p. A1, January 29, 1998.

Chudacoff, H. P., and Smith, J. E., *The Evolution of American Urban Society*, 6th ed. Englewood Cliffs, NJ: Prentice Hall, 2004.

Cronon, W., *Changes in the Land: Indians, Colonists, and the Ecology of New England*. New York: Hill and Wang, 1983.

Earle, R. L., and Wirth, J. D., *Identities in North America: The Search for Community*. Stanford, CA: Stanford University Press, 1995.

Friesen, G., *Citizens and Nation: An Essay on History, Communication, and Canada*. Toronto: University of Toronto Press, 2000.

Harris, C., and Warkentin, J., *Canada Before Confederation*. New York: Oxford University Press, 1974.

Hayden, D., *Building Suburbia: Green Fields and Urban Growth, 1820–2000*. New York: Vintage, 2004.

Hudson, J. C., *Across This Land: A Regional Geography of the United States and Canada*. Baltimore: The Johns Hopkins University Press, 2002.

Issel, W., "San Francisco, California," in L. Shumsky (ed.), *Encyclopedia of Urban America: The Cities and Suburbs*, Vol. 2 (pp. 688–91). Santa Barbara, CA: ABC-Clio, 1999.

Kerr, D., and Holdsworth, D. (eds.), *Historical Atlas of Canada. Volume 3: Addressing the Twentieth Century*. Toronto: University of Toronto Press, 1993.

Kotkin, J., *The New Geography: How the Digital Revolution Is Reshaping the American Landscape*. New York: Random House, 2000.

McCann, L. D. (ed.), *Heartland and Hinterland: A Geography of Canada*. Scarborough, Ontario: Prentice Hall, 1982.

Meinig, D. W., *The Shaping of America: A Geographical Perspective on 500 Years of History, Volume 1, Atlantic America, 1492–1800*. New Haven: Yale University Press, 1986.

Miller, J., *Shamanic Odyssey: The Lushootseed Salish Journey to the Land of the Dead*. San Francisco: Ballena Press, 1988.

Mitchell, R. D., and Groves, P. A. (eds.), *North America: The Historical Geography of a Changing Continent*. London: Hutchinson, 1987.

Moon, W. L. H., *River Horse: The Logbook of a Boat Across America*. New York: Penguin, 2001.

Morrison, R. B., and Wilson, C. R. (eds.), *Native Peoples: The Canadian Experience*, 2nd ed. Toronto: McClelland & Stewart, 1986.

Riebsame, W., *Atlas of the New West: Portrait of a Changing Region*. New York: W. W. Norton, 1997.

Smith, N., *The New Urban Frontier: Gentrification and the Revanchist City*. New York: Routledge, 1996.

Vázquez, F. H., and Torres, R. D., *Latino/a Thought: Culture, Politics, and Society*. Lanham, MD: Rowman & Littlefield, 2003.

Warkentin, J., *Canada: A Regional Geography*. Scarborough, Ontario: Prentice Hall, 1997.

Zelinsky, W., *The Cultural Geography of the U.S.: A Revised Edition*. Englewood Cliffs, NJ: Prentice Hall, 1992.

FILM, MUSIC, AND POPULAR LITERATURE

Film

A Day Without a Mexican. Directed by Sergio Arau, 2004. Story of what life would be like in Southern California without Mexican labor.

The Black Robe. Directed by Bruce Beresford, 1991. A tale of missionizing in 18th-century Canada.

Boyz N the Hood. Directed by John Singleton, 1991. Young men grow up in a Los Angeles ghetto.

Crash. Directed by Paul Haggis, 2005. Diversity, conflict, and redemption in Los Angeles.

Cul de Sac: A Suburban Story. Directed by Garrett Scott, 2001. A story of working-class life in decline in the suburbs of San Diego.

Dreamland. Directed by Lisanne Skyler, 2000. A portrait of Las Vegas beyond the grand casinos.

Gangs of New York. Directed by Martin Scorsese, 2002. Street conflict between "nativists" and Irish immigrants in New York City.

Giant. Directed by George Stevens, 1956. Conflicts arise between ranching and oil exploration in Texas.

In America. Directed by Jim Sheridan, 2002. A twenty-first century Irish immigrant family in New York City.

Lewis and Clark: The Journey of the Corps of Discovery. Directed by Ken Burns, 1993. Story of the famous expedition of Lewis and Clark across the United States.

Kanehsatake: 270 Years of Resistance. Directed by Alanis Obomsawin, 1993. Documents the 1990 crisis when Native Americans of the Mohawk Nation blocked access to reserve land that was being appropriated against the nation's will by the white community of Oka, Québec, Canada.

Mi Vida Loca. Directed by Allison Anders, 1993. Explores what life is like for girl gang members in a Los Angeles barrio.

My Father's Angel. Directed by Mark Bauche, 1999. A Muslim Serbian couple migrate to Vancouver.

Roger and Me. Directed by Michael Moore, 1989. Explores the closure of the General Motors plant at Flint, Michigan, which resulted in the loss of 30,000 jobs.

Well-Founded Fear. Directed by Michael Camarini and Shari Robertson, 2000. A story about refugee asylum in the U.S. Immigration Service.

Music

Bragg, Billy, and Wilco. *Mermaid Avenue, Vols. I and II*. Electra, 1998.

Four Mountain Nation Singers. *Navajo Chants, Vol. 1: Pow Wow Songs*. Astro Music, 2000.

Johnson, Robert. *The Robert Johnson Songbook*. King of Spades Music, 1998.

Monroe, Bill. *What Would You Give in Exchange for Your Soul?* Rounder, 2000.

NPR Radio. "American Routes." Radio program featuring varieties of American music.

Original Dixieland Jazz Band. *The Complete Original Dixieland Jazz Band*. BMG/RCA, 1995.

The Riverside History of Classic Jazz. Fantasy/Riverside, 1994.

Sugar Hill Gang. *Rapper's Delight: The Best of Sugar Hill Gang*. Rhino, 1996.

Various Artists. *Alligator Stomp 1: Cajun and Zydeco Classics*. Wea/Atlantic/Rhino, 1990.

Various Artists. *Masters of Tejano Music*. Sony Discos, 2000.

Various Artists. *Weaving the Strands: Music by Contemporary Native American Women*. Red Feather, 1990.

Popular Literature

Brown, Dee. *Bury My Heart at Wounded Knee: An Indian History of the American West*. New York: Henry Holt, 1991. Beginning with the Long Walk of the Navajos in 1860 and ending 30 years later with the massacre of Sioux men, women, and children at Wounded Knee in South Dakota, this book tells how the American Indians lost their land and lives to a dynamically expanding white society.

Bryson, Bill. *I'm a Stranger Here Myself: Notes on Returning to America After 20 Years Away*. New York: Broadway, 2000. A travel story of sorts about a man who returns to a small New Hampshire town after living in England for two decades.

Cather, Willa. *My Antonia*. Boston: Houghton Mifflin, 1954. Set in Nebraska in the late 19th century, this story of the immigrant settlers of the American plains is told through the experiences of the spirited daughter of a Bohemian immigrant family planning to farm on the untamed land.

Churchill, Ward. *A Little Matter of Genocide: Holocaust and Denial in the Americas, 1492 to the Present*. San Francisco: City Lights, 1998. An extremely well-documented historical accounting of targeted racial/ethnic killings from 1492 to the present, resulting in the near-extermination or genocide of the once-populous native North American Indians.

Coupland, Douglas. *Souvenir of Canada (1 and 2)*. Vancouver: Douglas & McIntyre, 2002 & 2004. Often reviewed as a "valentine" to Canada, the two volumes are a collection of stories about what it's like to be a Canadian now and what it might be like in the future.

Cronon, William. *Nature's Metropolis: Chicago and the Great West*. New York: W. W. Norton, 1992. History of 19th-century Chicago and the widespread effects it had on millions of square miles of ecological, cultural, and economic frontier.

Lee, Harper. *To Kill a Mockingbird*. Philadelphia: J. B. Lippincott, 1960. An eight-year-old girl named Scout, living in Maycomb County, Alabama, in the 1930s, is exposed to issues of class, justice, and race in the U.S. South.

McMurtry, Larry. *Lonesome Dove*. New York: Simon & Schuster, 1985. Pulitzer Prize-winning novel that depicts the degeneration of the myth of the American West through the story of cowboys herding cattle on a great trail-drive set in the 19th century.

Morrison, Toni. *Beloved*. New York: Knopf, 1987. Pulitzer Prize-winning novel about the years following the Civil War, focusing on a murdered child who haunts the Ohio home of a former slave.

Proulx, Annie. *The Shipping News*. New York: Scribner's, 1992. This darkly comic, wonderfully inventive work, winner of the 1993 National Book Award, transforms the lore of Newfoundland—including shipwrecks, nautical knotting, horrid weather, and family legend—into brilliant literary art.

Smiley, Jane. *A Thousand Acres*. New York: Knopf, 1991. Set in Zebulon County, Iowa, this novel is a portrait of an American family farm at the end of the 20th century.

Stegner, Wallace. *Angle of Repose*. New York: Doubleday, 1971. A novel of discovery—personal, historical, and geographical—that comes together in an enthralling portrait of four generations in the life of a U.S. family.

Steinbeck, John. *The Grapes of Wrath*. New York: Viking, 1939. Pulitzer Prize-winning novel about a family of dispossessed Oklahoma farmers who migrate to California to begin their lives anew.

Twain, Mark. *The Adventures of Huckleberry Finn*. New York: Signet Classics, 1959. A classic novel that tells the story of a teenaged misfit who finds himself floating on a raft down the Mississippi River with an escaping slave.

7 Latin America

ATLANTIC OCEAN

BAHAMAS
• Nassau

Gulf of Mexico

Tropic of Cancer

Tijuana ○

Ciudad Juárez ○

Monterrey •

MEXICO

Guadalajara ○

Mexico City ○
• Veracruz

Havana •

GREATER ANTILLES

CUBA
Santiago de Cuba

Cayman Is. (U.K.)
• George Town

BELIZE
• Belize City
• Belmopan
Guatemala City •
GUATEMALA
EL SALVADOR
San Salvador •

HONDURAS
• Tegucigalpa

Managua •

JAMAICA
Kingston •

Caribbean Sea

NICARAGUA

San José •

Cartagena •
• Panamá City
PANAMA

COSTA RICA

Medellín •

Cali ○
• Bogotá

COLOMBIA

Orinoco R.

Ciudad Bolívar •

Paramaribo •
• Cayenne

GUYANA
• Georgetown

French Guiana (Fr.)

SURINAME

Quito ○
ECUADOR

Guayaquil ○

Iquitos •

Amazon R.

Manaus •

Belém •

Equator

Galápagos Is. (Ec.)

PERU

ANDES

Lima ○

Fortaleza •

BRAZIL

Recife •

São Francisco R.

Salvador •

PACIFIC OCEAN

Arequipa •

BOLIVIA
La Paz •
Lake Titicaca

Santa Cruz •

Sucre •
Potosí •

Brasília •

Belo Horizonte •

PARAGUAY

Paraná R.

Rio de Janeiro ○

ANDES

Asunción •

Curitiba •

São Paulo ○

ARGENTINA

Uruguay R.

Porto Alegre •

N

More than 5 million

1–5 million

Fewer than 1 million

Capital cities are underlined

Departments are marked with protectorate in parentheses
Example: Puerto Rico (U.S.)

Juan Fernández Is. (Chile)

Valparaíso •
Santiago ○

Córdoba ○

Rosario •
Buenos Aires ○
La Plata •

URUGUAY
• Montevideo

Concepción •

Tropic of Capricorn

Río de la Plata

ATLANTIC OCEAN

CHILE
Bahía Blanca •

0   200   400 Miles
0   200   400 Kilometers

TIERRA DEL FUEGO

Punta Arenas •

Falkland Is. (U.K.)

South Georgia (U.K.)

FIGURE 7.1

Latin America is the southern part of the large landmass of the Americas that lies between the Pacific and Atlantic oceans (**Figure 7.1**) Traditionally, the Americas are divided into the two continents of North America (Canada, the United States, and Mexico) and South America (all the countries south of Mexico). Latin America includes all of the countries south of the United States from Mexico to the southern tip of South America in Chile and Argentina. It forms a world region of considerable physical and social coherence covering more than 20 million square kilometers (7.7 million square miles). The region includes 30 independent countries. Several islands and one mainland territory (French Guiana) are still under the political control of the United States, the United Kingdom, France, or the Netherlands.

The term *Latin America* was coined in the 19th century by the French, who sought to discourage British interests in the region and justify their own imperial ambitions there by asserting that the shared Romance languages of Spanish, French, and Portuguese—all of which were derived from Latin—were the defining characteristic of the region. In this book, we include the Caribbean islands in the Latin American region because of the physiographic links from the island chains to the South American mainland, because Spanish is spoken by many Caribbean inhabitants, and because of a shared legacy of European colonial domination.

Much of Latin America can be characterized by a common experience of colonialism that included the dominance of the Spanish and Portuguese languages, religion (Roman Catholicism), legal and political institutions, and European control of resource extraction, trade links, and other economic activity (**Figure 7.2**). Most of the region became independent in the 19th century and was drawn into global trade relations, especially with Britain and the United States. In the 20th century, the Latin American region experienced rapid integration into global markets and the transition from revolutionary and military governments to democratic ones.

Despite an apparent physical coherence and a shared historical experience of colonialism and economic development, as for many other world regions the definition of Latin America is contested and unclear. The clearest physical breaks between North America and South America occur at two narrow isthmuses (narrow necks of land between major seas)—in Mexico at the Isthmus of Tehuantepec and in Panama where the Panama Canal now cuts the Isthmus of Panama (see Geography Matters: The Panama Canal, p. 325).

FIGURE 7.2 Overlapping cultural landscapes of Mexico City At the Plaza of the Three Cultures in Tlatelolco in Mexico City, the ancient Aztec ruins, a Spanish colonial church, and modern apartment buildings stand together, symbolizing the links and overlaps from the past to the present in Latin America. The common themes illustrated here include the legacies of highly developed indigenous societies, the enduring economic and cultural imprint of Spanish (or other European) colonialism, and recent integration into a world economy of cities of modern architecture, business districts, and urban environmental problems.

Mexico is increasingly classified as part of North America, partly because of its physical location, and also as a result of the economic integration associated with the **North American Free Trade Agreement (NAFTA)** with the United States and Canada. It is still generally considered a Latin American country.

Several subregions have been defined in Latin America. Central America usually includes the countries of Belize, Costa Rica, El Salvador, Honduras, Guatemala, Nicaragua, and Panama. The Southern Cone encompasses Argentina, Chile, Paraguay, and Uruguay. The Caribbean region includes all of the volcanic and coral islands in the Caribbean Sea and a suboceanic basin of the western Atlantic Ocean called the Gulf of Mexico, encircled by the northern coast of South America to the south, Central America and Mexico to the west, and the United States to the northwest. The large islands of Cuba, Hispaniola, Jamaica, and Puerto Rico are included as a northern boundary, and the eastern edge includes the Lesser Antillean chain of islands from the Virgin Islands in the northeast to Trinidad, off the Venezuelan coast, in the southeast.

Sometimes the Latin American region is defined to include only those countries where either Spanish or Portuguese is the official language, thus excluding countries colonized by other European powers. Included in this latter

GEOGRAPHY MATTERS

The Panama Canal

The Panama Canal joined the world's two great oceans—the Atlantic and the Pacific—and shortened the ocean trade route between them by weeks, with considerable reduction in costs (**Figure 1**). Panamanian history has been shaped by the canal that crosses the Isthmus of Panama, a dream since the beginning of Spanish colonization. In November 1903, after the failure of a French attempt to build a canal, with U.S. encouragement and French financial support Panama proclaimed its independence from Colombia and concluded the Hay/Bunau-Varilla Treaty with the United States. The treaty conceded rights to the United States "as if it were sovereign," in a zone roughly 16 kilometers (10 miles) wide and 80 kilometers (50 miles) long. In that zone, the United States would build a canal, then administer, fortify, and defend it "in perpetuity." In 1914 the United States completed the existing 83-kilometer (50-mile) lock canal, one of the world's greatest engineering triumphs with three sets of locks lifting enormous ships up and across a lake 24 meters (80 feet) above sea level. Historian David McCullough, in his book *Path Between the Seas*, estimated that more than 25,000 people lost their lives trying to build the canal, mainly from tropical diseases such as malaria and yellow fever.

The early 1960s saw the beginning of sustained pressure in Panama for the renegotiation of the Hay/Bunau-Varilla Treaty. During the 1970s, negotiations between the United States and Panama over the status of the Panama Canal concluded with two new canal treaties in 1977, effective in 1979. These treaties handed control of the Canal Zone to Panama, with a joint U.S.–Panamanian Panama Canal Commission administering the canal until the end of 1999, at which time the U.S. forces in Panama would withdraw.

During the 1980s, when Panama's military government, led by Manuel Noriega, was implicated in drug trafficking and refused to recognize civilian elections supporting opposition candidates, the U.S. interests in the region were threatened. After economic sanctions failed, President George H. W. Bush ordered the U.S. military into Panama on December 20, 1989, citing the need to protect U.S. lives and property, to fulfill U.S. treaty responsibilities to operate and defend the canal, to assist the Panamanian people in restoring democracy, and to bring Noriega to justice.

Panama's celebrations upon the handover of the canal in 1999 reflected liberation from U.S. domination as well as acquisition of full control of an economic asset. Tolls for the canal bring in more than $500 million a year, and Panama plans to privatize the ports and invite foreign investors to build hotels, industrial parks, ecology-based tourism, ship-repair facilities, and private housing. Some environmentalists and engineers are concerned about the effects of these developments on the forests that border the canal, which are essential for the maintenance of the canal's hydrology and the protection of Panama's rich biodiversity.

FIGURE I Panama Canal The Panama Canal cuts through the isthmus that joins North and South America and is a critical transport route for both cruise ships and cargo.

group are the French-speaking islands of the Caribbean, such as Haiti, and the mainland country of French Guiana; the English-speaking islands of the Caribbean, such as Jamaica and Barbados, and the mainland countries Belize and Guyana; and the former Dutch mainland colony of Suriname and Caribbean islands still under Dutch political control, such as Bonaire and Curaçao. The Latin American region is also characterized by diversity. Even within the Spanish- and Portuguese-speaking countries, many people speak only indigenous languages or languages other than

Spanish or Portuguese, practice a religion other than Catholicism, and may have Asian or African heritage. While some women within the region work in globalized manufacturing and service industries, control land and wealth, and serve at the highest levels of government, others are marginalized within the household, labor force, and national politics. Furthermore, some Latin American countries are not well integrated into world economic markets and do not have democratic governments. Thus, the definition of the Latin American world region arose from the period of global integration associated with European colonialism, but it oversimplifies the physical and social diversity within the region and its links with many regions of the world other than Europe and North America. Although some dislike the colonial connotation and overgeneralization of the term *Latin America*, it is widely used to describe the region in international reports and organizations and is commonly used by people to identify their region within the world and by migrants to describe their "Latino" heritage and culture.

ENVIRONMENT AND SOCIETY IN LATIN AMERICA

Latin America's physical environments include vast areas of forests, grasslands, mountains, and deserts that, at first glance, seem minimally transformed by human activity. There are also areas of intensive human occupation where the physical limits of aridity and disease have been apparently overcome by modern technological innovations in irrigation, plant breeding, air conditioning, and medicine.

Latin American landscapes have long been transformed by humans. Research has shown that many of the seemingly pristine forests were cleared centuries ago, the grasslands selectively burned or grazed, the mountains carved into terraces, and the infrequent waters of the deserts stored or diverted. Similarly, studies show that human settlements and high-technology agriculture are extremely vulnerable to natural disasters and epidemics and, therefore, that the human geography of Latin America continues to be influenced by environmental conditions and events. An understanding of the physical geography and the ways in which people have modified their environmental surroundings is integral to appreciating the historical and contemporary human geography of the Latin American region and the challenges to its sustainable development.

Landforms and Landscapes

The physical landscape of Latin America varies widely and includes striking mountain ranges, high plateaus, and enormous river networks (**Figure 7.3**). The two largest-scale physical features in Latin America are the Andes Mountains and the Amazon basin or Amazonia, both easily seen from space (**Figure 7.4**). The Andes are an 8000-kilometer-long (5000-mile-long) chain of high-altitude peaks and valleys that for the most part run parallel to the west coast of South America (**Figure 7.5a**) with the highest peak, Aconcagua, at 6960 meters (22,830 feet). Amazon River tributaries flow downward and eastward from the Andes into an enormous river network that covers a basin of more than 6 million square kilometers (2.3 million square miles). The basin includes the river itself and the surrounding landscape, about two-thirds in Brazil and including parts of Peru, Ecuador, Bolivia, Colombia, Venezuela, Guyana, Suriname, and French Guiana. The Amazon River and its tributaries carry 20 percent of the world's fresh water and provides transport, sediment, and fish that support the agriculture, diets, and mobility of the peoples of the basin (**Figure 7.5b**). This watershed also nourishes the Amazon rain forest, which is home to more than 100,000 species. This rain forest is often termed the "lungs" of the world because of its key role in recycling the oxygen, carbon, and water resources that are critical to life on Earth.

Other important physical features include the mountainous spines of Mexico and Central America and the high-altitude flatter areas, or plateaus, that lie between or next to the mountain ridges. The high-elevation plateaus and basins that lie within

FIGURE 7.3 Physical regions and landforms of Latin America The Amazon basin and the Andes mountain range are the two largest physical features in Latin America. Major South American rivers such as the Plata and the Orinoco provide transport routes into the interior as well as water resources for agriculture and hydroelectricity generation. The two major deserts—the Sonoran and Atacama—are located along the Pacific coasts of Mexico and Chile, and important grasslands are located in the pampas region of Argentina and the llanos of northern South America. Past and current human populations settled on highland plateaus, such as the altiplano of the Andes and the Mesa Central of Mexico. The region has many active volcano and earthquake zones associated with the movements of tectonic plates. Older geological formations are associated with important mineral deposits, such as the silver mines of the Andes and central Mexico, copper in central and northern Chile and in northern Mexico, and gold and iron along the edges of the Brazilian and Guiana highlands. World-class oil deposits occur in the Gulf of Mexico and in Venezuela, especially Lake Maracaibo, and in the western Amazon basin.

FIGURE 7.4 Satellite image of Latin America Certain physical features of Central and South America are clearly visible in this satellite image, including the verdant green of the Amazon basin and the mountain ridges of the Andes and Central America as well as Lake Maracaibo on the northern coast of Venezuela.

even higher mountains, especially in Bolivia and Peru, at more than 3000 meters (9500 feet) in the Andes of Latin America are called the **altiplano**. This region, as well as the Mexican plateau, or Mesa Central, is an important area of human occupation because it provides flatter, cooler, and wetter environments for agriculture and settlement than do the adjacent steep-sloped mountains, dry lowland deserts, and humid lowlands. The Caribbean basin has large areas of limestone geology where water tends to flow underground and create large cave systems such as those in the Yucatán Peninsula of Mexico and in Puerto Rico (**Figure 7.5c**). Coral reefs, a key feature of the Caribbean landscape, are created when living coral organisms build colonies in warm, shallow oceans. These reefs, hosts to myriad other marine animals, are fragile ecosystems that are easily damaged by boats, divers, pollution, and environmental change.

Natural Disasters and Mineral Resources

The configuration of high-elevation and low-elevation land areas and the location of island chains is the result of a long history of tectonic activity in the region. Latin America is on and near several major tectonic plates (see Chapter 1, p. 20, and Figure 1.17) and Central America is one of the most tectonically active regions in the world. The region south of Panama sits on the South American plate, the slow westward drift of which causes it to collide with the adjacent Nazca plate. This activity results in a folding and uplifting of the western edge of the South American plate to form the Andes Mountains, thus forcing the Nazca plate downward and under South America in the process of subduction and producing active volcanoes and severe earthquakes. Simi-

(a)

(b)

FIGURE 7.5 The varied landscapes of Latin America (a) The snow-capped peaks of the Andes rise above a cemetery for silver miners near Potosi, Bolivia. (b) The Amazon River carries 20 percent of the world's fresh water across an extensive basin covered by tropical rain forests. The floodplain of the Amazon is important for agriculture, with soils renewed by annual floods, and the river provides a transport route and fishing ground. Adaptation to varying water levels includes seasonal floodplain farming and houses built on stilts, such as those in Belen, near the Peruvian town of Iquitos. (c) The Mayan city of Tulum on Mexico's Yucatán Peninsula is built of and on the white limestone rock associated with this region. Archaeological ruins, beaches of pale sand, and colorful offshore coral reef ecosystems bring millions of tourists to the Yucatán each year.

(c)

larly, Mexico sits on the North American continental plate, also drifting westward and causing the subduction of the Cocos plate and the uplift and folding of the Sierra Madre Mountains. The Caribbean plate, in contrast, is moving eastward, pulling away from the Cocos, moving under the South and North American plates, and causing geological tensions and cracks that produce earthquakes and volcanic activity in Central America. Similar plate motions have produced several volcanic islands in the Caribbean.

(a)

(b)

FIGURE 7.6 Natural disasters (a) The people of the island of Montserrat in the Caribbean have lived with the threat of volcanic eruptions for centuries. Eruptions in the 1990s in the Soufriere Hills forced the evacuation of more than two-thirds of the residents. Most left their homes, farms, beach houses, and hotels, abandoning their entire lives at the foot of the volcano. The capital city, Plymouth, was burned and half-buried by waves of gas and ash. Assistance was provided by the British government, which controls Montserrat as an overseas territory. (b) The 1985 earthquake in Mexico City killed as many as 10,000 people and devastated downtown buildings. The city is especially vulnerable because it is built on a former lake bed with sediments that act almost as liquids when shaken by earthquakes.

Volcanic activity poses threats to human activity when eruptions and ash destroy crops and lives (**Figure 7.6a**). The tensions associated with shifting tectonic plates have also produced devastating earthquakes that have ravaged the capital cities of some Latin American countries—for example, in Mexico City, Mexico; Managua, Nicaragua; Guatemala City, Guatemala; and Santiago, Chile (**Figure 7.6b**). Such natural disasters cannot be blamed solely on geophysical conditions. The greatest damages occur when people are forced to live in unsafe houses or on unstable slopes because they lack the money or power to live in safer places, cannot afford insurance, or are unable to obtain warnings of impending natural disasters such as volcanic eruptions and hurricanes.

This geological activity and history of Latin America has affected human history and activity in many ways. The mineral wealth of Latin America is typically found on the old crystalline Guiana shield (or highlands) and where crustal folding brings older rocks near the surface (see Figure 7.3). Major precious-metal mining districts in the region include the Peruvian and Bolivian Andes, where mountains of silver were excavated in the colonial period at Cerro de Pasco and Potosí (see Figure 7.5a), and lead, zinc, and tin are still important; the silver region of the Mexican Mesa Central; and the gold and iron mines at Carajas on the edge of the Brazilian plateau. World-class iron deposits are found on the southern edge of the Brazilian shield at Itabira, on the northern edge of the Guiana highlands at Cerro Bolivar, and in northern Mexico. Copper is the geological treasure of the southern Andes, especially northern Chile, and is also important in northern Mexico. The shores of the Caribbean, including the Guianas and Jamaica, have deposits of bauxite (a mineral used in the aluminum industry). These minerals, especially gold and silver, were foundations of the European colonial economies and now dominate the export economies of countries such as Chile and Bolivia. They are a focus of foreign interference and ownership and have often transformed local labor and environmental conditions.

The other critical resources associated with Latin America's geology are oil, gas, and coal. Coal is found in northern Mexico, Colombia, Brazil and Venezuela. The earliest oil booms and later gas developments occurred in Venezuela around Lake Maracaibo and on Mexico's Gulf Coast. Oil was discovered in Venezuela in 1917, and the country became one of the founding members of the Organization of Petroleum Exporting Countries (OPEC) in 1961. Oil became an important foundation of the national economy, and the oil industry was nationalized in 1976, but the economic benefits of oil production reached only about 20 percent of the population. Lake Maracaibo, the site of about 4 percent of world oil reserves, is now crowded with thousands of oil derricks that produce about two-thirds of Venezuela's oil output.

The Mexican oil deposits were first commercially exploited in the 1890s and were nationalized in the 1930s under the government oil company PEMEX (Petróleos Mexicanos). In all of Latin America's oil regions, environmental pollution has been a serious problem, leading to waterways contaminated with waste oil, widespread ecosystem damage, and serious health problems among local residents.

The most recent oil developments are in the Amazon, where oil was discovered in 1967. The Amazonian oil deposits are found mostly in remote forest areas where land rights of indigenous peoples are not secure, and as a result conflicts have erupted between Peru and Ecuador and among governments, corporations, and indigenous groups. Mining in the Amazon has also created controversy in regions where migrants have gathered to work in the gold mines. The mining process uses mercury, a hazardous chemical element that is now polluting ecosystems and causing health problems among the miners.

The $1.6-billion Camisea Natural Gas Project is the first major gas development in Peru. It includes a 700-kilometer (435-mile) pipeline, extending from gas fields in the Camisea and Lower Urubamba watershed, stretching from the Andes and cutting through biodiverse and sensitive rain forest, including an Amazon biodiversity hotspot, before reaching the Peruvian coast. Gas extraction in Camisea began in August 2004, and since that time there have been several spills of liquid petroleum. Bolivia is also expanding its gas pipeline network with plans to link to various markets, including Brazil, Argentina, Chile, Mexico, and the United States. Ecological concerns have surrounded the Bolivia-Brazil Pipeline, which traverses fragile and important ecosystems, including the Pantanal wetlands, Bolivia's Chaco forest, and Brazil's Mata Atlântica rain forest. The pipeline network also cuts through indigenous territories such as for the Yabog and Gasyrg pipeline, which crosses through Guaraní and Weenhayek ancestral homelands.

Climate

Latin America's geological configurations influence its climate and water systems. The overall climates of the region are determined by global atmospheric circulation, including the positions of the equatorial high- and tropical low-pressure zones and the major global wind belts (see Figure 1.20). Because Latin America straddles the equator, reaching north of the Tropic of Cancer in the Northern Hemisphere and south almost to the Antarctic, climatic patterns are relatively simple to understand and provide good general examples of how global circulation affects regional climate, vegetation, and human activity (**Figure 7.7**).

As we discussed in Chapter 1 (p. 22), the general circulation of the atmosphere is driven by the differential heating and rotation of Earth, with warm air rising at the equator at the intertropical convergence zone, then cooling as it rises, thereby producing high rainfall, then flowing poleward, and finally sinking over regions around the tropics of Capricorn and Cancer. The equatorial zones of high temperatures and rainfall provide conditions for the rapid growth of vegetation in the form of the rain forests of the Amazon. Annual rainfall in the Amazon basin ranges from 1.5 to 2 meters (60 to 80 inches). As the air sinks over the tropics, it becomes warmer and drier, holding so little moisture by the time it reaches ground level that these regions are characterized by the very low rainfall, sparse vegetation, and dry conditions of deserts. In Latin America, the

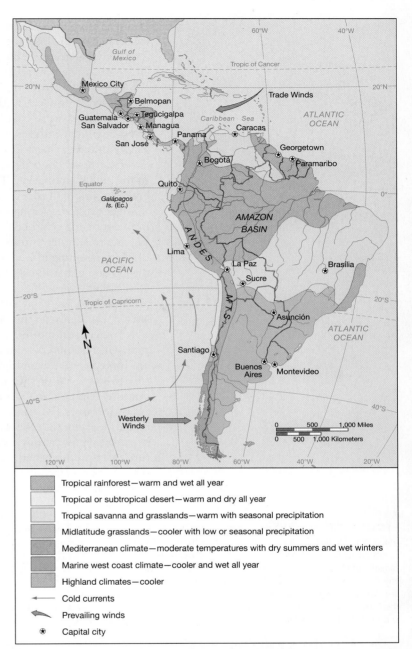

Tropical rainforest—warm and wet all year

Tropical or subtropical desert—warm and dry all year

Tropical savanna and grasslands—warm with seasonal precipitation

Midlatitude grasslands—cooler with low or seasonal precipitation

Mediterranean climate—moderate temperatures with dry summers and wet winters

Marine west coast climate—cooler and wet all year

Highland climates—cooler

Cold currents

Prevailing winds

Capital city

FIGURE 7.7 Climate regions of Latin America Latin America's climate is influenced by major wind and pressure belts and the configuration of land and oceans. The average pattern shown in this map tends to shift northward in June and southward in December, bringing seasonal changes to many regions.

Sonoran and Chihuahuan deserts of Mexico and the Atacama Desert of Chile are partly associated with this type of large-scale sinking of air in the atmosphere (subsidence). The convergence zone of high rainfall and the dry zones of sinking air shift north in the June–August season and south in the November–February period.

Air flowing from the tropics to the equator is dragged by the spinning Earth into an east–west flow called the *trade winds*, and air flowing poleward from the Tropics is dragged into a west–east flow called the *westerlies*.

The trade winds flowing across the Atlantic frequently produce rain on the Caribbean islands and east coasts of Central America in the Northern Hemisphere. In southern Latin America the trades bring rain to the east coast of Brazil but shift north and south because of the global circulation. The regions on the margins of the trades and at the edges of the equatorial rainfall zone have highly seasonal climates with a distinct rainy season.

The westerlies bring heavy rains to southern South America. In Chile, seasonal shifts in pressure and wind belts mean that the westerlies move southward in December, bringing rain to southernmost Chile, and northward in June, bringing rain to the central valley of Chile, resulting in wet and dry seasons on the margins of the westerly circulation. When the global circulation shifts southward in December, storms spinning out of the Northern Hemisphere westerlies also bring rain to northern Mexico. Latin America's extensive grasslands occur where seasonal shifts in wind and pressure belts result in a distinct rainy season, especially on the margins where the rains are fairly moderate.

The coastal mountain chains of Latin America clearly illustrate the role of topography in regional climate. First of all, ocean winds that encounter coastal mountains are forced to rise even higher, cooling to the point that they release most of their moisture in the form of rain and snow. This is a very clear feature of the Andean climate but also explains the rainfall of highland Central America and Mexico. The high precipitation over the Andes feeds the rivers that water the lowlands east of the mountains, most notably the Amazon. However, mountains also create a *rainshadow* effect because winds passing over mountains from the coast to the interior lose their moisture over the higher altitudes and then become warmer and drier as they descend to the interior, creating arid conditions to the leeward of mountain ranges (see Figure 1.21). Examples include the dry region of southern Argentina, known as Patagonia, in the lee of the Andes, and the drier regions of Chihuahua in northern Mexico in the lee of the Mexican Sierra Madre. Higher altitudes are also cooler, so despite the intensity of the sunlight, large regions of the Latin American tropics have cooler temperatures more conducive to human activities and agricultural crops, such as wheat, apples, and potatoes, generally found in colder climates.

Altitudinal zonation is a vertical classification of environment and land use according to elevation based mainly on changes in climate and vegetation from lower (warmer) to higher (cooler) elevations. In Latin America these changes are defined in a simple classification of Latin American mountain environments into the Tierra Caliente, Tierra Templada, and Tierra Fría. The very high altitudes are called the Tierra Helada. Each of these zones is associated with characteristic vegetation types and with agricultural activities (**Figure 7.8**). Communities locate fields at different elevations to take advantage of different climatic and soil conditions. At higher altitudes potatoes grow and animals graze; lower down, grains such

FIGURE 7.8 Altitudinal zonation   The altitudinal zonation of climate and vegetation in mountainous regions such as the Andes creates vertical bands of ecosystems and provides a range of microenvironments for agricultural production. The Tierra Caliente runs up to 900 meters (2950 feet), the Tierra Templada ranges from 900–1800 meters (2950–5900 feet), the Tierra Fría from 1800–3600 meters (5900–11,800 feet), and the very high altitudes (higher than 3600 meters, or 11,800 feet) are called the Tierra Helada. These zones are associated with characteristic vegetation types such as rain forest in the Tierra Caliente and grasslands in the Tierra Fría, and with agricultural activities such as growing sugar and bananas in the Tierra Caliente, coffee and cattle in the Tierra Templada, and potatoes and barley in the Tierra Fría.

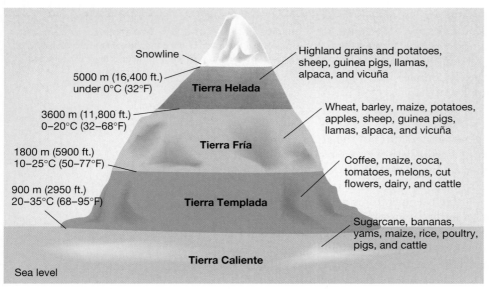

Snowline

5000 m (16,400 ft.) under 0°C (32°F)

Tierra Helada

Highland grains and potatoes, sheep, guinea pigs, llamas, alpaca, and vicuña

3600 m (11,800 ft.) 0–20°C (32–68°F)

Tierra Fría

Wheat, barley, maize, potatoes, apples, sheep, guinea pigs, llamas, alpaca, and vicuña

1800 m (5900 ft.) 10–25°C (50–77°F)

Tierra Templada

Coffee, maize, coca, tomatoes, melons, cut flowers, dairy, and cattle

900 m (2950 ft.) 20–35°C (68–95°F)

Sugarcane, bananas, yams, maize, rice, poultry, pigs, and cattle

Tierra Caliente

Sea level

as wheat and corn grow; and finally, vegetables and fruit are found at lower levels with more tropical climates.

Latin America also provides a classic case of how the temperatures of the ocean can influence the climate of adjacent landmasses. Colder air holds less moisture and promotes less evaporation than warm air. Winds flowing across the very cold ocean current that normally flows northward off the coast of Peru and Chile pick up very little moisture and exacerbate the already dry conditions promoted by descending air over the tropics. The Atacama Desert is one of the driest spots on Earth.

In contrast, easterly winds moving across the warm Caribbean absorb a lot of moisture, especially during the fall when the sea surface is warmest. When storms start to circulate, the warm sea fuels both the moisture and energy of the storms, producing the hurricanes that regularly cross the Atlantic coast of Latin America. The storms have some benefit to water resources but often threaten human settlements and lives with the power of their winds and the flooding from heavy rainfall.

Hurricane Mitch occurred in late October 1998, dumping a year's worth of rain (about 1.2 meters, or nearly 4 feet) on Central America in 48 hours (**Figure 7.9a**). Flash floods and mudslides on deforested slopes left nearly 10,000 people dead, almost 20,000 missing, and more than 2.5 million temporarily dependent on emergency aid. Honduras, the second-poorest nation in the Western Hemisphere, was the hardest hit. Of the 6 million people living in Honduras, nearly 2 million were affected by the storm, 1 million lost their homes, and 70 percent of the country's productive infrastructure was damaged or destroyed. This disaster created immediate food shortages and decimated the vital export crops of bananas, coffee, and shrimp, which are responsible for half the country's annual export revenue of $3 billion.

(a)

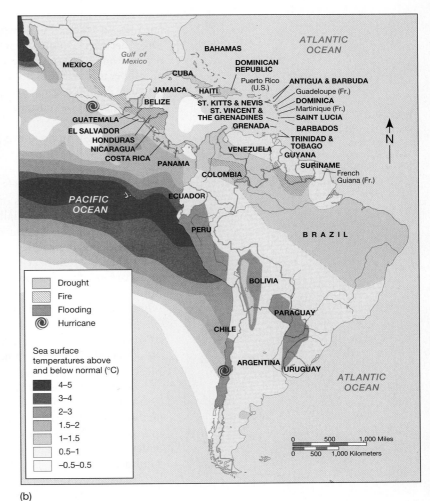

(b)

FIGURE 7.9 Climate hazards (a) Hurricane Mitch was one of the strongest hurricanes on record when it hit Central America after moving across the Caribbean in October 1998. With winds of more than 180 miles per hour, Mitch produced heavy rains that intensified over Central America's coastal mountains, causing severe flooding, especially below deforested hillslopes. Hurricane Mitch inundated vast areas of Honduras, dropping about 1.2 meters (4 feet) of rainfall over a 48-hour period and caused tremendous damage along the Nicaraguan coast, shown here. (b) During an El Niño, the ocean warms off the coast of Peru and causes heavy rain and flooding along the usually dry Peruvian coast. The Pacific warming is linked to other changes in atmospheric circulation that produce drought in northeast Brazil, the Caribbean, and the altiplano, floods on the Parana River, and droughts and fires in Mexico and Central America.

What turned Mitch from a natural hazard into a human disaster was a chain reaction of social vulnerabilities created by long-term climate change, environmental degradation, poverty, social inequality, sexism, racism, population pressure, rapid urbanization, and international debt. Deforestation increased the magnitude of the floods and the risk of landslides. When the forest is cleared, the ground is exposed; when rains come, the result is an increase in surface runoff and soil erosion. Geographers such as Piers Blaikie argue that the social, political, and economic environment is as much a cause of disasters as the natural environment. Nature creates hazards but it is humans who create *vulnerability*, through social inequality and unequal access to resources. Some 72 percent of the farmers of Honduras have access to only 12 percent of its arable land, whereas 1.5 percent control 40 percent. Large-scale beef ranching and banana plantations have displaced poor peasants over decades, forcing them to live in isolated valleys, on riverbanks, and on steep hillside farms. Forced to live in marginal areas, the peasants have carved out subsistence farms on surrounding hillsides and riverbanks, further destabilizing these areas. Poor people in poor states are the most vulnerable to natural hazards and are the least able to cope.

Disasters create long-term effects and vulnerabilities, which, like their causes, are not immediately visible. The most pervasive effect is that the poor get poorer because they lack the money or the social capital to rebuild. Almost 80 percent of the Honduran population already lives below the poverty line. With malnutrition and illiteracy rates higher than those of many African countries, the next generation in Honduras will suffer the effects of Hurricane Mitch for many decades.

One of the most significant features of Latin America's climate is that it does not remain constant from year to year. One of the most important causes of this climate variability is the phenomenon known as **El Niño**. El Niño, a periodic warming of sea surface temperatures in the tropical Pacific off the coast of Peru, results in worldwide changes in climate, including droughts and floods. The local effect of El Niño is to bring warmer and wetter winds to the coasts of Peru and Ecuador with high rainfall and flooding. But the sensitivity of the global atmospheric circulation is such that the links between Pacific Ocean temperatures and conditions elsewhere produce droughts in northeast Brazil, floods in southern Brazil and northern Mexico, and fewer Caribbean hurricanes as well as droughts in southern Africa, Australia, and Indonesia (**Figure 7.9b**). In some years, the ocean off Peru gets colder than normal, producing a contrasting global pattern called **La Niña** (the periodic abnormal cooling of sea surface temperatures in the tropical Pacific off the coast of Peru), with floods in northeast Brazil, drought in northern Mexico, and more intense Pacific hurricanes.

Environmental History

The natural environments of Latin America offer both constraints on and opportunities for human activity, especially agriculture. Geology affects soil fertility and agricultural potential through the influence of the underlying rock type and volcanic activity. Some mineral deposits produce soils that are toxic and cannot be used for agriculture. The older shields often bear less fertile soil, whereas volcanic ash provides nutrients. Some areas are much more productive than others, especially the flatter river valleys, with annual renewal of soils by sediment deposition and easy access to water, and regions where ash from volcanic activity provides nutrients to the soil.

A constraint on human development, particularly in the warm and wet climates of much of Latin America, is the large diversity and prevalence of pests and diseases that weaken and kill plants, animals, and humans in the tropics around the world. For example, malaria is endemic in much of the Amazon basin and lowland Central America.

Despite the constraints posed by the natural environment in Latin America, any assertion that human activity is determined by the environment (an argument called *environmental determinism*) is unwarranted, because the ability of humans to overcome many of these constraints is so clear throughout the region. Geographers such as Carl Sauer employed the approaches of *cultural ecology* (the study of the relationship between a cultural group and its natural environment) to show how native Latin American populations used technology and social organization to adapt the harsh physical environments to their needs and take full advantage of more favorable environments.

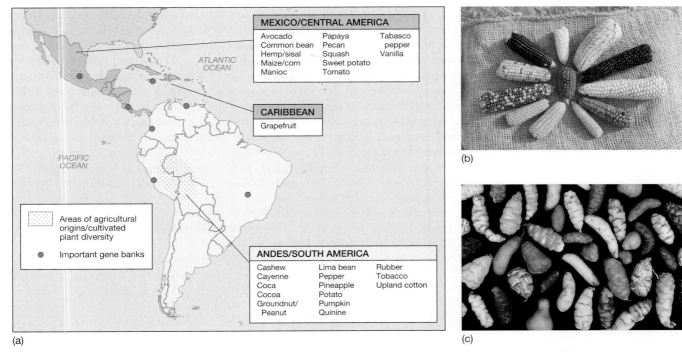

FIGURE 7.10 Domestication of food crops in Latin America (a) Latin America has two important centers of domestication in Mexico and the Andes. The red dots on the map denote research centers where attempts are being made to preserve crops' genetic diversity in "gene banks." (b) Maize (corn) was domesticated in Mexico from a wild grain called *teosinte*. Bred for a variety of microenvironments and tastes, traditional maize has many shapes and colors. (c) The many colors and shapes of potatoes grown in the Andes are indications of the diversity of varieties domesticated in these regions.

Domestication The most dramatic transformation of nature by early peoples in Latin America was domestication. Starting more than 10,000 years ago, wild plants and animals were domesticated into cultivated or tamed forms through selective breeding for preferred characteristics. Many of the world's major food crops were domesticated by native Latin Americans, including the staples of maize (corn), manioc, and potatoes, as well as vegetables and fruits such as tomatoes, peppers, squash, avocadoes, and pineapples (**Figure 7.10**). Tobacco, cacao (chocolate), vanilla, peanuts, and coca (cocaine) were also domesticated in Latin America. In dry areas, people tried to ensure water supplies by building small dams and channels to bring water to these crops. Latin America has very few indigenous domesticated animals. The camelids (llama and alpaca) were tamed and bred for wool, meat, or transport, and dogs and guinea pigs were also bred for pets and meat.

As in other regions of the world, the increased yields from domesticated crops created a surplus that permitted the specialization of tasks, the growth of settlements, and ultimately the development of highly complex societies and cultures. In Latin America, the complex societies included the great Mayan, Incan, and Aztec empires (**Figure 7.11a**). These groups all modified their environments to increase agricultural production and to exploit water, wood, and minerals to support their cities, metal production, and trade.

Mayan, Incan, and Aztec Adaptations to Environment

These environmental transformations were widespread, and in some cases—most notoriously the Mayan civilization—people placed so much pressure on regional landscapes that environmental degradation may have precipitated social collapse. The Mayas occupied the Yucatán Peninsula as well as a considerable portion of Guatemala and Honduras, with a period of expansion beginning about 3000 B.C. and reaching a peak of control and social development from about 600 B.C. to A.D. 800. Faced with rapid declines in the fertility of soils after clearing the rain forest, the Mayas adapted by burning the forest to capture the nutrients in the trees through the ash and then by moving on to clear another patch of forest once the declining fertility of the previously cleared area resulted in reduced yields. There is evidence that the Mayas cleared vast areas of forest during this period. It took up to 30 years for the forest to regrow on a plot that had been cleared, farmed, and then abandoned. This adaptation to rainforest environments mirrors those in other parts of the world and has been termed *slash and burn* (see p. 221 in Chapter 5), or *swidden*, agriculture. It is the agricultural system often used in tropical forests that involves cutting trees and brush and burning them so that crops can benefit from cleared ground and nutrients in the ash. The Mayas also developed methods for growing crops in wetland areas by building *raised fields* that lifted plants above flooding but took advantage of the rich soils and reliable moisture of wetland environments.

Between A.D. 500 and A.D. 1000 the great Mayan cities such as Copán, Palenque, Tulum, and Tikal were abandoned, and overall population declined dramatically (see Figure 7.5c). Many scholars believe that one reason for the Maya collapse was their overuse of the soils. Population growth and tribute demands by the Maya elites required increases in agricultural production, often involving the clearing of sloped lands, with no time to allow plots to recover before planting them again. Large-scale forest clearing has also been linked to regional changes in climate, with increases in temperature and decreases in rainfall that would threaten agriculture. Soil erosion, droughts, and declining soil fertility would have contributed to a decline in the amount of food available to feed the large population and would cause some of the nutritional stresses that archaeologists have detected in human skeletons from the period of collapse.

(a)

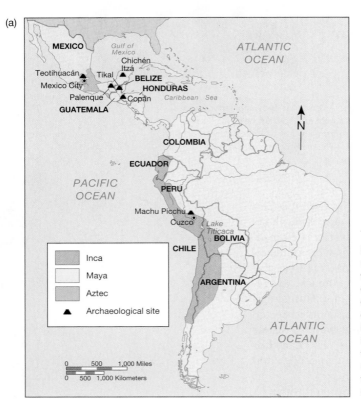

FIGURE 7.11 Maya, Aztec, and Inca adaptations to environment (a) Map of the extent of Maya, Inca, and Aztec empires. (b) The Inca constructed terraces, such as these around the Inca ruins at Machu Picchu, not only to reduce soil erosion and provide a flat area for planting, but also to decrease frost risks by breaking up downhill flows of cold air and allow for irrigation canals to flow across the slopes in efficient ways. Constructing and maintaining these terraces and irrigation systems required large-scale social organization in which the Incan empire excelled. People were organized into small groups called *ayullu*, and labor for agriculture and mines was commanded through the *mita* labor system by which communities were required to provide a certain number of days of work to the central authorities. In the 16th century, many terraces were abandoned as the native labor force was reduced due to the ravages of newly introduced European diseases and the need to shift laborers to the Spanish mines.

(b)

The Incas also responded to the difficulties of living in a mountain environment in a variety of ways, including through the construction of many miles of agricultural terraces on the steep hillslopes of the Andes during the height of their empire, which in A.D. 1400 stretched from northern Ecuador to central Chile (**Figure 7.11b**). The Aztecs, who settled in central Mexico in the 1300s, were experts in the control of water. They constructed an extensive network of dams, irrigation systems, and drainage canals in the basin of Mexico to cope with the highly seasonal and variable rainfall pattern that in some seasons and years produced droughts, and in other seasons and years produced large lakes and wetlands. They also developed the *chinampa* agricultural system, which permits agriculture in lake and wetland environments by building an island of soil and vegetation. Evidence suggests that as the Aztecs cleared forests in the basin of Mexico, they may have contributed to a drop in the water table and to a resulting water crisis that led to the abandonment of some settlements.

These widespread modifications of the environment of Latin America are evidence that has been used to debunk what geographer William Denevan has called the **pristine myth,** the erroneous belief that prior to European arrival in 1492 the Americas were mostly wild and untouched by humans and that native peoples lived in harmony with nature. In fact, large areas had been cultivated and deforested by indigenous populations. The environmental adaptations and impacts of the Mayas, Incas, and Aztecs still echo in the traditional technologies used in some regions of Latin America and in the continual efforts to use technology to benefit from the physical environment and avoid its hazards. Geographers are among those who have pointed to the ways in which overuse of their environment contributed to the collapse of Mayan society and to the warning that this implies for current patterns of widespread deforestation, overuse of the land, and depletion of water resources.

Water Resources

The three largest river basins in Latin America are the Amazon, the Plata, and the Orinoco, all flowing to the Atlantic Ocean (see Figure 7.1). The rivers in the Plata basin (including the Paraná, Paraguay, and Uruguay rivers) originate in the Andes and the Brazilian highlands. The Plata system has become a major source of energy through large hydroelectric dams such as the Itaipu dam on the Paraná, and there are controversial plans to dam and divert the water resources of the vast wetlands of the Pantanal. The Orinoco drains the *llanos* grasslands of Colombia and Venezuela, and the Amazon drains a vast basin that includes parts of Brazil, the Guianas, Venezuela, Colombia, Ecuador, Peru, and Bolivia. In cities such as Bogotá, Colombia, and Lima, Peru, increased water demands and climatic variations associated with El Niño and global warming have combined to threaten water and energy supplies with frequent droughts, water rationing, and electricity brownouts. The shrinking of Andean glaciers as a result of global warming poses serious risks to water resources.

Latin America has several large freshwater lakes, among them Lake Nicaragua in Nicaragua and Lake Titicaca at the border of Bolivia and Peru. Major waterfalls such as Iguaçu Falls—where Brazil, Argentina, and Paraguay meet (**Figure 7.12**)—and Angel Falls, Venezuela—the tallest waterfall in the world at a height of 985 meters (3230 feet), falling off the flat-topped mountain of Auyantepui—have become increasingly popular tourist destinations.

Biodiversity, Forests, and Conservation

The diversity of Latin America's physical environments has produced a large number of different species, or **biodiversity.** Latin America's biodiversity is substantial because of the size of the continent, the range in climates from north to south, altitudinal variations within short distances, and a comparatively long history of fairly stable climates and isolation from other world regions. Many tourists are attracted to the colorful birds and verdant plants associated with the ecological region between the tropics of the Americas, also called the **neotropics.**

FIGURE 7.12 Iguaçu Falls Iguaçu Falls, on the Paraná River, where Brazil, Argentina, and Paraguay meet, has become a major tourist destination.

Desert ecosystems, such as in the Atacama Desert of northern Chile and Peru, are associated with drier climates where species have developed many interesting adaptations to water scarcity (**Figure 7.13a**). Between the moist forests and dry deserts lie ecosystems where alternating wet and dry seasons produce vegetation ranging from scattered woodlands to dry grasslands. Grasslands are also found at higher altitudes where there is not enough precipitation or temperatures are too low to support highland forests. In Argentina the *pampas* grasslands cover more than 750,000 square kilometers

(a)

(b)

(c)

FIGURE 7.13 Latin American ecosystems Latin American ecosystems range from forests and grasslands to deserts and coastal mangroves. (a) The Atacama Desert of Peru and northern Chile is one of the driest locations on Earth. However, the area is economically important because of the copper and other minerals that lie beneath the surface and that support one of the world's most significant mining areas.
(b) The fertile soils of the extensive grasslands of *pampas* of southern South America traditionally supported a livestock economy associated with the *gaucho* cowboy. It was the wheat and beef of the *pampas* that made Argentina one of the richest countries in the world a century ago.
(c) Mangrove ecosystems protect coasts from storms and provide breeding areas for fish and other marine animals. In countries such as Honduras and Mexico, mangrove ecosystems are being destroyed to build shrimp farms for export (seafood farming or *mariculture*). The farms provide some local employment, yet often pollute the water and are vulnerable to disease.

338

(300,000 square miles) and have become important to the cattle economy (**Figure 7.13b**). Other large grassland ecosystems include the *llanos* of Colombia and Venezuela and the *cerrados* of Brazil. The high grasslands of the Andean altiplano provide habitat for grazing animals such as the llama, wild guanaco, and vicuña. Natural ecosystems vary with elevation and include the *páramo* of the northern Andes, with such unusual cold-adapted plants as the *frailejón*. The long coasts of Latin America and the islands of the Caribbean include about 50,000 square kilometers (about 19,000 square miles) of mangrove ecosystems, or about 25 percent of the world's total (**Figure 7.13c**).

Forests of Amazonia and Chile The wetter climates of Latin America are associated with magnificent forest ecosystems, including the tropical rain forests of the Amazon, Central America, and southern Mexico and the temperate rain forests of southern Chile. The Amazon forest ecosystems are notable for the sheer number of species found within small areas of forest.

Covering more than half a billion hectares (about 1.2 billion acres), the Amazon basin contains water, forest, mineral, and other resources of great value, yet has had relatively low population density until recent years (**Figure 7.14a**). The colonial image of the Amazon basin varied from a vision of a tropical Eden with untapped resources to an impenetrable, disease-ridden jungle hell of savage tribes. The region was of botanical

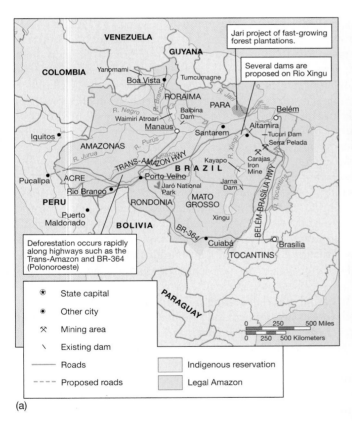

(a)

(b)

(c)

FIGURE 7.14 The Amazon basin (a) Map of development in the Amazon. This map shows some development projects that are causing deforestation and other environmental problems in the Amazon basin, including major roads such as the Trans-Amazon highway, dams such as Tucuri, and agricultural development around cities such as Acre. The basin also has many indigenous groups, some of which have gained reserve status for their lands. (b) Wide highways cut into the Amazon forest. (c) Satellite image of deforestation. This satellite image from the southern region of the Brazilian Amazon in the state of Rondonia shows how the forest is cleared as roads and people move into the Amazon area. The cleared areas are shown in lighter brown and the forest in green. A distinctive grid pattern is clear, as people farm rectangular plots along roads.. (*Source:* [a] Adapted from G. Knapp and C. Caviedes, *South America.* Englewood Cliffs, NJ: Prentice Hall, 1995, p. 233, and from "Controversial Infrastructure Projects Proposed or Underway in the Amazon Basin." Available at **http://www.amazonwatch.org**.)

interest, but it held little economic interest until the late 19th century, when development of the automobile industry in the United States and Europe exploded the demand for rubber, a product obtained by tapping the latex sap of scattered rubber trees in the forest. Local rubber tappers, or *seringuieros*, sold the rubber to middlemen. They in turn traded with the "rubber barons," who constructed enormous mansions and a magnificent opera house in the Amazonian port of Manaus. The end of the rubber boom is said to have occurred when Henry Wickham shipped thousands of rubber tree seeds from Brazil to Kew Gardens, in England, where they were cultured and the seedlings exported to Southeast Asia. The success of the more efficient Asian plantations, especially in Malaysia, drove the Amazon into decline, because Brazilian trees were too susceptible to disease when grown on plantations.

Although most people tend to associate the Amazon basin only with Brazil, the river basin and forests also include large parts of Bolivia, Peru, Ecuador, Colombia, Venezuela, and the Guianas (Guyana, Suriname, and French Guiana). Amazonian development became a focus of Brazilian government policy in the 1970s because the Amazon was seen as a pressure valve for landless and impoverished peasants in other regions and as a way of securing national territory through settlement. Several highways were built across the Amazon, including the Trans-Amazon from Recife to the Peruvian border and the Polonoreste from Brasilia to Belém at the mouth of the Amazon (**Figure 7.14b**).

Government policy was specifically designed to colonize the Amazon. Political leaders saw it as a frontier region similar to that of the western United States in the 19th century. Landless peasants were given title to plots of land if they promised to develop them productively, and peasants migrated in thousands along the new roads. As geographer Susannah Hecht has shown, much of the land was actually acquired by large landholders who took advantage of favorable incentives and tax breaks to develop ranches for speculation and tax havens. Hecht's fieldwork also found that when both small holders and large ranches cleared the land of forest, often by burning, soil fertility declined rapidly, leading to further deforestation as farms and pastures were abandoned.

In satellite images of the region, the process of Amazonian deforestation—the networks of new roads and associated forest clearance—can be clearly seen (**Figure 7.14c**). Satellites also show the thousands of fires that are set each year to clear land. These fires produce a dense layer of smoke that closes airports and chokes local residents. But the photos also show that the pattern of development and deforestation varies spatially, with some remote areas still relatively untouched and others along roads and around cities almost totally transformed to agriculture. At the southern margins of the Amazon basin, global and national markets for soybeans are driving deforestation and land use changes over large areas.

Estimates of the rate of Amazon basin deforestation do not always agree because of differences in the way in which forests are defined and satellite images are analyzed, and because clouds and smoke prevent accurate assessments in some regions. But the general consensus is that perhaps 15 percent of the Amazon forest has been cleared and that the current rate is about 130,000 square kilometers (50,000 square miles) a year. The fate of the Amazon has attracted global attention, led by scientists and environmental organizations concerned about the impacts of such large-scale forest loss on biodiversity and climate. The Brazilian government has responded by removing some of the tax breaks for development, by intensifying monitoring and control of deforestation, and by establishing parks and reserves. One of the best-known reserves is named for Chico Mendes, a rubber tapper, who organized resistance to deforestation by large ranchers and was murdered in 1988. He pushed for the establishment of areas that were protected for appropriate extractive uses called *extractive reserves*. Other parks and reserves, such as Manu in Peru and Cuyabeno in Ecuador, are becoming tourist destinations, where international tourists stay in jungle lodges and are able to observe the rich bird and animal life of the forest.

The Brazilian government has argued that it is inappropriate for other countries, like the United States and many in Europe, which cleared and developed their own territory in previous centuries, to criticize Brazil now for doing the same thing in an effort to grow its own economy. National and international campaigns have also sought to protect the indigenous peoples of the Amazon who have lost their traditional hunting and gathering lands to development and who are vulnerable to the diseases and cultures of new immigrants to the region.

The coastal zones of central and southern Chile are also important producers of timber for world markets. The forest industry has started to encroach on the groves of towering old-growth alerce trees that are similar to the redwoods of the western United States because both species rely on the heavy seasonal rains from westerly storms. Conservationists have been able to obtain some protection through environmental legislation and purchase of remaining forest land. One of the more controversial conservation efforts is that of U.S. millionaire Douglas Tompkins, who purchased a swath of 700,000 acres of forest land that cuts across almost the entire width of Chile. Tompkins established a national park there, called Pumalin Park, which the government of Chile declared a nature sanctuary on August 19, 2005.

Selling Nature to Save It: Market Solutions for Conservation   Led by Costa Rica, Latin America has seen a boom in tourism, often geared to the natural attractions of the coasts and rain forests. Environmentally oriented tourism, or **ecotourism**, is designed to protect the environment and provide employment opportunities for local people. Costa Rica has won high praise from environmentalists for protecting 30 percent of its territory in biosphere and wildlife preserves (**Figure 7.15a**). Costa Rica has more bird species (850) than are found in the United States and Canada combined and more varieties of butterflies than in all of Africa. It has 12 distinct ecosystems that contain more than 6000 kinds of flowering plants, more than 200 species of mammals, 200 species of reptiles, and more than 35,000 species of insects. The payoff for Costa Rica is the escalating number of tourists who come to visit its active volcanoes, palm-lined beaches, cloud forests, and tropical parks (**Figure 7.15b**). In 1995, when Costa Rica received more than 800,000 tourists, tourism exceeded banana exports as the country's main source of foreign exchange. Since 1995, the number of tourists visiting Costa Rica has increased by 10 percent each year.

Geographer Susan Place has shown that ecotourism has brought mixed benefits to rural areas of Costa Rica. The benefits are not shared equally among residents, and some regions are becoming so crowded that environmental degradation is occurring.

FIGURE 7.15 Conservation in Costa Rica (a) Costa Rica protects a higher percentage of its land in parks than any other Latin American or Caribbean country. (b) Ecotourism has become a source of income and employment, attracting thousands of tourists each year to forest and coastal ecosystems. This photo shows tourists on walkways high in the rain forest in the Arenal National Park, Costa Rica.

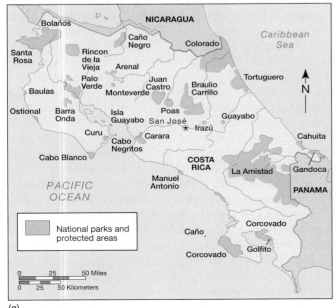

(a)

(b)

The ecological diversity of Latin America also supports biological prospecting, or **bioprospecting**, for new medicines and products with commercial uses. For example, Costa Rica has signed agreements with multinational pharmaceutical companies, such as Merck, that give the companies rights to prospect and develop in return for turning over a share of profits to the national government and to local people.

Other new approaches to conservation include *Payments for Environmental Services* (PES), a program that pays local residents to protect the environment because of its value to others. For example, in Costa Rica, upstream communities are paid to protect their forests because of the role they play in sustaining the flow of rivers for downstream water users such as plantations and hydroelectric schemes. Another market has been created as a result of the Kyoto agreement to reduce greenhouse gas emissions: Many Latin American communities are now receiving payments under Kyoto's Clean Development Mechanism (CDM) for energy efficiency, renewable energy, and sequestering carbon dioxide through reforestation schemes, growing carbon to create credits for northern countries to meet their commitments.

LATIN AMERICA IN THE WORLD-SYSTEM

The Colonial Experience in Latin America

The integration of Latin America into a global system of political, economic, ecological, and social relationships began more than 500 years ago with the arrival of Spanish and Portuguese explorers at the end of the 15th century and the onset of colonialism (the establishment and maintenance of political and legal domination by a state over a separate and alien society) that inexorably linked a Latin American periphery to a European core. As described in Chapter 2, the 15th and 16th centuries were a period of innovation in Europe with changes in manufacturing technology and the development of an economic policy in which government-controlled industry and trade (a system known as *mercantilism*; see Chapter 1, p. 33). Improvements in shipbuilding and navigation allowed Europe to explore—and then expand trade with—other regions of the world, including Asia to the east and Africa to the south. Europeans also sailed west in search of new routes to Asia.

The most famous of these European explorers was Christopher Columbus (known in Latin America as Cristóbal Colón), an Italian from Genoa who lived in Lisbon, Portugal, along with his brother Bartholomew, an expert chart maker. Under the sponsorship of Queen Isabella of Spain, Columbus was commissioned to search for new territory and trading opportunities on a western route to the Indies (as Asia was then known). Having set sail from southern Spain on August 3, 1492, with three small sailing ships—the *Santa María*, the *Pinta*, and the *Niña*—Columbus, commanding the *Santa María*, arrived in the Caribbean in October and landed on Watling Island, a small island in the Bahamas, to which he gave the name San Salvador (**Figure 7.16**). On his first voyage, Columbus also visited Cuba and another island that he called Hispaniola (now Haiti and the Dominican Republic). When the *Santa María* was wrecked on the north coast of Hispaniola, Columbus left behind 21 volunteers to found a colony and returned to Spain on the *Niña*, bringing with him six locals, several parrots, and some gold ornaments.

Columbus's second voyage in 1493 was much larger, with 17 ships and 1500 men, because he intended to establish permanent settlements, but he was frustrated by divisions within his team and by hostility from local residents. On his third and fourth voyages he explored the island of Trinidad and coasts of Venezuela and Central America. With the promise of new lands in the Western Hemisphere, the Spanish wanted a ruling that would assign the new lands to Spain rather than to Portugal. The resulting **Treaty of Tordesillas** was an agreement made by Pope Alexander VI in 1494 to divide the world between Spain and Portugal along a north–south line 370 leagues (about 1800 kilometers, or 1100 miles) west of the Cape Verde Islands. Portugal received the area east of the line, including much of Brazil and parts of Africa, and Spain received the area to the west.

Columbus was followed in subsequent decades by others seeking gold, territory, and other resources in Latin America. The most notable explorers, or *conquistadors*,

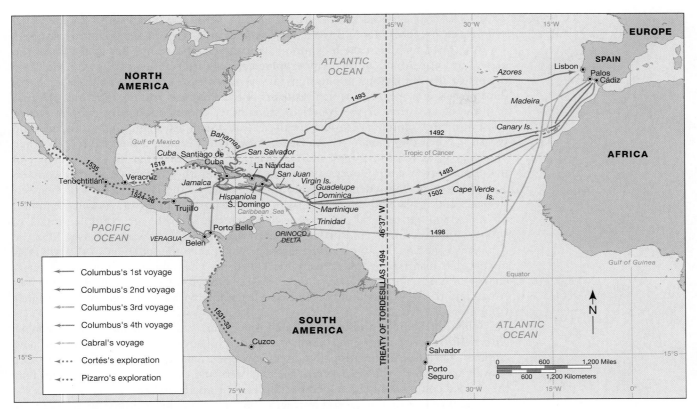

FIGURE 7.16 Colonial voyages and the Treaty of Tordesillas The map shows the major voyages and missions of Columbus, Pizarro, Cabral, and Cortés and the division of Latin America between Spain and Portugal under the Treaty of Tordesillas in 1494. The initial line set by the pope in 1493 was contested by Portugal and shifted farther west. (*Source:* Adapted from P. L. Knox and S. A. Marston, *Human Geography: Places and Regions in Global Context*, 3rd ed. Upper Saddle River, NJ: Prentice Hall, 2004.)

included Hernán Cortés, who landed in Veracruz, Mexico, in April 1519 and went on to conquer the Aztec empire and its capital of Tenochtitlán in the basin of Mexico; and Francisco Pizarro, who seized control of the Incan empire centered in Cuzco, Peru, in 1533. The Portuguese began their colonization of Brazil with the landing of Pedro Alvares Cabral in April 1500 at Porto Seguro in southeast Brazil.

The Spanish expanded and administered the new Latin American colonies through the **viceroyalty** system, the largest scale of Spanish colonial administration. In this system, Mexico City and Lima emerged as the headquarters of the viceroyalties of New Spain (Mexico and Central America) and Peru (Andean and southern South America), respectively. The Peruvian viceroyalty was subsequently divided into New Granada, Peru, and the Río de la Plata as colonial power expanded into the interior of the continent and new cities were established. These viceroyalties were subdivided into judicial regions called *audiencias*, administered from regional centers in the territories of Guatemala and Panama and in six cities that are now the capitals of Latin American countries: Bogotá (Colombia), Caracas (Venezuela), Quito (Ecuador), La Paz (Bolivia), Santiago (Chile), and Buenos Aires (Argentina). The contemporary significance of this political organization is dramatic in that these centers, and the boundaries of the *audiencias* that they controlled, are still important locations in Latin America.

The Spanish charged the new administrators with obtaining gold and silver for the Spanish crown, converting the native people to the Catholic religion, and making the colonies as self-sufficient as possible through the use of local land and labor. The Spanish crown demanded 20 percent of all mine profits, the so-called *Quinto Real*, or royal fifth. These objectives were based in concepts of nature as a commodity, with a secular identity to be governed by humans, and of land as a private property right.

The Demographic Collapse and the Columbian Exchange

The search for local labor to work in the mines and fields of the Spanish colonizers was frustrated by one of the most immediate and significant impacts of the European arrival in Latin America, the **demographic collapse** after about 1500, with the rapid die-off of the indigenous populations of the Americas as a result of diseases introduced by the Europeans to which residents of the Americas had no immunity. Because of the long isolation of the Americas from other continents, native peoples lacked resistance and immunity to European diseases such as smallpox, influenza, and measles. When they caught these diseases from Europeans and then from each other, mortality rates were very high. Researchers have estimated that up to 75 percent of the population of Latin America died in epidemics in the century or so after contact. This massive mortality demoralized local people, led to the abandonment of their settlements and fields, and meant that there was a scarcity of labor to work in the mines, missions, and agricultural activities with which the Spanish, for example, hoped to support their colonial enterprise. The introduction of European diseases into the Americas is just one example of the interaction between the ecologies of the two continents that historian Alfred Crosby has called the **Columbian Exchange**—the interchange of crops, animals, people, and diseases between the Old World of Europe and Africa and the New World of the Americas beginning with the voyages of Christopher Columbus in 1492.

When the Spanish and other colonial powers arrived in new lands, they brought with them favorite plants and animals that they planned to introduce into the new colonies, but also, unintentionally, diseases, weeds, and pests such as rats that were stowaways on their ships. In return, the explorers and colonists collected species that they hoped could be sold or traded back to Europe and elsewhere.

In Latin America, the Spanish introduced the crops and domesticated animals of their homeland—especially wheat and cattle, but also fruit and olive trees, horses, sheep, and pigs. Sugar, rice, citrus, coffee, cotton, and bananas, which had originally been brought to Spain from North Africa and the Middle East after the Moorish invasions of the sixth century, were also transported to the Americas. The Spanish colonizers took back to Europe corn, potatoes, tomatoes, tobacco, and possibly the human disease syphilis.

Over longer periods these exchanges had other effects. The clearing of land for European crops such as wheat and sugar and the overgrazing by cattle and sheep contributed to soil erosion and deforestation in Latin America and the Caribbean. Newly introduced rats, pigs, and cats ate the food that traditionally supported local species or consumed the species, especially ground-dwelling birds. One of many species of Andean potatoes carried back to Europe became the foundation of the Irish diet and one cause of a famine and migration to the Americas when disease destroyed potato harvests in Ireland in the mid-19th century. Corn and manioc were introduced into Africa and became new staples, whereas peanuts and cacao were the basis of new African export economies. Cotton was introduced to India and grown for British textile mills; pineapple was distributed to the Pacific, including Hawaii; and tobacco became an addictive habit, eventually throughout the world.

Colonial Landholding, Labor Relations, and Exports

In order to wrest profits and products from their new lands, the Spanish introduced several new forms of land tenure and labor relations into Latin America that still influence contemporary landscapes. Where the colonizers wished directly to control the land, they granted land rights over large areas to Spanish colonists, often military leaders, and to the Catholic Church, ignoring traditional local uses and establishing fixed property boundaries. These latifundia (large rural landholdings or agricultural estates) typically occupied the best land, forcing other farmers onto small plots of land or minifundia. **Haciendas** were established to grow crops such as olives and wheat, mainly for domestic consumption in mines, missions, and cities rather than for export. **Plantations** were large agricultural estates (usually tropical or semitropical and commercial- or export-oriented). Most were established in the colonial period, growing single crops (monocultures) such as sugar or tobacco for export, mainly in the wetter coastal areas. Labor for the haciendas, plantations, and mines was obtained initially through the institution of **encomienda**, a system by which groups of indigenous people were "entrusted" to Spanish colonists who could demand tribute in the form of labor, crops, or goods. The colonists in turn were responsible for the indigenous groups' conversion to the Catholic faith and for teaching them Spanish. These forms of labor control did not produce a large enough workforce, especially where the Europeans wanted to establish export plantations with high labor requirements and in the tropics where the demographic collapse had devastated local populations that may have been small to begin with. In this case, colonial trading routes were used to import slaves, mainly from Africa, to the Caribbean, Central America, and Brazilian plantations to work in the production of sugar. Slave imports from Africa to Latin America and the Caribbean eventually totaled more than 5 million people, including 3.5 million to Brazil and 750,000 to Cuba (see Geographies of Indulgence, Desire, and Addiction: Sugar, p. 346).

Colonialism as a Process and Legacy It is important to recognize that the colonial effort in Latin America was a process that took place over at least two centuries, with some places incorporated earlier than others and some regions never really coming under complete colonial control because of their remoteness (the Amazon) and local resistance (parts of the Andes). Many accounts have portrayed the Spanish in very negative terms—what historians have termed the "black legend" of a Spanish conquest characterized by greed, cruelty, environmental destruction, and insensitivity to local peoples. But there were also Spanish settlers, such as the conquistador-turned-priest Bartolomé de las Casas and Jesuits in Brazil and Paraguay, who were concerned about the rights of local people. There were also indigenous local leaders and groups who joined the Europeans in exploiting labor and conquering their rivals, such as the Tlaxcalans, who helped Cortés vanquish the Aztecs in Mexico. In some cases, the Spanish were able to capitalize on existing traditional hierarchies that demanded tribute and labor from local people, such as the Inca system of *mita* labor that required all communities in the empire to provide labor for mines and maintenance of terraces and other infrastructures. In many parts of Latin America the colonial legacy of land grabs, labor exploitation, and racism frames contemporary attitudes toward indigenous peoples, who are still trying to regain land and dignity lost during the colonial period.

As Europe consolidated colonial control of Latin America, changes occurred in global and regional economies and political geographies that brought new colonial powers, trading patterns, and institutions to the region. During the 16th century, the Portuguese expanded their interests in Brazil from a few trading stations on the coast, exporting wood used to produce dyes, to the development of large coastal sugar plantations using local (indigenous) forced labor. When disease and retreat of local populations into the interior created a labor scarcity, the Portuguese expanded their role in the slave trade along the African coast and started importing thousands of African slaves to Brazil.

The most important export commodities in Spanish colonial America were silver, produced mainly from mines in Mexico and Bolivia; sugar, grown on plantations in Cuba and southern Mexico; tobacco from Cuba; gold from Colombia; cacao (for chocolate) from Venezuela and Guatemala; and indigo, a deep blue dye, from Central America. In the first phase of the developed colonial economy (1540–1620), Spain derived enormous wealth from the bonanza of the silver mines at Potosí (now within Bolivia) that produced half of the world's silver in the 16th century. This rapid influx of money led to inflation in Europe and Spanish industry suffered as upper classes in both Spain and the colonies chose to purchase luxuries from other parts of Europe.

By 1620, Spain was embroiled in expensive wars with England, France, and Germany, partly over control of trade with the Americas. The demographic collapse and exhaustion of surface silver deposits was resulting in lower revenues from the colonies. Merchants and landowners in the colonies were also starting to resent the strict control of trade and taxation by Spain and were using positions of power and smuggling to keep revenue for themselves, thereby contributing to the overall weakening of Spanish power and economy.

Sugar

No other food has had the historical and geographical impact of sugar, a sweet substance prevalent in most contemporary diets, yet for much of human history unknown outside of some South Pacific islands and Asia. Millions of people now consume sugar in almost addictive quantities—in soft and alcoholic drinks and in candy and as an additive to most processed foods. Too much sugar can cause health problems such as diabetes and tooth decay, and sugar is especially appealing to children because it provides a quick boost of energy when it is absorbed into the bloodstream. About 60 percent of sugar is produced from a tropical grass known as *sugarcane*, and the remainder comes from sugar beets, which are grown in many of the world's temperate regions.

As demand for sugar, known as "white gold" because of its high value, grew in the 17th century, millions of Africans were transported to the Caribbean and Latin America and forced to work as slaves on sugarcane plantations. Sugarcane production is labor-intensive, especially the arduous process of burning the cane fields and then cutting the cane with machetes. The cane is then ground into pulp and boiled at the sugar mill to make sugar. The initial expansion of sugar production to the New World occurred in the 1500s when the Portuguese established plantations along the coast of northeast Brazil. Today the descendants of the African slaves who worked on those plantations make up a large segment of Brazil's large Afro-Brazilian population and dynamic culture. Geographer Jock Galloway describes how, by 1800, the Caribbean, under British and Dutch colonialism, had become the world's most important sugar production region, providing 80 percent of Europe's supply. It was also the primary destination of slave arrivals from Africa (**Figure 1a**).

Sugar provided enormous profits to those capitalists who controlled its production and who often gained considerable political power in the core countries. George Washington and Thomas Jefferson owned sugar plantations on the British Caribbean island of Barbados, for example. Anthropologist Sidney Mintz, in his book *Sweetness and Power*, argues that there is a clear but complex link between slavery, sugar plantations in the New World, and the rise of industrial capitalism in Europe. It is sugar, and the greed that sought slave labor to produce it, that is mostly responsible for the suffering of millions of slaves in the Americas and for the high proportion of people of African heritage in countries such as Brazil, Cuba, Jamaica, and Haiti. After slavery ended, sugar prompted another diaspora of indentured contract workers from Asia who were lured to Caribbean islands such as Trinidad and Jamaica. Sugar, in the form of rum, was the drug that propelled the British and French navies in their battles and colonizing expeditions into Asia and the Pacific. Sugar producers in Britain encouraged the consumption of sweetened tea and thus drove the development of tea plantations in Africa, Australia, and Southeast Asia, as well as on Pacific islands such as Hawaii and Fiji, and caused the shift from sugar as a luxury item to a virtual necessity in the diet of working-class Britain.

Slavery persisted longest in Cuba under Spanish control, and the sugar barons started to shift their operations there in the 19th century. The Cuban cane was of high quality, and before long the large island was covered with fields of sugarcane. By the mid-20th century, sugar dominated the economy, and many fields had foreign, and especially U.S., owners. After the Cuban Revolution in 1959, the sugar industry was nationalized by Fidel Castro's government, which found ready markets in the Soviet Union.

Independence

Independence movements arose in Latin America in 1808 when Napoleon conquered Spain and threatened to tighten trade controls. Revolutionaries, drawn from both Spanish-American and indigenous leaders, set out to liberate Latin America from Spain, partly inspired by the French and American revolutions. Between September 16, 1810, when priest and peasant leader Miguel Hidalgo called for Mexican independence in the famous *Grito* ("cry"), and 1824, when Simon Bolívar (**Figure 7.17**) finally led northern South America to independence, a series of regional revolts led to the formation of independent republics in Mexico, Argentina, Peru, Colombia, Chile, and Brazil. In the Caribbean, after several rebellions against France (inspired by the French Revolution), former slaves declared Haitian

FIGURE 7.17 Simon Bolívar Throughout Latin America, statues of Simon Bolívar, known as *the Liberator*, commemorate 19th-century independence movements in the region.

Brazil is now the world's major sugarcane producer, followed by India, China, and Thailand. Sugar consumption is very high within Latin America, especially in Brazil and Cuba. Sugar has had profound economic and social consequences on those parts of the world in which it became a major crop. It has created highly divided societies, with a wide gap between owners and workers, and has produced multi-ethnic societies with internal disparities and conflicts (**Figure 1b**). Where sugar remains a main export crop, it preserves a legacy of dependency and vulnerability to world markets, exacerbated by surpluses and new diet trends that have reduced the demand for sugar and depressed the price of sugar relative to other crops. The search for alternatives to oil is stimulating a new interest in fuels made from biomass, including from sugarcane.

FIGURE 1 Sugar production (a) This print shows workers on a sugarcane plantation in the 19th century in Cuba. Labor needs for the sugar plantations drove the importation of millions of Africans as slaves to Brazil and the Caribbean until the mid-19th century. The African diaspora to Latin America and the Caribbean is evident in the racial composition of contemporary populations of countries such as Jamaica, Cuba, Haiti, and Brazil. (b) A contemporary photo of sugarcane cutters from Marie Galante in the French West Indies shows that conditions remain very difficult.

(a)

(b)

independence in 1804 and occupied the rest of the island of Hispaniola until the Dominican Republic gained independence in 1844.

In the first half of the 19th century, the loss of colonial trade routes and protections against competition, civil wars led by regional strongmen, foreign reluctance to invest capital in the new and unstable republics, and a brain drain of skilled Spaniards back to Europe all combined to produce an economic decline in Latin America. But around 1850, as the political situation stabilized and industrialization in Europe and North America created investment profits and new demands and consumers, capital became available for the Latin American economies in which liberal political thought supported free trade and foreign investment.

The Export Boom Foreign capital helped develop export economies for nitrate (used to make fertilizer) and copper in Chile; livestock in Argentina; coffee in Brazil, Colombia, and Central America; bananas in Central America and Ecuador; tin in Bolivia; and silver and henequen (a fiber used in making sacks and matting) in Mexico. Foreign-owned companies, which were mostly British in the 19th century, ran many of the new export activities and developed railroads and banks. The subsequent export boom led to some modernization of production methods, improved transportation, and some investment in local light industries such as textiles and food processing. But many of the foreign companies made little effort to promote local markets and infrastructure, and the bulk of the profits were sent back to their home countries rather than reinvested locally. The basic mineral and agricultural exports did not command high prices in relation to the cost of manufactured imports (what is called poor *terms of trade*), and exports were very vulnerable to changes in world prices. Countries that relied on these exports developed economies highly dependent on, and closely linked to, a volatile world market—a condition still evident today in the vulnerabilities of Chile (14 percent of total export value between 2002 and 2005 from copper), the Dominican Republic (29 percent, bananas, including plantains), Ecuador (23 percent, bananas), and Venezuela (8 percent, crude petroleum).

Independence in the Caribbean Independence came much later to most of the Caribbean, especially to countries like Jamaica and Trinidad, which were under British control, and the Caribbean retains distinctive links to Britain, France, and the Netherlands, with Cuba and Puerto Rico characterized by their close and sometimes tense relationships with the mainland United States (see Signature Region: The Caribbean Islands, p. 350). When slavery was abolished by the British in 1807, many emancipated slaves eventually became small farmers. But a decline in sugar prices produced poverty and unemployment. These provoked rebellions in Jamaica beginning in 1865 that eventually resulted in a more representative government—but one still controlled by Britain as one of its crown colonies.

In 1958 an attempt was made to establish the West Indies Federation as an independent unit within the British Commonwealth, but the federation collapsed in 1962 when Jamaica seceded and became fully independent. The first phase of independence from Britain also included Trinidad and Tobago in 1962, Barbados in 1966, and Dominica and Grenada in 1967. The second phase included the Bahamas in 1973, after a typical decolonization period of internal self-government with a British governor. Other British island colonies such as Antigua and Barbados, St. Lucia, and St. Kitts and Nevis did not become fully independent until the beginning of the 1980s.

Cuba remained under Spanish control until after the Spanish-American War in 1898, when limited independence was granted under U.S. influence and frequent intervention. Puerto Rico also shifted from Spanish control to a U.S. territory after 1899 and is still currently part of the United States, with some residents desiring independence and others full status as a U.S. state. Six islands remain as Dutch protectorates with full autonomy for internal affairs (Aruba, Bonaire, Curaçao, St. Martin, Saba, and St. Eustatious), and Martinique and Guadeloupe are overseas departments of France. The British Virgin Islands, Turks and Caicos, Montserrat, Anguilla, and the Cayman Islands are still colonies of Britain, and the U.S. Virgin Islands are part of the United States.

U.S. Dominance, Latin American Revolutions, and the Cold War

The Monroe Doctrine and U.S. Interventionism A dramatic geopolitical step was taken in 1823 when U.S. President James Monroe issued his **Monroe Doctrine** stating that European military interference in the Western Hemisphere, including the Caribbean and Latin America, would no longer be acceptable, would be considered a threat to the peace and security of the United States, and would be considered a hostile act. It also stated that in return for European noninvolvement in the Western Hemisphere, the United States would not interfere in European affairs. This doctrine set the stage for subsequent U.S. involvement and intervention in Latin America and the growth of U.S. economic and political dominance in the region. In 1848 Mexico was defeated in its war with the United States and was forced to cede large portions of its territory to the state of Texas and to what would become the states of Arizona, California, Colorado, Nevada, and New Mexico, leaving in return an enduring Hispanic cultural legacy in these regions.

Latin America was drawn more explicitly into the new U.S. political and economic sphere of influence with U.S. interventions (**Figure 7.18**) to maintain stability and economic access in Cuba (1896–1922), Haiti (1915–34), Nicaragua (1909–33), and

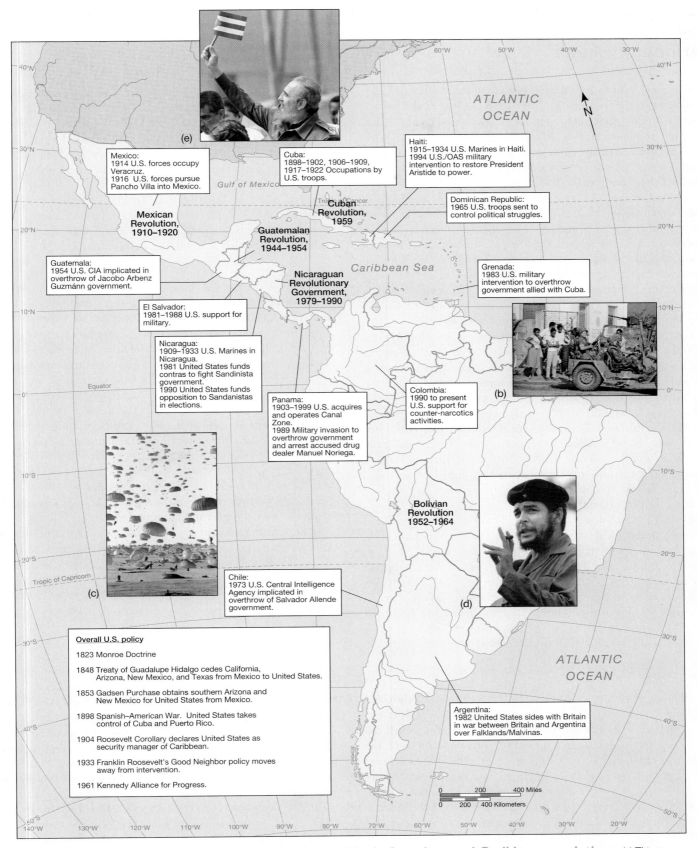

Mexico:
1914 U.S. forces occupy Veracruz.
1916 U.S. forces pursue Pancho Villa into Mexico.

Mexican Revolution, 1910–1920

Cuba:
1898–1902, 1906–1909, 1917–1922 Occupations by U.S. troops.

Cuban Revolution, 1959

Haiti:
1915–1934 U.S. Marines in Haiti.
1994 U.S./OAS military intervention to restore President Aristide to power.

Dominican Republic:
1965 U.S. troops sent to control political struggles.

Guatemalan Revolution, 1944–1954

Guatemala:
1954 U.S. CIA implicated in overthrow of Jacobo Arbenz Guzmánn government.

Nicaraguan Revolutionary Government, 1979–1990

Grenada:
1983 U.S. military intervention to overthrow government allied with Cuba.

El Salvador:
1981–1988 U.S. support for military.

Nicaragua:
1909–1933 U.S. Marines in Nicaragua.
1981 United States funds contras to fight Sandinista government.
1990 United States funds opposition to Sandanistas in elections.

Panama:
1903–1999 U.S. acquires and operates Canal Zone.
1989 Military invasion to overthrow government and arrest accused drug dealer Manuel Noriega.

Colombia:
1990 to present U.S. support for counter-narcotics activities.

Bolivian Revolution 1952–1964

Chile:
1973 U.S. Central Intelligence Agency implicated in overthrow of Salvador Allende government.

Overall U.S. policy

1823 Monroe Doctrine

1848 Treaty of Guadalupe Hidalgo cedes California, Arizona, New Mexico, and Texas from Mexico to United States.

1853 Gadsen Purchase obtains southern Arizona and New Mexico for United States from Mexico.

1898 Spanish–American War. United States takes control of Cuba and Puerto Rico.

1904 Roosevelt Corollary declares United States as security manager of Caribbean.

1933 Franklin Roosevelt's Good Neighbor policy moves away from intervention.

1961 Kennedy Alliance for Progress.

Argentina:
1982 United States sides with Britain in war between Britain and Argentina over Falklands/Malvinas.

0   200   400 Miles
0   200   400 Kilometers

FIGURE 7.18 U.S. interventions in Latin America, and Latin American and Caribbean revolutions (a) This map shows the dates and locations of U.S. intervention in Latin America and those areas where there were major Latin American revolutions in the 20th century. In most cases the United States intervened as a result of Cold War politics and in the interests of U.S. national security, desiring to prevent formation of governments perceived as allied with the Soviet Union. Most revolutionary movements have been inspired by calls for land reform and socialist policies. (b) U.S. marines in Grenada in 1983. (c) U.S. paratroopers during the invasion of Panama, December 21, 1989, ordered by U.S. President George H.W. Bush. The military were ordered to seize Manuel Noriega to face charges on drug trafficking in the United States. (d) Guerilla leader Che Guevara, who fought in the Cuban and Bolivian revolutions. (e) Cuban revolutionary leader Fidel Castro.

SIGNATURE REGION

Caribbean Islands

The Caribbean islands are a diverse mix of cultural traditions, political systems, and environments. They include some of the poorest countries in the region and some of the wealthiest, many linked closely to the international economy. The distinctive physical geographies include extensive coral reefs and mangrove forests, small islands dominated by active volcanic peaks, and vulnerability to the hurricanes that arrive each fall. The Caribbean is divided into several subregions: the *Greater Antilles*, which include the islands of Cuba, Hispaniola (divided into Haiti and the Dominican Republic), Jamaica, and Puerto Rico, and the *Lesser Antilles*, which include the British and U.S. Virgin Islands, the Windward Islands, the Leeward Islands, and the islands of the southern Caribbean Sea north of Venezuela. Political groupings and affiliations include the many islands of the Bahamas, the former British colonies that remain within the Commonwealth, the French protectorates of Guadeloupe and Martinique, and the U.S. territory of Puerto Rico.

Caribbean culture is heavily influenced by the African traditions of the millions of slaves who were brought to the region as labor for the colonial plantations. Many countries, such as Haiti and Jamaica, have a predominantly black population. Although most countries use the colonial languages of English, Dutch, French, and Spanish as official languages, millions of Caribbean residents speak versions of Creole, languages that blend English or French with African or even indigenous words to create distinct languages, such as Haitian patois. Reverberations of Africa are also found in Caribbean foods and music and in spiritual traditions such as Voodoo, Santería, and Rastafarianism.

Some islands, such as Barbados, have many residents of European origin, and several have significant populations of Asian descent. Most of the Commonwealth countries, such as Jamaica, Antigua, and Trinidad, share a passion for the British game of cricket; in Cuba and the Dominican Republic baseball is seen as the route to wealth and fame, with many players emigrating to work in the United States. The Caribbean has produced writers that provide fascinating insights into Caribbean life, such as V. S. Naipaul, Jamaica Kincaid, and Derek Walcott.

Caribbean Economies

The economy of the Caribbean still has strong echoes of the colonial past, with many islands specializing in plantation export crops, such as sugar, tobacco, and coffee. Sugarcane long dominated the land and economy of islands such as Cuba, Jamaica, and the Dominican Republic, but sugarcane has declined with competition from sugar beets—and in Cuba's case, the disintegration of Soviet markets—although the production of rum is still extremely important. Coffee is grown in the cooler highlands of countries such as Jamaica, Puerto Rico, and Haiti, with Jamaica's Blue Mountain coffee receiving premium prices on world markets. Tobacco is the basis of Cuba's renowned cigar industry. Bananas are grown on the British Caribbean islands of St. Vincent, St. Lucia, and Jamaica,

with preferential access to the European Union under the Lomé Agreements, which are intended to assist former British colonies with trade. Such preferences are likely to disappear with moves toward tariff removal and open markets within the European Union and under the World Trade Organization. In all cases, a country's primary exports are vulnerable to world market fluctuations and to the tastes of global consumers.

Jamaica and Trinidad and Tobago have economies partly reliant on mineral and energy resources. Jamaica exports bauxite for aluminum production; Trinidad and Tobago export oil and gas derivatives such as ammonia fertilizer and methanol.

Geopolitics

The Caribbean has both benefited and suffered from its location in "America's Backyard" as the impact of the Monroe Doctrine brought the region within the U.S. sphere of influence. U.S. political goals have included protecting the route to the Panama Canal, preventing the spread of communism, maintaining stability for U.S. corporations with assets in the region, and aligning trade in U.S. interests.

Using these and other goals as justification, the United States has intervened repeatedly in the Caribbean since the Spanish-American War of 1898, which freed Cuba from Spain and made Puerto Rico a U.S. colony. The United States sent troops to the Dominican Republic, Cuba, and Haiti several times in the earlier part of the 20th century; invaded Grenada in 1983 to oust a socialist government and rescue U.S. medical students; and sent troops as peacekeepers to Haiti in 1994.

Export manufacturing activities have developed in many Caribbean countries, especially where formal **free trade zones** have been established within which goods may be manufactured or traded without customs duties. The Caribbean Development Initiative (CDI), designed to promote development and discourage civil unrest and socialism, guaranteed access to U.S. markets and resulted in the growth of export industries such as textiles and clothing.

Although some countries and communities have benefited from export agriculture and new industrial development, there is serious poverty and inequality in many Caribbean countries. Haiti is the poorest country in the entire Latin American and Caribbean region, with high infant mortality, low life expectancy, and difficult living conditions for most of the population that many blame on the semi-feudal concentration of wealth and land under the Duvalier dictatorship from 1957 to 1976. High population densities and a search for land on which to grow a few subsistence crops has driven people to clear forests on steep slopes where soil erosion can be so serious that agriculture is impossible and the land is left desertified and degraded. In contrast to the poverty in Haiti, geographer Lydia Pulsipher links the high literacy and relatively good health in the islands connected with the British Commonwealth to well-established education and medical systems and to strong community networks that have created enduring **social capital** of networks and relationships that encourage trust, reciprocity, and cooperation.

Cuba is the largest island in the Caribbean and is distinctive as a result of the long period of communist rule under Fidel Castro (since the Cuban Revolution of 1959). The United States has taken an aggressive stance against the Cuban government, including the Bay of Pigs invasion in 1961 and a series of embargoes on trade. The United States maintains a large military base at Guantánamo Bay in eastern Cuba, where high-wire fences and mines separate the base from the rest of communist Cuba.

Most of the opposition to the Cuban government within the United States today is associated with Cuban-Americans based in Florida who left Cuba as a result of the revolution. Other U.S. groups, especially agricultural and pharmaceutical companies and states with economies based in these exports, are pressuring the federal government to open trade with Cuba. At one time, sugar and tobacco were the major Cuban exports, especially to the former Soviet Union. They were mostly produced on collective farms. Both scholars and politicians have debated the successes and failures of Cuban socialism, highlighting the positive elements of widespread access to health and education, reflected in favorable social indicators, and the negative aspects of the absence of free elections and inefficiencies of a centrally planned economy (**Figure 1**).

Tourism and Offshore Financial Services in the Caribbean

Tourism and offshore financial services are the two new foundations of the Caribbean economy. **Offshore financial services** include the provision of banking, investment, and services to foreign nationals and companies who wish to avoid taxes, oversight, or other regulations in their own countries. Such services are an important economic sector in the Bahamas and the Cayman Islands. The latter has thousands of registered companies and, with improved telecommunications, is integrally tied to the global financial sector. The sector does not employ a large number of people and is under suspicion of laundering drug money, but the fees support government programs that benefit local residents.

An image of the Caribbean as a paradise of golden sands, warm turquoise seas, and friendly festive people has been constructed to attract more than 25 million tourists each year, 10 million of them on cruise ships. Almost half the population of the Bahamas and the Virgin Islands is employed in tourism in hotels, restaurants, bars, casinos, ocean sports such as diving and fishing, and small shops (**Figure 2**). The downside of tourism includes pollution of oceans, reefs, and beaches by ships; competition for fresh water and higher food prices for local residents; cultural and social stresses from interactions between the wealthy visitors and poorer residents; and prostitution and drugs. Critics also point out that many profits flow out of the region because many tourist enterprises are foreign-owned.

FIGURE 1 Havana, Cuba Havana, located on the northern shore of the Caribbean's largest island, was one of Spain's most important ports and the gate to the wealth of the Americas. As trade in slaves, sugar, and tobacco grew during the colonial period, imposing buildings rose around the main plaza and along the harbor front. A recent resurgence in tourism, mainly from Europe and with modest investment from the Cuban government, has brought new prosperity to some sectors of Havana. These areas have seen construction of new hotels, the opening of stores accepting U.S. dollars, and renovation of older colonial architecture. Restrictions on vehicle imports mean that many are still driving old U.S. automobiles from the 1950s.

FIGURE 2 Tourism in the Caribbean Cruise ships tower over the town of Nassau on the island of New Providence in the Bahamas. The area near the cruise terminal is crowded with restaurants, bars, and souvenir shops catering to the tourists who may spend only a few hours on shore. But the Bahamas, like other Caribbean islands, also have large hotel resorts that entice visitors with beaches, warm weather, and exotic food and entertainment. Although tourism brings millions of dollars into the region, critics highlight the negative impact on culture and marine ecosystems.

Panama (from 1903 onward to control the canal). World War I (1914–18) was a positive stimulus to Latin America's industrial development because of an increased demand for raw materials and accelerated development of manufacturing industry to fill hemispheric demands.

Revolutions   Increasing the concentration of land and wealth in the hands of the few and expanding foreign ownership and export orientation at the beginning of the 20th century produced growing frustration among the poor, the landless, and opposition or regional factions in several countries. Internal tensions between elites and other groups, especially landless peasants, complicated relationships with the United States, especially as the Cold War between the democratic West and the Soviet Union intensified in the 1950s. A series of 20th-century revolutions in Mexico, Guatemala, Cuba, Bolivia, and Nicaragua reverberated around the hemisphere and the world (see Figure 7.18).

Urbanization and industrialization also created urban middle and working classes who wanted a role in governments that were dominated by *oligarchies*—small groups of powerful and wealthy families. In Central America these oligarchies included large coffee-producing landowners of El Salvador and the political elite that managed Guatemala and Honduras in the interests of the multinational fruit companies as so-called **banana republics** (small tropical countries, often run by dictators, dependent on the export of a few crops such as bananas).

The spread of socialist ideas about working-class activism and the need for land reform led to the election of socialist governments in Guatemala in 1954 and Chile in 1970. In both cases, redistribution of land and nationalization of key industries threatened the local elite and U.S. interests to the extent that the United States was implicated in assassinations and military coups that overthrew socialist leaders Jacobo Arbenz Guzmán in Guatemala and Salvador Allende in Chile within three years of their election.

In Nicaragua, concentration of wealth and land under the Somoza dictatorship fostered rebellion that resulted in the establishment of the socialist Sandinista government in 1979. Again, Cold War anticommunist sentiments led the United States to support—covertly—a counterrevolutionary movement of *contras*. When funding to the *contras* by the Reagan administration was linked to illegal arms deals with Iran, the resulting domestic and international opposition to U.S. covert operations led the U.S. government to change tactics: It supported opposition candidates in elections that ousted the Sandinistas in 1989. Guerilla movements inspired by socialist and communist ideas, which emerged in El Salvador, Colombia, Peru, and Bolivia, were severely and often violently repressed by ruling governments.

Economic Development in the 20th Century

Import Substitution   The 1929 stock market crash and ensuing world depression demonstrated the extent to which Latin America had become integrated into the global economy: Throughout the region there were declines in exports, restrictions on investment, and a general economic crisis. This, together with a general awareness that foreign ownership and poor terms of trade for unprocessed exports made Latin American economies vulnerable to world conditions, led to the development of the new economic strategy of import substitution, a process by which domestic producers provide goods or services that were formerly bought from foreign producers. Known as *Import Substitution Industrialization* (ISI) in Latin America, import substitution derived from critical views of global integration associated with the **dependency school of development theory** (see Chapter 1, p. 44).

Mexico, Brazil, and Argentina moved aggressively to implement import substitution policies from the 1930s to the 1960s, including protection of domestic industries through tariffs and import quotas. Government nationalization (the process of converting key industries from private to governmental organization and control) and investment in new manufacturing industries fostered production of chemicals, steel, automobiles, and electrical goods. Import substitution policies temporarily slowed Latin America's integration into global markets and stimulated the growth of domestic industry and workforce in regions such as northeastern Mexico (steel), Mexico's Gulf Coast (petrochemicals; **Figure 7.19**), and São Paulo, Brazil (automobiles). Growing criticisms of import substitution highlighted an oversized government bureaucracy and the high costs of subsidizing industries that were inefficient and produced goods of poor quality due to a lack of competition and government protectionism.

The Debt Crisis A new infusion of capital into the world economy, associated with the increased oil profits that followed the formation of the Organization of Petroleum Exporting Countries (OPEC), brought banks to Latin America seeking to invest in what they viewed as stable and rapidly growing economies. Mexico, with the promise of its own oil bonanza and industrial expansion, as well as the more industrialized countries of Brazil and Chile, were offered the largest loans, but almost all Latin American governments took advantage of the initially low-

FIGURE 7.19 Industrialization for import substitution in Latin America Between 1930 and 1970 many Latin American countries, especially Argentina, Brazil, and Mexico, implemented import substitution policies to develop national manufacturing capacity. Governments invested heavily in steel, automobile, and chemical plants and protected them against competition from imports through tariffs. This petrochemical plant in Mexico processes petroleum from the oil fields in the Gulf of Mexico.

interest loans to support development and other projects. When interest rates rose and debt payments soared in the early 1980s, Latin American governments were unwilling to cut back on popular subsidies and programs and instead borrowed more money, ran budget deficits, and overvalued their currencies. The resulting runaway inflation and debt reached unprecedented levels. By 1989 Brazil owed $111 billion; Mexico, $104 billion; and Venezuela, $33 billion—with annual payments reaching more than half of the annual gross national product (GNP). The 1980s have been called Latin America's "lost decade" because of the slowdown in growth and deterioration in living standards that occurred during that decade.

The resulting decline in purchasing power and living standards, and the likelihood that suspension of debt payments and default would destabilize the international financial system, prompted international financial institutions and the U.S. government to seek a solution to Latin America's debt crisis. The United States extended the repayment period for debts and lent more money, while the International Monetary Fund moved to restructure loans on condition that governments initiate stabilization and structural adjustment policies (see Chapter 1, p. 46). Mexico got a $48 billion bailout, paid mainly to its banking sector.

Structural Adjustment and Neoliberalism Stabilization policies set out to curb inflation by cutting public spending on government jobs and services, increasing interest rates, controlling wages, and devaluing currencies to increase exports. **Structural adjustment policies** required the removal of subsidies and trade barriers, the privatization of government-owned enterprises such as telephone and oil companies, reductions in the power of unions to demand higher wages, and an overall focus on export expansion. These policies, while reducing inflation and debt in a number of countries, had very negative effects on some people and sectors. Increased food prices and reduced health and education services due to the withdrawal of subsidies, as well as rising unemployment as government jobs were cut, hit the poor particularly hard with increases in malnutrition and destitution. As a result of structural adjustment in Peru in 1990, gas prices went from 10 cents to $2 per gallon.

Free-trade policies were introduced in many countries as political power shifted to those with a belief in *neoliberalism*, echoing the views of the 19th-century liberals who believed in free trade and reduced government. Neoliberalism promoted free trade and a reduction in the role and budget of government, including reduced subsidies and the privatization of formerly publicly owned and operated concerns such as utilities.

Neoliberal governments were open to the possibility of expanding free trade through regional agreements that would take down barriers among trading partners.

The most dramatic step was taken by Mexico, which in 1994 joined the North American Free Trade Agreement (NAFTA) with the United States and Canada. NAFTA set out to reduce barriers to trade among the three countries, through, for example, reducing customs tariffs, quotas, and other trade protections. Other initiatives include MERCOSUR (Spanish acronym for "southern common market"), initiated in 1991 and linking Chile, Argentina, Brazil, Paraguay, and Uruguay in a trade agreement, and CARICOM, formed in 1973 to create a trade zone in the Caribbean. The Andean Pact originally linked Peru, Ecuador, Colombia, Venezuela, Bolivia, and Chile in a 1969 agreement, but Chile and Venezuela have withdrawn leaving four countries in what is now called the Andean Community of Nations.

NAFTA   Advocates of NAFTA argued that free trade would create thousands of jobs in Mexico with higher wages and that these opportunities would reduce migration to the United States. Mexican agriculture would shift to growing high-value fruit and vegetables, where it had a comparative advantage during the winter, and Mexico would be able to reduce food prices by importing low-cost grain from the United States and Canada. Free trade was also linked to financial stabilization and to promises of more democratic government in Mexico.

The coalition to oppose NAFTA brought together environmentalists and labor activists in all three countries working within trinational coalitions that successfully petitioned for two side-agreements to be signed as part of NAFTA. The environmental side-agreement established the Commission for Environmental Cooperation (CEC) and led to the creation of two related institutions, the Border Environment Cooperation Commission (BECC) and the North American Development Bank (NADBank). The CEC would monitor environmental impacts and enforce regulations, the BECC would certify new water and sewage projects along the U.S.–Mexico border, and the NADBank would fund environmental infrastructure improvements certified by the BECC. The labor side-agreement included commitments regarding minimum wages, child labor, and rights to unionize and was matched by a U.S. program to compensate U.S. workers who could prove they had lost their jobs as a result of NAFTA.

FIGURE 7.20 NAFTA and neoliberalism A protester in Monterrey, Mexico, opposes U.S. imperialism in front of a banner that says "no to neoliberalism."

Studies suggest that NAFTA has led to the creation of thousands of new jobs in Mexico and to increased wages in some industries. However, many of the hoped-for benefits of NAFTA were frustrated by the economic crises that followed currency devaluation in 1994 and by continuing inequality in both urban and rural areas, which means the benefits have not reached the poor. The problems of pollution and waste associated with urban and industrial development along the border between the United States and Mexico have led a variety of nongovernmental organizations (NGOs) and community groups to demand improved environmental protection. In Nogales, Mexico, women in informal *colonia* settlements have organized to demand safe drinking water and the cleanup of wastes from factories, and they have also created a recycling and tree planting program. The new environmental agreements have created an important space for Mexicans to protest lack of environmental enforcement and to seek funding for water and sanitation projects, but this has not yet resulted in an overall improvement in environmental conditions in Mexico. Criticisms of NAFTA have fueled subsequent protests against neoliberalism and globalization in Mexico (**Figure 7.20**).

Contemporary Economic Conditions   The World Bank estimates the overall GNP of the Latin American region in 2004 at $2.0 trillion, about 5 percent of the world's total, higher than that of Africa, South and Southeast Asia, the Middle East, East Asia, and the Pacific. Per capita GNI at $3576 is also higher than that of any other low- or middle-income region (all world regions except Europe, Australia, New Zealand, Japan, the United States, and Canada). Brazil is ranked the world's ninth largest economy and Mexico is ranked eleventh.

Total exports in 2003 were valued at $378 billion and imports at $366 billion (each about 5 percent of the global total). The Latin American region also received more foreign investment in private capital than any other low- or middle-income region but also had the largest total debt—more than $774 billion. The strongest export economy was that of Mexico ($165 billion in 2002).

These data suggest that the Latin American region is highly linked into the global economic system, with considerable flows of capital and goods to other world regions, especially North America. Although its GNP makes this region rank higher than many others on economic indicators, as we will see, these indicators hide tremendous variations in economic conditions within the region and living conditions that do not always reflect seemingly favorable economic statistics.

The highest average incomes in 2003 are found in the Caribbean islands of the Bahamas and Barbados (more than $15,000 per year). The lowest per capita values in 2002 were reported for Haiti, Honduras, and Bolivia at less than $2600 per capita. As we will see later, some of these countries also have a very uneven distribution of wealth, with a large percentage of very poor people.

THE PEOPLES OF LATIN AMERICA
The History and Composition of the Peoples of Latin America

Prior to the arrival of the Europeans around 1500, Latin America is estimated to have had a population of approximately 50 million people, including large concentrations within the empires of the Aztecs and Incas and many smaller groups of hunters, gatherers, and agricultural communities. The demographic collapse dramatically reduced indigenous populations, but significant Indian populations remained in Mexico, northern Central America, and the Andes.

Colonialism changed the demographic profile of Latin America through the intermixing of European and Indian peoples and the importation of slaves from Africa to the Americas. Few European women accompanied the early Spanish and Portuguese explorers and settlers, and many of the newcomers fathered children with Indian women through force, cohabitation, or marriage. The resulting mixed-race populations were classified according to their racial mix. The most common category was that of **mestizo**, a person of mixed white (European) and American Indian ancestry. Others included *mulatto* (Spanish/African) and *zambo* (African/Indian). These racial categories reflected racist perceptions that permeated society and correlated strongly with social class and culture. Even the Spanish divided themselves between *peninsulares* (those born in Spain) and *criollos* (those born in the Americas), with the elite sending their pregnant wives to Spain so that their children would be born there and thus have the highest social status.

The African Diaspora to Latin America Slave imports to Latin America from Africa totaled more than 5 million people during the colonial period, including 3.5 million to Brazil and 750,000 to Cuba. Many of the Caribbean islands, including Haiti and Trinidad, with very small indigenous and European populations, had a large number of African slaves working on plantations, and African populations also settled along the *plantation* coasts of Mexico, Central America, northern South America, and Ecuador. Although slavery was not abolished until the mid-1800s (1888 in Brazil), escaped and freed slaves formed communities as early as 1605, most famously the African community of Palmares, which was an autonomous republic from 1630 to 1694 in the Brazilian interior. These settlements, also called *maroon communities*, were created by escaped and liberated slaves in other regions such as Jamaica. Racial mixing occurred among European, Indian, and African populations,

TABLE 7.1 Indigenous and Afro-American Population of Selected Latin American Countries (as percent of total population)

Country	Indigenous	Afro-American
Argentina	1	0
Bolivia	71	0
Brazil	1	50
Chile	8	0
Colombia	2	29
Costa Rica	1	0
Cuba	0	34
Ecuador	43	5
El Salvador	7	0
Guatemala	66	2
Guyana	8	0
Honduras	15	2
Mexico	14	0
Nicaragua	5	11
Panama	6	14
Paraguay	3	1
Peru	47	0
Suriname	6	0
Uruguay	0	2.5
Venezuela	2	8

Source: Cambridge Encyclopedia of Latin America, 1996, and Inter-American Development Bank, "Strategy for Indigenous Development for Indigenous Development," 2006. Available at **http://idbdocs.iadb.org/wsdocs/getdocument.aspx?docnum = 691275**.

especially in Brazil, where by the 20th century some scholars were promoting an image of Brazilian racial democracy and equality; skin color had merged to what was called "coffee"; and musical, religious, and dietary traditions had merged into a uniquely Brazilian culture.

This myth of racial democracy is contradicted by evidence of continuing racism in Brazil and other Latin American countries. Studies show that race and class correlate strongly, with Afro-Brazilians being on the whole poorer, less healthy, less educated, and more discriminated against in employment and housing. In Mexico, the media have tended to promote lighter skin as more desirable through the choice of more European-looking actors in commercials and other programs, and job advertisements still ask for "good appearance," hinting at a preference for nonindigenous features.

Other Diasporas   There is a legacy of other diasporas in contemporary Latin American populations. Asian immigration to the region began during the colonial period and picked up after the end of slavery, with Chinese, Indian, and Japanese workers brought to work on plantations and in construction. The workers had to pay off the cost of their travel and sustenance (*indentured* workers). Europeans other than the Spanish and Portuguese settled in the more temperate climates, especially in Argentina, where many families have Italian, German, or British names. Six million Italians and Spanish migrated to Argentina. Some regions, such as Patagonia, are associated with Welsh immigration and culture.

Recent population censuses have attempted to record race and ethnicity and show some general patterns that correlate with the population history described here. Brazil, Colombia, Cuba, and Haiti record large proportions of people of African heritage, and Argentina, Costa Rica, and Uruguay report significant numbers of Europeans (**Table 7.1**). Peru, Ecuador, Bolivia, and Guatemala have a significant percentage of their population defined as Indian, and Colombia, Chile, El Salvador, Mexico, Nicaragua, Panama, Paraguay, and Venezuela are more than half *mestizo.*

These numbers hide subtle differences in how different countries record, construct, and perceive race and ethnicity. For example, a tendency to identify with Europe may increase the proportion of those who report themselves as European in Argentina, whereas a national pride in *mestizo* heritage increases self-identification as being of mixed-race heritage in Mexico.

Population Growth and Migration

The overall population of contemporary Latin America totals about 561 million people, and the distribution is clustered around the historical highland settlements of Central America and the Andes and in the coastal colonial ports and cities (**Figure 7.21**).

Population Growth and Fertility   Population has grown rapidly since 1900, when the regional total was 100 million, mainly as a result of high birthrates and improvements in health care. Brazil (186 million) and Mexico (107 million) have the largest populations today. Fertility rates—the average number of children a woman in a particular population group is projected to have during the childbearing years, ages 15–49—reach four children per woman in Haiti. Many countries are still growing at more than 2 percent per year, and population-doubling times are at less than 35 years, placing pressure on food, water, housing, and infrastructure. Fertility rates have declined throughout much of the region. However, because a large percentage of the population is under age 15, especially in Central America, populations are likely to continue to grow as this cohort enters its reproductive years. For example, Guatemala's population is predicted to almost triple to 32 million people by 2050. The highest population densities (more than 200 people per square kilometer, or about 500 people per square mile) are found on the Caribbean islands and in El Salvador.

High fertility rates are characteristic of poorer, rural regions where infant mortality is high, children can contribute labor in the fields, and women do not have access

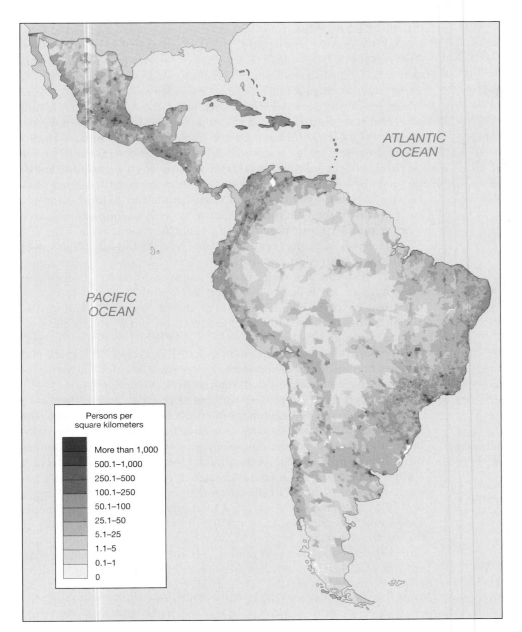

FIGURE 7.21 Population distribution of Latin America, 1995 The general distribution of population in Latin America includes sparsely settled interiors and high population densities around the historical highland regions of the Andes, Mesoamerica, and the coastal regions, especially former colonial ports and cities and their hinterlands. (*Source:* Center for International Earth Science Information Network [CIESIN], Columbia University; International Food Policy Research Institute [IFPRI]; and World Resources Institute [WRI]. *Gridded Population of the World* [GPW], Version 2. Palisades, NY: CIESIN, Columbia University, 2000. Available at **http://sedac.ciesin.org/plue/gpw**.)

to education, employment, or contraception. Fertility rates have tended to drop as people move into the cities, as health care improves, and as more women work and are formally educated. Mexico illustrates this pattern with lower fertility rates in urban, industrial, and higher-income states near Mexico City and the U.S. border and higher fertility rates in the poorer, more rural southern states. Attitudes toward family size in Latin America are also affected by the Catholic Church's position against contraception and the culture of machismo, which views high male fertility as a measure of status.

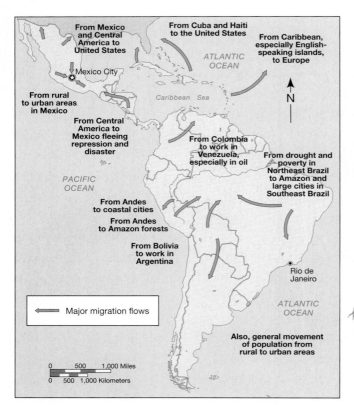

FIGURE 7.22 Major migration streams in Latin America There are major migration streams within countries and between countries in Latin America and to the rest of the world from Latin America. The most significant overall trend is rural-to-urban migration, but poor people are also moving into frontier regions in the Amazon and southern Mexico, from the Andes to work in Argentina and Venezuela, and away from political unrest and natural disasters. The Caribbean has flows to Europe, especially from the English-speaking islands, and to the United States, especially from Cuba, Haiti, the Dominican Republic, and Puerto Rico.

Migration More than 150 million people are estimated to have moved from rural areas to cities in Latin America in the 20th century. The reasons for this massive rural-urban migration include factors that tend to push people out of the countryside and others that pull people to the cities (**Figure 7.22**). People leave rural areas because wages are low; because services such as safe drinking water, health care, and education are absent or limited; or because they do not have access to land to produce food for home consumption or for sale. Unemployment as a result of agricultural mechanization, price increases for agricultural inputs, and the loss of crop and food subsidies have also driven people from rural areas to the cities. Other push factors have been environmental degradation and natural disasters, such as Hurricane Mitch in Honduras, as well as long-running civil wars or military repression of rural people as in Guatemala.

Cities pull migrants because they are perceived to offer high wages and more employment opportunities, as well as access to education, health, housing, and a wider range of consumer goods. Governments often have an urban bias in providing services and investment to cities that are seen as the engines of growth and the locus of social unrest. Social factors that encourage migration to the cities include the promotion of urban lifestyles and consumption habits through television and other media and long-standing social networks of friends and families that link rural communities with people in cities who can provide housing, contacts, and information to new migrants.

Although most people have migrated to cities within their own countries, there are several other important migration flows within the Latin American region. Several countries have encouraged the colonization of remote frontier regions by providing cheap land and other incentives to migrants. For example, the building of roads and availability of land in the Amazon created a stream of migrants from coastal regions of Brazil to the interior, and the development of irrigation in Mexico and Chile attracted migrants to desert regions. People have moved among countries in Latin America in search of work or fleeing from war and repression, with major population movements out of the Andes to work in mining, agriculture, and oil in Argentina and Venezuela and out of Central America to Mexico either as refugees or workers seeking higher wages. Some of the smaller migrant streams have included better-off sectors of society—for example, many intellectuals left Chile, Argentina, and Brazil for Mexico, Venezuela, and Costa Rica during times of repression of leftists and students by military governments.

Urbanization

Most people in Latin America now live in cities, and the levels of urbanization are among the highest in the world, ranging from about 50 percent in most of Central America to more than 90 percent in Argentina, Chile, Uruguay, and Venezuela. This compares to a regional average of only 10 percent in 1900. The region also hosts several of the world's largest metropolitan areas, including Mexico City at 19 million, São Paulo with about 18 million in the metropolitan area, Buenos Aires at 13 million, and Rio de Janeiro at 11.5 million. A major cause of urban growth is migration, although the redefinition of city boundaries (to include metropolitan regions) and internal population growth have also played a role. In many countries, the population of the largest city in an urban system is disproportionately large in relation to the second- and third-largest cities in that system and this so-called *urban primacy* is characteristic of Argentina (Buenos Aires has 38 percent of the national population), Peru (Lima, 40 percent), Chile (Santiago, 57 percent), and Mexico (Mexico City, 20 percent). This concentration of population and development in one or two cities within a country can create problems when physical and human resources, political power, and pollution are all focused in one major settlement. The challenges of urbanization in Latin America are clear when looking at the megacities of Mexico City, São Paulo, and Rio de Janeiro.

Major City: Mexico City Mexico City is the economic, cultural, and political center of Mexico and is one of the largest urban complexes in the world. The city contains almost 20 percent of the country's population, hosts most government functions, and produces 40 percent of the gross national product. On a clear day, the view from the top of the modern high-rise office building that dominates the urban skyline—the Torre Latina—includes elegant colonial plazas and administrative buildings, modern skyscrapers owned by international corporations, and the gleaming snowy peaks of the volcanoes that ring the basin (**Figure 7.23**).

FIGURE 7.23 Mexico City Mexico City is located in a high basin surrounded by mountains, including the volcanic pair of Popocatépetl on the left (5426 meters, 17,800 feet) and Iztaccihuatl on the right (5288 meters, 17,340 feet). Air pollution obscures the view of the volcanoes many days of the year.

As in most colonial cities, Mexico City's colonial center was designed around a main square or plaza formed by government buildings and the main Catholic cathedral. The plaza was in turn surrounded by the villas of the colonial elite and small specialized commercial zones for artisans. The 19th century saw the construction of wide avenues and elegant parks influenced by French urban design. The city grew very rapidly throughout the 20th century, from a population of 500,000 in 1900 to almost 20 million in 2000, expanding from 27 to 1000 square kilometers (10.4 to 386 square miles) as the city embraced many satellite communities. Migrants who were pushed out of rural areas and attracted by the opportunities of the city drove most of the growth.

As in other large Latin American cities, many of the new migrants to Mexico City could not afford to rent or purchase homes and settled in irregular settlements, or *barrios*, that surround the city. As much as 50 percent of Mexico City's housing stock is defined as self-help construction, ranging from cardboard and plastic shanties to sturdier wood and brick structures with aluminum or tile roofs. Many of these settlements occupy steep hillslopes, valley bottoms, and dry lake beds that are vulnerable to flooding, landslides, and dust storms. The *barrio* of Netzahualcóyotl houses more than 3 million people on the shores of Lake Texcoco.

The location of Mexico City on a former lake bed, with unconsolidated sediment, adds to the risks from earthquakes in this seismically active zone. The earthquake that woke residents in the early hours of October 19, 1985, killed as many as 10,000 people and destroyed more than 100,000 homes and other buildings (see Figure 7.6b). The city is also at risk from the volcano Popocatépetl, which overlooks the southern part of the basin (see Figure 7.23).

Mexico City's most infamous environmental problem is air pollution, which currently reaches levels that are dangerous to human health on more than 100 days a year. Thousands of automobiles, trucks, and buses, many with inadequate emission controls, are responsible for about 75 percent of the air pollution, with dust, fires, industrial plants, and miscellaneous energy use responsible for the remainder. The location of the city adds to the pollution problem because polluted air is often trapped in the basin by the surrounding mountains and by inversions where warm air traps cold air near the ground. The high altitude of the city at more than 2000 meters (6000 feet) means that fuel burns less efficiently and that humans must breathe more air because of the lower oxygen levels. Although the government has implemented air pollution controls, the continuing growth of the city and of car ownership has prevented any significant decline in pollution levels.

Major City: São Paulo Located on a high plateau about 50 kilometers (30 miles) from the Atlantic coast, the city of São Paulo has wide avenues and many skyscrapers around the central business district with surrounding neighborhoods of

FIGURE 7.24 São Paulo High-rise office buildings are surrounded by poorer slum housing called *favelas*.

FIGURE 7.25 Rio de Janeiro Rio de Janeiro has a stunning location with a harbor overlooked by Sugar Loaf Mountain and the beaches of Copacabana. The commercial harbor is now a center for shipbuilding and for agricultural exports from the southeast of Brazil, including soybeans and orange juice in specially constructed tankers.

poorer and slum housing (**Figure 7.24**). It has also become a major financial center for Brazilian and international banks and has recently developed a large telecommunications and information sector, with more than a million technical and scientific workers. Brazilian geographer Milton Santos reports that São Paulo employs more than 2 million manufacturing workers and produces 30 percent of Brazil's gross national product, having moved from a commercial center to a manufacturing hub to a service and information core for the global economy.

Major City: Rio de Janeiro While Rio de Janeiro has been overshadowed by the economic growth of its rival São Paulo, 250 kilometers (155 miles) to the southwest, it continues to be the cultural and media center of Brazil (**Figure 7.25**). Rio was the capital of Brazil from 1822 to 1960. The urban structure includes an older city center with a wealthier residential zone and beaches such as Copacabana toward the south and a poorer, more industrial zone to the north. The magnificent landscape of Rio's harbor and beaches draws worldwide attention during the festival of Carnival, a major tourist destination where the influence of African traditions emerges in music and dance. In both Rio and São Paulo, massive football (soccer) stadiums holding up to 200,000 people are a focus of city pride and entertainment.

Favelas Rio and São Paulo followed the same pattern as other Latin American cities, attracting millions of migrants who settled informally around the urban core. The **favelas**, a Brazilian term for informal settlements that grow up around the urban

core, lack good housing and services. In São Paulo, 28 percent of residents have no drinking water and 50 percent have no sanitation. The crowding, high land costs, violent crime, poverty, and pollution of the city are starting to cause economic development to shift to smaller neighboring cities.

The Latin American and Caribbean Diaspora

Latin American and Caribbean people have also left the overall region in considerable numbers, creating a global Latin American and Caribbean diaspora. The United States hosts the largest number of people who define themselves as being of Latin American or Hispanic heritage. Many Mexican families became part of the United States when the land they lived on became U.S. territory following the U.S.–Mexican War in 1848. They use the phrase "the border crossed us, we didn't cross the border" to emphasize that they are not migrants but long-standing residents. Between 1900 and 1930, 1.5 million Mexicans (10 percent of the total population) migrated to the United States to escape the chaos of the Mexican Revolution and partly to fill labor shortages created by World War I. Although 400,000 Mexicans (some of them U.S. citizens) were deported during the Great Depression in the early 1930s, the growth of the U.S. economy from about 1940 on and World War II created such a demand for low-cost labor, especially in agriculture, that the U.S. and Mexican governments introduced a formal guest farm worker program. This program distributed 4.6 million temporary permits for Mexicans to work in the United States between 1942 and 1964. Many **braceros** (defined as a guest worker from Mexico given a temporary permit to work as a farm laborer in the United States) never returned to Mexico, and migration continued after the program ended, even as U.S. immigration restrictions were tightened. Migrants are still drawn to the United States by higher wages, by jobs for women in the service sector, and by strong social networks that link communities in Mexico to family and friends in the United States.

In the last 50 years, Latin American and Caribbean migration to the United States has been dominated by Mexicans (about 40 percent of the total), but the total includes

FIGURE 7.26 Guatemalan handicrafts Tourists browse textiles and other crafts sold by indigenous Maya at a market in Guatemala.

large numbers of people from Cuba (15 percent) and Central America (10 percent). Significant Latin American populations can also be found in Canada and Europe (especially in Spain). The Caribbean diaspora includes migration to the United States (mainly from Cuba, Jamaica, and Puerto Rico), but because of colonial links to Britain, large numbers of Caribbeans have migrated to Europe and British Commonwealth countries, especially from Jamaica and Barbados to Britain and Canada.

The money that is sent back to Latin America from people working temporarily or permanently in other countries is called **remittances** and can make a significant contribution to national and local economies. Many communities in the Caribbean and Mexico rely on these funds to build houses, purchase agricultural inputs, or

FIGURE 7.27 Languages of Latin America This map shows the major regions of living indigenous languages in Latin America. Most of mainland Latin America uses Spanish as an official language, except for Brazil, which uses Portuguese; French Guiana, French; Suriname, Dutch; and Belize and Guyana, English. The Caribbean has more language variation than the mainland, and the dominant European languages reflect the colonial histories of the islands.

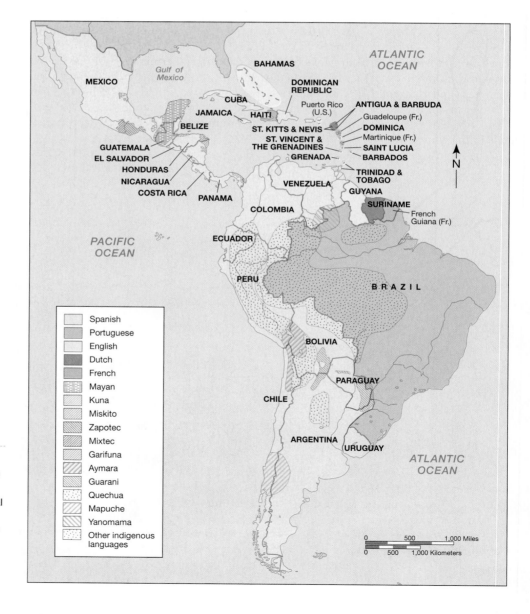

educate their children. They are one of the new but informal flows of international financial capital in the global economy.

Language and Cultural Traditions

The mixed racial and ethnic composition of Latin America is echoed in many aspects of cultural heritage and social practices in the region. Indigenous culture, including traditional dress, crafts, ceremonies, and religious beliefs, persists in regions such as highland Guatemala and Peru, partly as a result of colonial policies that kept Indian communities separate while demanding tribute and labor and partly due to resistance to the adoption of European culture by conservative indigenous religious and political leaders. Cultural traditions are now promoted to tourists and revalued through indigenous social movements seeking political rights and recognition. For example, indigenous Mayan centers such as Quetzaltenango in Guatemala are promoted as tourist destinations where traditional crafts may be purchased and photos taken (often for a price) of women and children in traditional colorful woven garments (**Figure 7.26**).

Indigenous languages endure in several regions of Latin America (**Figure 7.27**). The most widely spoken languages are *Quechua* in the Andean region (spoken by 13 million people), English Creole and French Creole in the Caribbean (10 million), *Guaraní* in Paraguay

FIGURE 7.28 Latin American art A self-portrait by Mexican artist Frida Kahlo standing on the United States–Mexico border contrasting the indigenous tradition of Mexico with modern industry in the U.S.

(4.6 million), *Aymara* in the Andes (2.2 million), *Mayan* in Guatemala and southern Mexico (1.7 million), and *Nahuatl* in Mexico (1.3 million). Spanish is the dominant language across most of Latin America, except for Brazil (Portuguese), Belize and Guyana (English), Suriname (Dutch), and French Guiana (French). The foods of Latin America blend indigenous crops such as corn or potatoes with European influences, especially from Spain. Although Mexico is associated with spicy dishes that include *chile*, the food is quite mild in the rest of Latin America. In livestock-producing areas, such as Argentina, grilled meat is extremely popular, but in much of Latin America, the poor eat simple meals of rice, corn, potatoes, and—for protein—beans. Modified versions of Mexican cuisine have diffused throughout North America and include many chain restaurants. Foods in the Caribbean reflect the medley of cultures in the region with African, Asian, and European influences combining to create dishes of fish, chicken, pork, a range of vegetables, fruits, and starch crops (rice, potatoes, and yuca).

Latin American and Caribbean art and literature have incredible variety and regional specialization. Traditional textiles, pottery, and folk art are sold to tourists and by import stores in North America and Europe. Literary traditions include magical realism (where authors such as Gabriel García Márquez blend imaginary and mystical themes into their fiction), and Latin American and Caribbean authors have won six Nobel prizes for literature. Works of noted Mexican muralists, including Diego Rivera, and the tortured paintings of his companion Frida Kahlo, are numbered among the masterpieces of 20th-century art (**Figure 7.28**).

In the 1990s several strands of Latin American and Caribbean music became popular. Traditional music, such as the Andean pipes of the groups Inti Illimani and Los Incas, has formed the soundtracks of documentary films and is available in music stores worldwide. The music of *Nueva Canción*, or New Song movement, with its social conscience, and singers such as Mercedes Sosa who have fled repression in their home countries, has become a part of the global folk music scene. Caribbean global

(a)

(b)

FIGURE 7.29 Latin Music (a) Years after his death, Bob Marley of Jamaica is still popular as a reggae artist and representative of the Rastafarian religion. (b) Gloria Estefan, who is originally from Cuba, is one of the superstars of Latin pop and rock based in Miami.

FIGURE 7.30 Michelle Bachelet The first female president of Chile was elected in 2006. A doctor, member of the Socialist party, and former minister of Defense, she has reformed the health service was detained and tortured by the military under General Pinochet in the 1970s.

influences include the reggae of Jamaica and steel-drum bands of Trinidad, which resonate with the rhythms of Africa (**Figure 7.29a**). Latin pop and rock music has become extremely popular, often produced from Miami, Latin America's business capital in the United States (**Figure 7.29b**).

Gender Relations

Certain cultural views of the family and gender roles are characteristic of Latin America. Multiple generations often live and work together, individual interests are subordinated to those of the family, and the traditions of machismo and marianismo define gender roles within the family and the society. *Machismo* constructs the ideal Latin American man as fathering many children, dominant within the family, proud, and fearless. *Marianismo* constructs the ideal woman in the image of the Virgin Mary as chaste, submissive, maternal, dependent on men, and closeted within the family. Latin American society is generally patriarchal, with institutions that have prohibited or limited women's right to own land, to vote, to get a divorce, and to secure a decent education.

These stereotypes are, of course, contradicted by individual cases and are breaking down in the face of new geographies and global cultures. Family links are weakened through migration and the isolation of many living spaces, from each other and from those of other family members in urban environments. Men's and women's roles are changing as fertility rates decline and women enter the workforce and politics. Latin American and Caribbean feminists have organized to obtain the right to vote; to effect changes in divorce, rape, and property laws; to gain access to education and jobs; and to elect women to political office (**Figure 7.30**).

Gender inequality is widespread in Latin America. Female literacy, on average, is 2 to 15 percent lower than that of male populations. Women tend to earn much less on average than men. In Latin America and the Caribbean, women earned 52 percent of the male rate in 2003. In Ecuador, for example, female GDP per capita was $1136 in 2003 compared to $1701 for men. This inequality has been associated with systematic institutional biases that denied women in many countries the right to vote or the right to marital property until the 1950s, with cultural traditions that discourage more than a few years of education for women, and with employment structures that pay women less than men or pay less for traditionally female work such as domestic service work and food processing.

Religion

One of the main objectives of Spanish and Portuguese colonialism was the conversion of indigenous peoples to Catholicism. While some indigenous people fiercely resisted missionary efforts, others found ways to blend their own traditions with those of the Catholic Church to create new *syncretic* religions. The process of conversion was facilitated by the reported appearance of the brown-skinned Virgin Mary of Guadalupe to an Indian convert in Mexico on December 9, 1531, and by the efforts of some priests to protect local communities from the Spanish efforts to obtain land, tribute, and labor by force. More than 400 million people in Latin America are followers of Catholicism, Islam and Judaism draw about 1 million people each, and more than 10 million people have traditional Mayan beliefs.

The slave trade brought African religious traditions to Latin America and the Caribbean, and these often merged with indigenous and Catholic beliefs to construct syncretic contemporary rituals, followed by more than 30 million people of Candomble and Umbanda in Brazil, Voodoo in Haiti, and Santería in Cuba and other islands. Candomble and Umbanda are both sects of the Macumba religion, with rituals that involve dances, offerings of candles and flowers, sacrifice of animals such as chickens, and mediums and priests who use trances to communicate with spirits that include several Catholic saints. Voodoo (also spelled Voudou) rituals include drumming, prayer, and animal sacrifice to important spirits based on traditional African gods and Catholic saints and are led by priests who act as healers and protectors against witchcraft. Santería, which is closely connected to the Yoruba religion of West Africa, blends Catholic saints with African spirits associated with nature, using rituals similar to other Latin American and Caribbean religions.

The emergence of a new form of Catholic practice, **liberation theology**, focused on the poor and disadvantaged. Liberation theology is informed by the perceived preference of Jesus for the poor and helpless and by the writings of Karl Marx and other revolutionaries on inequality and oppression. This new orientation to the poor was espoused by the Second Vatican Council, called by Pope John XXIII in 1962. Priests preached grassroots self-help to organized *Christian base communities* and often spoke out against repression and authoritarianism. In recent decades evangelical Protestant groups with fundamentalist Christian beliefs have grown and spread rapidly in Latin America. Their message of literacy, education, sobriety, frugality, and personal salvation has become very popular in many rural areas. Estimates suggest that up to 40 million Latin Americans are now members of such churches.

CONTEMPORARY CHALLENGES IN A GLOBALIZING WORLD

Latin America is a dynamic world region where economic, political, and social changes have been rapid in the 20th century and have varied in their nature and impact among and within countries. Latin American countries took divergent political paths that have included socialist and military governments; authoritarian, single-party, and multiparty systems; and highly centralized and localized administrations. The challenges of creating functioning national governments and promoting economic growth dominated the post-independence period in the 19th century. The 20th century saw regional factions, the working class and the poor demanding reform through revolution and populism, and threats to the distribution of wealth and elite power met by military and authoritarian rule. One of the most dramatic shifts was from a continent dominated by military and authoritarian governments in 1970 to almost region-wide democratic systems in 2000.

Politics: Transitions from Authoritarianism to Democracy

The dual threats of economic instability and communist ideas contributed to a rise in authoritarianism and military governments in the 1960s and 1970s. Seeking financial order and control of socialist movements, the military took control of government in Brazil in 1964, Chile and Uruguay in 1973, and Argentina in 1976. While central authoritarian control certainly provided some degree of economic stability and growth, the military governments aggressively kept social order by repressing dissent, especially among students and workers perceived as having socialist ideals. In Argentina, the military government's so-called *Dirty War* is alleged to have killed 15,000 people and forced many others to leave the country. In Chile, the military government of General Augusto Pinochet has been accused of similar disappearances and human rights abuses (see Figure 7.30).

Public and foreign outrage at authoritarian repression and human rights violations, the inability of military governments to solve economic problems, the end of the Cold War, and international and internal pressures that linked economic globalization to democratic governance resulted in gradual transitions to democratic governments in most Latin American countries—Argentina in 1983; Brazil in 1985; and Chile in 1989.

In Argentina the departure of the military government was hastened by the loss of a war with Britain when Argentina invaded the Falkland Islands in 1982 (called the *Islas Malvinas* in Latin America).

Political opposition and activism have often taken the form of organized **social movements** that have also pressured for specific resources and issues, such as housing, water, human rights, or environmental protection. Geographer Anthony Bebbington argues that social movements have also filled a gap in service provision and local administration created by the economic crisis and neoliberal policies that have shrunk government in many Latin American countries. Although many democratic governments adopted neoliberal policies by 1995, a backlash against budget cuts, privatization and inequality brought more left-wing, antiglobalization, and populist leaders to power after 2000, including Presidents Lula (Brazil), Chavez (Venezuela), and Morales (Bolivia).

Agriculture: The Green Revolution and Land Reform

For the first part of the 20th century, the yields of most agricultural crops in Latin America were very low (less than 1 ton per hectare) and farmers with small plots of land could not produce enough to feed themselves, let alone sell in the market. As population and urban-consumption demands increased, countries such as Mexico and Brazil had to import basic food crops such as wheat and corn. The legacy of large landholdings from the colonial period was compounded by the accumulation of land by the wealthy and by foreign companies in the late 19th century.

In Costa Rica, coffee was produced on small European- and mestizo-owned farms, but in El Salvador and Guatemala coffee land was consolidated into large operations controlled by a few families (known as the *oligarchies*). In Guatemala and Honduras, U.S.-owned companies such as Standard Fruit and United Fruit took over large areas of land to produce tropical fruit, especially bananas, for export. This led to widespread rural poverty, landlessness, and frustration that aided uprisings such as the Mexican and Cuban revolutions and the election of socialist governments in Chile and Guatemala. In addition, many large landholdings were being used for extensive ranching, for export crops, or for low-productivity crops and were not contributing to the food needs of the growing urban populations.

Land reform—a change in the way land is held or distributed, such as the division of large private estates into small private farms or communally held properties—was seen as a way to increase productivity and reduce social unrest and was implemented by revolutionary governments and others seeking to reduce the risk of rural uprising. Mexico's post-revolutionary land reform redistributed expropriated and government lands to 52 percent of rural households between 1917 and 1980. In many cases, the land was distributed in the form of *ejidos*, communal lands given to groups of landless peasants who could farm collectively or as individuals but could not rent or sell the land outside the ejido.

Bolivia redistributed land to 79 percent of rural households between 1953 and 1975. The socialist governments of Guatemala (1952), Chile (1972), and Nicaragua (1979) distributed land to at least 20 percent of rural households, but some of these lands were later returned to large landholders under military or more conservative governments.

Pressure for land reform continues throughout the region. For example, in Brazil, a landless movement with an estimated 1.5 million people is the largest social movement in Latin America. Since 1985, *Movimento dos Trabalhadores Rurais Sem Terra* or *MST*, Brazil's Landless Workers Movement, has won land titles for more than 350,000 families in 2,000 settlements. It has reformed land through forced land redistribution and by demanding legal rights and political change with considerable public support. The question of whether land reform in Latin America has been successful or not is hotly debated, with some believing that the reform sector is inefficient and that communal lands should be privatized and others arguing that land reform has increased rural stability and agricultural production. Most have recog-

FIGURE 7.31 Green Revolution in Mexico The International Center for Improvement of Maize and Wheat (CIMMYT) in Mexico. Scientists at the center, funded by the Rockefeller Foundation as well as the Mexican and U.S. governments, used advanced plant-breeding techniques to produce new varieties of grains that resisted disease and responded to fertilizer and irrigation with very high yields. Norman Borlaug, who led the plant-breeding effort, was awarded the Nobel Peace Prize in 1970 for his work to end world hunger. Farmers, especially in irrigation districts in northern Mexico, were quick to adopt the new crop varieties. National production of corn and wheat soared, turning Mexico into a major grain exporter by the 1970s.

nized that land reform on its own can be ineffective unless it is part of an overall agrarian reform package that also provides the new landowners with technical advice, inputs, credit, and market access.

A second solution to low productivity and poverty in rural areas was the **Green Revolution**—the process of agricultural modernization that used a technological package of higher yielding seeds, especially wheat, rice, and corn, that in combination with irrigation, fertilizers, pesticides, and farm machinery increased crop yields in several world regions from about 1950 to 1980. Mexico was a global center for Green Revolution technology, hosting the International Center for Improvement of Maize and Wheat (CIMMYT) near Mexico City (**Figure 7.31**). Other Latin American countries such as Argentina and Brazil also promoted Green Revolution agricultural modernization, including key crops such as rice and soybeans.

Although the Green Revolution increased crop production in many parts of Latin America, it was not an unqualified success because of its role in increasing inequality and in environmental degradation. The Green Revolution has been criticized because it increased dependence on imports of chemicals and machines from foreign companies and thus contributed to the debt problem. The benefits tended to accrue to wealthy farmers who could afford the new inputs and to irrigated regions, while poorer farmers on land watered only by rainfall fell behind or sold their land. In some cases, such as in southeastern Brazil, machines replaced workers, thus leading to unemployment, and Green Revolution technology and training also tended to exclude women, who play important roles in food production.

The new agricultural chemicals, especially pesticides, contributed to ecosystem pollution and worker poisonings, and the more intensive use of irrigation created problems of water scarcity and of salinization (buildup of salt deposits in soil due to evaporation of water that includes salts drawn up from the subsoil). The most serious criticism of the Green Revolution was that it contributed to the worldwide loss of genetic diversity by replacing a wide range of local crops and varieties with a narrow range of high-yielding varieties of a few crops. Planting single varieties over large areas (monocultures) also made agriculture vulnerable to disease and pests.

A second Green Revolution is now under way, involving crops engineered using biotechnology to resist pests and diseases and to produce even higher yields. This research is opposed by some who fear unanticipated consequences from such efforts, exemplified by concern that bioengineered corn pollen was negatively affecting monarch butterflies in Mexico. Brazil has planted large areas with genetically modified soya for export.

Economic crisis, the reduction of government programs, and opening of trade have slowed the progress of the Green Revolution in many countries. Fertilizer use in countries such as Brazil and Mexico has declined with high prices, fewer subsidies, and increased competition from imported corn and wheat, especially from the United States.

Many governments have shifted from giving top priority to self-sufficiency in basic grains to encouraging crops that are apparently more competitive in international

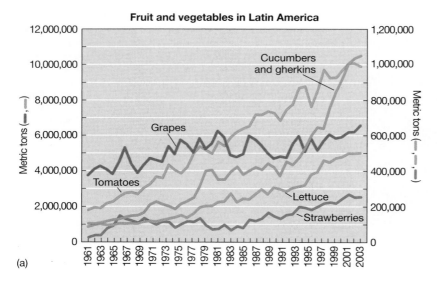

(a)

(b)

FIGURE 7.32 Nontraditional agricultural exports (a) Production of fruit and vegetables has increased in Latin America partly as a result of export of nontraditional crops. Tomato, cucumber, and lettuce production has grown rapidly in response to demand from North America and Europe. However, consumer demand for unblemished fruit and vegetables requires heavy applications of pesticides and water to meet export quality standards and distribution schedules. The crops are vulnerable to climatic variation and to the vagaries of the international market, including changing tastes for foods and health scares about pesticide or biological contamination. In countries such as Chile, annual pesticide use doubled between 1984 and 1998, from just under 6000 metric tons to more than 14,500 metric tons. (b) Spanish land grants distributed the fertile land of the Central Valley of Chile into large haciendas that produced wheat and raised cattle in the colonial period, especially to supply the growing cities of Santiago, Valparaíso, and Concepción. Wheat became an important export after independence, but the major boost to exports came in the 20th century with the development of refrigerated transport and shipment by air. This allowed Chile to take advantage of the hemispheric contrast in seasons, selling fruit and vegetables grown in the Chilean summer (November to March) to North American winter markets. Production and export of fruit and vegetables—especially fresh grapes, apples, peaches, and berries—grew dramatically, together with fruit packing and processing industries that employed thousands of people. Agricultural expansion has been aided by the Green Revolution package of technologies and by some land reforms that provided plots of land to those who would farm it intensively. Chile has also developed a wine industry that exported more than $800 million worth of wine in 2004. (*Source:* [a] UN Food and Agricultural Organization. Available at **http://faostat.fao.org/**.)

trade, such as fruit, vegetables, and flowers. These **nontraditional agricultural exports (NTAEs)** have become increasingly significant in areas of Mexico, Central America, Colombia, and Chile, replacing grain production and traditional exports such as coffee and cotton (**Figure 7.32a**). Rather than grow these and other crops on large company landholdings, the current strategy is **contract farming** for multinational corporations such as Del Monte. Farmers sign contracts with companies to produce crops to certain production and quality standards, in return for a guaranteed price. The increased use of imported pesticides on exports is associated with damage to ecosystems and workers' health. Using imported pesticides on export crops in developing countries, then exporting the contaminated crops to the regions where the pesticides were manufactured, is termed the **circle of poison**. Central Chile is one of the most productive agricultural export zones in Latin America and is increasingly compared to the U.S. state of California, with which it shares a moderate Mediterranean climate of warm, wet winters, and moderate summer temperatures (**Figure 7.32b**). Some farmers, especially of coffee and bananas, have turned to organic production and fair trade labels as a way to save on inputs and access new consumer markets in North America and Europe (**Figure 7.33**).

Fisheries are another critical component of Latin American and Caribbean food and export systems, and activities range from subsistence fisheries in small coastal villages to large-scale commercial exploitation of offshore fisheries. The overall catch in the region was more than 10 million metric tons in 1994, contributing on average about 10 percent of overall food supply and making a significant contribution to exports in Chile, Ecuador, and Costa Rica. But offshore catch has halved in Chile as a result of overfishing and climate variability. Aquaculture and mariculture (the cultivation of fish and shellfish under controlled conditions) in coastal lagoons has become an important export sector in countries such as Chile (salmon), Ecuador, and Honduras.

The Drug Economy

Latin America produces drugs that are illegal in many countries, including cocaine, heroin, and marijuana (**Figure 7.34a**). Many Latin American farmers grow drugs because of their high price compared to other agricultural products. In regions where crop yields are low, where people have only small plots of land, and where market prices for legal agricultural crops do not cover production costs, drug production is an attractive or even necessary survival option. The farmers receive only a fraction of the street value of the drugs when they are sold. In Bolivia a farmer might get $610 per kilogram (2.2 pounds) of coca leaves, whereas cocaine is sold for more than $100,000 per kilogram in the United States. Most of the drug exports are controlled by powerful families in Colombia and Mexico who manage the transport systems from rural Latin

FIGURE 7.33 Fair trade products Latin America is beginning to take advantage of markets for fair trade and organic products, especially for coffee.

America by land, air, and boat into the main distribution and consumption centers in the United States, such as Los Angeles and Miami.

In some areas the drug trade has exacerbated political conflicts. The situation is most severe in Colombia, where several guerilla movements control large zones despite opposition by government military units. The groups are alleged to have links with powerful drug lords and to offer protection to farmers involved in drug production. Because the conflicts are fueled by the drug economy, the United States has become involved in the strife through its support for the Colombian government's anti-drug activities. The United States sprays pesticides and provides military training and equipment to the Colombian army groups who repress rebel groups in the drug-producing regions (**Figure 7.34b**).

(a)

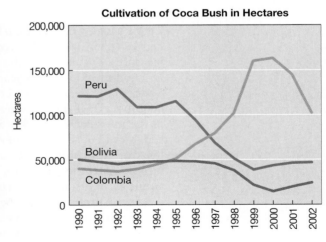

Cultivation of Coca Bush in Hectares

(b)

FIGURE 7.34 Drug production in Latin America (a) Cocaine derives from the coca plant, the leaves of which have been chewed by Andean residents for centuries to provide energy and alleviate the effects of high altitude. Peru, Colombia, and Bolivia produce about 98 percent of world cocaine supplies; Jamaica, Colombia, and Mexico are major producers of marijuana (cannabis). The coca-growing regions in Colombia are mostly located south of Bogota and near the border with Ecuador and Peru. In Peru and Bolivia coca has been grown on the eastern slopes of the Andes. (b) Because of aggressive eradication efforts, including herbicide spraying funded by the United States, the area in coca cultivation in Latin America has fallen from 210,000 hectares (741,000 acres) in 1990 to 173,000 hectares (445,000 acres) in 2002 and has shifted from Peru and Bolivia to Colombia. But production techniques have improved and the overall production has remained around 300,000 tons; the distribution is increasingly controlled by organized crime throughout the global world-system.

The drug economy threatens to destabilize other Latin American countries such as Bolivia, Peru, and Mexico because the drug traffickers increasingly control production areas and influence the police, the army, and political leaders through intimidation or bribery. Analysts contend that farmers will continue to produce crops that can be processed into drugs until they can obtain a better living from other crops or other means of employment or until the demand is controlled in the United States. They argue that the United States should be focusing on the control of demand within its own borders or even on limited legalization of consumption, rather than on fighting a "war on drugs" in Latin America.

Regional Development

Political change and economic restructuring have not necessarily resulted in reducing poverty and inequality in Latin America. In fact, some indicators of inequality show some Latin American and Caribbean countries as having greater concentrations of wealth and land in the hands of an elite few than in other parts of the world, with the vast majority of the population remaining poor and landless.

Income Inequality The highest average national incomes in Trinidad and Tobago and Venezuela are about 50 percent of those in the developed world, whereas in the poorest countries such as Haiti, there is a low-income economy of $875 or less. Recent reports from the Inter-American Development Bank suggest that 25 percent of all income in Latin America is received by only 5 percent of the population, compared to 16 percent in Southeast Asia and 13 percent in developed countries. At the other end of the scale, the poorest 30 percent of Latin Americans and Caribbeans receive only 7.5 percent of total income, compared to more than 10 percent in the rest of the world. Although income distribution became more equal from 1960 to 1982, conditions became more unequal during the late 1980s and have not recovered significantly since. These high levels of inequality are associated with high levels of poverty, with more than 132 million Latin Americans and Caribbeans earning less than a subsistence income of $2 U.S. per day and more than 20 percent of the population earning less than $1 per day in countries such as El Salvador, Venezuela, and Honduras.

Employment, Education, Health, and Literacy The vast gap between the richest 10 percent and the poorest 30 percent is reflected in other social measures. For example, the richest heads of households average 11.3 years of education and the poorest 4.3 years, with even larger gaps (of 9 years) in Mexico and Brazil. Those in the richest 10 percent tend to work in professional and technical occupations or to own their own businesses, whereas the majority of the poorest 10 percent work in the informal sector. The informal sector, or **informal economy**, includes economic activities that take place beyond official record and are not subject to formalized systems of regulation or remuneration. In Latin America this comprises a variety of income-generating activities of the self-employed that do not appear in standard economic accounts, including street selling, shoe shining, garbage picking, street entertainment, prostitution, crime, begging, and guarding or cleaning cars.

Social and health conditions are often considered a better measure of overall inequality within and between countries than are economic measures. National improvements in life expectancy, infant mortality, and literacy, for example, tend to reflect improvements at the lower end of the scale rather than for the better-off segments of the population. Latin America tends to compare more favorably to the rest of the world on social and health indicators than on measures of income and income inequality. For example, life expectancy averages 70 years, higher than any other region in the developing world and compared to a world average of 67 years. Literacy rates are also relatively high, averaging 89 percent, compared to 62 percent in Africa, 56 percent in South Asia, and 79 percent worldwide. According to the United Nations International Children's Fund (UNICEF), only 8 percent of children under age 5 are defined as underweight in Latin America, compared to 27 percent worldwide.

However, there are wide gaps in social and health conditions within Latin America. Haiti, Central America, and the Andes tend to have much worse conditions than do Argentina, Chile, Uruguay, northern South America, Costa Rica, Mexico, and the English-speaking Caribbean. For example, in 2003, the average Haitian lived only 52 years, and the literacy rate was only 52 percent, compared to a life expectancy of 78 years in Costa Rica with literacy reaching 96 percent.

These national indicators also hide large variations in economic and social conditions within Latin American and Caribbean countries. In Mexico, the southern regions of the country have lower incomes and life expectancies than do the northern and central areas of the country. In Brazil, the northeastern and Amazon zones have higher infant mortality, lower life expectancy, and lower average monthly incomes than the southern parts of the country. Each Latin American and Caribbean country has its own geography of inequality, with the more rural regions generally having lower social and economic conditions.

Subregions in Latin America face distinctive development challenges. Since urban development was already discussed earlier in this chapter, this section will focus on rural regions, in particular those of the Andes and Central America.

The Andes High elevations, indigenous cultures, distinctive agriculture, mining economy, and relative poverty characterize the Andean region. Andean residents include large populations of indigenous Aymara and Quechua speakers who have maintained traditional rituals, clothing, and crafts (**Figure 7.35a**). Most agricultural production is for subsistence or local markets except for coca, a traditional crop with leaves that are chewed to alleviate the effects of high altitude. Coca is grown on the eastern slopes, where it is turned into cocaine. Crop yields are low because of poor soils and cold, dry climates, but some groups still use the intensive raised-field and terrace systems of the Incas to reduce agricultural risks of frost, drought, and soil erosion.

Despite some efforts at land reform, the colonial legacy lingers in poverty, landlessness, and discrimination against many Andean Indians. Resentment has fueled rural revolt, illegal coca production, and some support for guerilla movements, such as the Shining Path (*Sendero Luminoso*) in Peru. Many young people now choose to migrate to the coastal cities, the tropical lowlands, or to countries such as Argentina to seek work and opportunities still not available in more remote Andean communities. Tourism has become an increasingly significant source of income near Inca sites and indigenous communities (**Figure 7.35b**).

The mining industry is important in many parts of the Andes and includes copper in Chile and Peru, tin in Bolivia, emeralds in Colombia, and silver and gold in several countries. Despite some unionization and attempts to improve technology and working conditions, many miners still face very difficult circumstances, and they endure high levels of respiratory diseases and accidents. The benefits of mining have also tended to concentrate in multinational corporations or in a few families that control the major companies. Prices have been very volatile, recently falling to low levels on world markets.

Development efforts in the Andean region have included large-scale government projects of road building, agricultural development in the Amazon lowlands, and tourism. But the collapse of many national economies during the 1980s and the subsequent restructuring to reduce government spending mean that in many areas, the only external assistance now comes from

(a)

(b)

(c)

FIGURE 7.35 The Andes (a) The Andean region has a high proportion of indigenous people living in traditional ways. The Uros people live on Lake Titicaca (at the border of Bolivia and Peru) on floating islands made from reeds and fish on the deep lake from canoelike boats. (b) Lake Titicaca is now a key stop on the international tourist route that includes a visit to the dramatic ruins of Machu Picchu. Tourists are attracted by the dazzling landscape, Inca ruins, and the indigenous cultures with their colorful woven clothing, pipe music, and fiestas. (c) Anti-globalization sentiments in Bolivia contributed to the election of indigenous leader Evo Morales as president.

NGOs. However, the mobilization of peasants against neoliberalism—especially water privatization and energy exports in countries such as Bolivia—has led to demands for equity and recognition of indigenous rights and in the election of Evo Morales, Latin America's first indigenous modern president (**Figure 7.35c**).

Central America   The landscapes of Central America include dense forests and vast export-crop plantations. They bear the social and ecological scars of recent civil wars and natural disasters in many parts of the region. Central America provides a rich biological corridor between North and South America and hosts large indigenous populations, including 3 million Mayas in Guatemala, 150,000 Miskito in Nicaragua, and the Kuna of Panama.

Costa Rica is generally an exception to highly unequal distribution of land and wealth in Central America and is noted for a long tradition of democracy since 1889, the lack of a standing army, and a higher standard of living than many other Latin American countries. In other Central American countries, repressive military regimes or dictatorships provoked unrest in the countryside that erupted into revolution in Nicaragua in 1979 and into guerilla movements in El Salvador in the 1980s. In El Salvador, the attempts of powerful oligarchies to retain power were associated with massacres and murders. After the Sandinistas took power and initiated socialist reforms in Nicaragua, the United States funded covert efforts to overthrow the government, including training counterrevolutionary forces, or *contras*, who crossed into Nicaragua from neighboring Honduras. Several decades of unrest in these countries slowed the development of agriculture and the economy, and it was not until political reforms and peace accords in the 1990s that funds and political will were generally available for economic and social development.

The difficulties faced by the indigenous populations of countries such as Guatemala are characteristic of the discrimination that persists against indigenous cultures in Latin America. Discrimination stems from the colonial period. It has been reinforced by a series of elites, who used an image of indigenous peoples as uncivilized, underdeveloped, and rebellious to take their lands, undermine their religion and language, and force them into low-paid occupations as farm workers, miners, or servants. In Guatemala, authoritarian governments forced Mayan populations to flee into neighboring Mexico or farther north or retreat into remote mountains. There the military, which did not differentiate between ordinary people and guerillas, often annihilated whole communities. New indigenous social movements have organized to promote language, culture, and land rights. Low wages in Central America have attracted labor-intensive manufacturing, such as garment industries, to urban areas in El Salvador and Honduras. Costa Rica, with a better-educated workforce and more stable economy, has lured high-technology companies such as Microsoft, General Electric, and Intel to build factories near San Jose. Central American governments are now seeking development through proposals for a Central American free trade agreement (CAFTA) and through infrastructure projects such as Plan Puebla Panama, which would link countries of the region through highways, hydroelectric developments, and tourist development.

SUMMARY AND CONCLUSIONS

The region of Latin America, with its diverse lands and peoples, has changed dramatically in recent years as the processes of market liberalization, economic integration, democratization, urbanization, and environmental degradation have transformed the region and changed its relationships with other world regions. Each of these processes has interacted with local conditions to produce a new mosaic of distinct regional geographies throughout the region and has produced new opportunities and challenges for people and policymakers. As this region entered the third millennium, the people there expressed considerable optimism and energy in their search for better lives and participation in political decision making. The challenge of sustainable development for Latin America faces the continuing legacy of inequality and vulnerability, the resource demands and pollution emissions of new industrial development and farming technologies, and the pressures of new consumption habits and growing populations.

KEY TERMS

altiplano (p. 328)
altitudinal zonation (p. 332)
banana republics (p. 352)
biodiversity (p. 337)
bioprospecting (p. 342)
braceros (p. 361)
circle of poison (p. 368)
Columbian Exchange (p. 344)
contract farming (p. 368)
demographic collapse
   (p. 344)

dependency school of
   development theory (p. 352)
ecotourism (p. 341)
El Niño (p. 334)
encomienda (p. 345)
favelas (p. 360)
free trade zone (p. 350)
Green Revolution (p. 367)
haciendas (p. 344)
informal economy (p. 370)
La Niña (p. 334)

land reform (p. 366)
liberation theology (p. 365)
mestizo (p. 355)
Monroe Doctrine (p. 348)
neotropics (p. 337)
nontraditional agricultural
   exports (NTAEs) (p. 368)
North American Free Trade
   Agreement (NAFTA) (p. 324)
offshore financial services
   (p. 351)

pristine myth (p. 337)
remittances (p. 362)
social capital (p. 351)
social movements (p. 366)
structural adjustment policies
   (p. 353)
Treaty of Tordesillas (p. 342)
viceroyalty (p. 343)

REVIEW QUESTIONS

Testing Your Understanding

1. How do deforestation, urban development, and poverty make regions vulnerable to natural disasters? What are the risks and benefits of living in volcanically active zones in Latin America?

2. Where were the Maya, Inca, and Aztec empires located and when did they flourish? How did they adapt to the physical environment and, in some cases, create environmental problems?

3. What was the Columbian Exchange? Please discuss with regard to (a) diseases, pests, and the demographic collapse; (b) the geography of crops and domesticated animals.

4. How did the Spanish organize the political administration of their colonies in Latin America, and how did this system influence the eventual boundaries of countries in the region? What were the two main forms of agricultural landholding and how did they differ? What role did *encomienda* and slavery play in the colonial economy? What were the most important exports from the colonies to Spain?

5. Compare the major goals and criticisms of import substitution and structural adjustment policies in Latin America in the 20th century. Identify the main partners in and goals of NAFTA, CARICOM, and MERCOSUR, and explain why some people are critical of these agreements, especially NAFTA.

6. Review the origins of the migrations into Latin America and how they affect the racial or ethnic composition of at least three countries. When people migrate from Latin America today, where do they go? What elements of Latin American culture have accompanied these migrants to other regions of the world? What are remittances and why are they important to local economies?

7. In what ways have the Green Revolution, land reform, and nontraditional export crops changed Latin American agriculture? Why do some Latin American farmers grow coca plants despite these agricultural innovations and new crops?

8. What is the role of the informal sector and informal settlements (*barrios, favelas*) in cities such as Mexico City and São Paulo? Which environmental problems do these cities face?

9. Explain how and where export crops, aquaculture, tourism, bioprospecting, offshore financial services, and U.S. involvement contribute to the economy of the Caribbean and Central America. Discuss the criticisms of some of these activities.

Thinking Geographically

1. Describe how the constraints and opportunities provided by the physical environment (for example, topography, climate, soils) help explain the geography of natural vegetation and agriculture in Latin America. What are some of the main ways in which humans have overcome the constraints of the environment to promote agriculture, and how and where has human activity altered the natural vegetation cover of the region?

2. During the colonial era, how did racial, ethnic, and class distinctions divide Latin American societies? Continued immigration during the 1800s and 1900s has made Latin America even more diverse. Which racial and indigenous issues do Latin American societies need to deal with today? Are they the same issues as in North America?

3. Identify the push and pull factors that motivate migration within Latin America. Why are these similar to or different from factors that stimulate migration into or out of Latin America? Describe the major patterns of migration within the region.

4. Why has the United States maintained such a strong interest in Panama and Cuba, and how has this interest affected the economic and political geographies of these countries?

5. Discuss how and where oil, road development, mining, dams, agricultural projects, and ranching have contributed to the deforestation of the Amazon basin. Why has forest loss in the Amazon attracted worldwide attention, and what role might satellite images, ecotourism, and extractive reserves play in reducing the rate of deforestation?

FURTHER READING

Bebbington, A., *Geographies of Development in Latin America*. New York: Routledge, 2005.

Caviedes, C., and Knapp, G., *South America*. Englewood Cliffs, NJ: Prentice Hall, 1995.

Clawson, D. L., *Latin America and the Caribbean: Lands and Peoples*, 3rd ed. New York: McGraw Hill, 2003.

Collier, S., Blakemore, H., and Skidmore, T. E. (eds.), *Cambridge Encyclopedia of Latin America and the Caribbean*. New York: Cambridge University Press, 1992.

Cravey, A. C., *Women and Work in Mexico's Maquiladoras*. Lanham, MD: Rowman and Littlefield, 1998.

Crosby, A., *The Columbian Exchange: Biological and Cultural Consequences of 1492*. Westport, CT: Greenwood Press, 1972.

Denevan, W. M., "The Pristine Myth: The Landscape of the Americas in 1492." *Annals of the Association of American Geographers*, 82(1992), 369–85.

Galloway, J., *The Sugar Cane Industry. An Historical Geography from Its Origins to 1914*. Cambridge, UK: Cambridge University Press, 1991.

Gilbert, A. G. (ed.), *The Megacity in Latin America*. New York: UNU Press, 1996.

Hecht, S. B., and Coburn, A., *The Fate of the Forest: Developers, Destroyers and Defenders of the Amazon*. London: Verso, 1989.

Herlihy, Peter H., "Indigenous Peoples and Biosphere Reserve Conservation in the Mosquitia Rain Forest Corridor, Honduras." In *Conservation Through Cultural Survival: Indigenous Peoples and Protected Areas* (pp. 99–130). Washington, DC: Island Press, 1997.

Klak, T. (ed.), *Globalization and Neoliberalism: The Caribbean Context*. Lanham, MD: Rowman and Littlefield, 1998.

Knapp, G. (ed.), *Latin America in the Twenty-First Century: Challenges and Solutions*. Austin, TX: University of Texas Press, 2002.

Latin American Network and Information Center (LANIC). Available at **http://www.lanic.utexas.edu**.

Mintz, S., and Price, S., *Caribbean Contours*. Baltimore, MD: Johns Hopkins University Press, 1985.

Momsen, J. J. (ed.), *Women and Change in the Caribbean: A Pan-Caribbean Perspective*. Bloomington, IN: Indiana University Press, 1993.

Pattullo, P., *Last Resorts: The Costs of Tourism in the Caribbean*. New York: Monthly Review Press, 2005.

Place, S. E., "Nature Tourism and Rural Development in Tortuguero." *Annals of Tourism Research* 18(1991), 186–201.

Preston, D. A., *Latin American Development: Geographical Perspectives*. Harlow, England: Longman, 1996.

Pulsipher, L. M., et al., *World Regional Geography*. New York: W. H. Freeman, 2002.

Richardson, B. C., *The Caribbean in the Wider World: 1492–1992*. Cambridge, UK: Cambridge University Press, 1992.

Roberts, J. T., and Thanos, N. D., *Trouble in Paradise: Globalization and Environmental Crises in Latin America*. New York: Routledge, 2003.

Santos, M., *A urbanização brasileira*, 3rd ed. São Paulo: Hucitec, 1996.

Sauer, C. O., *The Early Spanish Main*. Berkeley, CA: University of California Press, 1969.

Ward, P. M., *Mexico City*. New York: John Wiley and Sons, 1998.

West, R., and Augelli, J. P., *Middle America, Its Lands and Peoples*. Englewood Cliffs, NJ: Prentice Hall, 1989.

Wright, A. L., *The Death of Ramón González: The Modern Agricultural Dilemma*. Austin, TX: University of Texas Press, 1990.

FILM, MUSIC, AND POPULAR LITERATURE

Film

Americas. WGBH, 1993. In this series, the people of Latin America reflect on their lives, history, and society.

Amores Perros. Directed by Alejandro González Iñárritu, 2002. Three interconnected stories of life and violence in Mexico City.

Black Orpheus. Directed by Marcel Camus, 1958. This quintessential love story, based on the Greek myth of Orpheus and Eurydice, is set against the vivid backdrop of Carnival in Rio de Janeiro. Winner of the Grand Prize at Cannes as well as an Oscar for Best Foreign Film.

Buena Vista Social Club. Directed by Wim Wenders, 1996. This movie portrays Cuban musicians who revived their careers as a result of a best-selling album.

Central Station. Directed by Walter Salles, 1998. A letter writer in Rio de Janeiro sends a young boy to look for his father in northeast Brazil.

City of God. Directed by Kátia Lund and Fernando Meirelles, 2003. Life in a Rio *favela*.

Evita. Directed by Alan Parker, 1996. Musical account of the life of Evita Perón, wife of Argentinian president Juan Perón.

The Harder They Come. Directed by Perry Henzell, 1973. Reggae musicians in Jamaica.

Men with Guns. Directed by John Sayles, 1997. A doctor visits his former students working with indigenous people in a region of civil unrest.

Portrait of the Caribbean. Directed by Roger Mills, 1992. This six-hour series looks at the political, cultural, and social formation of the region.

Quilombo. Directed by Carlos Diegues, 1984. This historical saga of 17th-century Brazil documents the stories of groups of runaway black slaves who escaped to mountainous jungle strongholds, where they formed self-governing communities known as *Quilombos*.

Voices of Latin America. Directed by Andrian Malone, 1987. This video examines the cultural identity of Latin America through its writers and literature using dramatizations and interviews.

Music

Inti Illimani. *The Best of Inti Illimani*. Xenophile, 2000.

The Mexican Revolution. Folk Lyric, 1996.

Various Artists. *Beleza Tropical*. Emd/Luaka Bop, 1988.

Various Artists. *Forever Tango*. Bmg/RCA Victor, 1998.

Various Artists. *Tocando Tierra: A Tribute to Latin American Music*. Latin World Entertainment, 1999.

Various Artists. *Tougher Than Tough: The Story of Jamaican Music*. Uni/Mango, 1993.

Popular Literature

Allende, Isabel. *House of the Spirits*. New York: Bantam Books, 1986. The story of three generations of a family who experience political change in a country similar to Chile. Written by the niece of former socialist President Salvador Allende.

Alvarez, Julia. *In the Time of the Butterflies*. New York: Penguin USA, 1995. A tale of three sisters in the Dominican Republic during the rise of the Trujillo dictatorship.

da Cunha, Euclides. *Rebellion in the Backlands*. Chicago: University of Chicago Press, 1944. Classic account of a rebellion at the end of the 19th century in rural Brazil.

Fuentes, Carlos. *The Years with Laura Díaz*. New York: Farrar, Straus and Giroux, 2000. Follows one woman through the upheavals of 20th-century Mexico.

García Márquez, Gabriel. *One Hundred Years of Solitude*. New York: Harper Perennial Library, 1967. Magical realism novel from the Colombian Nobel Prize winner about the history of a family in the mythical town of Macondo.

Kinkaid, Jamaica. *A Small Place*. New York: Farrar, Straus and Giroux, 2000. Life on the Caribbean island of Antigua and the impacts of colonialism.

Llosa, Mario Vargas. *The War of the End of the World*. New York: Penguin USA, 1997. Revolutionary community in the 19th-century Brazilian backlands.

Menchu, Rigoberta. *I Rigoberta Menchu*. New York: Verso, 1987. Testimony from a Guatemalan Mayan woman about Mayan life and military repression.

Naipaul, V. S. *A House for Mr. Biswas*. New York: Vintage Books, 2001. A comic novel about the efforts of a Trinidad resident of Asian-Indian descent to own his own home.

Paz, Octavio. *Labyrinth of Solitude*. New York: Grove Press, 1985. Exploration and explanation of Mexico and Mexicans by a Nobel Prize winner.

Rulfo, Juan. *Pedro Paramo*. New York: Grove Press, 1994. A search for roots in rural Mexico.

Walcott, Derek. *Tiepolo's Hound*. New York: Farrar, Straus and Giroux, 2000. Nobel Laureate explores European domination of the West Indies.

East Asia

FIGURE 8.1

East Asia consists of China, Japan, Mongolia, North and South Korea, and Taiwan. This is the most populous of all world regions, containing 1.55 billion people. The region is dominated in both demographic and territorial terms by China, which occupies 9.6 million square kilometers (3.7 million square miles; about 6.5 percent of Earth's land surface) and has a population of 1.32 billion, about 22 percent of the world's population.

A glance at **Figure 8.1** shows that East Asia is naturally bounded by mountain ranges and oceans. To the northwest are the Elburz Mountains of northern Iran and the Tien Shan ("Mountains of Heaven") along the southern borders of the Central Asian countries. To the north are the Altay and Sayan Mountains, which separate Siberia from Mongolia, and the Yablonovyy and Khingan ranges, which separate southeastern Siberia from northern China. To the southwest are the Pamir Mountains and the Himalayas, while to the south and east are the coastal seas—the South China Sea, the East China Sea, and the Yellow Sea—of the Pacific Ocean.

East Asia is a region of tremendous contrasts in natural environments and history, while the human geography of the region has been subject to radical change during the modern era. China's vast and diverse domain has been restructured by a communist revolution whose objectives have been redirected several times. Japan, on the other hand, has been transformed by no fewer than two dramatic "economic miracles." East Asia is one of the most rapidly urbanizing of all world regions, yet traditional rural communities with a great variety of distinctive ways of life still characterize much of the region. Japan is already highly urbanized (almost 80 percent of the population lives in urban areas), but the pace and scale of urbanization in China is truly phenomenal. Overall, only 34 percent of China's population lives in urban areas, but 30 years ago the figure was only 17 percent, and 50 years ago it was 12 percent. China now has **96** cities with a population of 1 million or more, including 6 with a population in excess of 5 million.

ENVIRONMENT AND SOCIETY IN EAST ASIA

A great deal of East Asia consists of juxtaposed plateaus, basins, and plains separated by narrow, sharply demarcated mountain chains. These broad physiographic regions contain a great diversity of ecosystems, which in turn have evoked a variety of human responses and adaptations.

Landforms and Landscapes

The satellite photograph of East Asia in **Figure 8.2** suggests a broad, threefold physical division:

1. *The Tibetan Plateau, in the southwest, an uplifted* **massif** *(a mountainous block of Earth's crust) of about 2.5 million square kilometers (965,000 square miles).* Within the plateau are several mountain ranges—including the Himalaya Mountains—with peaks of 7000 meters (22,964 feet) or more. The Himalayas contain the world's highest peak, Mount Qomolangma (Mount Everest), at 8848 meters (29,027 feet). The Tibetan Plateau occupies about one-fourth of China's total land area. It is a unique physical environment, a vast area that has been violently uplifted in relatively recent geological time to produce the youngest, highest plateau in the world. The elevation of the entire plateau is at least 2500 meters (8202 feet), rising to between 4500 and 5000 meters (14,763 to 16,403 feet) in its northwestern part. It is surrounded by a series of lofty mountains that tower to heights of between 6000 and 8000 meters (19,684 to 26,245 feet): the Himalayas on the southwestern border, the Kunlun and Karakoram mountains on the northwestern border, the Hengduan Mountains on the southeastern border, and the Altun and Qilian mountains to the northeast. In addition, there are many imposing mountain ranges inside the plateau. The climate is harsh, with extreme variations in seasonal and daily temperatures. Glaciers cover a total of more than 47,000 square kilometers (18,147 square miles), much of the landscape is shaped by the

FIGURE 8.2 East Asia from space As this image shows, much of East Asia consists of vast areas of upland plateaus and mountain ranges.

raw features of glacial erosion and deposition, and permafrost is widespread. This "roof of the world" is also the source of many great rivers in East Asia and South Asia, including the Chang Jiang, the Huang He, the Mekong, the Indus, and the Yarlung Zangbo, which forms the upper reaches of the Brahmaputra.

2. *The central mountains and plateaus of China and Mongolia, a checkerboard of mountain ranges, plateaus, basins, and plains.* These include the Mongolian Plateau, the Ordos Plateau, the Loess Plateau, the Yunnan-Guizhou Plateau, and the Tarim, Sichuan, and Zunghaer basins. Most of these have elevations of 1000 to 2000 meters (3281 to 6562 feet) above sea level and are bordered by uplifted mountain ranges of about 3000 meters (9843 feet). This pattern is largely the consequence of the intersection of two sets of geological structures that underlie much of China: a series of roughly parallel upfolds that run south–southwest to north–northeast and a less-pronounced series of mountain ranges that run east–west (**Figure 8.3**).

3. *The continental margin of plains, hills, continental shelves, and islands.* The bulk of the population of East Asia live in this continental margin, which includes the great plains of China: the Northeast China (Manchurian) Plain, the North China Plain, and the plains of the Middle and Lower Chang Jiang (Yangtze River) valley. Most of these plains lie below 200 meters (656 feet) in elevation. South of the Chang Jiang is hill country with elevations of around 500 meters (1640 feet) and along the coast, including the Korean peninsula, are uplifted hills and mountains of 750–1250 meters (2460–4100 feet). The Japanese archipelago of Hokkaido, Honshu, Shikoku, and Kyushu forms the outer arc of East Asia's continental margin. Its backbone of unstable mountains and volcanic ranges that project from the shallow seafloor extends to the island of Taiwan and is part of the **Ring of Fire** that girdles the Pacific Ocean.

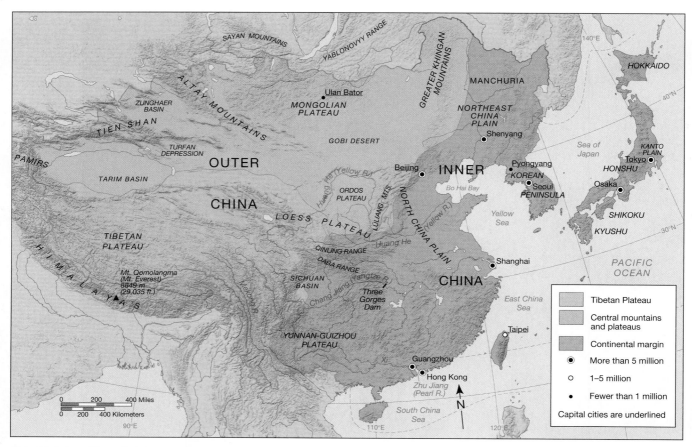

FIGURE 8.3 **East Asia's physiographic regions** East Asia can be divided into three broad physiographic units: the Tibetan Plateau and central mountains; plateaus corresponding to Outer China; and the continental margins approximating to Inner China, the Japanese archipelago, the Korean Peninsula, and Taiwan.

This broad division is the product of a long and complex geological history. The key to understanding the basic physiography of the region is the plate tectonics that have had a dramatic influence in recent geological times. The entire Tibetan Plateau was uplifted between 65 million years ago and 2 million years ago as the Indian-Australian plate moved northward and pushed up against the Eurasian plate, not only uplifting the Tibetan Plateau but also causing the mountain-building episode that resulted in the Himalayas. Subsequently, the weathering of the newly created mountains provided huge quantities of clay, silt, and other fluvial deposits that now blanket the plains. To the east, the movement of the Pacific plate toward the Eurasian plate caused the folding and faulting that have resulted in the mountains of the peninsulas and islands of the continental margin, including the Korean peninsula and the Japanese archipelago.

The geological uplift of the Tibetan Plateau also had consequences for geomorphic processes. It increased the gradient of the rivers that flowed off the borders of the plateau, enabling them to incise into the plateau and produce a great number of gorges and canyons of considerable length and depth. As geographer Yi-Fu Tuan has noted, the canyons at the southeastern edge of Tibet, clothed in dense vegetation, provided an effective barrier between the Chinese and South Asian civilizations. The rivers are still incising rapidly, and the Tibetan Plateau itself is still not stable: Seismic disturbances continually occur along the Himalayan foothills, often bringing disaster to settlements there.

The physical environments of East Asia are, in fact, relatively hazardous. In addition to regular earthquakes along the Himalayan foothills, much of the North China Plain is subject to seismic activity. Here, earthquakes along fault lines beneath the silty soils have the effect of loosening the soil, causing major landslides. In eastern Shaanxi, a destructive earthquake occurs, on average, every 15 to 20 years. The most ruinous of these took place in December 1921, when more than a quarter of a million people perished. Fifty-five years later, almost as many (242,000) were killed when a strong earthquake devastated the city of Tangshan in Hebei Province. (In Imperial China, natural disasters were thought to presage the death of an emperor who had lost the Mandate of Heaven; Mao Zedong, the communist leader of the People's Republic of China, died in September 1976, just two months after the Tangshan disaster.)

Much of Japan, too, is subject to earthquake hazards. The Japanese archipelago is situated within one of Earth's most geologically active zones, at the junction of three tectonic plates: the Eurasian, Philippine, and Pacific plates. In addition to volcanic activity—at least 60 volcanoes have been active within historic times in Japan—there is almost perpetual earthquake activity. Most of the 1000 or so earthquake events that occur in Japan each year are minor, but a few are serious enough to cause damage to property, and occasionally they can be devastating. In 1730 an earthquake in Hokkaido caused 137,000 deaths; in 1923 the Great Kanto earthquake resulted in 104,619 dead or missing. The most recent disaster was in Kobe in 1995, when a severe earthquake killed 6452.

Climate

The geological uplift of the Tibetan Plateau between 65 million and 2 million years ago is also key to understanding certain aspects of the climate of East Asia. The elevation of the Tibetan Plateau cut off the moisture that was formerly brought in to the interior of East Asia from the Indian Ocean by monsoonal winds. This contributed to the gradual dessication of the Tibetan Plateau, the numerous lakes of which are now much reduced in size. Protected by mountain barriers and sheer distance from the coast, much of western and northwestern East Asia today averages less than 125 millimeters (5 inches) of rain a year. On the Tibetan Plateau, high elevations make for cool summers and extremely cold winters. Further north, in Xinjiang, Qinghai, Gansu, and Mongolia, summer temperatures may be extremely hot. The Turfan Depression, some 154 meters (505 feet) below sea level, is one of the hottest places in East Asia, with recorded temperatures in excess of 45°C (113°F).

To the east of this vast arid region are two distinctive climatic regimes. The northern regime is subhumid (slightly or moderately humid, with relatively low rainfall). It is bounded to the west by the Lüliang Mountains and the Greater Khingan Mountains and extends southward as far as a latitude of about 35° N, encompassing the Northeast China Plain, the North China Plain, and the northern parts of the Korean peninsula, and the Japanese archipelago. Winters here are cold and very dry. Summers are warm, with moderate amounts of rain from the southeasterly summer monsoon winds. Rainfall, however, is very variable, so that both drought and flooding occur frequently. The southern regime is humid and subtropical. It extends west from the plains of the Middle and Lower Chang Jiang valley as far as the Sichuan basin and south as far as the southernmost coastlands of South China. Winters here are mild and rainy, and summers are hot with heavy monsoonal rains. Overall, annual rainfall is 1200 millimeters (47 inches) or more higher than it is in the north.

In the arid and subhumid regions of East Asia, drought is a critical natural hazard, causing widespread famine as a result of crop failures in drought years. In addition, the subhumid parts of East Asia tend to be prone to flooding. To some extent, this pattern is a result of the irregular summer monsoon rains, which can produce a sudden deluge. In addition, the rivers that flow through the plains carry a tremendous amount of silt, which is then deposited in their more sluggish lower reaches, building up the height of the riverbed and making their course unstable. The Huang He (Yellow River) is the largest and most notorious of these rivers, having changed its course several times in the last two centuries. In between these events, the Huang He regularly bursts its banks, flooding the farms and villages of the densely populated North China Plain.

Environmental History

Many of the landscapes of East Asia have been heavily modified by humankind. The principal human impact has been through clearing land for farming. Over the millennia, as the population grew and premodern civilizations flourished, much of humid and subhumid East Asia was cleared of its forest cover. At the same time, these landscapes were also modified by the Oriental passion for water control. Over the centuries, marshes were drained, irrigation systems constructed, lakes converted to reservoirs, and levees raised to guard against river floods. Even the topography was altered to suit the needs of growing and highly organized populations, with hills and mountainsides being sculpted into elaborate terraces to provide more cultivable land. Meanwhile, several of the world's most important food crops and livestock species were domesticated by the peoples of East Asia, beginning around 6500 B.C. Millet, soybeans, peaches, and apricots were domesticated in the more northerly subhumid regions, while rice, mandarin oranges, kumquats, water chestnuts, and tea were domesticated in the more humid regions to the south. Mulberry bushes were domesticated as silkworm fodder and hemp was domesticated as a source of fiber and oil. Chickens and pigs were among the livestock species domesticated.

Only in the arid western parts of East Asia and the inhospitable Tibetan Plateau—a broad region often referred to as "Outer China" (**Figure 8.4**)—do contemporary regional landscapes reflect large-scale natural environments that are relatively unmodified by human intervention. Outer China is an outback region that contains barely 4 percent of the population of East Asia. Large areas are effectively uninhabited, and in the greater part of it, population density does not exceed one person per square

FIGURE 8.4 Regional landscapes The landscapes of Outer China are relatively unmodified by human intervention. In contrast, the natural landscapes of Inner China and the continental margin have been greatly altered by human occupancy. (*Source:* Adapted from S. Zhao, *Geography of China.* New York: John Wiley & Sons, 1994, p. 31; and Y-F. Tuan, *China.* London: Longman, 1970, p. 25.)

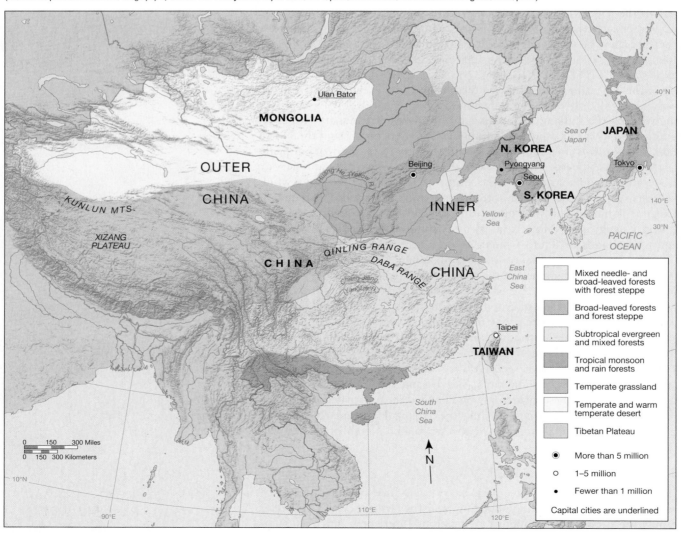

FIGURE 8.5 The Tibetan Plateau The highest and largest plateau in the world, the Tibetan Plateau occupies about 25 percent of China's land area but contains less than 1 percent of its population.

kilometer. The scenery is often spectacular, encompassing snow-clad mountains, vast swamps, endless steppes, and fierce deserts.

In broad terms, Outer China can be divided into three types of landscapes (see Figure 8.4). The Tibetan Plateau (**Figure 8.5**) is dominated by rugged mountains with intermontane basins of needle-leaf forests, alpine meadows, and marshes. Not surprisingly, the rugged terrain of the Tibetan Plateau is quite sparsely inhabited. Nomadic pastoralism remains the chief occupation within the region; the principal source of livelihood is the yak, along with sheep and goats. Yaks supply milk and wool as well as meat. Yak wool is the fabric used for the darkish, rectangular tent that is a distinctive component of the Tibetan landscape. In recent decades, Chinese reforms have brought an expansion of farming to the more sheltered valleys of the region, with wheat, highland barley, peanuts, and rapeseed as the principal crops. The mixed forests of Gaoshan pine, Manchurian oak, and Himalayan hemlock are increasingly being brought into timber production, accelerating a long history of deforestation in the region and extending the imprint of humankind on this wild region. At the eastern edge of the plateau, overgrazing, combined with a decade of hotter, drier weather, has destroyed the thin topsoil, with the result that legendary horse country is now gradually turning into desert. Perhaps the most distinctive aspects of the human landscape, though, are the shrines and temples of Tibetan Buddhism. Together with the spectacular scenery of the region, the picturesque, romantic, and mystical qualities of Tibet underpin a tourist industry that the Chinese authorities have allowed to develop, in controlled fashion, since the mid-1980s.

Northwestern China (**Figure 8.6**) and much of Mongolia is a territory of temperate desert—dunes, scrub-covered hillslopes, and basins with plant communities that are

FIGURE 8.6 Northwest China Surrounded by mountain ranges, the vast plains and deserts of northwest China stretch for thousands of kilometers.

tolerant of high levels of mineral salts in the soil—although dense forests of tall spruce clothe the cool, wet flanks of the Tien Shan and Altay mountains. Inner Mongolia is mostly a mixture of steppe and semidesert. As in the steppe lands of Central Asia (to the west of the Altay Mountains), a gradation of landscapes ranges from the wooded steppe through the steppe proper and desert steppe. Wooded steppe, where rolling grasslands are interspersed with stands of mixed woodland, accounts for 23 percent of Mongolia, mostly in valley bottoms and in the scenic basin complex of northern Mongolia known as the Great Lakes region. The wooded steppe quickly shades into the steppe proper, which accounts for a further 27 percent of the territory in Mongolia. The landscape is flat, treeless, and dominated by tall, hardy grasses. Here and there, small, stubby massifs mark the cones of extinct volcanoes. South of the steppe are equally extensive zones of desert steppe characterized by immense sweeps of boulder-strewn wastes and salt-pans, with patches of rough vegetation used by nomadic pastoralists.

Most of the remaining 22 percent of Mongolia is taken up by the Gobi Desert, where bare rock and extensive sand dunes predominate. Several spectacular natural features are found in the Gobi, including huge basalt columns arranged in clusters resembling groups of pencils. These natural landscapes were impacted significantly from the 1950s to the 1980s by an extensive virgin lands program similar to that in the Soviet Union (see Chapter 3), whereby hundreds of thousands of acres of virgin land were plowed and large-scale irrigation systems were installed to allow for farming—especially wheat, root vegetables, and fodder crops. Meanwhile, Mongolia's extensive mineral resources (including oil, coal, copper, lead, and uranium) began to be exploited, and an industrial sector emerged, stimulating urban growth.

The remainder of East Asia—"Inner China" plus the Korean peninsula, the Japanese archipelago, and Taiwan—can be divided broadly into the landscapes of the subhumid regions to the north of the Qinling and Daba mountain ranges and those of the humid and subtropical regions to the south (see Figure 8.4). The natural landscapes of the northern part of Inner China, along with the northern part of the Korean peninsula and the northern half of the Japanese archipelago, are dominated by mixed temperate broad-leaf and needle-leaf forests on the hills and mountains, with a forest-steppe mixture on the Loess Plateau. Higher elevations, and more northerly latitudes, are dominated by spruce, fir, and birch trees; lower elevations and more southerly latitudes are dominated by maple, basswood, and oak. The North China Plain has been modified by thousands of years of human occupancy. The capitals of the Shang and Qin dynasties were established here, and the Mongol Yuan dynasty established the imperial capital in Dadu, which was later renamed, under the Ming dynasty, as Beijing ("Northern Capital"). The North China Plain is a region of monotonous flatness. The original vegetation was probably a deciduous broad-leaf forest dominated by oaks. Today, the only significant wooded areas are along streams and riverbanks, where willows, poplars, and elms grow, much as they have for centuries. The flat, rolling landscape is a mosaic of rectangular fields (**Figure 8.7**) Geographer Yi-Fu Tuan notes that in summer "a bird's-eye view emphasizes the intricacy and the extreme fragmentation of the landscape for the crops are then in varying stages of growth, each farmer having planted at a slightly different time, and the fields are a glorious palette of yellows, browns, and different shades of green."[1] In contrast, the winter landscape of the North China Plain is brown and parched, and on windy days the air is thick with the dust that blows easily from the silty soils. The rivers that flow through the region—especially the Huang He and the Huai He—are the agents that have nourished the plains, a region of relatively low rainfall; they are also the agents of disaster, bringing occasional floods of devastating impact. The Huang He is the most important river. Before entering the North China Plain, it flows through the easily eroded Loess Plateau, carrying a silt load of about 1.6 billion tons annually. It then suddenly drops onto the North China Plain and starts building a gigantic delta of about 250,000 square kilometers (96,525 square miles). The rapid buildup of silt on the riverbed makes its course unstable, with the result that it regularly bursts its banks.

---

[1] Y-F. Tuan, *China*, London: Longman, 1970, p. 151.

FIGURE 8.7 Inner China's northern farming landscape   The Northeast China Plain, the initial core region of Chinese civilization, has the largest concentration of cultivated land in China. Winter wheat, corn, sorghum, millet, and cotton are the chief crops.

To the south of the Qinling and Daba ranges, including Taiwan, the southern part of the Korean peninsula, and the southern half of the Japanese archipelago, contemporary landscapes are dominated by low hills that are covered with a secondary growth of evergreen monsoon forest, leaving less than 10 percent of the land for agriculture. Nevertheless, the cultivable land is very productive, and the climate allows for double-cropping of paddy rice and for cash crops such as sugarcane, mulberry trees, and hemp. Water and waterways are of vital importance in this region (see Signature Region: Central China, p.386).

Parts of the southernmost regions of Inner China, such as the Guangxi Basin, have retained much of their traditional flavor as agricultural regions. Inland, the hills are higher and the forests are sparse, but the valleys are productive (**Figure 8.8**) The topography of the region, together with its relatively isolated location toward the southern margin of China and the absence of coal, oil, or mineral deposits, has left traditional ways of life relatively undisturbed. Around Guilin and in the Zuo River area to the

FIGURE 8.8 Inner China's southern interior   Lijiang, on the Chang Jiang, Yunnan province.

Central China

Central China—the middle and lower reaches of the Chang Jiang (**Figure 1**)—is a hearth area of Han China and of Chinese agricultural civilization. By the late 17th century, the middle reaches of the Chang Jiang had become the largest center of commercial food (mainly rice) production in China, while the Chang Jiang Delta flourished as a center of handicraft industries. Today, Central China accounts for almost a quarter of all cultivated land in China. It is one of the most densely populated regions of East Asia and contains China's largest city, Shanghai (population 13.1 million in 2005), and several other key metropolitan centers, including Wuhan (5.93 million), Nanjing (2.84 million), Hangzhou (1.96 million), Nanchang (1.99 million), Hefei (1.33 million), and Suzhou (1.36 million).

Central China has developed around waterways. A series of lake basins stretch from the Three Gorges in the middle reaches of the Chang Jiang (see Figure 8.3) eastward to the sea for a length of more than 1800 kilometers (1119 miles) and a total area of about 160,000 square kilometers (61,776 square miles, roughly the size of Michigan). The Chang Jiang has long been the west–east "Golden Waterway," while its tributaries, together with the Grand Canal, have provided north–south routeways. The Chang Jiang is prone to flooding, however. The flood of 1887 was probably the most disastrous ever recorded in the world; an estimated 7 million people lost their lives. In 1931 another disastrous flood claimed approximately 200,000 lives. More recently, floods in 1998 led to the loss of more than 3000 lives, the evacuation of 14 million people, and damage amounting to $24 billion. Throughout the region, levees must be continuously repaired and improved to guard against river floods.

Water dominates the landscapes of Central China. The large lakes that border the Chang Jiang occupy more than 18,000

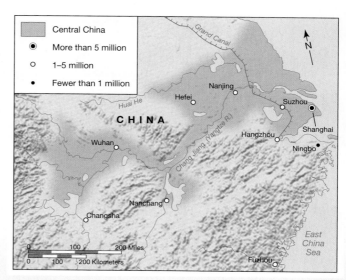

FIGURE 1 **Map of Central China** Reference map showing principal physical features and major cities.

square kilometers (6950 square miles), while all along the river itself are smaller lakes and ponds, together with tens of thousands of kilometers of canals, irrigation ditches, and thousands of linear ponds (**Figure 2**). The countryside is characterized by the rectilinear patterns of the drainage channels and the canals that link the smaller settlements of the region (**Figure 3**). This "land of rice and fish" is extremely productive; in many locales the humid subtropical climate allows for a triple-cropping system (two crops of rice,

south, near Nanning, erosion has dissolved areas of soft limestone, leaving spectacular pinnacles several hundred feet tall. These improbably shaped hills contrast with intermediate areas of intensely cultivated flatlands and winding rivers, making for some strikingly beautiful landscapes (**Figure 8.9**). The region is heavily populated and produces large crops of rice and cash crops of sugarcane and hemp. In the Zhu Jiang (Pearl River) Delta, extensive areas are devoted to an especially productive farming system involving fishponds along with rice paddies and fields of cash crops and vegetables.

EAST ASIA IN THE WORLD-SYSTEM

East Asia has been the setting for some of the world's most sophisticated civilizations and most extensive empires. Imperial China and Imperial Japan were both very inward-looking, but both eventually came into conflict with European and American imperialism. Both empires subsequently experienced revolutionary changes—though of a very different nature—before the modern states of China and Japan emerged to play key roles in the contemporary world economy.

Ancient Empires

China's Dynasties
China has had a continuous agricultural civilization for more than 8000 years. The first organized territorial state was that of the Xia dynasty, a Bronze Age state that occupied the eastern side of the Loess Plateau (in present-day

FIGURE 2 Central China Rice fields with fishponds in the Chang Jiang Delta region.

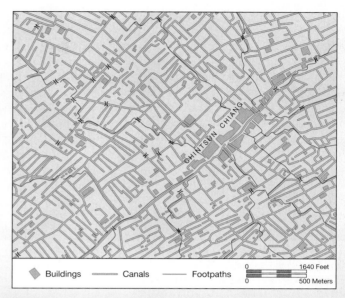

| Buildings | Canals | Footpaths | 0 — 1640 Feet / 0 — 500 Meters |

FIGURE 3 Central China: Rural settlement pattern
Settlements in the watery landscapes of Central China are dispersed along the rectilinear patterns of drainage channels and canals. Shown here is the settlement pattern of the Fengshien district of the Chang Jiang Delta. (*Source:* Redrawn from Y-F. Tuan, *China*. London: Longman, 1970, Fig. 24.)

plus one of winter wheat or barley). Since 1949, Central China has been developed as a core industrial region as well as a key food-producing region. The middle Chang Jiang plains contain one of the most important oil fields in China, and the region's energy resources will be significantly increased by hydroelectric power from the Three Gorges Dam, due for completion in 2009 (see p. 418). The industrial belt of the middle Chang Jiang includes two concentrations of heavy industry: steel, engineering, and shipbuilding in Wuhan and automobiles in western Hubei. It is the Delta region of the Chang Jiang that is the most important economic hub, however, with Shanghai standing at the center of an extensive industrial complex dominated by engineering, textiles, chemicals, and electronics.

FIGURE 8.9 The Guangxi Basin In this region a unique combination of geomorphology and agricultural development has led to one of the world's most spectacular landscapes. From classic old landscape paintings to contemporary tourist posters, the dramatic karst landscape of the Guangxi Basin has come to embody a stereotypical traditional Chinese landscape.

FIGURE 8.10 The Great Wall The Qin dynasty (316–209 B.C.) began construction of the Great Wall. The Wall that visitors see today dates from the Ming period and was built at various times between the late 14th and mid-16th centuries.

Shanxi Province) and the western parts of the North China Plain (northwestern Henan Province) between 2206 and 1766 B.C. It was succeeded by the Shang dynasty (1766–1126 B.C.), during which walled cities appeared. The first unified Chinese empire, though, was that of the Qin dynasty. Emperor Shih Huang-ti (221–209 B.C.) established an imperial system that lasted for 2000 years. He abolished feudalism, replacing the feudal hierarchy with a centralized bureaucratic administration, and had the Great Wall (**Figure 8.10**) built to protect China from "barbarian" nomads. The stability brought about by the Qin dynasty was a precondition for the success of the Silk Road (**Figure 8.11**) as an economic and cultural link among the civilizations of China, Central Asia, India, Rome, and, later, Byzantium.

The history of the Chinese empire is complex, with constantly shifting territorial boundaries and successive dynasties that tended to move from vigorous beginnings, with power concentrated around a strong center, followed by a slow loss of control as regional centers gained more power, and a final collapse as a forceful new dynasty was established. Sometimes, the empire was fragmented or subdivided for extended periods, but over two millennia the overall trend was for a larger and more consolidated continental empire.

The first major dynasty to run through the cycle was the Han dynasty, from 206 B.C. to A.D. 220. Han emperors extended the Great Wall westward, allowing the Chinese to control more trade routes along the Silk Road. Another important economic development took place early in the seventh century, under the Sui dynasty, when the northern and southern regions of Inner China were linked by the first of a series of Grand Canals. Its purpose was to bring the plentiful rice of the south to the Sui capital in the northwest (present-day Xi'an) and to the armies stationed in the northeast.

Over the next several centuries, the canal system was enlarged and modified. By the 15th century, China's canal system was more than 1000 kilometers (621 miles) in length. The imperial grain transportation system along the canals employed up to 150,000 soldiers to man its fleet and required the compulsory labor of many more to dredge and maintain the channels. (Canals of comparable scale only began to be cut in Europe—most notably in France—in the 18th century.)

FIGURE 8.11 The Silk Road The political and economic stability created by the Qin dynasty was a precondition for success of the Silk Road, the overland system of trade routes that connected China with Mediterranean Europe. The map shows the trade routes of the Silk Road as they existed between 112 B.C. and A.D. 100. (*Source:* Adapted from I. Barnes and R. Hudson, *History Atlas of Asia.* New York: Macmillan, 1998, pp. 45 and 46–47.)

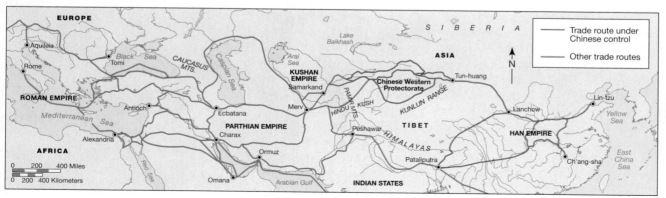

cultural productivity had helped finance an emergent industrial sector and in time to provide an expanding labor force and market for industrial products.

Several other factors helped foster rapid industrialization in Japan in the late 19th and early 20th centuries. First was the cultural order that allowed the Japanese to follow government leadership and accept new ways of life—a recurring theme in modern Japanese economic history. Second was the success of educational reforms: By 1905, 95 percent of all children of school age were receiving an elementary education. Third, Japanese sericulture (silk production) provided the basis for a lucrative export trade with which to help finance expenditure on overseas technology, materials, and expertise (see Geographies of Indulgence, Desire, and Addiction: Silk, p. 392). It has been estimated that between 1870 and 1930 the raw silk trade alone was able to finance as much as 40 percent of Japan's imports of raw materials and machinery. Finally, and most important, were the spoils of military aggression (**Figure 8.12**). Naval victories over China (1894–95) and Russia (1904–05) and the annexation of Taiwan (1895), Korea (1910), and Manchuria (1931) not only provided expanded markets for Japanese goods in Asia. They also provided indemnities from the losers (which paid for the costs of conquest) and stimulated the armaments industry, shipbuilding, industrial technology, and financial organization in general.

By the early 1900s, a broad base of industries had successfully been established from what had been a feudal economy in 1868—Japan's first "economic miracle." Most industries were geared toward the domestic market in a kind of preemptive import substitution strategy. The textile industry, however, had already begun to establish an export base. Unable to compete with Western nations in producing high-quality textiles, the Japanese concentrated on producing inexpensive goods, competing initially with Western producers for markets in Asia. Their success was based on labor-intensive processes in which high productivity and low wages were maintained through a combination of exhortations to personal sacrifice in the cause of national independence and strict government suppression of labor unrest.

Just as Japanese industry was becoming established, with a base in textiles and shipbuilding, World War I provided a timely opportunity to expand productive capacity. With much European and American industry diverted to supply war materials, Japanese textile manufacturers were able to expand into Asian and Latin American markets. Meanwhile, with a large portion of the world's merchant ships destroyed by the hostilities, Japanese shipping industries took the opportunity to expand their merchant fleets. The profits from this commercial activity paid for the rebirth of the Japanese navy, which by 1918 had 12 battleships and battle cruisers, with 16 more under construction. The United States at the time had only 14 battleships, with 3 under construction. *Within 50 years of the Meiji revolution, Japan had joined the core of the world-system.*

This pattern of progress was halted, however, by the stagnation of international trade that followed the stock market collapse of 1929 and the subsequent Great Depression. Once again, state intervention provided a critical boost. A massive devaluation of the yen in 1931 allowed Japanese producers to undersell on the world market, while a Bureau of Industrial Rationalization was set up to increase efficiency, lower costs, and weed out smaller, less-profitable businesses.

Although these interventions helped sustain Japanese industrialization and improve Japan's overall economic independence, they led directly to crisis. Western governments—particularly that of the United States—began seriously to resist the purchase of Japanese goods. At home, the austerity resulting from devaluation and "industrial rationalization" precipitated social and political unrest. The government response was to increase military expenditures and to adopt a more aggressive territorial policy.

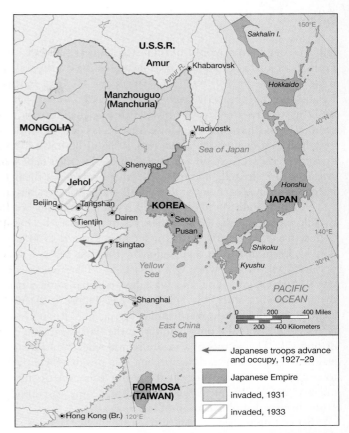

FIGURE 8.12 Japanese expansionism In the late 1920s and early 1930s, Japan deliberately pursued a policy of military aggression in order to secure a larger resource base for its growing military-industrial complex. (*Source:* Adapted from I. Barnes and R. Hudson, *History Atlas of Asia.* New York: Macmillan, 1998, p. 129.)

Silk

Silk has long been symbolic of opulence, luxury, and social status. From its origins in China, silk became one of the principal items of trade along the ancient trade routes between Asia and Europe. In Renaissance Europe, sericulture—the production of silk—and silk weaving were regarded as lucrative, leading-edge industries. Today, synthetic fibers have displaced lower-grade silks in most world markets, but good-quality silk fabrics remain highly desirable. Not only does their cost set them off as status symbols, but their light weight, sensuous feel, strength, and resistance to creasing make them a preferred indulgence of many of the world's more affluent consumers.

Silk is manufactured from the fibers of the cocoons produced by silkworms, which live on the leaves of mulberry bushes. Sericulture was first practiced in North China around 2700 B.C. and was well established in that region by the first century B.C. Silk was used as currency when Qin dynasty and Han dynasty envoys traveled in Central Asia and was the principal item carried by their merchants along the Silk Road (see Figure 8.11) through Central Asia and on toward India, Persia, and Rome. For centuries, China was the only country in the world capable of producing silk. The secrets of sericulture and silk manufacture were jealously guarded by early emperors: The penalty for attempting to export silkworm eggs or divulging the technique of silk weaving was death. Within China, silk fabrics came to embody the refinement and sophistication of the elite.

Sericulture reached Japan through Korea by the third century, thus facilitating the first development of silk production outside China. Shortly afterward, sericulture was established in India. According to legend, two monks smuggled silkworms from China to Europe in the sixth century A.D. Promoted by the Byzantine Emperor Justinian I (A.D. 527–65), sericulture spread to Syria, Turkey, and Greece. The more prosperous cities of the Mediterranean, pursuing an import substitution strategy, deliberately invested in silk manufacture, buying the raw silk from Greek and Arab merchants. By the end of the 14th century, silk production had been established in Bologna, Florence, Genoa, Lucca, and Venice. By the end of the 15th century, silk production played a vital economic role throughout the Italian peninsula, from the Alps to Sicily.

Chinese silk fabrics continued to be imported into Europe, however, because of their superior quality. Chinese governments under the Ming dynasty (1368–1681) vigorously promoted sericulture, and great quantities of Chinese silk were exported to Southeast Asia, Japan, and Spanish America as well as to Europe. By the 18th century, Britain led European silk manufacturing because of British innovations in silk-weaving looms, power looms, and roller printing. At the beginning of the 19th century, a Frenchman named Joseph Jacquard developed a machine for figured-silk weaving that gave French manufacturers an edge. Then, with the opening of the treaty ports in the 19th century, exports of silk from China more than doubled. This was partly because of a silkworm disease that devastated sericulture in France and Italy in 1847 and partly because of the expansion of the world economy.

Silk was also important in Japan's entry to the modern world economy. With the Meiji revolution in 1868, the Japanese government organized a domestic silk industry, deliberately developing it with modern technologies as a major export sector. This enabled Japan to earn a significant portion of the foreign exchange it needed to purchase the machinery and raw materials necessary for its industrialization. Between 1870 and 1930, Japan's raw silk trade financed about 40 percent of its imports of foreign machinery and raw materials.

Japan's success came at the expense of China. Silk continued to be China's major export until the 1930s, but the Chinese silk industry was undercapitalized and unresponsive to changing market conditions. Political instability, followed by Japanese invasions, further weakened the industry's effectiveness, and after 1949 it was relegated to a very low priority in Mao Zedong's communist regime.

China's silk industry bounced back with the overall liberalization of the economy under Deng Xiaoping's leadership in the late 1970s. Since that time, China has once again become the world's main producer of silk (**Figure 1**), while world silk production has almost doubled, despite the fact that synthetic fibers have displaced silk for many uses. Together, China and Japan are responsible for more than half the world's total annual production of silk fabrics.

FIGURE I Silk A woman waits for customers at a store on Silk Street, Beijing.

In 1931 the Japanese army advanced into Manchuria to create a puppet state. In 1936 a military faction gained full political power and, declaring a Greater East Asian Co-Prosperity Sphere, began a full-scale war with China the following year. Japan attacked British colonies in the Far East in 1939, and by 1940 the Japanese had become heavily committed to an industrial empire based on war. Also by this time, as the rest of the world quickly realized, Japan had attained the status of an advanced industrial nation. The military leadership overplayed its hand, however, by attacking the United States at Pearl Harbor in December 1941. With the defeat of Japan in 1945, Japanese industry lay in ruins. In 1946, output was only 30 percent of the prewar level, and the United States, having begun to dismantle the *zaibatsu* and to impose widespread social and political reforms, was preparing to impose punitive reparations.

Japan's Postwar Economic Miracle   Within five years, the Japanese economy had recovered to its prewar levels of output. Throughout the 1950s and 1960s the annual rate of growth of the economy held at around 10 percent, compared with growth rates of around 2 percent per year in North America and western Europe. Having begun the postwar period at the bottom of the ladder of international manufacturing, Japan found itself at the top by 1963. By 1980, Japan had outstripped the major industrial core countries in the production of automobiles and television sets, for example (**Figure 8.13**), and only the Soviet Union was producing more steel. The Japanese, in short, not only achieved a unique transition directly from feudalism to industrial capitalism, they presided over a postwar "economic miracle" of impressive dimensions.

Explanations of this second economic miracle have identified a variety of contributory factors. Once under way, reconstruction of the Japanese economy was able to draw on some of its previously established advantages: a well-educated, flexible, loyal, and relatively cheap labor force, a large national market with good internal communications, a good geographical situation for trade within Asia, a high degree of cooperation between industry and government, and a mode of industrial organization—derived from the *zaibatsu*—big enough to compete with the multinational corporations of western Europe and North America. In addition, several new factors helped transform reconstruction into spectacular growth. These included:

- Exceptionally high levels of personal savings (15 to 20 percent of personal disposable income through the 1960s and 1970s, compared with less than 5 percent in the United States), which helped fund high levels of capital investment.
- The acquisition of new technology: Between 1950 and 1969 Japan was able to acquire, for around $1.5 billion in royalties and licenses, a body of thoroughly tested U.S. technology that had cost the United States $20 billion *per year* in research and development (R&D).
- New means of government support: On one hand, a rigid and sophisticated system of import restrictions protected domestic markets from overseas competition. On the other hand, the growth of domestic industry was fostered by a multitude of tax concessions and by investment financing provided through the Japan Development Bank. Most important of all was the orchestration of industrial growth by the Ministry of International Trade and Industry (MITI). In particular, MITI identified key recovery sectors (for example, steel and shipbuilding) and potential growth sectors (for example, automobiles, electronics, and computers) and facilitated their development by providing financing, ensuring protection from foreign competition, subsidizing technological development, and arranging corporate mergers.

The economic miracle achieved by Japan was remarkable not only for its overall success in terms of economic performance but also because it represented a unique path to development, one that was able to combine economic growth with income distribution. Real wages (that is, the effective purchasing power of wages) rose substantially, while income inequality was reduced to one of the lowest levels in the world. Equally remarkable was the interdependence of government and industry, characterized by some as "Japan, Inc." Orchestrated by MITI, the state bureaucracy guided and coordinated Japanese corporations—organized in business networks (known as **keiretsu**)—setting up

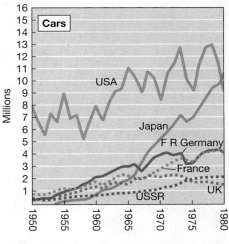

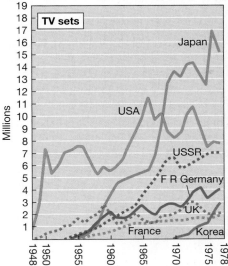

FIGURE 8.13 Japanese manufacturing growth   Between 1950 and 1980, Japanese manufacturing output grew at a phenomenal rate, outstripping other industrial countries by the early 1960s. (*Source*: P. Knox and J. Agnew, *Geography of the World Economy*, 3rd ed. London: Arnold, 1998, p. 175.)

FIGURE 8.14 **A Japanese family with their material possessions** The Ukita family from Tokyo, photographed with their possessions outside their home in the mid-1990s, represents a statistically average Japanese family in terms of family size, residence, and income.

favorable trade policies, technology policies, and fiscal policies to help Japanese industry compete successfully in the world economy. Also important was the exceptional degree of social stability and management-labor cooperation during this phase of tremendous change. This stability and cooperation was, like the interdependence of government and industry, a reflection of Japanese nationalism and people's commitment to rebuilding the nation. The same sense of national identity and purpose helped foster people's adherence to traditional values and lifestyles, their willingness to work many more hours than their European and American counterparts, and their willingness to defer consumption (**Figure 8.14**), thus providing a pool of savings that could be invested in Japanese industry.

Revolutionary China

Revolution came to China in 1911, when the Qing dynasty was overthrown and replaced by a republic under the leadership of Sun Yat-Sen's Nationalist Party (or Kuomintang). The overthrow of the imperial government in 1911 was the outcome of a long economic decline and a series of military defeats. A rising generation of intellectuals believed that the "dead hand" of imperial bureaucracy had retarded Chinese responses to the West. The intellectuals searched for new philosophies from abroad—including capitalism, communism, liberal democracy, and socialism—as possible solutions to China's many problems. But before any progress could be made, the country fell into disarray, with contending warlords struggling for power.

In the 1920s an alliance of China's fledgling Communist Party and the Nationalist Party, now led by Chiang Kai-shek, flourished for a while, but it ended abruptly in 1927 when Chiang Kai-shek, fearful of the growing power and ambitions of the Communist Party, attempted to quash its organization. The Communists organized a strategic retreat in what became known as the Long March (1934–35). They traveled more than 9600 kilometers (5965 miles) from the southeast, through the rugged interior, to the plains of Yanan in northern China. During the march, in which more than 100,000 people perished, Mao Zedong emerged as the leader of the party. Mao devised a new strategy, aimed at gaining support for revolution from China's rural peasantry—who made up 85 percent of China's population. This approach was in direct contradiction to the preferred strategy of Soviet advisors, who had insisted that the key to revolution, as in Russia, must be the urban proletariat.

Japanese military advances into China in 1937 temporarily caused the Communists and the Nationalists to set aside their differences and resist the Japanese, but with the defeat of the Japanese in World War II, the Communists and the Nationalists resumed their internal conflict. It was the Communist forces who had fought hardest and suffered most against the Japanese, and their experience proved crucial in fighting the Nationalists. Having won the support of the vast peasantry, Mao Zedong's troops surrounded China's cities until, one by one, they fell to Communist control. By October 1949 the Communist Party had control over almost all of China except for the island of Taiwan, where the Nationalist leadership had retreated under U.S. protection.

Meanwhile, the end of World War II brought about an important geopolitical change to Korea. Under the sponsorship of Soviet troops that had moved south from Manchuria into the northern part of Korea, Kim Il Sung, an anti-Japanese Marxist-Leninist nationalist, came to power in 1949. Almost immediately, U.S. troops occupied the southern part of the country. Like East and West Germany, Korea was suddenly divided into two. The 38th parallel was agreed upon as the border, and both Soviet and U.S. military forces withdrew.

In June 1950, just a few months after Mao Zedong's victory in China, Kim Il Sung's troops carried out a major attack on South Korea, seizing the capital, Seoul, and quickly extending control over almost the whole country. This led the United Nations to intervene, and U.S. forces rapidly rolled back the North Korean forces all the way to the Chinese border. This, in turn, prompted China to become involved on behalf of the North Koreans, and there followed a devastating war. Casualties were horrendous, with hundreds of thousands killed and much of the country destroyed. In 1953 the 38th parallel was finally restored as the border, but the two Koreas have remained bitter rivals, and China's relations with most Western countries, especially the United States, were so seriously damaged that they did not recover until the 1970s. North Korea, meanwhile, has remained locked in a time warp of self-imposed isolation.

The Great Leap Forward   Back in China, Mao Zedong faced the task of reshaping society after two millennia of imperial control. The first years were tentative, with land reform and the formation of agricultural collectives as the principal objectives. In 1958, in what became known as the Great Leap Forward, Mao launched a bold scheme to accelerate the pace of economic growth. Land was merged into huge communes and an ambitious Five-Year Plan was implemented. The fervor to industrialize led to the expectation that farmers would help industrialize the countryside by building their own "backyard furnaces" capable of producing steel.

The impact of the new Five-Year Plan on the landscape was dramatic. Whereas pre-Communist China had an average farm size of 1.4 hectares (3.5 acres), the new agricultural communes averaged 19,000 hectares (46,949 acres, or 73 square miles) in size, with between 30,000 and 70,000 workers. Instead of a patchwork of fields, each with a different crop and presenting a rich palette of browns, yellows, and shades of green, there now appeared vast unbroken vistas, planted with crops dictated by the central planners.

China's planners, however, were concerned only with increasing overall production. They paid little or no attention to whether a need for the products existed, whether the products actually helped advance modernization, or whether local production targets were suited to the geography of the country. The attempt to industrialize the countryside failed completely. Lacking iron ore, let alone any knowledge of how to make steel, peasants tore out metal radiators, pipes, and fences and sacrificed pots and pans in their zeal to produce steel in their backyard furnaces. Almost none of the final smelted product was usable. Meanwhile, several years of bad weather, combined with the rigid and misguided objectives of centralized agricultural planning, resulted in famine conditions throughout much of China.

It is estimated that between 20 and 30 million people died from starvation and malnutrition-related diseases between 1959 and 1962. When the central economic leadership ordered all peasants to eat in large, communal mess halls, what was optimistically called the Great Leap Forward fizzled out. For people who valued family above all else, being deprived of time alone with their families for meals was the final disillusionment.

Cultural Revolution   In an attempt to restore revolutionary spirit and to reeducate the privileged and increasingly corrupt Communist Party officials, Mao Zedong launched what he called a "Great Proletarian Cultural Revolution" in 1966. The Cultural Revolution brought a sustained attack on Chinese traditions and cultural practices and a relentless harassment of "revisionist" elites, the latter being defined broadly as anyone not belonging to the rural peasantry. Millions of people were displaced, tens of thousands lost their lives, and much of urban China was plunged into a terrifying climate of suspicion and recrimination. U.S. President Richard Nixon made a path-breaking visit to China in 1972 in an attempt to re-open China's relations with the Western world, but only with the death of Mao Zedong and the subsequent arrest of the politically extreme "Gang of Four" (which included Mao's wife) in 1976 did the Cultural Revolution come to an end. China's new leader, Deng Xiaoping, charted a more pragmatic course, gradually achieving stability and economic growth and opening China to Western science, technology, and trade.

In the aftermath of the Cultural Revolution, though, there remained little faith in Communist Party doctrine. Traditional values had been severely eroded. The result was that Western values of materialism, democracy, and individualism began to spread into the ideological vacuum along with a substantial revival of traditional Chinese culture. To combat the threat to established order, China's leadership therefore launched a series of mass campaigns—first a campaign against "spiritual pollution," then a repressive campaign against opponents of the ruling Communist Party (following the violent crackdown against protesters who challenged the legitimacy of the party in Beijing's Tiananmen Square in 1989), followed by a campaign against corruption, and then another to promote civil and respectful behavior. Despite all of this, China's leadership was able to keep the country on the path of economic liberalization, with the result that China's economy has been growing at double-digit rates for much of the past 20 years.

The Four Modernizations Under the leadership of Deng Xiaoping (1978–97), China embarked on a thorough reorientation of its economy, dismantling central planning in favor of private entrepreneurship and market mechanisms and integrating China into the world economy. Saying that he did not care whether the cat was black or white, as long as it caught mice, Deng Xiaoping elevated economic growth above the class struggle and established a program of "Four Modernizations" (industry, agriculture, science, and defense). He also established an "open-door policy," allowing trade with the rest of the world and integrating China with the interdependent circuits of the global economy. As a result, China completely reorganized and revitalized its economy. Agriculture was decollectivized, with Communist collective farms modified to allow a degree of private profit taking. State-owned industries were closed or privatized, and centralized state planning was dismantled in order to foster private entrepreneurship.

In the 1980s and early 1990s, when the world economy was sluggish, China's manufacturing sector grew by almost 15 percent each year. Almost all of the shoes once made in South Korea or Taiwan are now made in China. More than 60 percent of the toys in the world, accounting for $9 billion in trade, are made in China. Since 1992, China has extended its open-door policy, permitted foreign investment aimed at Chinese domestic markets, normalized trading relationships with the United States and the European Union, and joined the World Trade Organization.

China's national economic growth also resulted in some problems. Environmental degradation and pollution were inevitable consequences of the speed of industrialization. Meanwhile, the success of industrial modernization intensified the gap among different regions and between urban and rural areas. As a result, the most recent policy slogan has been to "Walk on Two Legs," that is, to facilitate the development not only of larger towns and cities but also of smaller towns and their surrounding rural areas.

East Asia in Today's World

Today, economic and cultural globalization is both cause and effect of the changing geography of East Asia. New technologies in freight movement, telecommunications, finance, and electronic media are changing long-established patterns of production, trade, and culture. Meanwhile, East Asia is rapidly becoming very important to patterns of global economic development. Japan's role as one of the established nodes of the triadic core of the world-system means that East Asia is well situated within the world economy. Japan itself is the world's second most powerful single economy and has developed extensive linkages not only within East Asia but also throughout the **Pacific Rim**, a loosely defined region of countries that border the Pacific Ocean.

In addition to Japan's established strength, East Asia has three of the so-called **Asian Tigers**, newly industrialized territories that have experienced rapid economic growth that has lifted them from the periphery of the world-system to the semiperiphery. These are Hong Kong, South Korea, and Taiwan (the fourth Asian Tiger is Singapore, in Southeast Asia; see Chapter 9). As we shall see, all of the Asian Tigers have developed specialized roles within the world economy and have become highly interdependent with places and regions throughout the Pacific Rim and in Europe.

China, while still a semiperipheral state in terms of per capita incomes, levels of industrialization, technological sophistication, and patterns of trade and investment, has the potential not only to dominate East Asia but also to play a key role in the world economy. Indeed, many observers predict a "Pacific Destiny" for the 21st century. In this scenario, China will be the hub of a world economy, the center of gravity of which is around the rim of the Pacific rather than the North Atlantic.

China certainly has the potential to join the core of the world-system. It has a vast territory with a comprehensive resource base and a long history of political, cultural, and economic integration. It has the largest population of any country in the world (1.32 billion in 2005) and an economy that has been growing very rapidly. China's increased participation in world trade has created an entirely new situation within the world economy, causing a deflationary trend in world prices for manufacturers (see Geography Matters: Made in China, p. 398). Not only does the Chinese economy's size make it a major producer, but its huge labor force guarantees that its wage levels will not approach Western levels for a long time. Overall, China's economy is already the third largest in the world after those of the United States and Japan.

Nevertheless, China's economy will remain largely agrarian for some time. The task of feeding, clothing, and housing its enormous population will also constrain its ability to modernize its economy to the point where it can compete for a dominant position within the world economy. Meanwhile, a great deal of social and political reform remains to be accomplished before free enterprise can truly flourish. In the short term, China mostly needs to develop its internal market and moderate its growth. In some respects, China has been following such a strategy, with a big program of infrastructure investment. Recently, China has also been trying to boost domestic demand by easing credit. It remains to be seen, however, whether the Chinese government can continue to control the situation. Managing things is not easy when capitalist energy is turning life upside-down and creating vast new wealth amidst a poor society based on different principles.

THE PEOPLES OF EAST ASIA

The most striking demographic characteristic of East Asia as a whole is the sheer size of its population. With a total population of some 1.55 billion in 2005 and almost 14 percent of Earth's land surface, East Asia contains about 22 percent of its population at an overall density of only 11 persons per square kilometer (28 per square mile). As **Figure 8.15** shows, the bulk of the population is distributed along coastal regions and in the more fertile valleys and plains of Inner China. Population densities in Outer China are very low, lower than 1 person per kilometer (between 2 and 3 per square mile) in most districts—the same as in the far north of Canada. In contrast, population densities throughout Inner China, and in Japan, North and South Korea, and Taiwan, are very high: between 200 and 500 per square kilometer (518 to 1295 per square mile) on average.

Crowding and Population Policy

Population Density High densities of population are in part a reflection of the very high levels of agricultural productivity in these regions, and in part a reflection of past population growth rates. High densities often mean overcrowding, especially in areas where farmland is valuable and where the topography restricts settlement. The most striking examples of crowding are from Japan, where mountainous regions preclude urban development in much of Honshu, the main island. The great majority of Japan's 127 million people live in crowded conditions in the towns and cities of the Pacific Corridor, where space is so tight and expensive that millions of adults live with their parents because they cannot afford places of their own. The average dwelling in metropolitan Tokyo is about 60 square meters (646 square feet). (By comparison, the

GEOGRAPHY MATTERS

Made in China

In 2001, China was admitted to the World Trade Organization, allowing China to trade more freely than ever before with the rest of the world. In 2005 the United States bought more than $243.5 billion worth of goods made in China. Wal-Mart was the single largest U.S. importer, according to a study by the Citizens Trade Campaign, procuring at bargain prices from China everything from t-shirts to car stereos. The Ford Foundation has estimated that within a few years China's new freedom to trade within the world economy will result in a 60 percent increase in China's exports of textiles and a 200 percent increase in exports of clothing.

The low cost of labor underpins the preponderance of "Made in China" apparel labels in U.S. stores. Whereas skilled clothing workers in Toronto's garment district, for example, are paid $350 to $400 a week, plus benefits, for a 33-hour week, their counterparts in Hong Kong are paid $250 for a 60-hour week, with no benefits; and in China skilled garment workers can be hired for $30 for a 60-hour week (**Figure 1**). Studies of the industry have shown that some of the female workers in Chinese garment factories are as young as 12 years old, girls from rural villages who have been sent to work as sewing machinists in city workshops, sleeping eight to a room, sewing seven days a week from 8 A.M. to 11 P.M. As a result of these conditions, the retail margin on clothing made in workshops in China and sold in Europe and the United States is 200 to 300 percent, compared to a margin of only 70 percent or so on domestic-made clothing.

Much of China's manufacturing growth has been based on a strategy of import substitution (see page 352 in Chapter 7). In spite of China's membership in the World Trade Organization (which has strict rules about intellectual property), a significant amount of China's industry is based on counterfeiting and reverse engineering (making products that are copied and then sold under different or altered brand names) and piracy (making look-alike products passed off as the real thing). Copies of everything from DVDs, movies, designer clothes and footwear, drugs, motorcycles, and automobiles to high-speed magnetic levitation (maglev) cross-country trains save Chinese industry enormous sums in research and development and licensing fees, while saving the country even greater sums in imports.

Foreign investors, meanwhile, have been keen to develop a share of China's rapidly expanding and increasingly affluent market. The automobile market is particularly attractive to Western manufacturers. Volkswagen was the first to establish a presence in China in 1985. By 2003, Volkswagen had claimed around 40 percent of China's annual production of almost 4 million cars and light trucks. General Motors, in partnership with Shanghai Automotive Industry Corporation, has a 10 percent market share. Other foreign manufacturers operating in China include Honda, Toyota, Nissan, and most recently, BMW and Mercedes.

Overall, most foreign investment in China comes from elsewhere within East Asia. Japan, Taiwan, and South Korea, having developed manufacturing industries that undercut those of the United States, now face deindustrialization themselves through the inexorable process of "creative destruction" (see p. 301 in Chapter 6). More than 50,000 Taiwanese firms have established operations in China, investing an estimated $90 billion. Pusan, the center of the South Korean footwear industry that in 1990 exported $4.3 billion worth of shoes, is now full of deserted factories. South Korean footwear exports are down to less than $700 million, while China's footwear exports have increased from $2.1 billion in 1990 to $13 billion in 2002. Several Japanese electronics giants, including Toshiba Corp., Sony Corp., Matsushita Electric Industrial Co., and Canon, Inc., have expanded operations in China even as they have shed tens of thousands of workers at home. Olympus manufactures its digital cameras in Shenzhen and Guangzhou. Pioneer has moved its manufacture of DVD recorders to Shanghai and Dongguan. Toshiba's factory in Dalian illustrates the logic. Toshiba is one of about 40 Japanese companies that have built large-scale production facilities in a special export-processing zone established by Dalian in the early 1990s with generous financial support from the Japanese government and major Japanese firms. By shifting production of digital televisions here from its plant in Saitama, Japan, in 2001, Toshiba cut labor costs per worker by 90 percent.

FIGURE 1 Chinese electronics factory
China's relatively inexpensive labor force has been a major comparative advantage in the globalizing world economy.

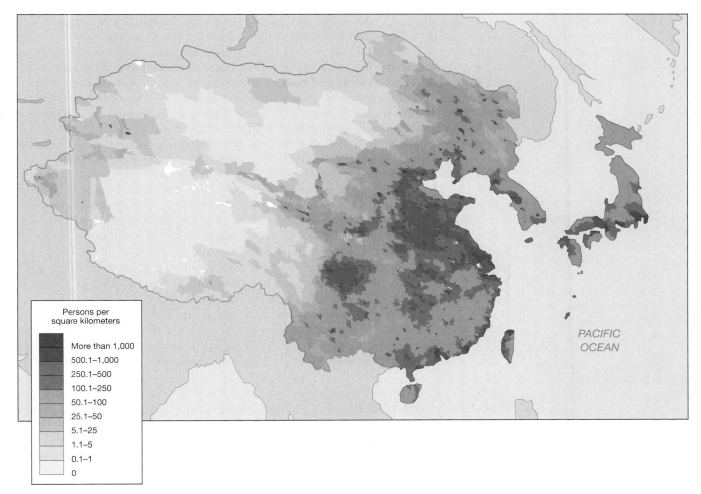

FIGURE 8.15 Population density in East Asia 1995 The density of population is very high throughout most of the continental margins of East Asia and in the fertile basins and river valleys of Inner China, but population densities are very low in the Tibetan Plateau, northwestern China, and Mongolia. (*Source:* Center for International Earth Science Information Network [CIESIN], Columbia University; International Food Policy Research Institute [IFPRI]; and World Resources Institute [WRI], 2000. *Gridded Population of the World [GPW],* Version 3. Palisades, NY: CIESIN, Columbia University, 2005. Available at **http://sedac.ciesin.columbia.edu/gpw/.**)

median dwelling size in metropolitan Los Angeles is just over 150 square meters, or 1615 square feet.)

These levels of crowding are reflected not only by crowded streets and tiny homes (**Figure 8.16**), but by people's behavior and social organization. Japanese daily life is filled with rules, and many of them have evolved because of space shortages. In many Tokyo neighborhoods, for example, trash is picked up four times a week, mainly because people have no place to store it. The trash itself must be sorted carefully into burnable and nonburnable loads and put out in government-approved see-through bags so that it is easy to spot violations.

Population Control In China, crowded towns and cities are more often a reflection of high rates of the rural-to-urban migration of low-income households than of a sheer lack of space. China

FIGURE 8.16 Small suburban homes, Japan High population densities have driven up the price of land so much that even suburban homes, such as these in Kyoto, are very small by Western standards.

certainly does not lack space, and until relatively recently China's population was officially regarded as being too small rather than too large. Mao Zedong wanted a large population with which to fully exploit China's large territory. When Ma Yinchu, an eminent economist and the president of Beijing University, cautioned the leadership in 1957 about the rapid growth of China's population, he was dismissed from his post and became a "non-person," his existence not recognized by the authorities, for the next 22 years. Between 1961 and 1972, China's population spurted by 210 million people as a demographic transition took effect (see Chapter 1, p. 10). Improved medical care and public health reduced death rates, while birthrates remained high, encouraged by the political leadership. In 1970 the average family size was 5.8 children, and China's population had been growing at 2.6 percent per year for the previous decade.

By the early 1970s, it had become clear that China's communal mode of production could not sustain such a large population. Increasingly, population growth was seen as a threat to the country's chances of economic development. In response, China's Communist Party instituted an aggressive program of population control. A sustained propaganda campaign (**Figure 8.17**) was reinforced in 1979 by strict birth quotas: one child for urban families, two for rural families, and up to three for families that belonged to ethnic minorities. The policy involved rewards for families giving birth to only one child, including work bonuses and priority in housing. The only child was later to receive preferential treatment in university admission and job assignments (an aspect of the policy that was later abandoned). In contrast, families with more than one child were to be penalized by a 10 percent decrease in their annual wages, and their children would not be eligible for free education and healthcare benefits.

In China's major cities, the one-child policy has been rigorously enforced, to the point where it has been almost impossible for a woman to get away with a second pregnancy. Who is allowed to have a child, as well as when she may give birth, is rigidly controlled by the woman's work unit. Workers are usually organized into groups of 10 to 30 individuals. If any woman in the group gives birth to more than one child, the entire group can lose its annual bonus. Neighborhood committees and "granny police" also watch over the families in their locale, adding social pressure and acting as distributors of birth-control devices. Abortions are freely available for unsanctioned and unwanted pregnancies.

In terms of reducing population growth, the policy has been very successful. The average family size in China in 2005 was 1.8 children, while the overall annual growth rate of the country's population between 1995 and 2005 was 0.9 percent. China, like Japan, Taiwan, and North and South Korea, has completed its demographic transition and now has low birthrates as well as low death rates. Without such an aggressive population policy, China's population today would have been more than 300 million larger.

Nevertheless, the policy has not been without problems. In addition to the personal and social coercion involved, the one-child policy has led to the problem of spoiled children—"little emperors" who are the center of attention of six anxious adults (the parents plus two sets of grandparents). One aspect of this is an increasing incidence of obesity in Chinese children. Being fat used to be considered a hedge against bad times, but it is now coming to be seen not only as unhealthy but also as symptomatic of the cultural shift that has produced so many spoiled children.

More serious is the practice of aborting female fetuses in response to the one-child policy. There has long been a cultural bias toward male children in China. Boys are not only considered inherently more worthy than girls but are also seen as insurance against hard times and providers for their parents in old age. In the past, this bias took the form of abandonment of girl children and even infanticide. Today, such practices are much less common, but widespread selective abortion means that, for every 100 female babies born in China, according to the 1999 census figures, there are 111.3 baby

FIGURE 8.17 China's population policy This billboard proclaiming the importance of family planning embodies the ideal of China's policy of limiting urban families to a single child.

boys. In Jiangxi Province, the *China Women's News* reported in 1999, the ratio of newborn boys to girls was 117.1 per 100 and, in some parts, as high as 120 per 100. One consequence of this is that within a few years there will be 50 million Chinese men who will have no prospect of finding a wife, simply because there will not be enough women to go around.

Today, China's population policies are beginning to be relaxed. Not only has the rate of growth of China's population slowed satisfactorily, but the sharp reduction in birthrates over the past two decades will mean that for the next three or four decades there will be a pronounced aging of the population, creating a top-heavy situation in which more and more elderly will have to be supported by fewer and fewer younger workers.

Migrations and Diasporas

Migrations For decades internal migration within East Asia has been dominated by the movement of people from peripheral, rural settings to the towns and cities of more prosperous regions. In China, however, migration has been strictly controlled for much of the past 50 years. In the immediate aftermath of the Communist revolution, there was a great deal of local movement as people were reorganized into communes. Then, in the late 1960s, the Cultural Revolution brought about the forced migration of millions of younger city dwellers, a program of "reverse urbanization" that was designed to purge the cities of "decadent" and "revisionist" thinkers and to inculcate a proletarian revolutionary zeal among the young men and women sent out to live and work in villages. According to Maoist thinking, cities tended to harbor materialist and counterrevolutionary values. A household registration program effectively operated as an internal passport system, allowing Mao's planners to restrict urbanization. Even after Mao's death and the end of the Cultural Revolution, Chinese authorities remained opposed to urbanization, seeking to keep rural labor forces in place and to prevent the kind of overurbanization typical of peripheral countries. Regulations aimed at restricting rural-to-urban migration included raising housing costs for migrants and fining employers who hire transient workers without permission.

The gradual liberalization of the Chinese economy has inevitably led to increased rural-to-urban migration, however (**Figure 8.18**). Between 1975 and 2005, the percentage of the Chinese population living in urban areas increased from 17.3 percent to 34.3 percent. Given the overall growth of population during that period, this meant an additional 277.7 million urban dwellers. To prevent the country's few big cities from swelling to unmanageable proportions, the Chinese government created several hundred buffer cities—smaller settlements with populations of fewer than 500,000 people. By 2000, satellite photos showed that China was losing at least 500,000 hectares (1.24 million acres) of arable land each year to housing, roads, and factories through the expansion of these smaller towns and cities.

Meanwhile, several megalopolitan areas had emerged in spite of the state's policy of giving priority to the development of smaller towns and cities. These megalopolitan areas include the Bo Hai Bay area centered on Beijing, Tianjin, Qingdao, Shenyang, and Dalian; the Yangtze River Delta around Shanghai, Nanjing, Hangzhou, and Ningbo; and the Zhu Jiang (Pearl River) Delta around Guangzhou, Shenzhen, and Hong Kong. (Chongqing, with a registered population of more than 30 million people, is an artificial megacity, created through merging Chongqing administratively with the settlements of the Three Gorges basin.) Faced with these realities, and wishing to accelerate urbanization in a bid to take advantage of economies of scale, in 2000 the government finally reversed its long-standing policy against creating megacities.

In Japan, levels of urbanization have increased dramatically since World War II. In 1950 almost half of Japan's population was dispersed throughout the country in farming households in rural areas. During the period of postwar

FIGURE 8.18 Migrants A migrant laborer and his daughter traveling to work in fields outside Beijing.

economic recovery and growth, rural-to-urban migration occurred very rapidly as manufacturing industries expanded, mainly along the Pacific Corridor from Tokyo to northern Kyushu. As in the United States, there was a brief phenomenon of **counterurbanization** (the net loss of population from cities to smaller towns and rural areas) during the 1970s, as some businesses sought to escape the congestion and inflated land prices of metropolitan areas and as some people sought out quieter and more traditional settings in which to pursue slower-paced lifestyles. This counterurbanization, however, was selective, affecting only a few places and regions.

By 1990 some 46.8 percent of Japan's total land area was officially designated as "depopulated" and eligible for special funding. With less than 7 percent of Japan's population, these rural areas were left with declining economies and aging populations. Japan's cities, in contrast, grew at a terrific pace—partly through migration and partly through natural increase of their younger populations. By 2005 nearly 80 percent of Japan's population was urbanized, the Pacific Corridor having become a megalopolitan region with several major metropolises.

South Korea has experienced a similar pattern of rural-to-urban migration, with Seoul the focus of a shift that has seen overall levels of urbanization increase from 21.4 percent in 1950 to 84.2 percent in 2005. Even North Korea, with a strictly controlled Communist regime and poor levels of productivity, experienced a steady increase in urbanization: from 31.0 percent in 1950 to 64.8 percent in 2005.

Diasporas East Asia is a world region that is distinctive insofar as it has few immigrant populations of any significant size. Dislike of—and disdain for—foreigners of all kinds has long been a strong cultural trait within East Asia. The Communist regimes of China and North Korea have resulted in tightly closed borders for several decades. In contrast, there has been considerable emigration from East Asia. The Chinese diaspora (**Figure 8.19**) dates from the 13th century, after the conquest of China by the Mongols in 1279. Some Chinese took refuge in Japan, Cambodia, and

FIGURE 8.19 The Chinese diaspora Most emigration from China has been from the heavily populated regions of Inner China. Chinese emigration began on a large scale during the 19th-century Industrial Revolution, when Chinese laborers found opportunities for employment in newly colonized lands. (*Source:* Redrawn from G. Chaliand and J-P. Rageau, *The Penguin Atlas of Diasporas.* New York: Viking, 1995, p. 143.)

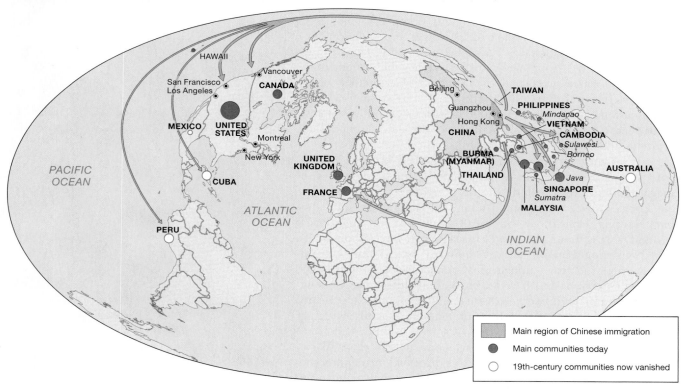

Vietnam, but it was the Yuan (Mongol) dynasty that promoted the basis for a wider Chinese diaspora through its trading colonies in Cambodia, Java, Sumatra, Singapore, and Taiwan. Under the Ming and Qing dynasties, Chinese communities developed around additional trading colonies, including several in Indonesia, the Philippines, and Thailand.

After defeat in the Opium War (1840–42) and the opening of trade with Western powers, many more Chinese emigrated, creating the basis for the modern Chinese diaspora. The Industrial Revolution and the opening of the world economy through imperialism and colonization provided many opportunities. Between 1845 and 1900, 400,000 Chinese are estimated to have emigrated to the United States, Canada, Australia, and New Zealand. Over the same period, an additional 1.5 million emigrated to Southeast Asia (Indonesia, Malaysia, Singapore, Thailand, and Vietnam), working in mines, on road- and railroad-building, and as farm laborers. Another 400,000 emigrated to the West Indies and Latin America, mainly Chile, Cuba (after 1847), and Peru (after 1848).

Chinese immigration to the United States began with the California gold rush of the 1850s. By 1860 there were 35,000 Chinese in the United States, concentrated in San Francisco, Los Angeles, Seattle, and Portland and scattered in the mines, railway construction projects, and ranches of California. Other significant concentrations of Chinese immigrants developed in Boston, New York, and Philadelphia. But intense discrimination against the Chinese—who were, as geographer Susan Craddock has shown, wrongly blamed for everything from outbreaks of cholera to the moral corruption of 19th-century cities—led to a decade of federal restrictions on Chinese immigration, beginning in 1882. It was only after World War II that Chinese immigration to the United States once more became a significant flow. Today, the Chinese diaspora is the largest in the world and one of the most prosperous. The past quarter-century has seen a great increase in Chinese emigration to the United States, Canada, and western Europe. In 2000 the Chinese population of the United States was 1.6 million.

The Korean and Japanese diasporas are much smaller but have become important elements of the contemporary geography of both East Asia and North America. Few people from Korea had left the country before Japanese colonization in 1910, but during the Japanese colonial period (1910–45), significant numbers of Korean workers emigrated to settle in Manchuria; Sakhalin, a large, formerly Japanese island north of Japan; and Japan itself. Following Japan's defeat in World War II, the Soviet occupation of Sakhalin stranded the Korean population there, while in Japan the Korean population has remained a discriminated minority, even after three generations. After the mid-1970s, a second burst of emigration occurred—this time from South Korea, with the destination of the emigrants focused on Hawaii and North America, mainly Los Angeles and Vancouver. Japanese emigration to its colonies in East Asia in the 1930s and 1940s was reversed with the Japanese defeat in World War II. The remaining component of the Japanese diaspora is in North America. Japanese immigration to the United States dates from the 1880s, when federal restrictions were placed on Chinese immigration. Today, the Japanese-American population numbers almost 900,000, with concentrations in Honolulu, San Francisco, and Los Angeles.

Ethnicity

Although East Asia has few immigrant populations of any significant size, there are some important ethnic variations. According to China's census of 2000, its population contains 56 different ethnic groups. The dominant group consists of Han people, who make up more than 91 percent of the population. The Han people originally occupied the lower reaches of the Huang He and the surrounding North China Plain. They spread gradually inland along river valleys, into present-day Korea, and toward the humid and subtropical south. With the Ming dynasty, Han colonialism and imperialism established them as the dominant group throughout the jungle lands of the south and southeast (as far as present-day Vietnam) and in Taiwan. In the 19th century, they spread north into Manchuria. Today there are more than a billion Han in China. The remaining 55 minority groups add up to fewer than 110 million people. They are mostly residual groups of indigenous peoples, such as the Miao, the Dong, Li, Naxi, and Qiang, and are found in the border regions, removed from central authority in Beijing, relatively remote, and economically disadvantaged.

Under these circumstances, it is not surprising to find that tensions exist between several of the larger minority groups and the dominant Han. Perhaps the best-known case is that of the Tibetans, who came under the rule of the Han as recently as 1950, when the Chinese People's Liberation Army marched into Tibet as "liberators." As early as the seventh and tenth centuries A.D., with the expansion and unification of the Chinese empire, the Han Chinese had begun to move into the margins of the Tibetan region. By that time, Tibet had developed a distinctive culture based on Tibetan Buddhism—developed from a fusion of the region's ancient animistic religion (known as Bon) with Tantric Buddhism imported from India. During the Ming (1368–1644) and Qing (1644–1911) dynasties, the entire Tibetan Plateau became part of the Chinese empire. Far away from the center of power, Tibet was divided into numerous small tribes and districts, with feudal chieftains ruling autocratically, generation after generation. As a result, Tibet became a highly repressive theocracy based on serfdom. In 1950 China seized on this fact as justification for its invasion of the strategically important region.

Between 1950 and 1970 the Chinese "liberated" the Tibetans, drove their spiritual leader, the Dalai Lama, into exile, destroyed much of Tibetan cultural heritage, and caused the death of an estimated 1 million Tibetans. In 1959 the Tibetans rose in an attempted revolt, and their spiritual leader, the Dalai Lama, fled into exile. In 1965, Tibet was granted the status of an autonomous region, called Xizang, but by that time large numbers of Han had flooded in, often taking positions of authority, leaving Tibetans as disadvantaged, second-class citizens. There were serious anti-Chinese disturbances in 1988, and since then the volatile situation has continued to simmer. Today in Xizang, all Buddhist monasteries are rigidly controlled by the police and Communist Party officials, and expressions of devotion to the Dalai Lama are banned. About 60 percent of the area's population is now of Han Chinese descent. These developments have given rise to significant ethnic tensions within the region, while the exiled Dalai Lama has acquired global celebrity as a result of his international tours promoting Buddhism and publicizing the "cultural genocide" committed by China in Tibet. The Dalai Lama does not want national independence for Tibet, but greater autonomy. For their part, the Chinese cannot understand the ingratitude of the Tibetans. As the Chinese see it, they have saved the Tibetans from feudalism and built roads, schools, hospitals, and factories.

Another region of tense interethnic relations is that of Xinjiang, a vast territory that occupies one-sixth of China. Its multiethnic population totals only 15 million, including an estimated 8 million Uighurs and a sizable number of Han colonists who arrived after 1950. The majority of Xinjiang's population are Muslim, but their agitation for greater autonomy and respect for Islamic values has been ruthlessly suppressed by the Chinese authorities. In 1962 minority factions rebelled against the Chinese, calling for the establishment of an independent East Turkestan Muslim Republic. Tens of thousands of nomadic peoples fled across the mountainous border with the Soviet Union, and for several decades now there has been ongoing feuding in the frontier region. In recent years, separatist sentiments in Xinjiang have been fueled by the collapse of the Soviet Union and the realignment of Central Asia's newly independent Muslim states that share borders with Xinjiang. Protests and bombings increased sharply in the 1990s, and the traffic of weapons, political literature, and insurgents has prompted the Chinese to increase surveillance in Xinjiang and, intermittently, to close its borders with Pakistan and neighboring Central Asian states.

Cultural Traditions

Language The dominance of Han peoples within China is reflected in the geography of language. Mandarin, the language of the old imperial bureaucracy, is spoken by Hui and Manchu people (as well as the people of Taiwan), together with almost all Han people, though significant regional variations still remain in the Mandarin dialects that people use. The other 53 ethnic minorities in China have their own languages.

Chinese writing dates from the time of the Shang dynasty (1766–1126 B.C.), with tens of thousands of characters, or ideographs, each representing a picture or a sound of a word. The Communist government has facilitated literacy by reducing the number of characters in use and by simplifying them. It has also adopted a new system, **pinyin**, for spelling Chinese words and names using the Latin alphabet of 26 letters. Previously, Chinese words and names had been translated into a Latin-based version using a Western system, known as the Wade-Giles system. Older textbooks, reference books, and atlases, for example, refer to Chongquing (pinyin) as Chunking (Wade-Giles), Mao Zedong as Mao Tse-Tung, and so on.

Religion   Chinese culture found spiritual expression in the philosophy of Confucianism. Unlike formal religions, Confucianism has no place for gods or an afterlife. Also distinctive is Confucianism's emphasis on ethics and principles of good governance, and on the importance of education as well as family and hard work. Confucianism proved to be ideally suited to Imperial China, and it remains the most widely recognized belief system in China, even after several decades of discouragement from the Communist regime. Formalized religions in China include Daoism (throughout much of the country), Tibetan Buddhism (in Xizang), and Islam (in large parts of Inner Mongolia and Xinjiang).

For most Chinese, however, folk religions are far more important than any organized religion. Animism—the belief that nonliving things have spirits that should be respected through worship—continues to be widely practiced, as does ancestor worship—based on the belief that the living can communicate with the dead and that the dead spirits, to whom offerings are ritually made, have the ability to influence people's lives. The costs of ancestor worship can be financially burdensome. The offerings involve burning paper money and hiring shamans and priests to perform rituals that will heal the sick, appease the ancestors, and exorcise ghosts at times of birth, marriage, and death.

Japanese indigenous culture found expression in Shinto, which does not have a distinctive philosophy but, rather, a belief in the nature of sacred powers that can be recognized in every individual existing thing. The traditions of Shinto may be thought of as the traditions of Japan itself. Seasonal and other festivals elicit widespread participation in present-day Japan, regardless of people's religious affiliation. These traditions usually entail ritual purification, the offering of food to sacred powers, sacred music and dance, solemn worship, and joyous celebration. Buddhism is also important in Japan. It was introduced to Japan in the sixth century A.D. from Korea. During the Nara period (A.D. 710–84), Buddhism was vigorously promoted, leading to the first blossoming of distinctive Japanese art and architecture. Later, between the 12th and 14th centuries, Zen Buddhism was introduced from China, adding new painting styles, new skills in ceramics, and the custom of tea drinking.

Feng Shui   Throughout East Asia there is widespread adherence to **feng shui** (pronounced *fung shway*)—not a religion but a belief that the physical attributes of places can be analyzed and manipulated in order to improve the flow of cosmic energy, or *qi*, that binds all living things. *Feng shui* involves strategies of siting, landscaping, architectural design, and furniture placement to direct energy flows and is often known as **geomancy**. The oldest school of *feng shui*, known as the Land Form (or simply Form) School, dates back to the Tang dynasty (A.D. 618–907). From its origin in the jagged mountains of southern China, the Form School used hills, mountains, rivers, and other geomorphological features as a basis to evaluate the quality of a location. Subsequent modifications introduced the idea that specific points of the compass exert unique influences on various aspects of life. For example, the south, with its orientation toward the Sun's path and away from cold north winds, was declared a most auspicious direction, conducive to longevity, fame, and fortune, while influence over career and business success was attributed to the north.

FIGURE 8.20 Feng Shui The principles of feng shui are as popular as ever throughout much of East Asia.

In East Asia today, *feng shui* practitioners focus most on the layout and interior design of homes and offices (**Figure 8.20**). The principles and beliefs are complex, but some of the key ideas are as follows: Water and mirrors enhance *qi* flow. Narrow openings or hallways cause *qi* to flow too quickly, negating its beneficial effects. Straight lines are a frequent cause of high-velocity *qi* that can be dangerous to health and well-being. The numbers 8 (representing "prosperity") and 9 (representing the fullness of heaven and earth) are good; but 4 is bad ("death"). The placement of furniture and other objects, as well as the use of certain colors (purple is popular) and motifs (birds are favored), are all believed to enhance *qi* flow, and, therefore, career success, strong family relationships, and good health. Ideally, each room should include some representation of each of the five fundamental elements (fire, metal, water, wood, and earth).

Regional Variations Traditional East Asian societies revolved around family, kin networks, clan groups, and language groups, with a strong bureaucracy enforcing social order. Society was rigidly hierarchical, and individuals were subsumed within the family unit, the village, and the domain of the local lord. In these environments, important social values were those of humility, understatement, and refined obsequiousness, with particular deference being shown to older persons and those of superior social rank.

These traditional values persist as a distinctive dimension of the cultural geography of the region. Not surprisingly, in rural areas and smaller towns, and among older people in general, traditional cultural values are held most strongly. Traditional rural communities with a great variety of distinctive ways of life still characterize much of the

(a)

(b)

(c)

FIGURE 8.21 Rural China The majority of China's population lives in rural settings, and rural ways of life remain dominant throughout much of the country. (a) Vegetable market in Shanxi, Xian. (b) Girl herding ducks, Guangdong province. (c) Women with cattle, Yunnan province.

region (**Figure 8.21**). There are, however, marked regional variations in cultural traditions within East Asia. In addition to the variations in religious adherence associated with different ethnic groups, there are some striking regional differences in diet, dress, and ways of life. Within China, for example, there are fundamental differences between the cuisines of Inner and Outer China and between those of the north and south within Inner China. In Outer China, milk-based dishes—yogurt, curds, and so on—are common, while herds of sheep, goats, cows, horses, camels, and yaks also provide meat dishes. Inner China, by contrast, has little stock-raising and, consequently, few milk-based dishes; its principal meat dishes derive from scavengers such as ducks, poultry, and pigs. Within Inner China, the humid and subtropical south has developed a cuisine based on rice, while in the subhumid north noodles form the staple diet.

In cities, and especially among youth, traditional ideas are giving way to new value systems and cultural practices, partly hybridized with imported Western cultural norms and partly original. The rise and commercialization of sports is one example, as evidenced by the popularity of baseball and golf in Japan and of soccer everywhere. Another is the emergence of distinctive youth cultures in the major metropolises of China, Japan, Taiwan, and South Korea. In Tokyo, for example, more than 70 percent of the single women live at home as "parasite singles." The number of Japanese women in their late twenties who have not married has risen from 30 percent to about 50 percent in the last 15 years—and their opinions and lifestyle help define a kind of Tokyo yuppie devoted to leisure and luxury (**Figure 8.22**). Another distinctive aspect of contemporary Japanese urban culture is the pachinko parlor (**Figure 8.23**), where individual players sit passively at noisy machines that are a cross between slot machines and pinball.

Globalizing East Asia While these traditions remain a dimension of the geography of East Asia, they are being increasingly drawn into the globalization of culture. Chinese art and artifacts were popularized in Europe and North America in the 19th century; Chinese and Japanese cuisines have been introduced to cities throughout the rest of the world; the simplicity of Japanese architecture and interior design has influenced Modernist design; religions such as Tibetan Buddhism and Zen Buddhism have a small but growing following in both Europe and North America; and *feng shui* has recently found adherents in many Western countries. Some new East Asian cultural products have become popular beyond the region. One example is Hong Kong movies, with their distinctive genre that mixes martial arts, metropolitan youth culture, and traditional values. Another is the Japanese Pokémon characters. At the same time, the cultural traditions of East Asia are themselves being modified, hybridized, and displaced by the globalization of culture. This is perhaps most striking in terms of the

FIGURE 8.22 Dining out Miki Takasu, foreground, and her girlfriends dine at a Tokyo restaurant. (*Source*: © 2000, *The Washington Post*. Photo by Kathryn Tolbert. Reprinted with permission.)

FIGURE 8.23 Pachinko parlor A typical pachinko parlor in the Shinjuku district of Tokyo.

FIGURE 8.24 The Great Leader A commune group visiting Pyongyang bows to the Grand Monument to Kim Il Sung, the "Great Leader."

growth of Western materialism and consumer culture in Japan, South Korea, and Taiwan but, as in most other world regions, globalization is rapidly diffusing new ideas, values, and social practices, as well as consumer products, to every corner.

CONTEMPORARY CHALLENGES IN A GLOBALIZING WORLD

Over the past 20 years, places and regions in most of East Asia have been increasingly linked to the circuits of the global economy. The economic, social, cultural, and political outcomes of these changes have already been profound, even though the change is still very much in motion. These outcomes have also been uneven in their impact. East Asia is a world region with a legacy of three very different economies: a huge rural economy based on 18th- and 19th-century agriculture; a large, urban 20th-century industrial economy; and a small but rapidly growing economy based on advanced technologies. As more and more places and regions in East Asia are drawn into the agricultural-, manufacturing-, and information-based circuits of the global economy, long-standing spatial patterns become blurred, new regional patterns emerge, and places develop new forms of interdependence. East Asia is a world region whose dominant motifs are its dynamism, its distinctive pathways to modernization, and the contradictions and disjunctures that have resulted from rapid economic and social change. East Asia also contains two of the world's geopolitical hotspots—Taiwan and North Korea—while North Korea is also notable as one of the world's most introverted economic and social systems.

Geopolitical Hotspot: North Korea

The partition of North and South Korea in 1953 left North Korea behind the world's most heavily militarized border. It reflected the leadership of Kim Il Sung, whose vision for North Korea was what he called *juche*: a mixture of Stalinist socialism, self-reliant nationalism, and the cult of the personality. The people soon learned to refer to Kim Il Sung as the "Great Leader" (**Figure 8.24**). With good natural resources, including significant reserves of coal and iron ore and good potential for hydropower, North Korea set out to become a major power within East Asia. For decades, more than one quarter of the country's GDP has been expended on the military, including the development of nuclear capability that could lead to nuclear weaponry.

To carry out this strategy of national development, the "Great Leader," Kim Il Sung imposed an austere regime that resulted in drab cities with bleak housing and a population whose bland and regimented quality of life was poisoned by the paranoia that was generated by a "Big Brother" government. The everyday landscapes of rural and small-town North Korea entered a time warp that, in 2006, has given them the appearance of late-1950s environments, with old buildings, old technologies, and clunky-looking consumer goods.

In 1994 Kim Il Sung died and was succeeded by his son Kim Jong Il, who immediately came to be referred to as the "Dear Leader." Soon afterward, in 1995 and 1996, North Korea experienced unusually bad floods, followed in 1997 by a severe drought. By 1998, agricultural production was down to 50 percent of its previous levels. Worse, the floods had affected the country's coal mines, so that industrial production was disrupted, along with supplies of coal for winter heating. North Korea's landscape became one of famine and distress (**Figure 8.25**). Estimates of the total number of deaths due to North Korea's food shortages between 1995 and 2005 range between 1 and 3 million.

FIGURE 8.25 Famine in North Korea Disastrous harvests in 1997 and 2000 left North Korea with only two-thirds of the food it needs. Shown here are children in a kindergarten in Pyongyang in 1997.

By 2005, after 52 years of sacrifice and austerity, personal incomes in North Korea were only one-tenth those in South Korea, and infant mortality rates were five times higher. Stories reached Western newspapers of starvation and of families so desperate for food that they were selling their daughters to Chinese farmers who were having trouble finding wives or to the brothels and karaoke halls that line the grimy streets of the small cities in neighboring northeastern China.

North Korea remains not only one of the world's most impoverished societies but also one of the most closed and rigid. Listening to foreign radio broadcasts is punishable by death, citizens can be detained arbitrarily, and there are an estimated 150,000 political prisoners. Society is stratified according to loyalty to the Communist Party, and citizens' level of commitment determines their access to housing, education, and health care.

North Korea is also one of the most highly militarized countries in the world. It has the world's fifth-largest standing army (after China, the United States, Russia, and India), even though it has a relatively small population (an estimated 23.1 million in 2005). North Korea's weapons and missiles are sold indiscriminately on world markets to raise badly needed foreign exchange, while its own arsenal—including possible nuclear capability—is pointed menacingly at South Korea and Japan. This threat represents a major geopolitical problem for the region, and it has been deliberately intensified and manipulated by the "Dear Leader" in an attempt to leverage economic aid and political concessions from both China and the United States.

Unresolved Geopolitics: Taiwan

When the Communist revolution created the People's Republic of China in mainland China, the ousted Nationalist government established itself in Taiwan (then called Formosa) as the Republic of China. Granted diplomatic recognition by Western governments but not by the People's Republic, Taiwan immediately became a potential geopolitical flashpoint in the Cold War. Large amounts of economic aid from the United States, provided because of Cold War geopolitics, helped prime Taiwan's economy. Strict currency controls, the creation of government corporations in key industries, and strong trade barriers to protect domestic industries from foreign competition were introduced by the Taiwanese government in an effort to establish a self-sufficient economy. An authoritarian regime suppressed opposition to government policies. By the early 1960s, Taiwan's political stability and cheap labor force provided a very attractive environment for export processing industries.

Taiwan lost its full international diplomatic status in 1971, when U.S. President Richard Nixon's rapprochement with the People's Republic led to its entrance into the United Nations. In 1987 Taiwan's government lifted martial law, began a phase of political liberalization, and relaxed its rules about contact with mainland China. Meanwhile, mainland China still claims Taiwan as a province of the People's Republic and has offered to set up a Special Administrative Region for Taiwan, with the sort of economic and democratic privileges that it has given Hong Kong.

Taiwan's geopolitical problems have not prevented it from achieving great economic success. With a land area of 36,000 square kilometers (13,900 square miles), only 25 percent of which is cultivable, and a population of 22 million, Taiwan would be the second smallest of China's provinces and seventh from the bottom in population. Yet Taiwan's per capita GDP (in PPP "international" dollars) in 2005, $27,572, was almost four times that of mainland China (excluding Hong Kong and Macao). In 2005 Taiwan was the world's 19th-largest exporter, with a total export trade of $189.4 billion. Taiwan's economic growth rate over the past three decades has been phenomenal, averaging more than 8 percent per year. Sometimes referred to as "Silicon Island," Taiwan has some 1.2 million small- and medium-sized enterprises. Most make components, or entire products, according to specifications set by other, often well-known international firms, whose brand names go on the final product. Because Taiwan's firms tend to be small, they have been able to be flexible in responding to changes in technology. They have also been able to move quickly to take advantage of China's "open door" policy. Between 1990 and 2005, Taiwanese businesspeople

FIGURE 8.26 Taipei As the capital of one of the newly industrialized "Asian Tigers," Taipei has grown rapidly, and in 2004 it could boast the world's tallest building, the Taipei 101.

invested more than $150 billion abroad, the greater share of it in mainland China. In South China and in Fujian Province, across the Taiwan Strait from Taiwan, Taiwanese enterprises operate what amounts to a parallel economy.

Taiwan's economic success as one of the newly industrialized "Asian Tigers" is not without growing pains. In Taipei and other cities, Taiwan's breathtakingly fast modernization has brought heavy pollution, acute housing shortages, and rampant corruption. The rapid acquisition of automobiles, motor scooters, and air conditioners has made the environment unbearable and transportation a nightmare. Growth has been so rapid that the government has been unable to solve the problems of water supply and waste disposal, and "garbage wars" over the issue of sanitary landfill placement have occasionally led to huge quantities of uncollected garbage. Within Taipei (**Figure 8.26**), the capital and the industrial and commercial heart of Taiwan (population 2.95 million in 2005), these problems have been intensified by an influx of young people from other parts of the island, drawn by the educational and economic opportunities and by the exciting sense of rapid change.

Regional Development

East Asia's economic development is concentrated along the continental margin, where the bulk of the population lives. Within this continental margin are the most productive agricultural regions and the most prosperous cities. The core regions of Imperial China were the plains of North and Central China and the fertile countryside of South China. China's recent transition toward market economies has intensified the comparative advantages of these regions, especially around the principal ports and river towns with good connections to the wider world. In Japan, the highly populated Kanto Plain around Tokyo became the platform for a core region—the Pacific Corridor—that was engineered to be the geographic basis of Japan's postwar "economic miracle." Meanwhile, the geopolitics of the Cold War, coupled with significant flows of investment by transnational corporations, helped Taiwan and South Korea become prosperous core regions within East Asia.

Japan's Pacific Corridor The Japanese pathway to economic development has been very distinctive. First, Japan is notably lacking in natural resources for large-scale manufacturing industries. The country's "economic miracle" of the 1960s was founded on the import of raw materials and the manufacturing and export of finished products. Japan's resurgent industries thus flourished best in coastal locations, close to deep-water ports. Second, Japan was able to prosper while keeping social institutions and cultural traditions more or less intact. Japan's economic and environmental landscapes, though, have been dramatically rearranged.

A particularly striking feature of the geography of industrialization in Japan is the sheer intensity of development that has been crammed into the relatively limited amount of suitable land. The logic of **agglomeration**—the clustering together of economic activities because of cost advantages that accrue to individual firms as a result of their location among functionally related activities—and economies of scale has been particularly evident in Japan, and has been strongly encouraged by government policies through MITI.

Within this overall transformation, one distinctive feature to emerge was the large company town. This was a consequence of the special role of *zaibatsu* and *keiretsu* in Japanese industrialization. The early leaders among the *zaibatsu*—Mitsui, Mitsubishi, and Sumitomo—inevitably came to dominate their host cities (which included Omuta, Niihama, Nobeoka, and Nagasaki), while later-established *keiretsu*, as well as some of the corporate giants spawned by postwar growth, sponsored new company towns in newly industrializing regions—for example, the city of Hitachi, northeast of Mito.

The megalopolitan Pacific Corridor between Tokyo and Kobe (**Figure 8.27**) is the embodiment of these developments. It developed into the core region of modern Japanese industrialization because it not only had several deep-water ports but also large pools of skilled labor and relatively large amounts of flat land. The entire region has developed into a megalopolitan area, known as the Tokaido Megalopolis, that is comparable in size and scope to the megalopolitan area in the United States that stretches from Boston through New York and Philadelphia to Washington. The Tokaido Megalopolis contains more than 50 million people and accounts for more than 80 percent of Japan's total GDP. In 2000, Osaka alone accounted for a GDP that was greater than those of all but eight countries in the world.

Transportation has been a key factor in the successful development of the Pacific Corridor. Though port facilities were a precondition for the region's success, internal connections within the region were poor, making it difficult for manufacturers and suppliers to exploit agglomeration economies and restricting the movement of workers and consumers. In response, the Japanese government undertook a massive program of infrastructure investment. The showpiece of this program is the Shinkansen railway system (**Figure 8.28**). First opened in 1964 to coincide with the Tokyo Olympic Games, the "bullet trains" of the Shinkansen were, for a long time, the fastest in the world. The Shinkansen has turned the entire Pacific Corridor into a daily commuter belt, with trains leaving at intervals of between 10 and 30 minutes throughout the day from each of the major cities of the Corridor, some of them carrying more than 1400 passengers each at 220 kilometers (125 miles) per hour.

The Pacific Corridor's prewar industrial base was dominated by cotton, silk, other textiles, toys, glass, and porcelain. These industries are still present in the region but have been dwarfed by the growth of iron and steel, heavy metal products and machinery, shipping and shipbuilding, petrochemicals, paper products, ceramics, automobile and truck manufacturing, cameras, scientific instruments, and electrical and electronics goods of all kinds. Tokyo has grown into a world city of the first rank, with a banking and financial sector that compares to those of London and New York. The population of the Tokyo metropolitan area in 2005 was 26.4 million. Nearby Yokohama (population 3.31 million) is first and foremost a port city and manufacturing center. Nagoya (3.38 million) is a center of heavy engineering, chemical, textile, and machinery manufacture and has a commercial port; Kyoto (1.85 million) is a major cultural and tourist center but also has electronics industries, including the manufacture of Nintendo games; Osaka (11.01 million) is a deep-water port with an industrial base of comparable size and diversity to Tokyo's but without Tokyo's international banking and finance; Kobe (1.42 million) is a center of shipping, shipbuilding, engineering, and manufacturing.

Most of these cities were almost entirely flattened by firebombing toward the end of World War II, with the exception of the old imperial capital, Kyoto. Unfortunately, it has not been possible to take advantage of building afresh to produce either more efficient or more livable cities. Growth has been so rapid, and Japanese land-use planning so weakly developed, that the entire region has the air of haphazard development. Tiny houses are wedged between tall hotels or modern offices or in the shadows of busy elevated highways; factories and warehouses sit amid private residences or next to gleaming office towers; and the sprawling mix is festooned with ugly power lines,

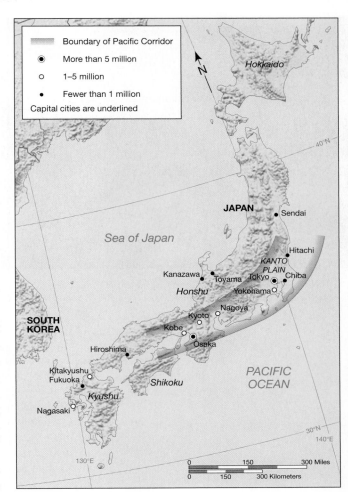

FIGURE 8.27 Japan's Pacific Corridor Reference map showing principal physical features, political boundaries, and major cities.

FIGURE 8.28 Shinkansen locomotives The 515-kilometer (320-mile) Pacific Corridor route between Tokyo and Osaka has 115 round-trip journeys per day.

FIGURE 8.29 Urban sprawl Japanese land-use planning has been notoriously weak, resulting in a high-density sprawl. Shown here is Yoshiwara.

punctuated by netted golf ranges, tall smokestacks, and cranes, and decorated with giant billboards and neon signs (**Figure 8.29**).

The growth of the Pacific Corridor has inevitably brought serious problems: crowding, congestion, environmental pollution, and ground subsidence. Meanwhile, the concentration of economic activity in the Pacific Corridor has resulted in a relative lack of development elsewhere. Japan is thus characterized, like Europe and North America, by a *center-periphery* pattern. In the Japanese case, the periphery consists of northern Hokkaido, Honshu, Kyushu, and Shikoku. Like peripheral regions within older core nations, they have experienced the **backwash effects** of metropolitan development: selective out-migration, restricted investment (both public and private), and limited employment opportunities. In addition, much of the periphery has a climate that most Japanese find severe, thus compounding feelings of deprivation and remoteness.

Meanwhile, the high costs of operating in Japan have begun to weigh on Japanese corporations, straining their allegiance to the nationalist project of economic development. Many larger Japanese corporations have moved production facilities elsewhere in East and Southeast Asia in search of lower production costs and expanding markets. MITI has attempted to counter the consequent loss of Japanese capital and technology by developing a Technopolis program that seeks to establish the infrastructure necessary to lure Japanese capital to domestic high-tech industries. However, MITI no longer has direct influence over Japanese corporations, nor do these corporations decide their strategies primarily within the framework of Japan's economic interests.

This decoupling of the systematic interdependence between Japanese government and industry means that places and regions in Japan are becoming much more interdependent with places and regions elsewhere. It also means that it is increasingly difficult to sustain the system of lifelong tenure for workers in large corporations that has distinguished Japanese employment practices for decades. Not surprisingly, people's willingness to work long hours and defer consumption in the cause of national economic development has also declined. This unraveling of Japan's successful system of economic development has been reflected in a series of recent economic and political crises. It is also beginning to be reflected in shifting values and lifestyles. Traditional patriarchal values and nationalistic bureaucratic indoctrination have little meaning for the generation that has grown up in affluence.

Major City: Tokyo   The central city, or "ward area," of Tokyo extends for approximately 15 kilometers (9.3 miles) from the center of the city, covering an area of just under 600 square kilometers (230 square miles) and containing a population of more than 8 million. Situated at the head of Tokyo Bay, the heart of the city is marked by the extensive grounds of the Imperial Palace, around which are clustered the main railway station and the office towers of the central business district (**Figure 8.30a**). The scarcity of land, together with the expense of building safe high-rise buildings in an earthquake zone, has driven growth outward, with concentrations of offices, retailing, and industry along the major transport arteries and at nodal points where railways and subway systems intersect (**Figure 8.30b**). The Tokyo metropolitan area extends for up to 50 kilometers (31 miles) from the center of the city.

The Tokyo metropolitan area accounts for more than 25 percent of Japan's population but handles more than 80 percent of the country's imports and exports (by value), and accounts for about 60 percent of the country's employment in business services. In addition to the many government agencies, half of all Japan's businesses, cultural organizations, and media firms are located in Tokyo. More than 1 million college students study in the several dozen colleges and universities in the metropolitan area and almost 90 percent of the foreign banks and transnational corporations have their offices in Tokyo. All this translates into an extremely high-energy environment. Crowds seem to be everywhere: Even at 11 P.M. on a weekday evening, there is often standing room only on downtown subways. Throughout the central city, road traffic moves slowly, if at all.

If modern Tokyo can be said to have an identifiable structure, then it is organized around the train and subway network that has evolved to cope with the millions of commuters who must pour into the central city each weekday. Where rail lines from the outer suburbs intersect with the circular Yamanote Line and the subway stations that serve the central city, nodes of office and retail development have sprung up, so that the central business district (CBD) is encircled by a series of secondary (but still very large) business districts, each at a distance of between 3 and 5 kilometers (1.9 to 3.1 miles) from the CBD. All of these centers are vibrant with people and blazing with neon long into the night. In contrast, the suburbs, though the housing is tightly packed, are relatively quiet. The suburbs are, however, very diverse. Some are effectively industrial towns in their own right; some are dominated by universities; some are dominated by company housing or public housing; and some are planned new towns with high-tech industries and research institutes. Some are exurban settlements, their residents taking advantage of the high-speed bullet trains that allow them to purchase larger homes amid paddy fields, orchards, or tea plantations, with mountainous backdrops.

Two characteristics of these suburbs are particularly striking in comparison to the suburbs of North American metropolises: first, the small size and high density of people's homes; and second, the relative lack of spatial segregation along lines of income or class. Even at the scale of individual streets, housing is often very mixed, with very modest homes adjacent to those of more affluent families. In part, this is the result of the absence of the kind of land-use planning and zoning regulations that are common in North American cities. More important, though, is a broader cultural difference: The refined understatement and strong sense of collective identity that have traditionally been valued within Japanese culture have led people to avoid ostentatious residential segregation.

Tokyo is particularly vulnerable to earthquake damage because much of the city, including most of the downtown and all of the waterfront districts, is built on loosely consolidated landfill. When severely shaken by an earthquake, this material behaves like liquid, causing the buildings on it to collapse. Tough building codes and sophisticated building technologies make it possible to erect structures that can withstand a severe earthquake, but 2 million of Tokyo's 2.6 million buildings were constructed before 1981, when building codes were significantly strengthened. In addition, the city's low elevation makes it vulnerable to tidal waves (*tsunami*) that would be triggered by an earthquake with an offshore epicenter. The threat of a major earthquake is very much part of the background of living in Tokyo and a major shaper of both the built environment and the city's personality. To protect against *tsunami*, there is an extensive pattern of breakwaters in Tokyo Bay, sea walls and river walls at the waterfront, and massive gates that can close off river mouths to prevent a flood tide from surging in. To protect against the spread of fires that are likely to occur after a major earthquake, city planners have built continuous ribbons of fire-resistant apartment blocks.

(a)

(b)

FIGURE 8.30 Tokyo With a population (in 2000) of more than 28 million, the Tokyo metropolitan area is highly congested. (a) The Imperial Palace (foreground) and downtown. (b) Pedestrian traffic at Shibuya Crossing.

Inner China At the heart of China's reforms since 1978 has been the dramatic economic development of Inner China. Deng Xiaoping initially sought to bring "world standards" to bear on the Chinese economy in a controlled way through the establishment of a few Special Economic Zones (SEZs) (**Figure 8.31**) and Economic and Technical

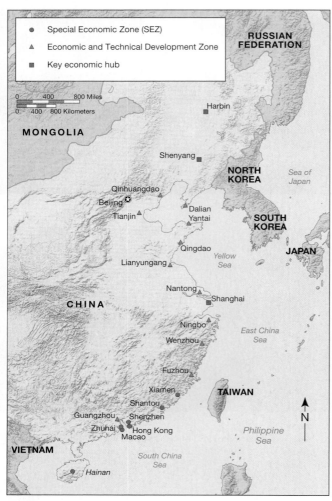

FIGURE 8.31 China's Special Economic Zones Since the 1980s, China has established a series of Special Economic Zones and Economic and Technical Development Zones as a way to attract foreign capital, technology, and management practices while maintaining political control.

Development Zones. The first four SEZs—Shantou, Shenzhen, Xiamen, and Zhuhai—were all located in South China, deliberately building on the prosperity of Hong Kong, the former British colony that was returned to China on July 1, 1997. The SEZs were experimental, as the Communist leadership in Beijing looked for ways to maintain political control while absorbing foreign capital, technology, and management practices. The zones were set up as carefully segregated export-processing areas that offered cheap labor and land, along with tax breaks, to transnational corporations. They have been only partially successful; transnational corporations can obtain similar conditions in a wide range of peripheral countries, often under more favorable and predictable political circumstances. What the transnational corporations really want is to penetrate the Chinese market, but the Chinese government remains wary of the potential damage to its fledgling domestic industries.

The SEZs did, however, signal China's openness to capitalist investment and trade, a signal to which investors from Hong Kong and Taiwan responded positively and enthusiastically. Networks of business connections quickly sprang up in the coastal cities and regions adjacent to Hong Kong and Taiwan. Once the business networks were in place, capital flowed in from all over the globe. The surge of investment in coastal China has been led by ethnic Chinese within networks that stretch across the Chinese diaspora in Southeast Asia and around the Pacific Rim. Common language and a common culture ease the flow of money, managers, and trade.

Taiwan and China are officially still on a war footing, and all economic relations are carried on through Hong Kong. But in 1992 China became the biggest single destination for Taiwanese foreign direct investment. Pressure is mounting on the Taiwan government to allow direct trade and investment with the mainland. Meanwhile, a new web of interdependent trade and investment has emerged, linking coastal China with Singapore, Bangkok, Penang, Kuala Lumpur, Jakarta, Los Angeles, Vancouver, New York, and Sydney.

The coastal regions of Inner China that have been infused with capital and business know-how from the Chinese diaspora have now become the nodal points for reforming the Chinese economy as a whole. Their dramatic success has influenced managers and bureaucrats elsewhere. Much of the investment is in joint ventures or corporate alliances between foreign firms and local enterprises operated by local governments and cooperatives. Throughout Inner China, the industrial structure increasingly resembles that of its more prosperous East Asian neighbors; Chinese manufacturing output is now dominated by a large number of small firms with mixed state and private (often foreign) participation rather than by giant state companies as in the past. Today, most enterprises, both private and collective, contract with one another rather than with the central government and deal directly with consumers. After they have fulfilled their contracts and paid their taxes, they are free to pay incentive bonuses and to invest any remaining profits in improved equipment or expanded production facilities. Some 80 percent of China's GDP is now generated by these nonstate enterprises.

Within the vast region that is Inner China there are several key industrial subregions. These are (**Figure 8.32**):

1. The Beijing-Tianjin-Tangshan region: Chief industries include steel and metallurgy, petroleum and chemicals, engineering, electrical equipment, electronics, and textiles. Altogether, this subregion accounts for almost 10 percent of China's total industrial production.
2. The Jinan-Qingdao railway belt: Chief industries include textiles, chemicals, porcelain, fertilizer, and steel.
3. The Shijiazhuang-Handan railway belt, located along the Beijing-Wuhan railway and along the foothills of the Taihang Mountains: Chief industries include textiles, engineering, steel, porcelain, and light manufacturing.

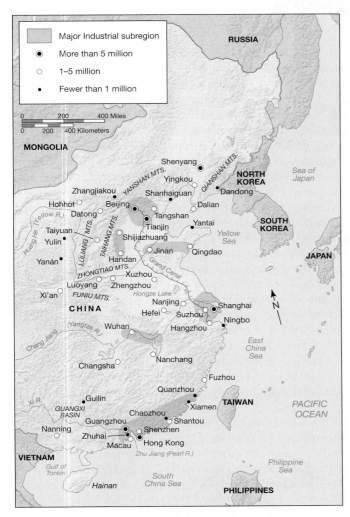

FIGURE 8.32 Inner China's industrial regions Inner China contains many cities of 1 million or more, together with all of China's principal industrial complexes.

(a)

(b)

FIGURE 8.33 Beijing (a) The Forbidden City. Now officially called the Palace Museum, the complex of the Forbidden City was the residence of two dynasties of emperors, the Ming and Qing, and during their reigns it was strictly off-limits to ordinary citizens. (b) A section of Beijing's Second Ring Road.

4. The industrial belt of the middle Chang Jiang, dominated by the steel, engineering and shipbuilding industries of Wuhan and served by the electricity generated by the giant Three Gorges Dam (see p. 418).

5. Shanghai and the Chang Jiang Delta region, an extensive industrial complex dominated by engineering, textiles, chemicals, and electronics (see Signature Region: Central China, p. 386).

6. The cities and Special Economic Zones of Guangdong province, in Southern China, that have become China's principal export-processing platform—largely for goods such as clothes, shoes, and toys—that has achieved double-digit annual economic growth for much of the past two decades. Exports from the province, funneled mostly through Hong Kong and Shenzhen, accounted for about 45 percent of China's total exports in 2005.

Major City: Beijing The popular image of Beijing is that of the Forbidden City (**Figure 8.33a**), the grounds of the Imperial Palace of the Ming and Qing dynasties. Modern Beijing, however, is almost entirely built in the image of Chinese socialism (**Figure 8.33b**). Mao Zedong's determination that Beijing would become a true "producing city" resulted in the extraordinary growth of heavy and manufacturing industries, with the result that the city has been transformed into one of China's key industrial centers. Ring roads and radiating highways provide the framework for a system of ten suburban industrial nodes, while new highways link the city to the international port of Tianjin and to Tangshan, a center of coal mining and heavy industry.

Meanwhile, Beijing's distinctive series of symmetrical walls-within-walls, which subdivided the imperial city into districts that were successively nearer to the centrally located Forbidden City, were torn down in the 1950s to make way for the ring roads. The Forbidden City itself was renamed as the Palace Museum, and a huge area in front of the Tiananmen entrance ("Gate of Heavenly Peace") to the palace was cleared to make the largest open square of any city in the world. Designed as a staging ground for vast spectacles, parades, and rallies organized by the government on national holidays, Tiananmen Square gained international notoriety in 1989 when army tanks and soldiers savagely repressed grassroots pro-democracy demonstrations, killing an unknown number of people (estimates range from 100 to 3000).

Today, Beijing is a vast metropolitan area with a large industrial base. As the capital of the country, it has a large white-collar service sector and has attracted a significant amount of foreign direct investment since Deng Xiaoping's "open door" policy was initiated in 1979. A concentration of universities and research institutes, in conjunction with a Special Economic Zone, has attracted the beginnings of a high-tech sector in the northwest of the city. Compared to most other Chinese cities, Beijing is remarkably affluent, with some excellent hotels and restaurants, good recreation facilities, and high levels of automobile ownership and consumer goods. Nevertheless, the city remains rather bleak and unattractive and suffers from serious levels of air and water pollution.

Major City: Shanghai Before the Communist revolution of 1949, Shanghai was one of the world's three largest manufacturing centers, the busiest international port in Asia. Standing on the Huangpu River near the mouth of the Chang Jiang, it was a city of extremes, with rich merchants, manufacturers, traders, and financiers and impoverished masses who worked in the city's sweatshops, factories, and docks. It was also a city of gangsters, get-rich-quick artists, drugs, and vice. Its growth had been the result of its role, organized by European merchants, as the principal entrepôt (transshipment port) for trade in opium, silk, and tea. The British were the first to develop Shanghai in this way, after the end of the Opium War in 1842. By 1847 the French had arrived, and by 1895 large sectors of the city had been parceled up into autonomous international settlements that were immune from Chinese law. The centerpiece of the city was the Bund, the riverfront development of monumental neoclassical buildings occupied by the major banks and trading houses.

By the time of the Communist revolution, Shanghai had a population of well over a million. Under Communist rule, however, very little was invested in the city, with the result that Shanghai developed a distinctly dour and shabby appearance: larger and more industrialized but with none of its former vibrancy. All of that changed dramatically in the 1990s, when the central government recognized the need for massive investments in the city's infrastructure. Favorable settings for investment were created through the establishment of a Shanghai Economic Zone and several Economic and Technical Development Zones. In addition, 350 square kilometers (137 square miles) of farmland and swampland to the east of the Huangpu River was turned into the Pudong industrial district (**Figure 8.34**), a massive, multibillion-dollar concentration of export-processing industries, commercial and financial office space, and scientific, research, and educational facilities.

Today, Shanghai is once more a very vibrant city. Once more, it is a city of extremes, with grinding poverty and vice alongside luxury apartment buildings and flashy luxury stores. Its phenomenal growth has not only reinforced its status as China's largest city but has propelled it to the role of a world city, a key node in the flows of capital, goods, and information that underpin the global economy.

Major City: Hong Kong In 1950 the prospects for Hong Kong looked bleak. Japanese occupation during World War II had prompted 1 million of its prewar population of 1.6 million to disperse, along with many of the trading companies that had been based there. The Communist revolution in China, the conflict in Korea, and Japan's derelict condition seemed to offer little prospect for the revival of a trading port. Yet today Hong Kong stands as a major world city, not only a thriving port city but a major manufacturing center and financial hub (**Figure 8.35**). Furthermore, it was able to grow into a metropolis of 6.1 million with few of the problems of inadequate infrastructure and illegal squatter housing that characterize the metropolises of the periphery.

One of the reasons for the transformation of Hong Kong was the arrival of refugee entrepreneurs from mainland China—and especially from Shanghai—as they fled the Communist takeover in 1949. With their expertise and their capital, together with Hong Kong's cheap labor, they established a thriving cotton textile industry, producing inexpensive jeans, t-shirts, and leisure wear for the expanding markets in the United States and western Europe. The British governors of Hong Kong assisted this economic revival by keeping taxes and regulations to a minimum and by investing in the infrastructure of roads and port facilities. Meanwhile, in a rather unusual mixture of socialism with free enterprise, the government undertook a massive program of housing development. Squatter housing and slums were cleared, and hundreds of high-rise apartment blocks were built for the city's growing population, many of them with highly subsidized rents. Following the initial success of the housing program in the city itself, the government followed another British town-planning initiative, setting up several New Towns in the New Territories to the north of the city.

The revitalized Hong Kong proved attractive to investors, and the city's entrepreneurs moved from producing cheap apparel to subcontracting for designer wear and producing cheap electronics. As the Asian region began to prosper and markets expanded, Hong Kong became a major center for finance, banking, and tourism. In the mid-1990s, there was some nervousness about the fate of the city on its return to China with the expiration of the 99-year lease to the British. Yet it did not stop the development of a major new airport or significantly stem the pace of development.

FIGURE 8.34 Shanghai The Pudong district, shown here, reflects the government's success in reestablishing Shanghai as a major international center.

FIGURE 8.35 Hong Kong Returned to China by the British at the expiration of their lease in 1997, Hong Kong remains a vibrant world city of critical importance to the economic development of South China.

China saw the wisdom of maintaining Hong Kong's position as a capitalist dynamo and agreed to create a Special Administrative Region for Hong Kong. This arrangement preserves Hong Kong's legal system, guarantees the rights of property ownership, gives residents the right to travel, permits Hong Kong to continue independent membership in international organizations, and guarantees the democratic rights of assembly, free speech, and academic research, the right to strike, and so on. The result is that Hong Kong continues to prosper, even after the 1998 financial crisis that affected most of East and Southeast Asia (and which sharply reduced the number of tourists from Japan and South Korea). Thousands of companies are located in Hong Kong for the purpose of doing business with China. Although most of its manufacturing has been transferred to neighboring Guangdong Province, where wages are much lower, Hong Kong remains the world's largest container port, the third-largest center for foreign exchange trade, the seventh-largest stock market, and the tenth-largest trading economy. Considering its size and its history, these are extraordinary achievements.

China's Regional Problems   The euphoria engendered by the recent economic transformation of Inner China should be tempered somewhat by recognizing that it has intensified the problem of regional inequality. The visible polarization of wealth, which was virtually eradicated in the first 30 years of Communist rule, has returned to China with the return of capitalism. Development along the south and east coasts is creating a significant disparity in growth and incomes between coastal and interior regions. This disparity will grow greater as the advantaged regions build up their external links. The central government may well have to intervene to prevent spatial polarization from generating internal political conflict.

The nine interior provinces and the autonomous regions have remained, for the most part, appallingly poor, the average income of their population of 285 million people having already fallen to less than 65 percent of the national average. Of the more than $300 billion in foreign investment that China attracted in the 1990s, only $9.9 billion went to these regions. Meanwhile, within coastal China the emergence of a crassly ostentatious wealthy class has begun to breed the kind of social and political problems that the Communists fought a revolution to eliminate. Street crime has become a serious problem, white-collar crime and corruption are on the rise, and social tensions are increasingly in evidence.

A second regional problem is the poor condition of the transportation infrastructure. The transportation system in the interior is poorly developed and the railways, in particular, need modernization and expansion (China has one of the world's smallest railway networks relative to population and arable land). The basic infrastructures for energy and water supplies are also woefully deficient throughout the interior regions. The central government has recognized these problems and has announced plans for a "Second Opening" of China, with 4000 kilometers (2485 miles) of new railway lines and 32,000 kilometers (19,885 miles) of new highways by 2010, including a new Sichuan-to-Guangxi expressway.

A massive public works program aimed at hydroelectric facilities, irrigation and drainage, and improved waterways has been the cornerstone of the central government's approach to the economic development of the interior. The Three Gorges Dam on the Chang Jiang (**Figure 8.36**) has become emblematic of this strategy and of China's ambitious determination to modernize. It has also, unfortunately, become emblematic of the problems of graft, corruption, and disregard for the social and environmental consequences of large-scale infrastructure development. The dam itself will span 2 kilometers (1.25 miles) from bank to bank. The reservoir will extend 650 kilometers (404 miles) upstream, submerging 19 cities, 150 towns, and 4500 villages and hamlets. On completion, 26 giant generators will provide for almost 10 percent of China's energy output, bringing electricity to mil-

FIGURE 8.36 Three Gorges Dam Construction of the Three Gorges Dam, scheduled for completion in 2009, is one of the world's largest-ever engineering projects. The dam is being built in central China at a spot where the Chang Jiang narrows to form the Xiling, Wu, and Qutang gorges.

lions of rural households and opening central China to a much broader range of industries. The increased water level in the enormous reservoir will improve river navigation and should help flood control along the Chang Jiang. One significant potential problem is that the dam sits on an active fault line. The weight of the water in the reservoir could trigger an earthquake, with devastating consequences. Critics also predict that the dam will threaten the region's ecosystem. The river blockage will endanger several species indigenous to the region, including the Chinese alligator, the white crane, and the Chinese sturgeon. Meanwhile conservationists have no hope of recovering more than a fraction of the historical artifacts and relics that will become permanently submerged.

Gender and Inequality   Just as economic reform in China has been accompanied by the reemergence of regional inequality, economic and social reforms have also led to changes in the status of women. Until Deng Xiaoping's reforms of the 1990s, gender equality was a central tenet of government policy. One of Mao Zedong's much-quoted slogans was that "Women hold up half the sky." During the Cultural Revolution, society was strictly gender-neutral, images of female beauty and ideas of romance were suppressed, and the participation of women in political and economic activities reached almost 100 percent.

The effects of economic and social reform were mixed. Competitive markets in education resulted in a fourfold expansion of women college students in the 1990s, and these better-educated women have gone on to make their mark in China's labor markets, earning high salaries and challenging traditional gender boundaries for top jobs. Between 1991 and 2001 the number of marriages in rural areas arranged by parents—a tradition that largely escaped the attention of the Cultural Revolution—fell from 36 percent to 16 percent. At the same time, there has been an explosion of femininity and sexuality in the media, not always with positive results for women. Traditional gender stereotypes have resurfaced, with women associated with domestic responsibilities and unskilled work. This has played out in labor markets as older and less well-educated women have borne the brunt of layoffs in the state sector and have been left with lower-paid occupations. As a result, there is a widening income gap between men and women. Urban women who made, on average, 70 percent of men's wages in 1990 made less than 63 percent of men's wages in 2005. Gender inequality is most marked in rural settings, where women's wages, on average, are only 40 percent of men's and where gender roles have regressed farthest toward traditional stereotypes.

South Korea   Like Taiwan, South Korea has become one of the newly industrialized "Asian Tigers" through a combination of an authoritarian regime that orchestrated economic development through land reform, protection of domestic industry, and creation of state enterprises; massive inputs of foreign aid (again because of the country's geopolitical importance); and the presence of a disciplined and well-educated but low-wage workforce. And like Taiwan, South Korea has moved through successive stages toward an increasingly balanced and liberalized economy. The initial emphasis was on import substitution, developing domestic industries, with government protection, to produce goods for the domestic market. The second stage, between the mid-1960s and mid-1970s, saw the growth of export-oriented, labor-intensive manufacturing. The South Korean government facilitated the development of these export industries by providing incentives, loans, and tax breaks to firms, and by encouraging the growth of giant, interlocking industrial conglomerates called **chaebol**. The success of this strategy was reflected in annual growth rates in the overall economy of more than 10 percent.

In the late 1970s, South Korean economic planners decided to diversify the economy with greater emphasis on heavy industry, chemicals, automobile assembly, and shipbuilding. To do this, the government worked with the *chaebol*, which were best placed not only to maximize internal and external economies of scale but also to acquire new technology from transnational partners. By the mid-1980s, about a dozen *chaebol* had come to dominate the economy, employing the majority of the workforce, controlling the banking system, and dominating government economic policy. Manufactured goods accounted for 91 percent of total exports, and more than half were in the form of ships, steel, and automobiles.

FIGURE 8.37 Seoul South Korea's capital city has more than doubled in size since the early 1970s and now has a population in excess of 12 million.

During the late 1980s and 1990s, the economy diversified still further, with the manufacture of semiconductors and electronics and the emergence of telecommunications and information processing. Giant South Korean conglomerates like Samsung and Hyundai became household names around the world, and the economy once again grew at more than 10 percent each year. South Korea was hit particularly hard, however, by the Asian financial crisis of 1998: The preceding boom had led South Korean banks to make loans to their parent companies for investments throughout Asia and, when the bubble burst, many of the investments had to be written off. South Korea's economy had to be propped up with loans and guarantees from the International Monetary Fund, which in turn has required the liberalization of the economy, including curbs on the power and influence of the *chaebol*.

In spite of the shock of the 1998 crisis, South Korea remains a core region within East Asia. With a total export trade of $288.2 billion in 2005, South Korea is the world's 12th-largest exporter. In terms of its overall economy, South Korea had a GDP (in PPP "international" dollars) of just under $986 billion, ranking 14th in the world. Seoul (**Figure 8.37**) has become one of the world's largest metropolitan areas (with a population of 9.89 million in 2005) and is a fast-paced city with a broad economic base. Other important centers are Pusan (population 3.83 million in 2005), an international port and major industrial center specializing in automobile production, electronics, chemicals, iron and steel, and shipbuilding; Inch'on (3.1 million), an entrepôt for Seoul and a center of electronics and iron and steel manufacture; Taegu (2.68 million), a textile manufacturing center; and Kwangju (1.38 million) and Taejon (1.6 million).

As in Taiwan, the pace of South Korean economic growth and urbanization has brought heavy pollution, acute housing shortages, and rampant corruption. Socioeconomic inequality is also a characteristic feature of South Korea, both within the cities and between the country's subregions. The government has attempted to improve equality among the subregions through spatial-planning policies that have directed industrial growth away from Seoul toward provincial towns and cities. Currently, the major priorities of domestic policy are keeping up with the need for basic infrastructure improvements to maintain economic efficiency, and keeping up with educational spending in order to be able to further develop a high-tech sector. Government spending on social and environmental issues remains minimal, however, so that there is little immediate prospect of a reduction in social inequalities or of improvements in the quality of life for the many millions who live in cramped housing and degraded environments.

SUMMARY AND CONCLUSIONS

East Asia is the most populous of all world regions, containing 1.55 billion people. Though dominated in territorial, demographic, and geopolitical terms by China, it is Japan—the world's second most powerful single economy and one of the established nodes of the triadic world-system—that is the key economic component of the region. In addition, Hong Kong, South Korea, and Taiwan in East Asia have developed as three of the Asian Tigers that have progressed from the periphery of the world-system to the semiperiphery.

The geopolitics of the Cold War, coupled with significant flows of investment by transnational corporations, helped both Taiwan and South Korea become prosperous core regions within East Asia. Together with Japan, they have come to occupy specialized roles within the world economy and are highly interdependent with places and regions throughout the Pacific Rim and in Europe.

All of the core regions and key cities of East Asia are situated along the continental margin, where the bulk of the population lives. Within this continental margin are the most productive agricultural regions and the most prosperous cities. In Japan, the Pacific Corridor was developed as the geographic basis of the country's postwar "economic miracle." In China, which has made a significant impact on the world economy since the death of Mao Zedong and the adoption of an "open door" policy, the transition toward market economies has intensified the comparative advantages of its coastal regions, where economic and cultural globalization are swiftly becoming both cause and effect of striking changes in long-established patterns of production, trade, and culture.

Nevertheless, East Asia remains a region of tremendous contrasts. Traditional rural communities with a great variety of distinctive ways of life still characterize much of the region, while Outer China is a dramatic "outback" region with extensive uninhabited areas and spectacular scenery encompassing snow-clad mountains, vast swamps, endless steppes, and fierce deserts. In contrast, most of the rest of East Asia has been heavily modified by humankind. East Asia has been cleared of its forest cover, while marshes have been drained, irrigation systems constructed, lakes converted to reservoirs, levees raised to guard against river floods, and hills and mountainsides sculpted into elaborate terraces in order to provide more cultivable land. These changes reflect the imprint of some of the world's most sophisticated civilizations and most extensive empires.

Today, East Asia is one of the most dynamic and most rapidly urbanizing of all world regions, but it still encompasses a rich mosaic of traditional landscapes and ways of life. As China—and perhaps even North Korea and Mongolia—become increasingly incorporated into the dynamics of global economic and cultural change, the pace of environmental, social, and political change is likely to increase, obliterating some elements of these long-standing local geographies while adding new elements and creating new regional patterns.

KEY TERMS

agglomeration (p. 410)
Asian Tigers (p. 396)
backwash effects (p. 412)
chaebol (p. 419)

counterurbanization (p. 402)
feng shui (p. 405)
geomancy (p. 405)
keiretsu (p. 393)

massif (p. 378)
Pacific Rim (p. 396)
pinyin (p. 405)
Ring of Fire (p. 379)

treaty port (p. 390)
zaibatsu (p. 390)

REVIEW QUESTIONS

Testing Your Understanding

1. When and why was the Great Wall of China built? Why were canal systems so important to Imperial China?
2. How did the Tokugawa dynasty keep foreign influences out of Imperial Japan? How did Japan change following the Meiji revolution of 1868?
3. What factors helped Japan industrialize rapidly before World War II? What factors helped Japan reconstruct and grow after the war?
4. After the fall of the last dynasty in 1911, which two groups fought for power in China? Who embarked on the Long March of 1934–35 and why was it a success by 1949?

5. What triggered the Korean War? What is the significance of the 38th Parallel? Who is Kim Jong Il?
6. In China, what were the results of the 1958 Great Leap Forward, the 1966 Cultural Revolution, and the 1979 "open door" policy?
7. In 1970, how many children were born to the average Chinese family? By 2005, what was the average number of children per family? Who helps enforce China's one-child policy? Aside from lower birthrates, what are two main results of the one-child policy?
8. During the 1800s, why did so many people emigrate from East Asia? Where did they migrate to?

9. How do Confucianism and Shinto differ from each other, and how have they influenced the cultural geography of East Asia? What is animism?

10. How has China increased farm production as well as peasant incomes since 1980? Where and what are Special Economic Zones?

11. Why is clothing made in China produced more profitably than in Hong Kong or Canada?

12. How do transportation routes help structure the city of Tokyo? How are Japanese suburbs different from American suburbs?

13. Compare Taiwan to South Korea with regard to their post-World War II economic development. What are *chaebol*?

Thinking Geographically

1. What are the three main physiographic provinces of East Asia? How do the Tien Shan and Himalaya mountains affect East Asia physically and culturally? How has human activity modified the landscape in East Asia?

2. Briefly discuss the territorial expansion of Imperial Japan from 1890 to 1945. What motivated Japan's acquisition of new territory? Having lost all of its colonial possessions in 1945, how did Japan achieve its postwar economic miracle?

3. Describe the factors that have led to urbanization and counterurbanization in East Asia during the 20th century.

4. What are some dominant East Asian cultural traditions? How is geomancy (*feng shui*) used in everyday life? How have East Asian beliefs and traditions affected other world regions?

5. State-assisted capitalism occurs frequently in East Asia. Please explain how the central government involves itself in corporate activities in China, Japan, and South Korea.

6. How are private investors in Hong Kong, Taiwan, and elsewhere changing the geography of China, especially in the Special Economic Zones? How has the People's Republic of China's attempt to create a classless society been affected by capitalist investment in China?

7. Beijing, like other cities modified or created during periods of state socialism, has been described as "a city primarily designed to express the government's power and control." Compare Beijing to Moscow and to Tokyo. How is Beijing changing in response to foreign investment?

8. Shanghai exemplifies the dichotomy of modern China. Freed from strict economic control by becoming a Special Economic Zone, Shanghai is now more disorderly and less equitable than it once was, but is also more productive and generates greater revenue. Compare Shanghai to Hong Kong—what factors make it possible for a city to have both strong social control and strong economic growth?

9. What physical and cultural factors make western China distinctive?

FURTHER READING

Armstrong, C., *The Koreas*. London: Routledge, 2006.

Barnes, I., and Hudson, R., *The History Atlas of China*. New York: Macmillan, 1999.

Benewick, R., and Donald, S., *The State of China Atlas*. London: Penguin Reference, 1999.

Blunden, C., and Elvin, M., *Cultural Atlas of China*. New York: Checkmark Books, 1999.

Cannon, T. (ed.), *China's Economic Growth: The Impact on Regions, Migration, and the Environment*. New York: St. Martin's Press, 2000.

Cartier, C., *Globalizing South China*. Cambridge, MA: Blackwell, 2001.

Chai, J., Jackson, S., and White, H., *Economic History of Modern China*. New York: Routledge, 2000.

Donald, S. H., and Benewick, R., *The State of China Atlas: Mapping the World's Fastest Growing Economy*. Berkeley, CA: University of California Press, 2005.

Guthrie, D., *China and Globalization*. London: Routledge, 2006.

Institute of Geography, Chinese Academy of Sciences, *The Atlas of Population, Environment, and Sustainable Development in China*. Beijing: Science Press, 2000.

Karan, P., *Japan in the 21st Century*. Lexington, KY: University Press of Kentucky, 2005.

Li, S-M., and Tang, W-S. (eds.), *China's Regions, Polity, and Economy*. Hong Kong: Chinese University Press, 2000.

Link, P., Madsen, R. P., and Pickowicz, P. G. (eds.), *Popular China. Unofficial Culture in a Globalizing Society*. Lanham, MD: Rowman and Littlefield, 2001.

Logan, J. R. (ed.), *The New Chinese City: Globalization and Market Reform*. Malden, MA: Blackwell, 2002.

Ma, L. J. C., and Cartier, C. (eds.), *The Chinese Diaspora: Space, Place, Mobility, and Identity*. Lanham, MD: Rowman and Littlefield, 2003.

Mather, C., Karan, P. P., and Iijima, S., *Japanese Landscapes*. Lexington, KY: University Press of Kentucky, 1999.

McDonogh, G., and Wong, C., *Global Hong Kong*. London: Routledge, 2005.

McGrew, A., and Brook, C. (eds.), *Asia-Pacific in the New World Order*. New York: Routledge, 1999.

Olds, K., Dicken, P., Kelly, P., Kong, L., and Yeung, H., *Globalisation and the Asia Pacific*. New York: Routledge, 1999.

Pyle, D. J., *China's Economy: From Revolution to Reform*. New York: St. Martin's Press, 1997.

Smil, V., *China's Environmental Crisis: An Inquiry into the Limits of National Development*. New York: M. E. Sharpe, 1997.

Smith, C. J., *China in the Post-Utopian Age*. Boulder: Westview Press, 2000.

Weightman, B. A., *Dragons and Tigers: A Geography of South, East, and Southeast Asia*. New York: John Wiley & Sons, 2002.

Zweig, D., *Internationalizing China: Domestic Interests and Global Linkages*. Ithaca: Cornell University Press, 2002.

FILM, MUSIC, AND POPULAR LITERATURE

Film

The Blue Kite. Directed by Tian Zhuangzhuang, 1993. The story of China's political upheavals is told from the point of view of a simple family trying desperately to survive.

China: Unleashing the Dragon. PBS Home Video Series, 1995. Documentary examines the social impact of China's experiment with a market economy.

Chungking Express. Directed by Kar-wei Wong, 1994. An acclaimed example of the Hong Kong movie industry.

Farewell My Concubine. Directed by Chen Kaige, 1993. The story of two men who met as apprentices in the Peking Opera and stayed friends for more than 50 years.

Great Wall Across the Yangtze. PBS Home Video Series, 1999. Documentary about the controversial Three Gorges Dam on China's Yangtze River.

Kokoro: The Heart Within. PBS Home Video series, 1999. A ten-part presentation of the land and people of Japan.

Not One Less. Directed by Yimou Zhang, 1999. Set in the remote, dry high plains of Hebei, China, the film depicts rural life in telling detail as it deals with the story of a young teacher in a village school.

Robert Thurman on Tibet. PBS Home Video series, 1999. Documentary reviews the history and culture of Tibet from ancient times to the present.

The Silk Road. PBS Home Video series, 1992. Eighteen-part documentary series on the Silk Road across China and Central Asia.

The Story of Qiu Ju. Directed by Yimou Zhang, 1992. Gong Li, China's top actress, plays a naive, young married woman from a remote farming village who has to make repeated trips to the city to seek justice over a domestic dispute.

Music

Dadawa. *Sister Drum*. Wea/Elektra Entertainment, 1996.

Kodo. *Ibuki*. Tristar Music, 1997.

Shanghai Chinese Traditional Orchestra. *Chi Gong*. Wind Records, 1997.

Tomoko Sunazaki. *Tegoto*. Fortuna Records, 1989.

Various Artists. *The Silk Road: A Musical Caravan*. Smithsonian Folkways, 2002.

Xiao-Lin, Yang. *I Take You There*. Kiigo, 2000.

Yo-Yo Ma and the Silk Road Ensemble. *Silk Road Journeys*. Sony, 2002.

Yuan, Lily. *Ancient Art Music of China*. Lyrichord, 1991.

Popular Literature

Buck, P. *The Good Earth*. New York: Washington Square Press, 1999. A fictional account of life in 19th-century China.

Dutton, M. (ed.). *Streetlife China*. Cambridge: Cambridge University Press, 2000. A collection of pieces about life in contemporary China, focusing on the lives of ordinary people and the rules and rituals that govern their daily existence, including the impact of the emergence of a consumer culture driven by market values.

Gao, M. C. F. *Gao Village: A Portrait of Rural Life in Modern China*. Honolulu: University of Hawaii Press, 1999. A good account of everyday life in a small Chinese village.

Guest, H. (ed.). *Travellers' Literary Companion—Japan*. Summary of literary works from and about Japan.

Hessler, P. *River Town. Two Years on the Yangtze*. New York: HarperCollins, 2001. An account of life in Fuling, in China's Sichuan province, by a Peace Corps teacher who was the first foreigner to stay in the region for 50 years.

Hopkirk, P. *Foreign Devils on the Silk Road: The Search for the Lost Cities and Treasures of Chinese Central Asia*. Amherst: University of Massachusetts Press, 1984. Fascinating insights into the history of the ancient Silk Road as well as its later intersection with the "Great Game"—European imperial powers' jockeying for influence in Central Asia.

Kristof, N., and Wudunn, S. *China Wakes*. New York: Vintage Books, 1995. An account of contemporary politics and society in China.

Kuhn, L. *Made in China: Voices from the New Revolution*. Boston: PBS Books, 2000. Explores how the Chinese are adapting to their new hybrid system of personal and economic freedoms combined with rigid political controls.

Lever-Tracy, C., and Ip, D. *The Chinese Diaspora and Mainland China*. London: Macmillan, 1996. Describes the emerging economic ties between China and the Chinese diaspora.

Ma, J. *Red Dust: A Path Through China*. London: Chatto & Windus, 2001. The account of dissident Ma Jian's travels through the hinterland of China.

Seagrave, S. *Lords of the Rim*. New York: Putnam, 1995. A fascinating insight into the world of the so-called "Overseas Chinese."

Seth, V. *From Heaven Lake: Travels Through Sinkiang and Tibet*. New York: Vintage Books, 1987. An award-winning account of a hitchhiking trip from China into Tibet.

Weston, T. B., and Jensen, L. M. (eds.). *China Beyond the Headlines*. New York: Rowman and Littlefield, 2000. A series of essays that seek to dispel stereotypes about China by describing China's society, economy, and culture under the stresses of modernization.

Wong, J. *Red China Blues: My Long March from Mao to Now*. New York: Anchor, 1997. The detailed recollections of the journeys of an observant and engaged traveler over several extended visits to China.

Yatsko, P. *New Shanghai. The Rocky Rebirth of China's Legendary City*. New York: John Wiley & Sons, 2001. A journalist's personal view of the turbulent change in contemporary Shanghai.

Southeast Asia

FIGURE 9.1

Tropic of Cancer

20°N

Capital cities are underlined

- ● More than 1 million
- ○ 500,000–1 million
- • Fewer than 500,000

| 0 | 200 | 400 Miles |
| 0 | 200 | 400 Kilometers |

10°N

PACIFIC OCEAN

Ternate

Halmahera

Equator 0°

Sorong

Jayapura

Moluccas

Ceram

Ambon

Irian Jaya

PAPUA NEW
GUINEA

Arafura Sea

Merauke

10°S

AUSTRALIA

140°E 150°E

The continent of Asia is often divided into three large regions: East Asia, South Asia, and Southeast Asia. East Asia (Chapter 8) is dominated demographically and geographically by China, and South Asia (Chapter 10) is dominated by India. Southeast Asia, the subject of this chapter, consists of a group of islands and peninsulas that lie between India and China (**Figure 9.1**). Although the region is strongly influenced by those two countries, it has its own distinctive cultures and landscapes. The long coasts of Southeast Asia's peninsulas and islands, and the narrow marine channels between them, have made Southeast Asia a crossroads for international maritime trade, first with India, the Middle East, and China, and later with Europe, Asia, and the Americas. The entire region has a tropical monsoon environment with warm temperatures and seasonal high rainfall, and the predominant land uses include irrigated rice cultivation in the lowlands and shifting agriculture in the highlands, as well as village gardens and plantation estate agriculture.

Southeast Asia is frequently divided into two main physical regions of approximately equal size: the mainland or peninsula region, which includes Burma, Cambodia, Laos, Thailand, and Vietnam, and the island or insular region, which includes Brunei, East Timor, Indonesia, the Philippines, and Singapore. Malaysia includes a mainland peninsula and the northern region of the island of Borneo and is usually considered within insular Southeast Asia (**Figure 9.2**).

Mainland or peninsular Southeast Asia stretches from Burma, bordering Bangladesh along the Bay of Bengal, to the long peninsula of Malaysia through Thailand and Cambodia to Vietnam and a border with China on the South China Sea. Landlocked Laos lies inland surrounded by Thailand, Burma, China, Vietnam, and Cambodia. Prior to World War II, Vietnam, Laos, and Cambodia were called French Indochina because of their location between India and China and their shared history of French colonization.

Island or insular Southeast Asia includes the island of Borneo, shared by the small nation of Brunei, Malaysia, and the Indonesian province of Kalimantan. It encompasses the arc of Indonesian islands from Sumatra in the west to Irian Jaya in the east and the new nation of East Timor (or Timor L'Este), the island of Singapore, and the Philippine islands, which face Vietnam on the east side of the South China Sea.

The region covers an area of 4 million square kilometers (1.5 million square miles), about the size of Europe but consisting mainly of ocean, with a 2005 population of about 557 million people. Indonesia dominates the region in both size and population, ranking as the fourth most populous nation in the world. The **Association of Southeast Asian Nations (ASEAN)** now links all of the countries (except East Timor) in a regional security and economic alliance.

There is tremendous economic, ethnic, linguistic, and environmental diversity among and within the countries of Southeast Asia. Only Thailand avoided the direct European colonial control that dominated the economies of the region from about 1500 to 1946. Colonialism in Southeast Asia built on existing networks of trade and on the labor and business expertise both of residents and of migrants from India and China. Because of the region's considerable geopolitical importance, Japanese forces invaded it during World War II, and U.S., British, and other Allied forces retook the region after a protracted war on land, air, and sea. At the end of

FIGURE 9.2 Southeast Asia from space This image clearly shows the many islands and major peninsulas that make up Southeast Asia.

World War II, the newly independent countries of the region faced Cold War tensions in the form of communist rebellions and various alliances with China, the Soviet Union, and the United States. The Vietnam War brought first France and then the United States into a regional conflict with the Chinese- and Soviet-supported forces of North Vietnam, a conflict that was based in South Vietnam and spilled over into Laos and Cambodia. Until relatively recently, communist and socialist governments of Vietnam, Laos, Cambodia, and Burma remained isolated within the region and from much of the Western world, with their economies focused on agriculture.

The socialist and communist experiences of Vietnam, Laos, Cambodia, and Burma contrast with the experience of countries such as Singapore, Thailand, Malaysia, Indonesia, and the Philippines, whose governments chose to open their economies to world capitalism in the latter half of the 20th century. In these countries, existing trade in traditional export commodities—such as rubber, rice, timber, and tin—expanded with the help of foreign investment to include textiles, clothing, and manufactured goods as well as new high-technology products for the telecommunications and computer industries. Agricultural intensification through new seeds and chemicals, as well as a growth in tourism, also contributed to economic prosperity, although the benefits of growth were not distributed equally.

Policies in both the socialist and capitalist economies of Southeast Asia were promoted through heavy state intervention in the economy and everyday life and included government subsidies, state-owned industry, and regulation of trade. Japan has become the major foreign investor in the region, and investment also flows within Southeast Asia from countries such as Singapore and Malaysia.

Those in favor of rapid globalization saw the economic and industrial boom as a success story. Critics of globalization highlighted the exploitation of cheap labor in factories and sex workers in tourism, the grave environmental problems that accompanied development, and the serious social and political impact of the financial crisis in 1997, which brought sudden recession to the region.

Standard measures of economic development, such as per capita GDP, rank oil-rich Brunei and the international port and business center of Singapore among the most developed nations. East Timor, Vietnam, Laos, Cambodia, and Burma are among the world's poorer nations on recent economic rankings, with Thailand, Malaysia, Indonesia, and the Philippines in the middle range of economies.

As in other regions, independence and subsequent changes in government have brought several changes in names of countries, territories, and key locations in Southeast Asia. Burma is called Myanmar by the current government, but we use the traditional name of Burma, which is proposed by the United Nations and the country's pro-democracy movement and used by many of the country's residents. From 1976 to 1989, Cambodia was called Kampuchea. North and South Vietnam were unified as Vietnam in 1976. The full name of Brunei is Brunei Darussalam; many islands and places in Indonesia are also known by their Indonesian names and spellings. The large island of New Guinea is split between the independent nation of Papua New Guinea to the east and the Indonesian province of Irian Jaya to the west. Some texts treat the whole island, with its tropical climate, lofty mountains, and diverse and scattered ethnic groups, as part of the Pacific island or Oceania region, but we include Irian Jaya in Southeast Asia. The newest nation in Southeast Asia is the island of East Timor.

ENVIRONMENT AND SOCIETY IN SOUTHEAST ASIA

Landforms and Landscapes

The physical geography of Southeast Asia is shaped by processes of plate tectonics that have influenced the configuration of land and oceans, highlands and lowlands, geological hazards and resources, and the development of ecosystems. The mainland of Southeast Asia and the island of Borneo occupy the Sunda shelf of the Eurasian tectonic plate. The Sunda shelf is now flooded by the shallow South China Sea between Borneo and the mainland, but it was exposed during the ice ages, forming a **land bridge** to Asia. The Indonesian island arc from Sumatra to East Timor lies along the edge of the Eurasian plate. To the south and east, the Australian, Pacific, and Philippine plates are moving toward, and colliding with, the Eurasian plate and are being forced downward in deep-sea

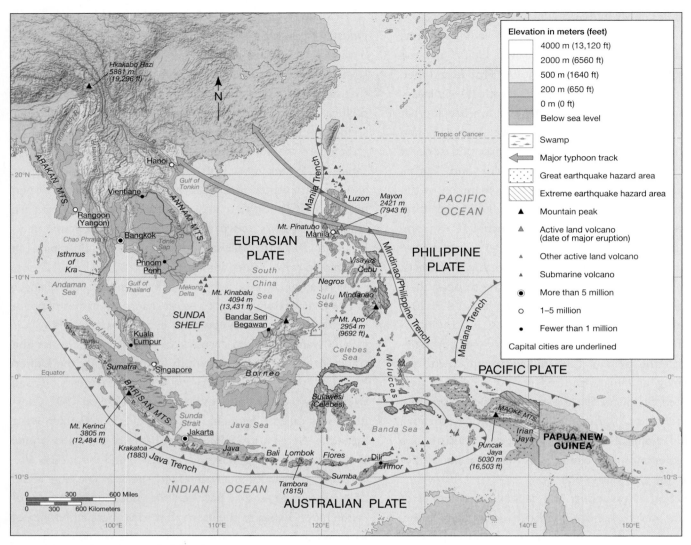

FIGURE 9.3 Southeast Asia's physiographic regions Southeast Asia, one of the most geologically active regions of the world, experiences many earthquakes and volcanoes because it lies at the intersection of active tectonic plates. The region is very mountainous except for the major valleys of the Irrawaddy, Chao Phraya, Red, and Mekong rivers and some coastal plains. (*Source:* Map is based on information from T. R. Leinbach and R. Ulack, *Southeast Asia: Diversity and Development.* Upper Saddle River, NJ: Prentice Hall, 2000, Map 2.1; and H. C. Brookfield and Y. Byron, *South-East Asia's Environmental Future: The Search for Sustainability.* New York: United Nations University Press, 1993, Figure 13.1.)

trenches along major subduction zones. The Mariana deep-sea trench, between the Pacific and Philippine plates in the Pacific Ocean southeast of the Mariana Islands, is the deepest in the world at 11,034 meters (36,201 feet). The collision zones are also associated with mountain building and volcanic activity and have created the thousands of islands that form the Indonesian and Philippine archipelagoes (**Figure 9.3**). The catastrophic potential of undersea tectonic activity was seen when in December 2004 an undersea earthquake off the island of Sumatra triggered **tsunamis** (large waves) that killed more than 230,000 people in South and Southeast Asia (see Geography Matters: The 2004 Indian Ocean Tsunami, p. 430).

The relatively young islands of the region have high mountains, steep slopes, and generally narrow coastal plains. Irian Jaya on the island of New Guinea has mountains reaching 5300 meters (16,000 feet); temperatures are so cold at these high elevations that these mountains are capped by permanent glaciers even at this tropical latitude. More than a dozen other mountains and volcanoes in insular Southeast Asia reach 3300 meters (10,000 feet). Many countries of Southeast Asia have very fragmented, elongated, or rugged geographies that have created immense challenges to national integration, transportation, and economic development. Indonesia has more than 13,600 islands (only half of them inhabited), and the Philippines is made up of more than 7000 islands. Burma, Thailand, and Vietnam all include long narrow segments less than 160 kilometers (100 miles) wide.

The economies and lifestyles of insular Southeast Asia have been oriented to the sea through ocean fishing and maritime trade for centuries (**Figure 9.4a**), and it has often been easier to use ocean or river transport rather than difficult overland routes.

(a)

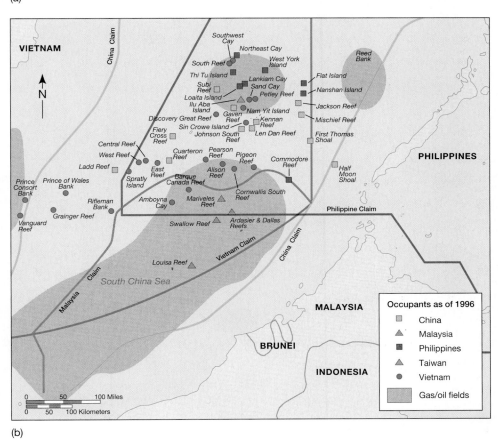

(b)

FIGURE 9.4 Physical landscapes of Southeast Asia (a) The many islands and long coastlines in much of Southeast Asia orient human activity toward the sea. These boats (called *junks*) in Halong Bay, Vietnam, are used for transport and fishing, for both subsistence and commercial sales. (b) This map shows the multitude of contradictory claims on the Spratly Islands in the South China Sea. (*Source:* [b] Redrawn from M. J. Valencia, J. M. Van Dyke, and N. A. Ludwig, *Sharing the Resources of the South China Sea.* Honolulu: University of Hawaii Press, 1999, Plate 1.)

But the complexity of coastlines and the many islands of some nations, together with the economic significance of ocean fishery and oil resources, have created conflicts over maritime territorial jurisdictions and boundaries.

The most disputed territories in Southeast Asia are the Spratly Islands, which lie between Vietnam and the Philippines in the South China Sea. The islands consist of several hundred treeless, sun-baked coral reef outcrops, many of them less than 1 square kilometer (less than half a square mile) in size. Brunei, China, Malaysia, the Philippines, Taiwan, and Vietnam each claim one or more of the Spratly Islands, and all except Brunei have established military posts on one or more of the islands (**Figure 9.4b**). China has invaded the seven islands claimed by Vietnam and also threatened those claimed by the Philippines.

The 2004 Indian Ocean Tsunami

On December 26, 2004, a massive earthquake registering 9.3 on the Richter scale ruptured the seabed off the western coast of Indonesia near Aceh along a line reaching northwesterly toward the Andaman Islands. The deep ocean seabed rose, displacing more than 30 cubic kilometers (7 cubic miles) of water and driving tidal waves across the Indian Ocean. As these tsunami waves moved into shallow water, they formed large destructive waves as high as 24 meters (80 feet) when they hit the shoreline. The coast of Sumatra was hit by waves within 15 minutes, but more distant regions such as Sri Lanka were affected up to two hours later (**Figure 1**).

FIGURE 1 Map of the 2004 tsunami (*Source:* UN World Food Program. Available at **http://www.ksg.harvard.edu/alum/images/ events/tsunami/tsunami_map.pdf.**)

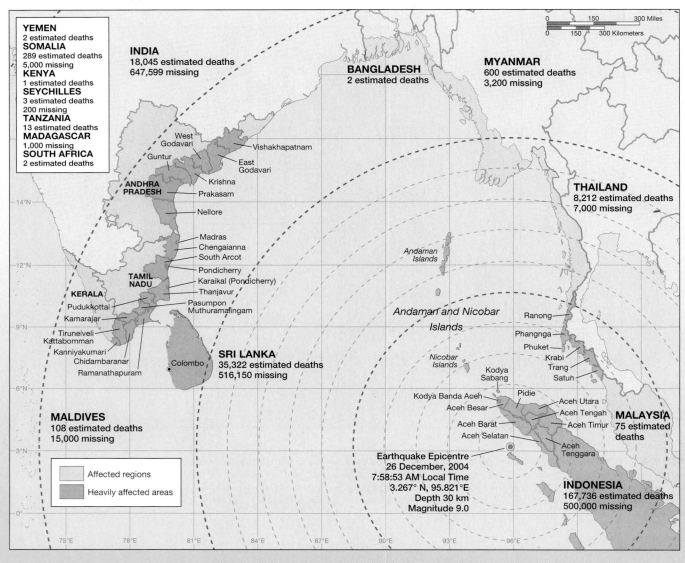

The Spratly dispute is an example of international conflicts over marine resources that usually center on rights for oil or fisheries. A 1958 United Nations conference began the process of allocating the oceans and their resources among countries, trying for years to reach agreement. The 1982 Convention on the Law of the Sea was signed by 117 nations but was not signed by several world powers, including the United States and Japan. However, most countries have agreed to a territorial limit of sovereignty that extends 19.3 kilometers (12 miles) from the coast and to an exclusive economic zone that

Despite the time lags between the earthquake and the waves hitting the coastline, almost all regions were taken by surprise by the enormous waves that surged inland along low-lying coasts around the Indian Ocean. There was no tsunami warning system in the Indian Ocean, in contrast to the Pacific System based in Hawaii, which uses seismic and oceanographic data, including tide gauges to issue warnings to at-risk areas.

Thousands of people in coastal communities were swept away and their houses and livelihoods destroyed in the deadliest tsunami in recorded history (**Figure 2**). The death toll included 167,000 in Indonesia, 35,000 in Sri Lanka, 18,000 in India and 8000 in Thailand, including more than 9000 tourists, mainly from northern Europe, who were enjoying a Christmas vacation. Many of the dead were children, who were more easily overtaken by the flood waters, and women who were waiting for returning fishermen and looking after children in their houses.

The impact on infrastructure and livelihoods was devastating, especially for the already poor fishing communities who lost two-thirds of their boats and fishing gear. More than half a million people were displaced in each of Indonesia, India, and Sri Lanka, and drinking water and agricultural fields were contaminated by seawater.

The Indian Ocean tsunamis illustrated many of the themes of vulnerability to natural disasters discussed in other chapters. Lack of financial resources and political will meant there was no Indian Ocean tsunami warning system—although in the aftermath the UN led an initiative to establish one. Women, children, and poorer communities were especially vulnerable, but vulnerability was also created by the construction of luxury coastal resorts in countries such as Thailand. And there are some indications that the impact of the tsunamis was more serious where protection against waves had been reduced by the clearing of mangroves and destruction of coral. There is even anecdotal evidence that the teaching of geography reduced the vulnerability of a few families. In Thailand and Sri Lanka, children who had studied geography recognized the warning sign of a tsunami—the recession of the sea exposing large areas of beach—and warned others, who evacuated the beach.

The outpouring of humanitarian relief was unprecedented, with more than $13 billion in assistance pledged especially from governments and charities in the United States, Australia, Germany, and the United Kingdom. Almost two years after the disaster, many communities were still trying to recover partly because of misallocation of relief to inappropriate fishing equipment and housing and because some of the pledged funds were never delivered.

FIGURE 2 Tsunami damage Damage caused by the December 26, 2004, tsunami in Banda Aceh, Indonesia, a region where thousands died in the tidal wave that day.

spreads a 370-kilometer (200-nautical-mile) limit around islands and coasts where a country has the sole right to exploit or rent its resources such as fish or oil. In November 2002 China and the ten member states of ASEAN signed a declaration agreeing on a code of conduct in the South China Sea in order to reduce tensions and armed disputes.

The mainland is geologically older, but it is still very mountainous. Peaks in the highlands of Burma and Thailand reach 4000 meters (12,000 feet), and ridges link to the Himalayas. Between these ridges lie areas of flatter land along the major river

SIGNATURE REGION

The Mekong Basin and Vietnam

The Mekong Basin region is the most recent zone of rapid economic development and political transformation in Southeast Asia. Cambodia, Laos, and Vietnam are linked by the Mekong River, share a history of conflict and communist rule, and are now integrating rapidly into the global economy.

The lower reaches of the Mekong River flow slowly past thatched villages and rice paddies, while the upper reaches rush through deep, forested gorges, linking the countries of Indochina in a legacy of past conflict and a promise of joint water development (**Figure 1**). It is the 12th longest river in the world and the 10th largest in terms of the volume of flow. It forms the main transportation and settlement corridor for the underdeveloped and conflict-torn countries of Laos and Cambodia. It provides water for irrigation and hydroelectric development and is a pro-

FIGURE 1 The Mekong River The Mekong River links the countries of mainland Southeast Asia as it flows from a source on the Tibetan Plateau to the delta in Vietnam and Cambodia. (*Source:* Redrawn from Probe International, Mekong Basin Project. Available at **http://www.probeinternational.org/pi/Mekong/images/mekongmap3.gif**.)

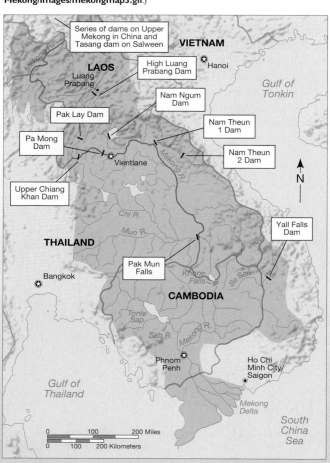

FIGURE 2 Mekong River dam Dams such as that at Manwan on the headwaters of the Mekong in Yunnan, China, are of great concern to the Southeast Asian countries and people who live downstream.

valleys and deltas of the Irrawaddy, Chao Phraya, Mekong, and Red rivers (the Red River is called the Yuan Jiang in China and Song Hong in Vietnam).

The Mekong River is Southeast Asia's longest waterway, flowing 4000 kilometers (2500 miles) from the highlands of Tibet to its delta in Vietnam and Cambodia. The river valleys and coastal plains are the focus of human activity and settlement, although swamps and disease have posed problems for humans and animals in the lowland tropical environments (see Signature Region: The Mekong Basin and Vietnam, p. 432).

ductive fishery. One of the most unusual physical features in the Mekong Basin is the lake of Tonle Sap in Cambodia. The lake acts as a safety-valve overflow basin for flooding on the Mekong River. During the dry season, water flows out of the lake along the Sab River into the Mekong, and during flooding on the Mekong, water flows back up into the lake, sometimes more than doubling its area.

Until recently, the Southeast Asian section of the Mekong was one of the world's last large untamed rivers, with no bridges or dams. The lower Mekong landscape and delta still show the scars of war, with mosquito-infested bomb craters, ruined bridges and roads, residues of defoliants, and thousands of unexploded anti-personnel mines. Vietnam is attempting to restore the landscape with the support of foreign assistance for reforestation, rebuilding, reclamation, and nature conservation. The delta has recovered to become the national granary for rice production, with boats carrying the harvest to the coast for export and upriver to domestic markets.

The Mekong provided a motive for cooperation among countries of the basin, even during times of tension, because of the potential for water resource development that could provide mutual benefits. The Mekong River Commission, established in 1957, has coordinated the planning of flood control and dam projects and has studied environmental issues within the basin with advice from geographer Gilbert White. The 1995 Chiang Rai accord provides mechanisms for resolving disputes within the basin. Several large dams have been constructed on the Mekong tributaries—among them the Manwan on the headwaters in China and Nam Ngum in Laos, which generates several million dollars of hydroelectric sales to Thailand—and many others are proposed (**Figure 2**).

Since the end of the Vietnam War and the Cambodian genocide, the Mekong basin has developed rapidly, especially in Vietnam. In 1986 the Vietnamese government began to move away from a centrally planned to a more market economy and to encourage foreign investment in a renovation policy called *Doi Moi*. Economic growth sectors include seafood, lumber, coffee, and construction and the economy grew 20 percent per year from 1990 to 2000 (**Figure 3**). Over the same period the population defined as poor fell from 58 percent to 29 percent. The Vietnamese economy is fuelled by cheap and efficient labor and has been especially attractive to the apparel industry with major U.S. brands producing sneakers and clothing. Criticisms of "sweat-shop" conditions for younger women have led to new labor laws and fair trade labeling for products from the region. Cambodia and Laos are now joining Vietnam by providing cheap labor to global garment companies and their economies are also starting to grow after years of stagnation (Figure 3).

FIGURE 3 Hanoi A merchant sells pots in front of an old French colonial mansion in Hanoi, Vietnam.

Volcanic Activity and Soils The active volcanoes and earth-quake zones of Southeast Asia pose great risks to the human populations of the region. The Indonesian and Philippine volcanoes are part of the Ring of Fire (see page 379 in Chapter 8) that surrounds the Pacific Ocean, linking this region with the seismically active regions of Japan, the western United States, and the Andes Mountains in South America. The island of Borneo sits on the Eurasian Plate and is of older and more stable geological composition. In 19th-century Indonesia, the eruptions of Tambora in

1815 and Krakatoa in 1883 had severe local and global effects. The Krakatoa volcano collapsed into the ocean during the eruption, leaving only the remnants of an island above sea level and causing a massive tsunami that killed more than 35,000 people on the adjacent Indonesian islands of Java and Sumatra. Both eruptions ejected ash and soot high into the atmosphere, causing temperatures to fall worldwide and creating a "year without a summer" in 1884 that caused crop failures from cool temperatures in Europe and North America. More recently, the eruption of Mount Pinatubo on the Philippine island of Luzon in June 1991 forced more than 100,000 people from their homes and destroyed 30,000 hectares (about 75,000 acres) of cropland (**Figure 9.5**).

The risks of volcanoes are balanced by the benefits they provide in terms of soil nutrients. As in other parts of the world, volcanic eruptions have deposited ash that contributes to fertile, less acidic soils that can sustain high crop yields and associated population densities. In Java, the rich volcanic soils have contributed to a productive agriculture and particularly dense populations. Soil fertility is also high in river valleys and deltas that receive regular replenishment of river sediment and nutrients in annual floods. Regions farther from volcanoes and rivers experience soil limitations typical of tropical climates around the world, where heavy rain and warm temperatures wash nutrients through the soil and organic material is broken down and recycled rapidly into forest vegetation. When forests are cleared, fertility declines rapidly as soil nutrients are washed out (leached) by heavy rains and the soil itself bakes in the hot tropical sun.

Energy and Mineral Resources The geology and tectonics of Southeast Asia have promoted the formation and development of mineral and energy resources, especially oil and tin, but generally the region is not as resource-rich as other regions, such as Africa or Latin America. Oil from Southeast Asia contributes about 5 percent to global production. Indonesia, Malaysia, and Brunei are the principal producers, exporting oil mainly to Japan from major oil fields off the north coast of Borneo, Sumatra, and Java. With foreign assistance, Vietnam is starting to expand oil production, and Burma is reinvigorating its energy sector through exploitation of gas reserves for domestic use and for sale to Thailand. From colonial times, tin has been a major export from Malaysia, but exports have dropped in the last 20 years as easily worked deposits are exhausted and competition has lowered prices. Thailand and Indonesia also have significant tin reserves and production. The Philippines has developed a wide range of mineral resources, including copper, nickel, silver, and gold, and Indonesia is developing new gold, silver, and nickel mines in Irian Jaya despite opposition from environmentalists and indigenous groups.

Mountainous topography, rivers, and high rainfall favor hydroelectric development in Southeast Asia, and there are a number of proposals to expand hydroelectric capacity beyond the current modest facilities. As little as 1 percent of the estimated 1-million-megawatt hydroelectric potential has been developed so far, with the greatest potential in Burma and Indonesia. The newest energy sources to be developed in Southeast Asia are biofuels, especially palm oil, which can be converted into biodiesel. Indonesia and Malaysia accounted for almost 90 percent of crude palm oil exports in 2006, and concern is growing about the conversion of tropical forests to palm oil plantations across the region (**Figure 9.6**).

FIGURE 9.5 Mount Pinatubo Mount Pinatubo erupted on the island of Luzon in the Philippines in 1991, forcing the evacuation of thousands of people, the closing of a major U.S. air base, and cooling global temperatures. Scientific monitoring provided predictions that allowed warning and evacuations, limiting the loss of life to about 700 people.

FIGURE 9.6 Palm oil A worker arranges oil palm fruits at a plantation near Kuala Lumpur, Malaysia. High crude oil prices and the drive for cleaner and renewable energy has boosted the development of alternative fuels, including biodiesel, made from palm oil.

Climate

Straddling the equator, most of Southeast Asia has a tropical monsoon climate, with warm temperatures all year and high, but seasonal, rainfall. Temperatures average above 27°C (80°F) because the sun is high in the sky for most of the year, but it is cooler at higher elevations in the mountains. Annual rainfall totals more than 200 centimeters (80 inches) across much of the region and is strongly associated with seasonal monsoon winds.

As the sun heats inland Asia from May to October, low pressure builds over the continental interior, and winds start to flow in from cooler high-pressure regions over the Indian and Pacific oceans (**Figure 9.7**). These winds are laden with moisture and produce heavy rain over land, particularly where air currents rise and cool to produce orographic precipitation on highlands and south-facing island slopes. The onset of the monsoon is a momentous event in many places. It brings some alleviation from the very high and oppressive temperatures as rains cool the air, and it brings water for crops and drinking. But the monsoons can also cause severe floods, and the constant heavy rain strains nerves and promotes the growth of molds and fungus.

On mainland Southeast Asia, the November-to-March period brings cooler temperatures and higher pressures. The ocean temperatures become warmer relative to land, and lower pressure prevails over the oceans. During this period, the monsoon winds reverse, now blowing out of the continental interiors and out across the ocean. On the mainland, this period is drier, resulting in lower overall annual rainfall totals, but the islands now receive a second sequence of monsoon rainfall, this time on the north-facing slopes. The Indonesian island of Sumatra, for example, receives the bulk

FIGURE 9.7 Climate map of Southeast Asia Southeast Asia has a hot, wet climate with equatorial convergence and seasonal monsoon winds that bring heavy precipitation. The mainland is drier with more seasonal rainfall, and regional climates can vary considerably from year to year as a result of El Niño conditions and the direction and intensity of tropical cyclones known as *typhoons*. (*Source:* Redrawn from R. Ulack and G. Pauer, *Atlas of Southeast Asia.* New York: Macmillan, 1988, p. 6.)

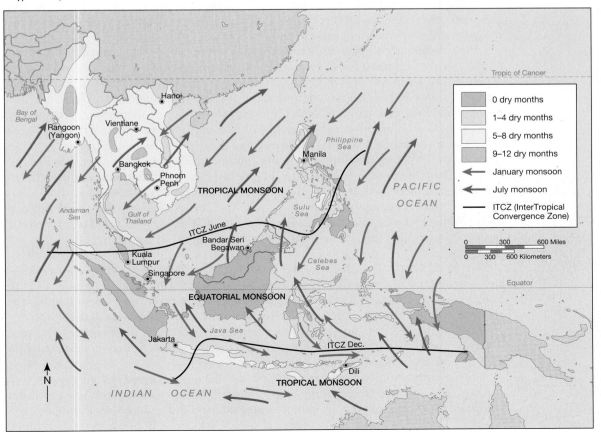

of its rain on north-facing slopes during the December–February period as winds blow southward from mainland Southeast Asia across the South China Sea but on south-facing slopes between June and August when monsoon winds sweep northward across from the Indian Ocean.

Historically important, the summer onshore winds brought traders and migrants to Southeast Asia, and with them their religious beliefs—Islam from Arabia and Hinduism from India. The shift in winds in winter carried the traders back home along with spices and other products.

The equatorial location of the Southeast Asian islands brings them within the influence of the intertropical convergence zone (ITCZ; see Chapter 1, p. 24), where intense sun means high evaporation and a vigorous hydrological cycle associated with daily tropical thunderstorms throughout the year. Warm ocean temperatures from August to October combine with eddies in the trade winds to produce the large rotating storms known as *typhoons* in Asia and *hurricanes* in the Americas. Typhoons most commonly develop east of the Philippines and move eastward into the South China Sea. The combined effect of monsoons, the ITCZ, and typhoons means that the islands of Southeast Asia are among the wettest regions in the world with lush forest vegetation.

Environmental History

Ecosystems The vegetation and ecosystems of Southeast Asia reflect the wet tropical climate, with a natural land cover of dense forests originally dominating the region. Indonesia is ranked second in the world in terms of its biodiversity, including at least 10 percent each of the world's plant, bird, and mammal species. The two major forest types are evergreen (with leaves year-round) tropical forests in the wetter areas and tropical deciduous, or monsoon, forests where rainfall is more seasonal or lower and trees lose their leaves in the dry season (**Figure 9.8**). In drier regions, these forests are less diverse, and vegetation cover changes to savanna and grasslands where rainfall is less or more seasonal, or at higher elevations. Mangroves and marshes are found along the long mainland and island coastlines, together with a rich offshore marine ecosystem that includes coral reefs and productive fisheries. Indonesia leads the world in mangrove area, with more than 4 million hectares (10 million acres).

Plate tectonics and climate change together produced a fascinating division in the ecology of the Southeast Asian region. The last ice age, when sea levels dropped as ice sheets locked up moisture, exposed the Sunda Shelf between the mainland and Indonesia until about 16,000 years ago, and many species, including tigers, elephants, and orangutans, migrated across this land bridge to the islands of Indonesia. To the south, animals such as kangaroos and opossums moved north across the Australian Plate to New Guinea and other islands. These mammals are called *marsupials,* because after birth the incompletely developed offspring continue to develop and nurse in an abdominal pouch on the mother (see Chapter 11). Between Bali and Lombok is a deep ocean trench that remained ocean, even during ice ages, and prevented these two very different types of species communities from mixing. This created an ecological division called **Wallace's Line,** named after naturalist Alfred Wallace, who traveled extensively in the region in the 19th century and first noted this striking contrast.

Human Use of the Environment About 5000 years ago the selective breeding of a grass with edible seeds produced rice, the basis of human diets in Southeast Asia. Domesticated in several parts of Asia, rice grew best where rainfall was evenly distributed through the year and totaled more than 120 centimeters (80 inches). Rice complemented fish and vegetables in a traditional diet, and the plant was also used for fodder and thatch in building. Other crops probably domesticated in Southeast Asia include taro, sago, bananas, mango, and sugar.

The modification of landscapes for rice production included the construction of terraces, paddies, and irrigation systems (**Figure 9.9**). Terraces cut into steep hillsides provided level surfaces that facilitated water control and reduced erosion. The construction of dikes (ridges) around fields allowed them to be flooded, plowed, planted,

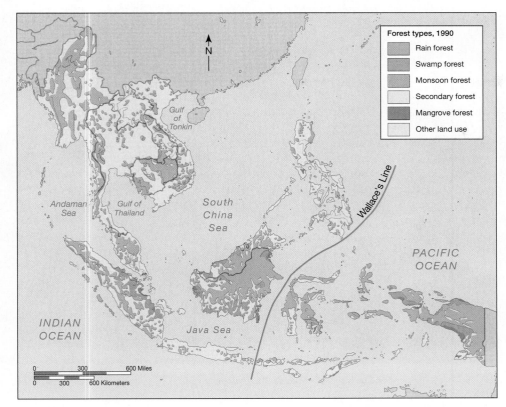

FIGURE 9.8 Southeast Asian vegetation and ecology The natural land cover of most of Southeast Asia is forest—evergreen in the wetter areas and tropical deciduous in drier regions. This map shows the actual land cover in 1990 and the extensive conversion of forests to agriculture and other land uses. Wallace's Line, named after 19th-century naturalist Alfred Wallace, indicates the location of a deep-ocean trench. The trench divided two sections of a great land bridge that rose above Southeast Asian oceans and seas 16,000 years ago. This line divides the two major biogeographical zones of Asia and Australia. (*Source:* Based on maps in R. Ulack and G. Pauer, *Atlas of Southeast Asia.* New York: Macmillan, 1988, p. 11; and T. R. Leinbach and R. Ulack, *Southeast Asia: Diversity and Development.* Upper Saddle River, NJ: Prentice Hall, 2000, Map 2.6b.)

and drained before harvest in a system called *paddy farming*. Rice, one of the few major crops that can grow in standing water, was suited to the flooding that accompanied heavy monsoon rains. Wet rice, or *sawah*, became the most important crop in Southeast Asia. Traditional rice production is highly labor-intensive, with work throughout the season in preparing and maintaining fields, transplanting seedlings, weeding, and harvesting each stalk by hand. Women perform much of the labor.

The main adaptation to the seasonal and yearly variability of rainfall in Southeast Asia is irrigation, ranging from small canal and pump systems to large water-diversion systems and dams. Adaptation to the constraints of the tropical environment in Southeast Asia, as in other tropical regions, has centered on managing soil fertility and controlling seasonal water supplies. The swidden, or slash and burn, agricultural system often used in tropical forests involves cutting trees and brush and burning them so that crops can benefit from nutrients in the ash and be grown on the cleared ground. When soil fertility in these agricultural clearings declines as a result of leaching of nutrients by rainfall and damage from the relentless tropical sun, subsistence migratory farmers move on to another patch of forestland. This process of extensive shifting cultivation was sustainable when widely scattered villages controlled large areas of land and could use fields for a few years and then leave them for 10 to 30 years to recover. If access to land decreases, or population and consumption increase, land may be cleared more frequently, causing long-term declines in environmental productivity.

The third traditional agricultural land use is the house garden. Many people plant vegetables and other crops, such as fruit trees, close to their homes.

FIGURE 9.9 Traditional agriculture in Southeast Asia Irrigated and terraced rice fields such as these in Luzon, the Philippines, have supported the food needs of Southeast Asia for hundreds of years.

Deforestation Deforestation is the most significant region-wide environmental problem in Southeast Asia (**Figure 9.10a**). The region was once dominated by forests that provided habitat for a diverse ecology and food, medicines, fuel, fiber, and construction materials to local peoples. As trade with countries such as China developed, demand for specialized products, such as aromatic sandalwood and teak, grew and resulted in some increased forest exploitation. Swidden farming cleared patches of forest for crops; widespread clearance began in the late 1800s with the expansion of rice production and export of tropical hardwoods under European colonial control. Most of the deforestation during this period was in lowland regions such as the Irrawaddy delta. After World War II, timber extraction expanded in the highlands, especially cutting teak in Thailand and Burma for export to the furniture industry. More recently, the growth of oil palm plantations, the pulp and paper industry, and cutting trees for plywood and veneers has placed even greater pressure on the forests. Japan is often blamed for deforestation in Southeast Asia because of the country's high demand for tropical hardwoods.

Deforestation has destroyed or is threatening the habitat of many species in Southeast Asia, including charismatic animals such as tigers and orangutans (**Figure 9.10b**). But the deep forests of mainland Southeast Asia are still relatively unexplored by biologists. New species are still being discovered, including relatively large animals such as the Vu Quang ox and giant Muntjac deer, identified as recently as the 1990s.

The driving forces for contemporary deforestation include export agricultural plantations, logging for tropical hardwoods and pulp, and land clearing by frontier migrants and traditional swidden farmers (**Figure 9.10c**). Swidden clearing has intensified in areas where population has increased, land is limited, and chainsaws are available. Forest has also been cleared by those resettled under Indonesia's transmigration program (see p. 451) and by Malaysia's Federal Land Development Authority (FELDA) programs to develop land for export crops.

Forest cutting increased as timber prices increased by 50 percent during the 1990s, at the same time that prices for many other commodities were falling. By 1996 more

than half of the original forests had been cleared—Thailand and Vietnam had about 20 percent of their forests left, whereas Cambodia, Malaysia, and Indonesia retained about 65 percent. Forest loss rates in Indonesia are 1.8 million hectares (almost 7000 square miles) a year, second only to Brazil. Only 40 percent of Burma's original forests remained. Timber exports are critical to the Burmese economy, making up 15 percent of export earnings, including earnings from concession of more than 18,000 square kilometers (6950 square miles) for virgin teak extraction by Thailand. The timber industry provides thousands of jobs and a significant amount of foreign exchange in Southeast Asia.

The impact of deforestation includes loss of species habitat and traditional cultures, flooding and soil erosion, and smoke and pollution from forest burning. In the Philippines, floods in Mindanao in 1981 killed 283 people and injured 14,000 below a region of major forest clearing, and deforestation has been associated with the near-extinction of the Manobo culture in northern Luzon.

Governments have responded by setting aside forest reserves and by banning logging in many regions, as well as by insisting on local processing rather than export of raw logs. But earlier patterns of "crony capitalism" (see p. 458) that gave generous timber concessions to friends and relatives of government in Indonesia, Malaysia, and the Philippines have not been rescinded. Multinational companies such as Weyerhaeuser, Georgia-Pacific, and Mitsubishi have also benefited from concessions.

Local people and international environmentalists have responded to deforestation in Southeast Asia by forming social movements and alliances to protect forests. In Thailand, Buddhist monks have helped to protect trees by wrapping them in saffron cloth and ordaining them, thus providing strong religious taboos against deforestation. The environmental movement is one of many organized grassroots efforts that also include action to support women, indigenous groups, factory workers, and religious minorities (**Figure 9.10d**).

The enormous islands of Borneo, Sulawesi, and Irian Jaya, the Indonesian portion of New Guinea, are frontier regions that have become a focus for resettlement, mineral

Deforestation in Southeast Asia

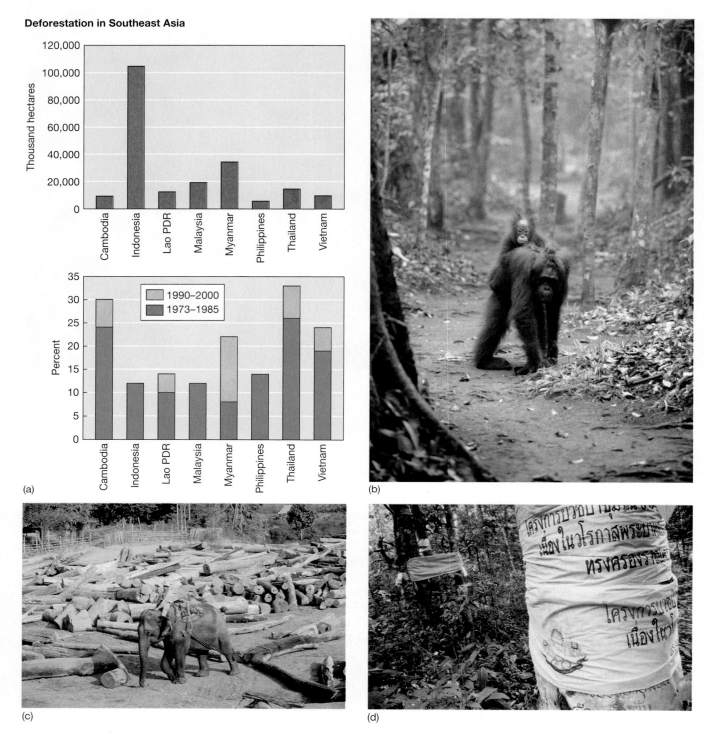

FIGURE 9.10 Deforestation in Southeast Asia (a) Forest cover in 2000 (in thousand hectares) and deforestation rates (for 1973–85 and 1990–2000 in percent) for selected countries and periods of years in Southeast Asia. (b) Forest loss in Southeast Asia threatens species such as the orangutan, shown here in the Indonesian province of East Kalimantan on the island of Borneo. (c) An elephant hauls valuable teakwood near Pak Lay in Laos. The use of elephants for logging and transport in countries such as Laos and Burma has less impact on the environment than mechanized deforestation. (d) Trees have traditionally been robed to propitiate the spirits believed to dwell in them, an example of the Thai blend of animism and Buddhism. In 1988, when loggers threatened to harvest a forest in northern Nan province, a monk named Phra Manasnati Pitak ordained trees in order to protect them. His action saved the forest, and soon other communities were following his example, such as in this region near Chiang Mai, Thailand. (*Sources:* [a] 1990–2000 percent forest loss and 2000 forest cover: FAO State of the World's Forests. Rome, FAO, 2003; 1973–85 percent forest loss: Rain Forest Report Card, East Lansing, MI: Michigan State University, 2000. Available at **http://bsrsi.msu.edu/rfrc/stats/seasia7385.html**.)

development, forest exploitation, and resistance by indigenous groups. Borneo, a stable zone of old crystalline rocks, covers more than 750,000 square kilometers (290,000 square miles) and includes territory controlled by Indonesia (Kalimantan), Malaysia (Sarawak and Sabah), and the country of Brunei. Borneo, Sulawesi, and Irian Jaya have more than 25,000 species of plants and 10 percent of the world's biodiversity. Elephants, tigers, rhinos, and orangutans reside in the mountainous and forested interiors, with human populations concentrated in the coastal plains and river valleys around Hulu Sungai in southern Kalimantan and Pontianak in western Kalimantan.

European explorers and writers such as Alfred Wallace and Joseph Conrad described Borneo as a luxuriant landscape inhabited by primitive tribes. This perception of primitive people and wild frontiers has persisted, with both Malaysian and Indonesian governments interested in developing the region that they portray as economically and politically isolated. Geographer Harold Brookfield argues that many of the indigenous peoples of Borneo have actually traded with others in the region and the world for centuries, selling forest products such as rattan, pepper, and camphor to traders. Collectively called the Dayak by outsiders, there are actually many different groups with individual names, such as the Kenyah and Iban.

Deforestation and the fate of indigenous populations on Borneo are two of the critical geographic issues that have garnered the attention of international environmental and human rights groups. Large-scale logging in Borneo increased after about 1960, when Japan shifted demand to Southeast Asia and altered preferences from teak on the mainland to hardwoods and trees used for plywood in the island regions. Harold Brookfield identifies agricultural clearing for transmigration settlements and the introduction of chainsaws and heavy logging equipment as additional causes of deforestation. The process has moved from zones along rivers into more remote areas. By the late 1990s, Borneo was providing more than half of the world's tropical hardwoods, mainly through concessions given to multinational timber corporations. The damage from forest clearing includes loss of biodiversity, erosion and flooding, and loss of forest benefits to indigenous populations. Although bans on export of raw logs were put in place in 2002, the corresponding increase in wood processing on Borneo, including more than 50 plywood mills, keeps the pressure on the forests.

SOUTHEAST ASIA IN THE WORLD-SYSTEM

Humans probably reached Southeast Asia through migrations from Europe and mainland Asia and over land bridges and oceans about 60,000 years ago. These people formed populations that were the ancestors of contemporary indigenous groups in New Guinea and Australia. A migration around 5000 years ago brought farmers and fisher people from southern China to the coast of Vietnam and to the islands of present-day Indonesia and the Philippines. Archaeological sites in Vietnam provide evidence of early hunting-and-gathering activities, including fishing and collecting forest products. Domesticated agriculture, including raising rice, cattle, pigs, and chickens, probably spread southward from China beginning in about 3000 B.C. By 700 B.C. the Dong Song culture had developed wet-rice cultivation and a metal industry that produced bronze artifacts.

Maritime trade brought merchants from the Middle East, China, and India about 2000 years ago, together with new religions, crops, and technologies. The most important interaction was with India, whose Hindu religion and related forms of government were attractive to local chiefs: They saw advantage in the divine privilege they could be granted as god-kings (*deva raja*). To claim this power, they needed the blessing of Hindu priests, who in return demanded the construction of temples in the Indian architectural tradition. Two types of urban settlement emerged: port cities focused on trade, and sacred religious and ceremonial capitals focused on elaborate temples. The earliest kingdoms inspired by Indian models included Langkasuka on the Malay peninsula and Fu-nan, centered in present-day Cambodia and Vietnam. By the tenth century there were large kingdoms, influenced by Indian culture and religion, along the Irrawaddy River in Burma and in the Chen-la and Champa kingdoms in what is now Vietnam. These kingdoms relied on state taxation of rice production and power structures based

FIGURE 9.11 Historical sites in Southeast Asia (a) The complex that includes the 12th-century temple of Angkor Wat and sacred city of Angkor Thom was constructed by the Khmer empire just north of the Tonle Sap Lake in present-day Cambodia. The design represents symbols from the Hindu cosmos, including mountains, artificial lakes, and sculptures. After years of conflict, the site is being restored and promoted as a major tourist destination. (b) A 19th-century print of the port and town of Malacca, founded in the 12th century. The strategically located colonial city controlled the spice trade to Europe and was ruled by the Portuguese, then the Dutch, and finally the British prior to Malaysian independence.

(a)

(b)

on kinship and religious and royal bureaucracies, and they built spectacular capitals, such as Pagan in Burma. In northern Vietnam, China influenced kingdoms at Annam on the Red River and Hanoi.

Two of the most powerful states to emerge in Southeast Asia were the mainland Khmer empire and the island Srivijaya culture of Sumatra. Srivijaya ruled Sumatra and the southern Malay peninsula from the 7th to 12th centuries by controlling the region's long-distance maritime trade through the Strait of Malacca. This powerful state had a capital at Palembang and Buddhist religious traditions. The Khmer kingdom emerged in the 9th century near Tonle Sap Lake and built the magnificent 12th-century temple compound of Angkor Wat, one of the largest religious structures ever built and a focus of tourism in contemporary Cambodia (**Figure 9.11a**).

An increasingly powerful Thai kingdom, centered on the city of Ayutthaya on the Chao Phraya River, conquered the Khmer empire in the 14th century and maintained control of the Malaysian peninsula for four centuries. A series of empires also flourished on Java and produced magnificent temples, such as the Buddhist temple Borobudur.

By the 15th century, the political geography of Southeast Asia had restructured around a series of sultanates such as Malacca (in present Malaysia) and Brunei (on the island of Borneo) and a new set of mainland empires. Malacca's strategic location controlling the trading route between India and China gave it great commercial power as a sea-based trading state, and after the rulers enthusiastically adopted Islam, Malacca disseminated Islamic beliefs and institutions in Southeast Asia (**Figure 9.11b**).

European Colonialism in Southeast Asia

Scholars usually divide the colonial period in Southeast Asia into two periods. The mercantile period, based on trade, spanned from about 1500 to 1800. The industrial period, concentrated on political and economic control of exports, lasted from about 1800 to 1945. A number of European powers sought to control Southeast Asia and its valuable trade: Portugal, Spain, the Netherlands, Britain, France, and the United States controlled different parts of the region at different times and often in competition (**Figure 9.12**).

Portugal dominated early mercantile trade with the region. The Portuguese sailed around Africa, established a headquarters at Goa in India, and then moved on to gain control of the vibrant and strategic port of Malacca in 1511. To obtain commodities such as cloves, nutmeg, and pepper from local producers in the scattered islands of Indonesia, they relied on indigenous and other Asian merchants. Other Europeans, such as the British, traded directly with local merchants on the outer islands. These local merchants often wished to avoid trading through Malacca because it was dominated by Portuguese Catholics who criticized Islam, imposed heavy taxes, and monopolized markets, thereby keeping prices down for producers and middlemen.

FIGURE 9.12 European expansion into Southeast Asia   This map shows the areas controlled by the major colonial powers in Southeast Asia. Note the dominance of the Dutch in the island subregion, the British and French in the peninsula/mainland region, and the Spanish in the Philippines. (*Source:* Redrawn from B. Crown and A. Thomas [eds.], *Third World Atlas*. Milton Keynes: Open University Press, 1984, p. 39.)

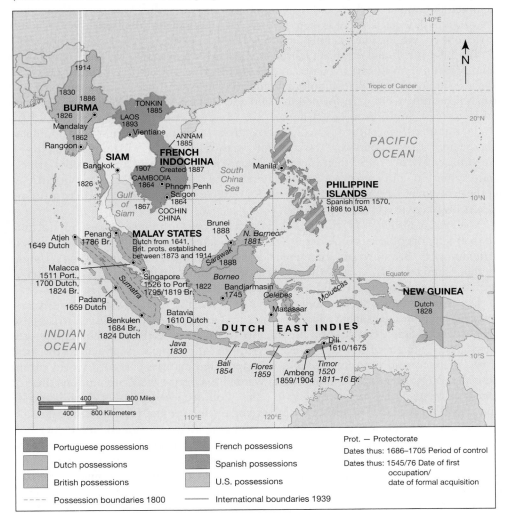

Meanwhile, the Spanish sailed across the Pacific and sought to conquer the Philippines in order to spread Catholicism, expand the Spanish empire, and gain access to trade in spices and other commodities in Southeast Asia. The country comprised the two large islands of Luzon to the north and Mindanao to the south, several other sizable islands, such as Cebu and Negros, and hundreds of smaller ones. The islands were originally covered with dense forests and were home to more than 75 distinct ethnic groups speaking hundreds of dialects. The city of Manila, founded in 1571, became the center of trade with Latin America, with galleons sailing regularly to Acapulco, Mexico, Spain's main Pacific port in the Americas. As in Latin America, Spanish colonial rule resulted in the dominance of Catholicism, the consolidation of land ownership under Spanish landowners, and the reorientation of land use to export crops—especially sugar—through Spanish-owned plantations or systems of tribute. The Spanish fostered creation of an elite landholding group, many of mixed Spanish and local ethnicity, dominated by families who were designated as *principales*. This group came to control land and, after independence, the economy and politics. Despite some attempts at land reform, Philippine land tenure still includes large export-oriented landholdings growing sugar, tobacco, and pineapples.

The third colonial power to move rapidly into Southeast Asia was the Netherlands. The Dutch dominated trade from about 1600 to 1750, with an initial focus on the Molucca Islands of Indonesia—the famous Spice Islands that produced the valuable commodities of nutmeg, cinnamon, and cloves. The formation of the Dutch East India Company in 1602 consolidated private commercial interests from the Netherlands to control trade in Indonesia (then called the East Indies). The coordinated effort was supported by the Dutch government and military. The privately chartered Dutch East India Company was based in Batavia on the island of Java, a city that later became the capital of independent Indonesia and was renamed Djakarta (now Jakarta). The Dutch attempted to control markets and increase commodity prices by restricting the production of valuable spices such as pepper and by destroying communities that ignored restrictions or participated in smuggling.

The British colonial effort in Southeast Asia was an extension of their activities in India. It focused on Burma, Malaya, and Borneo and on the control of strategic ports. As with the Dutch, the British colonial enterprise was led by a trading company, the British East India Company, formed in 1600 and focused for three centuries on British domination of South Asia (see Chapter 10, p. 486). For the most part the British waited until the 19th century to make a move from their empire in India into Southeast Asia, beginning with control of the strategic ports of Penang (1786), Singapore (1819), and Malacca (1824). They then fought two wars with the Burmese and used a protectorate system to gain control of the Malay peninsula. The British focused on reorienting the economies to exports of tin, rubber, and tropical hardwoods and on controlling trade routes between India and China.

The French influence originated in the 18th century with missionaries in Indochina and their support of local emperors. It was consolidated in the 19th century in response to rivalry with Britain over commercial links to China. French Indochina brought together Cambodia, Laos, and the districts of Tonkin, Annam, and Cochin China in Vietnam as the Union of French Indochina.

The United States was a colonial power in Southeast Asia for less than 50 years, acquiring the Philippines in 1898 after victory in the Spanish-American War, which also gave the United States control over Guam, Puerto Rico, and Cuba. The Philippines provide a good example of how the global geography of colonialism influenced the local culture, politics, and economy so as to differentiate countries within a world region (Figure 9.12). Spain and the United States wanted to control the Philippines because of their location as a gateway to trade with Asia. Four hundred years of domination by Spain and the United States resulted in several distinctive characteristics, including a majority Catholic religion, mainly Spanish names, highly concentrated land ownership, an agriculture oriented to exports of sugar, tobacco, and pineapples to the Americas, the widespread use of English, and a general orientation to the west, especially the United States. Even after the United States granted independence to the Philippines in 1946, it continued to treat the islands as a strategic location, maintaining several enormous military installations such as Clark Air Force Base and Subic Bay Naval Base.

As noted earlier, Thailand (called Siam until 1939) was able to maintain its political independence throughout the colonial period. It provided a buffer between British and French interests, losing territory to the British in Malaya and Burma and to the French in Cambodia and Laos but maintaining a core independent kingdom with tacit support of Britain. Although it remained independent, Siam was linked into colonial trading systems and vulnerable to the policies of the European powers.

The 19th century provides us with several insights into the processes and geography of colonial activities in Southeast Asia and the legacies of these activities for countries that became independent in the 20th century. The first general process was the integration of Southeast Asia into a global trading system, building on long-standing traditions of trade with the Middle East, India, and China. Spices (pepper, cloves, nutmeg, and cinnamon) were still important exports from the region in the 19th century; trade also included tortoise shell and tropical hardwoods, such as teak, and aromatic woods, such as sandalwood. Other key exports were tin, hemp, sugar, palm oil, tobacco, tea, and rubber. Economic developments in Europe and North America in the late 19th and early 20th centuries increased demand for many of these products.

For example, in the late 19th century, the economy of Malaya, under British control, focused on producing natural rubber and mining tin. Rubber production grew rapidly after 1876, when plants grown in Britain from seeds smuggled out of Brazil were introduced to Malaya. The area covered by rubber plantations grew from 800 hectares (2000 acres) in 1898 to 850,000 hectares (2.1 million acres) in 1920, as the explosion of automobile ownership in North America and Europe increased demand for rubber tires (**Figure 9.13**). Rubber was initially grown by expatriate planters on plantations, encouraged by enthusiasts such as "Rubber Ridley," who walked around Malaya at the turn of the century promoting rubber and distributing seeds from his pockets. Even though there was a ban on production by local people in Malaya in order to protect the profits and monopoly of European planters, rubber quickly became popular with local farmers because of the high price and low labor its production demanded. Tin mines used imported Chinese labor because local people were reluctant to abandon subsistence rice production.

A second set of processes directly changed the economies and land use of colonized countries. During the 19th century, Dutch control over the Indonesian economy tightened with the introduction of the notorious **Culture System** into Java in 1830. The Culture System required Javanese farmers to devote one-fifth of their land and their labor to export-crop production, especially coffee and sugar, with the profits going to the Dutch government. In many cases officials demanded more land and labor than specified, causing distress and food shortages in local populations. The British and French promoted rice production to feed laborers and growing populations, and expansion was especially dramatic in the Irrawaddy delta of Burma and in the Mekong Delta of French Indochina. Local and imported labor was employed to clear forests and build irrigation and drainage systems in these vast deltas, which became the rice bowls of Southeast Asia. This persistent stream of migrants from India and China accelerated in the 19th century, a third major process that changed the geography of Southeast Asia. Thousands of workers were brought in to convert the deltas to rice production, to mine tin and other minerals, to manage the services in major ports, and to develop small businesses to serve colonial and local demands for consumer goods. In some cases, a shortage of European administrators was filled when rights to collect taxes and harbor duties, to market opium, or to operate gambling were auctioned by colonial governments and purchased by the Chinese. Such activities were valuable revenue generators. These migrants, who were seen as more entrepreneurial and fit to govern by some colonial administrators, became a core of the colonial economies and are the ancestors of the large populations of South and East Asians, and especially Chinese, that live in Southeast Asia today.

The raw materials of Southeast Asia were very important to the industrialization of the core European economies and brought Southeast Asia into a peripheral relationship within the world-system. The colonial systems created spatial inequalities. Key port and trading cities such as Singapore, Batavia, and Manila

FIGURE 9.13 Rubber Rubber plantation in Sumatra. Rubber was introduced into Malaya by the British in the 19th century and the area under production grew rapidly in response to demand from North America and Europe. Although demand dropped with the development of synthetic substitutes, there are still a large number of plantations such as this one.

developed as regional cores and gateways to the world, with export agricultural regions oriented to these cores and with remote rural peripheries left in subsistence livelihoods with little investment in education or other services. Most of Southeast Asia remained under colonial control during the first part of the 20th century. As in other regions with strong links to the world economic system, the Great Depression of the 1930s had a serious economic impact in Southeast Asia and was associated with several anti-colonial uprisings. The price of rubber in 1932 dropped to 12 percent of what it was in 1928, tin was 20 percent, and sugar 26 percent, and many farmers shifted back into subsistence production.

Independence

European colonial power in Southeast Asia was diminished by the Japanese invasion of the region in World War II, which reduced the image of Western racial superiority, and by the costs of the war (**Figure 9.14**). Hastened by postwar global calls for decolonization, independence came relatively peacefully to most of the region except for Indochina and Indonesia, where extensive French and Dutch settlement and investments made the Europeans reluctant to hand over power.

FIGURE 9.14 Japan's occupation of Southeast Asia in World War II The Japanese occupation of Southeast Asia during World War II had severe effects on economies and local peoples. Japan sought access to the natural resources of the region, claiming legitimacy from a shared set of cultural values with the regions that they captured under the slogan "Asia for the Asiatics." But the Japanese occupation cut off many regions from trade revenues, used forced labor, and diverted food and other resources to Japan at the expense of local economies and food security. The destruction of bridges and roads by the Allies and by native populations as a means of preventing Japanese advances, and then by the Japanese as they retreated, left Southeast Asia's infrastructure in ruins. In Vietnam the Japanese requisitioned rice for their own use and also forced farmers to grow jute fiber rather than rice, resulting in a famine that killed more than 2 million people in 1944–45. The Japanese were particularly harsh on the Chinese population of Southeast Asia. (*Source:* Redrawn from M. Dockrill, *Atlas of 20th Century World History.* New York: Harper, 1991, pp. 74–75.)

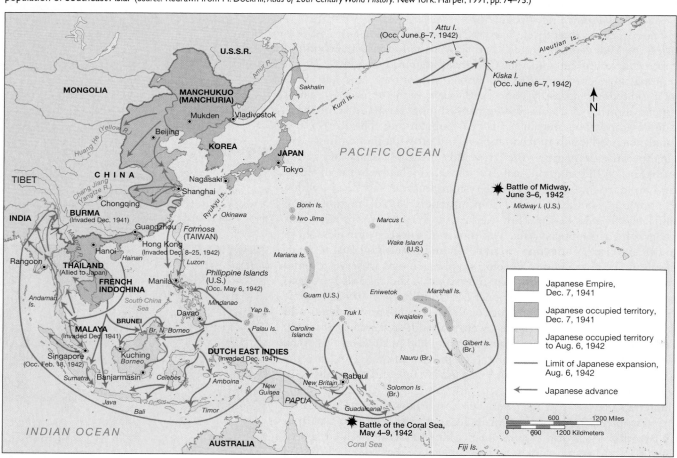

The Philippines was granted independence from the United States immediately after the war, in 1946. The British granted independence to Burma in 1948, after Indian independence and partition in 1947, and created the Federation of Malaysia in 1963. Singapore left the federation to become an independent country in 1965. Brunei converted from a British protectorate to an independent nation in 1983. Indonesia was granted independence by the Dutch in 1949 only after a violent struggle following a declaration of independence in 1945. Western New Guinea, formerly Dutch New Guinea, became part of Indonesia as Irian Jaya in 1963.

Indonesia faced great challenges in forging a sense of national unity among scattered islands and diverse cultures. The concept of *Pancasila*—unity in diversity through belief in one God, nationalism, humanitarianism, democracy, and social justice—as the national ideology and the promotion of a national Indonesian language were used to try to unify the country. However, fractures soon developed around religious differences and in response to government repression of criticism and political opposition.

Communist groups were part of the independence movements in several countries and continued to seek revolutionary change after independence. In 1965 a communist coup against Indonesian leader Sukarno was unsuccessful; at least 500,000 people associated with the communist movement were massacred in the aftermath (one perspective on this period is portrayed in the film *The Year of Living Dangerously*). In Burma, a military coup in 1962 resulted in a socialist form of government that isolated Burma from the world and nationalized land and industry.

The Vietnam War

It was in Indochina that the intersection of independence, communism, and the Cold War had the most global and long-lasting impacts. Communist groups had led resistance against Japanese occupation during World War II and against French recolonization at the end of the war. Led by Ho Chi Minh, the communists fought for a base in northern Vietnam. They established a separate government in Hanoi that supported guerilla war against the French in southern Vietnam with assistance from the Chinese and Soviet Union. When the French withdrew from Indochina after a devastating loss to Ho Chi Minh's forces at Dien Bien Phu in 1954, Laos and Cambodia became independent and the Geneva accords formally divided Vietnam into North Vietnam and South Vietnam. North Vietnam became an independent communist country, and thousands of refugees, especially Catholics, fled to South Vietnam, which had become an anti-communist partner of the United States with a capital in Saigon.

Communist rebels in Cambodia and Laos joined with North Vietnamese forces (called the *Vietcong*) to try to bring the whole region under communist control, with considerable success in several regions of South Vietnam. Subscribing to a **domino theory**, which held that the communist takeover of South Vietnam would lead to the spread of communism throughout Southeast Asia, the United States sent military advisors to South Vietnam in 1962. This was followed by the bombing of North Vietnam in 1964 and escalation to a full-scale land war, with more than half a million U.S. troops in 1965.

The Vietnam War, together with its aftermath, was probably the most serious global manifestation of Cold War competition and wrought terrible social and environmental effects in Southeast Asia as well as on U.S. domestic and international politics. More than a million Vietnamese people died, together with 58,000 Americans (**Figure 9.15**). U.S. forces sprayed 2 million hectares (5 million acres) of Vietnam with defoliants, such as Agent Orange, that poisoned ecosystems and caused irreparable damage to human health. Cambodia and Laos were also bombed with napalm and defoliated to disrupt communist supply lines and camps.

FIGURE 9.15 The Vietnam War U.S. troops waiting to be evacuated at Khe Sanh, Vietnam, in 1968—a year during which domestic opposition to U.S. involvement in Southeast Asia grew dramatically.

The media images of destruction, the loss of American lives, and the cost of the war created considerable opposition to the war in the United States, including protests on college campuses and marches on Washington. The United States gradually withdrew its forces in the early 1970s and left South Vietnam as the Vietcong approached Saigon in 1973; in 1975 Vietnam was unified under communist rule.

Two million people left South Vietnam fearing repression after unification, many (the so-called "Vietnamese boat people") sailing away in small, fragile boats. The communist government confiscated farms and factories from owners to create state- and worker-owned enterprises, resettled hill tribes into intensive agricultural zones, and moved 1 million people into new economic development regions. But U.S.–led economic sanctions from 1973 to 1993 limited the potential for exports and restricted some critical imports such as medicines.

In Cambodia, the Khmer Rouge communist revolutionaries overcame the U.S.–backed military government in 1975 and instituted a cruel regime under the leadership of Pol Pot. The Khmer Rouge suspended formal education, emptied the cities, and set out to eliminate the rich and educated and to isolate themselves from the world. They renamed the country Kampuchea. Mass murders in the so-called "killing fields" (depicted in the movie of the same name) and the brutal "death march" out of the capital Phnom Penh in 1975–76 killed at least 2 million people—a quarter of Cambodia's population, including most intellectuals and professionals—between 1975 and 1979, when Vietnam invaded and installed a new government.

Since 1990 the formerly conflict-ridden nations of Vietnam, Laos, and Cambodia have stabilized and embarked on new development paths that include trade, tourism, and integration with the global economy and culture similar to the wealthier countries of the region, such as Malaysia and Thailand.

Economic Development and New Export Economies

The wars and instability in the countries of Indochina limited their economic development and trade with the world for more than 30 years. Meanwhile, many other countries in Southeast Asia reoriented their economies, first of all to import substitution and later to export manufacturing. In the second half of the 20th century, Malaysia, Singapore, and Thailand provide regional examples of how government-led economic development policies brought Southeast Asia into a new relationship with the global system. Southeast Asia is a classic case of how changes in the international division of labor (see Chapter 1) fostered manufacturing in the global periphery.

The Shift from Import Substitution to Free Trade In the early years after independence in the 1960s, governments pursued import substitution industrialization (ISI; see Chapter 7) policies that sought to develop a domestic capability in manufacturing rather than rely on imported goods. For example, in Malaysia tariffs on imports such as clothing and plastics were increased dramatically to protect locally produced goods from global competition. Dominated by non-Malay (especially Chinese) investment and producing low-value goods that quickly saturated domestic markets or competed, in the case of steel, with global overcapacity, the economic gains of ISI did not benefit much of the population or the national trade balance. Malaysia, Singapore, and Thailand all made decisions to shift toward export-oriented industrialization. This meant trying to profit from their competitive advantages in the global economy, especially a low-cost but relatively well-educated workforce. Strong state involvement and incentives and high levels of foreign direct investment characterized economic development (**Figure 9.16**).

In 1971 Malaysia implemented a program for a New Economic Policy. It set out to shift the economy away from a dependence on tin and rubber exports to higher value exports and to distribute the benefits of economic development to the ethnic Malay population called *Bumiputra* ("those of the soil"). This program explicitly discriminated against ethnic Chinese populations. Incentives for foreign investment included tax breaks and freedom from customs tariffs when locating within a Free Trade Zone (FTZ) or

Export Processing Zone (EPZ; see Chapter 7). From 1980 onward, foreign investment flowed into a range of Malaysian economic sectors and the share of manufacturing in exports increased from 20 to 80 percent in 2003.

Manufacturing sectors that developed or relocated to Southeast Asia included automobile assembly, chemicals, and electronics. Japan was a major source of foreign investment in Southeast Asia, including the relocation of Japanese-owned firms seeking cheaper labor and land. This "offshore manufacturing" included 250 Japanese firms in Malaysia by 1990.

Thailand also attracted considerable Japanese investment and relocation of Japanese firms that were interested in the availability of cheap, well-educated labor, as well as comparative political stability and less discrimination against East Asians. Indonesia and the Philippines also pursued an export strategy, including electronics and apparel manufacturing in the Philippines and automobile manufacturing in Indonesia.

The Little Tigers

The rapid growth of these Southeast Asian economies, averaging 8 percent per year in the early 1980s, was seen as part of the larger East Asian economic miracle. The more successful countries—Thailand, Malaysia, and Singapore—joined the so-called *Asian tigers* (see Chapter 8) of Hong Kong, South Korea, and Taiwan. These "little tigers" were termed Newly Industrializing Economies (NIEs) rather than "developing" or "underdeveloped" countries. High rates of savings, balanced budgets, and low inflation were all indicators of a successful transition to modern industrial economies. Foreign investment flowed into Southeast Asia not only to benefit from cheap labor but also to take advantage of domestic markets for consumer goods, such as automobiles and soft drinks, and of valuable natural resources, such as oil and minerals.

The Asian Economic Crisis of 1997

The risks of such close financial and trade linkages to the global economy became dramatically evident in the 1997 collapse of Southeast Asian economies. The collapse was preceded by a slight decrease in competitiveness, as wages increased in Southeast Asia compared to low-cost labor in China, and by extensive international borrowing by governments and banks at low interest rates. Thailand was the first economy to fall: A decline in the value of the Japanese yen relative to the Thai baht (which was tied to the U.S. dollar) placed exports at a competitive disadvantage, and currency speculators on global markets began to bet on a currency devaluation. The Thai government raised interest rates and used up foreign exchange reserves in attempts to prop up the baht but was eventually forced to unlink from the dollar, causing a sharp fall in currency value. The high interest rates stopped economic development and the country fell into recession, with massive job layoffs.

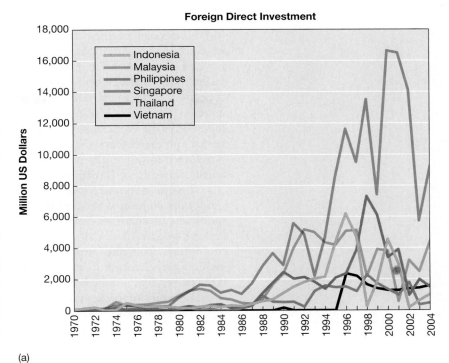

(a)

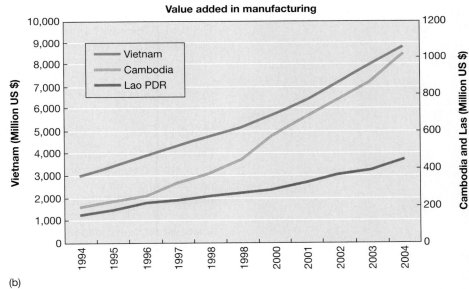

(b)

FIGURE 9.16 Foreign investment in Southeast Asia Foreign direct investment increased during the 1980s and early 1990s in many Southeast Asian countries but dropped suddenly in 1997 and again in 2001, precipitating serious financial crises. (*Source:* Data from World Bank, *World Development Indicators.* Washington, DC: World Bank, 2006.)

In the 1997 panic, $12 billion was withdrawn from the region. Malaysian markets lost 80 percent of their value over a two-year period. The crisis in the region was exacerbated by overinflation of stocks, speculative real estate development, and overlending by banks freed from government oversight. The effects of the 1997 crisis were most severe in Indonesia, where the rupiah currency lost 80 percent of its value as the country coped with a severe drought caused by El Niño. Food prices increased; government spending cuts resulted in the removal of subsidies on gas and kerosene. Public resentment focused on the ethnic Chinese, who fled the country, abandoning their shops and businesses and thereby creating further economic scarcities, and on President Suharto, who was forced to resign. Unemployment reached 40 percent. Those living below the poverty line increased from 10 percent to more than 50 percent of the population.

The International Monetary Fund agreed to help restructure debt and stabilize the economies so long as strict structural-adjustment policies were followed, including the reduction of corruption and removal of tariffs. Indonesia received the third largest bailout to date, requiring strict cutbacks in government spending and a reduction in corruption. Thailand and Malaysia responded to the crisis with austerity measures, including reductions in government spending and appeals to the public to accept reduced services and increased prices of basic goods.

The return of foreign investment has again brought the risks and benefits of globalization to the region. One overall indicator of linkage to the global economy is the relationship between the value of exports and the value of gross domestic product (GDP—the total value of all materials, foodstuffs, goods, and services produced in a country in a particular year; see Chapter 1). Singapore, with exports valued at 170 percent of GDP in 2004, and Malaysia, at 121 percent, are the most integrated into the global economy through exports, followed by Indonesia (31 percent), the Philippines (52 percent), and Thailand (71 percent). In terms of key global commodities, Southeast Asia produces more than half of the world's rubber, coconut, tin, palm oil, and hardwoods.

PEOPLES OF SOUTHEAST ASIA
Population and Fertility

The population of Southeast Asia was estimated at about 557 million in 2005. The country of Indonesia, with a population of 227 million, is the world's fourth largest. Vietnam and the Philippines each have about 84 million people, followed by Thailand at 65 million, Burma at 50 million, and Malaysia at 26 million. Although there is archaeological evidence of early humans in Southeast Asia, most contemporary Southeast Asians are descendants of migrants from East Asia.

Population growth and life expectancy in Southeast Asia surged with the eradication of malaria and improved medical care after about 1950. After several decades of growth at more than 2 percent a year, overall population growth has slowed to 1.5 percent a year, mainly as a result of significant fertility declines in Indonesia, Thailand, Singapore, and Vietnam. In these countries the total fertility rate (average number of children born to a woman of child-bearing age) has fallen from more than 6 to fewer than 3. In Singapore, where the fertility rate has fallen to 1.06—below the replacement level of 2.1—and population growth is negative, the government is now promoting marriage and childbearing, especially among the highly educated. Fertility rates have remained higher, at 3.11, in the Philippines, partly as a result of opposition to birth control by the Catholic Church, and in Malaysia, where the government encourages the ethnic and Muslim Malay population to have at least 5 children per married couple. Fertility rates are also higher in the poorer countries of the region, including Laos, where total fertility is 4.5 children per woman. Southeast Asian data support theories that fertility decline is associated with higher income, lower infant mortality, and higher status of women. Cambodia and Laos have lower GDP per capita, higher infant mortality, and lower levels of female literacy and schooling than do other countries in the region. Until recently, overall population growth in Cambodia, Laos, and Vietnam was reduced by high death rates from war and famine.

Indonesia's population policy is often promoted as a model for noncoercive family planning. Indonesia promotes two-child families through advertising, grassroots leadership training, and free distribution of birth-control pills and condoms. Population growth rates in Indonesia have fallen from 3 percent to 1.6 percent.

The map of population distribution shows that people are concentrated in the river valleys and deltas and on the island of Java (**Figure 9.17**). The highest population densities (people per hectare) are in Singapore, the Philippines, and Vietnam. Levels of urbanization range from 100 percent in the city-state of Singapore, to more than 60 percent in Malaysia and 40 percent in Indonesia and the Philippines to less than 30 percent in Cambodia, Laos, Thailand, and Vietnam.

According to UN estimates, at the end of 2001, more than 670,000 people in Thailand were infected with HIV/AIDS—about 2 percent of the adult population—and 55,000 people had died. This is by far the highest number of cases in Southeast Asia and is one result of the active sex industry. Local and international protests against the prevalence of child prostitution and a growing toll from HIV/AIDS prompted the Thai government in the 1990s to clamp down on the sex industry and to develop a strong anti-AIDS campaign that included distribution of condoms.

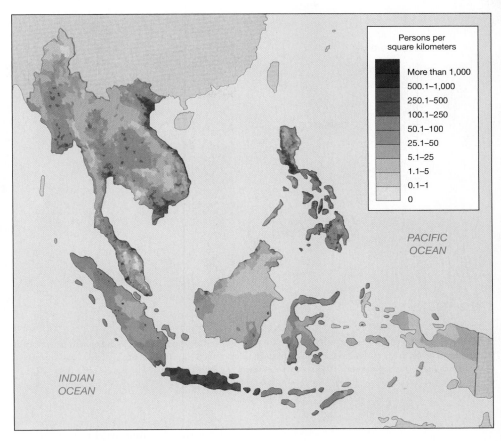

FIGURE 9.17 Population density in Southeast Asia 1995 The majority of the people of Southeast Asia live in or near river valleys and deltas and on the islands of Java, the Philippines, and Singapore. (*Source:* Center for International Earth Science Information Network [CIESIN], Columbia University; International Food Policy Research Institute [IFPRI]; and World Resources Institute [WRI]. 2000. *Gridded Population of the World [GPW]*, Version 2. Palisades, NY: CIESIN, Columbia University. Available at **http://sedac.ciesin.org/plue/gpw.**)

Migration and the Southeast Asian Diaspora

There are three major types of migration within the countries of Southeast Asia. The first is the worldwide phenomenon of people flowing into the cities from rural areas. They are driven by landlessness and agricultural stagnation or pulled by the attractions of urban areas, including job opportunities, education and health services, and access to consumer goods and popular culture. The second set of flows arises from war and civil unrest within countries, such as the mass evacuations from cities in Cambodia under the Khmer Rouge and from war zones in Vietnam. The third, and distinctively Southeast Asian, pattern is the resettlement of populations from urban to rural areas, especially in Indonesia. The Dutch moved thousands of people from Java and Bali to Sumatra, Kalimantan, and Sulawesi to work on plantations in 1904. This was dwarfed by massive relocation programs, or transmigration, initiated by the Indonesian government beginning in 1950.

Transmigration Indonesia's **transmigration** program was designed to redistribute population from densely settled Java and the city of Jakarta to reduce civil unrest, increase food production in peripheral regions, and further goals of regional development, national integration, and the spread of the official Indonesian language. It is estimated that more than 4 million people moved to the Moluccas, Sulawesi, Sumatra, and Kalimantan, with 1.7 million of the migrants receiving official government sponsorship

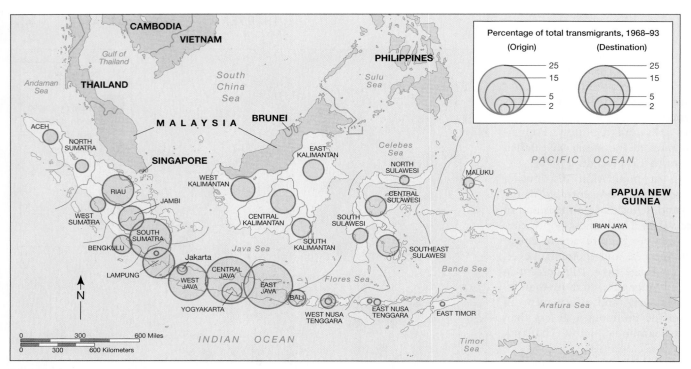

FIGURE 9.18 Transmigration flows in Indonesia The Indonesian government has relocated thousands of people from urban areas on Java to rural areas of the islands of the Moluccas, Sumatra, Sulawesi, and Borneo. (*Source:* Redrawn from T. R. Leinbach and R. Ulack, *Southeast Asia: Diversity and Development.* Upper Saddle River, NJ: Prentice Hall, 2000, Map 12.7.)

in the form of transport, land grants, and social services (**Figure 9.18**). The Philippines followed similar resettlement programs in subsidizing migration from Luzon to frontier regions such as Mindanao.

Geographer Thomas Leinbach identifies a number of problems with the transmigration program. He includes lack of infrastructure in the new settlements, conflict between the settlers and indigenous groups, and the destruction of forests as peasant farmers accustomed to the fertile soils of Java cleared more rain forests as their crops failed because soil degraded after deforestation. Malaria, pests, and weed invasion also hindered the success of the program.

Internal Refugees War, ethnic and religious conflict, and poverty within Southeast Asia forced thousands of people to move within the region between 1970 and 1995. Included in the total were more than 300,000 Laotians and 370,000 Cambodians to Thailand, about 300,000 Vietnamese to China and Hong Kong, 300,000 Muslims from Burma to Bangladesh, 200,000 Muslims from the Philippines to Malaysia, and 110,000 Burmese to Thailand. The UN High Commission for Refugees reports that in 2005 there were 120,000 Burmese in refugee camps in Thailand; 20,000 Burmese still refugees in Bangladesh; and 300,000 Vietnamese in China. There is also a flow of labor migrants among countries, with more than 500,000 Indonesians working in the Malaysian construction industry and 400,000 Thais working in Singapore and Malaysia.

International Migration to and from Southeast Asia International migration to and from the region has a long history. The most important flow into the region has been the centuries of movement of Chinese into Southeast Asia beginning as early as the 14th century. Driven by civil wars, famine, and revolution in China, more than 20 million Chinese moved to Southeast Asia during the colonial period to work as contract plantation laborers harvesting rubber and to work in mines and railways. Many of these migrants then shifted into jobs in retail and trading and as clerical employees of the colonial trading companies. These so-called **overseas Chinese** became essential to the success of the colonial economy, and upon independence they became the entrepreneurs who ran banks, insurance companies, and shipping and agricultural businesses. Explanations for the business success of the overseas Chinese include upholding the Confucian tradition of family and ethnic business links and providing children with a professional education, sending them overseas and to private schools when local facilities were not accessible.

As a result of this massive in-migration, ethnic Chinese make up a large percentage of the overall population in Singapore (77 percent), Malaysia (26 percent), and Thailand (10 percent). In other countries, such as Indonesia, ethnic Chinese make up a large percentage of the economic elite, even when they are a small percentage of total population. The overseas Chinese generally live in urban areas, in separate neighborhoods often known as Chinatowns, with their own social clubs and schools.

The economic dominance and closed societies of the overseas Chinese are some reasons why they have been a target of discrimination in Southeast Asia. Singled out for persecution by the Japanese in World War II, overseas Chinese have also been vulnerable to communist groups who see them as a symbol of capitalism. One of the main reasons for Singapore independence from the Malay Federation was the desire of many Malays to detach from this city dominated by ethnic Chinese. In contemporary Malaysia, where ethnic Malays are favored, the Chinese must have a Malay business partner and are restricted by quotas in government jobs and higher education. In Indonesia, anger during the economic crisis of 1997–98 was focused on looting and murder of Chinese business owners, many of whom fled the country.

Out-migration from Southeast Asia includes large refugee flows and many thousands of labor migrants (**Figure 9.19a**). Since 1974, 1.5 million people have left Vietnam as refugees from war and communism. About half of the Vietnamese refugees went to the United States; France, Canada, and Australia accepted others. U.S. cities such as San Francisco have large Vietnamese populations living in distinctive neighborhoods with a strong Vietnamese heritage. Some Vietnamese refugees remained in refugee camps in Hong Kong. After Vietnam invaded Laos in 1975, more than 300,000 Hmong people fled to Thailand, fearing persecution because they had supported the Americans; they were subsequently resettled in the United States. Recently, with peace and reform, many Vietnamese are returning to Vietnam, and some bring capital for investment.

The largest numbers of labor migrants from Southeast Asia work in the Middle East, especially in Saudi Arabia, Kuwait, and Oman, and in Hong Kong and Japan. Many Southeast Asians in the Middle East are Muslim women working in the service sector as nurses and maids. Philippine men have a tradition of joining the merchant marines of many countries and working as cooks, seamen, and mechanics. Thousands of Thais and Filipinos work in Hong Kong, where their wages are typically much lower than those of local laborers. Many Filipina women work as maids or nannies in North America, Europe, and Singapore.

The money sent back by these labor migrants (remittances) is very important to national and local economies. For example, it is estimated that $11 billion was sent back to the Philippines in 2005 by the 10 percent of the population working abroad (**Figure 9.19b**). Thailand's remittances are worth more than $1.5 billion each year.

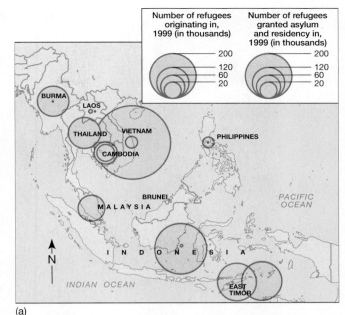

(a)

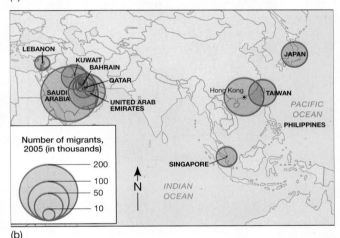

(b)

FIGURE 9.19 Migrations in Southeast Asia (a) Southeast Asia has experienced enormous refugee flows within and from the region, including out-migrations from Vietnam, Burma, Laos, and Cambodia to Thailand and beyond the region, from the Philippines to Malaysia, and from East Timor to Indonesia. In 1999 the total number of refugees registered with the UN in the region was more than 700,000, but was lower than in many previous years and has declined since. (b) This map shows where Philippine labor migrants were moving in 2005 and illustrates the significance of remittances from workers in Japan, Hong Kong, and the Middle East to the Philippine economy. (*Source:* [a] UN High Commission on Refugees, *Refugees and Others of Concern to UNHCR 1999 Statistical Overview.* Geneva, Switzerland: Statistical United Nations High Commissioner for Refugees, July 1998, Table I.2 and Table II.2; [b]: Philippine Overseas Employment Administration, 2000–2005. Available at **http://www.poea.gov.ph/html/statistics.html**.)

Urbanization

About half of Southeast Asia's people live in cities, most of which have grown rapidly since 1950. Most of this growth is driven by migration from rural areas, but Bangkok and Kuala Lumpur jumped in size as a result of annexing neighboring regions into the

(a)

(b)

FIGURE 9.20 Bangkok, Thailand (a) Bangkok is crossed by many canals (or *klong*) crowded with houseboats and floating markets such as this fruit market. Many of the canals are polluted. (a) The city developed along both sides of the Chao Phraya River in Thailand. It is a city of many temples, palaces, and canals. This view looks across the Wat Arun temple to the river.

metropolitan areas. Urban growth in Cambodia and Vietnam was slowed, or even reversed, under communist governments whose policy was to return people to rural areas to grow food or develop small rural industries.

Southeast Asia is dominated by several enormous cities with metropolitan-area populations estimated at about 5 million, among them Bangkok (8.5m), Ho Chi Minh City (5.4m), Manila (15 million), and Jakarta (16.5 million). These cities have grown so rapidly that they have serious problems of overurbanization (see Chapter 1), with insufficient employment opportunities, an inadequate water supply, sewerage problems, and inadequate housing.

The streets of Bangkok, Thailand (**Figure 9.20a and b**), are crowded with people, street vendors, and a variety of vehicles ranging from hand-pulled rickshaws, to tricycles, to minibuses. The golden spires of religious buildings and soaring towers of secular buildings dot the skyline. The city is crossed by dozens of polluted canals, called *klong,* packed with houseboats and floating markets. Bangkok's problems include serious air and water pollution and an AIDS epidemic associated with a sex industry that has become a focus for international tourism.

With a metropolitan population of more than 9 million people, Bangkok is the hub of mainland Southeast Asia and is a clear example of primacy (see Chapter 1, p. 14). The city dominates Thailand with 70 percent of the urban population (more than 30 times the size of the next largest city), 90 percent of the trade and industrial jobs, and 50 percent of the GDP. There are more than 25,000 factories in the Bangkok metropolitan region, many of them labor-intensive textile producers. Although manufacturing grew rapidly from 25 to more than 70 percent of national exports between 1980 and 1998, the economic development of Bangkok has been constrained by inadequate infrastructure, including the lack of mass transit and the need to upgrade the international airport.

The origins of Bangkok's notorious sex industry lie to some extent in a traditional acceptance of prostitution but also in the role that the city played as a major R&R ("rest and recreation") center for U.S. troops during the Vietnam War. Sex tourism was constructed around an image of Asian women as passive and exotic, and by the 1990s tours were being heavily advertised in places such as Japan and Germany. Sex tourism is estimated to generate more than $10 billion, a significant source of national foreign exchange, and to involve about half of the almost 15 million tourists who arrive in Thailand each year.

Several countries have two major urban centers. In the case of Burma, this resulted from the relocation of its capital, from Mandalay to Rangoon (now called Yangon). The unification of North and South Vietnam left the new country with two major urban centers—

Hanoi and Ho Chi Minh City (formerly called Saigon). New administrative capitals have been established to promote decentralization in Quezon City (Philippines) and Putrajaya (Malaysia), but their proximity to Manila and Kuala Lumpur creates one large urban region in each case. Key secondary cities with more than 500,000 residents include Palambang, Medan, Bandung, Ujung Pandang, and Surabaya in Indonesia and Cebu and Davao in the Philippines.

Cities in Southeast Asia mix traditional design with that of colonial and modern planning, but they are surrounded by unplanned growth, including desperately poor squatter settlements of recent migrants. The cities retain characteristics of earlier functions and include sacred cities such as Mandalay, trading/port cities such as Malacca, cities established as colonial centers such as Manila and Jakarta, and the post-socialist cities of Hanoi and Yangon. The traditional core of the city, symbolized by temples, was replaced by the fort or garrison under colonialism and by a high-rise central business district in modern times. Singapore is a world financial and trade center and a major gateway to Asia. It is the only true "world city" in Southeast Asia, where a disproportionate share of the world's business is transacted (see more on Singapore on page 463).

Geographer Terence McGee, who has written at length on cities in Southeast Asia, argues that the region has a distinctive urban landscape in the form of extended metropolitan regions (called *desakota*). Cities have extended out into intensively farmed agriculture, especially rice paddies; town, industry, and agricultural villages have become intermixed. McGee's work reminds us that boundaries between the city and the countryside in Southeast Asia are often blurred. There are many small industries, such as textiles, in rural areas, and considerable agricultural production in the cities.

Ethnicity, Language, and Cultural Traditions

Southeast Asia accommodates an incredibly diverse set of cultures, which is reflected in more than 500 distinct ethnic and language groups (**Figure 9.21**). Indonesia, for example, has more than 300 distinct ethnic groups and languages, and the population of Laos speaks more than 90 different languages. In general, the cultures have remained distinct from each other and from the cultures of migrants who arrived from India, China, Europe, and other world regions. No language has unified the region in the way that Arabic has in the Middle East or Spanish has in Latin America. The most common dialects are versions of Malay spoken in Malaysia, Indonesia, and Brunei and a version used as a *lingua franca* (trade language).

Some national boundaries of Southeast Asia do enclose relatively coherent cultural and language groups. Thailand (Thai), Burma (Burmese), Cambodia (Khmer), Vietnam (Vietnamese), Laos (Lao), and Malaysia (Malay) all have large majority populations that speak the same language and share cultural and religious traditions. The adoption of a common language in Indonesia and Pilipino in the Philippines as official national languages are attempts at integrating diverse cultural groups. However, there are significant minority populations in many of these countries, including the Karen and Shan in Burma and the Hmong in Laos, as well as large populations of Chinese and Indians in many countries. Even within these groups there are distinct cultural and regional differences. For example, the Indian populations include Bengalis and Sikhs in Burma and Tamils in Malaya.

The imprint of Indian and Chinese cultural traditions is strong in Southeast Asia. The monuments of the early Hindu kingdoms reflect the art and architecture of India, as do the crafts and rituals of contemporary Bali. Chinese business traditions were spread by the millions of overseas Chinese who settled in the region.

The global influence of Southeast Asia is considerable, although the music, literature, and art of the region is not well known in the United States, and culinary influences are often confused with Western versions of Chinese food. However, Thai and Vietnamese restaurants are becoming more popular worldwide with the distinctive use of spices, lemon grass, and coconut milk. Tourism is increasing awareness of the region.

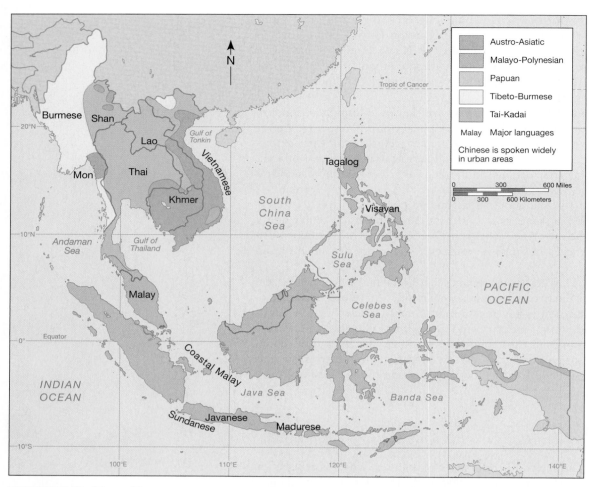

FIGURE 9.21 **Map of languages** Southeast Asia has hundreds of distinct languages, which fall into five major language families and are dominated by versions of Malay. The major language families are Austronesian (or Malayo-Polynesian), spoken in insular Southeast Asia and the Malay peninsula; Tibeto-Burmese in Burma; Tai-Kadai focused on Thailand; Papuan in New Guinea; and the Austro-Asiatic languages of Vietnam and Cambodia. (*Source:* Redrawn from R. Ulack and G. Pauer, *Atlas of Southeast Asia*. New York: Macmillan, 1988, p. 27.)

Religion The contemporary religious geography of Southeast Asia reflects centuries of evolution under Indian, Chinese, Arab, and European influence. Most generally, Buddhism tends to dominate the mainland region and Islam the islands (**Figure 9.22**). Islamic believers in Indonesia now outnumber those in the Middle East, although the practices are sometimes seen as more liberal than in the Middle East. Islam is also widespread in Malaya and is growing in the Philippines. Intensification of fundamentalist Islamic belief has resulted in the seclusion and veiling of women; in political conflict over the enforcement of Islamic law, especially in diverse populations; and in terrorism linked to tensions in the Middle East. In 2002 the bombing of a nightclub in Bali killed 202 people, and further terrorist attacks in Indonesia's tourist regions have been linked to radical Islamist groups.

Hinduism is common in Burma, Java, and Bali. Christianity is the religion of 85 percent of the Philippine population as a legacy of Spanish colonialism. It is also found among the hill tribes of Burma and in Vietnam, converted by French and British missionaries who could not make inroads into the Buddhist beliefs of lowland residents. Remote indigenous groups have maintained traditional animistic beliefs that imbue nature with spiritual meaning, especially in the mountains of Burma, Laos, and Vietnam and in Borneo and Irian Jaya.

Religion and cultural tradition intersect in the reverence for the monarchy in countries such as Thailand and Cambodia. The Thai royal family is held in high,

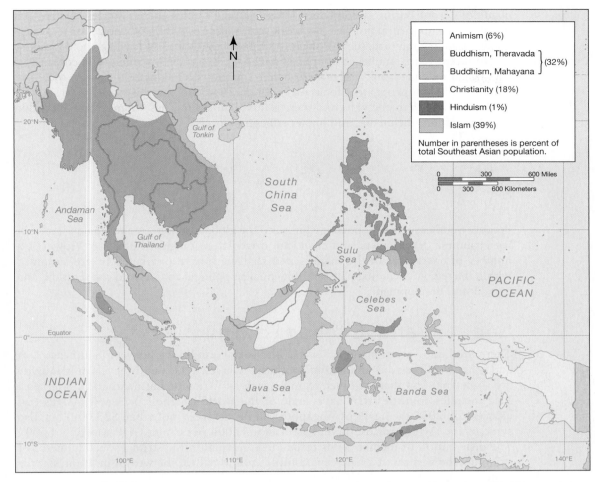

FIGURE 9.22 Religion The geography of religious belief in Southeast Asia is dominated by versions of Buddhism on the mainland and Islam on the islands. Buddhism includes both Theravada and Mahayana, the former more conservative and found mostly in Burma, Thailand, and Cambodia, and the latter associated with Vietnam. Catholicism is important in the Philippines. Indigenous groups maintain animist beliefs in remoter mountain and island areas. (*Source:* Redrawn from R. Ulack and G. Pauer, *Atlas of Southeast Asia.* New York: Macmillan, 1988, p. 29.)

almost godlike esteem, with pictures of the king in the majority of homes. The royal family has selectively intervened during times of political crisis and plays a balancing and leadership role.

Women's Roles In general, women have more power within Southeast Asian families and societies than in many other world regions. For example, couples often live with the wife's parents, with authority passing from father to son-in-law. This often gives women more power because they live with their own families rather than with in-laws. In Indonesia, women often manage the family money. The value of daughters is reflected in a more equal preference for female compared to male children than in either East or South Asia, where preferences are highly biased toward males. Women also have new employment opportunities in services and manufacturing and are preferred by many high-technology companies because they receive lower wages and are perceived as more careful and docile.

Nevertheless, cultures are patriarchal, and socioeconomic conditions are generally better for men than for women. Men tend to receive higher wages and more education. One of the more exploitative professions for women is as sex workers in the tourist industry, most notably in Thailand, one of the world's centers of prostitution. Millions of sex tourists, especially Germans and Japanese, visit Thailand each year. Some of the sex workers are very young women sold into bondage by rural families or smuggled in slavelike conditions from Burma. Geographer Jonathan Rigg quotes studies suggesting that for women from poor rural families, sex work may appear as a rational choice for making a living, providing opportunities for them to send money back to their villages and families.

In recent years families in Southeast Asia have become more nuclear, in contrast to traditional extended links. This has changed patterns of obligation from a focus on parents and older people to a focus on children. There are fewer arranged marriages or men with more than one wife, and there is less child labor. These changes are likely due to urbanization, the media, and higher education levels.

CONTEMPORARY CHALLENGES IN A GLOBALIZING WORLD

Because Southeast Asia is so closely linked to the global economy, many changes, including economic development and crisis, are driven from outside the region. However, a number of shared regional dynamics and challenges have originated or are sustained within the region, including patterns of inequality, political conflict and cooperation, and agricultural development.

Social and Economic Inequality

There are large variations in economic and social conditions between Southeast Asia and other world regions and within Southeast Asia itself. Generally, levels of inequality are somewhat less than in other regions, such as Africa or Latin America. Southeast Asia includes countries that have some of the world's highest per capita GDPs (for example, in 2005 the GDPs of Singapore and Brunei were more than $23,000) but also some of the lowest (for example, East Timor's 2004 per capita GDP was only $400). The distribution of income tends to be most unequal in the strongest economies. For example, the wealthiest 20 percent control around half of the wealth in Malaysia, the Philippines, Singapore, and Thailand.

There are wide variations in how poverty is defined in the region, but there do seem to be general improvements in overall conditions. For example, Malaysia reduced the proportion of people living in poverty from 60 percent in 1970 to 5 percent by 2002. Geographer Jonathan Rigg suggests that the poorest and most disadvantaged populations include those living in areas of extractive industry, such as timber and mining, indigenous groups, religious and ethnic minorities, guest workers, refugees, and the young and elderly. He points out that some are disadvantaged by who they are (ethnicity and religion) and others as a result of their occupation (in an urban informal sector such as sex worker or garbage picker) but that there is considerable variation within the region and within each group. Urban residents tend to be much better off than rural dwellers. In Malaysia and Thailand about a quarter of rural people live in poverty, compared to less than 10 percent of urban residents. Most Southeast Asian countries have considerable inequality within the nation.

Wealth concentration in Southeast Asia has been associated with crony capitalism, in which leaders allow friends and family to control the economy, and kleptocracy, in which leaders divert national resources for their personal gain. Evidence and public perception of such behavior by President Marcos in the Philippines led to uprisings and repression during his dictatorship.

Critics suggest that income and per capita GDP are inadequate measures of living conditions and that indicators of basic human development, such as life expectancy, infant mortality, and literacy, provide more appropriate insights into levels of development. For all three of these indicators, Southeast Asia is above the world averages and has shown great improvements over recent decades. Brunei, Malaysia, Singapore, and Thailand show much better conditions than Burma, Cambodia, and Laos. Indonesia, the Philippines, and Vietnam rank well above conditions in regions such as Sub-Saharan Africa and South Asia.

As noted earlier, women are more equal to men in Southeast Asia than in many other regions. Female literacy averages more than 85 percent, only 10 percent less than the male rate, compared to an average for women of less than 50 percent in Sub-Saharan Africa and South Asia. Despite these relatively positive measures, many workers in Southeast Asia are exploited in terms of wages and labor conditions compared to workers producing similar goods in North America and Europe. Many work 12-hour days and seven days a week without benefits or unions, making products such as clothing and electronics for global markets. International companies such as Nike have come under criticism for sweatshop labor practices in countries such as Vietnam and Cambodia, where wages are less than $2 a day and workers earn less than 5 percent of what workers earn producing similar goods in the United States.

Political Instability and Cooperation

Legacies of colonialism, territorial expansionism by some countries in the region after independence, and Cold War conflicts such as the Vietnam War contribute to continuing political instability in some parts of Southeast Asia. Some of the most long-lasting conflicts are those where ethnic minorities are seeking recognition and independence or where fractured physical and cultural geographies have made national unification more difficult (**Figure 9.23**).

Indonesia In Indonesia, the outer islands have long resisted the dominance of Java, with the most serious insurrections in East Timor, Irian Jaya, and Aceh. East Timor is mostly Christian, a former Portuguese colony that occupies the eastern portion of the

FIGURE 9.23 Map of conflict zones This map shows some of the major zones of conflict in Southeast Asia, including separatist movements in the outer islands of Indonesia and the Philippines. (*Source:* Adapted from T. R. Leinbach and R. Ulack, *Southeast Asia: Diversity and Development.* Upper Saddle River, NJ: Prentice Hall, 2000, Map 10.2.)

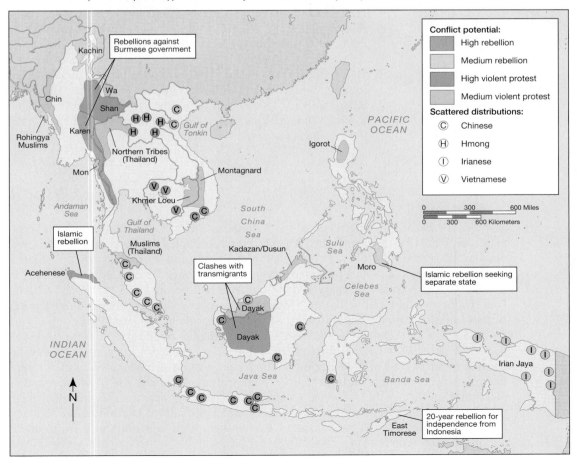

Opium

The mist-shrouded highlands of Burma, Laos, and Thailand contain much of mainland Southeast Asia's remaining forests, but they are also known for the fields of opium poppies that provided as much as half of the global supply of the addictive drug known as heroin. The drug economy has fueled rebellions and has even evolved a tourist industry in the exotically named Golden Triangle that centers on the region where Burma, Laos, and Thailand intersect (**Figure 1**).

FIGURE I **The Golden Triangle** Map of the region known as the *Golden Triangle*. (*Source:* Redrawn from "The Opium Kings," *PBS Frontline,* 1998. Available at **http://www.pbs.org/wgbh/pages/frontline/showsheroin/maps/shan.html**.)

The allure of the opium poppy as a narcotic is centuries old. It was a component of trade between China and Europe, with the exchange of opium for Chinese tea, silk, and spices, creating thousands of addicts in China (see Chapter 8, p. 390). Medical uses of opium expanded at the end of the 19th century with the isolation of morphine and heroin as powerful painkilling drugs. During the 19th century, literary figures such as John Keats and Elizabeth Barrett Browning popularized the recreational use of opium, and Britain and China went to war twice over control of the lucrative opium trade. Britain introduced opium production into its colonies in South and Southeast Asia to create an alternative supply. In 1905, as heroin addiction rose, the U.S. Congress banned opium and eventually prohibited both opium and heroin sales. Black markets for these narcotics developed worldwide and expanded with the popularity of drug consumption in the 1960s in North America and Europe.

Large markets for heroin now exist in the United States, Europe, and Australia, as well as in Thailand. However, production of opium in Southeast Asia has declined dramatically in recent years, from almost 2000 tons in 1990 to only 326 tons, almost all in Burma, in 2005. Afghanistan is now the largest producer at more than 4000 tons per year.

The sap inside the opium poppy seed pods provides the raw opium, which is then sold to a refinery and concentrated into morphine. Morphine can then be combined with chemicals and processed to create highly potent and addictive heroin worth more than $100,000 a kilogram. The United Nations estimates that there are 11 million heroin and opium addicts worldwide, many unable to work productively and turning to crime to fund the regular purchase of heroin. Addiction can result in overdoses and death from respiratory failure, and the use of shared needles to inject heroin has contributed to the transmission of HIV/AIDS among addicts. Opium and heroin production and distribution has been monopolized by international crime syndicates. It is an important source of funds for some rebel groups.

island of Timor, at the eastern end of the Indonesian archipelago. Initial hopes for independence in East Timor were dashed when Indonesia occupied the region as Portugal gave up colonial control in 1976. Twenty years of resistance and more than 200,000 deaths finally resulted in a local vote for independence in 1999. After the vote, anti-independence militias went on a violent rampage and thousands of refugees fled to West Timor. In 2000, East Timor was granted status as a newly independent country under initial United Nations administration. East Timor is now the 11th nation in Southeast Asia.

Irian Jaya was retained by the Dutch for more than a decade after Indonesian independence. A 1962 vote for union with Indonesia provoked a resistance movement because of suspicions of vote rigging by the Indonesian government, which then resettled many transmigrants on Irian Jaya despite local opposition. A rise of Islamic fundamentalism in Aceh, the far west region of Sumatra, is associated with an armed rebellion rooted in decades of resistance to Dutch colonialism. In Kalimantan, indigenous peoples, especially the Dayak, have clashed with transmigrants from other regions of Indonesia.

The opium poppies that are used to produce heroin are grown mainly by poorer farmers on small plots of land in the warmer and drier highlands that stretch from Turkey through Afghanistan and Pakistan to the Golden Triangle (**Figure 2**). The Golden Triangle provides a powerful example of a landscape and society transformed by opium production. In the early 1990s, before control policies in Thailand and Vietnam and the expansion of production in Afghanistan, the region produced about two-thirds of the world's opium. U.S. troops in Vietnam provided a major market for heroin produced in the Golden Triangle, and the Nationalist Chinese forces of the Kuomintang (K.M.T.), who had fled from Maoist China to Burma, fostered its production. The K.M.T. worked with indigenous groups rebelling against the Burmese government, including the Wa in northern Burma and the Shan on the northeastern plateau. The Shan taxed production and transportation of opium in order to purchase arms for their rebellion against the Burmese state. The Wa also produced millions of methamphetamine pills in remote laboratories.

An aggressive campaign to eradicate poppy production in northern Thailand was successful. It persuaded farmers to switch to growing alternative crops such as tobacco and soybeans by offering generous cash rewards. The opium crop in Thailand decreased by 90 percent over a ten-year period, and what is now grown is mainly for consumption by hill tribes. However, Thailand is still a major smuggling route, with the newest group of smugglers being Nigerians. Thailand has also developed a tourist industry centered on the Golden Triangle that includes treks operated from the city of Chiang Mai to indigenous villages to view local cultures, the opium museum, and specimen poppy fields (**Figure 3**). Bringing $2 million to the region each year, tourism is proposed as a more sustainable activity for the Golden Triangle than opium or logging. However, critics suggest that tourism exploits local culture, puts stress on local food supplies, and is still overly focused on the mystique of opium.

FIGURE 2 Opium harvest A woman of the Wa ethnic group harvests opium poppies in Burma.

FIGURE 3 Buddhist monks Monks pose in front of tourist sign for the Golden Triangle.

The Philippines Separatist movements are also found in the islands of the Philippines. The Islamic Moro liberation front on Mindanao has sought a separate state based on religious differences and opposes resettlement of migrants on the island. Communist rebels, the New People's Army, were active during the 1980s. Tribal peoples in northern Luzon have rebelled against dams and deforestation. Repression under the Marcos government has been replaced with attempts at mediation and concession with these groups.

Burma Ever since independence in 1948, the Burmese government has faced serious rebellion from hill tribes and religious minorities, who resist the political, linguistic, and religious domination of the Buddhist and Burmese-speaking authority. Muslims on the northern Arakan coast fled into neighboring Bangladesh. The Karen, who live along the border with Thailand and were favored by the British because of their Christian beliefs, were repressed by the independent Burmese government. With a population of more than 3 million, the Karen have been able to establish an insurgent state supported by smuggling diamonds and opium (see Geographies of Indulgence, Desire, and Addiction: Opium, p. 460). The Shan, with a population of 4.5 million in northern Burma, have similarly used drug profits to establish control of their territory and oppose the Burmese government.

The repressive authority of the Burmese military government is also opposed by Burmese who want a more democratic government. Popular protests in 1988 resulted in martial law and the establishment of the State Law and Order Restoration Council (SLORC—now known as the State Peace and Development Council). Elections were held in 1990 in which an opposition party, the National League for Democracy (NLD), won 60 percent of the vote, compared to 21 percent for the existing government party. SLORC cancelled the election results and remained in power. One of the leaders of the NLD is Aung San Suu Kyi, daughter of Burma independence hero General Aung San (**Figure 9.24**). Resolute in her quest for democracy and in her opposition to the authoritarian approach of SLORC, she has been kept under house arrest by the government and constitutionally barred from leading the country because she had lived abroad. She was awarded the Nobel Peace Prize in 1991.

Regional Values and Cooperation Defenders of more authoritarian styles of both military and elected governments in Southeast Asia claim that such systems are based on traditional Asian values. Among them are the Confucian idea of individual submission to authority, which emphasizes putting the nation and community before self, of consensus rather than conflict, of hard work and discipline, and of racial and religious harmony. This philosophy has been used to justify control of the press and constraints on freedom of expression by dominant parties that control government, the media, and sometimes even election outcomes. Calls for more open democracy and freedom of speech have increased with economic development, education, and a more diverse and international media.

Despite internal, regional, and international political conflicts, Southeast Asia provides a model for economic and political cooperation in the form of ASEAN—the Association of Southeast Asian Nations formed in 1967. ASEAN was formed with the goal of encouraging intraregional trade and reducing the political interference of both the United States and the Soviet Union. The initial alliance of Indonesia, Malaysia, Singapore, and Thailand was distinctly anti-communist and formed a defensive regional security group against China. The Asian Free Trade Association (AFTA) was created as part of ASEAN in 1993, reducing many tariffs within the region to less than 5 percent. A policy of constructive engagement with both military and socialist governments led to invitations to the rest of the region to join ASEAN (Brunei, 1994; Vietnam, 1995; Burma and Laos, 1997; Cambodia, 1999). Despite some resistance from Malaysia, ASEAN has generally been open to discussions with other nations and groups, including China and Australia.

Agricultural Development

Although agriculture has decreased in economic significance across most of the region, it is still a major employer and is essential to food security, employing more than 45 percent of the economically active population in Indonesia, Thailand, and Vietnam and almost 70 percent in Cambodia and Laos. Rice production continues to dominate the land area of Southeast Asia, but the traditional exports of spices and plantation crops, such as rubber, tea, coffee, and sugar, are still important. The area in plantations is only 15 percent of that in rice, with about half of the plantation area planted with rubber. Regional and international demand has increased the area planted with oil palm and pineapples, especially in Malaysia, the Philippines, and Thailand. Multinational corporations such as Del Monte and Dole are heavily involved in producing pineapples and other fruits in Thailand and the Philippines. Southeast Asian agriculture was trans-

FIGURE 9.24 Aung San Suu Kyi Nobel Peace Prize–winner Aung San Suu Kyi speaks to supporters while under house arrest in Burma.

formed by two major factors—the Green Revolution and land reform—in the last 50 years.

The Green Revolution comprised a technological package of higher yielding seeds, especially wheat, rice, and corn, that in combination with irrigation, fertilizers, pesticides, and farm machinery was able to increase crop production in the developing world. The Green Revolution contributed to dramatic increases in rice and other cereal production in Indonesia, the Philippines, and Thailand (**Figure 9.25**). As in other world regions, the benefits of the Green Revolution in Southeast Asia were unequally distributed. Communal land and rights to the rice harvest were lost in the new orientation to exports and wage labor, and the introduction of mechanical rice harvesting increased rural unemployment in countries such as Malaysia. The rate of successful adoption was higher among those with access to irrigation. When the new varieties were planted uniformly across large areas as monocultures, they became vulnerable to diseases and pests, such as the brown plant hopper. Rather than continue to use pesticides to combat such pests, the Indonesian government sponsored the use of integrated pest management, which uses less chemically intense techniques, by 2.5 million small farmers.

Land reform was a policy of new socialist governments—for example, in Vietnam—and of others seeking to reduce rural unrest in countries such as the Philippines, where land ownership was highly concentrated. In North Vietnam more than 70 percent of the land was redistributed and collectivized in 1954, although many peasants continued to farm small individual plots within larger collectives. Land reform in the Philippines has been partial and slow, with 7 percent of the crop area distributed to 9 percent of the mainly tenant population between 1972 and 1983. Landowners avoided reform by evicting tenants who might become eligible for land and by denying irrigation rights to new small holders.

Regional Development

The history, problems, and potential for regional development in Southeast Asia can be seen in two places: Singapore and Jakarta. In both cases the economic growth of the urban area has extended to transnational regions around the cities.

Singapore and the Strait of Malacca Singapore is a small, flat, marshy island that has been drained and developed to become the principal port and business center in Southeast Asia. It is one of the 25 wealthiest countries in the world in terms of per capita GDP and has the highest standard of living in Asia. Today, the international business executive flying into Singapore's modern airport sees towering high-rise offices, luxury hotels, and large-scale industrial facilities (**Figure 9.26**). When the British colonized the so-called Straits Settlements along the shores of the channel between the Malay peninsula and Indonesia, Singapore became the jewel of their Southeast Asian colonies, with its strategic location on the major route from the Indian Ocean to China. Northward from Singapore, along the west coast of the peninsula, the cities of Malacca, Kuala Lumpur, and Penang became the core of the British colonial administration and economy in the region (**Figure 9.27a**).

Although some equate Singapore and Hong Kong because they are both island Asian cities of great economic importance, Singapore appears much less chaotic and more modern than Hong Kong. It is more independent as a city-state, compared to Hong Kong's status as a British protectorate that recently became part of China.

The city of Singapore (effectively the same as the country) has a population of 4.5 million people and a high density of more than 6500

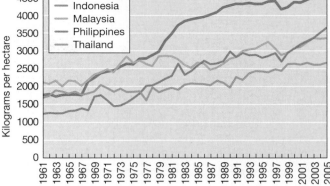

Rice yields

FIGURE 9.25 Green Revolution Growth in rice yields as countries adopted the Green Revolution in Southeast Asia. (*Source:* Data from UN Food and Agricultural Organization, available at **http://www.fao.org**.)

FIGURE 9.26 Singapore View of the city of Singapore looking across older colonial buildings to the modern high-rise city core with harbor cranes at loading docks in the distance.

(a)

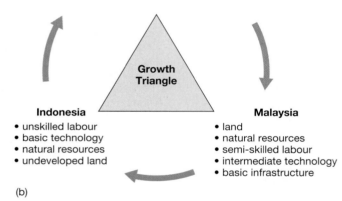

(b)

FIGURE 9.27 Malay peninsula and Singapore (a) The Malay peninsula and Singapore are a center for economic development in Southeast Asia, especially the Johor-Singapore-Riau growth triangle. (b) The economic complementarities of Singapore; Riau, Indonesia; and Johor, Malaysia. (*Source:* [a] Adapted from T. R. Leinbach and R. Ulack, *Southeast Asia: Diversity and Development.* Upper Saddle River, NJ: Prentice Hall, 2000, Map 14.1 and Map 14.6. [b] M. Sparke, J. Sidaway, T. Bunnell, and C. Grundy-Warr, "Triangulating the Borderless World: Geographies of Power in the Indonesia-Malaysia-Singapore Growth Triangle." *Transactions of the Institute of British Geographers,* NS29, 485–498.)

people per square kilometer. This is the second highest population density of any country in the world (only Monaco is higher). The superior infrastructure—especially the excellent port and international airport—has made Singapore the import and transshipment center for the region (often termed an *entrepôt*) and the busiest port in the world. Containers are moved from smaller feeder ships and planes onto larger ocean and air transport. It is one of the world's largest oil refining centers, where crude oil is unloaded and refined before shipment to the rest of Asia. These functions are complemented by a large variety of maritime service activities, including banking, insurance, communications, and consulting.

When Singapore became independent from Malaysia in 1965, the government immediately made the attraction of foreign firms and investment a priority. It offered a low-cost, hard-working, and compliant workforce for labor-intensive manufacturing and incentives to locate in new industrial parks. The country was successful in attracting companies that manufactured textiles and electronic equipment, such as stereos and TVs, and the economy began to grow at more than 10 percent a year.

As wages began to increase, labor shortages developed, and trade barriers grew internationally in the late 1970s, these industries became less competitive. The government of Singapore made the astute decision to move away from labor-intensive manufacturing to higher-technology activities that required a skilled workforce, such as precision engineering, aerospace, medical instruments, specialized chemicals, and, most importantly, the emerging computer industry. To support this policy, the government invested in advanced education, especially engineering and computing, in high-technology industrial parks, and in some state-owned pilot companies such as Singapore Aerospace. The strategy was successful. Singapore is now a center for information technology and aerospace, producing many of the world's computer hard drives and sound cards in companies like Seagate, as well as computer memory chips and software for Hewlett-Packard and Apple, among others.

Singapore has also diversified its service sector to include a wider range of financial, communications, and management activities and has attracted the regional headquarters of many multinational corporations. A number of Hong Kong businesspeople relocated to Singapore to avoid becoming part of China. Tourism has also become a significant industry. This diversification, as well as high consumption levels in the domestic market, allowed Singapore to cope with the 1983 oil crisis and 1997 Asian financial crisis somewhat more easily than other countries in the region.

Singapore has a population of diverse ethnicity and religion, but it is dominated (77 percent) by overseas Chinese, descendants of immigrants to Singapore in the colonial period who followed the religions of Buddhism and Taoism. Other groups include Malays (about 15 percent, mainly Muslim) and Indians (about 7 percent, mainly Hindu). As noted earlier, fertility rates are low in Singapore, and the government has tried to promote more births among the highly educated in order to reduce labor shortages and ensure a workforce to support the older population.

Colonial Singapore was residentially segregated, with the British living next to the government buildings on the east shore of the Singapore River, Chinatown on the west riverbank, and Indian and Malay neighborhoods farther toward the east. There are remnants of this structure in contemporary Singapore, but the city is now characterized by dozens of tall office buildings, housing complexes, "New Towns," and industrial parks such as Jurong on the western end of the island. The container ports stretch along the south shore of the island.

Singapore has avoided the poor sprawling squatter settlements of other Asian cities through high wages and employment, careful urban planning, a public transit system, and the construction of thousands of publicly funded housing units. Compulsory but flexible savings plans have allowed most residents to purchase their apartments.

The government has made serious attempts to foster harmony among ethnic groups and to create a sense of national identity by designating four official languages (Mandarin Chinese, English, Malay, and Indian Tamil) and requiring a mix of groups in housing developments. They promote an Asian identity (as well as government authority and a cooperative labor force) through schools and national military service that emphasize hard work, community consensus, and respect for authority. They also enforce Singapore's image of a clean and crime-free environment through very strict rules against litter and graffiti, media censorship, and licensing of satellite dishes and street entertainers.

In recent years Singapore has looked beyond the city to develop and invest in the wider region. Manufacturing has expanded to a new Growth Triangle (called SIJORI) that includes Johor Baharu in Malaysia and the Riau Islands (especially Batam) of Indonesia. It has been promoted as a "borderless" growth area and an example of how to prosper in a globalizing world. Geographer Matt Sparke suggests that the growth triangle has allowed Singaporean capital to escape the high wage, resource, and land costs of Singapore through moving to adjacent regions of Indonesia and Malaysia (**Figure 9.27b**). Trade restrictions have been eased within the triangle so that labor- and land-intensive activities are carried out in the province of Johor and Batam, with value and business services added in Singapore in a flexible production system. Singapore obtains half of its water supply from Johor and has developed agroprocessing industries in the Riau Islands that supply Singapore with pork, chicken, prawns, and flowers. Singapore investors are also active in Thailand and China.

Johor Baharu is the southernmost in a string of Malaysian cities along the western side of the Malay peninsula facing the Strait of Malacca. To the north, the island of Penang shares many characteristics with Singapore in that it has become a center for high-technology manufacturing for the computer industry and has a population made up mostly of Chinese. Government investment in training skilled labor (many young women) and generous tax and free trade incentives have attracted multinationals such as Intel, Sony, Philips, Motorola, and Hitachi to the island, which is connected to mainland Malaysia by a bridge. Penang has become known as Silicon Island. Kuala Lumpur, located about halfway between Penang and Singapore, originally developed as a center for the colonial tin industry. Now, as the capital of Malaysia, it has a population of about 1.5 million and is the center of a manufacturing region called the Klang Valley Conurbation that includes a free trade zone.

Java and Bali, Indonesia

Java is the most populous and economically significant island of Indonesia; Java, Bali, and Madura constitute the inner core of this island nation. Sixty-two percent of Indonesia's population and 25 percent of that of Southeast Asia—130 million people—live on Java at high population densities. Four cities have more than 1 million people, including Jakarta, with more than 10 million.

Java is famous for its fertile agricultural landscapes, carved with elaborate terraced rice paddies nurtured by centuries of human attention and by nutrient-rich volcanic soils. The island is about 1000 kilometers (650 miles) long from east to west, with a volcanic mountain chain creating its spine. More than two-thirds of the island is under cultivation, mainly irrigated rice. Early travelers from India brought both the Hindu and Buddhist religions to the island, producing the magnificent structures at Borobudur and a number of other temples. The Dutch established the headquarters of the Dutch East India Company in the 17th century at Batavia on the swampy northwest coast of Java, where there were several Muslim kingdoms and sultanates. Renamed Jakarta after independence, this became the capital of Indonesia and the focus of industrial development, especially an export textile industry and factories producing shoes, appliances, and lower-technology electronic goods.

Jakarta's downtown area includes the old city fort, the Portuguese church, many silver-roofed mosques reflecting Indonesia's Islamic tradition, a central business district, and spacious squares and parks, such as the Medan Merdeka. The Istiquial mosque is one of the largest in the world. The old Dutch port, Sunda Kelapa, hosts dozens of sailing ships. Many houses are built of wood and bamboo mats. The expanded metropolitan region around

FIGURE 9.28 Jakarta Waste pollutes canals in the slums of Jakarta as a woman carries drinking water home to her family.

Jakarta also includes the cities of Bogor, Tangerang, and Bekasi, with a total of 20 million people and thousands of factories representing 80 percent of Indonesia's industrial employment. The larger region combines the first letters of each city into the name *Jabotabek*.

The city is surrounded by unplanned squatter settlements that lack basic services, and it has a large informal sector. Informal-sector activities include street selling, charging fees for guarding parked cars, assisting traffic flow, and filling cars to the three occupants required to travel on some streets. The growing population of Jakarta moves around the city in an increasing number of automobiles as well as on public transportation, such as buses and pedal taxis (called *betjol*). Traffic congestion and air pollution can be a serious problem.

The majority of people in Jakarta use septic tanks and pit latrine facilities. A large proportion of the urban poor disposes of human waste directly into the canals, drains, and rivers (**Figure 9.28**). The rapid urbanization of the region has resulted in increased flooding downstream, especially in the low-lying areas of north Jakarta. The KIP (Kampung Improvement Programme) attempted to improve the welfare of the urban poor by upgrading their living environment and basic infrastructure. While the program improved the condition of large slum areas, a new pattern emerged as improvements increased property values, attracting higher-income groups and forcing the poor to create new slums.

As the capital of Indonesia, Jakarta is often a focus of social unrest. For example, in May 1998, after government budget cuts and price increases associated with the Asian economic crisis, rioters set fire to shops and other businesses owned by overseas Chinese and the family of President Suharto (who at the time had ruled for 32 years). Discontent was fueled by the cronyism of the Suharto family and by resentment of perceived Chinese wealth. Suharto was forced to resign, and in fiercely contested elections power passed through parliamentary selection to more democratic rule.

The island of Bali lies off the eastern coast of Java. With images of waving palm trees, soft breezes, towering volcanoes, and pristine beaches, Bali has been promoted to the world as a tropical paradise with a unique culture ideal for romantic vacations (**Figure 9.29**). This small island of 3 million residents in the Indonesian archipelago has become a major international tourist destination, with more than 4 million visitors a year.

Bali has maintained Hindu traditions within an increasingly Muslim Indonesia. It has a centuries-old landscape of rice terraces and temples. The cultural attractions include Hindu temples dating from the fourth century A.D., crafts such as batik cloth and wood carving, dance, traditional *gamelan* orchestras, and the retelling of Hindu and other legends with intricately carved shadow puppets.

FIGURE 9.29 The Ulu Danu temple
The Ulu Danu temple on Lake Bratan in Bali is one of the cultural attractions often visited on day trips to Bali's verdant interior.

More than 1 million tourists fly directly into Bali each year. Perhaps another million travel from Java and neighboring countries. Tourism makes up nearly 40 percent of the gross domestic product of the island economy. The standard of living in Bali is much higher on average than in other parts of Indonesia.

Tourism to Bali began to grow in the 1920s when Dutch steamships began to stop offshore and the luxurious Bali Hotel opened in the capital of Denpasar. An art colony grew up around the community of Ubud in the lush interior hills, and members of the international artistic and literary community who arrived to experience exotic culture introduced local artists to new techniques and opportunities. In 1937, Mexican author Miguel Covarrubias wrote a book on Bali in which he lamented that the island was "doomed to disappear under the merciless onslaught of modern commercialism and standardization." In 1972, the government of Indonesia drew up the Master Plan for the Development of Tourism in Bali to make Bali the "showcase" of Indonesia and to serve as the model of future tourism development for the rest of the country. The plan was financed by the UN Development Programme and carried out by the World Bank. The plan called for the focus of development in the southern peninsula of the island, Nusa Dua, with only day trips to the interior in order to protect cultural integrity.

Bali has become a focus for research on the costs and benefits of tourism. Critics charge that the culture has lost its authenticity in constructing images for international tourists, who come especially from Australia and Europe, and that economic development has placed unsustainable pressures on water supplies and coastal ecosystems. Coral reefs have been destroyed to build new tourist accommodations, and waste collection is inadequate. Some local people complain that the mass marketing of their culture is destroying their way of life; that communities are being forced to compete for tourists through lavish festivals; and that communities are ignoring the traditional laws (*adat*) that govern everything from land tenure to social relations.

SUMMARY AND CONCLUSIONS

This review of the geography and distinctive landscapes of Southeast Asia reveals a region of rapid change, complexity, and great economic, political, and environmental challenges. The region illustrates at least two major waves of integration into the global economic system—colonization by Europe (preceded by extensive trade with China and India) and 20th-century economic restructuring toward exports associated with foreign investment and industrialization. Demographic linkages to the rest of the world include a large population of labor migrants and refugees and significant historical immigration from other Asian regions, especially China.

There can be few fixed images of Southeast Asia, as is evident in the sudden collapse of the thriving industrial economies of Thailand, Malaysia, Indonesia, and Singapore in 1997 and in the new reforms that have opened markets to foreign investment in the socialist and war-weary countries of Cambodia, Laos, and Vietnam. The geopolitical and economic relationships with Europe and the United States fashioned by colonialism and the Cold War are being replaced by new linkages with Japan, China, and Australia and by the emergence of the independent regional network of ASEAN. The diversity of religious, ethnic, and political beliefs within Southeast Asian nations demands innovative approaches to national integration and recognition of local identity, but this diversity has also produced long-standing rebellions and demands for autonomy.

Future sustainable development in Southeast Asia must confront the impact of urban growth and land-use change in much of the region, especially air pollution, spreading slums, and inadequate infrastructure in the cities, and deforestation of the highlands of the mainland and many of the islands such as Borneo. The vulnerability of the region was illustrated tragically by the 2004 Indian Ocean tsunami. Managing the environment and land use more equitably and ecologically will contribute to maintaining and, it is hoped, improving social and economic conditions in this region.

KEY TERMS

Association of Southeast Asian Nations (ASEAN) (p. 426)
Culture System (p. 445)

domino theory (p. 447)
land bridge (p. 427)

overseas Chinese (p. 452)
transmigration (p. 451)

tsunami (p. 428)
Wallace's Line (p. 436)

REVIEW QUESTIONS

Testing Your Understanding

1. Southeast Asia is often divided into two main regions. What are these regions called and which countries are in each? What is the name of the newest independent nation emerging in Southeast Asia?

2. What is ASEAN and what role does it play in Southeast Asia?

3. Which countries in Southeast Asia have governments that followed socialist or communist ideas? Which countries have pursued more capitalist paths and open economies? How has the concept of "Asian values" been used to explain authoritarian tendencies in Southeast Asian politics?

4. What is the main crop in Southeast Asia and the main systems by which it is produced? How and where did the Green Revolution affect this crop?

5. What were the five main European colonial powers in Southeast Asia and what regions were under their control between about 1500 and 1890? Which country remained independent during the colonial period? Identify four key mineral or agricultural products that the colonial powers exported from Southeast Asia and the regions from which they came.

6. What factors led to the Vietnam War? What were some of the effects of the war on the peoples and environments of the region?

7. Which Southeast Asian countries participated in the so-called Asian economic miracle? What triggered the 1997 financial crisis? What were some of the responses to the crisis?

8. What is transmigration, and how does it contribute to ethnic tensions and environmental degradation in Indonesia?

9. What factors explain the geographical patterns of damage from the 2004 tsunami in Southeast and South Asia?

Thinking Geographically

1. How does the monsoon influence the climate and vegetation of Southeast Asia?
2. What roles did India and China play in Southeast Asia prior to the colonial period and how did this influence culture and religion? What political and economic roles have Japan and the United States played in Southeast Asia during the 20th century?
3. Who are the "overseas Chinese," and what are three Southeast Asian countries where they constitute more than 10 percent of the population? What are their traditional roles in the economy? How and where has this resulted in a backlash against ethnic Chinese?
4. How do the crops and commercial transactions of the Golden Triangle affect Southeast Asia and other regions of the world?
5. When and why have Burma and Cambodia been a focus of international concern about human rights in the last three decades?

FURTHER READING

Atkinson, J. M., and Errington, S. (eds.), *Power and Difference: Gender in Island Southeast Asia.* Stanford, CA: Stanford University Press, 1990.

Bahramitash, R., *Liberation from Liberalization: Gender and Globalization in Southeast Asia.* New York: Zed Books, 2005.

Bishop, R., Phillips, J., and Yeo, W. (eds.), *Postcolonial Urbanism: Southeast Asian Cities and Global Processes.* New York: Routledge, 2003.

Brookfield, H. C., and Byron, Y., *South-East Asia's Environmental Future: The Search for Sustainability.* New York: United Nations University Press, 1993.

Brookfield, H. C., Lian, F. J., Kwai-Sim, L., and Potter, L., *Borneo and the Malay Peninsula.* In B. L. Turner II, W. C. Clark, R. W. Kates, J. T. Mathews, and W. B. Meyer (eds.), *The Earth as Transformed by Human Action* (pp. 495–511). Cambridge: Cambridge University Press, 1990.

Brown, I., *Economic Change in South-East Asia c. 1830–1980.* Kuala Lumpur: Oxford University Press, 1997.

Cox, C. R., *Chasing the Dragon: Into the Heart of the Golden Triangle.* New York: Holt/Marion Wood, 1996.

Day, T., *Fluid Iron: State Formation in Southeast Asia.* Honolulu: University of Hawaii Press, 2002.

Dixon, C., and Drakakis-Smith, D. (eds.), *Uneven Development in South East Asia.* Brookfield, VT: Ashgate, 1998.

Dwyer, D. (ed.), *South East Asian Development: Geographical Perspectives.* Harlow, England: Longman Scientific & Technical, 1990.

Forbes, D. K., *Asian Metropolis: Urbanisation and the Southeast Asian City.* New York: Oxford University Press, 1996.

Funston, J. (ed.), *Government and Politics in Southeast Asia.* New York: Zed Books, 2001.

Geertz, C., *Agricultural Involution: The Processes of Ecological Change in Indonesia.* San Francisco: University of California Press, 1994.

Hill, R. D. (ed.), *South-East Asia: A Systematic Geography.* New York: Oxford University Press, 1979.

Hitchcock, M., King, V. T., and Parnwell, M. J. G. (eds.), *Tourism in South-East Asia.* London: Routledge, 1993.

Howe, L., *The Changing World of Bali: Religion, Society and Tourism.* New York: Routledge, 2005.

Kratoska, P. H., Nordhold, S., and Raben, R. (eds.), *Locating Southeast Asia: Geographies of Knowledge and Politics of Space.* Athens, OH: Ohio University Press, 2005.

Leinbach, T. R., and Ulack, R., *Southeast Asia: Diversity and Development.* Upper Saddle River, NJ: Prentice Hall, 2000.

McGee, T. G., "Eurocentrism in Geography: The Case of Asian Urbanization," *Canadian Geographer* 35(1991), 332–344.

Murray, G., and Perera, A., *Singapore: The Global City State.* New York: St. Martin's Press, 1996.

Palmujoki, E., *Regionalism and Globalism in Southeast Asia.* New York: Palgrave, 2001.

Parnwell, M. J. G., and Bryant, R. L. (eds.), *Environmental Change in South-East Asia: People, Politics and Sustainable Development.* New York: Routledge, 1996.

Resosudarmo, B. P. (ed.), *The Politics and Economics of Indonesia's Natural Resources.* Washington, D.C.: Resources for the Future, 2006.

Rigg, J., *Southeast Asia: The Human Landscape of Modernization and Development.* New York: Routledge, 2003.

Rodan, G., Hewison, K., and Robison, R., *The Political Economy of South-East Asia: Markets, Power and Contestation.* South Melbourne, Victoria: Oxford University Press, 2006.

Rosaldo, R. (ed.), *Cultural Citizenship in Island Southeast Asia: Nation and Belonging in the Hinterlands.* Berkeley: University of California Press, 2003.

SarDesai, D. R., *Southeast Asia: Past and Present.* Boulder: Westview Press, 1997.

Sarker, S., and Niyogi De, E. (eds.), *Trans-status Subjects: Gender in the Globalization of South and Southeast Asia.* Durham: Duke University Press, 2002.

Schmidt, J. D., Hersh, J., and Fold, N. (eds.), *Social Change in Southeast Asia.* New York: Longman, 1997.

Scott, J. C., *The Moral Economy of the Peasant: Rebellion and Subsistence in Southeast Asia.* New Haven: Yale University Press, 1976.

Tarling, N. (ed.), *The Cambridge History of Southeast Asia* (4 vols.). Cambridge: Cambridge University Press, 1999.

Ulack, R., and Pauer, G., *Atlas of Southeast Asia.* New York: Macmillan, 1988.

Wall, G., Mitchell, B., and Knight, D., "Bali: Sustainable Development, Tourism and Coastal Management," *Ambio* 26 (1997), 90–96.

Watters, R. F., and McGee, T. G., *Asia-Pacific: New Geographies of the Pacific Rim.* London: Hurst & Co., 1997.

Wong, T., Shaw, B. J., and Goh, K. C., *Challenging Sustainability: Urban Development and Change in Southeast Asia.* Singapore: Marshall Cavendish Academic, 2006.

FILMS, MUSIC, AND POPULAR LITERATURE

Films

Blue Collar and Buddha. Directed by Taggart Siegel, 1987. This documentary follows the mounting resentment toward the Laotian refugees who have settled in a small blue-collar American town.

Buffalo Boy. Directed by Minh Nguyen-Vo, 2004. Gender and family relationships are explored in this story about a young boy herding buffalos in Southern Vietnam.

Dekada '70. Directed by Chito S. Roño, 2002. Set in the Philippines, this film tells the story of a middle-class family and the ways in which their life is shaped by the political context. The film is an adaptation of the book *Dekada '70* by Lualhati Bautista.

Indochine. Directed by Regis Wargnier, 1992. A story of romance and separation during the transition from French colonial rule of Indochina to the U.S. presence in Vietnam.

The Killing Fields. Directed by Roland Joffé, 1984. The film traces the experiences of Cambodian Dith Pran, who was working for *The New York Times*, after he was forced by the Khmer Rouge to join the long march out of Phnom Penh into the countryside.

Memories of Gold, Memories of Silk. Directed by Catherine Choron-Baix, 2003. This documentary follows the life and art of Prince Nithakhong Somsanith, born in Laos and settling in France.

The Opium Kings. Directed by Adrian Cowell, 1998. This documentary, shot in the guerilla-held opium-producing regions of Burma, is a report on the black-market heroin that comes from the Shan States of Burma.

The Quiet American. Directed by Philip Noyce, 2003. Based on a novel by Graham Greene about a British journalist and the growing U.S. intervention in Vietnam.

The Scent of Green Papaya. Directed by Tran Anh Hung, 1993. The interior life of a Vietnamese household in the 1950s, as seen through the eyes of a young servant girl.

Suriyothai. Directed by Chatrichalerm Yukol, 2002. A Thai historical epic set in the 16th century depicting Queen Phra Suriyothai in combat against invasion from Burma.

The Year of Living Dangerously. Directed by Peter Weir, 1982. Set in Indonesia during the 1965 coup against President Sukarno, the film examines the chaos in Jakarta from the perspective of an Australian journalist.

Music

Bayanihan Dance Company. *Bayanihan Dance Company*. New York: Monitor, 1992.

Isan Slete. *The Flower Of Isan: Songs and Music from Northeast Thailand*. London: Globe Style, 1989.

Mustapha, Sabah Habas. *So-La-Li*. Minneapolis MN: Omnium, 2000.

Naam, Fong. *Ancient-Contemporary Music from Thailand*. Tucson, AZ: Celestial Harmonies Records, 1995.

Tiếng Hát Quê Húong Ensemble. *From Saigon to Hanoi, Traditional Songs and Music of Vietnam*. Milan Records, 2001.

Various Artists. *The Music of Vietnam* (3 vols.). Tucson, AZ: Celestial Harmonies Records, 1995.

Various Artists. *Rough Guide to the Music of Indonesia*. London: World Music Network, 2000.

Popular Literature

Ahmad, S. *No Harvest But a Thorn*. New York: Oxford University Press, 1972. Depicts the hardships of a farming family in Malaysia.

Ananta Toer, P. *The Buru Quartet*. New York: William Morrow, 1991. Pramoedya Ananta Toer's four-part epic encompasses the beginnings of the collapse of colonialism in Java nearly 100 years ago.

Bnounyavong, O. *Mother's Beloved: Stories from Laos*. Hong Kong: Hong Kong University Press, 1999. This book of 14 deceptively simple stories tells of ordinary Lao people, their customs, traditions, and values.

Burgess, A. *The Long Day Wanes: A Malayan Trilogy*. New York: Norton, 1965. Three novels about the Chinese, Indian, Malays, Eurasians, and British colonialists who inhabited the pre-independence Malaya of the 1950s.

Ghosh, A. *The Glass Palace: A Novel*. New York: Random House, 2001. Burma, Malaya, India, and the British Empire come together in this novel that follows the life of Rajkumar, an Indian in Burma, caught up in a history spanning the colonial period and repression under the SLORC regime.

Godshalk, C. S. *Kalimantaan*. New York: Henry Holt, 1998. This novel describes the lives and ambitions of the English in colonial Borneo, including one man, Gideon Barr, who sets himself up as a rajah.

Khoo Thwe, P. *From the Land of Green Ghosts: A Burmese Odyssey*. New York: Harper Perennial, 2003. A memoir that spans the latter half of the 20th century in Burma, from a childhood among the Karenni tribe to student rebellion and migration to England.

Lubis, M. *Twilight in Djakarta*. New York: Vanguard Press, 1964. A searing critique of corruption and poverty in 1950s Jakarta.

Orwell, G. *Burmese Days*. New York: Harcourt Brace, 1934. A novel about life and racism in a remote outpost of colonial Burma.

Phung, V. T. *Dumb Luck: A Novel*. P. Zinoman, (ed.), translated by N. N. Câm and P. Zinoman. Ann Arbor: University of Michigan Press, 2002. The first translation of Vu Trong Phung, this is a major work of Vietnamese fiction and satire that comments on modernity and colonialism.

Rizal, J. *Noli Me Tangere (The Lost Eden)*. Bloomington, IN: Indiana University Press, 1961. A classic account of Philippine suffering under Spanish rule that inspired independence struggles.

Sudham, P. *Monsoon Country*. St. John's, Newfoundland, Canada: Breakwater Books, 1990. This novel conveys the cultural tension between the East and West and the clashes between the new powers and the old values in Thailand.

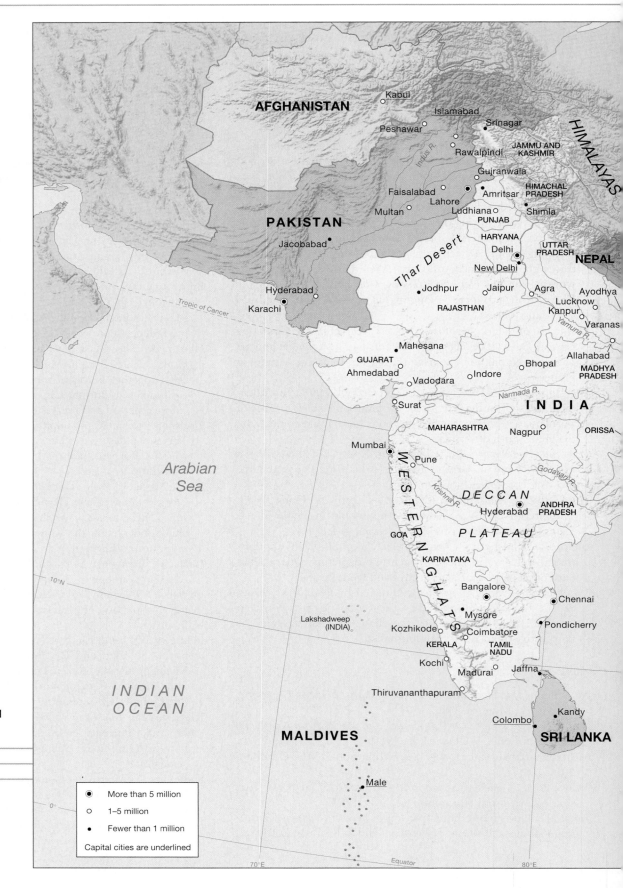

FIGURE 10.1

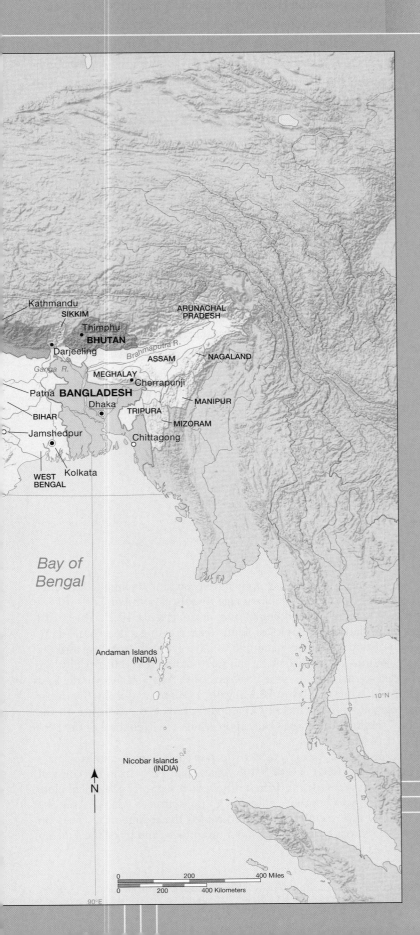

Kathmandu

SIKKIM

ARUNACHAL
PRADESH

Thimphu
● **BHUTAN**

● Darjeeling

Brahmaputra R.

ASSAM

NAGALAND

Ganga R.

MEGHALAY

Patna **BANGLADESH**

● Cherrapunji

Dhaka ◉

BIHAR

TRIPURA

MANIPUR

○ Jamshedpur ◉

MIZORAM

○ Chittagong

Kolkata

WEST
BENGAL

Bay of
Bengal

Andaman Islands
(INDIA)

10°N

Nicobar Islands
(INDIA)

↑
N

| 0 | 200 | 400 Miles |

| 0 | 200 | 400 Kilometers |

90°E

South Asia consists of Afghanistan, Bangladesh, Bhutan, India, the Maldives, Nepal, Pakistan, and Sri Lanka—a region that is naturally bounded by mountain ranges and seas **(Figure 10.1)**. To the north is the almost impenetrable mountain rim of the Karakoram range and the Himalayas, while to the northwest are the forbidding ranges of the Sulaiman and the Hindu Kush. The Indian Peninsula and its large offshore island of Sri Lanka are girdled by the seas of the Indian Ocean—the Arabian Sea to the west and the Bay of Bengal to the east. It is a very heavily populated world region, with 1.35 billion people, more than 1 billion of whom live in India.

South Asia is semiperipheral or peripheral and politically volatile, though it is also a region of great potential. It is still a land of villages: Only about 10 percent of the population of Bhutan and Nepal live in urban settlements, while in the greater part of the region, the urban population amounts to between 25 and 35 percent of the total. Not surprisingly, rural ways of life and traditional cultures remain extremely important throughout South Asia.

An even broader defining characteristic of the region is poverty. The majority of South Asia's rural population is desperately poor, as are millions of the region's city dwellers. Hunger and malnutrition are widespread; barely half the adult population is literate, and only a minority of the population lives in sound housing with electricity and piped water. The abiding image, as described by Indian author Pankaj Mishra, is "the broken road, the wandering cows, the open gutter, the low ramshackle shops, the ground littered with garbage, the pressing crowd, the dust."[1]

However, another defining characteristic of the region derives from the stark contrasts that exist within and among places and subregions. Amid hierarchical traditions and social conservatism are deeply rooted ideals of equity and social justice. Amid predominantly rural settings are megacities like Delhi, Kolkata (formerly Calcutta), and Mumbai (formerly Bombay) in India, Dhaka in Bangladesh, and Karachi in Pakistan. Furthermore, amid extreme economic backwardness and widespread illiteracy there exists intellectual refinement and world-class technological innovation. To the stereotypical image of slow-moving lifestyles of dusty poverty we must add the legacies of sophisticated civilizations and the imprint of a growing middle class—computer programmers, managers, engineers, shop owners, media consultants, and so on—whose social practices and material consumption are in line with those of the middle classes in Europe and North America.

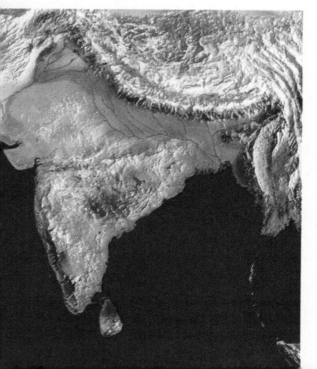

FIGURE 10.2 South Asia from space This image clearly shows how South Asia is naturally bounded by mountains and oceans.

ENVIRONMENT AND SOCIETY IN SOUTH ASIA

Two aspects of South Asia's physical geography have been fundamental to its evolution as a world region. First, as the satellite image reveals, South Asia is clearly set apart from the rest of Asia by a forbidding mountain rim (**Figure 10.2**). This arc of mountain ranges has isolated the peoples of South Asia, creating a large-scale natural setting in which distinctive human geographies have evolved. A second striking feature of the satellite image is the extent of the surrounding seas. Historically, the Arabian Sea provided a crucial trade route between South Asia and the Middle East and the Mediterranean, while the Bay of Bengal gave access to (and from) Southeast Asia. These seas, together with the Indian Ocean, also produce the moisture for the summer monsoons, seasonal torrents of rain upon which the livelihood of the peoples of South Asia depends.

In geological terms, South Asia is a recent addition to the continental landmass of Asia. The greater part of what is now South Asia broke away from the coast of Africa about 100 million years ago. It drifted slowly on a separate geological plate for more than 70 million years until it collided with the southern edge of Asia (see Figure 1.18). The slow but relentless impact crumpled the sedimentary rocks on the south coast of Asia into a series of lofty mountain ranges and lifted the Tibetan

[1]P. Mishra, *Butter Chicken in Ludhiana: Travels in Small Town India*, London: Penguin, 1995, p. 93.

Plateau more than 5 kilometers (3.1 miles) into the air. The Himalayas, which stand at the center of South Asia's mountain rim, are still rising (at a rate of about 25 centimeters—9.8 inches—per century) as a result of this geological event.

Landforms and Landscapes

Not surprisingly, the principal physiographic regions of South Asia—the Peninsular Highlands, the Mountain Rim, the Plains, and the Coastal Fringe—also reflect this major geological event. Between the mountain rim and the peninsular highlands of India—which stand on the ancient geological plate that drifted across from Africa—are alluvial plains of young sedimentary rocks and material that has been washed down from the surrounding mountain rim and plateau. The coastal fringe of peninsular India, together with the coastal plains of Sri Lanka, the Maldives, and the Andaman and Nicobar islands, constitutes a fourth physiographic region (**Figure 10.3**).

FIGURE 10.3 South Asia's physiographic regions The physical geography of South Asia is framed by the highland plateaus of an ancient continental plate and a young mountain rim, separated by broad plains of alluvium washed down from both. (*Source:* Adapted from B. L. C. Johnson, *South Asia,* 2nd ed. London: Heinemann, 1982, p. 9.)

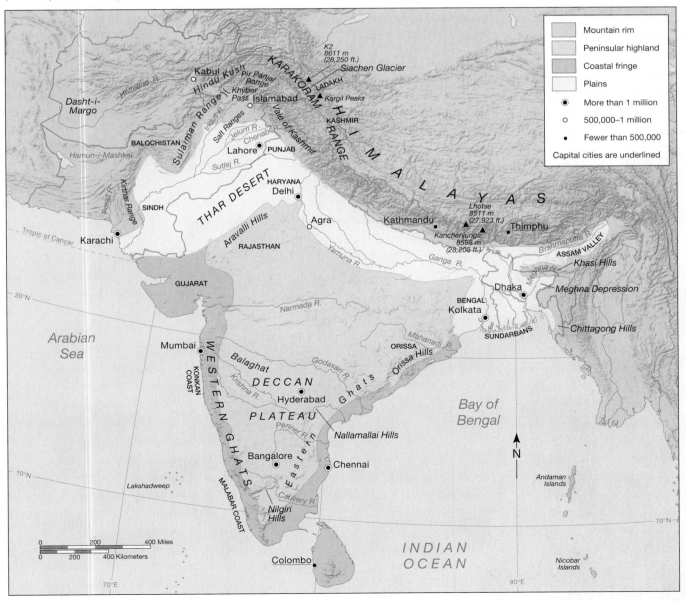

The Peninsular Highlands The Peninsular Highlands of India form a broad plateau flanked by two chains of hills and uplands. The highlands rest on an ancient shield of granites and other igneous and metamorphosed sedimentary material, together with some very old sedimentary rocks. This shield has remained a relatively stable landmass for much of the past 30 million years. However, between 65 and 55 million years ago, immense fissure eruptions of lava buried the northwestern part of the peninsula beneath up to 3000 meters (9842 feet) of basalt, a dense volcanic rock. Today, this lava plateau—the Deccan Lava Plateau—covers about one-third of the Peninsular Highlands (**Figure 10.4**). To the north and southeast of the lava plateau, the ancient shield has been shaped into a broad area of plateaus, basins, and escarpments (steep slopes resulting from erosion or faulting). Surrounding this central body of the Peninsular Highlands is a series of hills and uplands. These include Aravalli Hills, the Western Ghats (the steep westward-facing slope of the eastward-tilted shield of the Peninsular Highlands), the Nilgiri Hills, the Eastern Ghats, the Orissa Hills, the Nallamallai Hills, and the Balaghat (see Figure 10.3). These uplands are sparsely populated but have long provided refuge for many of India's tribal populations and for renegade princes, slopes on which to locate tea and coffee plantations, and shelter for wild game.

The rugged topography of the Peninsular Highlands has left the region somewhat isolated. Historically, it developed its own traditions and distinctive cultures, supporting a mosaic of local kingdoms. Because the only sources of water for farming are the seasonal and unpredictable annual rains of the monsoon, the peoples of the region have never enjoyed a rich agricultural economy, and subsistence farming and small villages still dominate the landscape throughout most of the region. There are, though, valuable deposits of iron ore, manganese, gold, copper, asbestos, and mica in the region, and thick seams of coal are present in the northeastern and east-central parts. The region is also the location of several of India's larger and most industrialized cities—including Ahmedabad, Bangalore, Bhopal, and Mysore.

FIGURE 10.4 Deccan Lava Plateau This landscape in the northern province of Madhya Pradesh is part of the vast landscape of the Deccan Lava Plateau.

FIGURE 10.5 Mountain Rim This photograph shows the Hunza Valley in Pakistan, with Mount Rakaposhi (25,550 feet), part of the Karakoram Range, in the distance.

The Mountain Rim The Mountain Rim is a vast region of spectacular mountain terrain, remote valleys, varied flora and fauna, ancient Buddhist monasteries, and fiercely independent tribal societies. The physical geography of the region is complex, with several mountain ranges together sweeping in a 2500-kilometer (1554-mile) arc that contains numerous high peaks (**Figure 10.5**). Among the highest are K2 (8611 meters; 28,250 feet), Kanchenjunga (8598 meters; 28,208 feet), Lhotse (8511 meters; 27,923 feet), and 19 others of 7000 meters or more (22,964 feet), all of them among the world's 30 highest peaks. In addition to these high peaks are parallel ranges of lower but still impressive mountains and bands of deeply incised, rugged foothills. The higher ranges are bare rock with glaciated features, but some of the lower ranges and foothills are forested with "chir" (*Pinus longifolia*), while the low outer ridges carry a sparse dry scrub. The Mountain Rim can be traversed only in a few key passes. These include the famous Khyber Pass in Pakistan's Northwest Frontier and the Rohtang La and Kunzum La between northern India and Tibet.

At the heart of the Mountain Rim are the young but spectacular Himalaya and Karakoram ranges. Arcing to the west are the structurally complex ridges, ranges, and basins of the Hindu Kush, the Sulaiman range, and the Kirthar range, and behind these are several basins of inland drainage containing shallow playa lakes, such as Dasht-i-Margo and Hamun-i-Mashkel. Arcing to the east is a series of parallel folded hills and valleys that reach the coast in the Chittagong Hills. Coal is found in workable quantities in parts of the mountain rim; oil-bearing ranges have been located in the Salt Ranges (also a source of rock salt), the Assam Valley, and Gujarat; and natural gas is present in Bangladesh and the Sindh region. Still slowly rising, the Mountain Rim suffers from earthquakes, and severe shocks have occurred at various places along the entire length of the rim. In 2005, an earthquake centered on the border between Pakistan's North-West Frontier province and Kashmir killed some 80,000 people and left hundreds of thousands more homeless.

Because of the high altitude and barren terrain, much of this region is uninhabitable. Yet interspersed among the high peaks and the foothills are protected gorges and fertile valleys that sustain isolated settlements of mountain peoples (**Figure 10.6**). The largest of the fertile valleys is the Vale of Kashmir, a verdant basin some 130 kilometers (81 miles) long and between 30 and 40 kilometers (19 to 25 miles) wide that is enclosed by the Himalayas to the east and the snow-capped ridges of the Pir Panjal range to the west. In this and other valleys it is possible to grow rice, with corn and wheat at higher elevations and orchards—especially of apricots and walnuts—on the valley slopes. Herds of sheep, yak, and goats are kept on the higher slopes of the valleys and in the more arid valleys and basins.

FIGURE 10.6 Mountain agriculture Human settlement within the Mountain Rim is largely confined to sheltered valleys, many of which are quite productive. Shown here is part of the Hindu Kush region, near Chitral, Pakistan.

The Plains Broad plains of young sedimentary rocks and alluvium have been created by the deposition of material eroded from both the Peninsular Highlands and the Mountain Rim. Three river systems—the Indus, the Ganga (Ganges), and the Brahmaputra—begin within 1600 kilometers (994 miles) of one another in the Himalayas but flow in three different directions through the mountains and into the plains. The Indus flows to the west, through Pakistan, to the Arabian Sea. The Brahmaputra flows eastward before doubling back through the Assam Valley and then flowing south to the Bay of Bengal. The Ganga flows southward before turning east, eventually merging with the Brahmaputra and forming a vast delta, more than 300 kilometers (186 miles) wide.

All three river systems provide the Plains region with a steady, if uneven, flow of melting snow. As a result, the Plains region has long been widely irrigated and has supported a high population density. The great dynasties of India—the Mauryan (320–125 B.C.), Gupta (A.D. 320–480), and Mughal (1526–1707)—all rose to prominence in this region, and the British moved their imperial capital here, to Delhi. Today, the Plains contain some of the most productive agricultural lands of South Asia (**Figure 10.7**). Cultivation of grains and rice is the predominant activity (see Signature Region: The Indus Plains, p. 478).

There are no significant mineral resources in the region, which is an immense plain built up from detritus eroded from the Himalayas. The monotony of the plains is broken up only by minor physical features: the *bhabar,* a tract of boulders and coarser gravels that skirts the hills to the north of the Ganga plains; the marshy *terai* areas that collect the drainage that falls freely through the *bhabar;* shallow salt-pans, known as *usar* plains, where chemical soil constituents have been deposited in dazzling sheets as water has evaporated from short-lived lakes and ponds; and occasional patches of low, sandy, undulating uplands known as *bhur.* Otherwise, most of the plains are very much as they were described almost 100 years ago in a government survey:

"... a level plain, the monotony of which is broken only by the numerous village sites and groves of dark-olive mango-trees which meet the eye in every direction. The great plain is, however, highly cultivated, and the fields are never bare except during the hot months, after the spring harvest has been gathered, and before the rainy season has sufficiently advanced for the autumn crops to have appeared above the ground. . . . With the breaking of the monsoon in the middle or end of June the scene changes as if by magic; the turf is renewed, and tall grasses begin to shoot in the small patches of jungle. Even the salt *usar* plains put on a green mantle, which lasts for a very short time after the close of the rains. A month later the autumn crops—rice, the millets, and maize [corn]—have begun to clothe the naked fields. These continue to clothe the ground until late in the year, and are succeeded by the spring crops—wheat, barley, and gram [a kind of chickpea]. In March they ripen and the great plain is then a rolling sea of golden corn [wheat], in which appear islands of trees and villages. . . ."[2]

Not all of the Plains are so productive, however. Within the Plains are subregions with harsh environments for human settlement. The Thar Desert, between the Indus Valley and the Aravalli Hills, is one. At the other end of the Plains is the Meghna Depression, an immense backswamp of the Brahmaputra system that provides a seasonal natural reservoir for the floods that regularly inundate lowland Bangladesh. In the Assam Valley, the shifting, braided course of the turbulent Brahmaputra discourages settlement.

The Bengal Delta, which covers a large portion of Bangladesh and extends into India, is a distinctive subregion of the Plains, dominated by water. The delta country is the product of three major rivers, the Ganga, the Brahmaputra, and the Meghna and their **distributaries** (river branches that flow away from the main stream), along with a number of lesser rivers and their tributaries that sluice down to the Bay of Bengal, creating a vast web of waterways. Because these rivers lie in deep deposits of sand and clay and carry such enormous quantities of water, especially in flood stage, they are almost impossible to control with engineering works; as a result, flooding is normal. In the monsoon season, about 70 percent of the delta region is flooded up to 1 to 2 meters (3 to 6 feet) deep (**Figure 10.8**). The entire region is flat and low-lying, the land never rising above 10 meters (33 feet). Entering this environment, the rivers meander and braid and often burst their banks to shift course. The history of the region is full of thriving towns that were permanently abandoned because the rivers on which they were situated silted up or changed course.

Nevertheless, humans adapted to the environment, and the region is rather densely populated (about 900 persons per square kilometer; 2340 persons per square mile). Annual floods are a part of life, and farmers rely on floods to water and fertilize the land. The natural landscape of the delta country is dominated by marshlands and dense jungle that is a haven for wildlife. Much of the youngest part of the delta is tidal, and

---

[2]*United Provinces Gazetteer,* Vol. 1, Calcutta: United Provinces, p. 8. Quoted in O. H. K. Spate and A. Learmonth, *India and Pakistan,* London: Methuen, 1972, p. 549.

FIGURE 10.7 The Ganga Plains Although the Plains have been the hearth of successive empires because of their agricultural productivity, most of the Plains farmers rely on irrigation for their crops, and some areas are very dry.

SIGNATURE REGION

The Indus Plains

The Indus Plains (**Figure 1**) have a long history of agricultural productivity that has supported a succession of empires. Harappan agriculturalists, flourishing between 3000 and 2000 B.C., produced enough surplus to sustain a civilization that was centered in the cities of Kot Diji (near present-day Sukkur), Moenjodaro (near Larkana), and Harappa (near Sahiwal). The center of gravity of later empires shifted north as it became more important to command access to the overland routes to Central Asia. For a thousand years, from the 6th century B.C. until around A.D. 450, the northern Indus Plains took over as the core area of civilization, where a fusion of Greek, Central Asian, and Indian art and culture developed. Taxila (near present-day Islamabad) was of particular significance as a cultural center.

From these earliest times, the region's productivity depended on irrigation, for the climate is hot, the rainfall irregular, and the soils sandy (**Figure 2**). The plains consist of a great mass of alluvium brought down by the Indus and its five tributaries (from west to east, these are the Jhelum, Chenab, Ravi, Beas, and Sutlej) that flow across the Punjab (*panj ab* means "five rivers"). The river floodplains are naturally fertile, but the interfluves (areas of runoff between river valleys, known in this region as *doabs*), though they have good soils, are semiarid and require irrigation.

There were two traditional methods of irrigation that established the plains as the granary of successive empires. One was a series of inundation canals—channels constructed to carry the floodwaters of the monsoon season beyond the regular floodplains

FIGURE 1 Indus Plains Reference map showing principal physical features, political boundaries, and major cities.

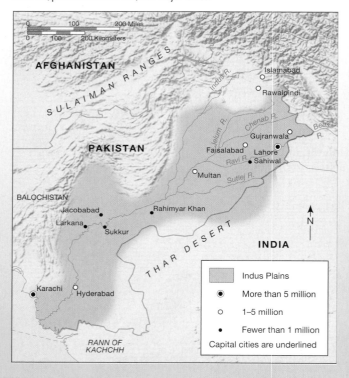

FIGURE 2 Indus Plains agriculture Centuries of labor-intensive investment in irrigation systems have made productive agriculture possible in the sandy soils and semiarid climate of the Indus Plains.

FIGURE 10.8 Monsoon season
Flooding occurs regularly during monsoon season in the Bengal Delta. Though the floods are troublesome, the silt deposited during the floods helps replenish soil nutrients. Serious problems occur when the rains are unusually heavy and when high tides and/or exceptionally high rainfall are accompanied by strong onshore winds.

of the rivers. The other was the tube well, a simple shaft sunk to the level of the water table, from which the water is raised by a variety of means, the most common being the "Persian Wheel," driven by bullocks or other farm animals (**Figure 3**). British colonial engineers extended the inundation canals in the 19th century and in the early 20th century they added a series of dams and irrigation schemes that extended irrigation to a greater portion of the doabs in the Punjab and to the lower Indus plains known as the Sindh. The new farmlands created by these irrigation schemes came to be called the Canal Colonies. Today they are distinctive within the landscape of the plains for their severely rectilinear field patterns, in contrast to the small, irregular-shaped field systems of the older-established areas.

With irrigation, farmers on the Indus Plains can grow two sets of crops. The first set of crops, sown to take advantage of the monsoon rains and harvested by early winter, includes rice, millet, corn, and cotton. The second, sown at the start of the cool, dry season and harvested in March or April, includes wheat, barley, rapeseed, mustard, and tobacco. This productivity has traditionally supported a high population density, mostly in large, nucleated villages. Recently, however, the Indus has become so overused that fishermen and farmers are being forced to migrate. A series of grandiose dams and barrages on the river, intended to boost irrigated crop production, have so damaged the water flow that Pakistan is now forced to import an increasing volume of grain.

As in the Ganga Plains, craft industries are present throughout the towns and villages of the region. In the Indus Plains these are dominated by the traditional manufacture of homespun and woven fabrics in cotton, silk, and wool, carpets, footwear, pottery, and metalworking. Modern manufacturing industry is dominated by cotton textiles and woolen knitwear and is concentrated in the larger cities. Lahore (population 6.5 million in 2006) is the cultural, educational, and artistic capital of Pakistan and has a relatively large engineering and electrical goods sector. Multan (metropolitan population 3.8 million) is situated at the center of the country's main cotton-growing region, and its manufacturing sector is dominated by cotton textiles. Gujranwala (population 2 million) is an engineering and metalworking center. Hyderabad is a tobacco-processing and textile-manufacturing center. Its economy has been particularly hard hit by the ethnic tensions between the indigenous (Sindhi) population and the *muhajirs*, Muslim refugees from India who settled in the Sindh in large numbers after 1947, when Britain partitioned colonial India into separate independent national states. Similar tensions exist in Karachi (population 11.9 million), though it is large and cosmopolitan enough that these tensions have not adversely affected its economy. Like all cities in this region, Karachi has a large informal economic sector and correspondingly extensive slums and squatter neighborhoods. But it also has a thriving commercial center with towering hotels, tourist shops, shopping centers, wide boulevards, and some exclusive residential districts.

FIGURE 3 Irrigation Raising water from tube wells in the Punjab is usually accomplished by "Persian Wheels."

in the southernmost reaches of the delta saltwater penetrates the channels, creating a distinctive ecology of untouched mangrove and tropical swamp forest—the Sundarbans ("beautiful forest")—that is home to crocodiles, Bengal tigers, and Chital deer.

The Coastal Fringe

The Coastal Fringe of South Asia consists of a mixed group of physical features. In places the Coastal Fringe is the product of marine erosion that has sawed into the edge of the ancient shield of the Peninsular Highlands. Elsewhere it is the product of marine deposits, and in some places the plains consist of alluvial deposits in the form of deltas and mudflats. For the most part, the Coastal Fringe is relatively narrow. Along India's western coast, outlying spurs from the

FIGURE 10.9 The Maldives Only 200 of the 1190 islands in the Maldives are inhabited. Most are small atolls, circular coral reefs that almost or entirely enclose a lagoon.

Western Ghats make it difficult to travel along the fringe by land. Far out into the Bay of Bengal are the Andaman Islands and the Nicobar Islands, both belonging to India but physiographically an extension of the Sumatran ranges of Southeast Asia (see Chapter 9). About 650 kilometers (404 miles) to the southwest of India in the Indian Ocean are the Maldives, an independent state of 1190 tiny islands (**Figure 10.9**). Parts of the Coastal Fringe are occasionally subject to earthquakes, and in 2001 a major tremor centered on Bhuj, in western Gujarat, killed about 30,000 people and left hundreds of thousands homeless.

The Coastal Fringe is fertile in places and has been hospitable for human settlement. During the rainy monsoon seasons, the Coastal Fringe is filled with luxuriant growth, especially along the southwest Malabar Coast of India and the southwest coast of Sri Lanka (**Figure 10.10**), where rich harvests of rice and fruit support rural populations of more than 1500 persons per square kilometer (3900 per square mile). Many of South Asia's largest and most prosperous cities developed from trading posts that were established along the Coastal Fringe in the 17th century. The largest among them—Chennai (formerly Madras), Colombo, Karachi, Kolkata, and Mumbai—were great centers of commerce under British imperialism.

FIGURE 10.10 Coastal Fringe
Hundreds of miles of the Coastal Fringe are covered with dense tropical vegetation. This photograph shows part of the southwestern coast of Sri Lanka.

Climate

The Mountain Rim and the surrounding seas that we have noted as having been funda-mental to South Asia's evolution as a world region also strongly influence climate. The Mountain Rim effectively bars the movement of surface-level airstreams between South Asia and the rest of Asia, and vice versa. By contrast, no relief feature to the south of the Mountain Rim stands high enough to prevent the free flow inland of airstreams from the surrounding seas. Rather, all of the hills and uplands exert a strong **orographic effect,** causing moist air from the sea to lift and condense and producing heavy rainfall.

Beyond these factors, the overall climates of South Asia are determined by global atmospheric circulation, as in other world regions. In South Asia, the dominant aspect of atmospheric circulation is the southwesterly summer monsoon. The word *monsoon* derives from the Arabic word *mausim*, meaning "season." Although now widely used to describe any seasonal reversal of wind flows in the lower-middle latitudes, *monsoon* was originally applied to the distinctive seasonal winds in the Indian Ocean on which Arab traders relied to power their sailing ships on their annual voyages to and from the East Indies (the name formerly applied loosely to present-day Malaysia and Indonesia) in quest of spices, ivory, and fine fabrics.

Seasonal Patterns   In most of South Asia, the seasonal pattern of climate is as follows: a cool and mainly dry winter, a hot and mainly dry season from March or April into June, and a wet monsoon that "bursts" in June and lasts into September or later. In winter, a major branch of the jet stream tends to fend off the low-pressure systems of the circumpolar atmospheric whirl, helping maintain stable high-pressure conditions over the Mountain Rim and the Tibetan Plateau. The prevailing winds are northeasterly, blowing from the interior toward the sea—these are the so-called "dry monsoon" winds (**Figure 10.11**). One exception to this pattern is in parts of Afghanistan, Pakistan, and northwest India, where shallow low-pressure systems move through from the eastern Mediterranean, bringing light but useful rainfall in late winter. Another is northern and eastern Sri Lanka, where trade winds bring some winter rains.

FIGURE 10.11 Summer and winter monsoons The wet summer monsoon "bursts" in June and lasts into September or later. In winter, the prevailing "dry monsoon" winds are then north-easterly.

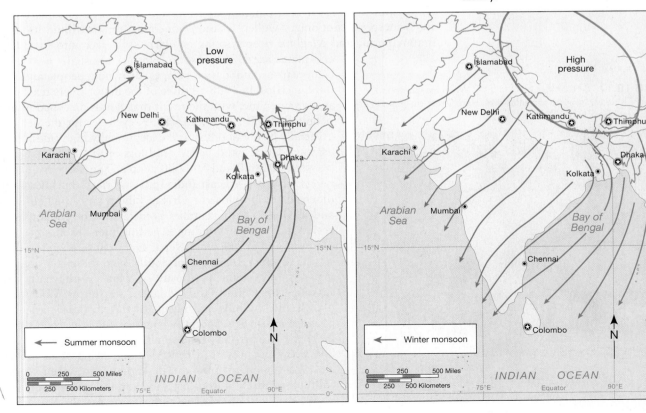

The southern part of Sri Lanka, the Maldives, and the Nicobar Islands are so far south as to be affected by intertropical convergence (see Chapter 1), and so rarely have a dry month all year.

In terms of atmospheric circulation, similar conditions persist into the early summer. By May, daytime temperatures reach between 30°C and 40°C (86°F and 104°F) across most of South Asia. This is the season of heat and dust. By June, the earth is scorched and farmers can grow nothing without irrigation. Everyone tends to become preoccupied with the discomfort of heat and humidity. One of the hottest places is Jacobabad, in Pakistan, where daytime temperatures in June average 45°C (113°F), with a maximum of 53°C (127°F) and a minimum of 29°C (84°F).

The Monsoons In mid-summer, the jet stream and the northern circumpolar atmospheric circulatory system move north of the Mountain Rim, allowing moist maritime air to invade the region. The southern circumpolar atmospheric circulation now produces strong trade winds that sweep north to become the southwest, or "wet" monsoon (see Figure 10.11). The arrival of the wet monsoon season is announced by violent storms and torrential rain. This is the "breaking" or "bursting" of the monsoon (**Figure 10.12**). The monsoon season typically brings almost daily downpours, giving life to farms and fields.

Where the low-pressure systems of the summer monsoon flow over hills and mountains, the monsoon rains are especially heavy. The Western Ghats and adjacent coastal plains typically receive between 2000 and 4000 millimeters (79 to 158 inches) of rainfall as the southwest monsoon winds meet the steep slope at the edge of the Peninsular Highlands. Similar levels of annual rainfall are received in the central and eastern parts of the Mountain Rim. Cherrapunji, in the Khasi Hills south of the Assam Valley, boasts the world's average annual rainfall record of 11,437 millimeters (450.6 inches). It once recorded as much as 924 millimeters (36.4 inches) in one day at the onset of the monsoon season.

Occasionally, two streams of monsoon air—one moving up the Ganga Valley from the Bay of Bengal, the other across Rajasthan from the Arabian Sea—converge over the Himalayan foothills to produce abnormally heavy rainfall and floods. This happened in August 2000, leaving more than 500 dead and more than 4.5 million homeless in a 1500-kilometer (932-mile) long, 500-kilometer (311-mile) wide swath of the Himalayan foothills. It is in Bangladesh, however, that monsoon rains produce regular and widespread flooding. Swollen by monsoon rains, the distributaries of the Ganga, Brahmaputra, and Meghna river systems regularly spill over into the low-lying delta and plains areas. If monsoon rains are unusually heavy, flooding can be disastrous, inundating villages, drowning people and livestock, and ruining crops. In 1988 all three of the major rivers reached flood stage at the same time, with the result that floods drowned more than 2000 people. In 1970, 1991, and 1999, cyclones hit the delta area during especially heavy flooding and exceptionally high tides, leading to devastating damage and widespread loss of life. The 1970 cyclone killed between 300,000 and 500,000 people. The 1999 cyclone hit the low-lying coast of northeast India, pushing rivers backward and flooding much of the province of Orissa, killing an estimated 20,000 people and leaving 278,000 families homeless. Some geographers have suggested that annual flooding is getting more pronounced, pointing to deforestation in India and Nepal as the cause of increased runoff.

In contrast, for much of South Asia, there is a significant risk of drought and famine as a result of a late or unusually dry monsoon season. The Peninsular Highlands, the Indus Valley and adjacent plains, and the hills and basins of the northwestern portion of the Mountain Rim are especially prone to drought. In 2000 and again in 2002 the late arrival of the summer monsoon left more than 50 million people in west and central India facing acute water shortages and widespread crop failure. In Afghanistan, seven years of drought culminated in 2004 in disastrous crop failures that drove an average of 500 families into refugee camps each day.

FIGURE 10.12 Breaking monsoon When the monsoon breaks, there is no escaping the torrential rains. Here, street children play in monsoon rainwater in New Delhi.

Environmental History

The first extensive imprint of human occupation in this region dates from at least 4500 years ago, when the peoples of the Harappan culture began to irrigate and cultivate large areas of the Indus Valley. Flourishing between 3000 and 2000 B.C., Harappan agriculturalists produced enough surplus, primarily in cotton and grains, to sustain an urban civilization. Harappan culture rivals its contemporary urban civilizations along the Euphrates and the Nile (see Chapter 4) for the tag of a "cradle of civilization." Archaeological evidence shows that Harappans carried on trade with these civilizations in the Fertile Crescent, as well as with peoples in Southeast Asia and China. Soon after 2000 B.C., floods obliterated Harappan cities, leaving them covered in mud. It is possible that environmental degradation—especially the loss of the natural vegetation and the silting-up of irrigation and drainage channels—contributed to the flooding, though it may have been due entirely to climate change or tectonic movement.

The next significant impact on the natural environments of South Asia came with the incursion of tribal herdsmen from Central Asia into the plains of the Ganga Valley. They were called Aryans (after the language that they spoke), and between 1500 and 500 B.C. they developed arable farming, assimilated or repulsed neighbors, adopted a settled life, organized into functional groups, opened trade links, built cities, and created a rich culture—the Vedic culture—whose mythic understanding of the world came to be a cornerstone of Hinduism. As their numbers grew, clans began to split away to annex new territory. In doing so, they began the transformation of the plains of the Ganga Valley from a moist green wilderness of forest and swamp to a dusty plain where tufts of trees survive only as shade for huddled villages and flocks of sheep (**Figure 10.13**). The deforestation of South Asia had begun. By 500 B.C. the Vedic peoples had spread eastward into present-day Bihar and had learned to cultivate rice, clearing land along valley slopes to build terraces.

FIGURE 10.13 Deforestation Although the Plains were originally covered with woodlands, 3000 years of agricultural clearing has left much of the region bereft of trees. This photograph was taken in the western plains, near Rajasthan.

While the Plains region remained the most intensively developed, human settlement spread throughout South Asia, and a succession of kingdoms, sultanates, and empires slowly brought more land under cultivation. For the most part, human occupation was sustainable. Subsistence farmers, herders, fisherfolk, and artisans drew on local resources for their food, traditional medicines, housing materials, and fuel, but apart from clearing part of the forest cover, their activities could be sustained from one generation to another without significant harm to the environment.

It was the arrival of European traders, and especially British rule, that accelerated the deforestation of South Asia. In 1750, when the British were beginning their imperial conquests, more than 60 percent of South Asia was still forested, from the dry alpine forests of the Himalayan foothills and the mangrove forests of Bengal to the acacia forests of the Peninsular Highlands and the evergreen rain forests of the tropical coastal plains. British imperial rule brought systematic clearing of land for plantations and the methodical exploitation of valuable tropical hardwoods for export to Europe and North America. As railways opened up the interior, deforestation gathered speed. By 1900, only 40 percent of South Asia remained forested.

Population Pressure and Resource Depletion The most rapid period of change has been the past 50 years, as the independent countries of South Asia have sought to modernize and expand their domestic economies. Between 1951 and 1976, for example, some 15 percent of India's land area was converted to cropland. Meanwhile, population growth in rural India has led to more and more wood being taken as fuel. Only 20 percent of India remains forested today, and less than half of that is intact, natural forest—the rest consists of forest plantations, which have displaced natural ecosystems with monocrops. About one-third of the forest plantations in India consist of eucalyptus, a fast-growing, nonindigenous species that is very demanding of soil moisture. India's forests still represent a valuable trove of biodiversity. Together, they house some 45,000 species of plants, 1250 species of birds, more than 350 species of mammals, and nearly 400 species of reptiles. However, they are under severe pressure, along with some of the key species that rely on them.

The combination of growing population and the desire on the part of newly independent countries to jump-start industry and agriculture has put pressure on other natural resources, especially water. In parts of Punjab and Haryana, the "breadbasket" of India where almost a third of the country's wheat is grown, the water table has fallen more than 4 meters (13 feet) in the last decade. In the southern Indian state of Tamil Nadu, groundwater levels have fallen more than 25 meters (82 feet) in the last decade as a result of overpumping, leaving Chennai, like many other large cities, dependent on supplementary water supplies hauled in by tanker.

Environmental Pollution In parallel with the acceleration of resource depletion, environmental pollution has accelerated. In India some 200 million people do not have access to safe and clean water; about 690 million lack adequate sanitation; and an estimated 80 percent of the country's water sources are polluted with untreated industrial and domestic wastes. The Asian Development Bank has estimated that fewer than 1 in 10 of the industrial plants in South Asia comply with pollution-control guidelines. Only 10 percent of all sewage in South Asia is treated. India alone generates about 50 million tons of solid waste each year, most of which is disposed in unsafe ways: burned, dumped into lakes or seas, or deposited into leaky landfills.

Air pollution has also become a serious issue. Little is known about the effects of acid rain on forests and cropland in South Asia, but the effects of air pollution in cities are clear. According to the Tata Research Institute in New Delhi, air pollution in India causes an estimated 2.5 million premature deaths each year. Motor vehicle emissions are a major contributor to urban air pollution. During the 1990s, the number of vehicles on Indian roads increased by 300 percent, and there has been a corresponding rise in rates of respiratory diseases.

Still, most people in South Asia—65 to 75 percent, in fact—are not city dwellers. Geographers Madhav Gadgil and Ramachandra Guha of the Indian Institute for Science estimate that some 400 to 500 million people remain what they call "ecosystem people," living at subsistence levels but in sustainable ways that have protected and preserved the environment. Increasingly, however, these ecosystem people are being pushed onto unproductive soils and arid hillsides as commercial forestry, mining, road and dam construction, and the spread of industry limit their access to the land. As the environmental commons diminishes and populations increase, a destructive cycle is set in motion. Ecosystem people are forced to use their limited resources in increasingly unsustainable ways, depleting sources of fuelwood, exhausting soils, and draining water resources.

SOUTH ASIA IN THE WORLD-SYSTEM

South Asia has developed distinctive cultures and generated influential concepts and powerful ideals that have spread around the world. From the hearth areas (the areas of origin) of Harappan and Vedic civilization in the Plains, sophisticated cultures and powerful political empires spread across vast sections of the region. South Asia's resources and its geographic situation on sea-lanes between Europe and the East Indies made it especially attractive to European imperial powers, and in modern times it has become a pivotal geopolitical region with an emergent industrial and high-tech sector and a large market for core-region products.

The Mauryan Empire (320–125 B.C.) was the first to establish rule across the greater part of South Asia. By 250 B.C. the emperor Asoka had established control over all but present-day Sri Lanka and the southern tip of India. Securing control had wrought such havoc and destruction, however, that Asoka renounced armed conquest and adopted a policy of "conquest by *dharma*," that is, through the example of spiritual rectitude and chivalrous obligations. *Dharma*, a key element of Buddhist teachings, is part of the legacy of Asoka's reign over Southwest Asia, which also includes Buddhist principles of vegetarianism, kindness to animals, nonacquisitiveness, humility, and nonviolence.

After Asoka's death in 232 B.C., the Mauryan Empire fell into decline, and northern India soon succumbed to invaders from Central Asia. After more than four centuries of division and political confusion, the Gupta Empire (A.D. 320–480) united northern India and came to control all but the northwestern hill country, the Peninsular Highlands, the southwestern coastlands (modern Kerala), and Sri Lanka. The Gupta period is generally regarded as the classical period of Hindu civilization. It produced the decimal system of notation, the golden age of Sanskrit and Hindu art, and contributions to science, medicine, and trade. The Mughal Empire (1526–1707) brought the most comprehensive and extensive economic, political, and administrative unification of South Asia, providing a framework that was absorbed into the British Empire in the 18th century.

Mughal India

Toward the end of the 15th century, a clan of militant Turks from Persia (now Iran) moved east in an attempt to evade the control of Timur's (Tamerlane's) Tartar Mongol empire. These Turks were the Mughals. Led by Babur, they conquered Kabul, in what is now Afghanistan, in 1504. By 1605, Babur's grandson Akbar had established control over most of the Plains, and in the next century Mughal rule extended to all but Sri Lanka and the southern tip of India (**Figure 10.14**).

Akbar's rule was an extraordinary time, his achievements driven by his personal desire to synthesize the best of the many traditions that fell within his domain while maintaining strict control. Traditional kingdoms and princely states were kept intact, but they were integrated in a highly organized administrative structure with an equitable taxation system and a new class of bureaucrats. Persian became the official language, yet Akbar abolished the tax on non-Muslims that had been instituted by his grandfather. Mughal rule did not seek to impose Islam on indigenous populations. However, Mughal commitment to the religious precepts of Islam, together with the equitable system of Mughal governance, gave great stature to Islam. Over time, Islam

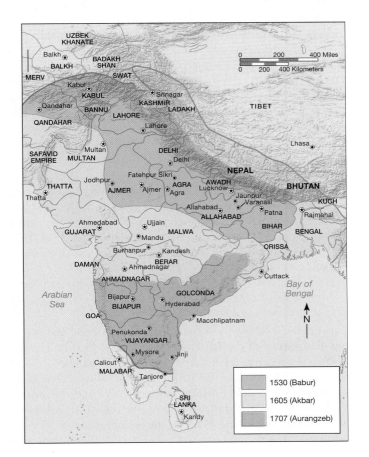

FIGURE 10.14 Mughal India Two centuries of Mughal rule began in 1504, with the conquest of Kabul, in present-day Afghanistan; by the time of Aurangzeb's death in 1707, Mughal rule had extended to almost all of the subcontinent. (*Source:* Redrawn from J. Keay, *India: A History.* New York: Atlantic Monthly Press, 2000, p. 314.)

FIGURE 10.15 Mughal architecture Mughal rulers expressed their wealth and power in the form of imposing palaces, forts, and mosques. This photograph shows the Majestic Fort at Mehrangarh, Jodhpur.

proved attractive to many, especially in the northwest (the Punjab) and the northeast (Bengal), both areas where Buddhism had previously been dominant. By 1700, mosques, daily calls to prayer, Muslim festivals, and Islamic law had become an integral part of the social fabric of South Asian life.

Mughal rule was also characterized by a luxurious court and by extensive support for creativity in art, architecture, music, and literature. Akbar led the way by building Fatehpur Sikri as the capital for his empire. The most famous legacy of Mughal architecture is the Taj Mahal. Spectacular architecture became a signature of Mughal rule, the landscape of the northern regions becoming punctuated not only with lavish mosques and palaces but also with forts and citadels, towers, and gardens (**Figure 10.15**). Most ambitious of all was Shahjahanabad (now known as Old Delhi), which was designed to supersede Agra as the imperial capital. Here was a whole new city, complete with processional thoroughfares, spacious squares, bazaars, caravansaries, shaded waterways, and massive stone walls that were pierced by 11 gates and guarded by 27 towers. Its rigid geometry has long since been blurred, but some of the walls and gates remain, as do the imperial complex known as the Red Fort and, nearby, the great Jama Masjid, which in its day was the largest mosque in India.

The last of the great Mughal emperors, Aurangzeb (1658–1707), provoked a series of rebellions and uprisings with his anti-Hindu policies and his reinstatement of the tax on non-Muslims. At the same time he had to deal with raids from the Marathas, a warlike people from the Konkan coast, and was forced to conduct military campaigns on several fronts. With his death in 1707, the Mughal Empire collapsed, leaving South Asia open to the increasing interest and influence of European traders and colonists.

British Imperialism

European traders were a regular presence along the coasts of South Asia long before the dissolution of the Mughal Empire. The Portuguese were the first, with the arrival of Vasco da Gama in India in 1498. Early in the 17th century the British East India Company (established in 1600) and the Dutch East India Company (established in 1602) set out to deliberately contest the Portuguese monopoly of the Indonesian spice trade. South Asia, situated as it was on the route between Europe and the East Indies, provided an attractive array of intermediate stops for trade in the calicos, chintzes, taffetas, brocades, batiks, and ginghams of Gujarat, Bengal, Golconda, and the Tamil country. Soon, the armed ships of the two East India companies had pushed aside the Portuguese and had begun to tap into the ancient trade between India's east coast ports and Southeast Asia. In the 1660s the French established the *Compagnie des Indies* and joined in the scramble for trade.

By the 1690s, European trading companies had established a permanent presence in several ports, though they had no interest in establishing colonies or exerting any kind of political authority, even when South Asia fell into disarray at the end of Mughal rule. But European wars in the 18th century (in particular the War of the Austrian Succession, 1740–48, and the Seven Years' War, 1756–63) spilled over into an imperial contest in South Asia. Initially, the armies of the East India Companies fought over territory simply to protect their trading areas. With its own navy, backed by the powerful Royal Navy and its superior weapons technology, the British East India Company was most successful. In 1773 the British government transformed its East India Company into an administrative agency. Soon afterward, during the French Revolution and Napoleonic Wars, the British pushed ahead with aggressive imperialist policies in South Asia, using a mixture of force, bribery, and political intrigue to gain control over more and more of the region, which by this time was riddled with political and religious disunity.

The *Raj* The focus of British imperialism now shifted beyond trade and territorial control to social reform and cultural imperialism. In a famous memo written by East India Company Supreme Council member Thomas Macaulay in 1853, British administrators were urged to create a special class of South Asian people who would be "Indian in blood and colour, but English in taste, in opinions, in morals, and in intellect." One by one, the territories of native rulers were annexed or brought under British protection (**Figure 10.16**).

Under the governor-generalship of Lord Dalhousie (1848–56), there was a push to bring Western institutions and a modern industrial infrastructure to South Asia. Railroads, roads, bridges, and irrigation systems were built and restrictions were placed on slave-trading, *suttee* (a widow's ritual suicide on her husband's funeral pyre), and other traditional practices. Western educational curricula flourished in private colleges; British-style public universities were established. All of this provoked a conservative and anti-colonial reaction, which came to a head in 1857, when an Indian Army unit rebelled because 85 of its soldiers were jailed for upholding their religious principles, refusing to use ammunition greased with animal fat. The incident quickly spread into a year-long civil uprising—the "Indian Mutiny"—throughout the north-central region. Massacres were carried out on both sides, but the mutiny was eventually quelled, and in 1858 the British Crown assumed direct control over India. In 1876 Queen Victoria was declared Empress of India.

Thus emerged the **Raj,** British rule over South Asia, which by 1890 extended to the entire region with the exception of present-day Afghanistan and Nepal (see Figure 10.16). The British brought plantation agriculture to South Asia, producing food crops for the British domestic population and commodity crops for British industry and British merchant traders. Among plantation crops were coconuts, coffee, cotton, jute, rubber, and tea (see Geographies of Indulgence, Desire, and Addiction: Tea, p. 490). The *Raj* also introduced Western industrial development and technology to South Asia, displacing indigenous crafts and industries. It fostered Western political ideas of social reform, democracy, freedom of expression, and the materialism that accompanies free markets in land, labor, and commerce along with the Western concept of national states. This was to be an explosive legacy at the conclusion of the *Raj* in 1947, when Britain partitioned colonial India into separate independent national states.

Partition Grassroots political resistance to British imperial rule had been institutionalized through the Indian National Congress Party, formed in 1887 to promote greater democracy and freedom, not only from imperial rule but from the traditional and autocratic rule of hereditary maharajas (leaders of the princely states that were under British protection). A leader and the inspirational figure of this movement was Mohandas Gandhi, whose vision of social justice and accountability and methods

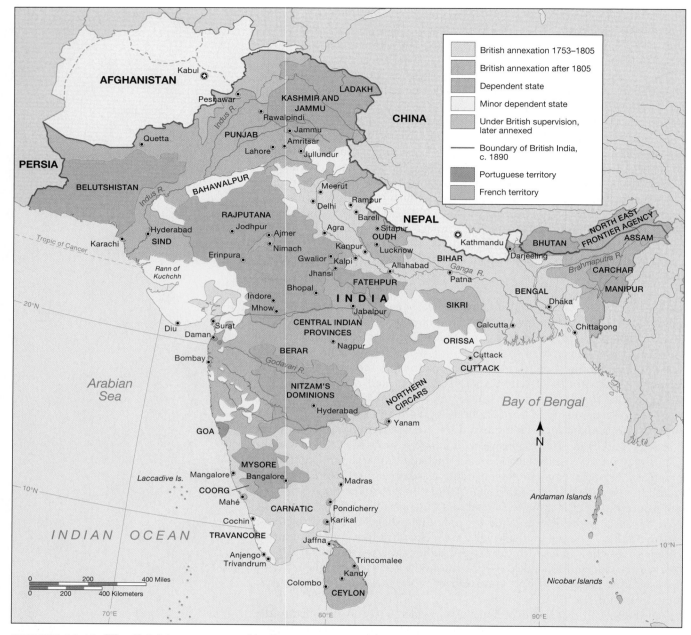

FIGURE 10.16 The British conquest of India British interest in India began as a consequence of merchant trade in the early 18th century, but by 1890 the British had come to control, directly or indirectly, most of South Asia. (*Source:* Adapted from I. Barnes and R. Hudson, *The History Atlas of Asia.* New York: Macmillan, 1998, pp. 118–19.)

of nonviolent protest (including boycotts and fasting) were inspired by the ancient Buddhist concept of *dharma*. Under Gandhi's leadership, the case for national independence became irrefutable. Soon after the conclusion of World War II, the British set about withdrawing from South Asia altogether.

In creating new, independent countries, Britain sought to follow the European model of building national states on the foundations of ethnicity, with particular emphasis on language and religion. As a result, it was decided to establish a separate Islamic country, called Pakistan ("Land of the Pure"). Administrative districts under direct British control that had a majority Muslim population were assigned to Pakistan, together with those princely states whose ruling maharajas wished to join Pakistan rather than India. The result was that Pakistan was created in two parts, East

Pakistan and West Pakistan, one on each shoulder of India, separated by 1600 kilometers (994 miles) of Indian territory.

In 1947, when Pakistan and India were officially granted independence, millions of Hindus and Sikhs found themselves as minorities in Pakistan, while millions of Muslims felt threatened as a minority in India. Communal violence erupted across the region. In desperation, more than 12 million people fled across the new national boundaries—the largest refugee migration ever recorded in the world. As Hindus and Sikhs moved toward India and Muslims moved toward Pakistan in opposite directions between the two countries, many hundreds of thousands were senselessly killed. Hyderabad, in the Peninsular Highlands, had a Hindu majority population but a Muslim leader who had volunteered Hyderabad to Pakistan. Hyderabad was quickly absorbed into India when riots broke out at the time of partition. In Kashmir the situation was reversed: A Hindu maharaja had elected to join India, but Pakistani forces intervened on partition to protect the majority Muslim population.

Having withdrawn from the greater part of South Asia, the British granted independence to the island of Ceylon as a Commonwealth dominion in 1948. In 1949 Britain handed to India its formal control over the external affairs of the kingdom of Bhutan, and in 1968 Britain granted independence to the Maldives. The *Raj* was finally over, but the legacy of partition remains a dimension of the geography of South Asia in today's world. In some ways, the states of South Asia are still adjusting to the 1947 partition of India and Pakistan. In Pakistan, divergent regional interests in East and West Pakistan quickly developed into regionalism, with East Pakistani leaders calling for secession. As a result, the country was split into two independent states in 1971: West Pakistan became Pakistan, and East Pakistan became Bangladesh. Meanwhile, neither India nor Pakistan could agree on the status of Kashmir, and the two countries briefly went to war over the region in 1948, in 1965, and again in 1971.

South Asia in Today's World

Geopolitics   South Asia occupies a significant level of importance in global geopolitics. South Asia's strategic location meant that it was of great interest to the superpowers during the Cold War. India took full advantage of this, playing both sides against one another in seeking aid, while following a hybrid approach to domestic policy, with a democratic form of governance but a socialist-style approach to economic development. Post-colonial ties to Britain were maintained by Bangladesh, India, Pakistan, and Sri Lanka through the British Commonwealth, a loose association of countries tied together by patterns of trade, a shared language, and a similarity of institutions.

Ironically, South Asia has become even more of a geopolitical hot spot since the end of the Cold War. Both India and Pakistan have developed the capability of producing nuclear weapons. With the territorial dispute over Kashmir still simmering, India announced in May 1998 that five nuclear tests had been carried out in the Thar Desert close to the Pakistani border. This triggered a fervent bout of national pride within India, but it prompted Pakistan to respond within a few weeks with its own series of nuclear tests. India and Pakistan, together with Israel, are among the few states not to have signed the Nuclear Non-Proliferation Treaty that was formulated by the superpowers during the Cold War in 1968.

Afghanistan has long occupied a situation of particular geopolitical significance because it is situated pivotally between Central Asia and South Asia. Control of its mountainous terrain and the passes—such as the Khyber Pass—has often been disputed, more often than not leaving its villages and its countryside in ruins. For much of the latter part of the 20th century, Afghanistan had economic and cultural ties to the Soviet Union and began to pursue a Soviet-style program of modernization and industrialization that ran counter to deeply rooted Islamic traditions. This provoked resistance from a zealous group of fundamentalist Islamic tribal leaders called the *mujahideen*, who were armed and trained by Pakistan. A total of more than 120,000 Soviet troops were subsequently sent to Afghanistan, but they were unable to establish authority outside Kabul.

Tea

Tea, a mild drug that makes a refreshing drink, was cultivated in China and Japan for centuries before becoming a commodity in international trade. Thereafter, tea became a catalyst of economic, social, and political change. The Opium War (see Chapter 8) was fought in large part over tea; the American Revolution was sparked by riots over a tax on tea; and the social and economic fabric of large parts of South Asia was destroyed by colonial mercantile forces that transformed land into tea plantations.

Tea was first brought to Europe by Portuguese traders and marketed as a medicine. Tea drinking was adopted by the royal court of King Charles II in England (1660–1685), and tea quickly became an indulgence of the European bourgeoisie. By 1700 more than 17 million pounds of tea were being exported to Europe each year, mostly to Holland, Portugal, and England. As East Asian trade came to be dominated over the next century by the British East India Company, the cost of tea fell and the taste for it spread. It soon became an addiction for the middle and working classes in Britain and a desirable indulgence for many in the American colonies. A significant market for tea had meanwhile developed in Russia and in many countries of the Middle East and North Africa.

South Asia became a source of tea only in the 19th century, when the British sought to find commercial advantage in their newly acquired territories in Assam. In 1848 the Assam Company hired botanist Robert Fortune to travel incognito to China to discover the secrets of cultivating and processing tea. After four expeditions, he brought to Assam not only the knowledge that the company needed but 12,000 seedlings, the specialized tools used in processing tea, and a skilled Chinese workforce. The British colonial government granted land on inexpensive leases to anyone who had the capital to establish a tea plantation. Inevitably, those with the capital were European settlers, and thousands of would-be planters flocked to Assam. Valuable timber was cut, forests were cleared, and the land not needed for tea plantations was rented to tribal peoples from Bihar and Orissa who were contracted to work—for miserably little pay and in dreadful conditions—as laborers in the plantations.

The opening of the Suez Canal in 1869 cut transport costs, made tea even cheaper, and allowed producers a bigger profit margin. Tea plantations in Assam and neighboring Bengal increased sixfold in size between 1870 and 1900, by which time there were half a million plantation workers in the region. In this same period, Ceylon—now Sri Lanka—emerged as a major tea-producing area. In the 1870s, 250,000 acres of coffee plantations in Ceylon were destroyed by blight, leaving coffee planters bankrupted and land extremely cheap. Thomas Lipton, a prosperous grocer from Glasgow, Scotland, arrived in Ceylon in 1871 while on a world cruise, bought dozens of the plantations at bargain prices, and turned them over to the production of tea.

Lipton was a pioneer of vertical economic integration, and by taking over all of the operations from growing tea to processing,

The guerilla war ended in 1989 with the withdrawal of the Soviet Union. With the demise of their common enemy, the militias' ethnic, clan, religious, and personality differences surfaced, and civil war ensued. Eventually, the hard-line Islamist faction of the *mujahideen,* the Taliban, gained control of Kabul and most of Afghanistan. The Taliban regime not only imposed harsh religious laws and barbaric social practices on the Afghan population but also harbored the source of an entirely new geopolitical factor with worldwide implications: Osama bin Laden and his Al Qaeda terrorist network, which was responsible for the September 11, 2001, attacks on the Pentagon and the World Trade Center. Consequently, Afghanistan became the focus of a U.S. military operation, "Enduring Freedom," that resulted in the defeat of the Taliban and installation of a U.S.–backed government in Kabul.

Economic Transition On a more positive note, South Asia—and India, in particular—has come to play an enlarging role within the world-system. India is the world's largest democracy and has maintained stable parliamentary and local government through elections and rule of law since adopting its Constitution in 1950. India has also developed a significant industrial base. Although two-thirds of the labor force is still engaged in agriculture, half of the country's GDP is accounted for by an industrial sector that is the tenth largest in the world, by value.

In 1992, after losing its major trading partner with the collapse of the Soviet Union, India embarked on a series of reforms as a condition of a structural adjustment program attached to a loan from the World Bank. Before these reforms, many key institutions—including banks, utilities, airlines, railways, radio, and television—were government owned and operated. High tariffs, restrictions on foreign ownership, high taxes, and widespread corruption all kept foreign investors away and suppressed the

management, transport, blending, packaging, and marketing, Lipton was able to cut the cost of tea to European consumers by 35 percent. Lipton and other tea planters brought in low-caste Tamil Hindus from famine-stricken areas of South India to work as laborers in the Ceylonese plantations. The conditions in which they were forced to work were atrocious, as bad as those of their counterparts in Assam and Bengal. Being low caste, low paid, isolated on estates in the highlands, and with no political voice, the "estate Tamils" were effectively enslaved on the plantations.

After independence in India, Bangladesh, and Sri Lanka, most European planters were forced to sell their tea plantations, either to the respective governments, under nationalization programs, or to indigenous business interests. The conditions for plantation workers have remained relatively unchanged, however. Plantation workers are still an impoverished group, a fact that is often belied by the image of smiling tea-pickers dressed in traditional costume, adorned with jewelry, working in sunshine amid beautiful scenery (**Figure 1**). Women, especially, are exploited. They are restricted to the lowest-paid jobs: plucking, sifting, and weeding. Many start monotonous, repetitive, and back-breaking work in the fields at age 12 or younger. Fieldwork takes place in searing heat and in pouring rain, with no protective clothing except, perhaps, a fertilizer bag over the head and shoulders, and with hands bandaged because of sores caused by pesticides.

FIGURE 1 Tea pickers At the beginning of the economic chain that links South Asian producer regions with consumers in Europe and North America, tea pickers work long hours in harsh conditions for meager pay.

energy of Indian entrepreneurs. Although more than three-quarters of the economy was in the private sector, government bureaucracy had developed a complex system of permits, licenses, quotas, and permissions that further restricted economic vitality.

The reforms created a more open and entrepreneurial economy. Key institutions have been privatized, and foreign investment has been flowing into the country, helping generate exceptionally high economic growth rates. The fact that India's middle class conducts business in English gives India a comparative advantage in today's world economy. Over the past 15 years, India has been the second-fastest growing country in the world—after China—averaging above 6 percent growth per year.

India now has an affluent middle class estimated at some 200 million—a huge, well-educated, and sophisticated consumer market that has become part of the "fast" world and an agent of globalization. The rapid growth of India's affluent middle classes serves not only to accentuate the contrasts within South Asia between the traditional and the modern but also to highlight the desperate situation of an even larger group: the extremely poor. According to the United Nations Development Fund, some 45 percent of India's population (that is, almost half a billion people) lives on less than a dollar a day—the World Bank's definition of dire poverty. In fact, most of India's poor (390 million of them) somehow exist with an income of a dollar a *week*.

The other countries of South Asia have not experienced the kind of economic boom enjoyed by India, though there have been attempts to foster regional economic integration. In 1985 the South Asian Association for Regional Cooperation (SAARC) was established. Although progress has been slow—mainly because of the friction between India and Pakistan—the member states did sign a South Asian Preferential Trade Agreement in 1996, which established some modest mutual tariff concessions. Impatient with the pace of SAARC, India also set up two subregional cooperation groups: one with

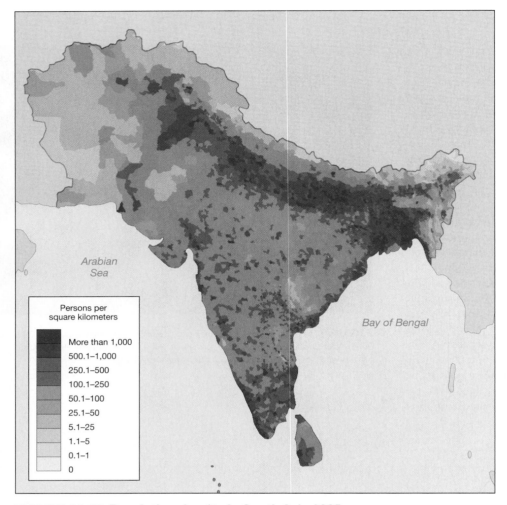

Nepal, Bhutan, and Bangladesh, and another with Sri Lanka and the Maldives. India has also signed a free-trade agreement with Sri Lanka and has pursued wider avenues of economic and diplomatic cooperation, becoming a "dialogue partner" in the Association of Southeast Asian Nations (ASEAN) and lobbying for a seat as a permanent member of an expanded United Nations Security Council.

THE PEOPLES OF SOUTH ASIA

South Asia has the second largest and the fastest-growing population of all world regions. The total population of South Asia in 2006 stood at 1.47 billion, with India accounting for just over 1 billion. With overall growth rates in the region of 1.7 percent per year (compared to 1.0 percent per year in China), South Asia is headed for a population of 1.63 billion by 2010.

Figure 10.17 shows the distribution of population within South Asia. The first thing to note about this map is the very high density of population throughout most of the region. The overall density of population in India is 316 persons per square kilometer (819 per square mile), compared to 131 persons per square kilometer (338 per square mile) in China and 29 persons per square kilometer (75 per square mile) in the United States. In detail, patterns of population density reflect patterns of agricultural productivity. The com-

FIGURE 10.17 Population density in South Asia 1995 The density of population is very high throughout most of South Asia, but especially so in the Plains and in subregions with good soils and humid climates. (*Source:* Center for International Earth Science Information Network [CIESIN], Columbia University; International Food Policy Research Institute [IFPRI] and World Resources Institute [WRI]. 2000. *Gridded Population of the World [GPW]*, Version 2. Palisades, NY: CIESIN, Columbia University. Available at **http://sedac.ciesin.org/plue/gpw.**)

bination of good soils with a humid climate or with extensive irrigation supports densities of more than 500 persons per square kilometer (1300 per square mile) in a belt extending from the upper Indus Plains and the Ganga Plains through Bengal and the Assam Valley. Similar densities are found along much of the Coastal Fringe.

Urbanization

In comparison with other world regions, South Asia is still very much a land of villages. Approximately 65 percent of Pakistan's population and 73 percent of India's live in rural settings; in Afghanistan, Bangladesh, and Sri Lanka the rural population is around 80 percent; and the tiny state of Bhutan is 94 percent rural. Rural-to-urban migration is shifting the balance toward towns and cities, however. This is largely a result of population pressure in rural areas, where natural population increase has reduced the amount of cropland per person to half of what it was in 1960. In that year, there were just 9 cities of 1 million or more in South Asia, and only one of these had more than 5 million inhabitants. In 2005 there were 50 cities of 1 million or more, including 9 of 5 million or more. Between 1960 and 2005, Mumbai, the largest metropolis in South Asia, grew from 4.1 million to 20 million; Dhaka, in Bangladesh, grew from fewer than 650,000 to more than 12.5 million; and in Pakistan, Karachi grew from 1.8 million to almost 12 million.

Population Policies

Both the overall rate of population growth and the rate of urbanization are cause for concern in South Asia. With hundreds of millions already living in extreme poverty, high rates of natural increase, intensified in urban areas by high rates of in-migration, bring the prospect of serious food and water shortages, mass starvation, and food riots. As a result, each country of the region has developed policies to try to limit population growth, with varying degrees of success. India was the first country to establish such policies, announcing an official family-planning program in 1952. Little attention was paid to the program until the mid-1960s, when the government announced specific demographic targets and opened "camps" around the country for the mass insertion of intrauterine devices (IUDs). The program soon failed, mainly because of negative public reaction to the poor training of health workers and unsanitary conditions in the camps.

Next came vasectomy camps. More than 10 million men were coerced into being sterilized in the 1970s in an "Emergency Drive" for family planning that saw all kinds of government administrators—from police to teachers and railway inspectors—given monthly quotas to recruit "volunteers" for vasectomy camps. Bureaucrats in some Indian states sought to reinforce the sterilization drive with harsh penalties. In Bihar state, for example, families with more than three children were denied public food rations; and in Uttar Pradesh, teachers who refused to volunteer for sterilization were fined a month's salary. Not surprisingly, a popular backlash put an end to the vasectomy program.

Today, the level of public mistrust remains high, the quality of family-planning services remains poor, and the demand for contraceptives is low. In 1998 the Indian government acknowledged the evidence of international experience—that female education is the single most influential determinant of lower birthrates—and finally abandoned targets for sterilization and contraception. Several Indian states are now following Kerala's successful example of emphasizing women's education and better infant and maternal care. While this policy shift seems likely to be successful in the long run, it means that India can expect population growth to continue for several decades before leveling off.

The South Asian Diaspora

The South Asian diaspora amounts to some 5 or 6 million people, most of them located in Europe, Africa, North America, and Southeast Asia (**Figure 10.18**). The origins of this diaspora can be traced to the abolition of slavery in the British Empire in 1833. The consequent demand for cheap labor in the plantations and on the railways of the British Empire was filled in part by emigrants from British India. In the mid-19th century, thousands of Indians left for the plantations of Mauritius (in the Indian Ocean), East Africa, the West Indies, and South Africa. The stream of emigration intensified in the early 20th century. By 1920 there were more than a million South Asian immigrants in Burma, about 600,000 in Malaya, 300,000 in the West Indies, 200,000 in South Africa, and 100,000 in East Africa. About 20,000 South Asians had made their way to Britain to work in factories and another 5000 or so had found their way to North America to work in railway building, in sawmills, and as farm workers.

After World War II the pattern changed significantly. Independence in former British colonies led to the exclusion of South Asian immigrants, and both Burma and Uganda expelled most South Asian immigrants. But a new destination for South Asian emigrants opened as the postwar economic recovery in Europe resulted in a severe shortage of labor on assembly lines and in transportation. Britain received more than 1.5 million South Asian immigrants, whose permanent presence not only filled a gap in the labor force but has also served to enrich and diversify British urban culture. About 800,000 South Asians moved to North America, mainly to larger metropolitan areas where most found employment in service jobs. From the 1970s onward there has also been a steady stream of South Asian immigrants to the oil-rich Persian Gulf states, recruited on temporary visas to fill manual and skilled manual jobs.

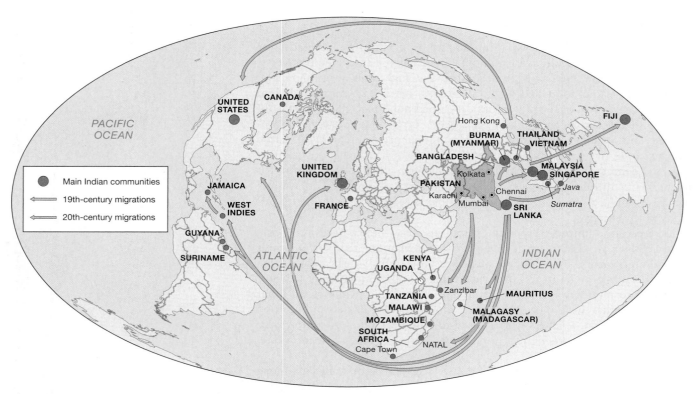

FIGURE 10.18 The South Asian diaspora Nineteenth-century migrations from South Asia were mainly to British colonies in East Africa, South Africa, and Southeast Asia, where there was a demand for cheap labor. In the 20th century the principal flows were to factory and service jobs in Britain and the United States. (*Source:* Redrawn from G. Chaliand and J-P. Rageau, *The Penguin Atlas of Diasporas.* New York: Viking, 1995, p. 155.)

South Asia has experienced a "brain drain" of significant proportions over the past several decades. Beginning with the emigration of physicians and scientists to Britain in the 1960s, the brain drain accelerated as South Asian students, having completed their studies in British and American universities, stayed to take better-paying jobs rather than return to South Asia. The idea of living abroad gained popularity among India's cosmopolitan and materialist middle-classes as newspaper and television features publicized the global successes of Indian emigrants. Geographer Pamela Shurmer-Smith comments that ". . . it is sobering to know that virtually the whole of the youth of a social fraction in India is now craving to live outside its own country and that this obsession has been largely constructed by the power of the international media."[3] In the 1990s the most distinctive aspect of the brain drain from South Asia was the emigration of computer scientists and software engineers from India to the United States and parts of Europe. By 2005, more than 2000 of the 15,000 employees on Microsoft's Redmond campus were South Asian immigrants.

Cultural Traditions

Diversity has to be the key word to describe the cultural geography of South Asia. The whole region has deep cultural roots, but these roots are often tangled. Even where traditions have not been mixed or hybridized, there are significant differences in the degree to which traditional cultures have accommodated or resisted globalization. In Afghanistan and Pakistan, powerful Islamist movements have resisted globalization, attempting to re-create certain aspects of traditional culture as the basis of contemporary social order. There is strong adherence in both countries, for example, to traditional forms of dress and public comportment (**Figure 10.19**). In Afghanistan the ultra-orthodox Taliban

[3]P. Shurmer-Smith, *India: Globalization and Change*, London: Arnold, 2000, p. 171.

FIGURE 10.19 Traditional dress
These women at prayer in a Mumbai mosque are wearing the typical everyday attire of Muslim women in the region.

rulers who controlled 90 percent of the country between 1996 and 2002 imposed a harsh version of Islamic law that followed a literal interpretation of the Muslim holy book, the Qu'ran. Under Taliban laws, murderers were publicly executed by the relatives of their victims. Adulterers were stoned to death, and the limbs of thieves were amputated. Lesser crimes were punished by public beatings.

In contrast to Afghanistan, India has successfully fostered democracy after its introduction through British colonial governance in the 19th century. In India, contemporary culture is open to the economic and cultural flows of globalization. The result is that traditional cultures, still strong, are juxtaposed vividly against modern global culture. For example, the tradition of parents seeking marriage partners for their children through newspaper advertisements continues relatively undiminished, but those same advertisements often provide an e-mail address or even a Web site for replies.

Religion Tradition is very important in South Asian cultures. Many different indigenous cultural threads have evolved into a variety of regional patterns. Over the centuries much has been added, while little appears to have been lost. As a result, the regional cultural geography of South Asia is extremely complex. At face value, one basis for regional differences in cultural traditions is religion. The two most important religions in South Asia are Hinduism and Islam. Hinduism is the dominant religion in Nepal (where about 90 percent of the population are Hindu) and India (about 80 percent). Islam is dominant in Afghanistan (99 percent), Bangladesh (more than 80 percent), the Maldives (100 percent), and Pakistan (about 80 percent).

Buddhism, though it originated in South Asia, is followed by only about 2 percent of the region's population. It is the predominant religion in Bhutan and Sri Lanka, and there is an enclave of Buddhism in Ladakh, the section of Kashmir closest to China. Jains are another distinctive religious group whose origins are in South Asia. Jains, like Buddhists, trace their faith to Prince Siddhartha, a religious leader who lived in northern India in the 6th century B.C. and who came to be known as Buddha, that is, the Enlightened One. Sikhs, whose religion was founded by Guru Nanak in the 16th century A.D., are concentrated in the Punjab, which straddles the India-Pakistan border (**Figure 10.20**).

The broad regional patterns reflected in Figure 10.20 are much more complex when considered in any detail. Underlying much of this complexity is the fact that Hinduism is not a single organized religion with one sacred text or doctrine; it has no unifying organizational structure, worship is not congregational, and there is no agreement as to the nature of the divinity. Rather, Hinduism exists in different forms in

FIGURE 10.20 The geography of religion in South Asia Partition between India and Pakistan in 1947 resulted in mass migrations of Hindus from Pakistan to India and of Muslims from India to Pakistan. There remain, however, more than 123 million Muslims in India, concentrated in a number of subregions.

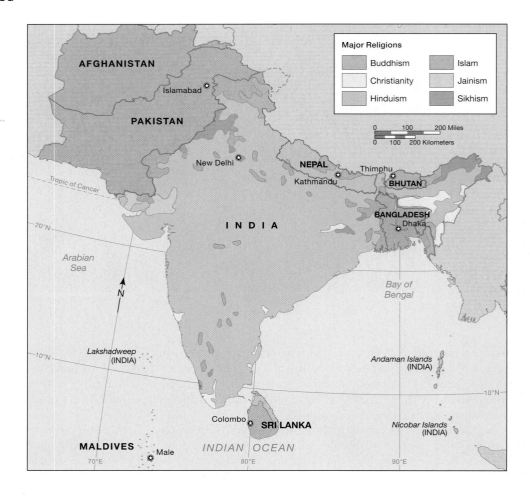

different communities as a combination of "Great Traditions" and "Little Traditions." The Great Traditions derive from the Rig Veda, a collection of 1028 Vedic poems that date from the tenth century B.C. A key aspect of this Great Tradition is the belief that human lives represent an episode of cosmic existence, followed after death by the transmigration of the soul to some other form of life. The "Little Traditions" of Hinduism consist of many local gods, beliefs, rituals, and festivals, and the sacred spaces that are associated with them.

In Hinduism, the number seven has special significance. There are seven especially sacred cities in India: Varanasi (**Figure 10.21**), associated with the god Shiva (the destroyer, but without whom creation could not occur); Haridwar (where the Ganga enters the Plains from the Himalayas); Ayodhya (birthplace of Rama, one of the incarnations of Vishnu, the preserver); Mathura (birthplace of Krishna, another incarnation of Vishnu, sent to Earth to fight for good and combat evil); Dwarka (legendary capital of Krishna thought to be located off the Gujarat coast); Kanchipuram (the great Shiva temple); and Ujjain (the site every 12 years of the Kumbh Mela, a huge religious fair). There are also seven sacred rivers: the Ganga, the Yamuna, the (mythical) Saraswati, the Narmada, the Indus, the Cauvery, and the Godavari. Hindus visit sacred pilgrimage sites for a variety of reasons, including to seek a cure for sickness, wash away sins, or fulfill a promise to a deity. The Ganga is India's holiest river, and many sacred sites are located along its banks, including Haridwar and Varanasi. Many important sacred sites, including thousands of temples and shrines, attract Hindu pilgrims.

A sizable minority population adheres to religions other than Hinduism. The most important of these is Islam. Although several million Muslims migrated from India to Pakistan at the time of partition, more than 123 million Muslims still reside in India today. There are also almost 20 million Christians in India. According to legend, Christianity was introduced to South Asia by the Apostle Thomas during the first

FIGURE 10.21 Varanasi Situated on the banks of the holy Ganga River, Varanasi is one of the most sacred places in India. Hindu pilgrims come to bathe in the waters of the Ganga, a ritual that is held to wash away all sins.

century. Silk traders passing through northwest Pakistan to China during the second century encountered Christians, but the small Christian community did not increase significantly until the arrival of colonial powers. The Portuguese brought Roman Catholicism to the west coast of India in the late 1400s, and Protestant missions, under the protection of the British East India Company, began to work their way through the region in the 1800s. Christianity is most widespread in the state of Kerala, in southwest India, where nearly one-third of the population is Christian.

Language A great diversity of languages is spoken in South Asia. In India alone there are some 1600 different languages, about 400 of which are spoken by 200,000 or more people. There is, however, a broad regional grouping of four major language families:

1. Indo-European languages, introduced by the Aryan herdsmen who migrated from Central Asia between 1500 and 500 B.C., prevail in the northern plains region, Sri Lanka, and the Maldives. This language family includes Hindi, Bengali, Punjabi, Bihari, and Urdu.
2. Munda languages, spoken among the tribal hill peoples who still inhabit the remoter hill regions of peninsular India.
3. Dravidian languages (which include Tamil, Telegu, Kanarese, and Malayalam), spoken in southern India and the northern part of Sri Lanka.
4. Tibeto-Burmese languages, scattered across the Himalayan region.

In India the boundaries of many of the country's constituent states were established after partition on the basis of language. No single language is spoken or understood by more than 40 percent of the people. Since India became independent, there have been efforts to establish Hindi, the most prevalent language, as the national language, but this has been resisted by many states within India, whose political identity is now closely aligned with a different language. In terms of popular media and literature, there is a thriving Hindi and regional language press, while film and television are dominated by Hindi and Tamil, with some Telegu programming.

English, spoken by fewer than 6 percent of the people, serves as the link language between India's states and regions. As in other former British colonies in South Asia, English is the language of higher education, the professions, and national business and government. Without English, there is little opportunity for economic or social mobility. Most children who attend school are taught only their local language and so are inevitably restricted in their prospects. A guard, sweeper, cook, or driver who speaks only Hindi or Urdu will likely do the same work all his or her life. In contrast, those who can speak English—by definition, the upper-middle classes—are able to practice their profession or do business in any region of their country or in most parts of the world. English-language South Asian literature has produced many excellent novels. Among the most familiar authors are Anita Desai, V. S. Naipaul, Arundhati Roy, and Salman Rushdie.

Caste   A very important—and often misunderstood—aspect of India's cultural traditions is that of caste. **Caste** is a system of kinship groupings, or *jati,* that are reinforced by language, region, and occupation. There are several thousand separate *jati* in India, most of them confined to a single linguistic region. Many *jati* are identified by a traditional occupation, from which each derives its name: *jat* (farmer), for example, or *mali* (gardener), or *kumbhar* (potter). Modern occupations such as assembly-line operators, clerks, and computer programmers, of course, do not have a traditional *jati*, but that does not mean that people doing these jobs cease to be members of the *jati* into which they were born. People within the same *jati* tend to sustain accepted norms of behavior, dress, and diet. They are also endogamous, which means that families are expected to find marriage partners for their children among other members of the *jati.*

In each village or region, *jati* exist within a locally understood social hierarchy—the caste system—that determines the accepted norms of interaction between members of different *jati*. In a normal village caste system, individuals will typically interact on a daily basis with others from about 20 different *jati*. Each individual person's *jati* is fixed by birth, but the position of the *jati* within the local caste system is not. Nevertheless, the broad structure of caste systems always places certain groups at the top and others at the bottom. Caste systems tend to hold in high esteem those who are religious and those who are especially learned. Those who pursue wealth or hold political power are typically less well regarded, and those who perform menial tasks are accorded least status of all. Priestly *jatis*—known as brahmins—are always at the very top of the caste hierarchy. Brahmins are expected to lead ascetic lives and revere learning.

At the opposite end of all caste systems are the so-called "untouchables"—*jatis* whose members deal with human waste and dead animals. Mohandas Gandhi, the inspirational leader of India before independence, crusaded to dissociate these *jatis* from the demeaning term *untouchable.* Gandhi called them Harijans, meaning "children of God," but today most people in these *jatis* prefer to be referred to as Dalits, meaning "the oppressed," and the Indian government refers to them as "Scheduled Castes" (**Figure 10.22**). Traditionally, the Dalits were forced to live outside the main community because they were deemed by the brahmins to be capable of contaminating food and water by their touch. They were denied access to water wells used by other *jatis*, refused education, banned from temples, and subject to violence and abuse.

FIGURE 10.22 Caste There are about 138 million Dalit, or "untouchables" in India, most of whom still live on the margins of society.

Although these practices were outlawed by India's constitution in 1950, discrimination and violence against Dalits is still routine in many rural areas.

Contemporary Culture Contemporary culture provides many sharp contrasts with the deep-rooted traditions of South Asia, although there are places and regions (in Afghanistan, in Bhutan, and in many of the more remote rural areas of South Asia) where contemporary culture finds few expressions. The growth of a large and affluent middle class in India since the country's 1992 economic reforms has brought the sights and sounds of Western-style materialism to India's larger towns and cities: fast-food outlets, ATMs, name-brand leisure wear, consumer appliances, video games, luxury cars, and a fast world of pubs, clubs, and shopping malls (**Figure 10.23**). Between 2001 and 2007 the number of shopping mall developments in India jumped from 3 to 345; and the Indian credit-card industry is growing at a rate of 35 percent a year. As of 2007, India's luxury goods market was estimated to be $14 billion annually, featuring international brands such as Rolex, Tag Heuer, Hermes, Gucci, Hugo Boss, and Armani. The preeminent sport in both

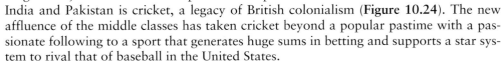

FIGURE 10.23 New malls The rapid growth of India's economy has spurred consumer spending for the country's growing middle class. This mall is in Gurgaon, just outside New Delhi.

India and Pakistan is cricket, a legacy of British colonialism (**Figure 10.24**). The new affluence of the middle classes has taken cricket beyond a popular pastime with a passionate following to a sport that generates huge sums in betting and supports a star system to rival that of baseball in the United States.

Cable television arrived in India in the early 1990s, at about the same time the government initiated its economic reforms. After years without access to popular Western culture, urban middle-class Indians could now watch, via Hong Kong–based Star TV, programming that included MTV, "Baywatch," and "The Oprah Winfrey Show." The expectation among many was that such programming would quickly displace Indian culture, at least among the young and the middle classes. The sheer size and market power of India's middle classes, however, has meant that this scenario of an externally imposed global culture has not occurred. Rather, Indian television and cable companies quickly began to produce films, musical shows, sitcoms, and soap operas in Hindi, Tamil, and some other local languages. The only Hollywood-made programs that earn

FIGURE 10.24 Cricket People in India and Pakistan are passionate about cricket. Shown here are young children with makeshift equipment, playing near the Taj Mahal.

FIGURE 10.25 Bollywood escapism
These billboards hint at the escapist themes common to Bollywood movies.

reasonable ratings are those that are dubbed, while the domestic Indian television and movie industry, based in Mumbai, has quickly grown to major proportions.

When Mumbai was still known as Bombay, the city developed a huge Hindi-language film industry, which acquired the nickname "Bollywood." Although revenues from the hundreds of movies produced in India each year do not compare to those of Hollywood, they nevertheless represent a significant industry within India. Equally important, they represent a unique cultural element. They provide a popular form of escapism from the harsh realities of daily life for the majority of the population (**Figure 10.25**), and they do so in a form that is culturally distinctive, drawing on classical Hindu mythology and traditional social values. The roots of the Bollywood approach lie in traditions of folk theater and performance that stretch back 2000 years, with familiar themes: good triumphing over evil, the struggle of the poor, the sins of the big city, and the melodrama of family life. Hindi-language movies have been a potent force in shaping Indian ideas of nationhood. At the same time, many of the Bollywood movies and TV productions deal with themes such as caste and modernization in ways that relate directly to the lives of Indian viewers.

Although India has produced avant-garde movies that have been recognized for their artistic and dramatic content, most Bollywood products are exuberant, spectacle-driven entertainment: melodramatic fantasies that mix action, violence, romance, music, dance, and moralizing into a distinctive, formulaic form. Bollywood stars such as Salman Khan, Amitabh Bachchan, Priyanka Chopra, Aishwarya Rai, Shilpa and Shamita Shetty, and Twinkle Khanna, have their careers and private lives monitored by adoring fans with an intensity that Hollywood agents would envy. Most Bollywood films have some sort of musical content, and the songs (lip-synched by the actors but sung by "playback artists" who are also stars) dominate Indian pop charts. Soundtracks include sitars, synthesizers, pianos, and violins to provide a score that moves effortlessly from classical Indian ragas to Mozart to hip-hop and rap music. Every taste is catered to, making a bridge between the traditional and the modern, and between East and West.

There is a large market for Bollywood films among the Indian diaspora, earning India more than $225 million in film exports each year. In addition to expatriate Indian markets, Bollywood movies are successful in the Persian Gulf states and in Russia. Nevertheless, Bollywood has its problems. Indian filmgoers, especially those in cities and those with access to satellite television, have become more and more difficult to satisfy with the standard Bollywood recipe. Meanwhile, India has become one of the largest markets for Hollywood films.

FIGURE 10.26 Street vending This scene is from the town of Bikaner, Rajasthan, India.

Just as the impact of globalization has been mediated and transformed by India's television and movie industry, other aspects of economic and cultural globalization have found mixed expression amid South Asia's traditional cultural patterns. Thus, for example, it is still common to see people dressed in traditional clothing—saris for women, dhotis (loin cloths) for Hindu men, turbans for Sikh men, and so on—often in combination with Nike or Adidas sneakers or some other nontraditional apparel. Similarly, despite the proliferation of fast-food outlets such as Domino's Pizza and vending machines selling soft drinks such as Pepsi and Coca-Cola, Western-style food retailing has little appeal to affluent households, most of whom still live in neighborhoods where street vendors sell high-quality fruits, vegetables, dairy products, and other basics (**Figure 10.26**). Appliances such as washing machines, dishwashers, and power tools are also less prevalent than might be expected among South Asia's affluent middle classes, simply because of the millions of people available to undertake domestic labor at very low wages.

Meanwhile, as in other world regions, the cultural shifts involved in globalization flow out as well as in. South Asian mysticism, yoga, and meditation found their way into Western popular culture during the "flower power" era of the 1960s after the Beatles had visited India. South Asian cuisine, with its spicy curries and unleavened breads, found its way into Britain at about the same time and has since become established in restaurants and supermarkets in much of Europe and North America. South Asian methods of nonviolent protest such as boycotts and fasting, inspired by the ancient Buddhist concept of *dharma* and developed in the 20th century by Gandhi, have spread all around the world. Contemporary South Asian literature from writers such as R. K. Narayan, Vikram Seth, Satyajit Ray, and Salman Rushdie has found a global readership. South Asian art and music have been less influential, though Indian singers and musicians are well represented in the "international music" sections of Western record stores and some artists, such as Sheila Chandra, have crossed over into a broader international audience.

Ethnicity and Nationalism

The Western concept of nation-states did not transfer very well to South Asia, where tremendous cultural diversity means that national political boundaries tend to encompass diverse groups in terms of ethnicity, language, religion, and cultural identity, while at the same time dividing some groups, leaving some in one country and some in another. The partition of British India in 1947 demonstrated this in relation to Hindus and Muslims, as did the subsequent secession of Bangladesh from Pakistan in relation to Bengali ethnic and cultural identity. But South Asia's cultural diversity, framed within national boundaries that have been relatively recently imposed, has also given

FIGURE 10.27 Regional and separatist movements in South Asia The imposition of modern political and administrative boundaries on centuries-old patterns of cultural and ethnic differentiation has led to ongoing tensions and a number of cases of regionalism, separatism, and irredentism.

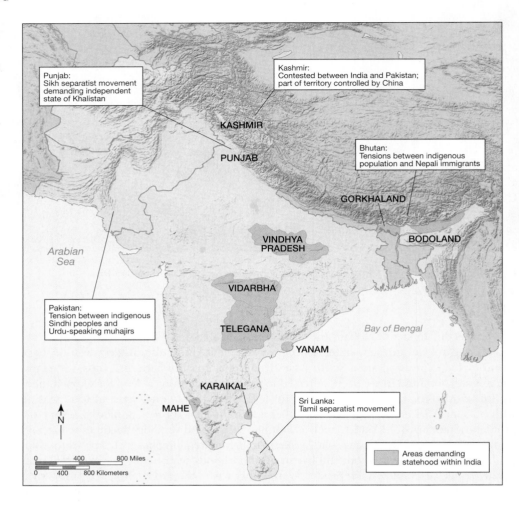

Punjab:
Sikh separatist movement demanding independent state of Khalistan

Kashmir:
Contested between India and Pakistan; part of territory controlled by China

KASHMIR

PUNJAB

Bhutan:
Tensions between indigenous population and Nepali immigrants

GORKHALAND

Arabian Sea

VINDHYA PRADESH

BODOLAND

Pakistan:
Tension between indigenous Sindhi peoples and Urdu-speaking muhajirs

VIDARBHA

TELEGANA

Bay of Bengal

YANAM

KARAIKAL

Sri Lanka:
Tamil separatist movement

MAHE

N

0   400   800 Miles
0   400   800 Kilometers

Areas demanding statehood within India

rise to several other cases of regionalism, separatism, and irredentism (**Figure 10.27**) that are a continuing basis for political tension, social unrest, and, occasionally, outright rioting or armed conflict.

Kashmir   Kashmir, whose predominantly Muslim population found itself isolated as a minority within India at partition, has three times been the cause of war between India and Pakistan (in 1948, in 1965, and 1971). Kashmir remains a contentious and complex arena. Kashmir's northern border is not an accepted international border—it is a "line of control" established after the 1971 war. Pakistan controls the northwestern portion of what India claims as Kashmir, and China controls the northeastern corner. In 1986 Muslim separatists began a renewed campaign of insurgency in the Indian-controlled portion of Kashmir. Since 1989, more than 30,000 people—separatist guerillas, policemen, Indian army troops, and civilians—have died in a guerilla campaign aimed at incorporating Kashmir into Pakistan as part of a larger Islamic state. The Pakistani-backed campaign culminated in Pakistan sending its own forces across the border into the Kargil Peaks district in 1999. Pakistani troops were withdrawn after India launched a full-scale military offensive to evict them and U.S. President Clinton put pressure on the Pakistani government, which subsequently fell to a military coup d'état, the fourth such coup since Pakistan became independent in 1947.

Pakistan   Within Pakistan, ethnic tensions have developed around linguistic differences. Most indigenous Pakistanis speak Punjabi or Sindhi, but families who migrated from India at the time of partition—known in Pakistan as *muhajirs*—have tended to retain Urdu as their language. To protect and maintain their distinctive identity, the *muhajirs* formed a political party, the Mohajir Quami Movement. This attracted a great deal of resentment among indigenous Pakistanis, and in 1995 more than 1800 people were killed in riots in Karachi. In 1998 continuing tensions led the government to impose martial law and to exile, in London, the leadership of the Mohajir Quami Movement.

Sri Lanka   Sri Lanka's ethnic tensions involve both language and religion. The majority population is Buddhist and Sinhalese-speaking. In the northeastern part of the country, however, the majority population is an enclave of Tamil-speaking and Hindu population that represents about 17 percent of Sri Lanka's total population. Ever since independence from Britain in 1948, the Sri Lankan government has pursued a nationalistic posture that has resulted in oppression of this Tamil population. The first casualties were 600,000 descendants of Tamil plantation workers who had been brought to Ceylon (as it was then called) from southern India to work in tea plantations. The deportation of these "plantation Tamils" led to the formation in the 1980s of a militant and bloody Tamil separatist movement that crystallized in 1983 into the "Tamil Tigers"—the Liberation Tigers for Tamil Eelam. In the early 1990s, more than a million Tamil villagers were displaced by fighting between the Tamil Tigers and the Sri Lankan army, becoming refugees in their own land. Since the mid-1990s the level of conflict has diminished, but Sinhalese and Tamil nationalism continues to result in sporadic terrorist attacks and outbreaks of violence.

India   India's ethnic tensions, in addition to those in the Punjab and Kashmir, include those related to separatist movements in Jharkand (an alliance of tribal peoples in southern Bihar, western Orissa, and eastern Madhya Pradesh), Vidarbha and Telegana (involving tribal peoples of the Peninsular Highlands), and Assam, where the Assamese-speaking indigenous population has long resented the Bengali administrators and business elite (see Figure 10.27). These tensions have provoked a strong reaction within India's majority Hindu population. A nationalistic form of Hinduism, *Hindutva,* emerged in the late 1980s, fanned by an epic television series (more than 100 30-minute episodes) based on the classic Hindu story, the *Ramayana.* This coincided with the emergence of a new political party committed to Hindu nationalism, the Bharatiya Janata Party, or BJP. The BJP quickly attracted popular support, and between 1999 and 2004 it was the key partner in a 24-party coalition that came to power after national elections.

CONTEMPORARY CHALLENGES IN A GLOBALIZING WORLD

South Asia is at a critical juncture in its development. On the one hand, it has considerable potential in its human and natural resource base and emerging new economy. Between 2000 and 2005, the region was able to sustain annual growth rates of between 6 and 7 percent. Food production in South Asia has shown a significant increase, and the region as a whole is now a net exporter of food (which is not to say that there are no food shortages). Most South Asian countries are opening up their economies, introducing financial discipline, and attempting to build technological capacity that will permit them to compete in the global economic system. Meanwhile, there is a 1-billion-strong domestic market waiting to be fully developed. India's middle class, at 200 million or more, is the largest in the world and a major consumer market in its own right. More important, perhaps, is India's strong tradition of democracy. India, with a billion people, is the world's largest democracy and a critical element in the region's overall stability.

On the other hand, the region is facing a potentially deep and multifaceted crisis that could well undermine this potential. In marked contrast to India, other countries in the region have struggled to sustain democracy, sometimes failing altogether. In Afghanistan, the Taliban regime reduced the country to a state of oppressive religious autocracy between 1978 and 2002. In the Maldives, Nepal, and Bhutan, traditional hierarchical systems are only slowly evolving toward democracy. Bangladesh and Pakistan have each fallen under military rule: Bangladesh between 1975 and 1989 and

TABLE 10.1 Indicators of Poverty in South Asia, 2005				
	Percentage of Total Population Not Expected to Survive to Age 40	Adult Illiteracy Rate	Percentage of Total Population without Access to Safe Water	Percentage of Total Population without Access to Sanitation	Percentage of Population with an Income of Less Than $1 a Day
Afghanistan	No data	31.5	88	92	No data
Bangladesh	21.4	68.7	5	47	29.1
Bhutan	20.2	53.0	42	31	No data
India	16.7	42.8	19	69	44.2
Maldives	12.5	3.3	40	44	No data
Nepal	22.5	58.2	29	73	37.7
Pakistan	20.1	56.8	21	39	31.0
Sri Lanka	6.4	8.4	15	17	6.6

Pakistan between 1958 and 1971, 1977 and 1988, and from 1999 until the time of this writing. Throughout South Asia, poverty threatens to swamp the gains of economic development, while extreme inequality threatens to undermine political stability. Meanwhile, both poverty and economic development pose a serious threat to South Asia's resource base and its fragile ecological system.

Gender and Inequality

Against the background of acute and chronic poverty in South Asia, the material wealth and Western lifestyles of the growing middle classes serve to highlight the extreme inequality that also characterizes the region. Official statistics reveal that hundreds of millions in South Asia live not just in poverty, but in ignorance and destitution (**Table 10.1**). If anything, poverty and inequality are increasing.

In rural South Asia, scarcity is the norm (**Figure 10.28**). Illiteracy is common, and even the most basic services and amenities are lacking. Life expectancy is low; hunger and malnutrition are constant facts of life. Cow dung is used for fuel (**Figure 10.29**), and most villagers brush their teeth with sticks from neem trees (which have a natural antibacterial sap). In urban areas, poverty is compounded by crowding and unsanitary conditions. In South Asia's largest cities, a third or more of the population lives in slums and squatter settlements, and hundreds of thousands are homeless. In Kolkata alone, it is estimated that more than 700,000 people sleep on the streets each night (**Figure 10.30**). Clean drinking water is limited, and most poor households do not have access to a latrine of any kind.

Poverty The worst concentrations of poverty are characterized by overcrowding, a lack of adequate sanitation, high levels of ill health and infant mortality, and rampant social pathologies. Consider, for example, the squatter settlement of Chheetpur in the city of Allahabad, India. The settlement's site is subject to flooding in the rainy season, and a lack of drainage means stagnant pools for much of the year. Two standpipes (outdoor taps) serve the entire population of 500. There is no public provision for sanitation or the removal of household wastes. In this community, most people eat less than the recommended mini-

FIGURE 10.28 An Indian family with their material possessions The Yadav family from Ahraura village, in Uttar Pradesh, photographed with their possessions outside their home in the mid-1990s, represents a statistically average Indian family in terms of family size, residence, and income.

FIGURE 10.29 Rural poverty Grinding poverty is the norm in rural South Asia. This woman ekes out a living cracking stones on the banks of the Mahananda River in northeastern India.

FIGURE 10.30 Urban poverty For many of the urban poor, poverty means homelessness. In Kolkata entire families dwell on the sidewalk.

mum of 1500 calories a day; 90 percent of all infants and children under age four have less than the minimum calories needed for a healthful diet. More than half of the children and almost half the adults have intestinal worm infections. Infant and child mortality is high—though nobody knows just how high—with malaria, tetanus, diarrhea, dysentery, and cholera the principal causes of death among children under age five.

A great deal of this poverty results from the lack of employment opportunities in cities that are swamped with people. In order to survive, people who cannot find regularly paid work must resort to various ways of gleaning a living. Some of these ways are imaginative, some desperate, some pathetic. Examples include street vending, shoe-shining, craftwork, street-corner repairs, and scavenging on garbage dumps (**Figure 10.31**). This informal economic sector consists of a broad range of activities

FIGURE 10.31 Informal economic activities In cities where jobs are scarce, people have to cope through the informal sector of the economy, which includes a broad variety of activities, including agriculture (backyard hens, for example), manufacturing (craftwork), and retailing (street vending). (a) Street barber, Gujarat, India. (b) A woman sells coconuts and vegetables on the sidewalk in Cochin, India.

(a)

(b)

FIGURE 10.32 Women's work In most households, women must not only raise children, prepare food, and do most of the domestic chores but also work in informal-sector activities or as unskilled laborers. Here, Bhil women work on widening the road to their village, Damodra, in Jaisalmer, Rajasthan, India.

that represent an important coping mechanism. For too many, however, coping means resorting to begging, crime, or prostitution. More than half a billion people in South Asia must feed, clothe, and house themselves entirely from informal sector occupations.

Women and Children Among South Asia's poor, women bear the greatest burden and suffer the most. South Asian societies are intensely patriarchal, though the form that patriarchy takes varies by region and class. The common denominator among the poor throughout South Asia is that women not only have the constant responsibilities of motherhood and domestic chores but also have to work long hours in informal-sector occupations (**Figure 10.32**). In many poor communities, 90 percent of all production is in the informal sector and more than half of it is the result of women's efforts. In addition, women's property rights are curtailed, their public behavior is restricted, and their opportunities for education and participation in the waged labor force are severely limited.

Women's subservience to men is deeply ingrained within South Asian cultures, and it is manifest most clearly in the cultural practices attached to family life, such as the custom of providing a dowry to daughters at marriage. The preference for male children is reflected in the widespread (but illegal) practice of selective abortion and female infanticide. Within marriages, many (but by no means all) poor women are routinely neglected and maltreated. More extreme are the cases—usually reported only when they involve middle-class families—of "bride burning," whereby a husband or mother-in-law reports the "accidental" death (kitchen fires are favored) or suicide of a bride whose parents had defaulted in their dowry payments. Several thousand such deaths are reported in India each year, and this is almost certainly only a fraction of the real number.

The picture is not entirely negative, however, and one of the most significant developments has been the emergence of women's self-help movements. Perhaps the best known of these is the Grameen Bank, a grassroots organization formed to provide small loans to the rural poor in Bangladesh. The Grameen Bank runs completely against the established principles of banking by lending to poor borrowers who have no credit. Since 1983, more than 5.7 million Bangladeshis, spread over 62,089 villages, have borrowed from the Grameen Bank, which now claims to be a financially sustainable, profit-making venture with 17,366 employees. Cumulatively, the bank has loaned more than $5.2 billion, 98 percent of which has been repaid, according to Grameen, a rate that is far higher than that for any conventional financial institution operating in the country. The average size of a Grameen loan is about $120, typically enough to purchase a cow, a sewing machine, or a silkworm shed. Studies have shown that the bank's operations have resulted in improvements in nutritional status, sanitation, access to food, health care, pure drinking water, and housing, and that more than one-third of all borrowers have risen above the poverty line, with another third close to doing so. The most distinctive feature of the Grameen Bank is that 96 percent of its borrowers are women (**Figure 10.33**).

FIGURE 10.33 Rural enterprise Microcredit programs such as those pioneered by the Grameen Bank have enabled tens of thousands of rural women to begin small businesses.

FIGURE 10.34 Child labor The exigencies of poverty mean that children are required to contribute to the household economy, often from a very early age. Here a ten-year-old girl from Jammu, India, works full time in a brick factory.

In India, the Self-Employed Women's Association (SEWA) has made a major contribution to building self-confidence and self-reliance among poor working women by mobilizing and organizing them. SEWA was formed in 1972 in Ahmedabad in the state of Gujarat. It evolved from a trade union of textile workers, but, unlike conventional trade unions, SEWA organizes women workers in the informal sector: vegetable vendors, rag and paper pickers, bamboo workers, cart-pullers, and garment workers. SEWA has given its members a degree of independence from middlemen and, consequently, an invaluable sense of independence. Following the example of the Grameen Bank in Bangladesh, SEWA has also established its own bank to finance income-generating projects for small groups of women, helping them meet the emergencies that would otherwise drive them to money-lenders.

A third example of women's self-help movements comes from Rajasthan, in India, where the Women's Development Programme, sponsored by the government, organizes rural women as volunteers to counter the deep-seated patriarchy of the region. Community-based groups, coordinated by these volunteers, disseminate information on women's legal rights, health and literacy programs, and income-generating schemes and occasionally organize campaigns to protest particularly extreme injustices to individual women.

Children in impoverished settings are even more vulnerable than women. Throughout South Asia, the informal labor force includes children (**Figure 10.34**). In environments of extreme poverty, every family member must contribute something, and so children are expected to do their share. Industries in the formal sector often take advantage of this situation. Many firms farm out their production under subcontracting schemes that are based not in factories but in home settings that use child workers. In these settings, labor standards are nearly impossible to enforce.

The International Labour Office has documented the extensive use of child labor in South Asia, showing that many children under 10 years of age are involved in a great variety of work—tending animals, carpet-weaving, stitching soccer balls, making bricks, handling chemical dyes, mixing the chemicals for matches and fireworks, sewing, and sorting refuse. Most of them work at least 6 and as many as 12 hours a day. A particularly cruel type of exploitation of child labor is **bonded labor.** This kind of bondage occurs when persons needing a loan but having no security to back up the loan pledge their labor, or that of their children, as security for the loan.

In addition, there are many street children, some of whom do casual work and beg but return to their families at night, while others live on the street and effectively have no families. UNICEF has estimated that there are more than 11 million of these street children in India. Finally, perhaps the cruelest exploitation of children is as sex workers. In parts of India—notably in the small towns of rural regions—there are prostitute *jati,* where the cycle of recruitment into sex work is an unavoidable legacy from mother to daughter. Meanwhile, in the red-light districts of every large city, there are hundreds of young bonded or kidnapped rural girls who have been sold into brothels.

Environmental Issues

As we have seen, South Asia's environmental history has left a legacy that includes deforestation, water shortages, and air and water pollution. Given the severe problems of population pressure and poverty in South Asia, it is not surprising that concepts of sustainable development and social responsibility for environmental protection are very weakly developed. Each country in the region has a set of environmental laws and regulations, but they are routinely flouted and only weakly enforced. One reason is corruption, but another reason is that governments simply do not have the institutional apparatus or the funds to enforce environmental laws. More important still, perhaps, is the short-term perspective that derives from the high priority given to economic development: Enforcing environmental laws would wipe out a significant part of South Asian countries' competitive advantage in world markets.

The long-term costs of this situation are certain to be measured in serious environmental degradation and loss of biodiversity (see Geography Matters: South Asia's Disappearing Megafauna, p. 510). Meanwhile, the short-term costs are significant. A 1998 World Bank study estimated that India loses $13.8 billion every year—equivalent to 6.4 percent of the country's gross domestic product (GDP)—as a result of environmental degradation. The largest share of this cost—$8.3 billion—is associated with the health effects of water pollution. The health impact of urban air pollution and consequent loss of productivity account for an estimated loss of $2.1 billion. Soil degradation and the consequent loss of agricultural output is estimated to cost $2.4 billion a year; and rangeland degradation, resulting in a loss of livestock carrying capacity, costs $417 million each year. Deforestation is estimated to cost $244 million annually.

Such estimates do not always take into account the disastrous effects of environmental problems on peoples' lives or, indeed, the raw cost in human lives of disasters such as flooding or the release of untreated toxic waste. One of the most horrific disasters of all time took place in Bhopal, India, in 1984, when lethal methyl isocyanate leaked overnight from a Union Carbide plant, killing more than 6000 people in nearby neighborhoods and permanently damaging the health of hundreds of thousands more. The exact causes and responsibility for the event have still not been settled conclusively. However, to many the Bhopal disaster is emblematic of the potentially disastrous effects of lax attitudes toward environmental planning and regulation on the part of plant owners and managers. Most of the time, such laxity does not involve loss of human life. Nevertheless, the results can be calamitous both to communities and to the environment.

Planning Disasters   Take, for example, the consequences of poor environmental planning in the case of the dams and irrigation schemes along the Porali River in Pakistan. The depth and spread of the river's delta, with its extensive mangrove swamps, made it a breeding ground for fish. For centuries, local villages earned their livings from this natural bonanza. But the river and its delta began to silt up due to a combination of upstream dams and badly applied irrigation techniques, all installed as part of an economic development program. In particular, the huge Tarbela Dam (which is itself suffering from sedimentation because of deforestation in the mountains) has been a major cause of silting by preventing the otherwise natural scouring out of mud during the rainy season. The result is that the rich ecology of the coastal mangrove forest belt of Sindh and Balochistan is dwindling, and the future of the coastal villages is seriously threatened. As fish habitat has shrunk and stocks fallen, fishermen have switched from traditional techniques—

catching large fish with long lines—to using fine-mesh nets. This quickly depleted stocks still further, reducing the average catch to small immature fish. Affluent fishing communities that previously paid their taxes in gold now find it a challenge to feed themselves.

The most dramatic case of poor environmental planning came to light in 2000, when it was discovered that millions of tube wells in Bangladesh are drawing arsenic-contaminated water. Tube wells are water wells that are lined with a durable and stable material, usually cement, that makes it possible to sink wells to a greater depth than traditional water wells. They were installed throughout the country as a result of a campaign in the 1970s by UNICEF, the United Nations children's fund. The purpose of the wells was to provide drinking water free of the bacterial contamination of the surface water that was killing more than 250,000 children each year in Bangladesh.

Unfortunately, the well water was never tested for arsenic contamination, which occurs naturally in the groundwater, and for many years the well water was believed to be completely safe. By the 1990s, high rates of certain types of cancer throughout much of Bangladesh led researchers to investigate, resulting in the identification of the cause as arsenic-contaminated water from tube wells. Medical statistics indicate that 1 in 10 people who drink such water over a prolonged period will ultimately die of lung, bladder, or skin cancer. In a 2000 report, the World Health Organization described the crisis as the largest mass poisoning of a population in history. The scale of the environmental disaster far exceeds those of Bhopal or Chernobyl (see Chapter 3, p. 118): As many as 85 million people still draw arsenic-contaminated water from their local wells, and although the technology is available to purify Bangladesh's plentiful supplies of surface water, it will take many years to replace the estimated 6 million tube wells that are affected.

Regional Development

India's market reforms of the early 1990s triggered a transformation in the country's economic development with implications for regional change and interdependence within South Asia. Since 1992, India's government has built on its structural economic reforms, bringing in a series of second-phase market reforms that have made it easier for free-enterprise capitalism to flourish. India's manufacturing productivity has increased, and the amount of foreign direct investment flowing into the country has increased dramatically: from $76 million in 1991 to $4 billion between 2004 and 2005. BMW, for example, is investing $23 million in a new assembly plant for 3-series and 5-series vehicles in Chennai; Cisco has announced plans to invest $1.1 billion in India between 2006 and 2009; and Nokia has announced plans to invest $100–$150 million in its production facilities in India. The results of this investment are most visible among India's newly affluent middle class. Market reforms have meanwhile triggered an associated cultural change: Flaunting success is no longer frowned upon, and so India's expanding middle class is increasingly unabashed about its cars, Palm Pilots, mobile phones, and vacations in Phuket and Singapore.

Breaking with socialist principles of centrally planned development and social and regional equality has unleashed the spatially uneven economic development processes of capitalism. The growth and the wealth have not been evenly distributed throughout India. Certain industries and certain places and regions have grown dramatically, while elsewhere there has been disinvestment and recession—the "creative destruction" inherent to capitalism. One of the most dramatic examples of regional growth is that of the software industry in south India. More generally, the growth has been centered in larger metropolitan areas and preexisting industrial centers in the Upper Ganga Plains, Damodar-Hooghlyside, and Mumbai-Pune, again following classic principles of capitalist economic development. Places and regions with an initial advantage in terms of factories, skilled labor, specialized business services, and affluent markets can attract more investment, faster, through "cumulative causation," the self-reinforcing spiral of regional growth. The corollary is that places and regions with a weak industrial base, with a weak or obsolescent infrastructure, and with an unskilled or poorly educated workforce tend

South Asia's Disappearing Megafauna

In 2000 a World Conservation Union (IUCN) study identified 11,046 plant and animal species from around the globe as being at risk, including 180 species of mammals and 182 species of birds that are critically endangered. Symbolic of this acute problem are the so-called "charismatic megafauna": large and exotic species such as the rhinoceros, the elephant, whales, and tigers. In South Asia, some charismatic megafauna have already disappeared. Cheetahs disappeared from the wild in India more than 50 years ago, the last sighting being in 1948, when three young males were shot dead by a hunting party in the jungles of Bastar in Madhya Pradesh, central India. Today, the Bengal tiger (**Figure 1**) and the Asian elephant (**Figure 2**) are emblematic of critically endangered species in South Asia.

Experts put remaining numbers of Bengal tigers somewhere between 3060 and 3985, although this could be an overestimate. Tiger populations are notoriously difficult to evaluate, despite recent technological advances that help keep track of their movements. What is clear is that the tiger is being lost. Animal by animal, its footprints are vanishing from South Asia's forests. The causes of the animal's decline are the same ones that are killing off many other species: loss of habitat and remorseless poaching.

In April 2000, the United Nations Convention on International Trade in Endangered Species (CITES) issued a report criticizing how India is caring for its tigers, claiming that the Indian government has displayed a lack of concern and effort. Tiger losses to poachers, concluded CITES, are being covered up by officials, and figures for the remaining animals are deliberately inflated. Poachers hunt tigers in response to the huge demand for tiger body parts in traditional Chinese and Japanese medicine. A single tiger is worth more than $50,000 to poachers. The skin alone fetches an estimated $11,000, while a 10-gram tablet containing tiger bone sells for $25 and a bowl of tiger penis soup sells for $53.

The Asian elephant is also under great pressure. In South Asia, elephants have long been valued for cultural and religious reasons. In countries like Sri Lanka and Nepal, elephants take the lead in many festivals and ceremonies, while in India Ganesha is the elephant-headed Hindu god of wisdom. Stables of domesticated elephants are still kept in parts of South Asia for heavy work, but the region's herds of wild elephants are under stress. There are still between 17,000 and 25,000 wild elephants in South Asia, but as the region becomes more crowded, the elephants are rapidly running out of space. Farmers clear elephants' habitat to grow crops, while roads and urban development claim still more habitat. As elephants trespass on agricultural land, they are sometimes trapped, shot, or poisoned by farm managers.

Asian elephants are also the target of poachers, who sell the animals' ivory tusks to make jewelry and their skin for shoes and bags. About 80 percent of the ivory goes to Japan, where it is used for making personal name seals (called *hankos*), which are considered an elegant substitute for a person's signature. Only male Asian elephants have tusks and the number of tuskers of breeding age is just 1000 to 1200. This small fraction of the elephant population is being targeted by poachers.

FIGURE 1 Bengal tiger The most charismatic of all "charismatic megafauna," the Bengal tiger is one of the most seriously endangered species: Its habitat is fast diminishing, and it is hunted by poachers, with inadequate protection from government agencies.

FIGURE 2 Asian elephant Like the Bengal tiger, the Asian elephant is endangered because of loss of habitat and indiscriminate killing by poachers. These elephants are at Pinnawala Elephant Orphanage, Kegalle, Sri Lanka.

to experience a downward spiral of recession. In India today, the remoter rural regions are experiencing most acutely the negative consequences of the country's economic reforms.

The liberalization of India's economy has shown less predictable consequences. As geographer Pamela Shurmer-Smith has noted, lifting export controls has enabled farmers with access to large amounts of capital to reorganize their production toward lucrative overseas markets, with the result that domestic consumers have to pay more for traditional staples. Thus, for example, many farmers are switching from growing grains for local consumption to cash crops like cotton and tobacco, while others are turning to the cultivation of flowers and strawberries to be shipped to newly affluent urbanites or to be air-freighted abroad. Now that a global market has become aware of high-quality local specialties, such as the fragrant Basmati rice of the Himalayan foothills and the short-season Alphonso mangoes of Maharashtra, their price within India has put them in the luxury class, out of reach of many of the consumers who have traditionally regarded them as occasional treats.

(a)

The Upper Ganga Plains The Upper Ganga Plains have historically constituted the most prominent region of India, and today they are the most heavily populated region of the country. The great empires of India rose to power here. The Ganga is the sacred river of Hinduism, and four of Hinduism's seven holy towns are located in the region, including Varanasi, the holiest of them all. The wealth of the Upper Ganga Plains came from its agricultural productivity, carefully nourished by irrigation canals and wells. It has proved sustainable, but it can carry only a certain density of population, and that density may well have been reached or surpassed in many parts of the plains. Industry has developed throughout the region, but for the most part on a relatively small scale, involving agricultural processing, textiles, glassmaking, crafts, and carpet weaving. Ludhiana (population 2.3 million in 2006), in the northwestern corner of the region, is a textile center and the location of the world's largest bicycle manufacturer, Hero Bicycles, which produces 3 million bicycles annually. Agra (population 1.2 million), Allahabad (1.1 million), Lucknow (2.6 million), and Patna (1.3 million) are all

(b)

FIGURE 10.35 Delhi The capital of India, its third-largest city, and north India's industrial hub, Delhi still has elements of its Mughal and colonial past, though both are swamped by the slums and squatter settlements resulting from over-urbanization. (a) Cows resting on a downtown street. (b) Delhi Metro, opened in 2004 and one of the most sophisticated transit systems in the world.

textile and light-engineering centers. Kanpur (formerly Cawnpore, population 2.7 million), the region's largest industrial city, rose to prominence as a textile center at the time of the U.S. Civil War. The war created a sudden demand for Indian cotton just as the city was linked by rail to Kolkata. Today, Kanpur is one of the most heavily polluted cities in the world. By far the largest and most important city of the Upper Ganga Plains, however, is Delhi.

Major City: Delhi Situated at a great crossroads, Delhi (**Figure 10.35**) occupies an important strategic location at the narrowest point of the Ganga Plains, the most productive agricultural regions of South Asia. For centuries, Delhi provided an essential base for controlling access to and from South Asia's northwestern frontier, and thereby the key overland routes to Central Asia and the Middle East. As a result, Delhi has been the site of the capital of at least eight different empires. Delhi also has seen many invaders throughout the ages. Timur (Tamerlane) plundered it in the 14th century; the Afghan Babur occupied it in the 16th century; and in 1739, Nadir Shah, the Persian emperor, sacked the city and made off with the famous Peacock Throne and with the 186-carat Kohinoor diamond (which was cut down to 108.93 carats and is now in what is known as Queen Mary's crown, part of the British royal family's crown jewels).

Delhi's golden age was in the 17th century under the Mughal emperor Shah Jahan (1628–58), when it was known as Shahjahanabad. Shah Jahan built the famous Red Fort with its palace and city walls, as well as the imposing Jama Masjid (Friday Mosque). Today, Shahjahanabad is part of Old Delhi, the central focus of which is Chandni Chowk—"Silver Street," the bazaar of goldsmiths and jewelers—which runs west from the Red Fort on the right bank of the River Yamuna. Old Delhi is characterized by narrow streets and alleys, low-rise buildings, outdoor markets, bazaars, mosques, temples, and crowds. To the north and west of Old Delhi, the modern metropolis (population 15.3 million in 2006) has spilled out into a sprawl of industrial suburbs and high-density slums and squatter settlements.

To the south is New Delhi, the planned capital of British India. Government administrative functions were moved to Delhi from Calcutta (now Kolkata) in 1912, but New Delhi was not completed until 1931. Designed by British architect-planner Edwin Lutyens, New Delhi was laid out with spacious roads and an impressive ensemble of imposing (but rather ungainly) government buildings in a modernistic geometric street pattern. The site originally stood separate from the unsanitary and congested environments of Old Delhi, but both Old and New Delhi are now engulfed by the vast sprawl of metropolitan Delhi. There is a marked contrast between the suburbs that surround Old Delhi and those that surround New Delhi. The southern suburbs around New Delhi have very little industry and are dominated by the middle-class neighborhoods of civil servants, interspersed with the spacious suburbs of New Delhi's diplomatic sector and with shopping centers and office complexes.

The Damodar Valley and Hooghlyside The initial development of the Damodar Valley and Hooghlyside resulted from European traders' desire to gain sea access to the wealth of the Ganga Plains (with their fine textiles and valuable crops of opium, tea, and indigo) and the jute supplies of Bengal (a world monopoly). Calcutta (now Kolkata) provided a port for ocean-going merchant vessels on the River Hooghly, with access to the river traffic of the Ganga. As commerce grew, so did industry, and in particular the manufacture of jute goods (rope and sacking) and engineering. By the mid-19th century, Hooghlyside had become the largest manufacturing region in India.

Opening of the Suez Canal in 1869 and the boost to the cotton-growing industry in western India that was triggered by the U.S. Civil War (which dried up Britain's supply of cotton) meant that Calcutta's preeminence as an industrial center was challenged by Bombay (now Mumbai). But by then the mineral wealth of the Damodar Valley had been discovered and linked by railway lines to Hooghlyside, just 75 kilometers (47 miles) away. By the 1920s the Damodar Valley and Hooghlyside together accounted for fully one-third of British India's manufacturing employment.

India's richest coalfields are found in the Damodar Valley, while extensive deposits of iron ore are found nearby in the Keonjhar Hills. These resources gave rise to an iron and steel industry. After independence, India, assisted by development aid from the Soviet Union, Britain, and West Germany, invested heavily in the Damodar Valley. The Damodar River and its principal tributaries were brought under control to reduce flooding, produce power, provide irrigation for the region's farmers, and provide water for the modern steelworks.

Today, the towns of the Damodar Valley remain important for iron and steel, and they export coal to many other regions within India. They have also developed a broad industrial base that includes mining copper and bauxite, refining zinc and lead, manufacturing fertilizers, and a range of heavy engineering and toolmaking. Meanwhile, Hooghlyside has lost some of its jute industry (at partition, the traditional jute-producing areas fell within East Pakistan—now Bangladesh—and synthetic fibers have replaced jute in many

(a)

(b)

FIGURE 10.36 Kolkata (a) Central Kolkata. (b) Kolkata is notorious for its slums.

applications) but has developed a mix of industries that includes engineering, metallurgy, food processing, petrochemicals, and publishing.

Major City: Kolkata   The second-largest metropolis in South Asia (population 13.5 million in 2006), Kolkata is spread along both banks of the Hooghly River for up to 80 kilometers (50 miles), covering an area of some 1300 square kilometers (507 square miles). As the capital of British India between 1772 and 1911, Kolkata acquired an impressive range of public buildings, broad streets, universities, and imposing homes. In the 19th century it was known as the "city of palaces."

As a major commercial and industrial city, Kolkata has acquired a Western-style central business district (CBD) with a large office sector housing banks, transnational corporations, and business services. Throughout its history, though, the positive aspects of Kolkata's development have been overshadowed by its problems. A victim of its own success—attracting many more migrants than the labor and housing markets could absorb—and handicapped by a low-lying site that is vulnerable to floods, Kolkata has long had a reputation for having some of the worst slums in South Asia (**Figure 10.36**). Kolkata's infrastructure came under exceptional stress when Hindu refugees from East Pakistan crowded into the city at the time of the 1947 partition, which also deprived Kolkata of a large portion of its economic sphere of influence. Since independence, overurbanization has compounded the problem of slums and urban decay. Today, tens of thousands of sidewalk dwellers crowd the CBD, while squatters have invaded many of the colonial-era parks and open spaces.

Mumbai-Pune   The Mumbai-Pune region is relatively small and isolated, but in terms of economic production it ranks as one of the most successful in South Asia. Its vitality stems from its history and its strategic location rather than its resource base. With the rise of the *Raj*, the trading port of Bombay (now Mumbai) became the chief British base on the west coast. The first railway in India was built from Bombay to nearby Thana in 1853, and by 1864 the railway had reached Poona (now Pune) and Ahmedabad. At the same time, Bombay's docks were modernized to accommodate larger freighters. This infrastructure enabled the region to take full advantage of the boom in cotton prices created by the blockade of the South during the U.S. Civil War. Prices fell sharply with the end of the Civil War in 1865, but by then a massive industrial base had been created. Just four years later the opening of the Suez Canal gave Bombay and its hinterland a huge locational boost, providing much-improved sea routes to Europe and the Middle East. Also significant in securing the economic well-being of the region was the influence of the Tata family, an economic dynasty whose members held a near-monopoly in several key industries based in the Mumbai-Pune region, including iron and steel. The Tata family also helped persuade the government to develop hydroelectric power for the region, exploiting the steep slope of the Western

(a)

FIGURE 10.37 Mumbai The largest metropolis in South Asia, Mumbai has many facets, from its British colonial legacy to the polarized extremes of contemporary metropolitan development. (a) Downtown Mumbai. (b) Mumbai slums.

(b)

Ghats. More recently, the Mumbai-Pune corridor has experienced significant growth in information technology industries, especially in systems software and systems tools.

Major City: Mumbai   When the Portuguese began trading along India's Konkan coast in the 1530s, they set up a fort on a series of seven islets that provided shelter for their merchant vessels. They called it Bon Bahia. The name was anglicized to Bombay in 1661, when the trading post was signed over to the British as part of the dowry for Portugal's Catherine of Braganza when she married England's Charles II. The port soon became the headquarters of the British East India Company. Thereafter it grew steadily until the cotton boom of the 1860s. The cotton boom not only provided Bombay with an industrial base, but also funded the reclamation of the tidal marshes surrounding the islets and transformed the cityscape with an impressive collection of Victorian buildings and parks.

Today, Mumbai (**Figure 10.37**) is by a comfortable margin the largest metropolis in South Asia (population almost 20 million in 2006). It is India's economic powerhouse and financial center. In addition to having a still-significant textile and apparel industry and an international port that handles more than one-third of India's trade, Mumbai is an industrial hub for a very broad spectrum of industry that includes the manufacture and assembly of automobiles, trucks, and buses, consumer durables, chemicals, petrochemicals, plastics, pharmaceuticals, precision instruments, food processing, printing, and filmmaking.

Many remnants of the British colonial era can still be seen in Mumbai—Victorian buildings and upscale residences, red double-decker buses, and cricket matches in the parks. But the city's economic growth and its limited site mean that skyscrapers, office blocks, and apartment complexes have crowded into the peninsula that was formerly the seven islets of Bon Bahia. Meanwhile, of course, Mumbai's prosperity has been a magnet for the rural poor from western and central India. Mumbai's metropolitan area has spread inland and along the coast for 30 kilometers (19 miles). Millions of people live in squalid shanty settlements that surround the corridors of industry radiating from the port and central area. These neighborhoods represent some of South Asia's largest and worst slums. Many are organized with a distinctive mixture of communalist local politics and underworld organizations. They are also congested to the point where much of the city's industry faces gridlock.

In response to Mumbai's congestion and the proliferation of slums, a completely new city—New Bombay, now called Navi Mumbai—was planned in 1973 for a greenfield site across the bay. The plan called for a series of 20 subdistricts with 2 million inhabitants by the year 2000. Each subdistrict was to house the entire range of income groups, with the poorest one-third of the population being provided "sites-and-services" rather than finished housing: plots with all basic infrastructure (streets, sewage and water lines, and foundations) but no construction. Households could build their own homes on these sites and have complete security of tenure. But the result has fallen short of the ideal, and the failure to provide affordable housing to the poor is considered the worst shortcoming of Navi Mumbai. Today around 1 million people live in about seven completed subdistricts, but slums have proliferated, and much of the speculatively built office space in Navi Mumbai's downtown remains vacant.

Congestion in Greater Mumbai (which includes Navi Mumbai) has stimulated economic growth in the Mumbai-Pune corridor. The corridor has recently experienced a good deal of growth in information technology industries as well as in longer-established industries such as electrical components, machine tools, pharmaceuticals, chemicals, rubber, paper, plastics, glass, and various packaged goods. Pune itself, with good infrastructure, a new expressway connection to Mumbai, and institutions such as the National Defence Academy, the Institute of Military Engineering, the Film and Television Institute, and the Armed Forces Medical College, is now growing much faster than Greater Mumbai.

Southern India   The towns and cities of southern India together account for about 20 percent of the country's industrial employment. Bangalore (population 6.1 million in 2006), in particular, has become a thriving industrial and business center. Following the location of key defense and telecommunications research establishments by the government in the 1960s, Bangalore became the premier science and technology center of India, attracting investment from a variety of transnational corporations as a result of the quality of its workforce. Industries here include the manufacture of aircraft, telecommunications equipment, watches, radios, and televisions. However, the city has become world famous for its software industry, the affluent employees of which have contributed to the city's progressive and liberal atmosphere and its lively commercial centers featuring fast-food restaurants, yuppie theme bars, and glitzy shopping malls (**Figure 10.38**).

First impressions of Bangalore are similar to those of other major cities in India: a sprawl of decaying single-story houses and shops, cramped apartment buildings, crumbling colonial offices, mile after mile of squatter slums, and the pervasive sights

(a)

(b)

FIGURE 10.38 Bangalore (a) A rave party at a Bangalore warehouse, organized by MTV and Kingfisher beer. (b) Downtown Bangalore at dusk.

and smells of poverty. Yet within Bangalore is a parallel universe of high-tech industry and the Western-style materialism and fast-world lifestyles of its workers. Koramangala, a south Bangalore neighborhood, is home to a wide variety of software companies, from local start-up operations to subsidiaries of Compaq, Motorola, Nexus, Oracle, Texas Instruments, and Verizon. Infosys Technologies, a Bangalore-based firm that writes and maintains software for hundreds of corporations worldwide, employs 6000 people, has a modern 17-hectare (42-acre) campus with a decidedly Silicon Valley feel, and was the first Indian company to be listed on the U.S. Nasdaq exchange. Daimler-Chrysler has a small center in Bangalore that produces communications technology for automobiles. Philips Research, a branch of the $34 billion Philips Electronics N.V., has established a research center for embedded and software technology. Altogether, Bangalore is now home to more than 500 high-tech companies that employ 100,000 people.

Bangalore is home to the Indian Institute of Science, a world-renowned technical school that has produced top scientists and engineers since 1910. In the 1960s the Indian government chose Bangalore as a site for one of its weapons and aeronautics laboratories, fostering a skilled labor force. After the structural economic reforms of the Indian government in the early 1990s, free-enterprise capitalism was able to flourish, and in Bangalore there was a pool of Indian programmers who had become experts at writing concise, elegant code on their rather limited hardware. When American software companies began to encounter rising costs in Silicon Valley, they found a large pool of highly trained, English-speaking, ambitious, and inexpensive software engineers. Transnational corporate investments, combined with local entrepreneurship, have enabled Bangalore to become a world-class engine of high-tech development.

SUMMARY AND CONCLUSIONS

Isolated and protected by an arc of mountain ranges, the peoples of South Asia have developed distinctive cultures and generated influential concepts and powerful ideals that have spread around the world. The Harappan culture that flourished between 3000 and 2000 B.C. was one of the world's hearth areas of urban civilization. South Asia's resources and its geographic situation on sea-lanes between Europe and the East Indies made it especially attractive to European imperial powers beginning in the 16th century. In the latter part of the 20th century, South Asia's strategic location—between the Middle East and Southeast Asia, and adjacent to China—meant that it was of great interest to the superpowers during the Cold War.

Today, South Asia has the fastest-growing—and the second largest—population of all world regions, with a diaspora that extends to Europe, Africa, North America, and Southeast Asia. In comparison with other world regions, South Asia is still very much a land of villages, though it contains several metropolises of global importance. The region has become even more of a geopolitical hot spot since the end of the Cold War as India and Pakistan, both with access to nuclear weapons, continue to struggle to come to terms with partition. Meanwhile, South Asia is at a critical juncture in its development. On the one hand, it has considerable potential in its human and natural resource base and

emerging new economy. India, in particular, is opening up its economy through reforms that have created a more open and entrepreneurial climate. Key institutions have been privatized, and foreign investment has flowed into the country, helping generate exceptionally high economic growth rates. India now has a huge, well-educated, and sophisticated consumer market of more than 200 million that has become an agent of globalization. With the world's largest democracy and a significant industrial base, India plays a growing role within the world-system, and the fact that India's middle class conducts business in English gives the country a comparative advantage in today's world economy.

On the other hand, the whole of South Asia is facing a potentially deep and multifaceted crisis that could well undermine this potential. In marked contrast to India, other countries in the region have struggled to sustain democracy, sometimes failing altogether. In Islamic Afghanistan and Pakistan, powerful fundamentalist movements have resisted globalization, attempting to re-create certain aspects of traditional culture as the basis of contemporary social order. Throughout South Asia, poverty threatens to swamp the gains of economic development; extreme inequality threatens to undermine political stability; and both poverty and economic development pose a serious threat to South Asia's fragile ecological system.

KEY TERMS

bonded labor (p. 507)

caste (p. 498)

orographic effect (p. 481)

Raj (p. 487)

REVIEW QUESTIONS

Testing Your Understanding

1. What are the three major river systems in the Plains region?

2. Who were the Harappans and the Aryans/Vedics?

3. Emperor Asoka of the Mauryan Empire helped spread which tenets of Buddhism? How did Mughal rule further transform the people of South Asia?

4. How did Imperial Britain change South Asia? How did tea cultivation affect the population of Sri Lanka (Ceylon)?

5. What were the principal consequences of the 1947 partition of India and Pakistan?

6. What is the Grameen Bank? How do its services operate, and are they successful?

7. What is the role of women in India's economy? How does the success of women's self-help movements transform Indian society?

8. Why is child labor so pervasive in South Asia?

9. Briefly discuss the environmental damage and risks to human health caused by the industrial chemical spill in Bhopal, India; the high sedimentation rates at Porbela Dam, Pakistan; and arsenic in groundwater from tube wells in Bangladesh.

10. Define caste, *jati*, brahmin, and Dalit.

11. Who are the Sikhs, Mujahirs, Tamil Tigers, Sinhalese, and the BJP?

12. The 2001 earthquake in Gujarat killed more than 20,000 people and left more than a million homeless. Why is eastern Gujurat such a densely populated area?

13. How does demand for medicinal products in Southeast Asia and for ivory in Japan affect tiger and elephant populations in South Asia?

Thinking Geographically

1. How do the Himalayan Mountains and monsoon season help define the character of South Asia? What is the orographic effect?

2. What challenges face the people of South Asia with regard to water and air pollution?

3. How did Britain transform the physical and cultural geographies of South Asia with plantations, manufacturing, preferential education, and cultural exchange?

4. Compare poverty in rural and urban South Asia. With malnutrition and illiteracy rates high, how do the poor manage to survive?

5. India provides outsourcing for core regions, especially in the high-tech industry where computer programmers at companies like Infosys create a large amount of computer code for far less money than it would cost in North America or Europe, yet for relatively high salaries in South Asia. How does that change the lives of programmers in the United States and in India?

6. How did the U.S. Civil War (1861–65) affect agricultural and industrial development in India? Which cities in India benefited most, and how?

7. Why is India so successful at retaining many of its local cultural traditions in the face of rising globalization since the 1992 market reforms?

8. As South Asians migrated worldwide, which occupations did they take? Which cultural traditions did they bring with them?

9. Why do China, India, and Pakistan all have a claim to the Kashmir region?

10. Bhutan strictly controls the number of visitors to the country in order to protect fragile ecosystems. Nepal, home to Mount Everest and other popular climbing destinations within the Himalayan Mountains, welcomes tourist revenue. Does this different attitude toward tourism have any bearing on relations between the countries or on the way each country treats its minority populations?

FURTHER READING

Barnes, I., and Hudson, R., *The History Atlas of Asia*. New York: Macmillan, 1998.

Bhagat, P., *India: An Oxfam Country Profile*. Oxford: Oxfam, 2004.

Chapman, G. P., *The Geopolitics of South Asia*, 2nd ed. London: Ashgate Publishing, 2003.

Corbridge, S., and Harriss, J., *Reinventing India: Liberalization, Hindu Nationalism, and Popular Democracy*. Cambridge: Polity Press, 2000.

International Labour Office, *Child Labour: Targeting the Intolerable*. Geneva: ILO, 1996.

Jha, V., Hewison, G., and Underhill, M., *Trade, Environment, and Sustainable Development: A South Asian Perspective*. New York: St. Martin's Press, 1997.

Keay, J., *India: A History*. New York: Atlantic Monthly Press, 2000.

Mitra, S. K. (ed.), *Subnational Movements in South Asia*. Boulder: Westview Press, 1994.

Norton, J., *India and South Asia*, 4th ed. Guilford, CT: Dushkin/McGraw-Hill, 1999.

Oza, R., *The Making of Neoliberal India*. London: Routledge, 2006.

Raju, S., Kumar, S., and Corbridge, S. (eds.), *Colonial and Post-Colonial Geographies of India*. Thousand Oaks, CA: Sage Publications, 2006.

Shurmer-Smith, P., *India: Globalization and Change*. London: Arnold, 2000.

Singh, J. P., and Mumtaz, K., *Mythical Space, Cosmology and Landscape: Towards a Cultural Geography of India*. Delhi: Manak, 2002.

Spate, O. H. K., and Learmonth, A. T. A., *India and Pakistan: A General and Regional Geography.* London: Methuen, 1967.

Standage, T., *A History of the World in Six Glasses.* New York: Walker & Co., 2005.

Thomas, G. C., "Competing Nationalisms: Secessionist Movements and the State," *Harvard International Review,* Summer 1996.

Weightman, B. A., *Dragons and Tigers: A Geography of South, East, and Southeast Asia.* New York: John Wiley & Sons, 2002.

Wolpert, S., *India,* rev. ed. Berkeley: University of California Press, 1999.

FILM, MUSIC, AND POPULAR LITERATURE

Film

Asoka. Directed by Santosh Sivan, 2001. The story of the emperor of the Mauryan dynasty who massacred thousands before becoming a Buddhist monk.

City of Joy. Directed by Roland Joffé, 1992. This movie depicts life in a Kolkata slum; it gives a good flavor of India and the monsoon season.

Gandhi. Directed by Richard Attenborough, 1982. Hit movie biography of the lawyer who became the famed leader of the Indian revolt against the British through his philosophy of nonviolent protest.

The Great Indian Railway. PBS Home Video, 1998. Documentary that describes journeys on India's vast railway network.

Kabhi Khushi Khabie Gham. Directed by Karan Johar, 2001. Bollywood romantic drama that made the box office top 10 in North America.

Kandahar. Directed by Mohsen Makhmalbaf, 2001. An independent film about a young journalist based in Canada who returns to her native Afghanistan to find the country in the grip of the Taliban.

Lagaan: Once Upon a Time in India. Directed by Ashutosh Gowariker, 2001. A Bollywood period epic about Indian farmers who best their colonial rulers in a cricket game. Academy Award nominee for Best Foreign Film.

Monsoon Wedding. Directed by Mira Nair, 2001. Contemporary story of a Punjabi wedding in New Delhi. A Bollywood movie that was a major hit in Europe and the United States.

My Beautiful Laundrette. Directed by Stephen Frears, 1985. Based on the novel by Hanif Kureishi, this movie tells the story of a romance between an Anglo-Pakistani and a London skinhead.

Salaam Bombay. Directed by Mira Nair, 1988. Portrays the life of street children in Mumbai.

Music

Chandra, Sheila. *Weaving My Ancestors' Voices.* Real World Records, 1993.

Jhaveri, Shweta. *Anahita*. Intuition Records, 2000.

Khan, Nusrat Fateh Ali. *Dust to Gold*. EMD/Real World, 2000.

Danna, Mychael. *Monsoon Wedding* (movie soundtrack). Milan Entertainment, 2002.

Musafir. *Dhola Maru*. Sounds True, 1999.

Shankar, Ananda. *Walking On*. EMD/Real World, 2000.

Shankar, Ravi, and Glass, Philip. *Passages*. BMG/Private, 1990.

Subramaniam, L. *Global Fusion*. Wea/Atlantic/Atrium, 1999.

The Sabri Brothers. *Greatest Hits*. Shanachie, 1997.

Popular Literature

Denker, D. *Sisters on the Bridge of Fire*. Los Angeles: Allstory.com, 1993. An account of solo travel through Pakistan, sharing the lives of local women.

Grewal, R. *In Rajasthan*. London: Lonely Planet Publications, 1997. A personal journey that takes in the traditional villages, palaces, and personalities of one of India's most exotic regions.

Hasan, M. "Partition: The Human Cost," *History Today*, September 1997. An account of the trauma and tragedy of partition through literature and personal histories.

Kipling, R. *Kim*. New York: Doubleday, 1966. A classic epic novel of India under the British by a great storyteller.

Mehta, G. *Karma Cola: The Marketing of the Mystic East*. London: Jonathan Cape, 1991. Describes the collision between India's desire for Western technology and methods and the West's fascination with India's ancient wisdoms.

Mishra, P. *Butter Chicken in Ludhiana: Travels in Small Town India*. London: Penguin, 1995. A popular account of travel through the "real" India.

Nasrin, T. *Lajja*. New York: Prometheus, 1997. The title of this novel means "shame"; it describes the 1992 Muslim-Hindu clash over the destruction of the Babri Masjid in India.

Newby, E. *Slowly Down the Ganges*. London: Lonely Planet Publications, 1998. Captures the sights and sounds of traveling down the river.

Novak, J. *Bangladesh: Reflections on the Water*. Dhaka: University Press, 1994. A penetrating overview of the country and its people.

Rushdie, S. *Midnight's Children*. New York: Penguin USA, 1995. A novel that tells of the lives of the children who were born, like modern India itself, in 1947.

Rushdie, S., and West, E. (eds.). *Mirrorwork: 50 Years of Indian Writing, 1947–1997*. London: Henry Holt, 1997. A celebration of Indian writing in English.

Sarkar, T. "Women in South Asia: The *Raj* and After," *History Today*, September 1997. Examines the evolving position of women.

Seth, V. *A Suitable Boy*. New York: HarperPerennial, 1993. An epic novel about post-independence India.

Tharoor, S. *India: From Midnight to the Millennium*. New York: HarperPerennial, 1998. A passionate but often agonized account of the history of India since independence that attempts to define what makes India one country and Indians of various ethnic, religious, and cultural backgrounds one nationality.

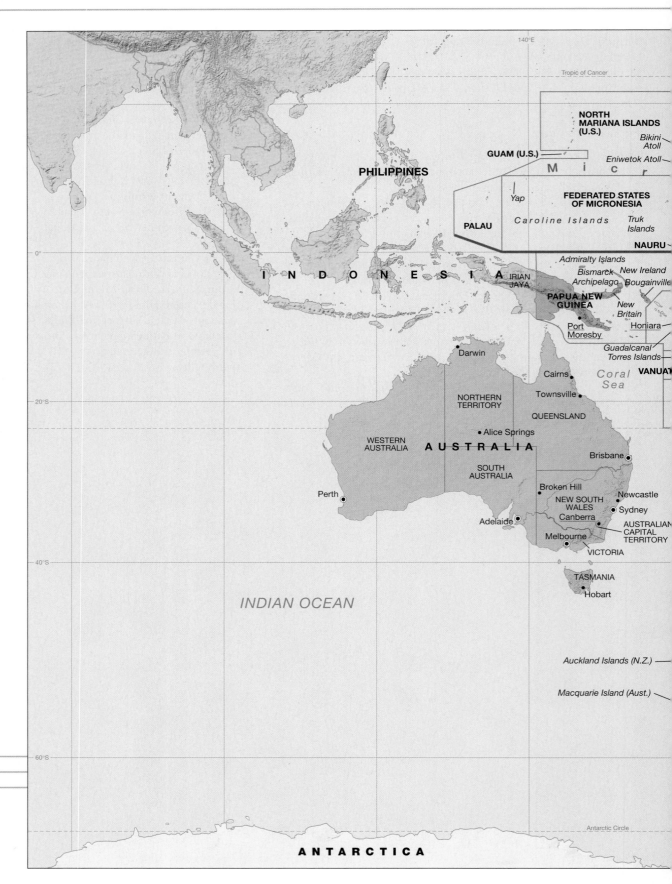

FIGURE 11.1

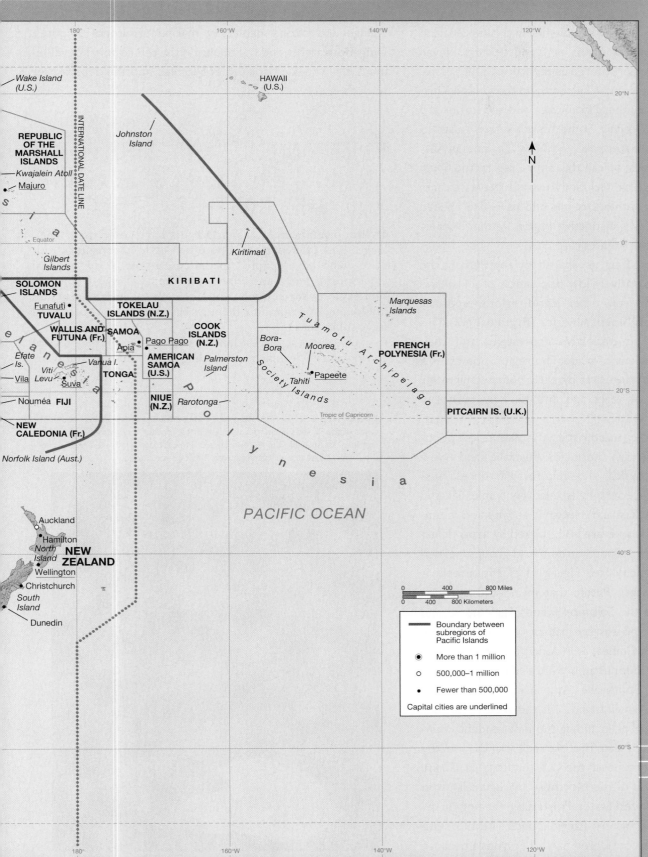

Wake Island
(U.S.)

HAWAII
(U.S.)

REPUBLIC OF THE MARSHALL ISLANDS

Johnston Island

Kwajalein Atoll
• Majuro

Equator

Kiritimati

Gilbert Islands

KIRIBATI

SOLOMON ISLANDS

Funafuti •
TUVALU

TOKELAU ISLANDS (N.Z.)

Marquesas Islands

WALLIS AND FUTUNA (Fr.)
SAMOA

COOK ISLANDS (N.Z.)

Pago Pago
Apia

Bora-Bora
Moorea

Efate Is.
Viti Levu
Vanua I.

AMERICAN SAMOA (U.S.)

Palmerston Island

FRENCH POLYNESIA (Fr.)

Vila
• Suva

TONGA

Tahiti
• Papeete

T u a m o t u   A r c h i p e l a g o

Society Islands

Nouméa
FIJI

NIUE (N.Z.)

Rarotonga

Tropic of Capricorn

PITCAIRN IS. (U.K.)

NEW CALEDONIA (Fr.)

Norfolk Island (Aust.)

P o l y n e s i a

M e l a n e s i a

INTERNATIONAL DATE LINE

PACIFIC OCEAN

Auckland
• Hamilton
North Island

NEW ZEALAND

• Wellington
• Christchurch
South Island

Dunedin

0	400	800 Miles
0	400	800 Kilometers

▬▬▬	Boundary between subregions of Pacific Islands
⊙	More than 1 million
○	500,000–1 million
•	Fewer than 500,000
Capital cities are underlined	

One-third of Earth's surface is occupied by the Pacific, an immense ocean that spans 16,000 kilometers (10,000 miles) between the Americas and Asia and reaches from Alaska to the Antarctic. More than 20,000 islands dot the Pacific Ocean (**Figure 11.1**). Most are in the southeastern Pacific, including the large countries of Papua New Guinea and New Zealand and 11 independent nation islands or island clusters. Eleven other island groups are constituted as territories of Australia, France, the United States, New Zealand, and the United Kingdom. As a world region, these countries and territories are commonly known as *Oceania*. Some texts exclude Australia from Oceania, designate Australia and New Zealand as Australasia or the Antipodes, or call this entire region the *South Pacific*. In this book we have included Australia, New Zealand, and the Pacific islands within Oceania and have also chosen to discuss Antarctica as a distinctive region within Oceania (see Geography Matters: Antarctica, p. 524).

The region is defined by its shared orientation to the ocean realm, its comparatively low population of 34 million people, and its isolation from other world regions, especially the core of Europe and North America (**Figure 11.2**). This isolation has resulted in distinctive ecosystems and challenges to the development of trade. The region possesses a lengthy history of migration, first by early humans migrating from Asia thousands of years ago and then by European colonists in the 19th century.

Despite their shared characteristics of isolation, low population density, and British heritage, Australia and New Zealand have many physical and cultural differences. Australia's ancient physical geography is relatively stable, flat, and low compared to New Zealand's tectonic activity and mountain ranges. The Pacific islands are also marked by many differences and are often divided into three broad groups, defined by geography and ethnicity (see Figure 11.1). **Melanesia** is the region of the western Pacific that includes the largest islands of New Guinea, the Solomon Islands, Fiji, Vanuatu, and New Caledonia. Only the eastern half of New Guinea (the country of Papua New Guinea) is included in Oceania, since the western half is the Indonesian province of Irian Jaya and is usually included in Southeast Asia (see Chapter 9). **Micronesia** (meaning "small islands") is the group of islands at, or north of, the equator, including the independent countries of Nauru, Kiribati, Palau, the Marshall Islands, and the Federated States of Micronesia; the U.S. territory of Guam; and the Commonwealth of the Northern Mariana Islands in association with the United States. Polynesia (meaning "many islands") comprises the eastern Pacific islands. The U.S. state of Hawaii is sometimes considered part of Polynesia because

of ethnic and linguistic links between the indigenous Maori, Hawaiiana, and people of the eastern Pacific islands.

This chapter examines the environment, history, and peoples of Oceania. It provides an opportunity to highlight some global issues and their regional impacts, including climate change and ozone depletion, marine territorial disputes, indigenous rights and multiculturalism, the regional development challenges of isolated economies, and the debate over nuclear energy.

ENVIRONMENT AND SOCIETY IN AUSTRALIA, NEW ZEALAND, AND THE SOUTH PACIFIC

Environmental conditions in Oceania have posed many challenges and offered many opportunities to the region's residents, who have adapted to the constraints of the physical environment and transformed it in dramatic ways. This section explores the environmental context for human activities in Oceania by examining the physical environments of several large subregions.

Australia, the largest landmass in the region, has several contrasting environments, including the dry interior and west-

FIGURE 11.2 Oceania from space This image conveys the importance of the Pacific Ocean to Oceania and the contrast among the large island continent of Australia, the larger islands of New Guinea and New Zealand, and the scattering of smaller islands across the southern Pacific.

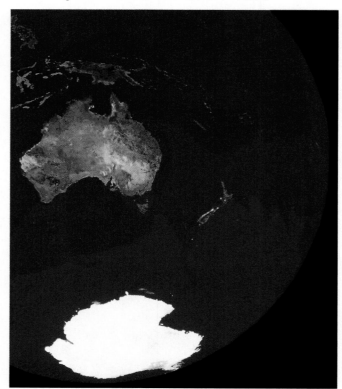

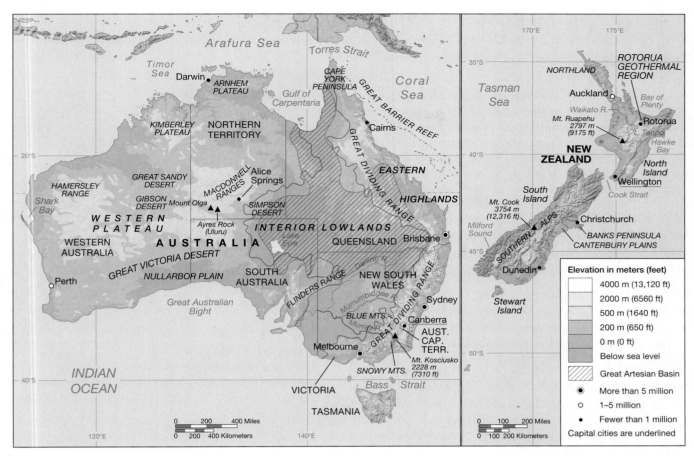

FIGURE 11.3 The physical landscape of Australia and New Zealand
Major physiographic regions and distinctive landforms of Australia and New Zealand are shown on these maps. For Australia, key features include the eastern highlands, central deserts, Great Artesian Basin, and Great Barrier Reef, and for New Zealand, the Southern Alps and west coast fjords, such as Milford Sound.

ern plateau and an eastern coastal lowland backed by uplands. The climate ranges from tropical conditions on the northern Queensland coast to cooler conditions in the southeast state of New South Wales and on the island of Tasmania. Australia is the only country in the world that also forms an entire continent, and it is the driest and flattest of all the continents. New Zealand has two major environmental regions, the more tropical North Island and the cooler South Island. The Pacific islands can be classified into two physical types, the higher volcanic islands and the low coral atolls. Antarctica covers an area of 8.8 million square kilometers (5.5 million square miles). It contains 70 percent of the world's fresh water and 90 percent of the world's ice. It is the highest, coldest, and windiest of all the continents.

Landforms and Landscapes

Geological history, especially tectonic activity, influences the nature of many of the major environmental regions of Oceania. Australia is a very old and stable landmass that was part of the Southern Hemisphere supercontinent called *Gondwanaland* (see Chapter 1), which broke away from Pangaea 200 million years ago and moved toward the South Pole. The Indo-Australian Plate separated about 50 million years ago and began moving northeast until it collided with the Pacific Plate. New Zealand now sits at the boundary where the Pacific Plate is moving under (subducting) the Indo-Australian Plate and producing high levels of volcanic and earthquake activity.

Australia The Australian landmass lies in the middle of the Indo-Australian Plate and forms a continental shield of ancient stable rock with very little volcanic, earthquake, or other mountain-building activity. Australia, which has an area of 7.7 million square kilometers (3 million square miles), is divided into three major physical regions by a series of interior, low-lying basins that divide the western Australian Plateau from the uplands of eastern Australia (**Figure 11.3**).

523

GEOGRAPHY MATTERS

Antarctica

Antarctica was once at the heart of a single supercontinent called *Gondwanaland* (see Chapter 1). Fossils of marine animals and forests found in Antarctica suggest that the Antarctic seas cooled about 65 million years ago, and most trees and reptiles disappeared by 5 million years ago. Today, Antarctica temperatures average −51°C (−60°F) during the six-month winter, when the sun does not rise above the horizon and the continent is in perpetual twilight. The world's lowest temperature was recorded on July 21, 1985, at the Russian Vostok base, at −89°C (−129°F). By September each year, half the surrounding ocean is frozen, creating a vast mantle of Antarctic pack ice with an area of 20 million square kilometers (32 million square miles) and a thickness of more than 2 meters (6.6 feet). The average elevation is above 2300 meters (7000 feet), and the highest mountains reach almost 5000 meters (16,000 feet).

It is always difficult to categorize Antarctica within the normal groupings of world regions, but in some ways it fits well within Oceania because of the importance of the marine environment, its isolation, the links to New Zealand and Australia as well as Great Britain and the United States, and the growing role of tourism.

Antarctica's landscapes are beautiful but sterile. There are few growing plants, surface lakes, and little running water. The vast polar ice cap, more than 3 kilometers (nearly 2 miles) thick in places, is pierced by mountain peaks called *nunataks*. Glaciers and snowfields cover most of the rest of Antarctica, though in the brief summer the snow in some coastal regions melts to reveal a lunar landscape of rock, boulders, and volcanic ash. The largest glaciers, such as the Lambert and the Beardmore glaciers, are so massive that they force great quantities of ice beyond the landmass onto the surrounding seas, where it floats as an ice shelf, terminating in towering ice cliffs.

Antarctica's landscapes are also striking for their near-silence. Because absolutely nothing grows in the region, there is no sound of wind in the vegetation. There is very little animal life or human habitation, no buzzing insects, and the crying of birds is localized in a few of the relatively more hospitable coastal locations. Because it is frozen for much of the year, even the sea is silent. As the ice melts along the coasts, the most active and noisy residents of Antarctica's landscapes are millions of seals and penguins and the occasional giant blue whale surfacing offshore (**Figure 1**).

Visually, the most striking aspect of Antarctica's landscapes is the sheer scale. In the clear, bright light of unpolluted air, the unbounded snow- and ice fields seem endless. The distances are indeed immense, and the atmosphere is so clear that one can easily be deceived: Mountains that seem no more than 20 kilometers (11.4 miles) away may in fact be 80 kilometers (49.7 miles) dis-

FIGURE 1 Antarctic landscape Antarctica is an ice-covered landscape populated by penguins and other species adapted to cold temperatures. The penguins feed on abundant fish in the oceans around the icecaps.

tant. And in the absence of haze, the colors of distant objects are different—mountains seen at a distance seem yellow rather than blue. In detail, the snowy, icy landscape is subject to constant change as ice features move and new snow blankets old features.

Along parts of the coast, stark granite promontories provide fixed landmarks, but much of the coastline of Antarctica is ephemeral. The latest maps of Antarctica are always out of date because of the changing configuration of glaciers as they reach the sea. In summer, the Antarctic pack ice breaks up and the coastal glaciers carve huge icebergs that shift, drift, and change shape by the hour.

Although scarcely inhabited by humans, there is a great deal of interest in Antarctica, both from the point of view of scientific research and from the point of view of the potential exploitation of reserves of natural resources such as deposits of iron ore, coal, gas, and oil that may lie beneath Antarctica and the seas around it. The 1911–12 race to the South Pole between Britain's Captain Robert F. Scott and Norwegian explorer Roald Amundsen has gained mythic proportions and inaugurated further scientific exploration and territorial claims on the continent. Amundsen reached the pole in December 1911, and Scott arrived on January 18, 1912. On their return trip, Scott and his companions perished when they were slowed by bad weather and ran out of food.

The eastern highlands of Australia are the remnants of an old folded mountain range with a steep escarpment on the eastern flanks. The range was created when New Zealand broke away from Australia about 80 million years ago. The highland crest is often called the Great Dividing Range because it separates the rivers that flow to the east coast from those flowing inland or to the south (**Figure 11.4a**). The highest moun-

International relations on the continent are governed by the **Antarctic Treaty**, which covers the area south of 60° S. The treaty, created in 1958 and now signed by 45 countries, bans nuclear tests and the disposal of radioactive waste and ensures that the continent can be used only for peaceful purposes and mainly for scientific research. In 1991 the treaty added a 50-year ban on mineral and oil exploration. Nevertheless, several countries—Australia, Argentina, Chile, France, New Zealand, Norway, and Great Britain—still claim specific slices of the Antarctic pie, hoping to be able to assert rights to offshore fisheries and onshore resource exploitation (**Figure 2**).

Small groups of military personnel, scientists, and support personnel have been based in Antarctica in pursuit of these scientific and national interests. There are no airports whatsoever in the entire continent and only one hotel (on King George Island), so these specialized personnel are flown in on aircraft equipped with skis. They are accommodated in camps and research institutes called *stations*. Odd-shaped buildings, domes, and antennas, seemingly arranged haphazardly, dot the landscape of these stations, where snowmobiles and vehicles with monster truck tires provide the only sign of outdoor activity. The stations are supplied by specialized icebreaking ships that are also used for scientific research. When the Soviet Union collapsed in 1989, most of the former Soviet Union's specialized ships were suddenly idle. But not for long: Entrepreneurial Western travel companies hired the ships and their crews, turning high-tech research vessels into ecotourist cruise ships. Each summer about 30,000 travelers visit Antarctica. Cruises are by far the most popular tourist activity in Antarctica, but organized tours also offer mountain climbing, kayaking, sailing, camping, and even scuba diving.

Though these numbers are minuscule on the overall scale of world tourism, the environmental impact is already giving cause for concern. Bird species such as petrels, penguins, and albatrosses are declining in number. Petrels are long-lived birds—the oldest on record survived 50 years—and they feed on a variety of foods, making them an ideal Antarctic "indicator species." Many ecologists believe that the increased human presence in Antarctica may

be disturbing these sensitive birds so much that they fail to breed. Another possible culprit is commercial fishing, which is booming, often illegally, throughout the southern oceans. Meanwhile, the efficiency, persistence, and greed of Russian, Japanese, and Norwegian whaling fleets have led to the near-extermination of the blue whale and the decimation of other species.

There is growing concern that global warming is threatening Antarctica, especially the Antarctic peninsula, where temperatures are warming and changing the ecology and ice cover is disappearing. In 2002 a 3250-square-kilometer (1225-square-mile) chunk of the Larsen B ice shelf broke away from the mainland. If Antarctic ice continues to melt as a result of climate change, it will contribute to a worldwide rise in sea levels.

FIGURE 2 Territorial claims in Antarctica Seven countries have territorial claims in Antarctica but more than 40 have signed the Antarctic Treaty. The treaty bans nuclear tests and the disposal of radioactive waste, ensures that the continent can be used only for peaceful purposes and mainly for scientific research, and includes a 50-year ban on mineral and oil exploration. Sixteen countries have maintained scientific research bases on the Antarctic continent, including the U.S. Amundsen-Scott base at the geographical South Pole and the Russian Vostok base at the magnetic South Pole. (*Source:* Based on G. Lean and D. Hinrichsen (eds.), *Atlas of the Environment.* Santa Barbara, CA: ABC-CLIO, 1994, pp. 182–83; and Terraquest, Virtual Antarctica Expedition. Available at http://www.terraquest.com/va/expedition/maps/cont.map.html.)

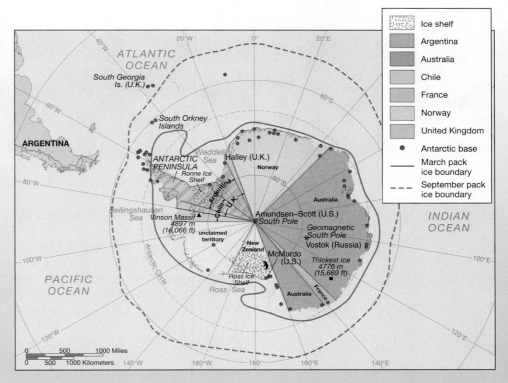

tain in the eastern uplands is Mount Kosciusko (2228 meters, 7310 feet) in the Snowy Mountains of New South Wales. The east coast is distinguished by the offshore presence of the world's largest coral reef, the Great Barrier Reef.

The interior lowlands were once flooded by a shallow ocean and now contain the Lake Eyre basin, filled only occasionally by inland-draining rivers. Waters in the Lake

(a)

(b)

Eyre basin are very salty because of the high levels of evaporation in the hot, dry climate. A large part of the lowlands is also called the **Great Artesian Basin** because it is underlain by the world's largest groundwater aquifer, a reservoir of underground water in porous rocks. The basin is artesian because overlying rocks have placed pressure on the underground water so that when a well is drilled, the water rises rapidly to the surface and discharges as if from a pressurized tap. The wells that tap the Great Artesian Basin are critical to the human settlements and livestock of arid east-central Australia, although the cost of drilling is high and the water is often very warm and salty. The southern part of the interior lowlands is drained by the Murray and Darling river systems, which flow west out of the eastern highlands toward the southern coast. These river basins have been transformed by irrigation projects.

Two-thirds of Australia is occupied by the western plateau of old shield rocks with a few low mountains, such as the Macdonnell and Hamersley ranges, and large areas of flatter desert plains and plateaus, such as the Simpson and Great Sandy deserts and the Kimberly and Arnhem plateaus. This region has numerous mineral deposits—the basis for Australia's mining industry—and old, weathered soils that are too nutrient-poor or salty for agriculture. Western Australia and the interior lowlands contain impressive examples of desert landforms, including wind-shaped undulating ridges of sand dunes, stony plains with varnished rock fragments called *desert pavement,* and dry interior drainage basins called *playas.* Centuries of erosion by wind and water have left erosion-resistant domes of rocks standing above the surrounding landscape. Cycles of extremes of heat and cold, combined with moisture and various chemical processes, can varnish the rocks or peel them off in concentric layers. The most famous of these isolated rock domes are Ayres Rock, called *Uluru* by the Aborigines, and the Olgas, called *Kata Tjuta* (**Figure 11.4b**). The remoter and drier inland areas of Australia are often called the "Outback" (see Signature Region: The Australian Outback, p. 528).

New Zealand   In contrast to Australia, New Zealand is a much younger and more tectonically active landscape, located where the Pacific Plate is moving under the Indo-Australian Plate, thrusting land upward into high relief and promoting volcanic activity. The New Zealand physical landscape includes two major islands spanning 1600 kilometers (976 miles) from north to south, with a combined area of just over 268,000 square kilometers (103,000 square miles). The South Island is about 25 percent larger than the North Island, from which it is separated by the narrow Cook Strait.

The South Island has rugged mountains rising to more than 3500 meters (11,500 feet) in the Southern Alps, dominated by Mount Cook at 3754 meters (12,316 feet) (**Figure 11.5a**). The South Island is far enough south (41 to 47 degrees south latitude) to have extensive permanent snowfields and more than 300 glaciers, some flowing

(a)

FIGURE 11.5 New Zealand landscapes (a) Mount Cook (Aoraki) National Park has more than 19 peaks that are over 3000 m (10,000 ft), with glaciers covering more than a third of the park area. The region is a popular ski destination. (b) The region around Rotorua, on the North Island of New Zealand, has numerous hot springs, geysers, and steam vents associated with volcanic activity. Geothermal energy sources such as the Wairakei power plant shown here have been developed and contribute 10 percent of New Zealand's electricity production. The region is also popular with tourists attracted by the landscape, spas, and thriving Maori culture.

(b)

The Australian Outback

The **Outback** is the term generally applied to the remote and drier inland areas of Australia. It carries an image of a reddish, dusty landscape occupied by a few cows, Aborigines, and mining enterprises. Although low rainfall and frequent drought are common in inland Australia, the exploitation of underground water from the Great Artesian Basin has allowed the development of scattered homesteads that raise livestock on sheep and **cattle stations** (**Figure 1**). In these enterprises, animals are raised on large grazing leases. Cattle are left to fend for themselves for the most part and are only brought into the stations once or twice a year. Sheep are raised where rainfall is higher to the east and west. Life on the cattle and sheep stations is often tough, exposed to the hazards of drought and wildfires and remote from schools, shops, and hospitals. Distance education was pioneered in these remote settlements, with children taught through radio broadcasts. The ill receive emergency medical care from the Flying Doctor service.

Many Aborigines still live somewhat traditional lives in the Outback, although many work on stations and mines or reside in small settlements known as *outstations* (**Figure 2**). Many receive government support. Some areas of inland Australia, especially in the Northern Territory and Western Australia, have been set aside for Aborigines.

Some of the earliest transportation routes into the Outback were roads and railways that connected mining centers with the coast. Mining centers developed across the interior at Broken Hill in New South Wales and Kalgoorlie in Western Australia, and more recently at new finds near Mount Isa (lead, zinc, copper) in Queensland and Pilbara (iron ore) in Western Australia. Uranium is also mined in the Outback. At the town of Coober Pedy, which is a center for the mining of opals valued for jewelry, the temperatures are so intense that much of the town has been built underground. Mining communities are the most important settlements in the Outback, together with the town of Alice Springs, which developed on the telegraph line and later the Stuart Highway from Adelaide in the south of the country to Darwin in the north. Goods are transported across the vast interior using "road trains," enormous trucks that pull a chain of trailers at rapid speeds.

Life in the Outback is vulnerable to several natural hazards, including frequent droughts that can decimate livestock herds and exacerbate problems of soil erosion and overgrazing. Droughts are also associated with severe wildfires that can race across the tinder-dry bush vegetation, especially where oily eucalyptus fuels the fire. Livestock operations are at risk from dingoes, which are called *warrigal* by the Aborigines, who sometimes tame the animals. Dingoes hunt alone or in small groups, preying on kangaroos, rabbits, sheep, and cattle. The world's longest fence was built in order to keep the dingoes out of southern Australia. The so-called Dog Fence is a straight wire-and-post fence 5322 kilometers (3307 miles) long, twice as long as the Great Wall of China (shown in the movie *Rabbit-proof Fence*). Another irritant in the Outback are the hordes of flies that land on any sign of moisture, especially the faces of humans and animals.

FIGURE 1 The Outback Wallara ranch, a cattle station in the Australian outback. The distances involved are so vast that helicopters and motorbikes are used to herd cattle, in addition to the traditional horses and dogs.

FIGURE 2 Aboriginal camp An elderly aboriginal landowner Lilly Billy, sits with a friend at her Outback camp at Anna Creek Station in Arnhem Land of the Northern Territories.

almost to sea level. The southern portion of the west coast is penetrated by magnificent fjords, such as Milford Sound, created when the sea flooded the deep valleys cut by glaciers. The spectacular alpine scenery is a major draw for tourists and was popularized, in digitally enhanced forms, in recent movies based on J. R. R. Tolkien's *Lord of the Rings* trilogy. The east coast of the South Island has much gentler relief, with rolling foothills, long valleys with braided rivers and freshwater lakes, and alluvial plains (formed from stream deposits), such as the Canterbury Plains, which are used for agriculture.

The North Island has much more volcanic activity than the South Island; many volcanoes, craters, and lava flows dot the central region. Recent eruptions, such as that of Mount Ruapehu in 1995–96, have ejected ash over a large area and caused damage to agriculture and property. Volcanically heated water that emerges from hot springs, geysers, and steam vents is captured in geothermal facilities and used as an energy resource (**Figure 11.5b**). The North Island also has extensive areas of rolling hills and valleys, where the warmer climate and rich volcanic and river-deposited soils nourish a productive agriculture.

New Guinea The island of New Guinea is the second-largest island in the world (after Greenland, because Australia is considered a continent rather than an island) and is much larger than the country of New Zealand at more than 800,000 square kilometers (309,000 square miles). The western portion is administered by Indonesia, but more than 57 percent of the island forms the independent nation of Papua New Guinea and is considered to be part of Oceania and Melanesia. The island is separated from Australia to the south by the Torres Strait. The mountain spine of the island of New Guinea rises to more than 4000 meters (13,000 feet), with many extinct volcanoes and high isolated basins. The southern part of the island has a large marshy lowland plain drained by the Fly River.

Pacific Islands The Pacific islands can be classified into the high volcanic islands and the low coral islands called **atolls**. The high islands, which are mostly volcanic in origin, rise steeply from the sea and have very narrow coastal plains and deep narrow valleys (**Figure 11.6a**). Many high islands, such as those of Hawaii and Samoa, are created in linear chains as tectonic plates move over hot spots where molten rock reaches the surface. Others, such as the Marianas and Vanuatu islands, form island arcs along the edge of tectonic plates. The heights of the islands promote heavy rainfall and are often capped by clouds, creating spectacular landscapes

FIGURE 11.6 Pacific islands (a) The higher islands of the Pacific are mostly volcanic in origin and rise steeply from the sea to forested mountain slopes. The island of Moorea in French Polynesia is a spectacular example of a volcanic high island with surrounding coral reefs that protect shallow lagoons. (b) Low islands and reefs surround a lagoon in Tetiaroa Atoll in French Polynesia.

(a)

(b)

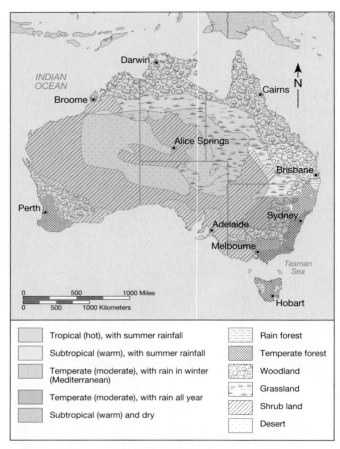

FIGURE 11.7 The climate and vegetation of Australia The climate of Australia is determined by proximity to the ocean and by latitude, with cooler temperatures in New South Wales, Victoria, and Tasmania; tropical warm and wet conditions in Queensland; and dry conditions in the Australian interior. Vegetation patterns are closely associated with climate and include rain forest in the northeast and desert vegetation in the interior. (*Source:* Based on T. McKnight, *Oceania: The Geography of Australia, New Zealand and the Pacific Islands.* Englewood Cliffs, NJ: Prentice Hall, 1995, Figure 2.2e; and G. M. Robinson, R. J. Loughran, and P. J. Tranter, *Australia and New Zealand: Economy, Society and Environment.* New York: Oxford University Press, 2000, Figure 3.1.)

such as those of Tahiti, where the mountains rise to 2100 meters (6900 feet), Bougainville (3000 meters or 9840 feet), or Hawaii, where the Mauna Loa volcano reaches 3900 meters (12,800 feet).

The low islands are mostly coral islands, or atolls, created from the buildup of skeletons of coral organisms that grow in shallow tropical waters. Atolls are usually circular, with a series of coral reefs or small islands ringing and sheltering an interior lagoon (**Figure 11.6b**). The lagoon may contain the remnants of earlier islands or a volcanic island that has sunk below the surface. Although in some cases, such as the islands of Nauru and Guam, tectonic activity may uplift coral reefs to create higher-elevation limestone plateaus, many of these islands are very low-lying, with most of the land within a meter of sea level, making them vulnerable to storms, tidal waves, and rising seas. Pacific atolls include Kiribati, the Marshall Islands, and Tuvalu. The Kwajalein Atoll in the Marshall Islands is the largest in the world, with 90 small coral islands circling a 650-square-kilometer (251-square-mile) lagoon.

Climate

Much of Oceania lies within the tropics and is dominated by the warm seas and moisture-bearing winds of these latitudes. Australia and New Zealand reach farther south and thus have climates that range from tropical to the cooler temperate climates of the southern westerly wind belts, with annual average temperatures declining from north to south. Australian climate is dominated by the very dry and hot conditions that parch the interior and define it as one of the most arid regions on Earth, with two-thirds of the country receiving less than 50 centimeters (20 inches) of rainfall a year (**Figure 11.7**). The dryness is created by the great distances from moisture sources and the dominance of the subtropical high-pressure zone with descending dry air. This harsh climate limits human activity and has required complex adaptations from both people and ecosystems.

Most of the coastal perimeter has higher precipitation. For example, northeastern Australia has heavy rainfall from the southeasterly trade winds that rise over the eastern uplands with associated orographic rainfall. The rainfall at Cairns in Queensland averages more than 460 centimeters (180 inches) a year. Northern Australia receives most of its rain from monsoon winds, drawn inland by the southward shift of the intertropical convergence zone (ITCZ) and heating of the landmass in the Southern Hemisphere summer from November to February. The rainy season is called the *Big Wet*, and it sometimes brings tropical cyclones, such as Cyclone Tracy, which devastated the city of Darwin in 1974. Southern Australia receives rainfall from storms associated with the westerly wind zone, especially during the winter (June to August) when the storm tracks shift northward. The southern coast, specifically the regions around the cities of Adelaide and Perth, has the mild temperatures and winter rainfall associated with the Mediterranean climate type that is also found at this latitude in California, Chile, southern Europe, and South Africa. The southernmost part of New South Wales, Victoria, and the island of Tasmania are wetter as a result of exposure to westerly rain-bearing winds for most of the year. These areas have considerable snowfall in the mountains.

New Zealand sits in the middle of the westerly wind belt, and frequent storms release heavy rain on the west coast as they rise over the high mountain ranges. The eastern coasts of New Zealand are much drier because they lie in the rain shadow to the east of the mountains, and this area can be sunny in summer when subtropical highs move southward and create clear and stable conditions. The North Island is generally much warmer than the South, but mountain climates are cooler and wetter throughout the country, often with heavy snow that favors ski tourism in the June–October period, drawing many skiers from North America.

The Pacific islands have warm temperatures associated with year-round high sun and the warmth of the tropical ocean. Islands with higher elevations experience substantial rainfall as moist winds rise over the land, cooling and releasing their moisture. Islands throughout the region receive rainfall from the towering cumulus clouds that occur at the ITCZ as intense heating creates rising air (convection) and heavy afternoon rains. The lower islands are much drier because they do not benefit from orographic uplift over mountain ranges and are small enough to elude the convective downpours. As a result, many low-lying islands experience near-desert conditions and shortages of fresh water.

Oceania extends into the region of the Pacific Ocean that is directly connected to El Niño, the periodic change in ocean temperature off the coast of Peru that affects weather worldwide (see Chapter 7). The 1997–98 El Niño caused severe drought in Papua New Guinea, Australia, and Micronesia, with crop failures and food shortages in New Guinea, expensive shipments of drinking water to smaller islands, and serious livestock loss and wildfires in Australia.

Environmental History

The long isolation of Oceania has contributed to the development of some of the world's most diverse and vulnerable ecosystems. Many of the species that evolved from the isolated populations have remarkable adaptations to the physical environment and are found only in that locality. Australia is beloved by biogeographers and conservationists for its great biodiversity and unusual species (**Figure 11.8**). There are more than 20,000 different plant species, 650 species of birds, and 380 different species of reptiles.

Australia has several remarkable species of marsupials and of monotremes, animals descended from mammals that died out on most other continents. A **marsupial** gives birth to a premature offspring that then develops and feeds from nipples in a pouch on the mother's body. Australian marsupials run in size from the large gray kangaroo (with adults reaching 2 meters—6 feet—tall) to koalas, wombats, and ferocious Tasmanian devils, to small mice and voles. Monotremes are very unusual mammals in that they lay eggs rather than gestate their young within the body but then nurture the young with milk from the mother. They include the platypus, with a ducklike bill and tail like a beaver, and the spiny anteater.

Australian ecosystems are defined by their growth form and dominant species and include several types of forest and shrubland with species well adapted to dry climates and frequent fires. The most important type of tree is the eucalyptus, commonly known as the *gum tree*. Eucalyptus trees have waxy leaves that hang vertically to reduce evaporation and moisture loss. The leaves contain strong-smelling oils that are used to treat respiratory illness. Eucalyptus has been introduced into many other world regions for reforestation and pulp plantations. Acacia, commonly called *wattle*, is another dominant tree and shrub type, especially in the drier woodlands.

FIGURE 11.8 Unusual Australian animals This road sign on the Nullarbor Plain warns drivers to beware of two of Australia's marsupials—the kangaroo and the wombat—as well as feral camels, an introduced domestic animal that now runs wild.

FIGURE 11.9 The Great Barrier Reef The undersea landscape of the Great Barrier Reef has become a major destination for tourists who swim among the corals and grasses to view the colorful tropical fish.

The densest forests are found along the wettest portion of the east coast, with the largest remnants in Queensland composed mainly of trees of Southeast Asian origin interspersed with woody vines (*lianas*). The forests of southeastern and southwestern Australia are dominated by drought-adapted eucalyptus, with more open woodlands in the transition to the dry interior. The northwestern and southern regions have a shrub vegetation called *mallee* that includes low, multibranching eucalyptus and plains covered with bushes similar to the sagebrush found in North America. The northern interior has extensive but sparse grasslands, and the driest zones have scattered grasses and shrubs characteristic of desert ecosystems (but without cacti).

The Great Barrier Reef is considered one of the natural wonders of the world (**Figure 11.9**). Fringing the northeast coast of Australia, the reef is more than 2000 kilometers (1250 miles) long and easily visible from space. The view from the air does not reveal the real beauty of the landscape because the most attractive parts of the reef are underwater. Diving below the surface, the visitor encounters intricate and colorful corals and waving sea grasses that are home to millions of brilliant fish and majestic marine animals such as turtles, whales, and dugong (large seal-like mammals).

The Great Barrier Reef actually consists of 3400 individual and fringing coral reefs, incorporating more than 300 species of coral and hosting more than 1500 species of fish and 4000 different types of mollusks. The reefs were formed over millions of years from the skeletons of marine coral organisms in the warm tropical waters of the Coral Sea.

The reef is Australia's second most popular foreign tourist destination, after Sydney, and the most popular for domestic tourists. Tourists visit the reef by boat or stay at resorts on the reef and participate in activities that include fishing, diving, snorkeling, and reef walking. Today the reef is under pressure from trawling in the lagoon, chemical and sediment pollution, climate change, and coastal development.

New Zealand was heavily forested prior to the arrival of humans about 1000 years ago, with towering *kauri* conifers in the north and beech in the cooler south. The remaining one-third of the land was covered with scrub, with grasses at drier, lower elevations, and with alpine grasslands (tundra) at high altitudes. Faunal evolution in New Zealand produced no predators or carnivores, and several birds remained flightless, including the now extinct moa, which was 3 meters (nearly 10 feet) tall, and the kiwi bird (**Figure 11.10**). The Pacific islands have also developed many different ecosystems and species, with the smaller islands generally less diverse than the larger ones; this pattern is in accordance with the **theory of island biogeography**, which holds that diversity increases with island size. Plant species that can be easily transported by ocean (for example, coconuts) or air (for example, fruit seeds eaten and excreted by birds) are more widely distributed. The variety declines as one moves eastward, away from the larger landmasses. Luxuriant rain forests are found on the wetter and higher islands, and marshes and mangroves thrive along the coastal margins. The larger islands, such as New Guinea and Hawaii, also have extensive middle-elevation grasslands. The smaller and drier coral islands have much sparser vegetation, but coconut palms are ubiquitous, are a basis of human subsistence, and grow along many beaches. There are few native mammals on the Pacific islands (with the exception of New Guinea). The richest fauna include the birds that have been able to fly from island to island and marine organisms, especially those of reefs and lagoons, including turtles, shellfish, tuna, sharks, and octopus.

Human Habitation The early human history of Oceania is usually divided into two main phases: the migration of humans from Southeast Asia into Australia, New Guinea, and nearby islands about 40,000 years ago, and a second dispersal to more remote Pacific islands such as Fiji, Tonga, and Samoa about 3500 years ago. The expansion eastward required difficult voyages against the trade winds, and Hawaii was settled only about 1500 years ago. Recent biological evidence from DNA analysis confirms Maori legends that suggest that migrants from Polynesia settled New Zealand about 1000 years ago. The early inhabitants of Australia are ancestors of today's Aborigines, who still preserve some traditions that reflect the early adaptations and modifications of the Australian environment. These traditions include a complex spiritual relationship to the land, a nomadic lifestyle, and the use of fire in hunting. Gathering roots, seeds, grubs, insects, and lizards contributed essential calories and proteins to traditional diets. People in some coastal areas constructed traps for stonefish and eel. As Aborigine populations grew, they may have reduced local populations of major game species such as kangaroos, but the most significant environmental change was the transformation of vegetation through the use of fire to improve grazing for game and to drive animals to hunters. Ecologists believe that over thousands of years, some Australian vegetation became more resistant to these fires. The only domesticated animal was the dingo, a dog that was probably imported from Southeast Asia. The Aborigine worldview linked people to each other, to ancestral beings, and to the land through rituals, art, and taboos. Their worldview is associated with the **Dreamtime**, a concept that joins past and future, people and places, in a continuity that ensures respect for the natural world.

FIGURE 11.10 Kiwi bird The kiwi is the national emblem of New Zealand. It has given its name to a popular fruit (formerly known as the Chinese gooseberry) and has become a nickname for New Zealanders.

The Maori arrived in New Zealand much more recently but are believed to have caused much more widespread environmental transformations than Australian Aborigines. They hunted the enormous moa bird to extinction, cleared as much as 40 percent of the original forests, and practiced agriculture based on shifting cultivation of sweet potatoes. The Maori migrated from Polynesia, where subsistence was based on fishing and the cultivation of root crops such as taro and yams and tree crops such as coconuts and breadfruit, all originally domesticated in Southeast Asia.

The next major stage in the environmental history of Oceania was associated with the incorporation of the region into the world economy during the later phases of European colonialism. This brought massive transformations of the environment through newly introduced species and new economic practices, including mining, extractive forestry, livestock raising, and large-scale crop production.

The Introduction of Exotics Beginning with the introduction of the dingo from Southeast Asia by Australian Aborigines about 3500 years ago, foreign species have devastated the native species of Oceania. The dingo, a canine similar to a coyote, probably out-competed and out-hunted the marsupial predators, such as the now-extinct Tasmanian wolf, as well as rodents. But it was **ecological imperialism**—the way in which European organisms were able to take over the ecosystems of other regions of the world—that led to the endangerment and extinction of numerous other native species through hunting, competition, and habitat destruction. These species are also called "exotics" because they come from elsewhere.

The flightless birds of Oceania were the most vulnerable to exotic predators such as rats, cats, dogs, and snakes. After centuries of such predation, several birds have become extinct and others are in danger. Conservation efforts to protect birds today include the establishment of reserves and the careful monitoring and elimination of predators. On the Pacific islands, there are great efforts to contain the spread of the introduced brown tree snake, the mongoose (a very aggressive small mammal), and a carnivorous snail, all of which prey on local species. Other changes included the introduction of European weeds, pests, and crops and the escape of domesticated livestock. These "feral" animals of Australia include horses, cattle, sheep, goats, and pigs, as well as camels that were introduced to provide transportation across vast deserts (see Figure 11.4b). The overall escaped populations are as large as 23 million pigs, 2.6 million goats, 300,000 horses (called Brumbys) and 300,000 camels and comprises the largest population of feral domestic animals in the world.

Another ecological disaster was the introduction of the European rabbit to Australia in 1859. Over the next 50 years, the rabbit population exploded to plague proportions that devastated pasturelands. The rabbit population was partially eradicated in the 1950s by the deliberate introduction of a disease called *myxomatosis*. The introduction of the prickly pear cactus in the 1920s to create hedges led to the infestation of more than 20 million hectares (50 million acres) of Australian pasture before the cactus was eradicated by introducing a beetle that fed on the plants. The cane toad, introduced to control pests in the sugarcane district of Queensland, has destroyed frogs, reptiles, and small marsupials; is highly toxic to predators; and has spread to northern Australia. The eucalyptus has become a widespread exotic on other continents, out-competing other species in places such as California and contributing to fire hazards.

Marine Ecosystems   Oceania is defined by its marine environment, and it is not surprising that the region shares many concerns about fisheries, territorial claims over ocean boundaries, and pollution of marine ecosystems. Pacific islanders eat more fish per person than any other population, and fishing and coastal tourism are critical to the majority of smaller island economies. Marine resources include not only fish and shellfish but also valuable exports such as pearls and shell (mostly for shirt buttons), as well as products made from whales, the species that initially attracted many Europeans to the Pacific. Because of the warm water, the southern Pacific is actually less biologically productive than the colder water that wells up near the continental shelves of Australia and New Zealand. The preponderance of reefs also limits the harvest of fish and other marine resources because coral organisms use up most of the nutrients and the coral reefs snag nets. Island societies consume a very wide range of fish species as well as other marine organisms, such as sea cucumbers (exported to China) and giant clams. They use many traditional methods to harvest marine resources, including spear diving, fish traps, and traditional poisons.

FIGURE 11.11 Tuna fishery Landing the tuna catch in Kolonia, Pohnpei, in the Federated States of Micronesia. Tuna are sold for thousands of dollars in markets in Japan, North America, and Europe.

The main fishery is tuna that live near the surface of the western Pacific, with most of the remaining commercial fish caught in the coastal waters of New Zealand and Australia (**Figure 11.11**). The Pacific tuna harvest is more than 2.7 million tons (5 billion pounds) of fish a year, of which 90 percent is caught in large nets towed by massive boats from Japan, Korea, China, and the United States. New Zealand has an economically important coolwater fishery that includes squid and roughy as well as coastal shellfish resources under Maori control.

The declaration of the international 200-nautical-mile (370-kilometer) *Exclusive Economic Zone* (EEZ) in the 1970s was of tremendous significance to Oceania because it allowed countries with a small land area but many scattered islands, such as Tonga and the Cook Islands, to lay claim to immense areas of ocean. The pattern of Pacific islands is such that most of the region is now covered by their EEZs, with relatively little unclaimed ocean (**Figure 11.12**). These island nations can demand licensing fees from the international fleet that seeks to catch tuna within their zones.

Oceania provides many interesting examples of how communities manage renewable resources such as fisheries. Fisheries are often thought of as **common property resources**; these are managed collectively by a community that has rights to the resource, rather than owned by individuals. Strategies for managing common property resources in the Pacific include traditional moratoriums, called *tabu* in the Pacific (periods or places where fishing is not permitted), and recognition of family or group access based on customary rights to harvest a resource. Recently, some countries have brought fisheries under government control or have regulated harvesting through permits and quotas. Beyond the EEZs, fisheries are open to all and are vulnerable to the so-called tragedy of the commons, in which an open-access common resource is overexploited by individuals who do not recognize

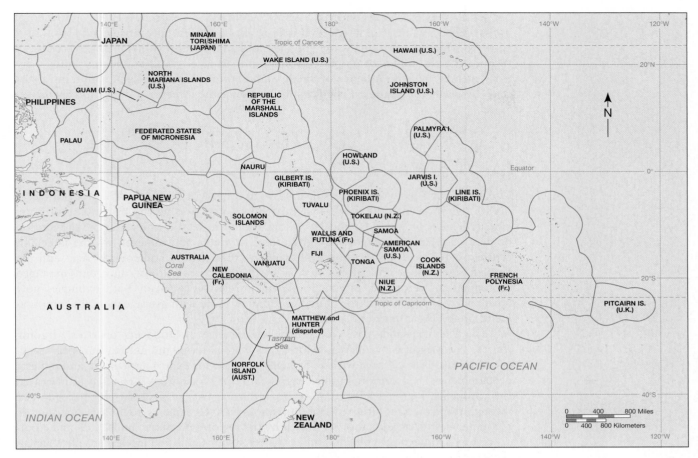

FIGURE 11.12 Marine territorial claims in the Pacific The Exclusive Economic Zones of Pacific nations and territories leave very little unclaimed ocean in the South Pacific. (*Source:* Redrawn from M. Rapaport (ed.), *The Pacific Islands: Environment and Society.* Honolulu: The Bess Press, 1999, Figure 30.3.)

how their own use of the resource can aggregate with that of many others to degrade the environment—for example, overfishing a given species to the point of extinction. One of the greatest challenges in the sustainable management of fisheries is the lack of information about fish numbers, movement, and reproduction, especially in the Pacific.

Climate Change and Ozone Depletion

Oceania is especially vulnerable to global environmental changes, particularly ozone depletion, global warming, and sea-level rise. Scientists first noticed a dramatic drop in the amount of ozone over the South Pole in the 1980s: the so-called "hole" in the ozone layer. **Ozone depletion**—the loss of the protective layer of ozone gas—can result in higher levels of ultraviolet radiation and associated increases in skin cancer, cataracts, and damage to marine organisms. Australia, with its southern latitude location, sunny days, and traditions of beach-going and sunbathing, is especially vulnerable and has a growing incidence of skin cancer. However, the Montreal Protocol—an international treaty to control chemicals that damage the ozone layer—has succeeded in preventing further ozone depletion.

Human activities have also caused an increase in carbon dioxide associated with global warming (see Chapter 1). In Oceania the impacts of global warming include drier conditions in the already drought-prone interior of Australia, increased risk of forest fires, and the melting of New Zealand's magnificent glaciers. A rise in global temperatures is also likely to produce a significant rise in sea levels, mainly because a warmer ocean takes up slightly more volume than a cooler one and secondarily because global warming may melt glaciers and ice sheets such as those in the Antarctic.

Sea-level rise is of urgent concern to many Pacific islands, especially those on low coral atolls where any increase in sea level may result in the disappearance of the land, salt-water moving into drinking water supplies, and an increased vulnerability to storms. In response to the threat of global warming and sea-level rise, the Pacific islands were early members of the **Alliance of Small Island States** (**AOSIS**), which maintains a sustained voice in international negotiations to reduce the threat of global climate change.

AUSTRALIA, NEW ZEALAND, AND THE SOUTH PACIFIC IN THE WORLD-SYSTEM

Oceania has played various roles in relation to other world regions. The story of Oceania's integration into the world-system is dominated first by the British colonization and settlement of Australia and New Zealand in the 19th century and the orientation of their economies to exporting agricultural products and minerals. In the late 20th century, a political and economic shift away from Britain and toward Asia and the United States occurred, along with a shift from protectionist and state-managed economies to free trade, privatization, and foreign investment. Both countries now have relatively high standards of living, commensurate with average incomes comparable to other core countries.

The Pacific islands rose to strategic significance as stopovers on ocean trading routes. Their significance increased after they were parceled out among European powers in the late 19th century, with some being targeted for export agriculture and mineral development. Their critical strategic significance in World War II resulted in increased U.S. influence in the Pacific islands, an influence that was subsequently reinforced through the growth of international tourism. Indeed, Oceania as a whole is emerging as a popular destination for tourists drawn by the region's dramatic landscapes and tropical retreats, indigenous cultures and exotic ecosystems, and the modern, mellow urban centers of Australia and New Zealand.

European Exploration and Early Settlement

Although Oceania had some early contact with other regions of the world, especially Southeast Asia, it was not until the mid-1700s that European explorers opened up the area for trade and eventually colonization. Spanish and Portuguese sailors controlled Guam as a stop for galleons traveling from Manila to Acapulco and may have encountered Australia. The Dutch explored the west coast and south coasts of Australia and claimed Van Diemen's Land in 1642, later named Tasmania after the Dutch explorer Abel Tasman (**Figure 11.13**). Tasman also made contact with the Maori in 1642, but the encounter was violent and the Dutch did not land, calling the region *Nieuw Zeeland* (after a region of the Netherlands). It was more than a hundred years later that the most enduring claim was advanced by explorer Captain James Cook, who landed at Botany Bay in 1770, claiming the land for Britain and calling the new territory New South Wales. Cook also explored New Zealand at this time and established harmonious relationships with the Maori.

Based on Cook's reports, the British government decided to people New South Wales by using it as a penal colony. The British sent boatloads of convicts in order to relieve pressure on their prisons but also to reinforce territorial claims and provide cheap labor for economic development. The First Fleet of 11 ships with about 730 male and female convicts arrived in 1788, settling at the site of the city of Sydney. From 1800 to 1830, the British established several settlements around the coast, including Hobart and Launceston in Tasmania. In mainland Australia, Newcastle and Brisbane were established on the east coast and Melbourne, Albany, and Perth along the southern coast. Eighty percent of Australians still live within 35 kilometers (22 miles) of the coast.

More than 160,000 convicts were eventually transported to Australia by 1868, half to New South Wales and half to Van Diemen's Land (Tasmania). Most were not

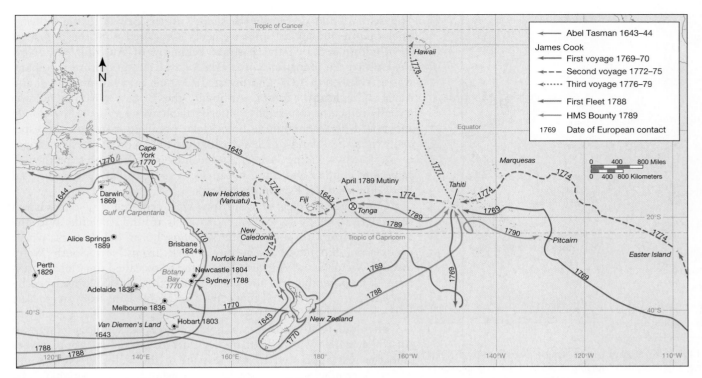

FIGURE 11.13 The European exploration of Oceania This map shows the sequence of European exploration and settlement of Oceania, including the voyages of Abel Tasman, Captain James Cook, and of the HMS *Bounty*. Cook made three voyages to Oceania, landing at Botany Bay and claiming Australia for Britain; he was ultimately killed in Hawaii. (*Source:* Based on C. McEvedy, *The Penguin Historical Atlas of the Pacific.* New York: Penguin Books, 1998, pp. 49, 63, 65, 90.)

serious criminals and many have been identified as petty thieves and Irish political activists. It has been argued that a strong Irish Catholic element among these early immigrants explains the more anti-British and anti-establishment tradition in Australia compared to New Zealand. The convicts worked for the government or were assigned to private employers. Many eventually gained freedom through pardons, often prompted by the desperate need for more farmers to produce food. Many other free settlers arrived in Australia. Some were given cash rewards for emigrating and were assigned convicts as laborers. The convicts' forced labor for colonists ended in eastern Australia by 1840 and in the west by 1868.

The initial goal of the settlements was self-sufficiency, but many, including Sydney, were unable to produce an adequate range of foodstuffs because of poor soils, plant disease, and a variable climate, even after convicts were released to increase the number of farmers. As a result, many settlements depended on imports of food and other goods from Britain. The most successful agricultural areas were in coastal valleys, such as the Derwent Valley in Tasmania, which produced wheat for Sydney. The main exports from the initial settlements were associated with the whaling trade, such as whale oil and seal pelts, with Hobart as the main base of the South Pacific whaling fleet.

Colonial Economies

Australia A momentous shift took place with the import of the first livestock to Australia, especially the Merino sheep, which thrived in central New South Wales and Tasmania. The first wool shipment to Britain took place in 1807, and high prices encouraged further expansion of the sheep industry. By 1831 more than 1 million kilograms (2.2 million pounds) of wool were being exported. By 1860 exports totaled 16 million kilograms (35 million pounds), and there were 21 million sheep in Australia.

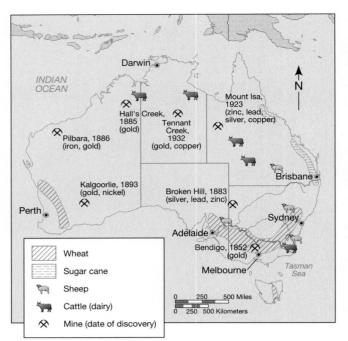

FIGURE 11.14 The development of livestock, wheat, and mining in Australia This map shows the main areas of settlement, agriculture, and mining development in 19th-century Australia, including the development of the "fertile crescent" of wheat production in southeastern Australia, the sugarcane region along the tropical east coast, and the mining centers of Broken Hill and Kalgoorlie. (*Source:* Based partly on T. McKnight, *Oceania: The Geography of Australia, New Zealand and the Pacific Islands.* Englewood Cliffs, NJ: Prentice Hall, 1995, Figures 4.1 and 4.2; J. M. Powell, *An Historical Geography of Modern Australia: The Restive Fringe.* New York: Cambridge University Press, 1988, pp. 3–55; and G. M. Robinson, R. J. Loughran, and P. J. Tranter, *Australia and New Zealand: Economy, Society and Environment.* New York: Oxford University Press, 2000, Figure 6.5.)

The demand was driven by the success of the British textile industry (including technological improvements associated with the Industrial Revolution) and tied the pastoral economy of Australia and New Zealand to the industrial core. The Australian Agriculture Company was established in 1824 and invested £1 million to promote wool and other agricultural exports. Although the British government was initially reluctant to permit frontier settlements away from the closely supervised port communities, stockmen began to move inland, especially to the grasslands, such as the Bathurst Plain on the western slopes of the Great Dividing Range. As the European frontier expanded, it came into conflict with the Aborigines, who defended their traditional lands and lost their lives in the process.

Commercial wheat production was centered in southeastern Australia, especially on the red-brown soils around Adelaide. With the use of fertilizers to compensate for phosphorus deficiencies, wheat production expanded, to occupy a belt from New South Wales through Victoria and Adelaide that came to be called the "fertile crescent." The potential area for wheat production was circumscribed by "Goyder's line" of rainfall that separated arable land from semidesert to the north (**Figure 11.14**).

The mid-1850s brought a great degree of self-government to Australia, with two-thirds of the legislatures elected by popular vote (and the rest appointed by the British) in the states of New South Wales, Victoria, South Australia, Queensland, and Tasmania. The boundaries between these states were mostly drawn as straight lines, regardless of physical features or indigenous land rights.

The next major transformation of the Australian economy occurred with the discovery of gold in 1851, first in New South Wales, next in Victoria, then in Queensland and the Northern Territory, and finally and most dramatically in Western Australia in the 1890s. Gold diggers were drawn by the thousands from all over Australia, England, and China in a gold rush fueled by rumors of giant nuggets weighing 30 kilograms (100 pounds) or more. The town of Broken Hill at the border of New South Wales and South Australia (see Figure 11.14) became one of Australia's busiest mining communities, producing lead, silver, and zinc that were exported to Europe to sustain industrial development. The Australian frontier based on livestock raising and mining development parallels that of western North America and has given rise to folklore similar to that of the U.S. Wild West. Stories of rural outlaws (called *bushrangers*) such as Ned Kelly, leader of a gang, captured the public imagination during the 1870s and continue to contribute to the image of the Australian frontier today.

Development of the Australian economy was facilitated by the construction of railroads, which radiated from ports to terminuses at livestock yards, grain elevators, and mines. This transportation pattern increased the importance of the port cities but hindered later national integration, especially when it became evident that three different rail gauges had been selected by different colonies.

The frost-free climate of the central coast of eastern Australia allowed for development of tropical agriculture around Brisbane beginning in the 1860s, especially sugar plantations, using indentured laborers brought in from Vanuatu and the Solomon Islands. Cattle were also introduced into the warmer and drier regions of central and northern Australia after wells were drilled into the Great Artesian Basin in the 1880s. Cattle grazed more lightly than sheep on the sparse vegetation.

New Zealand The history of European settlement and economic development in New Zealand is closely tied to that of Australia. A sealing station was established on the South Island of New Zealand in 1792, but British sovereignty and the first official settlers' colonies were not established until the 1840s, initially as part of New South Wales. Small whaling settlements had established trading relationships with the Maori, who

FIGURE 11.15 Sheep farming The landscapes of Australia and New Zealand are still characterized by extensive grazing lands for sheep, initially a colonial enterprise designed to provide Britain's factories with wool. The development of refrigerated shipping in the 1880s boosted sheep farming for meat production. This photograph is from Otago, New Zealand, which has a population of more than 6 million sheep.

through such contacts obtained access to firearms, were exposed to disease, and were brought into a capitalist economy. Missionaries had also established settlements in the early 1800s and contributed to the transformation of Maori culture. The British annexed New Zealand in 1840 through the **Treaty of Waitangi**, a pact with 40 Maori chiefs on the North Island. This treaty purported to protect Maori rights and land ownership if the Maori accepted the British monarch as their sovereign, granted a crown monopoly on land purchases, and became British subjects. At the last minute before the treaty was signed, land agents purchased large areas of land around the Cook Strait, often without identifying the true Maori owners. This land was held by the private New Zealand Association and included the sites of the cities of New Plymouth, Wellington, and Nelson.

Alarmed by European settlement, some Maori resisted the British and waged warfare for several years until suppressed in 1847. The introduction of sheep (**Figure 11.15**) prompted further settler expansion in search of pastures and a renewal of hostilities with the Maori during the Maori wars of the 1860s. The discovery of gold in 1861 on the South Island in the Otago region made Dunedin the largest settlement in New Zealand (with a population of 60,000) within ten years and fostered development of wheat production on the Canterbury Plains.

The next stage of the integration of Australia and New Zealand into a global economy was driven by a technological innovation, the development of refrigerated shipping, after 1882. This advance allowed both economies to expand or shift from producing nonperishables such as wool, metals, and wheat to the more valuable export of meat and dairy products. New Zealand became Britain's "farm in the South Pacific," trading its high-quality agricultural products for imported manufactured goods from Britain. Trade was facilitated by the opening of the Suez Canal in 1867 and the Panama Canal in 1914, which reduced the time and cost of ocean transport to Europe. Australia and New Zealand, like Canada, became staple economies that depended on the export of natural resources.

Colonization of the Pacific Islands Initially the Pacific islands were of little interest to European explorers, and they were drawn into the world economy more slowly than Australia and New Zealand. During the Age of Discovery (see Chapter 1), Guam, Palau, parts of the Federated States of Micronesia, and the Mariana Islands became Spanish colonies. More generally, explorers brought European diseases to local populations who had no resistance to them, so the most serious impact was mortality.

But as Britain and France rose to power in Europe in the 18th century, a series of explorations set out for the Pacific. British explorer Samuel Wallis and Luis Antoine de Bougainville of France were made welcome by the people of Tahiti in the 1760s, and

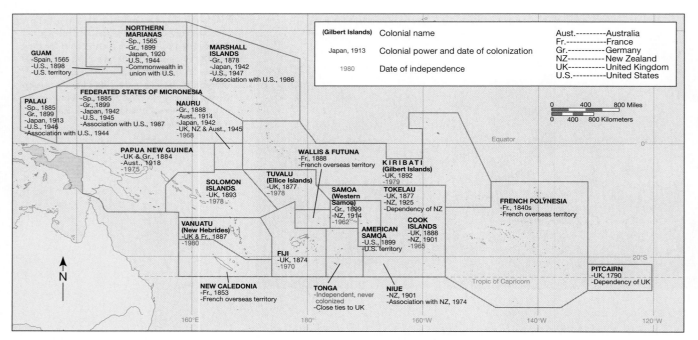

FIGURE 11.16 The colonization and independence of the Pacific Many Pacific islands are now independent from their former colonial rulers. This map shows the pattern and dates of colonial control, dates of independence of Pacific island countries, and current affiliations of territories. Note that only Tonga resisted colonization and that some countries, such as Nauru and Palau, were handed from one European power to another. (*Source:* Data from Australian Broadcasting Company. Available at http://www.abc.net.au/ra/carvingout/maps/statistics.htm.)

their reports of friendly people and abundance cultivated the myth of a tropical paradise (**Figure 11.16**).

At the beginning of the 19th century, the Pacific islands came into contact with missionaries, whalers, and traders. The London Missionary Society was very active in the Pacific, seeking conversions in Tahiti, Samoa, Tuamotu, Tuvalu, and the Cook Islands. The Methodists focused on Tonga and Fiji. The missionaries often worked through native chiefs who were advised to alter local laws and traditions to conform to European principles, sometimes provoking local rebellions. Missionary activity altered traditional social ties, beliefs, and political structures. Hundreds of whaling ships called regularly at islands such as Tahiti, Fiji, and Samoa for supplies and maintenance. The discovery of sandalwood, a valued aromatic wood, attracted traders to Fiji, Hawaii, and New Caledonia; they were ruthless in their treatment of local people.

Coconut, the staple product of the Pacific, became part of European trade from about 1840 in the form of copra, dried coconut meat used to make coconut oil for soaps, and food. Some Europeans sought to establish plantations on islands such as Fiji and Samoa. A scarcity of cotton during the U.S. Civil War prompted the establishment of cotton plantations on Fiji in the 1860s. The same scarcity increased the need for laborers for the cotton plantations in Queensland, Australia; workers came from the islands. Beginning in the 1840s, Pacific islanders had been kidnapped and enslaved in a process called *blackbirding* that brought thousands of laborers, collectively called *kanakas* (because many of them were of Kanak origin from the islands now known as Vanuatu), to Australian cotton and sugar plantations. This practice continued until 1904.

The islands were governed according to the different colonial styles of European nations modified to local conditions. Britain ruled through governors who incorporated native leadership into their administrations in a form of indirect rule. The Germans administered their Pacific colonies through commercial companies, and the French practiced direct rule and assimilation into French culture and institutions. The imposition of colonial rule met with resistance in the form of armed uprisings, alternative trading networks, political movements, and defiant behavior.

The colonial powers restructured the economies and peoples of the Pacific islands in ways that left enduring legacies. The British brought large numbers of contract workers from India to work on plantations in Fiji, creating a divided society of ethnic Asians and Pacific islanders that produces significant political tensions even today.

Political Independence and Economic Restructuring

Independence was granted to Australia in 1901. The Commonwealth of Australia was established with a federal structure governing the six states of Western Australia, South Australia, Queensland, New South Wales, Victoria, and Tasmania and administering the Federal territories of the Northern Territory and (after 1908) the Australian Capital Territory around Canberra. New Zealand declined to join this new nation and chose dominion status as a self-governing colony of Britain in 1907. Both countries soon gained their own colonies in the Pacific. In 1901, Britain turned over Papua New Guinea to Australia and the Cook Islands to New Zealand. New Zealand was granted a mandate over Samoa in 1920 and jurisdiction over Tokelau in 1925.

Thousands of Australians and New Zealanders fought for the Allies in World War I in the Australian and New Zealand Army Corps (Anzac), most notably at Gallipoli, Turkey, in 1915, when more than 33,000 of them died. The war contributed to the development of a steel and auto industry in Australia and to increased agricultural exports at higher prices because of difficulties the war created in international trade.

World War II influenced Australia's geopolitical orientation. Although Australia fought in defense of Britain in Europe and North Africa, the rapid advance of the Japanese in Asia and the Pacific, including the capture of 15,000 Australians in Singapore and the bombing of the northern Australian city of Darwin, caused Australia to look to the United States as an ally. American and Australian troops fought together in New Guinea and the Pacific islands, forging enduring bonds that were formalized in the ANZUS security treaty between Australia, New Zealand, and the United States, signed in San Francisco in 1951.

As the Cold War deepened after 1950, Southeast Asia became the focus of U.S. concern about communist expansion from China. As the United States became more involved in Indochina (see Chapter 9), both Australia and New Zealand sent troops to Vietnam.

Beginning in the 1920s, policies to substitute expensive imports with domestic production resulted in heavy subsidies of manufacturing and high tariffs on imported goods, especially in Australia. The goal was to create new jobs, diversify the economy, and reduce the sensitivity to global demand for wool and minerals. As in other regions, these import substitution policies had mixed success. Although Australia and New Zealand had middle-class populations with a demand for manufactured goods, the overall market was small, and labor costs were high as a result of a strong tradition of labor union activism. The new industries were often inefficient because they were protected from competition in the world market. New Zealand had a particularly high level of government involvement in the economy, with state-run marketing boards controlling the export of commodities, such as wool, meat, dairy products, and fruit, and government ownership of banking, telecommunications, energy, rail, steel, and forest enterprises.

World War II and Independence in the Pacific

World War II marked a critical turning point in the history of the Pacific, with thousands of foreign soldiers fighting across the islands and constructing military bases. In the process, many islanders lost their lives. The most significant impacts were in the western Pacific, where the Japanese advanced from their colonies in Micronesia (such as Palau) to Guam, New Guinea, and the Solomon Islands and then attacked the U.S. base at Pearl Harbor in Hawaii in 1941 (**Figure 11.17**). Three years of intense and bitter warfare on land, air, and sea included many famous battles such as those of Guadalcanal and Saipan, in which the Allies, especially the United States, retook the islands from Japan. The damage from bombing was extensive, and exposure to

FIGURE 11.17 The legacy of World War II in the Pacific War had a significant impact on the economies, cultures, and landscapes of the Pacific with thousands of Japanese and Allied troops stationed and fighting across the region. This photo shows warships from World War II rusting on a coastal reef in Micronesia.

Western values and goods also transformed the islands. For example, canned foods such as Spam™ and corned beef, as well as U.S.-style music, clothing, and sports, became popular.

The strategic and economic significance of the Pacific islands slowed their decolonization after the war. The United States was determined to maintain military bases in and control of the Pacific, especially in response to Cold War competition with China and the Soviet Union. High prices for primary products such as copra and sugar brought profits to colonial powers. Self-government began with elected governments and small independence movements. Western Samoa became independent from New Zealand in 1962 (and dropped the "Western" from its name in 1997), Nauru from Australia in 1968, Fiji and Tonga from the United Kingdom in 1970, Papua New Guinea from Australia in 1975, and the Solomons, Kiribati, Tuvalu (from the U.K.) and Vanuatu (from the U.K. and France) by 1980.

A number of smaller or resource-poor islands have maintained close associations with the United States (the Marshall Islands, the Federated States of Micronesia, and Palau) or New Zealand (the Cook Islands and Niue). The U.S. dependencies receive financial subsidies in return for military bases and security control. France has maintained its control over the islands of French Polynesia, New Caledonia, and Wallis and Futuna, insisting that they are integral parts of the French state and thus need no independent presence at the United Nations. The United States still controls American Samoa and Guam; Australia controls Norfolk Island; New Zealand controls Tokelau; and the U.K. controls Pitcairn. The money that is sent to these colonies, usually called *transfer payments*, is an important component of their economies but is also a relatively cheap way for the United States and other core powers to maintain political bases in the Pacific.

As in other regions, artificial lines were drawn during processes of colonialism and independence that cut across otherwise coherent geographic and ethnic regions. For example, the island of New Guinea was split by a boundary that gave the western half to Indonesia as Irian Jaya and the eastern half to Britain and Australia. Some of the Solomon Islands, including Bougainville and Buka, were placed under the control of newly independent Papua New Guinea in 1975, although the remainder of the island group gained independence as the Solomon Islands. The islands of Samoa were divided at the 171-degree line of longitude in 1899 and the eastern portion placed under U.S. jurisdiction, whereas the western group was allocated to the Germans and later to New Zealand. The Gilbert and Ellice islands were split during decolonization, with the Gilberts becoming the Micronesian nation of Kiribati and the Ellices the Polynesian nation of Tuvalu.

Globalization and Economic Change   Although Australia protected manufacturing and subsidized agriculture, there were few barriers to foreign investment. Many sectors had high levels of foreign ownership, including minerals and land, especially by British firms. During the 1970s, investment patterns began to change, with Asian, especially Japanese, capital starting to flow into Australia. Another major change occurred when the U.K. decided to enter the European Community in 1973 and was forced to end preferential trade relationships with British Commonwealth nations, including Australia and New Zealand. New Zealand was particularly hard hit by the loss of guaranteed markets, but the shock provided an impetus to seek new markets in Asia.

Both Australia and New Zealand decided to reduce government intervention in and regulation of the economy in the 1980s. The Australian government deregulated banking, reduced subsidies to industry and agriculture, and sold off public-sector energy industries beginning in about 1983. The move to the neoliberal policies of free trade and reduced government was even more dramatic in New Zealand. There, sweeping policy reversals eliminated agricultural subsidies, removed trade tariffs, reduced welfare spending, and privatized government-owned enterprises, including airlines, postal services, and forests. Although these policies succeeded in reducing the national debt, they also increased economic inequality and unemployment.

The most rapidly growing sector during the 1980s and 1990s was services, with employment in this sector increasing from 58 percent in 1980 to 71 percent in 2006 in Australia and from 58 percent to 66 percent in New Zealand. Finance, tourism, and business services expanded the most and were associated with an increase in female employment and considerable foreign investment. The region has become a major international tourist destination. Of the more than 6.4 million visitors in 2003, many came from Asia, especially Japan. Asia has also invested in hotels and other tourist facilities in the region.

The future of agriculture in Australia and New Zealand is unclear, as competition from Latin America and Asia, the high cost of inputs, the loss of subsidies, and the changing structure of demand create a new geography of international agricultural trade. In both Australia and New Zealand, agriculture has been transformed through horizontal integration in which smaller enterprises are merged to create larger units (for example, when adjacent farms are consolidated into one large landholding, resulting in the disappearance of small family-run farms) and through vertical integration, in which a single firm takes control of several stages in the production process (for example, when a company owns the fertilizer and seed companies as well as the food-processing plant and supermarkets). For example, the transnational agribusiness firm H. J. Heinz has purchased New Zealand agricultural processing enterprises with the goal of supplying growing Asian markets, while the international corporation ConAgra owns grain companies, feedlots, meat-processing, and wholesale distribution in Australia.

New Zealand agriculture, in particular, has changed significantly in response to the restructuring of the global food system. A dramatic change in agricultural policies in 1984 abruptly removed most price supports, trade protections, and farm subsidies and required farms to pay for extension services, water, and quality inspections. New Zealand agriculture was thrown into a global free market while most other developed countries, including the United States, Canada, and Europe, maintained considerable state regulation and support for their agricultural systems. Although New Zealand farmers coped by adjusting their herd sizes and changing their crop mix, some farmers went out of business and their properties were horizontally integrated into larger farms. The landscapes of agricultural regions such as the Hawkes Bay region of the North Island began to change, as farms switched into fruit production (**Figure 11.18**), often associated with increases in pesticide use. New Zealand was also one of the first countries to adopt certification for organic agricultural products, and there is a thriving domestic market for sustainably grown foods.

The Pacific Islands in the Contemporary World-System

Many Pacific islands are now integrated into the world-system through their dependence on imported goods, transfer payments, improvements in transportation, and the emergence of international tourism as the major source of foreign exchange. Fiji, for example, obtains most of its income from sugar exports, remittances from people working abroad and from the 400,000 tourists who visit each year. French Polynesia exports pearls but obtains most foreign exchange from tourism or employment in French government agencies, including the military. The Samoan economy is dependent on agricultural exports of coconut products and on tourism. Tuvalu seeks to make money from the new global communications economy partly by selling its Internet address, which is ".tv."

With their long experience of global trade, investment, and migration, the Pacific islands have in many ways been less affected by more recent globalization of trade, capital flows, culture, and labor than have other world regions. They are sometimes called *MIRAB* (migration, remittances, aid, and bureaucracy) economies because of their dependence on labor migration, jobs with foreign governments, and foreign aid.

Most of the nations in Polynesia spend twice as much on imports as they gain from exports, and they must finance the deficit through borrowing, foreign aid, or

FIGURE 11.18 Kiwi production These kiwi orchards on the North Island of New Zealand in the Bay of Plenty are surrounded by lines of trees that protect the delicate kiwi fruit from strong winds.

remittances from citizens working elsewhere. However, compared to countries in Latin America and the Caribbean or Southeast Asia, total international debt is relatively low in Oceania, with annual interest payments averaging less than 5 percent of GDP. This low level of debt has been maintained despite the trade deficits because of the large flows of official aid, remittances from overseas workers, and interest on savings held outside the country. Kiribati and Nauru finance their imports from offshore financial assets, including interest on profits saved from phosphate mining.

THE PEOPLES OF AUSTRALIA, NEW ZEALAND, AND THE SOUTH PACIFIC

Oceania is one of the least populated world regions, with just over 34 million people in 2006, of which 20.6 million live in Australia, 6 million in Papua New Guinea, and 4.1 million in New Zealand. Most people live along the coasts of the larger land areas, especially along the coast of southeast Australia and coastal Papua New Guinea. Overall population densities of the larger countries are very low: 2.5 people per square kilometer (6 per square mile) in Australia, 12 per square kilometer (31 per square mile) in Papua New Guinea, and 15 per square kilometer (39 per square mile) in New Zealand. The smaller islands, in contrast, can have fairly high population densities, reaching more than 150 per square kilometer (300 people per square mile) in Guam, the Marshall Islands, Nauru, and Tonga. The region is highly urbanized, with more than 73 percent of the population living in urban areas (**Figure 11.19**).

The overall population of the region is growing quite slowly (at 1 percent per year), and it will take 65 years for the population to double at current growth rates. This slow growth is in large part due to the very low growth and fertility rates in Australia and New Zealand. Women in these two countries bear an average of less than two children during their reproductive years. The low birthrate, combined with long life expectancy, is creating a growing proportion of older residents and raising concerns about the provision of services such as Social Security, health care, and pensions for the aging population. Fertility rates are higher in the Pacific islands, ranging from 2 children per woman during her child-bearing years in French Polynesia to 4.1 children per woman in Kiribati.

Migration and Ethnic Composition

It is estimated that when Europeans arrived in Oceania, there were at least half a million Australian Aborigines and perhaps a quarter of a million New Zealand Maori. The introduction of European diseases and the violence of some colonial encounters reduced native populations significantly and resulted in majority European populations in Australia and New Zealand within a century or so of initial settlement. Today, although tension exists between the majority population of European ancestry and the indigenous populations in both countries, and both countries are moving toward a more multicultural society, the Maori of New Zealand have more rights and power than the Aborigines of Australia. Some Aborigines prefer to be called *Koori* or *Murri*, but the term *Aborigine* is still commonly used as a self-description and in legislation. New Zealand is alternatively called by its Maori name *Aotearoa*, meaning "land of long white clouds."

Immigration and Ethnicity The contemporary ethnic composition of Australia and New Zealand is strongly influenced by the history of immigration. Almost a quarter of Australia's current residents were born elsewhere. As noted earlier, the first European settlers were mostly English. Some Chinese arrived in Australia during the gold rush of the 19th century. Migrants of Irish and Scottish origins, as well as some Germans, were also common.

Australia's immigration policy sought to maintain a European "look" through the adoption of the **White Australia policy** after independence in 1901. This policy essentially restricted immigration to people from northern Europe through a ranking that placed British and Scandinavians as the highest priority, followed by southern Europeans. By 1936 more people were coming from southern Europe, especially Italy and Greece. After World War II, the government made extra efforts to attract immigrants as labor for manufacturing, as a source of military volunteers, and in response to humanitarian pressure to resettle refugees from eastern Europe.

In 1973 the racist restrictions on immigration were removed and replaced with skills criteria, and a new wave of immigration from Asia began, with large numbers of migrants from Vietnam, Hong Kong, and the Philippines. By the end of the 20th century, Australia's population was much more diverse, with about 73 percent of the population of British or Irish heritage, 20 percent from elsewhere in Europe, 5 percent from Asia, and only 2 percent Aborigine.

New Zealand also practiced an immigration policy designed to attract white immigrants, and prior to World War II this included a bias not just against nonwhites but also against Irish Catholics. After the war, labor shortages were met by temporary labor migration from the Pacific islands. More recent changes in immigration policy have opened New Zealand to more permanent settlers from the Pacific as well as to Asian immigrants who can bring capital with them. In 2005, New Zealand was still dominated by people of English and Scottish ancestry, but with a growing percentage of people of Pacific island (around 6.5 percent) or Asian (around 6.6 percent) heritage and a significant (more than 15 percent who are full or part) Maori population.

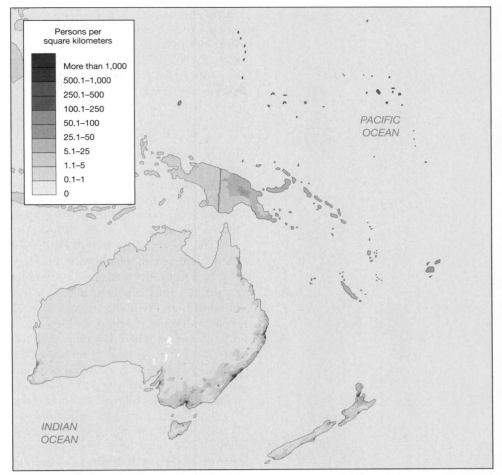

FIGURE 11.19 Population density map of Oceania 1995 Although most of Oceania appears thinly populated on this map, several small islands have high population density. Australian population is concentrated in the cities and in the southeastern region of the country. (*Source:* Center for International Earth Science Information Network [CIESIN], Columbia University; International Food Policy Research Institute [IFPRI]; and World Resources Institute [WRI]. 2000. *Gridded Population of the World [GPW],* Version 2. Palisades, NY: CIESIN, Columbia University. Available at http://sedac.ciesin.org/plue/gpw.)

The Pacific islands have a much higher proportion of indigenous people, averaging more than 80 percent, with Asians (14 percent) and Europeans (6 percent) representing the remainder. The exceptions are Fiji, which has a very large Asian Indian population associated with the importation of contract labor during colonial times; New Caledonia, where about 40 percent of the population are indigenous, 40 percent French, and 20 percent descendants of Southeast Asian contract workers; and Guam, where there are significant American and Filipino populations.

Oceanic Diasporas   One of the largest diasporas is internal to Oceania and is the emigration of Pacific islanders to work and live in New Zealand and Australia. This emigration has been encouraged in the last 50 years by labor needs, refugee movements, and lenient rules allowing migration from current and former colonies. More people from Niue, Tokelau, and the Cook Islands now live in the capital of New Zealand, Auckland, than remain on the islands, as well as about one-eighth of all Samoans and migrants from Tonga and Fiji. Australia has accepted thousands of refugees from East Timor in Indonesia and from Fiji.

A second diaspora is from the Pacific islands to North America, especially to Hawaii and California. Many Samoans and Tongans have moved to the United States, and recent unrest in Fiji sent a wave of several thousand Asian-Fijians to the United

States and Canada. There is a small emigration flow of Australians and New Zealanders to Europe and North America, including people of British heritage returning to retire in Britain and young people seeking educational and work opportunities in England, Canada, or the United States. Within Australia there is an internal migration flow from the population concentration in southeastern Australia northward along the east coast and to western Australia.

Language and Religion

British settlement in Australia and New Zealand resulted in English being the most widely spoken and official language. Of an estimated 260 interrelated languages spoken by Australian Aborigines, and unique to the continent, many have become extinct or have only a few surviving speakers. Only Mabuiag (the language of the Western Torres Strait islands) and the Australian Western Desert languages are spoken by more than a few hundred people. Many Aborigines no longer speak anything but English.

The British heritage of Australia and New Zealand is reflected in the dominance of the Christian religion—mostly Protestant in New Zealand, and about half Protestant and half Catholic in Australia—although many people report themselves as having no strong religious beliefs at all. As a result of Asian immigration, both Buddhism and Hinduism are growing in significance, and many Aboriginal communities maintain their traditional religions. In New Zealand, Maori communities abandoned many traditional beliefs when they converted to Christianity and lost their land in the 19th century, but there is now a revival of religion, ritual, and the teaching of the Maori language, which was made an official language of New Zealand in 1987. Almost all Maori speak English, and about 100,000 also speak or understand Maori, a language related to those of Polynesia and especially to Hawaiian and Samoan.

The Pacific islands have an enormous number and variety of languages, which can be divided into two general families—Austranesian and Papuan. It is believed that almost 20 percent of all living languages are spoken on the island of New Guinea and that most are not understood by even the people in the next valley. Papua New Guinea has 820 distinct living languages and a widespread trade language (or *lingua franca*) called *Tok Pisin*, which combines local and English words into pidgin. Some island groups also have a large number of languages. For example, Vanuatu has 110 living languages, many spoken by at least 500 people, and the Solomon Islands have 70 different languages, most with at least 500 speakers. This diversity of languages has been explained by the fragmentation and isolation of New Guinea's physical geography and Vanuatu's many islands. Linguistic diversity generally decreases toward the eastern Pacific. The missionaries were successful in converting most of the Pacific islanders to Christianity, with a range of Protestant denominations and Catholicism prevalent in French Polynesia. Hinduism is important in Fiji among the Asian Indian population.

Traditional beliefs are still important in more remote islands and regions, especially in Papua New Guinea, and some communities have fused traditional and Christian practices by combining harvest rituals with the celebration of Christmas, for example. Melanesia is associated with a set of religious movements that have been called **cargo cults**, in which the dawn of a coming new age was associated with the arrival of goods brought by spiritual beings or foreigners. In some cases, symbolic ship piers or airstrips for the arrival of the cargo were constructed. Anthropologists interpret these cults in several ways, including protests against European colonialism and oppression or as demands for a return to the tradition of reciprocal gift-giving. More recently, critical perspectives suggest that the idea of a cargo cult overgeneralizes many different kinds of movement and reflects a Western obsession with commodities and lack of understanding of local peoples.

Culture and Society

The traditional cultures of Australia, New Zealand, and the Pacific islands have been disrupted by contact with the rest of the world. They have sometimes become transformed into societies oriented to cultures based on the demands of tourism and the

(a)

(b)

FIGURE 11.20 Aborigine and Maori culture (a) Boomerangs decorated with traditional aboriginal patterns and symbols, displayed at the Keringke Arts Centre. (b) The New Zealand national rugby team—the All Blacks—perform a traditional Maori *haka* dance prior to an international match against South Africa.

need to strengthen political identity. In Australia, Aboriginal cultures, based on strong spiritual ties to land, were marginalized and homogenized when Aborigines were removed from their ancestral lands and resettled on reserves. Aboriginal art, often based on rock art designs in dotted forms, silhouettes, and so-called X-ray styles, has become very popular in contemporary markets (**Figure 11.20a**), and native dances and songs, such as those that are part of the social gathering known as *corroboree*, are performed for tourists. Aboriginal symbols have been appropriated for major events, such as the Sydney 2000 Olympic Games.

Maori tradition—such as the welcome ceremonies that include the *hongi* (pressing noses together) and the *haka* war dance (**Figure 11.20b**) now performed at international sporting events—is celebrated as integral to New Zealand's official bicultural identity. Maori architecture includes distinctive carved and decorated meeting houses called *whare*. Artistic expressions include intricate carvings such as those found on war canoes and decorative masks and tattoos (*moko*), which are also found on other Pacific islands.

Overall, society in Australia and New Zealand is still influenced by British legacies, including the significance of sports such as cricket and rugby, where the national teams, such as the New Zealand All Blacks rugby team (see Figure 11.20b), have gained international renown and have enthusiastic, if not fanatic, local support. Australia and New Zealand have also produced a series of award-winning films and novels as well as two of the world's most popular opera singers—Australian Joan Sutherland and New Zealander and part-Maori Kiri Te Kanawa. The echoes of the colonial relationship with Britain provoke considerable ambivalence, and there have been strong attempts to establish distinct identities by embracing indigenous traditions, new immigrant cultures such as those from Asia, or the particular livelihoods and landscapes of the Outback frontier or the surfing beach.

Gender roles in Oceania are influenced by stereotypes, but roles are as rapidly changing and complex as in any other world region. In Australia, the image of the frontier rancher or miner is associated with heavy drinking, gambling, male camaraderie, and a tough, laconic attitude epitomized by movie characters such as those in *Crocodile Dundee* or the lone outlaw portrayed in *Mad Max*. But other films, such as *Priscilla, Queen of the Desert*, celebrate an alternative image of Australia as a center for gay and other transsexual identities. Sydney's Mardi Gras parade has become a celebration of gay culture and a major tourist attraction. Many women in Australia and New Zealand have shifted from roles as traditional housewives into a multitude of careers and to senior political positions (such as Prime Minister Helen Clark of New Zealand) supported by a strong feminist movement.

It is nearly impossible to generalize about the cultures of the Pacific islands, which are as varied as the many languages. Some of the most distinctive social and material forms include the strict separation of the male and female in much of New Guinea and Melanesia; the tradition of ritual warfare and reciprocal gift exchange; the importance of local leaders, or "big men"; and close links with kin and extended families. Pigs are still considered a measure of wealth on many islands, including New Guinea, and a traditional plant, kava, is consumed as a recreational and ritual relaxant on many islands. Polynesian cultures have a strong orientation to the ocean. Natives have been stereotyped by some explorers, anthropologists, and tourists as sexually promiscuous and living an easy life of tropical abundance. Contemporary cultures on the Pacific islands reflect the tensions between the maintenance and revival of traditional cultures, their selective construction for the tourist industry, and the widespread penetration of global culture, especially formal education, television, and processed foods.

CONTEMPORARY CHALLENGES IN A GLOBALIZING WORLD

Oceania has seen regional changes in recent years, including the shift in alignment from Europe to North America and Asia discussed earlier and the challenges of coping with geographic isolation within a global economy. Within the region, the stability of some independent democracies and dependencies in the Pacific has been threatened by internal tensions, while political and economic integration has been sought through regional cooperation agreements. Glaring inequalities within generally wealthy countries such as Australia and New Zealand have highlighted the fate of indigenous groups, while at the same time the countries have embraced multicultural identities. Oceania is particularly vulnerable to human activities, such as the use of fossil fuels, marine overharvesting, and pollution, which are affecting global climate, sea levels, and fishery resources. The region also encapsulates critical examples of the impacts of international tourism and of the risks of nuclear energy (see Geographies of Indulgence, Desire, and Addiction: Uranium in Oceania, p. 550).

Political Stability

Oceania is relatively stable compared to many other regions. The most serious recent political conflicts in Oceania have involved encounters between ethnic groups in Fiji and demonstrations by independence or secessionist movements in New Caledonia and Papua New Guinea. But the region has also seen renewed attempts at regional integration and peacekeeping through a variety of regional and subregional cooperation agreements.

The conflict in Fiji is a legacy of British colonial policies that brought Asian Indians as indentured workers for sugar plantations from 1879 to 1920. By the 1960s, Indo-Fijians almost outnumbered the ethnic Fijian population, dominating commerce and urban life and maintaining a separate existence with little intermarriage and continued cultural and religious differences. The indigenous Fijians took over government at independence in 1970, but subsequent elections have produced contested wins for Indo-Fijian parties and coups in 1987 and 2000. As of 2006 a coalition dominated by indigenous Fijians is in power. In the nickel-rich islands of New Caledonia, the indigenous Melanesian population, known as *Kanaks*, has been militantly pressing for independence for years but has been outvoted by those of French descent (called *demis*), who prefer to remain part of France. The Nouméa Accord of 1998 promises to grant independence by 2018. In the Solomon Islands, residents of Bougainville are trying to secede from Papua New Guinea, claiming ethnic affiliation with the other Solomon Islands that are independent and complaining that they do not receive a fair share of the profits from mining. Within the Solomon Islands there are conflicts between ethnic groups over land, such as those between longtime residents of Guadalcanal and immigrants from the neighboring island of Malaita.

Regional cooperation agreements include the South Pacific Commission, founded in 1947, which focuses on social and economic development and includes 21 island nations and territories, Australia, New Zealand, the United States, France, and the United Kingdom. The **South Pacific Forum**, established in 1971, excludes France, the United Kingdom, the United States, and their colonies and promotes discussion and cooperation on trade, fisheries, and tourism among all of the independent and self-governing states of Oceania. It has supported maritime territorial rights and a nuclear-free Pacific as well as the independence goals of French Polynesia and New Caledonia. A summit in 2000 legitimized peacekeeping military operations led by New Zealand and Australia in the Solomon Islands and Papua New Guinea. There are also dozens of nongovernmental organizations and intergovernmental agencies that operate region-wide, especially among the smaller Pacific islands. For example, the University of the South Pacific fosters higher education across 12 countries through distance education and three main campuses in Fiji, Samoa, and Vanuatu.

Australia and New Zealand are members of larger economic and political alliances such as the Asia-Pacific Economic Cooperation group (APEC), which also includes Papua New Guinea and which focuses on improving transportation links and liberalizing regional trade. Both Australia and New Zealand have been able to take advantage of APEC to increase exports to Asia, especially to Japan. In attempts to foster regional markets as global trade liberalizes and restructures around them, Australia and New Zealand created the free trade focused **Closer Economic Relations (CER) agreement** in 1983, which built on an earlier New Zealand-Australia Free Trade Agreement (NZAFTA). CER set out to remove all tariffs and restrictions on trade between the two countries. The resulting increased trade has been especially beneficial to New Zealand, with its small domestic market, which has doubled its exports to Australia. Many manufacturing firms now operate in both countries.

Poverty and Inequality

Although Oceania has generally higher incomes and better living conditions than many other world regions, there are significant differences between and within countries of the region. Australia and New Zealand are distinctive for their very high average incomes as expressed by the per capita annual gross domestic product (GDP) at almost $32,000 (in PPP) for Australia and more than $25,000 for New Zealand in 2005. Some Pacific islands have an average GDP in PPP near or above $10,000 per person as a result of their associations with the United States (Guam) or France (French Polynesia, New Caledonia). Others, especially Kiribati and Vanuatu, register less than $2000 in GDP per capita per year. Although there is little published information on the distribution of incomes within most of the smaller countries, and although inequality is apparently less than in many other world regions, there is persistent poverty throughout the region, including in Australia and New Zealand, where the Aborigine and Maori populations are particularly disadvantaged. Australia and New Zealand were for many years reputed to have strong welfare systems and equitable societies, at least for the nonindigenous populations. However, income inequality has increased in the last two decades, and the government has reduced or privatized social services, especially in New Zealand. Larger populations of single parents, the elderly, refugees, and workers in low-paid service-sector jobs are also diminishing the overall ranking of Australia and New Zealand as places where everyone can make a good living.

Monetary measures such as GDP are of limited use where many people are living in economies based on exchanges and barter or on subsistence. The concept of **subsistence affluence** has been used to describe Pacific island societies: Monetary incomes may be low, but local resources such as coconut and fish provide a reasonable diet, and extended family and reciprocal support prevent serious deprivation. Adequate diets and relatively effective health and education systems contribute to comparatively high life expectancies and literacy and low infant mortality throughout the Pacific. Life expectancies range from 62 years in Kiribati and Vanuatu to more than 75 years in American Samoa, Australia, French Polynesia, Guam, the Northern Marianas, and New

Uranium in Oceania

As with oil in the Middle East, the extraction and use of uranium links Oceania to the global hunger for cheap energy and to geopolitical conflicts beyond the region. Uranium is a radioactive element that can be split in a process of nuclear fission to produce a chain reaction that releases large amounts of energy. Controlled reactions can be used to generate electricity in nuclear power plants, whereas uncontrolled reactions can be used in atomic bombs that release enormous amounts of thermal energy and radioactivity. Uranium became a desirable commodity after World War II demonstrated the power of atomic weapons at Hiroshima and Nagasaki, and the potential of nuclear-powered electrical generation became apparent.

This interest in uranium affected several regions of Oceania. The United States, Britain, and France all joined the Cold War arms race and the effort to develop even more powerful weapons based on uranium and related elements such as plutonium. They chose to test many of the atomic weapons in the Pacific, with devastating implications for local residents and environments. The United States tested its bombs in the Marshall Islands, relocating the residents of Bikini and Enewetak atolls to other islands and exploding several different types of nuclear weapons between 1946 and 1958 (**Figure 1**). Although the prevailing winds were supposed to carry the radioactive fallout from bomb testing away from inhabited islands, in 1954 radioactive ash dusted the island of Rongelap and its almost 100 residents, including several relocated from Bikini.

Radioactive exposure can have serious short- and long-term effects, including acute poisoning, leukemia, and birth defects, so the U.S. government evacuated the residents of Rongelap at short notice with little information about the hazard they had been exposed to or warning that they would not be able to return to their homelands. Years later, in 1968, the residents of Rongelap and Bikini were told it was safe to return; those on Bikini later had to be re-evacuated when scientists discovered that dangerous levels of radioactivity persisted in food gathered on the islands. Although the United States has monitored the health of the islanders and established a $90-million trust fund, many residents of the islands are angry and resentful about the experiments that disrupted their lives.

France conducted more than 150 bomb tests on the tiny atolls of Moruroa and Fangataufa in French Polynesia beginning in 1966. The first bombs showered the surrounding regions with radioactivity, reaching as far as Samoa and Tonga hundreds of miles to the west. Opposition from other Pacific islands, including New Zealand and Australia, culminated in boycotts of French products, including wine and cheese, during the 1970s. France moved to underground testing and refused to release information about accidents and monitoring of radioactive pollution or health in French Polynesia. While locals use the bomb tests as a reason to seek independence from France, international activists have tried to stop the French bomb tests (**Figure 2**). In 1985 the environmental group Greenpeace planned to protest tests by sailing their ship *Rainbow Warrior* to Moruroa, but French intelligence agents scuttled the ship while it was moored in the harbor of Auckland, New Zealand.

The international scandal prompted New Zealand to take a strong stand against nuclear proliferation, banning all nuclear-powered and nuclear-armed vessels from its harbors, breaking off

FIGURE 1 Bikini Atoll The atomic bomb test at Bikini Atoll in the Marshall Islands on July 25, 1946. Fallout from this and subsequent tests posed serious health risks to Pacific islanders and resulted in the evacuation of several atolls.

FIGURE 2 Greenpeace ship A Greenpeace ship moored off Tahiti during protests against nuclear testing. This ship replaced the *Rainbow Warrior*, scuttled by French agents in the harbor of Auckland, New Zealand, because of its role in protesting nuclear testing in French Polynesia. New Zealand has declared its ports as nuclear-free zones and has joined Pacific island nations in strongly protesting nuclear activities in Oceania. (*Source:* © 1985 Miller/Greenpeace.)

diplomatic relations with France, and taking a leadership role in the antinuclear movement in the Pacific. This created a long-term strain on relations between New Zealand and the United States because U.S. military vessels, which will not admit nuclear capability, were therefore banned from New Zealand. However, New Zealand's actions contributed to the announcement by France in 1996, after riots in Tahiti and declines in tourism, that it would end nuclear testing.

The British tested their bombs on Christmas Atoll, now within the nation of Kiribati, and also at several locations in Australia, including the Monte Bello islands off the coast of Western Australia and Maralinga in South Australia. Critics now claim that neither the Australian government nor its people were made fully aware of the risks of these tests and that the local Aborigines were heavily exposed to radiation and continue to wander into the contaminated test sites.

The consumption of uranium has also threatened Australian Aborigines through mining on or near their lands in northern Australia (**Figure 3**). The Ranger mine, for example, began operations in the Northern Territory in 1980 within the boundary of Kakadu National Park, a region of great natural beauty listed as a World Heritage site for both natural and cultural values. The mine has produced more than 16 million tons (35 billion pounds) of radioactive waste and has created serious water-pollution problems in the area. Great controversy has arisen over proposals to open another mine at Jabiluka on land belonging to the Mirrar Aboriginal Group; activists have blockaded the mine road, and protests have occurred around Australia. Australia has 40 percent of the world's uranium deposits and exports fuel to nuclear power stations in the United States, Japan, Europe, Canada, and South Korea. Australia itself does not produce electricity from uranium.

Thus, uranium links the countries of Oceania to the global geography of energy consumption and to the desire for geopolitical supremacy in a multitude of ways. Though nuclear testing has been halted in the Pacific, radioactivity persists for thousands of years and will continue to pose risks to people and ecosystems. Although uranium prices are currently low because few new nuclear power stations are under construction in the aftermath of the Chernobyl accident (see Chapter 3, p. 118), many countries are reconsidering the nuclear energy options and seeking to purchase uranium as other supplies become scarce or create environmental problems.

Zealand. Women live 2 to 4 years longer than men. Literacy is above 90 percent for both men and women in much of the region. Papua New Guinea, Kiribati, and Vanuatu have higher infant mortality and lower literacy than other parts of Oceania.

Some of the more serious social problems in the region include alcohol abuse and high levels of domestic violence. Papua New Guinea has some of the highest levels of violence against women in the world.

Indigenous Issues and Multiculturalism

Among the most passionately debated issues in contemporary Australia and New Zealand are those relating to the rights of their indigenous peoples and the creation of a multicultural society and national identity. The countries share a history of British colonialism and dispossession of indigenous lands and cultures. They have distinctly different contexts and contemporary approaches to intercultural relationships.

In New Zealand, Maori rights are framed by the 1840 Treaty of Waitangi. Although the Maori interpreted the treaty as guaranteeing their land and rights, the century that followed saw large-scale dispossession of Maori land and disrespect for Maori culture. Maori landholdings were reduced from 27 million hectares (100,000 square miles) to only 1.3 million hectares (5000 square miles), or 3 percent of the total area of New Zealand. A series of protests, court cases, and reawakening to Maori tradition led in 1975 to the establishment of the Waitangi tribunal, which eventually reinterpreted the Treaty of Waitangi as more favorable to the Maori and investigated a series of Maori land and fishery claims. The Maori were established as *tangata whenua* (the "people of the land") and Maori was recognized as an official language of New Zealand (**Figure 11.21**). Some land claims were settled or compensated through money or grants of government land. Others are too large or threatening to private interests to be easily recognized. A bicultural Maori and *Pakeha* (a Maori term for whites) society has been adopted rather than a multicultural policy that would encompass other immigrant groups, such as Pacific islanders and Asians, or recognize the differences within Maori and other cultures.

New Zealand's recognition of Maori rights and culture as part of a national identity has not solved some of the deeper problems of racism toward the Maori or of their poverty and alienation. Maori unemployment is twice that of white residents; average incomes, home ownership, and educational levels are less than half; and welfare dependence is much higher.

Australian Aborigines, in contrast, have had no recourse to a treaty to assert their rights. The European colonists saw the indigenous peoples as primitive and their land as *terra nullius*, owned by no one, and therefore freely available to settlers. Only in the 1930s were reserves set aside for Aboriginal populations, mostly in very marginal environments with little autonomy or access to services. In many ways the Aboriginal population had been made "invisible," not counted in the census or allowed to vote until the 1960s. It was also stereotyped as a primitive and homogeneous nomadic culture, when in fact there were many different cultures. One of the most misguided programs set out to assimilate the Aboriginal population by forcibly removing their children from their families and communities and placing them in white foster homes and institutions from 1928 to 1964. This **stolen generation** of as many as 100,000 Aboriginal children was given voice and officially acknowledged by the Australian government in a national inquiry in the 1990s.

Indigenous Australians are disadvantaged on almost all economic and social indicators, with unemployment at four times the national average, much lower average incomes,

FIGURE 11.21 Maoris demand that New Zealand honor the Treaty of Waitangi A group of Maori activists protest at the 1995 Waitangi Day celebrations, held each year to celebrate the signing of the 1840 Treaty of Waitangi in which the Maori yielded land ownership to the settlers. Activists contend that the European signatories did not honor their side of the treaty. The banner shows that Te Kawau Maro (a Maori indigenous organization) supports Rangatiratanga (or Maori control of all things Maori), a statement of sovereignty that was mentioned in the treaty.

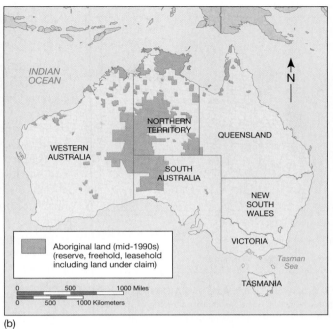

FIGURE 11.22 Aboriginal issues in Australia (a) Millions of Australians have apologized to the Aborigines for discrimination and the damage to the "stolen generation" of Aboriginal children who were taken forcibly from their homes. This apology was flown over the Sydney Opera House. (b) This map shows the current status of Aboriginal lands in Australia, with the majority in the Northern Territory. Key legal settlements such as the Mabo and Wik judgments have prompted Aborigine land claims to more than 35 percent of the country. (*Source:* [b] Adapted from G. M. Robinson, R. J. Loughran, and P. J. Tranter, *Australia and New Zealand: Economy, Society and Environment.* New York: Oxford University Press, 2000, Figure 5.5.)

housing quality, and educational levels, and higher levels of suicide, substance abuse, disease, and violence. Growing awareness and regret at the treatment of Aborigines has led to efforts at apology and reconciliation by many white Australians. In 2000, more than 300,000 people marched across the Sydney Harbor Bridge in a walk of reconciliation, and more than 1 million Australians signed "Sorry Books" that stated, "We stole your land, stole your children, stole your lives. Sorry," as a way of apologizing for the treatment of Aboriginal peoples (**Figure 11.22a**). The Aboriginal Land Rights Act of 1976 gave Aborigines title to almost 20 percent of the Northern Territory and opened government land to claims through regional land councils. The states of South Australia and Western Australia have also handed over land to Aboriginal ownership or leases. In 1992 the Australian High Court effectively overruled the doctrine of *terra nullius*, which has had the effect of encouraging Aboriginal claims for land and compensation. Aboriginal control now extends over about 15 percent of Australia, with claims to at least another 20 percent (**Figure 11.22b**). The more contentious claims surround land with valuable mineral resources, especially uranium, or where development threatens spiritual sites.

Australian Aborigines still have much less power and recognition than the Maori of New Zealand, and this is reflected in Australia's adoption of a multicultural rather than bicultural policy of national integration. Multiculturalism emerged in the 1970s and set out to embrace the distinctive cultures of many different ethnic and immigrant groups. The National Agenda for a Multicultural Australia (published in 1989) set out to promote tolerance and cultural rights and to reduce discrimination, while maintaining English as the official language and avoiding special treatment for any one group. In contrast to New Zealand, where Maori language and culture is an essential component of the national bicultural identity, Aborigines are just one of many ethnic groups in a multicultural society. Some have resented this status. There has also been considerable opposition to immigration, Aboriginal rights, and multiculturalism in the last decade. The government of Prime Minister John Howard declined to apologize formally for past offenses against Aborigines and set limits on land claims. In the 1990s a new political party, the One Nation party, emerged with a platform that opposed immigration, multiculturalism, and any special preferences for Aborigines, but the party has now lost favor.

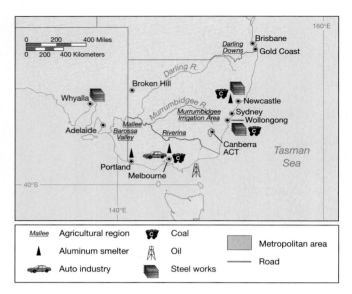

FIGURE 11.23 Southeastern Australia The most economically significant region of Oceania is the agroindustrial region of southeastern Australia with the dynamic cities of Sydney and Melbourne and the federal capital of Canberra.

REGIONAL DEVELOPMENT
Southeastern Australia

The most important economic region in Oceania is probably the area of southeastern Australia that stretches from the Gold Coast in southeastern Queensland, south along the coast to the cities of Newcastle, Sydney, Wollongong, Melbourne, and Adelaide and inland to Australia's capital city of Canberra and the agricultural regions of the Darling Downs, Murrumbidgee Irrigation Area, and the Barossa Valley (**Figure 11.23**). A moderate climate, a coastline of safe harbors and world-class beaches, and rich mineral and agricultural resources all make southeastern Australia a center of historical and contemporary economic development. The area is home to more than 60 percent of Australia's population (and more than one-third the population of Oceania).

The regional economy is now dominated by the service sector, although mining and agriculture provide the most important export sectors. The rich agricultural lands of southeastern Australia host a livestock industry of milk, beef, and lamb production, with animals that graze on pastures improved by fertilizer (especially phosphate) and introduced grasses. Southeastern Australia is also the heart of the Australian wheat industry in a "fertile crescent" that stretches with rolling farmland from the Darling Downs of southern Queensland to central South Australia. Wheat and other grains are often grown in rotation with pasture and sheep raising on larger farms. Wheat from this area combines with that from Western Australia to constitute an export wheat industry that ranks with that of Canada and France, with only the United States ahead of this group. The irrigated farms of the Murrumbidgee Irrigation Area and the grazing lands of the Riverina are also very important to agriculture. Cotton from New South Wales contributes to Australia's dominance in world cotton exports. Southeastern Australia also includes several areas of intensive horticulture (fruit and vegetables) and vineyards. Australian wine has gained an excellent reputation in world markets, especially the wines of the Barossa Valley north of Adelaide and the Hunter Valley of New South Wales. Australian wine exports are the fourth largest in the world (behind France, Italy, and Spain). Wine is produced with the most advanced technology and innovative marketing and supports a thriving tourist industry similar to that of the Napa Valley in the U.S. state of California. The city of Sydney, the capital of the state of New South Wales, has a spectacular location on the shore and low hills that surround an extensive natural harbor with many inlets (**Figure 11.24**). Two architectural symbols dominate the landscape—the Sydney Harbor Bridge completed in 1932 as one of the longest steel arch bridges in the world, and the Sydney Opera House with its brilliant white sail- or shell-shaped roof. These images became familiar to many worldwide during the broadcasts of the 2000 Summer Olympics, which brought thousands of visitors to the city. Although Sydney has some manufacturing, the city economy is overwhelmingly service oriented, focusing on trade, banking, and tourism.

With a population of almost 4 million people, the city has high levels of car ownership and sprawls into surrounding suburbs. The wealthier areas of the city are to the east, with poorer residents concentrated in the western suburbs. As immigrants from different regions settled in groups of similar origin, Sydney developed several ethnic neighborhoods, including Greek and Italian (Leichhardt) and Vietnamese (Cabramatta). Many Aborigines who migrated to the city settled in the suburb of Redfern, and poverty and discrimination has made this neighborhood a focus of indigenous action and social programs. A number of older downtown neighborhoods, such as Paddington, have been renovated by higher-income groups in a process of gentrification (the invasion of older, centrally located working-class neighborhoods by higher-income households). Some of the older warehouse and manufacturing districts near the harbor have been redeveloped into shopping, museum, convention, and entertainment structures, such as the Darling Harbor district. Sydney is surrounded by parks and protected areas and by magnificent beaches that encourage swimming, surfing, and sailing. The major industrial cities of Wollongong and Newcastle, with coal mines and steelworks, lie to the south and north of Sydney. Newcastle also has two major aluminum smelters in the Hunter Valley, which cuts inland from the coast.

The manufacturing center of southeastern Australia is Melbourne, the capital of the state of Victoria. Located on a sheltered harbor on Port Phillip Bay, Melbourne has a local population exceeding 2 million people. The city first developed as the transport hub for the 19th-century gold rush; it grew further when thousands of refugees and migrants were sponsored to come to Australia after World War II and were sent to work in Melbourne's industrial sector, which included textiles, clothing, and metal processing. Contemporary industry includes chemicals, food processing, automobiles, and computers. The Latrobe Valley, east of Melbourne, has the world's largest reserves of brown coal (or lignite) used to fuel Australia's thermoelectric power stations and for export. Australia is the world's biggest exporter of hard coal—one of the reasons the current government is reluctant to ratify the Kyoto Protocol to combat climate change.

The Islands of the Pacific

The islands of the Pacific form a distinctive image in the minds of most of the world—tropical paradises where local people fish, collect coconuts, and make crafts while tourists relax on beautiful beaches and swim in peaceful lagoons fringed with coral reefs. The reality of the Pacific islands is, as we have already seen, far more complex and in some cases more conflict-ridden and difficult than the popular image suggests. This, together with the islands' far-flung geography and isolation from each other, makes it difficult to treat the islands as a coherent distinctive landscape and to plan development of this complex region. Even the geographical classification into Melanesia, Micronesia, and Polynesia, or into high and low islands, clusters islands that are very different into subregional groups.

Another way to understand the distinctive landscapes of the Pacific islands is to focus on groups of islands that share distinct forms of integration into the global economy. These forms of integration have shaped their social and physical environments in similar ways. Two such categories are islands transformed by mineral extraction and islands transformed by international tourism. One further group, the islands transformed by nuclear testing, is described in Geographies of Indulgence, Desire, and Addiction: Uranium in Oceania, on p. 550.

Mining in the Pacific One distinctive set of islands contains those where the economy is almost wholly dependent on exports of mineral resources. Mining has destroyed the landscape and created social tensions over the wealth that flows from

FIGURE 11.24 Sydney This view of Sydney features the Sydney Opera House (left) and Sydney Harbor Bridge with the modern office skyline across the harbor.

FIGURE 11.25 Nauru The landscape of Nauru was devastated by mining phosphate rock that accumulated from the guano of roosting seabirds. This shows the dock where phosphate was loaded onto ships for export.

exports. Perhaps the most dramatic case is that of Nauru, an oval island with an area of only 21 square kilometers (8 square miles) consisting of an uplifted coral platform about 30 meters (100 feet) above sea level (**Figure 11.25**).

Centuries of roosting by seabirds covered most of Nauru with deep deposits of guano (bird droppings) that have created the highest-quality phosphate rock in the world. Exploitation of the phosphate for use as a fertilizer began in 1906, and Nauru phosphate was especially valuable in making the phosphorus-poor soils of Australia productive for crops and pasture. When Nauru became independent from Australia in 1968, its government took over control of the mining industry.

Phosphate dominated the economy and was strip-mined, crushed, and sent by conveyor belts to ships that anchor outside the reef that surrounds the island. The profits were divided among the government, local landowners, and a long-term trust fund. Many locals chose not to work, and the mining was done by temporary migrant contract workers from other islands. Nauru invested in real estate in Australia and in other enterprises as alternative sources of revenue after the phosphate income disappeared. Its other alternative income sources included offering its territory as an offshore detention center for asylum seekers trying to enter Australia. The phosphate ran out in the 1990s. The landscape of Nauru is now a desolate wasteland stripped of vegetation and soil, with cavernous pits dotting a rainless rocky plateau. Drinking water comes from an aging desalination plant or is shipped in from Australia. High levels of consumption and sedentary lifestyles among local people have brought the diseases of affluence to the island, including obesity, diabetes, and heart disease and a loss of traditional culture.

Banaba, an even smaller island north of Nauru that is part of Kiribati, had similar resources of guano-derived phosphate deposits that were exhausted by 1980, stripping 90 percent of the island's surface. Some money was set aside in a reserve fund that now supports the government of the sparsely inhabited and ecologically devastated island.

Mineral extraction also dominates the landscapes and livelihoods of larger islands in the Pacific. The main island of New Caledonia, located northwest of New Zealand, has one of the largest nickel reserves in the world, extensive mines, and an enormous, polluting nickel refinery located in the capital city of Nouméa. Nickel is used not only in coins but in many industrial alloys. Its value is one reason that France has held on to New Caledonia as an Overseas Territory, supported by the descendants of French immigrants but opposed by the indigenous Melanesian Kanaks, who seek independence.

Mining also exacerbates problems on the island of Bougainville, which is controlled by Papua New Guinea but is geographically and culturally part of the Solomon Islands. The giant Panguna copper mine owned by the multinational company Rio

Tinto was one of the world's largest open-pit mines and contributed as much as a quarter of Papua New Guinea's export earnings. The mine was developed in the forests without the participation of the resident indigenous Nasioi, and it has polluted several rivers that provided fish and drinking water to other groups. Local people seeking a share of the copper revenues, concerned about the mine's environmental impacts, and demanding independence from Papua New Guinea, have joined a rebel movement. The conflict over mining on indigenous lands in Bougainville parallels that surrounding the Ok Tedi copper and gold mine on the mainland of Papua New Guinea, where the pollution of rivers by mine tailings has prompted international environmental concern (**Figure 11.26**). In the 1990s the communities downstream sued the BHP company who owned the mine until 2002 and received US$28.6 million in an out-of-court settlement, which was the culmination of an enormous public-relations campaign against the company by environmental groups. The Ok Tedi case provides another example of how mineral exports and mining by foreign-owned companies can transform local environments, cultures, and politics in Oceania.

Tourism and the Pacific The widespread image of the Pacific islands as a vacation paradise has origins in the accounts of the first European visitors, who described tropical abundance and peaceful locals, including the romantic depiction of island women as exotic and available partners. The island of Bora-Bora in French Polynesia uses these images to advertise its luxury five-star resorts, describing the location as the "islands of dreams," an "emerald in a setting of turquoise, encircled by a necklace of pearls." Tourists are invited to purchase crafts and to view the traditional dances of "beautiful Polynesian women." Bora-Bora, a small mountainous island surrounded by coral reefs and lagoons, certainly has a stunning setting, but its beauty has attracted so many luxury hotels that it is rapidly becoming an expensive caricature of the typical Pacific island paradise (**Figure 11.27**).

FIGURE 11.27 **Bora-Bora** Luxury tourist resorts dot the coastline of Bora-Bora in French Polynesia. Visitors to these resorts bring valuable foreign exchange to the economy, but the resorts put pressure on the local resource base and encourage local peoples to modify their livelihoods and rituals to please foreign visitors.

The notion of the Pacific as a tourist destination grew as international air and cruise routes included stops at island groups such as Hawaii and Fiji, often en route to Australia or Asia. But the big boom in Pacific tourism occurred from about 1980 onward as air travel became more accessible and increased numbers of North Americans and Asians (especially Japanese) sought luxury and exotic vacations. The most popular Pacific island destinations, after the U.S. state of Hawaii, are Guam, Fiji, and Tahiti; the total number of tourists to the Pacific islands (Hawaii excepted) reached more than 3 million a year in the late 1990s. The significance of international tourism to economies and employment in individual countries is tremendous and is the major source of foreign exchange for the Cook Islands, Fiji, French Polynesia, Samoa, Tonga, Tuvalu, and Vanuatu. Challenges faced by these tourism-dependent economies include vulnerability to international trends in tourism, political unrest that dissuades tourists, the need to ensure that the benefits of tourism reach throughout the population, and the need to minimize negative effects on local cultures and environments.

Samoa is trying to build an image as the ecotourism capital of the South Pacific, promoting trips to waterfalls, lava flows, snorkeling, sea kayaking, rugby football matches, and accommodation in the traditional open thatched hut, or *fale*. The councils of village chiefs have decided that large-scale tourist development is inconsistent with Samoan values. They have promoted eco-villages that commit to protect their wildlife and culture and to adopt sustainable development policies. More than 88,000 people visited Samoa in 2002 and employment is rapidly shifting from agriculture to the service sector.

SUMMARY AND CONCLUSIONS

Oceania is the most geographically isolated of world regions, yet it is also closely connected by migration, trade, environment, politics, and tourism to the world-system. The historical geography of Oceania illustrates how ecological imperialism—especially the introduction of exotic species, together with European immigration and trade in staple agricultural and mineral commodities—transformed Australia, New Zealand, and the Pacific in the 19th century. Australia and New Zealand became two of the world's wealthiest countries in the 20th century, with preferred trading links to Britain succeeded by new export and investment relations with Asia. Immigration patterns paralleled this shift, with increased numbers of migrants from Asia and the Pacific arriving, especially in Australia. These new immigrants, together with increased awareness of the rights of indigenous Aborigines and Maori, challenged Australia and New Zealand to rethink their national identities. Australia promoted a multicultural society and New Zealand promoted a bicultural approach of a Maori-Pakeha (white) society.

The Pacific islands were strongly affected by World War II, and they continue to play a role in world politics. Countries such as France and the United States maintain territories and military bases in the region and tested nuclear weapons there until relatively recently. The world's last frontier, Antarctica, is protected from militarization under international agreements. The Pacific has also become the testing ground for the impacts of global pollution. It was the first world region to experience the effects of ozone depletion, and some of its low-lying islands have already disappeared as a result of sea-level rise associated with global warming.

Within the region there are great contrasts—between the densely populated core region of southeastern Australia and the remote, rural Outback; between the high-income districts of modern cities such as Sydney and their poorer neighborhoods; between the semitropical North Island and alpine South Island of New Zealand; between the high volcanic islands and low coral atolls of the Pacific; and among the Pacific islands variously dependent on mining, military bases, remittances, and tourism.

While there are many problems in the Pacific, including ethnic strife and struggles for greater autonomy, the region is peaceful and prosperous compared to many other world regions. Regional cooperation includes agreements on trade, environment, and security and the promotion of a Pacific way of self-determination, cultural esteem, and peace through consensus.

KEY TERMS

Alliance of Small Island States (AOSIS) (p. 536)
Antarctic Treaty (p. 525)
atoll (p. 529)
cargo cult (p. 546)
cattle station (p. 528)
Closer Economic Relations (CER) agreement (p. 549)

common property resources (p. 534)
Dreamtime (p. 533)
ecological imperialism (p. 533)
Great Artesian Basin (p. 526)
marsupial (p. 531)

Melanesia (p. 522)
Micronesia (p. 522)
Outback (p. 528)
ozone depletion (p. 535)
South Pacific Forum (p. 549)
stolen generation (p. 552)

subsistence affluence (p. 549)
theory of island biogeography (p. 532)
Treaty of Waitangi (p. 539)
White Australia policy (p. 544)

REVIEW QUESTIONS

Testing Your Understanding

1. Define: (a) Oceania; (b) Melanesia; (c) Micronesia; (d) Polynesia. Identify three factors that make Oceania a distinctive region.
2. Describe some of the physical differences between high volcanic islands and low coral atolls. (Discuss how they formed and what they look like, whether they receive a lot of rainfall, what the soils and vegetation are like, and so forth.)
3. How are marsupials and monotremes different from other mammals?
4. What is ecological imperialism and how did it transform the environment of Oceania?
5. Which European powers colonized which sections of Oceania and what are the legacies of the colonial period (for example, in terms of the official languages)?
6. Currently, why and where do the United States, Britain, France, and New Zealand maintain dependent territories in the Pacific?
7. How and where has nuclear weapons testing transformed the people and places of Oceania? Is nuclear weapons testing still going on today?
8. How does the term MIRAB summarize the basis of many modern Pacific island economies?
9. Why have the Maori generally been more successful than the Aborigines in reasserting their land rights and cultural heritage? What aspects of Maori and Aborigine culture are now part of mass-marketed popular culture?
10. What is Antarctica's unique political status? Why do some states maintain claims to the region? Why do scientists and environmentalists value Antarctica?

Thinking Geographically

1. What are some ways in which the large expanse of ocean has defined culture and economy in Oceania?

2. How, why, and when did Australia and New Zealand start to shift their economic and political orientations away from Great Britain toward Asia and North America?
3. Describe the differences between the ways in which Australia and New Zealand have dealt with their indigenous peoples, immigration, and multiculturalism in general. Include a discussion of the White Australia policy, the stolen generation, the Treaty of Waitangi, *terra nullius*, and any changes over time.
4. Why was Tahiti a key location in the colonial history of Pacific island states? How did the perceptions of early colonial explorers influence the image of the Pacific in other parts of the world? Is Tahiti an independent country today?
5. How did World War II affect the Pacific? Which regions of the Pacific are still strongly influenced by international geopolitical activities (for example, through military bases and bomb testing)?
6. What is ozone depletion and how does it relate to global warming? Why is Oceania particularly vulnerable to these environmental changes and what is the name of the organization that helps some of the smaller countries respond to these changes?
7. Using specific islands as examples, how do resource extraction and tourism pose regional development challenges for Pacific island states?
8. In what ways does southeastern Australia operate as a key region for Oceania, yet still not rank as a core region within the global economy?
9. In what ways do livestock, mining, and indigenous livelihoods make the Outback a distinctive but contested landscape?

FURTHER READING

Brookfield, H. C., and Hart, D., *Melanesia: A Geographical Interpretation of an Island World*. London: Methuen, 1971.

Cameron, I., *Lost Paradise: The Exploration of the Pacific*. Topsfield, MA: Salem House Publishers, 1987.

Colbert, E., *The Pacific Islands*. Boulder: Westview Press, 1997.

Cowlishaw, G., *Blackfellas, Whitefellas, and the Hidden Injuries of Race*. Oxford: Blackwell Publishers, 2004.

Crocombe, R., *The New South Pacific: An Introduction*. Suva, Fiji: The University of the South Pacific, 1990.

D'Arcy, P., *The People of the Sea: Environment, Identity and History in Oceania*. Honolulu: University of Hawaii Press, 2006.

Diamond, J., *Guns, Germs, and Steel: The Fate of Human Societies*. New York: W. W. Norton, 1997.

Firth, S., *Nuclear Playground*. Honolulu: University of Hawaii Press, 1987.

Forster, C., *Australian Cities: Continuity and Change*. Melbourne, Victoria, Australia: Meridian, 2004.

Freeman, O. W., *Geography of the Pacific*. New York: John Wiley & Sons, 1951.

Garden, D., *Australia, New Zealand, and the Pacific: An Environmental History*. Santa Barbara, CA: ABC-CLIO, 2005.

Horne, D., *The Lucky Country*. Ringwood, Victoria, Australia: Penguin, 1998.

Howe, K. R., Kiste, R. C., and Lal, B. (eds.), *Tides of History: The Pacific Islands in the Twentieth Century*. Sydney: Allen & Unwin, 1994.

Le Heron, R. B., *Globalized Agriculture: Political Choice*. New York: Pergamon Press, 1993.

Lockwood, V., *Tahitian Transformation: Gender and Capitalist Development in a Rural Society*. Boulder: Lynne Reiner, 1993.

Lyons, P., *American Pacificism: Oceania in the U.S. Imagination*. London: Routledge, 2006.

MacLeod, C. L., *Multiethnic Australia: Its History and Future*. Jefferson, NC: McFarland & Co., 2006.

Mageo, J. M. (ed.), *Cultural Memory: Reconfiguring History and Identity in the Postcolonial Pacific.* Honolulu: University of Hawaii Press, 2001.

McEvedy, C., *The Penguin Historical Atlas of the Pacific.* New York: Penguin Books, 1998.

McKnight, T., *Oceania: The Geography of Australia, New Zealand and the Pacific Islands.* Englewood Cliffs, NJ: Prentice Hall, 1995.

Mead, M., *Coming of Age in Samoa.* New York: Quill, 1928.

Moran, A., *Australia: Nation, Belonging, and Globalization.* New York: Routledge, 2005.

Patman, R., and Rudd, C. (eds.), *Sovereignty Under Siege?: Globalisation and New Zealand.* Burlington, VT: Ashgate, 2005.

Pawson, E., and Brooking, T. (eds.), *Environmental Histories of New Zealand.* Oxford: Oxford University Press, 2002.

Rapaport, M. (ed.), *The Pacific Islands: Environment and Society.* Honolulu: The Bess Press, 1999.

Rickard, J., *Australia: A Cultural History.* London: Longman, 1996.

Robinson, G. M., Loughran, R. J., and Tranter, P. J., *Australia and New Zealand: Economy, Society and Environment.* New York: Oxford University Press, 2000.

Russell, L. (ed.), *Boundary Writing: An Exploration of Race, Culture, and Gender Binaries in Contemporary Australia.* Honolulu: University of Hawaii Press, 2006.

Sinclair, K., *Maori Times, Maori Places: Prophetic Histories.* Oxford: Rowman & Littlefield, 2003.

South Pacific Regional Environment Programme, *Environment and Development: A Pacific Island Perspective.* Manila: Asian Development Bank, 1992.

Stratford, E. (ed.), *Australian Cultural Geographies.* Melbourne: Oxford University Press, 1999.

Sturma, M., *South Sea Maidens: Western Fantasy and Sexual Politics in the South Pacific.* Westport, CT: Greenwood Press, 2002.

Taylor, G. T., *Australia: A Study in Warm Environments and Their Effect on British Settlement.* London: Methuen, 1940.

Vaughn, B. (ed.), *The Unraveling of Island Asia? Governmental, Communal, and Regional Instability.* Westport, CT: Praeger, 2002.

Vayda, A., *Peoples and Cultures of the Pacific.* Garden City, NY: American Museum of Natural History, Natural History Press, 1968.

Waddell, E., Naidu, V., and Hau'ofa, E. (eds.), *A New Oceania: Redefining Our Sea of Islands.* Suva, Fiji: University of the South Pacific, Beake House, 1993.

Watters, R. F., and McGee, T. G. (eds.), *Asia-Pacific: New Geographies of the Pacific Rim.* London: Hurst and Co., 1997.

Young, D., *Our Islands, Our Selves: A History of Conservation in New Zealand.* Dunedin, New Zealand: University of Otago Press, 2004.

FILM, MUSIC, AND POPULAR LITERATURE

Films

Black Harvest. Directed by Robin Anderson and Bob Connolly, 1992. Presents the troubled relationship between the Ganiga tribe and Joe Leahy, the mixed-race owner of a coffee plantation in New Guinea built on land sold cheaply by the tribe.

Cannibal Tours. Directed by Dennis O'Rourke, 1987. Depicts the interaction between tourists on a luxury cruise in the South Pacific and the aboriginal people of Papua New Guinea.

Half Life: A Parable for the Nuclear Age. Directed by Dennis O'Rourke, 1985. Documents the official government cynicism behind U.S. nuclear testing in the Pacific and led to open debate on the morality of exposing the Marshall Islanders to fallout.

Once Were Warriors. Directed by Lee Tamahori, 1995. A family descended from New Zealand Maori warriors is devastated by a violent father and the societal problems of being treated as outcasts.

The Piano. Directed by Jane Campion, 1993. A young woman is sent from Scotland to a remote area of New Zealand's South Island in the mid-19th century for an arranged marriage.

Picnic at Hanging Rock. Directed by Peter Weir, 1975. Mysterious disappearance of Australian schoolgirls during a picnic in rural Victoria.

Priscilla, Queen of the Desert. Directed by Stephan Elliott, 1994. A comedy that follows a road trip by three drag queens through the landscape of Australia.

Rabbit-proof Fence. Directed by Phillip Noyce, 2002. In 1931, three aboriginal girls escape after being plucked from their homes to be trained as domestic staff and set off on a trek across the Australian Outback.

Rising Waters: Global Warming and the Fate of the Pacific Islands. Directed by Andrea Torrice, 2000. A documentary.

River Queen. Directed by Vincent Ward, 2005. An Irish family is split by involvement in the 19th century British-Maori wars.

Ten Canoes. Directed by Rolph De Heer, 2006. An adaptation of Australian aboriginal history and myth acted by aboriginal cast members.

Whale Rider. Directed by Niki Caro, 2002. The story of Pai, an 11-year-old girl in a patriarchal New Zealand Whangara community, who believes she is destined to be the new tribal chief.

Music

Kiri Te Kanawa. *Maori Songs*. Emd/EMI classics, 1999.

Oceania. *Oceania*. Phillips, 2000.

Tahitian Choir. *Rapa Iti*. Triloka Records, 1991.

Te Vaka. *Nukukehe*. New Zealand: Warm Earth Records.

Various Artists. *Australia: Our Land, Our Music*. EMI International, 2005.

Various Artists. *Dance Music of Tonga*. Pan, 1994.

Various Artists. *Music of Oceania: Samoan Songs*. Musicaphon, 1999.

Various Artists. *Rough Guide: Australian Aboriginal Music*. World Music Network, 1999.

Various Artists. *Spirit of Polynesia*. Saydisc, 1993.

Various Artists. *Tuvalu*. Pan, 1995.

Yothu Yindi. *Freedom*. Mushroom, 2000.

Popular Literature

Barclay, R. *Melal: A Novel of the Pacific*. Honolulu: University of Hawaii Press, 2002. Past and present, myth and history are interwoven in this novel set in the Marshall Islands.

Chatwin, Bruce. *The Songlines*. New York: Penguin, 1988. An exploration of Australian Aboriginal culture and the invisible pathways or Dreamtime tracks that are mapped and communicated through song.

Eri, Vincent. *The Crocodile*. Auckland: Longman Paul, 1970. One of the first published novels from Papua New Guinea.

Grace, Patricia. *Potiki*. Honolulu: University of Hawaii, 1995. A novel by a New Zealand Maori writer regarding Maori-Pakeha relations that explores how Maori are adapting to change while attempting to preserve a sense of cultural identity.

Hau'ofa, Epeli. *Tales of the Tikongs*. Honolulu: University of Hawaii, 1994. Short stories of Polynesian life by a Tongan writer.

Hulme, Keri. *The Bone People*. New York: Viking Press, 1986. A dreamlike novel about relationships among three individuals and the Maori culture in New Zealand.

Van Den Berg, Rosemary, Brewster, Anne, and O'Neill, Angeline. *Those Who Remain Will Always Remember: An Anthology of Aboriginal Writing*. Fremantle, W. Australia: Fremantle Arts Centre Press, 2000.

Wendt, Albert. *Leaves of the Banyan Tree*. Honolulu: University of Hawaii, 1994. A novel that explores colonialism and independence through three generations of Samoans.

White, Patrick. *The Tree of Man*. New York: Viking Press, 1955. An epic family saga, by a Nobel Prize-winning author, depicting an ordinary couple at the beginning of the 20th century who establish a farm in the Australian wilderness that is eventually engulfed by suburb.

Winton, Tim. *The Turning: Stories*. New York: Scribner, 2006. Short stories about small-town life in Western Australia.

12 Future Regional Geographies

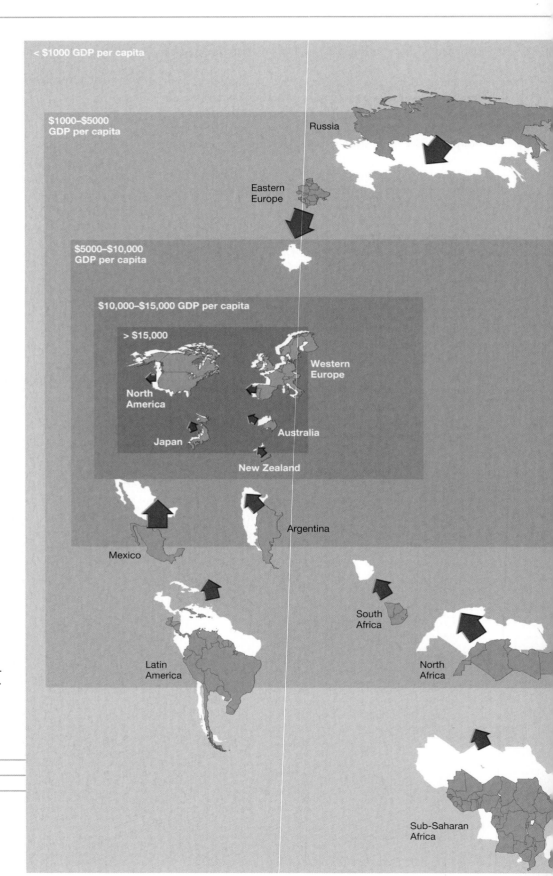

FIGURE 12.1 Projected changes to the world-system While the triadic core is likely to maintain its dominance of the world economy, up-and-coming countries with very large populations, such as China and India, are closing the gap as they are likely to move up from their peripheral or semiperipheral status. (*Source: Wired Magazine*, June 2003, p. 122.)

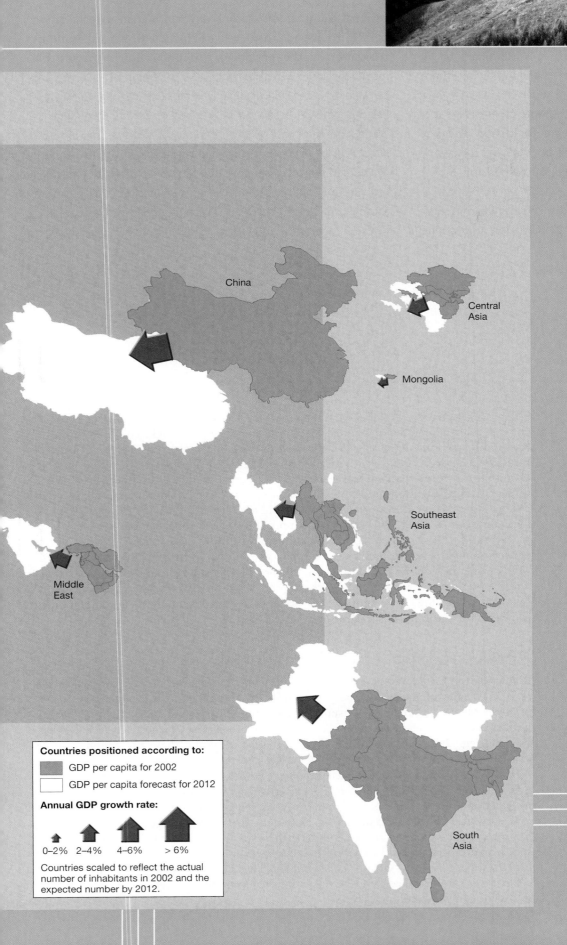

China

Central
Asia

Mongolia

Southeast
Asia

Middle
East

South
Asia

Countries positioned according to:

GDP per capita for 2002

GDP per capita forecast for 2012

Annual GDP growth rate:

0–2% 2–4% 4–6% > 6%

Countries scaled to reflect the actual
number of inhabitants in 2002 and the
expected number by 2012.

It is, of course, impossible to accurately predict the future of the very complex and diverse regions we have discussed in this text. Yet, for all sorts of reasons, it is important to be able to envisage what the future might hold for them (**Figure 12.1**). We have to live in the world for a while, and naturally we want to leave it in good shape for future generations. We therefore need to be able to identify the key changes that the future might bring so that we can work toward enabling the most desirable outcomes for future residents of planet Earth.

To attempt to look into the future means we must ask some very difficult questions. Will globalization undermine regional cultures? Will technology and human determination be able to cope with the environmental stresses that industrialization in the periphery and population increases will inevitably create? Will peripheral and semiperipheral regions be able to develop sustainably into core regions? Will new regions emerge based on new types of connectivity such as trade, the Internet, or any number of political movements such as mobilizations against globalization or the movement for human rights? What sort of limitations will global warming impose on global economic development? In this chapter, we attempt to address these and related questions to get a sense of the future of the ten world regions we have described.

GLOBALIZATION AND THE FUTURE OF REGIONS

The most effective way to approach the questions listed above is to explore how different aspects of globalization change the world and how they might continue to do so. As we discussed in Chapter 1, globalization of the capitalist world-system is a process that has been occurring for at least 500 years. But since World War II, world integration and transformation have been remarkably accelerated and dramatic. Among the forces driving integration and transformation are the strengthening of regional alliances such as the European Union (EU) and the Organization of Petroleum Exporting Countries (OPEC), the increasing connectivity of the most remote regions of the world due to telecommunications and transportation linkages, the emergence of the new economy in the core countries, and the rise of global institutions such as the World Trade Organization (WTO). How will the forces of broadening global connectivity—and the popular reactions to them—change the world regions whose current coherence owes more to 18th- and 19th-century European colonialism than to contemporary forces of integration or disintegration?

Predicting the Future

Predicting the future can be a tricky business. The uncertainties of geopolitical transformations, the unexpected impact of technological breakthroughs, and the complexity of environmental change all conspire to make our future seem, at first glance, highly unpredictable. Nevertheless, there is no shortage of visionary projections (see Geography Matters: Future Scenarios, p. 566). Broadly speaking, these projections can be divided into two sorts of extreme scenarios: optimistic and pessimistic. Optimistic futurists stress the potential for technological innovations to enable the harnessing of new resources, to provide faster and more effective means of transportation and communication, and to make possible new ways of living. This sort of futurism is characterized by science-fiction spaceship-style living pods, by bioecological harmony, and by unprecedented social and cultural progress through the information highways of cyberspace. It projects a world that will be stabilized and homogenized by supranational organizations or even "world" governments. The sort of geography implied by such scenarios is rarely spelled out. The relevance of the region, we are led to believe, will be transcended by technological fixes.

564

To pessimistic futurists, however, this is just "globaloney." They stress the finite limitations of Earth's resources, the fragility of its environment, and population growth rates that exceed the capacity of peripheral regions to sustain them. This sort of doomsday forecasting is characterized by scenarios that include irreversible environmental degradation, increasing social and economic polarization, and the breakdown of law and order (see Geography Matters: Dark Age Ahead?, p. 568). The sort of geography associated with these scenarios is rarely explicit, but it usually involves the probability of a sharp polarization between the haves and have-nots at every geographical scale.

Fortunately, we need not choose between these two extreme scenarios. To arrive at a more grounded understanding of future geographies, however, we must first glance back at the past. Then, looking at present trends and using what we know about processes of geographic change and principles of spatial organization, we can begin to map out the kinds of geographies the future most probably holds.

Understanding the Past

Looking back at how the geography of the world-system has unfolded, we can see now that a fairly coherent period of economic and geopolitical development occurred between the outbreak of World War I (in 1914) and the collapse of the Soviet Union (in 1991). Some historians refer to this period as the **short 20th century**. It was a period when the modern world-system developed its triadic core of the United States, Western Europe, and Japan; when geopolitics was based on an East–West divide; and when geoeconomics was based on a North–South divide. This was a time when the geographies of specific places and regions within these larger frameworks were shaped by the needs and opportunities of technology systems that were based on the internal combustion engine, oil and plastics, electrical engineering, aerospace industries, and electronics and by the political struggles of the Cold War. In this short century, the modern world was consolidated, along with its now-familiar landscapes and spatial structures: from the industrial landscapes of the core to the unintended metropolises of the periphery and from the voting blocs of the west to the newly independent nation-states of the south.

At present, much of the established familiarity of the modern world and its geographies seems to be disappearing. We have entered a period of transition, triggered by the end of the Cold War in 1989 and rendered more complex by the geopolitical and cultural repercussions of the terrorist attacks of September 11, 2001. The result is a series of unexpected developments and unsettling juxtapositions. The United States gives economic aid to Russia; Eastern European countries have joined NATO and the European Union; Germany has unified, but Czechoslovakia and Yugoslavia have disintegrated; South Africa has been transformed to black majority rule, through an unexpectedly peaceful revolution. Meanwhile, Islamist terrorists shoot up tourist buses, bomb office buildings, and sabotage aircraft; former communist Russian ultranationalists have become comradely with Austrian and German neo-Nazis; although open warfare between Hindus, Sikhs, and Muslims in South Asia has ceased, tensions continue to strain relations; the United States and the United Kingdom invaded Afghanistan and Iraq; and Sudanese military factions steal food from aid organizations in order to sell it to the refugees for whom it was originally intended (**Figure 12.2**).

These examples illustrate that we cannot simply project our future geographies from the regions and landscapes of the past. Rather, we must map them out from a combination of existing structures and budding trends. In other words, we have to anticipate how the shreds of tradition and the strands of contemporary change will be rewoven into new landscapes and new spatial structures.

FIGURE 12.2 Humanitarian aid, Darfur, Sudan In addition to killing and uprooting millions of men, women, and children from the southern part of Sudan, government and Janjaweed forces also have made it difficult for organizations like the United Nations and the World Food Program to deliver food and other types of aid to the displaced populations. The man shown here is guarding a shipment of food aid from the World Food Program.

GEOGRAPHY MATTERS

Future Scenarios

One way to think about the future is through scenarios that posit different outcomes based on the determining importance of different factors as they unfold in combination. Here we examine three such scenarios as they relate to our environmental future.

The Global Orchestration

This scenario depicts a global society that is well connected and in which global markets are well developed. Supranational institutions are well placed to deal with global environmental problems, such as climate change and fisheries (**Figure 1**). However, their reactive approach to ecosystem management makes them vulnerable to surprises arising from delayed action or unexpected

FIGURE 1 Mangroves These are areas of woody plants and shrubs able to thrive in coastal environments where fine sediments are deposited away from the effects of strong wave action. Mangrove habitats are among the most threatened in the world.

regional changes. The scenario is about global cooperation not only to improve the social and economic well-being of all people but also to protect and enhance global public goods and services (such as public education, health, and infrastructure). There is a focus on the individual rather than the state, inclusion of all impacts of development in markets (internalization of externalities), and use of regulation only where appropriate. Environmental problems that threaten human well-being (such as pollution, erosion, and climate change) are dealt with only after they become apparent. Problems that have little apparent or direct impact on human well-being are given a low priority in favor of policies that directly improve well-being. People are generally confident that the necessary knowledge and technology to address environmental challenges will emerge or can be developed as needed, just as it has in the past. The scenario highlights the risks from ecological surprises under such an approach such as emerging infectious diseases.

The Order from Strength

This scenario represents a regionalized and fragmented world concerned with security and protection, emphasizing primarily regional markets, and paying little attention to the common goods, and with an individualistic attitude toward ecosystem management. Nations see looking after their own interests as the best defense against economic insecurity. They reluctantly accept the argument that a militarily and economically strong liberal democratic nation could maintain global order and protect the lifestyles of the richer world and provide some benefits for any poorer countries that elect to become allies. Just as the focus of nations turns to protecting their borders and their people, so too their environmental policies focus on securing natural resources seen as critical for human well-being. But, as in Global Orchestration, people in this scenario see the environment as secondary to their other challenges. They believe in the ability of humans to bring technological innovations to bear as solutions to environmental challenges after these challenges emerge.

The Adapting Mosaic

This scenario depicts a fragmented world resulting from discredited global institutions. It sees the rise of local ecosystem management strategies and the strengthening of local institutions. Investments in human and social capital are geared toward improving knowledge about ecosystem functioning and management, resulting in a better understanding of the importance of resilience, fragility, and local flexibility of ecosystems. There is optimism that we can learn, but also humility about preparing for surprises and about our ability to know all there is to know about managing socioecological systems. Initially, trade barriers for goods and products are increased, but barriers for information (for those who are motivated to use it) nearly disappear due to improving communication technologies and rapidly decreasing costs of access to information. Eventually, the focus on local governance leads to failures in managing the global commons. Problems like climate change, marine fisheries, and pollution grow worse, and global environmental surprises become common (**Figure 2**). Communities slowly realize that they cannot manage their local areas because global problems are infringing, and they begin to develop networks among communities, regions, and even nations to better manage the global commons.

The TechnoGarden

This scenario depicts a globally connected world relying strongly on technology and on highly managed and often-engineered ecosystems to deliver needed goods and services. Overall, eco-efficiency improves, but it is shadowed by the risks inherent in large-scale human made solutions. Technology and market-oriented institutional reform are used to achieve solutions to environmental problems. In many cases, reforms and new policy initiatives benefit from the strong feel for international cooperation that is part of this scenario. As a result, conditions are good for finding solutions for global environmental problems such as climate change. These solutions are designed to benefit both the economy and the environment. Technological improvements that reduce the environmental impact of goods and services are combined with improvements in ecological engineering that optimize the production of ecosystem services. These changes co-develop with the expansion and development of property rights to ecosystem services, such as requiring people to pay for pollution they create or paying people for providing key ecosystem services through actions such as preservation of key watersheds. These property rights are assigned to a diversity of individuals, corporations, communal groups, and states that act to optimize the value of their property. This scenario assumes that ecological management and engineering can be successful, although it does produce some ecological surprises that affect many people due to an over-reliance on highly engineered systems.

As the assessment makes clear, each scenario might resemble some people's ideal world, but all four scenarios have both strengths and potentially serious weaknesses. An ideal future would probably involve a mix of all four,

with different elements dominating at different times and in different places. The future could be far better or far worse than any of the scenarios, depending on choices made by key decision-makers and other people in society who bring about change.

Source: Taken verbatim from Millennium Ecosystem Assessment Board, *Ecosystems and Human Well-being.* Washington, DC: Island Press, 2005, p. 225.

FIGURE 2 Increase in global temperature averages This graph shows dramatic projected temperature rise over this century. The Intergovernmental Panel on Climate Change (IPCC) represents these projections based on different scenarios of human behavior. (*Source:* Intergovernmental Panel on Climate Change, 2002. Available at http://www.maweb.org/en/products.aspx.)

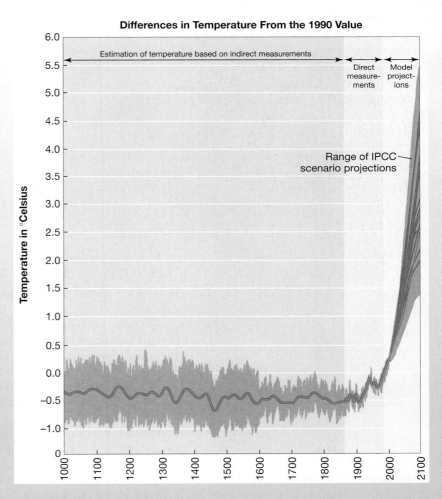

Dark Age Ahead?

Jane Jacobs, who died in April 2006 and was recognized in 2004 by *Business Week* magazine as one of the most influential public intellectuals in North America in the last 75 years, has argued that the United States is slipping toward the beginnings of a new "Dark Age." As the cause, she points to the deterioration of five pillars of modern society—community and family, higher education, the application of science and technology, the integrity of the professions, and the role of government in relation to society's needs and potential.

Jacobs was a passionate advocate of cities and urban life, and her views have been both influential and controversial. But Jacobs's fears for an incipient Dark Age go well beyond her past concerns for urban development, centering as they do on several important aspects of higher education, the application of knowledge, the role of the professions, and the role of government. "A culture is unsalvageable," writes Jacobs, "if stabilizing forces themselves become ruined." The roots of her concerns are based on evidence of:

- corporate immorality in the marketplace instead of entrepreneurship bonded to social justice;
- universities that serve employers and act as credential factories, stripping from education the music, art, ethics, idealism, and notion of the public good;
- scientific research increasingly and immorally being bought by corporations or suppressed and ignored by governments; and
- a neoliberal political economy that is intent on abandoning the stewardship of urban and regional development.

Jacobs has written that universities are complicit in allowing scientific research to be controlled by corporations and directed—and sometimes suppressed—by governments. Rather than serving as one of the cultural pillars of society, universities now serve employers and act as "colleges of heraldry," awarding graduates a "coat of arms" (i.e., university diploma) to distinguish them from those without marketable credentials.

She is equally direct about the professions. This time it is not so much planners and design professionals that are the focus of her concern but accountants, bankers, lawyers, and other financial professions whose ethics and practices have serially been called into question in relation to the vast corporate scandals of the past two decades. Nevertheless, the design and public policy professions are implicated in her critique of urban trends. Cities—vital economic engines and crucibles of cultural change and innovation—are being starved of the money they need by national, state, and local governments. Neoliberal policies are responsible for sagging public transit and public education systems, increasing pollution, increasing social polarization, the erosion of community, and the burgeoning sullenness of citizens. Families, she argues, are rigged to fail by public policies that, unintentionally, force both parents to work to meet the financial needs for themselves and their children. Communities are rigged to fail by public policies that foster sprawling, placeless, and automobile-dependent suburbs—a reprise of her earlier critique in *The Death and Life of Great American Cities*.

It behooves us to reflect critically on Jacobs's extended essay. She confides that "I have written this cautionary book in hopeful expectations that time remains for corrective actions." If we accept that corrective actions are in fact warranted, then a foundation of geographic knowledge will be fundamental to the incisive analysis that will be necessary in order to contribute effectively to countervailing forces.

Source: J. Jacobs, *Dark Age Ahead: Caution*, New York: Random House, 2004.

Future Geographies

As we look ahead to the future, we can appreciate that some dimensions of future geographies are more certain than others (**Table 12.1**). In some ways, the future is already here, embedded in the world's institutional structures and in the dynamics of its populations. We know, for example, a good deal about the demographic trends of the next quarter-century, given present populations, birth- and death rates, and so on (**Figure 12.3**). We also know a good deal about the distribution of environmental resources and constraints, about the characteristics of local and regional economies, and about the legal and political frameworks within which geographic change will probably take place.

On the other hand, we can only guess at some aspects of the future. Two of the most speculative realms are those of politics and technology. While we can foresee some of the possibilities (maybe a spread and intensification of ethnic and/or nationalist conflict; perhaps a new railway era based on high-speed trains), politics and technology are both likely to spring surprises at any time. The September 11, 2001, terror attack in the United States is a painful example of the sort of political surprises that are likely to occur. In a matter of about 100 minutes, terrorists who crashed two commercial jetliners into the towers of the World Trade Center, one into the Pentagon, and another into a field near Shanksville, Pennsylvania, were able to deliver a crippling blow to the U.S.

TABLE 12.1 The 2020 Global Landscape

Relative Certainties	Key Uncertainties
Globalization largely irreversible, likely to become less Westernized.	Whether globalization will pull in lagging economies; degree to which Asian countries set new "rules of the game."
World economy substantially larger.	Extent of gaps between "haves" and "have-nots"; backsliding by fragile democracies; managing or containing financial crises.
Increasing number of global firms facilitate spread of new technologies.	Extent to which connectivity challenges governments.
Rise of Asia and advent of possible new economic middleweights.	Whether rise of China/India occurs smoothly.
Aging populations in established powers.	Ability of EU and Japan to adapt workforces, welfare systems, and integrate migrant populations; whether EU becomes a superpower.
Energy supplies "in the ground" sufficient to meet global demand.	Political instability in producer countries; supply disruptions.
Growing power of nonstate actors.	Willingness and ability of states and international institutions to accommodate these actors.
Political Islam remains a potent force.	Impact of religiosity on unity of states and potential for conflict; growth of jihadist ideology.
Improved WMD capabilities of some states.	More or fewer nuclear powers; ability of terrorists to acquire biological, chemical, radiological, or nuclear weapons.
Arc of instability spanning Middle East, Asia, Africa.	Precipitating events leading to overthrow of regimes.
Great power conflict escalating into total war unlikely.	Ability to manage flashpoints and competition for resources.
Environmental and ethical issues even more to the fore.	Extent to which new technologies create or resolve ethical dilemmas.
U.S. will remain single most powerful actor economically, technologically, militarily.	Whether other countries will more openly challenge Washington; whether U.S. loses S&T edge.

Source: National Intelligence Council, *Mapping the Global Future.* Washington, DC: U.S. Government Printing Office, 2004, p. 8.

FIGURE 12.3 Population geography of the future Population projections for 2025 and 2050 show very marked disparities among world regions, with core countries and core regions growing very little in the next half-century compared with the periphery and semiperiphery.

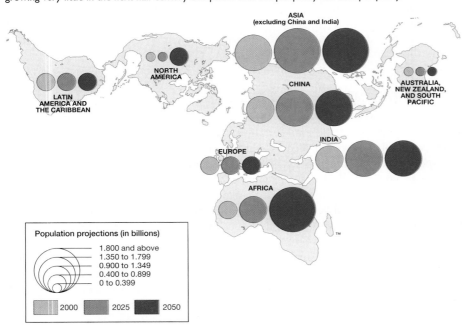

FIGURE 12.4 Pronuclear crowds in Tehran Thousands of Iranians have demonstrated in support of Iran's refusal to cease its uranium enrichment program. The banner shown here is directed at the United Nations. Iran also took out a full-page advertisement in the *New York Times* in November 2005 defending its nuclear activities.

economy, draw the country into full military alert, and profoundly transform the conduct of daily life in the United States. Other events—the production of nuclear weapons in Iran (**Figure 12.4**), political instability in Saudi Arabia, the detonation of a nuclear device in North Korea, or even unanticipated breakthroughs in biotechnology—can cause geographies to be rewritten suddenly and dramatically. As we review the prospects for regional transformations, therefore, we must always be mindful that our prognoses are all open to the unexpected. As painful as such surprises can be, we must remember that the unexpected can also be our biggest source of optimism.

The following section examines debates about contemporary globalization, offering a clearer sense of how globalization might affect the future of the world's regions. An important aspect of globalization is the widespread perception that the world, through economic and technological forces, is increasingly becoming one shared political and economic space where the events in one part of the globe will have repercussions for all other parts, whether near or far. The regionalization scheme we described in the previous chapters implies that flows, interactions, and networks are strongest *within* the geographical groupings of states we have identified as Europe; the Russian Federation, Central Asia, and the Transcaucasus; the Middle East and North Africa; Sub-Saharan Africa; the United States and Canada; Latin America; East Asia; Southeast Asia; South Asia; and Australia, New Zealand, and the South Pacific. Given that economic and technological forces are breaking down the barriers within and among both near and distant places, will the most recent phase of globalization strengthen some regional connections, weaken others, or make regions altogether irrelevant? Alternatively, will globalization enable some regions—core regions, for instance—to create even greater differences of wealth and power than already exist in the world-system? Understanding what the experts believe about globalization will give us a better glimpse of the future globalization is likely to make possible.

THE GLOBALIZATION DEBATES

The main participants in contemporary debates about globalization can be grouped into three general camps: the hyperglobalists, the skeptics, and the transformationalists. Although these three viewpoints do not exhaust the range of the debate, they do provide a clear sense of the spectrum of issues on which the experts on globalization agree and disagree.

The Hyperglobalists

One group of experts—the hyperglobalists—believes the current phase of globalization signals the beginning of the end for the nation-state and the "denationalization" of economies. What this would mean is that national boundaries will become irrelevant with respect to economic processes and that national governments will not control their once geographically bounded economies but will instead facilitate connections among different parts of the world. The wider implication of the hyperglobalist position is that the world will become borderless as national governments become increasingly meaningless or as they function as merely the facilitators of global capital flows and investments.

Hyperglobalists believe that the nation-state, as the primary political and economic unit of contemporary world society, will eventually be replaced by institutions of global governance in which individuals claim transnational allegiances that are founded on a commitment to neoliberal principles of free trade and economic integration. Politically, the global spread of liberal democracy will reinforce the emergence of a global civilization with its own mechanisms of global governance, replacing the outmoded nation-state with global institutions like the International Monetary Fund (IMF) or the WTO.

The Skeptics

A second broad argument within the globalization literature belongs to the skeptics, who believe that contemporary levels of global economic integration represent nothing particularly new and that globalization is an exaggerated myth. The skeptics look to the 19th century and draw on statistical evidence of world flows of trade, labor, and investment to fortify their position. They argue that contemporary economic integration is actually much less significant than it was in the late 19th century, when nearly all countries shared a common monetary system known as the gold standard. The skeptics are also dismissive of the idea that the nation-state is in decline. They argue that national governments are essential to regulating international economic activity and that the continuing liberalization of the world economy can be facilitated only by this regulatory power.

The skeptics assert that their analysis of 19th-century economic patterns demonstrates that we are today witnessing not globalization but rather "regionalization," as the world economy is increasingly dominated by three major financial and trading blocks—western Europe, the United States, and Japan. According to the skeptics, regionalization and globalization are contradictory tendencies. They believe that the world is actually less integrated than it once was because western Europe, the United States, and Japan control the world economy and limit the participation of other regions in that economy.

The Transformationalists

According to the transformationalist view, the contemporary processes of globalization are historically unprecedented as governments and peoples across the globe confront the absence of any clear distinction between what is global and what is local, between what are domestic affairs and what are international ones. Like the hyperglobalists, this group understands globalization as a profound transformative force that is changing societies, economies, and institutions of government—in short, the world order. In contrast to the hyperglobalists and the skeptics, however, the transformationalists make no claims about the future trajectory of globalization, nor do they see present globalization as a pale version of a more "globalized" 19th-century past. Instead, they see globalization as a long-term historical process underlain by crises and contradictions that are likely to shape it in all sorts of different and unpredictable ways. Moreover, unlike the skeptics, the transformationalists believe that the historically unprecedented contemporary patterns of economic, military, technological, ecological, migratory, political, and cultural flows have functionally linked all parts of the world into a larger global system. In fact, they see regionalism as a stepping stone to more global connectedness in which free trade agreements such as NAFTA or ASEAN help draw regions into a global, neoliberal economic framework.

The position of this book is closest to that of the transformationalists; we believe this approach to globalization can tell us a great deal about what we might expect in the future—especially the future of world regions. The transformationalists—mindful that no one can accurately predict the future, regardless of how reasonable and rational the theories—suggest that we are heading toward a period in which world regions will experience a range of internal changes at the same time that the strength of their connections with other parts of the world will increase. It is very difficult to determine whether those internal adjustments and external linkages will signal the wholesale transformations of the ten regions we have discussed in this book. We can, however, identify tendencies and how those tendencies might reshape the current world of regions.

What is most disturbing about the transformationalist view of globalization is the identification of global patterns of increasing disparities in wealth. Transformationalists believe that globalization is leading to increased social stratification, in which some

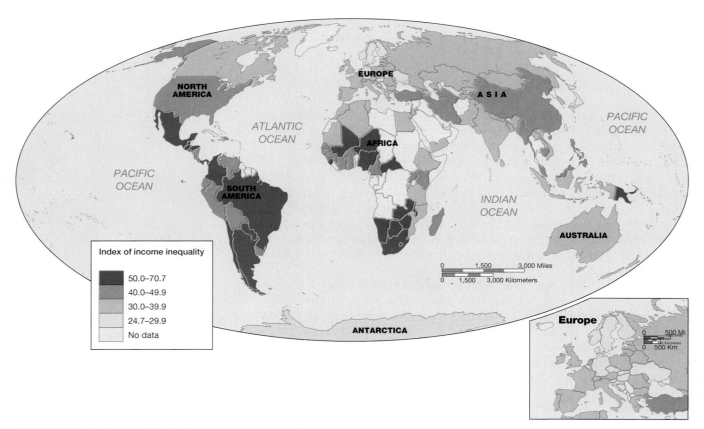

FIGURE 12.5 Inequality in the world-system This map shows the degree of inequality of income distributions within countries using the Gini coefficient, a commonly used indicator that compares actual income distributions to a hypothetical distribution of perfect equality. The higher the index score, the greater the degree of inequality within a country. (*Source:* United Nations Development Programme, *Cities in a Globalizing World.* Sterling, VA: Earthscan Publications, 2001, p. 18.)

states and societies are more tightly connected to the global order while others are becoming increasingly marginalized (**Figure 12.5**). They argue that the world will increasingly consist of a three-tiered system—the marginalized, the elites, and the embattled middle—that cuts across national, regional, and local boundaries. Thus within and between regions, disparities of wealth will increase just as they will increase across the world-system itself. The economic projections discussed in the following section can provide us with some sense of how and why this might be so.

GLOBAL STRATIFICATION, REGIONAL CHANGE

For many years now, organizations such as the United Nations and the World Bank have prepared forecasts of the world economy. These forecasts are based on models that take data on economic variables—for example, trends in countries' gross domestic product (GDP), their imports and exports, their economic structure, their investment and saving performance, and their demographic dynamism—and use known relationships among these variables to predict future outcomes. The problem is that economic projection is an inexact science. Economic models are not able to take into account the changes brought about by major technological innovations, significant geopolitical shifts, governments' willingness and ability to develop strong economic policies, or the rather mysterious longer-term ups and downs that characterize the world economy.

What is clear is that in *overall* terms the global economy is vastly richer, more productive, and more dynamic than it was just 15 or 20 years ago, and every prospect exists that, in the longer term, the world economy will continue to expand. The U.S. National Intelligence Council's 2004 report *Mapping the Global Future*—based on consultations with nongovernmental experts from around the world—concluded that the world economy is likely to continue growing impressively: By 2020, it is projected to be about 80 percent larger than it was in 2000, and average per capita income will be roughly 50 percent higher.

Uneven Development

Global economic expansion will be uneven, of course. The world in 2020 will change radically. Emerging powers—China, India, and perhaps others such as Brazil and Indonesia—have the potential to render obsolete the old categories of East and West, North and South, aligned and nonaligned, developed and developing. Traditional regional groupings may increasingly lose salience in international relations. A state-bound world and a world of mega-cities, linked by flows of telecommunications, trade, and finance will coexist. Competition for allegiances will be more open, less fixed than in the past.

In parallel with the world-system categorization of core, semiperipheral, and peripheral regions, we can think of the prospects of large sectors of the world's population as being in one of three categories: the elite, the embattled, and the marginalized. The elite are participants in—and beneficiaries of—a world of new transport and communications technologies, globalized production networks, and global consumer culture. The embattled are also participants, but in dependent roles, with fewer benefits and limited opportunities: assembly-line workers, for example, in offshore commodity chains. The marginalized have to survive, largely disconnected from formal economies and the dynamics of globalization.

The most significant point to keep in mind about the stratification of the world economy through contemporary globalization is that the elite, the marginalized, and the embattled are likely to be less concentrated in particular regions than they once were. It is no longer accurate to see Africa as a wholly embattled region, for instance, or its population as exclusively embattled. Instead, Africa, like Europe and most other countries, contains a range of stratified sub-regions and groups within its national boundaries such that elite, embattled, and marginalized social groups are all part of the larger whole. Moreover, the elite regions and social groups have more in common with elite regions and groups in other parts of the world than they do with the embattled and marginalized groups within their own national boundaries (**Figure 12.6**).

Nevertheless, future geographies seem likely to be structured by an even greater gap between the haves and have-nots of the world. The gap between the world's core areas and the periphery has already begun to widen significantly. Even within the United States, the degree of income inequality ranks with that in China, Bolivia, Malaysia, Senegal, and Russia. U.S. Census Bureau data, for example, show that the gap between the rich and poor in the United States in 2001 was the widest it had been since World War II. The United Nations has calculated that the ratio of GDP per capita (measured at constant prices and exchange rates) between the developed and developing areas of the world increased from 10:1 in 1970 to 12:1 in 1985

FIGURE 12.6 Wealth amidst poverty Finima, Nigeria, a poor village, without electricity, piped water, or sanitation facilities, is located in the shadow of a high-income-generating export facility and Mobil's liquid natural gas facility. While significant revenues flow into the national government's treasury, little of it is redistributed to the poor.

and 18:1 in 2005. Little hope exists that any future boom in the overall world economy will reverse this trend. In spite of the globalization of the world-system (and in many ways *because* of it), much of the world has been all but written off by the bankers and corporate executives of the core.

A New World Order?

The same factors that will consolidate the advantages of the core of the world-system as a whole—the end of the Cold War, the availability of advanced telecommunications, the transnational reorganization of industry and finance, the liberalization of trade, and the emergence of a global culture—will also open the way for a new geopolitical and geoeconomic order. This is likely to involve some new relationships between places, regions, and countries. As we have suggested, the old order of the "short" 20th century (1914–89), dominated both economically and politically by the United States, is rapidly disappearing. In our present transitional phase, the new world order is "up for grabs"; we are coming to the end of a geopolitical leadership cycle. This does not necessarily mean that the United States will be unable to renew or extend its position as the world's dominant power. Britain had two consecutive stints as the dominant world power—the hegemon that was able to impose its political view on the world and set the terms for a wide variety of economic and cultural practices.

The United States   The United States is the current reigning hegemon, and its economy is the largest in the world, with a broad resource base; a large, well-trained, and very sophisticated workforce; a domestic market that has greater purchasing power than any other single country; and a high level of technological sophistication. The United States also has the most powerful and technologically sophisticated military apparatus and spends more than any other country (**Table 12.2**), and it has the dominant voice and the last word in international economic and political affairs. It is at least as well placed as its rivals to exploit the new technologies and new industries of a globalizing economy. It also has a distinctive message as a global leader: free markets, personal liberty, private property, electoral democracy, and mass consumption.

For the moment, however, the United States is a declining hegemon, at least in relative terms. Its economic dominance is no longer unquestioned in the way it was in the 1950s, 1960s, and 1970s. A relatively sluggish rate of growth has brought the prospect of the U.S. economy being caught and overtaken by China. On some measures of economic development, the European Union has already overtaken the United States. More important, the globalization of the economy has severely constrained the ability of the United States to translate its economic might into the firm control of international financial markets that it used to enjoy.

The end of the Cold War, while a victory for the United States, robbed it of its image as Defender of the Free World and weakened the legitimacy of its role as global policeman. For a decade or so, the absence of a Cold War enemy and the globalization of economic affairs made it much more difficult for the United States to identify and define the national interest. Symptomatic of such problems was the hesitancy in the 1990s in U.S. policies toward Kosovo, East Timor, Somalia, Sudan, Bosnia, and Haiti. The terrorist Al-Qaeda attacks of 2001 gave a new focus for U.S. geopolitical strategy. But the invasion of Iraq in the absence of evidence of weapons of mass destruction, together with U.S. refusal to participate in high-profile international agreements such as the Kyoto Protocol and its lack of cooperation with the International Criminal Court and the United Nations, has resulted in a significant weakening of the political, cultural, and moral leadership of the United States in global affairs.

Growing numbers of ordinary people around the world, especially in the Middle East and the broader Muslim world, believe the United States is bent on regional domination—or direct political and economic domination of other states and their resources. In the future, growing distrust could prompt governments to take a more hostile approach to the United States, including resistance to support for U.S. interests in multinational forums and the development of military capabilities as a hedge against

TABLE 12.2 Top Fifty Countries in Military Expenditures, 2005		
Selected Countries	Military Budget ($ billions)	World Ranking
United States (including funding for Iraq and Afghanistan)	522	1
China (2004 Expenditures)	62.5	2
Russia (2004 Expenditures)	61.9	3
United Kingdom	51.1	4
Japan	44.7	5
France	41.6	6
Germany	30.2	7
India	22	8
Saudi Arabia	21.3	9
South Korea	20.7	10
Italy	17.2	11
Australia	13.2	12
Brazil	13.1	13
Canada	10.9	14
Turkey	9.8	15
Israel (2004 Expenditures)	9.7	16
Netherlands	9.7	16
Spain	8.8	18
Taiwan	8.3	19
Indonesia (2004 Expenditures)	7.6	20
Mayanmar	6.9	21
Ukraine (2004 Expenditures)	6.0	22
Singapore	5.6	23
Sweden	5.6	23
North Korea (2004 Expenditures)	5.5	25
Poland	5.2	26
Norway	4.7	27
Greece	4.5	28
Iran	4.9	29
Kuwait	4.3	30
Colombia (2004 Expenditures)	3.9	31
Switzerland	3.8	32
Pakistan	3.7	33
Vietnam	3.5	34
Belgium	3.4	35
Denmark	3.1	38
Egypt	2.5	45
Portugal	2.4	47
Czech Republic	2.2	50
Romania	2.2	50

Source: Center for Arms Control and Non-Proliferation. Available at *http://www.armscontrolcenter.org/archives/002244.php.*

the United States. As geographer Neil Smith has argued, this nationalism has undercut the ability of the United States to impose its vision of globalization in the past and may well do so again in the future.

In summary, although the United States must be considered the strongest contender, it is by no means a foregone conclusion that it will, in fact, become the leader for the next cycle of economic and political leadership. The United States has choices not dissimilar to those faced by the British at the end of the nineteenth century. It can either oppose its rivals or accommodate them. It can oppose by pressing for a seamless global system that remains under its own hegemony. Or it can try to accommodate by coaxing the others into a global sharing of power, with some mix of regional spheres of interest and collective world responsibilities.

Europe and the European Union Envisioning a successful European Union as the main contender for world leadership is not stretching things too far. In geopolitical terms, the collapse of the Soviet Union advanced the prospects of the European Union significantly. The European Union (EU), which began in 1952 as a trading bloc (the European Economic Community, or EEC), is now an economic union (with integrated economic policies among member states) and has moved a long way toward its goal of becoming a supranational political union (with a single set of institutions and policies). With the 2004 addition of Cyprus, the Czech Republic, Estonia, Hungary, Latvia, Lithuania, Malta, Slovakia, and Slovenia, the EU had a total population of 458 million (the U.S. population is 293 million) and an overall economy of $11.7 trillion (the GDP of the United States is just under $11 trillion). The proposed addition of Bulgaria, Croatia, Romania, and Turkey would mean a total population of 527 million and a GDP of $12.1 trillion. If and when the EU achieves full political union, its size will enable it to outvote the United States in the International Monetary Fund and the World Bank.

The EU has evolved dramatically since its start with six member nations in 1952. Now there is a common EU passport and a single currency, the euro, is used by many of its members. The EU regulates trade as well as coordinating energy, communications, and transportation. It has a president, a parliament, foreign policy powers, and a court whose decisions are binding on member countries and individuals. The EU is the world's largest internal market and largest exporting power. Of the world's 20 largest commercial banks, 14 are European. The EU also has one of the world's most vibrant and sophisticated industrial core regions, which stretches from southeast England to northern Italy; its economic policies and infrastructure investments have fostered emerging axes of economic growth that stretch east–west and north–south (**Figure 12.7**); and European industries are world leaders in chemicals, insurance, engineering,

---

FIGURE 12.7 European growth areas Most of Europe's major cities and advanced manufacturing regions lie along a crescent-shaped axis that extends from southeast England through southwest Germany to northern Italy, and along emerging axes that extend to southern France, Spain, eastern Austria, and southern Italy.

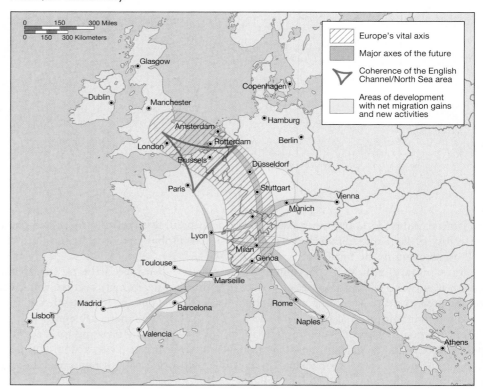

construction and aerospace industries. The EU also offers a distinctive message. In contrast to the American Dream,

> The European Dream emphasizes community relationships over individual autonomy, cultural diversity over assimilation, quality of life over the accumulation of wealth, sustainable development over unlimited material growth, deep play over unrelenting toil, universal human rights and the rights of nature over property rights, and global cooperation over the unilateral exercise of power.[1]

Successful enlargement, combined with already-successful monetary union and economic integration, would see the EU poised either to challenge U.S. hegemony or to become a senior partner among superpowers. EU citizens, however, have expressed reservations about establishing a Constitution to underpin a supranational political union. There are also concerns that the extension of the EU to 30 countries would risk destroying its own internal balance and cohesion. Europe's future international role also depends greatly on whether it undertakes major structural economic and social reforms to deal with the problem of its aging workforce. This will demand more immigration and better integration of workers, most of whom are likely to be coming from North Africa and the Middle East. Even if more migrant workers are not allowed in, western Europe will have to integrate a growing Muslim population. Barring increased legal entry may only lead to more illegal migrants who will be harder to integrate, posing a long-term problem. It is possible to imagine European nations successfully adapting their workforces and social welfare systems to these new realities, but it is harder to see some countries—Germany, for example—successfully assimilating millions of new immigrant workers in a short period of time.

East and South Asia According to the U.S. National Intelligence Council (NIC), the greatest benefits of globalization will accrue to countries and groups that can access and adopt new technologies. The Council's report on *Mapping the Global Future* concludes that China and India are well positioned to become technology leaders and that the expected next revolution in high technology—involving the convergence of nano-, bio-, information and materials technology—could further bolster the prospects of China and India. Both countries are investing in basic research in these fields and are well placed to be leaders in a number of key fields. As the NIC report puts it:

> The likely emergence of China and India, as well as others, as new major global players—similar to the advent of a united Germany in the 19th century and a powerful United States in the early 20th century—will transform the geopolitical landscape, with impacts potentially as dramatic as those in the previous two centuries. In the same way that commentators refer to the 1900s as the "American Century," the 21st century may be seen as the time when Asia, led by China and India, comes into its own. A combination of sustained high economic growth, expanding military capabilities, and large populations will be at the root of the expected rapid rise in economic and political power for both countries. . . . Barring an abrupt reversal of the process of globalization or any major upheavals in these countries, the rise of these new powers is a virtual certainty.[2]

Most forecasts indicate that by 2020 China's GNI will exceed that of individual Western economic powers except the United States. India's GNI will have overtaken or be on the threshold of overtaking the larger European economies. Because of the sheer size of China's and India's populations—projected by the U.S. Census Bureau to be 1.4 billion and almost 1.3 billion, respectively, by 2020—their standard of living need not approach Western levels for these countries to become important economic powers. How China and India exercise their growing power and whether they relate cooperatively or competitively to other powers in the international system, however, are key uncertainties.

[1]J. Rifkin, *The European Dream*, Los Angeles: J. P. Tarcher, 2004.
[2]National Intelligence Council, *Mapping the Global Future. Report of the National Intelligence Council's 2020 Project*, Washington, DC: U.S. Government Printing Office, 2004, p. 11.

So, although China is not currently part of the core of the world-system, many observers predict a "Pacific Destiny" for the 21st century. In this scenario, China will be the hub of a world economy whose center of gravity is around the rim of the Pacific rather than the North Atlantic. China certainly has the potential to be a contender. It has a vast territory with a comprehensive resource base and a long history of political, cultural, and economic integration. It has the largest population of any country in the world (1.3 billion in 2004), and an economy that has been growing very rapidly. Beginning in 1978, under the leadership of Deng Xiaoping, China completely reorganized and revitalized its economy. Agriculture was decollectivized, with communist collective farms modified to allow a degree of private profit taking. State-owned industries were closed or privatized, and centralized state planning was dismantled in order to foster private entrepreneurship.

Since 1992, China has extended its "open door" policy (that is, allowing trade with the rest of the world) beyond its special economic zones and allowed foreign investment aimed at Chinese domestic markets. In the 1980s and early 1990s, when the world economy was sluggish, China's manufacturing sector grew by almost 15 percent each year, and has continued into the 2000s with double-digit growth. China's increased participation in the world economy has created an entirely new situation, causing a deflationary trend in world prices for manufactures (**Figure 12.8**). Not only does the Chinese economy's size make it a major producer, but its huge labor force

FIGURE 12.8 China's changing role in the world economy China's reemergence as a significant player in the world economy is reflected in trends of inward investment, exports, manufacturing output, and oil consumption.

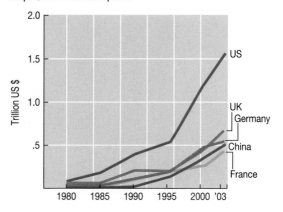

Stock of Inward Foreign Direct Investment, 1980 – 2003

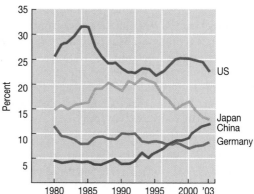

Share of World Manufacturing, 1980 – 2003

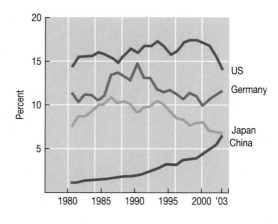

Share of World's Exports, 1980 – 2003

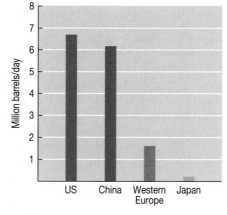

Growth in Demand for Oil, 2000 – 2020

ensures that its wage levels will not approach Western levels for a long time, thus guaranteeing a key competitive advantage. Overall, China's economy is already the fourth largest in the world after the European Union, the United States, and Japan.

Nevertheless, China's economy will remain largely agrarian for some time yet. The task of feeding, clothing, and housing its enormous population will also constrain its ability to modernize to the point where it can dominate the world economy. Meanwhile, a great deal of social and political reform remains to be accomplished before free enterprise can really flourish. Finally, before China can emerge as a hegemonic power it must resolve a major feature of its contemporary human geography: the dramatically uneven development that has been a consequence of its economic reforms. The positive spiral of cumulative causation has affected only the larger cities and coastal regions, while the vast interior regions of the country have become increasingly impoverished. Ironically, this is the very same geographical pattern of spatial polarization that motivated Chinese communists to revolt in the 1940s. Today, it is a source of potential unrest and of political instability among the central government, the provincial governments of the interior regions, and the provincial governments of the coastal regions.

In the short term, China mostly needs to develop its internal market and moderate its growth. In some respects, China has been following such a strategy with a big program of infrastructure investment. Recently, it has also been trying to boost domestic demand by easing credit. But it remains to be seen whether the Chinese government can continue to control the situation. Managing things is not easy when capitalist energy is turning life upside down, creating vast new wealth amidst a poor society based on different principles.

Alternatively, we may not see the same kind of hegemonic power in the new world order of the 21st century: There may not be a new hegemony at all. Instead, the globalization of economics and culture may result in a polycentric network of nations, regions, and world cities bound together by flows of goods and capital. Order may come not from military strength rooted in national economic muscle but from a mutual dependence on *trans*national production and marketing, with stability and regulation provided by powerful international institutions (such as the World Bank, the IMF, the World Trade Organization, the European Union, NATO, and the United Nations).

At the Margins Whatever the outcome of any new world order, the prospects for peripheral countries and marginalized populations are highly unfavorable. Notwithstanding the debt-relief packages and proclamations of the G8 group of the world's most affluent countries and the grassroots popularity of the Live8 concerts in 2005 (**Figure 12.9**), peripheral countries and marginalized populations face near-insurmountable obstacles to significant progress. It is not just that they have already been dismissed by investors in the core, nor that their domestic economies are simply threadbare. They face unprecedented levels of demographic, environmental, economic, and societal stress. In the worst-off regions—including much of West and Central Africa, for example—the events of the next 15 to 20 years are going to be played out from a starting point of scarce basic resources, serious environmental degradation, overpopulation, disease, unprovoked crime, refugee migrations, and criminal anarchy.

African countries will be further disadvantaged because the prices of commodities produced there and in other peripheral locations have been dropping, while imported goods from the core have become more expensive. This means that many peripheral countries, especially in Africa, have and will probably continue to have reduced purchasing power in the global marketplace because of the decline in the value of their exports. Continuing to disable the periphery's full participation in the global economy are the combined effects of external debt crisis, dwindling amounts of foreign aid, insufficient resources to purchase technology or develop indigenous technological innovations, and the high costs of marketing and transporting commodities.

FIGURE 12.9 Celebrity causes in Africa A recent article in the *New York Times* SundayStyles section described how Africa has recently become "hot" as a site for celebrities who may be promoting themselves as they align themselves with causes there. Shown here is Angelina Jolie, one of the best-known Hollywood stars, who has taken on the cause of orphaned African children. Other celebrities who have made public visits to Africa include Drew Barrymore, Don Cheadle, Matt Damon, Ashley Judd, Jessica Simpson, Oprah Winfrey, and Madonna.

Post-independence ideals of modernization and democracy now seem more remote than ever in these regions. Corrupt dictators, epitomized by The Democratic Republic of the Congo's former President Mobutu and Nigeria's former President General Abacha, have created "kleptocracies" (as in *kleptomania*: an irresistible desire to steal) in place of democracies. In early 2004, the anti-corruption watchdog Transparency International released a list of what it believes to be the ten most self-enriching leaders in recent years. In order of amount allegedly stolen, they are: former Indonesian President Suharto (U.S.$15 billion–$35 billion), former Philippine President Ferdinand Marcos ($5 billion–$10 billion), former Zairian President Mobutu Sésé Seko ($5 billion), former Nigerian President Sani Abacha ($2 billion–$5 billion), former Yugoslav President Slobodan Milosevic ($1 billion), former Haitian President Jean-Claude Duvalier ($300 million–$800 million), former Peruvian President Alberto Fujimori ($600 million), former Ukrainian Prime Minister Pavlo Lazarenko ($114 million–$200 million), former Nicaraguan President Arnoldo Alemán ($100 million), and former Philippine President Joseph Estrada ($78 million–$80 million).

Some governments, including those of Liberia, Sudan, and Sierra Leone, lost control of large parts of their territories: groups of unemployed youths plunder travelers; tribal groups war with one another; refugees trudge from war zones to camps and back again; environmental degradation proceeds unchecked (**Figure 12.10**). The U.S. State Department has estimated that during the 1990s, wars in Africa produced more than 8 million refugees and claimed 7 to 8 million lives, including about 2 million children. One of the bloodiest wars, between Eritrea and Ethiopia, was launched in May 1998 and centers on an ill-defined border region known as Badme. Most conflicts in Africa, however, are civil wars that have become complicated and intractable as guerilla groups have proliferated and divided into warring factions. Among the worst-affected countries are Algeria, Angola, Burundi, Congo, Democratic Republic of Congo (formerly Zaire), Guinea-Bissau, Rwanda, Sierra Leone, Somalia, Sudan, and Uganda.

Amid this chaos, disease has prospered. Parts of Africa may be more dangerously unhealthy today than they were 100 years ago. Malaria and tuberculosis are out of control over much of Sub-Saharan Africa, while AIDS is truly epidemic. In Uganda, where annual spending on health is less than $5 per person (compared with international debt repayments of almost $20 per person), one in five children die before their fifth birthday, and HIV/AIDS is epidemic among young adults. More than 23 million people in

FIGURE 12.10 Environmental degradation in Burma A small village where opium and rice farmers live can be seen behind the denuded landscape in the foreground that has been cleared by the slash-and-burn method. Deforestation is acute in this region, as a consequence of timber exploitation for export to China. Burma is one of the least environmentally protected countries in Southeast Asia.

Sub-Saharan Africa in 2002 were infected with HIV, or one in every 12 people. Almost 30 percent of Zimbabwe's population aged 15 to 49 is infected with HIV, followed by Botswana and Zambia, with rates of 25 percent and 19 percent, respectively. Eight other African countries have infection rates of more than 10 percent of their adult populations.

Altogether, Africa, with just 10 percent of the world's total population, is home to more than two-thirds of the world's 33 million HIV-infected people. HIV/AIDS has left 6 million African children orphaned, accounting for 7 percent of the world's HIV/AIDS orphans. In the nine most severely affected countries in the world, all of them in Africa, a child born in 2003 will have a life expectancy of 43 years instead of 60 years in the absence of HIV/AIDS. And while the rate of increase in HIV-positive cases in core countries has leveled off, it is still increasing dramatically in much of Africa. Given all this, it is not surprising that much of Africa is unattractive to the globalizing world economy.

CRITICAL ISSUES AND THREATS

To this review of future prospects for regional change, we must add the interdependent and less predictable dynamics of politics, culture, society, and environment. From what we have discussed already, it is clear that the immediate future will be characterized by a phase of geopolitical and geoeconomic transition, by the continued overall expansion of the world economy, and by the continued globalization of industry, finance, and culture. The processes of change involved in shaping this kind of future will inevitably bring forth critical issues, changes, conflicts, and threats. We can identify what several of these might involve: fault lines of cultural dissonance, complex security issues, and sustainability.

Globalizing Culture and Cultural Dissonance

At one level, globalization has brought a homogenization of culture through the language of consumer goods. This is the material culture of the core, enmeshed by Airbus jets, CNN, music video channels, cell phones, and the Internet; and swamped by Coca-Cola, Budweiser, McDonald's, GAP clothing, Nikes, Walkmans, Nintendos, Toyotas, Disney franchising, and formula-driven Hollywood movies. Furthermore, sociologists have recognized that a distinctive culture of "global metropolitanism" is emerging among the transnational elite. This is simply homogenized culture at a higher plane of consumption (French wines instead of Budweiser, Hugo Boss clothes instead of Levis, BMWs instead of Toyotas, and so on). The members of this new culture are people who hold international conference calls, who make decisions and transact investments that are transnational in scope, and who edit the news, design and market international products, and travel the world for business and pleasure.

These trends are transcending some of the traditional cultural differences around the world. We can, perhaps, more easily identify with people who use the same products, listen to the same music, and appreciate the same sports stars that we do. At the same time, however, sociocultural cleavages are opening up between the elites and the marginalized. By focusing people's attention on material consumption, these trends are also obscuring the emergence of new fault lines—between previously compatible cultural groups and between ideologically divergent civilizations.

Several reasons account for the appearance of these new fault lines. One is the release of pressure brought about by the end of the Cold War. The evaporation of external threats has allowed people to focus on other perceived threats and intrusions. Another is the globalization of culture itself. The more people's lives are homogenized through their jobs and their material culture, the more many of them want to revive subjectivity, reconstruct we/us feelings, and reestablish a distinctive cultural identity. For the marginalized, a different set of processes is at work, however. The juxtaposition of poverty, environmental stress, and crowded living conditions alongside the materialism of the fast world creates a fertile climate for gangsterism. The same juxtaposition also

FIGURE 12.11 Surveillance society Security cameras have become a fact of life in most major cities in the United States, Canada, and Europe and are becoming increasingly prevalent in the world's periphery. Pictured here is a closed-circuit television camera installed in New York's Times Square after the terrorist bombings in London in 2005.

provides the ideal circumstance for the spread and intensification of religious fundamentalism and for fundamentalist-inspired terrorism. This—perhaps more than anything else—represents a source of serious potential cultural dissonance.

The overall result is that cultural fault lines are opening up everywhere. Their presence poses the prospect of some very problematic dimensions of future regional geographies, from the city to the globe. Metropolitan areas face a prospect of fragmented and polarized communities, with outright cultural conflict suppressed only through electronic surveillance (**Figure 12.11**) and the "militarization" of urban space via security posts and "hardened" urban design using fences and gated streets. Of course, this scenario presupposes a certain level of affluence in order to meet the costs of keeping the peace across economic and cultural fault lines. In the unintended metropolises of the periphery, where unprecedented numbers of migrants and refugees will be thrown together, the genuine prospect of anarchy and intercommunal violence exists—unless intergroup differences can be submerged in a common cause, such as religious fundamentalism.

At the subnational level the prospect is one of increasing ethnic/racial rivalry, parochialism, and insularity. Examples of these phenomena can be found throughout the world. In Canada the secessionism of the French-speaking Quebeçois heightens ethnic rivalry. In the United States the insistence of some Hispanic groups on the installation of Spanish as an alternative official language has the same effect. In Europe, examples are the secessionism (from Spain) of the Basques, the separatist movement of the Catalans (also in Spain), the regional elitism of Northern Italy, and, recently, outright war among Serbs and Croats. In South Asia, examples are provided by the recurring hostility between Hindus and Muslims throughout the Indian subcontinent and between the Hindu Tamils and Buddhist Sinhalese of Sri Lanka. In Africa ethnic rivalry, parochialism, and insularity are reflected in the continuing conflict between the Muslim majority in northern Sudan and the Christian minority in the south and in widespread unrest in northeast Democratic Republic of Congo. Where the future brings prosperity, tensions and hostilities such as these will probably be muted; where it brings economic hardship or decline, they will undoubtedly intensify.

The prospect for the globe is of a rising consciousness of people's identities in terms of their broader historical, geographical, and racial "civilizations": Western, Latin American, Confucian, Japanese, Islamic, Hindu, and Slavic-Orthodox. According to some observers, deepening cleavages of this sort could replace the ideological differences of the Cold War era as the major source of tension and potential conflict in the world. And as many globalization experts have observed, they may also point the way toward new foundations for cooperation and unity as people see themselves less as citizens of a particular nation or state and more as world citizens sharing a common global cause.

Security

In addition to cultural fault lines, globalization will inevitably generate enormous economic and, consequently, political upheavals that will translate into a complex set of security issues. With the gradual integration of China, India, and other emerging countries into the global economy, hundreds of millions of working-age adults will become available for employment in a more integrated world labor market. This enormous workforce—a growing portion of which will be well educated—will be an attractive, competitive source of low-cost labor at the same time that technological innovation is expanding the range of globally mobile occupations. The transition will hit the middle classes of the core regions in particular, bringing more rapid job turnover and requiring professional retooling, while outsourcing on an increasing scale will intensify the anti-globalization movement. Where these pressures lead will depend on how political leaders respond, how flexible labor markets become, and whether overall economic growth is sufficiently robust to absorb a growing number of displaced workers. In some regions, it is quite possible that weak governments, lagging economies, religious extremism, and increasing numbers of young people will align to create a "perfect storm" for internal conflict, with far-reaching repercussions for security elsewhere.

Such internal conflicts, particularly those that involve ethnic groups straddling national boundaries, risk escalating into regional conflicts and the failure of states, with expanses of territory and populations devoid of effective governmental control. These territories can become sanctuaries for transnational terrorists (such as Al-Qaeda in Afghanistan) or for criminals and drug cartels (such as in Colombia). According to the U.S. National Intelligence Council, within the next 15 years Al-Qaeda itself will likely be superceded by similarly inspired Islamic extremist groups, and there is a substantial risk that broad Islamic movements akin to Al-Qaeda will merge with local separatist movements.[3] Information technology, allowing for instant connectivity, communication, and learning, will enable the terrorist threat to become increasingly decentralized, evolving into an eclectic array of groups, cells, and individuals that do not need a stationary headquarters to plan and carry out operations. Training materials, targeting guidance, weapons know-how, and fund-raising will become virtual (i.e., online). As biotechnology information becomes more widely available, the number of people who can potentially misuse such information and wreak widespread loss of life will increase. Moreover, as biotechnology advances become more ubiquitous, stopping the progress of offensive biological warfare programs will become increasingly difficult. Over the next 10 to 20 years, there is a risk that advances in biotechnology will allow the creation of advanced biological agents designed to target specific systems—human, animal, or crops.

Economic and political turbulence and instability will also be conducive to transnational crime. Transnational crime syndicates pose a considerable threat to global security. They distribute harmful materials, weapons, and drugs; exploit local communities; disrupt fragile ecosystems; and control significant economic resources. In 2003, transnational crime syndicates may have grossed up to $2 trillion—more than all national economies except the United States, Japan, and Germany.[4] The bulk of crime syndicates' revenue comes from drug trafficking, but other significant sources include environmental products—everything from protected plants and animals to hazardous waste and banned chemicals. Trafficking in humans—for labor, sex work, and even for the removal of kidneys or other organs for transplant purposes—is another aspect of transnational crime. The U.S. State Department estimates that at least 600,000 to 800,000 people are sold internationally each year. Weapons trafficking earns the syndicates comparatively little—estimated at less than $1 billion annually—but it contributes significantly to the complex security issues facing most countries. There are few international laws on arms trafficking, and UN arms embargoes often go unforced.

Another dimension of the security issues associated with globalization concerns the environmental and human health issues that have emerged as a result of increases in global commerce and tourism. As people and goods move around the world, so do other species, pathogens, and zoonotic diseases (transmitted between animals and people; **Figure 12.12**). New plant and animal species can invade ecosystems, choke pastures, disrupt water systems, drive other species to extinction,

FIGURE 12.12 Global disease This photo shows an example of reactions to the accelerated global movement of pathogens facilitated by the increased connectedness of the world. Shown are members of Hong Kong's Health Department at the International Airport wearing protective suits during a simulated scenario in which a passenger onboard a Cathay Pacific flight was suspected of carrying SARS or bird flu.

[3]*Ibid.*, p. 9.
[4]E. Assadourian, "Transnational Crime," in Worldwatch Institute, *State of the World 2005*, New York: W. W. Norton, 2005, p. 20.

and result in expensive and unanticipated consequences. In the United States, the European zebra mussel has invaded freshwater systems across almost half of the country, displacing other marine species and costing an estimated $1 billion in eradication costs during the 1990s. The total costs of losses from all kinds of invasive species in the United States now exceeds $138 billion annually (**Figure 12.13**). The diffusion of contagious diseases such as influenza, and of zoonotic diseases such as Anthrax, Avian Flu, Ebola, and West Nile Virus epidemics, also poses a much greater security risk as a result of the speed and intensity of global flows—yet another dimension of the "risk society" (see Chapter 1) associated with globalization.

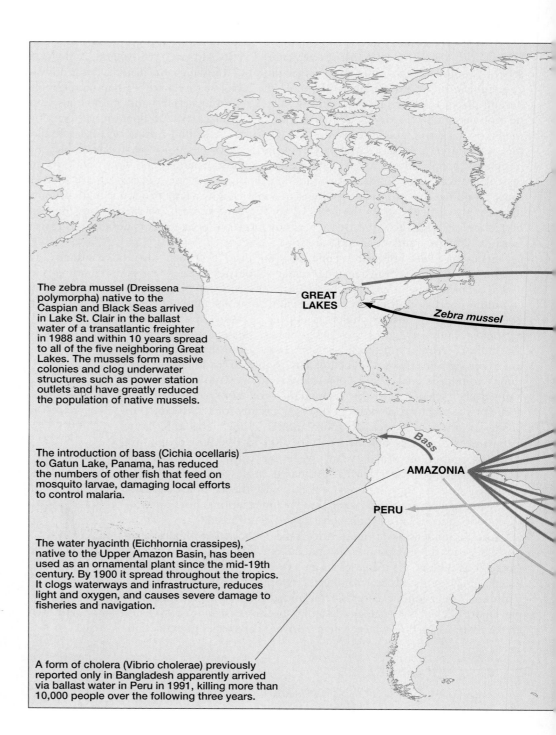

The zebra mussel (Dreissena polymorpha) native to the Caspian and Black Seas arrived in Lake St. Clair in the ballast water of a transatlantic freighter in 1988 and within 10 years spread to all of the five neighboring Great Lakes. The mussels form massive colonies and clog underwater structures such as power station outlets and have greatly reduced the population of native mussels.

The introduction of bass (Cichia ocellaris) to Gatun Lake, Panama, has reduced the numbers of other fish that feed on mosquito larvae, damaging local efforts to control malaria.

The water hyacinth (Eichhornia crassipes), native to the Upper Amazon Basin, has been used as an ornamental plant since the mid-19th century. By 1900 it spread throughout the tropics. It clogs waterways and infrastructure, reduces light and oxygen, and causes severe damage to fisheries and navigation.

A form of cholera (Vibrio cholerae) previously reported only in Bangladesh apparently arrived via ballast water in Peru in 1991, killing more than 10,000 people over the following three years.

FIGURE 12.13 Worldwide invasive species Shown is a sampling of the many invasive species that are changing the world's ecosystems. (*Source:* Millennium Ecosystem Assessment Board, *Living Beyond Our Means: Natural Assets and Human Well-being.* Washington, DC: World Resources Institute, 2005, p. 13.)

Sustainability

As we saw throughout this text, the world currently faces a daunting list of environmental threats: the destruction of tropical rain forests and the consequent loss of biodiversity; widespread, health-threatening pollution; the degradation of soil, water, and marine resources essential to food production; stratospheric ozone depletion; acid rain, and so on. Most of these threats are greatest in the world's periphery, where daily environmental pollution and degradation represent a catastrophe that will continue to unfold, in slow motion, in the coming years (see Geography Matters: The Asian Brown Cloud, p. 586).

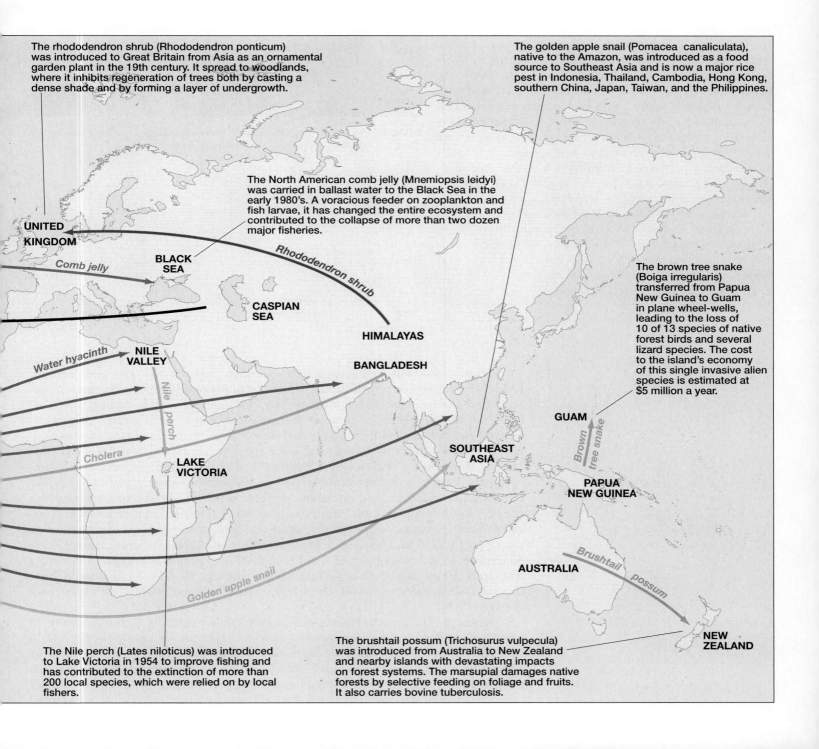

The rhododendron shrub (Rhododendron ponticum) was introduced to Great Britain from Asia as an ornamental garden plant in the 19th century. It spread to woodlands, where it inhibits regeneration of trees both by casting a dense shade and by forming a layer of undergrowth.

The golden apple snail (Pomacea canaliculata), native to the Amazon, was introduced as a food source to Southeast Asia and is now a major rice pest in Indonesia, Thailand, Cambodia, Hong Kong, southern China, Japan, Taiwan, and the Philippines.

The North American comb jelly (Mnemiopsis leidyi) was carried in ballast water to the Black Sea in the early 1980's. A voracious feeder on zooplankton and fish larvae, it has changed the entire ecosystem and contributed to the collapse of more than two dozen major fisheries.

The brown tree snake (Boiga irregularis) transferred from Papua New Guinea to Guam in plane wheel-wells, leading to the loss of 10 of 13 species of native forest birds and several lizard species. The cost to the island's economy of this single invasive alien species is estimated at $5 million a year.

The Nile perch (Lates niloticus) was introduced to Lake Victoria in 1954 to improve fishing and has contributed to the extinction of more than 200 local species, which were relied on by local fishers.

The brushtail possum (Trichosurus vulpecula) was introduced from Australia to New Zealand and nearby islands with devastating impacts on forest systems. The marsupial damages native forests by selective feeding on foliage and fruits. It also carries bovine tuberculosis.

UNITED KINGDOM

Comb jelly

BLACK SEA

Rhododendron shrub

CASPIAN SEA

HIMALAYAS

BANGLADESH

Water hyacinth

NILE VALLEY

Nile perch

Cholera

LAKE VICTORIA

Golden apple snail

GUAM

Brown tree snake

SOUTHEAST ASIA

PAPUA NEW GUINEA

Brushtail possum

AUSTRALIA

NEW ZEALAND

GEOGRAPHY MATTERS

The Asian Brown Cloud

At the heart of the World Summit on Sustainable Development in Johannesburg in September 2002 was the question: How can developing nations grow economically without overburdening Earth's environment and creating an uninhabitable planet for future generations? Emblematic of this issue is the Asian Brown Cloud, a blanket of air pollution 3 kilometers (nearly 2 miles) thick that hovers over most of the tropical Indian Ocean and South, Southeast and East Asia, stretching from the Arabian Peninsula across India, Southeast Asia, and China almost to Korea. The brown haze was first identified by U.S. Air Force pilots but is now clearly visible in satellite photographs and from the Himalayas (**Figure 1**).

The Asian Brown Cloud consists of sulfates, nitrates, organic substances, black carbon, and fly ash, along with several other pollutants. It is an accumulated cocktail of contamination resulting from a dramatic increase in the burning of fossil fuels in vehicles, industries, and power stations in Asia's megacities, from forest fires used to clear land, and from the emissions from millions of inefficient cookers burning wood or cow dung. A study of the Asian Brown Cloud sponsored by the UN Environment Programme and involving more than 200 scientists suggests that the Asian Brown Cloud not only influences local weather but also may have worldwide consequences.

The smog of the Asian Brown Cloud reduces the amount of solar radiation reaching the Earth's surface by 10 to 15 percent, with a consequent decline in the productivity of crops. But it can also trap heat, leading to warming of the lower atmosphere. It suppresses rainfall in some areas and increases it in others, while

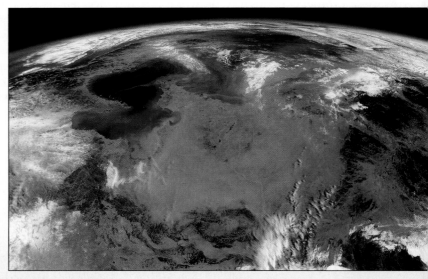

FIGURE I Asian Brown Cloud This view shows a dense haze over eastern China, looking east across the Yellow Sea toward Korea.

damaging forests and crops because of acid rain. The haze is also believed to be responsible for hundreds of thousands of premature deaths from respiratory diseases.

Source: P. L. Knox and S. A. Marston, *Human Geography: Places and Regions in Global Context*, 4th ed. Upper Saddle River, NJ: Prentice Hall, 2006.

Future trends will only intensify the contrasts between rich and poor regions. Environmental problems will be inseparable from processes of demographic change, economic development, and human welfare. In addition, it is becoming clear that environmental problems are going to be increasingly enmeshed in matters of national security and regional conflict. The spatial *interdependence* of economic, environmental, and social problems means that some parts of the world are ecological time bombs. The prospect of civil unrest and mass migrations resulting from the pressures of rapidly growing populations, deforestation, soil erosion, water depletion, air pollution, disease epidemics, and intractable poverty is real. These specters are alarming not only for the peoples of the affected regions but also for the peoples of rich and faraway countries, whose continued prosperity will depend on processes of globalization that are not disrupted by large-scale environmental disasters, unmanageable mass migrations, or the breakdown of stability in the world-system as a whole. U.S. policy effectively denied such concerns when President George W. Bush announced in 2001 that the United States would no longer honor its commitment to the Kyoto agreement (**Figure 12.14**).

Despite the fact that the United States appears to be excluding itself from efforts to solve some of Earth's most pressing environmental problems, we cannot simply wait to see what the future will hold. If we are to have a better future (and if we are to *deserve* a better future), we must use our understanding of the world—and of geographical patterns and processes—to work toward more desirable outcomes. No discipline is more relevant to the ideal of sustainable development than geography. As British geographer

W. M. Adams has observed, where else can the science of the environment (physical geography) be married to an understanding of economic, technological, social, political, and cultural change (human geography)? What other discipline offers insights into environmental change, and who but geographers can cope with the diversity of environments and the sheer range of scales at which it is necessary to manage global change?

Those of us in the richer countries of the world have a special responsibility for leadership in sustainable development, because our present affluence is based on a cumulative past (and present) exploitation of the world's resources that is disproportionate to our numbers. We also happen to have the financial, technical, and human resources to enable us to take the lead in developing cleaner, less resource-intensive technologies, in transforming our economies to protect and work with natural systems, in providing more equitable access to economic opportunities and social services, and in supporting the technological and political frameworks necessary for sustainable development in poor countries. We cannot do it all at once, but we will certainly deserve the scorn and resentment of future generations if we do not try.

ADJUSTING TO THE FUTURE

Resources and Development

The expansion of the world economy and the globalization of industry will undoubtedly boost the overall demand for raw materials of various kinds, and this will spur the development of some previously underexploited but resource-rich regions in Africa, Europe, and Asia. Raw materials, however, will be only a fraction of future resource needs. The main issue, by far, will be energy resources. World energy consumption has been increasing steadily over the recent past (**Figure 12.15**). As the periphery is industrialized and its population increases further, the global demand for energy will expand rapidly. Basic industrial development tends to be highly energy-intensive. The International Energy Agency, assuming (fairly optimistically) that energy in peripheral countries will be generated in the future as efficiently as it is today in core countries, estimates that developing-country energy consumption will more than double by 2025, lifting total world energy demand by almost 50 percent. By 2020, peripheral and semiperipheral regions will account for more than half of world energy consumption. Much of this will be driven by industrialization geared to meet the growing worldwide market for consumer goods, such as private automobiles, air conditioners, refrigerators, televisions, and household appliances.

Without higher rates of investment in exploration and extraction than at present, production will be slow to meet the escalating demand. Many experts believe that current levels of production in fact represent "peak oil" and that by 2020 global oil production may be only 90 percent of its current peak. The result might well be a temporary but significant increase in energy prices. Geographical ramifications would follow: Companies would be forced to seriously reconsider their operations, causing core households into a serious reevaluation of their residential preferences and commuting behavior; peripheral households would be forced further into poverty. If the oil-price crisis of 1973 is anything to go by (after crude oil prices were quadrupled by the OPEC cartel), the outcome could be a significant

FIGURE 12.14 Climate change activism At the 2005 UN Climate Change Conference in Montreal, Quebec, Canada, thousands of people marched in protest against global warming. The demonstrators urged the United States to join the 148 nations who have signed the Kyoto Protocol.

FIGURE 12.15 Trends in energy consumption Global commercial energy consumption is expected to continue to rise steadily over the next two decades as peripheral countries continue to develop economically and require a larger share of the global energy pie. (*Source:* History: Energy Information Administration, *International Energy Annual 2003*, and Projections: Energy Information Administration, *Systems for the Analysis of Global Energy Markets, 2006.* Available at http://www.eia.doe.gov/iea/.)

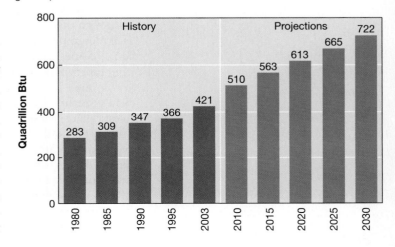

revision of patterns of industrial location and a substantial reorganization of metropolitan form. Significantly higher energy costs may change the optimal location for many manufacturers, leading to deindustrialization in some regions and to new occasions for economic advantage in others. Higher fuel costs will encourage some people to live nearer their places of work; others will be able to take advantage of telecommuting to reduce personal transportation costs. It is also relevant to note that almost all of the increase in oil production over the next 15 or 20 years is likely to come from outside the core economies. This means that the world economy will become increasingly dependent on OPEC governments, which control more than 70 percent of all proven oil reserves, most of them in the Middle East.

In countries that can afford research and development, new materials will reduce the growth of demand both for energy and for traditional raw materials such as aluminum, copper, and tin. Japan, for instance, may be able to reduce motor vehicle fuel consumption by 15 percent (and thereby reduce its total fuel oil consumption by 3 percent) by using ceramics for major parts of engines. It may also be possible to substitute ceramics for expensive rare metals in heat-resistant materials. Improved engineering and product design will also make it possible to reduce the need for the input of some resources. U.S. cars, for example, were almost 20 percent lighter in 2006 than they were in 1974. In addition, of course, the future may well bring technological breakthroughs that dramatically improve energy efficiency or make renewable energy sources (such as wind, tidal, and solar power) commercially viable. As with earlier breakthroughs that produced steam energy, electricity, gasoline engines, and nuclear power, such events would catalyze a major reorganization of the world's economic geographies.

The past 25 years have seen a growing awareness of how continued globalization will affect the regions in which we live. Increasingly, citizens, nongovernmental organizations, and environmental policymakers express concern over the negative outcomes of rapid and enduring global economic growth. However, because growth is so critically tied to improving the lives of poor people around the world, governments are reluctant to limit it. The response from the global community, hammered out during international meetings, through academic publications, and in response to social protest, is a different approach to development than previously existed. This approach is known as globalization, transnational governance, and the state.

Globalization, Transnational Governance, and the State

As we have noted, globalization has been as much about restructuring geoeconomics as it has been about reshaping geopolitics. In fact, the hyperglobalists believe that the impact of globalization on politics has been so profound that it is eroding the powers of the modern state, if not leading to its ultimate disappearance. The hyperglobalists believe that because the modern state is organized around a bounded territory and because globalization is creating a new economic space that is transnational, the state is increasingly unable to respond to the needs of the new transnational economy. Although this text does not subscribe to such a position, we do recognize that the state is undergoing dramatic changes that are restructuring its role with respect to both local, domestic concerns and global, transnational ones. Moreover, these changes are very much part of recent history.

In the 20th century, from the end of World War II until 1989, when the Berlin Wall was dismantled, world politics was organized around two superpowers. The capitalist West rallied around the United States and the communist East gathered around the Soviet Union. But with the fall of the Berlin Wall signaling the end of communism, a bipolar world order came to an end and a new world order, organized around global capitalism, emerged and has solidified around a new set of political powers and institutions that recast the role of the state in a new context. The new world order predicated on the fall of communism and enabled by the technological (particularly communication and transportation) changes of the last 25 years is restructuring the architecture as well as the conduct of contemporary politics at both the international and the domestic level.

This text has referred to regional and supranational organizations such as the EU, the North American Free Trade Agreement (NAFTA), the Association of Southeast Asian Nations (ASEAN), OPEC, and the WTO (see Chapter 1 for a more extended discussion). We have also noted that this type of organization is unique in modern history. These organizations aim to treat the world or the respective regions as seamless trading areas not hindered by the rules that ordinarily regulate national economies. The increasing importance of these trade-facilitating organizations is the most telling indicator that the world, besides being transformed into one global economic space, is also experiencing global geopolitical transformations. Another example of growing transnational governance is provided by the international response to the emergence of global environmental problems such as fisheries depletion, global warming, and the loss of biodiversity. The United Nations connects with other international organizations to develop treaties and agreements that seek to manage resources and pollution at a global level. But rather than disappearing altogether, the powers and roles of the modern state are changing as it is forced to interact with these sorts of organizations as well as with a whole range of other political institutions, associations, and networks.

The point is not that the state is disappearing but rather that it must now contend with a whole new set of processes and other political actors, not only on the international stage but also within its own territory. For instance, geographer Andrew Leyshon has shown how the financial revolution of the 1980s established a transnational financial network that is far beyond the control of any one state, even a very powerful state like the United States, to regulate effectively. In fact, the increasing importance of transnational flows and connections indicates that the state is less a container of political or economic power and more a site of flows and connections.

As we discussed in Chapter 1, the increasing importance of flows and connections means that contemporary globalization has enabled an increasingly shrinking world. Geographers call this phenomenon **time-space convergence**, which is the rate at which places move closer together in terms of travel or communications costs. In addition to allowing people and goods to travel farther faster and to receive and send information more quickly, time-space convergence means that politics and political action have also become global. In short, politics is able to move beyond the confines of the state and into the global arena, where rapid communications enable complex supporting networks to be developed and deployed, thereby facilitating interaction and decision making. A good example of this phenomenon is the protests that occurred in Seattle, Washington, in 1999 over the scheduled meeting of the WTO. Telecommunications, and especially the Internet, enabled the protest leaders to organize and deploy their actions with the participation of interested groups all over the world. These Seattle protests were an expression of truly global politics that matched the global politics of the WTO itself. Thus both institutionalized politics as well as popular political movements are able to be truly global in their reach. Another indication of the increasingly global nature of politics, outside of formal political institutions, is the increase in environmental organizations whose purview and membership are global (**Figure 12.16**).

The involvement of the state in new global activities, the growth of supranational and regional institutions and organizations, the critical significance of transnational corporations to global capital, and the proliferation of transnational social movements and professional organizations is captured by the term **international regime**. The term is meant to convey the idea that the orientation of contemporary politics is now directed to the international arena rather than the national one. This is so much the case that even city governments and local interest groups—from sister city organizations to car clubs—are making connections and conducting their activities beyond as well as within the boundaries of their own states. An example of this

FIGURE 12.16 Growth of international environmental initiatives, 2005 The graph shows the steady and most recent phenomenal growth of multilateral environmental agreements since the mid-1970s. (*Source:* Millennium Ecosystem Assessment Board, *Living Beyond Our Means: Natural Assets and Human Well-being.* Washington, DC: Island Press, 2006, pp. 79 and 80.)

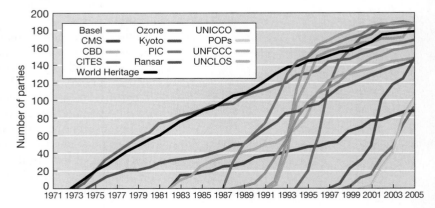

is the human rights movement that has gained ascendancy over the last four to five decades. Until World War II, safeguarding human rights was the provenance of states whose rules and regulations legislated the proper treatment of its citizens, from prisoners to schoolchildren. Since the late 1940s and 1950s, nearly all states have come to accept a comprehensive political and legal framework that focuses on human rights and that allows an international organization to intervene in the operations of a sovereign state that is in violation of the International Bill of Human Rights.

The changing role of the state and the emergence of new regimes of international governance are primary forces shaping the future of world regions. As a result, the contemporary world political order is one in which the state system persists at the same time that a growing number of international, supranational, and regional authority structures are emerging and gaining strength. Such a new political order can be seen to have both fragmenting and integrating influences on the present organization of world regions.

Regional Integration and Fragmentation

Will globalization bring about increased regional integration so that our current regions will remain the building blocks of the world order? Or will overall fragmentation lead to the emergence of new regions? The answers to these two questions are not easy, because for different parts of the world, there is evidence to support both successful integration and continued fragmentation. In Europe, for instance, regional integration has been remarkably successful. Since 1957, the various states of Europe have become increasingly integrated around political and economic concerns, so much so that the European Union (organized in 1957 as the European Economic Community, or EEC) is a shining global example of a coherent and prosperous world region. Elsewhere, however, especially in Africa and Latin America, attempts at regional integration have been far less successful, and in fact, subnational pressures have led to more fragmentation than integration. A helpful way to think about the possibilities for future regional integration is to consider why regional integration might be attractive for some states and troubling for others.

Probably the main reasons to pursue regional integration involve strategic and security issues. As we have discussed, regional trading blocks are created because they are understood to enable economic and trading advantages. The one variable that demonstrates the foundation of contemporary globalization is the increase in global trade linkages (**Figure 12.17**). Regional trading blocks are also believed to provide security for weaker states against economic and political threats. Following the devastation wreaked on Europe by World War II and compounded by the loss of their colonies, the member states of the EEC viewed the regional trading block as a way to increase political and economic leverage in world affairs. It was widely understood that no single state could have exercised the power that a cooperative union could. The perceived military threat of the Soviet Union was also a factor in the decision to establish a regional bloc among the founding, western European, members of the EEC. Finally, since its founding, the still-developing European Union has been seen by smaller and later-joining states—such as Denmark and Ireland—as a way to improve their political and market status, something they would lack if they remained isolated.

But just as there are strong incentives for forming regional blocks, there are also substantial obstacles that make it difficult for states to cooperate and intensify any blocks that already exist. These obstacles tend to revolve around difference and the desire by states to maintain control over their own affairs. The issue of difference centers on the fear that integration can undermine the cultural traditions of any particular nation because cooperation would necessarily require standardization of practices. Because nation-states are rarely homogeneous, the cultural and economic diversity that already exists is often used as a basis for demanding more local control rather than ceding a portion of control to an even more remote political unit.

It is commonly perceived that integration is likely to exacerbate the tensions surrounding difference and increase social problems. These are just the sorts of challenges

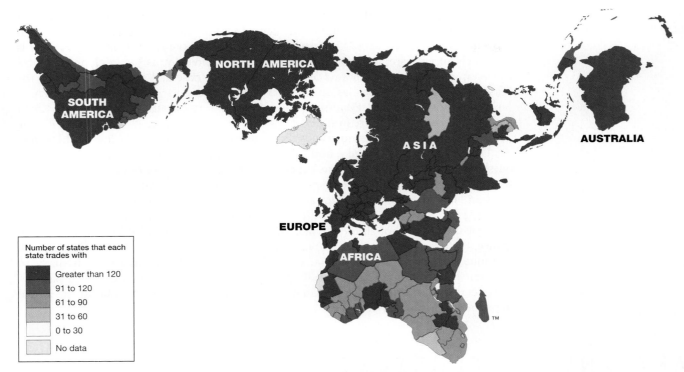

FIGURE 12.17 World trade interconnectedness Since World War II, a number of agreements have been put into place to help foster the multilateral trading patterns shown in this map. Bretton Woods and GATT were particularly important in providing the basis for a multilateral trading order. In 1995 the World Trade Organization transformed and superseded GATT as the primary international trade agency.

that the Latin American and African trading blocks have faced. But it is also important to recognize that even the very successful EU is not immune to these sorts of counterpressures. Britain is currently reluctant to enter into the single EU currency scheme, for instance. Attempts to expand the Asian trading blocks such as ASEAN as well as NAFTA have also raised fears about protecting local interests and maintaining local control.

Because regional integration represents both pros and cons, and mindful that predicting the future is a tricky business, our view is that the contemporary world order of regions is likely to continue over the next decade with some possibility for surprise. As you will recall from Chapter 1, the triadic core consists of Europe, the United States and Canada, and East Asia—even more precisely, the EU, the United States, and Japan. So while one world region is a dominant player on the world stage, the other two are actually states, which, although involved in regional alliances (NAFTA in the case of the United States and ASEAN in the case of Japan), are at the moment the strongest, most aggressively controlling players in their respective regions. We are convinced that the contemporary triadic core is likely to continue to dominate the global economy and, moreover, is more than likely to increase its strength over the first decades of the 21st century, with some additions and transformations.

The additions and transformations we anticipate include the possibility that Mexico may become increasingly integrated into the United States and Canada region through continued growth and expansion of NAFTA. While Mexico will not achieve the level of wealth of either Canada or the United States over this decade, it will probably increase its position in the world economy and alter and add to the strength of the region.

Europe, through the EU, will also continue to develop and gain strength as the current applicant states to the EU (Estonia, Latvia, Lithuania, Poland, Czech Republic, Slovakia, Hungary, Slovenia, Romania, Bulgaria, and Cyprus) become more economically strong and politically stable. And while there will still be an uneven distribution of wealth and development in the transforming EU, the new states will be better off than they were ten years ago, and Europe overall will be economically and politically stronger. East Asia is also likely to gain strength both politically and economically, as Japan climbs out of a recession and China continues to develop its economic base and open its markets to the West. Although China too has an uphill battle in raising its level of wealth to that of Japan, its enormous market and the industriousness of its population suggest that China has a bright economic future in store.

Yet, if we are fairly certain about the continued integration and growth of Europe, the United States and Canada, and East Asia, we must also acknowledge that regions outside the core are not likely to experience any dramatic economic transformations that will catapult them into core status. Latin America, Southeast Asia, South Asia, the Russian Federation, Central Asia, and the Transcaucasus, Sub-Saharan Africa, and the Middle East and North Africa will continue to press for special trading relationships with the core, and though there will certainly be changing fields of influence and allegiance, the relative economic disadvantage of these regions with respect to the core will continue. The region of Australia, New Zealand, and the South Pacific is likely to maintain its position as economically part of the core, though politically not particularly central to it, though the proximity of India and China may also boost the global importance of this region as well.

SUMMARY AND CONCLUSIONS

This chapter discussed the future of contemporary world regions in light of the likely transformations that globalization may bring. We reviewed the three positions in the globalization debate as a way to understand the different approaches to globalization's possible effects. One effect has been the changing role of the nation-state, which, though once the primary political actor on the world stage, must now contend with new transnational and international organizations and institutions in negotiating the fortunes of its national space. Others were issues of sustainability and cultural dissonance.

As the global integration of the world economy continues, we should expect to see that social stratification will continue to increase the gap between the haves and the have-nots of the world, and a three-tiered hierarchy that has already become established will deepen. This hierarchy consists of the elite, the marginalized, and the embattled, who have more in common with their counterparts in other parts of the world than with the other social strata of their own region.

The future of the worst-off peripheral regions could be very bad indeed. They face unprecedented levels of demographic, environmental, and societal stress, with the events of the next 50 years being played out from a starting point of scarce basic resources, serious environmental degradation, overpopulation, disease, unprovoked crime, refugee migrations, and criminal anarchy.

For the core regions, however, the long-term question is one of relative power and dominance. The same factors that consolidate the advantages of the core as a whole—the end of the Cold War, the availability of advanced telecommunications, the transnational reorganization of industry and finance, the liberalization of trade, and the emergence of a global culture—will also open the possibility of a new geopolitical and geoeconomic order, within which the economic and political relationships among core countries might change substantially.

Many aspects of future regional geographies will depend on trends in the demand for resources and on the exploitation of new technologies. The expansion of the world economy and the globalization of industry will undoubtedly boost the overall demand for raw materials of various kinds, and this will spur the development of previously underexploited but resource-rich regions in Africa, Central Asia, and East Asia. Raw materials will be only a fraction of future resource needs, however; the main issue, by far, will be energy resources. It also appears that the present phase of globalization has the potential to create such disparities between the haves and the have-nots (as well as between the core and the periphery) that social unrest will ensue.

At the same time that protests against globalization and new geographies are being waged, the products of a global economy and culture are being widely embraced. The market for blue contact lenses is growing in such unlikely places as Bangkok and Nairobi, and plastic surgery to make eyes more Western-looking is increasing in many Asian countries. CNN as well as American TV soap operas are eagerly viewed in even the most remote corners of the globe. Highway systems, airports, and container facilities are springing up throughout the periphery.

In short, future geographies are being negotiated at this very moment—from the board rooms of transnational corporations to the huts of remote villagers. The outcomes of these negotiations are still in the making as we all, in our daily lives, make seemingly insignificant decisions about what to wear, what to eat, where to work, how to travel, and how to entertain ourselves. These decisions help to either support or undermine the larger forces at work in the global economy, such as where to build factories, what products to make, or how to package and deliver them to the consumer. In essence, future geographies can be very much shaped by us through our understanding of the relatedness of people, places, and environments in a globalized economy.

KEY TERMS

international regime (p. 589)   time-space convergence
short 20th century (p. 565)   (p. 589)

REVIEW QUESTIONS

Testing Your Understanding

1. What is the "short 20th century"?
2. State the principal arguments of the hyperglobalists, skeptics, and transformationalists.
3. How does national debt affect the economic development potential of poor countries?
4. Who are the marginalized, the elite, and the embattled?
5. Describe the link between poverty and pollution.
6. What is sustainable development?
7. What is global metropolitanism?
8. Which trends characterize the modern state at the start of the 21st century?
9. Why is state fragmentation often a more likely outcome than regional integration?
10. If current trends continue, what does the near future hold for the geography of world regions?

Thinking Geographically

1. Identify some key factors behind the regional geographies that developed during the "short 20th century."
2. What may be some of the worldwide demographic trends of the next 25 years?
3. Why does Subcommandante Marcos of Mexico describe current trends in the global economy as "a death sentence for the poor"?
4. Why is sustainable development a global as well as a local issue?
5. Why is global warming considered not just an environmental issue but a security threat to countries like the United States?
6. How is the human rights movement an example of an "international regime"?

FURTHER READING

Allen, J., and Hamnett, C., *A Shrinking World: Global Unevenness and Inequality*. Milton Keynes: Open University Press, 1995.

Anderson, J., Brook, C., and Cochrane, A., *A Global World? Re-ordering Political Space*. Milton Keynes: Open University Press, 1995.

Berry, B. J. L., *Long-Wave Rhythms in Economic Development and Political Behavior*. Baltimore: Johns Hopkins University Press, 1991.

Chatterjee, P., and Finger, M., *The Earth Brokers: Power, Politics, and World Development*. London: Routledge, 1994.

Cohen, R., and Kennedy, P., *Global Sociology*. London: Macmillan, 2000.

De Alcantara, C. H. (ed.), *Social Futures, Global Visions*. Oxford: Blackwell, 1996.

Hammond, A., *Which World? Scenarios for the 21st Century*. Washington, DC: Island Press, 1998.

Held, D., McGrew, A., Goldblatt, D., and Perraton, J., *Global Transformations: Politics, Economics and Culture*. Cambridge: Polity, 1999.

Hirst, P., and Thompson, G., *Globalization in Question: The International Economy and the Possibility of Governance*, 2nd ed. Cambridge: Polity, 1999.

Hoddess, R. (ed.), *Global Corruption Report 2003*. Berlin: Transparency International, 2003.

Holdgate, M., *From Care to Action: Making a Sustainable World*. London: Earthscan, 1996.

Hoogvelt, A., *Globalization and the Postcolonial World: The New Political Economy of Development*. Baltimore: Johns Hopkins University Press, 1997.

Jacobs, J., *Dark Age Ahead: Caution*. New York: Random House, 2004.

Johnston, R. J., Taylor, P. J., and Watts, M. (eds.), *Geographies of Global Change*. Cambridge, MA: Blackwell, 1995.

Millennium Ecosystem Assessment Board, *Living Beyond Our Means: Natural Assets and Human Well-being*. Washington, DC: Island Press, 2006.

National Intelligence Council, *Mapping the Global Future*. Washington, DC: U.S. Government Printing Office, 2004.

O'Meara, P., Mehlinger, H. D., and Krain, M. (eds.), *Globalization and the Challenges of a New Century*. Bloomington: Indiana University Press, 2000.

O'Riordan, T., *Environmental Science for Environmental Management*, 2nd ed. Harlow: Longman, 1998.

ÓTuathail, G., and Luke, T., "Present at the (Dis)integration: Deterritorialization and Reterritorialization in the New Wor(l)d Order," *Annals of the Association of American Geographers* 84(1994), 381–98.

Pearson, I. (ed.), *The Macmillan Atlas of the Future*. New York: Macmillan, 1998.

Smith, N., *The Endgame of Globalization*. New York: Routledge, 2005.

Worldwatch Institute, *State of the World 2005*. New York: W. W. Norton, 2005.

APPENDIX

Maps and Geographic Information Systems

Maps are representations of the world. They are usually two-dimensional, graphic representations that use lines and symbols to convey information or ideas about spatial relationships. Maps express particular interpretations of the world, and they affect how we understand the world and see ourselves in relation to others. As such, all maps are social products. In general, maps reflect the power of the people who draw them. Just including things on a map—literally "putting something on the map"—can be empowering. The design of maps—what they include, what they omit, and how their content is portrayed—inevitably reflects the experiences, priorities, interpretations, and intentions of their authors. The most widely understood and accepted maps—"normal" maps—reflect the view of the world that is dominant in universities and government agencies.

Maps that are designed to represent the *form* of Earth's surface and to show permanent (or at least long-standing) features such as buildings, highways, field boundaries, and political boundaries are called *topographic maps* (see, for example, **Figure A.1**). The usual device for representing the form of Earth's surface is the *contour*, a line that connects points of equal vertical distance above or below a zero data point, usually sea level.

Maps that are designed to represent the spatial dimensions of particular conditions, processes, or events are called *thematic maps*. These can be based on any of a number of devices that allow cartographers or map makers to portray spatial variations

FIGURE A.1 Topographic maps
Topographic maps represent the form of Earth's surface in both horizontal and vertical dimensions. This extract is from a Swiss map of Lugano at the scale of 1: 25,000. The height of landforms is represented by contours (lines that connect points of equal vertical distance above sea level), which on this map are drawn every 20 meters. Features such as roads, power lines, built-up areas, and so on are shown by stylized symbols. Note how the closely spaced contours of the hill slopes represent the shape and form of the land. (*Source:* Extract from Carta Nazionale Della Svizzera, Sheet 1353, 1: 25,000 series, Ufficio Federale di Topografia, 3084 Wabern, Switzerland. Edizione 1998.)

or spatial relationships. One device is the *isoline*, a line (similar to a contour) that connects places of equal data value (for example, air pollution, as in **Figure A.2**). Maps based on isolines are known as *isopleth maps*.

Another common device used in thematic maps is the *proportional symbol*. For example, circles, squares, spheres, cubes, or some other shape can be drawn in proportion to the frequency of occurrence of some phenomenon or event at a given location. Figure 9.19, p. 453 shows an example using proportional circles. Symbols such as arrows or lines can also be drawn proportionally to portray flows between particular places. Simple distributions can be effectively portrayed through *dot maps*, in which a single dot represents a specified number of occurrences of some phenomenon or event.

Yet another type of map is the *choropleth map*, in which tonal shadings are graduated to reflect area variations in num-

bers, frequencies, or densities (see, for example, Figure 1.13, p. 16). Finally, thematic maps can be based on *located charts*, in which graphs or charts are located by place or region. In this way, a tremendous amount of information can be conveyed in one map (see Figure 1.38, p. 43).

MAP SCALES

A *map scale* is simply the ratio between linear distance on a map and linear distance on Earth's surface. It is usually expressed in terms of corresponding lengths, as in "one centimeter equals one kilometer," or as a *representative fraction* (in this case, 1/100,000) or ratio (1:100,000). *Small-scale* maps are based on small representative fractions (for example, 1/1,000,000 or 1/10,000,000). They cover a large part of Earth's surface on the printed page. A map drawn on this page to the scale of 1:10,000,000 would cover about half of the United States; a map drawn to the scale of 1:16,000,000 would easily cover the whole of Europe. *Large-scale* maps are based on larger representative fractions (e.g., 1/25,000 or 1/10,000). A map drawn on this page to the scale 1:10,000 would cover a typical suburban subdivision; a map drawn to the scale of 1:1,000 would cover just a block or two.

MAP PROJECTIONS

A **map projection** is a systematic rendering on a flat surface of the geographic coordinates of the features found on Earth's surface. Because Earth's surface is curved and not a perfect sphere, it is impossible to represent on a flat plane, sheet of paper, or monitor screen without some distortion. Cartographers have devised a number of techniques for projecting **latitude** and **longitude** (**Figure A.3**) onto a flat surface, and the resulting representations each have advantages and disadvantages. None can represent distance correctly in all directions, though many can represent compass bearings or area without distortion. The choice of map projection depends largely on the purpose of the map.

Projections that allow distance to be represented as accurately as possible are called **equidistant projections**. These can represent distance accurately in only one direction (usually north–south), although they usually provide accurate scale in the perpendicular direction (which in most cases is the equator). Equidistant projections are often more aesthetically pleasing for representing Earth as a whole, or large portions of it. An example is the Polyconic projection (**Figure A.4**).

Projections on which compass directions are rendered accurately are known as **conformal projections**. On the Mercator projection (see Figure A.4), for example, a compass bearing between any two points is plotted as a straight line. As a result, the Mercator projection has been widely used in navigation for hundreds of years. The Mercator projection was also widely used as the standard classroom wall map of the world for many years, and its image of the world has entered deeply into general consciousness. As a result, many Europeans and North Americans have an exaggerated sense of the size of the northern continents and underestimate the size of Africa.

FIGURE A.2 Isoline maps Isoline maps portray spatial information by connecting points of equal data value. Contours on topographic maps (see Figure A.1) are a type of isoline. This map shows one type of air pollution in the eastern United States. (*Source: Reprinted with permission of Prentice Hall, from J. M. Rubenstein, The Cultural Landscape: An Introduction to Human Geography, 1996, p. 584. Adapted from William K. Stevens, "Study of Acid Rain Uncovers Threat to Far Wider Area," New York Times, January 16, 1990, p. 21, map.)*

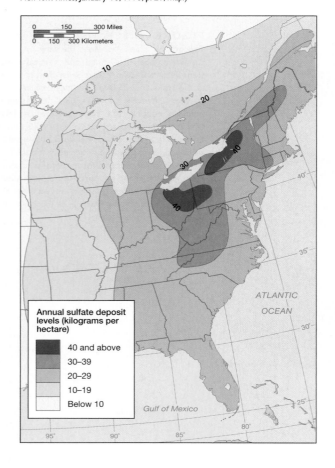

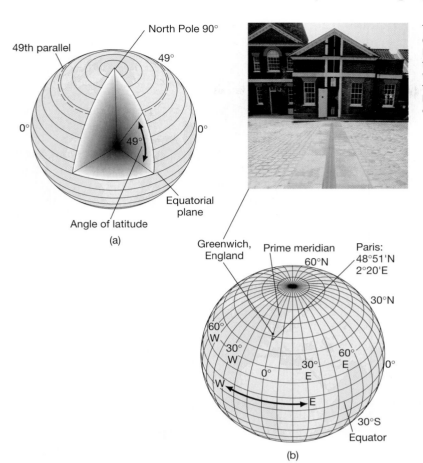

The prime meridian at the Royal Observatory in Greenwich, England. The observatory was founded by Charles II in 1675 with the task of setting standards for time, distance, latitude, and longitude—the key components of navigation.

FIGURE A.3 Latitude and longitude Lines of latitude and longitude provide a grid that covers Earth, allowing any point on Earth's surface to be accurately referenced. Latitude is measured in terms of angular distance (that is, degrees and minutes) north or south of the equator, as shown in (a). Longitude is measured in the same way, but east and west from the prime meridian, a line around Earth's surface that passes through both poles (North and South) and the Royal Observatory in Greenwich, just to the east of central London, in England. Locations are always stated with latitudinal measurements first (c). The location of Paris, France, for example, is 48°51' N and 2°20' E, as shown in (b).

Some projections are designed such that compass directions are correct from only one central point. These are known as **Azimuthal projections**. They can be equidistant, as in the Azimuthal Equidistant projection (see Figure A.4), which is sometimes used to show air-route distances from a specific location.

Projections that portray areas on Earth's surface in their true proportions are known as **equal-area** or **equivalent projections**. Such projections are used when the cartographer wishes to compare and contrast distributions on Earth's surface—the relative area of different types of land use, for example. Examples of equal-area projections include the Eckert IV projection, Bartholomew's Nordic projection (used in Figure 1.1) and the Mollweide projection (see Figure A.4). Equal-area projections such as the Mollweide are especially useful for thematic maps showing economic, demographic, or cultural data. Unfortunately, preserving accuracy in terms of area tends to result in world maps on which many locations appear squashed.

For some applications, aesthetic appearance is more important than conformality, equivalence, or equidistance, so cartographers have devised a number of other projections. Examples include the Times projection, which is used in many world atlases, and the Robinson projection, which is used by the National Geographic Society in many of its publications. The Robinson projection (**Figure A.5**) is a compromise projection that distorts both area and directional relationships but provides a general-purpose world map.

There are also political considerations. Countries may appear larger and so more important on one projection than on another. The Peters projection, for example (**Figure A.6**), is a deliberate attempt to give prominence to the underdeveloped countries of the equatorial regions and the Southern Hemisphere. As such, it has been officially adopted by the World Council of Churches and numerous agencies of the United Nations and other international institutions. Its unusual shapes give it a shock value that gets people's attention. For some, however, those shapes are ugly.

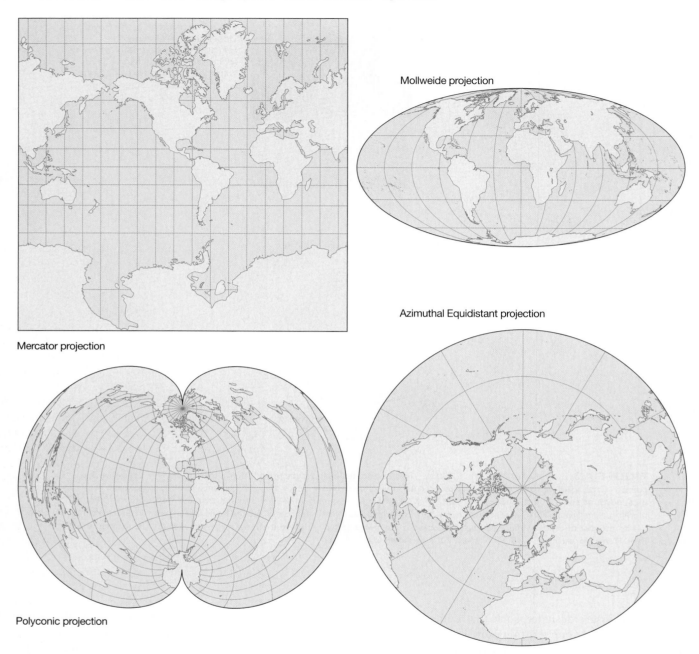

Mollweide projection

Azimuthal Equidistant projection

Mercator projection

Polyconic projection

FIGURE A.4 Comparison of map projections Different map projections have different properties. The Polyconic projection is true to scale along each east–west parallel and along the central north–south meridian. It is free of distortion only along the central meridian. On the Mercator projection, compass directions between any two points are true, and the shapes of land masses are true, but their relative size is distorted. On the Azimuthal Equidistant projection, distances measured from the center of the map are true, but direction, area, and shape are increasingly distorted with distance from the center point. On the Mollweide projection, relative sizes are true but shapes are distorted.

In this book we have occasionally used another striking projection, the Dymaxion projection devised by Buckminster Fuller (**Figure A.7**). Fuller was a prominent modernist architect and industrial designer who wanted to produce a map of the world with no significant distortion to any of the major land masses. The Dymaxion projection does this, though it produces a world that at first may seem disorienting. This is not necessarily a bad thing, for it can force us to take a fresh look at the world and at the relationships among places. Because Europe, North America, and Japan are all located toward the center of this map projection, it is particularly useful for illustrating two central themes of this book: the relationships among these prosperous regions and the relationships between this prosperous core group and the less prosperous, peripheral countries of the world. Fuller's projection shows the economically peripheral countries of the world as cartographically peripheral, too.

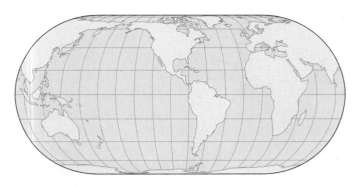

FIGURE A.5 The Robinson projection On the Robinson projection, distance, direction, area, and shape are all distorted in an attempt to balance the properties of the map. It is designed purely for appearance, and is best used for thematic and reference maps at the world scale. (*Source:* Reprinted with permission of Prentice Hall from E. F. Bergman, *Human Geography: Cultures, Connections, and Landscapes,* © 1995, p. 12.)

One kind of projection that is sometimes used in small-scale thematic maps is the *cartogram.* In this projection, space is transformed according to statistical factors, with the largest mapping units representing the greatest statistical values. **Figure A.8a** shows a cartogram of the world in which countries are represented in proportion to their population. This sort of projection is particularly effective in helping us visualize relative inequalities among the world's populations. **Figure A.8b** shows a cartogram of the world in which the cost of telephone calls made from the United States has been substituted for linear distance as the basis of the map. The deliberate distortion of the shapes of the continents in this sort of projection dramatically emphasizes spatial variations.

Finally, the advent of computer graphics has made it possible for cartographers to move beyond two-dimensional representations of Earth's surface. Computer software that renders three-dimensional statistical data onto the flat surface of a monitor screen or a piece of paper facilitates the **visualization** of many aspects of human geography in innovative and provocative ways (**Figure A.9**).

GEOGRAPHIC INFORMATION SYSTEMS

Geographic information systems (GIS)—organized collections of computer hardware, software, and geographic data that are designed to capture, store, update, manipulate, and display geographically referenced information—have rapidly grown to become a predominant method of geographic analysis, particularly in the military and commercial worlds. The software in GIS incorporates programs to store and access spatial data, to manipulate those data, and to draw maps.

Between 1999 and 2005, GIS services grew at a rate of around 10 percent per year. In 2005, estimates of global investment in GIS technologies ranged from $5 billion to more than $8 billion. In the United States, employment in GIS is now one of the 10 fastest-growing technical fields in the private sector. The U.S. government spends more than $4 billion per year on geographic data acquisition, and the total annual market for GIS services in North America is valued at around $3 billion.

The primary requirement for data to be used in GIS is that the locations for the variables are known. Location may be annotated by x, y, and z coordinates of longitude, latitude, and elevation, or by such systems as zip codes or highway mile markers. Any variable that can be located spatially can be fed into a GIS. Data capture—putting the information into the system—is the most time-consuming component of GIS work. Different sources of data, using different systems of measurement, scales, and systems of representation, must be integrated with one another; changes must be tracked and updated. Many GIS operations in the United States, Europe, Japan, and Australia have begun to contract out such work to firms in countries where labor is cheaper; India has emerged as a major data conversion center for GIS.

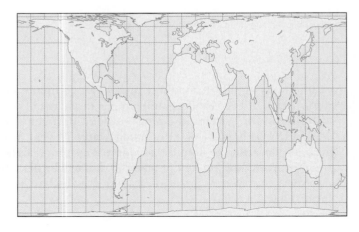

FIGURE A.6 The Peters projection This equal-area projection offers an alternative to traditional projections which, Arno Peters argued, exaggerate the size and apparent importance of the higher latitudes—that is, the world's core regions—and so promote the "europeanization" of Earth. While it has been adopted by the World Council of Churches, the Lutheran Church of America, and various agencies of the United Nations and other international institutions, it has been criticized by cartographers in the United States on the grounds of aesthetics: One consequence of equal-area projections is that they distort the shape of land masses. (*Source:* Reprinted with permission of Prentice Hall from E. F. Bergman, *Human Geography: Cultures, Connections, and Landscapes,* © 1995, p. 13.)

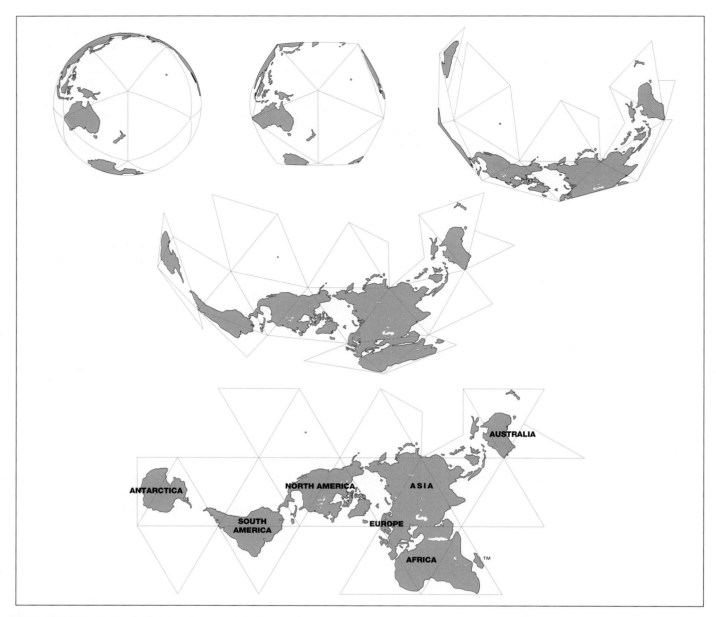

FIGURE A.7 Fuller's Dymaxion projection In this striking map projection, Buckminster Fuller (1895–1983) created a map with the minimum of distortion to the shape of the world's major land masses by dividing the globe into triangular areas. Those areas not encompassing major land masses were cut away, allowing the remainder of the globe to be "unfolded" into a flat projection. (*Source:* Buckminster Fuller Institute and Dymaxion Map Design, Santa Barbara, CA. The word *Dymaxion* and the Fuller Projection Dymaxion™ Map design are trademarks of the Buckminster Fuller Institute, Santa Barbara, California, © 1938, 1967 & 1992. All rights reserved.)

Applications of GIS

The most important aspect of GIS, from an analytical point of view, is that they it allows the merger of data from several different sources, on different topics, and at different scales. This capability allows analysts to emphasize the spatial relationships among the objects being mapped. A geographic information system makes it possible to link, or integrate, information that is difficult to associate through any other means. For example, using GIS technology and water-company billing information, it is possible to simulate the discharge of materials in the septic systems in a neighborhood upstream from a wetland. The bills show how much water is used at each address. Because the amount of water a customer uses will roughly predict the amount of material that will be discharged into the septic systems, areas of heavy septic discharge can be located using a GIS.

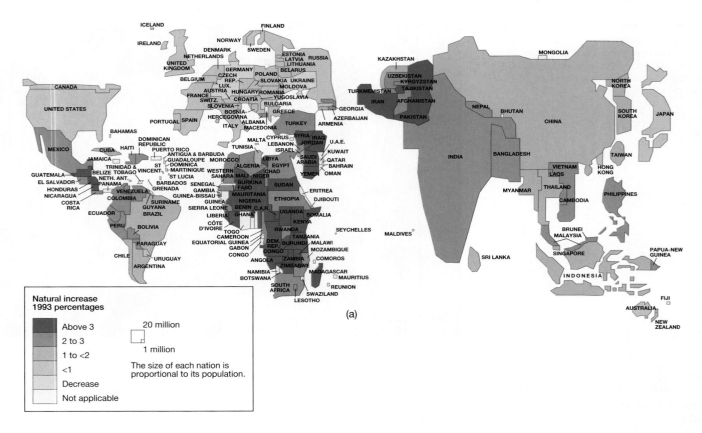

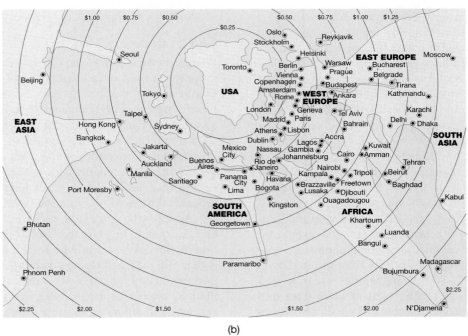

FIGURE A.8 Cartograms In a cartogram, space is distorted to emphasize a particular attribute of places or regions. (a) This example shows the relative size of countries based on their population rather than their area; the cartographers have maintained the shape of each country as closely as possible to make the map easier to read. As you can see, population-based cartograms are very effective in demonstrating spatial inequality. (b) In this example, the cost of telephone calls is substituted for linear distance as the basis of the map, thus deliberately distorting the shapes of the continents to dramatic effect. Countries are arranged around the United States according to the cost per minute of calls made from the United States in 1998. (*Source:* (a) M. Kidron and R. Segal (eds.), *The State of the World Atlas*, rev. 5th ed. London: Penguin Reference, 1995, pp. 28–29; (b) G. C. Staple (ed.), *TeleGeography 1999*. Washington, DC: TeleGeography, 1999, p. 82.)

FIGURE A.9 Visualization This example shows the spatial structure of the Internet backbone and associated traffic flows within the United States. (*Source:* Donna Cox and Robert Patterson, http://www.ncsa.uiuc.edu/SCMS/DigLib/text/technology/ Visualization-Study-NSFNET-Cox.html.)

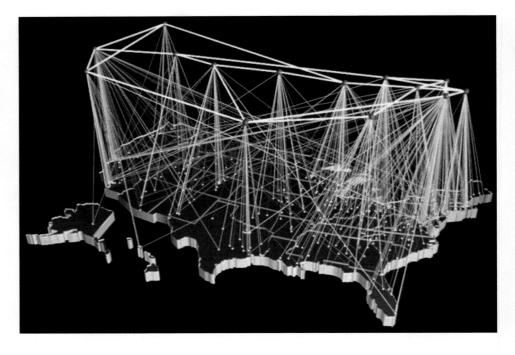

GIS technology can render visible many aspects of geography that were previously unseen. For example, GIS can produce incredibly detailed maps based on millions of pieces of information—maps that could never have been drawn by human hands. At the other extreme of spatial scale, GIS can put places under the microscope, creating detailed new insights using huge databases and effortlessly browsable media (**Figure A.10**).

Many advances in GIS have come from military applications. GIS allows infantry commanders to calculate line of sight from tanks and defensive emplacements, allows cruise missiles to fly below enemy radar, and provides a comprehensive basis for military intelligence. Beyond the military, GIS technology allows an enormous range of problems to be addressed. It can be used, for example, to decide how to manage farmland; to monitor the spread of infectious diseases; to monitor tree cover in metropolitan areas; to assess changes in ecosystems; to analyze the impact of proposed changes in the boundaries of legislative districts; to identify the location of potential business customers; to identify the location of potential criminals; and to provide a basis for urban and regional planning. Some of the most influential applications of GIS have resulted from geodemographic research. **Geodemographic research** uses census data and commercial data (such as sales data and property records) about the populations of small districts in creating profiles of those populations for market research. The digital media used by GIS make such applications very flexible.

With GIS it is possible to zoom in and out, evaluating spatial relationships at different spatial scales. Similarly, it is possible to vary the appearance and presentation of maps, using different colors and rendering techniques.

Critiques of GIS

Within the past five years, GIS has resulted in the creation of more maps than were created in all previous human history. One result is that, as maps have become more commonplace, more people and more businesses have become more spatially aware. Nevertheless, some critics have argued that GIS represents no real advances in geographers' understanding of places and regions. The results of GIS, they argue, may be useful but are essentially mundane. This misses the point that, however routine their subjects may be, all maps constitute powerful and influential ways to represent the world.

A more telling critique, perhaps, is that the real impact of GIS has been to increase the level of surveillance of the population by those who already possess power and control. The fear is that GIS may be helping create a world in which people are not treated and judged by who they are and what they do, but more by where they live. People's credit ratings, ability to buy insurance, and ability to secure a mortgage, for example, are all routinely judged, in part, by GIS-based analyses that take into account the attributes and characteristics of their neighbors.

FURTHER READING

Dorling, D., and D. Fairbairn, *Mapping: Ways of Seeing the World.* London: Addison Wesley Longman, 1977.

Greene, R. W., *GIS in Public Policy.* Redlands, CA: ESRI Press, 2000.

O'Looney, J., *Beyond Maps: GIS and Decision Making in Local Government.* Redlands, CA: ESRI Press, 2000.

Thrower, N. J. W., *Maps & Civilization: Cartography in Culture and Society*, 2nd edition. Chicago: University of Chicago Press, 1999.

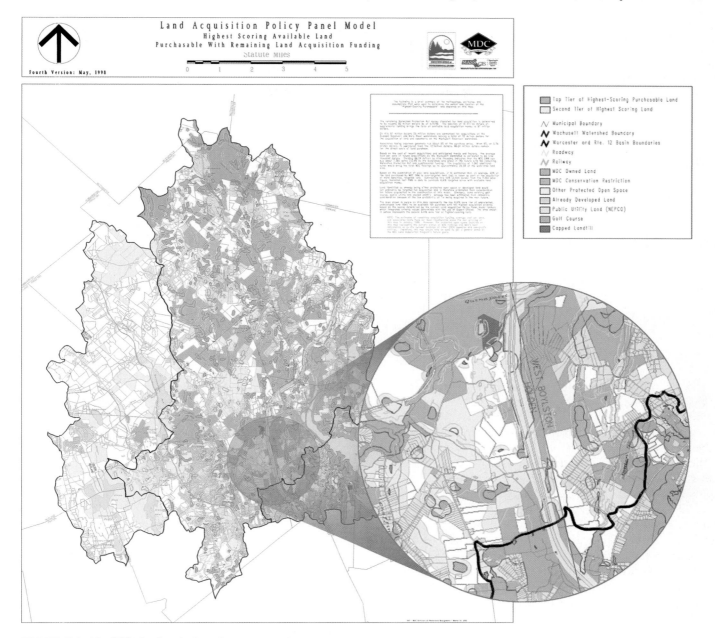

FIGURE A.10 GIS-derived planning map This map of the Wachusett Reservoir watershed in Massachusetts was prepared from a composite of 12 layers of GIS maps, each depicting a key aspect of land use and topography. The map is used to show in detail the parcels of land that the Commonwealth of Massachusetts needs to buy in order to keep development from damaging the watershed and the quality of the reservoir water. (*Source:* R. W. Greene, *GIS in Public Policy.* Redlands, CA: ESRI Press, 2000, p. 67.)

GLOSSARY

Aborigines: indigenous peoples of Australia.

acid rain: precipitation that has mixed with air pollution to produce rain that contains levels of acidity—often in the form of sulfuric acid—that are harmful to vegetation and aquatic life.

afforestation: converting previously unforested land to forest by planting trees or seeds.

agglomeration: clustering together of economic activities at the scale of metropolitan areas or industrial subregions.

agglomeration economies: cost advantages that accrue to individual firms because of their location among functionally related activities.

Alliance of Small Island States (AOSIS): association of more than 40 low-lying, mostly island, countries that have formed an alliance to combat global warming, which threatens their existence through sea-level rise.

altiplano: high-elevation plateaus and basins that lie within even higher mountains, especially in Bolivia and Peru, at more than 3000 meters (9500 feet) in the Andes of Latin America.

altitudinal zonation: vertical classification of environment and land use according to elevation based mainly on changes in climate and vegetation from lower (warmer) to higher (cooler) elevations.

americanization: process by which a generation of individuals born in the British American colonies felt less loyalty and fewer cultural ties to Great Britain and developed a new indigenous ethos.

Antarctic Treaty: international agreement to demilitarize the Antarctic continent, delay mineral exploration, and preserve it for scientific research.

apartheid: South Africa's policy of racial separation that prior to 1994 structured space and society to keep separate black, white, and colored populations.

archipelago: group of islands or expanse of water with many islands.

aridity: climate with insufficient moisture to support trees or woody plants.

Asian Tigers: newly industrialized territories of Hong Kong, Taiwan, South Korea, and Singapore that have experienced rapid economic growth and become semiperipheral within the world-system.

aspect: the direction in which a sloping piece of land faces.

assimilation: process by which peoples of different cultural backgrounds who occupy a common territory achieve sufficient cultural solidarity to sustain a national existence.

Association of Southeast Asian Nations (ASEAN): international organization of the nations of Southeast Asia established to promote economic growth and regional security.

atoll: low-lying island landform consisting of a circle of coral reefs around a lagoon, often associated with the rim of a submerged volcano or mountain.

Azimuthal projection: map projection on which compass directions are correct only from one central point.

backwash effects: negative impacts on a region (or regions)—including outmigration and the loss of capital—due to the economic growth of some other region.

Balfour Declaration: 1917 British mandate that required the establishment of a Jewish national homeland.

balkanization: division of a territory into smaller and often mutually hostile units.

banana republics: term used to describe small tropical countries, often run by a dictator, dependent on the export of a few crops such as bananas.

barchan: crescent-shaped sand dune, concave on the side sheltered from the prevailing wind.

Berlin Conference: meeting convened by German chancellor Bismark in 1884–85 to divide Africa among European colonial powers.

biodiversity: variety in the types and numbers of species in particular regions of the world.

biogeography: study of the spatial distribution of vegetation, animals, and other organisms.

biome: largest geographic biotic unit, a major community of plants and animals or similar ecosystems.

bioprospecting: search for plants, animals, and other organisms that may be of medicinal value or may have other commercial use.

bonded labor: labor that is pledged against an outstanding debt.

bracero: guest worker from Mexico given temporary permit to work as a farm laborer in the United States between 1942 and 1964.

British Commonwealth: group of former British colonies and other countries allied with Britain that cooperate on political, economic, and cultural activities.

buffer zone: group of smaller or less powerful countries situated between larger or more powerful countries that are geopolitical rivals.

bush fallow: modification of shifting cultivation where crops are rotated around a village and fallow periods are shortened.

capitalism: form of economic and social organization characterized by the profit motive and the control of the means of production, distribution, and exchange of goods by private ownership.

cargo cult: Pacific island religious movements in which the dawn of a coming new age was associated with the arrival of goods brought by spiritual beings or foreigners.

cartogram: map projection that is transformed in order to promote legibility or to reveal patterns not readily apparent on a traditional base map.

caste: system of kinship groupings that is reinforced by language, religion, and occupation.

cattle station: livestock enterprises where cattle (or sheep) are raised on large grazing leases in the remote regions of Australia.

chador: loose, usually black robe worn by Muslim women that covers the body, including the face, from head to toe.

chaebol: South Korean term for the very large corporations in that country that, with government help, control numerous businesses and dominate the national economy.

chernozem: thick, dark grassland soils (also called Black Earths) that are neutral in terms of acidic content and rich in humus.

circle of poison: use of imported pesticides on export crops in developing countries that then export back the contaminated crops to the regions where the pesticides were manufactured.

circular migration: traditional and long-standing population movements that respond to seasonal availability of pasture, droughts, and wage employment.

civil society: network of social groups and cultural traditions that operate independently of the state and its political institutions.

climate: typical conditions of the weather expected at a place often measured by long-term averages of temperature and precipitation (e.g., a rainy place).

Closer Economic Relations (CER) Agreement: agreement in 1983 that built upon an earlier New Zealand-Australia Free Trade Agreement (NZAFTA) and set out to remove all tariffs and restrictions on trade between the two countries.

cognitive image (mental map): psychological representation of locations that are made up from people's individual ideas and impressions of these locations.

colonialism: establishment and maintenance of political and legal domination by a state over a separate and alien society.

colonization: establishment of settlement in a place or region.

Columbian Exchange: interchange of crops, animals, people, and diseases between the Old World of Europe and Africa and the New World of the Americas beginning with the voyages of Christopher Columbus in 1492.

command economy: national economy in which all aspects of production and distribution are centrally controlled by government agencies.

commodity: anything useful that can be bought or sold.

commodity chains: networks of labor and production processes that originate in the extraction or production of raw materials. The end result is the delivery and consumption of a finished commodity.

common market: market in which internal restrictions on the movement of capital, labor, and enterprise are also removed from the basic framework of a customs union.

common property resources: resources such as fish or forests that are managed collectively by a community that has rights to the resource rather than it being owned by individuals.

communism: form of economic and social organization characterized by the common ownership of the means of production, distribution, and exchange.

comparative advantage: principle whereby places and regions specialize in activities for which they have the greatest advantage in productivity relative to other regions—or for which they have the least disadvantage.

conformal projection: map projection on which compass bearings are rendered accurately.

continental drift: slow movement of the continents over long periods of time across Earth's surface (*see* plate tectonics).

core regions: regions that dominate trade, control the most advanced technologies, and have high levels of productivity within diversified economies.

counterurbanization: net loss of population from cities to smaller towns and rural areas.

creative destruction: withdrawal of investments from activities (and regions) that yield low rates of profit, in order to reinvest in new activities (and new places).

culture: shared set of meanings that are lived through the material and symbolic practices of everyday life.

Culture System: Dutch colonial policy from 1830 to 1870 that required farmers in Java to devote one-fifth of their land and their labor to production of an export crop.

deindustrialization: decline in industrial employment in core regions as firms scale back their activities in response to lower levels of profitability.

demographic collapse: after about 1500, the rapid die-off of the indigenous populations of the Americas as a result of diseases introduced by the Europeans to which residents of the Americas had no immunity.

demographic transition: replacement of high birth and death rates by low birth and death rates.

dependency school (of development theory): school of thought based on the premise that the economic progress of peripheral or less-developed countries is constrained by the economic and political power of affluent, core countries.

desertification: process by which arid and semiarid lands become degraded and less productive, leading to more desertlike conditions.

development theory: analysis of social change that assesses the economic progress of individual countries in an evolutionary way.

diaspora: spatial dispersion of a previously homogeneous group.

disinvestment: sale of assets such as factories and equipment.

distributary: river branch that flows away from the main stream.

division of labor: separation of productive processes into individual operations, each performed by different workers or groups of workers.

domestication: adaptation of wild plants and animals through selective breeding by humans for preferred characteristics into cultivated or tamed forms.

domino theory: (also known as the domino effect) view that political unrest in one country can destabilize neighbors and start a chain of events like the fall of a stack of dominos.

Dreamtime: aboriginal worldview that links past and future, people and places, in a continuity that ensures respect for the natural world.

dry farming: arable farming techniques that allow the cultivation of crops without irrigation in regions of limited moisture (50 centimeters, or 20 inches per year).

Earth system science: integrated approach to the study of Earth that stresses investigation of the interactions among Earth's components in order to explain Earth and atmosphere dynamics, Earth evolution and ecosystems, and global change.

ecological imperialism: concept developed by historian Alfred Crosby to describe the way in which European organisms, including diseases, pests, and domestic animals, were able to take over the ecosystems of other regions of the world, often with devastating impacts on local peoples, flora, and fauna.

ecosystem: complex of living organisms, their physical environment, and all their relationships in a particular place.

ecotourism: environmentally oriented tourism designed to protect the environment and often to provide economic opportunities for local people.

egalitarian society: society based on belief in equal social, political, and economic rights and privileges.

El Niño: periodic warming of sea surface temperatures in the tropical Pacific off the coast of Peru that results in worldwide changes in climate, including droughts and floods.

enclave: culturally distinct territory that is encompassed by a different cultural group or groups.

encomienda: system by which groups of indigenous people were "entrusted" to Spanish colonists who could demand tribute in the form of labor, crops, or goods and in turn were responsible for the indigenous groups' conversion to Catholic faith and for teaching them Spanish.

Enlightenment: 18th-century movement marked by a belief in the sovereignty of reason and empirical research in the sciences.

entrepôt: seaport that is an intermediary center of trade and transshipment.

equal-area (equivalent) projection: map projection that portrays areas on Earth's surface in their true proportions.

equidistant projection: map projection that allows distance to be represented as accurately as possible.

ethnic cleansing: systematic and forced removal of members of an ethnic group from their communities in order to change the ethnic composition of a region.

ethnic group: group of people whose members share cultural characteristics.

ethnocentrism: attitude that one's own race and culture is superior to that of others.

europeanization: highly selective process involving the mixing of native and imported practices that eventually created distinct colonial cultures and societies.

exclave: portion of a country or a cultural group's territory that lies outside its contiguous land area.

farm crisis: financial failure and foreclosure of thousands of family farms across the U.S. Midwest.

fascism: political philosophy characterized by a centralized, autocratic government that values nation and race over the individual.

favela: Brazilian term for informal settlements lacking good housing and services that grow up around the urban core.

federal state: form of government in which power is allocated to units of local government within the country.

feminization of poverty: likelihood that women will be poor, malnourished, and otherwise disadvantaged because of inequalities within the household, the community, and the country.

feng shui: application of a collection of ancient principles of geomancy that are believed by adherents to ensure health, wealth, happiness, long life, and healthy offspring through the spatial organization of cities, buildings, and furniture.

feudal systems: regional hierarchies composed, at the bottom, of local nobles and at the top of lords or monarchs owning immense stretches of land. In these systems, landowners delegated smaller parcels of land to others in return for political allegiance and economic obligations in the form of money dues or labor.

fjord: steep-sided, narrow inlet of the sea, formed when deeply glaciated valleys are flooded by the sea.

flexible production region: region within which there is a concentration of small- and medium-sized firms whose production and distribution practices take advantage of computerized control systems and local subcontractors in order to quickly exploit new market niches for new product lines.

formal region: region with a high degree of homogeneity in terms of particular distinguishing features.

free trade association: association whose member countries eliminate tariff and quota barriers against trade from other member states but continue to charge regular duties on materials and products coming from outside the association.

free trade zone: area within which goods may be manufactured or traded without customs duties.

functional region: area characterized by a coherent functional organization of human occupancy.

G8: Group of Eight countries (Canada, France, Germany, Italy, Japan, Russia, the United Kingdom, and the United States) whose heads of state meet each year to discuss issues of mutual and global concern.

gender: social differences between men and women rather than the anatomical differences related to sex.

gender and development (GAD): approach to development that links women's productive and reproductive roles and an approach to understanding the gender-related differences and barriers to better lives of both men and women.

gender division of labor: separation of productive processes based on gender.

gentrification: invasion of older, centrally located working-class neighborhoods by higher-income households.

geodemographic research: use of census data and commercial data (such as sales data and property records) for small districts in creating profiles of the populations of those districts for market research.

geographic information systems (GIS): integrated computer tools for the handling, processing, and analyzing of geographical data.

geomancy: belief that the physical attributes of places can be analyzed and manipulated in order to improve the flow of cosmic energy, or *ch'i*.

geomorphology: study of landforms.

global warming: increase in world temperatures and change in climate associated with increasing levels of carbon dioxide and other gases resulting from human activities such as deforestation and fossil-fuel burning.

globalization: increasing interconnectedness of different parts of the world through common processes of economic, environmental, political, and cultural change.

Great Artesian Basin: world's largest reserve of underground water located in central Australia and under pressure so that water rises to the surface when wells are bored.

Green Revolution: technological package of higher yielding seeds, especially wheat, rice, and corn, that in combination with irrigation, fertilizers, pesticides, and farm machinery was able to increase crop production in the developing world after about 1950.

greenhouse effect: trapping of heat within the atmosphere by water vapor and gases, such as carbon dioxide, resulting in the warming of the atmosphere and surface.

gross domestic product (GDP): estimate of the total value of all materials, foodstuffs, goods, and services that are produced in a country in a particular year.

gross national product (GNP): similar to GDP, but also includes the value of income from abroad.

guest worker: foreigner who is permitted to work in another country on a temporary basis.

hacienda: large agricultural estate in Latin America and Spain that grows crops mainly for domestic consumption (for example, for mines, missions, and cities) rather than for export.

hajj: pilgrimage to Mecca required of all Muslims.

harmattan: hot, dry wind that blows out of inland Africa.

hate crime: act of violence committed because of prejudice against women; homosexuals; and ethnic, racial, and religious minorities.

heathland: open, uncultivated land with poor soil and scrub vegetation.

hegemony: domination over the world economy, exercised through a combination of economic, military, financial, and cultural means, by one national state in a particular historical epoch.

homelands: areas set aside in South Africa for black residents as tribal territories where they were given limited self-government but no vote and limited rights in the general politics of South Africa.

imperialism: extension of the power of a nation through direct or indirect control of the economic and political life of other territories.

import substitution: process by which domestic producers provide goods or services that were formerly bought from foreign producers.

indentured servant: individual bound by contract to the service of another for a specified term.

informal economy: economic activities that take place beyond official record and not subject to formalized systems of regulation or remuneration (e.g., street selling, petty crime).

intermontane: lying between or among mountains.

internal migration: movement of populations within a national territory.

internally displaced person: individuals who are uprooted within their own countries due to civil conflict or human rights violations, sometimes by their own governments.

international division of labor: specialization of different people, regions, and countries in certain kinds of economic activities.

International Monetary Fund (IMF): organization that provides loans to governments throughout the world.

international regime: orientation of contemporary politics around the international arena rather than the national one.

intertropical convergence zone (ITCZ): region where air flows together and rises vertically as a result of intense solar heating at the equator, often with heavy rainfall, and shifting north and south with the seasons.

intifada: the violent uprising of Palestinians against the rule of Israel in the Occupied Territories.

irredentism: assertion by the government of a country that a minority living outside its borders belongs to it historically and culturally.

Islam: religion that is based on submission to God's will according to the Qur'an.

Islamism: anti-colonial, anti-imperialist, and overall anticore political movement.

jihad: sacred struggle or striving to carry out God's will according to the tenets of Islam.

keiretsu: Japanese business networks facilitated after World War II by the Japanese government in order to promote national recovery.

kinship: shared notion of relationship among members of a group often but not necessarily based on blood, marriage, or adoption.

La Niña: periodic abnormal cooling of sea surface temperatures in the tropical Pacific off the coast of Peru that results in worldwide changes in climate, including droughts and floods that contrast with those produced by El Niño.

land bridge: dry land connection between two continents or islands, exposed, for example, when sea level falls during an ice age.

land reform: change in the way land is held or distributed, such as the division of large private estates into small private farms or communally held properties.

latitude: angular distance of a point on Earth's surface, measured north or south from the equator, which is 0°.

law of diminishing returns: tendency for productivity to decline, after a certain point, with the continued addition of capital and/or labor to a given resource base.

leadership cycles: periods of international power established by individual states through economic, political, and military competition.

liberation theology: Catholic movement, originating in Latin America, focused on social justice and on helping the poor and oppressed.

loess: surface cover of fine-grained silt and clay deposited by wind action and usually resulting in deep layers of yellowish, loamy soils.

longitude: angular distance of a point on Earth's surface, measured east or west from the prime meridian (the line that passes through both poles and through Greenwich, England, and is given the value of 0°).

Main Street: dominant urban corridor of Canada, extending from Québec City to Windsor, Ontario.

mandate: delegation of political power over a region, province, or state.

map projection: systematic rendering on a flat surface of the geographic coordinates of the features found on Earth's surface.

maquiladora: industrial plant in Mexico, originally within the border zone with the United States and often owned or built with foreign capital, that assembles components for export as finished products free from customs duties.

market economies: economy in which goods and services are produced and are distributed through free markets.

Marshall Plan: strategy (named after U.S. Secretary of State George Marshall) of quickly rebuilding the West German economy after World War II in order to prevent the spread of socialism or a recurrence of fascism.

marsupial: Australian mammal such as the kangaroo, koala, and wombat that gives birth to premature infants that then develop and feed from nipples in a pouch on the mother's body.

massif: mountainous block of Earth's crust bounded by faults or folds and displaced as a unit.

Megalopolis: dominant urban corridor of the United States that extends along the eastern seaboard from Boston to Washington, DC.

Melanesia: region of the western Pacific that includes the westerly and largest islands of Papua New Guinea, the Solomon Islands, Fiji, Vanuatu, and New Caledonia.

mercantilism: economic policy in which government controls industry and trade.

merchant capitalism: form of capitalism characterized by trade in commodities and a highly organized system of banking, credit, stock, and insurance services.

mestizo: term used in Latin America to identify a person of mixed white (European) and American Indian ancestry.

microfinance programs: programs that provide credit and savings to the self-employed poor, including those in the informal sector, who cannot borrow money from commercial banks.

Millennium Development Goals (MDGs): eight goals to be met by the year 2015, agreed to by members of the United Nations, that include the eradication of poverty, universal primary education, gender equality, the reduction of child mortality, the improvement of maternal health, the combating of disease, environmental sustainability, and the creation of global partnerships.

mikrorayon: neighborhood-scale planning unit of the Soviet era.

minifundia: very small parcels of land farmed by tenant farmers or peasant farmers.

minisystem: society with a single cultural base and a reciprocal social economy.

Modernity: forward-looking view of the world that emphasizes reason, scientific rationality, creativity, novelty, and progress.

modernization theory: economic development occurs when investment rates enable higher levels of industrialization, thus raising labor productivity and increasing the GDP per capita levels.

monoculture: agricultural practice in which one crop is grown intensively over a large area of land.

Monroe Doctrine: proclamation of U.S. President James Monroe in 1823 stating that European military interference in the Western Hemisphere, including the Caribbean and Latin America, would no longer be acceptable.

monsoon: seasonal reversal of wind flows in parts of the lower to middle latitudes. During the cool season, a dry monsoon occurs as dry offshore winds prevail; in hot summer months a wet monsoon occurs as onshore winds bring large amounts of rainfall.

moraine: accumulation of rock and soil carried forward by a glacier and eventually deposited at its frontal edge or along its sides.

multiculturalism: process of immigrant incorporation in which each ethnic group has the right to enjoy and protect their officially recognized "native" culture.

municipal housing: rental housing that is owned and managed by a local government or municipality; a form of *social housing*.

Muslim: member of the Islamic religion.

nation: group of people often sharing common elements of culture, such as religion, language, a history, or political identity.

nationalism: feeling of belonging to a nation as well as the belief that a nation has a natural right to determine its own affairs.

nationalist movement: organized groups of people, sharing common elements of culture, such as language, religion, or history, who wish to determine their own political affairs.

nationalization: process of converting key industries from private to governmental organization and control.

nation-state: ideal form consisting of a homogeneous group of people governed by their own state.

Near Abroad: independent states that were formerly republics of the Soviet Union.

neocolonialism: economic and political strategies by which powerful states in core economies indirectly maintain or extend their influence over other areas or people.

neoliberalism: economic doctrine based on a belief in a minimalist role for the state, assuming the desirability of free markets as the ideal condition not only for economic organization but also for social and political life.

neoliberal policies: economic policies that are predicated on a minimalist role for the state and the reduction in the role and budget of government, including reduced subsidies and the privatization of formerly publicly owned and operated concerns, such as utilities.

neotropics: ecological region of the tropics of the Americas.

new international division of labor: decentralization of manufacturing production from core regions to some peripheral and semiperipheral countries.

nontraditional agricultural exports (NTAEs): new export crops, such as vegetables and flowers, that contrast with the traditional exports such as sugar and coffee, and often require fast refrigerated transport to market.

North American Free Trade Agreement (NAFTA): 1994 agreement among the United States, Canada, and Mexico to reduce barriers to trade among the three countries, through, for example, reducing customs tariffs and quotas.

oasis: spot in the desert made fertile by the availability of surface water.

offshore financial services: provision of banking, investment, and other services to foreign nationals and companies who wish to avoid taxes, oversight, or other regulations in their own countries.

orographic effect: influence of hills and mountains in lifting airstreams, cooling the air, and thereby inducing precipitation.

Outback: dry and thinly populated interior of Australia.

overseas Chinese: migrants from China who settled in Southeast Asia as early as the 14th century, but mainly during the period of European colonialism, when they arrived as contract plantation, mine, and rail workers and then moved into clerical and business roles.

ozone depletion: loss of the protective layer of ozone gas that prevents harmful ultraviolet radiation from reaching Earth's surface and causing increases in skin cancer and other ecological damage.

Pacific Rim: loosely defined region of countries that border the Pacific Ocean.

pastoralism: system of farming and way of life based on keeping herds of grazing animals—cattle, sheep, goats, horses, camels, yaks, and so on, depending on the environment.

peripheral regions: regions that are characterized by dependent and disadvantageous trading relationships, by inadequate or obsolescent technologies, and by undeveloped or narrowly specialized economies with low levels of productivity.

permafrost: permanently frozen subsoil, which may extend for several meters below the surface layer and may defrost up to a depth of a meter or so during summer months.

petrodollar: revenues generated by the sale of oil.

physiographic region: broad region within which there is a coherence of geology, relief, landforms, soils, and vegetation.

pinyin: system of writing Chinese language using the Roman alphabet.

place: specific geographic setting with distinctive physical, social, and cultural attributes.

plantation: large agricultural estate that is usually tropical or semitropical, monocultural (one crop), and commercial- or export-orientated, most of which were established in the colonial period.

plate tectonics: theory that Earth's crust is divided into large solid plates that move relative to each other and cause mountain building, volcanic, and earthquake activity when they separate or meet.

pluralist democracy: society in which members of a diverse group continue to participate in their traditional cultures and special interests.

polder: area of low land reclaimed from a body of water by building dikes and draining the water.

Polynesia: central and southern Pacific islands that include the independent countries of Samoa, Tonga, the Cook Islands, Niue, and Tuvalu; the U.S. territory of American Samoa; the French territories of Wallis and Fortuna and French Polynesia (including the island of Tahiti, the Society Islands, the Tuamotu archipelago, and the Marquesas Islands); the New Zealand territory of Tokelau; and the British territory of the Pitcairn Islands. Polynesia sometimes includes New Zealand and the Hawaiian islands.

primacy: condition in which the population of the largest city in an urban system is disproportionately large in relation to the second- and third-largest cities in that system.

primary activity: economic activity that is concerned directly with natural resources of any kind.

pristine myth: erroneous belief that the Americas were mostly wild and untouched by humans prior to European arrival. In fact, large areas had been cultivated and deforested by indigenous populations.

privatization: turnover or sale of state-owned industries and enterprises to private interests.

quaternary activity: economic activity that deals with the handling and processing of knowledge and information.

Raj: rule of the British in India.

region: large territory that encompasses many places, all or most of which share similar attributes in comparison with the attributes of places elsewhere.

regional geography: study of the ways in which unique combinations of environmental and human factors produce territories with distinctive landscapes and cultural attributes.

regionalism: strong feelings of collective identity shared by religious or ethnic groups that are concentrated within a particular region.

regionalization: geographer's classification of individual places or areal units.

remittances: money sent home to family or friends by people working temporarily or permanently in other countries.

remote sensing: collection of information about parts of Earth's surface by means of aerial photography or satellite imagery designed to record data on visible, infrared, and microwave sensor systems.

Richter scale: logarithmic scale ranging from 1 to 10 used to measure the amount of energy released by an earthquake.

rift valley: block of land that drops between two others, forming a steep-sided trough, often at faults on a divergent plate boundary.

Ring of Fire: chain of seismic instability and volcanic activity that stretches from Southeast Asia through the Philippines, the Japanese archipelago, the Kamchatka Peninsula, and down the Pacific coast of the Americas to the southern Andes in Chile. It is caused by the tension built up by moving tectonic plates.

salinization: salt deposits caused when water evaporates from the surface of the land and leaves behind salts that it has drawn up from the subsoil.

satellite state: national state that is economically dependent and politically and militarily subservient to another—in its orbit, figuratively speaking.

savanna: grassland vegetation found in tropical climates with pronounced dry season and periodic fires.

sawah: Indonesian term used in Southeast Asia that means irrigated or wet rice cultivation.

secondary activity: economic activity involving the processing, transformation, fabrication, or assembly of raw materials, or the reassembly, refinishing, or packaging of manufactured goods.

sectionalism: extreme devotion to local interests and customs.

semiperipheral regions: regions that are able to exploit peripheral regions but are themselves exploited and dominated by the core regions.

sense of place: feelings evoked among people as a result of the experiences and memories that they associate with a place and to the symbolism that they attach to it.

shifting cultivation: agricultural system that preserves soil fertility by moving crops from one plot to another.

short 20th century: expression often used to describe the period from the outbreak of World War I in 1914 until the collapse of the Soviet Union in 1991, a time of distinctive economic and geopolitical development.

Silk Road: ancient east–west trade route between Europe and China.

site: physical attributes of a location that could include terrain, soil, vegetation and water sources.

situation: location of a place relative to other places and human activities.

slash and burn: agricultural system often used in tropical forests that involves cutting trees and brush and burning them so that crops can benefit from cleared ground and nutrients in the ash.

social capital: networks and relationships that encourage trust, reciprocity, and cooperation.

social housing: rental housing that is owned and managed by a public institution or nonprofit organization.

social movements: organized movements of people with an agenda of political opposition and activism.

South Pacific Forum: institution that promotes discussion and cooperation on trade, fisheries, and tourism between all of the independent and self-governing states of Oceania.

sovereignty: exercise of state power over people and territory, recognized by other states and codified by international law.

spatial diffusion: way that things spread through geographic space over time.

spatial justice: fairness of the distribution of society's burdens and benefits, taking into account spatial variations in people's needs and in their contribution to the production of wealth and social well-being.

staples economy: economy based on natural resources that are unprocessed or minimally processed before they are exported to other areas where they are manufactured into end products.

state: independent political unit with territorial boundaries that are internationally recognized by other states.

state socialism: form of economy based on principles of collective ownership and administration of the means of production and distribution of goods, dominated and directed by state bureaucracies.

steppe: semiarid, treeless, grassland plains.

stolen generation: Aboriginal children that were forcibly removed from their homes in Australia and placed in white foster homes or institutions.

structural adjustment policies: economic policies, mostly associated with the International Monetary Fund, that required governments to cut budgets and liberalize trade in return for debt relief.

subsistence affluence: achievement of a good standard of living through reliance on self-sufficiency in local foods and with little cash income.

suburbanization: growth of population along the fringes of large metropolitan areas.

superfund site: locations in the United States officially deemed by the federal government as extremely polluted and requiring extensive, supervised, and subsidized cleanup.

supranational organization: collection of individual states with a common economic and/or political goal that diminishes, to some extent, individual state sovereignty in favor of the collective interests of the membership.

sustainable development: vision of development that seeks a balance among economic growth, environmental impacts, and social equity.

taiga: ecological zone of boreal coniferous forest.

technology system: cluster of interrelated energy, transportation, and production technologies that dominates economic activity for several decades.

territorial production complex: regional groupings of production facilities based on local resources that were suited to clusters of interdependent industries.

tertiary activity: economic activity involving the sale and exchange of goods and services.

theory of island biogeography: theory that smaller islands will generally be less biologically diverse than larger ones.

time-space convergence: rate at which places move closer together in travel or communication time or costs.

total fertility rate: average number of children a woman will bear throughout her childbearing years, approximately ages 15 through 49.

trade creation effects: positive economic effects of transnational integration.

trade diversion effects: negative economic effects of transnational integration.

transform boundary: process of plates sliding past each other horizontally.

transhumance: movement of herds according to seasonal rhythms: warmer, lowland areas in the winter, and cooler, highland areas in the summer.

transmigration: policy of resettling people from densely populated areas to less populated, often frontier regions.

transnational corporation: corporation that has investments and activities that span international boundaries, with subsidiary companies, factories, offices, or facilities in several countries.

Treaty of Tordesillas: agreement made by Pope Alexander VI in 1494 to divide the world between Spain and Portugal along a north–south line 370 leagues (about 1800 kilometers, or 1100 miles) west of the Cape Verde Islands. Portugal received the area east of the line, including much of Brazil and parts of Africa, and Spain received the area to the west.

Treaty of Waitangi: 1840 agreement in which 40 Maori chiefs gave the Queen of England governance over their land and the right to purchase it in exchange for protection and citizenship. Reinterpreted by the Waitangi tribunal in the 1990s, it provides the basis for Maori land rights and New Zealand's bicultural society.

treaty ports: ports in Asia, especially China and Japan, that were opened to foreign trade and residence in the mid-19th century because of pressure from powers such as Britain, France, Germany, and the United States.

tribe: form of social identity created by groups who share a common set of ideas about collective loyalty and political action.

tundra: Arctic wilderness where the climate precludes any agriculture or forestry. Permafrost and very short summers mean that the natural vegetation consists of mosses, lichens, and certain hardy grasses.

unitary state: form of government in which power is concentrated in the central government.

viceroyalty: largest scale of Spanish colonial administration leading to the emergence of Mexico City and Lima as the headquarters of the viceroyalties of New Spain and Peru, respectively.

visualization: computer-assisted representation of spatial data, often involving three-dimensional images and innovative perspectives, in order to reveal spatial patterns and relationships more effectively.

Wallace's Line: division between species associated with the deep-ocean trench between the islands of Bali and Lombok in Indonesia that could not be crossed even during low sea levels of the ice ages.

watershed: drainage area of a particular river or river system.

weather: instantaneous or immediate state of the atmosphere (e.g., it is raining).

welfare state: institution with the aim of distributing income and resources to the poorer members of society.

White Australia policy: Australian policy, until 1975, that restricted immigration to people from northern Europe through a ranking that placed British and Scandinavians as the highest priority, followed by southern Europeans, with the goal of attaining a homogenized-looking and culturally similar population.

World Bank: development bank and the largest source of development assistance in the world.

world city: city in which a disproportionate share of the world's most important business—economic, political, and cultural—is transacted.

world region: large-scale geographic division based on continental and physiographic settings that contain major clusters of humankind with broadly similar cultural attributes.

world religion: belief system with worldwide adherents.

world-system: interdependent system of countries linked by political and economic competition.

xenophobia: hate and/or fear of foreigners.

yurt: circular tent used by nomadic groups in Mongolia, northwest China, and Central Asia, constructed from collapsible wooden frames and felt made from sheep's wool.

zaibatsu: large Japanese conglomerate corporation.

zionism: movement whose chief objective has been the establishment for the Jewish people of a legally recognized home in Palestine.

PHOTO CREDITS

5-9b: © Nik Wheeler/CORBIS
5-10b: Joe McDonald/Corbis/Bettmann
5-10c: © Reuters NewMedia Inc./CORBIS
5-10d: © Jeffrey L. Rotman/CORBIS
5-11b: Chris Hellier/Corbis/Bettmann
5-12c: FAO Photo/R. Faidutti
5-15: Nik Wheeler/Corbis/Bettmann
5-16a: Robert Holmes/Corbis/Bettmann
5-16b: © Nik Wheeler/CORBIS All Rights Reserved
5-18a: © Hulton-Deutsch Collection/CORBIS
5-18b: © Hulton-Deutsch Collection/CORBIS
5-22a: Chinch Gryniewicz; Ecoscene/Corbis/Bettmann
5-22b: Bernard and Catherine Desjeux/Corbis/Bettmann
5-22c: Peter Cunliffe-Jones/Agence France Presse/Getty Images
5-23b: Corbis/Bettmann
5-24c: David Turnley/Corbis/Bettmann
5-24d: Ian Hodgson/Reuters NewMedia Inc./Corbis/Bettmann
5-26: Steven Cashmore www.live8.us
5-30: Charles O'Rear/Corbis/Bettmann
5-31: © James Marshall/CORBIS All Rights Reserved
5-33: Liba Taylor/Corbis/Bettmann
5-35a: SEYLLOU/Agence France Presse/Getty Images
5-35b: John Elk III/Bruce Coleman Inc.
5-36b: Agence France Presse/Getty Images
5-37b: © Vince Streano/CORBIS
5-37c: © Earl & Nazima Kowall/CORBIS
5-37d: © Wolfgang Kaehler/CORBIS
5-38: International Potato Center (CIP)
5-39b: AP Wide World Photos
5-40a: © Reuters NewMedia Inc./CORBIS
5-40b: Greenpeace/AP Wide World Photos
5-40c: © Reuters NewMedia Inc./CORBIS
5-B1-1: Radhika Chalasani/SIPA Press
5-B2-2: Robert Holmes/Corbis/Bettmann
5-B3-1: David Turnley/Corbis/Bettmann
5-B3-2: © Wendy Stone/CORBIS
5-B3-3: © Wendy Stone/CORBIS

CHAPTER 6

6-3: Getty Images Inc. - Image Bank
6-7: Eastcott/Momatiuk/Valan Photos
6-9: Ron Garnett/Ursus Photography
6-10: James Quine/Alamy Images
6-11: Judith Canty/Stock Boston
6-12: © Bo Zaunders/CORBIS All Rights Reserved
6-13: Miguel Gandert/Corbis/Bettmann
6-15: © Underwood & Underwood/CORBIS All Rights Reserved
6-16: © John Zich/zrImages/CORBIS All Rights Reserved
6-19: © Barry Lewis/CORBIS All Rights Reserved
6-20: © Jan Butchofsky-Houser/CORBIS All Rights Reserved
6-22: Getty Images/Time Life Pictures
6-25a: Peter Ginter
6-25b: Robb Kendrick/Kendrick-Ralston CS, Inc.
6-27a: © Royalty-free/CORBIS
6-27b: © Richard Cummins/CORBIS All Rights Reserved
6-27c: © Robert Holmes/CORBIS
6-27d: Rolf W. Hapke/Corbis Zefa Collection
6-28: © C. Moore/CORBIS All Rights Reserved
6-29: Corbis Royalty Free
6-30: © Jim Richardson/CORBIS All Rights Reserved
6-32: © Dennis Degnan/CORBIS All Rights Reserved
6-33: © Richard Hamilton Smith/CORBIS All Rights Reserved
6-34: Michael S. Yamashita/Corbis/Bettmann
6-B1-1: Chris Hellier/Corbis/Bettmann
6-B2-1: Christinne Muschi/Corbis/Reuters America LLC
6-B2-2: © Staffan Widstrand/CORBIS All Rights Reserved

CHAPTER 7

7-2: Robert Frerck/Woodfin Camp & Associates
7-4: Tom Van Sant/Geosphere Project/Photo Researchers, Inc.

7-5a: © Eberhard Hummel/zefa/CORBIS All Rights Reserved
7-5b: Alison Wright/Corbis/Bettmann
7-5c: Richard A. Cooke/Corbis/Bettmann
7-6a: Kevin West/Getty Images, Inc - Liaison
7-6b: © Owen Franken/CORBIS All Rights Reserved
7-9: Pensa Nicarabua/Corbis/Sygma
7-10b: Ted Spiegel/Corbis/Bettmann
7-10c: International Potato Center (CIP)
7-11b: Getty Images, Inc.
7-12: © Joseph Sohm; Visions of America/CORBIS All Rights Reserved
7-13a: Charles O'Rear/Corbis/Bettmann
7-13b: Kit Houghton Photography/Corbis/Bettmann
7-13c: Tim Wright/Corbis/Bettmann
7-14b: Herve Collart/Corbis/Bettmann
7-14c: © CNES/Spot Image/Science Source/Photo Researchers, Inc.
7-15b: © Bob Krist/CORBIS All Rights Reserved
7-17: Joachim Messerschmidt/Bruce Coleman Inc.
7-18b: Cobis/Bettmann
7-18c: Cobis/Brttmann
7-18d: Roberto & Osvaldo Salas/Getty Images, Inc.-Liaison
7-18e: Reuters NewMedia, Inc./Corbis Bettmann
7-19: © Keith Dannemiller/CORBIS All Rights Reserved
7-20: Mariana Bazo/Reuters/Corbis/Reuters America LLC
7-23: Tom Jacobi/Black Star
7-24: Paulo Whitaker/Reuters/Corbis/Reuters America LLC
7-25: © Sergio Pitamitz/CORBIS All Rights Reserved
7-26: © Buddy Mays/CORBIS All Rights Reserved
7-28: Frida Kahlo, Self-Portrait at the Border Between Mexico and the United States. 1932. Museo Nacional de Arte Moderno, © 2001 Banco de Mexico Diego Rivera & Frida Kahlo Museums Trust. Av. Cinco de Mayo No. 2, Col. Centro, Del. Cuauhtemoc 06059, Mexico,
7-29a: Jeff Albertson/Corbis/Bettmann
7-29b: Corbis/Bettmann
7-30: © Nancy Coste/CORBIS All Rights Reserved
7-31: Diana Liverman
7-32b: Charles O'Rear/Corbis/Bettmann
7-33: The Fairtrade Foundation
7-34a: Reuters NewMedia Inc./Corbis/Bettmann
7-35a: Nik Wheeler/Corbis/Bettmann
7-35b: John Van Hasselt/Corbis/Bettmann
7-35c: © Martin Alipaz/EPA/CORBIS All Rights Reserved
7-B1-1: © Serbio Pitamitz/CORBIS All Rights Reserved
7-B2-1a: © Bettmann/Walter Yeager/CORBIS All Rights Reserved
7-B2-1b: © Kelly-Mooney Photography/CORBIS All Rights Reserved
7-B3-1: Jeremy Horner/Corbis/Bettmann
7-B3-2: Dave G. Houser/Corbis/Bettmann

CHAPTER 8

8-2: Getty Images Inc. - Stone Allstock
8-5: © Keren Su/CORBIS All Rights Reserved
8-6: Bruno Morandi/Getty Images - Robert Harding World Imagery
8-7: © Keren Su/CORBIS All Rights Reserved
8-8: Getty Images/Digital Vision
8-9: Keren Su/Taxi/Getty Images
8-10: Photographer's Choice/Getty Images, Inc.
8-14: Peter Menzel/Peter Menzel Photography
8-16: Paul L. Knox
8-17: Yann Layma/Image Bank/Getty Images
8-18: Guang Niu/Getty Images, Inc.
8-20: Photodisc/Getty Images
8-21a: Keren Su/Riser/Getty Images, Inc.
8-21b: David Hume Kennerly/Getty Images, Inc.
8-21c: China Tourism Press/Riser/Getty Images, Inc.
8-22: © 2000, *The Washington Post*. Reprinted with permission.
8-23: © Niels Alpert/ZUMA/CORBIS All Rights Reserved
8-24: Tony Waltham/Getty Images - Robert Harding World Imagery
8-25: © KILCULLEN/TROCAIRE/CORBIS SYGMA
8-26: Jeremy Woodhouse/Image Bank/Getty Images
8-28: DAJ/Photodisc/Getty Images
8-29: Ursula Gahwiler/Getty Images - Robert Harding World Imagery

INDEX

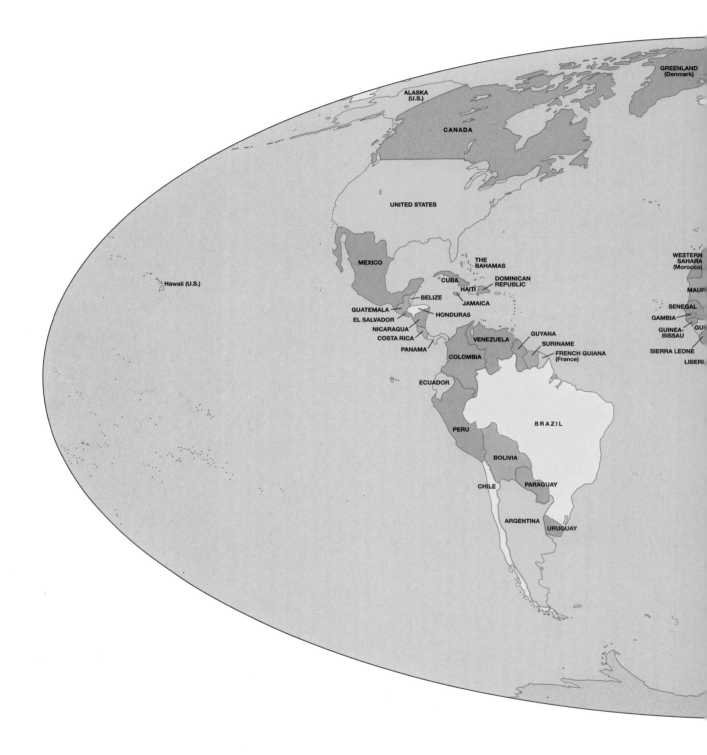

World States

RUSSIA

KAZAKHSTAN

MONGOLIA

GEORGIA
ARMENIA
TURKEY

UZBEKISTAN   KYRGYZSTAN

TURKMENISTAN   TAJIKISTAN

AZERBAIJAN

NORTH
KOREA

SOUTH
KOREA   JAPAN

CHINA

ISIA

LEBANON
ISRAEL

SYRIA   IRAQ   IRAN

AFGHANISTAN

LIBYA   EGYPT

JORDAN   KUWAIT

BAHRAIN   QATAR

UNITED
ARAB
EMIRATES

PAKISTAN

NEPAL   BHUTAN

TAIWAN

BANGLADESH

INDIA

BURMA
(MYANMAR)   LAOS

SAUDI
ARABIA

OMAN

CHAD

ERITREA   YEMEN

SUDAN

DJIBOUTI

THAILAND

CAMBODIA

VIETNAM

PHILIPPINES

CENTRAL
AFRICAN
REPUBLIC

ETHIOPIA

SRI
LANKA

EROON

SOMALIA

BRUNEI

RWANDA   UGANDA

DEMOCRATIC
REPUBLIC
OF THE CONGO

KENYA

MALAYSIA

SINGAPORE

ON

BURUNDI   TANZANIA

I N D O N E S I A

PAPUA
NEW
GUINEA

SOLOMON
ISLANDS

ANGOLA   MALAWI

ZAMBIA

MOZAMBIQUE

EAST
TIMOR

ZIMBABWE

MADAGASCAR

VANUATU

BOTSWANA

New
Caledonia
(France)

NAMIBIA

SWAZILAND

AUSTRALIA

SOUTH
AFRICA   LESOTHO

RCTICA

NEW
ZEALAND

Europe

ICELAND

FINLAND

NORWAY

SWEDEN

ESTONIA

DENMARK

LATVIA
LITH.

RUSS.

RUSSIA

IRELAND

UNITED
KINGDOM

NETH.

BELARUS

POLAND

BELG.

GERMANY

LUX.

CZH.
REP.

UKRAINE

FRANCE

SWITZ.

AUS.   SLVK.

HUN.

MOLDOVA

SLOVE.

ROMANIA

ITALY

CRO.   BOS. &
HERZ.   SERBIA

BULGARIA

GEORGIA

MONT.

MAC.
ALB.

PORTUGAL   SPAIN

GREECE

TURKEY

MOROCCO   ALGERIA   TUNISIA

CYPRUS   SYRIA